This is a complimentary review
copy from
Gale Research
For ordering information, call
(800) 877-4253

WHAT MYSTERY DO I READ NEXT?

A Reader's Guide to Recent Mystery Fiction

Explore your options!

Gale databases are offered in a variety of formats

GALE The information in this Gale publication is also available in some or all of the formats described here. Your Gale Representative will be happy to fill you in. Call toll-free 1-800-877-GALE.

GaleNet℠ *your information community*

GaleNet
A number of Gale databases are now available on GaleNet, our new online information resource accessible through the Internet. GaleNet features an easy-to-use end-user interface, the powerful search capabilities of BRS/SEARCH retrieval software and ease of access through the World Wide Web.

Diskette/Magnetic Tape
Many Gale databases are available on diskette or magnetic tape, allowing systemwide access to your most-used information sources through existing computer systems. Data can be delivered on a variety of mediums (DOS-formatted diskettes, 9-track tape, 8mm data tape) and in industry-standard formats (comma-delimited, tagged, fixed-field).

CD-ROM
A variety of Gale titles are available on CD-ROM, offering maximum flexibility and powerful search software.

Online
For your convenience, many Gale databases are available through popular online services, including DIALOG, NEXIS, DataStar, ORBIT, OCLC, Thomson Financial Network's I/Plus Direct, HRIN, Prodigy, Sandpoint's HOOVER, the Library Corporation's NLightN and Telebase Systems.

WHAT MYSTERY DO I READ NEXT?

A Reader's Guide to Recent Mystery Fiction

STEVEN A. STILWELL

GALE

Detroit
New York
Toronto
London

Steven A. Stilwell

Gale Research Staff

Coordinating Editor: Charles B. Montney
Contributing Editors: Victoria A. Coughlin, Kathleen Dallas, Shelly Dickey, Lydia Fink,
William Harmer, Arlene Johnson, Debra M. Kirby, Rebecca Mansour, Dana Shonta
Managing Editor: Ann V. Evory

Production Director: MaryBeth Trimper
External Production Assistant: Shanna P. Heilveil
Product Design Manager: Cynthia Baldwin
Senior Art Director: Mary Krzewinski
Cover Photography: Policeman Typing Report by Syd Greenberg/FPG International Corp.;
Man in Hat by Mary Krzewinski/Gale Research

Manager Data Entry Services: Eleanor Allison
Data Entry Coordinator: Gwendolyn S. Tucker
Senior Data Entry Associate: Beverly Jendrowski
Data Entry Associate: Stephanie Pearson

Manager, Technical Support Services: Theresa Rocklin
Programmer/Analyst: Joshua E. Cohen

Library of Congress Cataloging-in-Publication Data

Stilwell, Steven A.
    What mystery do I read next? : a reader's guide / Steven A.
Stilwell.
      p. cm.
    Includes indexes.
    ISBN 0-7876-1592-7 (alk. paper)
    1. Detective and mystery stories--Bibliography. 2. Detective and
mystery stories--Stories, plots, etc. I. Title.
Z5917.D5S85   1997
[PN3448.D4]
016.80883'872--dc21   96-47713
                                                                                     CIP

While every effort has been made to ensure the reliability of the information presented in this publication, Gale Research does not guarantee the accuracy of the data contained herein. Gale accepts no payment for listing; and inclusion in the publication of any organization, agency, institution, publication, service, or individual does not imply endorsement of the editors or publisher. Errors brought to the attention of the publisher and verified to the satisfaction of the publisher will be corrected in future editions.

This publication is a creative work fully protected by all applicable copyright laws, as well as by misappropriation, trade secret, unfair competition, and other applicable laws. The authors and editors of this work have added value to the underlying factual material herein through one of more of the following: unique and original selection, coordination, expression, arrangement, and classification of the information.

All rights to this publication will be vigorously defended.

Copyright © 1997
Gale Research
645 Griswold St.
Detroit, MI 48226-4094

All rights reserved including the right of reproduction in whole or in part in any form.

∞™ This book is printed on acid-free paper that meets the minimum requirements of
American National Standard for Information Sciences—Permanence Paper for Printed
Library Materials, ANSI Z39.48-1984.

ISBN 0-7876-1592-7

Printed in the United States of America

Contents

Introduction vii

Key to Story Types xi

Award Winners xiii

What Mystery Do I Read Next?

    Mystery Titles 3

Indexes:

    Series Index 375

    Time Period Index 385

    Geographic Index 395

    Story Type Index 409

    Character Name Index 421

    Character Description Index 449

    Author Index 481

    Title Index 507

Introduction

Year after year, mystery and crime fiction continues to enjoy huge popularity among readers. The number of titles available each year proves the enduring strength of the genre, and in many large cities bookstores specializing in mysteries cater to the needs of ardent mystery buffs. And of course librarians find whodunits circulating widely among their patrons. *What Mystery Do I Read Next?* aims to help the reader of mysteries as well as librarians and booksellers by pointing the way to the best fiction in the genre published in the 1990s.

What Mystery Do I Read Next? compiles the descriptions for the mystery titles listed in Gale's acclaimed series *What Do I Read Next? A Reader's Guide to Current Genre Fiction*, which has been published annually since 1989. In the seven editions of *WDIRN?* have appeared 1,800 entries describing mystery books in detail. These entries also recommend, on average, five other books that are similar to the described title. Thus, *What Mystery Do I Read Next?* unlocks the door to thousands of books, pointing the way to many more hours of reading pleasure for mystery aficionados.

Highlights

- "Other books you might like," included in each entry, leads to the exploration of new authors or titles recommended by the genre expert.

- Key to story types provides information on the classification of stories within the mystery genre.

- A list of award-winning books, another clue to further reading enjoyment offered by our genre expert, follows the Introduction.

- Eight indexes help locate specific titles or offer suggestions for reading in favorite time periods or geographic locations or about characters in specific professions.

- All authors and titles listed in entries under "Other books you might like" are indexed, allowing easy access to thousands of books recommended for further reading by the genre expert.

Introduction

Titles Recommended by Mystery Expert Steven Stilwell

The 1,800 entries in this volume were originally selected by noted authority Steven A. Stilwell, who owns Once Upon a Crime Mystery Bookstore in Minneapolis. He was the compiler of *The Armchair Detective Index, 1967-1977* (Mysterious Press, 1979) and was the co-compiler, with William F. Deeck, of *The Armchair Detective Index: Volumes 1-20, 1967-1987*. He has contributed to several mystery publications, including *Mystery Scene Magazine, The Armchair Detective, The Mystery Fancier,* and *Twentieth Century Crime and Mystery Writers, 3rd ed.* 1991. He is also co-owner of Crossover Press, a small press specializing in books about crime and detective fiction. Steven and his assistants have spent countless hours reading and comparing mysteries in the process of finding the ones to recommend in the *What Do I Read Next?* series.

Details on 1,200 Titles...

What Mystery Do I Read Next? details 1,800 recommended mystery and crime titles published between 1989 and 1996. The entries are listed alphabetically by author, so that an author's entries all appear together. Readers will find the following information:

- **Author or editor's name** and real name if a pseudonym is used. Co-authors and co-editors are also listed where applicable.

- **Book title.**

- **Date and place of publication; name of publisher.**

- **Series name.**

- **Story type:** Specific categories within the Mystery genre, identified by the compiling expert. Definitions of these types are listed in the "Key to Genre Terms" section following the Introduction.

- **Major characters:** Names and brief descriptions of up to three characters featured in the title.

- **Time period:** Tells when the story takes place.

- **Locale**: Tells where the story takes place.

- **What the book is about:** A brief (usually two- or three-sentence) plot summary.

- **Other books you might like:** Titles by other authors written on a similar theme or in a similar style. These titles further the reader's exploration of the genre. The titles mentioned in this rubric range from contemporary books to classics in the genre, all sharing one or several components similar to the main title.

What Mystery Do I Read Next? — Introduction

Indexes Answer Readers' Questions

The eight indexes in *What Mystery Do I Read Next?*, used separately or in conjunction with each other, create many pathways to the featured titles, answering general questions or locating specific titles. For example:

"What *Kate Delafield* books have I missed?"
　The SERIES INDEX lists entries by the name of the series of which they are a part.

"I like books about amateur detectives featuring a woman as the detective. Can you recommend any new ones?"
　The STORY TYPE INDEX breaks the mystery genre down into more specialized areas. For example, there is a story type heading "Amateur Detective--Female Lead." For the definitions of story types, see the "Key to Story Types Terms" beginning on page xi.

"Are there any mysteries set in ancient Rome?"
　The GEOGRAPHIC INDEX lists titles by their locale. This can help readers pinpoint an area in which they may have a particular interest, such as their hometown, another country, or even Cyberspace.

"Do you know of any crime stories set during the 1920s?"
　The TIME PERIOD INDEX is a chronological listing of the time settings in which the main entry titles take place.

"What mysteries are available that feature lawyers?"
　The CHARACTER DESCRIPTION INDEX identifies the major characters by occupation (e.g. Accountant, Editor, Librarian) or persona (e.g. Historical Figure, Noblewoman).

"Has anyone written any new books in the last few years with Sherlock Holmes in them?"
　The CHARACTER NAME INDEX lists the major characters named in the entries. This can help readers who remember some information about a book, but not an author or title.

"What has Tony Hillerman written recently?"
　The AUTHOR INDEX contains the names of all authors featured in the entries and those listed under "Other books you might like."

"What books are like *J is for Judgment*?"
　The TITLE INDEX includes all main entry titles and all titles recommended under and "Other books you might like" in one alphabetical listing. Thus, a reader can find a specific title, new or old, then go to that entry to find out what new titles are similar.

The indexes can also be used together to narrow down or broaden choices. A reader interested in mysteries set in New York during the 19th century would consult the TIME PERIOD INDEX and GEOGRAPHIC INDEX to see which titles appear in both. With the

AUTHOR and TITLE indexes, which include all books listed under "Other books you might like," it is easy to compile an extensive list of recommended reading, beginning with a recently published title or a classic from the past.

Suggestions Are Welcome

The editors welcome any comments and suggestions for enhancing and improving *What Mystery Do I Read Next?*. Please address correspondence to:

> Editors
> *What Mystery Do I Read Next?*
> Gale Research
> 835 Penobscot Bldg.
> Detroit, MI 48226-4094
> Phone: 313-961-2242
> Toll-free: 800-347-4253
> Fax: 313-961-6083

Key to Story Types

The following is a list of terms used to classify the story type of each novel included in *What Mystery Do I Read Next?* along with brief definitions of the terms. To find books that fall under a particular story type heading, see the Story Type Index.

Action/Adventure - Minimal detection; not usually espionage, but can contain rogue police or out of control spies.

Alternate History - A story in which the author has created a history different from that which actually happened.

Amateur Detective - Detective work is performed by a non-professional rather than by police or a private detective. This story type has been divided into **Amateur Detective—Female Lead** and **Amateur Detective—Male Lead**, for readers wishing to explore fiction concentrating on female or male characters. Books in which male and female characters share the lead will be found under the general **Amateur Detective** heading.

Anthology - A collection of short stories by different authors, often sharing a common theme.

Collection - A book of short stories by the same author.

Espionage - Involving the CIA, KGB, or other organizations whose main focus is the collection of information from the other side. Can be either violent or quiet.

Historical - Usually detection set in an earlier time frame than the present.

Humor - A mystery with a strong focus on humorous elements.

Legal - Main focus is on a lawyer, though it does not always involve courtroom action.

Police Procedural - A story in which the action is centered around a police officer. This story type has been divided into **Police Procedural—Female Lead** and **Police Procedural—Male Lead**, for readers wishing to explore fiction concentrating on female or male characters. Books in which male and female characters share the lead will be found under the general **Police Procedural** heading.

Private Detective - Usually detection involving a professional for hire. This story type has been divided into **Private Detective—Female Lead** and **Private Detective—Male Lead**, for readers wishing to explore fiction concentrating on female or male characters. Books in which male and female characters share the lead will be found under the general **Private Detective** heading.

Psychological Suspense - Main focus is on the workings of the mind, usually with some danger involved.

Romantic Suspense - A mystery with elements of suspense and romance.

Serial Killer - The investigation centers on tracking and apprehending a mass murderer.

Techno-Thriller - A relatively new term used to describe books where the main focus is on machinery, usually weaponry, rather than on the characters.

Traditional - Usually means the classic British mystery, but is coming to mean non-private detective fiction.

Award Winners

Edgar Allan Poe Awards

Known as the Edgars, they are presented by the Mystery Writers of America. Nominees and winners are selected by committees made up of members of that organization.

1996

Best Novel: *Come to Grief* by Dick Francis
Other Nominees: *The Bookman's Wake* by John Dunning; *The Shadow Man* by John Katzenbach; *The Summons* by Peter Lovesey; *The Roaring Boy* by Edward Marston

Best First Novel by an American Author: *Penance* by David Housewright
Other Nominees: *Tight Shot* by Kevin Allman; *Murder in Scorpio* by Martha C. Lawrence; *The Harry Chronicles* by Allan Pedrazas; *Fixed in His Folly* by David J. Walker

Best Paperback Original: *Tarnished Blue* by William Heffernan
Other Nominees: *Deal Breaker* by Harlan Coben; *High Desert Malice* by Kirk Mitchell; *Charged with Guilt* by Gloria White; *Hard Frost* by R.D. Wingfield

Best Short Story: "The Judge's Boy" by Jean B. Cooper
Other Nominees: "Rule of Law" by K.K. Beck; "Death in a Small Town" by Larry Beinhart; "When Your Breath Freezes" by Kathleen Dougherty; "A Plain and Honest Death" by Bill Pomidor

1995

Best Novel: *The Red Scream* by Mary Willis Walker
Other Nominees: *Lights Out* by Peter Abrahams; *A Long Line of Dead Men* by Lawrence Block; *Miami, It's Murder* by Edna Buchanan; *Wednesday's Child* by Peter Robinson

Best First Novel by an American Author: *The Caveman's Valentine* by George Dawes Green
Other Nominees: *One for the Money* by Janet Evanovich; *Mallory's Oracle* by Carol O'Connell; *Suspicion of Innocence* by Barbara Parker; *Big Town* by Doug J. Swanson

Best Paperback Original: *Final Appeal* by Lisa Scottoline
Other Nominees: *The Broken-Hearted Detective* by Milton Bass; *Viper Quarry* by Dean Feldmeyer; *Power of Attorney* by Walter Sorrells; *Sunrise* by Chassie West

1994

Best Novel: *The Sculptress* by Minette Walters
Other Nominees: *Free Fall* by Robert Crais; *Smilla's Sense of Snow* by Peter Hoeg; *Wolf in the Shadows* by Marcia Muller; *The Journeyman Tailor* by Gerald Seymour.

Best First Novel by an American Author: *A Grave Talent* by Laurie King

Other Nominees: *The List of Seven* by Mark Frost; *Criminal Seduction* by Darian North; *The Ballad of Rocky Ruiz* by Manuel Ramos; *Zaddick* by David Rosenbaum

Best Paperback Original: *Dead Folks' Blues* by Steven Womack
Other Nominees: *The Servant's Tale* by Margaret Frazer; *Tony's Justice* by Eugene Izzi; *Beyond Sura* by T.A. Roberts; *Everywhere That Mary Went* by Lisa Scottoline

1993

Best Novel: *Bootlegger's Daughter* by Margaret Maron
Other Nominees: *Backhand* by Lisa Cody; *32 Cadillacs* by Joe Gores; *White Butterfly* by Walter Moseley; *Pomona Queen* by Kem Nunn

Best First Novel by an American Author: *The Black Echo* by Michael Connelly
Other Nominees: *Trail of Murder* by Christine Andreae; *Trick of the Eye* by Jane Stanton Hitchcock; *Ladystinger* by Craig Smith

Best Paperback Original: *A Cold Day for Murder* by Dana Stabenow
Other Nominees: *The Good Friday Murder* by Lee Harris; *Principal Defense* by Gina Hartzmark; *Shallow Graves* by William Jeffries; *Night Cruise* by Billie Sue Mosiman

1992

Best Novel: *A Dance at the Slaughterhouse* by Lawrence Block
Other Nominees: *Don't Say a Word* by Andrew Klavan; *Prior Convictions* by Lia Matera; *I.O.U.* by Nancy Pickard; *Palindrome* by Stuart Woods

Best First Novel by an American Author: *Slow Motion Riot* by Peter Blauner
Other Nominees: *Deadstick* by Terence Flaherty; *Deadline* by Marcy Heidish; *Zero at the Zone* by Mary Willis Walker; *A Cool Breeze on the Underground* by Don Winslow

Best Paperback Original: *Dark Maze* by Thomas Adcock
Other Nominees: *Murder in the Dog Days* by P.M. Carlson; *Cracking Up* by Ed Naha; *Midtown North* by Christopher Newman; *Fine Distinctions* by Deborah Valentine

1991

Best Novel: *New Orleans Mourning* by Julie Smith

Best First Novel by an American Author: *Postmortem* by Patricia Daniels Cornwell

Best Paperback Original: *The Man Who Would Be F.Scott Fitzgerald* by David Handler.

1990

Best Novel: *Black Cherry Blues* by James Lee Burke

Best First Novel by an American Author: *The Last Billable Hour* by Susan Wolfe

Best Paperback Original: *The Rain* by Keith Peterson

Shamus Awards

Presented by the Private Eye Writers of America to honor the best in private detective fiction. Nominated and voted on by committees of members of that organization.

1996

Best P.I. Novel: *Concourse* by S.J. Rozan
Other Nominees: *The Vanishing Smile* by Earl Emerson; *Come to Grief* by Dick Francis; *Movie* by Parnell Hall; *The Neon Smile* by Dick Lochte

Best First P.I. Novel: *The Innocents* by Richard Barre
Other Nominees: *Who in Hell Is Wanda Fuca?* G.M. Ford; *If Looks Could Kill* by Ruthe Furie; *Penance* by David Housewright

Best Original P.I. Paperback Novel: *Native Angels* by William Jaspersohn
Other Nominees: *Zero Tolerance* by J.D. Knight; *Interview with Mattie* by Shelly Singer; *Charged with Guilt* by Gloria White; *Way Past Dead* by Steven Womack

Best P.I. Short Story: "And Pray Nobody Sees You" by Gar Anthony Haywood
Other Nominees: "Trial by Fire" by David Dean; "A Plain and Honest Death" by Bill Pomidor; "Home Is the Place Where" by Bill Pronzini; "Enigma" by D.H. Redall

1995

Best P.I. Novel: *K Is for Killer* by Sue Grafton
Other Nominees: *A Long Line of Dead Men* by Lawrence Block; *Carnal Hours* by Max Allan Collins; *The Killing of Monday Brown* by Sandra West Prowell; *The Lake Effect* by Les Roberts

Best First P.I. Novel: *A Drink Before the War* by Dennis LeHane
Other Nominees: *The Heaven Stone* by David Daniel; *One for the Money* by Janet Evanovich; *The Fall-Down Artist* by Thomas Lipinski; *When Death Comes Stealing* by Valerie Wilson Wesley

Best Original P.I. Paperback Novel: *Served Cold* by Ed Goldberg
Other Nominees: *Double Plot* by Leo Axler; *Lament for a Dead Cowboy* by Catherine Dain; *Dead Ahead* by Bridget McKenna; *Deadly Devotion* by Patricia Wallace

Best P.I. Short Story: "A Necessary Brother" by Brendan DuBois
Other Nominees: "A Matter of Character" by Michael Collins; "Split Decision" by Clark Howard; "Slipstream" by Loren Estleman; "The Romantics" by John Lutz

1994

Best P.I. Novel: *The Devil Knows You're Dead* by Lawrence Block
Other Nominees: *The Lies That Bind* by Judith Van Gieson; *Wolf in the Shadows* by Marcia Muller

Best First P.I. Novel: *Satan's Lambs* by Lynn Hightower
Other nominees: *Brotherly Love* by Randye Lorden; *By Evil Means* by Sandra West Prowell

Best Original P.I. Paperback: *Brothers and Sinners* by Rodman Philbrick
Other Nominees: *The Half-Hearted Detective* by Milton Bass; *A Minyan for the Dead* by Richard Fliegel; *Shadow Games* by Ed Gorman; *Torch-Town Boogie* by Steven Womack

Best P.I. Short Story: "The Merciful Angel of Death" by Lawrence Block

1993

Best P.I. Novel: *The Man Who Was Taller Than God* by Harold Adams

Other Nominees: *Cassandra in Red* by Michael Collins; *Lullaby Town* by Robert Crais; *Shallow Graves* by Jeremiah Healy; *Special Delivery* by Jerry Kennealy

Best First P.I. Novel: *The Woman Who Married a Bear* by John Straley
Other Nominees: *Return Trip Ticket* by David C. Hall; *Switching the Odds* by Phyllis Knight; *The Long-Legged Fly* by James Sallis

Best Original P.I. Paperback: *The Last Tango of Delores Delgado* by Marele Day
Other Nominations: *Lay It on the Line* by Catherine Dain; *Dirty Money* by Mark Davis; *The Brutal Ballet* by Wayne Dundee

Best P.I. Short Story: "Mary, Mary, Shut the Door" by Benjamin Schutz

1992

Best P.I. Novel: *Stolen Away* by Max Allan Collins
Other Nominees: *A Dance at the Slaughterhouse* by Lawrence Block; *Where Echoes Live* by Marcia Muller; *A Fistful of Empty* by Benjamin Schutz; *Second Chance* by Jonathan Valin

Best First P.I. Novel: *Suffer the Little Children* by Thomas Davis
Other Nominees: *The January Corpse* by Neil Albert; *Dead on the Island* by Bill Crider; *Best Performance by a Patsy* by Stan Cutler; *A Cool Breeze on the Underground* by Don Winslow

Best Original P.I. Paperback: *Cool Blue Tomb* by Paul Kemprecos
Other Nominees: *Black Light* by Daniel Hearn; *House of Cards* by Kay Hooper; *The Thousand Yard Stare* by Rob Kantner

Best P.I. Short Story: "Discards" by Faye Kellerman

1991

Best P.I. Novel: *"G" Is for Gumshoe* by Sue Grafton

Best First P.I. Novel: *Devil in a Blue Dress* by Walter Moseley

Best Original P.I. Paperback: *Rafferty: Fatal Sisters* by W. Glenn Duncan

Best P.I. Short Story: "Final Resting Place" by Marcia Muller

1990

Best P.I. Novel: *Extenuating Circumstances* by Jonathan Valin

Best First P.I. Novel: *Katwalk* by Karen Kijewski

Best Original P.I. Paperback: *Hell's Only Half Full* by Rob Kantner

Best P.I. Short Story: "The Killing Man" by Mickey Spillane

The Agatha Awards

Presented by the annual Malice Domestic Convention to celebrate the best in "traditional" mysteries. Nominated and voted on by attending members of the current year's convention.

1995

Best Novel: *She Walks These Hills* by Sharyn McCrumb

Other Nominees: *Scandal in Fair Haven* by Carolyn G. Hart; *The Beekeeper's Apprentice* by Laurie R. King; *Angel of Death* by Rochelle Majer Krich; *Night Train to Memphis* by Elizabeth Peters

Best First Novel: *Do Unto Others* by Jeff Abbott
Other Nominees: *One for the Money* by Janet Evanovich; *Fool's Puzzle* by Earlene Fowler; *Writers of the Purple Sage* by Barbara Burnett Smith; *Until Death* by Polly Whitney

1994

Best Novel: *Dead Man's Island* by Carolyn G. Hart
Other Nominees: *Old Scores* by Aaron Elkins; *O Little Town of Maggody* by Joan Hess; *Fair Game* by Rochelle Majer Krich; *Southern Discomfort* by Margaret Maron; *To Live and Die in Dixie* by Kathy Hogan Trocheck

Best First Novel: *Track of the Cat* by Nevada Barr
Other Nominees: *Goodnight, Irene* by Jan Burke; *A Share in Death* by Deborah Crombie; *Death Comes as Epiphany* by Sharan Newman; *Child of Silence* by Abigail Padgett

1993

Best Novel: *Bootlegger's Daughter* by Margaret Maron
Other Nominees: *Southern Ghost* by Carolyn G. Hart; *The Hangman's Beautiful Daughter* by Sharyn McCrumb; *Defend and Betray* by Anne Perry; *The Snake, the Crocodile and the Dog* by Elizabeth Peters

Best First Novel: *Blanche on the Lam* by Barbara Neely
Other Nominees: *Decked* by Carol Higgins Clark; *Thyme of Death* by Susan Wittig Albert; *Seneca Fall Inheritance* by Grace Hall Monfredo; *Drink of Deadly Wine* by Kate Charles

1992

Best Novel: *I.O.U.* by Nancy Pickard
Other Nominees: *Make No Bones* by Aaron Elkins; *The Christie Caper* by Carolyn G. Hart; *An Owl Too Many* by Charlotte MacLeod; *The Last Camel Died at Noon* by Elizabeth Peters

Best First Novel: *Zero at the Bone* by Mary Willis Walker
Other Nominees: *Carpool* by Mary Cahill; *Just Desserts* by Mary Daheim; *The Bulrush Murders* by Rebecca Rothenberg; *Flowers for the Dead* by Ann Williams

1991

Best Novel: *Bum Steer* by Nancy Pickard

Best First Novel: *The Body in the Belfry* by Katherine Hall Page

1990

Best Novel: *Naked Once More* by Elizabeth Peters

Best First Novel: *Grime and Punishment* by Jill Churchill

Best Short Story: "A Wee Doch and Doris" by Sharyn McCrumb

Award Winners

What Mystery Do I Read Next?

The Anthony Awards

Presented by the annual World Mystery Convention, called Bouchercon, and voted on by attending and supporting members of that year's convention. The awards and the convention are named in honor of author and critic Anthony Boucher.

1996
Best Novel: *She Walks These Hills* by Sharyn McCrumb

Best First Novel: *The Alienist* by Caleb Carr

1995
Best Novel: *Wolf in the Shadows* by Marcia Muller

Best First Novel: *Track of the Cat* by Nevada Barr

1994
Best Novel: *Bootlegger's Daughter* by Margaret Maron

Best First Novel: *Blanche on the Lam* by Barbara Neely

1993
Best Novel: *The Last Detective* by Peter Lovesey

Best First Novel: *Murder on the Iditarod Trail* by Sue Henry

1992
Best Novel: *G Is for Gumshoe* by Sue Grafton

Best First Novel: *Postmortem* by Patricia Daniels Cornwell

Best Paperback Original (tie): *Grave Undertaking* by James McCahery and *Where's Mommy Now?* by Rochelle Majer Krich

1991
Best Novel: *The Sirens Sang of Murder* by Sarah Caudwell

Best First Novel: *Katwalk* by Karen Kijewski

Best Paperback Original: *Honeymoon with Murder* by Carolyn G. Hart

1990
Best Novel: *A Silence of Lambs* by Thomas Harris

Best First Novel: *A Great Deliverance* by Elizabeth George

Best Paperback Original: *Something Wicked* by Carolyn G. Hart

The Macavity Awards

Established in 1986, the Macavity Awards are presented by Mystery Readers International to recognize excellence in the mystery writing field

1996
    Best Mystery Novel: *Under the Beetle's Cellar* by Mary Willis Walker

    Best First Mystery Novel: *The Strange Files of Fremont Jones* by Dianne Day

    Best Mystery Short Story: "Evans Tries an O-Level" by Colin Dexter

1995
    Best Novel: *She Walks These Hills* by Sharyn McCrumb

    Best First Novel: *Do Unto Others* by Jeff Abbott

    Best Short Story (tie): "Cast Your Fate to the Wind" by Deborah Adams; "Unharmed" by Jan Burke

1994
    Best Novel: *The Sculptress* by Minette Walters

    Best First Novel: *Death Comes as Epiphany* by Sharan Newman

    Best Short Story: "Checkout" by Susan Dunlap

1993
    Best Novel: *Bootlegger's Daughter* by Margaret Maron

    Best First Novel: *Blanche on the Lam* by Barbara Neely

    Best Short Story: "Henrie O's Holiday" by Carolyn G. Hart

1992
    Best Novel: *I.O.U.* by Nancy Pickard

    Best First Novel (tie): *Murder on the Iditarod Trail* by Sue Henry; *Zero at the Bone* by Mary Willis Walker

    Best Short Story: "Deborah's Judgement" by Margaret Maron

1991
    Best Novel: *If Ever I Return Pretty Peggy-O* by Sharyn McCrumb

    Best First Novel: *Postmortem* by Patricia Cornwell

    Best Short Story: "Too Much to Bare" by Joan Hess

1990
    Best Novel: *A Little Class on Murder* by Carolyn G. Hart

    Best First Novel: *Grime and Punishment* by Jill Churchill

    Best Short Story: "Afraid All the Time" by Nancy Pickard

WHAT MYSTERY DO I READ NEXT?

A Reader's Guide to Recent Mystery Fiction

Mystery Titles

1
Jeff Abbott
Do Unto Others (New York: Ballantine, 1994)
Story type: Amateur Detective—Male Lead
Major character(s): Jordan Poteet, Librarian
Time period(s): 1990s
Locale(s): Mirabeau, Texas
What the book is about: Jordan Poteet has returned to his hometown to help care for his ailing mother. He is now the town librarian and has run afoul of the town's self-appointed judge of morality and virtue, Beta Harcher. When Beta is found dead in the library soon after attacking Jordan with a D.H. Lawrence book, Jordan realizes he is the prime suspect and decides he'd better find the real murderer. His only clue is a list of the town's leading citizens with a bible verse for each. First novel.
Other books you might like:
Leo Axler, *Final Viewing*, 1994
Jo Dereske, *Miss Zukas and the Library Murders*, 1994
Charlaine Harris, *Real Murders*, 1991
Justin Scott, *Hardscape*, 1993
Susan Steiner, *Library: No Murder Aloud*, 1993

2
Jeff Abbott
The Only Good Yankee (New York: Ballantine, 1995)
Series: Jordon Poteet
Story type: Amateur Detective—Male Lead
Major character(s): Jordan Poteet, Librarian
Time period(s): 1990s
Locale(s): Mirabeau, Texas
What the book is about: Somebody seems to be trying to blow up the town of Mirabeau, starting with doghouses and toolsheds. When some developers come to town wanting to buy up river property and build condos, the town is divided and tempers run short. It doesn't help Jordon that one of the developers is a former girlfriend who wants him back. When another of the developers is killed, the former girlfriend is a prime suspect and his current lover is not terribly thrilled that Jordan is helping her.
Other books you might like:
Deborah Adams, *The Jesus Creek Series*, 1992-
Leo Axler, *The Bill Hawley Series*, 1994-
Sally Gunning, *The Peter Bartholomew Series*, 1990-
Justin Scott, *The Ben Abbott Series*, 1993-
Stephen F. Wilcox, *The NIMBY Factor*, 1992

3
Kenneth Abel
Bait (New York: Delacorte, 1994)
Story type: Action/Adventure; Police Procedural—Male Lead
Major character(s): Jack Walsh, Police Officer (recently resigned); Johnny D'Angelo, Criminal (local crime boss)
Time period(s): 1990s
Locale(s): Althol, Massachusetts
What the book is about: Jack Walsh's partner has been killed in a drug bust gone bad. This has caused Jack to hit the bottle quite heavily. When he wakes up in the hospital after a car accident he discovers that he has killed a man, but not just any man. The man he killed was the only son of the local Mafia kingpin, Johnny D'Angelo. This means that Walsh himself will most likely soon be dead. He resigns from the police force and moves to his hometown of Althol, Massachusetts and waits. What he doesn't know is that the D.A.'s office is using him as bait to get the goods on D'Angelo. Can he stay alive when all seem to be aligned against him? First novel.
Other books you might like:
Michael Connelly, *The Black Ice*, 1993
Stanley Ellin, *The Luxembourg Run*, 1977
Joe Gores, *Dead Man*, 1994
Thomas Perry, *Sleeping Dogs*, 1992
Les Standiford, *Done Deal*, 1993

4
Peter Abrahams
Lights Out (New York: Mysterious, 1994)
Story type: Action/Adventure
Major character(s): Eddie "Nails" Nye, Criminal, Convict (ex-con); Jack Nye, Businessman (Wall Street investor)
Time period(s): 1990s
Locale(s): New York, New York

5 | Abrahams

What the book is about: Eddie Nye is just out of jail after serving all fifteen years of his sentence for drug possession. He was innocent of the crime for which he was convicted, but while in prison he did take revenge on the three cons who raped him. Now he wants to find his brother and learn what really happened fifteen years earlier. He is also obsessed with learning the meaning of *The Rime of the Ancient Mariner*, which somehow reflects his life.

Other books you might like:
K. Patrick Connor, *Kingdom Road*, 1991
James W. Hall, *Hard Aground*, 1993
Tom Kakonis, *Michigan Roll*, 1988
Sin Soracco, *Edge City*, 1992
Tim Willocks, *Green River Rising*, 1994

5

Peter Abrahams
Pressure Drop (New York: Dutton, 1989)

Story type: Action/Adventure

Major character(s): Nina Kitchener, Public Relations; N.H. Mattias, Businessman (owner of a Bahamas' club)

Time period(s): 1980s

Locale(s): New York, New York

What the book is about: After undergoing artificial insemination and the birth of a son, Nina Kitchener is plunged into a nightmare when her newborn is kidnapped. She determines to investigate the institute she was involved with and eventually hooks up with Mattias who is looking into the institute for reasons of his own.

Other books you might like:
Mary Higgins Clark, *The Cradle Will Fall*, 1980
Robin Cook, *Harmful Intent*, 1989
Brian Garfield, *Necessity*, 1984
David Morrell, *Testament*, 1975

6

Peter Abrahams
Revolution #9 (New York: Mysterious, 1992)

Story type: Action/Adventure

Major character(s): Charlie Ochs, Fisherman (lobsterman)

Time period(s): 1990s

Locale(s): Cape Cod, Massachusetts (and across the USA)

What the book is about: Charlie Ochs used to be Blake Wrightman, 60s radical, but when a young boy was killed in a bomb explosion he was forced to go underground and take on a new identity. But now he's made a mistake - he's fallen in love. Just when he has something to lose, a government agent working on his own agenda shows up and wants Charlie to get in touch with members of his old radical group.

Other books you might like:
Daniel Hearn, *Black Light*, 1991
Frederick D. Huebner, *The Joshua Sequence*, 1986
Lia Matera, *A Radical Departure*, 1987
Marcia Muller, *Trophies and Dead Things*, 1990
Jim Weikart, *Casualty Loss*, 1991

7

Richard Abshire
The Dallas Deception (New York: Morrow, 1992)

Series: Jack Kyle

Story type: Private Detective—Male Lead

Major character(s): Jack Kyle, Detective—Private (former police officer)

Time period(s): 1990s

Locale(s): Dallas, Texas

What the book is about: Jack is doing a favor for a friend. Eddie Cochran is in love but the lady's daughter, Liz, is in big trouble. Someone has taken a pornographic video of her and is demanding money. Jack quickly finds the blackmailer and retrieves the tape. But Liz knows more than she is saying. When she disappears, Jack goes to the blackmailer's apartment and finds him dead and Liz there covered in blood and high on drugs. Solving the case involves Jack with Asian gangs, designer drugs, virtual reality and an odd house with an even odder owner.

Other books you might like:
W. Glenn Duncan, *The Rafferty Series*, 1987-
Edward Mathis, *The Dan Roman Series*, 1985-
James Reasoner, *Texas Wind*, 1980
Roger L. Simon, *California Roll*, 1985
Ned White, *The Very Bad Thing*, 1990

8

Richard Abshire
Turnaround Jack (New York: Morrow, 1990)

Series: Jack Kyle

Story type: Private Detective—Male Lead

Major character(s): Jack Kyle, Detective—Private (former cop)

Time period(s): 1990s

Locale(s): Dallas, Texas

What the book is about: Hired by businessman Guy Borodin to find out if his wife is cheating on him, Dallas P.I. Jack Kyle is immediately suspicious when he calls on the client and finds a naked woman in the client's pool—supposedly his niece. From there Kyle gets involved in an international smuggling conspiracy in which it is not easy to tell who the players are.

Other books you might like:
Bill Crider, *Dead on the Island*, 1991
W. Glenn Duncan, *Rafferty's Rules*, 1987
Edward Mathis, *The Dan Roman Series*, 1985-
Robert J. Ray, *Cage of Mirrors*, 1980
James Reasoner, *Texas Wind*, 1980

9

Bronte Adams
Margin for Murder (New York: Carroll & Graf, 1993)

Story type: Amateur Detective—Female Lead

Major character(s): Aphra Colquhoun, Editor (for a book publisher)

Time period(s): 1990s

Locale(s): London, England

What the book is about: Aphra Colquhoun is a commissioning editor for Gilman Press and thinks she is doing a good job but her boss, Adrian Lynch, is hinting otherwise and what's more he's made it clear that he knows Aphra's secret past. When Aphra is found over Adrian's dead body with the murder weapon in her hand she knows she is in big trouble. The police will never believe she is innocent so she and her friends will have to discover the truth. First novel.

Other books you might like:
Robert A. Carter, *Casual Slaughters*, 1992
John Dunning, *Booked to Die*, 1992
M.K. Lorens, *Sweet Narcissus*, 1990
Jennifer Rowe, *Murder by the Book*, 1989
Elizabeth Travis, *Under the Influence*, 1989

10
Deborah Adams
All the Great Pretenders (New York: Ballantine, 1992)

Series: Kate Yancy

Story type: Amateur Detective—Female Lead

Major character(s): Kate Yancy, Innkeeper; Owen Komelecki, Photographer (psychic)

Time period(s): 1990s

Locale(s): Jesus Creek, Tennessee

What the book is about: Heiress Lynne Hampton has disappeared from the Twin Elms Inn. Between the police and reporters, Kate is being driven crazy. Now the Hampton family has hired the well-known psychic, Owen Komelecki, to investigate. Owen holds a seance, announces Lynne is dead and that he knows where the body is. Then he disappears and another man shows up saying he is Owen Komelecki. First novel.

Other books you might like:
Mary Kittredge, *Murder in Mendocino*, 1990
Janet LaPierre, *Children's Games*, 1989
Sharyn McCrumb, *The Elizabeth MacPherson Series*, 1984-
Nancy Pickard, *Bum Steer*, 1989
Gillian Roberts, *Philly Stakes*, 1989

11
George Adams
Swindle (New York: Pocket, 1989)

Story type: Amateur Detective—Male Lead

Major character(s): Charlie Byrne, Photographer (high-fashion); Henry Stein, Con Artist

Time period(s): 1980s

Locale(s): New York, New York

What the book is about: When someone swindles Charlie's friend out of $50,000, he decides to help her get it back. This is Adams' first mystery.

Other books you might like:
William Bayer, *Blind Side*, 1989
Liza Bennett, *Madison Avenue Murder*, 1989
Lary Crews, *Extreme Close-up*, 1989
Donald E. Westlake, *God Save the Mark*, 1967
Robert Winder, *No Admission*, 1988

12
Harold Adams
The Ditched Blonde (New York: Walker, 1995)

Series: Carl Wilcox

Story type: Amateur Detective—Male Lead; Historical

Major character(s): Carl Wilcox, Businessman (odd-job fellow; painter)

Time period(s): 1930s

Locale(s): Greenhill, South Dakota

What the book is about: Carl finds himself in Greenhill, South Dakota, where he gets involved in a four-year-old unsolved murder case, this time with the approval of the local constabulary. The pregnant teenager who was killed still has a hold over some of the boys and men in town. But someone doesn't want the truth discovered.

Other books you might like:
Bill Crider, *The Sheriff Dan Rhodes Series*, 1986-
Terence Faherty, *Live to Regret*, 1992
Vince Kohler, *Rainy North Woods*, 1990
Troy Soos, *Murder at Ebbets Field*, 1995

13
Harold Adams
The Man Who Missed the Party (New York: Mysterious Press, 1989)

Series: Carl Wilcox

Story type: Amateur Detective—Male Lead

Major character(s): Carl Wilcox, Hotel Worker (ne'er-do-well)

Time period(s): 1930s (1934)

Locale(s): Corden, South Dakota

What the book is about: When the 1924 Corden High School football team gathers for its ten year reunion, murder strikes.

Other books you might like:
Robert Campbell, *Red Cent*, 1989
A.B. Guthrie Jr., *No Second Wind*, 1980
Doug Hornig, *Waterman*, 1987
David Stout, *Carolina Skeletons*, 1988
Ted Wood, *Live Bait*, 1985

14
Harold Adams
A Perfectly Proper Murder (New York: Walker, 1993)

Series: Carl Wilcox

Story type: Amateur Detective—Male Lead; Historical

15

Major character(s): Carl Wilcox, Businessman (sign painter; ne'er-do-well)

Time period(s): 1930s

Locale(s): Podunkville, South Dakota

What the book is about: As sign painting has dried up a bit in Carl Wilcox's hometown of Corden, he has moved his base of operations to Podunkville. No sooner does he arrive in town and start to solicit business than the local bully turns up dead next to Carl's car. Initially Carl is the prime suspect as he had a run-in with the fellow soon after arrival, but eventually it becomes clear that he is innocent and the local law asks for his assistance in finding out what really happened. With time out for romancing the Widow Bower, Carl does just that.

Other books you might like:
Bill Crider, *The Sheriff Dan Rhodes Series*, 1986-
Mary Daheim, *The Alpine Advocate*, 1992
Vince Kohler, *Rainy North Woods*, 1990
James Reasoner, *Texas Wind*, 1980

15

Lydia Adamson
A Cat in a Glass House (New York: Signet, 1993)

Series: Alice Nestleton

Story type: Amateur Detective—Female Lead

Major character(s): Alice Nestleton, Actress (part-time cat sitter)

Time period(s): 1990s

Locale(s): New York, New York

What the book is about: Alice is dining with her agent in a trendy Chinese restaurant when gunmen show up and start shooting. When it's over a young waitress is dead. What intrigues Alice even more is the glimpse of a beautiful red cat that disappears and no one will admit to knowing anything about. She and an Asian detective become involved in more than mystery solving as they try to find out who and why.

Other books you might like:
Lilian Jackson Braun, *The Cat Who Series*, 1966-
Rita Mae Brown, *Wish You Were Here*, 1990
Jane Dentinger, *First Hit of the Season*, 1984
Gillian B. Farrell, *Alibi for an Actress*, 1993
Dorian Yeager, *Cancellation by Death*, 1992

16

Lydia Adamson
A Cat in Fine Style (New York: Signet, 1995)

Series: Alice Nestleton

Story type: Amateur Detective—Female Lead

Major character(s): Alice Nestleton, Actress (part-time cat sitter)

Time period(s): 1990s

Locale(s): New York, New York

What the book is about: Alice has been offered a job by two cat-sitting clients to pose in lingerie for some high-fashion photographs. The scene of the shoot is a Soho loft and Alice is wondering how she got talked into this when she finds one of the loft's owners dead in the kitchen. He apparently died of an allergic reaction to almonds. However, he knew he had this allergy and had prepared the food himself, so what gives? His wife thinks it's murder and asks Alice to investigate.

Other books you might like:
Lilian Jackson Braun, *The Cat Who Series*, 1966-
Jane Dentinger, *The Queen Is Dead*, 1994
Selma Eichler, *Murder Can Kill Your Social Life*, 1994
Gillian B. Farrell, *Murder and a Muse*, 1994
Dorian Yeager, *Eviction by Death*, 1993

17

Lydia Adamson
A Cat in the Manger (New York: Signet, 1990)

Series: Alice Nestleton

Story type: Amateur Detective—Female Lead

Major character(s): Alice Nestleton, Actress (cat owner)

Time period(s): 1990s (1990)

Locale(s): Long Island, New York

What the book is about: When Alice Nestleton arrives to catsit on a Long Island estate, she finds the estate's owner dead. This is Adamson's first mystery.

Other books you might like:
Lilian Jackson Braun, *The Cat Who Series*, 1966-
Rita Mae Brown, *Wish You Were Here*, 1990
Kay Hooper, *Crime of Passion*, 1991
Susan Conant, *A New Leash on Death*, 1990
Barbara Moore, *The Doberman Wore Black*, 1984

18

Lydia Adamson
A Cat in the Wings (New York: Signet, 1992)

Series: Alice Nestleton

Story type: Amateur Detective—Female Lead

Major character(s): Alice Nestleton, Actress

Time period(s): 1990s

Locale(s): New York, New York

What the book is about: The shooting death of a former famous ballet dancer turned derelict sends Alice behind the scenes in the ballet world. One of her friends, who is one of the dead man's former lovers, is arrested for the murder. Alice is hired by the woman's attorney to investigate because of her past successes.

Other books you might like:
Carole Berry, *Good Night, Sweet Prince*, 1990
Edgar Box, *Death in the Fifth Position*, 1952
Lucy Cores, *Corpse de Ballet*, 1941
Diana Ramsay, *Four Steps to Death*, 1990

19

Lydia Adamson
A Cat in Wolf's Clothing (New York: Signet, 1991)
Series: Alice Nestleton
Story type: Amateur Detective—Female Lead
Major character(s): Alice Nestleton, Actress (expert on cats)
Time period(s): 1990s
Locale(s): New York, New York
What the book is about: Alice has established herself as an expert on cats and crime. This time the police seek her out. They need her help. Two brothers have been murdered and the police computer has indicated that this may be the latest in a series of killings going back fifteen years. The only common denominator is that all the victims owned cats and there was always a toy mouse left at the crime scene.
Other books you might like:
Lilian Jackson Braun, *The Cat Who Series*, 1966-
Rita Mae Brown, *Wish You Were Here*, 1990
Jeffrey Wilds Deaver, *Manhattan Is My Beat*, 1989
Jane Dentinger, *Death Mask*, 1989
Kay Hooper, *Crime of Passion*, 1991

20

Lydia Adamson
A Cat on the Cutting Edge (New York: Signet, 1994)
Series: Alice Nestleton
Story type: Amateur Detective—Female Lead
Major character(s): Alice Nestleton, Actress (cat-sitter)
Time period(s): 1990s
Locale(s): New York, New York
What the book is about: Alice Nestleton is having trouble with one of her cats so she contacts the Village Cat People for help. When the help arrives it's in the shape of a young woman, who has her throat slashed and dies on Alice's doorstep. She is asked to use her crime-solving abilities to help find the killer, but she is reluctant. Another killing gets Alice involved—too involved—and may threaten her and her niece, Allison.
Other books you might like:
Lilian Jackson Braun, *The Cat Who Series*, 1966-
Rita Mae Brown, *The Mrs. Murphy Series*, 1990-
Carole Nelson Douglas, *The Midnight Louie Series*, 1992-
Gillian B. Farrell, *Alibi for an Actress*, 1993
Dorian Yeager, *Cancellation by Death*, 1992

21

Lydia Adamson
Dr. Nightingale Goes the Distance (New York: Signet, 1995)
Series: Dr. Nightingale
Story type: Amateur Detective—Female Lead
Major character(s): Deirdre "Didi" Quinn Nightingale, Veterinarian; Allie Voegler, Police Officer (deputy)
Time period(s): 1990s
Locale(s): Hillsbrook, New York
What the book is about: Didi Nightingale has been invited to the social event of the year, the gala at Avignon Horse Farms celebrating the start of the summer racing season. At the party, Dr. Samuel Hull, a respected horse veterinarian, commits suicide after drugging a race horse. The owner of the farm asks Didi to investigate; her fee is to be beautiful horse. Soon, however, the owner is brutally murdered. Didi has her job cut out for her—find a murderer and protect the horses.
Other books you might like:
Virginia Anderson, *Blood Lies*, 1989
L.L. Blackmur, *Love Lies Slain*, 1989
Laura Crum, *Cutter*, 1994
Mary Willis Walker, *Zero at the Bone*, 1991
Karen Ann Wilson, *The Samantha Holt Series*, 1994-

22

Lydia Adamson
Dr. Nightingale Rides the Elephant (New York: Signet, 1994)
Series: Dr. Nightingale
Story type: Amateur Detective—Female Lead
Major character(s): Deirdre "Didi" Quinn Nightingale, Veterinarian; Allie Voegler, Police Officer
Time period(s): 1990s
Locale(s): Hillsbrook, New York
What the book is about: Didi Nightingale is finally getting used to being back in Hillsbrook, the rural community where she grew up. Now she is contemplating joining the circus—or at least being their vet while they are in town. But on her first visit, she witnesses an elephant crush one of the young dancers to death. This is followed by the suicide of the elephant trainer. Several other strange incidents follow. Didi begins to suspect that all is not as it seems under the big top. Adamson also writes a series about Alice Nestleton.
Other books you might like:
Mary Daheim, *The Emma Lord Series*, 1992-
Joan Hess, *The Maggody Series*, 1987-
Leslie Meier, *Mail-Order Murder*, 1991
Patricia Houck Sprinkle, *Somebody's Dead in Snellville*, 1992
Mary Willis Walker, *Zero at the Bone*, 1991

23

Thomas Adcock
Drown All the Dogs (New York: Pocket, 1994)
Series: Neil Hockaday
Story type: Action/Adventure
Major character(s): Neil Hockaday, Police Officer; Ruby Flagg, Actress (Neil's lover)
Time period(s): 1990s
Locale(s): New York, New York; Dublin, Ireland

24

What the book is about: Neil Hockaday is off to Dublin to visit his uncle, who is rumored to be dying. Neil wants his lady friend, Ruby Flagg, to meet his family and maybe help him learn more about his father, who disappeared in World War II. Before leaving, Neil talks to his "rabbi," NYPD Captain Davy Mogaill and his priest, Father Kelly. Soon after their arrival in Ireland, Neil and Ruby are witnesses to a murder, then Neil learns that Father Kelly has committed suicide and Davy has disappeared. There seems to be a connection between the events in New York and the murder in Ireland. What started out to be a pleasant vacation is turning into something else.

Other books you might like:
Sheila MacGill Callahan, *Death in a Far Country*, 1993
Norman Flood, *To Killashea*, 1990
Bartholomew Gill, *The McGarr Series*, 1977-
Ken Gross, *Hell Bent*, 1992

24

Jack Adrian, Editor
Detective Stories from the Strand (New York: Oxford University Press, 1992)

Story type: Anthology

What the book is about: A collection of short fiction, all published by the *Strand Magazine*, noted mostly for publishing the Sherlock Holmes short stories. There was much more detective fiction published in their pages, as this anthology attests. Authors include Agatha Christie, Maugham, Huxley, Wallace, Chesterton and many others not as well known.

Other books you might like:
Hugh Greene, *The Rivals of Sherlock Holmes*, 1970
Alan Russell, *The Rivals of Sherlock Holmes*, 1979

25

Catherine Aird
The Body Politic (New York: Doubleday, 1991)

Series: C.D. Sloan

Story type: Police Procedural—Male Lead

Major character(s): C.D. Sloan, Police Officer (detective inspector C.I.D.)

Time period(s): 1990s

Locale(s): East Berebury Calleshire, England

What the book is about: Alan Ottershaw is an embarrassment. While working in the Sheikdom of Lassera he was involved in a traffic accident. Unless he is returned Lassera will nationalize all British holdings, cutting off the supply of the rare mineral, queremite. Fortunately, while taking part in a reenactment of the Battle of Lewes, Ottershaw falls dead—fortunately for all but C.D. Sloan. When Ottershaw is cremated, a hollow pellet made of queremite is discovered. Was Ottershaw murdered and how can Sloan prove it?

Other books you might like:
Colin Dexter, *The Inspector Morse Series*, 1975-
Martha Grimes, *The Old Fox Deceiv'd*, 1982
Mary Monica Pulver, *Murder at the War*, 1987
Dorothy Simpson, *The Inspector Luke Thanet Series*, 1981-
Susannah Stacey, *Goodbye, Nanny Gray*, 1988

26

Marvin Albert
The Riviera Contract (New York: Fawcett, 1993)

Series: Stone Angel

Story type: Private Detective—Male Lead

Major character(s): Pete Sawyer, Detective—Private (French-born, raised in the US)

Time period(s): 1990s

Locale(s): The Riviera, France

What the book is about: Pete Sawyer has been hired to find Sandrine Tally, a beautiful and famous courtesan of the Riviera. What he finds is the body of a dead man in her bedroom. It seems obvious that Sandrine is the killer, although it may have been self-defense. Pete becomes involved with deposed dictators, death squads and mercenaries, all looking for Sandrine. Can Pete find her before she is killed?

Other books you might like:
Jack Barnao, *The John Locke Series*, 1987-
Peter Corris, *The Cliff Hardy Series*, 1980-
Miles Tripp, *The John Samson Series*, 1973-

27

Marvin Albert
The Zig-Zag Man (New York: Fawcett, 1991)

Series: Stone Angel

Story type: Private Detective—Male Lead

Major character(s): Pete Sawyer, Detective—Private

Time period(s): 1990s

Locale(s): Cote D'Azur, France

What the book is about: When Helen Marsh was ten, she was kidnapped and held for ransom. In the process the kidnappers cut off two of her fingers. The only clue she had was the voice of the kidnapper. Now, eight years later, she has heard the voice again. She wants Pete to find out the identity of the man and prove he was the kidnapper. The investigation will lead Pete to an international drug cartel and worse.

Other books you might like:
Peter Corris, *The Cliff Hardy Series*, 1980-
Philip Kerr, *March Violets*, 1989
John Milne, *Dead Birds*, 1986
Paco Ignacio Taibo II, *An Easy Thing*, 1990
Miles Tripp, *The John Samson Series*, 1973-

28

Neil Albert
Burning March (New York: Dutton, 1994)

Series: Dave Garrett

Story type: Private Detective—Male Lead

Major character(s): Dave Garrett, Detective—Private (ex-lawyer)

Time period(s): 1990s

Locale(s): Philadelphia, Pennsylvania

What the book is about: Dave Garrett has been called by Emily Voss, the bookkeeper of his old law firm, who hints that something is wrong. When Dave arrives for his appointment, he finds that Emily has died in a mysterious apartment fire. Dave's old friend and the firm's senior partner asks him to continue the investigation. If something is wrong, he wants to know it. Someone else will do anything to stop that from happening.

Other books you might like:
Stephen Greenleaf, *The John Marshall Tanner Series*, 1979-
Jeremiah Healy, *The John Francis Cuddy Series*, 1985-
Frederick D. Huebner, *The Matt Riordan Series*, 1986-
Benjamin M. Schutz, *The Leo Haggerty Series*, 1984-
William G. Tapply, *The Brady Coyne Series*, 1983-

29
Neil Albert
Cruel April (New York: Dutton, 1995)
Series: Dave Garrett
Story type: Private Detective—Male Lead
Major character(s): Dave Garrett, Detective—Private, Lawyer (disbarred)
Time period(s): 1990s
Locale(s): Philadelphia, Pennsylvania

What the book is about: Dave Garrett is finally going to be reunited with Kate McMahan, a woman he met and fell in love with on a previous case. She says she is leaving her husband and flying to meet him. However when the plane arrives, Kate is a no show. She was seen leaving with a mysterious couple and Garrett realizes she has been kidnapped. With Kate's husband in the background urging him on, Dave follows a trail of violence and death, hoping that Kate's body isn't at the end.

Other books you might like:
Stephen Greenleaf, *The John Marshall Tanner Series*, 1979-
Jeremiah Healy, *The John Francis Cuddy Series*, 1984-
Arthur Lyons, *The Jacob Asch Series*, 1974-
Benjamin M. Schutz, *The Leo Haggerty Series*, 1984
Jonathan Valin, *The Harry Stoner Series*, 1980-

30
Neil Albert
The February Trouble (New York: Walker, 1992)
Series: Dave Garrett
Story type: Private Detective—Male Lead
Major character(s): Dave Garrett, Detective—Private (ex-lawyer)
Time period(s): 1990s
Locale(s): Lancaster, Pennsylvania

What the book is about: Garrett has been hired to provide security for a new franchise fast-food Chinese restaurant that seems to be having more than its share of problems. Garrett is suspicious because the corporation has its own security force but needs the money. More sabotage is attempted and then the owner's wife is kidnapped and her next door neighbor and good friend is killed.

Other books you might like:
Stephen Greenleaf, *The John Marshall Tanner Series*, 1979-
Jeremiah Healy, *The John Francis Cuddy Series*, 1985-
Arthur Lyons, *The Jacob Asch Series*, 1974-
Benjamin M. Schutz, *The Leo Haggerty Series*, 1984-
Jonathan Valin, *The Harry Stoner Series*, 1980-

31
Neil Albert
The January Corpse (New York: Walker, 1991)
Series: Dave Garrett
Story type: Private Detective—Male Lead
Major character(s): Dave Garrett, Detective—Private (disbarred lawyer)
Time period(s): 1990s
Locale(s): Philadelphia, Pennsylvania

What the book is about: Garrett is hired by the Wilson family's attorney to try and prove that David Wilson, who disappeared seven years ago, is either dead or alive. A court hearing is in three days and the family wants the matter settled, one way or another. However, before Garrett even gets started, he is threatened to stay off the case. Why? And does the threat extend to Wilson's sister Lisa who has secrets of her own? First novel.

Other books you might like:
Stephen Greenleaf, *Book Case*, 1991
Frederick D. Huebner, *The Matt Riordan Series*, 1986
Arthur Lyons, *The Jacob Asch Series*, 1977
William G. Tapply, *Spotted Cats*, 1991
Jonathan Valin, *The Harry Stoner Series*, 1981-

32
Susan Wittig Albert
Hangman's Root (New York: Scribners, 1994)
Series: China Bayles
Story type: Amateur Detective—Female Lead
Major character(s): China Bayles, Businesswoman (ex-lawyer); Mike McQuaid, Teacher (of criminology; China's lover)
Time period(s): 1990s
Locale(s): Pecan Springs, Texas

What the book is about: China Bayles has witnessed the hatred Frank Harwick has for Dottie Riddle. Frank and Dottie are rivals in the university biology department; Dottie is an animal rights activist and Frank wants to establish an animal research lab. When Frank is found hanged, Dottie is the prime suspect. She asks China to help prove her innocence. China is also being pressured by her lover, Mike McQuaid, to—as he romantically puts it—"fish or cut bait".

Other books you might like:
Claudia Bishop, *A Taste for Murder*, 1994
Carol Brennan, *The Liz Wareham Series*, 1992-
Diane Mott Davidson, *Dying for Chocolate*, 1992
Patricia Houck Sprinkle, *The Sheila Travis Series*, 1988-
Judith Van Gieson, *The Wolf Path*, 1992

33
Susan Wittig Albert
Thyme of Death (New York: Scribners, 1992)
Story type: Amateur Detective—Female Lead
Major character(s): China Bayles, Businesswoman (owner of a herb shop); Ruby Wilcox, Businesswoman (owner of New Age shop)
Time period(s): 1990s; 4th century (B.C.)
Locale(s): Pecan Springs, Texas
What the book is about: China Bayles, once a high-powered lawyer, opts for the quiet life so she moves to a small town and opens an herb shop. Now a close friend, Jo Gilbert, has been found dead. Since she was dying of cancer, the police rule it a suicide. China and her friend Ruby are not so sure. Jo had political enemies for her fight against a new airport and she had a collection of letters that people are anxious to get back - especially Jo's friend, Roz. Was it murder and if so, can China and Ruby prove it? First novel.
Other books you might like:
Muriel Resnick Jackson, *The Garden Club*, 1992
Marlys Millhiser, *Murder at Moot Point*, 1992
Yvonne Montgomery, *Scavengers*, 1987
B.J. Oliphant, *Death and the Delinquent*, 1993
Judith Van Gieson, *The Other Side of Death*, 1991

34
Gary Alexander
Kiet Goes West (New York: St. Martin's, 1992)
Series: Bamsan Kiet
Story type: Police Procedural—Male Lead
Major character(s): Bamsan Kiet, Police Officer (superintendent); Bihn, Police Officer (captain)
Time period(s): 1990s
Locale(s): Seattle, Washington
What the book is about: The Southeast Asian country of Luong has lost 20 million dollars in a computer swindle. Bihn was sent to the U.S. to arrest the hacker who stole the money. Now Kiet is sent to the U.S. to help Bihn who is being sought for the murder of the thief and for attacking Donald Duck at Disneyland—obviously the more serious crime.
Other books you might like:
Carl Hiaasen, *Native Tongue*, 1991
H.R.F. Keating, *The Inspector Ghote Series*, 1964-
William Marshall, *Yellowthread Street*, 1976-

35
Gary Alexander
Unfunny Money (New York: Walker, 1989)
Series: Bamsan Kiet
Story type: Police Procedural—Male Lead
Major character(s): Bamsan Kiet, Police Officer
Time period(s): 1980s
Locale(s): Luong, Fictional Country

What the book is about: Someone is counterfeiting Luonganian currency and Kiet must find out why.
Other books you might like:
K.P. Bahadur, *Murder in the Dehli Mail*, 1976
Lawrence G. Blochman, *Red Snow at Darjeeling*, 1938
H.R.F. Keating, *The Inspector Ghote Series*, 1964
William Marshall, *Yellowthread Street*, 1976
B.N. Sidwa, *The Crow Eaters*, 1981

36
Lawrence Alexander
The Strenuous Life (New York: Knightsbridge, 1991)
Series: Theodore Roosevelt
Story type: Historical
Major character(s): Theodore Roosevelt, Historical Figure (police commissioner, New York)
Time period(s): 1890s (1895)
Locale(s): New York, New York; Fort Sill, Oklahoma
What the book is about: Trying to deal with John D. Rockefeller, Geronimo and the Marquis de Mores while worrying about a theft at the armory brings Teddy Roosevelt all kinds of grief.
Other books you might like:
William L. DeAndrea, *The Lunatic Fringe*, 1980
Brian Garfield, *Manifest Destiny*, 1989
H. Paul Jeffers, *The Adventure of the Stalwart Companions*, 1978
Robert J. Randisi, *The Ham Reporter*, 1986
James Sherburne, *Death's Clenched Fist*, 1983

37
Ted Allbeury
The Lantern Network (New York: Mysterious, 1989)
Story type: Espionage
Major character(s): Nick Bailey, Spy (intelligence officer); Charles Parker, Spy (resistance worker)
Time period(s): 1980s; 1940s
What the book is about: The suicide of a non-descript Englishman has its roots buried in the French resistance during World War II.
Other books you might like:
Eric Ambler, *Epitaph for a Spy*, 1952
R. Wright Campbell, *The Spy Who Sat and Waited*, 1975
Brian Garfield, *The Paladin*, 1980
Bill Granger, *The British Cross*, 1983
Jack Higgins, *The Eagle Has Landed*, 1975

38
Ted Allbeury
A Time Without Shadows (New York: Mysterious, 1991)
Story type: Espionage; Historical

Major character(s): Philip Maclean, Military Personnel (fighting with the resistance); Harry Chapman, Spy (investigator for MI6)

Time period(s): 1940s; 1980s (alternates between time periods)

Locale(s): France; England

What the book is about: Harry Chapman, MI6 investigator, is asked to look into allegations that to keep Stalin happy, Churchill compromised a network of spies working with the French underground during WWII. The repercussions on Britain today could be staggering but what happened to the people involved is what really touches Harry deeply.

Other books you might like:
Len Deighton, *SS-GB*, 1979
Brian Garfield, *The Paladin*, 1980
Bill Granger, *The British Cross*, 1986
John Le Carre, *The Russia House*, 1989
Anthony Price, *Sion Crossing*, 1985

39
Michael Allegretto
Blood Relative (New York: Scribners, 1992)

Series: Jacob Lomax

Story type: Private Detective—Male Lead

Major character(s): Jacob Lomax, Detective—Private

Time period(s): 1990s

Locale(s): Denver, Colorado

What the book is about: Jake has just come back from vacation and needs money. Otherwise he would never have taken the case. He is hired to find three witnesses that might clear Samuel Butler, accused of murdering his beautiful but unfaithful wife. Jake thinks Butler is guilty, but as he starts to investigate, he realizes that somebody doesn't want Butler cleared and will do anything to see he is convicted.

Other books you might like:
Rex Burns, *Parts Unknown*, 1990
Earl Emerson, *The Thomas Black Series*, 1985-
William J. Reynolds, *The Nebraska Series*, 1984-
Les Roberts, *The Milan Jacovich Series*, 1988-
Jonathan Valin, *The Harry Stoner Series*, 1980-

40
Michael Allegretto
The Dead of Winter (New York: Scribners, 1989)

Series: Jacob Lomax

Story type: Private Detective—Male Lead

Major character(s): Jacob Lomax, Detective—Private

Time period(s): 1980s

Locale(s): Denver, Colorado

What the book is about: Joseph Bellano, bookie, hires Lomax to find his daughter. Soon Bellano is killed, but Lomax chooses to stay on the case.

Other books you might like:
Rex Burns, *The Alvarez Journal*, 1975
Jack Early, *A Creative Kind of Killer*, 1984
Jeremiah Healy, *Yesterday's News*, 1989
Robert B. Parker, *Promised Land*, 1976
Robert J. Randisi, *No Exit From Brooklyn*, 1987

41
Michael Allegretto
Grave Doubt (New York: Carroll & Graf, 1995)

Series: Jacob Lomax

Story type: Private Detective—Male Lead

Major character(s): Jacob Lomax, Detective—Private

Time period(s): 1990s

Locale(s): Denver, Colorado

What the book is about: Jake is asked by Roger Armis for help. Roger and his wife Vivian are being blackmailed by Vivian's former husband. The real problem is that the husband has been dead for four years. Did he fake his own death or is someone else being clever. Jake's investigation involves him with a powerful televangelist and organized crime. Apparently when the husband vanished so did a lot of money and someone is willing to kill to get it back.

Other books you might like:
Rex Burns, *Parts Unknown*, 1990
Loren D. Estleman, *The Amos Walker Series*, 1983-
R.R. Irvine, *Pillar of Fire*, 1995
Les Roberts, *The Milan Jacovich Series*, 1988-
Walter Satterthwait, *A Flower in the Desert*, 1992

42
Michael Allegretto
Night of Reunion (New York: Scribners, 1990)

Story type: Psychological Suspense

Major character(s): Christine Helstrum, Criminal (escapee from an asylum); Sarah Whitaker, Businesswoman (owner of a beauty salon)

Time period(s): 1980s

Locale(s): Colorado

What the book is about: Years ago Christine Helstrum killed Alex Whitaker's first wife and adopted son. Now she's escaped and is on her way to injure his current family.

Other books you might like:
Jay Brandon, *Predator's Waltz*, 1989
Charlaine Harris, *A Secret Rage*, 1984
John Katzenbach, *Day of Reckoning*, 1989
Sharyn McCrumb, *If Ever I Return, Pretty Peggy-O*, 1990

43
Michael Allegretto
The Suitor (New York: Simon & Schuster, 1992)

Story type: Psychological Suspense

Major character(s): Valerie Rowe, Artist (painter), Single Parent (divorced); Leonard Tully, Antiques Dealer

Time period(s): 1990s

Locale(s): Denver, Colorado

What the book is about: When Valerie Rowe has her purse stolen, Leonard Tully inadvertantly helps stop the thief. When Valerie treats him to lunch to thank him, Leonard takes this act of kindness as a sign of romantic interest. Leonard begins a campaign of harassment that leads to innocent people being hurt and makes Valerie fear for her life.

Other books you might like:
Gary Amo, *Silent Night*, 1991
Mary Higgins Clark, *Loves Music, Loves to Dance*, 1991
Diane Johnson, *The Shadow Knows*, 1974
Patricia MacDonald, *Stranger in the House*, 1983

44
Michael Allegretto
The Watchman (New York: Simon & Schuster, 1991)

Story type: Action/Adventure; Psychological Suspense

Major character(s): Lauren Caylor, Architect (landscape); Richard Caylor, Businessman

Time period(s): 1990s

Locale(s): San Miguel, California

What the book is about: Lauren, divorcee and mother of five-year old Emily has recently remarried. She is successful and happy, but strange things start to happen. Why doesn't anybody know or even see the new neighbors across the street? Why does Lauren keep seeing the same person everywhere she goes? Why is Richard acting so scared and lying about his past?

Other books you might like:
Mary Higgins Clark, *A Cry in the Night*, 1983
Caroline Crane, *The Girls Are Missing*, 1980
Susan Trott, *The Housewife and the Assassin*, 1979

45
Irene Allen
Quaker Silence (New York: Villard, 1992)

Series: Elizabeth Elliot

Story type: Amateur Detective—Female Lead

Major character(s): Elizabeth Elliot, Widow(er) (Quaker)

Time period(s): 1990s

Locale(s): Cambridge, Massachusetts

What the book is about: Elizabeth Elliot has just been elected to be Clerk of the Meeting of Friends of Cambridge. At one of the meetings, a time of quiet meditation and prayer, John Hoffman announces that he is changing his will and leaving his estate to charity. Soon after he is found dead in his garden. The police concentrate on a homeless man who worked on and off for Hoffman and had an argument with him not long before he died. Elizabeth knows other people including his relatives and gay activists had motives - can she find the truth? First novel.

Other books you might like:
Richard Barth, *The Margaret Binton Series*, 1978-
Dorothy Gilman, *The Mrs. Pollifax Series*, 1966-
Robert Nordan, *All Dressed Up to Die*, 1989
David Osborn, *Murder on the Chesapeake*, 1992
James Yaffe, *The Mom Series*, 1987-

46
Irene Allen
Quaker Witness (New York: Villard, 1993)

Series: Elizabeth Elliot

Story type: Amateur Detective—Female Lead

Major character(s): Elizabeth Elliot, Religious (clerk of the Quaker meeting), Widow(er); Janet Stevens, Student

Time period(s): 1990s

Locale(s): Cambridge, Massachusetts

What the book is about: Janet Stevens, graduate student in paleontology at Harvard, has put up with an escalating campaign of sexual harassment from her advisor, Professor Chadwick. Finally she files a complaint and, seeking peace, finds her way to the Quaker Meeting. Elizabeth is sympathetic and tries to help. When Chadwick is murdered, Janet is the chief suspect and Elizabeth is determined to find the truth but Harvard seems determined to cover up the entire affair.

Other books you might like:
Eleanor Boylan, *The Clara Gamadge Series*, 1989-
Robert Nordan, *The Mavis Lashley Series*, 1989-
David Osborn, *The Margaret Barlow Series*, 1990-
Jennifer Rowe, *Grim Pickings*, 1988
John Sherwood, *The Celia Grant Series*, 1984-

47
Douglas Allyn
The Cheerio Killings (New York: St. Martin's, 1989)

Story type: Police Procedural—Female Lead

Major character(s): Lupe Garcia, Detective—Police; Lamont Yarborough, Musician (guitar player)

Time period(s): 1980s

Locale(s): Detroit, Michigan

What the book is about: A serial killer is murdering women and Lupe Garcia is assigned to the case. She fixates on guitarist Yarborough who plays at a tavern near the site of the killings. First book.

Other books you might like:
Katherine V. Forrest, *The Beverly Malibu*, 1989
Margaret Maron, *Baby Doll Games*, 1988
Lee Martin, *Deficit Ending*, 1990
Lillian O'Donnell, *A Good Night to Kill*, 1988
L.V. Sims, *Murder Is Only Skin Deep*, 1987

48
Douglas Allyn
Icewater Mansions (New York: St. Martin's, 1995)

Story type: Action/Adventure; Amateur Detective

Major character(s): Michelle "Mitch" Mitchell, Worker (underwater construction), Single Parent

Time period(s): 1990s

Locale(s): Huron Harbor, Michigan

What the book is about: Michelle "Mitch" Mitchell is back in Huron Harbor from the Gulf oil rigs to settle the affairs of her father who recently died under mysterious circumstances. At first she only wants to sell everything and get out, but while resurrecting his rundown bar and tackle shop, she finds herself thinking of settling down. First she has to settle with the people who had some deal going with her father involving illegal salvage. They think she knows something and will stop at nothing to find out what she knows.

Other books you might like:
Sarah Andrews, *Tensleep*, 1994
Nevada Barr, *Track of the Cat*, 1993
Tony Gibbs, *Landfall*, 1992
Dana Stabenow, *The Kate Shugak Series*, 1992-
Dorian Yeager, *Murder Will Out*, 1994

49
Gary Amo
Silent Night (New York: Pinnacle, 1991)

Story type: Psychological Suspense

Major character(s): Cassandra Morgan, Journalist (television anchor); Simon Bartlett, Criminal

Time period(s): 1990s

Locale(s): Phoenix, Arizona

What the book is about: Cassandra is covering a serial killer story and the serial killer is stalking her. Nominated for MWA best novel.

Other books you might like:
Mary Higgins Clark, *Loves Music, Loves to Dance*, 1991
Patricia D. Cornwell, *Postmortem*, 1990
Frank De Felitta, *Funeral March*, 1991
David L. Lindsey, *Mercy*, 1990
Nicholas Sarazen, *Family Reunion*, 1990

50
Douglas Anderson
First and Ten (New York: Crown, 1993)

Story type: Amateur Detective—Male Lead; Action/Adventure

Major character(s): Santa Arkwright, Sports Figure (professional football player); Cramer McKenzie, Art Dealer

Time period(s): 1990s

Locale(s): Buffalo, New York

What the book is about: Santa Arkwright is a veteran football player for the Buffalo Bills but he is not doing much playing these days—the players are on strike and tempers are getting short. Santa gets a cryptic note that seems to suggest that if he doesn't end the strike people will die. He doesn't take it seriously at first, but then his teammates and friends start to die. Among those who seem to be involved on one level or another are the daughter of an ex-girlfriend, a journalism professor and a doctor. All have secrets of some sort, but why would any of them be killing off football players? First mystery.

Other books you might like:
Paul Engleman, *Dead in Center Field*, 1983
Dave Klein, *Blind Side*, 1980
John Stephen Strange, *Murder on the Ten-Yard Line*, 1931
Fran Tarkenton, *Murder at the Superbowl*, 1982
Jonathan Valin, *Life's Work*, 1986

51
Jack Albin Anderson
The Society Ball Murders (New York: Walker, 1990)

Story type: Amateur Detective—Female Lead

Major character(s): Patty Nottingham, Journalist (society columnist); Rex Murphy, Musician (professional pianist), Boyfriend (of Patty)

Time period(s): 1990s (1990)

Locale(s): San Francisco, California

What the book is about: A woman is found dead at a society ball and Patty Nottingham doesn't believe it was an accident. When there is another death at another ball it appears she was right. This is Anderson's first novel.

Other books you might like:
Joyce Christmas, *Suddenly in Her Sorbet*, 1988
Gloria Dank, *Friends till the End*, 1989
Jacqueline Girdner, *Adjusted to Death*, 1990
Gabrielle Kraft, *Screwdriver*, 1988
Susan Wolfe, *The Last Billable Hour*, 1989

52
Virginia Anderson
Blood Lies (New York: Bantam, 1989)

Story type: Amateur Detective—Male Lead

Major character(s): Ted Whysse, Heir, Horse Trainer

Time period(s): 1980s

Locale(s): Kentucky

What the book is about: Ted returns home, shocked to learn of the death of his friend, a jockey. A valuable horse provides the motivation for more murder.

Other books you might like:
L.L. Blackmur, *Love Lies Slain*, 1989
Dave Burkey, *Rain Lover*, 1985
Dick Francis, *Bolt*, 1986
Anne McCaffrey, *Ring of Fear*, 1971

53
Virginia Anderson
Storm Front (New York: Doubleday, 1992)

Story type: Police Procedural—Male Lead; Psychological Suspense

Major character(s): Joe Hope, Police Officer

Time period(s): 1990s

Locale(s): Florida

What the book is about: Florida lawman Joe Hope is part of a task force assigned to find the "sinkhole killer", a serial murderer who has killed at least fourteen women.

Other books you might like:
Thomas Harris, *Red Dragon*, 1981
John Katzenbach, *In the Heat of the Summer*, 1982
John Leslie, *Killer in Paradise*, 1990
David L. Lindsey, *A Cold Mind*, 1983
Ridley Pearson, *Probable Cause*, 1989

54
Christine Andreae
Grizzly (New York: St. Martin's, 1994)

Series: Lee Squires

Story type: Amateur Detective—Female Lead

Major character(s): Lee Squires, Professor (of English; part-time cook)

Time period(s): 1990s

Locale(s): Choteau, Montana

What the book is about: Lee Squires is once again out west acting as a cook, taking a break from boring English compositions. She has answered a call for help from the owners of a dude ranch where she visited every year as a child. Due to the rising costs of insurance, the ranch is in trouble and looking for a bail-out from Japanese investors who want real western cooking. The owners of the ranch are two brothers who are at odds over environmental issues. Lee is drawn to the handsome radical, Mac Fife. Then she discovers a body with no hands, feet, or head.

Other books you might like:
Nevada Barr, *Track of the Cat*, 1993
Karin McQuillan, *Deadly Safari*, 1990
Elizabeth Quinn, *Murder Most Grizzly*, 1993
Judith Van Gieson, *The Wolf Path*, 1992
Lee Wallingford, *Cold Tracks*, 1992

55
Christine Andreae
Trail of Murder (New York: St. Martin's, 1992)

Series: Lee Squires

Story type: Amateur Detective—Female Lead

Major character(s): Lee Squires, Professor (of English)

Time period(s): 1990s

Locale(s): Montana (Bob Marshall Wilderness area)

What the book is about: Lee Squires is spending a quiet summer in D.C., housesitting, when she gets an unusual offer from a friend of a friend. Would she like to be a cook on a trail ride in the Rockies? She accepts but begins to have second thoughts when she meets the people she is to cook for, a family with too many secrets. First novel.

Other books you might like:
Karin McQuillan, *Deadly Safari*, 1990
B.J. Oliphant, *Dead in the Scrub*, 1990
Nancy Pickard, *Bum Steer*, 1990
Judith Van Gieson, *Raptor*, 1990
Lee Wallingford, *Cold Tracks*, 1992

56
Sarah Andrews
A Fall in Denver (New York: Scribners, 1995)

Series: Em Hansen

Story type: Amateur Detective—Female Lead

Major character(s): Emily "Em" Hansen, Scientist (geologist)

Time period(s): 1990s

Locale(s): Denver, Colorado

What the book is about: During Em's first hour on her new job as a geologist for Blackfeet Oil a man jumps to his death. She decides to look into the suicide of the accountant who worked for a competing oil company. She finally gets an assignment that may have ties to the dead man. She also finds herself attracted to another geologist who happens to be married to an old friend. Then another co-worker falls to his death.

Other books you might like:
Carole Berry, *The Bonnie Indermill Series*, 1988-
Trella Crespi, *The Simona Griffo Series*, 1991-
Marlys Millhiser, *Death of the Office Witch*, 1993
Dianne G. Pugh, *Cold Call*, 1993
Dana Stabenow, *A Cold-Blooded Business*, 1994

57
Sarah Andrews
Tensleep (New York: Penzler, 1994)

Series: Em Hansen

Story type: Amateur Detective—Female Lead

Major character(s): Emily "Em" Hansen, Oil Industry Worker (on an oil rig); Alix Chadwick, Scientist (geologist)

Time period(s): 1990s

Locale(s): Meeteetse, Wyoming

What the book is about: Em Hansen's friend, Bil Kretzmeer, an oil company geologist, is killed in an accident that seems highly suspicious to Em. She has no proof though, and has her hands full with work, putting up with the unwanted advances of her boss, and getting to know the new geologist, the beautiful and sophisticated Alix Chadwick. Then there is another fatal accident. Something seems to be very wrong and Em wants to find out what it is. First novel.

Other books you might like:
Christine Andreae, *Trail of Murder*, 1992
B.J. Oliphant, *Dead in the Scrub*, 1990
Dana Stabenow, *A Cold-Blooded Business*, 1994
Elizabeth Atwood Taylor, *The Northwest Murders*, 1992
Lee Wallingford, *Clear-Cut Murder*, 1993

58
Jeff Andrus
Tracer, Inc. (New York: Scribners, 1994)

Story type: Private Detective—Male Lead

Major character(s): John Tracer, Detective—Private; Chris Tracer, Secretary, Spouse (John's wife); Shorty Tracer, Student (John's daughter)

Time period(s): 1990s

Locale(s): Salinas, California

What the book is about: John Tracer is hired by Anne Walker to find the runaway daughter of her housekeeper. What Anne doesn't know is that this is John's first case and that his family thinks that what he is doing is crazy. What Tracer doesn't know is that there is a lot more going on than what his client has told him, such as the involvement in the case of drug dealers and a psychotic killer. Reluctantly his family pitches in to help him solve the big case but it may put them all in danger. First novel.

Other books you might like:
Rick Boyer, *Yellow Bird*, 1991
L.L. Enger, *Swing*, 1991
Jon Katz, *Death by Station Wagon*, 1993
Michael Z. Lewin, *And Baby Will Fall*, 1990

59
John Angus
The Monster Squad (New York: St. Martin's, 1994)

Story type: Police Procedural—Female Lead

Major character(s): Caitlin O'Neil, Police Officer

Time period(s): 1990s

Locale(s): Madison, Oregon

What the book is about: Caitlin O'Neil was a Los Angeles vice cop for six years until she decked her boss for making unwanted sexual suggestions. Now she is moving to Oregon to work for a semi-rural sheriff's department. She thinks it will be easy after Los Angeles vice until she is placed in charge of the "Monster Squad," the midnight shift of goof-offs and misfits. Then one of the squad is found murdered in his police car with a live but naked hooker in the trunk. First novel.

Other books you might like:
Susan Dunlap, *The Jill Smith Series*, 1981-
Catherine O'Connell, *Skins*, 1993
Jack O'Connell, *Box Nine*, 1992
Soledad Santiago, *Undercover*, 1988
James Schermerhorn, *Night of the Cat*, 1993

60
Michael David Anthony
The Becket Factor (New York: St. Martins, 1991)

Story type: Amateur Detective—Male Lead

Major character(s): Richard Harrison, Businessman (former intelligence officer)

Time period(s): 1990s

Locale(s): Canterbury, England

What the book is about: Do the death of an elderly canon and the finding of the lost remains of Thomas Becket have anything to do with the forthcoming investiture of the Archbishop of Canterbury? Is he in danger? Recently retired intelligence officer Richard Harrison must find out. First book.

Other books you might like:
Frederick Forsyth, *The Day of the Jackal*, 1974
Thomas Gifford, *The Assassini*, 1990
Isabelle Holland, *A Death at St. Anselm's*, 1984
William F. Love, *The Chartreuse Clue*, 1990
W.J. Wetherby, *Coronation*, 1990

61
Michael David Anthony
Dark Provenance (New York: St. Martin's, 1995)

Series: Richard Harrison

Story type: Action/Adventure; Amateur Detective—Male Lead

Major character(s): Richard Harrison, Aged Person (former soldier, colonel)

Time period(s): 1990s

Locale(s): Canterbury, England

What the book is about: Richard and his wife have just returned from vacation to find a lot has happened in their absence. The new Archdeacon is instituting radical cost-cutting procedures, causing a furor with everyone. Richard, as head of the Dilapidations Board responsible for building upkeep is sought as an ally by both sides. Additionally, a man who sought an appointment with Richard apparently committed suicide before they could meet. The man's daughter thinks he was murdered, and when Richard realizes that the man was a post-war colleague and expatriated Jew, he agrees to look into the death.

Other books you might like:
Kate Charles, *A Drink of Deadly Wine*, 1992
D.M. Greenwood, *Clerical Errors*, 1992
Robert Richardson, *The Latimer Mercy*, 1985
J.G. Sandom, *Gospel Truths*, 1992
Barbara Whitehead, *The Dean It Was That Died*, 1991

62
William Appel
Whisper.He Might Hear You (New York: Fine, 1991)

Series: Kate and Josh Berman

Story type: Psychological Suspense; Serial Killer

Major character(s): Kate Berman, Doctor (psychologist); Carl Nasson, Serial Killer

63
Appel

Time period(s): 1990s

Locale(s): New York, New York

What the book is about: Kate Berman used to be a consulting pyschologist for the city of New York until she was attacked. Now one of her former colleagues has asked her to come back and help catch another killer.

Other books you might like:
Marc Berrenson, *Perfection*, 1991
Patricia D. Cornwell, *Postmortem*, 1990
Frank De Felitta, *Funeral March*, 1991
Thomas Harris, *The Silence of the Lambs*, 1988
Marcel Montecino, *The Cross Killer*, 1988

63
William Appel
Widowmaker (New York: Walker, 1994)

Series: Kate and Josh Berman

Story type: Police Procedural

Major character(s): Kate Berman, Criminologist; Josh Berman, Doctor (retired medical examiner); Nina Benanti, Serial Killer, Mentally Ill Person (multiple personality)

Time period(s): 1990s

Locale(s): New York, New York

What the book is about: Their policeman friend, Casey, asks Kate and Josh Berman to help him catch a serial killer who seems to be murdering men by giving them a fatal dose of digitalis. They suspect it's a woman, but the FBI says there are no women serial killers. Nina Benanti is unaware that at times she becomes another person who delights in killing unfaithful husbands.

Other books you might like:
Patricia D. Cornwell, *The Kay Scarpetta Series*, 1990-
Rochelle Majer Krich, *Fair Game*, 1993
Marsha Landreth, *The Holiday Murders*, 1992
Paul Levine, *Night Vision*, 1991
David L. Lindsey, *Mercy*, 1991

64
Anthony Appiah
Avenging Angel (New York: St. Martin's, 1991)

Story type: Amateur Detective—Male Lead

Major character(s): Sir Patrick Scott, Lawyer (barrister)

Time period(s): 1990s

Locale(s): Cambridge, England

What the book is about: David Glen Tannock is found dead of an allergic reaction to penicillin. Sir Patrick knew and liked the young man and feels it could not be suicide or an accident. As David was a member of the "Apostles"—an exclusive society—and Sir Patrick is a former "Apostle" he is privy to facts the police are unaware of. When a second death occurs he realizes the "Apostles" may have a Judas in their midst. First novel.

Other books you might like:
Gillian Linscott, *Unknown Hand*, 1989
Dilwyn Rees, *The Cambridge Murders*, 1941
Robert Robinson, *Landscape with Dead Dons*, 1956
Dorothy L. Sayers, *Gaudy Night*, 1935
Howard Shaw, *Death of a Don*, 1981

65
John Armistead
A Homecoming for Murder (New York: Carroll & Graf, 1995)

Series: Grover Bramlet

Story type: Police Procedural—Male Lead

Major character(s): Grover Bramlet, Police Officer (sheriff)

Time period(s): 1990s

Locale(s): Sheffield, Mississippi

What the book is about: A popular high school teacher is killed and the killer was seen by two people in the area who may be able to identify him. One of the witnesses is Sheriff Bramlet's grandson. Although the boy hasn't really seen anything the killer may not be taking any chances as the other witness soon turns up dead. Meanwhile, the investigation shows that the teacher was involved in more than a few shady deals and quite a few people wanted him dead. To save his grandson, the sheriff better find out who did it—and quickly.

Other books you might like:
K.C. Constantine, *The Mario Balzac Series*, 1974-
Susan Rogers Cooper, *The Milt Kovak Series*, 1988-
Steven F. Havill, *The Sheriff Bill Gastner Series*, 1991-
D.R. Meredith, *The Sheriff Charles Matthews Series*, 1984-
Susan Oleksiw, *The Joe Silva Series*, 1993-

66
Harrison Arnston
Trade-Off (New York: Harper, 1991)

Story type: Legal; Psychological Suspense

Major character(s): Laura Scott, Lawyer (public defender); John Slocum, Defendant, Serial Killer

Time period(s): 1990s

Locale(s): Orlando, Florida

What the book is about: Laura's life is a real mess; her husband is an alcoholic, her young daughter is in a coma, and now a judge has asked her to defend a drifter accused of killing one of the best-liked girls in town. Before the case is over, Laura will be faced with the hardest decisions of her life.

Other books you might like:
Miriam Borgenicht, *Undue Influence*, 1989
Philip Friedman, *Reasonable Doubt*, 1990
Richard Harris, *Honor Bound*, 1982
Colin Harrison, *Break and Enter*, 1990
Paul Levine, *To Speak for the Dead*, 1990

67

Jeffrey Ashford (Pseudonym of Roderic Jeffries)
The Honourable Detective (New York: St. Martin's, 1989)
Story type: Police Procedural—Male Lead
Major character(s): Frederick Brice, Detective—Police (Inspector)
Time period(s): 1980s
What the book is about: When two men witness a hit and run accident, both are offered a bribe—one refuses, the other accepts.
Other books you might like:
Alan Hunter, *Gently Through the Woods*, 1975
Roderic Jeffries, *Three and One Make Five*, 1984
Elizabeth Lemarchand, *Troubled Waters*, 1982
June Thomson, *Dying Fall*, 1986
Margaret Yorke, *Intimate Kill*, 1985

68

Nancy Atherton
Aunt Dimity and the Duke (New York: Viking, 1994)
Series: Aunt Dimity
Story type: Amateur Detective—Female Lead
Major character(s): Emma Porter, Computer Expert, Gardener (amateur); Grayson Alexander, Nobleman (Duke of Penford)
Time period(s): 1990s
Locale(s): Cornwall, England
What the book is about: Emma Porter is on a tour of England after being left by her long-time boyfriend. She is guided to the Bransley manor by Aunt Dimity and the odd Pym sisters. Apparently it is her destiny to restore the manor's gardens and help find the Lady's Lantern. There are several mysteries connected with Grayson Alexander, lord of the manor. What is the source of his money? Did he kill the famous rock singer, Rex Lex? And what happened to his cousin, the beautiful model, who was found almost dead after a fall?
Other books you might like:
Carol Higgins Clark, *Decked*, 1993
Judith Eubank, *Crossover*, 1992
Laura Hastings, *The Peacock's Secret*, 1994
Barbara Michaels, *Black Rainbow*, 1982
Robin Paige, *Death at Bishop's Keep*, 1994

69

Nancy Atherton
Aunt Dimity's Death (New York: Viking, 1992)
Series: Aunt Dimity
Story type: Amateur Detective—Female Lead
Major character(s): Lori Shepherd, Office Worker; Bill Willis, Lawyer
Time period(s): 1990s
Locale(s): Boston, Massachusetts; The Cotswolds, England

What the book is about: Lori Shepherd loved the Aunt Dimity stories her mother told her when she was a young girl. Now Lori is not doing well - her mother, who she loved very much, is recently dead, she is newly divorced and almost broke. Now a prestigious law firm has informed her that Aunt Dimity was a real person, living in England, an old friend of her mother and on her recent death has left a considerable estate to Lori. The only problem is that Lori has to solve a mystery if she is to inherit. First novel.
Other books you might like:
K.K. Beck, *A Hopeless Case*, 1992
Judith Eubank, *Crossover*, 1992
Tony Gibbs, *Shadow Queen*, 1991
Charlaine Harris, *A Bone to Pick*, 1992
Robert Specht, *The Soul of Betty Fairchild*, 1991

70

Leo Axler
Double Plot (New York: Berkley, 1994)
Series: Bill Hawley
Story type: Amateur Detective—Male Lead
Major character(s): Bill Hawley, Undertaker (funeral home owner/director)
Time period(s): 1990s
Locale(s): Cleveland, Ohio
What the book is about: Bill Hawley has the job of arranging the funeral of Alexander Kane, victim of a car crash. Due to his reputation as an amateur sleuth, Bill is asked by Kane's son to investigate a mysterious tape recording wherein Kane says he is going to commit suicide. The son says the tape is a fake but if so, who made it and why? When Bill's wife is attacked, he realizes he may be involved in something he may not survive.
Other books you might like:
Jeff Abbott, *Do Unto Others*, 1994
Richard Barth, *Furnished for Murder*, 1990
Sally Gunning, *Hot Water*, 1990
A.J. Orde, *The Jason Lynx Series*, 1989-
Justin Scott, *Hardscape*, 1993

71

Leo Axler
Grave Matters (New York: Berkley, 1995)
Series: Bill Hawley
Story type: Amateur Detective—Male Lead; Private Detective—Male Lead
Major character(s): Bill Hawley, Undertaker, Detective—Private (part-time)
Time period(s): 1990s
Locale(s): Cleveland, Ohio

What the book is about: Bill Hawley has earned his reputation as "The Sleuthing Undertaker." The powers that be are not happy about it however, and are threatening to take away his undertaking license. His newest client is Ellie Lyttle who wants him to bury her husband Frank, who died from dog bites. Things become more interesting when a friend tells him that, according to dental records, Frank Lyttle died two years ago. Bill becomes involved in the deadly worlds of dogfighting, organized crime, and city politics.

Other books you might like:
Jeff Abbott, *The Jordan Poteet Series*, 1994-
Jeff Andrus, *Tracer, Inc.*, 1994
Jon Katz, *The Kit Deleeuw Series*, 1993-
Michael Z. Lewin, *The Albert Samson Series*, 1971-
John Lutz, *The Alo Nudger Series*, 1976-

72
E.C. Ayres
Eye of the Gator (New York: St. Martin's, 1995)

Series: Tony Lowell

Story type: Private Detective—Male Lead

Major character(s): Tony M.C. Lowell, Detective—Private, Photojournalist (part-time); Lena Bedrosian, Police Officer (detective)

Time period(s): 1990s

Locale(s): Manatee City, Florida

What the book is about: Timothy Cross, a young African-American environmental activist, has been murdered. As the Manatee police department is a bit short-handed, Tony has been hired by his sometime friend, sometime adversary, Lena Bedrosian, to help investigate. What Lena doesn't know is that Tony would have done it for free because the dead man is the nephew of a long-time friend. What Tony finds is that a lot of people might have wanted him dead, for both personal and professional reasons.

Other books you might like:
Philip R. Craig, *The J.W. Jackson Series*, 1990-
James W. Hall, *Tropical Freeze*, 1989
Paul Levine, *To Speak for the Dead*, 1990
John Lutz, *The Fred Carver Series*, 1986-
Justin Scott, *The Ben Abbott Series*, 1993

73
E.C. Ayres
Hour of the Manatee (New York: St. Martin's, 1994)

Series: Tony Lowell

Story type: Private Detective—Male Lead

Major character(s): Tony M.C. Lowell, Detective—Private (unlicensed), Photographer (retired photojournalist); Lena Bedrosian, Police Officer (detective-sergeant)

Time period(s): 1990s

Locale(s): Florida (Gulf coast)

What the book is about: Anthony Lowell, Vietnam veteran and famous photojournalist, is now a recluse living in Florida. For money, he teaches a class or two and acts as an unlicensed private detective. He is called by Maureen Fitzgerald, who tells him she was just released from an institution where she has been confined because she witnessed a murder many years ago. Before she can explain more fully, she is shot and killed. Lowell feels obligated to find the killer, but it will involve his past and a woman he loved and left. First mystery.

Other books you might like:
Lawrence Block, *The Matt Scudder Series*, 1976-
Paul Levine, *To Speak for the Dead*, 1991
John Lutz, *The Fred Carver Series*, 1986-
John D. MacDonald, *The Travis McGee Series*, 1965-1985
Ed McBain, *The Matthew Hope Series*, 1978-

74
Noreen Ayres
Carcass Trade (New York: Morrow, 1994)

Series: Smokey Brandon

Story type: Police Procedural—Female Lead

Major character(s): Samantha "Smokey" Brandon, Police Officer (forensic investigator)

Time period(s): 1990s

Locale(s): Los Angeles, California

What the book is about: Smokey Brandon, ex-stripper, is now a forensic investigator for the Orange County Sheriff's Department. She is called to investigate a car crash that seems routine at first. Soon, however, evidence points to murder, and the victim, burned beyond recognition, may be the ex-wife of Smokey's brother. When a local biker gang is found to be involved, Smokey asks to go undercover where she finds a lot more than she bargained for.

Other books you might like:
Patricia D. Cornwell, *The Kay Scarpetta Series*, 1990-
Rochelle Majer Krich, *Angel of Death*, 1994
Jack O'Connell, *Box Nine*, 1992
Soledad Santiago, *Undercover*, 1988
Kim Wozencraft, *Rush*, 1990

75
Jacqueline Babbin
Bloody Soaps: A Tale of Love and Death in the Afternoon (New York: International Polygonics, 1989)

Story type: Police Procedural—Male Lead

Major character(s): Clovis Kelley, Police Officer (Homicide)

Time period(s): 1980s

Locale(s): New York, New York

What the book is about: Wally Krog, producer of a soap opera called *Key to Life*, is found murdered. Detective Kelley, whose girlfriend works on the program, is put on the case. First book.

Other books you might like:
Steve Allen, *The Talk Show Murders*, 1982
William L. DeAndrea, *Killed in the Ratings*, 1978
R.R. Irvine, *Ratings Are Murder*, 1985
Marvin Kaye, *The Soap Opera Slaughters*, 1982
Judy Miller, *Murder of the Soap Opera*, 1988

76
Marian Babson
Encore Murder (New York: St. Martin's, 1990)
Series: Evangeline Sinclair/Trixie Dolan
Story type: Amateur Detective—Female Lead
Major character(s): Evangeline Sinclair, Actress; Trixie Dolan, Actress
Time period(s): 1990s (1990)
Locale(s): London, England
What the book is about: Trixie is planning the wedding of her daughter Martha, to Hugh. Suddenly Martha calls off the wedding when she discovers Hugh had been married before to a radical feminist. When murder happens, Martha is the prime suspect.
Other books you might like:
Simon Brett, *The Charles Paris Series*, 1982-
P.M. Carlson, *The Maggie Ryan Series*, 1985-
Caroline Graham, *Death of a Hollow Man*, 1990
Anne Morice, *The Tessa Crichton Series*, 1970-1990
Patricia Moyes, *Falling Star*, 1964

77
William Babula
According to St. John (New York: Lyle Stuart, 1989)
Series: Jeremiah St. John
Story type: Private Detective—Male Lead
Major character(s): Jeremiah St. John, Detective—Private; Mickey Farabaugh, Detective—Private (ex-cop)
Time period(s): 1980s
Locale(s): San Francisco, California
What the book is about: When Mickey's former roommate is the prime suspect in the murder of a fellow actress, St. John and partners have to try to find the real killer. Is it the roommate?
Other books you might like:
Jerry Kennealy, *Polo Solo*, 1987
W.R. Philbrick, *Slow Dancer*, 1984
Bill Pronzini, *The Nameless Detective Series*, 1971
J.W. Rider, *Jersey Tomatoes*, 1986
Chelsea Quinn Yarbro, *Ogilvie, Tallant, and Moon*, 1976

78
James Baddock
The Faust Conspiracy (New York: Walker, 1989)
Story type: Espionage
Major character(s): Paul Koenig, Spy (German); Karl Vogel, Military Personnel (SS major)
Time period(s): 1940s (World War II)
What the book is about: An expert marksman is sent to England to assassinate King George VI. Another group of Germans send Paul Koenig to stop him. First book.
Other books you might like:
R. Wright Campbell, *The Spy Who Sat and Waited*, 1975
Len Deighton, *SS-GB*, 1978
Ken Follett, *Eye of the Needle*, 1978
Frederick Forsyth, *The Day of the Jackal*, 1971
Jack Higgins, *The Eagle Has Landed*, 1975

79
Jo Bailey
Bagged (New York: St. Martin's, 1991)
Story type: Amateur Detective—Female Lead
Major character(s): Jan Gallagher, Security Officer (in a hospital); Frank White, Police Officer
Time period(s): 1990s
Locale(s): Abilene, Texas
What the book is about: When the body of the head neurologist of General Jackson Hospital shows up in the morgue, security chief Gallagher—though under pressure to stop investigating—is determined to find out who killed the doctor and why. To do this she teams up with police detective Frank White, who quickly falls in love with her. First novel.
Other books you might like:
Patricia D. Cornwell, *Postmortem*, 1990
Susan Dunlap, *Pious Deception*, 1989
Mary Kittredge, *Fatal Diagnosis*, 1990
Mary Kittredge, *Rigor Mortis*, 1991
Joyce Anne Schneider, *Darkness Falls*, 1989

80
Jo Bailey
Recycled (New York: St. Martins, 1993)
Series: General Jack Hospital
Story type: Action/Adventure
Major character(s): Jan Gallagher, Security Officer, Single Parent
Time period(s): 1990s
Locale(s): Minnesota
What the book is about: A woman is coming to "General Jack" Hospital for a liver transplant. The problem is that she is a key witness for the DEA against the Colombian drug lords and they don't want her testifying. When an ambulance is blown up, Jan Gallagher is put in charge of protection. But she is up against an assassin who has not failed in 83 times.
Other books you might like:
Robin Cook, *Blindsight*, 1992
Patricia D. Cornwell, *All That Remains*, 1992
Susan Dunlap, *Rogue Wave*, 1991
M.D. Lake, *The Peggy O'Neill Series*, 1989-
Marsha Landreth, *The Holiday Murders*, 1992

81
Abbey Penn Baker
In the Dead of Winter (New York: St. Martin's, 1994)
Story type: Historical; Amateur Detective—Female Lead
Major character(s): Myrl Adler Norton, Professor (of logic, at Smith College); Faye Tullis, Student (teaching assistant)
Time period(s): 1910s (1918)
Locale(s): Northampton, Massachusetts
What the book is about: While going to help a student whose rooms have been tossed, Myrl Adler Norton and her teaching assistant, Faye Tullis, hear a shot from the house. They find the landlady dead. But for how long was she dead? It seems that she has been stuffed and mounted and the drapes and record player that gave the illusion of her being alive are run by weights and pulleys. Norton recognizes the voice on the record and she and her assistant are soon involved in blackmail, smuggling, and more murder. First novel.
Other books you might like:
Carole Nelson Douglas, *Irene's Last Waltz*, 1994
William Hjortsberg, *Nevermore*, 1994
John T. Lescroart, *Son of Holmes*, 1986
Sam Siciliano, *The Angel of the Opera*, 1994
Daniel D. Victor, *The Seventh Bullet*, 1992

82
Nikki Baker
In the Game (Tallahassee: Naiad, 1991)
Series: Virginia Kelly
Story type: Amateur Detective—Female Lead
Major character(s): Virginia Kelly, Stock Broker, Lesbian
Time period(s): 1990s
Locale(s): Chicago, Illinois
What the book is about: After meeting her former college roommate, Bev, for drinks, Ginny Kelly is distressed to find that the roomie's former lover has turned up dead. Fearing that Bev is implicated in the crime Ginny sets out to find the killer. Complicating matters are her relationships with her live-in lover and a highpowered lawyer she meets while investigating. Soon she finds that she is a target. First novel.
Other books you might like:
Ellen Hart, *Vital Lies*, 1990
Sara Paretsky, *The V.I. Warshawski Series*, 1982-
Deborah Powell, *Bayou City Secrets*, 1990
Karen Saum, *Murder Is Relative*, 1989
Pat Welch, *Murder by the Book*, 1990

83
Nikki Baker
The Lavender House Murder (Tallahasse, Florida: Naiad, 1992)
Series: Virginia Kelly
Story type: Amateur Detective—Female Lead
Major character(s): Virginia Kelly, Stock Broker, Lesbian
Time period(s): 1990s
Locale(s): Provincetown, Massachusetts
What the book is about: While on vacation in Provincetown, Virginia Kelly discovers the corpse of a gay newspaper writer. Was she killed because she was in the business of outing closeted gays or was there something in her personal life that caused her death? Virginia and her traveling companion, Naomi, get involved in trying to find out the truth.
Other books you might like:
Katherine V. Forrest, *Murder at the Nightwood Bar*, 1986
Ellen Hart, *Hallowed Murder*, 1989
Delores Klaich, *Heavy Gilt*, 1987
Claire McNab, *Cop-Out*, 1991
Eve Zaremba, *Beyond Hope*, 1988

84
Susan Baker
My First Murder (New York: St. Martin's, 1989)
Story type: Private Detective—Female Lead
Major character(s): Mavis Davis, Detective—Private
Time period(s): 1980s
Locale(s): Houston, Texas
What the book is about: When Carl Singleton hires Mavis to find out who killed one of his employees, Mavis finds that the dead woman was not who she seemed to be. First book.
Other books you might like:
Linda Grant, *Random Access Murder*, 1988
Edward Mathis, *From a High Place*, 1985
T.J. MacGregor, *On Ice*, 1989
D. Miller Morgan, *Money Leads to Murder*, 1987

85
Robert Ballard
Co-Author: Tony Chiu
Bright Shark (New York: Delacorte, 1992)
Story type: Techno-Thriller; Espionage
Major character(s): Edna Haddix, Military Personnel (Navy lieutenant); Wendell Trent, Government Official, Troubleshooter (for the Department of Energy)
Time period(s): 1980s (1988)
Locale(s): At Sea
What the book is about: While doing underwater research off the coast of Greece, a U.S. vessel finds traces of an Israeli submarine, the *Dakar*, that has been reported lost in 1967. This is big news, not only to the Israelis and the U.S. but to the U.S.S.R. as well. In fact, Israel and the Soviets join forces to keep the *Dakar's* secret from the U.S. First novel by Ballard.
Other books you might like:
Tom Clancy, *The Hunt for Red October*, 1984
Michael Crichton, *Sphere*, 1987
Stuart Woods, *Deep Lie*, 1987

86
Jo Bannister
Death and Other Lovers (New York: Doubleday, 1991)

Story type: Action/Adventure

Major character(s): Mickey Flynn, Photojournalist; Laura Wade, Girlfriend (of Mickey Flynn)

Time period(s): 1990s

Locale(s): London, England

What the book is about: Someone is trying to kill Mickey Flynn. Given the number of people he has indicted with his camera, this is not a surprise. There seem to be four top suspects - but which one? Or is it someone closer to him?

Other books you might like:
Don Flynn, *A Suitcase in Berlin*, 1989
Keith Peterson, *The Rain*, 1990
Mike Phillips, *Blood Rights*, 1989
Stephen Robinett, *Final Option*, 1990
S.K. Wolf, *The Harbinger Effect*, 1989

87
Jo Bannister
The Going Down of the Sun (New York: Doubleday, 1989)

Series: Clio and Harry Marsh

Story type: Amateur Detective

Major character(s): Clio Marsh, Doctor (wife of Harry); Harry Marsh, Police Officer (husband of Clio)

Time period(s): 1980s

What the book is about: While sailing near the coast of Scotland, the Marshes witness an explosion on a nearby yacht that kills the owner. They rescue the sole passenger who is then accused of murder.

Other books you might like:
George Bellairs, *All Roads to Sospel*, 1974
Lionel Black, *The Eve of the Wedding*, 1980
Anne Morice, *Death in the Round*, 1980
Patricia Moyes, *Down Among the Dead Men*, 1961

88
Robert Barnard
A City of Strangers (New York: Scribners, 1990)

Story type: Traditional

Major character(s): Jack Phelan, Unemployed; Carol Southgate, Teacher

Time period(s): 1990s

Locale(s): Burtle, England (Yorkshire)

What the book is about: When the infamous Phelans look to move up in the world, the neighborhood into which they intend to move is appalled. Someone is looking to stop them and may go so far as murder. Or is there another crime afoot? Meanwhile Carol Southgate has taken on one of the Phelan children as a reclamation project.

Other books you might like:
Patricia Highsmith, *People Who Knock on the Door*, 1985
Ruth Rendell, *Live Flesh*, 1986

89
Robert Barnard
Death and the Chaste Apprentice (New York: Scribners, 1989)

Story type: Police Procedural—Male Lead

Major character(s): Dundy, Police Officer (Inspector); Charlie Peace, Police Officer

Time period(s): 1980s

Locale(s): England (Outside London)

What the book is about: When the owner of the Saracen's Head Inn is murdered, it appears that everyone who was present had cause to kill him. Can Peace and Dundy find the real culprit?

Other books you might like:
W.J. Burley, *Wycliffe and the Scapegoat*, 1979
Colin Dexter, *Service of All the Dead*, 1980
Reginald Hill, *Ruling Passion*, 1977
Colin Watson, *Lonelyheart 4122*, 1967

90
Robert Barnard
The Masters of the House (New York: Scribners: 1994)

Story type: Psychological Suspense

Major character(s): Matthew Heenan, Teenager; Annie Heenan, Teenager

Time period(s): 1970s

Locale(s): Leeds, England

What the book is about: Their mother has died in childbirth and their father has fallen apart, physically and emotionally, so teenagers Matthew and Annie Heenan begin to raise themselves, their younger brothers, and take care of their invalid father. One day Carmen O'Keefe shows up at their home. It appears she was having an affair with their father. Soon after, Carmen turns up dead on their doorstep. Matthew and Annie handle that problem, but then Carmen's mother-in-law shows up. She doesn't really want to know what happened to Carmen, but moves in and starts to take care of the family. Some years later Carmen's killer is revealed.

Other books you might like:
Patricia Highsmith, *People Who Knock on the Door*, 1985
Barbara Vine, *The Dark-Adapted Eye*, 1986
Julian Symons, *Something Like a Love Affair*, 1992
Donna Tartt, *The Secret History*, 1992
Steven Yount, *Wandering Star*, 1994

91
Robert Barnard
A Scandal in Belgravia (New York: Scribners, 1991)

Story type: Historical; Amateur Detective—Male Lead

Major character(s): Peter Proctor, Political Figure

Time period(s): 1990s; 1950s

Locale(s): United States; England

What the book is about: After being put out to pasture by the Thatcher government, statesman Peter Proctor starts to work his memoirs. This process takes him back to the 1950's and the murder of a friend that was never solved. Disappointed in himself because of his lack of concern at time, Peter determines to find out the truth.

Other books you might like:
Tony Cape, *The Cambridge Theorem*, 1991
Kate Green, *Night Angel*, 1990

92
Linda Barnes
Coyote (New York: Delacorte, 1990)

Series: Carlotta Carlyle

Story type: Private Detective—Female Lead

Major character(s): Carlotta Carlyle, Detective—Private, Taxi Driver

Time period(s): 1990s (1990)

Locale(s): Boston, Massachusetts

What the book is about: A mysterious Hispanic woman hires Carlotta to find her lost green card. Then she disappears and another woman is found dead with the missing green card on her body.

Other books you might like:
Susan Dunlap, *Pious Deception*, 1989
Sue Grafton, *The Kinsey Millhone Series*, 1982-
Karen Kijewski, *Katwalk*, 1989
Marcia Muller, *The Sharon McCone Series*, 1977-
Sara Paretsky, *The V.I. Warshawski Series*, 1982-

93
Linda Barnes
Snapshot (New York: Delacorte, 1993)

Series: Carlotta Carlyle

Story type: Private Detective—Female Lead

Major character(s): Carlotta Carlyle, Detective—Private

Time period(s): 1990s

Locale(s): Boston, Massachusetts

What the book is about: Emily Woodrow thinks that her daughter's death from leukemia shouldn't have happened. She hires Carlotta Carlyle to help her find the truth. Then Emily disappears. While investigating the hospital Carlotta is also concerned with her "little sister" who has started to hang out with an older thug.

Other books you might like:
Mary Higgins Clark, *The Cradle Will Fall*, 1980
Dick Cluster, *Obligations of the Bone*, 1992
Barbara D'Amato, *The Cat Marsala Series*, 1989-
Jeremiah Healy, *Act of God*, 1994
Sara Paretsky, *Bitter Medicine*, 1987

94
Linda Barnes
Steel Guitar (New York: Delacorte, 1991)

Series: Carlotta Carlyle

Story type: Private Detective—Female Lead

Major character(s): Carlotta Carlyle, Detective—Private, Taxi Driver (part-time); Dee Willis, Singer (former best friend of Carlotta)

Time period(s): 1990s

Locale(s): Boston, Massachusetts

What the book is about: Singer Dee Willis, once Carlotta's best friend, is in Boston to start a tour and looks up Carlotta, but not just for old time's sake. She wants Carlotta to find a former mutual friend and musician, but won't tell Carlotta the real reason why. Carlotta is less than ethusiastic about the whole venture as her relationship with Dee brings back a lot of bad memories, but when someone turns up dead and Carlotta's home is ransacked she decides to investigate anyway.

Other books you might like:
Sue Grafton, *The Kinsey Millhone Series*, 1984-
Jeremiah Healy, *The John Francis Cuddy Series*, 1984-
Karen Kijewski, *Katapult*, 1990
Marcia Muller, *Trophies and Dead Things*, 1990
Gloria White, *Murder on the Run*, 1991

95
Trevor Barnes
A Pound of Flesh (New York: Morrow, 1993)

Series: Blanche Hampton

Story type: Police Procedural—Female Lead

Major character(s): Blanche Hampton, Police Officer (detective superintendent); David Parker, Accountant, Serial Killer

Time period(s): 1990s

Locale(s): London, England

What the book is about: Accountant David Parker goes quietly crazy after the death of his mother and starts killing and cannibalizing women. It falls to Detective Superintendent Blanche Hampton to find him and put an end to the slaughter. Blanche must also fight sexism at work while trying to track him down.

Other books you might like:
Liza Cody, *Dupe*, 1984
Deborah Crombie, *All Shall Be Well*, 1994
P.D. James, *An Unsuitable Job for a Woman*, 1972
Lydia LaPlante, *The Prime Suspect Series*, 1992-
Jennie Melville, *The Charmian Daniels Series*, 1988-

96
Nevada Barr
A Superior Death (New York: Putnam, 1994)

Series: Anna Pigeon

Story type: Amateur Detective—Female Lead

Major character(s): Anna Pigeon, Ranger (national park ranger)

Time period(s): 1990s

Locale(s): Isle Royale National Park, Michigan (in Lake Superior)

What the book is about: Soon after Anna Pigeon's arrival on Isle Royale, a body is discovered on the submerged wreck of an old ship. The body, however, is recent and belongs to the fellow who ran the commercial diving concession in the park. The wife of another ranger is missing and Anna fears for her life. The relationships among those who work and live in the park are not easy to understand and people keep hiding things from Anna as she tries to find out the truth behind the death and disappearance.

Other books you might like:
Philip R. Craig, *A Beautiful Place to Die*, 1990
Alison Drake, *Tango Key*, 1988
Sue Grafton, *The Kinsey Millhone Series*, 1984-
Gunnard Landers, *The Deer Killers*, 1990
Mary Willis Walker, *Zero at the Bone*, 1991

97
Nevada Barr
Track of the Cat (New York: Putnam, 1993)

Series: Anna Pigeon

Story type: Amateur Detective—Female Lead

Major character(s): Anna Pigeon, Ranger (national park ranger)

Time period(s): 1990s

Locale(s): Texas (West Texas; Guadaloupe Mountains National Park)

What the book is about: When another ranger is found dead, ostensibly killed by a mountain lion, Ranger Anna Pigeon is convinced that the woman was actually murdered. Though her superiors tell her she's wrong, she is determined to find the truth. Then there is another supposedly accidental death and Anna herself seems to be at risk. First mystery.

Other books you might like:
B.J. Oliphant, *The Unexpected Corpse*, 1990
Abigail Padgett, *Child of Silence*, 1993
Sandra West Prowell, *By Evil Means*, 1993
Bernard Schopen, *The Desert Look*, 1990
Judith Van Gieson, *North of the Border*, 1988

98
Neal Barrett Jr.
Pink Vodka Blues (New York: St. Martin's, 1992)

Story type: Amateur Detective—Male Lead; Action/Adventure

Major character(s): Russell Murray, Editor (of a literary magazine), Alcoholic; Sherry Lou Winn, Heiress

Time period(s): 1990s

Locale(s): United States (Chicago to Wisconsin to Dallas to Miami to Chicago)

What the book is about: Alcoholic Russell Murray takes what he is told is a manuscript from Chicago to Dallas and back. After he's been back a few days he wakes up next to a woman he doesn't know and while he is in the bathroom, two men come in and kill the woman and try to shoot him. Naturally he runs but when he checks back later he finds he is wanted for the woman's murder. After winding up in a detox center he escapes and takes another inmate with him, or rather she takes him. On the run from who knows what they go from Dallas to Miami and back to Chicago trying to find out what's going on. First crime novel.

Other books you might like:
Lawrence Block, *After the First Death*, 1969
James W. Hall, *Bones of Coral*, 1991
Carl Hiaasen, *Native Tongue*, 1992
Jerome Stanford, *Miami Heat*, 1991
Stuart Woods, *Santa Fe Rules*, 1992

99
Adam Barrow
Flawless (New York: Dutton, 1995)

Story type: Psychological Suspense; Action/Adventure

Major character(s): Michael Woodrow, Businessman, Criminal (serial killer); Victor Flam, Detective—Private

Time period(s): 1990s

Locale(s): United States

What the book is about: Michael Barrow is killing women who remind him of his mother. Private detective Victor Flam is on his trail. Michael's father, who killed his mother, is now out of prison and they are living together, though his father has no idea that Michael is a serial killer. Michael wants to quit killing and it appears that the love of a good woman might bring him out of it, but Flam is closing in. First novel under this name. Supposedly a pseudonym for a famous writer.

Other books you might like:
Thomas Harris, *The Silence of the Lambs*, 1988
John Katzenbach, *The Traveler*, 1987
Joe R. Lansdale, *Act of Love*, 1981
David L. Lindsey, *Mercy*, 1990
Bill Pronzini, *The Eye*, 1984 (John Lutz, co-author)

100
Richard Barth
Deathics (New York: St. Martins, 1993)

Series: Margaret Binton

Story type: Amateur Detective—Female Lead

Major character(s): Margaret Binton, Aged Person

Time period(s): 1990s

Locale(s): New York, New York

What the book is about: When Margaret Binton's partner in her Smoke Stoppers group, Adrian Lavin, is stabbed to death in what police are calling a random murder, she thinks otherwise. She had just spoken with him before he was killed and thought he sounded nervous and frightened. She soon discovers that in researching a book on a church Adrian had uncovered some secrets about some of the parishioners that some people might kill to keep hidden. She sets out to find the killer.

Other books you might like:
M.C. Beaton, *Agatha Raisin and the Quiche of Death*, 1992
Susanna Hofmann McShea, *The Pumpkin-Shell Wife*, 1992
A.J. Orde, *A Little Neighborhood Murder*, 1989
David Osborn, *The Margaret Barlow Series*, 1989-
Celestine Sibley, *Ah, Sweet Mystery*, 1991

101
Richard Barth
Furnished for Murder (New York: St. Martins, 1990)

Story type: Amateur Detective—Male Lead

Major character(s): Leo Perkins, Businessman (furniture salesman); Jakob Barzeny, Sports Figure (chess master; former Soviet po)

Time period(s): 1990s (1990)

Locale(s): Westchester, New York

What the book is about: Leo discovers his daughter's piano teacher was supplementing his income by stealing from the houses of his pupils. When the teacher is found dead, Leo is the prime suspect and his wife may have been having an affair with the teacher. Leo, with Jakob's help, tries to find the real killer.

Other books you might like:
Al Guthrie, *Private Murder*, 1989
A.J. Orde, *A Little Neighborhood Murder*, 1989
Valerie Wolzien, *Murder at the PTA Luncheon*, 1988
Victor Wuamett, *Teardown*, 1990

102
Frederick Barton
With Extreme Prejudice (New York: Villard, 1993)

Story type: Amateur Detective—Male Lead; Action/Adventure

Major character(s): Michael Barnett, Critic (film reviewer)

Time period(s): 1980s (1988-1989)

Locale(s): New Orleans, Louisiana

What the book is about: When Michael Barnett returns home after a trip he finds that his house has been burgled. The only thing missing, however, is a file that his late wife had been working with at the time of her "accidental" death a year earlier. When Barnett finds that files regarding this case are missing from her former law firm as well, he determines to find out what was in the files to cause someone to steal them and maybe kill his wife. First mystery.

Other books you might like:
Robert Ferrigno, *The Cheshire Moon*, 1993
J.F. Freedman, *Against the Wind*, 1992
John Grisham, *The Pelican Brief*, 1992
Carl Hiaasen, *Native Tongue*, 1991
Joe R. Lansdale, *The Savage Season*, 1990

103
Bernard Bastable (Pseudonym of Robert Barnard)
To Die Like a Gentleman (New York: St. Martins, 1993)

Story type: Historical; Psychological Suspense

Major character(s): Jane Hudson, Teenager; Richard Hudson, Landowner

Time period(s): 1840s (1842)

Locale(s): England

What the book is about: Sir Richard Hudson is dying and the machinations of his family and servants are what drive this novel. His manservant is scheming, his wife is contemplating an affair, his young son Andrew is becoming estranged from him, his doctor is eying his wife, and his daughter is a budding feminist. There is also the governess and the tutor and all their private intrigues. First book under this name.

Other books you might like:
James Anderson, *The Affair of the Blood-Stained Egg Cosy*, 1975
John Dickson Carr, *The Burning Court*, 1937
Kate Kingsbury, *Service for Two*, 1994
Peter Lovesey, *Bertie and the Seven Bodies*, 1990
Kate Ross, *Cut to the Quick*, 1993

104
Colin Bateman
Divorcing Jack (New York: Arcade, 1995)

Story type: Action/Adventure

Major character(s): Dan Starkey, Writer (columnist)

Time period(s): 1990s

Locale(s): Belfast, Northern Ireland

What the book is about: Dan Starkey is cheating on his wife—again—but this time the consequences may be deadly. While out for food after his latest dalliance he returns to find the woman's bullet-ridden body. Then he kills her mother accidently while struggling in the dark. It turns out the dead woman, Margaret McBride, was the daughter of a politician and may have held the key to the upcoming election for prime minister. Others, including the IRA, think Dan may now be that key and he's in serious trouble because he hasn't a clue. First novel.

Other books you might like:
Thomas Adcock, *Drown All the Dogs*, 1994
Sheila McGill Callahan, *Death in a Far Country*, 1993
Norman Flood, *To Killashea*, 1990
Ken Gross, *Hell Bent*, 1992
Jack Higgins, *Angel of Death*, 1995

105

William Bayer
Blind Side (New York: Villard, 1989)

Story type: Psychological Suspense

Major character(s): Geoffrey Barnett, Photographer; Kimberly Yates, Model

Time period(s): 1980s

Locale(s): New York, New York

What the book is about: Geoffrey Barnett is a photographer who hasn't been able to take pictures of people for a number of years. Suddenly Kimberly Yates enters his life, helps him break his block and just as suddenly disappears. Where did she go and why?

Other books you might like:
Franklin Bandy, *Deceit and Deadly Lies*, 1978
Stanley Ellin, *Mirror on the Wall*, 1972
Thomas Gifford, *The Cavanaugh Quest*, 1976
Brian Lysaght, *Special Circumstances*, 1983
Thomas Maxwell, *The Saberdene Variations*, 1987

106

Gregory Bean
No Comfort in Victory (New York: St. Martin's, 1995)

Story type: Police Procedural—Male Lead

Major character(s): Harry Starbranch, Police Officer (sheriff)

Time period(s): 1990s

Locale(s): Victory, Wyoming

What the book is about: Harry Starbranch leaves his job as a Denver homicide detective thinking that the sheriff's job in Victory, Wyoming will provide him with a slower pace and less angst. When a teenage girl is found raped and murdered with a couple of dead guys nearby it appears that he should have settled elsewhere. Is it a case of cattle rustling gone bad or are more sinister forces at work? First mystery.

Other books you might like:
Jameson Cole, *A Killing in Quail County*, 1996
Bill Crider, *The Sheriff Dan Rhodes Series*, 1986-
D.R. Meredith, *The Homefront Murders*, 1995
Kirk Mitchell, *High Desert Malice*, 1995
B.J. Oliphant, *A Ceremonial Death*, 1996

107

M.C. Beaton
Agatha Raisin and the Quiche of Death (New York: St. Martin's, 1992)

Series: Agatha Raisin

Story type: Amateur Detective—Female Lead

Major character(s): Agatha Raisin, Advertising (retired)

Time period(s): 1990s

Locale(s): Carsley, England (the Cotswolds)

What the book is about: Agatha Raisin has realized her dream, she has sold her business and bought a cottage in the Cotswolds. Unfortunately, after a week she is in tears and the villagers while civil, are not very friendly. To break the ice Agatha enters a quiche tasting contest but she can't boil water so she cheats and enters a store-bought quiche. The judge takes the quiche home with him, and the next day is found dead of poison from Agatha's quiche.

Other books you might like:
Natasha Cooper, *Poison Flowers*, 1991
Ann Granger, *A Season for Murder*, 1992
Hazel Holt, *Mrs. Malory Investigates*, 1992
Betty Rowlands, *A Little Gentle Sleuthing*, 1991
John Sherwood, *The Celia Grant Series*, 1984-

108

M.C. Beaton
Agatha Raisin and the Vicious Vet (New York: St. Martins, 1993)

Series: Agatha Raisin

Story type: Amateur Detective—Female Lead

Major character(s): Agatha Raisin, Advertising (retired); James Lacey, Writer (Agatha's neighbor)

Time period(s): 1990s

Locale(s): Carsley, England (the Cotswolds)

What the book is about: Agatha Raisin is bored and looking for some male companionship. Her pursuit of her neighbor, James Lacey, has been unproductive so she turns to the new veterinarian. He proves to be something of a disappointment. He is charming but treats pets roughly and is more concerned with his own advancement. When he turns up dead, the apparent victim of an accident, Agatha and the now-interested James decide to investigate.

Other books you might like:
Natasha Cooper, *The Willow King Series*, 1990-
Hazel Holt, *The Mrs. Malory Series*, 1990-
David Osborn, *Murder on Martha's Vineyard*, 1990
Betty Rowlands, *The Melissa Craig Series*, 1991
John Sherwood, *The Celia Grant Series*, 1984-

109

M.C. Beaton
Death of a Charming Man (New York: Mysterious, 1994)

Series: Hamish MacBeth

Story type: Police Procedural—Male Lead

Major character(s): Hamish MacBeth, Police Officer; Priscilla Halburton-Smythe, Hotel Worker (manager)

Time period(s): 1990s

Locale(s): Lochdubh, Scotland

What the book is about: Hamish MacBeth's life seems to be working out fine—he's newly promoted and unofficially engaged to his long-loved Priscilla. Why then isn't he happy? Priscilla seems to want him to change and be somebody. Hamish was happy being a nobody. Also, an outlander has moved into Drim, a nearby backward farming community. He is charming to the women of the area, which doesn't endear him to the men. When he disappears, Hamish is convinced there was foul play.

Other books you might like:
Leo Bruce, *The Sergeant Beef Series*, 1937-1952
Barry Cork, *The Angus Straum Series*, 1989-
Colin Dexter, *The Inspector Morse Series*, 1975-
Gerald Hammond, *The Keith Calder Series*, 1979-
Frank Parrish, *The Dan Mallett Series*, 1978-1986

110
M.C. Beaton
Death of a Hussy (New York: St. Martins, 1990)
Series: Hamish MacBeth
Story type: Police Procedural—Male Lead
Major character(s): Hamish MacBeth, Police Officer (small town constable)
Time period(s): 1990s
Locale(s): Lochdubh, Scotland
What the book is about: Hamish is assigned to city duty but wants to return to his belove Lochdubh. Maggie Baird hatches a plot to get him reassigned. When Hamish returns, Maggie leaves. When she returns she announces she will marry one of several suitors accompanying her. She is murdered first.

Other books you might like:
Barry Cork, *Dead Ball*, 1989
Colin Dexter, *Last Bus to Woodstock*, 1975
Frank Parrish, *Snare in the Dark*, 1981
Robert Richardson, *The Dying of the Light*, 1990
Susannah Stacey, *Goodbye, Nanny Gray*, 1987

111
M.C. Beaton
Death of a Nag (New York: Mysterious, 1995)
Series: Hamish MacBeth
Story type: Police Procedural—Male Lead
Major character(s): Hamish MacBeth, Police Officer (constable)
Time period(s): 1990s
Locale(s): Skag, Scotland
What the book is about: Since Hamish's demotion and his break-up with Priscilla, the villagers have been treating him like a pariah. Deciding this would be a good time to take a vacation, he ends up at an inn in Skag known as Friendly House. It is anything but, however, due mostly to the presence of the obnoxious Bob Harris, who has nothing good to say about anybody or anything. He so infuriates Hamish that Hamish punches him in the nose. When Harris is killed, Hamish finds himself a suspect.

Other books you might like:
Marten Claridge, *Nobody's Fool*, 1992
Barry Cork, *The Angus Straum Series*, 1989-
Bill Knox, *The Colin Thane Series*, 1961-
Ian Rankin, *The Inspector Rebus Series*, 1978-
Susannah Stacey, *Bone Idle*, 1995

112
M.C. Beaton
Death of a Perfect Wife (New York: St. Martin's, 1989)
Series: Hamish MacBeth
Story type: Police Procedural—Male Lead
Major character(s): Hamish Macbeth, Police Officer (constable)
Time period(s): 1980s
Locale(s): Lochdubh (Scottish Highlands)
What the book is about: A woman new to the village is murdered. There is no dearth of suspects as she has managed to irritate most everyone in a fairly short time.

Other books you might like:
Barry Cork, *Dead Ball*, 1989
Bill Knox, *Who Shot the Bull*, 1970
William McIlvanney, *Laidlaw*, 1977
Jack S. Scott, *The View from Deacon Hill*, 1981
John Wainwright, *All on a Summer's Day*, 1981

113
M.C. Beaton
Death of a Traveling Man (New York: St. Martin's, 1993)
Series: Hamish MacBeth
Story type: Police Procedural—Male Lead
Major character(s): Hamish Macbeth, Police Officer (sergeant)
Time period(s): 1990s
Locale(s): Lochdubh, Scotland
What the book is about: Hamish Macbeth has been so successful that he has received a promotion. He is now a sergeant and as such rates an assistant, a very mixed blessing. To add to his troubles, an itinerant trouble-maker has moved into town. Hamish knows he is no good but has no proof. When the man is killed Hamish must discover what secrets the man had uncovered and who would kill to hide them.

Other books you might like:
Barry Cork, *Dead Ball*, 1989
Gerald Hammond, *The Keith Calder Series*, 1979-
Bill Knox, *The Colin Thane Series*, 1961-
William McIlvanney, *Strange Loyalties*, 1992
Ian Rankin, *The Inspector John Rebus Series*, 1978-

114
K.K. Beck (Pseudonym of Kathrine Marris)
Amateur Night (New York: Mysterious, 1993)
Series: Jane Da Silva

Story type: Amateur Detective—Female Lead

Major character(s): Jane Da Silva, Singer

Time period(s): 1990s

Locale(s): Vancouver, British Columbia, Canada

What the book is about: Jane is still trying to secure her inheritance by solving hopeless cases. She becomes involved with Kevin Shea, a young hoodlum, who was convicted of holding up a pharmacy and shooting the owner's wife. He says he didn't do it and there is slim evidence that there may have been a witness who could clear him.

Other books you might like:
Susan Kelly, *Until Proven Innocent*, 1990
Sharyn McCrumb, *The Elizabeth MacPherson Series*, 1984-
Nancy Pickard, *The Jenny Cain Series*, 1984-
Gillian Roberts, *The Amanda Pepper Series*, 1987-
Minette Walters, *The Sculptress*, 1993

115

K.K. Beck (Pseudonym of Kathrine Marris)
Electric City (New York: Mysterious, 1994)

Series: Jane Da Silva

Story type: Amateur Detective—Female Lead

Major character(s): Jane Da Silva, Singer, Detective—Private (investigator for a foundation)

Time period(s): 1990s

Locale(s): Seattle, Washington

What the book is about: Jane Da Silva is still working for the Foundation for Righting Wrongs. She gets a salary and a place to stay only if she can find hopeless cases and solve them. A strange pair shows up asking for her help. Monica and Clark work for a clipping service and one of their co-workers, Irene March, has disappeared. Jane finds that Irene has a knack for collecting odd facts and unearthing secrets—secrets that a lot of people don't want uncovered.

Other books you might like:
Susan Wittig Albert, *The China Bayles Series*, 1992-
Mary Daheim, *The Emma Lord Series*, 1992-
Jaqueline Girdner, *The Kate Jasper Series*, 1991-
Marlys Millhiser, *The Charlie Green Series*, 1992-
Janet L. Smith, *The Annie MacPherson Series*, 1990-

116

K.K. Beck (Pseudonym of Kathrine Marris)
A Hopeless Case (New York: Mysterious, 1992)

Series: Jane Da Silva

Story type: Action/Adventure; Amateur Detective—Female Lead

Major character(s): Jane Da Silva, Singer

Time period(s): 1990s

Locale(s): Seattle, Washington

What the book is about: Expatriate singer Jane Da Silva is offered an inheritance from her late uncle if she will take on his profession of solving hopeless cases. No publicity is allowed and the bankers will make the final determination as to whether she succeeds. Her first attempt is for a young woman who wishes to recover some money her mother had given to a cult many years before. It appears that someone is less than enthusiastic about this quest as Jane soon finds herself embroiled with a murder.

Other books you might like:
Susan Conant, *A New Leash on Death*, 1990
Janet Dawson, *Kindred Crimes*, 1990
Kay Hooper, *Crime of Passion*, 1991
Nancy Baker Jacobs, *The Turquoise Tattoo*, 1991
Karen Kijewski, *Katwalk*, 1989

117

K.K. Beck (Pseudonym of Kathrine Marris)
Peril under the Palms (New York: Walker, 1989)

Series: Iris Cooper

Story type: Amateur Detective—Female Lead

Major character(s): Iris Cooper, Student (college); Jack Clancey, Journalist

Time period(s): 1920s

Locale(s): Hawaii

What the book is about: When Iris Cooper visits Hawaii with her aunt and a fellow student from Stanford—the heiress of a Hawaiian fortune—she gets involved in murder.

Other books you might like:
Marian Babson, *The Cruise of a Deathtime*, 1983
Peter Lovesey, *The False Inspector Dew*, 1982
Peter Lovesey, *Keystone*, 1983
Charlotte MacLeod, *The Family Vault*, 1979
Barbara Paul, *A Cadenza for Caruso*, 1984

118

Jack Becklund
Golden Fleece (New York: St. Martins, 1990)

Story type: Police Procedural—Male Lead; Action/Adventure

Major character(s): Ray MacNulty, Police Officer (sheriff); Nels Dahlstrom, Businessman (owner of a charter service); Graham Jackson, Businessman (works with Nels)

Time period(s): 1990s

Locale(s): Minnesota (on the shores of Lake Superior)

What the book is about: Did Harry Potter and his ship really disappear into the depths of Lake Superior? And what does the Amazon-like girlfriend of a murdered logger have to with the alleged disappearance? This is Becklund's first novel.

Other books you might like:
L.L. Enger, *Comeback*, 1990

119
Sophie Belfort
The Marvell College Murders (New York: Fine, 1991)

Series: Molly Rafferty/Nick Hannibal

Story type: Amateur Detective; Police Procedural

Major character(s): Molly Rafferty, Professor (of history); Nick Hannibal, Police Officer

Time period(s): 1990s

Locale(s): Boston, Massachusetts

What the book is about: A candidate for a position at Scattergood College is stabbed at the Boston Public Library with a jewel-encrusted dagger belonging to one of the professors at the college. Molly and Nick must discover whether the reason behind the killing is academic or personal. Then there is another murder. Is Molly in danger?

Other books you might like:
Bob Fenster, *The Last Page*, 1989
Carolyn G. Hart, *A Little Class on Murder*, 1989
Joan Hess, *Strangled Prose*, 1986
Susan Kelly, *And Soon I'll Come to Kill You*, 1991
M.D. Lake, *Poisoned Ivy*, 1992

120
Dick Belsky
South Street Confidential (New York: St. Martin's, 1989)

Story type: Amateur Detective—Female Lead

Major character(s): Jenny McKay, Journalist (television reporter)

Time period(s): 1980s

Locale(s): New York, New York

What the book is about: While covering the disappearance of a young heiress, Jenny discovers a mystery that has been covered up for nearly 20 years.

Other books you might like:
Sophie Belfort, *The Lace Curtain Murders*, 1986
J.S. Borthwick, *The Down-East Murders*, 1985
Lucille Kallen, *Introducing C.B. Greenfield*, 1979
Michael J. Katz, *Last Dance in Redondo Beach*, 1989
Nancy Pickard, *The Jenny Cain Series*, 1985

121
Laurien Berenson
A Pedigree to Die For (New York: Kensington, 1995)

Story type: Amateur Detective—Female Lead

Major character(s): Melanie Travis, Teacher (special education), Single Parent; Sam Driver, Businessman (dog breeder)

Time period(s): 1990s

Locale(s): Stamford, Connecticut

What the book is about: Melanie's Uncle Max, well-known poodle breeder, has died of a heart attack and his champion breeder poodle Beau is missing. Aunt Pee, Max's widow, has a plan and asks Melanie for help. Melanie is to pose as a poodle breeder and see if she can find out who has taken Beau. Melanie, whose life is on the down-side at the moment, reluctantly agrees. She meets the various members of the doggie community including the exasperating, but incredibly handsome, Sam Driver. Then another breeder is killed. Is there a connection to Max's death and the missing dog?

Other books you might like:
Lydia Adamson, *Dr. Nightingale Goes to the Dogs*, 1995
Rita Mae Brown, *Murder at Monticello*, 1994
Melissa Cleary, *The Jackie Walsh Series*, 1992-
Susan Conant, *Black Ribbon*, 1995
Karen Ann Wilson, *Eight Dogs Flying*, 1994

122
Barry Berg
Hide and Seek (New York: St. Martin's, 1989)

Story type: Action/Adventure

Major character(s): Richard Knowles, Student (14 years old), Teenager; Lisa Frank, Prostitute (15 years old), Teenager

Time period(s): 1980s

Locale(s): New York, New York

What the book is about: When 14 year old Richard Knowles returns from Colombia, he does not know that his father has sewn cocaine into his coat. Soon he is on the run from his father, among others. First book.

Other books you might like:
Dick Lochte, *Sleeping Dog*, 1985

123
David Berlinski
A Clean Sweep (New York: St. Martins, 1993)

Story type: Private Detective—Male Lead

Major character(s): Aaron Asherfeld, Detective—Private

Time period(s): 1990s

Locale(s): San Francisco, California

What the book is about: Hired by a black mobster to find a missing businessman, who owes the mobster big money, Asherfeld finds himself involved with pornography, computer software, the businessman's wife and girlfriend and murder. That the man who hired him is killed doesn't discourage Asherfeld. First novel.

Other books you might like:
Joe Gores, *The D.K.A. Series*, 1973-
John T. Lescroart, *The Dismas Hardy Series*, 1990-
John Leslie, *Killing Me Softly*, 1994
David M. Pierce, *Write Me a Letter*, 1994
Collin Wilcox, *Silent Witness*, 1990

124
Carole Berry
Death of a Dancing Fool (New York: Berkley, 1995)
Series: Bonnie Indermill
Story type: Amateur Detective—Female Lead
Major character(s): Bonnie Indermill, Businesswoman, Detective—Amateur
Time period(s): 1990s
Locale(s): New York, New York
What the book is about: Bonnie's life is looking up. She is engaged to be married and has a steady job. However Sam, her fiance, is out of town and there is a lull in the moving business. In other words, she is bored. Even so, her old "friend" Eddie can't talk her into working at his new upscale dancing club, even when a TV star commits suicide. Finally, though, when an actor pretending to be a janitor is killed, Bonnie takes up sleuthing again. But it may be her last dance.
Other books you might like:
Carol Brennan, *The Liz Wareham Series*, 1993-
Trella Crespi, *The Simona Griffo Series*, 1991-
Marlys Millhiser, *The Charlie Green Series*, 1991-
Dianne G. Pugh, *The Iris Thorne Series*, 1993-
Kerry Tucker, *Cold Feet*, 1992

125
Carole Berry
The Death of a Difficult Woman (New York: Berkley, 1994)
Series: Bonnie Indermill
Story type: Amateur Detective—Female Lead
Major character(s): Bonnie Indermill, Office Worker (temporary)
Time period(s): 1990s
Locale(s): New York, New York
What the book is about: Although she swore never to work for another law firm, Bonnie Indermill is back at one, assisting the firm's move to a new building. Almost immediately, by hook or by crook, she is placed in charge of the move. She does a fine job until a strange laughing man starts some vicious practical jokes aimed at the cantankerous and difficult Kate Hamilton. Bonnie also has some trouble with Kate and when Kate is found murdered Bonnie knows the police will suspect her. She better find the real killer quickly or he may find her.
Other books you might like:
Susan Rogers Cooper, *Funny as a Dead Comic*, 1993
Trella Crespi, *The Trouble with a Small Raise*, 1991
Marlys Millhiser, *Death of the Office Witch*, 1993
Dianne G. Pugh, *Cold Call*, 1993
Kathy Hogan Trocheck, *Every Crooked Nanny*, 1992

126
Carole Berry
Good Night, Sweet Prince (New York: St. Martin's, 1990)
Series: Bonnie Indermill
Story type: Amateur Detective—Female Lead
Major character(s): Bonnie Indermill, Dancer (temporary worker)
Time period(s): 1980s
Locale(s): New York, New York
What the book is about: While working as an assistant at the Gotham Ballet, Bonnie Jean Indermill is involved in the defection of a visiting Soviet dancer. When he is killed in a fall during his debut performance, Bonnie Jean doesn't believe the KGB was responsible.
Other books you might like:
Edgar Box, *Death in the Fifth Position*, 1952
Lucy Cores, *Corpse de Ballet*, 1941
Jeffrey Wilds Deaver, *Manhattan Is My Beat*, 1989
Nancy Pickard, *Say No to Murder*, 1985
Elizabeth Powers, *On Account of Murder*, 1984

127
Carole Berry
Island Girl (New York: St. Martin's, 1991)
Series: Bonnie Indermill
Story type: Amateur Detective—Female Lead
Major character(s): Bonnie Indermill, Worker (temporary worker at odd jobs)
Time period(s): 1990s
Locale(s): Bahamas
What the book is about: Bonnie is asked to fill in as an assistant fitness counselor at a resort in the Bahamas. She jumps at the chance to escape wintery New York. When she gets to the Bahamas, however, she is less than thrilled. Instead of the fancy resort she thought she'd find, she finds instead a run-down hotel, a crime wave and a roommate from hell. Then the roommate drowns and Bonnie suspects foul-play.
Other books you might like:
Toni Brill, *Date with a Dead Doctor*, 1991
Susan Conant, *The Holly Winter Series*, 1989-
Jeffrey Wilds Deaver, *Manhattan Is My Beat*, 1989
Janet Laurence, *A Deepe Coffyn*, 1990
Meg O'Brien, *The Jessica James Series*, 1990-

128
Carole Berry
Nightmare Point (New York: St. Martins, 1993)
Story type: Psychological Suspense
Major character(s): Joyce Neuhauser, Housewife, Mentally Ill Person; Ronnie Haddon, Criminal
Time period(s): 1990s
Locale(s): Cape Cod, Massachusetts
What the book is about: Vacationing in Cape Cod after her release from a hospital where she was receiving treatment for depression, Joyce Neuhauser spots someone she feels she knows from her past. With a feeling of dread, she probes her memories to try and figure it out. Then this man, Ronnie Haddon, murders a woman and kidnaps Joyce's daughter and as things become clear she realizes she must face her past to rescue her daughter in the present.

129 Bickham

Other books you might like:
Mary Higgins Clark, *Where Are the Children?*, 1975
Joy Fielding, *Kiss Mommy Goodbye*, 1982
Beverly Hastings, *Don't Look Back*, 1991
Judith Kelman, *The House on the Hill*, 1992
Marlys Millhiser, *Murder at Moot Point*, 1993

129
Jack Bickham
Dropshot: A Brad Smith Novel (New York: Tor, 1990)
Series: Brad Smith
Story type: Action/Adventure
Major character(s): Brad Smith, Sports Figure (ex-Wimbledon champ and ex-spy)
Time period(s): 1980s
Locale(s): St. Maarten, West Indies
What the book is about: After refusing an offer from his old doubles partner to visit the partner's tennis camp, Brad Smith discovers that the CIA would like him to go anyway. When his old doubles partner dies in an "accident" Smith decides he'd better check it out.
Other books you might like:
Frank Deford, *The Spy on the Deuce Court*, 1986
Thomas Gifford, *The Man from Lisbon*, 1977
Ilie Nastase, *Tie-Break*, 1986

130
Bob Biderman
The Genesis Files (New York: Walker, 1991)
Story type: Action/Adventure; Amateur Detective—Male Lead
Major character(s): Joseph Radkin, Journalist, Unemployed
Time period(s): 1990s
Locale(s): San Francisco, California
What the book is about: Unemployed reporter Joseph Radkin agrees to investigate an outbreak of salmonella at a San Francisco hospital. The outbreak coincides with an explosion and death at the same hospital's research laboratory. The dead man was a popular doctor, head of the People's Medical Clinic, and Radkin wonders what he was doing at the research clinic in the middle of the night. First novel published in the U.S.
Other books you might like:
Don Flynn, *Ed Fitzgerald Series*, 1983-
Keith Peterson, *Rough Justice*, 1990
Mike Phillips, *Blood Rights*, 1989
John R. Riggs, *Wolf in Sheep's Clothing*, 1989
Noel Vreeland Carter, *The Mooncalf Murders*, 1989

131
Lloyd Biggle Jr.
The Glendower Conspiracy (Tulsa: Council Oak, 1990)
Series: Sherlock Holmes and Edward Porter Jones
Story type: Private Detective—Male Lead; Historical
Major character(s): Edward Porter Jones, Detective—Private (assistant to Sherlock Holmes); Sherlock Holmes, Detective—Private
Time period(s): 1900s (1904)
Locale(s): Wales
What the book is about: Sherlock Holmes sends his assistant Edward Porter Jones, who was formerly a Baker Street irregular, to Wales to do preliminary work on the murder of a Welsh landowner. Did someone want the land—or his daughter?
Other books you might like:
Rick Boyer, *The Giant Rat of Sumatra*, 1976
Carole Nelson Douglas, *Good Night, Mr. Holmes*, 1990
John Gardner, *The Return of Moriarty*, 1974
L.B. Greenwood, *Sherlock Holmes and the Thistle of Scotland*, 1989
H. Paul Jeffers, *The Adventure of the Stalwart Companions*, 1978

132
Lloyd Biggle Jr.
A Hazard of Losers (Tulsa: Council Oaks, 1991)
Story type: Private Detective—Male Lead
Major character(s): J. Fletcher, Detective—Private
Time period(s): 1990s
Locale(s): Las Vegas, Nevada
What the book is about: Summoned to Las Vegas to investigate a scam at one of the casinos, Fletcher soon discovers a murder—which may have been committed to forestall his investigation. Or maybe not. With the help of frustrated detective Leda Rauchman, Fletcher uncovers both the murderer and the brains behind the scam.
Other books you might like:
W.T. Ballard, *Pretty Miss Murder*, 1961
William Goldman, *Heat*, 1985
J.J. Lamb, *Nickel Straight*, 1976
Bernard Schopen, *The Desert Look*, 1990
Mark Schorr, *Ace of Diamonds*, 1984

133
John Birkett
The Queen's Mare (New York: Avon, 1990)
Series: Michael Rhinehart
Story type: Private Detective—Male Lead
Major character(s): Michael Rhinehart, Detective—Private
Time period(s): 1990s
Locale(s): Louisville, Kentucky
What the book is about: Someone has stolen a valuable brood mare and its foal from a Louisville farm and has asked a million dollars ransom. Rather than call in the police, the Beaumont family calls in P.I. Michael Rhinehart. Does the theft have anything to do with the forthcoming visit of the Queen of England—or something even more sinister?

What Mystery Do I Read Next?

Other books you might like:
Jon L. Breen, *Listen for the Click*, 1983
Stephen Dobyns, *Saratoga Longshot*, 1976
Dick Francis, *Dead Cert*, 1962
Kin Platt, *The Princess Stakes Murder*, 1973
Robert J. Randisi, *The Disappearance of Penny*, 1980

134
Claudia Bishop (Pseudonym of Mary Stanton)
A Dash of Death (New York: Berkley, 1995)
Series: Sarah Quilliam
Story type: Amateur Detective—Female Lead
Major character(s): Sarah "Quill" Quilliam, Artist, Hotel Owner; Meg Quilliam, Cook (Sarah's sister and partner)
Time period(s): 1990s
Locale(s): Hemlock Falls, New York
What the book is about: Famed arbiter of culture for the rich and famous Helena Houndswood is staying at the Hemlock Falls Inn. She is in town to bestow a million dollars on the winner of a china design contest. Quill thinks it would be great if the ceremony was televised from the inn. The winner of the contest turns out to be a group of five women working for the local paint company. The publicity may not be quite what Quill wants when the winners start to disappear or show up dead.
Other books you might like:
Mary Daheim, *The Bed-and-Breakfast Series*, 1991-
Jean Hager, *The Iris House Series*, 1994-
Kate Kingsbury, *The Pennyfoot Hotel Series*, 1993-
Tamar Myers, *Too Many Cooks Spoil the Broth*, 1994
Joanne Pence, *Something's Cooking*, 1993

135
Claudia Bishop
A Taste for Murder (New York: Berkley, 1994)
Series: Sarah Quilliam
Story type: Amateur Detective—Female Lead
Major character(s): Sarah "Quill" Quilliam, Innkeeper; Meg Quilliam, Cook (Sarah's sister)
Time period(s): 1990s
Locale(s): Hemlock Falls, New York
What the book is about: Sarah Quilliam has her hands full just trying to keep her guests happy during the History Days Festival, what with an obnoxious salesman and a litigious older woman. When the litigious older woman's companion is almost killed in a fall, is involved in a fatal accident to her boyfriend and finally is killed in a reenactment of the witch trials, that is too much. Sarah is determined to find out who is responsible and protect the inn's reputation. First novel.
Other books you might like:
Mary Daheim, *The Bed-and-Breakfast Series*, 1991-
Denise Dietz, *Throw Darts at a Cheesecake*, 1993
Jean Hager, *Blooming Murder*, 1994
Janet Laurence, *Hotel Morgue*, 1992
Katherine Hall Page, *The Body in the Bouillon*, 1991

136
Veronica Black
A Vow of Chastity (New York: St. Martin's, 1992)
Series: Sister Joan
Story type: Amateur Detective—Female Lead
Major character(s): Sister Joan, Religious (nun), Teacher
Time period(s): 1990s
Locale(s): England
What the book is about: Why did someone kill one of Sister Joan's students, an immigrant Romanian? When Sister Joan and Sister Margaret investigate, Sister Margaret ends up bludgeoned to death with a candlestick. The police are at sea in this semi-closed society, so Sister Joan is on her own.
Other books you might like:
D.M. Greenwood, *Clerical Errors*, 1992
Lee Harris, *The Yom Kippur Murder*, 1992
Isabelle Holland, *A Death at St. Anselm's*, 1984
Sister Carol Anne O'Marie, *Advent of Silence*, 1986
Monica Quill, *Sine Qua Nun*, 1986

137
Veronica Black
A Vow of Obedience (New York: Fawcett, 1994)
Series: Sister Joan
Story type: Amateur Detective—Female Lead
Major character(s): Sister Joan, Religious (nun)
Time period(s): 1990s
Locale(s): Cornwall, England
What the book is about: Sister Joan finds the strangled body of a teenage girl dressed in a wedding gown. The next day another teenager is found, killed in the same way and also dressed in a wedding gown. Then Sister Hilaria, the nun in charge of the younger nuns, is injured in a hit-and-run accident. Are these incidents related? Sister Joan is determined to help the police in their investigation of the likely suspects, one of whom is a cop.
Other books you might like:
D.M. Greenwood, *Clerical Errors*, 1991
Lee Harris, *The Saint Patrick's Day Murder*, 1994
David Willis McCullough, *Think on Death*, 1991
Sister Carol Anne O'Marie, *The Sister Mary Helen Series*, 1984-
Monica Quill, *The Sister Mary Teresa Series*, 1981-

138
Veronica Black
A Vow of Sanctity (New York: St. Martins, 1993)
Series: Sister Joan
Story type: Amateur Detective—Female Lead
Major character(s): Sister Joan, Religious (nun)
Time period(s): 1990s
Locale(s): Scotland (western)

139 Blackmur

What the book is about: In Scotland for a month-long retreat, Sister Joan is soon involved in the mysteries of the locals. There seem to be a lot of them, including the disappearance of a local Catholic six years earlier who may or may not have been killed by his wife for having an affair; the apparent suicide some months later of the woman with whom he was having the affair; late night rendevouzes between a young woman and what may be one of the monks; and finally the disppearance of a body—supposedly of a long dead priest—from the monastery crypt. But this priest appeared to be wearing modern shoes.

Other books you might like:
D.M. Greenwood, *Clerical Errors*, 1991
Lee Harris, *The Christening Day Murder*, 1993
David Willis McCullough, *The Ziza Todd Series*, 1990-
Sister Carol Anne O'Marie, *The Sister Mary Helen Series*, 1984-
Monica Quill, *The Sister Mary Teresa Series*, 1981-

139
L.L. Blackmur
Love Lies Slain (New York: St. Martin's, 1989)

Story type: Psychological Suspense

Major character(s): Galen Shaw, Writer, Journalist (former reporter); Henry Baugh, Artist

Time period(s): 1980s

Locale(s): Massachusetts

What the book is about: After meeting and befriending elderly artist Henry Baugh, former reporter Galen Shaw is asked to write his biography. Soon she is involved in murder and with Baugh's son.

Other books you might like:
Mary Higgins Clark, *While My Pretty One Sleeps*, 1989
Nickolae Gertsner, *Dark Veil*, 1989
Velda Johnston, *Flight to Yesterday*, 1990
Harriet La Barre, *The Florentine Win*, 1988
Phyllis Whitney, *The Singing Stones*, 1990

140
W. Edward Blain
Passion Play (New York: Putnam, 1990)

Story type: Psychological Suspense

Major character(s): Thomas Boatwright, Student (at a prep school)

Time period(s): 1980s

Locale(s): Virginia; New York

What the book is about: What does a murder in New York City have to do with a suspicious death at a Virginia prep school? First book.

Other books you might like:
S.F.X. Dean, *By Frequent Anguish*, 1982
Michael T. Hinkemeyer, *Fourth Down, Death*, 1985
William Maner, *Die of a Rose*, 1970
Victoria Silver, *Death of a Harvard Freshman*, 1984

141
Eleanor Taylor Bland
Dead Time (New York: St. Martin's, 1992)

Series: Marti MacAlister

Story type: Police Procedural—Female Lead

Major character(s): Marti MacAlister, Police Officer (African-American), Widow(er)

Time period(s): 1990s

Locale(s): Lincoln Prairie, Illinois

What the book is about: A murder victim found in a flop house turns out to be the schizophrenic daughter of a wealthy family from which she's been estranged for many years. Recently relocated police detective Marti MacAlister, widowed and black, is determined to find the truth. It appears that some homeless children may have witnessed the murder and Marti needs to find them before the killer does. First novel.

Other books you might like:
Barbara D'Amato, *The Cat Marsala Series*, 1989-
Wayne Dundee, *The Burning Season*, 1988
Margaret Maron, *The Sigrid Harald Series*, 1985-
Barbara Neely, *Blanche on the Lam*, 1992
Dorothy Uhnak, *The Ledger*, 1970

142
Eleanor Taylor Bland
Slow Burn (New York: St. Martins, 1993)

Series: Marti MacAlister

Story type: Police Procedural—Female Lead

Major character(s): Marti MacAlister, Police Officer (African-American)

Time period(s): 1990s

Locale(s): Lincoln Prairie, Illinois

What the book is about: The search through a burned-out medical clinic turns up the bodies of the receptionist and an unidentified twelve year old. Was the clinic torched on purpose and if so, who was responsible? Lincoln Prairie police officer Marti MacAlister must sift through the lies and cover-ups to find the guilty parties.

Other books you might like:
Nikki Baker, *The Virginia Kelly Series*, 1991-
Margaret Maron, *The Sigrid Harald Series*, 1985-
Lee Martin, *The Deb Ralston Series*, 1984-
Barbara Neely, *Blanche on the Lam*, 1992
Lillian O'Donnell, *The Norah Mulcahaney Series*, 1972-

143
Martin Blank
Shadowchase (New York: St. Martin's, 1989)

Story type: Psychological Suspense

Major character(s): Paul Lazzeri, Recluse; Owen Anderson, Doctor

Time period(s): 1980s (story is told in flashback)

Locale(s): Chicago, Illinois

What the book is about: What is the motive for the murders of a middle-aged brother and sister? Paul Lazzeri thinks he knows the motive and the murderer. First book.

Other books you might like:
Joe Gash, *Newspaper Murders*, 1985
Sara Paretsky, *Burn Marks*, 1990
Ruth Rendell, *Death Notes*, 1981

144

Peter Blauner
Slow Motion Riot (New York: Morrow, 1991)

Story type: Action/Adventure

Major character(s): Steven Baum, Probation Officer; Darryl King, Drug Dealer, Murderer

Time period(s): 1990s

Locale(s): New York, New York

What the book is about: Steven Baum, probation officer, gets more than he bargained for when he gets involved with the charming, but lethal, Darryl King. As Baum tries to control and keep track of Darryl, his life becomes more interesting and deadly. First novel. Edgar nominee for best first novel of 1991.

Other books you might like:
John Farris, *The Trouble at Harrison High*, 1970
J.P. Hailey, *The Underground Man*, 1990
Evan Hunter, *The Blackboard Jungle*, 1954
Jonathan Kellerman, *Time Bomb*, 1990
Keith Peterson, *The Rain*, 1989

145

Lawrence Block
The Burglar Who Traded Ted Williams (New York: Dutton, 1994)

Series: Bernie Rhodenbarr Mystery

Story type: Amateur Detective—Male Lead

Major character(s): Bernie Rhodenbarr, Store Owner (bookstore), Criminal (burglar)

Time period(s): 1990s

Locale(s): New York, New York

What the book is about: Business is adequate at the bookstore though his landlord is trying to raise his rent enough to put him out of business, but still Bernie Rhodenbarr has the urge to burgle and when he does there's a dead body. Stolen baseball cards, insurance scams, poetry readings, and his bookstore cat all seem to be causing Bernie problems.

Other books you might like:
M.C. Beaton, *Agatha Raisin and the Quiche of Death*, 1992
K.K. Beck, *The Body in the Cornflakes*, 1992
John Camp, *The Fool's Run*, 1989
Mary Daheim, *Fowl Prey*, 1991
Donald E. Westlake, *The Dortmunder Series*, 1970-

146

Lawrence Block
A Dance at the Slaughterhouse (New York: Morrow, 1991)

Series: Matt Scudder

Story type: Private Detective—Male Lead

Major character(s): Matt Scudder, Detective—Private, Alcoholic (recovering); Mick Ballou, Criminal (friend of Scudder's)

Time period(s): 1990s

Locale(s): New York, New York

What the book is about: Scudder is hired to investigate the brutal murder of Amanda Thurman that took place during a robbery. The woman's brother thinks it wasn't really a robbery but that her husband had her killed. While trailing the husband Scudder gets involved in an earlier case involving a snuff film, as he sees a familiar face. The two cases meld together as Scudder learns about the sex for sale world. Edgar winner for best Novel of 1991.

Other books you might like:
Jack Early, *A Creative Kind of Killer*, 1986
Keith Peterson, *Rough Justice*, 1990
Benjamin M. Schutz, *Embrace the Wolf*, 1985
Stephen Solomita, *A Twist of the Knife*, 1988
Jonathan Valin, *The Lime Pit*, 1980

147

Lawrence Block
The Devil Knows You're Dead (New York: Morrow, 1993)

Series: Matt Scudder

Story type: Private Detective—Male Lead

Major character(s): Matt Scudder, Detective—Private (unlicensed)

Time period(s): 1990s

Locale(s): New York, New York

What the book is about: Neither the widow of a man gunned down seemingly at random on the street, nor the brother of the man accused of doing the shooting, believe that what appears to be an open and shut case is, in fact, not as clear cut as it appears to be. Asked by the brother to investigate, Matt Scudder soon finds himself emotionally involved with the widow—who has turned up a box of cash which makes her think she didn't really know her husband. It also makes her even more sure that his death wasn't random.

Other books you might like:
Neal Barrett Jr., *Pink Vodka Blues*, 1992
James Lee Burke, *The Dave Robicheaux Series*, 1986-
Loren D. Estleman, *The Amos Walker Series*, 1980-
Alice Hoffman, *Turtle Moon*, 1992
Stephen Solomita, *A Good Day to Die*, 1993

148

Lawrence Block
Out on the Cutting Edge (New York: Morrow, 1989)

149
Series: Matt Scudder

Story type: Private Detective—Male Lead

Major character(s): Matt Scudder, Detective—Private, Alcoholic (recovering)

Time period(s): 1980s

Locale(s): New York, New York

What the book is about: Matt is hired to find a missing girl from Indiana. He's also trying very hard to stay sober as he is a recovering alcoholic.

Other books you might like:
Robert Campbell, *Alice in La-La Land*, 1987
Tucker Coe, *A Jade in Aries*, 1970
James Crumley, *The Last Good Kiss*, 1978
Timothy Harris, *Kyd for Hire*, 1977
Philip Lee Williams, *Slow Dance in Autumn*, 1988

149
Lawrence Block
A Ticket to the Boneyard (New York: Morrow, 1990)

Series: Matt Scudder

Story type: Private Detective—Male Lead; Psychological Suspense

Major character(s): Matt Scudder, Detective—Private, Alcoholic (recovering); James Leo Motley, Criminal

Time period(s): 1980s (1987)

Locale(s): New York, New York

What the book is about: James Leo Motley, who Scudder helped put in prison years ago, is coming after him. But before he gets to Scudder he is killing off all of "Scudder's women."

Other books you might like:
Gary Amo, *Silent Night*, 1991
Joe R. Lansdale, *The Savage Season*, 1990
John Sandford, *Rules of Prey*, 1990
Benjamin M. Schutz, *A Fistful of Empty*, 1991
Stephen Solomita, *Bad to the Bone*, 1991

150
Lawrence Block
A Walk Among the Tombstones (New York: Morrow, 1992)

Series: Matt Scudder

Story type: Private Detective—Male Lead

Major character(s): Matt Scudder, Detective—Private (unlicensed)

Time period(s): 1990s

Locale(s): New York, New York

What the book is about: The dismembered body of the kidnapped wife of a drug dealer gets Scudder involved with some serious undesirables. But, because the woman killed was a total innocent, he agrees to help find the killers.

Other books you might like:
Jack Early, *Donato and Daughter*, 1988
Andrew Klavan, *Don't Say a Word*, 1991
Benjamin M. Schutz, *Embrace the Wolf*, 1985
Stephen Solomita, *Bad to the Bone*, 1991
Jonathan Valin, *Extenuating Circumstances*, 1991

151
Michael Bond
Monsieur Pamplemousse Investigates (New York: Fawcett, 1990)

Series: Monsieur Pamplemousse

Story type: Amateur Detective—Male Lead; Humor

Major character(s): Pamplemousse, Writer, Critic (restaurant critic)

Time period(s): 1980s

Locale(s): Paris, France

What the book is about: Someone is trying to ruin *Le Guide*, the world famous restaurant directory—fake death reports, killer fish—and now someone has taken over the computer. Can M. Pamplemousse find out who is doing this and why?

Other books you might like:
Dorothy Cannell, *The Thin Woman*, 1986
Fred Halliday, *Murder in the Kitchen*, 1979
Janet Laurence, *A Deepe Coffyn*, 1990
Nan Lyons, *Someone Is Killing the Great Chefs of Europe*, 1976 (Ivan Lyons, co-author)
Virginia Rich, *The Cooking School Murders*, 1982

152
Michael Bond
Pamplemousse Rests His Case (New York: Fawcett, 1991)

Series: Monsieur Pamplemousse

Story type: Amateur Detective—Male Lead

Major character(s): Pamplemousse, Writer (food writer; retired inspector)

Time period(s): 1990s

Locale(s): Vichy, France

What the book is about: Monsieur Pamplemousse arrives in Vichy to cover a mystery dinner based on one once hosted by Alexandre Dumas. Once there he finds himself embroiled in more than good food. There are two fake murders, an amorous American publisher, false arrest and one genuine murder.

Other books you might like:
Dorothy Cannell, *The Thin Woman*, 1986
Fred Halliday, *Murder in the Kitchen*, 1979
Nan Lyons, *Someone Is Killing the Great Chefs of Europe*, 1976 (Ivan Lyons, co-author)
Virginia Rich, *The Cooking School Murders*, 1982

153
Miriam Borgenicht
Undue Influence (New York: St. Martin's, 1989)

Story type: Psychological Suspense

Major character(s): Lydia Ness, Lawyer, Single Parent

Time period(s): 1980s

Locale(s): New York, New York

What the book is about: Lydia Ness agrees to defend an alleged rapist/murderer and gets him off. The family of the victim kidnaps Lydia's daughter in retaliation.

Other books you might like:
Paul Levine, *To Speak for the Dead*, 1990
Lia Matera, *The Good Fight*, 1990
Julie Smith, *The Sourdough Wars*, 1984
Michael Underwood, *The Hidden Man*, 1985

154
J.S. Borthwick
The Bridled Groom (New York: St. Martin's, 1994)

Series: Sarah Deane & Alex McKenzie

Story type: Amateur Detective

Major character(s): Sarah Deane, Teacher (of English; Ph.D. candidate); Alex McKenzie, Doctor

Time period(s): 1990s

Locale(s): Maine

What the book is about: While planning their wedding, Sarah Deane and her fiance, Alex McKenzie, get distracted while trying to find out who is sending anonymous, threatening notes to Sarah's Aunt Julia. The notes get more and more threatening until finally there is a death, though it is not the one that was expected. Who is the guilty party—the Colonel who wants to marry Aunt Julia, the librarian, or a representative of a mining company that wants Julia's property? Sarah and Alex try to find out.

Other books you might like:
Gerry Boyle, *Deadline*, 1993
Susan Kelly, *The Liz Connors Series*, 1985-
Charlotte MacLeod, *The Sarah Kelling Series*, 1980-
Mary Monica Pulver, *The Kori and Peter Brichter Series*, 1988-
Gillian Roberts, *The Amanda Pepper Series*, 1987-

155
D.B. Borton
Four Elements of Murder (New York: Berkley, 1995)

Series: Cat Caliban

Story type: Private Detective—Female Lead

Major character(s): Catherine "Cat" Caliban, Widow(er), Detective—Private; Louella Simmons, Real Estate Agent

Time period(s): 1990s

Locale(s): Cincinnati, Ohio; Cayter, Tennessee

What the book is about: Cat Caliban is still learning how to be a private detective, a career she decided to try after turning sixty. She is asked to investigate the death of Louella Simmons' uncle, Red McIntyre. Red was coming to Cincinnati to protest the building of a trash incinerator when he died in a car accident. Cat finds the circumstances suspicious. Was there a conspiracy among the chemical companies in his home town to quiet Red who was asking embarrassing questions about their methods of disposing of toxic chemicals? Cat may need nine lives to find the answers.

Other books you might like:
Jill Churchill, *The Jane Jeffry Series*, 1990-
Janet Evanovich, *One for the Money*, 1994
Jaqueline Girdner, *The Kate Jasper Series*, 1990-
Charlotte MacLeod, *The Sarah Kelling Series*, 1979-
Meg O'Brien, *The Jessica James Series*, 1989-

156
D.B. Borton
Three Is a Crowd (New York: Berkley, 1994)

Series: Cat Caliban

Story type: Private Detective—Female Lead

Major character(s): Catherine "Cat" Caliban, Detective—Private, Widow(er)

Time period(s): 1990s

Locale(s): Cincinnati, Ohio

What the book is about: With Cat's husband dead and her children grown and gone, she decides on a new career. She becomes a private detective and acquires a strange group of friends while doing so. One of them, a streetperson and ex-veteran, approaches her for help. He had been at a protest rally when someone was murdered and he is afraid he will be accused. When Cat investigates, she finds he has good reason to worry. The trail leads back to the 1960s and an antiwar group of radicals.

Other books you might like:
Charlaine Harris, *The Aurora Teagarden Series*, 1990-
Meg O'Brien, *The Jessica James Series*, 1990-
B.J. Oliphant, *The Shirley McClintock Series*, 1990-
Jennifer Rowe, *The Verity Birdwood Series*, 1991-
Shelley Singer, *The Barrett Lake Series*, 1993-

157
D.B. Borton
Two Points for Murder (New York: Berkley, 1993)

Series: Cat Caliban

Story type: Private Detective—Female Lead

Major character(s): Catherine "Cat" Caliban, Detective—Private (in training), Single Parent (of three)

Time period(s): 1990s

Locale(s): Cincinnati, Ohio

What the book is about: Cat Caliban is trying to get experience as a private detective so she can get her license. Her latest case is to find a lost kitten. She finds the kitten and a notebook written by Jules Kay, a local teen basketball star until he was murdered. She offers to look into the case for his mother and finds that Jules wasn't the first member of the team to die.

Other books you might like:
Jill Churchill, *The Jane Jeffry Series*, 1990-
Jon Katz, *Death by Station Wagon*, 1993
Katherine Hall Page, *The Body in the Belfry*, 1990
Shelley Singer, *Following Jane*, 1993
Valerie Wolzien, *The Susan Henshaw Series*, 1988-

158
Michael Bowen
Act of Faith (New York: St. Martins, 1993)
Series: Thomas Curry and Sandine Cadette
Story type: Amateur Detective; Historical
Major character(s): Thomas Curry, Businessman (independently wealthy); Sandy Cadette, Spouse (French)
Time period(s): 1960s (1963)
Locale(s): Burundi
What the book is about: While on photo safari, Thomas Curry and his wife Sandrine get involved in the murder of an American. The American's roommate is charged with the killing but insists that he is innocent. The murder may have something to do with the military and political situation. Or it may not.

Other books you might like:
J.N. Catanach, *Brideprice*, 1989
Elspeth Huxley, *Murder on Safari*, 1938
M.M. Kaye, *Death in Zanzibar*, 1983
Karin McQuillan, *Deadly Safari*, 1990

159
Michael Bowen
Faithfully Executed (New York: St. Martin's, 1992)
Series: Richard Michaelson
Story type: Amateur Detective—Male Lead
Major character(s): Richard Michaelson, Diplomat (political advisor)
Time period(s): 1990s
Locale(s): Washington, District of Columbia
What the book is about: After a government execution appears to have failed, Michaelson is appointed to head a commission to try and discover what happened and why. The plot may involve a stolen election and the Japanese.

Other books you might like:
Jerome Doolittle, *Stranglehold*, 1991
Lawrence Meyer, *A Capitol Crime*, 1977
William D. Pease, *Playing the Dozens*, 1990
Ross Thomas, *The Fools in Town Are on Our Side*, 1970

160
Michael Bowen
Fielder's Choice (New York: St. Martin's, 1991)
Series: Thomas Curry and Sandine Cadette
Story type: Amateur Detective; Historical
Major character(s): Thomas Curry, Businessman (independently wealthy); Sandy Cadette, Spouse (of Thomas Curry)
Time period(s): 1960s (1962)
Locale(s): New York, New York
What the book is about: When a friend is murdered Thomas and Sandy decide to investigate. It seems the friend was a con man—though small time—and his murder may have something to do with a swindle he was working on at the time.

Other books you might like:
William L. DeAndrea, *Five O'Clock Lightning*, 1986
Paul Engleman, *Dead in Center Field*, 1987
Alison Gordon, *The Dead Pull Hitter*, 1989
Carolyn G. Hart, *Death on Demand*, 1986
Richard and Frances Lockridge, *The Mr. and Mrs. North Series*, 1940-1963 (Frances Lockridge, co-author)

161
Elisabeth Bowers
No Forwarding Address (Seattle, Washington: Seal, 1991)
Series: Meg Lacey
Story type: Private Detective—Female Lead
Major character(s): Meg Lacey, Detective—Private (middle-aged), Single Parent (divorced)
Time period(s): 1990s
Locale(s): Vancouver, British Columbia, Canada
What the book is about: Meg has been hired by Vicky Fischer to find her sister who has left her husband and taken her four-year old son along. Meg finds them hiding and terrified, in a less than exciting part of town. Meg is not sure whether to believe the woman but when she is found beaten to death, Meg knows she must find the killer.

Other books you might like:
Linda Barnes, *Coyote*, 1990
Barbara D'Amato, *Hardball*, 1990
Sue Grafton, *The Kinsey Millhone Series*, 1982-
Karen Kijewski, *Katwalk*, 1989
Sara Paretsky, *Burn Marks*, 1990

162
Rick Boyer
Yellow Bird (New York: Fawcett, 1991)
Series: Doc Adams
Story type: Amateur Detective—Male Lead
Major character(s): Charlie "Doc" Adams, Dentist
Time period(s): 1990s
Locale(s): Massachusetts

What the book is about: While visiting Cape Cod Doc and his wife Mary think they hear a shot from a deserted mansion. When they investigate the house seems empty. Then, weeks later, a body is found, shot, in the house, which belongs to Northrup Chesterton, one of the upper crust. The body turns out to be a former neighbor of Doc's. What is behind the murder and when and where did it really take place?

Other books you might like:
L.L. Enger, *Swing*, 1991
Richard Forrest, *Bea and Lyon Wentworth Series*, 1974-
Mary Monica Pulver, *The Unforgiving Minutes*, 1988
William G. Tapply, *The Brady Coyne Series*, 1984-
Elizabeth Travis, *Under the Influence*, 1988

163
Gerry Boyle
Deadline (Belfast, Maine: North Country, 1993)

Story type: Amateur Detective—Male Lead

Major character(s): Jack McMorrow, Journalist (newspaper editor)

Time period(s): 1990s

Locale(s): Androscoggin, Maine

What the book is about: The discovery of the body of a free-lance photographer floating in a canal causes newspaper editor Jack McMorrow all kinds of grief. He is kidnapped, threatened, beaten and almost killed as he tries to find the truth behind the death of the photographer. First novel.

Other books you might like:
Mary Daheim, *The Alpine Advocate*, 1992
Andrew Klavan, *Corruption*, 1994
Vince Kohler, *Rainy North Woods*, 1990
Keith Peterson, *The John Wells Series*, 1988-
John R. Riggs, *Let Sleeping Dogs Lie*, 1985

164
Lynn Bradley
Stand-In for Murder (New York: Walker, 1994)

Story type: Private Detective—Male Lead

Major character(s): Cole January, Detective—Private

Time period(s): 1990s

Locale(s): Houston, Texas

What the book is about: Cole January awakens one morning to find himself stepping on a dead woman as he gets out of bed. The police are on the scene almost instantly, but Cole manages to talk himself out of the current situation so he can try and figure out why someone would try to set him up. The dead woman is supposed to be socialite Molly Jones-Heitkamp. However, a woman soon calls up Cole's office claiming to be the dead woman, only this one is very obviously alive. What is going on? First novel.

Other books you might like:
Neil Albert, *The January Corpse*, 1990
Richard Barre, *The Innocents*, 1995
Neal Barrett Jr., *Pink Vodka Blues*, 1993
James Crumley, *Dancing Bear*, 1983
Ron Ely, *Night Shadows*, 1994

165
Jay Brandon
Predator's Waltz (New York: St. Martin's, 1989)

Story type: Action/Adventure

Major character(s): Daniel Greer, Businessman (pawnshop owner); Tranh Van Khai, Criminal (Vietnamese)

Time period(s): 1980s

Locale(s): Houston, Texas

What the book is about: Soon after Daniel Greer asks Trang Van Khai for help in eliminating a business rival, Greer realizes he has made a mistake. Greer's wife is then kidnapped and he must try to rescue her.

Other books you might like:
Joe Gores, *A Time of Predators*, 1969
David L. Lindsey, *A Cold Mind*, 1983
Edward Mathis, *Another Path, Another Dragon*, 1988
T. Jefferson Parker, *Little Saigon*, 1988

166
Nat Brandt
Co-Author: Yanna Brandt
Land Kills (Woodstock, Vermont: Countryman, 1991)

Story type: Amateur Detective—Male Lead

Major character(s): Mitch Stevens, Journalist

Time period(s): 1990s

Locale(s): Southborough, Vermont

What the book is about: In Southborough to cover a summer music festival reporter Mitch Stevens stumbles across the body of a local woman who has been missing since the previous fall. Not believing that she died by accident he decides to investigate. He discovers other unusual deaths and almost becomes a victim himself. First novel.

Other books you might like:
Don Flynn, *Murder on the Hudson*, 1985
Douglas Kiker, *Murder on Clam Pond*, 1987
Vince Kohler, *Rainy North Woods*, 1990
Keith Peterson, *The Trapdoor*, 1988
John R. Riggs, *The Garth Ryland Series*, 1984-

167
Lilian Jackson Braun
The Cat Who Moved a Mountain (New York: Putnam, 1992)

Series: Cat Who.

Story type: Amateur Detective—Male Lead

Major character(s): Jim Qwilleran, Journalist (reporter); Koko, Animal (cat)

Time period(s): 1990s

Locale(s): Spudsboro, North Carolina

What the book is about: Having collected his inheritance, Jim Qwilleran—along with his cats, Koko and Yum-Yum—is off to the Potato Mountains to reevaluate his life. Once there he cannot help getting involved in a development issue and in trying to solve the murder of the town's leading resident over a year ago. It just so happens that Jim is living in the man's house. Was he killed because of his pro-development stance or were there other, deeper issues involved?

Other books you might like:
Lydia Adamson, *A Cat in the Manger*, 1990
Rita Mae Brown, *Wish You Were Here*, 1990
Carole Nelson Douglas, *Catnap*, 1992
Ed Gorman, *Cat Crimes*, 1990 (editor)
M.K. Wren, *The Conan Flagg Series*, 1974-

168
Lilian Jackson Braun
The Cat Who Talked to Ghosts (New York: Putnam, 1989)

Series: Cat Who.

Story type: Amateur Detective—Male Lead

Major character(s): Jim Qwilleran, Journalist; Koko, Animal (Siamese cat)

Time period(s): 1980s

Locale(s): Midwest

What the book is about: When the curator dies of a supposed heart attack after telling Qwilleran that she was seeing ghosts, he is suspicious and moves into the museum to find out the truth.

Other books you might like:
Lesley Grant-Adamson, *Wild Justice*, 1988
Carolyn G. Hart, *A Little Class on Murder*, 1989
Lucille Kallen, *No Lady in the House*, 1982
Constance Little, *The Black Paw*, 1941 (Gwenyth Little, co-author)

169
Lilian Jackson Braun
The Cat Who Went into the Closet (New York: Putnam, 1993)

Series: Cat Who.

Story type: Amateur Detective—Male Lead

Major character(s): Jim Qwilleran, Journalist (newspaperman); Koko, Animal (Siamese cat); Yum Yum, Animal (Siamese cat)

Time period(s): 1990s

Locale(s): Pickax City, Michigan

What the book is about: Currently renting a mansion from his managing editor at the newspaper, Jim Qwilleran and the cats, Koko and Yum Yum, soon find themselves trying to find out the truth behind the death of the mansion's former owner, Euphonia Gage, a supposed suicide in her Florida retirement community. Before her death she appears to have gambled away a fortune, but her grandson, the aforementioned managing editor, doesn't believe it.

Other books you might like:
Lydia Adamson, *A Cat in the Manger*, 1990
Lawrence Block, *The Burglar Who Traded Ted Williams*, 1994
Rita Mae Brown, *Wish You Were Here*, 1990
Carole Nelson Douglas, *The Midnight Louie Series*, 1990-
M.K. Wren, *The Conan Flagg Series*, 1974-

170
Jon L. Breen
Hot Air (New York: Simon & Schuster, 1991)

Series: Jerry Brogan

Story type: Amateur Detective—Male Lead

Major character(s): Jerry Brogan, Sports Figure (race track announcer)

Time period(s): 1990s

Locale(s): Los Angeles, California

What the book is about: Jockey Brad Roark is set to retire and the race track director has set up a surprise family reunion—though Roark is not fond of his family. Someone will be surprised, as murder pays a visit. Jerry Brogan, the track announcer, decides to try and find out what happened.

Other books you might like:
Virginia Anderson, *King of the Roses*, 1983
John Birkett, *The Queen's Mare*, 1990
Michael Geller, *Dead Last*, 1986
William Murray, *Tip on a Dead Crab*, 1984
Robert J. Randisi, *The Disappearance of Penny*, 1980

171
Jon L. Breen
Loose Lips (New York: Simon & Schuster, 1990)

Series: Jerry Brogan

Story type: Amateur Detective—Male Lead

Major character(s): Jerry Brogan, Sports Figure (race track announcer)

Time period(s): 1980s

Locale(s): Los Angeles, California

What the book is about: When a track journalist, who was also a blackmailer, is killed, Jerry is asked by the LAPD to assist their investigation. Breen has won two Edgar awards for his critical works.

Other books you might like:
Virginia Anderson, *King of the Roses*, 1983
Dave Burkey, *Rain Lover*, 1985
Stephen Dobyns, *Saratoga Swimmer*, 1981
Michael Geller, *Dead Last*, 1986
William Murray, *Tip on a Dead Crab*, 1984

172
Carol Brennan
Full Commission (New York: Carroll & Graf, 1993)

Series: Liz Wareham

Story type: Amateur Detective—Female Lead

Major character(s): Liz Wareham, Public Relations; Ike O'Hanlon, Police Officer, Detective—Homicide

Time period(s): 1990s

Locale(s): New York, New York

What the book is about: One of Liz Wareham's clients thinks someone is trying to destroy their real estate business with dirty tricks. One of her other clients is having trouble with his rent-controlled building. When people involved in both situations begin to die, Liz decides she needs to involve her boyfriend, homicide detective Ike O'Hanlon.

Other books you might like:
Susan Wittig Albert, *Thyme of Death*, 1992
Mary Kittredge, *Poison Pen*, 1990
Annette Meyers, *The Smith and Wetzon Series*, 1987-
Marlys Millhiser, *Murder at Moot Point*, 1992
Ann M. Williams, *Flowers for the Dead*, 1991

173
Carol Brennan
In the Dark (New York: Putnam, 1994)

Story type: Amateur Detective—Female Lead; Psychological Suspense

Major character(s): Emily Silver, Actress (motion picture); Dev Hannigan, Writer

Time period(s): 1990s

Locale(s): New York; Florida; California

What the book is about: Emily Silver hears the voice of the man who killed her parents twenty years ago. With the help of her lover, Mike Florio, she sets out to find the truth about their deaths. When Mike is killed she goes to a friend of his, Dev Hannigan, in hopes that he will help her. A cross-country search ensues.

Other books you might like:
Mary Higgins Clark, *Weep No More, My Lady*, 1987
Kate Green, *Shooting Star*, 1992
Faye Kellerman, *False Prophet*, 1992
Susan Kelly, *Out of the Darkness*, 1992
Stuart Woods, *Santa Fe Rules*, 1992

174
Simon Brett
Corporate Bodies (New York: Scribners, 1992)

Series: Charles Paris

Story type: Amateur Detective—Male Lead

Major character(s): Charles Paris, Actor

Time period(s): 1990s

Locale(s): England

What the book is about: Actor Charles Paris is the initial suspect when a woman is found dead, crushed by a fork-lift he was supposed to drive in a corporate video. It soon turns out that the woman had no shortage of enemies, most of whom were former bedmates she was blackmailing on the way up the corporate ladder. Paris discovers she was video-taping her lovers and was probably killed for one of the tapes. The killer doesn't like Paris investigating and takes a bead on him.

Other books you might like:
Margot Arnold, *Exit Actors Dying*, 1979
Linda Barnes, *Blood Will Have Blood*, 1982
Jane Dentinger, *Murder on Cue*, 1983
William Campbell Gault, *Blood on the Boards*, 1953
Michael Innes, *Hamlet, Revenge!*, 1937

175
Simon Brett
Mrs. Pargeter's Package (New York: Scribners, 1991)

Series: Mrs. Pargeter

Story type: Amateur Detective—Female Lead

Major character(s): Melita Pargeter, Widow(er) (husband was a criminal)

Time period(s): 1990s

Locale(s): Greece

What the book is about: Going to Greece on vacation with a friend, things are going along quite well until her friend asks Mrs. Pargeter to smuggle a package through customs. The friend soon turns up dead and Mrs. Pargeter must find out what happened and why.

Other books you might like:
Heron Carvic, *The Miss Seeton Series*, 1968-
Dorothy Gilman, *The Mrs. Pollifax Series*, 1966-
Remar Sutton, *Long Lines*, 1989
Patricia Wentworth, *The Miss Silver Series*, 1928-1968
James Yaffe, *The Mom Series*, 1987-

176
Simon Brett
A Series of Murders (New York: Scribners, 1989)

Series: Charles Paris

Story type: Amateur Detective—Male Lead

Major character(s): Charles Paris, Actor, Alcoholic

Time period(s): 1980s

What the book is about: When Paris gets temporary work on a TV series, murder, of course, follows him there. The TV series is based on a fictional group of Golden Age mystery novels.

Other books you might like:
Margot Arnold, *Exit Actors Dying*, 1979
Linda Barnes, *Blood Will Have Blood*, 1982
Jane Dentinger, *Murder on Cue*, 1983
William Campbell Gault, *Blood on the Boards*, 1953
Michael Innes, *Hamlet, Revenge!*, 1937

177
Toni Brill
Date with a Dead Doctor (New York: St. Martins, 1991)

Story type: Amateur Detective—Female Lead

Major character(s): Margaret Midge Cohen, Writer (of young adult books; Russian); Russo, Police Officer (homicide detective)

Time period(s): 1990s

Locale(s): New York, New York

What the book is about: A blind date with a doctor turns into murder when the doctor asks Midge to translate a letter from some Russian relatives. Before she can finish translating, the doctor is murdered. Midge finds herself a suspect and attracted to the policeman investigating the case. First mystery under this name.

Other books you might like:
Bob Fenster, *The Last Page*, 1989
Melodie Johnson Howe, *The Mother Shadow*, 1989
Meg O'Brien, *The Jessica James Series*, 1990-
Elizabeth Peters, *Naked Once More*, 1990
James Yaffe, *The Mom Series*, 1987-

178
D.C. Brod
Murder in Store (New York: Walker, 1989)

Story type: Amateur Detective—Male Lead

Major character(s): Quint McCauley, Security Officer (Chief of Security for a dept.)

Time period(s): 1980s

Locale(s): Chicago, Illinois

What the book is about: The owner of the department store where Quint works is murdered. The victim's wife is the primary suspect. Quint knows her as a chronic shoplifter from her own store. First book.

Other books you might like:
Lawrence Block, *Burglars Can't Be Choosers*, 1977
Spencer Dean, *Credit for a Murder*, 1961
S.F.X. Dean, *By Frequent Anguish*, 1982

179
Dale Brown
Day of the Cheetah (New York: Fine, 1989)

Story type: Techno-Thriller

Major character(s): Patrick McLanahan, Pilot (Lt. Colonel); Ken James, Pilot, Spy (Soviet)

Time period(s): 1990s (1996)

What the book is about: Captain James, test pilot for an experimental American fighter plane with guidance systems that literally merge with the mind of the pilot, is actually a Soviet mole bent on stealing the revolutionary new plane. Lt. Col. McLanahan appears to be the only man with the skill to catch James.

Other books you might like:
Tom Clancy, *The Hunt for Red October*, 1984
Stephen Paul Cohen, *Night Launch*, 1989 (Senator Jake Garn, co-author)
Clive Cussler, *Night Probe*, 1981
Dean Ing, *The Ransom of Black Stealth One*, 1989
Basil Jackson, *Crooked Flight*, 1985

180
Rita Mae Brown
Illustrator: Wendy Wray
Murder at Monticello (New York: Bantam, 1994)

Series: Mrs. Murphy

Story type: Amateur Detective—Female Lead

Major character(s): Mrs. Murphy, Animal (cat); Mary Minor "Harry" Hairsteen, Postal Worker (Mrs. Murphy's owner)

Time period(s): 1990s

Locale(s): Crozet, Virginia

What the book is about: Everyone is happy when money is raised to conduct an archaeological investigation of the slave quarters of Monticello. Everyone is not happy when the skeleton of an apparently rich white man is discovered after having been hidden for over 170 years. Many people trace their ancestry back to Jefferson and do not want any scandal. Soon a fresh corpse turns up and it's up to Mrs. Murphy to set things right.

Other books you might like:
Lydia Adamson, *The Alice Nestleton Series*, 1990-
Lilian Jackson Braun, *The Cat Who Series*, 1966-
Carole Nelson Douglas, *The Midnight Louie Series*, 1992-
Akif Pirincci, *Felidae*, 1993
Christopher Reed, *The Big Scratch*, 1988

181
Rita Mae Brown
Rest in Pieces (New York: Bantam, 1992)

Series: Mrs. Murphy

Story type: Amateur Detective—Female Lead

Major character(s): Mary Minor "Harry" Hairsteen, Postal Worker (post mistress in Crozet); Mrs. Murphy, Animal (cat)

Time period(s): 1990s

Locale(s): Crozet, Virginia

What the book is about: Blair Bainbridge, male model, moves onto the farm next door to Harry and the gossip mongers and matchmakers set to work. Then pieces of body turn up on Bainbridge's land and talk turns to murder not to matchmaking. This happens among the animals as well as the humans. Part of the book is told from the animals' point of view.

Other books you might like:
Lydia Adamson, *A Cat in the Manger*, 1990
Lilian Jackson Braun, *The Cat Who Series*, 1966-
Carole Nelson Douglas, *Catnap*, 1992
Christopher Reed, *The Big Scratch*, 1988

182
Rita Mae Brown
Wish You Were Here (New York: Bantam, 1990)

Series: Mrs. Murphy

Story type: Amateur Detective—Female Lead; Humor

Major character(s): Mary Miner "Harry" Hairsteen, Postal Worker (post mistress in the town of C); Mrs. Murphy, Animal (cat)

Time period(s): 1990s

Locale(s): Crozet, Virginia

What the book is about: Someone is sending "poison postcards" to the residents of Crozet and then following through on the threats. "Harry" and Mrs. Murphy work together - sort of - to solve the crimes. Part of the book is told from the point of view of the cat. First mystery.

Other books you might like:
Lydia Adamson, *A Cat in the Manger*, 1990
Lilian Jackson Braun, *The Cat Who Series*, 1966-
Christopher Reed, *The Big Scratch*, 1988
M.K. Wren, *The Conan Flagg Series*, 1974-

183
Howard Browne
Scotch on the Rocks (New York: St. Martins, 1991)

Story type: Historical

Major character(s): Lee Vance, Criminal (con man)

Time period(s): 1930s (1932)

Locale(s): United States (on the road from Texas to Kansas)

What the book is about: The Dawson family, recent victims of a farm foreclosure, find a bootlegger's cache of booze. Unfortunately con man Lee Vance finds them and convinces them to go on the road to Kansas City to sell the stuff. Their adventures on the road include a crooked cop, a bank robbery and gambling. Will they make it?

Other books you might like:
Max Allan Collins, *The Nate Heller Series*, 1983-
Loren D. Estleman, *Red Highway*, 1988
Paul Kavanaugh, *Not Comin' Home to You*, 1974

184
Anthony Bruno
Bad Apple (New York: Delacorte, 1994)

Series: Gibbons and Tozzi

Story type: Police Procedural—Male Lead; Action/Adventure

Major character(s): Mike Tozzi, FBI Agent; Bert Gibbons, FBI Agent

Time period(s): 1990s

Locale(s): New York, New York

What the book is about: FBI agents Gibbons and Tozzi again find that things just do not go according to plan. First an undercover agent is shot and killed just as he is about to meet an important mobster. Tozzi, also undercover, gets involved with another mobster who is set free by the FBI so he can introduce Tozzi to a big-time loan shark. One thing leads to another and Tozzi finds himself kidnapped, along with his current love interest (the sister of yet another mobster), with another mobster, who has kidnapped Gibbons and his wife, in hot pursuit. This all climaxes at the Macy's Thanksgiving Day Parade.

Other books you might like:
Larry Beinhart, *You Get What You Pay For*, 1988
Robert Campbell, *Juice*, 1988
Thomas H. Cook, *Flesh and Blood*, 1989
Robert K. Tanenbaum, *Depraved Indifference*, 1989
Ross Thomas, *The Porkchoppers*, 1972

185
Anthony Bruno
Bad Blood (New York: Putnam, 1989)

Series: Gibbons and Tozzi

Story type: Action/Adventure

Major character(s): Cuthbert Gibbons, Police Officer (FBI agent); Mike Tozzi, Police Officer (FBI agent)

Time period(s): 1980s

Locale(s): New York, New York

What the book is about: A Japanese couple is found floating in the Hudson River-they have been neatly sliced in half. Things seem to point to a Japanese slave ring that imports menial workers.

Other books you might like:
James Ellroy, *Blood on the Moon*, 1984
Eugene Izzi, *The Take*, 1987
Elmore Leonard, *Glitz*, 1985
Gerald Petievich, *To Live and Die in L.A.*, 1984
John Westermann, *High Crimes*, 1988

186
Anthony Bruno
Bad Moon (New York: Delacorte, 1992)

Series: Gibbons and Tozzi

Story type: Police Procedural—Male Lead; Action/Adventure

Major character(s): Cuthbert Gibbons, Police Officer (FBI agent); Mike Tozzi, Police Officer (FBI agent)

Time period(s): 1990s

Locale(s): New York; New Jersey

What the book is about: Mafia man Sal Immordino wants to be the Boss of the Mistretta family to which end he has himself committed to an asylum. Unfortunately FBI agent Tozzi has figured out Sal is not crazy, so Sal decides that Tozzi must die. The hit goes wrong and Sal decides to make the hit himself—with the help of a psychopath from the asylum. Things do not go as planned.

Other books you might like:
Thomas H. Cook, *Flesh and Blood*, 1989
David L. Lindsey, *Spiral*, 1986
Jerry Oster, *Fixing to Die*, 1992
Gerald Petievich, *Paramour*, 1991
Stephen Solomita, *Force of Nature*, 1989

187
Edna Buchanan
Nobody Lives Forever (New York: Random, 1990)

Story type: Police Procedural—Male Lead

Major character(s): Rick Barrish, Detective—Police; Laurel Trevlyn, Criminal (Rick's live-in lover)

Time period(s): 1980s

Locale(s): Miami, Florida

What the book is about: Violence breaks out near Rick's house. Is it possible his beautiful live-in girlfriend is involved? This is Buchanan's first novel, though she has written true crime books.

Other books you might like:
Art Bourgeau, *The Seduction*, 1988
John Leslie, *Killer in Paradise*, 1990
Robert B. Parker, *Crimson Joy*, 1988
Bill Pronzini, *The Running of Beasts*, 1976 (Barry Mazberg, co-author)

188
William F. Buckley Jr.
Tucker's Last Stand (New York: Random House, 1990)

Series: Blackford Oakes

Story type: Espionage; Historical

Major character(s): Blackford Oakes, Spy; Tucker Montana, Spy

Time period(s): 1960s (1964)

Locale(s): Vietnam; Washington, District of Columbia

What the book is about: Blackie and Tucker are assigned to Vietnam - their mission is to stop the flow of supplies to the Viet Cong coming from Hanoi down the Ho Chi Minh trail. Everyone seems to have his own agenda, however, including Oakes' one time mentor.

Other books you might like:
Len Deighton, *The Harry Palmer Series*, 1962-
Ian Fleming, *The James Bond Series*, 1959-
Bill Granger, *Schism*, 1982
Charles McCarry, *The Tears of Autumn*, 1975

189
Thomas Bunn
Closing Costs (New York: Holt, 1990)

Series: Jack Bodine

Story type: Private Detective—Male Lead

Major character(s): Jack Bodine, Detective—Private

Time period(s): 1980s

Locale(s): Washington, District of Columbia

What the book is about: Jack's old partner, Ed Quinn, is dying and just wants to be left alone, but Ed's lawyer is worried someone is trying to cheat him. When Ed disappears, Jack investigates and finds a link to a powerful Washington, D.C. family.

Other books you might like:
James Grady, *Runner in the Street*, 1984
William J. Reynolds, *The Nebraska Quotient*, 1984
J.W. Rider, *Jersey Tomatoes*, 1986
Les Roberts, *Pepper Pike*, 1988
Jonathan Valin, *Fire Lake*, 1987

190
Thomas Bunn
Worse than Death (New York: Holt, 1989)

Series: Jack Bodine

Story type: Private Detective—Male Lead

Major character(s): Jack Bodine, Detective—Private

Time period(s): 1980s

Locale(s): Michigan

What the book is about: When some friends ask Bodine's wife to find their stolen adopted child, Jack is unwillingly drawn into the netherworld of baby-selling.

Other books you might like:
Wayne Dundee, *The Skintight Shroud*, 1989
Loren D. Estleman, *The Amos Walker Series*, 1980
Sara Paretsky, *The V.I. Warshawski Series*, 1982
Robert B. Parker, *The Spenser Series*, 1973

191
Pat Burden
Screaming Bones (New York: Doubleday, 1990)

Story type: Amateur Detective—Male Lead

Major character(s): Henry Bassett, Farmer (retired detective); Jack "the Poacher" Carter, Writer (former soldier)

Time period(s): 1980s

Locale(s): The Cotswolds, England

What the book is about: The discovery of a dead body in a church sends retired detective Bassett on a search for the killer. The truth about this murder is buried somewhere in the past. First novel.

Other books you might like:
M.C. Beaton, *Death of a Perfect Wife*, 1989
Elizabeth George, *A Great Deliverance*, 1988
Martha Grimes, *The Old Silent*, 1989
Elizabeth Lemarchand, *The Glade Manor Murder*, 1989
Henry Wade, *A Dying Fall*, 1955

192
Alan Dennis Burke
Dead Wrong (New York: St. Martins, 1990)

Story type: Amateur Detective—Male Lead; Action/Adventure

Major character(s): Kevin Bourque, Businessman (building contractor)

Time period(s): 1990s

Locale(s): Norham, Massachusetts

What the book is about: Everything seems to be going well for newly divorced Kevin Bourque, his business is starting to do well and he has met Terri Pratt, a very sexy divorcee. His business partner, Larry Dexter, is cutting corners, money is disappearing and Terri has a secret past. When Larry is found dead, killed with Kevin's nail gun, nobody believes Kevin is innocent.

Other books you might like:
William Bayer, *Blind Side*, 1989
Brian Lysaght, *Special Circumstances*, 1983
A.J. Orde, *A Little Neighborhood Murder*, 1989
Victor Wuamett, *Teardown*, 1990

193
James Lee Burke
Black Cherry Blues (New York: Little, Brown, 1989)

Series: Dave Robicheaux

Story type: Amateur Detective—Male Lead

Major character(s): Dave Robicheaux, Detective—Amateur, Veteran

Time period(s): 1980s

Locale(s): Montana; Louisiana (Bayou)

What the book is about: After Dave Robicheaux agrees to help an old friend investigate some men, a murder is committed and Dave becomes the prime suspect. He must go to Montana to get at the truth in order to clear himself.

Other books you might like:
James Crumley, *The Last Good Kiss*, 1978
James Crumley, *The Wrong Case*, 1975
Frederick D. Huebner, *Judgement by Fire*, 1988
Robert Sims Reid, *Big Sky Blues*, 1988
Daniel Woodrell, *Under the Bright Lights*, 1986

194
James Lee Burke
Burning Angel (New York: Hyperion, 1995)

Series: Dave Robicheaux

Story type: Police Procedural—Male Lead; Action/Adventure

Major character(s): Dave Robicheaux, Police Officer

Time period(s): 1990s

Locale(s): New Orleans, Louisiana

What the book is about: An old woman, descended from sharecroppers, comes to Dave for help in claiming property that was promised to her family years earlier. The current owner of the property, Mollen Bertrand, is planning to develop it and wants to have nothing to do with the claims of an old woman. As Dave begins to try to help the woman an old compatriot resurfaces and wants Dave to hold a journal that seems to interest some people with whom Dave would rather not deal. Bad folks abound and it's sometimes hard to tell the good guys from the bad.

Other books you might like:
Robert Crais, *Voodoo River*, 1995
Tony Dunbar, *Crooked Man*, 1994
James Sallis, *The Long-Legged Fly*, 1992
Julie Smith, *New Orleans Mourning*, 1990
Mary Willis Walker, *The Red Scream*, 1994

195
James Lee Burke
Dixie City Jam (New York: Hyperion, 1994)

Series: Dave Robicheaux

Story type: Police Procedural—Male Lead

Major character(s): Dave Robicheaux, Police Officer (detective)

Time period(s): 1990s

Locale(s): New Orleans, Louisiana

What the book is about: A sunken German submarine, crime kingpins, and a man who thinks the Holocaust was a hoax all come together to cause Dave Robicheaux and his family serious problems. Being a police officer may not help him with this.

Other books you might like:
Lawrence Block, *The Matt Scudder Series*, 1976-
John Clarkson, *And Justice for One*, 1992
John Sandford, *Winter Prey*, 1992
Julie Smith, *New Orleans Mourning*, 1990

196
James Lee Burke
In the Electric Mist with Confederate Dead (New York: Hyperion, 1993)

Series: Dave Robicheaux

Story type: Police Procedural—Male Lead; Psychological Suspense

Major character(s): Dave Robicheaux, Police Officer

Time period(s): 1990s

Locale(s): New Orleans, Louisiana

What the book is about: The filming of a movie and the discovery of a skeleton wrapped in chains combine to get Dave Robicheaux involved in a case that will threaten him and his family with events from the past.

Other books you might like:
Lawrence Block, *A Dance at the Slaughterhouse*, 1992
John Clarkson, *And Justice for One*, 1992
John Sandford, *Rules of Prey*, 1989
Julie Smith, *New Orleans Mourning*, 1990
Jonathan Valin, *Life's Work*, 1986

197
James Lee Burke
A Morning for Flamingos (New York: Little, Brown, 1990)

Series: Dave Robicheaux

198

Burke

Story type: Action/Adventure; Police Procedural—Male Lead

Major character(s): Dave Robicheaux, Police Officer (former private detective)

Time period(s): 1990s

Locale(s): New Orleans, Louisiana

What the book is about: After being shot while transporting a prisoner, Robicheaux goes undercover to catch a drug dealer and, maybe, the man who shot him.

Other books you might like:
J. Madison Davis, *White Rook*, 1990
Julie Smith, *New Orleans Mourning*, 1990
Stephen Solomita, *Force of Nature*, 1989
Chris Wiltz, *The Emerald Lizard*, 1991
Daniel Woodrell, *Under the Bright Lights*, 1987

198

Jan Burke
Goodnight, Irene (New York: Simon & Schuster, 1993)

Story type: Amateur Detective—Female Lead

Major character(s): Irene Kelly, Journalist; Frank Harriman, Police Officer

Time period(s): 1990s

Locale(s): Las Piernas, California

What the book is about: Shocked when one of her friends is killed by a package bomb, reporter Irene Kelly gets herself re-employed by the newspaper and, with the help of her ex-lover, police officer Frank Harriman, sets out to solve the case. It seems to center around the unidentified body of a woman discovered years ago, a case that obsessed the murdered man. First novel.

Other books you might like:
Susan Wittig Albert, *Thyme of Death*, 1992
K.K. Beck, *A Hopeless Case*, 1992
Elizabeth Quinn, *Murder Most Grizzly*, 1993
Sarah Shankman, *First Kill All the Lawyers*, 1988
Kerry Tucker, *Still Waters*, 1992

199

Rex Burns
Body Guard (New York: Viking, 1991)

Series: Devlin Kirk

Story type: Private Detective—Male Lead

Major character(s): Devlin Kirk, Detective—Private (industrial security specialist)

Time period(s): 1990s

Locale(s): Denver, Colorado

What the book is about: Three cases involve Kirk and his associates. A corporation wants a possible drug connection checked out, a wealthy man wants a bodyguard for him and his wife, and an insurance company wants some suspicious claims checked out. When one of the operatives is killed and tortured while on the drug case, Kirk puts the other cases on the back burner while he and his partner go after the killers.

Other books you might like:
Robert Crais, *Lullaby Town*, 1992
Warwick Downing, *A Clear Case of Murder*, 1990
Joe Gores, *The DKA Series*, 1974-
Ed McBain, *The 87th Precinct Series*, 1956-
Donald Zochert, *The Man of Glass*, 1982

200

Rex Burns
Parts Unknown (New York: Viking, 1990)

Series: Devlin Kirk

Story type: Private Detective—Male Lead

Major character(s): Devlin Kirk, Detective—Private

Time period(s): 1990s

Locale(s): Denver, Colorado

What the book is about: What do three missing persons, two of them pregnant women, have in common? They are all illegal aliens from El Salvador and were living at a seedy rooming house, the landlord of which has ties to a local doctor. Spare parts? Has someone used these people for spare parts?

Other books you might like:
Michael Allegretto, *Death on the Rocks*, 1987
Warwick Downing, *The Player*, 1974
Gary Paulsen, *Night Rituals*, 1989
Donald Zochert, *The Man of Glass*, 1982

201

Ron Burns
Roman Nights (New York: St. Martin's, 1991)

Story type: Historical; Amateur Detective—Male Lead

Major character(s): Livinius Severus, Lawyer

Time period(s): 2nd century

Locale(s): Rome, Italy (Roman Empire)

What the book is about: A beautiful young woman has asked Severus to investigate her husband. Reluctantly he agrees. But shortly she turns up dead at an orgy with her husband standing over her with a knife. This is just the beginning of a terrible time for Severus. First novel.

Other books you might like:
Lindsey Davis, *The Silver Pigs*, 1989
Margaret Doody, *Aristotle, Detective*, 1980
John Maddox Roberts, *The SPQR Series*, 1990-
Steven Saylor, *Roman Blood*, 1991

202

Agnes Bushnell
Shadow Dance (Freedom, CA: Crossing, 1989)

Story type: Private Detective—Female Lead

Major character(s): Johannah Wilder, Detective—Private, Lesbian; Ruth Wilson, Detective—Private (Partner of Johannah)

Time period(s): 1980s

Locale(s): Portland, Maine; New York, New York

What the book is about: Acting as bodyguard to some Russian women who are visiting Portland plunges Johannah into her past life. First book.

Other books you might like:
Katherine V. Forrest, *The Beverly Malibu*, 1989
Marion Foster, *The Monarchs Are Flying*, 1987
Sara Paretsky, *Burn Marks*, 1989
Mary Wings, *She Came in a Flash*, 1989
Eve Zaremba, *Work for a Million*, 1987

203
Gwendoline Butler
Coffin on Murder Street (New York: St. Martin's, 1992)
Series: Inspector Coffin
Story type: Police Procedural—Male Lead
Major character(s): John Coffin, Police Officer (Inspector)
Time period(s): 1990s
Locale(s): London, England

What the book is about: American actress Nell Casey, appearing in London in a theatre festival—run by Inspector Coffin's lover—appeals to the police when she feels her son is in danger. His teddy bear was stolen and buried in their yard under a marker with her son's name on it. Then the boy disappears. Was he kidnapped? Did his mother arrange it as a publicity stunt? Did a pederast just released from prison have anything to do with it?

Other books you might like:
Catherine Aird, *The Body Politic*, 1991
Ann Cleeves, *A Day in the Death of Dorothea Cassidy*, 1991
Jennie Melville, *Witching Murder*, 1991
Janet Neel, *Death of a Partner*, 1991
Peter Robinson, *A Dedicated Man*, 1992

204
Gwendoline Butler (Pseudonym of Jennie Melville)
Coffin Underground (New York: St. Martins, 1989)
Series: Inspector Coffin
Story type: Police Procedural—Male Lead
Major character(s): John Coffin, Police Officer (inspector)
Time period(s): 1970s (1978)

What the book is about: Assigned to do some undercover work checking on a possible dirty cop, Coffin ends up in a small town with a house where tragedy has struck more than once.

Other books you might like:
Margaret Erskine, *The Septimus Finch Series*, 1939
Nicholas Freeling, *Inspector Van Der Valk Series*, 1962
June Thomson, *A Question of Identity*, 1977
Colin Watson, *Plaster Sinners*, 1981

205
Max Byrd
Fuse Time (New York: Bantam, 1991)

Story type: Police Procedural—Male Lead; Action/Adventure
Major character(s): David Renner, Police Officer (former top cop in Britain); Simon Caute, Criminal (mad bomber)
Time period(s): 1990s
Locale(s): Los Angeles, California

What the book is about: David Renner is convinced that a series of bombings in Los Angeles is the work of one man. The police think otherwise and remove him from the task force. He is forced to use his own resources to track the bomber. Complicating the issue is his love for a woman who may be connected to the bomber.

Other books you might like:
Drew Mallory, *Target Manhattan*, 1975
Eric Sauter, *Skeletons*, 1990
David Wiltse, *The Fifth Angel*, 1985

206
Carol Cail
Unsafe Keeping (New York: St. Martin's, 1995)
Series: Maxey Burnell
Story type: Amateur Detective—Female Lead
Major character(s): Maxey Burnell, Journalist (co-owner of newspaper)
Time period(s): 1990s
Locale(s): Boulder, Colorado

What the book is about: Someone is stealing vans and turning them loose on the hills. Maxey is almost a victim of one of these dangerous pranks. Then her landlady, apparently in the wrong place at the wrong time, is killed by one of the vans. However, when it is revealed that the landlady owned some property that is a bone of contention among residents and eagerly sought by developers, Maxey's suspicions are aroused. Could it have been a clever murder?

Other books you might like:
Mary Daheim, *The Alpine Series*, 1992
Leona Karr, *Murder in Bandora*, 1993
Mary Kittredge, *Poison Pen*, 1990
Celestine Sibley, *Ah, Sweet Mystery*, 1991
Triss Stein, *Murder at the Class Reunion*, 1993

207
Sheila MacGill Callahan
Forty Whacks (New York: St. Martin's, 1994)
Series: Brian Donodio
Story type: Amateur Detective—Male Lead
Major character(s): Brian Donodio, Professor (retired); Liza Borden, Veterinarian
Time period(s): 1990s
Locale(s): Fall River, Massachusetts

208 | Cambray

What the book is about: Liza Borden is a veterinarian in Fall River, Massachusetts, home of the infamous Lizzie Borden. She works for the Delaney Institute, concerned with saving threatened animals. The institute seems to be the target of someone with a grudge because animals are being kidnapped, mutilated, and killed. Then Liza's friend, Abby Meyer, is killed and Liza is found by the body holding a bloody ax. Someone seems to have taken advantage of her name to plot an elaborate and deadly frame. Brian Donodio is asked by Liza's family to prove her innocence.

Other books you might like:
Richard Timothy Conroy, *Mr. Smithson's Bones*, 1993
Desmond Cory, *The Catalyst*, 1991
Warren Murphy, *Leonardo's Law*, 1978
Walter Satterthwait, *Miss Lizzie*, 1989
Michael W. Sherer, *Little Use for Death*, 1992

208
C.K. Cambray (Pseudonym of Dimitri Gat)
Personal (New York: Pocket, 1990)

Story type: Psychological Suspense

Major character(s): Amanda Walker, Businesswoman (restaurant owner); Evan Dent, Criminal

Time period(s): 1980s

Locale(s): Connecticut

What the book is about: When Amanda Walker answers a personal ad, she gets more than she bargained for. Cambray has also written under his real name, Dimitri Gat.

Other books you might like:
Karin Berne, *Bare Acquaintances*, 1985
Art Bourgeau, *The Seduction*, 1988
Trish Janeshutz, *Hidden Lake*, 1987
Faye Kellerman, *The Ritual Bath*, 1986

209
Sara Cameron
Natural Enemies (New York: Turner, 1993)

Story type: Action/Adventure

Major character(s): Sam Hawthorne, Journalist

Time period(s): 1990s

Locale(s): Kenya

What the book is about: While working in Kenya, American reporter Sam Hawthorne stumbles on the murdered bodies of the head of the Kenya Wildlife Services and his wife. Initially accused of the crimes, he is soon contacted by members of an environmental terrorist group claiming credit for the murders. They tell him their plan, which is to keep killing members of the wildlife service, one of whom is Hawthorne's former lover.

Other books you might like:
Karin McQuillan, *Deadly Safari*, 1990

210
John Camp
The Empress File (New York: Holt, 1991)

Series: Kidd

Story type: Action/Adventure

Major character(s): Kidd, Artist, Computer Expert; LuEllen, Criminal (burglar)

Time period(s): 1990s

Locale(s): Longstreet, Mississippi

What the book is about: When a fourteen-year-old black child is shot by to mistake in the town of Longstreet, one of Kidd's computer friends gets him involved in tryingn to uncover the coverup and, while he's doing that, crush the machine that runs the town. Camp also writes as John Sandford.

Other books you might like:
Lawrence Block, *The Bernie Rhodenbarr Series*, 1977-
Max Allan Collins, *The Nolan Series*, 1973-
Ross Thomas, *The Fools in Town Are on Our Side*, 1971
Donald E. Westlake, *Butcher's Moon*, 1974

211
Harlen Campbell
Monkey on a Chain (New York: Doubleday, 1993)

Story type: Action/Adventure

Major character(s): Rainbow Porter, Veteran (Vietnam veteran); April Bow, Student (Eurasian)

Time period(s): 1990s

Locale(s): Southwest

What the book is about: Rainbow Porter lives by himself in the mountains near Albuquerque and accepts jobs to do "crisis management." In situations where everyone is wrong, he chooses to help the least wrong. April, the adopted daughter of an old war buddy, shows up asking for help. Her father has been killed by a booby-trapped claymore mine and she wants to know why. Rainbow feels obligated to help and subsequently is led into the past and life-threatening danger for him and April. First novel.

Other books you might like:
E.C. Ayres, *Hour of the Manatee*, 1994
Michael Connelly, *The Black Echo*, 1992
David Debin, *Nice Guys Finish Dead*, 1992
Joe R. Lansdale, *Mucho Mojo*, 1994
Al Sarrantonio, *Summer Cool*, 1993

212
Robert Campbell
The Gift Horse's Mouth (New York: Pocket, 1990)

Series: Jimmy Flannery

Story type: Amateur Detective—Male Lead

Major character(s): Jimmy Flannery, Worker (sewer inspector), Political Figure

Time period(s): 1990s

Locale(s): Chicago, Illinois

What the book is about: Death by misadventure, say the cops about the death of the secretary of the head of the Chicago Democratic Party. Was she killed and if so, why? The head of the party wants Jimmy to poke around and see what he can come up with. What he finds are secrets, some of them 40 years old and some of them hitting very close to home.

Other books you might like:
Harold Adams, *The Carl Wilcox Series*, 1981-
Robert Campbell, *The Jake Hatch Series*, 1988-
Warren Murphy, *The Trace Series*, 1983-

213
Robert Campbell
Nibbled to Death by Ducks (New York: Pocket, 1989)

Series: Jimmy Flannery

Story type: Amateur Detective—Male Lead

Major character(s): Jimmy Flannery, Maintenance Worker (sewer inspector)

Time period(s): 1980s

Locale(s): Chicago, Illinois

What the book is about: While trying to rescue his old friend Chips Delvin from a nursing home, Flannery stumbles on a scheme involving murder and money.

Other books you might like:
Harold Adams, *The Carl Wilcox Series*, (1981-)
Robert Campbell, *The Jake Hatch Series*, (1988-)
Joe Gores, *Gone, No Forwarding*, 1978
Warren Murphy, *The Trace Series*, (1983-)

214
Dorothy Cannell
Femmes Fatal (New York: Bantam, 1992)

Series: Ellie Haskell

Story type: Amateur Detective—Female Lead; Humor

Major character(s): Ellie Haskell, Housewife; Roxie Malloy, Servant (cleaning lady)

Time period(s): 1990s

Locale(s): Chitterton Falls, England

What the book is about: Ellie is feeling down - she is fat again after giving birth to twins and thinks the fire may have gone out of her marriage. She sees an advertisement for *Fully Female*, a club that says it will make a woman reach her full sexual potential. She is undecided when her cleaning lady, Mrs. Malloy, threatens suicide because of unrequited love. Forming a mutual support group they both enroll in the "Fully Female" plan. Unfortunately a murder interrupts their plans.

Other books you might like:
Joyce Christmas, *The Lady Margaret Priam Series*, 1988-
Jill Churchill, *A Quiche Before Dying*, 1993
Diane Mott Davidson, *Catering to Nobody*, 1990
Jaqueline Girdner, *Adjusted to Death*, 1991
Stefanie Matteson, *The Charlotte Graham Series*, 1990-

215
Dorothy Cannell
How to Murder Your Mother-in-Law (New York: Bantam, 1994)

Series: Ellie Haskell

Story type: Amateur Detective—Female Lead

Major character(s): Ellie Haskell, Housewife; Roxie Malloy, Servant (cleaning lady)

Time period(s): 1990s

Locale(s): Chitterton Falls, England

What the book is about: Ellie Haskell has made a horrible mistake. She has planned an anniversary party for her in-laws and has asked an estranged friend of theirs to join the festivities. Disaster follows disaster until it is finally revealed that the couple were never really married. This leads to "Mum" moving in with Ellie and settling down for a long stay. When Ellie and her friends get together, they compare mother-in-law stories and come up with four ways to kill them, all in fun, of course. Then someone starts carrying out the plans.

Other books you might like:
Jill Churchill, *A Farewell to Yarns*, 1991
Jaqueline Girdner, *Adjusted to Death*, 1990
Joan Hess, *A Diet to Die For*, 1989
Sarah Shankman, *Now Let's Talk of Graves*, 1990
Valerie Wolzien, *A Good Year for a Corpse*, 1994

216
Taffy Cannon
A Pocketful of Karma (New York: Carroll & Graf, 1993)

Story type: Amateur Detective—Female Lead; Legal

Major character(s): Nan Robinson, Lawyer

Time period(s): 1990s

Locale(s): Los Angeles, California

What the book is about: When Nan Robinson tries to get in touch with her former secretary, Debra, she finds her missing. As Nan tries to track her down she gets involved with a number of odd characters, some of them from the Past Lives Institute. Then Debra's body turns up and her estranged husband seems to have killed himself. Nan turns up Debra's journal which seems to point in other directions. First mystery.

Other books you might like:
Harrison Arnston, *Trade-Off*, 1992
Patricia D. Cornwell, *Postmortem*, 1990
Lia Matera, *Hidden Agenda*, 1988
Nancy Taylor Rosenberg, *Interest of Justice*, 1993
Janet L. Smith, *Practice to Deceive*, 1992

217
Tony Cape
The Cambridge Theorem (New York: Doubleday, 1990)

Story type: Police Procedural—Male Lead

Major character(s): Derek Smailes, Police Officer (CID detective)

Time period(s): 1980s

Locale(s): Cambridge, England

What the book is about: The apparent suicide of a Cambridge student is soon diagnosed to have been murder. It seems that the student had recently begun to get close to identifying the "Fifth Man" in the group of Soviet spies recruited from Cambridge in the 1930s. First book.

Other books you might like:
Joseph Hone, *The Oxford Gambit*, 1977
John Le Carre, *Call for the Dead*, 1962

218
P.M. Carlson
Bad Blood (New York: Doubleday, 1991)

Series: Maggie Ryan

Story type: Amateur Detective—Female Lead

Major character(s): Maggie Ryan, Businesswoman (statistical consultant); Nick O'Connor, Actor (husband of Maggie)

Time period(s): 1970s (1979)

Locale(s): New York, New York

What the book is about: Ginny Marshall is a teenager having trouble at home. When a murder occurs and Ginny is a suspect, she decides to find her real mother-Maggie Ryan. Nick and Maggie decide to help find the real culprit while trying to work out what to do with Ginny.

Other books you might like:
Carolyn G. Hart, *The Annie Laurance Series*, 1987-
Joan Hess, *The Claire Malloy Series*, 1986
Wendy Hornsby, *Half a Mind*, 1990
Sharyn McCrumb, *The Elizabeth MacPherson Series*, 1984
Nancy Pickard, *I.O.U.*, 1991

219
P.M. Carlson
Gravestone (New York: Pocket, 1993)

Story type: Police Procedural—Female Lead

Major character(s): Marty Hopkins, Police Officer (deputy)

Time period(s): 1990s

Locale(s): Dunning, Indiana (Nichols County)

What the book is about: Marty Hopkins is investigating a mysterious fire that turns out to be a burning cross near a shallow grave that holds a mutilated corpse. Marty's boss doesn't want her involved in this case and assigns her to investigate the threats to a local judge who is dying of a brain tumor. The judge swears he is being harassed by his long-lost daughter. Marty thinks he is crazy and wants back on the murder case, but both cases may be connected to the Klan.

Other books you might like:
Susan Dunlap, *The Jill Smith Series*, 1981-
Joan Hess, *The Maggody Series*, 1987-
M.D. Lake, *The Peggy O'Neill Series*, 1989-
Lee Martin, *The Deb Ralston Series*, 1984-
Charlene Weir, *Consider the Crows*, 1993

220
Jennifer Carnell
Murder, Mystery and Mayhem (New York: Harper, 1989)

Story type: Amateur Detective—Female Lead

Major character(s): Esmerelda Fry, Spinster; Pierre Du Bois, Businessman (his job may be a cover story)

Time period(s): 1930s (1936; Holiday season)

Locale(s): Waddington (Fictional village)

What the book is about: After the death of her father, Miss Fry feels liberated and sets out to live life. But when she arrives at an exclusive inn that becomes snowbound, it appears that her new life may be short indeed. First book.

Other books you might like:
James Anderson, *The Affair of the Blood-Stained Egg Cosy*, 1975
Marion Babson, *The Twelve Days of Christmas*, 1980
Agatha Christie, *And Then There Were None*, 1940
Alisa Craig, *Murder Goes Mumming*, 1981
Runa Fairleigh, *An Old-Fashioned Mystery*, 1983

221
John Dickson Carr
Fell and Foul Play (New York: International Polygonics, 1991)

Story type: Amateur Detective—Male Lead

Major character(s): Gideon Fell, Doctor

Time period(s): 1930s; 1940s

Locale(s): England

What the book is about: A collection of short fiction, most involving impossible crimes and starring Carr's character Dr. Gideon Fell. Edited by Douglas Greene.

Other books you might like:
R.C.S. Adey, *Death Locked In*, 1987 (Douglas Greene, co-author)
R.C.S. Adey, *Murder Impossible*, 1990 (Jack Adrian, co-author)
Edmund Crispin, *Beware of Trains*, 1963

222
Noel Vreeland Carter
The Mooncalf Murders (New York: Walker, 1989)

Story type: Amateur Detective—Female Lead

Major character(s): Miranda Fay, Journalist (investigative journalist)

Time period(s): 1980s

Locale(s): New York, New York

What the book is about: After stumbling upon the strangled corpse of a deformed baby, Miranda Fay hopes to use the story to further her career.

Other books you might like:
Robert J. Bowman, *The House of Blue Lights*, 1987
Charlaine Harris, *Sweet and Deadly*, 1981
Susan Kelly, *Trail of the Dragon*, 1988
Keith Peterson, *The John Wells Series*, (1988-)

223
Robert A. Carter
Casual Slaughters (New York: Mysterious, 1992)
Series: Nicholas Barlow
Story type: Amateur Detective—Male Lead
Major character(s): Nicholas Barlow, Publisher (head of Barlow and Company); Joseph Scanlon, Police Officer
Time period(s): 1990s
Locale(s): New York, New York
What the book is about: Nicholas Barlow, publisher, bonvivant and mystery afficianado is now involved in a real mystery. He is called by the police to identify the body of one of his best-selling authors, Jordan Walker. Walker was the author of celebrity tell-alls and he had just finished his latest - about Graham Farrar, famous actor. When copies of the manuscript start disappearing, Nicholas is drawn into the investigation. First mystery.
Other books you might like:
John Dunning, *Booked to Die*, 1992
Bob Fenster, *The Last Page*, 1989
Will Harriss, *The Bay Psalm Book Murder*, 1983
M.K. Lorens, *Sweet Narcissus*, 1990
Elizabeth Travis, *Finders Keepers*, 1990

224
Robert A. Carter
Final Edit (New York: Mysterious, 1994)
Series: Nicholas Barlow
Story type: Amateur Detective—Male Lead
Major character(s): Nicholas Barlow, Publisher; Timothy Barlow, Handicapped (Nicholas' paraplegic brother)
Time period(s): 1990s
Locale(s): New York, New York
What the book is about: Nicholas Barlow seems to be a suspect in the murder of one of his editors, just because the editor was obnoxious and outspoken, was causing other talented people to quit, was costing the firm a small fortune, and Nicholas was the one to discover the body after his public argument with the victim. Nicholas figures he and his brother Timothy had better find the real killer before he finds himself in jail. He also finds himself falling in love with one of the murder victim's former lovers.
Other books you might like:
Nicholas Blake, *End of the Chapter*, 1957
John Dunning, *Booked to Die*, 1992
Jennifer Rowe, *Murder by the Book*, 1992
Barbara Burnett Smith, *Writers of the Purple Sage*, 1994
Elizabeth Travis, *Finders Keepers*, 1990

225
Dennis Casley
Death Underfoot (New York: St. Martin's, 1994)
Story type: Police Procedural—Male Lead
Major character(s): James Odhiambo, Police Officer (inspector)
Time period(s): 1990s
Locale(s): Nairobi, Kenya
What the book is about: Inspector Odhiambo has accepted an invitation to Hawk's Nest, a tourist attraction built in a tree for the wealthy to observe animals at a salt lick. He also meets another group, including the sensuous Diana Farwell, who seems to be the center of the men's attention and the women's jealousy. When she is found crushed after an elephant stampede, the inspector assumes it was murder, especially since Diana knew a lot of secrets and enjoyed teasing people with her knowledge. First novel.
Other books you might like:
Sara Cameron, *Natural Enemies*, 1993
Agatha Christie, *Evil under the Sun*, 1941
Karin McQuillan, *The Cheetah Chase*, 1994

226
J.N. Catanach
Brideprice (Vermont: Foul Play, 1989)
Story type: Amateur Detective—Female Lead
Major character(s): Stephanie Duncan, Detective—Amateur; Wellington Waki Oloo, Detective—Private (Kenyan)
Time period(s): 1960s (1967)
Locale(s): Kenya
What the book is about: Upon her return to Kenya after 11 years, Stephanie Duncan sets out to find the truth behind the death of her parents.
Other books you might like:
Matthew Head, *The Cabinda Affair*, 1949
Elspeth Huxley, *The African Poison Murders*, 1940
M.M. Kaye, *Death in Zanzibar*, 1983
James McClure, *The Artful Egg*, 1985
James McClure, *The Steam Pig*, 1971

227
J.N. Catanach
The Last Rite of Hugo T (New York: St. Martin's, 1992)
Story type: Psychological Suspense; Action/Adventure
Major character(s): Hugo T, Aged Person (Polish emigre; octagenerian)
Time period(s): 1990s
Locale(s): New York, New York; Paris, France
What the book is about: Hugo T has decided to commit suicide, his "last rite," but strange things are happening around him. A burglar steals clothes, a stretch limo seems to follow him around, and a young neighbor and his mysterious friend want to involve him in a Free Poland Society. The past and the present are coming together and Hugo will be forced to make some unpleasant decisions.

Other books you might like:
William Bayer, *Blind Side*, 1989
Robert Ferrigno, *The Horse Latitudes*, 1990
Thomas Maxwell, *The Suspense Is Killing Me*, 1990
Don Winslow, *A Cool Breeze on the Underground*, 1990

228
Sarah Caudwell (Pseudonym of Sarah Cockburn)
The Sirens Sang of Murder (New York: Delacorte, 1989)
Series: 62 New Square Lawyers
Story type: Amateur Detective
Major character(s): Hilary Tamar, Lawyer; Michael Cantrip, Lawyer
Time period(s): 1980s
Locale(s): Channel Islands, England; London, England
What the book is about: When Michael Cantrip is sent to the Channel Islands to do some legal work, things turn out to be not as they seem. His colleagues back in London must do what they can to stop him from becoming the next victim.
Other books you might like:
Edmund Crispin, *The Gervase Fen series*, (1945-1978)
Jocelyn Davey, *The Ambrose Usher Series*, 1956
Michael Gilbert, *Smallbone Deceased*, 1950
B.M. Gill, *Death Drop*, 1979
Cyril Hare, *Tragedy at Law*, 1942

229
William J. Caunitz
Exceptional Clearance (New York: Crown, 1991)
Story type: Police Procedural—Male Lead
Major character(s): John Vinda, Detective—Police
Time period(s): 1990s
Locale(s): New York, New York
What the book is about: John Vinda was once happily married and head of a top unit. Now his wife is dead of cancer, the unit has been disbanded for excessive force and John is a glorified file clerk. He is called back to investigate a possible serial killer and to keep the lid on to prevent panic. This becomes impossible when the violence escalates. Can Vinda find the killer before a lot more people die?
Other books you might like:
Thomas Harris, *Red Dragon*, 1981
David L. Lindsey, *Heat From Another Sun*, 1984
Rex Miller, *Stone Shadow*, 1989
Gary Paulsen, *Night Rituals*, 1989
John Sandford, *Silent Prey*, 1992

230
Tony Caxton
Murder in a Quiet Place (New York: St. Martin's, 1994)
Story type: Police Procedural—Male Lead
Major character(s): Denis Bowker, Police Officer (detective inspector); Jack Knight, Police Officer (detective sergeant)
Time period(s): 1990s
Locale(s): Long Slaughter, England
What the book is about: Lynn Hurst's brutally murdered body has been discovered by her fiance, Mark Stanhope. There is no lack of suspects as the beautiful Miss Hurst seems to have slept with half the men in the area. It's up to Inspector Bowker to sort it out. Bowker has the looks, and apparently the personality, of a professional wrestler. His new partner hopes he is smarter than he looks. Then two more bodies show up and Bowker's bosses want an answer before there is more killing. First novel.
Other books you might like:
Ann Cleeves, *A Day in the Death of Dorothea Cassidy*, 1992
Marjorie Eccles, *Death of a Good Woman*, 1986
Lucretia Grindle, *The Killing of Ellis Martin*, 1993
Kay Mitchell, *A Lively Form of Death*, 1990
Peter Robinson, *Past Reason Hated*, 1993

231
Zev Chafets
Inherit the Mob (New York: Fawcett, 1993)
Story type: Action/Adventure
Major character(s): William Gordon, Journalist; John Flanagan, Journalist
Time period(s): 1990s
Locale(s): New York, New York
What the book is about: William Gordon's Uncle Max has just died and left him his business if he wants it. Unfortunately the business is Max's share of the mob. Max was one of the last of the once powerful "Jewish Mafia" and the catch is that the other bosses want to take over Max's territory. John Flanagan convinces William to give it a try but John has his own plans. William may not survive the double and triple dealing of New York City's criminal elite. First novel.
Other books you might like:
Milton Bass, *The Moving Finger*, 1986
Carl Hiaasen, *Strip Tease*, 1993
Dick Lochte, *Blue Bayou*, 1992
Laurence Shames, *Florida Straits*, 1992

232
Sally Chapman
Love Bytes (New York: St. Martin's, 1994)
Story type: Private Detective
Major character(s): Julie Blake, Detective—Private, Computer Expert; Vic Paoli, Detective—Private (Julie's partner and lover), Computer Expert
Time period(s): 1990s
Locale(s): Silicon Valley, California

What the book is about: Julie Blake and Vic Paoli have opened their own investigation firm, specializing in computer crime, but business is slow. That's why Julie is anxious to take the case of the missing computer expert. Bail bondswoman Lorna Donatello wants them to find Arnie Lufkin, who has skipped bail, not because of the money but because she's in love. What they find is that Arnie may have been a genius but he was not a very nice person and that someone does not want him found.

Other books you might like:
Denise Danks, *User Deadly*, 1992
Linda Grant, *A Woman's Place*, 1994
C.A. Haddad, *Caught in the Shadows*, 1992
Rob Kantner, *Concrete Hero*, 1994
Maynard F. Thomson, *Trade Secrets*, 1994

233
W.J. Chaput
Dead in the Water (New York: St. Martin's, 1991)

Story type: Amateur Detective—Male Lead

Major character(s): Ozzie Barrett, Fisherman (commercial; ex-banker); Wilson Malone, Professor, Friend (of Ozzie)

Time period(s): 1990s

Locale(s): Strike's Landing, Massachusetts

What the book is about: Ozzie's Uncle Barry has a strange habit - he collects keys and wanders through people's houses. Now he has wandered through one too many and discovered the body of pretty and wealthy widow Veronica Hammond. Of course, the police suspect Barry. Ozzie and his friend Wilson want to find the real killer.

Other books you might like:
Rick Boyer, *Billingsgate Shoal*, 1982
Philip R. Craig, *A Beautiful Place to Die*, 1989
Paul Kemprecos, *Cool Blue Tomb*, 1991
John Walter Putre, *A Small and Incidental Murder*, 1990
John Smolens, *Winter by Degrees*, 1988

234
Louis Charbonneau
The Ice (New York: Fine, 1991)

Story type: Action/Adventure

Major character(s): Kathy McNeely, Scientist (marine biologist); Brian Hurley, Explorer (ex-lover of McNeely)

Time period(s): 1990s (1991)

Locale(s): Antarctica, Poland

What the book is about: Marine biologist Kathy McNeely is trying to discover what caused the oil spill that killed a multitude of penguins. Unknown forces try to stop her - while her former lover, Hurley, is also in Antartica preparing for an assault of a glacier, further complicating her life.

Other books you might like:
Bob Langley, *Precipice*, 1991
Alistair MacLean, *Ice Station Zebra*, 1963
Martin Cruz Smith, *Polar Star*, 1989

235
Kate Charles
A Drink of Deadly Wine (New York: Mysterious, 1992)

Story type: Amateur Detective—Male Lead

Major character(s): David Middleton-Brown, Lawyer; Gabriel Neville, Religious (priest; former lover of David)

Time period(s): 1990s

Locale(s): London, England

What the book is about: Father Gabriel has received a blackmail note about an incident in his past that he thought long buried. He turns to his former lover, David, to help him find the blackmailer and save his position and his marriage. David is torn because he still loves Gabriel and doesn't want to help the woman who stole him away. Things get complicated when he meets the wife, Emily, and develops a respect and liking for her, and an attraction for her friend, Lucy. Then one of the prime suspects meets a suspicious death. First novel.

Other books you might like:
Anthony Appiah, *Avenging Angel*, 1991
D.M. Greenwood, *Clerical Errors*, 1992
Robert Richardson, *The Augustus Maltravers Series*, 1985-
J.G. Sandom, *Gospel Truths*, 1992
Barbara Whitehead, *Playing God*, 1989

236
David Charnee
Party Till You Die (New York: St. Martin's, 1991)

Series: D.L. Blacker

Story type: Amateur Detective—Male Lead; Legal

Major character(s): D.L. Blacker, Lawyer, Entertainer (part-time clown); Pat Arnold, Entertainer (juggler)

Time period(s): 1990s

Locale(s): New York, New York

What the book is about: Pat Arnold meets D.L. on the way to perform at a party booked by Gary Johnson, successful promoter and all-around sleaze. By the end of the night, Gary is dead, killed with one of Pat's juggling machetes. D.L. figures the best way to clear Pat is to find the real murderer and there is no lack of suspects - to know Gary was to hate him. First novel.

Other books you might like:
J.P. Hailey, *The Naked Typist*, 1991
Parnell Hall, *Juror*, 1991
Ralph McInerny, *The Andrew Broome Series*, 1987-
Haughton Murphy, *The Reuben Frost Series*, 1986-
William G. Tapply, *The Brady Coyne Series*, 1984-

237
David Charnee
To Kill a Clown (New York: St. Martin's, 1992)

Series: D.L. Blacker

Story type: Amateur Detective—Male Lead; Legal

Major character(s): D.L. Blacker, Lawyer, Entertainer (part-time clown); Pat Arnold, Entertainer (clown and juggler)

Time period(s): 1990s

Locale(s): New York, New York

What the book is about: Pat Arnold has been hired to be one of the Terry Town clowns. While attending the annual clown seminar, a clown is killed and the police quickly solve the crime - or do they? More clowns begin to die and Blacker has to solve the case before Pat becomes a victim.

Other books you might like:
Lawrence Block, *The Topless Tulip Caper*, 1974
J.P. Hailey, *The Steve Winslow Series*, 1988-
Lia Matera, *Where Lawyers Fear to Tread*, 1986
Ralph McInerny, *The Andrew Broome Series*, 1987-
Susan Wolfe, *The Last Billable Hour*, 1990

238
Jerome Charyn
Elsinore (New York: Mysterious, 1991)

Series: Sidney Holden

Story type: Psychological Suspense

Major character(s): Sidney Holden, Criminal (hit-man, trying to retire); Howard Phipps, Businessman, Wealthy

Time period(s): 1990s

Locale(s): New York, New York

What the book is about: Retired hit-man Sidney Holden has given up his hit-man's life but then his true love is stolen away. Until he gets involved with Howard Phipps, one of Manhattan's richest men, he is powerless to do anything. A surreal novel.

Other books you might like:
Paul Auster, *City of Glass*, 1985
Thomas Berger, *Who Is Teddy Villinova?*, 1977
George C. Chesbro, *The Beasts of Valhalla*, 1985
Max Allan Collins, *The Quarry Series*, 1972-
Loren D. Estleman, *Kill Zone*, 1984

239
Thomas Chastain
Perry Mason in The Case of Too Many Murders (New York: Morrow, 1989)

Series: Perry Mason

Story type: Legal

Major character(s): Perry Mason, Lawyer

Locale(s): Los Angeles, California

What the book is about: Gil Adrian shoots a man in a bar, goes home and is shot himself. His wife Laura is accused of his murder. She hires Mason and the search is on for the truth. This is the first of the continuation of Erle Stanley Gardner's original Perry Mason series.

Other books you might like:
Erle Stanley Gardner, *The Perry Mason Series*, (1933-1973)
Joe L. Hensley, *Robak's Cross*, 1985
Scott Turow, *Presumed Innocent*, 1986

240
Thomas Chastain
The Prosecutor (New York: Morrow, 1992)

Story type: Legal

Major character(s): Ann Gilman, Lawyer (district attorney); John Holland, Police Officer (lieutenant)

Time period(s): 1990s

Locale(s): New York, New York

What the book is about: Ann Gilman is the newly appointed District Attorney for Manhattan and she has problems. She has a man who she is convinced has killed many women but she can't get a conviction because there are no bodies. She has a woman whose husband is dead, supposedly shot by a burglar who was then shot by the wife, but the wife has a meeting with a man who knew the burglar. Gilman has a gangland power struggle and charges of police corruption. All this threatens her life as well as her career.

Other books you might like:
Harrison Arnston, *Trade-Off*, 1991
Warwick Downing, *A Clear Case of Murder*, 1990
Warwick Downing, *The Water Cure*, 1992
Walter Walker, *The Immediate Prospect of Being Hanged*, 1989
Kate Wilhelm, *Death Qualified: A Mystery of Chaos*, 1991

241
George C. Chesbro
In the House of Secret Enemies (New York: Mysterious, 1990)

Series: Mongo

Story type: Private Detective—Male Lead

Major character(s): Robert "Mongo" Frederickson, Detective—Private (dwarf), Professor (of criminology, formerly); Garth Frederickson, Police Officer (Mongo's brother)

Time period(s): 20th century (1970-90)

Locale(s): United States

What the book is about: A collection of short stories about Chesbro's series character Mongo, a dwarf private detective. Some have strong science fiction and fantasy elements.

Other books you might like:
Richard Bowker, *Marlborough Street*, 1987
Harlan Ellison, *No Doors, No Windows*, 1975
F. Paul Wilson, *Dydeetown World*, 1989

242
George C. Chesbro
The Language of Cannibals (New York: Mysterious, 1990)

Series: Mongo

Story type: Private Detective—Male Lead

Major character(s): Robert "Mongo" Frederickson, Detective—Private (dwarf), Professor (of criminology, formerly)

Time period(s): 1980s

Locale(s): Cairn, New York

What the book is about: Coming together in the small town of Cairn, New York are such elements as a drowned FBI agent, a right-wing demagogue, a former folksinger from the 60's, and Mongo.
Other books you might like:
Michael Collins, *Minnesota Strip*, 1987
Jack Livingston, *The Nightmare File*, 1986
Sharyn McCrumb, *If Ever I Return, Pretty Peggy-O*, 1990
Simon Ritchie, *The Hollow Woman*, 1987

243
P.F. Chisholm
A Famine of Horses (New York: Walker, 1995)
Story type: Historical; Amateur Detective—Male Lead
Major character(s): Sir Robert Carey, Nobleman (cousin of Queen Elizabeth I)
Time period(s): 16th century (1592)
Locale(s): Carlisle, England (on the border with Scotland)
What the book is about: Sir Robert has been asked by the Queen to accept the post of Deputy Warden of the West March in the troubled borderland, which is ruled by his incompetent brother-in-law. No sooner does he arrive than there is a murder. The victim is the favorite son of the head of the Graham Clan. He must also deal with the man who thought he should have been the new Deputy Warden, and answer the question of the missing horses. First novel under this name. Unknown pseudonym.
Other books you might like:
P.C. Doherty, *The Hugh Corbett Series*, 1987-
Anne Dukthas, *A Time for the Death of a King*, 1994
Ian Morson, *Falconer's Crusade*, 1994
Candace M. Robb, *The Owen Archer Series*, 1993-
Kate Sedley, *The Roger the Chapman Series*, 1992-

244
Jill Churchill (Pseudonym of Janice Young Brooks)
The Class Menagerie (New York: Avon, 1994)
Series: Jane Jeffry
Story type: Amateur Detective—Female Lead
Major character(s): Jane Jeffry, Widow(er), Housewife; Shelley Nowack, Friend, Housewife
Time period(s): 1990s
Locale(s): Chicago, Illinois
What the book is about: Jane has been coerced into helping Shelley organize a reunion of the ewe-lambs, an exclusive club from high school days. Someone starts playing nasty jokes on the members soon after they arrive for the reunion. Then one of them is killed—Lila, who had a notebook filled with information about the others, past and present. It's obvious to Jane that somebody has a secret worth killing to protect.
Other books you might like:
Mary Cahill, *Carpool*, 1991
Diane Mott Davidson, *The Goldy Bear Series*, 1990-
Jean Hager, *Blooming Murder*, 1994
Katherine Hall Page, *The Faith Fairchild Series*, 1990-
Valerie Wolzien, *The Susan Henshaw Series*, 1988-

245
Jill Churchill (Pseudonym of Janice Young Brooks)
A Farewell to Yarns (New York: Avon, 1991)
Series: Jane Jeffry
Story type: Amateur Detective—Female Lead
Major character(s): Jane Jeffry, Housewife (mother of three), Widow(er); Mel Van Dyne, Police Officer, Detective—Homicide
Time period(s): 1990s
Locale(s): Chicago, Illinois
What the book is about: Phyllis Wagner, an old friend of Jane's whom she hasn't seen in years, invites herself to spend Christmas. When she arrives, she is accompanied by her obnoxious teenaged son. Soon this irritating but well-meaning woman is murdered. Why would anyone want to kill her?
Other books you might like:
Diane Mott Davidson, *Catering to Nobody*, 1990
Jaqueline Girdner, *Adjusted to Death*, 1991
Robert Nordan, *Death Beneath the Christmas Tree*, 1991
Katherine Hall Page, *The Body in the Belfry*, 1990
Valerie Wolzien, *We Wish You a Merry Murder*, 1991

246
Jill Churchill (Pseudonym of Janice Young Brooks)
From Here to Paternity (New York: Avon, 1995)
Series: Jane Jeffry
Story type: Amateur Detective—Female Lead
Major character(s): Jane Jeffry, Widow(er), Single Parent; Mel Van Dyne, Police Officer, Detective—Homicide
Time period(s): 1990s
Locale(s): Colorado (the Rockies)
What the book is about: Jane and her children have been asked by Jane's friend Shelley and her husband to join them at a Colorado ski resort. Jane talks Mel into joining the party and off they go. They meet a group of genealogists, one of whom is the highly disagreeable Doris Schmidtheiser, who thinks the resort's owner is the heir to the Russian throne. Doris is soon discovered dead and Jane suspects it may be murder. Then Jane literally runs into the owner's dead body disguised as a snowman.
Other books you might like:
Jaqueline Girdner, *The Kate Jasper Series*, 1990-
Nancy Gladstone, *Mommy and the Murder*, 1995
Katherine Hall Page, *The Faith Fairchild Series*, 1990-
Gillian Roberts, *The Amanda Pepper Series*, 1987-
Valerie Wolzien, *The Susan Henshaw Series*, 1988-

247
Jill Churchill (Pseudonym of Janice Young Brooks)
A Quiche Before Dying (New York: Avon, 1993)
Series: Jane Jeffry
Story type: Amateur Detective—Female Lead
Major character(s): Jane Jeffry, Housewife, Widow(er)
Time period(s): 1990s

Locale(s): Chicago, Illinois

What the book is about: Jane's mother has talked her into taking a creative writing course specializing in autobiography. Also in the class is Agnes Pryce - one of the most hateful women that Jane has ever met. The first night of class she has something nasty to say to everyone. When she has a pot-luck supper at her house she suddenly drops dead from poison. Everyone in the class had a reason to kill her. To protect herself and her mother, Jane tries to find the killer.

Other books you might like:
Diane Mott Davidson, *Catering to Nobody*, 1990
M.D. Lake, *A Gift for Murder*, 1992
Katherine Hall Page, *The Body in the Belfry*, 1990
Gillian Roberts, *Caught Dead in Philadelphia*, 1987
Valerie Wolzien, *The Susan Henshaw Series*, 1988

248
Tom Clancy
The Sum of All Fears (New York: Putnam, 1991)

Series: Jack Ryan

Story type: Action/Adventure; Techno-Thriller

Major character(s): Jack Ryan, Spy

Time period(s): 1990s (Late)

Locale(s): Washington, District of Columbia; Middle East

What the book is about: A small nuclear explosion at the Super Bowl sets the stage for a series of terrorist actions that are all aimed at exacerbating East-West tensions, as well as doing everything possible to exploit the Middle-East crisis. Is there a central power behind these actions? It's up to Jack Ryan to find out.

Other books you might like:
Larry Bond, *Red Phoenix*, 1989
Sean Flannery, *Counterstrike*, 1991
Thomas Harris, *Black Sunday*, 1976
A.J. Quinnell, *The Mahdi*, 1982
Ridley Pearson, *Hard Fall*, 1991

249
Marten Claridge
Nobody's Fool (New York: Walker, 1991)

Story type: Police Procedural—Male Lead; Psychological Suspense

Major character(s): Frank McMorran, Detective; Dominic Bain, Criminal

Time period(s): 1990s

Locale(s): Edinburgh, Scotland

What the book is about: Dominic Bain is exorcising his demons by hanging children. Frank McMorran has been suspended pending a fatal accident inquiry. Political maneuvering has given him one last chance to save his career but he must be the one to find and bring in the hangman. He must outwit not only the killer, but his colleagues too. First novel.

Other books you might like:
M.C. Beaton, *The Hamish MacBeth Series*, 1985-
Bill Knox, *The Colin Thane Series*, 1961-
William McIlvanney, *Laidlaw*, 1977
Peter Turnbull, *The "P" Division Series*, 1982-

250
Carol Higgins Clark
Decked (New York: Warner, 1992)

Series: Regan Reilly

Story type: Private Detective—Female Lead

Major character(s): Regan Reilly, Detective—Private

Time period(s): 1990s (1992)

Locale(s): Oxford, England; At Sea

What the book is about: Regan Reilly is back in Oxford for a tenth reunion. Her stay at Oxford had only one bad time, the disappearance of her roommate. Now the body has been discovered, dead all these years. Regan has no time to investigate however, as she has been hired to be a companion to an old woman on a sea voyage. Incidents seem to indicate that the killer has followed Regan on board ship. First novel. Carol Higgins Clark is the daughter of best-selling author Mary Higgins Clark.

Other books you might like:
K.K. Beck, *Death in a Deck Chair*, 1984
Laura Frankos, *St. Oswald's Niche*, 1991
Orania Papazoglou, *Death's Savage Passion*, 1986
Elizabeth Peters, *Die for Love*, 1984

251
Carol Higgins Clark
Snagged (New York: Warner, 1993)

Series: Regan Reilly

Story type: Private Detective—Female Lead

Major character(s): Regan Reilly, Detective—Private; Richie Blossom, Inventor

Time period(s): 1990s

Locale(s): Miami Beach, Florida

What the book is about: Regan Reilly is in Miami Beach for the wedding of an old friend and to visit her parents. She renews her friendship with the bride's favorite relative, Uncle Richie Blossom, a lovable inventor who has just invented pantyhose guaranteed not to run or snag. However, someone seems to be trying to kill Uncle Richie and Regan is determined to find out who. The motive is unclear. Could it have something to do with the pantyhose?

Other books you might like:
Lydia Adamson, *The Alice Nestleton Series*, 1990-
K.K. Beck, *The Jane Silva Series*, 1992-
Catherine Dain, *Lay It on the Line*, 1992
Kay Hooper, *Crime of Passion*, 1991
Margaret Lucke, *A Relative Stranger*, 1991

252
Mary Higgins Clark
All Around the Town (New York: Simon & Schuster, 1992)

Story type: Psychological Suspense

Major character(s): Laurie Kenyon, Student; Sarah Kenyon, Lawyer

Time period(s): 1990s

Locale(s): Ridgewood, New Jersey

What the book is about: Laurie Kenyon, having been horribly abused as a child, is now a college senior with multiple personalities. Now she, or one of her personalities, is accused in the death of her college professor. Under pressure she may implicate her childhood abusers, not in the death, but in her abuse. They are now successful television evangelists. They are worried about her talking and they look to ensure her silence.

Other books you might like:
Michael Allegretto, *The Watchman*, 1991
Marjorie Dorner, *Blood Kin*, 1992
Tony Gibbs, *Shadow Queen*, 1991
Kate Green, *Shooting Star*, 1992
Marilyn Wallace, *A Single Stone*, 1991

253
Mary Higgins Clark
Loves Music, Loves to Dance (New York: Simon & Schuster, 1991)

Story type: Psychological Suspense

Major character(s): Davey Scott, Interior Decorator; Chris Sheridan, Antiques Dealer

Time period(s): 1990s

Locale(s): New York, New York

What the book is about: Davey Scott's best friend is killed after answering a personal ad. Evidence suggests that she was killed by the same person who killed Chris Sheridan's sister some fifteen years earlier. Davey and Chris get involved with each other as well as with the killer who has targeted Davey for his next victim.

Other books you might like:
Gary Amo, *Silent Night*, 1991
Patricia D. Cornwell, *Postmortem*, 1990
Kate Green, *Night Angel*, 1989
David L. Lindsey, *A Cold Mind*, 1983

254
John Clarkson
And Justice for One (New York: Crown, 1992)

Story type: Private Detective—Male Lead; Action/Adventure

Major character(s): Jack Devlin, Detective—Private (ex-cop; ex-Secret Service)

Time period(s): 1990s

Locale(s): New York, New York

What the book is about: The savage beating of his brother leads Jack Devlin into an investigation of after hours clubs in New York City. What he finds isn't pretty and is certainly dangerous, but he perseveres, determined to find out who injured his brother. Along the way he gets help from a couple of beautiful women. First novel.

Other books you might like:
Robert Campbell, *Alice in La-La Land*, 1987
Jon A. Jackson, *The Blind Pig*, 1977
Paul Levine, *To Speak for the Dead*, 1990
Jerry Oster, *Violent Love*, 1991
Gerald Petievich, *Shakedown*, 1988

255
Jon Cleary
Babylon South (New York: Morrow, 1990)

Series: Scobie Malone

Story type: Police Procedural—Male Lead

Major character(s): Scobie Malone, Detective—Police

Time period(s): 1980s

Locale(s): New South Wales, Australia

What the book is about: The discovery of a long-missing High Court justice reopens the investigation of his disappearance. This causes murder now.

Other books you might like:
Peter Corris, *The Dying Trade*, 1986
E.X. Ferrars, *The Crime and the Crystal*, 1985
Arthur W. Upfield, *The Inspector Napoleon Bonaparte Series*, (1929-1966)

256
Jon Cleary
Murder Song (New York: Morrow, 1990)

Series: Scobie Malone

Story type: Police Procedural—Male Lead; Action/Adventure

Major character(s): Scobie Malone, Police Officer (detective-inspector); Brian O'Brien, Businessman, Criminal

Time period(s): 1990s

Locale(s): Sydney, Australia

What the book is about: A construction worker, a cop, and a singer are all killed by a sniper. What does all of that have to do with the prime minister, his wife and businessman Brian O'Brien (who's seeing the prime minister wife on the sly)? Scobie Malone, O'Brien and the construction worker all went to the police academy together and this makes Scobie's wife very nervous.

Other books you might like:
Peter Corris, *The Dying Trade*, 1980
Claire McNab, *Cop-Out*, 1991
Arthur W. Upfield, *The Scribner Crime Classic Series*, 1929-1970
Charles West, *Funnelweb*, 1989

257
Melissa Cleary
First Pedigree Murder (New York: Berkley, 1994)
Series: Jackie Walsh
Story type: Amateur Detective—Female Lead
Major character(s): Jackie Walsh, Teacher (single parent), Actress
Time period(s): 1990s
Locale(s): Palmer, Massachusetts
What the book is about: Jackie Walsh is teaching a film class at Rodgers University and is present at the celebration of the opening of the new Radio Arts Building where the guests of honor are the Goodwillie brothers. The festivities are interrupted when Mannheim Goodwillie's pacemaker literally explodes inside him. Jackie, who is gaining a reputation as a crime solver, is asked to lend a hand in the investigation. Then another person who was present at the party is killed.
Other books you might like:
Susan Conant, *The Holly Winter Series*, 1990-
David Handler, *The Stewart Hoag Series*, 1988-
Barbara Moore, *The Doberman Wore Black*, 1984
Dallas Murphy, *Lover Man*, 1987
Karen Ann Wilson, *Eight Dogs Flying*, 1994

258
Melissa Cleary
The Maltese Puppy (New York: Berkley, 1995)
Series: Jackie Walsh
Story type: Amateur Detective—Female Lead
Major character(s): Jackie Walsh, Teacher (film); Maury, Animal (dog)
Time period(s): 1990s
Locale(s): Palmer, Ohio
What the book is about: Jackie has a major problem—somehow she has acquired Maury, the puppy from hell. He is well-meaning but has been know to roll a jeep in his enthusiasm. He also involves Jackie in the murder of visiting medical researcher Linus Munch. Munch may have been brilliant, but before his death he was an embittered old man with a deadly agenda of revenge. Can Jackie survive the misadventures of Maury long enough to find a killer?
Other books you might like:
Laurien Berenson, *A Pedigree to Die For*, 1995
Rita Mae Brown, *Wish You Were Here*, 1990
Susan Conant, *The Holly Winter Series*, 1989-
Barbara Moore, *The Doberman Wore Black*, 1984
Karen Ann Wilson, *Eight Dogs Flying*, 1994

259
Melissa Cleary
A Tail of Two Murders (New York: Diamond, 1992)
Series: Jackie Walsh
Story type: Amateur Detective—Female Lead
Major character(s): Jackie Walsh, Professor, Single Parent (divorced); Michael McGowan, Police Officer (homicide lieutenant)
Time period(s): 1990s
Locale(s): Palmer, Massachusetts
What the book is about: Jacky Walsh, newly divorced, has returned to her hometown to teach in the film department of Rodgers University. She is just settling in when her son Peter rescues an Alsatian shepherd who has apparently been shot. The next morning Jacky discovers the body of the chairman of her department. Jacky is a prime suspect, can she and ex-police dog Jake, with the help of Lt. McGowan, find the real killer? First novel.
Other books you might like:
Susan Conant, *The Holly Winter Series*, 1989-
David Handler, *The Man Who Would Be F. Scott Fitzgerald*, 1990
Barbara Moore, *The Doberman Wore Black*, 1984
Dana Stabenow, *A Cold Day for Murder*, 1992
Ted Wood, *The Reid Bennett Series*, 1985-

260
Ann Cleeves
A Day in the Death of Dorothea Cassidy (New York: Fawcett, 1992)
Series: Inspector Stephen Ramsey
Story type: Police Procedural—Male Lead
Major character(s): Stephen Ramsey, Police Officer (inspector); Gordon Hunter, Police Officer (sergeant)
Time period(s): 1990s
Locale(s): Northumberland, England
What the book is about: The vicar's wife turns up dead. Though one would not expect her to be a natural murder victim, there is, nonetheless, no shortage of suspects: the stepson, his girlfriend, the village idiot, a dying widow and the Vicar himself. Soon there is a second murder which eliminates at least one of the suspects.
Other books you might like:
Catherine Aird, *Henrietta Who?*, 1968
W.J. Burley, *To Kill a Cat*, 1970
Colin Dexter, *The Dead of Jericho*, 1981
Reginald Hill, *A Killing Kindness*, 1980
P.D. James, *Cover Her Face*, 1966

261
Edward Cline
Whisper the Guns (Milpitas, California: Atlantean, 1992)
Story type: Action/Adventure
Major character(s): Merritt Fury, Businessman (entrepreneur); Amber Lee, Economist
Time period(s): 1990s
Locale(s): Hong Kong

What the book is about: Fury is involved in an investment group that supposedly mines tungsten but actually uses that as a cover for large business deals of all kinds. There seems to be a conspiracy among some of the group to take over and cut out the others. Fury tries to protect his investment which involves him with mainland China, people trying to kill him, and the beautiful Amber Lee.

Other books you might like:
Charlotte Epstein, *Murder at the Friendship Hotel*, 1990
Stephen Leather, *The Fireman*, 1990
Wayne Warga, *Singapore Transfer*, 1991
Don Winslow, *The Trail to Buddha's Mirror*, 1992

262
John Cline
The Forever Beat (New York: Dutton, 1990)

Story type: Action/Adventure

Major character(s): Luke Byman, Writer (aspiring screenwriter); Stanley Cussone, Police Officer

Time period(s): 1990s

Locale(s): New York, New York; Los Angeles, California

What the book is about: Luke Byman helps his neighbor deliver her baby, then watches in horror as her older son is shot to death and the newborn is stolen. Luke, too, has been shot and left for dead and when he regains consciousness he vows to find out what happened and why. Even if he wanted out he couldn't escape because someone is killed in his apartment, he is pistol-whipped and his ex-girlfriend is murdered. He must find out what's going on for his own self-preservation. First novel.

Other books you might like:
William Bayer, *Blind Side*, 1989
Gary Devon, *Bad Desire*, 1990
Edwin Gage, *Phoenix No More*, 1978
Timothy Hallinan, *Everything but the Squeal*, 1990
Reed Stephens, *The Man Who Killed His Brother*, 1980

263
Dick Cluster
Obligations of the Bone (New York: St. Martin's, 1992)

Series: Alex Glauberman

Story type: Private Detective—Male Lead

Major character(s): Alex Glauberman, Detective—Private, Mechanic (cancer patient in remission)

Time period(s): 1990s

Locale(s): Boston, Massachusetts

What the book is about: When Doctor Jay Harrison receives a note from an old acquaintence demanding money, he is puzzled. According to him there is nothing in his past he is afraid of. Alex is hired to investigate. At the same time an irreplaceable sample of bone marrow is stolen and held for ransom. If it is not recovered the patient will die. This becomes Alex's first priority but he wonders if the cases are connected. Is someone more concerned with money or destroying Dr. Harrison?

Other books you might like:
Jerome Doolittle, *Body Scissors*, 1990
Stephen Greenleaf, *Blood Type*, 1992
Nancy Baker Jacobs, *The Turquoise Tattoo*, 1991
Sara Paretsky, *Bitter Medicine*, 1987

264
Michael Clynes
The Poisoned Chalice (New York: Otto Penzler, 1994)

Series: Roger Shallot

Story type: Historical; Amateur Detective—Male Lead

Major character(s): Roger Shallot, Secretary; Benjamin Daunbey, Nobleman

Time period(s): 16th century (1521)

Locale(s): Paris, France

What the book is about: Benjamin Daunbey and his young secretary, Roger Shallot, have been dispatched to Paris by Benjamin's uncle to investigate the brutal murder of the chief secretary of the English Embassy. Of course, since Benjamin's uncle is the devious Cardinal Wolsey, it is not that simple. Roger has already been involved with the Luciferi, a French group of spies, an involvement that almost got him hanged for murder. Is this same group involved in the secretary's death? Clynes also writes as P.C. Doherty, Paul Harding, and C.L. Grace.

Other books you might like:
Faye Kellerman, *The Quality of Mercy*, 1990
Edward Marston, *The Nicholas Bracewell Series*, 1988-
Candace M. Robb, *The Apothecary Rose*, 1993
Kate Sedley, *The Roger the Chapman Series*, 1992-
Leonard Tourney, *The Matthew Stock Series*, 1980-

265
Michael Clynes
The White Rose Murders (New York: St. Martins, 1993)

Series: Roger Shallot

Story type: Historical; Amateur Detective—Male Lead

Major character(s): Roger Shallot, Secretary

Time period(s): 16th century (1517)

Locale(s): London, England

What the book is about: Roger Shallot is the secretary and friend of Benjamin Daunby who is the nephew of Cardinal Wolsey. Wolsey has asked his nephew to help restore Henry VIII's sister, Margaret, to the throne of Scotland. To do so Benjamin and Roger must solve several murders including the locked room murder of Mad Driselkirk and defeat an assassin of the White Rose Society. First novel as Clynes. Also writes as P.C. Doherty.

Other books you might like:
P.C. Doherty, *The Crown in Darkness*, 1988
C.L. Grace, *The Fate of the Princes*, 1989
Paul Harding, *The Nightingale Gallery*, 1991
Candace M. Robb, *The Apothecary Rose*, 1993
Kate Sedley, *Death and the Chapman*, 1992

266
Harlan Coben
Play Dead (New York: British American, 1990)

Story type: Action/Adventure

Major character(s): Laura Ayars, Model; David Baskin, Sports Figure (Professional basketball player)

Time period(s): 1980s

What the book is about: David Baskin fakes his death while on his honeymoon with model Laura Ayars. Laura doesn't believe his death was an accident and when she starts to snoop, problems arise. First book.

Other books you might like:
Joe Gores, *Dead Skip*, 1972
William H. Hallahan, *The Search for Joseph Tully*, 1974
Elmore Leonard, *Unknown Man No. 89*, 1977

267
Andrew Coburn
No Way Home (New York: Dutton, 1992)

Series: James Morgan

Story type: Police Procedural—Male Lead

Major character(s): James Morgan, Police Officer (chief of police); Lydia Lapham, Nurse

Time period(s): 1990s

Locale(s): Bensington, Massachusetts

What the book is about: Lydia Lapham is just saying goodbye to her parents before going go work when a shot kills her mother instantly and her father dies of a heart attack. The state police believe it was Lydia's boyfriend trying to kill her and missing. Chief Morgan is sure it was an old man who has gotten away with murder before. Who is right? Or are they both wrong?

Other books you might like:
Susan Rogers Cooper, *Other People's Houses*, 1990
S.K. Epperson, *Dumford Blood*, 1991
David Martin, *Lie to Me*, 1990
Sharyn McCrumb, *The Hangman's Beautiful Daughter*, 1992
Anne Wingate, *Death by Deception*, 1988

268
Andrew Coburn
Voices in the Dark (New York: Dutton, 1994)

Series: James Morgan

Story type: Police Procedural—Male Lead; Psychological Suspense

Major character(s): James Morgan, Police Officer (chief of police)

Time period(s): 1990s

Locale(s): Bensington, Massachusetts

What the book is about: Sixteen-year-old Glen Bodine is dead, shoved in front of a speeding train. His death sends ripples through a suburban community and affects the lives of several well-to-do couples, who have troubles and secrets of their own. And what of the vague vagrant, Dudley, who when asked what he does, replies, "I kill kids?"

Other books you might like:
Susan Rogers Cooper, *Other People's Houses*, 1990
S.K. Epperson, *Dumford Blood*, 1991
Paula Gosling, *A Few Dying Words*, 1994
Susan Oleksiw, *Murder in Mellingham*, 1992
L.R. Wright, *Fall From Grace*, 1991

269
Liza Cody
Backhand (New York: Doubleday, 1992)

Series: Anna Lee

Story type: Private Detective—Female Lead

Major character(s): Anna Lee, Detective—Private

Time period(s): 1990s

Locale(s): London, England; Florida

What the book is about: Anna's personal life is a mess. Her job has become not much more than selling home security systems, her boyfriend is pressuring her, and her longtime home has been sold. When Lara Crowther, one of her security clients, asks her to help a friend she jumps at the chance. Penny Gardner, fashion designer, has gone bankrupt. Her husband has disappeared with the financial records, Penny's daughter Cynthia, and possibly her designs that have recently been showing up in other stores.

Other books you might like:
Antonia Fraser, *The Jemima Shore Series*, 1977-
Lesley Grant-Adamson, *Too Many Questions*, 1991
P.D. James, *An Unsuitable Job for a Woman*, 1973
Joan Smith, *Don't Leave Me This Way*, 1990
Hannah Wakefield, *The Price You Pay*, 1987

270
Liza Cody
Bucket Nut (New York: Doubleday, 1993)

Series: Eva Wylie

Story type: Amateur Detective—Female Lead; Action/Adventure

Major character(s): Eva Wylie, Sports Figure (wrestler; small-time thief)

Time period(s): 1990s

Locale(s): London, England

What the book is about: Eva Wylie is large, mean and ugly. As a wrestler she is one of the villains and is known as Bucket Nut—among other things. She is also a security guard, a part-time thief, and errand person for Mr. Cheng, the unofficial boss of Chinatown. She gets involved with a young girl with a drug problem and inadvertently ends up in the middle of a protection war. First in this series. Cody's other series character, Anna Lee, makes a brief appearance.

Other books you might like:
Sin Soracco, *Edge City*, 1992

271
Liza Cody
Monkey Wrench (New York: Mysterious Press, 1995)
Series: Eva Wylie
Story type: Action/Adventure; Amateur Detective—Female Lead
Major character(s): Eva Wylie, Sports Figure (wrestler)
Time period(s): 1990s
Locale(s): London, England
What the book is about: Eva Wylie, professional wrestler—billed as the London Lassassin, but known to the audience as Bucketnut—is a hardcase. Why should she care that one of her old street-mates wants her help. Crystal wants Eva to help her find out who killed her sister, Dawn. Dawn was a bitter and used-up hooker, but Crystal wants revenge. A group of hookers also want Eva's help to learn self-defense. For some reason, Eva agrees to both requests and ends up in more trouble than ever before.

Other books you might like:
Jeffrey Wilds Deaver, *Manhattan Is My Beat*, 1989
Ron Faust, *Fugitive Moon*, 1995
George Dawes Green, *The Caveman's Valentine*, 1994
Sin Soracco, *Edge City*, 1992

272
James Colbert
All I Have Is Blue (New York: Atheneum, 1992)
Series: Skinny
Story type: Police Procedural—Male Lead; Action/Adventure
Major character(s): Skinny, Police Officer; Ruth, Secretary (head of typing pool)
Time period(s): 1990s
Locale(s): New Orleans, Louisiana
What the book is about: Skinny and Ruth are collecting driftwood near the levee when a passing boat explodes. Skinny manages to rescue a young boy, Dwayne Charles, but the boy's father is dead. When the boy is given to his aunt, more violence ensues and the boy disappears. Soon several rival government agents are involved, along with a prominent black gangster.

Other books you might like:
James Lee Burke, *The Neon Rain*, 1986
Jon A. Jackson, *Grootka*, 1990
John Lawrence Reynolds, *Whisper Death*, 1992
M.K. Shuman, *Deep Kill*, 1991
Daniel Woodrell, *Under the Bright Lights*, 1988

273
James Colbert
Skinny Man (New York: Atheneum, 1991)
Series: Skinny
Story type: Action/Adventure; Police Procedural—Male Lead
Major character(s): Skinny, Police Officer (currently on suspension); Karen Hodges, Criminal
Time period(s): 1990s
Locale(s): New Orleans, Louisiana
What the book is about: Though currently on suspension for destroying his fourth squad car in a year, Skinny, who always refers to himself in the third person, manages to get involved in an arson investigation. He also gets involved with a blonde and a redhead.

Other books you might like:
Anthony Bruno, *Bad Guys*, 1989
James Lee Burke, *The Neon Rain*, 1986
James Crumley, *The Wrong Case*, 1975
Chris Wiltz, *The Emerald Lizard*, 1991
Daniel Woodrell, *Under the Bright Lights*, 1988

274
Anna Ashwood Collins
Deadly Resolutions (New York: Walker, 1989)
Story type: Private Detective—Female Lead
Major character(s): Abigail Doyle, Detective—Private; Margaret Standish, Detective—Police
Time period(s): 1980s
Locale(s): New York, New York
What the book is about: After finding the body of a murdered general while on a nature walk, P.I. Abby Doyle gets thoroughly involved in finding out what happened.

Other books you might like:
Linda Barnes, *The Snake Tattoo*, 1988
Karin Berne, *Bare Acquaintances*, 1985
D. Miller Morgan, *A Lovely Night to Kill*, 1988
Maxine O'Callaghan, *Death Is Forever*, 1981
Mary Wings, *She Came in a Flash*, 1989

275
Judy Collins
Shameless (New York: Pocket, 1995)
Story type: Psychological Suspense
Major character(s): Catherine Saint, Photojournalist
Time period(s): 1990s
Locale(s): New York, New York
What the book is about: Catherine Saint, former groupie turned photojournalist, is having trouble in her life. Her lover is having an affair, her favorite band is heavily into the drug scene, and someone may be trying to kill her. It may be one of her friends. First novel.

Other books you might like:
Edna Buchanan, *Suitable for Framing*, 1995
Mary Higgins Clark, *Loves Music, Loves to Dance*, 1991
Joy Fielding, *Don't Cry Now*, 1995
Melodie Johnson Howe, *Beauty Dies*, 1994
Rochelle Majer Krich, *Where's Mommy Now*, 1989

276
Max Allan Collins
Blood and Thunder (New York: Dutton, 1995)
Story type: Private Detective—Male Lead; Historical
Major character(s): Nate Heller, Detective—Private; Huey Long, Historical Figure
Time period(s): 1930s (1935)
Locale(s): Louisiana
What the book is about: Nate Heller is hired as an additional bodyguard by Huey Long, who likes Nate's style. Nate appreciates the "Kingfish" as well, though there is the added fillip of attractive young females to keep Nate occupied when he's not bodyguarding. But when Long is assassinated the fun and games stop and Nate is asked by Long's widow to find out who did the killing.
Other books you might like:
Howard Browne, *Pork City*, 1988
James Ellroy, *American Tabloid*, 1995
Loren D. Estleman, *Whiskey River*, 1990
Stuart M. Kaminsky, *Bullet for a Star*, 1977
Walter Mosley, *A Red Death*, 1991

277
Max Allan Collins
Carnal Hours (New York: Dutton, 1994)
Series: Nate Heller
Story type: Private Detective—Male Lead; Historical
Major character(s): Nate Heller, Detective—Private
Time period(s): 1940s (1943)
Locale(s): Bahamas
What the book is about: Chicago private detective Nate Heller is asked to go to the Bahamas to do some work for Sir Harry Oakes, millionaire and philanthropist. Sir Harry wants him to get proof that his son-in-law, Alfred de Marigny, is a philandering thief. Before Nate can do much investigating, Sir Harry is murdered. Alfred is the leading suspect and in fact is arrested for the crime. Sir Harry's daughter asks Nate to stay on and earn his money by proving her husband innocent of her father's murder. With some trepidation, Nate agrees. Among the people he gets involved with are the Duke and Duchess of Windsor, Meyer Lansky, and Erle Stanley Gardner, who shows up as a journalist to write about the case and ends up being helpful to Heller in his investigation.
Other books you might like:
Howard Browne, *Pork City*, 1988
James Ellroy, *American Tabloid*, 1995
Loren D. Estleman, *Whiskey River*, 1990
Stuart M. Kaminsky, *The Toby Peters Series*, 1977-
Walter Mosley, *Devil in a Blue Dress*, 1990

278
Max Allan Collins
Murder by the Numbers (New York: St. Martins, 1993)
Series: Eliot Ness
Story type: Historical; Police Procedural—Male Lead
Major character(s): Eliot Ness, FBI Agent, Historical Figure; Toussaint Johnson, Police Officer (African American)
Time period(s): 1930s (1938)
Locale(s): Cleveland, Ohio
What the book is about: After taking care of Al Capone, Eliot Ness goes from Chicago to Cleveland to try and break up the Mayfield Road Mob. A white-backed mob group, they have taken over the black numbers game and Ness wants to eliminate them. With the help of black detective Toussaint Johnson, Ness is able to break the back of the Mayfield group. A mixture of fact and fiction.
Other books you might like:
Max Allan Collins, *True Crime*, 1985
John Peyton Cooke, *Torsos*, 1993
James Ellroy, *The Black Dahlia*, 1987

279
Max Allan Collins
Murder in the Post-War World (Woodstock, Vermont: Countryman, 1991)
Series: Nate Heller
Story type: Private Detective—Male Lead; Historical
Major character(s): Nate Heller, Detective—Private
Time period(s): 1940s
Locale(s): Chicago, Illinois; Cleveland, Ohio
What the book is about: A collection of one novella and 5 long short stories. Stories are mostly about actual cases with fictional or alternate solutions.
Other books you might like:
Howard Browne, *Pork City*, 1988
James Ellroy, *The Black Dahlia*, 1988
Loren D. Estleman, *Whiskey River*, 1990
Thomas Maxwell, *Kiss Me Once*, 1986
Walter Mosley, *Devil in a Blue Dress*, 1990

280
Max Allan Collins
Stolen Away (New York: Bantam, 1991)
Series: Nate Heller
Story type: Historical; Private Detective—Male Lead
Major character(s): Nate Heller, Detective—Private; Charles Lindbergh, Historical Figure, Pilot
Time period(s): 1930s (1932-1936)
Locale(s): New Jersey

What the book is about: Heller is sent from Chicago to New Jersey to assist the police on the Lindbergh kidnapping case because of his connections to the underworld. Initially, it is thought that the mob is involved in the snatch. When he arrives he is hamstrung at every turn by resentment and suspicion. Then a child's body turns up. It is assumed that it is the Lindbergh baby. Years later Heller finds out the truth—or does he? Shamus nominee for Best Novel.

Other books you might like:
James Ellroy, *The Black Dahlia*, 1987
Walter Mosley, *Devil in a Blue Dress*, 1990
Steve Thayer, *Saint Mudd*, 1992

281
Michael Collins (Pseudonym of Dennis Lynds)
Cassandra in Red (New York: Fine, 1992)

Series: Dan Fortune

Story type: Private Detective—Male Lead

Major character(s): Dan Fortune, Detective—Private, Handicapped (has only one arm)

Time period(s): 1990s

Locale(s): Santa Barbara, California

What the book is about: Fortune has been hired by a homeless activist to find out who stabbed Cassandra Reilly, a smart and loud street person who had a lot of friends and an equal number of enemies. Among the enemies were the local merchants association, a spooky boyfriend and the militant street people, who didn't like her slower approach. When two more people die there is evidence pointing to a para-military unit.

Other books you might like:
Stephen Greenleaf, *Book Case*, 1991
Jack Livingston, *A Piece of the Silence*, 1982
Bill Pronzini, *The Nameless Detective Series*, 1971-
M.K. Shuman, *The Micah Dunn Series*, 1989-

282
Michael Collins (Pseudonym of Dennis Lynds)
Chasing Eights (New York: Fine, 1990)

Series: Dan Fortune

Story type: Private Detective—Male Lead

Major character(s): Dan Fortune, Detective—Private, Handicapped (has only one arm)

Time period(s): 1980s

Locale(s): Santa Barbara, California

What the book is about: When Angela Price hires Fortune to investigate her husband's business dealings, Fortune can't find the husband and finds another person involved already dead.

Other books you might like:
Jack Early, *A Creative Kind of Killer*, 1984
Loren D. Estleman, *Motor City Blues*, 1980
Jack Livingston, *A Piece of the Silence*, 1982
Bill Pronzini, *Jackpot*, 1990
Robert J. Randisi, *The Steinway Collection*, 1983

283
Michael Collins (Pseudonym of Dennis Lynds)
Crime, Punishment and Resurrection (New York: Fine, 1992)

Series: Dan Fortune

Story type: Private Detective—Male Lead; Collection

Major character(s): Dan Fortune, Detective—Private, Handicapped (has only one arm)

Time period(s): 20th century (1970s-1990s)

Locale(s): New York; California

What the book is about: A collection of short stories and one novella about private detective Dan Fortune. They occur at various times in his career and take place in both New York and California.

Other books you might like:
George C. Chesbro, *In the House of Secret Enemies*, 1990
Max Allan Collins, *Dying in the Post-War World*, 1991
William F. Nolan, *The Black Mask Boys*, 1985
Bill Pronzini, *Casefile*, 1988

284
B. Comfort (Pseudonym of Barbara Comfort)
The Cashmere Kid (Woodstock, Vermont: Foul Play, 1993)

Series: Tish McWhinny

Story type: Amateur Detective—Female Lead

Major character(s): Tish McWhinny, Artist (painter); Sophie Beaumont, Photographer

Time period(s): 1990s

Locale(s): Lofton, Vermont

What the book is about: Sophie Beaumont, Tish McWhinny's unofficial niece, has decided to try her hand at raising goats. Her herd includes a prime stud goat named William the Conqueror. Tish is conned into taking care of them for a few days and everything does not go well. She discovers the body of a neighbor beaten to death with a golf club and then returns to find William missing. Is there a connection?

Other books you might like:
Eleanor Boylan, *The Clara Gamadge Series*, 1989-
Mary Bowen Hall, *The Emma Chizzit Series*, 1989-
Charlotte MacLeod, *The Sarah Kelling Series*, 1979-
Stephanie Matteson, *The Charlotte Graham Series*, 1990-
David Osborn, *The Margaret Barlow Series*, 1990-

285
B. Comfort (Pseudonym of Barbara Comfort)
Elusive Quarry (Woodstock, Vermont: Foul Play, 1995)

Series: Tish McWhinny

Story type: Amateur Detective—Female Lead

Major character(s): Tish McWhinny, Artist (painter), Aged Person; Sophie Beaumont, Businesswoman (goat farmer)

Time period(s): 1990s

Locale(s): Lofton, Vermont

What the book is about: Sophie has two men interested in her, quarry owner Sid Colt and computer magnate Graham Gray. They are both also interested in Tish's neighbor, Hilary Oats, and his property. But a mysterious series of accidents and explosions, including the destruction of Sophie's house, indicate that all is not right in this sleepy Vermont village. Then Sid Colt's body is found in Hilary's house. Hilary is the obvious suspect but he swears he is innocent. Tish believes him and looks for the real killer.

Other books you might like:
Eleanor Boylan, *The Clara Gamadge Series*, 1989-
Mary Bowen Hall, *The Emma Chizzit Series*, 1989-1993
Stephanie Matteson, *The Charlotte Graham Series*, 1990-
David Osborn, *The Margaret Barlow Series*, 1990-
Corinne Holt Sawyer, *The Benbow and Wingate Series*, 1987-

286
B. Comfort (Pseudonym of Barbara Comfort)
Grave Consequences (Vermont: Landgrove, 1989)

Series: Tish McWhinny

Story type: Amateur Detective—Female Lead

Major character(s): Tish McWhinny, Artist (painter); Sophie Beaumont, Photographer (Tish McWhinny's niece)

Time period(s): 1980s

Locale(s): Lofton, Vermont (fictional town)

What the book is about: Tish McWhinny thinks she sees the murdered body of a friend, but when she goes to get help the body disappears. Was the friend really murdered or did something else happen?

Other books you might like:
Richard Barth, *The Rag Bag Clan*, 1978
Margaret Logan, *Deathampton Summer*, 1988
Charlotte MacLeod, *The Family Vault*, 1979
Sister Carol Anne O'Marie, *Novena for Murder*, 1984
Virginia Rich, *The Cooking School Murders*, 1982

287
Susan Conant
A Bite of Death (New York: Diamond, 1991)

Series: Holly Winter

Story type: Amateur Detective—Female Lead

Major character(s): Holly Winter, Journalist (writer for a dog magazine); Kimi, Animal (Malamute)

Time period(s): 1990s

Locale(s): Cambridge, Massachusetts

What the book is about: When psychologist Elaine Walsh is found dead Holly Winter agrees to adopt her malamute, Kimi. Then some questions arise about the death - was it suicide or murder? Kimi holds the clue to the truth.

Other books you might like:
Gerald Hammond, *Whose Dog Is It?*, 1991
David Handler, *The Man Who Would Be F. Scott Fitzgerald*, 1990
Dallas Murphy, *Lover Man*, 1987

288
Susan Conant
Black Ribbon (New York: Doubleday, 1995)

Series: Holly Winter

Story type: Amateur Detective—Female Lead

Major character(s): Holly Winter, Journalist (writer for a dog magazine); Rowdy, Animal (Malamute)

Time period(s): 1990s

Locale(s): Maine

What the book is about: Holly is on assignment at an upscale, down-east dog camp that also offers luxurious accomodations for humans. Soon after arriving, Holly and the other guests start receiving condolence notes for the deaths of their pets, ads for pet coffins and warnings of danger for dogs. An obnoxious woman, Eva Spitteler, is suspected of perpetrating these pranks. When Eva is killed, there is no lack of suspects and Holly and Rowdy try to sniff out the killer.

Other books you might like:
Laurien Berenson, *A Pedigree to Die For*, 1995
Melissa Cleary, *The Jackie Walsh Series*, 1992-
Barbara Moore, *The Doberman Wore Black*, 1984
Dallas Murphy, *Lover Man*, 1987
Karen Ann Wilson, *Eight Dogs Flying*, 1994

289
Susan Conant
Bloodlines (New York: Doubleday, 1992)

Series: Holly Winter

Story type: Amateur Detective—Female Lead

Major character(s): Holly Winter, Journalist (writer for a dog magazine)

Time period(s): 1990s

Locale(s): Cambridge, Massachusetts

What the book is about: Holly has become involved with the "rescue" of a malamute puppy from Puppy Luv - a local pet store. This puppy, along with other dogs for sale, are apparently from a puppy mill. Just as Holly gets involved, Diane Sweet, the owner of the store, is murdered. Trying to protect the dogs draws Holly into a web of fraud and murder.

Other books you might like:
Melissa Cleary, *A Tail of Two Murders*, 1992
Barbara Moore, *The Doberman Wore Black*, 1984
Dana Stabenow, *A Cold Day for Murder*, 1992

290
Susan Conant
Paws Before Dying (New York: Berkley, 1991)

Series: Holly Winter

Story type: Amateur Detective—Female Lead

Major character(s): Holly Winter, Animal Trainer (dog trainer); Leah Whitcomb, Student (Holly's cousin)

Time period(s): 1990s

Locale(s): Cambridge, Massachusetts

What the book is about: Leah, sweet sixteen, smart and beautiful, is staying with Holly for the summer and immediately falls in love with Holly's dogs, Rowdy and Kimi. Holly's friend and fellow dog lover, Rose Engleman, takes an interest in Leah, but then Rose is killed in a storm, supposedly hit by lightning. When the police suspect murder Holly and Leah start to snoop—which may prove to be fatal.

Other books you might like:
Gerald Hammond, *Whose Dog Is It?*, 1991
Barbara Moore, *The Doberman Wore Black*, 1983
Barbara Moore, *The Wolf Whispered Death*, 1986
Dallas Murphy, *Lover Man*, 1987

291
Susan Conant
Ruffly Speaking (New York: Doubleday, 1994)

Series: Holly Winter

Story type: Amateur Detective—Female Lead

Major character(s): Holly Winter, Journalist (writer for a dog magazine)

Time period(s): 1990s

Locale(s): Cambridge, Massachusetts

What the book is about: Holly Winter's friend and fellow dog person, Morris Lamb, dies from eating a salad he made from local plants, some of which were highly toxic—a tragic accident. A month later Holly meets Stephanie Benson, a hearing impaired cleric with a hearing guide dog, Ruffly. Ruffly seems to be acting rather strangely at times. Then another death occurs and there may be a connection between these incidents. It's up to Holly to determine what's going on.

Other books you might like:
Melissa Cleary, *The Jackie Walsh Series*, 1992-
Barbara Moore, *The Doberman Wore Black*, 1984
Dana Stabenow, *A Cold Day for Murder*, 1992
Karen Ann Wilson, *Eight Dogs Flying*, 1994
Ted Wood, *The Reid Bennett Series*, 1985-

292
Michael Connelly
The Black Echo (New York: Little, Brown, 1992)

Series: Harry Bosch

Story type: Police Procedural—Male Lead; Action/Adventure

Major character(s): Harry Bosch, Police Officer (detective), Veteran (Vietnam)

Time period(s): 1990s

Locale(s): United States

What the book is about: Called out on what he thinks is a routine drug overdose, Harry Bosch is more than distressed to find the body of an old Army buddy—a fellow tunnel-rat named Dan Meadows. He soon realizes that Meadows did not kill himself, either intentionally or by accident. He vows to find his friend's killer. First novel. Nominated for Best First Novel by the Mystery Writers of America.

Other books you might like:
Peter Blauner, *Slow Motion Riot*, 1991
Lawrence Block, *A Dance at the Slaughterhouse*, 1991
Robert Campbell, *The La-La Land Series*, 1986-
James Ellroy, *Blood on the Moon*, 1984
Joe R. Lansdale, *Cold in July*, 1989

293
Michael Connelly
The Black Ice (New York: Little, Brown, 1993)

Series: Harry Bosch

Story type: Police Procedural—Male Lead

Major character(s): Harry Bosch, Police Officer (detective), Veteran (Vietnam)

Time period(s): 1990s

Locale(s): Los Angeles, California

What the book is about: It's Christmas and Harry Bosch is the on-call officer. But when a dead body is found in a hotel room the higher-ups move in and start a massive cover-up. The body is that of an undercover police officer who was suspected of dealing a new drug called Black Ice. They call it suicide, but Harry shows up anyway and thinks it's the oddest suicide note he has ever seen.

Other books you might like:
Peter Blauner, *Slow Motion Riot*, 1991
Bruce Jones, *In Deep*, 1991
Bill Kent, *Down by the Sea*, 1993
Jack O'Connell, *Box Nine*, 1991
Roderick Thorp, *Rainbow Drive*, 1986

294
Michael Connelly
The Concrete Blonde (New York: Little, Brown, 1994)

Series: Harry Bosch

Story type: Police Procedural—Male Lead

Major character(s): Harry Bosch, Police Officer (detective), Veteran (Vietnam)

Time period(s): 1990s

Locale(s): Los Angeles, California

What the book is about: LAPD detective Harry Bosch is being sued by the widow of Norman Church, the Dollmaker, whom Harry shot to death. She is suing for violation of her husband's civil rights, as he was never convicted of being a murderer. Just as the trial gets underway, another body is unearthed. Is it another Dollmaker victim or is there a copycat killer out there? The answer could cost Harry his job.

Other books you might like:
Kenneth Abel, *Bait*, 1994
Harlen Campbell, *Monkey on a Chain*, 1993
Patricia D. Cornwell, *Cruel and Unusual*, 1992
Robert Crais, *Free Fall*, 1993
Ted Wood, *Snow Job*, 1993

295
K. Patrick Conner
Kingdom Road (New York: St. Martin's, 1991)

Story type: Action/Adventure

Major character(s): Winn Cahill, Musician (rock guitarist); Liana Harris, Widow(er)

Time period(s): 1990s

Locale(s): California (Central Valley area)

What the book is about: Winn Cahill is haunted by the memory of Liana, the young woman he loved. He finally decides to go back and find her. When he hits town he finds she is a rich widow with a jealous boyfriend. When he gets together with Liana, the boyfriend shows up and Liana shoots him. Winn takes the blame. But has Liana set him up as a patsy? Did Liana kill her husband?

Other books you might like:
William Bayer, *Blind Side*, 1989
James M. Cain, *The Postman Always Rings Twice*, 1934
Robert Ferrigno, *The Horse Latitudes*, 1990
Tom Kakonis, *Double Down*, 1991
Jim Thompson, *Nothing More Than Murder*, 1949

296
Richard Timothy Conroy
The India Exhibition (New York: St. Martin's, 1992)

Series: Smithsonian

Story type: Action/Adventure

Major character(s): Henry Scruggs, Diplomat (seconded to the Smithsonian); Violet Strauss, Designer (exhibit designer)

Time period(s): 1970s (1972)

Locale(s): Washington, District of Columbia; India

What the book is about: Henry Scruggs has spent his life being prim and proper, but when he begins working at the Smithsonian helping to set up the Chandra Exhibit, he finds himself seduced. First by the excitement and second by the young, sexy Violet Strauss. Her objective is to gain possession of a statue - 1100 pounds of gold covered with rubies, worth over $10 million. First novel.

Other books you might like:
Jonathan Gash, *Jade Woman*, 1989
Charles A. Goodrum, *A Slip of the Tong*, 1992
Margaret Truman, *Murder at the Smithsonian*, 1983

297
Richard Timothy Conroy
Mr. Smithson's Bones (New York: St. Martins, 1993)

Series: Smithsonian

Story type: Amateur Detective—Male Lead

Major character(s): Henry Scruggs, Diplomat (seconded to the Smithsonian)

Time period(s): 1970s (1972)

Locale(s): Washington, District of Columbia

What the book is about: Henry Scrugg's career as a diplomat has hit a snag and he is now liaison to the Smithsonian, overseeing their foreign department. Since no one really knows what his job is or what the Smithsonian's policy is, Henry has a lot of time on his hands. Then the officious Dr. Kraft is murdered and some literal skeletons come to light. A prequel to *The India Exhibition*.

Other books you might like:
Gary Alexander, *Kiet Goes West*, 1992
Alison Glen, *Showcase*, 1992
Charles A. Goodrum, *A Slip of the Tong*, 1992
Margaret Truman, *Murder at the Smithsonian*, 1983

298
K.C. Constantine (Pseudonym of Carl Kosak)
Sunshine Enemies (New York: Mysterious, 1990)

Series: Mario Balzic

Story type: Police Procedural—Male Lead

Major character(s): Mario Balzic, Police Officer (chief)

Time period(s): 1980s

Locale(s): Rocksburg, Pennsylvania

What the book is about: A man is murdered in the parking lot of a porn dealer. Balzic must deal with this at the same time his mother is dying.

Other books you might like:
Bill Crider, *Too Late to Die*, 1986
Joan Hess, *Malice in Maggody*, 1987
John Holbrook Vance, *The Fox Valley Murders*, 1966
Anne Wingate, *Death by Deception*, 1988

299
Bruce Cook
Death as a Career Move (New York: St. Martin's, 1992)

Series: Chico Cervantes

Story type: Private Detective—Male Lead

Major character(s): Antonio "Chico" Cervantes, Detective—Private (studio security consultant)

Time period(s): 1990s

Locale(s): Los Angeles, California

What the book is about: The studio Chico Cervantes works for is planning a big picture on the life of a late sixties rock star who died in a car crash in 1971. When someone assigned to the picture is killed, Chico is assigned to the picture as well. Soon he is involved with people from the rocker's life and music. A number of people are eager to jump back on the bandwagon.

Other books you might like:
Arthur Lyons, *Fast Fade*, 1987
George R.R. Martin, *The Armageddon Rag*, 1978
Thomas Maxwell, *The Suspense Is Killing Me*, 1990
Jim Stinson, *Low Angles*, 1986
L.J. Washburn, *Wild Night*, 1989

300
Bruce Cook
Rough Cut (New York: St. Martins, 1990)
Series: Chico Cervantes
Story type: Private Detective—Male Lead
Major character(s): Antonio "Chico" Cervantes, Detective—Private (studio security consultant)
Time period(s): 1990s
Locale(s): Los Angeles, California
What the book is about: "Chico" Cervantes is hired to guard Ursula Toller, daughter of movie producer Heinrich Toller, and to protect the film she is depending on to save the company.
Other books you might like:
Jack Barnao, *Locke Step*, 1987
Arthur Lyons, *Fast Fade*, 1987
Robert J. Ray, *Bloody Murdock*, 1986
Les Roberts, *An Infinite Number of Monkeys*, 1987
Jim Stinson, *Low Angles*, 1986

301
Bruce Cook
The Sidewalk Hilton (New York: St. Martin's, 1994)
Series: Chico Cervantes
Story type: Private Detective—Male Lead
Major character(s): Antonio "Chico" Cervantes, Detective—Private (studio security consultant)
Time period(s): 1990s
Locale(s): Los Angeles, California; Chicago, Illinois
What the book is about: Chico Cervantes has been hired to find Chicago millionaire Benjamin Sterling who has disappeared while visiting Los Angeles. Soon a body shows up in Sterling's room, shot three times in the back of the head. It turns out not to be Sterling, who was living among the homeless, but a stand-in. Sterling shows up alive and well, but another attempt is soon made on his life. When he returns to Chicago, someone is finally successful. The police arrest one of Sterling's Los Angeles homeless "consultants," but Chico doesn't think the man is guilty and tries to prove it.
Other books you might like:
Robert Crais, *The Monkey's Raincoat*, 1987
Timothy Hallinan, *The Simeon Grist Series*, 1989-
Arthur Lyons, *The Jacob Asch Series*, 1977-
Les Roberts, *The Saxon Series*, 1988-
Jim Stinson, *The Stoney Winston Series*, 1985-1988

302
Robin Cook
Blindsight (New York: Putnam, 1992)
Story type: Amateur Detective—Female Lead
Major character(s): Laurie Montgomery, Doctor (pathologist); Lou Soldano, Police Officer
Time period(s): 1990s
Locale(s): New York, New York
What the book is about: Laurie Montgomery is intrigued by a series of cocaine overdoses of yuppies whose relatives swear they never used drugs. When she tries to investigate further, she is ordered not to. She also becomes involved with Lou Soldano who is investigating a series of gangland slayings.
Other books you might like:
Jo Bailey, *Bagged*, 1991
Patricia D. Cornwell, *Postmortem*, 1990
Susan Dunlap, *Rogue Wave*, 1991
Mary Kittredge, *Rigor Mortis*, 1991
Leah Ruth Robinson, *Blood Run*, 1988

303
Robin Cook
Vital Signs (New York: Putnam, 1990)
Story type: Action/Adventure
Major character(s): Marissa Blumenthal, Doctor (epidemiologist)
Time period(s): 1990s
Locale(s): United States
What the book is about: When Marissa discovers she is infertile, she begins to investigate causes and cures. What she discovers threatens her marriage and her life.
Other books you might like:
Patricia D. Cornwell, *Postmortem*, 1990
D.J. Donaldson, *Cajun Nights*, 1988
Sarah Kemp, *What Dread Hand*, 1987
Richard Platt, *Letting Blood*, 1989 (Orah Platt, co-author)
R.D. Zimmerman, *Mindscream*, 1988

304
Stephen Cook
Dead Fit (New York: St. Martin's, 1993)
Story type: Police Procedural—Female Lead
Major character(s): Judy Best, Police Officer
Time period(s): 1990s
Locale(s): London, England
What the book is about: PC Judy Best has joined her boyfriend Clinton's health club to work out. Clinton introduces her to investor Duncan Stock. Stock is interested in Judy and persists until she goes to one of his parties where he makes lewd advances. The next day Stock is found dead, his head crushed by exercise weights. Clinton finds himself a prime suspect and Judy must try and clear him and find the real murderer.
Other books you might like:
Liza Cody, *The Anna Lee Series*, 1980-
Sarah Dunant, *Birthmarks*, 1992
P.D. James, *The Cordelia Gray Series*, 1973-
Jennie Melville, *The Charmian Daniels Series*, 1962-
Erica Quest, *Model Murder*, 1991

305

Thomas H. Cook
The City When It Rains (New York: Putnam, 1991)

Story type: Psychological Suspense; Amateur Detective—Male Lead

Major character(s): David Corman, Photographer (free-lance)

Time period(s): 1990s

Locale(s): New York, New York

What the book is about: A woman throws herself out of a fifth floor window in New York's Hell's Kitchen. Free-lance photographer David Corman, a man on the edge himself, sees in her story the possiblity of a new life for himself.

Other books you might like:
Ed Gorman, *The Night Remembers*, 1991
Keith Peterson, *The John Wells Series*, 1988-
Sam Reaves, *A Long Cold Fall*, 1991
Benjamin M. Schutz, *A Fistful of Empty*, 1991
S.K. Wolf, *Long Chain of Death*, 1987

306

Thomas H. Cook
Streets of Fire (New York: Putnam, 1989)

Story type: Police Procedural—Male Lead

Major character(s): Ben Wellman, Detective—Police (homicide)

Time period(s): 1960s (1963)

Locale(s): Birmingham, Alabama

What the book is about: Wellman is assigned to investigate the rape-murder of a 12 year-old black girl. During the investigation he uncovers a larger conspiracy.

Other books you might like:
William Bayer, *Switch*, 1984
William J. Caunitz, *One Police Plaza*, 1984
William Diehl, *Sharky's Machine*, 1978
Bill Granger, *Public Murders*, 1980
Stephen Solomita, *A Twist of the Knife*, 1988

307

Natasha Cooper (Pseudonym of Daphne Wright)
Bitter Herbs (New York: Crown, 1994)

Series: Willow King

Story type: Amateur Detective—Female Lead

Major character(s): Willow King, Writer (romances), Civil Servant; Tom Worth, Police Officer (Willow's lover)

Time period(s): 1990s

Locale(s): London, England

What the book is about: Willow King has finally come to terms with her alter ego, romance writer Cressida Woodruffe. As a change of pace, she accepts a commission to write a remembrance of famous author Gloria Grevinger who has just died of a heart attack. As she digs into Gloria's life she discovers that nobody is sorry that she is dead; in fact many are overjoyed. Could it have been murder? And why is Willow's lover, Tom Worth, so mad at her theories?

Other books you might like:
Robert Barnard, *Death of a Mystery Writer*, 1978
Ann Granger, *The Meredith Mitchell/Allan Markby Series*, 1991-
Janet Neel, *Death's Bright Angel*, 1988
Jennifer Rowe, *Murder by the Book*, 1989
Joan Smith, *Don't Leave Me This Way*, 1990

308

Natasha Cooper (Pseudonym of Daphne Wright)
Bloody Roses (New York: Crown, 1993)

Series: Willow King

Story type: Amateur Detective—Female Lead

Major character(s): Willow King, Writer (romance writer); Tom Worth, Police Officer (Willow's lover)

Time period(s): 1990s

Locale(s): London, England

What the book is about: Willow King is on holiday with her boyfriend, Tom Worth, when a call from an old friend asks for help. Richard Crescent has been arrested for the murder of a co-worker, the beautiful Sarah Allfarthing. Willow doesn't think her gentle banker friend could be capable of murder but the evidence is damning. She decides to go undercover at the bank and find the real murderer.

Other books you might like:
Sarah Dunant, *Birthmarks*, 1992
Frances Fyfield, *Deep Sleep*, 1992
Ann Granger, *A Season for Murder*, 1992
Lesley Grant-Adamson, *Too Many Questions*, 1991
Patricia Hall, *The Poison Pool*, 1993

309

Natasha Cooper (Pseudonym of Daphne Wright)
Rotten Apples (New York: St. Martin's, 1995)

Series: Willow King

Story type: Amateur Detective—Female Lead

Major character(s): Willow King, Writer (romance writer), Civil Servant; Tom Worth, Police Officer (Willow's husband)

Time period(s): 1990s

Locale(s): London, England

What the book is about: Willow, also known as romance writer Cressida Woodruffe, is trying to come to terms with a third identity—Mrs. Tom Worth. She has been asked by the new government to investigate an office of the Inland Revenue. A famous art historian has committed suicide after being accused of tax fraud. Willow doesn't think much of the case but when the office is burned and the case officer is found dead, obviously something is seriously wrong.

Other books you might like:
Sarah Dunant, *Under My Skin*, 1995
Sarah Lacey, *File Under: Arson*, 1994
Janet Neel, *Death on Site*, 1989
Audrey Peterson, *Death Too Soon*, 1994
Joan Smith, *What Men Say*, 1993

310
Susan Rogers Cooper
Dead Moon on the Rise (New York: St. Martin's, 1994)

Series: Milt Kovak

Story type: Police Procedural—Male Lead

Major character(s): Milt Kovak, Police Officer (deputy sheriff); Jean McDonnell, Doctor (psychiatrist; Milt's wife)

Time period(s): 1990s

Locale(s): Prophesy County, Oklahoma

What the book is about: Milt Kovak has made two major decisions. He is marrying his slightly pregnant lover and he is running for sheriff. He is running unopposed until his old buddy, Wade Moon, shows up and decides that he wants to be sheriff too. When Wade shows up dead Milt has to investigate, which is a little sticky as he makes a pretty good suspect as well. If that's not enough, someone is stealing and mutilating animals.

Other books you might like:
Bill Crider, *The Sheriff Dan Rhodes Series*, 1986-
Jean Hager, *The Mitch Bushyhead Series*, 1989-
D.R. Meredith, *The Sheriff Charles Matthews Series*, 1983-
Ted Wood, *The Reid Bennett Series*, 1983-
L.R. Wright, *The Karl Alberg Series*, 1986-

311
Susan Rogers Cooper
Doctors, Lawyers and Such (New York: St. Martin's, 1995)

Series: Milt Kovak

Story type: Police Procedural—Male Lead

Major character(s): Milt Kovak, Police Officer (deputy sheriff)

Time period(s): 1990s

Locale(s): Prophesy County, Oklahoma

What the book is about: Milt has just successfully run for county sheriff when trouble starts. The latest in an inexplicable rash of suicides is the wife of Milt's best friend, the chief of police. Then a famous TV newscaster who has recently settled down in the county is brutally murdered. Finally Milt's wife is undergoing a difficult pregnancy. Milt is beginning to wonder if being sheriff is worth it.

Other books you might like:
Bill Crider, *The Sheriff Dan Rhodes Series*, 1986-
Jean Hager, *The Mitch Bushyhead Series*, 1989-
Sharyn McCrumb, *The Spencer Arrowood Series*, 1990-
D.R. Meredith, *The Sheriff Charles Matthews Series*, 1984-
Anne Wingate, *The Mark Shigata Series*, 1988-

312
Susan Rogers Cooper
Funny as a Dead Comic (New York: St. Martins, 1993)

Series: Kimmey Kruse

Story type: Amateur Detective—Female Lead

Major character(s): Kimmey Kruse, Entertainer (stand-up comic); Sal Pucci, Police Officer, Detective—Homicide

Time period(s): 1990s

Locale(s): Chicago, Illinois

What the book is about: Kimmey Kruse hasn't made the big time yet, she is still the opening act for stars like Cab Neusberg. Cab is an old friend and lover and after the show they take up where they left off. But Cab dies at a most embarrassing moment. Worse, after an autopsy it is discovered that Cab was poisoned. Then more people die and Kimmey is in the middle of it all. Detective Pucci seems to think she knows more than she is telling.

Other books you might like:
K.K. Beck, *A Hopeless Case*, 1992
Toni Brill, *Date with a Dead Doctor*, 1991
Jeffrey Wilds Deaver, *Manhattan Is My Beat*, 1989
Leslie Meier, *Mail-Order Murder*, 1991
Kathy Hogan Trocheck, *Every Crooked Nanny*, 1992

313
Susan Rogers Cooper
Funny as a Dead Relative (New York: St. Martin's, 1994)

Series: Kimmey Kruse

Story type: Amateur Detective—Female Lead

Major character(s): Kimmey Kruse, Entertainer (stand-up comic); Sal Pucci, Police Officer, Detective—Homicide

Time period(s): 1990s

Locale(s): Port Arthur, Texas

What the book is about: Kimmey Kruse has been invited (ordered by her grandmother) to show up at the family reunion to help take care of her grandfather who has broken his leg. Her grandmother hasn't let him in *her* house for years. At the reunion Kimmey meets her Aunt Letitia, long estranged from the family because of a "bad" marriage and Letitia's drop-dead gorgeous son, Willard. When Letitia is found dead of wasp stings, nobody thinks much about it until Kimmey finds a jar with wasps still in it. Then it's thought the death might not be accidental. Sal Pucci, Chicago detective, shows up to pursue Kimmey and is enlisted to probe family secrets and find a killer.

Other books you might like:
Connie Fedderson, *Dead in the Cellar*, 1994
Toni L.P. Kelner, *Dead Ringer*, 1994
Sarah Shankman, *He Was Her Man*, 1993
Patricia Houck Sprinkle, *Death of a Dunwoody Matron*, 1993
Kerry Tucker, *Still Waters*, 1991

314
Susan Rogers Cooper
Houston in the Rearview Mirror (New York: St. Martin's, 1990)

315 Cooper

Series: Milt Kovack

Story type: Police Procedural—Male Lead

Major character(s): Milt Kovak, Police Officer (chief deputy)

Time period(s): 1980s

Locale(s): Houston, Texas

What the book is about: When Kovack's sister supposedly kills her husband and then shoots herself, he travels to Houston to find the truth.

Other books you might like:
Michael T. Hinkemeyer, *Fourth Down, Death*, 1980
Sharyn McCrumb, *If Ever I Return, Pretty Peggy-O*, 1990
Anne Wingate, *Death by Deception*, 1988
Ted Wood, *Live Bait*, 1985
L.R. Wright, *The Suspect*, 1985

315
Susan Rogers Cooper
One, Two, What Did Daddy Do? (New York: St. Martin's, 1992)

Story type: Amateur Detective—Female Lead

Major character(s): E.J. Pugh, Housewife; Willis Pugh, Businessman (husband of E.J.)

Time period(s): 1990s

Locale(s): Black Cat Ridge, Texas (suburb of Codderville)

What the book is about: E.J. and Willis Pugh and their kids are a typical suburban family and their best friends are the next door Lester family. One morning E.J. enters the Lester house and finds four of the five Lesters dead and the young daughter in shock. The police call it murder/suicide but E.J. knows better and is determined to prove it.

Other books you might like:
Mary Cahill, *Carpool*, 1991
Mary Anne Kelly, *Park Lane South, Queens*, 1990
Janice Law, *Infected Be the Air*, 1991
B.J. Oliphant, *Dead in the Scrub*, 1990

316
Susan Rogers Cooper
Other People's Houses (New York: St. Martins, 1990)

Series: Milt Kovak

Story type: Police Procedural—Male Lead

Major character(s): Milt Kovak, Police Officer (chief deputy)

Time period(s): 1990s

Locale(s): Prophesy County, Oklahoma

What the book is about: Lois Bell, a bankteller, and her family are found dead of carbon monoxide poisoning. Who did it and why is the government so interested?

Other books you might like:
Bill Crider, *Too Late to Die*, 1986
Sharyn McCrumb, *If Ever I Return, Pretty Peggy-O*, 1990
D.R. Meredith, *The Sheriff and the Panhandle Murders*, 1984
Anne Wingate, *Death by Deception*, 1988
Ted Wood, *Dead in the Water*, 1983

317
Barry Cork
Unnatural Hazard (New York: Scribners, 1990)

Series: Angus Straun

Story type: Action/Adventure

Major character(s): Angus Straun, Police Officer (inspector), Sports Figure (golfer)

Time period(s): 1980s

What the book is about: On the way to play in a golf tournament, Angus is shoved off the train. He survives but upon arrival he discovers a corpse and more murder.

Other books you might like:
M.C. Beaton, *Death of a Gossip*, 1985
Charlotte Elkins, *A Wicked Slice*, 1989 (Aaron Elkins, co-author)
John Logue, *Follow the Leader*, 1979
Keith Miles, *Bullet Hole*, 1986
Robert Upton, *Dead on the Stick*, 1986

318
Barry Cork
Winter Rules (New York: Scribners, 1992)

Series: Angus Straun

Story type: Police Procedural—Male Lead; Action/Adventure

Major character(s): Angus Straun, Police Officer (inspector), Sports Figure (golfer); Laurie Wilson, Businesswoman (literary agent; lover of Angus)

Time period(s): 1990s

Locale(s): London, England

What the book is about: Angus has two great interests in life - golf and cars. Both lead him into trouble. First his car is stolen, then he is seconded to the Foreign Office to act as bodyguard for the leader of an African nation whose main concern is the building of a golf course in his country. Things heat up when the leader's car is stolen and a man is murdered. Then while playing a round of golf with their lady friends, somebody shoots at Angus and the leader.

Other books you might like:
James Y. Bartlett, *Death Is a Two-Stroke Penalty*, 1990
Charlotte Elkins, *A Wicked Slice*, 1989 (Aaron Elkins, co-author)
John Logue, *Follow the Leader*, 1979
Keith Miles, *Bullet Hole*, 1986
Robert Upton, *Dead on the Stick*, 1986

319
Michael Cormany
Red Winter (New York: Lyle Stuart, 1989)

Series: Dan Kruger

Story type: Private Detective—Male Lead

Major character(s): Dan Kruger, Detective—Private

Time period(s): 1980s (1983)

Locale(s): Chicago, Illinois

What the book is about: A building contractor hires P.I. Kruger to find out who's blackmailing him about his past. The job quickly becomes much more complex than Kruger expects.

Other books you might like:
James Crumley, *The Wrong Case*, 1974
Wayne Dundee, *The Burning Season*, 1988
Loren D. Estleman, *Sugartown*, 1986
John Lutz, *The Right to Sing the Blues*, 1987
Jonathan Valin, *Life's Work*, 1986

320
Michael Cormany
Skin Deep Is Fatal (New York: Birch Lane, 1992)

Series: Dan Kruger

Story type: Private Detective—Male Lead

Major character(s): Dan Kruger, Detective—Private, Musician (sometime rock musician)

Time period(s): 1990s

Locale(s): Chicago, Illinois

What the book is about: Dan Kruger is just out of three days of detox, recovering from drug and alcohol abuse. He has been hired by another patient to deliver a message to cosmetic heiress Shannon Harper to return what she has taken or a videotape will be sent to the police. Kruger is wary but does as he is asked. This involves him with a militant animal rights group and starts a chain of violence and murder that threatens him and his girlfriend and many others.

Other books you might like:
James Crumley, *The Wrong Case*, 1974
Kinky Friedman, *The Kinky Friedman Series*, 1980-
Jesse Sublett, *The Martin Fender Series*, 1989-
Philip Lee Williams, *Slow Dance in Autumn*, 1988
Sharon Zukowski, *Dancing in the Dark*, 1992

321
Patricia D. Cornwell
All That Remains (New York: Scribners, 1992)

Series: Kay Scarpetta

Story type: Amateur Detective—Female Lead; Police Procedural—Female Lead

Major character(s): Kay Scarpetta, Doctor (medical examiner); Pete Marino, Police Officer (homicide detective)

Time period(s): 1990s

Locale(s): Richmond, Virginia

What the book is about: A serial killer has been kidnapping and killing young couples in cars traveling the highways of Virginia. The latest victims are the daughter of the President's drug czar and her boyfriend, whose empty car has been found abandoned. Kay tries to find evidence to catch the killer but he is very careful and everything runs into a dead-end. Can the police catch the killer before he kills again and why is the CIA involved?

Other books you might like:
Susan Dunlap, *Rogue Wave*, 1991
Thomas Harris, *The Silence of the Lambs*, 1988
Sarah Kemp, *No Escape*, 1984
David L. Lindsey, *Mercy*, 1990
Julie Smith, *The Axeman's Jazz*, 1991

322
Patricia D. Cornwell
The Body Farm (New York: Scribners, 1994)

Series: Kay Scarpetta

Story type: Police Procedural—Female Lead; Psychological Suspense

Major character(s): Kay Scarpetta, Doctor (medical examiner); Pete Marino, Police Officer (homicide captain)

Time period(s): 1990s

Locale(s): Black Mountain, North Carolina; Quantico, Virginia

What the book is about: Kay Scarpetta and Pete Marino have been asked to help in the investigation of the kidnapping and murder of a young North Carolina girl. There are indications that the crime may have been committed by a serial killer that they have investigated before. Problems arise in determining the actual time and cause of death. Kay also has to worry about her niece, Lucy, and Marino, who both seem to be becoming personally involved with the case.

Other books you might like:
Noreen Ayres, *A World the Color of Salt*, 1992
Susan Dunlap, *Rogue Wave*, 1991
Louise Hendricksen, *With Deadly Intent*, 1993
Marsha Landreth, *The Holiday Murders*, 1992
David L. Lindsey, *Mercy*, 1990

323
Patricia D. Cornwell
Body of Evidence (New York: Scribners, 1991)

Series: Kay Scarpetta

Story type: Amateur Detective—Female Lead

Major character(s): Kay Scarpetta, Doctor (medical examiner)

Time period(s): 1990s

Locale(s): Richmond, Virginia

What the book is about: A young woman who was being harassed and has fled to escape reruns is slain the night of her return. From all appearances she let the attacker into her house. Kay Scarpetta must trace back her life to find out the truth behind her death. At the same time an ex-lover drops back into Scarpetta's life and he may have something to do with the murder.

Other books you might like:
Susan Dunlap, *Pious Deception*, 1989
Sue Grafton, *The Kinsey Millhone Series*, 1982-
Thomas Harris, *The Silence of the Lambs*, 1988
Herbert Lieberman, *City of the Dead*, 1976
Joyce Anne Schneider, *Darkness Falls*, 1989

324
Patricia D. Cornwell
Cruel and Unusual (New York: Scribners, 1992)

Series: Kay Scarpetta

Story type: Police Procedural—Female Lead; Amateur Detective—Female Lead

Major character(s): Kay Scarpetta, Doctor (medical examiner); Pete Marino, Police Officer (homicide captain)

Time period(s): 1990s

Locale(s): Richmond, Virginia

What the book is about: A young boy is shot and left for dead after having strange wounds inflicted on him. There seems to be a connection to just-executed murderer Ronnie Joe Waddell. When Kay Scarpetta performs an autopsy on Waddell, she finds some strange inconsistencies and an envelope to be buried with him containing recent receipts. There seems to be a conspiracy of some sort, but what is its purpose, who are the players and why is Kay at the center of it?

Other books you might like:
Noreen Ayres, *A World the Color of Salt*, 1992
Susan Dunlap, *Rogue Wave*, 1991
Marsha Landreth, *The Holiday Murders*, 1992
David L. Lindsey, *Mercy*, 1990
Rochelle Majer Krich, *Fair Game*, 1993

325
Patricia D. Cornwell
From Potter's Field (New York: Scribners, 1995)

Series: Kay Scarpetta

Story type: Police Procedural—Female Lead; Psychological Suspense

Major character(s): Kay Scarpetta, Doctor (medical examiner); Benton Wesley, FBI Agent

Time period(s): 1990s

Locale(s): New York, New York; Richmond, Virginia

What the book is about: The brilliant and dangerous serial killer, Temple Brooks Gault, has returned. This time his first victim is a strange bald woman who cannot be identified. Kay works with the local police as part of an FBI task force trying to track down Gault. Soon Gault kills again, but seems really to be after Kay's niece, Lucy, and ultimately, Kay herself. Can she find him before he finds them?

Other books you might like:
Noreen Ayres, *The Smokey Brandon Series*, 1992-
Louise Hendricksen, *The Amy Prescott Series*, 1993-
Marsha Landreth, *The Samantha Turner Series*, 1992-
David L. Lindsey, *Mercy*, 1990
Rochelle Majer Krich, *Fair Game*, 1993

326
Patricia D. Cornwell
Postmortem (New York: Scribners, 1990)

Series: Kay Scarpetta

Story type: Amateur Detective—Female Lead

Major character(s): Kay Scarpetta, Doctor (medical examiner)

Time period(s): 1980s

Locale(s): Richmond, Virginia

What the book is about: There is a serial killer loose in Richmond and Dr. Scarpetta must bring all her skills to bear in trying to solve the case. But in doing so she becomes a target. First book.

Other books you might like:
Susan Dunlap, *Pious Deception*, 1989
Thomas Harris, *The Silence of the Lambs*, 1988
John Katzenbach, *The Traveler*, 1987
Herbert Lieberman, *City of the Dead*, 1976
Joyce Anne Schneider, *Darkness Falls*, 1989

327
Peter Corris
Matrimonial Causes (New York: Dell, 1994)

Series: Cliff Hardy

Story type: Private Detective—Male Lead

Major character(s): Cliff Hardy, Detective—Private

Time period(s): 1960s

Locale(s): Sydney, Australia

What the book is about: Cliff Hardy is reminiscing about his first case as a private detective. He is just out of the army and still married when he is hired to get some pictures of a man committing adultery. Just as he is about to snap the pictures, the man is killed. He is then hired by the 'other woman,' Virginia Shaw, a professional adulteress. She wants protection and her money. Cliff is drawn into a big time racket with a lot of dangerous people who dislike snoopy private eyes.

Other books you might like:
Marvin Albert, *The Stone Angel Series*, 1986-
John Milne, *Dead Birds*, 1986
Paco Ignacio Taibo III, *An Easy Thing*, 1990
Miles Tripp, *The John Samson Series*, 1973-
Charles West, *Stonefish*, 1991

328
Peter Corris
O'Fear (New York: Doubleday, 1991)

Series: Cliff Hardy

Story type: Private Detective—Male Lead

Major character(s): Cliff Hardy, Detective—Private

Time period(s): 1990s

Locale(s): Sydney, Australia

What the book is about: Barnes Toff, war vet and slightly shady businessman was recently married and seemed to have gone straight. Now he is dead, killed in a car crash. In his will is a bequest to Hardy for ten thousand dollars for the purpose of finding who killed him. Among others Cliff meets the pretty widow Felicia and the gangster Kevin O'Fearna, aka O'Fear.

Other books you might like:
Marvin Albert, *The Zig-Zag Man*, 1991
Jon Cleary, *The Scobie Malone Series*, 1966
Paula Gosling, *Death Penalties*, 1991
Arthur W. Upfield, *The Inspector Napoleon Bonaparte Series*, 1929-1966
Charles West, *Stonefish*, 1991

329
Peter Corris
Wet Graves (New York: Bantam, 1995)

Series: Cliff Hardy

Story type: Private Detective—Male Lead

Major character(s): Cliff Hardy, Detective—Private

Time period(s): 1990s

Locale(s): Sydney, Australia

What the book is about: Cliff Hardy has been hired to find Louise Madden's elderly father, a harmless, well-liked man. Somehow his disappearance may be linked to Sydney Harbor Bridge and other mysterious disappearances. Cliff must also confront personal problems as his license is being threatened by a very clever frame-up. Someone really doesn't like him.

Other books you might like:
Marvin Albert, *The Stone Angel Series*, 1985-
Jon Cleary, *The Scobie Malone Series*, 1966-
Miles Tripp, *The John Samson Series*, 1973-
Arthur W. Upfield, *The Inspector Napoleon Bonaparte Series*, 1929-1966
Charles West, *Stonefish*, 1991

330
Desmond Cory
The Catalyst (New York: St. Martin's, 1991)

Series: John Dobie

Story type: Amateur Detective—Male Lead

Major character(s): John Dobie, Professor (of mathematics); Kate Coyle, Doctor (police pathologist)

Time period(s): 1990s

Locale(s): Cardiff, Wales

What the book is about: Dobie hears that a former student has committed suicide. He investigates, not because he liked Sammy Cantwell but because he doesn't remember him at all and feels he should. Sammy, an expert with computers, has links to Dobie's wife Jenny and her friend Jane Corder. When a break-in at Dobie's ends with both Jane and Jenny dead, Dobie is the prime suspect.

Other books you might like:
Tony Cape, *The Cambridge Theorem*, 1990
V.C. Clinton-Baddeley, *The Dr. Davie Series*, 1967-1972
Edmund Crispin, *The Gervase Fen Series*, 1944-1978
Michael W. Sherer, *Little Use for Death*, 1992
Ned White, *The Very Bad Thing*, 1990

331
Desmond Cory
The Dobie Paradox (New York: St. Martin's, 1994)

Series: John Dobie

Story type: Amateur Detective—Male Lead

Major character(s): John Dobie, Professor (of mathematics); Kate Coyle, Doctor (police pathologist)

Time period(s): 1990s

Locale(s): Cardiff, Wales

What the book is about: John Dobie and Kate Coyle are on their way to the Tongwylais Rehabilitation Center to help a former acquaintance, Adrian Seymour. However, on the way they find the barely alive body of a teenage girl, apparently the victim of a hit-and-run. The girl dies and there are indications it may not have been an accident. There may be more going on at the center than rehabilitation. Dobie starts to investigate, much to the consternation of the local police.

Other books you might like:
Sheila MacGill Callahan, *Death in a Far Country*, 1993
V.C. Clinton-Baddeley, *The Dr. Davie Series*, 1967-1972
Edmund Crispin, *The Gervase Fen Series*, 1944-1978
Robert Richardson, *The Augustus Maltravers Series*, 1985-

332
Gordon Cotler
Shooting Script (New York: Morrow, 1992)

Story type: Amateur Detective—Male Lead; Police Procedural—Male Lead

Major character(s): Byron Saldinger, Writer (television scriptwriter), Divorced Person; Al Vecchi, Police Officer (retired; movie consultant)

Time period(s): 1990s

Locale(s): Los Angeles, California; New York, New York

What the book is about: Byron Saldinger is ready to finalize selling the first script of what could be a hit TV series when a man claims that the series was his idea and Byron has stolen it. The next day the man is murdered and Byron is the prime suspect. Al Vecchi, who was consulting on the series as an expert in police procedure and is bored, decides to look into the matter. When a man tries to kill Byron, he realizes he needs all the help he can get.

Other books you might like:
Pamela Chais, *Final Cut*, 1981
Bruce Cook, *Rough Cut*, 1990
Stan Cutler, *Shot on Location*, 1993
Kate Green, *Shooting Star*, 1992
Richard Nehrbass, *A Perfect Death for Hollywood*, 1991

333
William J. Coughlin
Shadow of a Doubt (New York: St. Martin's, 1991)
Story type: Action/Adventure; Legal
Major character(s): Charley Sloan, Lawyer (on the skids)
Time period(s): 1990s
Locale(s): Detroit, Michigan
What the book is about: Charley Sloan—on the skids because of alcohol—is offered the chance for redemption by an older lover. The daughter of her current lover, multimillionaire Harrison Harwell, has been arrested for his murder. Charley sees this case as an opportunity to salvage his life. Can Charley stay sober and beat back the challenges from the politically motivated district attorney? Is the daughter really innocent?
Other books you might like:
William Bernhardt, *Primary Justice*, 1992
J.F. Freedman, *Against the Wind*, 1991
John Grisham, *The Firm*, 1991
Robert K. Tanenbaum, *Immoral Certainty*, 1991
Scott Turow, *Presumed Innocent*, 1987

334
Alisa Craig (Pseudonym of Charlotte MacLeod)
The Wrong Rite (New York: Morrow, 1992)
Series: Madoc Rhys
Story type: Police Procedural—Male Lead
Major character(s): Madoc Rhys, Police Officer (RCMP inspector); Jenny Rhys, Spouse (wife of Madoc)
Time period(s): 1990s
Locale(s): Wales
What the book is about: Madoc and Jenny are in Wales for the 90th birthday of great-uncle Cardoc when death interrupts the festivities. Madoc is asked to join in the investigation and untangles a web involving blackmail, prostitution, a jewel theft, and an old murder.
Other books you might like:
Laurence Gough, *Hot Shots*, 1990
Carolyn G. Hart, *The Annie Laurance/Max Darling Series*, 1984-
Sharyn McCrumb, *The Windsor Knot*, 1990
Eric Wright, *A Question of Guilt*, 1988

335
Philip R. Craig
A Beautiful Place to Die (New York: Scribners, 1989)
Series: Jeff Jackson/Martha's Vineyard Mystery
Story type: Private Detective—Male Lead
Major character(s): Jeff Jackson, Detective—Private (former police officer), Fisherman; Zee Madieras, Nurse (lover of Jeff Jackson)
Time period(s): 1980s
Locale(s): Martha's Vineyard, Massachusetts
What the book is about: Susie Martin asks Jeff to investigate the explosion of her father's boat. First book.
Other books you might like:
Rick Boyer, *The Penny Ferry*, 1984
Jeremiah Healy, *Yesterday's News*, 1989
Douglas Kiker, *Murder on Clam Pond*, 1987
Neal Stephenson, *Zodiac*, 1988

336
Philip R. Craig
A Case of Vineyard Poisoning (New York: Scribners, 1995)
Series: Jeff Jackson/Martha's Vineyard Mystery
Story type: Private Detective—Male Lead
Major character(s): Jeff Jackson, Detective—Private (former police officer); Zee Madieras, Nurse (fiance of Jeff Jackson)
Time period(s): 1990s
Locale(s): Martha's Vineyard, Massachusetts
What the book is about: Jeff and Zee are planning their wedding, entertaining visiting friends, and, of course, doing a lot of fishing. When Zee's bank account briefly registers an extra $100,000, they wonder about it but pass it off as a temporary glitch. Then Jeff finds a young woman dying of poison in his driveway and it is discovered that she had just withdrawn $100,000 from her bank. Another young woman who made a similar withdrawal is missing. Is Zee also in danger?
Other books you might like:
E.C. Ayres, *Hour of the Manatee*, 1994
Rick Boyer, *The Doc Adams Series*, 1982-
Sally Gunning, *The Peter Bartholomew Series*, 1990-
Paul Kemprecos, *The Aristotle Socarides Series*, 1991-
Justin Scott, *Hardscape*, 1993

337
Philip R. Craig
Cliff Hanger (New York: Scribners, 1993)
Series: Jeff Jackson/Martha's Vineyard Mystery
Story type: Private Detective—Male Lead
Major character(s): Jeff Jackson, Detective—Private (former police officer); Zee Madieras, Nurse (lover of Jeff Jackson)
Time period(s): 1990s
Locale(s): Martha's Vineyard, Massachusetts

What the book is about: Jeff Jackson is worried that his lover Zee is going to leave him and now somebody is trying to kill him and he has no idea who. True, he has enemies but this person seems very determined. Is it the man he almost killed when he caught the man beating a young woman, somebody from his past as a policeman, or something more subtle?

Other books you might like:
Sally Gunning, *Ice Water*, 1993
Jeremiah Healy, *The John Francis Cuddy Series*, 1985-
Paul Kemprecos, *Neptune's Eye*, 1990
Justin Scott, *Hardscape*, 1993
William G. Tapply, *Spotted Cats*, 1991

338
Philip R. Craig
The Double Minded Men (New York: Scribners, 1992)

Series: Jeff Jackson/Martha's Vineyard Mystery

Story type: Private Detective—Male Lead

Major character(s): Jeff Jackson, Detective—Private (former police officer), Fisherman; Zee Madieras, Nurse (lover of Jeff Jackson)

Time period(s): 1990s

Locale(s): Martha's Vineyard, Massachusetts

What the book is about: Jeff and Zee are fishing when they are run down by a motorboat owned by the Padishah of Sarofim. Zee is mad and insults the Padishah who, with his head of security, is known for tyranny and torture. The Padishah is in town to retrieve an old family treasure, a priceless emerald necklace. Jeff is further involved when he accepts a job to help provide security. Then the necklace is stolen and Zee is kidnapped.

Other books you might like:
Paul Kemprecos, *Neptune's Eye*, 1991
Douglas Kiker, *Death Below Deck*, 1991
Don Matheson, *Ninth Life*, 1989
John Walter Putre, *A Small and Incidental Murder*, 1990
William G. Tapply, *Spotted Cats*, 1991

339
Philip R. Craig
Off Season (New York: Scribners, 1994)

Series: Jeff Jackson/Martha's Vineyard Mystery

Story type: Private Detective—Male Lead

Major character(s): Jeff Jackson, Detective—Private (former police officer), Fisherman; Zee Madieras, Nurse (lover of Jeff Jackson)

Time period(s): 1990s

Locale(s): Martha's Vineyard, Massachusetts

What the book is about: It's the off-season and Jeff Jackson is relaxing, contemplating his upcoming marriage to Zee Madieras. But it is also hunting season and the animal rights activists, led by Mimi Bettencourt, are after the hunters—Nash Cortez in particular—to stop hunting. First Mimi shoots Nash in the head with a dye-filled water pistol. Then a messenger from a local Mafioso threatens Nash. Jeff predicts that tempers will flare and sure enough, soon there is a murder. Strangely though, the victim had no connection with either faction—or did he?

Other books you might like:
Rick Boyer, *The Whale's Footprints*, 1988
Sally Gunning, *The Peter Bartholomew Series*, 1990-
Paul Kemprecos, *The Aristotle Socarides Series*, 1991-
John Walter Putre, *Death Among the Angels*, 1991
Justin Scott, *Hardscape*, 1993

340
Philip R. Craig
The Woman Who Walked into the Sea (New York: Scribners, 1991)

Series: Jeff Jackson/Martha's Vineyard Mystery

Story type: Amateur Detective—Male Lead

Major character(s): Jeff Jackson, Detective—Private (former police officer), Fisherman

Time period(s): 1990s

Locale(s): Martha's Vineyard, Massachusetts

What the book is about: A 70 year old Shakespeare scholar is murdered on Martha's Vineyard. Another professor who is putting the moves on Jeff Jackson's girlfriend is just one of many suspects. Jeff wouldn't mind if the professor was guilty.

Other books you might like:
Rick Boyer, *Billingsgate Shoal*, 1982
Jeremiah Healy, *Yesterday's News*, 1989
Douglas Kiker, *Murder on Clam Pond*, 1987
John Walter Putre, *A Small and Incidental Murder*, 1990
Neal Stephenson, *Zodiac*, 1988

341
Robert Crais
Free Fall (New York: Bantam, 1993)

Series: Elvis Cole

Story type: Private Detective—Male Lead

Major character(s): Elvis Cole, Detective—Private; Joe Pike, Detective—Private (Cole's partner)

Time period(s): 1990s

Locale(s): Los Angeles, California

What the book is about: Jennifer Sheridan asks P.I. Elvis Cole to find out what is troubling her fiance, who is a member of the LAPD. The fiance is an undercover cop and recently has become more secretive and touchy. The cop does not take kindly to Elvis's snooping and warns him off, telling Elvis that he is seeing another woman and that's why he has been distant with Jennifer. Jennifer doesn't believe it and persuades Elvis to keep looking. Soon the truth comes out and all hell breaks loose.

342 Crais

Other books you might like:
Harlen Campbell, *Monkey on a Chain*, 1993
Jeremiah Healy, *The John Francis Cuddy Series*, 1984-
Robert B. Parker, *The Spenser Series*, 1974-
Bill Pronzini, *The Nameless Detective Series*, 1971-
Wayne Warga, *Hardcover*, 1988

342
Robert Crais
Lullaby Town (New York: Bantam, 1992)
Series: Elvis Cole
Story type: Private Detective—Male Lead
Major character(s): Elvis Cole, Detective—Private; Joe Pike, Detective—Private (Cole's partner)
Time period(s): 1990s
Locale(s): Los Angeles, California
What the book is about: Elvis is hired by Peter Alan Nelson, the king of adventure movies, to find his ex-wife and their son, whom he hasn't seen in over ten years. With work and a little luck, Elvis finds them, but of course, things can't be that simple.
Other books you might like:
James Crumley, *The Wrong Case*, 1975
Timothy Harris, *Kyd for Hire*, 1977
Arthur Lyons, *The Jacob Asch Series*, 1975-
Robert B. Parker, *The Spenser Series*, 1974-
Jonathan Valin, *The Harry Stoner Series*, 1980-

343
Robert Crais
Stalking the Angel (New York: Bantam, 1989)
Series: Elvis Cole
Story type: Private Detective—Male Lead
Major character(s): Elvis Cole, Detective—Private; Joe Pike, Detective—Private (Cole's partner)
Time period(s): 1980s
Locale(s): Los Angeles, California
What the book is about: Elvis is hired by a wealthy executive to find a first edition of a samurai classic that has been stolen. Then the client's daughter is kidnapped.
Other books you might like:
Michael Collins, *The Dan Fortune Series*, (1967-)
Jeremiah Healy, *The John Francis Cuddy Series*, (1984-)
Robert B. Parker, *The Spenser Series*, (1974-)
Bill Pronzini, *The Nameless Detective Series*, (1971-)
Jonathan Valin, *The Harry Stoner Series*, (1980-)

344
Robert Crais
Voodoo River (New York: Hyperion, 1995)
Series: Elvis Cole
Story type: Private Detective—Male Lead
Major character(s): Elvis Cole, Detective—Private; Lucille Chenier, Lawyer, Single Parent
Time period(s): 1990s
Locale(s): Los Angeles, California; Louisiana
What the book is about: Elvis has been hired by Jodi Taylor, star of a popular television series, to find her birth mother. Elvis is off to Louisiana and quickly becomes involved with Lucy Chenier, Jodi's lawyer in Baton Rouge. Just as quickly he becomes involved in the affairs of Milt Rossier, a Cajun crime boss. Just what is Milt's connection to Jodi's search for her birth parents? He is apparently willing to kill anyone and everyone to protect that secret.
Other books you might like:
E.C. Ayres, *Hour of the Manatee*, 1994
James Lee Burke, *The Dave Robicheaux Series*, 1987-
Jerome Doolittle, *Bear Hug*, 1992
Jeremiah Healy, *The John Francis Cuddy Series*, 1984-
Robert B. Parker, *The Spenser Series*, 1974-

345
Camilla T. Crespi
The Trouble with Going Home (New York: HarperCollins, 1995)
Series: Simona Griffo
Story type: Amateur Detective—Female Lead
Major character(s): Simona Griffo, Advertising (native of Italy)
Time period(s): 1990s
Locale(s): Rome, Italy
What the book is about: Simona has returned home to Rome to find out why her mother has moved out on her father and is now living with her friend Mirella. Just as she arrives, she is witness to a purse snatching that leaves a young art student dead. The student, Tamar Deaton, had stayed at Mirella's, and Mirella and her family as well as Simona's mother and ex-husband are soon suspects. Rumor has it that Tamar had discovered a lost da Vinci drawing—a treasure that someone might be willing to kill for.
Other books you might like:
Carolyn Coker, *The Balmoral Nude*, 1990
Aaron Elkins, *A Glancing Light*, 1991
Katherine Hall Page, *The Body in the Vestibule*, 1992
Sheila Simonson, *Skylark*, 1992
Joan Smith, *Follow That Blonde*, 1990

346
Trella Crespi
The Trouble with Moonlighting (New York: Zebra, 1991)
Series: Simona Griffo
Story type: Amateur Detective—Female Lead
Major character(s): Simona Griffo, Advertising (native of Italy)
Time period(s): 1990s
Locale(s): New York, New York

What the book is about: Simona is moonlighting as a dialogue coach for some old friends making a movie in New York. The first day she witnesses an almost fatal accident to super-star actress, Johanna Gayle. Later Johanna is strangled and her boyfriend is arrested. Simona doesn't think he's guilty and tries to find the real murderer.

Other books you might like:
Liza Bennett, *Madison Avenue Murder*, 1989
Karin Berne, *Bare Acquaintances*, 1985
Carole Berry, *Good Night, Sweet Prince*, 1990
Maureen O'Brien, *Close-Up on Death*, 1989
Elizabeth Powers, *On Account of Murder*, 1984

347
Trella Crespi
The Trouble with Too Much Sun (New York: Zebra, 1992)

Series: Simona Griffo

Story type: Amateur Detective—Female Lead

Major character(s): Simona Griffo, Advertising (native of Italy)

Time period(s): 1990s

Locale(s): Pointe-a-Pitre, Guadeloupe

What the book is about: Simona is in Guadeloupe, at Club-Med, to shoot an ad for suntan lotion. She acquires a young boy and goes looking for his mother, the strangely named Iguana. She finds her once, loses her and finds her again. The second time she has a machete buried in her. Trying to help the police solve the murder leads Simona into drugs, guns, voodoo and more murder.

Other books you might like:
Liza Bennett, *Madison Avenue Murder*, 1989
Karin Berne, *False Impressions*, 1986
Carole Berry, *The Bonnie Indermill Series*, 1988-
Carol Brennan, *Headhunt*, 1991
Patricia Houck Sprinkle, *Murder on Peachtree Street*, 1991

348
Michael Crichton
Rising Sun (New York: Knopf, 1992)

Story type: Police Procedural—Male Lead

Major character(s): Peter Smith, Police Officer; John Connor, Police Officer (retired)

Time period(s): 1990s

Locale(s): Los Angeles, California

What the book is about: Pete Smith works for Special Services, a division to deal with celebrities and diplomats. At the opening of the Nakamoto Building, the body of a young woman is discovered in the board room and the Japanese are demanding a liaison officer be present. Smith has the help of John Connor, an expert in Japanese culture. He needs all the help he can get as the case quickly escalates to one of industrial espionage and intrigue.

Other books you might like:
John Brown, *Zaibatsu*, 1985
Anthony Bruno, *Bad Blood*, 1989
William J. Caunitz, *One Police Plaza*, 1984
David Morrell, *The Fifth Profession*,

349
Bill Crider
Blood Marks (New York: St. Martins, 1991)

Story type: Psychological Suspense

Major character(s): Casey Buckland, Teacher (unemployed), Single Parent (with young daughter); Dan Romain, Police Officer (serial killer expert)

Time period(s): 1990s

Locale(s): Houston, Texas

What the book is about: There is a serial killer at work in Texas. He leaves no clues and doesn't kill the same way twice. He is also one of the narrators of this book. He is stalking Casey Buckland for his next victim. Is it someone she knows?

Other books you might like:
John Katzenbach, *The Traveler*, 1987
Joe R. Lansdale, *Act of Love*, 1981
David L. Lindsey, *Mercy*, 1990
Bill Pronzini, *The Running of Beasts*, 1976 (Barry Malzberg, co-author)

350
Bill Crider
Dead on the Island (New York: Walker, 1991)

Series: Truman Smith

Story type: Private Detective—Male Lead

Major character(s): Truman Smith, Detective—Private

Time period(s): 1990s

Locale(s): Galveston, Texas

What the book is about: Private eye Truman Smith has given up the detective business since he failed to find his own missing sister. However, an old friend pleads with him to find another friend's missing teenage daughter. Seems the daughter has just discovered that her mother used to be a whore and didn't react well. But is that really why she's missing?

Other books you might like:
Austin Bay, *The Coyote Cried Twice*, 1985
R.D. Brown, *Hazzard*, 1986
Edward Mathis, *From a High Place*, 1985
Jesse Sublett, *Tough Baby*, 1990
Martha G. Webb, *Darling Corey's Dead*, 1984

351
Bill Crider
Dying Voices (New York: St. Martin's, 1989)

Series: Carl Burns

Story type: Amateur Detective—Male Lead

Major character(s): Carl Burns, Professor (college English professor); "Boss" Napier, Police Officer (sheriff)

Time period(s): 1980s

Locale(s): Pecan City, Texas (Fictional city)

What the book is about: Burns is asked to organize a seminar for Edward Street, formerly a teacher at the college who is now a best-selling writer. This proves to be the least of Burns's problems when Street is murdered shortly after arriving for the seminar.

Other books you might like:
P.M. Carlson, *Murder Is Academic*, 1985
Aaron Elkins, *Fellowship of Fear*, 1982
M.D. Lake, *Amends for Murder*, 1989

352
Bill Crider
Gator Kill (New York: Walker, 1992)

Series: Truman Smith

Story type: Private Detective—Male Lead

Major character(s): Truman Smith, Detective—Private

Time period(s): 1990s

Locale(s): Eagle Lake, Texas

What the book is about: After the death of his sister Truman Smith gave up being a private investigator and became a house painter. Now he's ready to try again, maybe. When Fred Benton asks him to find out who killed and skinned an alligator on his land, Truman is intrigued. This seems to be part of a campaign to harass Fred into selling his land. Then another land owner is found dead.

Other books you might like:
Richard Abshire, *Dallas Drop*, 1988
R.D. Brown, *Hazzard*, 1986
W. Glenn Duncan, *The Rafferty Series*, 1987-
Edward Mathis, *The Dan Roman Series*, 1985
James Reasoner, *Texas Wind*, 1980

353
Bill Crider
The Texas Capitol Murders (New York: St. Martin's, 1992)

Story type: Police Procedural—Male Lead; Amateur Detective

Major character(s): Ray Hartnett, Police Officer (Texas ranger); Jane Kettler, Administrator (of the Texas state capitol), Widow(er)

Time period(s): 1990s

Locale(s): Austin, Texas

What the book is about: A cleaning woman at the capitol is strangled. The only witness is a homeless flasher who won't talk and isn't sure what he saw. Enter Ray Hartnett to investigate and Jane Kettler to deal with the fallout.

Other books you might like:
Michael Bowen, *Washington Deceased*, 1990
Robert Campbell, *The Jimmy Fannery Series*, 1986-
Edward Mathis, *Dark Streets and Empty Places*, 1986
D.R. Meredith, *Murder by Deception*, 1989
D.R. Meredith, *The Sheriff and the Branding Iron Murders*, 1985

354
Bill Crider
When Old Men Die (New York: Walker, 1994)

Series: Truman Smith

Story type: Private Detective—Male Lead

Major character(s): Truman Smith, Detective—Private

Time period(s): 1990s

Locale(s): Galveston, Texas

What the book is about: Truman Smith hates missing person cases, but he relents and takes one for his old friend Dino who wants him to find Outside Harry, a local businessman who hasn't been seen in weeks. Soon one of the people Truman has questioned is murdered and Truman himself is ambushed and nearly killed. It appears someone doesn't want Harry located.

Other books you might like:
Richard Abshire, *Turnaround Jack*, 1990
W. Glenn Duncan, *The Rafferty Series*, 1987-
Jerry Kennealy, *Beggar's Choice*, 1994
Edward Mathis, *Natural Prey*, 1987
D.R. Meredith, *Murder by Masquerade*, 1990

355
C. Clark Criscuolo
Wiseguys in Love (New York: St. Martins, 1993)

Story type: Action/Adventure

Major character(s): Michael Bonello, Criminal (former law student); Lisa Johnson, Secretary

Time period(s): 1990s

Locale(s): New York, New York

What the book is about: Though he didn't plan to end up working for his mob-involved uncle, failed law student Michael Bonello has limited options. Now he finds he has to kill a man to make his bones. In addition to helping out against a union boss, he and his cousin are asked to help his aunt, who has been fired from her accounting job, just short of retirement. She wants them to kill her boss. This is not as easy as it sounds, especially since Michael is falling in love with the guy's secretary.

Other books you might like:
Zev Chafets, *Inherit the Mob*, 1991
Elmore Leonard, *Rum Punch*, 1992
D. Keith Mano, *Topless*, 1991
Donald E. Westlake, *The Fugitive Pigeon*, 1965

356
Deborah Crombie
All Shall Be Well (New York: Scribners, 1994)
Series: Duncan Kincaid/Gemma James
Story type: Police Procedural
Major character(s): Duncan Kincaid, Police Officer (superintendent, Scotland Yard); Gemma James, Police Officer (sergeant)
Time period(s): 1990s
Locale(s): Hampstead, England
What the book is about: Duncan Kincaid's downstairs neighbor, Jasmine Dent, is dying of cancer. It comes as no surprise when Kincaid finds her dead in bed, but the autopsy reveals she died of morphine poisoning. Many feel she took her own life to ease the pain, but Kincaid is not convinced. Since several people benefit from her death, he and Sergeant Gemma James begin a quiet investigation in search of a subtle killer.
Other books you might like:
Elizabeth George, *The Inspector Lynley Series*, 1988-
Caroline Graham, *The Inspector Barnaby Series*, 1987-
Martha Grimes, *The Inspector Jury Series*, 1981-
John Harvey, *The Inspector Resnick Series*, 1989-
Peter Robinson, *The Inspector Banks Series*, 1990-

357
Deborah Crombie
Leave the Grave Green (New York: Scribners, 1995)
Series: Duncan Kincaid/Gemma James
Story type: Police Procedural
Major character(s): Duncan Kincaid, Police Officer (superintendent, Scotland Yard); Gemma James, Police Officer (sergeant)
Time period(s): 1990s
Locale(s): Chiltern Hills, England
What the book is about: When the body of Connor Swann is found floating in the Thames, Kincaid and James are called in. While not normally a case for Scotland Yard, especially since murder cannot be proven, Swann was the son-in-law of a famous operatic conductor and an equally famous soprano. While investigating, Kincaid finds himself drawn to Swann's widow, Julia. She seems somehow indifferent to the death and is still preoccupied with the drowning death of her brother years before in the same river.
Other books you might like:
Caroline Graham, *Death of a Hollow Man*, 1989
Ann Granger, *A Fine Place for Death*, 1995
Elizabeth George, *The Inspector Lynley Series*, 1988-
Susan B. Kelly, *Hope Will Answer*, 1993
Jill McGown, *The Inspector Lloyd & Judy Hill Series*, 1983-

358
Deborah Crombie
A Share in Death (New York: Scribners, 1993)
Series: Duncan Kincaid/Gemma James
Story type: Police Procedural
Major character(s): Duncan Kincaid, Police Officer (superintendent, Scotland Yard); Gemma James, Police Officer (sergeant), Single Parent
Time period(s): 1990s
Locale(s): London, England; Woolsey-under-Bank, England (Yorkshire)
What the book is about: Superintendent Duncan Kincaid is on vacation in Yorkshire at an elegant estate when he gets embroiled in murder. First one death and then others cause him to forget about relaxation and try to solve the crimes. He is singularly unimpressed with the local police so he gets his Sergeant back in London, single mother Gemma James, involved as well. First mystery.
Other books you might like:
Elizabeth George, *A Great Deliverance*, 1988
Caroline Graham, *Death in Disguise*, 1993
Ann Granger, *Cold in the Earth*, 1992
Ruth Rendell, *A Sleeping Life*, 1978
Peter Robinson, *The Hanging Valley*, 1994

359
Virginia Crosby
The Fast-Death Factor (Tulsa: Council Oak, 1990)
Story type: Amateur Detective—Female Lead
Major character(s): Mary Walker, Artist (disabled—in a wheelchair); Thad Walker, Police Officer (chief of police)
Time period(s): 1990s
Locale(s): California (southern)
What the book is about: Someone has murdered the president of Tipton College. The available suspects are numerous and include disgruntled faculty, ambitious administrators, the president's wife, and the beautiful dean of the college. Then Mary Walker's friend is murdered. She had helped Mary out of her doldrums after her car accident. Though her brother is the chief of police, Mary is driven to get involved in finding the murderer. First Novel.
Other books you might like:
P.M. Carlson, *Murder Misread*, 1990
Bill Crider, *One Dead Dean*, 1988
Amanda Cross, *The Question of Max*, 1976
W.R. Philbrick, *Paint It Black*, 1989
Kevin Robinson, *Split Seconds*, 1991

360
Amanda Cross
An Imperfect Spy (New York: Ballantine, 1995)
Series: Kate Fansler
Story type: Amateur Detective—Female Lead
Major character(s): Kate Fansler, Professor; Blair Whitson, Professor
Time period(s): 1990s
Locale(s): New York, New York

361 Crowleigh

What the book is about: While teaching a course entitled "Women in Law and Literature" at Schuyler Law School, Kate becomes involved in trying to decide whether the recent death of a feminist professor was murder rather than the accident it was originally thought to be. Her teaching partner and a secretary at the school certainly think it was murder.

Other books you might like:
Bartholomew Gill, *Death of a Joyce Scholar*, 1989
M.D. Lake, *A Gift for Murder*, 1992
Robert B. Parker, *The Godwulf Manuscript*, 1973
Triss Stein, *Murder at the Class Reunion*, 1993
Janice Steinberg, *Death of a Postmodernist*, 1995

361
Ann Crowleigh (Pseudonym of Barbara Cummings and Jo-Ann Power)
Clively Close: Dead as Dead Can Be (New York: Zebra, 1993)
Story type: Amateur Detective—Female Lead; Historical
Major character(s): Miranda Clively, Spinster; Clare Clively-Murdoch, Widow(er)
Time period(s): 1870s (1875)
Locale(s): London, England

What the book is about: Due to the fall of the pound in recent years the Clively twins have had to rent out part of their family homes. The renovations have uncovered a horrible family secret, the skeleton of a baby. They must call the family together to figure out what to do. But when a fresh corpse shows up, they realize somebody desperately wants to hide the truth. First novel.

Other books you might like:
B. Comfort, *Grave Consequences*, 1989
Hazel Holt, *Mrs. Malory Investigates*, 1990
Susanna Hofmann McShea, *The Pumpkin-Shell Wife*, 1992
Betty Rowlands, *A Little Gentle Sleuthing*, 1991
Corinne Holt Sawyer, *The Benbow and Wingate Series*, 1987-

362
Laura Crum
Cutter (New York: St. Martin's, 1994)
Story type: Amateur Detective—Female Lead
Major character(s): Gail McCarthy, Veterinarian
Time period(s): 1990s
Locale(s): Salinas, California

What the book is about: Casey Brooks, local horse trainer, calls Gail McCarthy with an emergency. Several of his horses are in trouble. When three of them die, Casey blames George, a famous trainer of cow horses and Casey's competitor. Another accident, a cut saddle strap, furthers Gail's unease. When George is killed in a riding accident, she is sure it is murder and it is up to her to convince the police and find the killer. First novel.

Other books you might like:
Lydia Adamson, *Dr. Nightingale Comes Home*, 1994
Earlene Fowler, *Fool's Puzzle*, 1994
Karin McQuillan, *The Cheetah Chase*, 1994
Mary Willis Walker, *Zero at the Bone*, 1991
Karen Ann Wilson, *Eight Dogs Flying*, 1994

363
James Crumley
The Mexican Tree Duck (New York: Mysterious, 1993)
Series: C.W. Sughrue
Story type: Action/Adventure; Private Detective
Major character(s): C.W. Sughrue, Detective—Private, Veteran
Time period(s): 1990s
Locale(s): Montana; Texas; Mexico

What the book is about: Private detective C.W. Sughrue is hired to find the missing Mexican wife of a Texas politician. Did she run away on her own or was she kidnapped? It is not nearly as simple as that. The FBI, drug dealers, and Mexican outlaws are just a few of the things that Sughrue runs up against. Not to mention betrayal.

Other books you might like:
John Clarkson, *One Man's Law*, 1994
Michael Connelly, *The Black Echo*, 1992
Thomas Perry, *Metzger's Dog*, 1983
Scott Smith, *A Simple Plan*, 1993
Stuart Woods, *White Cargo*, 1988

364
Chris Crutcher
The Deep End (New York: Morrow, 1992)
Story type: Amateur Detective—Male Lead
Major character(s): Wilson Corder, Psychologist (specialist in children), Single Parent (divorced)
Time period(s): 1990s
Locale(s): Three Forks, Washington

What the book is about: Dr. Corder is treating Jerry Parker for child abuse and neglect when Jerry's sister Sabrina is kidnapped. Trying to find out what happened is difficult as Jerry won't talk and his alcoholic mother tells several different stories. Somebody doesn't want Jerry helped and the truth to come out. Then Corder's cat is killed and his daughter is threatened. First mystery.

Other books you might like:
Linda Barnes, *Coyote*, 1990
Faye Kellerman, *False Prophet*, 1992
Jonathan Kellerman, *The Alex Delaware Series*, 1985-
Donna Levin, *California Street*, 1990
Stephen White, *Private Practices*, 1992

365
Robert Cullen
Cover Story (New York: Atheneum, 1994)

Series: Colin Burke

Story type: Action/Adventure; Espionage

Major character(s): Colin Burke, Journalist (foreign correspondent); Ronit Evron, Teacher

Time period(s): 1990s

Locale(s): Moscow, Russia

What the book is about: Colin Burke, hardworking reporter, is onto a new story along with everyone else in Moscow—Russian nuclear scientists working with the Syrians to give them a nuclear capability. Burke has inside contacts however and may be able to find out what is going on. He also becomes involved with a beautiful Israeli teacher who may be an intelligence agent. The CIA seems to be interested as well.

Other books you might like:
Sean Flannery, *Moving Targets*, 1992
Stuart M. Kaminsky, *The Inspector Rostnikov Series*, 1984-
Philip Kerr, *Dead Meat*, 1994
Anthony Olcott, *Murder at the Red October*, 1981
Douglas Skeggs, *The Talinin Madonna*, 1992

366
Clare Curzon
Cat's Cradle (New York: St. Martin's, 1992)

Series: Yeadings and Mott

Story type: Police Procedural—Male Lead

Major character(s): Mike Yeadings, Police Officer (detective—superintendent); Angus Mott, Police Officer (detective—inspector)

Time period(s): 1990s

Locale(s): Berkshire, England (Thames River Valley)

What the book is about: Yeadings and his crew are called when elderly recluse Lorely Pelling is found shot to death. At first it seems to be suicide but the crime lab is able to determine that the body had been rearranged after death. Who would want to kill an old woman who never saw anyone?

Other books you might like:
Catherine Aird, *The Inspector Sloane Series*, 1966-
Douglas Clark, *The Masters and Green Series*, 1969-
Paula Gosling, *Death Penalties*, 1991
Reginald Hill, *The Dalziel and Pascoe Series*, 1970-
Elizabeth George, *A Great Deliverance*, 1988

367
Clare Curzon
Death Prone (New York: St. Martin's, 1994)

Series: Yeadings and Mott

Story type: Police Procedural—Male Lead

Major character(s): Mike Yeadings, Police Officer (detective—superintendent); Angus Mott, Police Officer (detective—inspector)

Time period(s): 1990s

Locale(s): Thames River Valley, England

What the book is about: Hadrian Bascombe is 91 and has decided to leave his fortune to one member of his family, but hasn't decided to whom. After interviewing all the relatives at a family gathering, a car crash leaves a grandnephew in a coma and a grandniece hurt. The police become involved and find that it was no accident. Then more members of the family start to die. Is one of them eliminating the competition—permanently? Superintendent Mike Yeadings finds himself strangely attracted to the young niece.

Other books you might like:
Marjorie Eccles, *The Inspector Gil Mayo Series*, 1986-
Paula Gosling, *The Wychford Murders*, 1986
Kay Mitchell, *The Inspector Morrissey Series*, 1991-
Dorothy Simpson, *The Inspector Luke Thanet Series*, 1981-
June Thomson, *The Inspector Rudd Series*, 1971-

368
Clare Curzon
Three-Core Lead (New York: Doubleday, 1990)

Series: Yeadings and Mott

Story type: Police Procedural—Male Lead

Major character(s): Mike Yeadings, Police Officer (inspector); Felicity Marlow, Actress

Time period(s): 1980s

Locale(s): Maidenhead; Prague, Czechoslovakia; Thames River Valley, England

What the book is about: After the death of a friend and former spy in Prague, the man's daughter turns up with a letter for Mike from her father. The death seems to tie in with the murder of a 16-year-old girl. This is the first of Curzon's books to be published in the U.S.

Other books you might like:
Nicholas Blake, *The Whisper in the Gloom*, 1954
Douglas Clark, *Storm Center*, 1986
Reginald Hill, *Child's Play*, 1987
Patricia Moyes, *A Six-Letter Word for Death*, 1983
June Thomson, *The Long Revenge*, 1974

369
Stan Cutler
Shot on Location (New York: Dutton, 1993)

Series: Goodman/Bradley

Story type: Private Detective—Male Lead

Major character(s): Rayford Goodman, Detective—Private; Mark Bradley, Writer, Homosexual

Time period(s): 1990s

Locale(s): Los Angeles, California

What the book is about: Rayford Goodman has been summoned to jury duty and try as he might to get out of it, he is on the jury of the murder trial of the year—Carey Jaeger, son of famous actor Stacy Jaeger is accused of killing his sister's lover. Mark Bradley is approached to write a book with Goodman about the case. When a bomb scare interrupts the trial they start to investigate on their own. Then Carey's girlfriend and possible alibi is killed.

370

Other books you might like:
Bruce Cook, *Rough Cut*, 1990
Robert Crais, *Lullaby Town*, 1992
Arthur Lyons, *Fast Fade*, 1987
Les Roberts, *The Saxon Series*, 1987-
Jim Stinson, *The Stoney Winston Series*, 1985-

370
Mary Daheim
The Alpine Advocate (New York: Ballantine, 1992)

Series: Emma Lord

Story type: Amateur Detective—Female Lead

Major character(s): Emma Lord, Journalist (owner of a newspaper), Single Parent; Vida Runkel, Secretary (Emma's assistant)

Time period(s): 1990s

Locale(s): Alpine, Washington (fictional town that actually existed but was abandoned in the twenties)

What the book is about: Emma Lord is the new owner of the *Alpine Advocate*, a small-town newspaper. Now, Chris, a friend of her son, has quit college and returned to Alpine where he was born, seeking the reason why his mother's family had abandoned them and why his father had disappeared years ago. When Chris's cousin is murdered, the police are sure Chris is guilty. Emma senses something deeper going on and is determined to uncover all the old scandals.

Other books you might like:
Mary Kittredge, *Murder in Mendocino*, 1987
Vince Kohler, *Rainy North Woods*, 1990
Marlys Millhiser, *Murder at Moot Point*, 1992
Elizabeth Atwood Taylor, *The Northwest Murders*, 1992
Lee Wallingford, *Cold Tracks*, 1991

371
Mary Daheim
The Alpine Christmas (New York: Ballantine, 1993)

Series: Emma Lord

Story type: Amateur Detective—Female Lead

Major character(s): Emma Lord, Journalist (newspaper owner)

Time period(s): 1990s

Locale(s): Alpine, Washington

What the book is about: It's a white Christmas for Alpine but not much news is happening except for a series of break-ins and vandalism against the Nyquist family. Then a fisherman reels in a strange catch - a woman's leg still wearing a sneaker. Then another woman's intact body is found. This is more news than Emma wanted. Who were these women, why are they being killed and who is the killer?

Other books you might like:
Judith Garwood, *Make Friends with Murder*, 1992
M.S. Karl, *Killer's Ink*, 1988
Marlys Millhiser, *Murder at Moot Point*, 1992
John R. Riggs, *Hunting Ground*, 1987
Celestine Sibley, *Ah, Sweet Mystery*, 1991

372
Mary Daheim
The Alpine Decoy (New York: Ballantine, 1994)

Series: Emma Lord

Story type: Amateur Detective—Female Lead

Major character(s): Emma Lord, Journalist (owner of a newspaper); Vida Runkel, Journalist (gossip columnist)

Time period(s): 1990s

Locale(s): Alpine, Washington

What the book is about: A new nurse, Marilynn Lewis, has come to the rural town of Alpine, Washington. She is smart, beautiful, and black. Someone in town is not happy about the latter and is sending her such things as dead crows. Emma Lord is outraged and she and Vida Runkel are determined to put a stop to it. Then a young black man arrives and is soon found shot to death. They find that this is not the first violent death around Marilynn Lewis.

Other books you might like:
Lydia Adamson, *Dr. Nightingale Comes Home*, 1994
K.K. Beck, *Electric City*, 1994
Kathryn Lasky Knight, *The Calista Jacobs Series*, 1986-
Marlys Millhiser, *Murder at Moot Point*, 1992
Kerry Tucker, *Death Echo*, 1993

373
Mary Daheim
The Alpine Fury (New York: Ballantine, 1995)

Series: Emma Lord

Story type: Amateur Detective—Female Lead

Major character(s): Emma Lord, Journalist (owner of a newspaper); Vida Runkel, Journalist (gossip columnist)

Time period(s): 1990s

Locale(s): Alpine, Washington

What the book is about: Emma is wondering why a Seattle banker is in town talking to Marv Petersen, the president of the Alpine Bank. She is told it is just a vacation, but Marv seems to be avoiding answering questions. The bank is very important to the town and the Petersen family has run it since it's founding. Then Marv's daughter Linda, the bank's bookkeeper, is found murderd. Emma, with the help of Vida, who seems to know where most of the town's skeletons are buried, try to find a killer.

Other books you might like:
Carol Cail, *The Maxey Burnell Series*, 1994-
Alison Glen, *Showcase*, 1992
Leona Karr, *Murder in Bandora*, 1993
Meg O'Brien, *The Jessica James Series*, 1990-
Celestine Sibley, *The Kate Mulcay Series*, 1991-

374
Mary Daheim
Bantam of the Opera (New York: Avon, 1993)

Series: Bed-and-Breakfast Mystery

Story type: Amateur Detective—Female Lead

Major character(s): Judith McMonigle, Innkeeper (owner of a bed and breakfast); Joe Flynn, Police Officer (Judith's husband)

Time period(s): 1990s

Locale(s): Washington

What the book is about: Judith's Hillside Manor bed and breakfast is being graced by the presence of famed opera tenor Mario Pacetti and his entourage. She is not happy, however, for Mario is imperious and disagreeable. He is also cursed with a series of accidents. When he dies of poison, Judith has to protect the reputation of the Manor, but she finds very few people who wouldn't have wanted to kill Mario.

Other books you might like:
Deborah Adams, *All the Great Pretenders*, 1992
Dorothy Cannell, *The Thin Woman*, 1986
Diane Mott Davidson, *Catering to Nobody*, 1990
Janet Laurence, *Hotel Morgue*, 1992
Kathy Hogan Trocheck, *Every Crooked Nanny*, 1992

375

Mary Daheim
A Fit of Tempera (New York: Avon, 1994)

Series: Bed-and-Breakfast Mystery

Story type: Amateur Detective—Female Lead

Major character(s): Judith McMonigle, Innkeeper (owner of a bed and breakfast); Serena "Renie" Grover, Designer (graphic designer)

Time period(s): 1990s

Locale(s): Glacier Falls, Washington

What the book is about: Judith McMonigle and Renie Grover are visiting their family's old cabin in the woods, which they have loved since they were children. One of their neighbors is the world famous Tobias Riley, whose paintings are worth a fortune. He gives Judith one of his early works when they visit him. Soon after they find him murdered and the police suspect Judith. She knows she is innocent and sets out to prove it.

Other books you might like:
Susan Wittig Albert, *Thyme of Death*, 1992
Claudia Bishop, *A Taste for Murder*, 1994
Jean Hager, *Blooming Murder*, 1994
Janet Laurence, *Hotel Morgue*, 1992
Tamar Myers, *Too Many Crooks Spoil the Broth*, 1994

376

Mary Daheim
Holy Terrors (New York: Avon, 1992)

Series: Bed-and-Breakfast Mystery

Story type: Amateur Detective—Female Lead

Major character(s): Judith McMonigle, Innkeeper (owner of bed and breakfast)

Time period(s): 1990s

Locale(s): Pacific Northwest

What the book is about: An elderly widow dies, precipitating one crisis after another. Who will inherit her million dollar estate? Who are the natural parents of an adopted child? Why is the wife of the supposed heir murdered? Will Judith marry the policeman investigating the case?

Other books you might like:
Mary Bowen Hall, *Emma Chizzit and the Queen Anne Killer*, 1989
Carolyn G. Hart, *The Annie Laurance Series*, 1987-
Vince Kohler, *Rainy North Woods*, 1991
Bernie Lee, *Murder Without Reservation*, 1990
Marlys Millhiser, *Murder at Moot Point*, 1992

377

Mary Daheim
Murder, My Suite (New York: Avon, 1995)

Series: Bed-and-Breakfast Mystery

Story type: Amateur Detective—Female Lead

Major character(s): Judith McMonigle, Innkeeper (owner of a bed and breakfast)

Time period(s): 1990s

Locale(s): Heraldsgate Hill, Washington; Canada

What the book is about: Judith is fed up with her latest guests, gossip columnist Dagmar Chatsworth, her entourage, and her really annoying dog. When they leave, Judith decides to take up her cousin Renie's offer of a vacation at a ski resort in Canada. Unluckily they run into Dagmar and company again. To know Dagmar is to despise her and no one would be surprised if she showed up dead. But it is her mousy secretary who dies instead. Why?

Other books you might like:
Susan Wittig Albert, *The China Bayles Series*, 1993-
Claudia Bishop, *The Sarah Quilliam Series*, 1994-
Jean Hager, *The Iris House Series*, 1994-
Janet Laurence, *Hotel Morgue*, 1992
Joanne Pence, *Cooking Up Trouble*, 1995

378

Catherine Dain (Pseudonym of Judith Garwood)
Bet Against the House (New York: Berkley, 1995)

Series: Freddie O'Neal

Story type: Private Detective—Female Lead

Major character(s): Freddie O'Neal, Detective—Private

Time period(s): 1990s

Locale(s): Reno, Nevada

What the book is about: Gloria Scope has inherited a controlling interest in her husband's computer chip company. Her children and other board members want control and hire Freddie to dig up some dirt on the widow to give them a bargaining position. Freddie is immediately involved in saving Gloria from a sniper attack. Gloria may be brash, opinionated, and loud but Freddie likes her and has second thoughts about the job. When someone murders Gloria, Freddie wants to find the guilty party. The killer doesn't want to be found and will kill again.

379 Dain

Other books you might like:
Linda Barnes, *The Carlotta Carlyle Series*, 1987-
Sue Grafton, *The Kinsey Millhone Series*, 1982-
Karen Kijewski, *The Kat Colorado Series*, 1989-
Shelley Singer, *The Barrett Lake Series*, 1993-
Gloria White, *The Ronnie Ventana Series*, 1991-

379
Catherine Dain (Pseudonym of Judith Garwood)
Lay It on the Line (New York: Jove, 1992)

Series: Freddie O'Neal

Story type: Private Detective—Female Lead

Major character(s): Freddie O'Neal, Detective—Private; Deacon "Deke" Adams, Guard (security), Friend (sometime partner of Freddie)

Time period(s): 1990s

Locale(s): Reno, Nevada

What the book is about: Freddie was born and raised in Reno and has heard all the jokes about her name, but she loves being a private detective. She is first involved with Joan Halliday when a couple hired to care for Joan's father trashes his house and skips with his car. Freddie recovers the car and a trunkload of drugs. Later a hit-and-run driver attacks Joan's father and kills her sister, Lois. The police think Joan was the driver. Freddie is hired to clear Joan and find the real killer. First novel.

Other books you might like:
Linda Barnes, *The Carlotta Carlyle Series*, 1987-
Karen Kijewski, *The Kat Colorado Series*, 1990-
J.J. Lamb, *The Zach Rolfe Series*, 1976-1979
Margaret Lucke, *A Relative Stranger*, 1991
Maxine O'Callaghan, *The Delilah West Series*, 1982-

380
Catherine Dain (Pseudonym of Judith Garwood)
Sing a Song of Death (New York: Jove, 1993)

Series: Freddie O'Neal

Story type: Private Detective—Female Lead

Major character(s): Freddie O'Neal, Detective—Private

Time period(s): 1990s

Locale(s): Reno, Nevada; Lake Tahoe, Nevada

What the book is about: Freddie O'Neal is talked into accompanying her friend Sandra on an interview of a famous singer Vince Marina. Vince has been attacked several times by his ex-wife and may be in the market for a bodyguard and Sandra hopes Freddie will be hired so she can get an inside story. Freddie wants nothing to do with it but is charmed into doing a little nosing around. Then Vince is murdered and the ex-wife, the obvious suspect, hires Freddie to prove her innocence.

Other books you might like:
Linda Barnes, *The Carlotta Carlyle Series*, 1987-
Valerie Frankel, *Prime Time for Murder*, 1993
Nancy Baker Jacobs, *The Devon MacDonald Series*, 1991
Karen Kijewski, *The Kat Colorado Series*, 1990-
Maxine O'Callaghan, *The Delilah West Series*, 1977-

381
Catherine Dain (Pseudonym of Judith Garwood)
Walk a Crooked Mile (New York: Jove, 1994)

Series: Freddie O'Neal

Story type: Private Detective—Female Lead

Major character(s): Freddie O'Neal, Detective—Private

Time period(s): 1990s

Locale(s): Reno, Nevada

What the book is about: Freddie O'Neal has accepted a case she doesn't want but can't refuse. Her mother has hired her to find her father who disappeared many years ago. The trail leads Freddie to a group of bikers, sleazy bars, and worse. Apparently the reason her father disappeared is a secret that someone is still willing to kill to keep.

Other books you might like:
Linda Barnes, *The Carlotta Carlyle Series*, 1987-
Nancy Baker Jacobs, *The Devon MacDonald Series*, 1991-
Karen Kijewski, *The Kat Colorado Series*, 1990-
Maxine O'Callaghan, *The Delilah West Series*, 1982-
Sara Paretsky, *The V.I. Warshawski Series*, 1982-

382
Barbara D'Amato
Hard Tack (New York: Scribners, 1991)

Series: Cat Marsala

Story type: Amateur Detective—Female Lead

Major character(s): Cat Marsala, Journalist (free-lance)

Time period(s): 1990s

Locale(s): Chicago, Illinois; Great Lakes (Lake Michigan)

What the book is about: Accepting an assignment to do a story on the life-styles of the rich and famous turns out to be a bigger deal than Cat expected. She goes on a cruise across Lake Michigan that quickly turns deadly. A crew-member turns up dead in a locked cabin and it could not have been suicide.

Other books you might like:
Lesley Grant-Adamson, *The Rain Morgan Series*, 1984-
Susan Kelly, *The Liz Connors Series*, 1986-
Meg O'Brien, *The Jessica James Series*, 1989-
Sara Paretsky, *Deadlock*, 1984
Sarah Shankman, *The Samantha Adams Series*, 1987-

383
Barbara D'Amato
Hard Women (New York: Scribners, 1993)

Series: Cat Marsala

Story type: Amateur Detective—Female Lead

Major character(s): Cat Marsala, Journalist (free-lance)

Time period(s): 1990s

Locale(s): Chicago, Illinois

What the book is about: Cat Marsala is doing a piece for television about women in prostitution. One of the prostitutes she meets is Sandra Lupica, who agrees to be on the show if Cat will put her up for a while. Shortly thereafter, Sandra turns up dead in the alley outside Cat's apartment. The police show little interest in the death of a prostitute, so it is left to Cat to investigate what she thinks is murder.

Other books you might like:
Linda Barnes, *The Carlotta Carlyle Series*, 1987-
Mary Daheim, *The Alpine Advocate*, 1992
Susan Kelly, *The Liz Connors Series*, 1986-
Meg O'Brien, *The Jessica James Series*, 1989-
Sarah Shankman, *The Samantha Adams Series*, 1987-

384
Barbara D'Amato
Hardball (New York: Scribners, 1990)

Series: Cat Marsala

Story type: Amateur Detective—Female Lead

Major character(s): Cat Marsala, Journalist (free-lance); Harold McCoo, Police Officer (captain)

Time period(s): 1980s

Locale(s): Michigan

What the book is about: While doing research for a story on the legalization of drugs, Cat witnesses a murder.

Other books you might like:
Linda Barnes, *A Trouble of Fools*, 1987
Richard Forrest, *A Child's Garden of Death*, 1975
Stuart M. Kaminsky, *When the Dark Man Calls*, 1983
Karen Kijewski, *Katwalk*, 1989
Marie Reno, *Final Proof*, 1976

385
Jeanne M. Dams
The Body in the Transept (New York: Walker, 1995)

Story type: Amateur Detective—Female Lead

Major character(s): Dorothy Martin, Widow(er), Aged Person; Alan Nesbitt, Police Officer (chief constable), Widow(er)

Time period(s): 1990s

Locale(s): Sherebury, England (fictional town)

What the book is about: American Dorothy Martin and her husband were planning to retire to Sherebury when his sudden death put a crimp in their plans. She goes ahead with the move. Not long after her arrival, she finds the body of the local minister in the cathedral. Though he was widely disliked she finds it difficult to believe anyone in the small village would do murder. Not so for Chief Constable Alan Nesbitt, who is not eager for Dorothy's assistance—which of course doesn't stop Dorothy. First novel.

Other books you might like:
Nancy Atherton, *Aunt Dimity and the Duke*, 1994
Robert Barnard, *The Skeleton in the Grass*, 1987
Agatha Christie, *The Miss Marple Series*, 1930-1976
Mary Daheim, *Auntie Mayhem*, 1995
Caroline Graham, *The Inspector Barnaby Series*, 1987-

386
David Daniel
The Heaven Stone (New York: St. Martin's, 1994)

Story type: Private Detective

Major character(s): Alex Rasmussen, Detective—Private (ex-police officer); Ada Chan Stewart, Social Worker

Time period(s): 1990s

Locale(s): Lowell, Massachusetts

What the book is about: Alex Rasmussen is asked by Ada Stewart to look into the murder of Cambodian refugee Bhuntan Tran. The police have dismissed it as drug related, but Ada says that Bhuntan was a hard worker, well-liked by everyone and appeared to have no relation to drugs. The only clue Alex has is that other Cambodians in the U.S. have mysteriously died recently. First novel.

Other books you might like:
Philip R. Craig, *A Beautiful Place to Die*, 1990
Jeremiah Healy, *The John Francis Cuddy Series*, 1985-
Zachary Klein, *Still Among the Living*, 1990
Robert B. Parker, *The Spenser Series*, 1974-
Maynard F. Thomson, *Trade Secrets*, 1994

387
Gloria Dank
Friends till the End (New York: Bantam, 1989)

Story type: Amateur Detective—Male Lead

Major character(s): Bernard Woodruff, Writer (children's books author); Arthur B. "Snooky" Randolph, Heir (brother-in-law of Bernard)

Time period(s): 1980s

Locale(s): Ridgewood, Connecticut (Fictional city)

What the book is about: Laura Sloane drinks a deadly cocktail at a party. This leads to more murder among rich friends.

Other books you might like:
Richard Forrest, *A Child's Garden of Death*, 1975
Carolyn G. Hart, *A Little Class on Murder*, 1989
Frances and Richard Lockridge, *The Mr. and Mrs. North Series*, (1940-1963)
Charlotte MacLeod, *Something the Cat Dragged In*, 1983
Nancy Pickard, *Marriage Is Murder*, 1987

388
Denise Danks
User Deadly (New York: St. Martin's, 1992)

Story type: Amateur Detective—Female Lead

Major character(s): Georgina Powers, Journalist (magazine reporter); Warren Graham, Computer Expert

Time period(s): 1980s (1987)

Locale(s): England

What the book is about: Just before he is to leave for a new job in California, reporter Georgina Power's cousin is found nude and hanged. Georgina doesn't believe he killed himself so she and her computer hacker friend, Warren Graham, set out to find the truth behind his death. First novel.

Other books you might like:
John Camp, *The Empress File*, 1991
Jerome Doolittle, *Stranglehold*, 1991

389
Diane Mott Davidson
The Cereal Murders (New York: Bantam, 1993)
Series: Goldy Bear
Story type: Amateur Detective—Female Lead
Major character(s): Goldy Bear, Caterer, Divorced Person (single parent); Tom Schulz, Police Officer, Detective—Homicide (Goldy's lover)
Time period(s): 1990s
Locale(s): Aspen Meadow, Colorado
What the book is about: While catering the senior class dinner for a prep school, Goldy Bear discovers the class valedictorian strangled with one of her extension cords. She and her lover, homicide detective Tom Schulz, soon discover that the boy may have been involved in extortion. And so might other members of the class. But who killed the scholar?
Other books you might like:
Susan Wittig Albert, *Thyme of Death*, 1992
M.C. Beaton, *Agatha Raisin and the Quiche of Death*, 1992
Michael Bond, *The Monsieur Pamplemousse Series*, 1986-
Janet Laurence, *The Darina Lisle Series*, 1990
Nancy Pickard, *The 27 Ingredient Chili Con Carne Murders*, 1993

390
Diane Mott Davidson
Dying for Chocolate (New York: Bantam, 1992)
Series: Goldy Bear
Story type: Amateur Detective—Female Lead
Major character(s): Goldy Bear, Caterer, Divorced Person (single parent)
Time period(s): 1990s
Locale(s): Aspen Meadow, Colorado
What the book is about: Although Goldy is still being harassed by her ex-husband, her life is looking up - the catering business is succeeding and she has two men in her life. One of them is old flame Philip Miller, a local shrink. Unfortunately Philip dies in a peculiar traffic accident while Goldy is following him. She is suspicious. Why did Philip's car start weaving all over the road and why didn't Philip stop the car?
Other books you might like:
Susan Wittig Albert, *Thyme of Death*, 1992
Michael Bond, *The Monsieur Pamplemousse Series*, 1986-
Dorothy Cannell, *The Thin Woman*, 1984
Janet Laurence, *The Darina Lisle Series*, 1990-
Virginia Rich, *The Mrs. Potter Series*, 1982-

391
J. Madison Davis
Red Knight (New York: Walker, 1992)
Series: Dub Greenert
Story type: Private Detective
Major character(s): Dub Greenert, Detective—Private
Time period(s): 1990s
Locale(s): New Orleans, Louisiana
What the book is about: A mail bombing at the home of civil rights leader Raleigh Lee Menzies brings Greenert to investigate. Is it rednecks who hate Menzies' decades long stand toward intergration or perhaps former allies who are angered by his recent book about the early years and leaders of the movement? When Menzies is kidnapped things get really messy. The Mafia is involved as is the FBI and a mystery women.
Other books you might like:
D.J. Donaldson, *Cajun Nights*, 1989
Warwick Downing, *The Water Cure*, 1992
Jerry Oster, *Fixing to Die*, 1992
Julie Smith, *New Orleans Mourning*, 1990

392
J. Madison Davis
White Rook (New York: Walker, 1990)
Story type: Private Detective
Major character(s): Dub Calabrese, Detective—Private (Pittsburgh based); Vonna Saucier, Detective—Private (working undercover on a murder)
Time period(s): 1980s
Locale(s): New Orleans, Louisiana
What the book is about: While working to discover whether Eddie Viek killed his business partner, Calabrese and Saucier—who have become lovers—discover Viek has a connection to a white supremacist group.
Other books you might like:
A.E. Maxwell, *Just Another Day in Paradise*, 1985
James Patterson, *The Thomas Berryman Number*, 1976

393
Kenn Davis
Blood of Poets (New York: Fawcett, 1990)
Series: Carver Bascombe
Story type: Private Detective—Male Lead
Major character(s): Carver Bascombe, Detective—Private (African—American); Royal Blue, Writer (poet)
Time period(s): 1990s
Locale(s): San Francisco, California
What the book is about: Police Lieutenant De Anza'a wife is accused of murdering a fellow poet. De Anza goes to his friend Carver Bascombe for help in proving her innocence.
Other books you might like:
John Ball, *In the Heat of the Night*, 1965
Gar Anthony Haywood, *Fear of the Dark*, 1988
Walter Mosley, *Devil in a Blue Dress*, 1990

394
Lindsey Davis
The Silver Pigs (New York: Crown, 1989)
Story type: Historical
Major character(s): M. Didius Falco, Detective—Amateur
Time period(s): 1st century (70)
Locale(s): Rome, Italy
What the book is about: After Falco rescues a senator's niece from a kidnapping attempt, the niece is then murdered. The family hires Falco to find out the truth behind her death. First book.
Other books you might like:
Margaret Doody, *Aristotle, Detective*, 1980
Wallace Irwin, *The Julius Caesar Murder Case*, 1935

395
Robert Davis
Kimura (New York: Walker, 1989)
Story type: Action/Adventure
Major character(s): Harry Edwards, Police Officer; Patti Kimura, Student, Activist
Time period(s): 1970s (1970)
Locale(s): San Francisco, California
What the book is about: When his father is killed after reopening a 1943 case, Harry tries to find the truth. First book.
Other books you might like:
Brian Garfield, *Recoil*, 1977
David Morrell, *Testament*, 1975
Michael Nava, *Little Death*, 1986
Ross Thomas, *Briarpatch*, 1984

396
Thomas D. Davis
Suffer Little Children (New York: Walker, 1991)
Story type: Private Detective—Male Lead
Major character(s): Dave Strickland, Detective—Private
Time period(s): 1990s
Locale(s): Azalea, California
What the book is about: Dave Strickland is asked to help find the Reverend Bauer's son, Billy, a sufferer of Tourette's Syndrome. At first the reverend and his wife offer to help Strickland but then turn against him. When a ransom demand is received for Billy's return they agree that Strickland should help with the transfer of money. Then Billy's body is found and Strickland must track down the killer. This case is harder than usual for Strickland because it causes him to deal with his own loss of faith. First novel.
Other books you might like:
Ed Gorman, *The Night Remembers*, 1991
Sue Grafton, *H Is for Homicide*, 1991
Ross Macdonald, *The Lew Archer Series*, 1949
Bill Pronzini, *The Nameless Detective Series*, 1971-

397
Janet Dawson
Kindred Crimes (New York: St. Martins, 1990)
Series: Jeri Howard
Story type: Private Detective—Female Lead
Major character(s): Jeri Howard, Detective—Private
Time period(s): 1990s
Locale(s): San Francisco, California
What the book is about: Jeri Howard suspects that her ex-husband, the policeman, only sent the missing-persons case in her direction in hopes she'd fail. Jeri is determined not to, but the case isn't as simple as it first appears. First novel. Winner of the St. Martins/PWA Best First Private Eye Novel contest.
Other books you might like:
Robert J. Bowman, *The House of Blue Lights*, 1988
Susan Dunlap, *Pious Deception*, 1989
Linda Grant, *Random Access Murder*, 1988
Karen Kijewski, *Katapult*, 1989
Marcia Muller, *The Sharon McCone Series*, 1977-

398
Janet Dawson
Nobody's Child (New York: Fawcett, 1995)
Series: Jeri Howard
Story type: Private Detective—Female Lead
Major character(s): Jeri Howard, Detective—Private
Time period(s): 1990s
Locale(s): Oakland, California; San Francisco, California
What the book is about: Jeri is hired to determine whether the body of a woman found in a burned-out building is the missing daughter who ran away three years ago. Yes, it is, but while investigating Jeri discovers that the missing daughter had a young daughter. The woman who hired her expresses no interest in this supposed granddaughter, but that doesn't stop Jeri from trying to find her.
Other books you might like:
Linda Barnes, *The Carlotta Carlyle Series*, 1987-
Catherine Dain, *The Freddie O'Neal Series*, 1992-
Karen Kijewski, *The Kat Colorado Series*, 1988-
Marcia Muller, *The Sharon McCone Series*, 1977-
Maxine O'Callaghan, *The Delilah West Series*, 1980-

399
Deforest Day
August Ice (New York: St. Martin's, 1990)
Story type: Action/Adventure
Major character(s): Chase Defoe, Spy (former navel officer)
Time period(s): 1970s
Locale(s): Pennsylvania
What the book is about: Chase Defoe arrives in a Pennsylvania town after a solitary canoe trip. He has discovered a dead body and is arrested for the murder. He soon clears himself and determines to find out what really happened. This crime has its roots in a crime from the '50s. First book.

400 Day

Other books you might like:
James Lee Burke, *The Neon Rain*, 1986
John Walter Putre, *A Small and Incidental Murder*, 1990

400
Dianne Day
The Strange Files of Fremont Jones (New York: Doubleday, 1995)

Story type: Amateur Detective—Female Lead; Historical

Major character(s): Caroline Fremont Jones, Businesswoman (owner of a typing business); Justin Cameron, Lawyer

Time period(s): 1900s (1905)

Locale(s): San Francisco, California

What the book is about: Fremont Jones has fled Boston and a failed relationship to come to San Francisco. She opens her own business doing typing for hire. This brings her in contact with some very strange people—and murder. One client, attorney Justin Cameron, expresses serious jealousy over Fremont's work for another. Someone else brings three manuscripts for typing and never returns to pick them up. Then another client turns up dead and her office is tossed. Are all of these incidents related? And how much danger is she in? First mystery.

Other books you might like:
Abbey Penn Baker, *In the Dead of Winter*, 1994
Caleb Carr, *The Alienist*, 1993
William L. DeAndrea, *The Lunatic Fringe*, 1980
Carole Nelson Douglas, *The Irene Adler Series*, 1990-
Mark Frost, *The List of 7*, 1994

401
William L. DeAndrea
Killed on the Rocks (New York: Mysterious, 1990)

Series: Matt Cobb

Story type: Amateur Detective—Male Lead

Major character(s): Matt Cobb, Journalist (television trouble-shooter)

Time period(s): 1990s

Locale(s): New York

What the book is about: Asked to oversee negotiations about the purchase of a network, Matt and the rest of the parties involved go to an estate in upstate New York where they are soon snowbound. Murder occurs, but how can it be murder when the body is in the middle of an unmarked snowbank?

Other books you might like:
James Anderson, *The Affair of the Blood-Stained Egg Cosy*, 1977
Barbara D'Amato, *Hard Tack*, 1991
Runa Fairleigh, *An Old-Fashioned Mystery*, 1984
Caryl Rivers, *Indecent Behavior*, 1990
Donald E. Westlake, *Trust Me on This*, 1988

402
William L. DeAndrea
The Manx Murders (New York: Penzler, 1994)

Series: Niccolo Benedetti

Story type: Amateur Detective; Private Detective—Male Lead

Major character(s): Niccolo Benedetti, Professor; Ron Gentry, Detective—Private; Janice Gentry, Psychologist

Time period(s): 1990s

Locale(s): Pennsylvania

What the book is about: Professor Niccolo Benedetti and his entourage of Ron and Janice Gentry get involved with twin brothers Clyde and Henry Pembroke. Clyde loves bird watching, but the birds have fled. Could brother Henry's Manx cats have anything to do with their disappearance? One of the brothers goes missing and then a secretary turns up dead. What *is* going on?

Other books you might like:
Robert Barnard, *Death of a Literary Widow*, 1980
Lawrence Block, *The Burglar Series*, 1978-
Peter Dickinson, *The Last House-Party*, 1982
Warren Murphy, *Leonardo's Law*, 1978
Rex Stout, *The Nero Wolfe Series*, 1934-1976

403
Jeffrey Wilds Deaver
Hard News (New York: Doubleday, 1991)

Series: Rune

Story type: Amateur Detective—Female Lead

Major character(s): Rune, Television (camerawoman for a tv station)

Time period(s): 1990s

Locale(s): New York, New York

What the book is about: Rune thinks she has a story about a man in prison for a murder he didn't commit. Unfortunately the person he was convicted of killing was the head of the network for which Rune works and no one at the network seems to be interested in helping her pursue the story. In fact, just the opposite. Someone doesn't want her to do the story bad enough that they will kill her.

Other books you might like:
Liza Bennett, *Seventh Avenue Murder*, 1988
Barry Berg, *Hide and Seek*, 1989
Carole Berry, *The Bonnie Indermill Series*, 1987
Dick Lochte, *Sleeping Dog*, 1988
Robert B. Parker, *Stardust*, 1990

404
Jeffrey Wilds Deaver
Manhattan Is My Beat (New York: Bantam, 1989)

Series: Rune

Story type: Amateur Detective—Female Lead

Major character(s): Rune, Clerk (sales)

Time period(s): 1980s

Locale(s): New York, New York

What the book is about: An old man is killed, possibly because of a movie he rented. Rune, a punker who works in a video store, is determined to find out what happened and why. This is Deaver's first mystery.

Other books you might like:
Liza Bennett, *Seventh Avenue Murder*, 1988
Barry Berg, *Hide and Seek*, 1989
Dorothy Salisbury Davis, *A Death in the Life*, 1976
Joseph Mathewson, *Alicia's Trump*, 1980

405
Jeffrey Wilds Deaver
Mistress of Justice (New York: Doubleday, 1992)

Story type: Amateur Detective—Female Lead; Legal

Major character(s): Taylor Lockwood, Paraprofessional (paralegal), Musician (jazz pianist); Mitchell Reece, Lawyer

Time period(s): 1990s

Locale(s): New York, New York

What the book is about: Taylor Lockwood is a paralegal for the old and prestigious law firm of Hubbard, White and Willis. When a note for twenty five million dollars needed as evidence in a case disappears, Mitchell Reece asks Taylor to help him recover it. When Taylor investigates she finds almost everyone in the firm is involved in greed, power-plays, strange secrets and maybe murder.

Other books you might like:
Karin Berne, *Bare Acquaintances*, 1985
John Grisham, *The Pelican Brief*, 1991
Gini Hartzmark, *Principal Defense*, 1992
Michael A. Kahn, *Grave Designs*, 1991
Susan Wolfe, *The Last Billable Hour*, 1989

406
David Debin
Nice Guys Finish Dead (New York: Random, 1992)

Story type: Amateur Detective—Male Lead; Action/Adventure

Major character(s): Albie Marx, Businessman (former '60s radical); Joe Danno, Police Officer

Time period(s): 1990s

Locale(s): United States (from Los Angeles to Florida to the Caribbean)

What the book is about: The murder of Albie Marx's girlfriend, Linda, sets Albie and Linda's daughter, Mariah, on a quest for the killer. Lieutenant Joe Danno thinks Albie did it. In the search for the truth Albie, Mariah and Joe get involved with the U.S. government, Janis Joplin's death 20 years ago, designer drugs, record producers and a Revolutionary War buff.

Other books you might like:
Peter Abrahams, *Revolution #9*, 1992
Daniel Hearn, *Black Light*, 1991
George R.R. Martin, *The Armageddon Rag*, 1983
Thomas Maxwell, *The Suspense Is Killing Me*, 1990
Jesse Sublett, *Boiled in Concrete*, 1992

407
Jim DeBrosse
Hidden City (New York: St. Martin's, 1991)

Series: Rick Decker

Story type: Amateur Detective—Male Lead; Action/Adventure

Major character(s): Rick Decker, Journalist

Time period(s): 1990s

Locale(s): Cincinnati, Ohio

What the book is about: Is a redevelopment scheme the reason behind the bubonic plague scare? Are the homeless really dying of the plague? Is the health comissioner involved in a coverup? These questions and more must be answered by reporter Rick Decker.

Other books you might like:
Sean Hanlon, *The Cold Front*, 1989
Vince Kohler, *Rainy North Woods*, 1990
Keith Peterson, *The John Wells Series*, 1988-
Les Roberts, *The Milan Jacovich Series*, 1988-
Jonathan Valin, *The Harry Stoner Series*, 1980-

408
Jim DeBrosse
Southern Cross (New York: St. Martin's, 1994)

Series: Rick Decker

Story type: Action/Adventure; Amateur Detective—Male Lead

Major character(s): Rick Decker, Journalist; Rebo Johnson, Photojournalist

Time period(s): 1990s

Locale(s): British Virgin Islands

What the book is about: Rick Becker's editor sends Rick and photojournalist Rebo Johnson to the Caribbean to find out the truth about the disappearance of the son of Cincinnati's richest man, who refuses to talk about it. The son disappeared while sailing on the *Southern Cross*, a ship that seems to be hiding more than it shows. While partying with the missing son's shipmates, Rick and Rebo find themselves getting in deeper and deeper. Can they get out in time?

Other books you might like:
Robert Ferrigno, *The Cheshire Moon*, 1993
James W. Hall, *Bones of Coral*, 1991
Carl Hiaasen, *Native Tongue*, 1991
Vince Kohler, *Rising Dog*, 1993
Stephen F. Wilcox, *All the Dead Heroes*, 1993

409
Jim DeFelice
Coyote Bird (New York: St. Martin's, 1992)

Story type: Techno-Thriller; Espionage

Major character(s): Tom Wright, Military Personnel (lieutenant colonel), Pilot; Jennifer Fitzgerald, Scientist, Computer Expert

Time period(s): Indeterminate Future

410 Deighton

What the book is about: A new, super-secret spy plane, mostly computer-controlled, is in danger of being sabotaged by the machinations of the Russians and the Japanese. The Japanese are looking to re-arm their country and their computer-controlled spy plane is on a collison course with the one from the U.S. Pilot Tom Wright and computer whiz Jennifer Fitzgerald are the only ones who can stop what's happening. First novel.

Other books you might like:
Dale Brown, *Day of the Cheetah*, 1989
Stephen Coonts, *Minotaur*, 1989
Dean Ing, *The Ransom of Black Stealth One*, 1989
Basil Jackson, *Crooked Flight*, 1985
Douglas Terman, *Free Flight*, 1980

410
Len Deighton
City of Gold (New York: HarperCollins, 1992)

Story type: Historical; Espionage

Major character(s): Jimmy Ross, Military Personnel (accused of murder)

Time period(s): 1940s (1942)

Locale(s): Egypt

What the book is about: While enroute to prison in Cairo, Jimmy Ross has the opportunity to take over his captor's identity when the man dies of a heart attack. He also takes over the dead man's other assignment—to ferret out the German spy who is feeding General Rommel information allowing him to anticipate British strategy.

Other books you might like:
James Baddock, *The Faust Conspiracy*, 1989
Ken Follett, *Eye of the Needle*, 1978
Brian Garfield, *The Paladin*, 1982
Thomas Gifford, *Praetorian*, 1993
Jack Higgins, *The Eagle Has Landed*, 1975

411
David Delman
The Last Gambit (New York: St. Martins, 1991)

Series: Jacob & Helen Horowitz

Story type: Police Procedural; Private Detective

Major character(s): Jacob Horowitz, Police Officer (homicide lieutenant); Helen Horowitz, Detective—Private

Time period(s): 1990s

Locale(s): Philadelphia, Pennsylvania; Chicago, Illinois

What the book is about: Jacob is in Philadelphia to play in a chess tournament while Helen is in Chicago searching for a missing daughter. The tournament has murder as well as chess and Helen's missing person may be connected to Jacob's murder.

Other books you might like:
Susan Kelley, *The Liz Connors Series*, 1985-
Carol Jerina, *The Tall Dark Alibi*, 1988
T.J. MacGregor, *The St. James and McCleary Series*, 1984-
Rex Stout, *Gambit*, 1962
James Yaffe, *The Mom Series*, 1988-

412
Nelson DeMille
The Gold Coast (New York: Warner, 1990)

Story type: Action/Adventure

Major character(s): John Sutter, Lawyer (member of a Wall Street firm)

Time period(s): 1980s

Locale(s): New York, New York; Long Island, New York

What the book is about: His wife is the mistress of his mobster client (and next door neighbor), the IRS is after him, and his law firm wants to dump him. John Sutter has problems.

Other books you might like:
Philip Freidman, *Reasonable Doubt*, 1990
Richard Nusser, *Walking After Midnight*, 1989
Scott Turow, *Presumed Innocent*, 1988

413
Jane Dentinger
Dead Pan (New York: Viking, 1992)

Series: Jocelyn O'Roarke

Story type: Amateur Detective—Female Lead

Major character(s): Jocelyn O'Roarke, Actress; Jack Breedlove, Hairdresser

Time period(s): 1990s

Locale(s): Los Angeles, California

What the book is about: Jocelyn has been in a funk for months so she accepts the offer from long-time friend, Austin Frost, to come to Hollywood to be in a TV movie. Austin wants her for her acting but also to help the troubled young starlet of the movie trying to make a comeback from drug addiction. Soon the director of photography, an all-around much hated man, is murdered. Jocelyn, with the help of Jack Breedlove and an ex-surfer cop, tries to find the killer.

Other books you might like:
Trella Crespi, *The Trouble with Moonlighting*, 1991
Gillian B. Farrell, *Alibi for an Actress*, 1992
Maureen O'Brien, *Close-Up on Death*, 1989
Jim Stinson, *Double Exposure*, 1985
Dorian Yeager, *Cancellation by Death*, 1992

414
Jane Dentinger
The Queen Is Dead (New York: Viking, 1994)

Series: Jocelyn O'Roarke

Story type: Amateur Detective—Female Lead

Major character(s): Jocelyn O'Roarke, Actress; Phillip Gerrard, Police Officer (homicide; Jocelyn's ex-lover)

Time period(s): 1990s

Locale(s): Corinth, New York

What the book is about: Jocelyn O'Roarke has been asked to take over for Tessa Grant in a college production of *The Winter's Tale*. Tessa has died and Jocelyn, who thought of Tessa as friend and mentor, agrees to help. She finds herself back in her old college with many old friends, but some things she learns make her wonder if Tessa's death was a natural one. With the help of Phillip Gerrard, who has showed up to try and win Jocelyn back, she tries to find the truth.

Other books you might like:
Lydia Adamson, *The Alice Nestleton Series*, 1991-
P.M. Carlson, *Rehearsal for Murder*, 1988
Gillian B. Farrell, *Murder and a Muse*, 1994
Anne Morice, *The Tessa Crichton Series*, 1973-1993
Dorian Yeager, *Cancellation by Death*, 1992

415
Jo Dereske
Miss Zukas and the Island Murders (New York: Avon, 1995)

Series: Miss Zukas

Story type: Amateur Detective—Female Lead

Major character(s): Helma Zukas, Librarian

Time period(s): 1990s

Locale(s): Bellehaven, Washington

What the book is about: Helma has received an anonymous note reminding her of her promise to organize a twenty-year reunion for her high school class. It also hints that a boy's death was not an accident as believed. Helma decides to honor her commitment and bring everyone from Scoop River, Michigan out to Washington. She has misgivings, though, when she gets a second anonymous letter telling her to cancel the reunion. Ruth, her friend and classmate, convinces her to continue and soon Ruth, Helma, and the class find themselves at an isolated island resort with a very determined murderer.

Other books you might like:
Jeff Abbott, *Do Unto Others*, 1994
Jean Hager, *Dead and Buried*, 1995
Charlaine Harris, *Real Murders*, 1991
Triss Stein, *Murder at the Class Reunion*, 1993
Susan Steiner, *Library: No Murder Aloud*, 1993

416
Jo Dereske
Miss Zukas and the Library Murders (New York: Avon, 1994)

Story type: Amateur Detective—Female Lead

Major character(s): Helma Zukas, Librarian; Ruth Winthrop, Artist; Wayne Gallant, Police Officer (chief of police)

Time period(s): 1990s

Locale(s): Bellehaven, Washington

What the book is about: Helma Zukas arrives at work at the Bellehaven Public Library to find it swarming with police. A body has been discovered in the stacks. Helma can't help but be interested, and she and her friend Ruth Winthrop decide to conduct their own investigation. When another body shows up, Helma realizes the killer may be one of her collegues, and if she gets too close she may be the next victim. First mystery.

Other books you might like:
Charity Blackstock, *Dewey Death*, 1977
Terrie Curran, *All Booked Up*, 1989
Charles A. Goodrum, *The Werner-Bok Library Series*, 1977-
Charlaine Harris, *The Aurora Teagarden Series*, 1991-
Susan Steiner, *Library: No Murder Aloud*, 1993

417
Gary Devon
Bad Desire (New York: Random, 1990)

Story type: Psychological Suspense

Major character(s): Henry Lee Slater, Political Figure (mayor); Faith Slater, Spouse (wife of Henry)

Time period(s): 1990s

Locale(s): Meridan, California

What the book is about: Henry Lee Slater is obsessed with 17-year-old Sheila Bonner and will let nothing get in the way of his having her. Soon the girl's grandmother is murdered—then the police chief. Who will be next?

Other books you might like:
Elizabeth George, *A Suitable Vengeance*, 1991
Melodie Johnson Howe, *The Mother Shadow*, 1989
M.D. Lake, *Cold Comfort*, 1990
Ruth Rendell, *Going Wrong*, 1990

418
Colin Dexter
The Wench Is Dead (New York: St. Martin's, 1990)

Series: Inspector Morse

Story type: Historical

Major character(s): Morse, Police Officer (inspector)

Time period(s): 1980s

Locale(s): Oxford, England

What the book is about: While laid up with an ulcer, Inspector Morse decides to try to solve a murder case that is a century old.

Other books you might like:
Josephine Tey, *The Daughter of Time*, 1952

419
Peter Dickinson
Skeleton-in-Waiting (New York: Pantheon, 1990)

Series: Alternate Royal Family

Story type: Amateur Detective—Female Lead; Alternate History

Major character(s): Princess Louise, Royalty (daughter of King Victor), Administrator; Victor II, Ruler (King of England), Doctor

Time period(s): 1980s (1987 in an alternate time-line)

Locale(s): England

What the book is about: In an alternate universe, Edward VII's eldest son survived to become king and engender a radically different royal line from the Windsors we know. Here Princess Louise must try her best to control things, including scandalous secrets in her late grandmother's private papers, rising terrorism, the potential nervous breakdown of the Prince of Wales, and a possible murderer in the palace itself. Sequel to *King and Joker*, 1976.

Other books you might like:
William F. Buckley Jr., *Saving the Queen*, 1976
Len Deighton, *SS-GB*, 1979
Michael Bishop, *The Secret Ascension*, 1988
Kingsley Amis, *The Alteration*, 1976
Philip K. Dick, *The Man in the High Castle*, 1962
Keith Roberts, *Pavane*, 1968

420
Peter Dickinson
The Yellow Room Conspiracy (New York: Mysterious, 1994)

Story type: Psychological Suspense

Major character(s): Lucy Vereker, Young Woman; Paul Ackerly, Businessman

Time period(s): 20th century (1930s-1990s)

Locale(s): England

What the book is about: Not an easy book to describe (as with much of Dickinson's work), this is a story told in flashbacks about the lives of five daughters who live and love at Blatchards, an old mansion in England and how the fire that destroyed the house in 1956 may have been set by any one of them. It is really the story of people in pre- and post-war England, centered around one household.

Other books you might like:
Ted Allbeury, *The Lantern Network*, 1989
Reginald Hill, *The Collaborators*, 1989
John Lawton, *Blackout*, 1995
Ruth Rendell, *Kissing the Gunner's Daughter*, 1992

421
William Diehl
Primal Fear (New York: Villard, 1992)

Story type: Legal; Psychological Suspense

Major character(s): Martin Vail, Lawyer (defense attorney); Molly Arrington, Doctor (psychiatrist)

Time period(s): 1990s

Locale(s): Chicago, Illinois

What the book is about: Appointed by the court—as punishment—to defend what appears to be an ironclad case against the accused killer of a priest, attorney Martin Vail puts together a team, including private detective Tommy Goodman and psychiatrist Molly Arrington, that he thinks can find out the truth since his feeling is that the accused man is innocent.

Other books you might like:
William Bayer, *Blind Side*, 1989
John Clarkson, *And Justice for One*, 1993
Richard Harris, *Honor Bound*, 1982
Nancy Taylor Rosenberg, *Mitigating Circumstances*, 1992
Scott Turow, *Presumed Innocent*, 1987

422
Denise Dietz
Beat Up a Cookie (New York: Walker, 1994)

Series: Ellie Bernstein

Story type: Amateur Detective—Female Lead

Major character(s): Ellie Bernstein, Businesswoman (director of Weight Winners); Peter Miller, Police Officer (Ellie's lover), Detective—Homicide

Time period(s): 1990s

Locale(s): Colorado Springs, Colorado

What the book is about: Twenty years ago a young woman died at "A Farewell to M*A*S*H" party. Ellie Bernstein was there then, and still loves "M*A*S*H" now, but someone seems to be killing people who look like the stars of the show. She becomes involved with a strange group of real "M*A*S*H" fanatics, many potential victims and maybe the killer too. Ellie has a good reason to find the killer—she looks an awful lot like "Hot-Lips" Houlihan.

Other books you might like:
Susan Wittig Albert, *The China Bayles Series*, 1992-
Dorothy Cannell, *The Ellie Haskell Series*, 1984-
Jill Churchill, *The Jane Jeffry Series*, 1989-
Diane Mott Davidson, *The Goldy Bear Series*, 1990-
Lora Roberts, *Murder in a Nice Neighborhood*, 1994

423
Denise Dietz
Throw Darts at a Cheesecake (New York: Walker, 1992)

Story type: Amateur Detective—Female Lead; Police Procedural

Major character(s): Ellie Bernstein, Businesswoman (director of Weight Winners); Peter Miller, Police Officer (Ellie's lover), Detective—Homicide

Time period(s): 1990s

Locale(s): Colorado Springs, Colorado

What the book is about: Ellie Bernstein's Weight Winners group seems to be having a run of bad luck—as people reach their goal weights they die of mysterious accidents. Only the police don't think they are accidents and as the deaths continue, Ellie is also convinced that someone is killing memebers of her group. With her knowledge of the people involved and her growing attraction to Detective Miller she decides to help him. Then someone decides to make her the next victim. First mystery.

Other books you might like:
Toni Brill, *Date with a Dead Doctor*, 1991
Dorothy Cannell, *Femmes Fatal*,
Jill Churchill, *A Quiche Before Dying*, 1993
Jaqueline Girdner, *Adjusted to Death*, 1991
Gillian Roberts, *Philly Stakes*, 1989

424
P.C. Doherty (Pseudonym of Paul Harding)
The Fate of Princes (New York: St. Martins, 1991)

Story type: Historical

Major character(s): Francis Lovell, Nobleman (viscount); Richard III, Ruler (King of England)

Time period(s): 15th century (1483-1487)

Locale(s): England

What the book is about: Francis, Viscount Lovell, is asked by his close friend Richard III to investigate the disappearance of the two princes from the Tower of London.

Other books you might like:
Elizabeth Peters, *The Murders of Richard III*, 1974
Josephine Tey, *The Daughter of Time*, 1952
Guy M. Townsend, *To Prove a Villain*, 1985

425
P.C. Doherty (Pseudonym of Paul Harding)
The Masked Man (New York: St. Martin's, 1991)

Story type: Historical; Amateur Detective—Male Lead

Major character(s): Ralph Croft, Criminal (forger)

Time period(s): 15th century

Locale(s): France

What the book is about: Pulled out of prison by the French regent, forger Ralph Croft is told he must find out who the mysterious Man in the Iron Mask was. He uncovers a plot against the crown that involves the Knights Templar and a disgraced cabinet minister.

Other books you might like:
Alexandre Dumas, *The Man in the Iron Mask*, 1885
Faye Kellerman, *The Quality of Mercy*, 1989
Edward Marston, *The Trip to Jerusalem*, 1990

426
P.C. Doherty (Pseudonym of Paul Harding)
Murder Wears a Cowl (New York: St. Martin's, 1994)

Series: Hugh Corbett

Story type: Historical; Amateur Detective—Male Lead

Major character(s): Hugh Corbett, Secretary (master of the clerks)

Time period(s): 14th century (1302)

Locale(s): London, England

What the book is about: Someone dressed in a monk's cowl is killing people in London and Edward I suggests that Hugh Corbett look into the matter before things begin to reflect badly on the church. There is also the problem of a break-in at the royal treasury.

Other books you might like:
Michael Clynes, *The Poisoned Chalice*, 1994
C.L. Grace, *The Eye of God*, 1994
Edward Marston, *The Nicholas Bracewell Series*, 1988-
Kate Sedley, *The Weaver's Tale*, 1994
Leonard Tourney, *The Matthew Stock Series*, 1980-

427
P.C. Doherty (Pseudonym of Paul Harding)
The Prince of Darkness (New York: St. Martins, 1993)

Series: Hugh Corbett

Story type: Amateur Detective—Male Lead; Historical

Major character(s): Hugh Corbett, Secretary (master of the clerks)

Time period(s): 14th century

Locale(s): Oxfordshire, England

What the book is about: When the body of Eleanor Belmont is found in the nunnery to which she had been sent to keep her away from the Prince of Wales, the king sends his clerk, Hugh Corbett, to investigate as the king fears that either the prince or his lover had her killed. Doherty also writes as Paul Harding.

Other books you might like:
Faye Kellerman, *The Quality of Mercy*, 1989
Edward Marston, *The Queen's Head*, 1989
Sharan Newman, *Death Comes as Epiphany*, 1993
Kate Sedley, *Death and the Chapman*, 1992
Leonard Tourney, *The Player's Boy Is Dead*, 1980

428
Anabel Donald
The Glass Ceiling (New York: St. Martin's, 1995)

Series: Alex Tanner

Story type: Private Detective—Female Lead

Major character(s): Alex Tanner, Detective—Private

Time period(s): 1990s

Locale(s): London, England

429 **Donaldson**

What the book is about: Alex has placed an advertisement stating "special rates for interesting cases" and receives a mysterious list of four 'wimmin' and the phrase "Stop me if you can...please stop me." She finds that the women were an early feminist group at Oxford and that one of them is recently dead. The others are strangely reticent to discuss the old days, but someone seems to be killing their pets—and sending them to Alex.

Other books you might like:
Liza Cody, *The Anna Lee Series*, 1986-
Sarah Dunant, *Birthmarks*, 1992
Nora Kelly, *My Sister's Keeper*, 1992
Janet Neel, *Death Among the Dons*, 1994
Michelle Spring, *Every Breath You Take*, 1994

429
D.J. Donaldson
Blood on the Bayou (New York: St. Martins, 1991)
Series: Andy Broussard/Kit Franklyn
Story type: Amateur Detective
Major character(s): Andy Broussard, Doctor (medical examiner); Kit Franklyn, Psychologist (criminal/forensic)
Time period(s): 1990s
Locale(s): New Orleans, Louisiana (and in the Bayou)
What the book is about: Could the murder of a stripper, a homeless man and a tourist really be the work of a loup garou - a werewolf? A family that Andy Broussard has know for years also seems to be involved.

Other books you might like:
George C. Chesbro, *The Fear in Yesterday's Rings*, 1991
Patricia D. Cornwell, *Postmortem*, 1990
Julie Smith, *New Orleans Mourning*, 1990
Les Whitten, *Moon of the Wolf*, 1967

430
D.J. Donaldson
New Orleans Requiem (New York: St. Martin's, 1994)
Series: Andy Broussard/Kit Franklyn
Story type: Police Procedural; Amateur Detective
Major character(s): Kit Franklyn, Psychologist (criminal/forensic); Andy Broussard, Doctor (medical examiner)
Time period(s): 1990s
Locale(s): New Orleans, Louisiana
What the book is about: There seems to be a surplus of corpses at a forensic medical convention that has come to town. All of the corpses have similar markings and all of them have had Scrabble tiles found nearby. It falls to Andy Broussard and Kit Franklyn to find out just what is going on.

Other books you might like:
Patricia D. Cornwell, *The Kay Scarpetta Series*, 1989-
Susan Dunlap, *Rogue Wave*, 1991
Aaron Elkins, *The Gideon Oliver Series*, 1984-
Julie Smith, *New Orleans Mourning*, 1991
Joyce Thompson, *Bones*, 1991

431
D.J. Donaldson
No Mardi Gras for the Dead (New York: St. Martin's, 1992)
Series: Andy Broussard/Kit Franklyn
Story type: Police Procedural; Amateur Detective
Major character(s): Kit Franklyn, Psychologist (criminal/forensic); Andy Broussard, Doctor (medical examiner)
Time period(s): 1990s
Locale(s): New Orleans, Louisiana
What the book is about: Kit Franklyn has moved into a new house and is doing some landscaping. During some digging her dog discovers a human jawbone. Calling her friend and boss, Andy Broussard, they soon discover the rest of the body, a young woman who was killed thirty years ago. Kit is professionally and personally determined to find out who she was and who killed her.

Other books you might like:
Patricia D. Cornwell, *Postmortem*, 1990
Susan Dunlap, *Rogue Wave*, 1991
Aaron Elkins, *Make No Bones*, 1991
M.K. Shuman, *The Last Man to Die*, 1992
Joyce Thompson, *Bones*, 1991

432
Jerome Doolittle
Bear Hug (New York: Pocket, 1992)
Series: Tom Bethany
Story type: Private Detective—Male Lead
Major character(s): Tom Bethany, Detective—Private (unlicensed)
Time period(s): 1990s
Locale(s): Boston, Massachusetts; Houston, Texas
What the book is about: A friend of Bethany's asks him to help a group of retired men who have been cheated out of most of their life savings in a junk bond scam. Unfortunately the head of the scam, Dr. Denton Somerville, died of a heart attack while out on bail and the money has disappeared. Bethany investigates and finds an awful lot of people are either after the money or covering up what happened to it.

Other books you might like:
Robert Crais, *Lullaby Town*, 1992
Jeremiah Healy, *The John Francis Cuddy Series*, 1985-
John D. MacDonald, *The Travis McGee Series*, 1964-1985
Robert B. Parker, *The Spenser Series*, 1973-
Thomas Perry, *Metzger's Dog*, 1983

433
Jerome Doolittle
Body Scissors (New York: Pocket, 1990)
Series: Tom Bethany
Story type: Action/Adventure; Private Detective—Male Lead
Major character(s): Tom Bethany, Detective—Private (unlicensed)

Time period(s): 1990s

Locale(s): Boston, Massachusetts

What the book is about: Tom Bethany is hired to look for skeletons in the closet of a potential secretary of state candidate. The main skeleton seems to be the unsolved murder of the candidate's daughter a few years earlier. First mystery.

Other books you might like:
Robert Crais, *The Monkey's Raincoat*, 1987
Joe Gores, *Wolf Time*, 1989
Thomas Perry, *Metzger's Dog*, 1983
John Walter Putre, *A Small and Incidental Murder*, 1989
Ross Thomas, *The Fourth Durango*, 1989

434

Jerome Doolittle
Kill Story (New York: Pocket, 1995)

Series: Tom Bethany

Story type: Action/Adventure; Private Detective—Male Lead

Major character(s): Tom Bethany, Detective—Private (unlicensed); Thurman Boucher, Publisher (newspaper owner)

Time period(s): 1990s

Locale(s): Boston, Massachusetts

What the book is about: Tom has been asked by friends of the late Linda Cushing to try and regain control of the paper she had sold to media mogul Thurman Boucher. He had made promises that were quickly broken and drove Linda to suicide. Now he is destroying the small but prestigious *Daily Banner*. Tom soon works his way into Boucher's confidence as a security consultant and right-hand man, but now what? Boucher is too cagey to be conned easily and too dangerous to leave alone.

Other books you might like:
Robert Crais, *Stalking the Angel*, 1989
Elmore Leonard, *Stick*, 1983
A.E. Maxwell, *The Fiddler Series*, 1984-
Thomas Perry, *Metzger's Dog*, 1983
Ross Thomas, *The Mordida Man*, 1981

435

Jerome Doolittle
Stranglehold (New York: Pocket, 1991)

Series: Tom Bethany

Story type: Private Detective—Male Lead; Action/Adventure

Major character(s): Tom Bethany, Detective—Private (unlicensed)

Time period(s): 1990s

Locale(s): Boston, Massachusetts

What the book is about: Bethany is asked by the ACLU to look into the death of a wealthy young man. If the man killed himself while in the act of autoeroticism then the ACLU will not inherit a lot of money. If the man was murdered then they do get the money. Bethany's lover is the top lawyer for the ACLU and this along with the victim's mother complicates his investigation.

Other books you might like:
Robert Crais, *The Monkey's Raincoat*, 1987
Jeremiah Healy, *Right to Die*, 1991
Thomas Perry, *Metzger's Dog*, 1983
John Walter Putre, *Death Among the Angels*, 1991
Ross Thomas, *Briarpatch*, 1984

436

Marjorie Dorner
Blood Kin (New York: Morrow, 1992)

Story type: Psychological Suspense; Amateur Detective—Female Lead

Major character(s): Kate Lundgren, Adoptee; Jack Kramer, Businessman (developer)

Time period(s): 1990s

Locale(s): Woodard, Minnesota

What the book is about: Searching for her birth mother Kate Lungren tracks the woman down in a small Minnesota town. The woman doesn't deny her but insists Kate leave her alone. Feeling that there is more to the rejection she starts to spy on the woman and soon discovers her dead body. Was Kate's mother killed to protect the identity of her natural father? Or was it because she was involved in criminal activity?

Other books you might like:
Frances Fyfield, *Shadows on the Mirror*, 1991
Isabelle Holland, *The Long Search*, 1990
Velda Johnston, *Shadow Behind the Curtain*, 1985
Lia Matera, *Prior Convictions*, 1991
Marcia Muller, *Dark Star*, 1989

437

Kathleen Dougherty
Moth to the Flame (New York: Berkley, 1991)

Story type: Action/Adventure; Psychological Suspense

Major character(s): Charlie Silverthorne, Computer Expert (former government worker); Vincent McKenna, Computer Expert, Criminal

Time period(s): 1990s

Locale(s): Baltimore, Maryland

What the book is about: Someone has broken into a government computer program and is using it to kill people. Charlie, who worked on the program initially, is asked to come back and help stop the infiltration. Little does she know that this will put her in grave personal danger. First novel.

Other books you might like:
Christopher Buckley, *Wet Work*, 1991
John Camp, *The Fool's Run*, 1989

438
Carole Nelson Douglas
Cat on a Blue Monday (New York: Tor, 1994)
Series: Midnight Louie
Story type: Amateur Detective
Major character(s): Midnight Louie, Animal (cat), Detective—Private; Temple Barr, Public Relations (free-lance); Matt Devine, Counselor (on a help-line)
Time period(s): 1990s
Locale(s): Las Vegas, Nevada
What the book is about: Temple Barr has been talked into doing the P.R. for the local cat show, and maybe looking into the threatening phone calls members have been getting. Matt Devine has been asked to help his old teacher, Sister Serafina, because the nuns of Our Lady of Guadalupe Church have been getting obscene phone calls. Meanwhile Midnight Louie has been warned that many cats are in danger. The trouble seems to center on the church and a nearby cat lady. Can the three find out who is responsible before felines and humans begin to die?
Other books you might like:
Lydia Adamson, *The Alice Nestleton Series*, 1990-
Lilian Jackson Braun, *The Cat Who Series*, 1966-
Rita Mae Brown, *Wish You Were Here*, 1990
Akif Pirincci, *Felidae*, 1993
Christopher Reed, *The Big Scratch*, 1988

439
Carole Nelson Douglas
Catnap (New York: Tor, 1992)
Story type: Amateur Detective; Private Detective
Major character(s): Temple Barr, Businesswoman, Public Relations (free-lance); Midnight Louie, Animal (cat), Detective—Private
Time period(s): 1990s
Locale(s): Las Vegas, Nevada
What the book is about: Temple Barr is in charge of the publicity for the American Booksellers Convention. Two cats she needs have disappeared and when she spots another cat she is giving chase when she literally trips over the corpse of the editor of Pennyroyal Press. The cat turns out to be a tough talking feline private detective named Midnight Louie—who narrates parts of the book. Louie and his newly adopted person set out to solve the crime.
Other books you might like:
Lilian Jackson Braun, *The Cat Who Series*, 1966-
Rita Mae Brown, *Wish You Were Here*, 1990
Akif Pirincci, *Felidae*, 1993
Christopher Reed, *The Big Scratch*, 1988

440
Carole Nelson Douglas
Good Morning, Irene (New York: Irene, 1991)
Series: Irene Adler
Story type: Historical; Amateur Detective—Female Lead
Major character(s): Irene Adler, Singer (opera star); Penelope (Nell) Huxleigh, Companion (to Irene)
Time period(s): 1880s (1888)
Locale(s): Paris, France
What the book is about: After besting Sherlock Holmes, Irene—along with her husband Geoffrey Norton and her faithful companion, Penelope Huxleigh—retires to Paris where she delights in reading her own obituaries after her presumed death in a railway accident. Soon though she is involved with a corpse and Bram Stoker and Sarah Benhnardt and.
Other books you might like:
Lloyd Biggle Jr., *The Glendower Conspiracy*, 1990
Loren D. Estleman, *Sherlock Holmes vs. Dracula*, 1978
L.B. Greenwood, *Sherlock Holmes and the Thistle of Scotland*, 1989
Nicholas Meyer, *The Seven-Percent Solution*, 1974
Elizabeth Peters, *The Amelia Peabody Series*, 1975-

441
Carole Nelson Douglas
Good Night, Mr. Holmes (New York: Tor, 1990)
Story type: Historical; Amateur Detective—Female Lead
Major character(s): Irene Adler, Singer, Adventurer; Penelope (Nell) Huxleigh, Servant (former governess)
Time period(s): 1890s
Locale(s): London, England
What the book is about: The retelling of the Irene Adler story—to Sherlock Holmes "The Woman"-by Penelope Huxleigh, a woman rescued from despair by Irene and allowed to be her "Watson". In addition to retelling the "Scandal in Bohemia" story from Irene's point of view, Irene also gets involved with Lily Langtry, Bram Stoker, Oscar Wilde and Antonin Dvorak, among others. Author's first straight mystery. She has written numerous SF and Fantasy novels.
Other books you might like:
John Gardner, *The Return of Moriarty*, 1975
L.B. Greenwood, *Sherlock Holmes and the Thistle of Scotland*, 1989
H. Paul Jeffers, *The Adventure of the Stalwart Companions*, 1978
Nicholas Meyer, *The Seven-Percent Solution*, 1974
Elizabeth Peters, *The Amelia Peabody Series*, 1975

442
Carole Nelson Douglas
Irene at Large (New York: Tor, 1992)
Series: Irene Adler
Story type: Historical; Amateur Detective—Female Lead
Major character(s): Irene Adler, Singer; Penelope (Nell) Huxleigh, Companion (to Irene)
Time period(s): 1890s
Locale(s): France

What the book is about: A disheveled man collapses on a Paris street in front of Irene and Nell. It turns out Nell had once known the man, Quentin Stanhope. He tells a story of treachery and murder during the Afghan campaign, particularly the battle of Maiwand. He also tells of another secret agent, code name Tiger, who was probably a double agent and is still a threat to both Quentin and a physician named Watson, who had saved Quentin's life in Afghanistan. The name Watson is slightly familiar to Irene.

Other books you might like:
Lloyd Biggle Jr., *The Glendower Conspiracy: A Memoir of Sherlock Holmes*, 1990
L.B. Greenwood, *Sherlock Holmes and the Thistle of Scotland*, 1989
Edward B. Hanna, *The Whitechapel Horrors*, 1992
Nicholas Meyer, *The Seven-Percent Solution*, 1974
Elizabeth Peters, *The Amelia Peabody Series*, 1975-

443
Carole Nelson Douglas
Pussyfoot (New York: Tor, 1993)

Series: Midnight Louie

Story type: Amateur Detective

Major character(s): Midnight Louie, Animal (cat), Detective—Private; Temple Barr, Public Relations (free-lance)

Time period(s): 1990s

Locale(s): Las Vegas, Nevada

What the book is about: The death of the PR man for a Las Vegas stripper competition and the ensuing deaths of a couple of the strippers combine to get Midnight Louie and his "owner", Temple Barr, involved in the investigation, though the police think they should stay out. While Barr takes over the PR for the contest, Louie continues to carouse, while trying to provide Temple with the necessary clues to solve the murders.

Other books you might like:
Lydia Adamson, *A Cat in the Manger*, 1990
Lilian Jackson Braun, *The Cat Who Series*, 1966-
Rita Mae Brown, *Rest in Pieces*, 1992
Christopher Reed, *The Big Scratch*, 1988

444
Lauren Wright Douglas
Ninth Life (Tallahasse: Naiad, 1990)

Series: Caitlin Reece

Story type: Private Detective—Female Lead

Major character(s): Caitlin Reece, Detective—Private, Lesbian

Time period(s): 1990s

Locale(s): Vancouver, British Columbia, Canada

What the book is about: Hired by an animal rights organization, Ninth Life, to expose a cosmetics company thought to be using live animals in research, Caitlin soon becomes involved in murder, eco-terrorism, and with a rival rights group which appears to have as their goal a competing cosmetics company.

Other books you might like:
Kelly Bradford, *Footprints*, 1988
Vicki McConnell, *Double Daughter*, 1988
Eve Zaremba, *Beyond Hope*, 1988

445
Warwick Downing
A Clear Case of Murder (New York: Pocket, 1990)

Story type: Amateur Detective—Male Lead; Legal

Major character(s): David Reddman, Lawyer

Time period(s): 1990s

Locale(s): Sopris County, Colorado

What the book is about: An ex-rodeo star runs over a female lawyer. Was he drunk or homicidal—or both? The district attorney thinks it was murder but he is against a town that likes the rodeo star and didn't like the attorney. Enter David Reddman, newest attorney for the National Association of Special Prosecutors.

Other books you might like:
Philip Friedman, *Reasonable Doubt*, 1990
Fredrick D. Huebner, *Picture Postcard*, 1990
Douglas J. Keeling, *A Case of Innocence*, 1989
Ronald Levitsky, *The Love That Kills*, 1991
William G. Tapply, *Spotted Cats*, 1990

446
Warwick Downing
The Water Cure (New York: Pocket, 1992)

Story type: Police Procedural; Action/Adventure

Major character(s): Frances "Frankie" Rommel, Lawyer (special prosecutor); Doug Swift, Police Officer, Detective—Homicide

Time period(s): 1990s

Locale(s): Atlanta, Georgia; Denver, Colorado

What the book is about: A beautiful police informant is killed and this sets off a series of other killings which appear to be revenge motivated. Special procurator Frankie Rommel is called in on the case and she, along with homicide detective Doug Swift, soon discover that the case is personal.

Other books you might like:
Harrison Arnston, *Trade-Off*, 1992
Deborah Gordon, *Beating the Odds*, 1992
Zachary Klein, *Still Among the Living*, 1990
Ronald Levitsky, *The Love That Kills*, 1990

447
Alison Drake (Pseudonym of Trish Janeschutz)
High Strangeness (New York: Ballantine, 1992)

Series: Tango Key

Story type: Police Procedural; Private Detective

Major character(s): Aline Scott, Police Officer (detective); Ryan Kincaid, Detective—Private (lover of Aline)

Time period(s): 1990s

448 Dreyer

Locale(s): Tango Key, Florida

What the book is about: A mental patient, Margaret Wickerd, has escaped, killing a doctor and an orderly in the process. When Aline and her partner Bernie investigate they find discrepancies in the scenario that the staff of the hospital are propagating. Margaret was also involved with a flying saucer cult, all of whom are convinced they have been kidnapped by UFOs. When Kincaid is asked to go undercover at the hospital he uncovers more strange facts. What is going on and why is the government involved?

Other books you might like:
Douglas Allyn, *The Cheerio Killings*, 1990
Susan Dunlap, *The Jill Smith Series*, 1986
Ruby Horansky, *Dead Ahead*, 1990
Margaret Maron, *The Sigrid Harald Series*, 1982-
Julie Smith, *The Skip Langdon Series*, 1990-

448
Eileen Dreyer
A Man to Die For (New York: Harper, 1991)

Story type: Amateur Detective—Female Lead

Major character(s): Dale Hunsacker, Doctor (gynecologist); Casey McDonough, Nurse

Time period(s): 1990s

Locale(s): St. Louis, Missouri

What the book is about: New doctor Dale Hunsacker impresses everyone at work with his smile and charm—everyone that is except emergency room nurse Casey McDonough. When a nurse disappears and another one is killed—both soon after run-ins with Hunsacker—Casey's suspicions are aroused. When a prostitute, who Hunsacker also knew, is murdered, Casey goes to the police where she gets the brushoff. As she seeks evidence of his guilt, he acckowledges her suspicions with threats. First mystery.

Other books you might like:
Jo Bailey, *Bagged*, 1991
Robin Cook, *Vital Signs*, 1991
Patricia D. Cornwell, *Body of Evidence*, 1991
Susan Isaacs, *Compromising Positions*, 1978
Mary Kittredge, *Fatal Diagnosis*, 1990

449
John Keith Drummond
Mass Murder (New York: St. Martins, 1991)

Series: Matilda Worthing

Story type: Amateur Detective—Female Lead

Major character(s): Matilda Worthing, Businesswoman (retired); Martha Shaw, Businesswoman (retired)

Time period(s): 1990s

Locale(s): Jolliston, California

What the book is about: Someone has poisoned a priest during communion and the bishop asks Matilda Worthing to see what she can find out. She uncovers unexpected secrets in the church including dabblers in the occult.

Other books you might like:
Joyce Christmas, *Suddenly in Her Sorbet*, 1988
Isabelle Holland, *A Death at St. Anselm's*, 1984
Melodie Johnson Howe, *The Mother Shadow*, 1989
Sister Carol Anne O'Marie, *Advent of Dying*, 1986
Virginia Rich, *The Nantucket Diet Murders*, 1985

450
Bruce Ducker
Bankroll (New York: Dutton, 1989)

Story type: Psychological Suspense

Major character(s): Spector, Businessman (Wall Street hotshot)

Time period(s): 1980s

What the book is about: Bored with Wall Street, Spector decides to forge a new life for himself involving fraud and new identities.

Other books you might like:
Patricia Highsmith, *The Talented Mr. Ripley*, 1955

451
Margaret Duffy
Man of Blood (New York: St. Martin's, 1992)

Story type: Action/Adventure; Police Procedural—Male Lead

Major character(s): Piers Ashley, Police Officer (undercover)

Time period(s): 1990s

Locale(s): London, England (Ashleigh Coombe)

What the book is about: Piers Ashley is a member of F9, a secret undercover department that infiltrates gangs and even serve prison terms to gain favor with gang leaders. Piers has just finished one such term and is in ill-favor with his family. He returns to the family home just in time to be a suspect in the murder of a local. Then strange accidents start happening to his family.

Other books you might like:
Jeffrey Ashford, *The Honourable Detective*, 1989
Ruth Dudley Edwards, *The English School of Murder*, 1990
Michael Gilbert, *End-Game*, 1982
Noah Webster, *The Jonathan Gaunt Series*, 1977

452
Margaret Duffy
Rook-Shoot (New York: St. Martin's, 1991)

Series: Langley and Gillard

Story type: Espionage; Action/Adventure

Major character(s): Ingrid Langley, Spy (retired MI5 agent), Writer; Patrick Gillard, Spy (retired MI5 agent)

Time period(s): 1990s

Locale(s): Wales

What the book is about: An appeal for help from Patrick's brother Larry takes Ingrid and Patrick to Wales to investigate a series of bizarre and malicious events, one of which is the hit and run killing of a couple. They soon find themselves involved with a survival school that trains international terrorists.

Other books you might like:
Paul Myers, *The Mark Holland Series*, 1986-
Peter O'Donnell, *The Modesty Blaise Series*, 1965-
David Williams, *The Mark Treasure Series*, 1972-

453
Margaret Duffy
Who Killed Cock Robin? (New York: St. Martins, 1990)

Series: Langley and Gillard

Story type: Espionage

Major character(s): Ingrid Langley, Spy (retired MI5 agent), Writer; Patrick Gillard, Spy (retired MI5 agent)

Locale(s): London, England

What the book is about: Ingrid and Patrick's friend and colleague Terry, code name "Robon," is killed in a bombing. While still mourning, they are assigned to investigate the murder of a higher-up. Ingrid is kidnapped and learns Terry may be alive.

Other books you might like:
Palma Harcourt, *Dance for Diplomats*, 1976
John Le Carre, *Tinker, Tailor, Soldier, Spy*, 1974
S.K. Wolf, *The Harbinger Effect*, 1989

454
Harris Dulaney
One Kiss Led to Another (New York: HarperCollins, 1994)

Story type: Private Detective—Male Lead

Major character(s): Cornelius Leeds, Detective—Private

Time period(s): 1990s

Locale(s): Atlantic City, New Jersey; New York, New York (Brooklyn)

What the book is about: Private eye Cornelius "Connie" Leeds is hired by wealthy Ben Arnold to look for his runaway 17-year-old granddaughter Bonnie. Connie finds her and gets her back to her family but soon thereafter she is found dead of a drug overdose in a Brooklyn park. Not believing that her death was self-inflicted, Connie sets out to find the truth. First novel.

Other books you might like:
James Lee Burke, *A Stained White Radiance*, 1992
Robert Crais, *Free Fall*, 1993
Zachary Klein, *Still Among the Living*, 1990
Benjamin M. Schutz, *A Fistful of Empty*, 1991
Philip Lee Williams, *Slow Dance in Autumn*, 1988

455
Sarah Dunant
Birthmarks (New York: Doubleday, 1992)

Story type: Private Detective—Female Lead

Major character(s): Hannah Wolfe, Detective—Private

Time period(s): 1990s

Locale(s): London, England

What the book is about: Hannah is hired by Carolyn Hamilton's former ballet teacher to find her—she has disappeared and left no forwarding address. Just as Hannah starts her investigation, Carolyn's body is found in the Thames. An autopsy reveals she was pregnant and when the police find a suicide note in her apartment they consider the case closed. But it is not closed to Hannah because she knows that the note was not in the apartment until after Carolyn was already dead.

Other books you might like:
Liza Cody, *The Anna Lee Series*, 1980-
Lesley Grant-Adamson, *Too Many Questions*, 1991
Jennie Melville, *The Charmian Daniels Series*, 1962-
Susan Moody, *The Penny Wanawake Series*, 1984-
Erica Quest, *The Kate Maddox Series*, 1988-

456
Sarah Dunant
Under My Skin (New York: Scribners, 1995)

Story type: Private Detective—Female Lead

Major character(s): Hannah Wolfe, Detective—Private

Time period(s): 1990s

Locale(s): Berkshire, England

What the book is about: There are nefarious doings at the Castle Dean health spa. Reluctant to take the case, Hannah nonetheless perseveres and quickly discovers what's going on. This convinces the spa's owner, Olivia Marchant, that Hannah is just the person to look into a series of threatening notes that her husband, a well-known plastic surgeon, has been receiving. This case may be as easy to solve—suicide and murder lay ahead for some people.

Other books you might like:
Liza Cody, *The Anna Lee Series*, 1981-
P.D. James, *An Unsuitable Job for a Woman*, 1972
Val McDermid, *Crack Down*, 1994

457
Sophie Dunbar
Behind Eclaire's Doors (New York: St. Martins, 1993)

Story type: Amateur Detective

Major character(s): Claire Claiborne, Hairdresser (owner of a beauty salon); Dan Claiborne, Lawyer (Claire's ex-husband and fiance)

Time period(s): 1990s

Locale(s): New Orleans, Louisiana

What the book is about: Claire Claiborne has just opened her beauty salon and is trying to get it established. She has also become engaged to her ex-husband, Dan, who swears his womanizing is a thing of the past. However, there is a strange relationship between him and the beautiful French manicurist, Angie. Most people think they are having an affair. Then Claire discovers Dan standing over Angie's dead body covered in her blood. First novel.

458
Duncan

Other books you might like:
Deborah Adams, *All the Great Pretenders*, 1992
Denise Dietz, *Throw Darts at a Cheesecake*, 1992
Charlaine Harris, *A Bone to Pick*, 1992
Leslie Meier, *Mail-Order Murder*, 1991
Patricia Houck Sprinkle, *Murder in the Charleston Manner*, 1990

458
W. Glenn Duncan
Rafferty: Fatal Sisters (New York: Fawcett, 1990)
Series: Rafferty
Story type: Private Detective
Major character(s): Rafferty, Detective—Private; Hilda Gardner, Businesswoman (antiques dealer)
Time period(s): 1990s
Locale(s): Dallas, Texas
What the book is about: Patty Aleister thinks her missing husband, Sherm, is a secret agent on a mission. Rafferty thinks he is a philandering husband who forgot to come home. They're both wrong. And when Sherm turns up dead, the case turns very ugly.

Other books you might like:
Richard Abshire, *Dallas Drop*, 1988
Edward Mathis, *The Dan Roman Series*, 1985-
Robert B. Parker, *Promised Land*, 1976
Robert J. Ray, *Cage of Mirrors*, 1980
James Reasoner, *Texas Wind*, 1980

459
Wayne Dundee
The Skintight Shroud (New York: St. Martin's, 1989)
Series: Joe Hannibal
Story type: Private Detective—Male Lead
Major character(s): Joe Hannibal, Detective—Private
Time period(s): 1980s
Locale(s): Rockford, Illinois
What the book is about: After two porn stars are murdered, Hannibal is hired to find out who killed them and why.

Other books you might like:
Max Allan Collins, *The Baby Blue Rip Off*, 1983
Rob Kantner, *The Back Door Man*, 1986
Michael Z. Lewin, *Ask the Right Question*, 1971
John Lutz, *The Right to Sing the Blues*, 1985
Sara Paretsky, *Burn Marks*, 1990

460
Susan Dunlap
Death and Taxes (New York: Delacorte, 1992)
Series: Jill Smith
Story type: Police Procedural—Female Lead
Major character(s): Jill Smith, Detective—Homicide
Time period(s): 1990s
Locale(s): Berkeley, California
What the book is about: Is anyone sorry about the murder of IRS auditor Philip Drem? It seems not, as he has quite a reputation as the auditor from hell and there are no shortage of suspects—including a prominent tax consultant and one of Jill Smith's collegues, another police officer.

Other books you might like:
M.D. Lake, *The Peggy O'Neill Series*, 1989-
Margaret Maron, *One Coffee With*, 1982
Lee Martin, *Deficit Ending*, 1990
Lillian O'Donnell, *No Business Being a Cop*, 1979
Martha G. Webb, *Darling Corey's Dead*, 1984

461
Susan Dunlap
Diamond in the Buff (New York: St. Martin's, 1990)
Series: Jill Smith
Story type: Police Procedural—Female Lead
Major character(s): Jill Smith, Detective—Homicide
Time period(s): 1980s
Locale(s): Berkeley, California
What the book is about: What caused the nude, sunbathing dentist to claim that he was attacked by a branch of a eucalyptus tree?

Other books you might like:
M.D. Lake, *Amends for Murder*, 1989
Margaret Maron, *Death of a Butterfly*, 1984
Marcia Muller, *The Shape of Dread*, 1989
Martha G. Webb, *Darling Corey's Dead*, 1984

462
Susan Dunlap
Pious Deception (New York: Villard, 1989)
Series: Kiernan O'Shaughnessy
Story type: Private Detective—Female Lead
Major character(s): Kiernan O'Shaughnessy, Detective—Private, Doctor (forensic pathologist)
Time period(s): 1980s
Locale(s): Phoenix, Arizona (harsh desert community outside Phoenix); La Jolla, California
What the book is about: Dr. O'Shaughnessy is called from her base in La Jolla, California to Phoenix to decide if a dead young priest committed suicide or hanged himself accidently—or maybe was murdered.

Other books you might like:
Mary Higgins Clark, *The Cradle Will Fall*, 1980
John R. Feegel, *Death Sails the Bay*, 1980
Marcia Muller, *The Shape of Dread*, 1989
Shelley Singer, *Free Draw*, 1984
Julie Smith, *Death Turns a Trick*, 1982

463
Susan Dunlap
Rogue Wave (New York: Villard, 1991)
Series: Kiernan O'Shaugnessy
Story type: Private Detective—Female Lead
Major character(s): Kiernan O'Shaughnessy, Detective—Private, Doctor (former medical examiner)
Time period(s): 1990s
Locale(s): San Francisco, California
What the book is about: Kiernan is called back to San Francisco to investigate a drowning that may not be a drowning and a hit and run from three years before that may be connected to the drowning that may not be a drowning. In doing this she also has to confront her own past and that of a former lover.
Other books you might like:
Patricia D. Cornwell, *Body of Evidence*, 1991
Herbert Lieberman, *City of the Dead*, 1976
Marcia Muller, *Where Echoes Live*, 1991
Joyce Anne Schneider, *Darkness Falls*, 1989

464
Susan Dunlap
Time Expired (New York: Delacorte, 1993)
Series: Jill Smith
Story type: Police Procedural—Female Lead
Major character(s): Jill Smith, Detective—Homicide
Time period(s): 1990s
Locale(s): Berkeley, California
What the book is about: Someone is preying on meter maids and after the report of a kidnapping turns out to be only a rubber-maid doll, detective Jill Smith is seriously annoyed. She visits a nursing home near the site of the alleged kidnapping in hopes that one of the residents noticed something. There she finds lawyer Madeleine Riordan dying of cancer. Convinced that Riordan knows something but isn't telling she decides to come back the next evening. Before she can, Riordan is smothered. The meter maid crimes continue while Smith searches for the killer and the connection between the crimes.
Other books you might like:
M.D. Lake, *The Peggy O'Neill Series*, 1989-
Margaret Maron, *The Sigrid Harald Series*, 1985-
Lee Martin, *The Deb Ralston Series*, 1987-
Lillian O'Donnell, *The Norah Mulcahaney Series*, 1972-
Martha G. Webb, *Darling Corey's Dead*, 1984

465
Carola Dunn
The Winter Garden Mystery (New York: St. Martin's, 1995)
Series: Daisy Dalrymple
Story type: Historical; Amateur Detective—Female Lead
Major character(s): Daisy Dalrymple, Writer; Alec Fletcher, Police Officer
Time period(s): 1920s (1923)
Locale(s): Occleswich, England
What the book is about: Daisy, much to the scandal of her family, has taken a job as a magazine writer and has left home to live on her own. She has recently wangled a stay at Occle's Hall and is planning on writing a story about it and the local village. Soon after her arrival, the body of a young maid is found, buried in the winter garden. The maid, who was thought to have run off with a peddler, was pregnant at the time of her death. A young gardener is arrested for the crime, but Daisy senses that there is much more to the crime and enlists the aid of her friend, Inspector Fletcher, to investigate.
Other books you might like:
K.K. Beck, *The Iris Cooper Series*, 1984-
Carole Nelson Douglas, *The Irene Adler Series*, 1991-
Marian J.A. Jackson, *The Abigail Danforth Series*, 1990-
Dianne Day, *The Strange Files of Fremont Jones*, 1995
Robin Paige, *Death at Gallows Green*, 1995

466
John Dunning
Booked to Die (New York: Scribners, 1992)
Series: Cliff Janeway
Story type: Amateur Detective—Male Lead
Major character(s): Cliff Janeway, Store Owner (rare book dealer; former cop)
Time period(s): 1990s
Locale(s): Denver, Colorado
What the book is about: Cliff Janeway has quit the police force and opened up a used and rare bookstore. When one of Denver's book scouts (a person who makes part of his or her living from selling books to booksellers) is killed, Janeway finds himself thrown back into the role of crime-solver. Was the book scout killed as a warning to Janeway by an old nemesis, or did the killing have something to do with the book business?
Other books you might like:
Jon L. Breen, *Touch of the Past*, 1988
Wayne Warga, *Hardcover*, 1987

467
John Dunning
The Bookman's Wake (New York: Scribners, 1995)
Series: Cliff Janeway
Story type: Private Detective—Male Lead
Major character(s): Cliff Janeway, Detective—Private, Businessman (bookseller; rare book dealer); Trish Aandahl, Journalist (reporter)
Time period(s): 1990s
Locale(s): Seattle, Washington (cross-country)

What the book is about: Janeway has been hired to bring back bail-jumper Eleanor Rigby from Seattle. He was chosen because the case involves rare books, specifically an unknown book from a small press that only exists in rumor. Or does it? Janeway, Rigby (after she disappears on him), and reporter Trish Aandahl team up to try and track down the truth and the book. There are pitfalls along the way—including murder.

Other books you might like:
Lawrence Block, *The Burglar Who Traded Ted Williams*, 1994
Gerry Boyle, *Deadline*, 1993
Robert A. Carter, *Casual Slaughters*, 1992
Andrew Klavan, *Corruption*, 1993
Richard A. Lupoff, *The Cover Girl Killer*, 1995

468
Joseph Eastburn
Kiss Them Goodbye (New York: Morrow, 1993)

Story type: Police Procedural—Male Lead; Action/Adventure

Major character(s): Nick Fowler, Police Officer; Maureen McCauley, Journalist (reporter)

Time period(s): 1990s

Locale(s): Ravenstown, New York (upstate)

What the book is about: There is a serial killer stalking the students at an exclusive boy's prep school in upstate New York. Detective Nick Fowler arrives to take charge of the case and almost immediately alienates all involved. Included in this group is reporter Maureen McCauley, who may be trying to undermine his investigation with her stories. At least that is their effect. Their antagonism soon turns to attraction, further complicating things. First novel.

Other books you might like:
W. Edward Blain, *Passion Play*, 1990
Richard LaPlante, *Mantis*, 1993
James Patterson, *Along Came a Spider*, 1993
Michael Weaver, *Impulse*, 1993
David Wiltse, *Prayer for the Dead*, 1991

469
Marjorie Eccles
Late of This Parish (New York: St. Martin's, 1994)

Story type: Police Procedural—Male Lead

Major character(s): Gil Mayo, Police Officer (detective chief inspector); Martin Kite, Police Officer (detective sergeant)

Time period(s): 1990s

Locale(s): Lavenstock, England

What the book is about: Chief Inspector Mayo and his crew are investigating the murder of the Reverend Cecil Willard, the retired headmaster of the Uplands House School. He was a man of strong convictions and moral rectitude, just the kind of man to be hated. He was keeping his daughter from marrying the man she loved and was creating enemies in choosing the new headmaster of the school. But are these motives for murder? And who or what is the cryptic reference to S A R A found in his diary?

Other books you might like:
Catherine Aird, *The Inspector Sloane Series*, 1966-
Clare Curzon, *The Yeadings and Mott Series*, 1979-
Caroline Graham, *The Inspector Barnaby Series*, 1988-
Cynthia Harrod-Eagles, *The Inspector Slider Series*, 1991-
Susannah Stacey, *The Superintendent Bone Series*, 1987-

470
Marjorie Eccles
More Deaths than One (New York: Doubleday, 1991)

Story type: Police Procedural—Male Lead

Major character(s): Gil Mayo, Police Officer (detective chief inspector); Martin Kite, Police Officer (detective sergeant)

Time period(s): 1990s

Locale(s): Coventry, England

What the book is about: Freelance journalist Rupert Fleming is found dead of a shotgun blast - an apparent suicide complete with note. When the post mortem reveals that he had been drugged, Mayo realizes he has a murder on his hands.

Other books you might like:
Catherine Aird, *Some Die Eloquent*, 1980
Douglas Clark, *The Masters and Green Series*, 1969-1988
Reginald Hill, *The Dalziel and Pascoe Series*, 1970-
Dorothy Simpson, *Puppet for a Corpse*, 1983
Susannah Stacey, *Grave Responsibility*, 1990

471
A.E. Eddenden
Murder on the Thirteenth (Chicago: Academy Chicago, 1992)

Series: Albert Tretheway

Story type: Police Procedural—Male Lead

Major character(s): Albert Tretheway, Police Officer (assigned to air raid duty)

Time period(s): 1940s (1943)

Locale(s): Fort York, Ontario, Canada

What the book is about: On January 13th, 1943, during a practice blackout, a strange fire is noticed in the marsh near town. When Tretheway, who has been appointed head of air raid wardens for the area, investigates he finds evidence of someone conducting rites involved with witchcraft. Nobody gives it much notice but on the 13th of the following months, strange things happen, finally culminating in the suspicious death of two of the air raid wardens.

Other books you might like:
Nicholas Blake, *The Nigel Strangeways Series*, 1935-1966
Christianna Brand, *Green for Danger*, 1944
John Dickson Carr, *The Gideon Fell Series*, 1933-1968
Carter Dickson, *The Sir Henry Merrivale Series*, 1935-1954

472
Ruth Dudley Edwards
Clubbed to Death (New York: St. Martin's, 1992)

Series: Robert Amiss

Story type: Police Procedural—Male Lead; Humor

Major character(s): Robert Amiss, Unemployed (ex-civil servant); Ellis Pooley, Police Officer (sergeant, C.I.D.)

Time period(s): 1990s

Locale(s): London, England

What the book is about: Robert Amiss is once again approached by his friend, Ellis Pooley, to do some undercover work for the police. He is to get a job at the Ffeatherstonehaugh (pronounce Fanshaw) Club and investigate the death of the club secretary, which could be suicide or murder. He becomes involved with the strangest and most eccentric group of people he has ever known. But is one of them the murderer?

Other books you might like:
Catherine Aird, *The Inspector Sloane Series*, 1966-
Robert Barnard, *Death by Sheer Torture*, 1981
Joyce Porter, *The Inspector Dover Series*, 1964-1990
Colin Watson, *The Inspector Purbright Series*, 1958-1982
R.D. Wingfield, *The Frost Series*, 1984-

473
Selma Eichler
Murder Can Kill Your Social Life (New York: Signet, 1994)

Story type: Private Detective—Female Lead

Major character(s): Desiree Shapiro, Detective—Private, Widow(er)

Time period(s): 1990s

Locale(s): New York, New York

What the book is about: Desiree Shapiro doesn't normally take murder cases. She specializes in divorce and insurance work. She is talked into one by her niece, Ellen. Desiree is staying with Ellen while her apartment is being painted and during the night an old lady one floor above them is robbed and killed. The police suspect a local delivery boy and Desiree is hired by the boy's boss to prove his innocence. Then another murder occurs in the same building. First novel.

Other books you might like:
Valerie Frankel, *Deadline for Murder*, 1991
Lillian O'Donnell, *The Gwen Ramadge Series*, 1990-
Marissa Piesman, *Unorthodox Practices*, 1989
Dorian Yeager, *Eviction by Death*, 1993
Sharon Zukowski, *Dancing in the Dark*, 1992

474
Randy Lee Eickoff
The Gombeen Man (New York: Walker, 1992)

Story type: Action/Adventure

Major character(s): Con Edwards, Journalist; Maeve Nolan, Widow(er)

Time period(s): 1970s (1979)

Locale(s): England; Ireland

What the book is about: Retired IRA shooter Conor Larkin is gunned down on the docks on Manchester. His friend, American journalist Con Edwards, shows up with Maeve, Larkin's widow and Con's former lover, to find a motive for the shooting. The British security service is also interested. When there are two attempts on their lives Con and Maeve run to Ireland. There they try to sort out friends from enemies.

Other books you might like:
Tom Clancy, *Patriot Games*, 1986
Norman Flood, *To Killashea*, 1989
James Graham, *The Run to Morning*, 1974
Jack Higgins, *Touch the Devil*, 1982

475
Bill Eidson
Dangerous Waters (New York: Holt, 1991)

Story type: Amateur Detective—Male Lead; Action/Adventure

Major character(s): Riley Burke, Advertising

Time period(s): 1990s

Locale(s): Boston, Massachusetts

What the book is about: Riley Burke is about to end ten years of fidelity to his wife, Ellen. While waiting for Rachel to ride out to his boat, a young man, also waiting for the launch, is attacked. Riley intervenes and manages to save the man. The next day the man's body is found beneath Riley's boat. The police think Riley knows more than he is telling and when Ellen is attacked he realizes the attacker thinks so too.

Other books you might like:
Alan Dennis Burke, *Dead Wrong*, 1990
W.J. Chaput, *Dead in the Water*, 1991
Doug Hornig, *Waterman*, 1986
Don Matheson, *Stray Cat*, 1987
John Walter Putre, *A Small and Incidental Murder*, 1990

476
Aaron Elkins
Dead Men's Hearts (New York: Mysterious, 1994)

Series: Gideon Oliver

Story type: Amateur Detective—Male Lead

Major character(s): Gideon Oliver, Anthropologist (forensic anthropologist)

Time period(s): 1990s

Locale(s): Valley of the Nile, Egypt

What the book is about: Gideon Oliver and his wife, Julie, have been offered a free trip to the Valley of the Nile and an archaeological dig if Gideon will do the narration for a documentary being shot at the same time. He accepts and is soon involved in the discovery of some bones in a storage shed at the dig. They prove to be ancient, but how did they get there? Is somebody involved in a joke? It isn't long before there is a much fresher corpse to examine—the much despised head of the expedition. Gideon is once again drawn into trying to solve the murder.

477 Elkins

Other books you might like:
Patricia D. Cornwell, *The Kay Scarpetta Series*, 1990-
D.J. Donaldson, *Blood on the Bayou*, 1991
Louise Hendricksen, *With Deadly Intent*, 1993
Linda Mariz, *Body English*, 1992
Elizabeth Peters, *The Amelia Peabody Series*, 1975-

477
Aaron Elkins
A Glancing Light (New York: Scribners, 1991)
Series: Chris Norgren
Story type: Amateur Detective—Male Lead
Major character(s): Chris Norgren, Museum Curator (of the Seattle Art Museum)
Time period(s): 1990s
Locale(s): Bologna, Italy
What the book is about: When a stolen Reubens shows up in a shipment of cheap reproductions from Bologna, Chris, who is traveling to Bologna to oversee the shipping of a collection of paintings to the U.S., is enlisted by the FBI as an information source. He is to ask questions about a series of art thefts and report to the Italian police.
Other books you might like:
Peter Clothier, *Chiaroscuro*, 1985
Carolyn Coker, *The Balmoral Nude*, 1990
John Malcolm, *A Back Room in Somers Town*, 1984
Joan Smith, *Follow That Blonde*, 1990
Wayne Warga, *Fatal Impressions*, 1989

478
Aaron Elkins
Make No Bones (New York: Mysterious, 1991)
Series: Gideon Oliver
Story type: Amateur Detective—Male Lead
Major character(s): Gideon Oliver, Anthropologist (forensic anthropologist); John Lau, Police Officer (FBI agent)
Time period(s): 1990s
Locale(s): Bend, Oregon
What the book is about: Ten years ago, the dean of forensic anthropology, Albert Jasper, died after a party with his students. Now his former students and colleagues are gathering for a seminar. The highlight will be the donating of Jasper's bones to a museum. The bones are stolen before they can be viewed. Then Dr. Oliver discovers a grave with a body that seems to have been killed ten years ago. Before Gideon and Lau can determine what happened years ago, they have a much fresher corpse to work on.
Other books you might like:
Patricia D. Cornwell, *Postmortem*, 1990
D.J. Donaldson, *Blood on the Bayou*, 1991
Susan Dunlap, *Rogue Wave*, 1991
Thomas T. Noguchi, *Unnatural Causes*, 1988 (Arthur Lyons, co-author)
Walter Satterthwait, *At Ease with the Dead*, 1990

479
Aaron Elkins
Old Scores (New York: Scribners, 1993)
Series: Chris Norgren
Story type: Amateur Detective—Male Lead
Major character(s): Chris Norgren, Museum Curator (of the Seattle Art Museum)
Time period(s): 1990s
Locale(s): France
What the book is about: Seattle Art Museum curator Chris Norgren has been offered a Rembrandt for the museum. There are a couple of catches, however. He must go to France to get it, the person offering it is less than reputable, and he is forbidden to get scientific authentication. And then, soon after Chris' arrival in France the dealer turns up dead. Chris must find the killer if he wants to keep the painting.
Other books you might like:
Jonathan Gash, *The Very Last Gambado*, 1990
Charles A. Goodrum, *A Slip of the Tong*, 1992
Marcia Muller, *Dark Star*, 1989
Elizabeth Peters, *Street of the Five Moons*, 1978
Wayne Warga, *Fatal Impressions*, 1989

480
Aaron Elkins
Co-Author: Charlotte Elkins
A Wicked Slice (New York: St. Martin's, 1989)
Story type: Police Procedural; Amateur Detective
Major character(s): Lee Ofsted, Sports Figure (professional golfer); Graham Sheldon, Police Officer (Lee's lover)
Time period(s): 1980s
Locale(s): Carmel, California
What the book is about: When the star of the women's pro golf tour is murdered, Lee Ofsted is the prime suspect. Detective Sheldon falls for her in the course of the investigation and together they go about finding the real murderer.
Other books you might like:
Brian Ball, *Death of a Low-Handicap Man*, 1978
Caroline Cooney, *Sand Trap*, 1984
Janice Law, *Death under Par*, 1981
Keith Miles, *Bullet Hole*, 1986
Keith Miles, *Double Eagle*, 1988

481
Charlotte Elkins
Co-Author: Aaron Elkins
Rotten Lies (New York: Mysterious, 1995)
Series: Lee Ofsted
Story type: Amateur Detective—Female Lead
Major character(s): Lee Ofsted, Sports Figure (professional golfer); Graham Sheldon, Police Officer (Lee's lover)
Time period(s): 1990s
Locale(s): Los Alamos, New Mexico

What the book is about: Lee has just finished a dream round on the first day of the High Desert Classic, setting a course record. During the second round, however, she discovers a body and injures her arm trying to revive the man. He was apparently struck by lightning, but the police think it might have been murder. Meanwhile, Lee has been offered a job doing color commentary for television since her arm injury has forced her to withdraw. Soon after, another body shows up. Lee asks for Graham's help when it seems she might be the next victim.

Other books you might like:
James Y. Bartlett, *Death Is a Two-Stroke Penalty*, 1990
Alison Gordon, *Night Game*, 1993
John Logue, *Murder on the Links*, 1996
Martina Navratilova, *The Total Zone*, 1995 (Liz Nickles, co-author)
Robert Upton, *Dead on the Stick*, 1986

482
Thorton Elliott
Hard Guy (New York: Fine, 1992)

Story type: Action/Adventure

Major character(s): Glenn Odum, Veteran, Criminal

Time period(s): 1990s

Locale(s): Tennessee

What the book is about: Glenn Odum, trying to stay straight, takes over a friend's pit bull operation - and the guy's beautiful friend. It seems life is finally going his way when his ex-wife shows up asking for his help and protection. Seems she robbed a small time crime boss and his son and is now trying to blackmail them. First novel.

Other books you might like:
Tom Kakonis, *Criss Cross*, 1990
Joe R. Lansdale, *The Savage Season*, 1990
Elmore Leonard, *Stick*, 1983
Timothy Watts, *Cons*, 1993
Charles Willeford, *Cockfighter*, 1972

483
James Ellroy
L.A. Confidential (New York: Mysterious, 1990)

Series: L.A. Quartet

Story type: Action/Adventure

Major character(s): Ed Exley, Police Officer (father was a cop); Bud White, Police Officer (watched father kill mother)

Time period(s): 1950s

Locale(s): Los Angeles, California

What the book is about: Set in the 1950s this book follows the careers of three policemen as they work with and against each other to eliminate, or at least control, corruption.

Other books you might like:
Max Allan Collins, *True Detective*, 1983
Ross Thomas, *The Fourth Durango*, 1989
Teri White, *Tightrope*, 1986

484
James Elward
Monday's Child Is Dead (New York: Carroll & Graf, 1995)

Story type: Amateur Detective—Male Lead

Major character(s): Horace Livsey, Professor (retired history professor); Ginny Karr, Student (acting; Horace's niece)

Time period(s): 1990s

Locale(s): New York, New York

What the book is about: Ginny is coming to New York to study acting. Fortunately for Horace's peace of mind, she doesn't want to stay with him. She is sharing an apartment with a well-known model. Before Ginny arrives, however, the model is murdered. Prior to her death she had sent Horace a package—an album of photographs. Bright and bubbly Ginny leads Horace into investigating the murder. First mystery.

Other books you might like:
Robert A. Carter, *The Nicholas Barlow Series*, 1992-
Desmond Cory, *The John Dobie Series*, 1991-
David Handler, *The Stewart Hoag Series*, 1988-
M.K. Lorens, *The Winston Sherman Series*, 1990-1993
Michael W. Sherer, *Little Use for Death*, 1992

485
Ron Ely
East Beach (New York: Simon & Schuster, 1995)

Series: Jake Sands

Story type: Action/Adventure; Private Detective—Male Lead

Major character(s): Jake Sands, Detective—Private (retired)

Time period(s): 1990s

Locale(s): Santa Barbara, California

What the book is about: Jake has retired from the business after his wife and child were murdered. He is trying to take it easy on the beach in Santa Barbara. However, when a young and pretty waitress that he has just been talking with is found murdered, he is drawn back into investigating. He is also drawn into the worlds of high-stakes beach volleyball and international finance. More people start to die and Jake may be next.

Other books you might like:
Jerome Doolittle, *The Tom Bethany Series*, 1990-
John D. MacDonald, *The Travis McGee Series*, 1964-1985
A.E. Maxwell, *The Fiddler Series*, 1985-
William Sanders, *The Taggert Roper Series*, 1991-
Benjamin M. Schutz, *Mexico Is Forever*, 1994

486
Ron Ely
Night Shadows (New York: Simon & Schuster, 1994)

Series: Jake Sands

Story type: Private Detective—Male Lead

Major character(s): Jake Sands, Detective—Private (ex-soldier)

Time period(s): 1990s

Locale(s): Santa Barbara, California

What the book is about: Ex-soldier, ex-spy, part-time bounty hunter, and private eye Jake Sands has two cases on his hands. He discovers a dead jogger and is asked to find a good looking blonde's husband. It may turn out that the two cases are connected. Could it be that someone is trying to set Jake up for a fall? First novel.

Other books you might like:
Jack Barnao, *The John Locke Series*, 1987-
Michael Collins, *The Dan Fortune Series*, 1967-
Sue Grafton, *The Kinsey Millhone Series*, 1984-
Thomas Perry, *Sleeping Dogs*, 1992
Robert J. Ray, *The Matt Murdock Series*, 1987-

487
Earl Emerson
Help Wanted: Orphans Preferred (New York: Morrow, 1990)

Series: Mac Fontana

Story type: Police Procedural—Male Lead

Major character(s): Mac Fontana, Fire Fighter (part-time sheriff)

Time period(s): 1980s

Locale(s): Washington

What the book is about: Someone is harassing, and killing, Fontana's men. As he tries to figure out what's going on he finds himself attracted to a married woman, which doesn't make things any easier.

Other books you might like:
Richard Hoyt, *Decoys*, 1980
J.A. Jance, *Until Proven Guilty*, 1985
Dennis Smith, *Glitter and Ash*, 1980
Kay Nolte Smith, *Catching Fire*, 1982

488
Earl Emerson
Morons and Madmen (New York: Morrow, 1993)

Series: Mac Fontana

Story type: Police Procedural—Male Lead

Major character(s): Mac Fontana, Fire Fighter (arson investigator); Laura Sanderson, Journalist (writer)

Time period(s): 1990s

Locale(s): Seattle, Washington

What the book is about: Mac Fontana has been approached by fire fighter Diane Cooper to investigate a fire in which three other fire fighters died. Diane survived and while there was no official action, Diane can't remember what happened and this has put the entire affirmative action program under a cloud. Mac, survivor of a similar fatal fire, is sympathetic and agrees to investigate. What he finds is a strange wall of silence from the officials involved. Can he find the truth?

Other books you might like:
Richard Hoyt, *The John Denson Series*, 1980-
Frederick D. Huebner, *Judgement by Fire*, 1988
J.A. Jance, *The J.P. Beaumont Series*, 1985-
Kay Nolte Smith, *Catching Fire*, 1982

489
Earl Emerson
The Portland Laugher (New York: Ballantine, 1994)

Series: Thomas Black

Story type: Private Detective—Male Lead

Major character(s): Thomas Black, Detective—Private; Elmer "Snake" Slezak, Detective—Private; Kathy Birchfield, Lawyer

Time period(s): 1990s

Locale(s): Seattle, Washington

What the book is about: Thomas Black is lying in a coma, with little memory of how he got that way. Unable to speak or move, he tries to reconstruct what happened. It started when "Snake" Slezak introduced him to Rosiland Lake and her foster son. They wanted Thomas to follow Philip Bacon, who may have been harassing an ex-con named Billy Battle. Thomas would like to get something on Philip because he is engaged to Kathy Birchfield, the woman Thomas loves.

Other books you might like:
Richard Hoyt, *The John Denson Series*, 1980-
Frederick D. Huebner, *The Matt Riordan Series*, 1986-
Rob Kantner, *The Ben Perkins Series*, 1987-
Bill Pronzini, *The Nameless Detective Series*, 1971-
Benjamin M. Schutz, *The Leo Haggerty Series*, 1984

490
Earl Emerson
The Vanishing Smile (New York: Ballantine, 1995)

Series: Thomas Black

Story type: Private Detective—Male Lead

Major character(s): Thomas Black, Detective—Private; Kathy Birchfield, Lawyer

Time period(s): 1990s

Locale(s): Seattle, Washington

What the book is about: Thomas' relationship with Kathy, the woman he loves, has been strained at best ever since he accidently shot and killed her fiance. Now Kathy asks Thomas to meet with one of her clients, Marian Wright. On the way to the meeting, Kathy hits a person with her car. When the victim turns out to be her client, Kathy is distraught. Thomas suspects all is not as it seems and begins to investigate. Marian had been helping several women track down men in their lives and maybe one of them really doesn's want to be found.

Other books you might like:
Richard Hoyt, *The John Denson Series*, 1980-
Frederick D. Huebner, *The Matt Riordan Series*, 1986-
Robert R. Irvine, *The Moroni Traveler Series*, 1988-
Rob Kantner, *The Ben Perkins Series*, 1986-
Walter Satterthwait, *The Joshua Croft Series*, 1988-

491
Earl Emerson
Yellow Dog Party (New York: Morrow, 1991)
Series: Thomas Black
Story type: Private Detective—Male Lead
Major character(s): Thomas Black, Detective—Private; Kathy Birchfield, Lawyer
Time period(s): 1990s
Locale(s): Seattle, Washington
What the book is about: What seems to be Thomas Black's simplest case turns deadly. Black was asked to set up dream dates for four businessmen which seemed simple at the time, but one of them has an ulterior motive and things soon turn ugly. An attempted hanging and double murder soon let Black know that things aren't what they seem.
Other books you might like:
Stuart Brock, *Killer's Choice*, 1956
Richard Hoyt, *Decoys*, 1980
Fredrick D. Huebner, *Picture Postcard*, 1990
Richard Hugo, *Death and the Good Life*, 1981

492
L.L. Enger (Pseudonym of Leif Enger and Len Enger)
Strike (New York: Pocket, 1992)
Series: Gun Pedersen
Story type: Amateur Detective—Male Lead
Major character(s): Gun Pedersen, Sports Figure (former baseball player); Carol Long, Journalist (reporter)
Time period(s): 1990s
Locale(s): Stony Lake, Minnesota
What the book is about: While hunting, Gun comes across the body of Julian Marks, frozen in the ice of Stony Lake. Julian's friend, Babe, the son of Gun's friend Dick Chandler, seems to be involved and when Babe disappears, Gun is drawn into a confusing affair of Native American activists, big time mining and more murder. Can Gun, with the help of Carol, keep more people from dying?
Other books you might like:
Ron Handberg, *Savage Justice*, 1992
Geoff Peterson, *Medicine Dog*, 1989
Dana Stabenow, *A Cold Day for Murder*, 1992
John Straley, *The Woman Who Married a Bear*, 1992
Lee Wallingford, *Cold Tracks*, 1991

493
L.L. Enger (Pseudonym of Leif Enger and Lin Enger)
Swing (New York: Pocket, 1991)
Series: Gun Pedersen
Story type: Amateur Detective—Male Lead
Major character(s): Gun Pedersen, Sports Figure (former baseball player)
Time period(s): 1990s
Locale(s): West Palm Beach, Florida; St. Paul, Minnesota
What the book is about: Gun Pedersen is called by an old team mate, Moses Gates, who is down in Florida with the Senior League. Moses had, years ago, been involved with a death by hanging, earning him the nickname Hangman Gates. Although the death was ruled a suicide there were always doubts. Now a reporter who was interested in Gates and the old scandal has been found hanged. Gates wants Gun to figure out what is going on.
Other books you might like:
Paul Engleman, *Dead in Center Field*, 1983
Crabbe Evers, *Murder in Wrigley Field*, 1991
David Everson, *Suicide Squeeze*, 1991
Michael Geller, *Major League Murder*, 1988
David F. Nighbert, *Strikezone*, 1989

494
Paul Engleman
The Man with My Name (New York: St. Martin's, 1994)
Story type: Private Detective—Male Lead
Major character(s): Phil Moony, Detective—Private (unlicensed; retired paramedic); Frankie Martin, Journalist (retired newspaper reporter)
Time period(s): 1990s
Locale(s): Chicago, Illinois
What the book is about: Phil Moony has an office—Moony Enterprises—but no income and he isn't sure what he wants to do or even if he wants to do anything. When he gets a call for another Phil Moony he offers to find him for a fee. Later he is asked to meet another man looking for the elusive Phil Moony. However all he finds is a dead body and a fortune in old baseball cards. He knows he is being set up, but by whom—the Chicago politicians he exposed or someone closer to home?
Other books you might like:
Lawrence Block, *The Burglar Who Traded Ted Williams*, 1994
Loren D. Estleman, *Peeper*, 1989
Parnell Hall, *The Stanley Hastings Series*, 1987-
Michael Z. Lewin, *The Albert Samson Series*, 1974-
Steven Womack, *Murphy's Fault*, 1990

495
Paul Engleman
Who Shot Longshot Sam? (New York: Mysterious, 1989)
Series: Mark Renzler
Story type: Private Detective—Male Lead
Major character(s): Mark Renzler, Detective—Private
Time period(s): 1970s (1974)
Locale(s): New York, New York
What the book is about: When a track handicapper is killed, Renzler just happens to be on the scene.
Other books you might like:
Lawrence Block, *The Matt Scudder Series*, (1976-)
Stephen Dobyns, *The Charlie Bradshaw Series*, (1981-)
William Murray, *Tip on a Dead Crab*, 1984

496

Charlotte Epstein
Murder at the Friendship Hotel (New York: Doubleday, 1990)

Story type: Amateur Detective—Female Lead

Major character(s): Janet Eldine, Professor (consultant)

Time period(s): 1990s

Locale(s): Beijing, China

What the book is about: In China to set up an English department at a provincial university, Janet Eldine is asked to assist the police in tracking down the murder of an abrasive American woman who has been knifed to death in her hotel room.

Other books you might like:
Dorothy Gilman, *Mrs. Pollifax on the China Station*, 1983
Margaret Jones, *The Confucious Enigma*, 1982
Vincent Starrett, *Murder in Peking*, 1946

497

Loren D. Estleman
King of the Corner (New York: Bantam, 1992)

Series: Detroit Trilogy

Story type: Action/Adventure

Major character(s): Doc Miller, Criminal (former major league pitcher); Maynard Ance, Businessman (bail bondsman)

Time period(s): 1990s

Locale(s): Detroit, Michigan

What the book is about: Bail bondsman Maynard Ance asks the just released from prison Doc Miller if he wants to come along while he, Maynard, looks for a skipped out client. Soon the missing client turns up dead, maybe a suicide. As he was the leader of band of dope-selling revolutionaries this opens up some interesting possiblities for the characters involved.

Other books you might like:
Jon A. Jackson, *Grootka*, 1991
Tom Kakonis, *Michigan Roll*, 1988
Rob Kantner, *Made in Detroit*, 1990
Elmore Leonard, *City Primeval*, 1980
John Lutz, *The Right to Sing the Blues*, 1985

498

Loren D. Estleman
Motown (New York: Bantam, 1991)

Series: History of Detroit

Story type: Historical

Major character(s): Rick Amery, Police Officer (fired in disgrace); Lew Canada, Police Officer (head of a special taskforce); Quincy Springfield, Criminal

Time period(s): 1960s (1966)

Locale(s): Detroit, Michigan

What the book is about: This book follows three main characters through a time of turbulence in Detroit. Rick Amery is hired to go undercover in a consumer safety group that is threatening the Big Three auto makers. Lew Canada is trying to find evidence to convict the head of a large labor union that has ties to organized crime. Quincy Springfield, one of the leaders of the black controlled numbers racket, is trying to prevent the Mafia from taking over his territory. This is the second of a trilogy of the history of Detroit. The first was *Whiskey River*, 1990.

Other books you might like:
Max Allan Collins, *The Nate Heller Series*, 1983-
Thomas H. Cook, *Streets of Fire*, 1989
James Ellroy, *The Big Nowhere*, 1989
Jon A. Jackson, *The Blind Pig*, 1978
Walter Mosley, *Devil in a Blue Dress*, 1990

499

Loren D. Estleman
Peeper (New York: Bantam, 1989)

Story type: Private Detective—Male Lead

Major character(s): Ralph Poteet, Detective—Private (unscrupulous)

Time period(s): 1980s

Locale(s): Detroit, Michigan

What the book is about: When the hooker who lives in Poteet's building asks for help in removing the dead priest from her bed, Poteet finds more trouble than he dreamed existed.

Other books you might like:
Dick Lochte, *Sleeping Dog*, 1985
Warren Murphy, *The Trace Series*, (1983-)
Ross H. Spencer, *The Missing Bishop*, 1985

500

Loren D. Estleman
Sweet Women Lie (New York: Houghton Mifflin, 1990)

Series: Amos Walker

Story type: Private Detective—Male Lead

Major character(s): Amos Walker, Detective—Private

Time period(s): 1990s

Locale(s): Detroit, Michigan

What the book is about: Walker is hired by a former B-movie queen to deliver a large sum of money to a once-notorious money man. How this all relates to a government assassin who just happens to be married to Walker's ex-wife and why the assassin wants Walker to help him disappear is made clear by an unexpected death. At which point Walker starts taking a serious interest in what's going on.

Other books you might like:
Thomas Bunn, *Worse than Death*, 1989
Wayne D. Dundee, *The Skintight Shroud*, 1989
Rob Kantner, *The Back Door Man*, 1986
Elmore Leonard, *Unknown Man #89*, 1977
John Lutz, *The Right to Sing the Blues*, 1985

501
Loren D. Estleman
Whiskey River (New York: Bantam, 1990)

Series: History of Detroit

Story type: Historical

Major character(s): Constantine Minor, Journalist (newspaper reporter); John "Jack Dance" Danzig, Criminal

Time period(s): 20th century (1928-1932)

Locale(s): Detroit, Michigan

What the book is about: An account of fictional gangster John "Jack Dance" Danzig and others during prohibition in Detroit, as seen through the eyes of reporter "Connie" Minor. Set against the real background of bootlegging, police corruption, gang wars and the depression.

Other books you might like:
Harold Adams, *Paint the Town Red*, 1982
Howard Browne, *Pork City*, 1988
Max Allan Collins, *The Dark City*, 1987
Max Allan Collins, *True Detective*, 1983
L.J. Washburn, *Dead-Stick*, 1989

502
Judith Eubank
Crossover (New York: Carroll & Graf, 1992)

Story type: Action/Adventure; Psychological Suspense

Major character(s): Meredith Blake, Student (American); Peter Graham, Professor (Meredith's tutor)

Time period(s): 1990s

Locale(s): Exeter, England

What the book is about: Meredith Blake is staying in Edwards Hall at Exeter University doings post-graduate work. As an American and outsider she seems to be senitive to strange voices and apparitions that reside in the 17th century hall. To maintain her sanity she may have to solve a 150 year old mystery. First mystery.

Other books you might like:
Lillian Stewart Carl, *Ashes to Ashes*, 1990
Daphne Du Maurier, *Rebecca*, 1938
Marjorie Dorner, *Freeze Frame*, 1990
Velda Johnston, *The Underground Stream*, 1991
Barbara Michaels, *Ammie, Come Home*, 1968

503
Janet Evanovich
One for the Money (New York: Scribners, 1994)

Story type: Amateur Detective—Female Lead; Private Detective—Female Lead

Major character(s): Stephanie Plum, Businesswoman (unemployed lingerie buyer), Divorced Person; Joe Morelli, Police Officer (vice cop)

Time period(s): 1990s

Locale(s): Trenton, New Jersey

What the book is about: Stephanie Plum is unemployed—nobody seems to be hiring lingerie buyers these days. When her car is repossessed, she decides to get a job, any job. She asks her cousin Vinnie to hire her as a bounty hunter, also known as an apprehension agent. Her first assignment is to find Joe Morelli, a cop accused of murder. He just happens to be the good-looking man who took Stephanie's virginity and who she later ran down with her car. She's very motivated to find him. First mystery.

Other books you might like:
K.K. Beck, *A Hopeless Case*, 1992
D.B. Borton, *One for the Money*, 1993
Wendi Lee, *The Good Daughter*, 1994
Shelley Singer, *Following Jane*, 1993
Kathy Hogan Trocheck, *To Live and Die in Dixie*, 1993

504
Geraldine Evans
Dead Before Morning (New York: St. Martins, 1993)

Story type: Police Procedural—Male Lead

Major character(s): Joseph Rafferty, Police Officer (detective inspector); Dafyd Llewellyn, Police Officer (detective sergeant)

Time period(s): 1990s

Locale(s): Elmhurst, England

What the book is about: Newly promoted Joseph Rafferty is in charge of his first investigation. The naked body of a young woman has been found at a private psychiatric hospital with her face mutilated. The owner of the hospital is an officious snob who has no use for a mere inspector. The young woman is identified as a London prostitute, giving a lot of people a possible motive for murder. First novel.

Other books you might like:
Douglas Clark, *The Masters and Green Series*, 1969-
Clare Curzon, *The Yeadings and Mott Series*, 1990-
Marjorie Eccles, *The Mayo and Kite Series*, 1986-
Reginald Hill, *The Dalziel and Pascoe Series*, 1970-
Kay Mitchell, *The Morrissey and Barrett Series*, 1991-

505
Crabbe Evers (Pseudonym of William Brashler and Reinder Van Til)
Bleeding Dodger Blue (New York: Bantam, 1991)

Series: Duffy House

Story type: Amateur Detective—Male Lead

Major character(s): Duffy House, Journalist (sports writer)

Time period(s): 1990s

Locale(s): Los Angeles, California

What the book is about: Duffy House, who sometimes investigates for the commissioner of baseball, is in Los Angeles to get material for his memoirs. He wants to interview Jack Remsen, glad-handing manager of the L.A. Dodgers. There is also a serial killer at work-the Sunset Slasher. After a game, Jack is killed-seemingly by the Slasher but why was he in that part of town? Duffy, with his inside knowledge of baseball, decides to help with the investigation.

506 Evers

Other books you might like:
Paul Engleman, *Dead in Center Field*, 1983
L.L. Enger, *Swing*, 1991
Michael Geller, *Major League Murder*, 1988
Alison Gordon, *The Dead Pull Hitter*, 1988
Richard Rosen, *Strike Three, You're Dead*, 1984

506

Crabbe Evers (Pseudonym of William Brashler and Reinder Van Til)
Fear in Fenway (New York: Morrow, 1993)
Series: Duffy House
Story type: Amateur Detective—Male Lead
Major character(s): Duffy House, Journalist (sports writer)
Time period(s): 1990s
Locale(s): Boston, Massachusetts
What the book is about: Rooting for the Red Sox is a heartbreaking experience. The true Red Sox fan knows that no matter how well things are going, something will always go wrong. Duffy House is in town to attend an old-timers' game and look into the impending sale of the Red Sox. At the game two old-timers who are bidding for the team are killed. Duffy and his irrepressible niece are once again tracking a murderer—who may be tracking them.

Other books you might like:
David Everson, *Suicide Squeeze*, 1991
Michael Geller, *Major League Murder*, 1986
Alison Gordon, *The Dead Pull Hitter*, 1988
David F. Nighbert, *Squeezeplay*, 1992
Richard Rosen, *Strike Three, You're Dead*, 1987

507

Crabbe Evers (Pseudonym of William Brashler)
Murder in Wrigley Field (New York: Bantam, 1991)
Series: Duffy House
Story type: Amateur Detective—Male Lead
Major character(s): Duffy House, Journalist (sports writer); Petrinella Biggers, Student (niece of Duffy)
Time period(s): 1990s
Locale(s): Chicago, Illinois
What the book is about: Someone has shot "Dream" Weaver, ace pitcher for the Chicago Cubs. The baseball commissioner wants Duffy to investigate, while keeping things fairly quiet. One complicating factor—aside from the list of potential suspects (which would fill Wrigley Field)—is Duffy's niece. She's staying with him while waiting for law school to start and decides to be involved in the investigation. First novel.

Other books you might like:
William L. DeAndrea, *Five O'Clock Lightning*, 1982
Paul Engleman, *Dead in Center Field*, 1983
Michael Geller, *Major League Murder*, 1986
Alison Gordon, *The Dead Pull Hitter*, 1989
Robert B. Parker, *Mortal Stakes*, 1975

508

Crabbe Evers (Pseudonym of William Brashler and Reinder Van Til)
Tigers Burning (New York: Morrow, 1994)
Series: Duffy House
Story type: Amateur Detective—Male Lead
Major character(s): Duffy House, Journalist (sports writer)
Time period(s): 1990s
Locale(s): Detroit, Michigan
What the book is about: Someone has set Tiger Stadium on fire. Was it an accident or arson? When the body of Kit Gleason, rich lady and leader of a group trying to save the old stadium, is found in the ruins, it appears to be murder. Duffy House begins to investigate the fire and death.

Other books you might like:
Paul Engleman, *Dead in Center Field*, 1983
David Everson, *Suicide Squeeze*, 1991
Michael Geller, *Major League Murder*, 1986
Richard Rosen, *Strike Three, You're Dead*, 1984
Troy Soos, *Murder at Fenway Park*, 1994

509

David Everson
False Profits (New York: St. Martin's, 1992)
Series: Robert Miles
Story type: Private Detective—Male Lead
Major character(s): Robert Miles, Detective—Private
Time period(s): 1990s
Locale(s): Springfield, Illinois
What the book is about: Robert Miles has been asked by U.S. Senator "Tree" Courtney to look into some documents about Abraham Lincoln that are being offered for sale by Joseph X. Smith, a descendent of Joseph Smith, founder of the Morman Church. The papers may cause embarrassment to a prestigious Lincoln society and Senator Courtney wants them certified and Smith checked out. The first prospective buyer dies in a mysterious plane crash and more violence follows Smith and the Lincoln papers. Can Miles stop it?

Other books you might like:
Michael Bowen, *The Richard Michaelson Series*, 1990-
Thomas H. Cook, *Tabernacle*, 1983
R.R. Irvine, *The Moroni Traveler Series*, 1988-
William J. Reynolds, *The Nebraska Series*, 1984-
Gary Stewart, *The Zarahembla Vision*, 1986

510

David Everson
Suicide Squeeze (New York: St. Martins, 1991)
Series: Robert Miles
Story type: Private Detective—Male Lead
Major character(s): Robert Miles, Detective—Private (former baseball player)
Time period(s): 1980s (1989)
Locale(s): Chicago, Illinois

What the book is about: Robert Miles jumps at the opportunity to play and coach in a fantasy baseball camp. He's really there to keep an eye on Dewey Farmer, a pitcher trying to make a comeback after being suspended for gambling. At the same time Miles is asked to look into a hit-and-run accident involving an important politician's son.

Other books you might like:
Paul Benjamin, *Squeeze Play*, 1982
Paul Engleman, *Dead in Center Field*, 1983
Crabbe Evers, *Murder in Wrigley Field*, 1991
Robert B. Parker, *Mortal Stakes*, 1974

511
Robert Eversz
False Profit (New York: Viking, 1990)

Series: Marston/Cantini Mystery

Story type: Private Detective

Major character(s): Paul Marston, Detective—Private (corporate investigator); Angel Cantini, Detective—Private (corporate investigator), Companion (of Paul)

Time period(s): 1980s

Locale(s): California; Paris, France

What the book is about: Taking on separate cases, Paul hires out as a bodyguard and Angel searches for a client's missing brother. Their cases merge after Paul's client is murdered.

Other books you might like:
William Babula, *St. John's Baptism*, 1988
Linda Grant, *Blind Trust*, 1990
Arthur Lyons, *Three with a Bullet*, 1984
A.E. Maxwell, *Gatsby's Vineyard*, 1987
Roger L. Simon, *California Roll*, 1985

512
Elizabeth Eyre (Pseudonym of Susannah Stacey)
Death of the Duchess (New York: Harcourt, 1992)

Story type: Historical; Amateur Detective—Male Lead

Major character(s): Sigismondo, Mercenary; Benno, Servant

Time period(s): 16th century (renaissance)

Locale(s): Italy

What the book is about: The Duchy of Rocca is in turmoil as two of the leading families are feuding - the Di Torres and the Bandinis. When Jacob Di Torres' daughter is kidnapped and her maid and dog killed, the Bandinis are blamed. Sigismondo is assigned by the Duke to investigate. Then the Duchess is found dead in her bedroom with a Bandini found drunk in the same room. Sigismondo is sure all is so simple. This may be part of a much more complex plot. First book using this name.

Other books you might like:
P.C. Doherty, *The Hugh Corbett Series*, 1985-
Faye Kellerman, *The Quality of Mercy*, 1989
Edward Marston, *The Nicholas Bracewell Series*, 1988
Kate Sedley, *Death and the Chapman*, 1992
Leonard Tourney, *The Matthew Stock Series*, 1980-

513
Terence Faherty
Deadstick (New York: St. Martin's, 1991)

Series: Owen Keane

Story type: Amateur Detective—Male Lead

Major character(s): Owen Keane, Researcher (legal)

Time period(s): 1990s

Locale(s): New Jersey

What the book is about: Owen Keane is asked to investigate a plane crash from 1941. The brother of one of the victims—wealthy and reclusive Robert Cateret—is looking for the truth about the crash. Or so Harry is told. It seems that war injuries did some serious damage to Robert's mental health and it may not really be he that is requesting the investigation. Edgar nominee for Best First novel of 1991.

Other books you might like:
Tony Gibbs, *Shadow Queen*, 1991
John Katzenbach, *Day of Reckoning*, 1988
Keith Peterson, *The Scarred Man*, 1990
S.K. Wolf, *Long Chain of Death*, 1987
Steven Womack, *Murphy's Fault*, 1990

514
Terence Faherty
Die Dreaming (New York: St. Martin's, 1994)

Series: Owen Keane

Story type: Amateur Detective—Male Lead

Major character(s): Owen Keane, Saloon Keeper/Owner, Student (seminary drop-out)

Time period(s): 1970s (1978); 1980s (1988)

Locale(s): Boston, Massachusetts; Atlantic City, New Jersey

What the book is about: In 1978, while attending his 10th high school reunion, Owen Keane gets involved in solving a mystery that dates from his senior year. A classmate also involved became a drug user and served in Vietnam because of what happened then. Ten years later Owen again becomes involved with this classmate, this time to solve the mystery of his death.

Other books you might like:
Kate Green, *Night Angel*, 1989
Lia Matera, *A Hard Bargain*, 1992
Sharyn McCrumb, *If Ever I Return, Pretty Peggy-O*, 1990
Marcia Muller, *Trophies and Dead Things*, 1990
Brian Tobin, *The Missing Person*, 1994

515
Terence Faherty
The Lost Keats (New York: St. Martins, 1993)

Series: Owen Keane

Story type: Amateur Detective—Male Lead; Historical

Major character(s): Owen Keane, Student (of divinity); Father Jerome, Religious (advisor)

Time period(s): 1970s (1973)

Locale(s): Indiana (southern)

What the book is about: A fellow seminarian of Owen Keane has disappeared. Father Jerome thinks that Owen would be the perfect person to search for the missing Michael Crosley. It appears that Michael may have disappeared after finding an unknown Keats sonnet. As well as searching for Michael, Owen is on a quest to find his own truth. A prequel to *Deadstick* from 1991.

Other books you might like:
W. Edward Blain, *Passion Play*, 1990
S.F.X. Dean, *By Frequent Anguish*, 1982
Michael T. Hinkemeyer, *Fourth Down, Death*, 1984
Gillian Roberts, *Caught Dead in Philadelphia*, 1987

516
Gillian B. Farrell
Alibi for an Actress (New York: Pocket, 1992)

Series: Annie McGrogan

Story type: Private Detective—Female Lead

Major character(s): Annie McGrogan, Actress (part-time investigator); Duke DeNobili, Detective—Private

Time period(s): 1990s

Locale(s): New York, New York

What the book is about: Having left Hollywood for New York City, actress Annie McGrogan is disappointed in the job market. So she applies for a job as an investigator for Duke DeNobili. He, though less than enthusiastic about her qualifications, hires her to be a night-time bodyguard for soap opera actress Lucinda Merrill. Ms. Merrill is separated from her husband and when he is murdered she is the prime suspect—particularly when a witness says she was seen leaving the scene. But Annie says Lucinda never left her home the night of the murder. Who is telling the truth? First novel.

Other books you might like:
Lydia Adamson, *A Cat in the Manger*, 1990
Jane Dentinger, *Murder on Cue*, 1991
Ellen Hart, *Vital Lies*, 1991
Stefanie Matteson, *Murder on the Cliff*, 1991
Anne Morice, *Fatal Charm*, 1989

517
Gillian B. Farrell
Murder and a Muse (New York: Pocket, 1994)

Series: Annie McGrogan

Story type: Private Detective—Female Lead

Major character(s): Annie McGrogan, Detective—Private, Actress; Sonny Gondolfo, Detective—Private (ex-cop)

Time period(s): 1990s

Locale(s): New York, New York

What the book is about: Annie McGrogan is using her experience as a private detective to good advantage in forming the character of Glenda, the long-suffering wife of a private eye, for an audition for a new movie. She catches the attention of Alan DeLuca, the director of the movie and gets the part as well as a more personal offer. She accompanies Alan (the Italian Woody Allen) on a location inspection and meets his wife and family. Soon Alan's body is discovered in Annie's room.

Other books you might like:
Trella Crespi, *The Trouble with Moonlighting*, 1991
Jane Dentinger, *Dead Pan*, 1992
Maureen O'Brien, *Close-Up on Death*, 1989
Denise Osborne, *Murder Offscreen*, 1994
Dorian Yeager, *Eviction by Death*, 1993

518
Ron Faust
When She Was Bad (New York: Forge, 1994)

Story type: Action/Adventure

Major character(s): Dan Stark, Journalist; Christine Terry, Criminal

Time period(s): 1990s

Locale(s): Aspen, Colorado; At Sea

What the book is about: Dan Stark is a reporter who falls in love with the wrong woman. When Christine Terry, supposed shipwreck survivor, asks Dan to sail with her to recover some jewels that went down with her ship, he is only too happy to oblige. After they find the jewels, Christine leaves him marooned on a reef to die. He is rescued and he sets out to track her down. It takes him seven years but he tracks her to Aspen where she is set up as a cocaine boss. Pretending to be a drug dealer, Dan tries to bring her to justice—his justice.

Other books you might like:
John Clarkson, *And Justice for One*, 1993
Robert Ferrigno, *The Cheshire Moon*, 1993
David Morrell, *Assumed Identity*, 1993
Darian North, *Criminal Seduction*, 1993
Mark T. Sullivan, *The Fall Line*, 1994

519
Quinn Fawcett
Napoleon Must Die (New York: Avon, 1993)

Story type: Amateur Detective—Female Lead; Historical

Major character(s): Victoire Vernet, Spouse (wife of Major Vernet); Lucien Vernet, Military Personnel (aide to Napoleon Bonaparte)

Time period(s): 1800s

Locale(s): Egypt

What the book is about: Napoleon has just won a grand victory in Egypt and liberated a vast quantity of priceless treasure. However, when a guard is killed and a priceless artifact disappears, suspicion falls on Major Vernet. His wife knows he is innocent and vows to prove it. At first she thinks it is mere greed and a cover-up by some of the officers but it may be quite a bit more. Can a "mere woman" defeat such powerful forces and clear her husband? First mystery.

Other books you might like:
John Dickson Carr, *Captain Cutthroat*, 1955
Carole Nelson Douglas, *Good Morning, Irene*, 1991
Richard Grayson, *The Inspector Gautier Series*, 1987
Gillian Linscott, *The Nell Bray Series*, 1979-
Elizabeth Peters, *The Amelia Peabody Series*, 1974-

520
Connie Fedderson
Dead in the Cellar (New York: Zebra, 1994)

Series: Amanda Hazard

Story type: Amateur Detective—Female Lead

Major character(s): Amanda Hazard, Accountant (CPA); Nick Thorn, Police Officer (Amanda's lover)

Time period(s): 1990s

Locale(s): Vamoose, Oklahoma

What the book is about: Once again Amanda Hazard has found a body. This time it is her elderly client, Elmer Jolly. It looks like an accident, but Amanda thinks it's murder. Her boyfriend, Nick Thorn, is not convinced. Amanda is the executor of Elmer's will but the will is nowhere to be found and someone else is desperately looking for it. To complicate her life further, Nick is tired of sneaking visits with Amanda and wants a commitment.

Other books you might like:
Mary Daheim, *The Alpine Betrayal*, 1993
Toni L.P. Kelner, *Down Home Murder*, 1993
Eve K. Sandstrom, *The Devil Down Home*, 1991
Elizabeth Daniels Squire, *Who Killed What's-Her-Name?*, 1994
Kerry Tucker, *Still Waters*, 1991

521
John Feinstein
Running Mates (New York: Villard, 1992)

Story type: Amateur Detective—Male Lead; Action/Adventure

Major character(s): Bobby Kelleher, Journalist (newspaper reporter); Maureen McGuire, Journalist (reporter)

Time period(s): 1990s

Locale(s): Maryland

What the book is about: Investigating the assassination of the Maryland governor, Bobby Kelleher finds evidence of a feminist plot to have the female lieutenant governor installed. He also finds, however, evidence that rabid anti-abortionists might have had a hand in the killing. In fact, it appears that the feminists and the womb warriors might be working together to further their own agenda. First novel.

Other books you might like:
Jerome Doolittle, *Body Scissors*, 1990
Nancy Baker Jacobs, *Slash of Scarlet*, 1993
Mary Logue, *Still Explosion*, 1993
Ridley Pearson, *Hard Fall*, 1992

522
Dean Feldmeyer
Viper Quarry (New York: Pocket, 1994)

Story type: Amateur Detective—Female Lead

Major character(s): Daniel Thompson, Religious (Methodist minister); Ray Hall, Police Officer (town constable)

Time period(s): 1990s

Locale(s): Baird, Kentucky

What the book is about: The Reverend Daniel Thompson has just been reinstated as a Methodist minister and has been assigned a congregation in the small Appalachian town of Baird, Kentucky. His goal is to stay sober and out of trouble. The sober part is fairly easy, the out of trouble less so. Soon after his arrival in town a couple of people are burned to death in what appears to have been arson and their foster daughter is missing. Baird may not be the sleepy, peaceful town it first appeared to be. And then there are the temptations of the flesh... First novel.

Other books you might like:
Joan Hess, *Roll Over and Play Dead*, 1991
Sharyn McCrumb, *The Hangman's Beautiful Daughter*, 1993
Sharyn McCrumb, *Lovely in Her Bones*, 1985
Eve K. Sandstrom, *Death Down Home*, 1990
Sarah Shankman, *He Was Her Man*, 1993

523
Jean Femling
Hush, Money (New York: St. Martin's, 1989)

Story type: Amateur Detective—Female Lead

Major character(s): Martha "Moz" Brant, Insurance Investigator (half-Filipino, assertive)

Time period(s): 1980s

Locale(s): California (southern)

What the book is about: Investigating the blowing up of a yacht and its owner, "Moz" finds that someone doesn't want the truth to come out.

Other books you might like:
M.F. Beal, *Angel Dance*, 1977
Dolores Komo, *Clio Browne, Private Investigator*, 1988
Marcia Muller, *The Tree of Death*, 1983

524
Bob Fenster
The Last Page (Menlo Park: Perseverance, 1989)

Story type: Police Procedural—Male Lead

Major character(s): Brian Skiles, Detective—Police (NYPD homicide); Anne Baker, Writer, Editor

525 Ferrigno

Time period(s): 1980s

Locale(s): New York, New York

What the book is about: A frustrated writer is killing off the mystery editors in New York. Using lovely editor Anne Baker as bait, Detective Brian Skiles hopes to catch a killer. First book.

Other books you might like:
Isaac Asimov, *Murder at the A.B.A.*, 1976
Edward D. Hoch, *The Shattered Raven*, 1969
Kin Platt, *Dead as They Come*, 1972
Marie Reno, *Final Proof*, 1976
Donald E. Westlake, *A Likely Story*, 1984

525
Robert Ferrigno
The Cheshire Moon (New York: Morrow, 1993)

Story type: Action/Adventure

Major character(s): Quinn, Journalist; Jen Takamura, Photojournalist

Time period(s): 1990s

Locale(s): Los Angeles, California

What the book is about: After he quits a newspaper and goes to work for a gossip magazine, Quinn finds himself working with sexy photojournalist Jen Takamura and covering a "Musclemen for Jesus" rally. Soon, however he finds that he and Jen are involved in more than covering the rally. They find themselves trying to solve a murder and trying to stay alive.

Other books you might like:
James W. Hall, *Bones of Coral*, 1991
Carl Hiaasen, *Native Tongue*, 1991
Bruce Jones, *In Deep*, 1991
Charles King, *Mama's Boy*, 1992
Thomas Perry, *Metzger's Dog*, 1984

526
Robert Ferrigno
The Horse Latitudes (New York: Morrow, 1990)

Story type: Action/Adventure

Major character(s): Danny DeMedici, Drug Dealer (reformed)

Time period(s): 1980s

Locale(s): California

What the book is about: Danny DeMedici is searching for his ex-wife. The police are searching for her as well, as the suspect in a murder. This is Ferrigno's first novel.

Other books you might like:
Eugene Izzi, *The Take*, 1987
Elmore Leonard, *La Brava*, 1983
Richard North Patterson, *Private Screening*, 1985
Bill Pronzini, *Games*,
Andrew Vachss, *Strega*, 1987

527
Sidney Filson
Nightwalker (New York: NAL, 1989)

Story type: Action/Adventure

Major character(s): Grey Coltrane, Heiress, Martial Arts Expert (student)

Time period(s): 1980s

What the book is about: When Grey Coltrane's mentor and teacher is taken from her, she searches the world to seek revenge. First book.

Other books you might like:
David Morrell, *First Blood*, 1972
Trevanian, *Shibumi*, 1979
Andrew Vachss, *Flood*, 1985
Eric Van Lustbader, *The Ninja*, 1980

528
Sean Flannery (Pseudonym of David Hagberg)
Crossed Swords (New York: Jove, 1989)

Story type: Espionage

Major character(s): Wallace Mahoney, Spy (retired); Yuri Chernov, Spy (KGB)

Time period(s): 1980s

What the book is about: When Chernov discovers a plot to kill millions he must call on his old adversary, Mahoney, to help stop it.

Other books you might like:
William L. DeAndrea, *Cronus*, 1984
Bill Granger, *The November Man Series*, 1980
Winona Kent, *Skywatcher*, 1989

529
Sean Flannery (Pseudonym of David Hagberg)
Moving Targets (New York: Tor, 1992)

Story type: Espionage

Major character(s): Anatoli Kaplin, Spy (KGB dissident); Albert Tyson, Government Official (national security advisor)

Time period(s): 1990s

Locale(s): United States; Union of Soviet Socialist Republics

What the book is about: Soviet KGB dissident Anatoli Kaplin and national security advisor Albert Tyson - whose mistress is a top Soviet agent - find themselves working together to stop both their governments from fouling up the growing healthy relationship between their countries.

Other books you might like:
Ralph Peters, *Flames of Heaven*, 1993
Bob Reiss, *The Last Spy*, 1993
Tim Sebastian, *The Spy in Question*, 1988

530
Norman Flood
To Killashea (New York: St. Martin's, 1990)

Story type: Police Procedural—Male Lead

Major character(s): Dermot Quaid, Detective—Police

Time period(s): 1980s

What the book is about: Filmmaker Jack O'Shay is found dead and Detective Dermot Quaid has no dearth of suspects to choose from. First book.

Other books you might like:
Ellis Dillon, *Death at Crane's Court*, 1963
Bartholomew Gill, *McGarr and the Method of Descartes*, 1984
Michael Innes, *The Case of the Journeying Boy*, 1949
Patrick McGinley, *Goosefoot*, 1982

531
Kate Clark Flora
Death in a Funhouse Mirror (New York: Forge, 1995)

Series: Thea Kozak

Story type: Amateur Detective—Female Lead

Major character(s): Thea Kozak, Businesswoman (educational consultant); Andre Lemieux, Police Officer

Time period(s): 1990s

Locale(s): Massachusetts

What the book is about: Kate's friend, Eve Paris, is trying to convince Eve to investigate the death of her mother. She says that her father killed her mother so that he could be with his lover. Would that this was the only thing going on in her life. Her business partner is less than helpful (she's getting married and is just slightly self-absorbed), she's having trouble with her love life, and she is trying to get Eve's father to hire her firm. She doesn't need a murder right now. Then someone sets her house on fire.

Other books you might like:
Wendy Hornsby, *Midnight Baby*, 1993
Susan Kelly, *The Liz Connors Series*, 1985-
Katherine Hall Page, *The Faith Fairchild Series*, 1990-
Nancy Pickard, *The Jenny Cain Series*, 1986-
Dianne G. Pugh, *Cold Call*, 1993

532
Don Flynn
A Suitcase in Berlin (New York: Walker, 1989)

Series: Ed Fitzgerald

Story type: Amateur Detective—Male Lead

Major character(s): Ed "Fitz" Fitzgerald, Journalist (reporter)

Time period(s): 1980s

Locale(s): Berlin, Germany (both east and west)

What the book is about: Is Fitz actually going to help a woman steal a painting from a museum in East Berlin?

Other books you might like:
Douglas Kiker, *Murder on Clam Pond*, 1986
Gregory McDonald, *Fletch*, 1974
Keith Peterson, *Rough Justice*, 1989
Wayne Warga, *Fatal Impressions*, 1989

533
Katherine V. Forrest
The Beverly Malibu (Tallahassee: Naiad, 1989)

Series: Kate Delafield

Story type: Police Procedural—Female Lead

Major character(s): Kate Delafield, Police Officer, Lesbian; Paula Grant, Actress (former)

Time period(s): 1980s

Locale(s): Los Angeles, California

What the book is about: When former movie director Owen Sinclair is murdered at the Beverly Malibu, none of the other tenants, who were also involved in the film industry, show much concern. Since Owen Sinclair was a "friendly witness" before the House Un-American Activities Committee (HUAC) this is not too surprising, particularly as the others were all affected in some way by the blacklist. Homicide detective Kate Delafield's investigation is furthur complicated by her attraction to one of the suspects in the murder.

Other books you might like:
Antoinette Azolakov, *The Contactees Die Young*, 1989
Kelly Bradford, *Footprints*, 1988
Vicki McConnell, *Double Daughter*, 1988
Claire McNab, *Lessons in Murder*, 1988
Diane McRae, *All the Muscle You Need*, 1988
Lillian O'Donnell, *A Good Night to Kill*, 1988
Rosie Scott, *Glory Days*, 1988
Barbara Wilson, *The Dog Collar Murders*, 1989
Eve Zaremba, *Beyond Hope*, 1988
Eve Zaremba, *Work for a Million*, 1987

534
Katherine V. Forrest
Murder by Tradition (Tallahassee: Naiad, 1991)

Series: Kate Delafield

Story type: Police Procedural—Female Lead

Major character(s): Kate Delafield, Police Officer, Lesbian

Time period(s): 1990s

Locale(s): Los Angeles, California

What the book is about: While investigating what she believes is a gay-bashing hate crime, Kate discovers that the lawyer for the accused knows her sexual preference. She is concerned about her job and how her testimony will be affected if the court finds out she is gay.

Other books you might like:
Margaret Maron, *The Sigrid Harald Series*, 1978-
Lee Martin, *Hal's Own Murder Case*, 1989
Claire McNab, *Cop-Out*, 1991
Barbara Wilson, *The Dog Collar Murders*, 1989
Eve Zaremba, *Beyond Hope*, 1988

535
Richard Forrest
Death on the Mississippi (New York: St. Martin's, 1989)

Series: Bea and Lyon Wentworth

Story type: Amateur Detective

Major character(s): Bea Wentworth, Political Figure (state senator); Lyon Wentworth, Writer (writes children's books)

Time period(s): 1980s

Locale(s): Murphysville, Connecticut (fictional city)

What the book is about: A friend of Lyon's, who saved his life in Korea, comes to visit. This man is also a practical joker and when he and his houseboat disappear, the Wentworths aren't sure whether or not to take the disappearance seriously.

Other books you might like:
Jon L. Breen, *Touch of the Past*, 1988
Carolyn G. Hart, *Death on Demand*, 1987
Nancy Pickard, *Generous Death*, 1984
Edith Skom, *The Mark Twain Murders*, 1989

536
Earlene Fowler
Fool's Puzzle (New York: Berkley, 1994)

Series: Benni Harper

Story type: Amateur Detective—Female Lead

Major character(s): Benni Harper, Widow(er), Museum Curator (of a folk art museum); Gabe Ortiz, Police Officer (chief of police)

Time period(s): 1990s

Locale(s): San Celina, California

What the book is about: Benni Harper is still recovering from the death of her husband and now has a job as curator of the folk art museum, where local artists work and display their wares. One of the artists is killed at the museum while working late and Benni is the one to discover the body. Her cousin seems to be a suspect, and while trying to protect her, Benni runs afoul of the new police chief, enigmatic and handsome Gabe Ortiz. Trying to show him up, she investigates and eventually realizes this may have all started with her husband's death. First novel.

Other books you might like:
Laura Crum, *Cutter*, 1994
Sara Hoskinson Frommer, *Buried in Quilts*, 1994
Marcia Muller, *The Tree of Death*, 1983
Katherine Hall Page, *The Body in the Basement*, 1994
Charlene Weir, *The Winter Widow*, 1992

537
Earlene Fowler
Irish Chain (New York: Berkley, 1995)

Series: Benni Harper

Story type: Amateur Detective—Female Lead; Police Procedural

Major character(s): Benni Harper, Widow(er), Museum Curator (of a folk art museum); Gabriel Otiz, Police Officer (acting chief)

Time period(s): 1990s

Locale(s): San Celina, California

What the book is about: Benni has been talked into running a "Senior" prom for the local retirement home. One of the residents, Brady O'Hara, has been causing trouble and seems to be a thoroughly unpleasant man. Benni finds his strangled body in a room of one of the other residents—her old teacher, Miss Violet, who has also been murdered. Who would want to kill them? When Benni's new boyfriend, Chief Ortiz, orders her to stay away from the case, of course she has to snoop.

Other books you might like:
Laura Crum, *Cutter*, 1994
Marcia Muller, *The Tree of Death*, 1983
B.J. Oliphant, *The Shirley McClintock Series*, 1991-
Katherine Hall Page, *The Body in the Basement*, 1994
Barbara Burnett Smith, *Dust Devils of the Purple Sage*, 1995

538
Dick Francis
Come to Grief (New York: Putnam, 1995)

Series: Sid Halley

Story type: Private Detective—Male Lead

Major character(s): Sid Halley, Detective—Private (former jockey), Handicapped (missing a hand)

Time period(s): 1990s

Locale(s): England

What the book is about: Someone is mutilating horses by amputating their left front hooves and Sid Halley is investigating the attacks. It appears that the man behind the crimes is a friend of Sid's, Ellis Quint, a former jockey and now a television host beloved by all. Public sentiment is not in Sid's favor and one scurrilous rag in particular seems to have it in for him. When there is another mutilation and Ellis seems to have an ironclad alibi, Sid thinks he may have been intentionally mislead and finds some interesting connections between the owner of the tabloid and Ellis Quint. Edgar nominee for Best Novel of 1995.

Other books you might like:
Virginia Anderson, *Blood Lies*, 1989
Laura Crum, *Cutter*, 1994
Mark Daniel, *The Devil to Pay*, 1992
John Francome, *Outsider*, 1993
Bill Shoemaker, *Stalking Horse*, 1994

539
Dick Francis
Comeback (New York: Putnam, 1991)

Story type: Amateur Detective—Male Lead; Action/Adventure

Major character(s): Peter Darwin, Diplomat

Time period(s): 1990s

Locale(s): England

What the book is about: On his way back to England for a new job in the Foreign Office, Peter Darwin comes to the aid of an older couple who are being mugged. This friendly act involves him in their lives to a degree that begins to threaten his life. Murder, suicide, swindling, and cruelty to horses all cause him trouble.

Other books you might like:
L.L. Blackmur, *Love Lies Slain*, 1989
Jerome Doolittle, *Stranglehold*, 1991
Doug Hornig, *Waterman*, 1987
Sam Llewellyn, *Dead Reckoning*, 1987
Ted Wood, *On the Inside*, 1990

540
Dick Francis
Longshot (New York: Putnam, 1990)

Story type: Action/Adventure

Major character(s): John Kendall, Writer (writer of survival books); Tremayne Vickers, Businessman, Horse Trainer

Time period(s): 1990s

Locale(s): Shellerton Berkshire, England

What the book is about: John Kendall, a writer of survival books, is convinced to write the memoirs of horsetrainer Tremayne Vickers. He becomes involved with Vickers' family and friends. Then the body of a groom who had disappeared turns up.

Other books you might like:
Virginia Anderson, *Blood Lies*, 1989
Stephen Dobyns, *Saratoga Swimmer*, 1981
Sam Llewellyn, *Dead Reckoning*, 1987
Michael Maguire, *Shot Silk*, 1975
William Murray, *Tip on a Dead Crab*, 1984

541
Dick Francis
Straight (New York: Putnam, 1989)

Story type: Action/Adventure

Major character(s): Derek Franklin, Sports Figure (steeplechase jockey)

Time period(s): 1980s

What the book is about: While recovering from a broken ankle, Franklin learns of the death of his older, estranged brother. He is the heir and executor now and soon finds that his brother's death may not have been an accident.

Other books you might like:
Virginia Anderson, *Blood Lies*, 1989
Bernard Cornwell, *Killer's Wake*, 1989
Michael Geller, *Dead Fix*, 1989
Sam Llewellyn, *Blood Orange*, 1989
William Murray, *Tip on a Dead Crab*, 1985

542
Valerie Frankel
Prime Time for Murder (New York: Pocket, 1993)

Series: Wanda Mallory

Story type: Private Detective—Female Lead

Major character(s): Wanda Mallory, Detective—Private; Alex Beaudine, Detective—Private (Wanda's partner)

Time period(s): 1990s

Locale(s): New York, New York

What the book is about: Sabrina Delorean is the hostess of the somewhat sleazy TV dating game show, "Party Girls." When someone tries to kill her and shoots one of the contestants instead, she hires Wanda Mallory to provide protection and find the killer. This involves Wanda in the world of network television, a cut-throat business, and someone is taking that phrase literally.

Other books you might like:
Catherine Dain, *Sing a Song of Death*, 1993
Michael Hendricks, *Friends in High Places*, 1991
Janice Law, *Time Lapse*, 1992
Lillian O'Donnell, *The Gwen Ramadge Series*, 1990-
Sharon Zukowski, *Dancing in the Dark*, 1992

543
Antonia Fraser
The Cavalier Case (New York: Bantam, 1991)

Series: Jemima Shore

Story type: Amateur Detective—Female Lead

Major character(s): Jemima Shore, Journalist (investigative journalist)

Time period(s): 1990s

Locale(s): England

What the book is about: Jemima Shore has fallen in love with a ghost—or at least the picture of someone that people say is a ghost. This ghost appears to have committed murder, but Jemima doesn't believe it for a moment and sets out to find the real murderer.

Other books you might like:
Anne Morice, *The Tessa Crichton Series*, 1970-1990
Patricia Moyes, *Angel Death*, 1981
Dorothy L. Sayers, *Strong Poison*, 1930
Michael Underwood, *A Compelling Case*, 1989

544
Margaret Frazer (Pseudonym of Mary Monica Pulver and Gail Bacon)
The Bishop's Tale (New York: Berkley, 1994)

Series: Sister Frevisse

Story type: Historical; Amateur Detective—Female Lead

Major character(s): Sister Frevisse, Religious (nun); Henry Beaufort, Religious (Cardinal Bishop of Winchester)

Time period(s): 15th century (1435)

Locale(s): Ewelme Manor, England

What the book is about: Sister Frevisse gets word that her beloved uncle, Thomas Chaucer, is dying. She rushes to his side but arrives too late. At the funeral feast, a local tyrant, Sir Clement Sharpe, dares God to strike him dead if he is wrong. An hour later he is dead. The abbot's opinion is that God got tired of him, but Thomas' great friend, Bishop Henry Beaufort, thinks someone may have poisoned him and asks Frevisse to investigate.

545 Frazer

Other books you might like:
Umberto Eco, *The Name of the Rose*, 1986
C.L. Grace, *A Shrine of Murders*, 1992
Paul Harding, *The Brother Athelstan Series*, 1994-
Sharan Newman, *Death Comes as Epiphany*, 1993
Ellis Peters, *The Brother Cadfael Series*, 1977-

545

Margaret Frazer (Pseudonym of Mary Monica Kuhfeld)
Co-Author: Gail Bacon
The Boy's Tale (New York: Berkley, 1995)
Series: Sister Frevisse
Story type: Amateur Detective—Female Lead; Historical
Major character(s): Sister Frevisse, Religious (nun)
Time period(s): 15th century (1430s)
Locale(s): England
What the book is about: Mistress Maryon has arrived at St. Fridewide's with two young children after being beset by a group of mercenaries. The children turn out to be the half-brothers of the young King Henry VI. Their existence could threaten the crown, and someone wants them dead. They seek sanctuary from Sister Frevisse, but somehow fatal accidents keep happening. Someone inside St. Fridewide's must be in league with the assassins. Can Sister Frevisse keep them safe?
Other books you might like:
Umberto Eco, *The Name of the Rose*, 1986
C.L. Grace, *The Katherine Swinbrooke Series*, 1992-
Paul Harding, *The Brother Athelstan Series*, 1994-
Sharan Newman, *The Cathe LeVendeur Series*, 1993-
Ellis Peters, *The Brother Cadfael Series*, 1977-1994

546

Peter Freeborn
Hollywood Requiem (New York: Simon & Schuster, 1991)
Story type: Psychological Suspense
Major character(s): Dan Springer, Writer (ghost writer); Nina Hardy, Actress
Time period(s): 1990s
Locale(s): Los Angeles, California
What the book is about: Dan Springer is hired to ghost-write the memoirs of actress Nina Hardy, but it appears that someone - perhaps Nina herself-doesn't really want them finished.
Other books you might like:
L.L. Blackmur, *Love Lies Slain*, 1989
William Goldman, *The Color of Light*, 1984
David Handler, *The Man Who Series*, 1989-
Elizabeth Peters, *Naked Once More*, 1989
Benjamin Stein, *Her Only Sin*, 1985

547

J.F. Freedman
Against the Wind (New York: Viking, 1991)
Story type: Legal; Action/Adventure
Major character(s): Will Alexander, Lawyer
Time period(s): 1990s
Locale(s): Santa Fe, New Mexico
What the book is about: Put on indefinite leave by his law partners, threatened by his ex-wife with the loss of visitation rights to his daughter, womanizing, hard-drinking lawyer Will Alexander is back on his pins. He thinks the case of the four bikers accused of murder can provide him with a way out of the bottle. But he forgets that there are people who don't want the bikers found innocent. First novel.
Other books you might like:
John Grisham, *The Firm*, 1991
Richard Harris, *Honor Bound*, 1982
Scott Turow, *Presumed Innocent*, 1987
Walter Walker, *The Immediate Prospect of Being Hanged*, 1989
Stuart Woods, *Santa Fe Rules*, 1992

548

Nicholas Freeling
Not as Far as Velma (New York: Mysterious, 1989)
Series: Henri Castang
Story type: Police Procedural—Male Lead
Major character(s): Henri Castang, Police Officer (inspector); Robert Marklake, Artist (painter)
Time period(s): 1980s
What the book is about: When the female owner of a small hotel vanishes, Castang is sent to investigate. Then a bomb destroys the local convent. Are the two things related?
Other books you might like:
E.V. Cunningham, *The Case of the One-Penny Orange*, 1977
Mark Hebden, *Pel and the Bombers*, 1985
Paul Orum, *Scapegoat*, 1975
Georges Simenon, *The Inspector Maigret Series*, (1932-)
Janwillem Van De Wetering, *The Rattle-Rat*, 1985

549

Nicholas Freeling
Sand Castles (New York: Mysterious, 1990)
Series: Inspector Van Der Valk
Story type: Police Procedural—Male Lead
Major character(s): Piet Van Der Valk, Police Officer (inspector); Arlette Van Der Valk, Spouse
What the book is about: While on vacation, Arlette and Piet get involved in numerous mysteries.
Other books you might like:
Bartholomew Gill, *The Inspector McGarr Series*, (1977-)
Mark Hebden, *The Inspector Pel Series*, (1979-)
Magdalen Nabb, *The Marshall Guarnaccia Series*, (1981-)

550

Brian Freemantle
The Run Around (New York: Bantam, 1989)

Series: Charlie Muffin

Story type: Espionage

Major character(s): Charlie Muffin, Spy

Time period(s): 1980s

Locale(s): Geneva, Switzerland

What the book is about: News of a probable assassination at a scheduled Middle East peace conference sends Charlie off to Geneva. Charlie is rebuffed at every turn as he tries to tighten security and stop the assassin.

Other books you might like:
Sean Flannery, *The Hollow Men*, 1982
Brian Garfield, *Hopscotch*, 1975
John Le Carre, *Tinker, Tailor, Soldier, Spy*, 1974
Marc Lovell, *Good Spies Don't Grow on Trees*, 1986
Hugh Munro, *The Man Who Sold Death*, 1965

551
James N. Frey
Came a Dead Cat (New York: St. Martin's, 1991)

Story type: Private Detective—Female Lead

Major character(s): Odyssey Gallagher, Detective—Private

Time period(s): 1990s

Locale(s): San Francisco, California

What the book is about: Odyssey Gallagher has been hired by Aletha Holmcroft to find her husband's latest paramour who, Aletha believes, is behind the dead cat on their doorstep. When Odyssey finds the woman she denies all knowledge of said cat and in fact is afraid for her life, but won't say why. Soon the wayward husband is killed and Odyssey's ex-boyfriend is involved in some way. More murders follow along with blackmail, adultery and suicide.

Other books you might like:
Karen Kijewski, *Katwalk*, 1989
Marcia Muller, *The Sharon McCone Series*, 1977-
Bill Pronzini, *The Nameless Detective Series*, 1973-
Robert J. Randisi, *Separate Cases*, 1990

552
James N. Frey
Winter of the Wolves (New York: Holt, 1992)

Story type: Espionage; Action/Adventure

Major character(s): Tom Croft, Spy (assassin); Theodore Fairweather, Spy (assassin, code name Gray Wolf)

Time period(s): 1990s

Locale(s): United States

What the book is about: Tom Croft has retired from "The Exchange", a secret group of assassins working for the U.S. Government. The agency wants him to come back and kill Gray Wolf, a top agent going freelance. Tom is happy living in peace and has even found a woman he cares about. But Gray Wolf doesn't know he has turned down the assignment and may try to kill him first.

Other books you might like:
Bill Granger, *The November Man Series*, 1981
Robert Ludlum, *The Bourne Identity*, 1980
David Morrell, *The Brotherhood of the Rose*, 1984
Robert Rostand, *The Killer Elite*, 1973
Trevanian, *The Loo Sanction*, 1973

553
Gary Friedman
Gun Men (New York: Morrow, 1993)

Story type: Action/Adventure

Major character(s): Elliot Brod, Criminal (professional hit man); Jamison Connors, Security Officer

Time period(s): 1990s

Locale(s): California

What the book is about: After an elementary school massacre, one of the victim's parents hires hit man Elliot Brod to assassinate someone from the NAGO, a gun owners rights group, the people the parent feels are partially responsible for his child's death. The organization gets wind of this and sets their security chief, Jamison Conners, on the trail of the assassin. First novel.

Other books you might like:
Loren D. Estleman, *Roses Are Red*, 1985
James N. Frey, *Winter of the Wolves*, 1992
John Grisham, *The Pelican Brief*, 1992
Stephen Hunter, *Point of Impact*, 1993
Eric Sauter, *Predators*, 1987

554
Kinky Friedman
God Bless John Wayne (New York: Simon & Schuster, 1995)

Series: Kinky Friedman

Story type: Private Detective—Male Lead

Major character(s): Kinky Friedman, Detective—Private

Time period(s): 1990s

Locale(s): New York, New York; Florida

What the book is about: Kinky's friend Ratso decides he needs to explore his past and find his parents. Not easy, as no one appears eager to claim Ratso as their own. Violence erupts and Kinky travels from New York to Florida and back again to help his ne'er-do-well friend—and to save his life.

Other books you might like:
Jerome Charyn, *Blue Eyes*, 1974
George C. Chesbro, *An Incident at Bloodtide*, 1993
James Crumley, *The Last Good Kiss*, 1974
Valerie Frankel, *A Body to Die For*, 1995
Warren Murphy, *Digger Smoked Out*, 1982

555
Kinky Friedman
Musical Chairs (New York: Morrow, 1991)

Series: Kinky Friedman

556 Friedman

Story type: Private Detective—Male Lead
Major character(s): Kinky Friedman, Detective—Private, Musician (former)
Time period(s): 1980s (1989)
Locale(s): New York, New York
What the book is about: Someone is killing the members of Kinky's former band. Kinky decides to get all the former Jewboys together in one place figuring there's safety in numbers. He's wrong. Why is this happening? Surely their music wasn't that bad.
Other books you might like:
Douglas Allyn, *The Cheerio Killings*, 1989
Jesse Sublett, *Rock Critic Murders*, 1989
Jesse Sublett, *Tough Baby*, 1990

556
Mickey Friedman
A Temporary Ghost (New York: Viking, 1989)
Series: Georgia Lee Maxwell
Story type: Amateur Detective—Female Lead
Major character(s): Georgia Lee Maxwell, Writer (ghost writer), Journalist; Vivien Howard, Widow(er) (suspected of killing husband)
Time period(s): 1980s
What the book is about: After accepting a ghost writing job for an accused murderess, Maxwell finds more than she bargained for as she becomes a member of the household.
Other books you might like:
Dorothy Salisbury Davis, *A Death in the Life*, 1976
Melodie Johnson Howe, *The Mother Shadow*, 1989
Helen McCloy, *Two Thirds of a Ghost*, 1956
Elizabeth Peters, *Naked Once More*, 1989
L.A. Taylor, *Footnote to Murder*, 1983

557
Philip Friedman
Inadmissible Evidence (New York: Fine, 1992)
Story type: Legal
Major character(s): Joe Estrada, Lawyer (assistant district attorney)
Time period(s): 1990s
Locale(s): United States
What the book is about: Hispanic real estate developer Roberto Morales, has just had his original guilty verdict for rape set aside on appeal. The district attorney decides on a retrial - though three years have passed - and assigns the task to Joe Estrada. Trying to build a solid case after this long a time is tough, plus Estrada has some doubts about Morales guilt himself.
Other books you might like:
Jay Brandon, *Fade the Heat*, 1990
Richard Harris, *Honor Bound*, 1982
Paul Levine, *To Speak for the Dead*, 1990
Steve Martini, *Compelling Evidence*, 1992
Scott Turow, *Presumed Innocent*, 1988

558
Philip Friedman
Reasonable Doubt (New York: Fine, 1990)
Story type: Legal
Major character(s): Michael Ryan, Lawyer (former U.S. prosecutor); Kassia Miller, Lawyer
Time period(s): 1980s
Locale(s): New York, New York
What the book is about: Michael Ryan is asked to defend his daughter-in-law who is accused of killing his son.
Other books you might like:
Richard Harris, *Honor Bound*, 1982
Joe L. Hensley, *Color Him Guilty*, 1988
Paul Levine, *To Speak for the Dead*, 1990
Robert Traver, *Anatomy of a Murder*, 1958
Scott Turow, *Presumed Innocent*, 1988

559
Sara Hoskinson Frommer
Buried in Quilts (New York: St. Martin's, 1994)
Series: Joan Spencer
Story type: Amateur Detective—Female Lead
Major character(s): Joan Spencer, Musician (viola player); Fred Lundquist, Police Officer
Time period(s): 1990s
Locale(s): Oliver, Indiana
What the book is about: Joan Spencer has enough to think about with her job at the senior center, managing and playing with the Oliver Orchestra and dealing with her daughter, Rebecca, who is back home again after two years away. Then Edna Ellett dies and the relatives are desperate to find her will. This is all happening as the town is getting ready for the Oliver Quilt Show, the most prestigious small town show in the country. Then Mary Sue Ellett is murdered. Now everyone is worried about a homicidal maniac, but Joan thinks there may be no madness in the killer's method.
Other books you might like:
Earlene Fowler, *Fool's Puzzle*, 1994
Joan Higgins, *A Little Death Music*, 1987
Lucille Kallen, *The Tanglewood Murder*, 1981
Katherine Hall Page, *The Body in the Basement*, 1994
Audrey Peterson, *Deadly Rehearsal*, 1990

560
Mark Frost
The 6 Messiahs (New York: Morrow, 1995)
Series: Jack Sparks
Story type: Action/Adventure; Historical
Major character(s): Jack Sparks, Spy; Arthur Conan Doyle, Historical Figure (writer)
Time period(s): 1990s
Locale(s): United States

What the book is about: Jack Sparks, Doyle's inspiration for Sherlock Holmes, has resurfaced ten years after their first meeting—just in time to save Doyle from death aboard ship as he embarks for an American tour. Doyle has unwittingly gotten involved in a scheme to form a new religion in the Arizona desert. Threats will follow him across America, finally landing him and Sparks outside of Phoenix where they must put an end to the situation.

Other books you might like:
Abbey Penn Baker, *In the Dead of Winter*, 1994
Caleb Carr, *The Alienist*, 1993
William L. DeAndrea, *The Lunatic Fringe*, 1980
Walter Satterthwait, *Escapade*, 1995
Daniel Stashower, *The Adventure of the Ectoplasmic Man*, 1985

561

Frances Fyfield (Pseudonym of Frances Hegerty)
Deep Sleep (New York: Pocket, 1992)

Series: Helen West

Story type: Legal; Police Procedural

Major character(s): Helen West, Lawyer (Crown prosecutor); Geoffrey Bailey, Police Officer

Time period(s): 1990s

Locale(s): London, England

What the book is about: The death from apparent natural causes of the wife of a pharmacist makes Helen West suspicious. Over the objections of her lover, policeman Geoffrey Bailey, she is determined to investigate. What she finds will please nobody.

Other books you might like:
Sarah Caudwell, *Thus Was Adonis Murdered*, 1981
Lesley Grant-Adamson, *Curse the Darkness*, 1990
Michael Underwood, *Seeds of Murder*, 1992
Hannah Wakefield, *The Price You Pay*, 1989
Sara Woods, *Nor Live So Long*, 1986

562

Frances Fyfield (Pseudonym of Frances Hegerty)
A Question of Guilt (New York: Pocket, 1989)

Story type: Traditional

Major character(s): Helen West, Lawyer (Crown prosecutor); Geoffrey Bailey, Police Officer (superintendent)

Time period(s): 1980s

What the book is about: West and Bailey must work together to try to tie Eileen Cartwright to the murder of her lawyer's wife. This first novel by Fyfield was nominated for an Edgar.

Other books you might like:
Michael Gilbertod, *Death Has Deep Roots*, 1951
Martha Grimes, *The Anodyne Necklace*, 1983
John Sherwood, *Flowers of Evil*, 1988
Michael Underwood, *Rosa's Dilemma*, 1990
Sara Woods, *The Law's Delay*, 1977

563

Frances Fyfield (Pseudonym of Frances Hegerty)
Shadows on the Mirror (New York: Pocket, 1991)

Story type: Psychological Suspense

Major character(s): Sarah Fortune, Lawyer (unhappy); Malcolm Cook, Lawyer (lover of Sarah); Ryan, Police Officer (detective sergeant)

Time period(s): 1990s

Locale(s): London, England

What the book is about: Lonely Sarah Fortune assuages her loneliness by giving comfort to men of like temperment. One she won't give comfort to is Charles Tysall - who, the police suspect, had murdered his wife some years ago.

Other books you might like:
Marjorie Dorner, *Freeze Frame*, 1990
Elizabeth George, *Well-Schooled in Murder*, 1990
Michael Gilbert, *The Body of a Girl*, 1972
Martha Grimes, *The Richard Jury Series*, 1981-
Sara Woods, *The Anthony Maitland Series*, 1962-1989

564

Kate Gallison
Bury the Bishop (New York: Dell, 1995)

Story type: Amateur Detective—Female Lead

Major character(s): Lavinia Grey, Religious (Episcopalian priest); David Dogg, Police Officer, Detective—Homicide

Time period(s): 1990s

Locale(s): Fisherville, New Jersey

What the book is about: Mother Lavinia's first assignment is to take over as vicar of St. Bede's Episcopical Church. The bishop's idea is to close the church and sell the land. Lavinia would like to keep the church open but her entire congregation consists of five people. When she discovers the murdered body of the bishop, she becomes a prime suspect. The unfortunately named Detective Dogg is interested in Lavinia as more than a suspect but things look bad when another murder implicates her again. Can she save the church and herself?

Other books you might like:
D.M. Greenwood, *The Theodora Braithwaite Series*, 1991-
Lee Harris, *The Christine Bennett Series*, 1992-
Isabelle Holland, *The Claire Aldington Series*, 1983-
David Willis McCullough, *The Ziza Todd Series*, 1990-
Sister Carol Anne O'Marie, *The Sister Mary Helen Series*, 1984-

565

Kate Gallison
Jersey Monkey (New York: St. Martin's, 1992)

Series: Nick Magaracz

Story type: Private Detective—Male Lead

Major character(s): Nick Magaracz, Detective—Private

Time period(s): 1990s

Locale(s): Trenton, New Jersey

What the book is about: Nick is hired by Howard Strass, CEO of Porcineau Pharmaceuticals, because he thinks someone is trying to poison him. Two people have already died from taking drugs from the company's private stock-which the police don't know.

Other books you might like:
Robert Eversz, *False Profit*, 1990
Richard Hilary, *Behind the Fact*, 1989
Robert J. Randisi, *The Miles Jacoby Series*, 1982-
J.W. Rider, *Jersey Tomatoes*, 1986
Les Roberts, *The Milan Jacovich Series*, 1988-

566
Joseph R. Garber
Vertical Run (New York: Bantam, 1995)

Story type: Action/Adventure

Major character(s): David Elliot, Businessman, Veteran (Vietnam)

Time period(s): 1990s

Locale(s): New York, New York

What the book is about: The day starts out badly for David Elliot when his boss walks into his office and tries to kill him. That is bad enough but then other men show up in his office building and try to kill him as well. He is trapped in the building and there is no one he can turn to for help—everyone he knows, including his family, seems to want him dead. Can he get out of the building alive? Why does everyone have it in for him?

Other books you might like:
Chuck Hogan, *The Standoff*, 1995
Craig Holden, *The Last Sanctuary*, 1996
Philip Kerr, *The Grid*, 1996
Chuck Logan, *Hunter's Moon*, 1995
John Sandford, *Fool's Run*, 1989

567
John Gardner
Win, Lose or Die (New York: Putnam, 1989)

Series: James Bond

Story type: Espionage

Major character(s): James Bond, Spy

Time period(s): 1980s

Locale(s): At Sea

What the book is about: Bond is sent to protect the heads of state of Russia, Great Britain, and the U.S., who are having a top-secret summit aboard the HMS Invicible, from the clutches of BAST (Brotherhood of Anarchy and Secret Terror). This book is a continuation of the James Bond series created by Ian Fleming.

Other books you might like:
Len Deighton, *The Ipcress File*, 1962
Ian Fleming, *The James Bond Series*, (1959-)
Donald Hamilton, *Death of a Citizen*, 1960
Kenneth Royce, *The XYZ Man*, 1970
Andrew York, *The Eliminator*, 1966

568
Ray Garton
Trade Secrets (Shingletown, CA: Ziesing, 1990)

Story type: Action/Adventure

Major character(s): Gerard Brady, Businessman (department store executive); Kendra Singer, Runaway (from an organization)

Time period(s): 1990s

Locale(s): Annapolis, Maryland

What the book is about: Finding a beat-up woman on his doorstep is the start of a nightmare for Gerry Brady. His girlfriend is killed and the woman he found has disappeared. A clinic and psychiatrist appear to be connected. First mystery, though he has written some horror novels.

Other books you might like:
Carl Hiaasen, *Skin Deep*, 1989
Joseph Koenig, *Smuggler's Notch*, 1989
Ira Levin, *The Stepford Wives*, 1972
John D. MacDonald, *Nightmare in Pink*, 1964

569
Judith Garwood
Make Friends with Murder (New York: St. Martin's, 1992)

Story type: Amateur Detective—Female Lead

Major character(s): Morgan Reeves, Journalist (writer for a magazine)

Time period(s): 1990s

Locale(s): Santa Clarissa, California

What the book is about: Morgan is assigned to do an article on the southern California wine industry. When she and her ex-boyfriend go on a tour of the up and coming Novelli winery, one of the first things they notice is a dead body in the wine cellar. Now Morgan has a real story. First novel.

Other books you might like:
Linda Barnes, *Bitter Finish*, 1983
Barbara D'Amato, *Hardball*, 1990
A.E. Maxwell, *Gatsby's Vineyard*, 1987
Meg O'Brien, *The Daphne Decisions*, 1990
Sarah Shankman, *Now Let's Talk of Graves*, 1990

570
Jonathan Gash
The Great California Game (New York: St. Martin's, 1991)

Series: Lovejoy

Story type: Action/Adventure

Major character(s): Lovejoy, Antiques Dealer

Time period(s): 1990s

Locale(s): New York, New York; Malibu, California

What the book is about: Lovejoy is an antiques "divvy"-somehow he just knows the real things from the fakes. Right now he is down on his luck in New York City, forced to tend bar. Soon his talent has him involved with three beautiful women all trying to use him in shady deals. As usual Lovejoy lets himself be used.

Other books you might like:
Eliza G.C. Collins, *Going, Going, Gone*, 1986
Nan Lyons, *Sold!*, 1982 (Ivan Lyons, co-author)
John Malcolm, *The Tim Simpson Series*, 1985
Neville Steed, *The Peter Marklin Series*, 1986

571
Jonathan Gash
The Lies of Fair Ladies (New York: St. Martin's, 1992)

Series: Lovejoy

Story type: Amateur Detective—Male Lead

Major character(s): Lovejoy, Antiques Dealer

Time period(s): 1990s

Locale(s): East Anglia, England

What the book is about: Lovejoy, the perpetually broke, disreputable antiques dealer, is in trouble with the law. They think he had something to do with the gutting of an old house. Lovejoy knows who did do it but keeps quiet. When the real culprit is murdered, Lovejoy wants to know why. Does it have to do with a large-scale scam that seems to be brewing? And who is scamming whom?

Other books you might like:
James Leasor, *Frozen Assets*, 1989
Roy Harley Lewis, *A Cracking of Spines*, 1982
John Malcolm, *The Tim Simpson Series*, 1983-
Neville Steed, *The Peter Marklin Series*, 1987-
Martin Sylvester, *A Lethal Vintage*, 1988

572
Jonathan Gash
The Sin Within Her Smile (New York: Viking, 1994)

Series: Lovejoy

Story type: Amateur Detective—Male Lead

Major character(s): Lovejoy, Antiques Dealer

Time period(s): 1990s

Locale(s): East Anglia, England; Wales

What the book is about: Lovejoy has agreed to be a "slave for a day" and have his services auctioned off for charity. Two high-class women seem to really want his services, with the winner bidding more than 2,000 pounds. And she wants her money's worth. It, of course, involves antiques and crooked schemes. Lovejoy wants to know more and hires a friend to do a bit of car theft, but the friend turns up murdered. What now?

Other books you might like:
Eliza G.C. Collins, *Going, Going, Gone*, 1986
John Malcolm, *The Tim Simpson Series*, 1983-
A.J. Orde, *The Jason Lynx Series*, 1990-
Neville Steed, *The Peter Marklin Series*, 1987-

573
Michael Geller
Dead Fix (New York: St. Martin's, 1989)

Story type: Amateur Detective—Male Lead

Major character(s): Ken Eagle, Sports Figure (Jockey); Tricia Martin, Sports Figure (Jockey)

Time period(s): 1980s

What the book is about: Jockey Ken Eagle blames the horse trainer when his girlfriend and fellow jockey Tricia Martin is injured in a fall. When the trainer turns up murdered and Eagle is framed, he must do some quick work to find the real killer.

Other books you might like:
Jon L. Breen, *Listen for the Click*, 1983
Stephen Dobyns, *Saratoga Swimmer*, 1981
Dick Francis, *Blood Sport*, 1968
Michael Maguire, *Scratchproof*, 1977
Robert J. Randisi, *The Disappearance of Penny*, 1980

574
Michael Geller
Three Strikes, You're Dead (New York: St. Martin's, 1992)

Series: Slots Resnick

Story type: Private Detective—Male Lead

Major character(s): Slots Resnick, Detective—Private (ex-chief of detectives, NYPD)

Time period(s): 1990s

Locale(s): Norville, Colorado

What the book is about: Slots has been hired by the New York Mets to investigate a million dollar prospect in the small town of Norville. Billy Joe Howlett is a natural ballplayer but has two problems. Billy Joe is really Billy Jo and she is a prime suspect in the murder of her step-mother. Slots finds this is only the latest death in her tragic life.

Other books you might like:
Paul Benjamin, *Squeeze Play*, 1982
L.L. Enger, *Swing*, 1991
Paul Engleman, *Dead in Center Field*, 1983
David Everson, *Suicide Squeeze*, 1991
David F. Nighbert, *Strikezone*, 1989

575
Elizabeth George
Missing Joseph (New York: Bantam, 1993)

Series: Inspector Lynley

Story type: Police Procedural—Male Lead; Psychological Suspense

Major character(s): Thomas Lynley, Police Officer (detective inspector); Simon St. James, Doctor; Deborah St. James, Spouse

Time period(s): 1990s

Locale(s): Winslough, England (Lancashire)

What the book is about: Deborah St. James is in London fighting depression over her failure to have a child and establish her career. A chance remark and conversation with a stranger starts her recovery. The stranger, the Vicar of Winslough, seems to be a very nice man and Deborah convinces her husband Simon to take a holiday in the area. When they try to visit the Vicar they discover he is dead of poisoning. It was ruled accidental but Simon is not sure. Soon they and their friend, Inspector Thomas Lynley, are investigating.

Other books you might like:
Caroline Graham, *The Inspector Barnaby Series*, 1987-
Martha Grimes, *The Inspector Jury Series*, 1981-
P.D. James, *The Inspector Dagliesh Series*, 1962-
Sheila Radley, *The Inspector Quantrill Series*, 1978-
Ruth Rendell, *The Inspector Wexford Series*, 1964-

576
Elizabeth George
Payment in Blood (New York: Bantam, 1989)

Series: Inspector Lynley

Story type: Police Procedural—Male Lead

Major character(s): Thomas Lynley, Detective—Police (detective inspector); Barbara Havers, Police Officer (sergeant)

Time period(s): 1980s

What the book is about: When Inspector Lynley is sent to Scotland to investigate a murder that involves a former lover, he loses control and tries to find evidence to convict her current lover.

Other books you might like:
Christianna Brand, *Fog of Doubt*, 1953
Douglas Clark, *Sick to Death*, 1971
Michael Gilbert, *The Killing of Katie Steelstock*, 1980
Martha Grimes, *The Old Fox Deceiv'd*, 1982
P.D. James, *Death of an Expert Witness*, 1977

577
Elizabeth George
Playing for the Ashes (New York: Bantam, 1994)

Series: Inspector Lynley

Story type: Police Procedural—Male Lead

Major character(s): Thomas Lynley, Police Officer (detective inspector); Barbara Havers, Police Officer (sergeant)

Time period(s): 1990s

Locale(s): Greater Springburn, England

What the book is about: The milkman has found the remains of a strange fire at the home of the beautiful Gabriella Patten. Upstairs is a body dead from asphyxiation. The body is soon identified as that of Kenneth Fleming, the famous cricketeer. When the fire proves to be arson, Inspector Lynley and Sergeant Havers need to find out if the fire was set to cause the death. The investigation soon involves a woman, Olivia Whitelaw, who knew Fleming most of his life and is still affected by him after his death.

Other books you might like:
Caroline Graham, *The Inspector Barnaby Series*, 1988-
Martha Grimes, *The Inspector Jury Series*, 1981-
P.D. James, *The Inspector Dagliesh Series*, 1962-
Sheila Radley, *The Inspector Quantrill Series*, 1978-
Peter Robinson, *The Inspector Banks Series*, 1990-

578
Elizabeth George
A Suitable Vengeance (New York: Bantam, 1991)

Series: Inspector Lynley

Story type: Police Procedural—Male Lead; Psychological Suspense

Major character(s): Thomas Lynley, Police Officer (detective inspector)

Time period(s): 1980s

Locale(s): Nanrunnet, England (Cornwall)

What the book is about: Lynley arrives at the family home with his fiancee Deborah. Tensions are high. Thomas is estranged from his mother; his brother is a violent drug addict; his best friend, Simon, is in love with Deborah; and Simon's sister is involved with another addict. When a murder in the nearby town points back to the family estate, Lynley has to investigate the most complicated and personal case of his career. Prequel to the other books in the series.

Other books you might like:
Caroline Graham, *The Killings at Badger's Drift*, 1987
Martha Grimes, *The Inspector Jury Series*, 1981-
P.D. James, *The Inspector Adam Dalgliesh Series*, 1962-
Sheila Radley, *The Inspector Quantrill Series*, 1978
Ruth Rendell, *The Inspector Wexford Series*, 1964-

579
Jack Gerson
Death Squad London (New York: St. Martin's, 1990)

Series: Ernst Lohmann

Story type: Amateur Detective—Male Lead

Major character(s): Ernst Lohmann, Refugee (former Berlin police inspector)

Time period(s): 1930s (1936)

Locale(s): London, England

What the book is about: Former Berlin policeman Ernst Lohmann, now a refugee in London, is asked by a Jewish friend to investigate the suicide of a reporter. She may have been killed because of a story she was working on about the funneling of money from England to Hitler.

Other books you might like:
Christianna Brand, *Green for Danger*, 1944
Len Deighton, *SS-GB*, 1979
Ken Follett, *Eye of the Needle*, 1978
Hans Hellmut Kirst, *The Night of the Generals*, 1963

580
Tony Gibbs
Capitol Offense (New York: Mysterious, 1995)

Story type: Amateur Detective—Female Lead; Action/Adventure

Major character(s): Diana Speed, Businesswoman (manager); Eric Szabo, Security Officer, Alcoholic

Time period(s): 1990s

Locale(s): New York, New York

What the book is about: Billionaire Roger Channing asks Diana Speed to solve a problem for him. It seems he is being threatened by a woman, but he won't tell Diana anything about her except that she is a danger to the publishing house he and Diana are involved with. With the assistance of Eric Szabo, she sets out to find what's going on. The murder of a congressman in Times Square seems to have some bearing on their quest.

Other books you might like:
Robert Carter, *Final Slaughter*, 1993
Jerome Charyn, *Montezuma's Man*, 1993
Michael Connelly, *The Concrete Blonde*, 1994
Bill Granger, *Public Murders*, 1981
Orania Papazoglou, *Charisma*, 1992

581
Tony Gibbs
Landfall (New York: Morrow, 1992)

Story type: Amateur Detective; Action/Adventure

Major character(s): Gillian Verdean, Businesswoman (boat owner), Sailor; Jeremy Barr, Sailor (boat captain)

Time period(s): 1990s

Locale(s): Caribbean

What the book is about: Jake Adler has chartered the Glory. He, his mistress Isabel, and four others want to get away for a while. However a death sentence has been passed on all but Isabel. Four are dead and an attempt has been made on Adler. Gillian and Jeremy have finally realized they are in love and are looking forward to their new relationship when Jeremy is approached by a former friend—a government agent—threatening him into spying on Adler. What are they involved in and will they survive?

Other books you might like:
Jo Bannister, *The Going Down of the Sun*, 1989
J.H. Hull, *Nicole*, 1985
Sam Llewellyn, *Dead Reckoning*, 1988
Stirling Silliphant, *Steel Tiger*, 1983
Stuart Woods, *White Cargo*, 1988

582
Tony Gibbs
Running Fix (New York: Random, 1990)

Story type: Action/Adventure

Major character(s): Gillian Verdean, Sailor

Time period(s): 1980s

Locale(s): At Sea

What the book is about: Convinced that his daughter is still alive, despite evidence of being lost at sea, the father of Gillian's former roommate asks Gillian to do a search for the daughter.

Other books you might like:
Bernard Cornwell, *Killer's Wake*, 1989
Peter Foy, *Challenge*, 1988
Sam Llewellyn, *Dead Reckoning*, 1988
Stuart Woods, *Run Before the Wind*, 1986
Stuart Woods, *White Cargo*, 1987

583
Tony Gibbs
Shadow Queen (New York: Mysterious, 1991)

Story type: Amateur Detective—Female Lead; Psychological Suspense

Major character(s): Diana Speed, Businesswoman (financial officer); Marie McIntyre, Young Woman

Time period(s): 1990s

Locale(s): New York, New York

What the book is about: A cache of letters from Mary, Queen of Scots, has surfaced in the possession of Marie McIntyre, a young woman living in Queens. A famous author is interested in publishing them as they will rewrite history. The publisher put Diane in charge of verifying the letters' provenance and taking charge of Marie. This is going to be more difficult than she thought because some ruthless people are after the letters and Marie seems to be inhabited by the persona of Mary, Queen of Scots.

Other books you might like:
Amanda Cross, *The James Joyce Murder*, 1967
Thomas Gifford, *The Glendower Legacy*, 1978
Linda Mariz, *Body English*, 1992
Jennifer Rowe, *Murder by the Book*, 1989
Edith Skom, *The Mark Twain Murders*, 1989

584
Thomas Gifford
Praetorian (New York: Bantam, 1993)

Story type: Historical; Action/Adventure

Major character(s): Rodger Godwin, Journalist (columnist and radio reporter)

Time period(s): 1940s

Locale(s): Europe

What the book is about: Journalist Rodger Godwin gets involved in an assassination operation against Rommel, all the while having an affair with the wife of the operations leader. When the operation is betrayed and the leader is killed and Rodger wounded, he vows to find the traitor. Double-crossing and double-double-crossing abound and the truth is not what Rodger thinks it to be.

585 Gilbert

Other books you might like:
Ted Allbeury, *The Lantern Network*, 1978
Ken Follett, *Night over Water*, 1991
Gillian Freeman, *Diary of a Nazi Lady*, 1978
Alan Furst, *Night Soldiers*, 1988
Jack Higgins, *Night of the Fox*, 1986

585
Dale L. Gilbert
Murder Begins at Home (New York: St. Martin's, 1989)
Series: Matt Doyle/Carter Winfield
Story type: Private Detective—Male Lead
Major character(s): Matt Doyle, Detective—Private; Carter Winfield, Detective—Private (doesn't like to leave home)
Time period(s): 1980s
Locale(s): San Diego, California
What the book is about: When Doyle is hired to live with and protect a mobster's family, they expect trouble but not as much as they get.
Other books you might like:
Lawrence Block, *The Topless Tulip Caper*, 1974
Rex Stout, *The Nero Wolfe Series*, (1934-1975)

586
B.M. Gill (Pseudonym of Barbara Trimble)
The Fifth Rapunzel (New York: Scribners, 1991)
Series: Inspector Maybridge
Story type: Police Procedural—Male Lead
Major character(s): Tom Maybridge, Police Officer (detective chief inspector)
Time period(s): 1990s
Locale(s): England
What the book is about: Professor Peter Bradshaw and his wife are killed in a car accident abroad. Tom Maybridge is at the funeral of his friends when he notices a bloody pig's foot in one of the floral displays. A note with the foot may relate to one of forensic pathologist Bradshaw's most famous cases, the Rapunzel murders. Is this revenge, a guilty person covering his tracks or something deeper?
Other books you might like:
Christianna Brand, *Fog of Doubt*, 1953
Peter Dickinson, *The Glass-Sided Ant's Nest*, 1968
Elizabeth George, *A Great Deliverance*, 1988
Ruth Rendell, *The Inspector Wexford Series*, 1964-

587
B.M. Gill (Pseudonym of Barbara Trimble)
Time and Time Again (New York: Scribners, 1990)
Story type: Psychological Suspense
Major character(s): Maeve Barclay, Housewife, Activist (political); Rene Dudgeon, Criminal (shoplifter)
Time period(s): 1980s

What the book is about: After 18 months in prison, Maeve Barclay feels alienated from everyone except her fellow inmates. When one of them is killed and another injured, she is forced to reexamine her life.
Other books you might like:
Joan Fleming, *Kill or Cure*, 1968
Michael Gilbert, *The Black Seraphim*, 1984
Ruth Rendell, *The Lake of Darkness*, 1980
Barbara Vine, *The Dark-Adapted Eye*, 1986

588
Dorothy Gilman
Mrs. Pollifax and the Whirling Dervish (New York: Doubleday, 1990)
Series: Mrs. Pollifax
Story type: Espionage
Major character(s): Emily Pollifax, Spy (grandmother and part-time spy)
Time period(s): 1980s
What the book is about: Sent to Morocco to provide a cover for another agent, Mrs. Pollifax soon discovers that the agent is not who he seems to be.
Other books you might like:
Richard Barth, *The Condo Kill*, 1985

589
Noreen Gilpatrick
The Piano Man (New York: St. Martins, 1991)
Story type: Amateur Detective—Male Lead
Major character(s): Paul Whitman, Musician (former concert pianist)
Time period(s): 1990s
Locale(s): Washington (island in Puget Sound)
What the book is about: Hired to restore three valuable pianos stored on an island in Puget Sound, Whitman finds the pianos in exceptionally bad shape. What's more, one of the strings is arranged in the form of a noose as if to welcome him. An earlier piano man has disappeared and soon turns up dead, the ferry to and from the island has gone into dry dock and he has no choice but to try and find the killer. First novel and winner of the St. Martins/Malice Domestic contest for best first traditional novel.
Other books you might like:
Kenn Davis, *The Forza Trap*, 1979
James Gollin, *Broken Consort*, 1989
Paul Myers, *Deadly Cadenza*, 1986
Bill Pronzini, *Games*, 1976

590
T.G. Gilpin
Death of a Fantasy Life (New York: St. Martins, 1993)
Story type: Amateur Detective—Male Lead

Major character(s): Anthony Ponton, Professor (of linguistics); Sylvia Mothersill, Stripper

Time period(s): 1980s

Locale(s): London, England

What the book is about: Professor Ponton was the legal guardian of Eric Wells until Wells reached maturity. Ponton is still concerned about him and finds that Eric has a fascination with strippers. A stripper that Eric liked was killed a month ago and now his current favorite has been found murdered. Eric is the obvious suspect and Ponton teams with a sympathetic stripper to clear him.

Other books you might like:
V.C. Clinton-Baddeley, *The Dr. Davie Series*, 1967-1972
Desmond Cory, *The Catalyst*, 1991
Edmund Crispin, *The Gervase Fen Series*, 1944-1978
D. Keith Mano, *Topless*, 1991
Robert Reeves, *Peeping Thomas*, 1990

591
T.G. Gilpin
Is Anybody There? (New York: St. Martin's, 1992)

Story type: Psychological Suspense; Amateur Detective—Male Lead

Major character(s): Thomas Wiggins, Police Officer (retired)

Time period(s): 1990s

Locale(s): England

What the book is about: Mrs. Hathaway is a medium and has a regular group of elderly ladies who want to talk to their departed relatives. When one of them is murdered, Wiggins is enlisted to join the group under the pretext of talking to his dead wife. Another woman of the group is killed and, more importantly, Wiggins' daughter becomes involved in the group. Can he keep her from becoming the next victim?

Other books you might like:
Marten Claridge, *Nobody's Fool*, 1991
Nancy Livingston, *The G.D.H. Pringle Series*, 1986
Molly McKittrick, *The Medium Is Murder*, 1992
Mignon Warner, *A Medium for Murder*, 1976

592
James Preston Girard
The Late Man (New York: Atheneum, 1993)

Story type: Psychological Suspense; Police Procedural—Male Lead

Major character(s): L.J. Loomis, Police Officer (captain); Sam Haun, Journalist (older reporter); Stosh Babicki, Journalist (younger reporter)

Time period(s): 1990s (1993)

Locale(s): Wichita, Kansas

What the book is about: A college student is found murdered and the method seems to be that of a known serial killer. It may, however, be the work of a copycat. Three people become obsessed with finding the killer: Sam Haun, a reporter who recently lost his wife and daughter in a car crash; Stosh Babicki, a young reporter who is determined to make a name for herself; and police Captain L.J. Loomis who is having a crisis in his own life as his ex-wife is moving in with a professor of hers. The relationships among these three and the people they are investigating form the crux of this novel. First novel under this name.

Other books you might like:
Frederick Barton, *With Extreme Prejudice*, 1993
Jay Brandon, *Loose Among the Lambs*, 1993
Richard Harris, *Honor Bound*, 1982
Christina Baker Kline, *Sweet Water*, 1993
Andrew Klavan, *Corruption*, 1994
Jeffrey Tharp, *A Killing in Kansas*, (pseudonym of James Preston Girard)

593
Jaqueline Girdner
Adjusted to Death (New York: Diamond, 1991)

Series: Kate Jasper

Story type: Amateur Detective—Female Lead

Major character(s): Kate Jasper, Store Owner (novelties); Wayne Caruso, Bodyguard (factotum to the murdered man)

Time period(s): 1990s

Locale(s): Mill Valley, California (Marin County)

What the book is about: On a visit to her chiropractor Kate discovers a dead body. She and the murdered man's friend/bodyguard team up to try and find the guilty party. First mystery.

Other books you might like:
P.M. Carlson, *The Maggie Ryan Series*, 1987-
Joan Hess, *The Claire Malloy Series*, 1987-
Susan Isaacs, *Compromising Positions*, 1978
Gillian Roberts, *Caught Dead in Philadelphia*, 1987
Marilyn Wallace, *A Case of Loyalties*, 1986

594
Jaqueline Girdner
The Last Resort (New York: Berkeley, 1991)

Series: Kate Jasper

Story type: Amateur Detective—Female Lead

Major character(s): Kate Jasper, Store Owner; Wayne Caruso, Boyfriend (Kate's lover)

Time period(s): 1990s

Locale(s): Delores, California (southern California)

What the book is about: Kate has just received her final divorce papers when she gets a call from her ex, Craig. His new girlfriend, beautiful, blonde lawyer Suzanne Sorenson, has been found murdered at the swank health spa where they were staying. Craig is the prime suspect and he needs Kate for moral support. When Kate arrives she finds a strange collection of guests and a threatening series of "accidents".

595

Other books you might like:
Jill Churchill, *Grime and Punishment*, 1989
Susan Isaacs, *Compromising Positions*, 1978
Mary Kittredge, *Poison Pen*, 1990
Gillian Roberts, *Caught Dead in Philadelphia*, 1987
Valerie Wolzien, *Murder at the PTA Luncheon*, 1988

595

Jaqueline Girdner
A Stiff Critique (New York: Berkley, 1995)

Series: Kate Jasper

Story type: Amateur Detective—Female Lead

Major character(s): Kate Jasper, Store Owner (novelties); Carrie Yates, Lawyer

Time period(s): 1990s

Locale(s): Marin County, California

What the book is about: When Kate mentions to her friend Carrie that she is thinking of writing poetry, Carrie suggests that Kate join a writers' critique group that Carrie belongs to. The group is not what Kate expects; there seems to be an awful lot of bickering and jealousy. A few hours after the meeting, Kate and Carrie find Slade Skinner, the only successfully published member of the group, beaten to death.

Other books you might like:
Jill Churchill, *The Jane Jeffry Series*, 1990-
Nancy Gladstone, *Mommy and the Murder*, 1995
Jean Hager, *Dead and Buried*, 1995
M.D. Lake, *A Gift for Murder*, 1992
Barbara Burnett Smith, *Writers of the Purple Sage*, 1994

596

Jaqueline Girdner
Tea-Totally Dead (New York: Berkley, 1994)

Series: Kate Jasper

Story type: Amateur Detective—Female Lead

Major character(s): Kate Jasper, Store Owner (novelties); Wayne Caruso, Restauranteur (Kate's lover)

Time period(s): 1990s

Locale(s): Marin County, California

What the book is about: Family reunions can be murder. Wayne Caruso's mother, recently released from a mental institution after 20 years confinement caused by over-medication, is bitter and wants revenge. She threatens the rest of the family at the reunion with revealing some secret. Of course before that can happen she is found dead—poisoned. Kate Jasper is determined to find the killer.

Other books you might like:
Susan Wittig Albert, *The China Bayles Series*, 1992-
Carole Berry, *The Bonnie Indermill Series*, 1987-
Trella Crespi, *The Simona Griffo Series*, 1990-
Gillian Roberts, *The Amanda Pepper Series*, 1987-
Lora Roberts, *Murder in a Nice Neighborhood*, 1994

597

E.X. Giroux (Pseudonym of Doris Shannon)
A Death for a Dancing Doll (New York: St. Martin's, 1991)

Series: Robert Forsythe

Story type: Amateur Detective—Male Lead; Legal

Major character(s): Robert Forsythe, Lawyer (barrister); Sandy Sanderson, Secretary (Forsythe's secretary)

Time period(s): 1990s

Locale(s): Vancouver, British Columbia, Canada

What the book is about: Robert and Sandy are on vacation in British Columbia. A friend offers them the use of his hotel suite but there turns out to be a price tag - they have to talk to Rebecca Holly. Rebecca wants an investigation of her grandmother's death that the police have called a suicide. Investigating involves the rest of the Holly-Pulos family and some mysterious deaths from the past.

Other books you might like:
Sarah Caudwell, *The Hilary Tamar Series*, 1981-
Anthony Gilbert, *The Arthur Crook Series*, 1936-1972

598

E.X. Giroux (Pseudonym of Doris Shannon)
A Death for a Dodo (New York: St. Martins, 1993)

Series: Robert Forsythe

Story type: Amateur Detective—Male Lead; Legal

Major character(s): Robert Forsythe, Lawyer; Sandy Sanderson, Secretary (Forsythe's secretary)

Time period(s): 1990s

Locale(s): London, England

What the book is about: Robert Forsythe has finally had knee surgery and must spend time recuperating. Because of his fear of hospitals he chooses the Damien Day Health Home (known as the DODO) which is run by some acquaintances from a previous case. He meets the other guests who all center around the international beauty queen Kate Kapiche, as sort of a reunion. There is suicide and a mass murder in their past and soon a new murder occurs.

Other books you might like:
Anthony Appiah, *Avenging Angel*, 1991
Sarah Caudwell, *The Hilary Tamar Series*, 1981-
Frances Fyfield, *A Question of Guilt*, 1991
Anthony Gilbert, *The Arthur Crook Series*, 1936-1972
Michael Underwood, *Seeds of Murder*, 1992

599

E.X. Giroux (Pseudonym of Doris Shannon)
The Dying Room (New York: St. Martins, 1993)

Story type: Psychological Suspense

Major character(s): Karen Dancer, Advertising, Single Parent (widow)

Time period(s): 1990s

Locale(s): Hampton, Ontario, Canada

What the book is about: Karen Dancer has left her job and returned home with her daughter Jamie, hoping that Jamie will recover from her illness. Karen is in need of emotional healing as well. Everything seems the same at first but soon she realizes that things have changed. Now someone seems to be out to get her and her daughter. A program of harassment escalates until people around her start to die.

Other books you might like:
Martha Grimes, *The End of the Pier*, 1992
Mary Anne Kelly, *Foxglove*, 1992
Janet LaPierre, *Old Enemies*, 1993
D.F. Mills, *Deadline*, 1991
Nancy Pickard, *I.O.U.*, 1991

600
Nancy Gladstone
Mommy and the Murder (New York: HarperCollins, 1995)

Story type: Amateur Detective—Female Lead

Major character(s): Elizabeth Halperin, Businesswoman (ex-Wall Street trader), Single Parent

Time period(s): 1990s

Locale(s): The Berkshires, Massachusetts

What the book is about: When Elizabeth Halperin decided to quit her high-paying Wall Street job and moved to the Berkshires to care for her daughter, Emily, her writer husband decided to look for greener fields. Apparently he found them and got a million dollar advance for his next book. Now he's dead—murdered at a Halloween party. Since Elizabeth was also at the party and is now a wealthy widow, the police consider her the prime suspect. Fortunately, Elizabeth has the help of the mothers of Emily's play group, but can they find the real killer? First mystery.

Other books you might like:
Jill Churchill, *The Jane Jeffry Series*, 1990-
Jaqueline Girdner, *A Stiff Critique*, 1995
M.D. Lake, *A Gift for Murder*, 1992
Barbara Burnett Smith, *Writers of the Purple Sage*, 1994
Valerie Wolzien, *The Susan Henshaw Series*, 1988-

601
Leslie Glass
Hanging Time (New York: Bantam, 1995)

Story type: Police Procedural—Female Lead

Major character(s): April Woo, Police Officer; Jason Frank, Doctor (psychoanalyst)

Time period(s): 1990s

Locale(s): New York, New York

What the book is about: A shop assistant at a Manhattan dress shop is found hanging from a chandelier. April Woo is unconvinced by a suspect's confession, nor by the threatening message on the victim's answering machine. Psychoanalyst Jason Frank is also withholding what could be vital evidence from the police.

Other books you might like:
Carol O'Connell, *Killing Critics*, 1996
Lillian O'Donnell, *The Norah Mulcahaney Series*, 1972-
S.J. Rozan, *China Trade*, 1994
Julie Smith, *The Skip Langdon Series*, 1990
Dorothy Uhnak, *The Christie Opera Series*, 1968-

602
Leslie Glass
To Do No Harm (New York: Doubleday, 1992)

Story type: Action/Adventure

Major character(s): Aaron Simon, Doctor (psychiatrist); Bettina Dunne, Artist (children's book illustrator); Peter Balkan, Lawyer

Time period(s): 1990s

Locale(s): Chester, New Jersey

What the book is about: Bettina and Tom Dunne are expecting a baby soon when Tom has to go overseas. Dr. Simon has a patient who cannot bring a child to term and is desperate to have a baby. Peter Balkan is in debt to some dangerous people due to a coke habit and has taken up baby-brokering to make some quick money. Soon these people will become involved in kidnapping and murder. First mystery.

Other books you might like:
Peter Abrahams, *Pressure Drop*, 1989
Mary Higgins Clark, *The Cradle Will Fall*, 1980
Robin Cook, *Harmful Intent*, 1989
Stephen Lewis, *And Baby Makes None*, 1991
Joyce Anne Schneider, *Darkness Falls*, 1989

603
Alison Glen (Pseudonym of Cheryl Meredith Lowry and Louise Vetter)
Showcase (New York: Simon & Schuster, 1992)

Story type: Amateur Detective—Female Lead

Major character(s): Charlotte Sams, Journalist (free-lance); Lou Torenson, Psychologist

Time period(s): 1990s

Locale(s): Columbus, Ohio

What the book is about: Charlotte has been talked into covering the 'Son of Heaven' oriental art exhibit. Also there is her cousin, Melanie and her obnoxious husband Phil. Phil is even worse that usual, denouncing the show as a fraud, saying at least one of the exhibits is a fake. The next day Phil is dead of a heart attack. Charlotte decides to look into the matter further and discovers this isn't the first 'heart attack' connected with the exhibit. First novel.

Other books you might like:
Jack Albin Anderson, *The Society Ball Murders*, 1990
Barbara D'Amato, *The Cat Marsala Series*, 1990-
Judith Garwood, *Make Friends with Murder*, 1992
Susan Kelly, *The Liz Connors Series*, 1986-
Kathryn Lasky Knight, *Mortal Words*, 1990

604

Alison Glen (Pseudonym of Cheryl Meredith Lowry)
Co-Author: Louise Vetter
Trunk Show (New York: Simon & Schuster, 1995)

Series: Charlotte Sams

Story type: Amateur Detective—Female Lead

Major character(s): Charlotte Sams, Journalist (magazine writer); Lou Toreson, Psychologist (retired)

Time period(s): 1990s

Locale(s): Columbus, Ohio

What the book is about: Lions and tigers and murders, oh my! Charlotte is writing a series of articles on the Columbus Zoo, and on the day she is to interview the elephant trainer, his body is found in the elephant compound. It is soon discovered that he was murdered and Charlotte, with the help of her friend Lou Toreson, begins to track the killer. Another death makes it clear that someone is desperate and Charlotte may be the next victim if she gets too close.

Other books you might like:
Barbara D'Amato, *The Cat Marsala Series*, 1990-
Kathryn Lasky Knight, *The Calista Jacobs Series*, 1988-
Sarah Shankman, *The Samantha Adams Series*, 1989-
Triss Stein, *Murder at the Class Reunion*, 1994
Mary Willis Walker, *Zero at the Bone*, 1991

605

Kenneth W. Goddard
Wildfire (New York: Forge, 1994)

Series: Henry Lightstone

Story type: Action/Adventure

Major character(s): Henry Lightstone, Police Officer, Government Official (U.S. Fish and Wildlife agent)

Time period(s): 1990s

Locale(s): Yellowstone National Park, Wyoming; Sequoia National Park, California

What the book is about: A number of forces are plotting both the destruction and saving of Yellowstone and Sequoia National Parks—and each other. U.S. Fish and Wildlife agent Henry Lightstone must sort out the good guys from the bad, all the while trying to keep himself and his staff alive.

Other books you might like:
Sarah Andrews, *Tensleep*, 1994
Nevada Barr, *Track of the Cat*, 1993
Les Standiford, *Spill*, 1991
Lee Wallingford, *Clear-Cut Murder*, 1993

606

Lee Goldberg
My Gun Has Bullets (New York: St. Martin's, 1995)

Story type: Action/Adventure

Major character(s): Charles Willis, Police Officer, Actor; Sabrina Bishop, Actress

Time period(s): 1990s

Locale(s): Los Angeles, California

What the book is about: Charles Willis stopped a speeding car driven by the beloved star of "Miss Agatha," television's top rated show. When he tries to give her a ticket, she shoots him. In order to keep Miss Agatha out of jail, the TV people offer Charlie a series of his own. He becomes the star of "My Gun Has Bullets." Unfortunately organized crime is trying to take over the industry and introducing some of their time-honored methods of eliminating competition. Charlie and his show are one of the prime targets as is Sabrina Bishop, an actress in whom Charlie is interested. First mystery.

Other books you might like:
Zev Chafets, *Inherit the Mob*, 1993
Carl Hiaasen, *Strip Tease*, 1994
Vince Kohler, *Banjo Boy*, 1994
Thomas Perry, *Metzger's Dog*, 1984

607

Robert Goldsborough
Fade to Black (New York: Bantam, 1990)

Series: Nero Wolfe

Story type: Private Detective—Male Lead

Major character(s): Nero Wolfe, Detective—Private; Archie Goodwin, Detective—Private, Sidekick (assistant to Nero Wolfe)

Time period(s): 1990s

Locale(s): New York, New York

What the book is about: This is a continuation of the series written by Rex Stout from 1934-1974. When rival ad agencies produce almost identical ads for competing soft drink companies, the result is murder. Nero Wolfe is persuaded to take the case.

Other books you might like:
Lawrence Block, *Make Out with Murder*, 1974
Dale Gilbert, *The Black Star Murders*, 1988
Melodie Johnson Howe, *The Mother Shadow*, 1989
William F. Love, *The Chartreuse Clue*, 1990
Herbert Resnicow, *The Gold Solution*, 1983

608

Robert Goldsborough
Silver Spire (New York: Bantam, 1992)

Series: Nero Wolfe

Story type: Private Detective—Male Lead

Major character(s): Nero Wolfe, Detective—Private; Archie Goodwin, Detective—Private, Sidekick (assistant to Nero Wolfe)

Time period(s): 1990s

Locale(s): New York, New York

What the book is about: Wolfe is approached by the business manager of the Reverend Barnabas Bay, televangelist of the Tabernacle of the Silver Spire, because someone is slipping threatening notes into the collection pouch. Wolfe decides not to take the case so Archie recommends Fred Durkin. Two weeks later Fred is under arrest for the murder of an assistant pastor. Now Wolfe has to take the case to save Fred. This is the continuation of the series done by Rex Stout from 1934-1974.

Other books you might like:
Lawrence Block, *The Topless Tulip Caper*, 1974
Dale L. Gilbert, *The Carter Winfield Series*, 1988-1990
Melodie Johnson Howe, *The Mother Shadow*, 1989
William F. Love, *The Bishop Regan Series*, 1990-
Herbert Resnicow, *The Gold Solution*, 1983

609
James Gollin
Broken Consort (New York: St. Martin's, 1989)

Series: Antiqua Players

Story type: Amateur Detective

Major character(s): Alan French, Musician; Jackie French, Musician

Time period(s): 1980s

Locale(s): At Sea; Caribbean

What the book is about: When the Antiqua Players are invited to play on the private yacht of Jeremiah Boyle as it cruises the Caribbean, they accept with pleasure. The cruise becomes less pleasurable when their host is murdered and there are further attacks on the passengers including one on Jackie.

Other books you might like:
Robert Barnard, *Death on the High C's*, 1978
V.C. Clinton-Baddeley, *Only a Matter of Time*, 1969
Kenn Davis, *The Forza Trap*, 1979
Paula Gosling, *Solo Blues*, 1981
Thomas Hauser, *The Beethoven Conspiracy*, 1984
Lucille Kallen, *The Tanglewood Murder*, 1980
Ngaio Marsh, *Overture to Death*, 1939

610
Gloria Gonzalez
The Thirteenth Apostle (New York: St. Martin's, 1993)

Story type: Amateur Detective—Female Lead; Action/Adventure

Major character(s): Geraldine St. Claire, Journalist (newspaper reporter); Owen Ryder, Businessman (charter boat owner)

Time period(s): 1990s

Locale(s): Key West, Florida; Cleveland, Ohio; New York, New York

What the book is about: Geraldine St. Claire is in Las Vegas losing money when she is approached by Owen Ryder who tells her that her lover, writer Hal Landry, is dead and that he was murdered. Hal had written a story about random Tylenol poisonings. Now there are coffee poisonings and Hal and Owen had discovered a link to some Asian businessmen. Revenge and a big story are irresistible lures to Geraldine, but many more will die before the story is finished. First novel.

Other books you might like:
Barbara D'Amato, *The Cat Marsala Series*, 1990-
Denise Danks, *User Deadly*, 1992
Wendy Hornsby, *Telling Lies*, 1992
Susan Kelly, *The Liz Connors Series*, 1985-
Kerry Tucker, *Still Waters*, 1991

611
Charles A. Goodrum
A Slip of the Tong (New York: St. Martin's, 1992)

Series: Werner-Bok Library

Story type: Amateur Detective—Male Lead

Major character(s): Crighton Jones, Librarian (assistant director); Edward George, Librarian (librarian emeritus)

Time period(s): 1990s

Locale(s): Washington, District of Columbia

What the book is about: Two staff members of the Prestigious Werner-Bok Library have been murdered in the Asian section of the library. There are also rumors that among the uncatalogued manuscripts is a rare treasure looted during the Boxer Rebellion. The mainland Chinese and the Taiwan governments are interested. Crighton calls on Edward and her lover Stephen to help her solve the mystery and preserve the reputation of the library.

Other books you might like:
Charity Blackstock, *Dewey Death*, 1977
Jon L. Breen, *Touch of the Past*, 1988
John Dunning, *Booked to Die*, 1992
Will Harriss, *The Bay Psalm Book Murder*, 1983
Gillian Linscott, *Unknown Hand*, 1989

612
Alison Gordon
The Dead Pull Hitter (New York: St. Martin's, 1989)

Series: Kate Henry

Story type: Amateur Detective—Female Lead

Major character(s): Kate Henry, Journalist (baseball writer)

Time period(s): 1980s

Locale(s): Toronto, Ontario, Canada

What the book is about: As the Toronto Titans are about to clinch the pennant, two of their star players turn up dead. Kate Henry decides to pursue the story. First book.

613 Gordon

Other books you might like:
Elizabeth Fackler, *Barbed Wire*, 1986
Michael Geller, *Major League Murder*, 1988
Alexander Law, *To an Easy Grave*, 1986
Dominic Stansberry, *The Spoiler*, 1987
Alice Storey, *First Kill All the Lawyers*, 1988

613
Alison Gordon
Night Game (New York: St. Martins, 1993)
Series: Kate Henry
Story type: Amateur Detective—Female Lead
Major character(s): Kate Henry, Journalist (sportswriter)
Time period(s): 1990s
Locale(s): Sunland, Florida

What the book is about: It's a new year for the Toronto Titans baseball team and they are at spring training in sunny Florida. Kate Henry is, of course, covering the team and once again murder interrupts the game. This time "Juicy Lucy" Cartwright, a good-looking reporter who is famous for checking out the new talent in the bedroom, is found shot to death. The prime suspect is a rookie, Domingo Avila, but Kate doesn't think he's guilty and sets out to prove it.

Other books you might like:
L.L. Enger, *Swing*, 1991
Paul Engleman, *Dead in Center Field*, 1983
Crabbe Evers, *The Duffy House Series*, 1990-
David Everson, *Suicide Squeeze*, 1991
David F. Nighbert, *Strikezone*, 1989

614
Alison Gordon
Safe at Home (New York: St. Martin's, 1991)
Series: Kate Henry
Story type: Amateur Detective—Female Lead
Major character(s): Kate Henry, Journalist (sportswriter); Andy Monroe, Police Officer, Detective—Homicide (Kate's lover)
Time period(s): 1990s
Locale(s): Toronto, Ontario, Canada

What the book is about: Kate Henry's boyfriend, homicide detective Andy Monroe, is investigating a serial killer who preys on young boys. At the same time Kate is pursuing a story involving homosexuality on the Toronto Titans baseball team. Is it possible that one of the ballplayers is the killer?

Other books you might like:
Charlotte Elkins, *A Wicked Slice*, 1989 (Aaron Elkins, co-author)
Michael Hendricks, *Money to Burn*, 1989
Janice Law, *Death under Par*, 1981
Shannon O'Cork, *Sports Freak*, 1980
Eric Wright, *A Sensitive Case*, 1990

615
Alison Gordon
Striking Out (Toronto: McClelland and Stewart, 1995)
Series: Kate Henry
Story type: Amateur Detective—Female Lead
Major character(s): Kate Henry, Journalist (sportswriter); Andy Munro, Detective—Homicide (Kate's lover)
Time period(s): 1990s
Locale(s): Toronto, Ontario, Canada

What the book is about: Kate is temporarily out of a job—the baseball strike abruptly ended the season and she refused to cover the negotiations. Soon she has plenty to do. First her lover policeman, Andy, is shot in the line of duty, then her tenant's son asks her to investigate the disappearance of Maggie, a homeless woman who has been living nearby. Did Maggie witness something she was not supposed to or has her violent past that she was running away from finally caught up to her?

Other books you might like:
Edna Buchanan, *Suitable for Framing*, 1995
Barbara D'Amato, *Hard Women*, 1993
Wendy Hornsby, *Midnight Baby*, 1993
Mary Logue, *Still Explosion*, 1993
Kerry Tucker, *Cold Feet*, 1992

616
Joe Gores
32 Cadillacs (New York: Mysterious, 1992)
Series: DKA
Story type: Private Detective—Male Lead; Action/Adventure
Major character(s): Dan Kearny, Detective—Private (owner of DKA)
Time period(s): 1990s
Locale(s): San Francisco, California; Steubenville, Iowa

What the book is about: The king of the gypsies has had an accident in Steubenville and may be dying. He calls the rest of the families to him to announce his successor. The Bay area gypsies decide to go in style and pull off a giant scam ending up with 31 Cadillacs. Dan Kearny and his group are hired by the bank to get the cars back. They get involved in the gypsies' quest for the 32nd Cadillac—a pink, 1958 El Dorado. The one who presents it to the dying king may be the next leader of the gypsies.

Other books you might like:
Gary Alexander, *Kiet Goes West*, 1992
Jonathan Gash, *The Great California Game*, 1991
Ken Grissom, *Big Fish*, 1991
Ross Thomas, *The Fools in Town Are on Our Side*, 1970
Donald E. Westlake, *Don't Ask*, 1971

617
Joe Gores
Dead Man (New York: Mysterious, 1993)

Story type: Action/Adventure; Private Detective—Male Lead

Major character(s): Eddie Dain, Detective—Private

Time period(s): 1990s

Locale(s): San Francisco, California; Chicago, Illinois; New Orleans, Louisiana

What the book is about: Eddie Dain is a low-key, high tech private detective who doesn't take his job very seriously. His latest case ends when the man he was investigating is blown up on his boat. Eddie is still looking into it using his computer skills when two men with shotguns kill his wife and son and leave him for dead. Two years later Dain is back, hard and haunted and looking for revenge.

Other books you might like:
Jay Brandon, *Deadbolt*, 1985
Stanley Ellin, *The Luxembourg Run*, 1977
Joseph Koenig, *Floater*, 1986
Les Standiford, *Done Deal*, 1993

618
Joe Gores
Menaced Assassin (New York: Mysterious, 1994)

Story type: Police Procedural—Male Lead; Psychological Suspense

Major character(s): Dante Stagnaro, Police Officer (lieutenant, organized crime); Will Dalton, Anthropologist (paleoanthropologist); Raptor, Criminal (assassin)

Time period(s): 1990s

Locale(s): San Francisco, California

What the book is about: Will Dalton's wife is having an affair and learns something she shouldn't have. When she is killed, Lieutenant Dante Stagnaro is concerned that her husband may also be a target. Soon he realizes that a brilliant assassin calling himself "Raptor" is killing anyone who had anything to do with the murder of the dead woman. Who is Raptor, why is he doing this, and can Dante keep him from making Will Dalton the final victim?

Other books you might like:
Harlen Campbell, *Monkey on a Chain*, 1993
Michael Connelly, *The Black Echo*, 1992
Gary Friedman, *Gun Men*, 1993
Stephen Hunter, *Point of Impact*, 1993
Bill Pronzini, *The Running of Beasts*, 1976 (Barry Malzberg, co-author)

619
Ed Gorman, Editor
Co-Editor: Martin H. Greenberg
Cat Crimes (New York: Fine, 1991)

Story type: Anthology

Time period(s): 1990s

What the book is about: A collection of stories, all involving cats in one form or another. Authors include Peter Lovesey, Bill Pronzini, Joan Hess, Jon Breen, Dorothy B. Hughes, Barbara Paul, Bill Crider, Les Roberts, John Lutz, J.A. Jance, Barbara D'Amato, Barbara Collins and others.

Other books you might like:
Lilian Jackson Braun, *The Cats Who Series*, 1991 (editor)
Carol-Lynn Rossel Waugh, *Purrfect Crime*, 1989 (Martin Greenberg and Isaac Asimov, co-editors)
Bill Fawcett, *Cats in Space*, 1992
Stella Whitelaw, *The Cat That Wasn't There*, 1992
Rita Mae Brown, *Wish You Were Here*, 1990

620
Ed Gorman, Editor
Co-Editor: Martin H. Greenberg
Cat Crimes II (New York: Fine)

Series: Cat Crimes

Story type: Anthology

Time period(s): 1990s

What the book is about: The second collection of all original stories starring cats. Authors include Charlotte MacLeod, Margaret Maron, Joan Hess, Sharyn McCrumb, Les Roberts, Bill Pronzini and Barbara Collins.

Other books you might like:
Lilian Jackson Braun, *The Cat Who Series*, 1991 (editor)
Carol-Lynn Rossel Waugh, *Purrfect Crime*, 1989 (Martin Greenberg and Isaac Asimov, co-editors)

621
Ed Gorman, Editor
Dark Crimes: Great Noir Fiction From the '50's to the '90's (New York: Carroll & Graf, 1991)

Story type: Anthology

What the book is about: A collection of nineteen short stories and two novellas in the hardboiled tradition. Authors include Ed McBain, Lawrence Block, Bill Pronzini, John Lutz, Andrew Vachss, Loren D. Estleman, Joe R. Lansdale, Peter Rabe and Marcia Muller.

Other books you might like:
William F. Nolan, *The Boys in the Black Mask*, 1980

622
Ed Gorman
Night Kills (New York: Ballantine, 1990)

Story type: Amateur Detective—Male Lead; Action/Adventure

Major character(s): Frank Brolan, Advertising; Greg Wagner, Handicapped, Computer Expert (wheel-chair bound)

Time period(s): 1990s

Locale(s): Minneapolis/St. Paul, Minnesota

What the book is about: Ad man Frank Brolan finds a murdered woman in his freezer - a woman he had recently had a confrontation with - so he is loathe to go to the police. He decides to try, with the help of Greg Wagner - who loved the dead woman - to find the killer himself.

623 Gorman

Other books you might like:
John Camp, *The Fool's Run*, 1989
Bill Crider, *The Carl Burns Series*, 1988-
Joel Helgerson, *Slow Burn*, 1987
Tom Kakonis, *Michigan Roll*, 1988
Joe R. Lansdale, *Cold in July*, 1989

623
Ed Gorman
The Night Remembers (New York: St. Martins, 1991)
Story type: Private Detective—Male Lead
Major character(s): Jack Walsh, Detective—Private (retired police officer)
Time period(s): 1990s
Locale(s): Cedar Rapids, Iowa
What the book is about: The wife of a man Walsh helped put in prison 12 years earlier comes to him to ask for his help in proving her recently released husband innocent. As Walsh is trying to decide what to do, there's a murder involving the same family.
Other books you might like:
Max Allan Collins, *Kill Your Darlings*, 1984
Stephen Greenleaf, *Book Case*, 1991
Bill Pronzini, *The Nameless Detective Series*, 1971-
John Sandford, *Eyes of Prey*, 1991
Benjamin M. Schutz, *A Fistful of Empty*, 1991

624
Paula Gosling
The Body in Blackwater Bay (New York: Mysterious, 1992)
Series: Jack Stryker
Story type: Police Procedural—Male Lead
Major character(s): Jack Stryker, Police Officer (detective lieutenant); Kate Trevorne, Professor (Jack's lady friend)
Time period(s): 1990s
Locale(s): Great Lakes
What the book is about: Jack is recuperating from a gunshot wound with his love Kate at her summer home on Paradise Island. Also there is Daria Grey, a famous artist. Daria says she is being harassed by her estranged husband. She says she is being stalked and has received threatening notes. Most people think she is crazy, but Kate asks Jack to help. Then the husband is killed and Daria is the main suspect.
Other books you might like:
Deforest Day, *August Ice*, 1990
L.L. Enger, *Comeback*, 1990
Frederic Huber, *Axx Goes South*, 1989
J.R. Levitt, *Ten of Swords*, 1991
Celestine Sibley, *Straight as an Arrow*, 1992

625
Paula Gosling
Death Penalties (New York: Mysterious, 1991)
Series: Luke Abbot
Story type: Police Procedural—Male Lead
Major character(s): Luke Abbot, Police Officer (chief inspector, CID); Tim Nightingale, Police Officer (detective sergeant, CID)
Time period(s): 1990s
Locale(s): London, England
What the book is about: Tim Nightingale is investigating the routine death of a retired police officer. He finds that the dead man had witnessed an auto crash in which Roger Leland had died under suspicious circumstances. When Tim investigates Leland's widow, he realizes she is suffering a strange series of harassments. His instinct tells him to investigate further, even against the advice of his superior, Luke Abbot.
Other books you might like:
Reginald Hill, *The Dalziel and Pascoe Series*, 1971-
Roger Ormerod, *Hung in the Balance*, 1991
Peter Robinson, *Gallows View*, 1990

626
Paula Gosling
A Few Dying Words (New York: Mysterious, 1994)
Series: Blackwater Bay Mystery
Story type: Police Procedural—Male Lead
Major character(s): Matt Gabriel, Police Officer (sheriff); Dominic Pritchard, Lawyer
Time period(s): 1990s
Locale(s): Blackwater Bay (Great Lakes region)
What the book is about: It's the off-season and the tourists have gone home, but that doesn't mean Sheriff Matt Gabriel can relax. It's Halloween and time for The Howl, where prizes are given for the best prank and all hell breaks loose. Matt's friend, Tom Finnegan, calls and wants to meet with Matt but Tom never makes the meeting. He is involved in a car crash and Matt gets there just in time for Tom's last words. They hint that an old accident may not have been so accidental. Stirring up the past may cause more tragedy in the present.
Other books you might like:
Andrew Coburn, *Voices in the Dark*, 1994
Susan Rogers Cooper, *Chasing Away the Devil*, 1992
Sharyn McCrumb, *She Walks These Hills*, 1994
Susan Oleksiw, *Double Take*, 1994
Anne Wingate, *Death by Deception*, 1988

627
Laurence Gough
Hot Shots (New York: Viking, 1990)
Series: Jack Willows/Claire Parker
Story type: Police Procedural
Major character(s): Jack Willows, Detective—Police; Claire Parker, Detective—Police
Time period(s): 1980s
Locale(s): Vancouver, British Columbia, Canada

What the book is about: Willows and Parker are out to solve a drug-related murder.

Other books you might like:
Alisa Craig, *Murder Goes Mumming*, 1981
Ted Wood, *An Inside Job*, 1990
Eric Wright, *A Question of Guilt*, 1988

628
Ron Goulart
Even the Butler Was Poor (New York: Walker, 1990)
Series: Mavity and Spanner
Story type: Humor; Action/Adventure
Major character(s): H.J. Mavity, Artist (paperback covers); Ben Spanner, Actor (TV/radio "voice"; ex-husband)
Time period(s): 1990s
Locale(s): Brimstone, Connecticut
What the book is about: Mavity's ex-boyfriend is to meet her and repay a loan. He shows up late, manages to talk about a large stash of money, utters his final words, "ninety-nine clop clop," and dies. Mavity turns to her ex-husband, Ben Spanner, for help to find the money. But she may not stay alive to spend it if she finds it.

Other books you might like:
Edward Ronns, *The Art Studio Murders*, 1950
J.M. Ryan, *Brooks Wilson Ltd.*,
Donald E. Westlake, *God Save the Mark*, 1969

629
Ron Goulart
Now He Thinks He's Dead (New York: Walker, 1992)
Series: Mavity and Spanner
Story type: Action/Adventure; Humor
Major character(s): H.J. Mavity, Artist (paperback covers); Ben Spanner, Actor (a voice man for TV and radio)
Time period(s): 1990s
Locale(s): Brimstone, Connecticut
What the book is about: Another friend has died in the arms of H.J. This time it's a well-known publisher who buys her artwork. A week ago he hinted that somebody was trying to kill him. Now he's dead from a hit-and-run driver wearing a ski mask - obviously murder. The only clue is a group of photographs that relate to a famous kidnapping of years ago.

Other books you might like:
Al Guthrie, *Murder by Tarot*, 1992
Bernie Lee, *Murder Without Reservation*, 1991
Charlotte MacLeod, *The Silver Ghost*, 1988
Joshua Quittner, *Shoofly Pie to Die*, 1992
Michael Thall, *Let Sleeping Afghans Lie*, 1990

630
Ron Goulart
The Tijuana Bible (New York: St. Martin's, 1990)
Story type: Amateur Detective—Male Lead

Major character(s): Jack Deacon, Artist (cartoonist); Sally Westerland, Young Woman (Jack's beautiful ex-roommate)
Time period(s): 1980s
Locale(s): Connecticut; California
What the book is about: A fellow cartoonist shows up in Deacon's yard shot full of holes and dying. Does this have anything to do with the beautiful woman hiding in Jack's closet, or the pornographic comic that soon shows up in his mailbox?

Other books you might like:
Dashiell Hammett, *The Thin Man*, 1989
Richard A. Lupoff, *The Comic Book Killer*, 1988
Robert J. Randisi, *The Steinway Collection*, 1985

631
C.L. Grace
The Eye of God (New York: St. Martin's, 1994)
Series: Kathryn Swinbrooke/Colum Murtagh
Story type: Historical
Major character(s): Kathryn Swinbrooke, Doctor (physician); Colum Murtagh, Military Personnel (soldier)
Time period(s): 15th century (1471)
Locale(s): Canterbury, England
What the book is about: The Yorkists are victorious—Henry VI and Warwick have been killed and Edward IV has assumed the crown. Before Warwick died he sent a soldier away with the precious Eye of God. The soldier is captured and mysteriously dies in jail and the Eye is nowhere to be found. King Edward asks Kathryn Swinbrooke and Colum Murtagh to look into it, but each of them has another problem as well. Colum is being pursued by a band of Irish assassins and Kathryn's husband, who may be dead, has been declared a traitor. C.L. Grace also writes as Paul Harding, Michael Clynes, and P.C. Doherty.

Other books you might like:
Margaret Frazer, *The Sister Frevisse Series*, 1993-
Sharan Newman, *Death Comes as Epiphany*, 1993
Ellis Peters, *The Brother Cadfael Series*, 1977-
Kate Sedley, *The Roger the Chapman Series*, 1992-
Leonard Tourney, *The Matthew Stock Series*, 1980-

632
James Grady
River of Darkness (New York: Warner, 1990)
Story type: Espionage; Action/Adventure
Major character(s): Jud Stuart, Spy (retired; former CIA agent); Nick Kelly, Journalist, Writer (novelist); Wes Chandler, Military Personnel (Marine major)
Time period(s): 1990s
Locale(s): United States
What the book is about: Wes Chandler has been asked by the new CIA director to see if alcoholic former agent Jud Stuart is a threat to national security. Before he can really get started, however, it seems that someone is trying to kill Stuart. While on the run Stuart manages to involve his friend, reporter Nick Kelly, who then becomes the object of someone's wrath.

633 Grady

Other books you might like:
Carl Hiaasen, *Skin Tight*, 1989
R. Lance Hill, *The Evil That Men Do*, 1978
Joe Gores, *Wolf Time*, 1989
James W. Hall, *Bones of Coral*, 1991
Gerald Petievich, *Paramour*, 1991

633
James Grady
Thunder (New York: Warner, 1994)

Story type: Action/Adventure

Major character(s): John Lang, Spy (CIA agent)

Time period(s): 1990s

Locale(s): United States (across the country)

What the book is about: What do the bombing of a New York skyscraper and the "accidental" shooting of a CIA agent in Washington, D.C. have in common? The government says nothing. But the dead agent's partner, John Lang, doesn't believe it. Lang sets out to prove that his partner was murdered. He starts by following up on a mysterious letter about the death of an American in Europe, which leads to a shipment of explosives, which leads to him being stalked by an assassin and set up for a crime he didn't commit. It seems that the Agency, among others, wants Lang to stop or be killed.

Other books you might like:
Brian Garfield, *Hopscotch*, 1974
John Grisham, *The Pelican Brief*, 1992
David Morrell, *Assumed Identity*, 1993
Warren Murphy, *Jericho Day*, 1989
Gerald Petievich, *Paramour*, 1991

634
Sue Grafton
F Is for Fugitive (New York: Holt, 1989)

Series: Kinsey Millhone

Story type: Private Detective—Female Lead

Major character(s): Kinsey Millhone, Detective—Private

Time period(s): 1980s

Locale(s): California (Southern)

What the book is about: Kinsey is hired to clear a man imprisoned for the murder of a teenager seventeen years earlier.

Other books you might like:
Robert Crais, *The Monkey's Raincoat*, 1987
Susan Dunlap, *Pious Deception*, 1989
Katherine V. Forrest, *The Beverly Malibu*, 1989
Marcia Muller, *The Shape of Dread*, 1989
Sara Paretsky, *Blood Shot*, 1988

635
Sue Grafton
G Is for Gumshoe (New York: Holt, 1990)

Series: Kinsey Millhone

Story type: Private Detective—Female Lead

Major character(s): Kinsey Millhone, Detective—Private

Time period(s): 1980s

Locale(s): Santa Teresa, California (Fictional city)

What the book is about: Kinsey Millhone is hired to track down a missing mother. At the same time she discovers she is on the hit list of a criminal she helped put in jail.

Other books you might like:
Janice Law, *The Shadow of the Palms*, 1980
Marcia Muller, *The Sharon McCone Series*, (1977-)
Sara Paretsky, *The V.I. Warshawski Series*, (1982-)

636
Sue Grafton
H Is for Homicide (New York: Holt, 1991)

Series: Kinsey Millhone

Story type: Private Detective—Female Lead

Major character(s): Kinsey Millhone, Detective—Private

Time period(s): 1990s

Locale(s): Los Angeles, California

What the book is about: Kinsey Millhone goes undercover to investigate possible insurance fraud and finds himself caught up with and kidnapped(?) by Los Angeles gang members. Jail is just one of the possible fates that may be ahead for her.

Other books you might like:
Linda Barnes, *Coyote*, 1990
Barbara D'Amato, *Hardball*, 1990
Karen Kijewski, *Katwalk*, 1989
Marcia Muller, *Trophies and Dead Things*, 1990
Sara Paretsky, *Burn Marks*, 1990

637
Sue Grafton
I Is for Innocent (New York: Holt, 1992)

Series: Kinsey Millhone

Story type: Private Detective—Female Lead

Major character(s): Kinsey Millhone, Detective—Private

Time period(s): 1990s

Locale(s): Santa Teresa, California (Santa Teresa is a thinly disguised Santa Barbara)

What the book is about: Taking over a case for a dead private detective, Kinsey finds herself involved in a six-year-old murder case. Though architect David Barney was acquitted of killing his wealthy wife, an earlier husband of said wife has filed a wrongful death suit in civil court. As she gets further into the investigation she finds that, among other things, the dead PI may not have died of natural causes after all. Who was the original murderer, if not Barney?

Other books you might like:
Linda Barnes, *Steel Guitar*, 1991
Barbara D'Amato, *The Cat Marsala Series*, 1990-
Linda Grant, *Love nor Money*, 1991
Karen Kijewski, *The Kat Colorado Series*, 1989-
Marcia Muller, *Trophies and Dead Things*, 1990

638
Sue Grafton
K Is for Killer (New York: Holt, 1994)
Series: Kinsey Millhone
Story type: Private Detective—Female Lead
Major character(s): Kinsey Millhone, Detective—Private
Time period(s): 1990s
Locale(s): Santa Teresa, California
What the book is about: Haunted by her daughter Lorna's death, Janice Kepler is drawn to Kinsey Millhone's office. When Lorna was found, her body was so badly decomposed police couldn't even tell if the cause of death was natural, accidental, or murder. Janice wants answers so she hires Kinsey to find them. She finds out more than she bargained for.
Other books you might like:
Linda Barnes, *The Carlotta Carlyle Series*, 1987-
Janet Dawson, *The Jeri Howard Series*, 1990-
Marcia Muller, *The Sharon McCone Series*, 1977-
Maxine O'Callaghan, *The Delilah West Series*, 1982-
Sara Paretsky, *The V.I. Warshawski Series*, 1982-

639
Sue Grafton
L Is for Lawless (New York: Henry Holt, 1995)
Series: Kinsey Millhone
Story type: Private Detective—Female Lead
Major character(s): Kinsey Millhone, Detective—Private
Time period(s): 1990s
Locale(s): Santa Teresa, California; Portland, Kentucky
What the book is about: Kinsey innocently does a small favor, helping her neighbor Bucky Lee try and find out the service record of his grandfather. Nobody seems to have heard of him. However, she meets an old friend of his, Ray Rawson. Kinsey slowly becomes involved with Ray and his family and in a cross-country treasure hunt for stolen loot. But someone else is after the money and may try to eliminate the competition permanently.
Other books you might like:
Linda Barnes, *The Carlotta Carlyle Series*, 1987-
Janet Dawson, *The Jeri Howard Series*, 1990-
Karen Kijewski, *The Kat Colorado Series*, 1988-
Marcia Muller, *The Sharon McCone Series*, 1977-
Sara Paretsky, *The V.I. Warshawski Series*, 1982-

640
Caroline Graham
Death in Disguise (New York: Morrow, 1993)
Series: Inspector Barnaby
Story type: Police Procedural—Male Lead
Major character(s): Thomas Barnaby, Police Officer (detective chief inspector)
Time period(s): 1990s
Locale(s): Compton Dando, England
What the book is about: The death of a member of a cult, the Lodge of the Golden Windhorse, is ruled an accident. As things slowly return to normal after this death, the father of another of the members visits. Soon after the master of the cult is killed in a mysterious manner. The father is the obvious suspect but is he really guilty? Detective Chief Inspector Barnaby is going to find out.
Other books you might like:
Deborah Crombie, *A Share in Death*, 1993
Ann Granger, *Cold in the Earth*, 1992
Martha Grimes, *Help the Poor Struggler*, 1985
Peter Robinson, *The Hanging Valley*, 1992
Margaret Yorke, *Admit to Murder*, 1990

641
Caroline Graham
Death of a Hollow Man (New York: Morrow, 1990)
Series: Inspector Barnaby
Story type: Police Procedural—Male Lead
Major character(s): Thomas Barnaby, Police Officer (inspector)
Time period(s): 1980s
What the book is about: When Barnaby's wife gets involved in an amateur theatrical troupe, she also gets involved with murder.
Other books you might like:
P.M. Carlson, *Rehearsal for Murder*, 1988
Jane Dentinger, *First Hit of the Season*, 1984
Ngaio Marsh, *Killer Dolphin*, 1967
Patricia Moyes, *Falling Star*, 1964
Barbara Paul, *The Fourth Wall*, 1979

642
Ann Granger
Cold in the Earth (New York: St. Martins, 1993)
Series: Mitchell and Markby
Story type: Police Procedural
Major character(s): Alan Markby, Police Officer; Meredith Mitchell, Diplomat (foreign service)
Time period(s): 1990s
Locale(s): Bamford, England (the Cotswolds)
What the book is about: Inspector Markby has more dead bodies than he wants, first a young woman dead of a drug overdose and now the body of a man that had been bludgeoned to death and buried at a construction site. The body has been stripped to make identification difficult and what's more the small farming village is closing ranks and being very uncooperative. Meredith Mitchell is bored in London and decides to visit her friend Markby and is lured into the case.
Other books you might like:
Deborah Crombie, *A Share in Death*, 1993
Frances Fyfield, *Deep Sleep*, 1992
Susan B. Kelly, *Hope Against Hope*, 1991
Janet Neel, *Death's Bright Angel*, 1991
Medora Sale, *Murder in a Good Cause*, 1990

643
Ann Granger
A Fine Place for Death (New York: St. Martin's, 1995)
Series: Mitchell and Markby
Story type: Police Procedural
Major character(s): Alan Markby, Police Officer (chief inspector); Meredith Mitchell, Diplomat
Time period(s): 1990s
Locale(s): Bamford, England (The Cotswolds)
What the book is about: When the body of fifteen-year-old Lynne Wills is found, Markby begins to investigate. He finds that Lynne was part of a wild group involved in drinking and sex, but no one in the group will talk to the police. He asks for Meredith's help to get information from one of the other girls in the group who seems to like Meredith, but she seems to have family problems of her own. Then death strikes again.
Other books you might like:
Deborah Crombie, *The Kincaid and James Series*, 1993-
John Harvey, *The Charlie Resnick Series*, 1989-
Susan B. Kelly, *Kidstuff*, 1994
Janet Neel, *Death of a Partner*, 1991
Peter Robinson, *The Inspector Banks Series*, 1990-

644
Ann Granger
Murder Among Us (New York: St. Martin's, 1994)
Series: Mitchell and Markby
Story type: Police Procedural
Major character(s): Alan Markby, Police Officer (chief inspector); Meredith Mitchell, Diplomat (foreign service)
Time period(s): 1990s
Locale(s): Bramford, England (the Cotswolds)
What the book is about: Chief Inspector Alan Markby is hoping to have a pleasant time visiting with Meredith Mitchell. No such luck. First the gala opening of the Springwood Hotel Restaurant is interrupted by a streaker, the resolute Hope Mapple, head of the Society For Preserving Historic Bramford. Then Meredith discovers the dead body of Ellen Bryant in the hotel's wine cellar. There are no clues or apparent motives for killing the harmless owner of a needlecraft shop.
Other books you might like:
Deborah Crombie, *All Shall Be Well*, 1994
Elizabeth George, *Payment in Blood*, 1989
Susan B. Kelly, *Hope Will Answer*, 1993
Janet Neel, *Death on Site*, 1989
Medora Sale, *Murder in a Good Cause*, 1990

645
Ann Granger
A Season for Murder (New York: St. Martin's, 1992)
Series: Mitchell and Markby
Story type: Amateur Detective; Police Procedural
Major character(s): Meredith Mitchell, Diplomat (foreign service); Alan Markby, Police Officer (chief inspector, CID)
Time period(s): 1990s
Locale(s): Bamford, England
What the book is about: Meredith is back in England and, with some misgivings, back in the Cotswolds. She has seen Markby socially and is wondering whether she likes him when her young and pretty neighbor, Harriet Needham, dies in what seems to be a tragic accident. Meredith doesn't think it was an accident and wants Markby to investigate. When he won't, she does and finds several people with reason to kill.
Other books you might like:
Pat Burden, *Screaming Bones*, 1990
Susan B. Kelly, *Hope Against Hope*, 1991
Janet Neel, *Death's Bright Angel*, 1988
Roger Ormerod, *Hung in the Balance*, 1991
Peter Robinson, *Gallows View*, 1987

646
Bill Granger
Drover and the Zebras (New York: Morrow, 1992)
Series: Jimmy Drover
Story type: Amateur Detective—Male Lead; Action/Adventure
Major character(s): Jimmy Drover, Journalist (ex-sportswriter, now bookie)
Time period(s): 1990s
Locale(s): Chicago, Illinois
What the book is about: An old girlfriend asks Jimmy Drover to help her brother, the coach of a nationally ranked college basketball team. He is suspected of recruiting and point-shaving violations. The apparent suicide of a referee, also mentioned in the charges, lends credence to the allegations.
Other books you might like:
Crabbe Evers, *Murder in Wrigley Field*, 1991
David Everson, *Rebound*, 1988
David Everson, *Suicide Squeeze*, 1991
Michael J. Katz, *Murder Off the Glass*, 1987
Robert B. Parker, *Playmates*, 1989

647
Bill Granger
The Last Good German (New York: Warner, 1991)
Series: November Man
Story type: Espionage
Major character(s): Devereaux, Spy (retired; code name "November"); Kurt Heinemann, Spy (East German agent)
Time period(s): 1990s (1990); 1970s (1976)
Locale(s): Washington, District of Columbia; New York, New York

What the book is about: 15 years ago, Heinemann set up Devereaux with a fake defection that ended with two men dead and Devereaux almost dead. Now, after reunification, Heinemann has really come to the United States and is being used by the section to obtain a Japanese super code machine. Devereaux is blackmailed to help but will he and the woman he loves survive the double and triple crosses?

Other books you might like:
Ian Stuart Black, *The Man on the Bridge*, 1975
William F. Buckley Jr., *The Blackford Oakes Series*, 1976-
Andrew Coburn, *Company Secrets*, 1986
Len Deighton, *The Bernard Samson Series*, 1983-1990
Charles McCarry, *The Paul Christopher Series*, 1973-1991

648
Linda Grant
Love nor Money (New York: Scribners, 1991)
Series: Catherine Sayler
Story type: Private Detective—Female Lead
Major character(s): Catherine Sayler, Detective—Private
Time period(s): 1990s
Locale(s): San Francisco, California

What the book is about: An old friend of Catherine's calls and asks a favor. His cousin has been killed in what looks like a mugging. The cousin had been molested as a young boy and the aftermath had ruined his life. He decided to try and get evidence on the man who did it but he is now a powerful judge with heavy influence. With the help of her police contacts Catherine looks into the case and soon realizes this one incident may be only the tip of the iceberg.

Other books you might like:
Janet Dawson, *Kindred Crimes*, 1990
Karen Kijewski, *Katwalk*, 1989
Margaret Lucke, *A Relative Stranger*, 1991
Marcia Muller, *Trophies and Dead Things*, 1990
Gloria White, *Murder on the Run*, 1991

649
Linda Grant
A Woman's Place (New York: Scribners, 1994)
Series: Catherine Sayler
Story type: Private Detective—Female Lead
Major character(s): Catherine Sayler, Detective—Private
Time period(s): 1990s
Locale(s): San Francisco, California

What the book is about: Catherine Saylor goes undercover at a software company to try and find a sexual harrasser. Would that it were that simple. Though she was hired by the owner of the company, he is being less than cooperative, and when things begin to escalate, Catherine finds herself in danger.

Other books you might like:
Janet Dawson, *The Jeri Howard Series*, 1990-
Karen Kijewski, *The Kat Colorado Series*, 1989-
Margaret Lucke, *A Relative Stranger*, 1991
Marcia Muller, *The Sharon McCone Series*, 1977-
Gloria White, *Murder on the Run*, 1991

650
A.W. Gray
Bino's Blues (New York: Simon & Schuster, 1995)
Series: Bino Phillips
Story type: Amateur Detective—Male Lead; Legal
Major character(s): Bino Phillips, Lawyer
Time period(s): 1990s
Locale(s): Dallas, Texas

What the book is about: Defending a cop accused of misconduct, Bino Phillips must contend with, among other things, a ruthless U.S. attorney, a corrupt judge and attorney, a hit man, an ex-wife, and a jealous secretary. He manages to prevail however, exposing corruption, conspiracy, and murder.

Other books you might like:
John Grisham, *The Chamber*, 1994
Frederick D. Huebner, *Methods of Execution*, 1994
Michael A. Kahn, *Firm Ambitions*, 1994
Paul Levine, *Mortal Sin*, 1994
Robert K. Tanenbaum, *Justice Denied*, 1994

651
A.W. Gray
Killings (New York: Dutton, 1993)
Series: Bino Phillips
Story type: Legal; Action/Adventure
Major character(s): Bino Phillips, Lawyer; Hardy Cole, Detective
Time period(s): 1990s
Locale(s): Dallas, Texas

What the book is about: When two college girls who were going to be witnesses in a drug case are murdered, Bino Phillips gets involved in the search for the killer, who also drank the blood of his victims. He must also deal with what he considers obstructionist local and federal officials and the danger to those close to him when the killer decides to target them.

Other books you might like:
Bill Crider, *Blood Marks*, 1991
William Diehl, *Primal Fear*, 1993
J.F. Freedman, *Against the Wind*, 1992
Thomas Harris, *The Silence of the Lambs*, 1986
Paul Levine, *To Speak for the Dead*, 1990

652
A.W. Gray
The Man Offside (New York: Dutton, 1991)

653 Gray

Story type: Action/Adventure; Amateur Detective—Male Lead

Major character(s): Rick Bannion, Sports Figure, Convict (ex-con)

Time period(s): 1990s

Locale(s): Texas

What the book is about: After serving time for selling drugs, former football star Rick Bannion is released only to find himself right back in the middle of another drug deal. When one of his friends is murdered he needs to find the killer before he is sent back to prison.

Other books you might like:
Michael Geller, *Major League Murder*, 1986
E. Richard Johnson, *The Inside Man*, 1969
Dave Klein, *Blind Side*, 1980
Richard Rosen, *Saturday Night Dead*, 1988
Jonathan Valin, *Life's Work*, 1986

653
A.W. Gray
Prime Suspect (New York: Dutton, 1992)

Story type: Action/Adventure

Major character(s): Lackey Ferguson, Businessman (construction); Everett Wilson, Criminal

Time period(s): 1990s

Locale(s): Fort Worth, Texas

What the book is about: Lackey Ferguson has just met Marissa Hardin, having been hired by her husband to do some construction. Soon after he leaves, Everett Wilson attacks Marissa, raping and killing her. The police, not knowing about Wilson, consider Lackey their prime suspect. Has Lackey been set up? In trying to clear himself, he and his girlfriend, Nancy, will have to contend with the psychopathic Wilson, as well as the police.

Other books you might like:
Alan Dennis Burke, *Dead Wrong*, 1990
K. Patrick Connor, *Kingdom Road*, 1991
Robert Ferrigno, *The Horse Latitudes*, 1990
James W. Hall, *Tropical Freeze*, 1988
Charles Willeford, *Sideswipe*, 1987

654
Gallagher Gray
Hubbert and Lil: Partners in Crime (New York: Fine, 1991)

Story type: Amateur Detective

Major character(s): T.S. Hubbert, Businessman (retired bank personnel manager); Lil Hubbert, Aged Person (T.S.'s aunt)

Time period(s): 1990s

Locale(s): New York, New York

What the book is about: The day after his retirement T.S. gets a frantic call from his former boss. One of the executives has been stabbed and the boss wants Hubbert to deal with the publicity. Not satisfied with the job the police are doing, T.S. and his 84-year-old aunt take up the chase. First novel.

Other books you might like:
Richard Barth, *The Margaret Binton Series*, 1981-
Emma Lathen, *The John Putnam Thatcher Series*, 1964-
Annette Meyers, *The Smith and Wetzon Series*, 1988-
Haughton Murphy, *The Reuben Frost Series*, 1986-

655
Richard Grayson
Death Off Stage (New York: St. Martin's, 1992)

Series: Inspector Gautier

Story type: Historical; Police Procedural—Male Lead

Major character(s): Jean-Paul Gautier, Police Officer (chief inspector, Sureté)

Time period(s): 1900s (1905)

Locale(s): Paris, France

What the book is about: The Russian Ballet is on tour in Paris. A judge caught with one of the dancers is attacked by a jealous lover. The judge wants an arrest. Then the judge is murdered. Gautier must handle the case, which may be complicated by the fact that the tour's sponsor is his mistress.

Other books you might like:
Ray Harrison, *The Bragg and Morton Series*, 1984-
Alanna Knight, *The Inspector Faro Series*, 1989-
Peter Lovesey, *The Prince of Wales Series*, 1988-
Peter Lovesey, *The Sergeant Cribb Series*, 1970-1978
Anne Perry, *The Thomas and Charlotte Pitt Series*, 1979-

656
Andrew M. Greeley
Happy Are the Merciful (New York: Jove, 1992)

Series: Blackie Ryan

Story type: Amateur Detective—Male Lead

Major character(s): Blackie Ryan, Religious (priest; bishop)

Time period(s): 1990s

Locale(s): Chicago, Illinois

What the book is about: Is beautiful, rich, death row inmate Clare Turner innocent of the crime for which she was convicted—slitting the throats of her adopted parents? The prosecutor who put her away has come to believe so. Of course, he's also fallen in love with her. It falls to Father Blackie Ryan to ferret out the truth. This comes to involve the Mafia, Clare's real parents, and an attempt to murder Ryan himself.

Other books you might like:
John Katzenbach, *Just Cause*, 1992
Harry Kemelman, *The Rabbi Small Series*, 1964-
William F. Love, *The Chartreuse Clue*, 1990
Ralph McInerny, *The Father Dowling Series*, 1977-
Jack Webb, *The Father Shanley Series*, 1953-1963

657

Andrew M. Greeley
Irish Gold (New York: Forge, 1994)

Story type: Action/Adventure; Amateur Detective—Male Lead

Major character(s): Dermot Coyne, Businessman (commodities trader); Nuala McGrail, Student, Entertainer (singer and actress)

Time period(s): 1990s

Locale(s): Dublin, Ireland

What the book is about: Dermot Coyne is in Dublin to find out why his grandparents left Ireland in 1922. It appears that someone or some group does not want him doing this research, as he is soon waylaid and attacked by three hoodlums who suggest he let the dead sleep in peace. This only makes him more determined to find the truth and he soon uncovers a plot to reunite Ireland and England. Involved with him is lovely student and actress Nuala McGrail, whom he has hired to translate his grandmother's diaries. Dermot soon finds himself falling for her, but they may not live to love.

Other books you might like:
Thomas Adcock, *Drown All the Dogs*, 1993
Randy Lee Eickoff, *The Gombeen Man*, 1992
Norman Flood, *To Killashea*, 1989
James Graham, *The Run to Morning*, 1974
Jack Higgins, *Touch the Devil*, 1982

658

Christine Green
Deadly Admirer (New York: Walker, 1993)

Series: Kate Kinsella

Story type: Private Detective—Female Lead

Major character(s): Kate Kinsella, Detective—Private (part-time), Nurse

Time period(s): 1990s

Locale(s): Longborough, England

What the book is about: Kate Kinsella has been hired by a nurse who says she is being followed by a mysterious man. Kate takes the case but has reservations about her client. She has attempted suicide, has a history of violent encounters with boyfriends and has accused a policeman of rape. When one of the client's patients is killed, Kate is convinced that someone is after her, but who and why?

Other books you might like:
Eileen Dreyer, *A Man to Die For*, 1991
Louise Hendricksen, *With Deadly Intent*, 1994
Mary Kittredge, *The Edwina Crusoe Series*, 1990-
Janet McGiffin, *Emergency Murder*, 1992
C.F. Roe, *A Nasty Bit of Murder*, 1990

659

Christine Green
Deadly Errand (New York: Walker, 1992)

Story type: Private Detective—Female Lead

Major character(s): Kate Kinsella, Detective—Private (part-time), Nurse; Hubert Humberstone, Undertaker (Kate's landlord)

Time period(s): 1990s

Locale(s): Longborough, England

What the book is about: Bored with nursing, Kate Kinsella has just started her own detective agency, "Medical and Nursing Investigations". Her first client, Nina Marburg, wants Kate to find out who murdered her niece, Jacky Byfield, who was stabbed while working at St. Dymphna's Hospital. Kate gets herself assigned to the hospital and the more she finds out, the more she realizes several people might have wanted Jacky dead.

Other books you might like:
Jo Bailey, *Bagged*,
Robin Cook, *Coma*, 1977
Mary Kittredge, *Fatal Diagnosis*,
Sara Paretsky, *Bitter Medicine*, 1987

660

Christine Green
Deadly Practice (New York: Walker, 1995)

Series: Kate Kinsella

Story type: Private Detective—Female Lead

Major character(s): Kate Kinsella, Nurse, Detective—Private (part-time)

Time period(s): 1990s

Locale(s): Longborough, England

What the book is about: The recession has hit Kate hard. She can't find a job as a nurse or as an investigator. When Jenny Martin, a local nurse, is found murdered Kate leaps at the opportunity to apply for the job. However, her landlord, Hubert Humberstone, arranges for her to get involved in her capacity as an investigator. She is hired by the mother of Nick Fenny, the prime suspect in Jenny's murder. Nick apparently stole Jenny's car while her body was in the trunk. Another woman, a friend of Jenny's, has now disappeared. Kate may be in over her head.

Other books you might like:
Jo Bailey, *Bagged*, 1992
Mary Kittredge, *The Edwina Crusoe Series*, 1990-
Marsha Landreth, *The Holiday Murders*, 1992
Janet McGiffin, *The Dr. Maxene St. Clair Series*, 1992-
C.F. Roe, *The Jean Montrose Series*, 1990-

661

Christine Green
Die in My Dreams (New York: Bantam, 1995)

Series: Wilson and O'Neill

Story type: Police Procedural

Major character(s): Fran Wilson, Police Officer (sergeant, C.I.D.); Connor O'Neill, Police Officer (chief inspector, C.I.D.)

Time period(s): 1990s

Locale(s): Fowchester, England

662 Green — What Mystery Do I Read Next?

What the book is about: Fran Wilson's career is on hold. She is distrusted by her colleagues because she turned in her former partner and lover for beating a suspect. Her new boss, Connor O'Neill, seems to be interested in her but has a drinking problem. They become involved in a high profile case when a body is discovered, stabbed to death. Suspicion falls on Carol Ann Forbes, a newly released, self-confessed murderer who stabbed a man to death ten years earlier. Does Carol Ann just like killing or is someone being clever?

Other books you might like:
Stephen Cook, *Dead Fit*, 1993
Lydia LaPlante, *The Prime Suspect Series*, 1993-
Jill McGown, *The Inspector Lloyd & Judy Hill Series*, 1983-
Jennie Melville, *The Charmian Daniels Series*, 1962-
Erica Quest, *Cold Coffin*, 1990

662
George Dawes Green
The Caveman's Valentine (New York: Warner, 1994)
Story type: Amateur Detective—Male Lead; Psychological Suspense
Major character(s): Romulus Ledbetter, Streetperson (homeless former musican)
Time period(s): 1990s
Locale(s): New York, New York

What the book is about: Romulus Ledbetter, known as the Caveman, has a difficult time connecting with reality. He thinks people are out to get him, particularly one Cornelius Gould Stuyvesant. When Romulus finds a corpse outside his cave one morning, he believes the kid, for it is just a boy, was murdered. Everyone else thinks the kid just froze to death. Now people are out to get him and he must connect with reality more than he has for years to save his life and the life of his daughter. First novel.

Other books you might like:
Todd Komarnicki, *Free*, 1994

663
Jen Green
Reader, I Murdered Him (New York: St. Martin's, 1989)
Story type: Anthology

What the book is about: Collection of crime stories, all by women. Includes stories by Amanda Cross, Sara Paretsky, Susan Dunlap, Margaret Yorke, Val McDermid and others.

Other books you might like:
Marie Smith, *Ms. Murder*, 1989 (editor)
Marilyn Wallace, *Sisters in Crime*, 1989 (editor)
Marilyn Wallace, *Sisters in Crime 2*, 1990 (editor)
Irene Zahava, *The Womansleuth Anthology Series*, 1988 (editor)

664
Kate Green
Night Angel (New York: Dell, 1991)
Story type: Psychological Suspense
Major character(s): Maggie Shea, Counselor (worker at a hospice, on leave)
Time period(s): 1980s
Locale(s): San Francisco, Minnesota

What the book is about: Is the recent drowning of one of Maggie's old roommates tied to their lives in the sixties? As friends gather for the funeral it seems that all who lived together in their old house are in danger. Originally published in 1989.

Other books you might like:
Deidre S. Laiken, *Killing Time in Buffalo*, 1990
Sharyn McCrumb, *If Ever I Return, Pretty Peggy-O*, 1990
Keith Peterson, *The Scarred Man*, 1990

665
Kate Green
Shooting Star (New York: HarperCollins, 1992)
Story type: Psychological Suspense; Private Detective—Male Lead
Major character(s): Nyia Wyatt, Actress; Harmon Bohland, Detective—Private, Bodyguard
Time period(s): 1990s
Locale(s): Santa Fe, New Mexico

What the book is about: While on location in Santa Fe for a movie, Nyia Wyatt feels that the plot of the movie is too closely paralleling her own life. She is also receiving letters from what appears to be a crazed fan. Feeling her life is in danger she forces the film's director to hire a bodyguard detective, Harm Bohland. When a woman is killed in a scene that Nyia was supposed to do, Harm wonders who was supposed to die.

Other books you might like:
Mary Higgins Clark, *Weep No More, My Lady*, 1987
Bruce Cook, *Death as a Career Move*, 1992
Arthur Lyons, *Fast Fade*, 1987
Robert Specht, *The Soul of Betty Fairchild*, 1991
Stuart Woods, *Santa Fe Rules*, 1992

666
Vincent Green
The Price of Victory (New York: Walker, 1992)
Story type: Legal
Major character(s): Jack Hayes, Lawyer, Military Personnel; Billy Frazier, Military Personnel
Time period(s): 1990s
Locale(s): Europe

What the book is about: Decorated veteran Billy Frazier stands accused of drug smuggling—something the army frowns upon very strongly. He asks Jack Hayes—who has problems of his own—to defend him. This won't be easy as the judge on the case is known as "The Whopper" for his sentences and courtroom demeanor. First novel.

Other books you might like:
William Bernhardt, *Primary Justice*, 1992
William J. Coughlin, *Shadow of a Doubt*, 1991
J.F. Freedman, *Against the Wind*, 1991
Herman Wouk, *The Caine Mutiny*, 1954

667
Stephen Greenleaf
Blood Type (New York: Morrow, 1992)
Series: John Marshall Tanner
Story type: Private Detective—Male Lead
Major character(s): John Marshall Tanner, Detective—Private (former lawyer)
Time period(s): 1990s
Locale(s): San Francisco, California
What the book is about: Tanner's good friend and drinking buddy, Tom Crandall, has a problem. One of the richest men in the country wants Tom's wife to leave him and Tom doesn't know what to do. When Tom is found dead in an alley, the police think it's suicide but Marsh doesn't agree. Investigating involves Tanner with Tom's younger brother, a dangerous schizophrenic, whose paranoid delusions may turn out to be true.
Other books you might like:
Thomas B. Dewey, *The "Mac" Series*, 1947-1970
Arthur Lyons, *The Jacob Asch Series*, 1974-
Bill Pronzini, *The Nameless Detective Series*, 1971-
Benjamin M. Schutz, *The Leo Haggerty Series*, 1985-
Jonathan Valin, *The Harry Stoner Series*, 1980-

668
Stephen Greenleaf
Book Case (New York: Morrow, 1991)
Series: John Marshall Tanner
Story type: Private Detective—Male Lead
Major character(s): John Marshall Tanner, Detective—Private (former lawyer)
Time period(s): 1990s
Locale(s): San Francisco, California
What the book is about: Tanner is asked by an old friend - the owner of a small publishing house - to find the author of an unsolicited manuscript the publisher received. The manuscript purports to tell truth about a crime committed years earlier for which an innocent man was imprisoned.
Other books you might like:
Max Allan Collins, *Kill Your Darlings*, 1984
Jeremiah Healy, *Yesterday's News*, 1989
Bill Pronzini, *Hoodwink*, 1981
Rex Stout, *Murder by the Book*, 1951
Jonathan Valin, *The Lime Pit*, 1980

669
Stephen Greenleaf
Southern Cross (New York: Morrow, 1992)
Series: John Marshall Tanner
Story type: Private Detective—Male Lead
Major character(s): John Marshall Tanner, Detective—Private (former lawyer); Seth Hartman, Lawyer
Time period(s): 1990s
Locale(s): Charleston, South Carolina
What the book is about: John Marshall Tanner is feeling old and alone when he attends his college reunion where his old friend Seth Hartman asks for his help. Seth has been receiving threatening notes from the Alliance for Southern Pride, a new racist hate group. Seth, a true southern gentleman of an old family, is torn between loyalty to family and friends and the fight for equal rights. Marsh wants to help but finds it hard to crack the tight-knit society.
Other books you might like:
Neil Albert, *The Dave Garrett Series*, 1991-
Jeremiah Healy, *The John Francis Cuddy Series*, 1984-
Zachary Klein, *The Matt Jacob Series*, 1990-
Bennie Lee Sinclair, *The Lynching*, 1992
David Stout, *Carolina Skeletons*, 1989

670
D.M. Greenwood
Clerical Errors (New York: St. Martin's, 1992)
Story type: Amateur Detective—Female Lead
Major character(s): Theodora Braithwaite, Religious (deaconess); Julia Smith, Secretary
Time period(s): 1990s
Locale(s): Medewich, England
What the book is about: Julia is at Medewich Cathedral to be interviewed for the job of typist for the tyrannical Canon Wheeler. While walking in the church she finds a cleaning woman screaming and a severed head in the font. The head turns out to belong to the pastor of a nearby parish. Theodora and Julia become involved in murder and black magic.
Other books you might like:
Veronica Black, *A Vow of Silence*, 1990
Isabelle Holland, *A Death at St. Anselm's*, 1984
Sister Carol Anne O'Marie, *Advent of Dying*, 1986
Monica Quill, *Sine Qua Nun*, 1986
Barbara Whitehead, *The Dean It Was That Died*, 1991

671
D.M. Greenwood
Idol Bones (New York: St. Martin's, 1993)
Series: Theodora Braithwaite
Story type: Amateur Detective—Female Lead
Major character(s): Theodora Braithwaite, Religious (Reverend, Church of England)
Time period(s): 1990s
Locale(s): London, England

What the book is about: Theodora Braithwaite has been assigned to Bow St. Aelfric to "stretch her talents." She arrives right after the new dean, Vincent Stream, a very unpleasant man who antagonizes everyone he meets. Soon after the unearthing of an old Roman statue, the body of the dean is found near it. Is it the work of one of many enemies or a pagan cult?

Other books you might like:
Veronica Black, *A Vow of Silence*, 1990
Isabelle Holland, *The Claire Aldington Series*, 1984-
David Willis McCullough, *The Ziza Todd Series*, 1990-
Winona Sullivan, *A Sudden Death at the Norfolk Cafe*, 1993
Barbara Whitehead, *The Dean It Was That Died*, 1991

672
D.M. Greenwood
Unholy Ghosts (New York: St. Martin's, 1992)
Series: Theodora Braithwaite
Story type: Amateur Detective—Female Lead
Major character(s): Theodora Braithwaite, Religious (deaconess, Church of England)
Time period(s): 1990s
Locale(s): Norfolk, England
What the book is about: Theodora is on vacation, house-sitting for some friends, when the local pastor is found dead at the bottom of a pit he himself had dug. Theodora becomes involved because she had been counseling the pastor's despondent wife, Amy, and wants to help. Then Amy disappears.

Other books you might like:
Veronica Black, *A Vow of Silence*, 1990
Isabelle Holland, *The Claire Aldington Series*, 1984-
David Willis McCullough, *The Ziza Todd Series*, 1990-
Sister Carol Anne O'Marie, *The Sister Mary Helen Series*, 1984-
Barbara Whitehead, *The Dean It Was That Died*, 1991

673
Julia Grice
The Cutting Hours (New York: Forge, 1993)
Story type: Psychological Suspense
Major character(s): Shay Wyoming, Artist (sculptress; divorced); Mickey McGee, Criminal (biker)
Time period(s): 1990s
Locale(s): Michigan
What the book is about: Shay Wyoming is trying hard to raise her children after her divorce but her sixteen year old daughter Kelly is at the age of rebellion and is running around with Mickey McGee, biker. What they don't know is that McGee really has designs on Shay and walks a fine line between love and hate.

Other books you might like:
Michael Allegretto, *The Suitor*, 1992
Mary Higgins Clark, *Loves Music, Loves to Dance*, 1991
J.A. Jance, *Hour of the Hunter*, 1991
Diane Johnson, *The Shadow Knows*, 1974
Samuel M. Key, *I'll Be Watching You*, 1994

674
Martha Grimes
The End of the Pier (New York: Knopf)
Story type: Psychological Suspense
Major character(s): Maud Chadwick, Waiter/Waitress; Sam De Gheyn, Police Officer (sheriff)
Time period(s): 1990s
Locale(s): United States
What the book is about: Maud Chadwick is at a turning point in her life. A divorcee and single parent, her son is going off to college and Maud is wondering what she will do now. There must be more to life than her job and the people of the Rainbow Cafe. Her friend Sam, though married, is interested in her, but he is also haunted by the deaths of three women and the fear that the wrong man may be in jail.

Other books you might like:
Kate Green, *Night Angel*, 1991
Deidre S. Laiken, *Killing Time in Buffalo*, 1990
Sharyn McCrumb, *If Ever I Return, Pretty Peggy-O*, 1990
Celestine Sibley, *Straight as an Arrow*, 1992

675
Martha Grimes
The Old Contemptibles (New York: Little, Brown, 1991)
Series: Richard Jury
Story type: Police Procedural—Male Lead; Amateur Detective—Male Lead
Major character(s): Richard Jury, Police Officer (superintendent); Melrose Plant, Nobleman (Lord Ardry)
Time period(s): 1990s
Locale(s): Lake District, England
What the book is about: Richard Jury's fiancee is murdered and he is a suspect. Since he is a suspect and also can't leave London, he sends his friend Melrose Plant to the household, obstensibly to catalogue the library, but really to ferret about for the truth.

Other books you might like:
Elizabeth George, *Payment in Blood*, 1989
Reginald Hill, *Bones and Silence*, 1990
Elizabeth Lemarchand, *Alibi for a Corpse*, 1986
Ruth Rendell, *The Inspector Wexford Series*, 1965-
June Thomson, *The Spoils of Time*, 1989

676
Martha Grimes
The Old Silent (New York: Little, Brown, 1989)
Series: Richard Jury
Story type: Police Procedural—Male Lead
Major character(s): Richard Jury, Police Officer
Time period(s): 1980s
Locale(s): Yorkshire, England; London, England
What the book is about: Jury witnesses a murder in an inn called the Old Silent, but all is not as it appears and the widow is not what she seems.

Other books you might like:
Elizabeth George, *A Great Deliverance*, 1988
Reginald Hill, *A Pinch of Snuff*, 1978
Elizabeth Lemarchand, *The Glade Manor Murder*, 1989
Sheila Radley, *Who Saw Him Die?*, 1988
Ruth Rendell, *Speaker of Mandarin*, 1983

677
Lucretia Grindle
The Killing of Ellis Martin (New York: Pocket, 1993)
Series: Inspector Ross
Story type: Police Procedural—Male Lead
Major character(s): Hubert Ross, Police Officer (chief inspector), Widow(er); Owen Davies, Police Officer (detective inspector)
Time period(s): 1990s
Locale(s): Wildesham, England (Kent)
What the book is about: A young girl is walking in the local wood with her dog when the dog finds a human hand. The hand proves to be attached to the bludgeoned body of Ellis Martin, a rich, young woman who seemed to lead a life of quiet desperation. Suspects include a former fiance and his ex-girlfriend, and a local businessman. Other than those people, Inspector Ross has very little to work with. First novel.
Other books you might like:
Ann Cleeves, *A Day in the Death of Dorothea Cassidy*, 1992
Elizabeth George, *For the Sake of Elena*, 1992
P.D. James, *Cover Her Face*, 1962
Susan B. Kelly, *Time of Hope*, 1992
Sheila Radley, *Death in the Morning*, 1978

678
Lucretia Grindle
So Little to Die For (New York: Pocket, 1994)
Series: Inspector Ross
Story type: Police Procedural—Male Lead
Major character(s): Hubert Ross, Police Officer (detective superintendent, CID), Widow(er); Owen Davies, Police Officer (detective inspector, CID)
Time period(s): 1990s
Locale(s): Gleneagles, Scotland
What the book is about: Inspector Ross is on vacation when he meets an acquaintance of his deceased wife. She tells him that there are mysterious thefts happening at their cottage. Ross doesn't think much of it but soon learns the woman, her sister and their husbands have been brutally murdered. The local police soon decide that a young sheepherder is guilty, but Ross doesn't think so and asks Inspector Davies to come up and help him look into it unofficially. He finds more than he bargained for.
Other books you might like:
Deborah Crombie, *A Share in Death*, 1993
Marjorie Eccles, *The Inspector Gil Mayo Series*, 1986-
John Harvey, *The Inspector Resnick Series*, 1989-
Reginald Hill, *The Dalziel and Pascoe Series*, 1970-
Peter Robinson, *The Inspector Banks Series*, 1990-

679
John Grisham
The Chamber (New York: Doubleday, 1994)
Story type: Legal; Amateur Detective—Male Lead
Major character(s): Adam Hall, Lawyer; Sam Crayhall, Convict
Time period(s): 1990s
Locale(s): Mississippi
What the book is about: Sam Crayhall has been tried three times and has finally been convicted of the 1967 Ku Klux Klan bombing that killed two young boys. Now he is on death row and Adam Hall, a young midwestern attorney, is determined to save his life. The catch is that Adam Hall is Sam Crayhall's grandson.
Other books you might like:
Andrew Klavan, *True Crime*, 1995
Keith Peterson, *The Trapdoor*, 1988
Mary Willis Walker, *The Red Scream*, 1994

680
John Grisham
The Client (New York: Doubleday, 1993)
Story type: Legal; Action/Adventure
Major character(s): Mark Sway, Child (precocious 11 year old); Reggie Love, Lawyer
Time period(s): 1990s
Locale(s): Memphis, Tennessee
What the book is about: 11 year old Mark Sway witnesses the suicide of a man who, before he dies, confides to Mark a deadly secret. The police, the Mafia and the FBI are all after this secret, so for protection Mark engages the services of female lawyer Reggie Love. This does not protect him as he thinks it will and soon Mark and Reggie are both in danger of losing their lives.
Other books you might like:
Brian Garfield, *The Paladin*, 1980
Dick Lochte, *Laughing Dog*, 1988
Dick Lochte, *Sleeping Dog*, 1985

681
John Grisham
The Pelican Brief (New York: Doubleday, 1992)
Story type: Action/Adventure; Legal
Major character(s): Darby Shaw, Student (law student); Gray Grantham, Journalist (reporter)
Time period(s): 1990s
Locale(s): Washington, District of Columbia
What the book is about: What and who is behind the assassination of two Supreme Court justices? The assumption is that the killings are part of a larger plot and Darby Shaw appears to have some insight into this. So much insight that she becomes the target of the killers. She goes underground with the only person she can trust - reporter Gray Grantham.

682 Grissom

Other books you might like:
Fletcher Knebel, *Seven Days in May*, 1964 (Charles Bailey, co-author)
David Morrell, *The Covenant of the Flame*, 1991
Warren Murphy, *Jericho Day*, 1989
Gerald Petievich, *Paramour*, 1991

682
Ken Grissom
Big Fish (New York: St. Martins, 1991)

Series: John Rodrique

Story type: Action/Adventure

Major character(s): John Rodrigue, Veteran (salvage expert)

Time period(s): 1990s

Locale(s): Galveston, Texas

What the book is about: Against his better judgement, John Rodrique lets the stunningly beautiful wife of a rich developer talk him into helping to fix a fishing contest in favor of her husband. This leads to many other complications, not the least of which is his lust for the wife.

Other books you might like:
James W. Hall, *Bones of Coral*, 1991
Carl Hiaasen, *Double Whammy*, 1988
Joe R. Lansdale, *The Savage Season*, 1990
Brian Lysaght, *Special Circumstances*, 1983
John Walter Putre, *Death Among the Angels*, 1990

683
Ken Grissom
Drowned Man's Key (New York: St. Martin's, 1992)

Series: John Rodrigue

Story type: Action/Adventure

Major character(s): John Rodrigue, Veteran (salvage expert)

Time period(s): 1990s

Locale(s): Texas (Gulf Coast)

What the book is about: The space shuttle Columbia is scheduled to land soon but due to a massive hurricane and sabotage, it and its crew are in danger. Meanwhile Rodrigue has been asked by a beautiful "niece" to reclaim the body of a drowned computer expert and dispose of it out at sea. This involves John in a network of spies, government agents and just plain greedy people, all of whom may be more deadly than the storm.

Other books you might like:
Rick Boyer, *Billingsgate Shoal*, 1982
James W. Hall, *Tropical Freeze*, 1989
Paul Kemprecos, *Cool Blue Tomb*, 1991
W.R. Philbrick, *The Crystal Blue Persuasion*, 1989
John Walter Putre, *Death Among the Angels*, 1990

684
Ken Gross
Hell Bent (New York: Tor, 1992)

Story type: Action/Adventure

Major character(s): Jack Mann, Police Officer (retired); Nora Burns, Companion (lover of Jack)

Time period(s): 1990s

Locale(s): Galway, Ireland; New York, New York

What the book is about: Jack and Nora are hiding out in Ireland because the police and Mafia are looking for them. The Mafia wants back three million dollars that disappeared at the same time as Jack and Nora. When Nora's son is killed by two policeman in the pay of the mob, she goes to New York to get revenge. She finds her brother Michael, a fanatical IRA terrorist, but he has a bloody agenda of his own. Jack follows, trying to keep Nora safe.

Other books you might like:
Jack Barnao, *Locke Step*, 1987
Max Byrd, *Fuse Time*, 1991
Tom Clancy, *Patriot Games*, 1987
Ridley Pearson, *Hard Fall*, 1992

685
Jan Guillou
Enemy's Enemy (New York: Knopf, 1992)

Story type: Espionage

Major character(s): Carl Hamilton, Spy (Swedish intelligence agent)

Time period(s): 1990s

Locale(s): Sweden; Russia

What the book is about: Suspected by his boss of being a KGB agent, Carl Hamilton must prove his innocence while trying to rescue two Swedish doctors kidnapped by the PLO. His love life is also a mess as he tries to juggle an old California flame, a female cop and a beautiful Palestinian. First novel. Translated from Swedish.

Other books you might like:
Tom Clancy, *Patriot Games*, 1987
Sean Flannery, *The Hollow Men*, 1982
David Hagberg, *Crossfire*, 1991
S.K. Wolf, *The Harbinger Effect*, 1989

686
Sally Gunning
Hot Water (New York: Pocket, 1990)

Series: Peter Bartholomew

Story type: Amateur Detective—Male Lead

Major character(s): Peter Bartholomew, Businessman (does odd jobs); Martha Hitchcock, Young Woman (daughter of the murdered woman)

Time period(s): 1990s

Locale(s): Nashtoba, Massachusetts (fictionalized Cape Cod)

What the book is about: Who killed Edna Hitchcock and tried to make it look like suicide? Peter Bartholomew, who found the body, is convinced it was murder. He gets involved with the victim's prodigal daughter in trying to solve the crime. First novel.

Other books you might like:
Rick Boyer, *Billingsgate Shoal*, 1982
Philip R. Craig, *A Beautiful Place to Die*, 1989
Jeremiah Healy, *Yesterday's News*, 1989
Douglas Kiker, *Murder on Clam Pond*, 1986
Margaret Logan, *Deathampton Summer*, 1988

687
Sally Gunning
Rough Water (New York: Pocket, 1994)

Series: Peter Bartholomew

Story type: Amateur Detective—Male Lead

Major character(s): Peter Bartholomew, Businessman (does odd jobs); Connie Bartholomew, Spouse (Peter's ex-wife)

Time period(s): 1990s

Locale(s): Close Harbor, Massachusetts

What the book is about: Peter Bartholomew has been asked by his sister Polly to go on a weekend whale watching cruise so he can meet her new fiance, Jackson Beers. Peter talks his ex-wife Connie into going with him in hopes of getting back together. After meeting the fiance he isn't sure the trip is worth it. Somebody else seems to share his opinion of Jackson Beers when he's found with an antique harpoon sticking through him.

Other books you might like:
Rick Boyer, *The Whale's Footprints*, 1988
Philip R. Craig, *The J.W. Jackson Series*, 1990-
Ken Grissom, *Big Fish*, 1991
Paul Kemprecos, *The Aristotle Socarides Series*, 1991-
Justin Scott, *Hardscape*, 1993

688
Sally Gunning
Still Water (New York: Pocket, 1995)

Series: Peter Bartholomew

Story type: Amateur Detective—Male Lead

Major character(s): Peter Bartholomew, Businessman (does odd jobs)

Time period(s): 1990s

Locale(s): Nashtoba, Massachusetts

What the book is about: Peter and his ex-wife Connie are trying to get back together, but both are somewhat hesitant to commit to anything permanent. It doesn't help that Peter finds himself drawn to his latest client's wife. He has been hired to look into two almost fatal accidents that could have killed the young bride. Initially he thinks it's just coicidence, but two more near-fatal incidents convince him that something is wrong. Then, in a house full of suspects, the wrong person dies.

Other books you might like:
Jeff Abbott, *The Jordan Poteet Series*, 1994-
Leo Axler, *The Bill Hawley Series*, 1994-
Rick Boyer, *The Doc Adams Series*, 1984-
Justin Scott, *The Ben Abbott Series*, 1993-
Stephen F. Wilcox, *The Elias Hackshaw Series*, 1991-

689
Sally Gunning
Troubled Water (New York: Pocket, 1993)

Series: Peter Bartholomew

Story type: Amateur Detective—Male Lead

Major character(s): Peter Bartholomew, Businessman (does odd jobs)

Time period(s): 1990s

Locale(s): Nashtoba, Massachusetts (Cape Cod)

What the book is about: Peter Bartholomew has taken a job to clean up the house and garden of two elderly sisters. One morning he arrives to find them both dead. The doctor says natural causes but Peter is not so sure. Pete's ex-wife, who he still loves, inherits part of the estate and the other heir is not at all happy about it. The sisters had a lot of secrets involving a lot of people - did one of them decide to silence the sisters once and for all?

Other books you might like:
W.J. Chaput, *Dead in the Water*, 1991
Philip R. Craig, *A Beautiful Place to Die*, 1989
Paul Kemprecos, *Cool Blue Tomb*, 1991
John Walter Putre, *A Small and Incidental Murder*, 1990
John Smolens, *Winter by Degrees*, 1988

690
Batya Gur
Murder on a Kibbutz (New York: HarperCollins, 1994)

Series: Michael Ohayon

Story type: Police Procedural—Male Lead

Major character(s): Michael Ohayon, Police Officer (Serious Crimes Unit)

Time period(s): 1990s

Locale(s): Israel

What the book is about: Detective Michael Ohayon sets out to find the murderer of kibbutz secretary Osnat Harel. His quest is hindered by politics—she had had an affair with a member of the Knesset; conflicts on the police force; and Ohayon's romantic interest in a colleague.

Other books you might like:
Jonathan Kellerman, *The Butcher's Theater*, 1988
Harry Kemelman, *Monday the Rabbi Took Off*, 1972
Philip Kerr, *The Pale Criminal*, 1989
Georges Simenon, *The Inspector Maigret Series*, 1932-1989
Maj Sjowall, *The Martin Beck Series*, 1966-1976 (Per Wahloo, co-author)

691
Batya Gur
The Saturday Morning Murder (New York: HarperCollins, 1992)

Series: Michael Ohayon

Story type: Police Procedural—Male Lead; Psychological Suspense

Major character(s): Michael Ohayon, Police Officer (chief inspector)

Time period(s): 1990s

Locale(s): Jerusalem, Israel

What the book is about: A researcher at the Jerusalem Psychoanyalytic Institute is shot right before a lecture. Is someone using her as an example? Inspector Ohayon's investigation leads him away from the Institute into the military and the world of commerce and then back to the Institute. First novel.

Other books you might like:
Jonathan Kellerman, *The Butcher's Theater*, 1988
Philip Kerr, *The Pale Criminal*, 1989
Maj Sjowall, *The Martin Beck Series*, 1966-1976 (Per Wahloo, co-author)

692
David Guterson
Snow Falling on Cedars (New York: Harcourt Brace, 1994)

Story type: Legal; Historical

Major character(s): Ishmael Chambers, Journalist (newspaper owner), Veteran; Hatsue Miyomoto, Spouse

Time period(s): 1950s (1954, with many flashbacks to 1941)

Locale(s): San Piedro Island, Washington (in Puget Sound)

What the book is about: Japanese-American Kabuo Miyomoto is accused of the murder of Carl Heine, a fisherman found trapped in his nets. They had had words earlier and means and motive were both available. Covering the trial for his newspaper is Ishmael Chambers, a native islander whose feelings are complicated because of the relationship he had before the war with the accused man's wife, Hatsue. What happened during the war looms large during the trial because Chambers lost an arm in combat and the Miyomotos were interned. First novel.

Other books you might like:
John E. Keegan, *Clearwater Summer*, 1994
Richard Parrish, *The Dividing Line*, 1993

693
Al Guthrie
Murder by Tarot (New York: Zebra, 1992)

Series: Abby & Mac McKenzie

Story type: Private Detective—Male Lead

Major character(s): Abby McKenzie, Businesswoman (craft store owner), Artist; Mac McKenzie, Detective—Private

Time period(s): 1990s

Locale(s): Sarahville, Illinois

What the book is about: Mac is trying to retire but he takes one last case, finding a lost dog. Meanwhile Abby is mad at city hall. One of the Mayor's people has tried to get money for approving her business permit. Both cases lead to a psychic named Madame Gladys. Then at a fair the mayor is found murdered in Madame Gladys tent.

Other books you might like:
Richard Forrest, *Death on the Mississippi*, 1989
Bernie Lee, *Murder at Musket Beach*, 1990
Charlotte MacLeod, *The Sarah Kelling Series*, 1979-
Eve K. Sandstrom, *Death Down Home*, 1990
Elizabeth Travis, *Under the Influence*, 1989

694
C.A. Haddad
Caught in the Shadows (New York: St. Martin's, 1992)

Story type: Private Detective—Female Lead

Major character(s): Becky Belski, Computer Expert, Divorced Person; Michael Rosen, Lawyer

Time period(s): 1990s

Locale(s): Chicago, Illinois

What the book is about: Becky Belski is employed by a computer research firm, a sort of private investigation by computer company. She's a "hacker". She becomes involved in a divorce of two of the rich and famous. The case involves her with her own past and the mysterious death of her mother.

Other books you might like:
Denise Danks, *User Deadly*, 1992
Marjorie Dorner, *Family Closets*, 1988
D.F. Mills, *Deadline*, 1991
Nancy Pickard, *I.O.U.*, 1991

695
Jane Haddam (Pseudonym of Orania Papazoglou)
Not a Creature Was Stirring (New York: Bantam, 1990)

Series: Gregor Demarkian

Story type: Amateur Detective—Male Lead

Major character(s): Gregor Demarkian, Troubleshooter (former FBI agent); Bennis Hannaford, Writer

Time period(s): 1990s

Locale(s): Philadelphia, Pennsylvania

What the book is about: Someone is killing off members of the Hannaford family. Demarkian, as a favor to his former priest, gets involved.

Other books you might like:
James Anderson, *The Affair of the Blood-Stained Egg Cosy*, 1976
Robert Barnard, *Death of a Mystery Writer*, 1979
Jeremiah Healy, *Right to Die*, 1991
Melodie Johnson Howe, *The Mother Shadow*, 1989
Rex Stout, *Where There's a Will*, 1940

696

Jane Haddam (Pseudonym of Orania Papazoglou)
Quoth the Raven (New York: Bantam, 1991)
Series: Gregor Demarkian
Story type: Amateur Detective—Male Lead
Major character(s): Gregor Demarkian, Troubleshooter (former FBI agent)
Time period(s): 1990s
Locale(s): Pennsylvania
What the book is about: The secretary of a missing professor is poisoned at dinner. Demarkian decides that this means the professor is also dead and that the secretary knew—or thought she knew—what had happened. Since this is talking place at Halloween, it is making the investigation a bit more complicated than it would be normally—what with witches and ravens and costumed students running about.
Other books you might like:
Simon Brett, *A Scandal in Belgravia*, 1990
Bill Crider, *One Dead Dean*, 1989
Sally Gunning, *Hot Water*, 1990
M.D. Lake, *Poisoned Ivy*, 1991
A.J. Orde, *A Little Neighborhood Murder*, 1989

697

Jane Haddam (Pseudonym of Orania Papazoglou)
A Stillness in Bethlehem (New York: Bantam, 1992)
Series: Gregor Demarkian
Story type: Amateur Detective—Male Lead
Major character(s): Gregor Demarkian, Police Officer (former FBI agent)
Time period(s): 1990s
Locale(s): Bethlehem, Vermont
What the book is about: In Bethlehem, Vermont for their famous nativity celebration Gregor Demarkian gets involved in helping the police solve the riddle of the deaths of two women shot on the same day with different rifles. He also manages to involve himself in the domestic crisis between a biker and his wife.
Other books you might like:
Simon Brett, *A Scandal in Belgravia*, 1990
Charlotte MacLeod, *Rest You Merry*, 1979
Katherine Hall Page, *The Body in the Bouillon*, 1991
Gillian Roberts, *Philly Stakes*, 1989
James Yaffe, *Mom Meets Her Maker*, 1990

698

Jean Hager
Blooming Murder (New York: Avon, 1994)
Series: Iris House Mystery
Story type: Amateur Detective—Female Lead
Major character(s): Tess Darcy, Innkeeper (bed-and-breakfast owner)
Time period(s): 1990s
Locale(s): Victoria Springs (near the Ozarks)
What the book is about: Tess Darcy has inherited Iris House from her aunt and she has decided to turn it into a bed-and-breakfast. For the opening she has been talked into putting up the members of the Victoria Springs Garden Club—or The Club as it's known to the locals. Then the local femme fatale, Lana Morrison, is found murdered. Inadvertantly at first, and later because she decides to solve the murder, Tess uncovers deceit, jealousy, and intrigue in The Club. First in what appears to be a series.
Other books you might like:
Jill Churchill, *The Class Menagerie*, 1994
Mary Daheim, *The Bed-and-Breakfast Series*, 1991-
Diane Mott Davidson, *The Goldy Bear Series*, 1990-
Muriel Resnick Jackson, *The Garden Club*, 1992
Janet Laurence, *The Darina Lisle Series*, 1990-

699

Jean Hager
Dead and Buried (New York: Avon, 1995)
Series: Iris House Mystery
Story type: Amateur Detective—Female Lead
Major character(s): Tess Darcy, Innkeeper (bed-and-breakfast owner)
Time period(s): 1990s
Locale(s): Victoria Springs, Missouri
What the book is about: Tess is hosting a class reunion at Iris House. One of the attendees is Francine Alexander, a well-known romance novelist. Her career is on the decline but she says that her new book, based on real life, will be her comeback. Soon after, she is poisoned. Several people seem to have secrets in their past that they don't want revealed but would one of them commit murder to keep it quiet? Tess is in a perfect position to find out.
Other books you might like:
Claudia Bishop, *The Sarah Quilliam Series*, 1994-
Mary Daheim, *The Bed-and-Breakfast Series*, 1991-
Jo Dereske, *Miss Zukas and the Island Murders*, 1995
Janet Laurence, *Hotel Morgue*, 1992
Triss Stein, *Murder at the Class Reunion*, 1993

700

Jean Hager
Ghostland (New York: St. Martin's, 1992)
Series: Mitchell Bushyhead
Story type: Police Procedural—Male Lead
Major character(s): Mitchell Bushyhead, Police Officer (chief of police)
Time period(s): 1990s
Locale(s): Buckskin, Oklahoma
What the book is about: The investigation of the death of a Cherokee child at her boarding school is hampered by the principal who seems to be afraid of something else. One of the teachers seems to have a suspicious background and when the teacher's daughter and the murdered girl disappear there would seem to be a connection.

701
Hager

Other books you might like:
Bill Crider, *The Sheriff Dan Rhodes Series*, 1986-
Brian Garfield, *The Threepersons Hunt*, 1974
Tony Hillerman, *The Blessing Way*, 1970

701
Jean Hager
Ravenmocker (New York: Mysterious, 1992)
Series: Molly Bearpaw
Story type: Police Procedural; Private Detective—Female Lead
Major character(s): Molly Bearpaw, Detective—Private, Indian; D.J. Kennedy, Police Officer (deputy sheriff)
Time period(s): 1990s
Locale(s): Tahlequah, Oklahoma
What the book is about: Molly Bearpaw is an investigator for the N.A.A.L., the Native American Advocacy League, and is paid by the Cherokee Nation to protect the rights of tribal members. Now Woodrow Mouse has asked her to look into the death of his father at a local retirement home. When the autopsy reveals he died of botulism poisoning, the authorities become involved but no source can be found. When a second resident dies, Molly and her one-time boyfriend, Deputy Sheriff Kennedy, suspect they have a murderer on their hands.
Other books you might like:
Brian Garfield, *The Threepersons Hunt*, 1974
Tony Hillerman, *The Joe Leaphorn Series*, 1970-
John Miles, *A Permanent Retirement*, 1993
Dana Stabenow, *The Kate Shugak Series*, 1992-
Chelsea Quinn Yarbro, *The Charlie Moon Series*, 1990-

702
Jean Hager
The Redbird's Cry (New York: Mysterious, 1994)
Series: Molly Bearpaw
Story type: Private Detective—Female Lead
Major character(s): Molly Bearpaw, Detective—Private, Indian
Time period(s): 1990s
Locale(s): Tahlequah, Oklahoma
What the book is about: It's time for the annual Heritage celebration in Tahlequah and tensions are running high because there is a power struggle between the Cherokee Nation and the True Echota Band. Tom Battle, storyteller and lawyer, has recently been involved in several legal decisions against the Echota faction, plus he is dating the ex-wife of one of the Echota activists. When he is murdered the ex-husband is the prime suspect, but Molly Bearpaw knows there are other things going on and tries to find the truth.
Other books you might like:
Cecil Dawkins, *Clay Dancers*, 1994
Tony Hillerman, *The Joe Leaphorn Series*, 1970-
Linda Mariz, *Body English*, 1992
Dana Stabenow, *The Kate Shugak Series*, 1992-
J.F. Trainor, *The Angela Biwaban Series*, 1993-

703
Isidore Haiblum
Bad Neighbors (New York: St. Martin's, 1990)
Series: James Shaw
Story type: Private Detective—Male Lead
Major character(s): James Shaw, Detective—Private (Jewish)
Time period(s): 1980s
Locale(s): New York, New York
What the book is about: Hired to find out who is trying to force elderly tenants out of a rent-controlled building, Shaw discovers that the mob is probably involved.
Other books you might like:
Jack Early, *A Creative Kind of Killer*, 1984
Robert J. Randisi, *No Exit From Brooklyn*, 1987
J.W. Rider, *Jersey Tomatoes*, 1986

704
J.P. Hailey (Pseudonym of Parnell Hall)
The Naked Typist (New York: Fine, 1990)
Series: Steve Winslow
Story type: Amateur Detective—Male Lead; Legal
Major character(s): Steve Winslow, Lawyer
Time period(s): 1990s
Locale(s): New York, New York
What the book is about: Why does the retired business tycoon insist that the woman hired to type his memoirs do so naked? Not for the reasons you might think. What does this have to do with his murder?
Other books you might like:
Bill S. Ballinger, *The Tooth and the Nail*, 1955
Erle Stanley Gardner, *The Perry Mason Series*, 1933-1973
Stephen Greenleaf, *State's Evidence*, 1982
Joe L. Hensley, *The Don Roback Series*, 1974-

705
J.P. Hailey (Pseudonym of Parnell Hall)
The Underground Man (New York: Fine, 1990)
Series: Steve Winslow
Story type: Legal
Major character(s): Steve Winslow, Lawyer
Time period(s): 1980s
Locale(s): New York, New York
What the book is about: Steve Winslow is hired to defend a teenager who is accused of killing his wealthy uncle.
Other books you might like:
Joe L. Hensley, *The Don Roback Series*, (1974-)
Ed Lacy, *Breathe No More, My Lady*, 1958
John Mortimer, *Rumpole of the Bailey*, 1980

706
Adam Hall (Pseudonym of Elleston Trevor)
Quiller KGB (New York: Charter, 1989)

Series: Quiller

Story type: Espionage

Major character(s): Quiller, Spy

Time period(s): 1980s

What the book is about: Quiller and his old adversary, Colonel Victor Yasolev of the KGB, must combine forces to prevent the assassination of Gorbachev.

Other books you might like:
Sean Flannery, *Broken Idols*, 1985
Brian Freemantle, *The Run Around*, 1989
Brian Garfield, *Hopscotch*, 1974
John Le Carre, *The Spy Who Came in from the Cold*, 1963
Marc Lovell, *The Spy with His Head in the Clouds*, 1982

707
James W. Hall
Bones of Coral (New York: Knopf, 1991)

Story type: Action/Adventure

Major character(s): Douglas Barnes, Criminal (landfill owner, former soldier); Shaw Chandler, Health Care Professional (paramedic)

Time period(s): 1990s

Locale(s): Key West, Florida

What the book is about: Called to the scene of an apparent suicide, Shaw Chandler is stunned to discover the body of his father—and it's not suicide, it's murder. This discovery leads him into a labyrinth of deceits and lies involving a twenty-year-old murder and the cover-up of a toxic waste dump.

Other books you might like:
Carl Hiaasen, *Double Whammy*, 1987
Carl Hiaasen, *Skin Tight*, 1989
Carl Hiaasen, *Tourist Season*, 1986
John Katzenbach, *In the Heat of the Summer*, 1982
James Patillo, *Skim*, 1991

708
James W. Hall
Gone Wild (New York: Delacorte, 1995)

Series: Thorn

Story type: Action/Adventure; Private Detective—Male Lead

Major character(s): Allison Farleigh, Businesswoman; Thorn, Detective—Private

Time period(s): 1990s

Locale(s): Florida; Malaysia

What the book is about: Thorn finds himself involved with wildlife smuggling when his childhood friend Allison Farleigh's daughter is killed while on a wildlife census. The people who did the killing knew who Allison was and were really after her. Allison vows vengeance on those who killed her daughter and Thorn agrees to help her.

Other books you might like:
Rick Hanson, *Spare Parts*, 1994
Carl Hiaasen, *Native Tongue*, 1991
Stephen Hunter, *Dirty White Boys*, 1994
Jonathan Kellerman, *The Web*, 1996
John Straley, *The Curious Eat Themsleves*, 1993

709
James W. Hall
Hard Aground (New York: Delacorte, 1993)

Story type: Action/Adventure

Major character(s): Hap Tyler, Veteran (former mental patient); Marguerite Rawlings, Journalist (newspaper columnist)

Time period(s): 1990s

Locale(s): Miami, Florida

What the book is about: The Carmelita, a Spanish treasure ship that sank over 350 years ago, has been sought by many people. Now a ruthless group has information that the Tyler family knows the ship's location and has been slowly selling off the treaure. When Daniel Tyler dies during questioning, his brother Hap and his girlfriend Marguerite Rawlings want to know why. Hap, who hears voices, was never entrusted with the family secret and the Rawlings family has a strange history of its own.

Other books you might like:
Robert Ferrigno, *The Horse Latitudes*, 1990
Carl Hiaasen, *Double Whammy*, 1987
Tom Kakonis, *Double Down*, 1991
John Katzenbach, *Just Cause*, 1992
Charles Willeford, *Sideswipe*, 1987

710
James W. Hall
Mean High Tide (New York: Delacorte, 1994)

Series: Thorn

Story type: Action/Adventure; Private Detective—Male Lead

Major character(s): Thorn, Detective—Private

Time period(s): 1990s

Locale(s): Florida (Florida Keys)

What the book is about: When Thorn's lover, Darcy Richards, is murdered, he vows revenge. She dies in what appears to be a diving accident but was really killed by a method known only to covert assassins. Why was she killed? Was it to get at Thorn? Has his past caught up with him?

Other books you might like:
Robert Ferrigno, *The Cheshire Moon*, 1993
Carl Hiaasen, *Native Tongue*, 1991
Bruce Jones, *In Deep*, 1991
Tom Kakonis, *Double Down*, 1991
John Katzenbach, *Just Cause*, 1992

711
Mary Bowen Hall
Emma Chizzit and the Mother Lode Marauder (New York: Walker, 1993)

Series: Emma Chizzit

Story type: Amateur Detective—Female Lead

Major character(s): Emma Chizzit, Businesswoman (owner of a salvage business)

Time period(s): 1990s

Locale(s): Buckeye, California

What the book is about: Emma Chizzit is in Buckeye to look in on the son of an old friend who says he seems to be having trouble. The town of Buckeye is split between people who want to preserve it and those who want to turn it into a tourist attraction. Things heat up when a rattlesnake shows up in a picnic basket, the first in a series of not-so-harmless pranks. Emma digs around trying to stop what's happening before someone gets hurt.

Other books you might like:
Eleanor Boylan, *Working Murder*, 1989
B. Comfort, *Grave Consequences*, 1989
Charlaine Harris, *Real Murders*, 1991
B.J. Oliphant, *The Shirley McClintock Series*, 1990-
David Osborn, *Murder in the Napa Valley*, 1993

712
Mary Bowen Hall
Emma Chizzit and the Napa Nemesis (New York: Walker, 1992)

Series: Emma Chizzit

Story type: Amateur Detective—Female Lead

Major character(s): Emma Chizzit, Businesswoman (owner of a salvage business)

Time period(s): 1990s

Locale(s): Napa Valley, California

What the book is about: Everyone in the area is in an uproar because a rumor has started saying there is a unpublished Robert Louis Stevenson novel hidden somewhere in the neighborhood. Emma's friend Frannie has talked Emma into looking for it too. When they start to look for it, they become involved with the mysterious Wulff twins and other strange treasure seekers. Then people connected with the local Stevenson museum start to disappear or show up dead.

Other books you might like:
Eleanor Boylan, *Working Murder*, 1989
Stefanie Matteson, *The Charlotte Graham Series*, 1990-
Corinne Holt Sawyer, *The J. Alfred Prufrock Murders*, 1987
Edith Skom, *The Mark Twain Murders*, 1989
Julie Smith, *Huckleberry Fiend*, 1986

713
Mary Bowen Hall
Emma Chizzit and the Queen Anne Killer (New York: Walker, 1989)

Series: Emma Chizzit

Story type: Amateur Detective—Female Lead

Major character(s): Emma Chizzit, Businesswoman (owner of a salvage business)

Time period(s): 1980s

Locale(s): Sacramento, California

What the book is about: While cleaning out a Queen Anne house, Emma finds a mummified baby in a cradle. After reporting this to the police, she finds herself very involved in a mystery that goes back 20 years or more but appears to be just as deadly today. First book.

Other books you might like:
B. Comfort, *Grave Consequences*, 1989
Dorothy Salisbury Davis, *A Death in the Life*, 1976
Jane Dentinger, *Murder on Cue*, 1983
Haughton Murphy, *Murder for Lunch*, 1986
Susan Trott, *Pursued by the Crooked Man*, 1988

714
Parnell Hall (Pseudonym of J.P. Hailey)
Juror (New York: Fine, 1990)

Series: Stanley Hastings

Story type: Private Detective—Male Lead; Humor

Major character(s): Stanley Hastings, Detective—Private (failed writer, failed actor)

Time period(s): 1990s

Locale(s): New York, New York

What the book is about: Stanley gets called for jury duty, can't get out of it, and gets involved with one of his fellow jurors. When she turns up dead, Stanley is a suspect so he must try and find out who really killed her. All of this may have something to do with the case for which he's been impaneled. Hall also writes as J.P. Hailey.

Other books you might like:
Lawrence Block, *The Bernie Rhodenbarr Series*, 1977-
Bill Crider, *One Dead Dean*, 1988
Gregory McDonald, *The Fletch Series*, 1974-
Donald E. Westlake, *God Save the Mark*, 1967

715
Parnell Hall (Pseudonym of J.P. Hailey)
Strangler (New York: Fine, 1989)

Series: Stanley Hastings

Story type: Amateur Detective—Male Lead

Major character(s): Stanley Hastings, Writer (works for a law firm)

Time period(s): 1980s

Locale(s): New York, New York

What the book is about: When a number of potential clients of the law firm Stanley works for are strangled, Stanley is the chief suspect. So he is forced to play detective to find out the truth.

Other books you might like:
Lawrence Block, *Burglars Can't Be Choosers*, 1977
Max Allan Collins, *Kill Your Darlings*, 1984
Bill Crider, *One Dead Dean*, 1988
Les Roberts, *Not Enough Horses*, 1988
Donald E. Westlake, *God Save the Mark*, 1967

716
Timothy Hallinan
Everything but the Squeal (New York: NAL, 1990)

Series: Simeon Grist
Story type: Private Detective—Male Lead
Major character(s): Simeon Grist, Detective—Private
Time period(s): 1980s
Locale(s): Los Angeles, California

What the book is about: Grist is hired to look for a runaway teenage girl from Kansas. He has little hope of finding her alive, particularly after a body, not hers, shows up in the morgue. The marks on the dead girl are very similar to marks seen in pictures of the girl Grist has been hired to find. Can he find and break up the child-selling ring before it's too late? Or is it always too late?

Other books you might like:
Robert Crais, *Stalking the Angel*, 1989
Robert B. Parker, *Ceremony*, 1982
Benjamin M. Schutz, *Embrace the Wolf*, 1985
Andrew Vachss, *Blossom*, 1990
Jonathan Valin, *The Lime Pit*, 1980

717
Timothy Hallinan
Incinerator (New York: Morrow, 1992)

Series: Simeon Grist
Story type: Private Detective—Male Lead
Major character(s): Simeon Grist, Detective—Private
Time period(s): 1990s
Locale(s): Los Angeles, California

What the book is about: Hired by the daughter of billionaire Abraham Winston to discover who torched her father, Grist begins to get notes from someone calling himself the Incinerator claiming credit for the murder. More burning deaths soon follow and it appears that Grist himself may be being set up to be a victim.

Other books you might like:
Robert Campbell, *In La-La Land We Trust*, 1987
Robert Crais, *Stalking the Angel*, 1989
James Ellroy, *Brown's Requiem*, 1981
Les Roberts, *An Infinite Number of Monkeys*, 1987
Jonathan Valin, *Second Chance*, 1991

718
Timothy Hallinan
Skin Deep (New York: Dutton, 1991)

Series: Simeon Grist
Story type: Private Detective—Male Lead
Major character(s): Simeon Grist, Detective—Private
Time period(s): 1990s
Locale(s): Los Angeles, California

What the book is about: After intervening between TV star Tony Vane and his date to stop Vane from beating her up, Grist is hired by Vane's producers to keep an eye on Vane to help curb his predilection for beating up women. All is well and good until Vane begins to slip away and battered bodies begin to show up.

Other books you might like:
Robert Campbell, *In La-La Land We Trust*, 1987
Robert Crais, *Stalking the Angel*, 1989
Michael J. Katz, *Last Dance in Redondo Beach*, 1989
Les Roberts, *An Infinite Number of Monkeys*, 1987
Jim Stinson, *Truck Shot*, 1989

719
Gerald Hammond
A Brace of Skeet (New York: St. Martins, 1990)

Series: Keith Calder
Story type: Amateur Detective—Male Lead
Major character(s): Keith Calder, Businessman (gunsmith); Deborah Calder, Businesswoman (gunsmith, daughter of Keith)
Time period(s): 1990s
Locale(s): Newton Lauder, Scotland

What the book is about: Keith Calder decides to go on vacation and let his daughter run the shop. No sooner has he left than the police need Deborah's expertise with firearms. The steward at a local gun club is found dead, seemingly killed by a skeet trap.

Other books you might like:
M.C. Beaton, *Death of a Gossip*, 1985
Barry Cork, *Dead Ball*, 1989
Bill Knox, *The Colin Thane Series*, 1958-

720
Gerald Hammond
Home to Roost (New York: St. Martin's, 1991)

Series: Keith Calder
Story type: Amateur Detective; Police Procedural
Major character(s): Deborah Calder, Businesswoman (gunsmith); Ian Fellowes, Police Officer (detective—sergeant)
Time period(s): 1990s
Locale(s): Newton Lauder, Scotland

What the book is about: Murder and poaching are the staples in this book which serves to introduce detective—sergeant Ian Fellowes to the series. He and Deborah Calder get involved with murder while investigating poaching.

721
Handberg

Other books you might like:
M.C. Beaton, *The Hamish MacBeth Series*, 1985-
Barry Cork, *Dead Ball*, 1989
Bill Knox, *The Colin Thane Series*, 1958-
William McIlvanney, *Laidlaw*, 1977-

721
Ron Handberg
Savage Justice (New York: Birch Lane, 1992)

Story type: Action/Adventure; Amateur Detective—Male Lead

Major character(s): Alex Collier, Journalist, Television Personality (anchorman); Pat Hodges, Housewife (former girlfriend of Collier)

Time period(s): 1990s

Locale(s): Minneapolis/St. Paul, Minnesota

What the book is about: At the urging of old girlfriend Pat Hodges, Alex Collier begins an investigation of a most esteemed judge—now a state supreme court nominee—but a man Pat suggests may be a pedophile. She is also worried that her husband, another judge, may be involved in a cover-up. As he gets into the investigation, Collier discovers that a reporter who had earlier been investigating the judge has disappeared. First novel.

Other books you might like:
Elmore Leonard, *Maximum Bob*, 1991
Mike Lupica, *Limited Partner*, 1990
Keith Peterson, *The Scarred Man*, 1990
Mike Phillips, *Blood Rights*, 1989
Stephen F. Wilcox, *The Dry White Tear*, 1989

722
David Handler
The Man Who Cancelled Himself (New York: Doubleday, 1995)

Series: Stewart Hoag

Story type: Amateur Detective—Male Lead

Major character(s): Stewart Hoag, Writer (ghostwriter); Lyle Hudnut, Actor (television star)

Time period(s): 1990s

Locale(s): New York, New York

What the book is about: Stewart "Hoagy" Hoag is under contract to ghostwrite the autobiography of self-destructive children's television star Lyle "Uncle Chubby" Hudnut. Hudnut is attempting a comeback after being arrested for indecent exposure. He also thinks someone is out to get him. When a series of accidents occur on the set of the show, it appears he may be right. As usual, it is up to Hoagy to discern the truth.

Other books you might like:
Susan Conant, *Gone to the Dogs*, 1992
Bill Crider, *Dying Voices*, 1990
Stan Cutler, *The Face on the Cutting Room Floor*, 1991
Jon Katz, *The Last Housewife*, 1995
James Yaffe, *Mom Among the Liars*, 1992

723
David Handler
The Man Who Would Be F. Scott Fitzgerald (New York: Bantam, 1990)

Series: Stewart Hoag

Story type: Amateur Detective—Male Lead

Major character(s): Stewart Hoag, Writer (ghostwriter); Lulu Hoag, Animal (basset hound)

Time period(s): 1990s

Locale(s): New York, New York

What the book is about: Hoag is hired to ghostwrite Cam Noyes' new expose of the book business. Many people don't want the book written, but it's people around Noyes who are dying, and Hoag's ex-wife, the lovely Merilee, is threatened.

Other books you might like:
P.J. Coyne, *Manuscript for Murder*, 1987
Stephen Greenleaf, *Book Case*, 1991
Mary Kittredge, *Poison Pen*, 1990
Warren Murphy, *The Trace Series*, 1983-
Michael Thall, *Let Sleeping Afghans Lie*, 1990

724
David Handler
The Woman Who Fell From Grace (New York: Bantam, 1991)

Series: Stewart Hoag

Story type: Amateur Detective—Male Lead

Major character(s): Stewart Hoag, Writer (ghostwriter); Lulu Hoag, Animal (bassett hound)

Time period(s): 1990s

Locale(s): United States

What the book is about: Hoagy has been hired to write the sequel to the best-selling novel of all time—the Revolutionary War epic, *Oh, Shenandoah*. The heir and other relatives of dead author Alma Glaze all have their own ideas of what should be written but these ideas become unimportant after a murder, the reason for which may be buried in the past. Maybe it has something to do with an earlier death. It seems that one of the stars of the film died mysteriously right after the movie was done. But why has it taken 50 years for someone to become afraid of the truth?

Other books you might like:
Mickey Friedman, *A Temporary Ghost*, 1989
Douglas Kiker, *The Mac McFarland Series*, 1987
Dallas Murphy, *Lover Man*, 1987
Warren Murphy, *The Trace Series*, 1983-
Elizabeth Peters, *Naked Once More*, 1988

725
Sean Hanlon
The Frozen Franklin (New York: Pocket, 1990)

Series: Prester John Riordan

Story type: Amateur Detective—Male Lead

Major character(s): Prester John Riordan, Journalist, Radio Personality (radio station owner)

Time period(s): 1990s

Locale(s): Alaska

What the book is about: While doing his radio show, Pres is intrigued by a caller's story of a land deed buried with the body of an explorer in the Artic. Unfortunately he's not the only one who is interested.

Other books you might like:
Louis Charbonneau, *The Ice*, 1991
Sue Henry, *Murder on the Iditarod Trail*, 1991
Alistair MacLean, *Ice Station Zebra*, 1963
Martin Cruz Smith, *Polar Star*, 1989

726
Joseph Hansen
The Boy Who Was Buried This Morning (New York: Viking, 1990)

Series: Dave Brandstetter

Story type: Amateur Detective—Male Lead

Major character(s): Dave Brandstetter, Insurance Investigator (retired), Homosexual

Time period(s): 1980s

Locale(s): California

What the book is about: Brandstetter comes out of retirement to find the killer of a wealthy young man, killed while playing paintball.

Other books you might like:
Nathan Aldyne, *Vermillion*, 1980
Tony Fennelly, *The Glory Hole Murders*, 1985
Dan Kavanagh, *Duffy*, 1980
Arthur Lyons, *Hard Trade*, 1981
Richard Stevenson, *On the Other Hand, Death*, 1984

727
Joseph Hansen
A Country of Old Men (New York: Viking, 1991)

Series: Dave Brandstetter

Story type: Amateur Detective—Male Lead

Major character(s): Dave Brandstetter, Insurance Investigator (retired), Homosexual; Jack Helmers, Writer (mystery writer)

Time period(s): 1990s

Locale(s): Los Angeles, California

What the book is about: Dave is talked into taking on the case of the dead pop musician, Cricket Shales. The police think it was a drug deal gone bad but Dave finds many people who might have wanted Cricket dead. A sub-plot involves a writer friend struggling with his life.

Other books you might like:
Nathan Aldyne, *Vermillion*, 1980
Arthur Lyons, *Hard Trade*, 1981
Grant Michaels, *A Body to Dye For*, 1990
Michael Nava, *How Town*, 1990
Richard Stevenson, *Ice Blues*, 1986

728
Rick Hanson
Mortal Remains (New York: Kensington, 1995)

Series: Adam McCleet

Story type: Amateur Detective—Male Lead

Major character(s): Adam McCleet, Artist (sculptor), Veteran (Vietnam)

Time period(s): 1990s

Locale(s): Portland, Oregon

What the book is about: Adam is watching a psychiatrist friend use hypnosis on a Vietman veteran to help him deal with post-traumatic stress syndrome. Suddenly the patient turns violent and kills Adam's friend. The police assume the patient just went temporarily nuts, but Adam thinks differently. He suspects that the patient was drugged and that killing was premeditated by someone.

Other books you might like:
G.M. Ford, *Who the Hell Is Wanda Fuca?*, 1995
James N. Frey, *Winter of the Wolves*, 1992
Brian Harper, *Deadly Pursuit*, 1995
Robert Upton, *Fade Out*, 1984
Kate Wilhelm, *The Hamlet Trap*, 1987

729
Mollie Hardwick
The Bandersnatch (New York: St. Martin's, 1989)

Series: Doran Fairweather

Story type: Amateur Detective—Female Lead

Major character(s): Doran Fairweather, Businesswoman (antique dealer)

Time period(s): 1980s

What the book is about: After successfully bidding for a carved cherub for her new baby, Doran Fairweather finds that someone else wants it more than she does and is willing to resort to crime to get it.

Other books you might like:
Marion Babson, *Death Warmed Up*, 1982
Eliza G.C. Collins, *Going, Going, Gone*, 1986
Antonia Fraser, *A Splash of Red*, 1981
Anne Morice, *Scared to Death*, 1978
Erica Quest, *The October Cabaret*, 1979

730
William Harrington
Town on Trial (New York: Fine, 1994)

Story type: Legal

Major character(s): Bill McIntyre, Judge

Time period(s): 1990s

Locale(s): Ohio

731
Harris

What the book is about: Judge Bill McIntyre is presiding over the trial of wealthy art patron, Marietta Rheinlander, who is accused of shooting three people—one of them a congressman. Because of the congressman, the trial has turned into a media circus. Did Marietta actually do the killing and will she be convicted—innocent or not?

Other books you might like:
William J. Coughlin, *Death Penalty*, 1992
Joe L. Hensley, *Color Him Guilty*, 1987
John T. Lescroart, *The 13th Juror*, 1994
Kate Wilhelm, *Justice for Some*, 1993

731
Charlaine Harris
A Bone to Pick (New York: Walker, 1992)

Series: Aurora Teagarden

Story type: Amateur Detective—Female Lead

Major character(s): Aurora Teagarden, Librarian (crime buff)

Time period(s): 1990s; 17th century (1670's)

Locale(s): Lawrenceton, Arkansas

What the book is about: Aurora's love life is the pits - her ex-boyfriend was just married - and her job as a librarian has just been cut. Out of the blue her friend Jane Engle dies and leaves Aurora her house and over half a million dollars. Why? They were not that friendly, only sharing an interest in true crime. Aurora starts to suspect a hidden motive when someone breaks in and searches the house. Then she finds a hidden skull that is obviously that of someone who has been murdered.

Other books you might like:
Joan Hess, *The Claire Malloy Series*, 1986-
Sharyn McCrumb, *The Elizabeth MacPherson Series*, 1984-
Sarah Shankman, *Then Hang All the Liars*, 1989
Celestine Sibley, *Ah, Sweet Mystery*, 1991
Patricia Houck Sprinkle, *Murder in the Charleston Manner*, 1990

732
Charlaine Harris
The Julius House (New York: Scribners, 1995)

Series: Aurora Teagarden

Story type: Amateur Detective—Female Lead

Major character(s): Aurora Teagarden, Aged Person (former librarian); Martin Bartell, Businessman

Time period(s): 1990s

Locale(s): Lawrenceton, Georgia

What the book is about: Aurora is engaged to Martin, and in an exchange of gifts, she gets the deed to the beautiful and mysterious Julius House. The mystery comes from the fact that the former owner, the Julius family, disappeared one night and have never been heard from again. Aurora, with her interest in crime, fictional and true, is intrigued. But why is Martin being so secretive and who are the couple living in the garage—helpers or keepers?

Other books you might like:
Jo Dereske, *The Miss Zukas Series*, 1994-
Carolyn G. Hart, *The Annie Laurence Series*, 1987-
Joan Hess, *The Claire Malloy Series*, 1986-
Sharyn McCrumb, *The Elizabeth MacPherson Series*, 1984-
Elizabeth Daniels Squire, *The Peaches Dann Series*, 1994-

733
Lee Harris
The Christening Day Murder (New York: Fawcett, 1993)

Series: Christine Bennett

Story type: Amateur Detective—Female Lead

Major character(s): Christine Bennett, Religious (ex-nun); Jack Brooks, Police Officer (Christine's lover)

Time period(s): 1990s

Locale(s): Studberg, New York

What the book is about: Christine Bennett's old friend Maddie has asked her to the christening of her baby. But this is not just any christening. It is to take place in the town of Studberg, a town that until the recent drought had been under water for thirty years. What Chris discovers is a body that has been hidden for all those years but now threatens to expose secrets that are best left under water.

Other books you might like:
Isabelle Holland, *The Claire Aldington Series*, 1984-
David Willis McCullough, *The Ziza Todd Series*, 1990-
Sister Carol Anne O'Marie, *The Sister Mary Helen Series*, 1984-
Barbara Whitehead, *The Dean It Was That Died*, 1991

734
Lee Harris
The Christmas Night Murder (New York: Fawcett, 1994)

Series: Christine Bennett

Story type: Amateur Detective—Female Lead

Major character(s): Christine Bennett, Housewife (ex-nun); Jack Brooks, Police Officer (Christine's husband)

Time period(s): 1990s

Locale(s): Oakwood, New York

What the book is about: Although Christine Bennett has left the order and is now happy as a housewife, she still has a fondness for St. Stephen's Convent and for Sister Joseph. She is looking forward to seeing Father McCormick who will be visiting on Christmas Day. But Father never arrives and his car is found abandoned. Has he changed his mind, been kidnapped, or worse? Sister Joseph asks Christine and her husband to help. They find this may be linked to the suicide of a young woman years ago.

Other books you might like:
Isabelle Holland, *The Claire Aldington Series*, 1984-
Frank McConnell, *Liar's Poker*, 1993
Katherine Hall Page, *The Body in the Belfry*, 1990
Carey Roberts, *Pray God to Die*, 1993
Winona Sullivan, *A Sudden Death at the Norfolk Cafe*, 1993

735
Colin Harrison
Break and Enter (New York: Crown, 1990)

Story type: Legal

Major character(s): Peter Scattergood, Lawyer (assistant district attorney)

Time period(s): 1980s

Locale(s): Philadelphia, Pennsylvania

What the book is about: Assistant D.A. Peter Scattergood's life is falling apart as he is trying to put together a case involving the murder of the mayor's nephew and the nephew's girlfriend. First book.

Other books you might like:
Richard Harris, *Honor Bound*, 1982
Brian Lysaght, *Special Circumstances*, 1983
Michael Malone, *Time's Witness*, 1989
Walter Walker, *A Dime to Dance By*, 1984

736
Jamie Harrison
The Edge of the Crazies (New York: Hyperion, 1995)

Story type: Police Procedural—Male Lead; Action/Adventure

Major character(s): Jules Clement, Police Officer (sheriff)

Time period(s): 1990s

Locale(s): Blue Deer, Montana

What the book is about: Someone has taken serious umbrage at the continued existence of George Blackwater. Suspects would seem to include his ex-wife, his brother, and a few of the townsfolk. Before Jules can do much, the wife shows up dead, which effectively eliminates her as a suspect. It appears that the answer to the current crimes may lie in the past—perhaps with Jules' own father, who was killed in the line of duty at about the same time that George's then-girlfriend died suspiciously. First novel.

Other books you might like:
James Crumley, *The Last Good Kiss*, 1978
Joe Gores, *32 Cadillacs*, 1992
Richard Hugo, *Death and the Good Life*, 1981
Sandra West Prowell, *By Evil Means*, 1993
William S. Slusher, *Shepherd of the Wolves*, 1995

737
Ray Harrison
Patently Murder (New York: St. Martin's, 1991)

Series: Bragg/Morton

Story type: Historical; Police Procedural—Male Lead

Major character(s): Joseph Bragg, Police Officer (sergeant); James Morton, Police Officer (constable)

Time period(s): 1890s

Locale(s): London, England

What the book is about: Was the weapon used to kill a child prostitute the same as the one used to kill wealthy Andrew Livesey, whose widow is the daughter of a member of Parliament? When Bragg and Morton attempt to reopen the Livesey case they are threatened by the MP. What can be the connection between the two deaths and why is the MP so adamant in his opposition?

Other books you might like:
Evelyn Hervey, *The Man of Gold*, 1985
Peter Lovesey, *The Sergeant Cribb Series*, 1970-
Anne Perry, *The Inspector Monk Series*, 1990-
Anne Perry, *The Thomas and Charlotte Pitt Series*, 1980-

738
Ray Harrison
Tincture of Death (New York: St. Martin's, 1989)

Series: Bragg/Morton

Story type: Historical

Major character(s): Joseph Bragg, Police Officer (sergeant); James Morton, Police Officer (constable)

Time period(s): 1890s (Victorian times)

Locale(s): England

What the book is about: The current case for Bragg and Morton involves the opium trade and the crimes, including murder, that result from that trade.

Other books you might like:
Kenneth Giles, *Murder Pluperfect*, 1970
Peter Lovesey, *Wobble to Death*, 1970
Anne Perry, *The Cater Street Hangman*, 1980
Anne Perry, *Resurrection Row*, 1981

739
Will Harriss
Noble Rot (New York: St. Martins, 1993)

Story type: Amateur Detective; Police Procedural

Major character(s): Vinnie Letessier, Businessman (bankrupt); Holly Shelton, Police Officer (detective)

Time period(s): 1990s

Locale(s): Napa Valley, California

What the book is about: Returning to his Uncle Francis's wine business to help out, Vinnie Letessier soon finds that there is more than a fungus causing trouble. First he finds a dead body in a fermentation tank, then his uncle dies in a suspicious car fire. There is no shortage of suspects in either death and Vinnie and Detective Holly Shelton set out to find who's responsible for all the action.

Other books you might like:
Mary Bowen Hall, *Emma Chizzit and the Napa Nemesis*, 1992
Martin Sylvester, *A Dangerous Age*, 1986
Martin Sylvester, *A Lethal Vintage*, 1988
Bruce Zimmerman, *Full-Bodied Red*, 1993

740
Cynthia Harrod-Eagles
Death Watch (New York: Scribners, 1993)
Series: Inspector Bill Slider
Story type: Police Procedural—Male Lead
Major character(s): Bill Slider, Police Officer (Inspector)
Time period(s): 1990s
Locale(s): London, England
What the book is about: After a fire at a motel, a body is discovered that turns out to be a fire alarm salesman, Richard Neal. When the police discover that he was a former fireman once involved in the suspicious death of a colleague, they realize it must be murder. Inspector Slider and his assistant, Atherton, set out to find the guilty parties, all the while trying to keep their own lives from falling apart.
Other books you might like:
M.C. Beaton, *Death of a Charming Man*, 1994
Deborah Crombie, *A Share in Death*, 1992
John Harvey, *Off Minor*, 1992
Peter Robinson, *Wednesday's Child*, 1994
R.D. Wingfield, *A Touch of Frost*, 1990

741
Carolyn G. Hart
The Christie Caper (New York: Bantam, 1991)
Series: Annie Laurance/Max Darling
Story type: Amateur Detective—Female Lead
Major character(s): Annie Laurance Darling, Store Owner (mystery bookstore)
Time period(s): 1990s
Locale(s): Broward Rock, South Carolina
What the book is about: Annie is holding a mystery weekend to honor Agatha Christie's centenary. An obnoxious hard-boiled aficionado shows up and is soon at risk. One just does not impugn the Queen of Crime. But someone else is killed. Is the conference a cover for crime of a more serious sort?
Other books you might like:
Max Allan Collins, *A Nice Weekend for Murder*, 1986
Joan Hess, *Murder at the Mimosa Inn*, 1988
Bernie Lee, *Murder at Musket Beach*, 1990
Annette Roome, *A Second Shot in the Dark*, 1992

742
Carolyn G. Hart
Dead Man's Island (New York: Bantam, 1993)
Story type: Amateur Detective—Female Lead
Major character(s): Henrietta O'Dwyer Collins, Journalist (former reporter), Widow(er)
Time period(s): 1990s
Locale(s): South Carolina (an island off the coast of South Carolina)
What the book is about: Former lover and media bigwig, Chase Prescott, calls on Henrietta O'Dwyer Collins (known as Henrie-O) to try and find out who has tried to kill him. He invites Henrie-O and all the suspects to his private island off the coast of South Carolina and there, with a hurricane threatening, Henrie-O must try and find out the truth. Among the possiblities are Chase's lawyer, his sons, his third wife and his second wife's sister. Then there are two murders which help reduce the number of suspects. With the hurricane coming Henrie-O must find the truth quickly. First in this series.
Other books you might like:
Harold Adams, *The Man Who Was Taller than God*, 1992
Agatha Christie, *And Then There Were None*, 1940
Charlaine Harris, *A Bone to Pick*, 1992
Sharyn McCrumb, *The Hangman's Beautiful Daughter*, 1993
Celestine Sibley, *Ah, Sweet Mystery*, 1991

743
Carolyn G. Hart
A Little Class on Murder (New York: Doubleday/Bantam, 1989)
Series: Annie Laurance/Max Darling
Story type: Amateur Detective—Female Lead
Major character(s): Annie Laurance, Businesswoman (mystery bookstore owner); Max Darling, Lawyer (investigator)
Time period(s): 1980s
Locale(s): Broward Rock, South Carolina (Fictional city)
What the book is about: While trying to teach a course on mystery literature at the nearby college, Annie, of course, gets involved in murder.
Other books you might like:
Jon L. Breen, *The Gathering Place*, 1984
Joan Hess, *Strangled Prose*, 1985
Charlotte MacLeod, *The Sarah Kelling Series*, (1979-)

744
Carolyn G. Hart
Mint Julep Murder (New York: Bantam, 1995)
Series: Annie Laurance/Max Darling
Story type: Amateur Detective—Female Lead
Major character(s): Annie Laurance Darling, Store Owner (bookstore owner)
Time period(s): 1990s
Locale(s): Hilton Head, South Carolina
What the book is about: The subject is writing at the annual Dixie Book Festival and Annie Darling has agreed to be the shepherd for the five honored writers. Little does she realize that the subject will soon be murder. A publisher has announced plans to write a roman a clef about the southern writing scene and when he turns up dead, it appears that Annie and her writers are the chief suspects. She must turn sleuth, again, to find out who killed the Mint Julep Press man.

Other books you might like:
Jeff Abbott, *Do Unto Others*, 1994
Bill Crider, *Dying Voices*, 1989
Mary Daheim, *Bantam of the Opera*, 1993
Jaqueline Girdner, *A Stiff Critique*, 1995
M.D. Lake, *A Gift for Murder*, 1992

745
Ellen Hart
Hallowed Murder (Seattle: Seal, 1989)

Story type: Amateur Detective—Female Lead

Major character(s): Jane Lawless, Restauranteur, Lesbian; Cordelia Thorn, Actress (artistic director of a theatre)

Time period(s): 1980s

Locale(s): Minneapolis, Minnesota; St. Paul, Minnesota

What the book is about: Jane Lawless is alumni advisor to a sorority. When one of its members is murdered, she and Cordelia Thorn get involved in trying to catch the killer. First book.

Other books you might like:
Amanda Cross, *The Question of Max*, 1976
Victoria Silver, *Death of a Harvard Freshman*, 1984
L.A. Taylor, *Footnote to Murder*, 1983
Barbara Wilson, *Murder in the Collective*, 1984

746
Ellen Hart
Vital Lies (Seattle: Seal, 1991)

Series: Jane Lawless/Cordelia Thorn

Story type: Amateur Detective—Female Lead

Major character(s): Jane Lawless, Restauranteur, Lesbian; Cordelia Thorn, Lesbian, Actress (artistic director of a theatre)

Time period(s): 1990s (1990)

Locale(s): Repentance River, Minnesota

What the book is about: Jane Lawless and her partner Cordelia Thorn have been invited to spend Christmas week at the Fothergill Inn, lately the site of some pranks that have gotten gradually more serious. Jane and Cordelia are destined to get very involved in finding out the who and why of the pranks before someone gets hurt.

Other books you might like:
Kate Green, *Night Angel*, 1989
Joan Hess, *Murder at the Mimosa Inn*, 1986
M.D. Lake, *Cold Comfort*, 1990
B.J. Oliphant, *The Unexpected Corpse*, 1990
Eve Zaremba, *Work for a Million*, 1987

747
Jeanne Hart
Threnody for Two (New York: St. Martins, 1991)

Series: Carl Pedersen

Story type: Police Procedural—Male Lead

Major character(s): Carl Pedersen, Police Officer (homicide detective); Freda Pedersen, Housewife (wife of Carl, and his sounding)

Time period(s): 1990s

Locale(s): Bay Cove, California

What the book is about: Two elderly women, totally different except for their ages and apparently unrelated, are both stabbed in their beds - with identical knives. Is there a common thread that connects the murders? Can detective Pedersen find a thread?

Other books you might like:
Carolyn G. Hart, *The Annie Laurance/Max Darling Series*, 1987-
Jane Langton, *The Homer Kelly Series*, 1964-
Bernie Lee, *Murder at Musket Beach*, 1990
Dell Shannon, *The Luis Mendoza Series*, 1960-

748
Roy Hart
Breach of Promise (New York: St. Martins, 1990)

Series: Inspector Roper

Story type: Police Procedural—Male Lead

Major character(s): Douglas Roper, Police Officer (inspector)

Time period(s): 1990s

Locale(s): Upper Gorton, England

What the book is about: Who would have a reason to kill a harmless old man unless, of course, the harmless old man wasn't what he appeared to be. Inspector Roper needs to find out what happened and why.

Other books you might like:
W.J. Burley, *Guilt Edged*, 1972
Ruth Rendell, *A Guilty Thing Surprised*, 1970
Jonathan Ross, *Dark Blue and Dangerous*, 1981
Dorothy Simpson, *Last Seen Alive*, 1985
June Thomson, *The Habit of Loving*, 1979

749
James Neal Harvey
By Reason of Insanity (New York: St. Martin's, 1990)

Story type: Police Procedural—Male Lead

Major character(s): Peter Barrows, Businessman (marketing executive), Murderer; Ben Tolliver, Police Officer (homicide detective)

Time period(s): 1980s

Locale(s): New York, New York

What the book is about: Peter Barrows is killing women and sending the pictures to a television anchorwoman. Ben Tolliver is the cop trying to catch him. First book.

Other books you might like:
Jeffrey Wilds Deaver, *Manhattan Is My Beat*, 1989
Joanne Fluke, *Video Kill*, 1989
Herbert Lieberman, *Nightbloom*, 1984
Stephen Solomita, *A Twist of the Knife*, 1988

750

James Neal Harvey
Painted Ladies (New York: St. Martin's, 1992)
Series: Ben Tolliver
Story type: Police Procedural—Male Lead; Action/Adventure
Major character(s): Ben Tolliver, Police Officer (homicide detective)
Time period(s): 1990s
Locale(s): New York, New York
What the book is about: A high class escort service comes under investigation when one of the hookers is killed and bizarrely painted. Because she is the daughter of a rich man more pressure than usual comes to bear on Tolliver - some to pursue the investigation to the fullest, some to stay away from some areas. Two more women are murdered and it appears that a missing computer disk could provide the answers.
Other books you might like:
William Bayer, *Switch*, 1984
Lawrence Block, *A Dance at the Slaughterhouse*, 1991
William J. Caunitz, *Suspects*, 1986
Michael Crichton, *Rising Sun*, 1990

751

John Harvey
Cold Light (New York: Holt, 1994)
Series: Charlie Resnick
Story type: Police Procedural—Male Lead
Major character(s): Charlie Resnick, Police Officer (detective inspector)
Time period(s): 1990s
Locale(s): Nottingham, England
What the book is about: As always in Nottingham police officer Charlie Resnick's life, there are many things going on. A social worker is missing and Charlie finds himself attracted to her roommate. There are a rash of cab driver robberies and beatings, and a killer is on the loose. Charlie is his usual depressed, jazz-loving self.
Other books you might like:
Liza Cody, *Bucket Nut*, 1994
Frances Fyfield, *Shadows on the Mirror*, 1989
Elizabeth George, *A Great Deliverance*, 1988
Ruth Rendell, *The Best Man to Die*, 1969
R.D. Wingfield, *A Touch of Frost*, 1990

752

John Harvey
Cutting Edge (New York: Holt, 1991)
Series: Charlie Resnick
Story type: Police Procedural—Male Lead
Major character(s): Charlie Resnick, Police Officer (detective inspector)
Time period(s): 1990s
Locale(s): Nottingham, England
What the book is about: The stabbings of a nurse, a doctor and a student are related. Charlie must find out how. Other things that threaten to take up his time are a rape case, another officer's love life and his own life, which is still a mess.
Other books you might like:
Reginald Hill, *The Dalziel and Pascoe Series*, 1974-
Elizabeth Lemarchand, *Nothing to Do with the Case*, 1981
Peter Robinson, *The Inspector Banks Series*, 1989-
June Thomson, *The Spoils of Time*, 1989
Colin Watson, *Charity Ends at Home*, 1968

753

John Harvey
Off Minor (New York: Holt, 1992)
Series: Charlie Resnick
Story type: Police Procedural—Male Lead
Major character(s): Charlie Resnick, Police Officer (detective inspector)
Time period(s): 1990s
Locale(s): England
What the book is about: Still saddened by the breakdown of his marriage, Charlie Resnick must put aside his personal feelings to work on the disappearances of two little girls less than a month apart. One of the girls has turned up dead—what of the other?
Other books you might like:
Catherine Aird, *Passing Strange*, 1981
Reginald Hill, *Recalled to Life*, 1992
Jonathan Ross, *Daphne Dead and Done For*, 1991
June Thomson, *Rosemary for Remembrance*, 1988
Colin Watson, *Charity Ends at Home*, 1968

754

John Harvey
The Wasted Years (New York: Holt, 1993)
Series: Charlie Resnick
Story type: Police Procedural—Male Lead
Major character(s): Charlie Resnick, Police Officer (detective inspector)
Time period(s): 1990s
Locale(s): Nottingham, England
What the book is about: There are a series of armed robberies being committed in Nottingham, some by a group of professionals and some by a couple of teenagers. The two groups don't seem to be connected but Charlie Resnick needs to know for sure. At the same time, a criminal from Charlie's past is released and seems bent on taking revenge on those he holds responsible for his time in prison.
Other books you might like:
Robert Barnard, *Bodies*, 1986
Thomas Boyle, *Only the Dead Know Brooklyn*, 1985
Reginald Hill , *Bones and Silence*, 1990
Philip Kerr, *The Pale Criminal*, 1990
Lydia LaPlante, *Prime Suspect*, 1992

755
Gustav Hasford
A Gypsy Good Time ()
Story type: Action/Adventure
Major character(s): Dowdy Lewis Jr., Businessman (co-owner of a bookstore), Veteran
Time period(s): 1990s
Locale(s): Los Angeles, California
What the book is about: Alcoholic veteran Dowdy Lewis, Jr. convinces sexy producer Yvonna Lablaine to have a fling with him. Soon after it starts, a secretary at Yvonna's studio is murdered - throat slit - and Yvonna is arrested for heroin possession. After Dowdy posts her bail, she disappears. Dowdy searches all over Los Angeles for her, running afoul of the film community, the cops and the mob. First crime novel.
Other books you might like:
Jeffrey Wilds Deaver, *Manhattan Is My Beat*, 1989
Robert Ferrigno, *The Horse Latitudes*, 1990
Tom Kakonis, *Criss Cross*, 1990
Stephen Robinett, *Final Option*, 1990
Andrew Vachss, *Shella*, 1993

756
Thomas Hauser
The Hawthorne Group (New York: Tor, 1991)
Story type: Action/Adventure; Espionage
Major character(s): Anne Rhodes, Actress (retired), Administrator (for an energy cartel); Ned Connor, Spy
Time period(s): 1990s
Locale(s): New York, New York
What the book is about: Retired stage actress Anne Rhodes takes an administrative position with an energy cartel. When the first friend she makes on the job dies, the verdict is suicide. Then a government agent shows up to tell Anne her friend was murdered because she was an undercover agent investigating the cartel. Anne agrees to go undercover to continue the investigation. But is she being told the truth?
Other books you might like:
Kathleen Dougherty, *Moth to the Flame*, 1991
David Hagberg, *Countdown*, 1990
David Morrell, *The Covenant of the Flame*, 1991
Warren Murphy, *Jericho Day*, 1989
S.K. Wolf, *The Harbinger Effect*, 1989

757
Steven F. Havill
Bitter Recoil (New York: St. Martin's, 1992)
Series: Bill Gastner
Story type: Police Procedural—Male Lead
Major character(s): Bill Gastner, Police Officer (sheriff); Estelle Guzman, Police Officer
Time period(s): 1990s
Locale(s): New Mexico
What the book is about: Though he should be taking it easy after heart surgery, Sheriff Bill Gastner decides to take a trip instead. He drives cross-state to visit an old deputy of his and gets involved in the investigation of the beating and death of a young pregnant woman. Suspects include a priest, who may have been the father of her child and her current lover, an aging hippie.
Other books you might like:
Bill Crider, *The Sheriff Dan Rhodes Series*, 1989-
A.B. Guthrie Jr., *Playing Catch-Up*, 1985
Michael T. Hinkemeyer, *A Time to Reap*, 1984
Walter Satterthwait, *Wall of Glass*, 1989
Frank C. Strunk, *Jordon's Wager*, 1990

758
Steven F. Havill
Heartshot (New York: St. Martins, 1991)
Series: Bill Gastner
Story type: Police Procedural—Male Lead
Major character(s): Bill Gastner, Police Officer (sheriff; 70 years old), Widow(er)
Time period(s): 1990s
Locale(s): Posadas County, New Mexico
What the book is about: Gastner is depressed after three teenagers he has known for years die in a police chase. He is even more distressed to find that there was a quarter million dollars worth of cocaine in the car. He sets out to break-up the drug ring responsible. First mystery.
Other books you might like:
Tony Hillerman, *Talking God*, 1989
Michael T. Hinkemeyer, *A Time to Reap*, 1984
A.B. Guthrie Jr., *Playing Catch-Up*, 1985
Walter Satterthwait, *Wall of Glass*, 1989
Frank C. Strunk, *Jordon's Wager*, 1990

759
S.T. Haymon
A Very Particular Murder (New York: St. Martins, 1989)
Series: Inspector Jurnet
Story type: Police Procedural—Male Lead
Major character(s): Benjamin Jurnet, Detective—Police (detective inspector); Max Flaschner, Scientist (physicist)
Time period(s): 1980s
What the book is about: Assigned to watch over a meeting of scientists from the world over, Jurnet meets and is quite taken with the scientist Flaschner. Invited to a dinner by him, Jurnet goes, only to have Flaschner die before the dinner is over.
Other books you might like:
W.J. Burley, *Wycliffe and the Scapegoat*, 1979
P.D. James, *Unnatural Cause*, 1967
Elizabeth Lemarchand, *Unhappy Returns*, 1978
Sheila Radley, *Who Saw Him Die?*, 1988
Ruth Rendell, *An Unkindness of Ravens*, 1985

760
Sparkle Hayter
What's a Girl Gotta Do? (New York: Soho, 1994)
Story type: Amateur Detective—Female Lead
Major character(s): Robin Hudson, Journalist (TV investigative reporter)
Time period(s): 1990s
Locale(s): New York, New York
What the book is about: Robin Hudson works for ANN, the All News Network, but is now on the third team thanks to two on-air screw-ups (belching at a presidential news conference and asking an air-crash survivor who had resorted to cannibalism how her boyfriend tasted). Robin is contacted by a man who seems to know too much about her past and wants to meet at a party. When the man is killed at the party—an all ANN party—all clues point to Robin as the killer. The man turns out to be a disreputable private eye who knew an awful lot about most of the ANN stars, so it seems that someone decided to shut him up permanently. Robin knows she didn't do it and needs to find out who did. First novel.
Other books you might like:
Barbara D'Amato, *Hard Women*, 1993
William L. DeAndrea, *Killed in the Act*, 1981
Jeffrey Wilds Deaver, *Hard News*, 1991
John Bartholomew Tucker, *He's Dead-She's Dead: Details at Eleven*, 1990
Polly Whitney, *Until Death*, 1994

761
Gar Anthony Haywood
Bad News Travels Fast (New York: Putnam, 1995)
Series: Dottie and Joe Loudermilk
Story type: Amateur Detective
Major character(s): Dottie Loudermilk, Aged Person (former professor); Joe Loudermilk, Aged Person (former cop)
Time period(s): 1990s
Locale(s): Washington, District of Columbia
What the book is about: Dottie and Joe have arrived in Washington DC to visit their son. Soon after their arrival, he is accused of the murder of his former roommate. Though witnesses place him at the scene, Joe and Dottie believe him when he says he is innocent and set out to find the real killer. The dead man had said something about having some books that would blow the lid off the city and that is Joe and Dottie's only clue.
Other books you might like:
Nikki Baker, *The Lavender House Murder*, 1992
Terris McMahan Grimes, *Somebody Else's Child*, 1996
Mary Bowen Hall, *The Emma Chizzit Series*, 1990-1993
Barbara Neely, *Blanche Among the Talented Tenth*, 1994
Chassie West, *Sunrise*, 1994

762
Gar Anthony Haywood
Not Long for This World (New York: St. Martin's, 1990)
Series: Aaron Gunner
Story type: Private Detective—Male Lead
Major character(s): Aaron Gunner, Detective—Private (African-American)
Time period(s): 1980s
Locale(s): Los Angeles, California
What the book is about: P.I. Aaron Gunner is asked to find the driver in a drive-by drug shooting. He soon finds it isn't that easy. Haywood won the St. Martin's Press Best First P.I. Novel contest for the first book in this series.
Other books you might like:
J.F. Burke, *Death Trick*, 1975
Kenn Davis, *Words Can Kill*, 1984
Richard Hilary, *Snake in the Grasses*, 1987
Ed Lacy, *Room to Swing*, 1957
Percy Spurlark Parker, *Good Girls Don't Get Murdered*, 1974

763
Tim Heald
Business Unusual (New York: Doubleday, 1990)
Series: Simon Bogner
Story type: Amateur Detective—Male Lead; Humor
Major character(s): Simon Bogner, Insurance Investigator (for the Board of Trade)
Time period(s): 1980s
Locale(s): Scarpinton, England
What the book is about: Simon has been assigned to Scarpinton as a place to put his finger on the pulse of English commerce. Unfortunately he must also put his finger on the cause of a series of murders.
Other books you might like:
Sarah Caudwell, *The Sirens Sang of Murder*, 1989
Alisa Craig, *The Terrible Tide*, 1985
Edmund Crispin, *The Moving Toyshop*, 1946
Nancy Livingston, *Death in Close-Up*, 1990

764
Jeremiah Healy
Act of God (New York: Pocket, 1994)
Series: John Francis Cuddy
Story type: Private Detective—Male Lead
Major character(s): John Francis Cuddy, Detective—Private
Time period(s): 1990s
Locale(s): Boston, Massachusetts
What the book is about: John Francis Cuddy is asked by two clients to split a case. One of them is Pearl Rivkind, who wants Cuddy to solve her husband, Abe's, murder. The other is the brother of Abe Rivkind's secretary who has gone missing. The brother figures that Cuddy can find his sister, or as the brother hopes, find her dead, while trying to find Abe's murderer.

Other books you might like:
Rick Boyer, *The Doc Adams Series*, 1984-
Robert Crais, *The Elvis Cole Series*, 1987-
Jerome Doolittle, *The Tom Bethany Series*, 1989-
Robert B. Parker, *The Spenser Series*, 1974-
William G. Tapply, *The Brady Coyne Series*, 1984-

765
Jeremiah Healy
Foursome (New York: Pocket, 1993)

Series: John Francis Cuddy

Story type: Private Detective—Male Lead

Major character(s): John Francis Cuddy, Detective—Private

Time period(s): 1990s

Locale(s): Maine

What the book is about: John Cuddy is hired to find out the truth behind the cross-bow shooting deaths of three out of four members of a group of friends at a summer house in Maine. The one who wasn't killed is the obvious suspect, but is he the actual guilty party? It appears so, as his dead wife and one of the others were having an affair, which certainly gave him motive. On the other hand, there are financial shenanigans to investigate and drug-dealing possibilites and even an arms deal. So there certainly appears to be more here than simple adultery.

Other books you might like:
Rick Boyer, *The Whale's Footprints*, 1988
B. Comfort, *Grave Consequences*, 1989
Robert Crais, *Lullaby Town*, 1991
Archer Mayor, *Open Season*, 1988
Robert B. Parker, *Playmates*, 1989

766
Jeremiah Healy
Yesterday's News (New York: Harper, 1989)

Series: John Francis Cuddy

Story type: Private Detective—Male Lead

Major character(s): John Francis Cuddy, Detective—Private

Time period(s): 1980s

Locale(s): Nasharbor, Massachusetts (Fictional city)

What the book is about: Cuddy is asked to go to Nasharbor by investigative reporter Jane Rust to find out if the police there are involved in the murder of her confidential source. Before Cuddy can do much, Jane dies in what the police label a suicide. Did she kill herself or was she murdered?

Other books you might like:
Robert Crais, *The Monkey's Raincoat*, 1987
Robert Crais, *Stalking the Angel*, 1989
Robert B. Parker, *Valediction*, 1984
Bill Pronzini, *Bones*, 1985
William G. Tapply, *Dead Winter*, 1989

767
Daniel Hearn
Black Light (New York: Dell, 1991)

Series: Joe Noonan

Story type: Private Detective—Male Lead

Major character(s): Joe Noonan, Detective—Private

Time period(s): 1990s

Locale(s): New York, New York

What the book is about: Trying to find out who killed an old college friend, Joe Noonan lands in a world of radical 60's politics, drugs and the record business.

Other books you might like:
Lawrence Block, *A Ticket to the Boneyard*, 1990
Kate Green, *Night Angel*, 1989
Lia Matera, *A Radical Departure*, 1986
Marcia Muller, *Trophies and Dead Things*, 1990
Sam Reaves, *A Long Cold Fall*, 1990

768
Mark Hebden (Pseudonym of John Harris)
Pel and the Missing Persons (New York: St. Martin's, 1991)

Series: Inspector Pel

Story type: Police Procedural—Male Lead

Major character(s): Evariste Pel, Police Officer (inspector)

Time period(s): 1990s

Locale(s): France (the Burgandy region)

What the book is about: Pel is unhappy about a series of robberies, about losing some of his staff and about a hit-and-run victim. Do the robberies and the hit-and-run have anything to do with one another? There was no blood at the scene and the victim had no identification. A history of blackmail, murder and greed permeate this case.

Other books you might like:
Michael Bond, *The Monsieur Pamplemousse Series*, 1985
Joyce Porter, *The Inspector Dover Series*, 1964-1990
Georges Simenon, *The Inspector Maigret Series*, 1932-1990

769
Jonellen Heckler
Circumstances Unknown (New York: Pocket, 1993)

Story type: Psychological Suspense

Major character(s): Paul Kincaid, Artisan (jewelry designer); Martin Trayne, Artist (courtroom sketch artist)

Time period(s): 1990s

Locale(s): New York

What the book is about: Tim Reuschel brings his wife, Deena, and son to New York to show them scenes from his childhood. While there they come in contact with two friends from his childhood, Martin Trayne and Paul Kincaid. Paul falls in love with Deena and follows the family to upstate New York where he begins to stalk her. There is soon a death and Martin and Deena both think Paul is responsible but cannot prove it. Can they prove it before Paul kills Deena?

Other books you might like:
Mary Higgins Clark, *Loves Music, Loves to Dance*, 1991
Joy Fielding, *Tell Me No Secrets*, 1994
Kate Green, *Shooting Star*, 1992
Judith Kelman, *While Angels Sleep*, 1988
Barbara Michaels, *Search the Shadows*, 1987

770
Jonellen Heckler
Final Tour (New York: Pocket, 1994)
Story type: Psychological Suspense; Amateur Detective—Female Lead
Major character(s): Sass Lindsey, Singer
Time period(s): 1990s
Locale(s): New York, New York
What the book is about: Sass Lindsey is at the peak of her career, but she's tired, in body and spirit. She is determined to retire, but her backers are less than pleased. Then her manager dies in an apparent suicide and her attorney is murdered in what seems to be a mugging gone wrong. Is someone sending her a message? She and her sisters, who have abusive pasts, are determined to find out who or what is behind the threat to Sass's peace of mind and maybe her life.
Other books you might like:
K.K. Beck, *Amateur Night*, 1993
Mary Higgins Clark, *While My Pretty One Sleeps*, 1980
Susan Rogers Cooper, *Funny as a Dead Comic*, 1993
Gillian B. Farrell, *Alibi for an Actress*, 1992
Martha Smilgis, *Fame's Peril*, 1992

771
Michael Hendricks
Friends in High Places (New York: Scribners, 1991)
Series: Rita Noonan
Story type: Private Detective—Female Lead
Major character(s): Rita Noonan, Detective—Private
Time period(s): 1990s
Locale(s): New York, New York
What the book is about: Rita is following a husband suspected of philandering - and she's also attracted to him. At the same time she is involved with her former husband's former partner who ends up dead in her apartment. He had fallen a long way - from golden boy cop to junkie, thief and pimp. He died with a lot of police secrets that scared many people.
Other books you might like:
Susan Baker, *My First Murder*, 1989
Susan Dunlap, *As a Favor*, 1984
Marcia Muller, *Trophies and Dead Things*, 1990
Maxine O'Callaghan, *Hit and Run*, 1989
Lillian O'Donnell, *A Good Night to Kill*, 1989

772
Michael Hendricks
Money to Burn (New York: Dutton, 1989)
Series: Rita Noonan
Story type: Private Detective—Female Lead
Major character(s): Rita Noonan, Detective—Private
Time period(s): 1980s
Locale(s): New York, New York
What the book is about: Rita Noonan, chief operative for a New York detective firm, takes on a missing persons case against her boss's wishes. Her personal feelings for her client cause her to pay less attention to things than she should, and when she finds that it's more than a simple disappearance, she has some problems. First book.
Other books you might like:
Susan Dunlap, *As a Favor*, 1984
Marcia Muller, *There's Something About a Sunday*, 1989
Maxine O'Callaghan, *Hit and Run*, 1989
Geoff Peterson, *Medicine Dog*, 1989
Nancy Pickard, *Marriage Is Murder*, 1987

773
Vicki Hendricks
Miami Purity (New York: Pantheon, 1995)
Story type: Action/Adventure; Psychological Suspense
Major character(s): Sherry Parley, Criminal; Payne Mahoney, Businessman
Time period(s): 1990s
Locale(s): Miami, Florida
What the book is about: Sherry Parley wants money and sex—and not necessarily in that order. And she'll do anything to get them. She is currently working in a Miami dry cleaning establishment to try and get a respite from stripping, but soon finds herself sleeping with the owner's son and trying to convice him that, without mom around, their lives would be very much better. The fact that the son is sleeping with his mother doesn't make Sherry's task any easier—so she decides to take matters into her own hands. First novel.
Other books you might like:
James M. Cain, *The Postman Always Rings Twice*, 1934
Carl Hiaasen, *Strip Tease*, 1994
Tom Kakonis, *Michigan Roll*, 1989
Andrew Klavan, *Don't Say a Word*, 1993
Jim Thompson, *The Grifters*, 1963

774
Louise Hendricksen
Grave Secrets (New York: Zebra, 1994)
Series: Amy Prescott
Story type: Private Detective—Female Lead
Major character(s): Amy Prescott, Doctor, Detective—Private (forensic investigator); Nathan Blackthorne, Detective—Private, Indian
Time period(s): 1990s
Locale(s): Rock Springs, Idaho

What the book is about: Amy Prescott's former boyfriend, Simon Kittredge, an investigative reporter, has disappeared in the wilds of Idaho while trying to track down a swindler. His last known location was Rock Springs, where Amy goes to try to find him. What she finds is a town that doesn't like strangers. She also meets the mysterious Nathan Blackthorne who is in town on some mission of his own. Then the dead bodies start to appear.

Other books you might like:
K.K. Beck, *Electric City*, 1994
Patricia D. Cornwell, *The Kay Scarpetta Series*, 1990-
Susan Dunlap, *The Kiernan O'Shaughnessy Series*, 1989-
Mary Kittredge, *The Edwina Crusoe Series*, 1990-
Marsha Landreth, *The Samantha Turner Series*, 1992-

775
Sue Henry
Murder on the Iditarod Trail (New York: Atlantic Monthly, 1991)

Story type: Police Procedural—Male Lead; Action/Adventure

Major character(s): Alex Jensen, Police Officer (state trooper); Jessie Arnold, Sports Figure (dog sledder in Iditarod)

Time period(s): 1990s

Locale(s): Alaska (on the race trail)

What the book is about: During Alaska's famous dogsled race, the Iditarod, someone is killing the top competitors. Sergeant Jensen and competitor Jessie Arnold work together to find out who's behind the killings - and get involved with each other as well. First mystery.

Other books you might like:
Sean Hanlon, *The Cold Front*, 1989
Ted Wood, *The Reid Bennett Series*, 1984-
Scott Young, *Murder in a Cold Climate*, 1989

776
Joan Hess
A Diet to Die For (New York: St. Martin's, 1989)

Series: Claire Malloy

Story type: Amateur Detective—Female Lead

Major character(s): Claire Malloy, Businesswoman (bookstore owner); Peter Rosen, Police Officer

Time period(s): 1980s

What the book is about: When an overweight heiress moves back to town, Claire and her friends conspire to remake the woman. This leads to complications regarding the diet and fitness center to which they take the woman.

Other books you might like:
Bill Crider, *Dying Voices*, 1989
Bill Crider, *One Dead Dean*, 1987
Carolyn G. Hart, *Something Wicked*, 1988
Charlotte MacLeod, *The Peter Shandy Series*, 1978
Dorothy Sucher, *Dead Men Don't Give Seminars*, 1987

777
Joan Hess
Madness in Maggody (New York: St. Martins, 1991)

Series: Arly Hanks

Story type: Police Procedural—Female Lead

Major character(s): Arly Hanks, Police Officer (female chief of police)

Time period(s): 1990s

Locale(s): Maggody, Arkansas (Ozarks)

What the book is about: At the grand opening of a supermarket that none of the other merchants want, someone has poisoned the food. But someone may have also used the food poisoning as a cover for murder. Also writes as Joan Hadley.

Other books you might like:
A.B. Guthrie Jr., *The Chick Charleston Series*, 1973-
Carolyn G. Hart, *Death on Demand*, 1987
Joe L. Hensley, *The Don Roback Series*, 1971-
M.D. Lake, *Amends for Murder*, 1989

778
Joan Hess
Miracles in Maggody (New York: Dutton, 1995)

Series: Arly Hanks

Story type: Police Procedural—Female Lead

Major character(s): Arly Hanks, Police Officer (female chief of police); Malachi Hope, Religious (televangelist)

Time period(s): 1990s

Locale(s): Maggody, Arkansas

What the book is about: Televangelist Malachi Hope has come to Maggody set on developing a Christian theme park in the area. Though a lot of the residents are believers in the Reverend's vision, Arly is skeptical. She becomes even more so when the girl's basketball coach is murdered and another killing quickly follows. Is someone among Hope's flock or family a murderer?

Other books you might like:
Stephen Cook, *Dead Fit*, 1993
Jean Hager, *The Molly Bearpaw Series*, 1992-
Wendy Hornsby, *Midnight Baby*, 1993
M.D. Lake, *The Peggy O'Neill Series*, 1989-
Lee Martin, *The Deb Ralston Series*, 1984-

779
Joan Hess
Mortal Remains in Maggody (New York: Dutton, 1991)

Series: Arly Hanks

Story type: Police Procedural—Female Lead

Major character(s): Arly Hanks, Police Officer (female chief of police)

Time period(s): 1990s

Locale(s): Maggody, Arkansas

What the book is about: Glittertown Productions decides that Maggody would be a good place to shoot their current epic. Unfortunately this epic turns out to be closer to an X-rated Romeo and Juliet. When a once-famous actress is murdered and her husband disappears Arly is thrown into trying to find the murderer. At the same time there is an arsonist loose who appears to be stalking Arly.

Other books you might like:
A.B. Guthrie Jr., *The Chick Charleston Series*, 1973-1990
Carolyn G. Hart, *Death on Demand*, 1987
Joe L. Hensley, *The Don Roback Series*, 1971-
M.D. Lake, *Cold Comfort*, 1990
Lee Martin, *The Deb Ralston Series*, 1984-

780
Joan Hess
O Little Town of Maggody (New York: Dutton, 1993)
Series: Arly Hanks
Story type: Police Procedural—Female Lead
Major character(s): Arly Hanks, Police Officer (female chief of police)
Time period(s): 1990s
Locale(s): Maggody, Arkansas
What the book is about: Country music star Matt Montana was born in Maggody and plans to return to his hometown to give a Christmas concert and visit his only surviving relative, his Aunt Adele. Unfortunately, the aunt has disappeared from her nursing home. When Matt arrives, the town has produced a stand-in for the missing aunt while Sheriff Arly Hanks searches for the missing woman. While on the search, Arly discovers the body of a record executive serving as the mannequin in the general store.

Other books you might like:
Bill Crider, *The Sheriff Dan Rhodes Series*, 1986-
A.B. Guthrie Jr., *The Chick Charleston Series*, 1973-1990
Joe L. Hensley, *The Don Roback Series*, 1971-
M.D. Lake, *The Peggy O'Neill Series*, 1989-
Lee Martin, *The Deb Ralston Series*, 1984-

781
Joan Hess
Roll Over and Play Dead (New York: St. Martin's, 1991)
Series: Claire Malloy
Story type: Amateur Detective—Female Lead
Major character(s): Claire Malloy, Businesswoman (bookstore owner)
Time period(s): 1990s
Locale(s): Farberville, Arkansas
What the book is about: Having being dragooned into taking care of Miss Emily Parchester's bassett hounds, Claire is extremely distressed to discover that they have disappeared. Her search for the dogs leads her into murder and into investigating the practice of stealing and selling animals to research laboratories. And it leads her into danger.

Other books you might like:
Bill Crider, *The Sheriff Dan Rhodes Series*, 1986-
Carolyn G. Hart, *Something Wicked*, 1988
Charlotte MacLeod, *The Sarah Kelling Series*, 1979-
Sara Paretsky, *Guardian Angel*, 1992

782
Carl Hiaasen
Native Tongue (New York: Knopf, 1991)
Story type: Action/Adventure
Major character(s): Joe Winder, Journalist (investigative reporter), Public Relations (for a theme park)
Time period(s): 1990s
Locale(s): Florida (South Florida Keys)
What the book is about: This wild and crazy tale involves the Amazing Kingdom of Thrills theme park, blue—tongued voles, an environmental group called the Mothers of Wilderness, the former governor of Florida—who lives in the swamp and survives on road kill-and an amorous rogue dolphin. Burnt-out investigative reporter Joe Winder is trying to find out the truth behind the theme park and a proposed golf course. All the rest of the elements are there to make his life more interesting.

Other books you might like:
John D. MacDonald, *A Flash of Green*, 1962
Thomas Perry, *Island*, 1987
Thomas Perry, *Metzger's Dog*, 1984
Ross Thomas, *The Fourth Durango*, 1989

783
Carl Hiaasen
Skin Tight (New York: Putnam, 1989)
Story type: Action/Adventure
Major character(s): Mick Stranahan, Detective (retired state investigator); Rudy Graveline, Doctor (plastic surgeon)
Time period(s): 1980s
Locale(s): Florida
What the book is about: A quack plastic surgeon whose patients have a habit of dying, Dr. Graveline fears that retired state investigator Mick Stranahan has evidence that could put him out of business. Graveline puts out a contract on Mick, who then has to face a variety of deranged hitmen.

Other books you might like:
Robert Campbell, *Juice*, 1989
John D. MacDonald, *The Last One Left*, 1967
Thomas Perry, *Island*, 1987
Thomas Perry, *Metzger's Dog*, 1983
Ross Thomas, *Out on the Rim*, 1987

784
Carl Hiaasen
Stormy Weather (New York: Knopf, 1995)
Story type: Action/Adventure
Major character(s): Skink, Streetperson (former governor); Edie March, Criminal

Time period(s): 1990s

Locale(s): Florida (southern)

What the book is about: The aftermath of a hurricane is the setting for this madcap adventure bringing together such characters as a former governor gone wild who kidnaps a citizen taking pictures of the destruction, a scam artist named Edie, and her partner named Snapper. All have varied and various adventures and their paths cross while the scenes get more and more bizarre.

Other books you might like:
James W. Hall, *Bones of Coral*, 1990
John Lutz, *Flame*, 1990
Barbara Parker, *Suspicion of Guilt*, 1995
Laurence Shames, *Florida Straits*, 1992
Robert Ward, *The Cactus Garden*, 1995

785
Carl Hiaasen
Strip Tease (New York: Knopf, 1993)

Story type: Action/Adventure

Major character(s): Erin Grant, Stripper (former FBI secretary); Gerald L. "Shad" Shaddick, Bouncer

Time period(s): 1990s

Locale(s): Fort Lauderdale, Florida

What the book is about: Part-time exotic dancer (at the Eager Beaver), Erin Grant is trying to earn lawyer fees to fight her ex-husband in court for the custody of her daughter. One evening a fight breaks out over her and one of the combatants is a U.S. congressman. One of the other patrons recognizes the congressman and sets out to blackmail the man on Erin's behalf but without her knowledge. This innocent act leads to murder, more blackmail, and election fixing, among other things. Meanwhile the bouncer at the Eager Beaver is involved in scams to bilk multi-national corporations out of money, but he also wants to help Erin.

Other books you might like:
James W. Hall, *Bones of Coral*, 1991
Elmore Leonard, *Maximum Bob*, 1991
James Patillo, *Skim*, 1991
Thomas Perry, *Metzger's Dog*, 1985
Ross Thomas, *The Fourth Durango*, 1989

786
Jack Higgins
Angel of Death (New York: Putnam, 1995)

Story type: Action/Adventure

Major character(s): Sean Dillon, Spy (former criminal/actor/assassin); Grace Browning, Actress, Criminal

Time period(s): 1990s

Locale(s): England

What the book is about: Sean Dillon finds himself pitted against a most intriguing foe. Grace Brown, who is Britain's greatest actress, is also an assassin for hire. She really doesn't care whom she kills as long as it creates chaos for Great Britain. She is working for someone who is in government, and while Dillon tracks her, his compatriots try and find the traitor.

Other books you might like:
Thomas Adcock, *Drown All the Dogs*, 1993
Colin Bateman, *Divorcing Jack*, 1995
Frederick Forsyth, *The Day of the Jackal*, 1977
Evelyn E. Smith, *The Miss Melville Series*, 1986-
Tom Wilson, *Black Wolf*, 1995

787
Jack Higgins
The Eagle Has Flown (New York: Simon & Schuster, 1991)

Series: Liam Devlin

Story type: Historical; Espionage

Major character(s): Liam Devlin, Criminal (IRA gunman, poet, and scholar); Kurt Steiner, Military Personnel (nazi assassin)

Time period(s): 1940s (1943-1944)

Locale(s): England; Germany

What the book is about: Liam Devlin is asked by the Germans to parachute into England to rescue Kurt Steiner, in prison for the attempted assassination of Churchill. It seems the Germans want him back to prevent the assassination of Hitler, to keep Himmler and the SS from taking over.

Other books you might like:
Ted Allbeury, *The Lantern Network*, 1989
James Baddock, *The Faust Conspiracy*, 1989
Ken Follett, *Eye of the Needle*, 1978
Jack Gerson, *Death's Head Berlin*, 1989
W.J. Weatherby, *Coronation*, 1990

788
Richard Hilary
Behind the Fact (New York: Bantam, 1989)

Series: "Easy" Barnes

Story type: Private Detective—Male Lead

Major character(s): Ezell "Easy" Barnes, Detective—Private (African-American)

Time period(s): 1980s

Locale(s): Newark, New Jersey

What the book is about: Someone is paying big money for the illegal garbage dumping rights off the Jersey shore and Easy finds himself involved in sorting things out.

Other books you might like:
Kenn Davis, *As October Dies*, 1987
Gar Anthony Haywood, *Fear of the Dark*, 1988
Chester Himes, *The Real Cool Killers*, 1959
Ed Lacy, *Room to Swing*, 1957
Mike Phillips, *Blood Rights*, 1989

789
Reginald Hill
Bones and Silence (New York: Delacorte, 1990)

Series: Dalziel and Pascoe

Story type: Police Procedural—Male Lead

790
Hill

Major character(s): Andrew Dalziel, Police Officer (detective superintendent); Peter Pascoe, Police Officer (inspector)

Time period(s): 1990s

Locale(s): Yorkshire, England

What the book is about: After witnessing what appears to be a rather straightforward murder, Dalziel is disgruntled to discover it's not as simple as that. At the same time he is receiving anonymous letters from a woman threatening suicide. These he passes on to Pascoe who is convinced that both he and Dalziel know the writer. Then Dalziel is asked to perform in a local mystery play which seems to catch the letter writer's attention.

Other books you might like:
Catherine Aird, *Passing Strange*, 1981
Douglas Clark, *Dead Letter*, 1985
Elizabeth Lemarchand, *The Glade Manor Murder*, 1989
Jonathan Ross, *Burial Deferred*, 1986
Colin Watson, *Charity Ends at Home*, 1968

790
Reginald Hill
Recalled to Life (New York: Delacorte, 1992)

Series: Dalziel and Pascoe

Story type: Police Procedural—Male Lead

Major character(s): Andrew Dalziel, Police Officer (detective superintendent); Peter Pascoe, Police Officer (inspector)

Time period(s): 1990s

Locale(s): United States; England

What the book is about: What appears to be new evidence brings about the release of a woman, an American, convicted for murder in 1963. The murder distantly touched the Royal Family and the new evidence seems to have piqued the current interest of the CIA and MI services. Pascoe follows the newly released woman across the ocean to New York and Williamsburg in hopes of finding the truth behind the old crime. Dalziel was involved in the original case.

Other books you might like:
Catherine Aird, *The Inspector Sloane Series*, 1967-
Elizabeth George, *Well-Schooled in Murder*, 1990
Martha Grimes, *The Inspector Jury Series*, 1981-
Sheila Radley, *The Inspector Quantrill Series*, 1978-
Ruth Rendell, *Kissing the Gunner's Daughter*, 1991

791
Richard Hill
Shoot the Piper (New York: St. Martin's, 1994)

Series: Randall Sierra

Story type: Private Detective—Male Lead

Major character(s): Randall Sierra, Detective—Private (ex-soldier; ex-hippie)

Time period(s): 1990s

Locale(s): England

What the book is about: Private eye Randall Sierra is hired to track down an old crony of his, one Jock MacLeod, who has disappeared in England with a huge advance from his publisher. While on the road, Sierra gets involved with hippies at Stonehenge, nuclear protests, and other mind-boggling experiences. But does he find Jock?

Other books you might like:
Robert Crais, *The Elvis Cole Series*, 1987-
James Crumley, *The Last Good Kiss*, 1978
Jonathan Gash, *The Great California Game*, 1989
Robert B. Parker, *The Judas Goat*, 1979
Les Roberts, *The Milan Jacovich Series*, 1989-

792
Tony Hillerman
Sacred Clowns (New York: HarperCollins, 1993)

Series: Joe Leaphorn and Jim Chee

Story type: Police Procedural—Male Lead

Major character(s): Joe Leaphorn, Police Officer (Navajo Tribal Police), Indian (Navajo); Jim Chee, Police Officer (Navajo Tribal Police), Indian (Navajo)

Time period(s): 1990s

Locale(s): Navajo Reservation, Arizona

What the book is about: A number of cases are being investigated by Lt. Joe Leaphorn and Officer Jim Chee. A white woodshop teacher is beaten to death in his workshop, a student from the school is missing, the missing boy's uncle is stabbed to death, and an old man is killed on the highway in a hit-and-run. Some of these incidents may be related—or they may not be. It is up to Leaphorn and Chee, who have an uneasy working relationship, to find out the truth or truths.

Other books you might like:
Nevada Barr, *Track of the Cat*, 1993
Brian Garfield, *The Threepersons Hunt*, 1974
Sandra West Prowell, *The Killing of Monday Brown*, 1994

793
Tony Hillerman
Talking God (New York: Harper, 1989)

Series: Joe Leaphorn and Jim Chee

Story type: Police Procedural—Male Lead

Major character(s): Jim Chee, Police Officer (Navajo Tribal Police), Indian (Navajo); Joe Leaphorn, Police Officer (Navajo Tribal Police), Indian (Navajo)

Time period(s): 1980s

Locale(s): New Mexico; Washington, District of Columbia

What the book is about: Two different cases involving desecration of graves and the murder of an unidentified man converge for Leaphorn and Chee in Washington, D.C.

Other books you might like:
Warwick Downing, *The Mountains West of Town*, 1975
Brian Garfield, *Relentless*, 1972
Brian Garfield, *The Threepersons Hunt*, 1974
Richard Martin Stern, *Death in the Snow*, 1973
Chelsea Quinn Yarbro, *Ogilvie, Tallant, and Moon*, 1976

794
Tami Hoag
Night Sins (New York: Bantam, 1995)

Story type: Police Procedural; Psychological Suspense

Major character(s): Megan O'Malley, Police Officer; Mitch Holt, Police Officer (chief of police)

Time period(s): 1990s

Locale(s): Deer Lake, Minnesota

What the book is about: The young son of a local woman doctor is kidnapped by someone who is leaving cryptic notes around. They are not ransom notes, but notes that seem to indicate that there is more behind the snatch than might first appear. There is no shortage of suspects for Megan and Chief Mitch Holt to choose from including the doctor's husband. Can they find the right bad guy before it's too late? First mystery. Hoag has written many romances.

Other books you might like:
Mary Higgins Clark, *Where Are the Children?*, 1975
George Dawes Green, *The Juror*, 1995
Martha Johnson, *Deadly Secret*, 1994
Jon Katz, *The Family Stalker*, 1994
Constance Rauch, *A Deep Disturbance*, 1990

795
Alice Hoffman
Turtle Moon (New York: Putnam, 1992)

Story type: Psychological Suspense

Major character(s): Julian Cash, Police Officer; Lucy Rosen, Single Parent

Time period(s): 1990s

Locale(s): Verity, Florida

What the book is about: Someone tries to kidnap a baby and ends up killing its mother. The baby is still missing even after the kidnapper turns up dead. Then a twelve year old boy also turns up missing. Police officer Julian Cash and the boy's mother, Lucy Rosen, work together to find the missing children. First crime novel.

Other books you might like:
Nancy Atherton, *Aunt Dimity's Death*, 1993
K.K. Beck, *A Hopeless Case*, 1992
Michael Malone, *Uncivil Seasons*, 1983

796
Chuck Hogan
The Standoff (New York: Doubleday, 1995)

Story type: Police Procedural—Male Lead; Action/Adventure

Major character(s): Glenn Ables, Criminal (white supremacist); John Banish, FBI Agent

Time period(s): 1990s

Locale(s): Montana

What the book is about: White supremacist Glenn Ables is holed up on a Montana mountaintop with his wife and five children. When agents come to arrest him, he vows not to be taken alive. Hostage negotiator and alcoholic John Banish is sent to defuse the situation. It will not be easy. First novel.

Other books you might like:
Harlen Campbell, *Monkey on a Chain*, 1993
Jeffrey Wilds Deaver, *Praying for Sleep*, 1995
Stephen Hunter, *Dirty White Boys*, 1995
Chuck Logan, *Hunter's Moon*, 1995
Mary Willis Walker, *Under the Beetle's Cellar*, 1995

797
Isabelle Holland
A Fatal Advent (New York: Doubleday, 1989)

Series: Claire Aldington

Story type: Amateur Detective—Female Lead

Major character(s): Claire Aldington, Religious (assistant rector at NY parish); O'Neill, Police Officer (lieutenant)

Time period(s): 1980s

Locale(s): New York, New York

What the book is about: A former dean at St. Paul's in London is killed in St. Anselm's parish house. Claire's husband of less than a year is a suspect.

Other books you might like:
William X. Kienzle, *Deathbed*, 1986
Sister Carol Anne O'Marie, *Advent of Dying*, 1986
Monica Quill, *Sine Qua Nun*, 1986
Charles Merrill Smith, *The Reverend Randollph Series*, (1974-1986)

798
Isabelle Holland
The Long Search (New York: Doubleday, 1990)

Story type: Psychological Suspense

Major character(s): Janet Covington, Businesswoman, Editor

Time period(s): 1990s

Locale(s): New York, New York

What the book is about: Janet appears to be happy and successful with a good job and loving boyfriend, but she harbors secrets and her past is beginning to catch up with her. Claire Aldington and St. Anselm's appear briefly.

Other books you might like:
K.K. Beck, *Unwanted Attentions*, 1988
Samantha Chase, *Needlepoint*, 1989
Velda Johnston, *Shadow Behind the Curtain*, 1985
Susan Kelly, *The Gemini Man*, 1985
Diana Ramsey, *Four Steps to Death*, 1990

799
Gerelyn Hollingsworth
Murder at St. Adelaide's (New York: St. Martin's, 1995)

Story type: Private Detective—Female Lead

Major character(s): Frances Finn, Detective—Private

Time period(s): 1990s

Locale(s): Braddock, Kansas

What the book is about: Frances has been asked back to her hometown by a former teacher—Mother Celeste of St. Adelaide's Academy. Celeste is dying, and to make peace, she wants Frances to confirm her belief that a young nun did not commit the sin of suicide thirty years ago, but was murdered. What Frances finds is that the old and powerful families of Braddock have many secrets. The threat of discovery drives someone to commit a present-day murder. First novel.

Other books you might like:
D.M. Greenwood, *The Theodora Braithwaite Series*, 1991-
Lee Harris, *The Christmas Night Murder*, 1995
Isabelle Holland, *The Claire Aldington Series*, 1984-
Sister Carol Anne O'Marie, *The Sister Mary Helen Series*, 1984-
Winona Sullivan, *A Sudden Death at the Norfolk Cafe*, 1993

800
Hazel Holt
The Cruellest Month (New York: St. Martins, 1991)

Series: Sheila Malory

Story type: Amateur Detective—Female Lead

Major character(s): Sheila Malory, Writer, Widow(er)

Time period(s): 1990s (1990)

Locale(s): Oxford, England

What the book is about: While in Oxford to do research at the Bodleian Library Sheila Malory gets involved in a mystery involving people and events from her past.

Other books you might like:
Colin Dexter, *The Wench Is Dead*, 1990
Gillian Linscott, *Unknown Hand*, 1989
Dorothy L. Sayers, *Busman's Honeymoon*, 1937
Dorothy Simpson, *Dead by Morning*, 1989

801
Hazel Holt
Mrs. Malory and the Festival Murders (New York: St. Martins, 1993)

Series: Sheila Malory

Story type: Amateur Detective—Female Lead

Major character(s): Sheila Malory, Writer

Time period(s): 1990s

Locale(s): Taviscombe, England

What the book is about: The annual Taviscombe Festival is the setting for the murder of new resident Adrian Palgrave. An undistinguished poet and biographer, Palgrave has recently been named literary executor of famous writer Lawrence Meredith and intends to milk this opportunity for all it's worth, including taking over the festival to suit his needs. Before he can do much however, someone puts him to death. There is no scarcity of suspects, including a television documentary maker and the treasurer of the festival. There are two more deaths and an attempt to destroy the Meredith papers which lead Sheila Malory to think that maybe the murder of Palgrave had less to do with his obnoxious personality and more to do with his literary executorship.

Other books you might like:
Eleanor Boylan, *Murder Machree*, 1992
B. Comfort, *Phoebe's Knee*, 1986
Mollie Hardwick, *The Bandersnatch*, 1989
Charlaine Harris, *A Bone to Pick*, 1992
Joan Smith, *Don't Leave Me This Way*, 1990

802
Hazel Holt
Mrs. Malory Investigates (New York: St. Martin's, 1990)

Series: Sheila Malory

Story type: Amateur Detective—Female Lead

Major character(s): Sheila Malory, Widow(er)

Time period(s): 1980s

Locale(s): Taviscombe (Fictional village)

What the book is about: A newcomer to Taviscombe is killed shortly after being introduced to Sheila and her friends. Sheila feels responsible and so sets out to find the killer. First book.

Other books you might like:
Gwen Moffat, *Over the Sea to Death*, 1976
Ellis Peters, *The Grass-Widow's Tale*, 1968
John Sherwood, *The Celia Grant Series*, (1985-)
Patricia Wentworth, *The Miss Silver Series*, (1929-1961)

803
Susan Holtzer
Curly Smoke (New York: St. Martin's, 1995)

Series: Anneke Haagen

Story type: Amateur Detective—Female Lead

Major character(s): Anneke Haagen, Businesswoman (computer maven; art collector); Karl Gennesko, Police Officer (former NFL player)

Time period(s): 1990s

Locale(s): Ann Arbor, Michigan

What the book is about: After losing her house in a fire, Anneke moves to a small cottage in an area that is the future home of a development. A few of her neighbors are less than enthusiastic about the proposal and one of them has just died, apparently of natural causes. When another, one of the more vocal opponents, turns up dead, Anneke tries to convince her policeman lover, Karl, that all is not kosher. He is not quick to believe her, but when someone tries to burn her out, he thinks she may be right.

Other books you might like:
Cecil Dawkins, *The Santa Fe Rembrandt*, 1993
Kate Clark Flora, *Chosen for Death*, 1993
Jean Hager, *Dead and Buried*, 1995
Joan Hess, *Strangled Prose*, 1986
Elizabeth Daniels Squire, *Memory Can Be Murder*, 1995

804
Ruby Horansky
Dead Ahead (New York: Scribners, 1990)

Series: Nikki Trakos

Story type: Police Procedural—Female Lead

Major character(s): Nikki Trakos, Detective—Homicide; Dave Lawton, Detective—Homicide

Time period(s): 1990s (1990)

Locale(s): New York, New York

What the book is about: Newly promoted Detective Nikki Trakos has "caught" her first homicide investigation. The body of Frankie Sunmann, a small-time horse player, is found and the only clue is the address of a businessman killed two days earlier in a boat explosion. Complicating things are the homicide expert she is assigned to work with who has another case on his mind and Nikki's boss who doesn't think women should be cops and gives her three days to solve the case. First novel.

Other books you might like:
Alison Drake, *Tango Key*, 1988
Susan Dunlap, *The Jill Smith Series*, 1981-
Margaret Maron, *The Sigrid Harald Series*, 1982-
Lillian O'Donnell, *The Norah Mulcahaney Series*, 1973-
Dorothy Uhnak, *Policewoman*, 1964

805
Ruby Horansky
Dead Center (New York: Scribners, 1994)

Series: Nikki Trakos

Story type: Police Procedural—Female Lead

Major character(s): Nikki Trakos, Police Officer, Detective—Homicide; Dave Lawton, Police Officer, Detective—Homicide

Time period(s): 1990s

Locale(s): New York, New York

What the book is about: Nikki Trakos catches the call to investigate a dead body in a car. She finds the man has been murdered, and what's more, he was a New York City councilman. For a politician who was well thought of by most, there seem to be plenty of suspects, particularly among those who knew him well, including his wife, son, and mistress. The pressure is on for a quick arrest and Nikki can't ask Dave Lawton for help. Dave wants to get married and Nikki isn't sure she does, so she has him removed from the case. Then the killer strikes again.

Other books you might like:
Jack Early, *Donato and Daughter*, 1988
Rochelle Majer Krich, *Fair Game*, 1993
Margaret Maron, *The Sigrid Harald Series*, 1982-
Carol O'Connell, *Mallory's Oracle*, 1994
Lillian O'Donnell, *The Norah Mulcahaney Series*, 1979-

806
Phyllis Horn
The Chesapeake Project (Tallahassee, FL: Naiad, 1990)

Story type: Action/Adventure

Major character(s): Jessie Andrews, Worker (fisherwoman), Lesbian; Meredith Tompkins, Lesbian (lover of Jessie)

Time period(s): 1990s

Locale(s): Maryland

What the book is about: Someone has murdered Jessie Andrews' father and now they're after her. But she doesn't know why. She and her lover Meredith run away but are pursued by her father's killer and federal agents. It appears her father's murder has something to do with the government. First novel.

Other books you might like:
Doug Hornig, *Waterman*, 1987
Diana McRae, *All the Muscle You Need*, 1988
John Walter Putre, *A Small and Incidental Murder*, 1990
Rosie Scott, *Glory Days*, 1988
Eve Zaremba, *A Reason to Kill*, 1987

807
Wendy Hornsby
Half a Mind (New York: NAL, 1990)

Series: Roger Tejeda and Kate Teague

Story type: Police Procedural

Major character(s): Roger Tejeda, Police Officer (lieutenant); Kate Teague, Professor

Time period(s): 1980s

Locale(s): Santa Angelica, California

What the book is about: When they discover a head on their beach, Roger and Kate are drawn back into a case they thought was finished.

Other books you might like:
Faye Kellerman, *Milk and Honey*, 1990
Mary Anne Kelly, *Park Lane South, Queens*, 1990
Janet LaPierre, *Children's Games*, 1989
T.J. MacGregor, *On Ice*, 1989
Dave Pedneau, *A.P.B.*, 1987

808
Wendy Hornsby
Midnight Baby (New York: Dutton, 1993)

Series: Maggie MacGowen

Story type: Amateur Detective—Female Lead; Police Procedural

Major character(s): Maggie MacGowen, Journalist, Filmmaker (of documentaries); Mike Flint, Police Officer, Detective—Homicide

Time period(s): 1990s

Locale(s): Los Angeles, California; Long Beach, California

What the book is about: While in Los Angeles to film a documentary about children, Maggie MacGowen meets a 14 year old hooker who calls herself Pisces. Maggie convinces a friend to take the girl into her home but Pisces turns up dead the next day. With the help of her sometime boyfriend, homicide detective Mike Flint, Maggie sets out to find out who the girl really was and who would want her dead.

Other books you might like:
Linda Barnes, *Snapshot*, 1993
Barbara D'Amato, *Hard Women*, 1993
Alice Hoffman, *Turtle Moon*, 1992
Nancy Pickard, *Confession*, 1994
Gillian Roberts, *I'd Rather Be in Philadelphia*, 1992

809
Wendy Hornsby
Telling Lies (New York: Dutton, 1992)

Series: Maggie MacGowen

Story type: Amateur Detective—Female Lead

Major character(s): Maggie MacGowen, Filmmaker (of documentaries), Single Parent; Aleda Weston, Activist (60s radical)

Time period(s): 1990s

Locale(s): Los Angeles, California

What the book is about: Maggie's sister, Emily, has asked to get together, saying she has a surprise. Emily never makes the meeting. Instead she is found shot in an alley and is now in an irreversible coma. Trying to find out what happened leads Maggie back to a radical protest group of the 1960s and who and what they've become. The focus seems to be Aleda Weston who has been hiding for twenty years, and may now want to surrender.

Other books you might like:
Peter Abrahams, *Revolution #9*, 1992
Lia Matera, *The Good Fight*, 1990
Marcia Muller, *Trophies and Dead Things*, 1990
Kerry Tucker, *Still Waters*, 1991
Jim Weikart, *Casualty Loss*, 1991

810
John Horton
A Black Legend (New York: Ivy, 1989)

Story type: Espionage

Major character(s): Ted Oliver, Spy (CIA station chief, Mexico City); Gennadi Alexeyev, Spy (Oliver's KGB counterpart)

Time period(s): 1980s

Locale(s): Mexico City, Mexico

What the book is about: Someone is circulating a false story about Oliver's part in the assassination of a rebel leader while in his previous post.

Other books you might like:
William F. Buckley Jr., *The Blackford Oakes Series*, (1976-)
Sean Flannery, *The Hollow Men*, 1982
Bill Granger, *The November Man Series*, (1979-)

811
Carolyn Hougan
Blood Relative (New York: Fawcett, 1992)

Story type: Action/Adventure; Psychological Suspense

Major character(s): Rolando Carrera, Criminal; Mariah Ebinger, Teenager

Time period(s): 1990s

Locale(s): Alexandria, Virginia

What the book is about: Blaming his niece - now Americanized teenager Mariah Ebinger - for the death of his family in Argentina, Rolando Carrera and his hired assassin stalk her to America intending to kill her and anyone who gets in their way. Meanwhile, Mariah - who has no memory of her birthplace or heritage - is coming to the realization that she is not what she appears to be.

Other books you might like:
James Grady, *River of Darkness*, 1990
Kate Green, *Shattered Moon*, 1987
Stephen Leather, *The Fireman*, 1990
Sharyn McCrumb, *If Ever I Return, Pretty Peggy-O*, 1990
Keith Peterson, *The Scarred Man*, 1990

812
David Housewright
Penance (Woodstock, Vermont: Countryman, 1995)

Story type: Private Detective—Male Lead

Major character(s): Holland Taylor, Detective—Private (ex-cop)

Time period(s): 1990s

Locale(s): Minneapolis/St. Paul, Minnesota

What the book is about: Holland Taylor is suspected of killing the drunk driver who killed his wife and child a few years earlier. While working to clear himself, he stumbles across skullduggery in the current election campaign for governor. The attractive female candidate seems to have more than one skeleton in her closet—including a hit-and-run death, blackmail, and a video tape that shows more of her than would be thought healthy for a politician. A campaign worker is soon dead and Holland sets out to find the killer. First novel. Edgar nominee for best first novel.

Other books you might like:
Becky Bohan, *Fertile Betrayal*, 1995
Ron Handberg, *Cry Vengeance*, 1993
John Sandford, *Rules of Prey*, 1989
Steve Thayer, *The Weatherman*, 1995
R.D. Zimmerman, *Closet*, 1995

813
Melodie Johnson Howe
Beauty Dies (New York: Viking, 1994)
Series: Claire Conrad/Maggie Hill
Story type: Private Detective
Major character(s): Claire Conrad, Detective—Private, Wealthy (upper-class); Maggie Hill, Detective—Private (Claire's assistant)
Time period(s): 1990s
Locale(s): New York, New York
What the book is about: Maggie Hill, assistant to the well-known aristocratic private investigator, Claire Conrad, is approached by a young woman who says that famous ex-model Cybella did not kill herself. Maggie and Claire aren't interested until the girl is killed after talking to them. Now they decide to investigate and their only clue is a pornographic videotape starring the young victim and Cybella's daughter.

Other books you might like:
Joyce Christmas, *The Lady Margaret Priam Series*, 1988-
Lucille Kallen, *The C.B. Greenfield Series*, 1979-1986
Meg O'Brien, *The Jessica James Series*, 1990-
Evelyn Smith, *The Miss Melville Series*, 1986-
Dorothy Sucher, *The Vic Newman/Sabina Swift Series*, 1988-

814
Melodie Johnson Howe
The Mother Shadow (New York: Viking, 1989)
Series: Claire Conrad/Maggie Hill
Story type: Private Detective
Major character(s): Maggie Hill, Writer; Claire Conrad, Detective—Private
Time period(s): 1980s
Locale(s): Los Angeles, California
What the book is about: When Maggie Hill's current employer, Ellis Kenilworth, commits suicide shortly after changing his will, Maggie is forced to go to Claire Conrad, the beneficiary of the change (which is missing), for help in finding out what's really going on.

Other books you might like:
Dorothy Salisbury Davis, *Lullaby of Murder*, 1984
Dale L. Gilbert, *The Black Star Murders*, 1988
Lucille Kallen, *Introducing C.B. Greenfield*, 1979
Lucille Kallen, *The Tanglewood Murder*, 1980
Rex Stout, *The Nero Wolfe Series*, (1934-1975)

815
Richard Hoyt
Bigfoot (New York: Tor, 1993)
Series: John Denson
Story type: Private Detective—Male Lead; Action/Adventure
Major character(s): John Denson, Detective—Private; Willie Prettybird, Detective—Private, Indian (shaman)
Time period(s): 1990s
Locale(s): Mt. St. Helens, Washington
What the book is about: Hired to guide Russian primatologist Sonja Popoleyev on her hunt for Bigfoot—and the reward offered for same—Denson and Prettybird encounter murder and other skullduggery even before the hunt begins.

Other books you might like:
Frederick D. Huebner, *The Matt Riordan Series*, 1986-
Earl Emerson, *The Thomas Black Series*, 1985-
J.A. Jance, *The J.P. Beaumont Series*, 1985-
Robert Crais, *The Monkey's Raincoat*, 1987
Richard Hugo, *Death and the Good Life*, 1981

816
Richard Hoyt
Whoo? (New York: Tor, 1991)
Series: John Denson
Story type: Private Detective—Male Lead
Major character(s): John Denson, Detective—Private
Time period(s): 1990s
Locale(s): Washington
What the book is about: Convinced by a Native American, John Denson gets involved in a dispute regarding the owl population of the Great Northwest. He was a little bit in love with a woman who appears to have a been a murder victim. Complications include an election, a wildlife photographer, and owls being taken across state lines.

Other books you might like:
Noreen Gilpatrick, *The Piano Man*, 1990
Stephen Greenleaf, *Book Case*, 1991
Jeremiah Healy, *The John Francis Cuddy Series*, 1984-
Fred Zackel, *Cinderella After Midnight*, 1980

817
Frederic Huber
Axx Goes South (New York: Walker, 1989)
Story type: Police Procedural—Male Lead

818
Major character(s): Brad Axx, Police Officer (NYPD cop on vacation)

Time period(s): 1980s

Locale(s): Gulf Shores, Florida (Fictional city)

What the book is about: While on vacation in Florida, Axx meets an attractive woman who shortly thereafter dies. The police call it accidental, but Axx is sure she was murdered and sets out to prove it.

Other books you might like:
Steve Knickmeyer, *Straight*, 1976
John Lutz, *The Fred Carver Series*, (1986-)
John D. MacDonald, *The Travis McGee Series*, (1963-1985)
Tom Pace, *Fisherman's Luck*, 1971

818
Frederick D. Huebner
Methods of Execution (New York: Simon & Schuster, 1994)

Series: Matt Riordan

Story type: Amateur Detective—Male Lead; Legal

Major character(s): Matt Riordan, Lawyer; Liz Kleinfeldt, Lawyer

Time period(s): 1990s

Locale(s): Seattle, Washington

What the book is about: Matt Riordan is burned-out and has withdrawn from the practice of law. He is drawn back in when an ex-lover, Liz Kleinfeldt, asks him to help her prove that a man facing execution for a series of prostitute killings is actually innocent. Matt is skeptical but agrees to help. He finds that the air-tight case actually has more than a few holes in it, and there are several people who have something to hide. Maybe Liz is right.

Other books you might like:
Neil Albert, *The Dave Garrett Series*, 1991-
Earl Emerson, *The Thomas Black Series*, 1985-
Stephen Greenleaf, *The John Marshall Tanner Series*, 1979-
Jeremiah Healy, *The John Francis Cuddy Series*, 1985-
Ed McBain, *The Matthew Hope Series*, 1978-

819
Fredrick D. Huebner
Picture Postcard (New York: Fawcett, 1990)

Series: Matt Riordan

Story type: Amateur Detective—Male Lead

Major character(s): Matt Riordan, Lawyer

Time period(s): 1980s

Locale(s): Seattle, Washington

What the book is about: Is the famous painter grandfather of Matt's current client still alive?

Other books you might like:
Earl Emerson, *Fat Tuesday*, 1987
Stephen Greenleaf, *Death Bed*, 1980
Richard Hoyt, *30 for a Harry*, 1981
Don Matheson, *Ninth Life*, 1989
William G. Tapply, *A Void in Hearts*, 1988

820
Evan Hunter
Criminal Conversation (New York: Warner, 1994)

Story type: Action/Adventure

Major character(s): Sarah Welles, Teacher; Andrew Farrell, Criminal (aka Andrew Faviola)

Time period(s): 1990s

Locale(s): New York, New York

What the book is about: Sarah Welles falls in love with businessman Andrew Farrell, not realizing he is really Mafia kingpin Andrew Faviola. He is also the target of a special rackets investigation headed by Sarah's husband. What nobody expects is that Andrew will fall in love with Sarah. Death, duplicity and disaster will all happen. Hunter also writes as Ed McBain.

Other books you might like:
Steve Martini, *Undue Influence*, 1994
Christine McGuire, *Until Proven Guilty*, 1993
Barry Reed, *The Indictment*, 1994
Robert Robin, *Above the Law*, 1992
Robert K. Tanenbaum, *Justice Denied*, 1994

821
Jessie Prichard Hunter
Blood Music (New York: Turtle Bay, 1993)

Story type: Psychological Suspense

Major character(s): Zelly Wyche, Housewife; Pat Wyche, Businessman (small-business owner)

Time period(s): 1990s

Locale(s): New York, New York; New Jersey

What the book is about: New Jersey housewife and amateur detective wannabe Zelly Wyche has been following murders—now up to five—of young women in New York City. It slowly dawns on her that it may be her husband who is responsible for the deaths. Meantime one of the victim's brother and a near-victim start to track the killer as well. First novel.

Other books you might like:
Mary Higgins Clark, *Loves Music, Loves to Dance*, 1991
Martha Conley, *Growing Light*, 1993
Carol Davis Luce, *Night Prey*, 1992
John Lutz, *Single White Female*, 1990

822
Stephen Hunter
Point of Impact (New York: Bantam, 1993)

Story type: Action/Adventure

Major character(s): Bob Lee Swagger, Veteran (former sniper in Vietnam); Nick Memphis, FBI Agent

Time period(s): 1990s

Locale(s): United States

What the book is about: Called out of his self-imposed retirement to help prevent a presidential assassination, Bob Lee Swagger finds himself the patsy for a real assassination. With the help of the only person who thinks he is innocent, FBI agent Nick Memphis, he must trace the real assassin before he himself is killed or imprisoned.

Other books you might like:
Harlen Campbell, *Monkey on a Chain*, 1993
James N. Frey, *Winter of the Wolves*, 1992
Gary Friedman, *Gun Men*, 1993
David Morrell, *Testament*, 1974
Gerald Petievich, *Paramour*, 1991

823

Anthony Hyde
China Lake (New York: Knopf, 1992)

Story type: Action/Adventure; Espionage

Major character(s): Jack Tannis, Military Personnel

Time period(s): 1990s

Locale(s): California

What the book is about: Years ago Jack Tannis helped prove a British scientist innocent of selling secrets to the Soviet Union. Now this has come back to haunt him. After a mysterious phone call asking for a meeting to discuss the case, Tannis goes and discovers a corpse. From this he must run for his life to Germany, Wales and back to the United States.

Other books you might like:
Peter Abrahams, *Hard Rain*, 1988
Thomas Gifford, *The Cavanaugh Quest*, 1976
Joe Gores, *Wolf Time*, 1989
James Grady, *River of Darkness*, 1990
James W. Hall, *Bones of Coral*, 1991

824

Greg Iles
Spandau Phoenix (New York: Dutton, 1993)

Story type: Action/Adventure; Historical

Major character(s): Hans Apfel, Police Officer (sergeant); Jonas Stern, Spy (rogue Mossad agent)

Time period(s): 1980s (1987); 1940s (1941)

Locale(s): Berlin, Germany; South Africa

What the book is about: During the destruction of Spandau prison, after the death of Rudolf Hess, German police sergeant Hans Apfel stumbles upon some yellowing documents. What he has discovered are the Spandau papers, evidence of a plot begun in 1941 to kill Churchill and replace him with the Duke of Windsor. It contains names of British Nazi sympathizers in Parliament and may also contain evidence of a present-day plot to annihilate Israel. When word of the papers gets out, quite a few folks are interested in having them for themselves, including the KGB, a rogue Mossad agent and the German secret police. First novel.

Other books you might like:
Ted Allbeury, *A Time Without Shadows*, 1991
Len Deighton, *SS-GB*, 1979
Bill Granger, *The British Cross*, 1986
John Le Carre, *The Russia House*, 1989
Anthony Price, *Sion Crossing*, 1985

825

Dean Ing
The Ransom of Black Stealth One (New York: St. Martin's, 1989)

Story type: Techno-Thriller

Major character(s): Kyle Corbett, Pilot; Petra Leigh, Student

Time period(s): 1980s (1989)

What the book is about: Someone steals Black Stealth One, America's most secret airplane, along with a hostage. Why?

Other books you might like:
Dale Brown, *Day of the Cheetah*, 1989
Tom Clancy, *The Hunt for Red October*, 1985
Stephen Coonts, *Minotaur*, 1989
David E. Fisher, *Hostage One*, 1989
Douglas Terman, *Free Flight*, 1980

826

R.R. Irvine
The Angel's Share (New York: St. Martin's, 1989)

Series: Moroni Traveler

Story type: Private Detective—Male Lead

Major character(s): Moroni Traveler, Detective—Private

Time period(s): 1980s

Locale(s): Salt Lake City, Utah

What the book is about: Soon after the Mormon Church asks Traveler to give up his search for a missing missionary, they ask him back to help solve the murders and mutilations of several women, suggesting that the cases are connected.

Other books you might like:
Michael Cormany, *Lost Daughter*, 1988
Cleo Jones, *Prophet Motive*, 1984
Rob Kantner, *Hell's Only Half Full*, 1989
Michael Z. Lewin, *Ask the Right Question*, 1971
Jonathan Valin, *The Lime Pit*, 1980

827 Irvine

827
R.R. Irvine
Barking Dogs (New York: St. Martin's, 1994)

Story type: Action/Adventure; Amateur Detective

Major character(s): Kevin Manwaring, Television (producer); Vicki Garcia, Journalist (television reporter)

Time period(s): 1990s

Locale(s): Idaho

What the book is about: TV producer Kevin Manwaring and reporter Vicki Garcia are investigating an Idaho fire that killed the members of a Morman splinter group. Since there were children killed, their bosses foresee big TV ratings, but Kevin and Vicki think there is more to discover.

Other books you might like:
Thomas H. Cook, *Tabernacle*, 1983
Michael J. Katz, *The Big Freeze*, 1991
Vince Kohler, *Rainy North Woods*, 1990
J.R. Levitt, *Ten of Swords*, 1991

828
R.R. Irvine
Called Home (New York: St. Martins, 1991)

Series: Moroni Traveler

Story type: Private Detective—Male Lead

Major character(s): Moroni Traveler, Detective—Private (lapsed Morman); Martin Traveler, Detective—Private (Moroni's father)

Time period(s): 1990s

Locale(s): Salt Lake City, Utah

What the book is about: Ellis Nibley wants to know why his wife of many years committed suicide - or was she murdered? The Church doesn't want Moroni investigating but that doesn't stop him.

Other books you might like:
Thomas H. Cook, *Tabernacle*, 1983
Cleo Jones, *Prophet Motive*, 1984
J.R. Levitt, *Carnivores*, 1990
Gary Stewart, *The Tenth Virgin*, 1983
Gary Stewart, *The Zarahembla Vision*, 1986

829
R.R. Irvine
The Great Reminder (New York: St. Martin's, 1993)

Series: Moroni Traveler

Story type: Private Detective—Male Lead

Major character(s): Moroni Traveler, Detective—Private; Martin Traveler, Detective—Private (Moroni's father)

Time period(s): 1990s

Locale(s): Salt Lake City, Utah

What the book is about: Major Lewis Stiles is dying of cancer and wants to put his affairs in order so he hires Moroni Traveler to find a German POW who disappeared 50 years ago. It sounds impossible but Moroni agrees to try. His personal life is also getting complicated. He is being pursued by Lael Woolley, niece of the Prophet. She is urging him to find his son who Moroni isn't even sure exists.

Other books you might like:
Thomas H. Cook, *Tabernacle*, 1983
J.R. Levitt, *Ten of Swords*, 1991
M.K. Shuman, *The Last Man to Die*, 1992
Gary Stewart, *The Zarahembla Vision*, 1986

830
R.R. Irvine
Pillar of Fire (New York: St. Martin's, 1995)

Series: Moroni Traveler

Story type: Private Detective—Male Lead

Major character(s): Moroni Traveler, Detective—Private; Martin Traveler, Detective—Private (Moroni's father)

Time period(s): 1990s

Locale(s): Utah (the Southwest)

What the book is about: Moroni has been asked by John Ellsworth, an apostle of the Church of Mormon, to investigate a possible Messiah who has come to the town of Fire Creek. Ellsworth's daughter and terminally ill grandson have gone to Fire Creek to seek healing. Meanwhile, Martin is looking for the retarded son of a friend. The boy wandered away from a strange government installation involved in drug and radiation testing. His path also leads to Fire Creek. What Moroni finds there are a religious cult, a woman he could love, and death.

Other books you might like:
Michael Allegretto, *Grave Doubt*, 1995
Thomas H. Cook, *Tabernacle*, 1983
J.R. Levitt, *Ten of Swords*, 1991
Walter Satterthwait, *A Flower in the Desert*, 1992
Gary Stewart, *The Zarahembla Vision*, 1986

831
Eugene Izzi
King of the Hustlers (New York: Bantam, 1989)

Story type: Action/Adventure

Major character(s): Tony Nello, Criminal; George Alessi, Police Officer

Time period(s): 1980s

Locale(s): Chicago, Illinois

What the book is about: Tony Nello is trying to set up one last score after years of being a small-time hustler. He is being harassed by Alessi, a cop whose father has been murdered. Alessi thinks that Tony knows the identity of the killer. Nominated for the best paperback original novel Edgar.

Other books you might like:
George V. Higgins, *The Friends of Eddie Coyle*, 1972
Elmore Leonard, *City Primeval*, 1980
Gerald Petievich, *To Live and Die in L.A.*, 1984
Andrew Vachss, *Hard Candy*, 1989

832
Jon A. Jackson
Grootka (Vermont: Foul Paly, 1990)

Series: "Fang" Mulheisen

Story type: Police Procedural—Male Lead

Major character(s): "Fang" Mulheisen, Police Officer (detective sergeant); Grootka, Police Officer (retired)

Time period(s): 1990s

Locale(s): Detroit, Michigan

What the book is about: Mulheisen's old mentor, Grootka, is involved in finding a body in a trunk of an old car. His identification of the corpse leads him to a thirty-year-old murder. His obsession with this old case leads to trouble for Mulheisen, who is trying to solve his own case, the murder of a widow. Is it possible they are connected?

Other books you might like:
Eugene Izzi, *King of the Hustlers*, 1989
Percy Spurlark Parker, *Good Girls Don't Get Murdered*, 1974
Gerald Petievich, *To Live and Die in L.A.*, 1984
Roderick Thorp, *Rainbow Drive*, 1986

833
Jon A. Jackson
Hit on the House (New York: Atlantic, 1993)

Series: "Fang" Mulheisen

Story type: Police Procedural—Male Lead

Major character(s): "Fang" Mulheisen, Police Officer (detective sergeant)

Time period(s): 1990s

Locale(s): Detroit, Michigan

What the book is about: While trying to find a hit man recently escaped from jail, Mulheisen meets up with a woman from his past. Her current husband may have links to the hit man, which means Mulheisen should not be falling in love with her again. He is not the only one searching for the hit man—there is also another hit man out there.

Other books you might like:
Douglas Allyn, *The Cheerio Killings*, 1989
Loren D. Estleman, *The Amos Walker Series*, 1980-
Rob Kantner, *The Ben Perkins Series*, 1986-
Elmore Leonard, *City Primeval*, 1980
Walter Mosley, *Black Betty*, 1994

834
Marian J.A. Jackson
Diamond Head (New York: Walker, 1992)

Series: Abigail Danforth

Story type: Private Detective—Female Lead; Historical

Major character(s): Abigail Danforth, Detective—Private (called a consulting detective); Maude Cunningham, Companion

Time period(s): 1900s

Locale(s): Oahu, Hawaii

What the book is about: Abigail Patience Danforth is the world's first woman consulting detective, in the manner of Sherlock Holmes. She has been asked to look into the suspected poisoning of the young heir of a wealthy family. Then her servant, Kincaid, is suspected of murder in the death of Lilliana, a member of the former Hawaiian royal family. Why does Kincaid confess to the murder of a woman whose life he had saved?

Other books you might like:
K.K. Beck, *Peril under the Palms*, 1989
Carole Nelson Douglas, *Good Night, Mr. Holmes*, 1990
Anne Perry, *The Thomas and Charlotte Pitt Series*, 1979-
Elizabeth Peters, *The Amelia Peabody Series*, 1975-

835
Marian J.A. Jackson
The Sunken Treasure (New York: Walker, 1994)

Series: Abigail Danforth

Story type: Private Detective—Female Lead; Historical

Major character(s): Abigail Danforth, Detective—Private (called a consulting detective); Maude Cunningham, Companion

Time period(s): 1900s (1900)

Locale(s): At Sea (Caribbean)

What the book is about: Abigail Danforth, the world's first female consulting detective, and her companion, Maude Cunningham, have been asked on a Caribbean cruise on millionaire Malcolm Tibault's yacht. Also along are Tibault's wife and son, a treasure hunter, and Erich Weiss, better known as Harry Houdini. When people start to die mysteriously, Miss Danforth is on the case.

Other books you might like:
Abbey Penn Baker, *In the Dead of Winter*, 1994
K.K. Beck, *Peril under the Palms*, 1989
Carole Nelson Douglas, *The Irene Adler Series*, 1990-
Laurie R. King, *The Beekeeper's Apprentice*, 1994
Gillian Linscott, *The Nell Bray Series*, 1991-

836
Muriel Resnick Jackson
The Garden Club (New York: St. Martin's, 1992)

Story type: Amateur Detective—Female Lead

Major character(s): Merrie Lee Spencer, Housewife; Warren Spencer, Writer, Stock Broker (ex-Wall Street broker)

Time period(s): 1990s

Locale(s): Davis Landing, North Carolina

What the book is about: Merrie and Warren are New York yuppies with a penthouse, boat, paintings—the whole ball of wax. But when Warren's firm goes broke they are forced to sell most of it and rent out the penthouse. They move to a house in Davis Landing, population 3000, in North Carolina. The town is suspicious of these "Damn Yankees" but Merrie makes friends with the town matriarch, Miss Emily. When Miss Emily dies of a swollen ankle Merrie wants an investigation but nobody is interested. Then more people die. It's up to Merrie to figure it out, but nobody wants to talk to an outsider. First mystery.

Other books you might like:
Joan Hess, *The Claire Malloy Series*, 1986-
Richard Forrest, *Death on the Mississippi*, 1989
Carolyn G. Hart, *The Annie Laurance Series*, 1987-
Patricia Houck Sprinkle, *Somebody's Dead in Snellville*, 1992
Elizabeth Daniels Squire, *Kill the Messenger*, 1990

837
Nancy Baker Jacobs
The Silver Scapel (New York: Putnam, 1993)
Series: Devon MacDonald
Story type: Private Detective—Female Lead
Major character(s): Devon MacDonald, Detective—Private
Time period(s): 1990s
Locale(s): Minneapolis/St. Paul, Minnesota
What the book is about: Devon MacDonald is hired by Monica Hammond to find her 16-year-old sister who has disappeared. This disappearance may or may not be related to the firebombing of a clinic where abortions are performed and where two women died in a bombing.

Other books you might like:
Linda Barnes, *The Carlotta Carlyle Series*, 1987-
Sue Grafton, *I Is for Innocent*, 1992
Mary Logue, *Still Explosion*, 1993
Marcia Muller, *The Sharon McCone Series*, 1977-
Sara Paretsky, *Bitter Medicine*, 1987

838
Nancy Baker Jacobs
The Turquoise Tattoo (New York: Putnam, 1991)
Series: Devon MacDonald
Story type: Private Detective—Female Lead
Major character(s): Devon MacDonald, Detective—Private (her son recently died); Sam Sherman, Detective—Private (older partner of Devon)
Time period(s): 1990s
Locale(s): Minneapolis, Minnesota; St. Paul, Minnesota
What the book is about: Benjamin and Gloria Levy, whose son has leukemia, come to Devon for help in tracing possible half-siblings that might be out there. Levy was a sperm donor while in medical school and it's possible he may have children he doesn't know about. Devon soon gets involved with neo-Nazis and murder. First mystery.

Other books you might like:
Kathryn Lasky Knight, *Mortal Words*, 1990
Marcia Muller, *The Sharon McCone Series*, 1977-
Keith Peterson, *The Trapdoor*, 1988

839
Jody Jaffe
Horse of a Different Killer (New York: Fawcett, 1995)
Story type: Amateur Detective—Female Lead
Major character(s): Natalie Gold, Journalist (fashion writer), Equestrian (amateur); Henry Goode, Journalist (investigative reporter)
Time period(s): 1990s
Locale(s): Charlotte, North Carolina
What the book is about: Natalie Gold wants to break into hard news and uses the beating death of horse trainer Wally Hempstead to further that goal. As a horsewoman herself whose horse is boarded at the same farm, she has insider knowledge that makes her invaluable to investigative reporter Henry Goode. The person arrested proclaims his innocence—he was the murdered man's lover—and Natalie thinks he's telling the truth. But that may mean one of her friends is guilty. First novel.

Other books you might like:
Virginia Anderson, *Blood Lies*, 1989
Laura Crum, *Cutter*, 1994
Mark Daniel, *The Devil to Pay*, 1994
Dick Francis, *Whip Hand*, 1979
John Francome, *Outsider*, 1993

840
Michael Jahn
City of God (New York: St. Martin's, 1992)
Series: Bill Donovan
Story type: Police Procedural—Male Lead; Action/Adventure
Major character(s): Bill Donovan, Police Officer (head of major crime unit); Marcie Barnes, Police Officer (African-American)
Time period(s): 1990s
Locale(s): New York, New York
What the book is about: St. John's Cathedral in New York provides the setting for this novel about the search for a serial killer. At the same time Bill Donovan's relationship with Officer Barnes is endangered because of the murder of her best friend during the New York City Marathon. Both of them get obsessed, he with capturing the Cathedral Killer, she with seeking revenge on the killer of her friend.

Other books you might like:
Eleanor Taylor Bland, *Dead Time*, 1992
Michael Blodgett, *Hero and the Terror*, 1982
William J. Caunitz, *Suspects*, 1986
Thomas Chastain, *Spanner*, 1977
John Sandford, *Silent Prey*, 1991

841

P.D. James
Devices and Desires (New York: Knopf, 1990)

Series: Adam Dalgliesh

Story type: Psychological Suspense

Major character(s): Adam Dalgliesh, Police Officer (commander, New Scotland Yard)

Time period(s): 1980s

Locale(s): Larsoken, England (Norfolk)

What the book is about: Dalgliesh is in Larsoken to settle the estate of a relative and is soon drawn into the investigation of a serial killer.

Other books you might like:
Colin Dexter, *Service of All the Dead*, 1980
Elizabeth George, *A Great Deliverance*, 1988
Elizabeth Lemarchand, *Buried in the Past*, 1975
Sheila Radley, *This Way Out*, 1989
Ruth Rendell, *From Doon with Death*, 1964

842

J.A. Jance
Desert Heat (New York: Avon, 1993)

Story type: Action/Adventure; Amateur Detective—Female Lead

Major character(s): Joanna Brady, Office Worker; Tony Vargas, Criminal (hit-man)

Time period(s): 1990s

Locale(s): Bisbee, Arizona (Sonora desert country)

What the book is about: Joanna Brady finds her husband, Andy, shot in the desert. He's a police officer and the other cops think he tried to commit suicide, because he was involved in drug-dealing. When he dies in the hospital the police are quick to close the case. Joanna doesn't believe it and sets out to find the truth.

Other books you might like:
Nevada Barr, *Track of the Cat*, 1993
William Bayer, *Blind Side*, 1989
Andrew Coburn, *Goldilocks*, 1989
Craig Holden, *The River Sorrow*, 1994
S.K. Wolf, *Long Chain of Death*, 1987

843

J.A. Jance
Hour of the Hunter (New York: Morrow, 1991)

Story type: Action/Adventure

Major character(s): Diana Ladd, Widow(er); Andrew Carlisle, Criminal (former professor)

Time period(s): 1990s

Locale(s): Southwest

What the book is about: Just released from prison, Andrew Carlisle is seeking vengeance on those he deems responsible for putting him behind bars. One of those he is after is Diana Ladd, the widow of one of his former students. She and another victim's grandmother band together to fight Carlisle off.

Other books you might like:
Michael Allegretto, *The Watchers*, 1991
Mary Higgins Clark, *All Around the Town*, 1992
Tony Hillerman, *Coyote Waits*, 1990
Robert R. McCammon, *Mine*, 1990

844

J.A. Jance
Minor in Possession (New York: Avon, 1990)

Series: J.P. Beaumont

Story type: Police Procedural—Male Lead

Major character(s): J.P. Beaumont, Detective—Police

Time period(s): 1980s

Locale(s): Arizona

What the book is about: While in treatment for alcoholism, Beaumont is suspected of killing one of the other patients.

Other books you might like:
James Lee Burke, *The Neon Rain*, 1987
Rex Burns, *The Alvarez Journal*, 1976
Trish Janeshutz, *Shadow*, 1985
David L. Lindsey, *A Cold Mind*, 1983

845

Roderic Jeffries
Too Clever by Half (New York: St. Martins, 1990)

Series: Inspector Alvarez

Story type: Police Procedural—Male Lead

Major character(s): Enrique Alvarez, Police Officer (inspector)

Time period(s): 1990s

Locale(s): Majorca, Spain

What the book is about: Alvarez is called on to investigate a shooting death that seems to be suicide. The victim's sister insists it is murder. She may be right as another death follows and both victims had connections to a mysterious Trojan treasure. Also writes under the name of Jeffrey Ashford.

Other books you might like:
M.J. Adamson, *Not Till a Hot January*, 1986
A.Z.H. Carr, *Finding Maubee*, 1971
H.R.F. Keating, *The Inspector Ghote Series*, 1965-
Magdalen Nabb, *Death of a Dutchman*, 1982

846

Bruce Jones
In Deep (New York: Crown, 1991)

Story type: Police Procedural—Male Lead; Psychological Suspense

847

Major character(s): Eustes Tully, Detective—Homicide; Mitch Spencer, Insurance Investigator (ex-cop)

Time period(s): 1990s

Locale(s): California (southern)

What the book is about: A woman's nude, mutilated body is found on a Southern California beach. Eustes Tully is assigned to the case. When a second murder occurs Tully is reassigned to a drug investigation. There he hooks up with an old friend, Mitch Spencer, and discovers that the drugs and the murders may be connected. First novel.

Other books you might like:
Kate Green, *Shattered Moon*, 1986
Thomas Harris, *Red Dragon*, 1981
Charles King, *Mama's Boy*, 1992
John Sandford, *Rules of Prey*, 1989

847

Hazel Wynn Jones
Death and the Trumpets of Tuscany (New York: Doubleday, 1989)

Story type: Amateur Detective—Female Lead

Major character(s): Emma Shaw, Writer (script supervisor on a film); Hal Halliwell, Director (assistant director on the film)

Time period(s): 1950s

Locale(s): Venice

What the book is about: Even though the star of the medieval epic being filmed is murdered, the shooting must go on. Then there is another death. First book.

Other books you might like:
Gavin Lyall, *Shooting Script*, 1966
Jim Stinson, *Double Exposure*, 1985
Michael Tolkin, *The Player*, 1989
L.J. Washburn, *Dead-Stick*, 1989

848

Lee Jordan
The Toy Cupboard (New York: Walker, 1990)

Story type: Action/Adventure; Psychological Suspense

Major character(s): Joanna Townsend, Businesswoman (antique dealer)

Time period(s): 1980s (1988)

Locale(s): England; France

What the book is about: Joanna Townsend finds herself being watched at market and when she runs home finds someone waiting for her there. The stranger beats her and gives her a message for her husband. Though she doesn't understand what it means, her husband says it involves black market merchandise and that she must go with the merchandise to France, her childhood home. Meanwhile the man convicted of murdering her father, on her testimony twenty years earlier, is out of prison and may be seeking revenge.

Other books you might like:
Peter Abrahams, *Pressure Drop*, 1989
Barry Berg, *Hide and Seek*, 1989
Marian Borgenicht, *Undue Influence*, 1989
Patricia MacDonald, *No Way Home*, 1989
Marcia Muller, *Dark Star*, 1989

849

Christine T. Jorgensen
A Love to Die For (New York: Walker, 1994)

Story type: Amateur Detective—Female Lead

Major character(s): Jane Smith, Accountant, Psychic (astrologer)

Time period(s): 1990s

Locale(s): Denver, Colorado

What the book is about: Jane Smith considers her life as boring as her name. She bulldozes her way into becoming Stella the Stargazer, an advice/astrologer columnist. The first letter she receives triggers a psychic flash showing the writer's dead body. She soon realizes that the writer is an aquaintance, a young woman named Grace who is looking for a "love to die for." Jane knows Grace has died for love but can't get the police to take her seriously. First novel.

Other books you might like:
Susan Rogers Cooper, *One, Two, What Did Daddy Do?*, 1992
Diane Mott Davidson, *The Goldy Bear Series*, 1990-
Denise Dietz, *The Ellie Bernstein Series*, 1993-
Linda Mather, *Blood of an Aries*, 1994
Ann M. Williams, *Flowers for the Dead*, 1991

850

Alex Juniper
A Very Proper Death (New York: Scribners, 1991)

Story type: Police Procedural—Male Lead; Action/Adventure

Major character(s): Jake Murphy, Police Officer (former seminarian); Marni Verstak, Real Estate Agent

Time period(s): 1990s

Locale(s): Boston, Massachusetts

What the book is about: Marni Verstak's plan to turn a ghetto property into a decent housing project runs her afoul of a drug syndicate. At the same time she is getting calls threatening her son. She thinks the two things are unrelated but Sergeant Murphy thinks differently. When she is framed for murder, Murphy must find the link. First novel.

Other books you might like:
Rick Boyer, *The Whale's Footprints*, 1989
Jerome Doolittle, *Stranglehold*, 1991
Jeremiah Healy, *Right to Die*, 1991
Robert B. Parker, *Promised Land*, 1976
Robert Reeves, *Peeping Thomas*, 1990

851
Michael A. Kahn
Death Benefits (New York: Dutton, 1992)
Series: Rachel Gold
Story type: Amateur Detective—Female Lead; Legal
Major character(s): Rachel Gold, Lawyer; Benny Goldberg, Lawyer, Professor
Time period(s): 1990s
Locale(s): St. Louis, Missouri
What the book is about: Rachel has been asked by her former boss, chairman of a nationwide law firm, to look into "an awkward matter", the head of his St. Louis office has committed suicide. Rachel must prove that the man was insane at the time so the widow can collect the full amount of his insurance. When Rachel investigates, she finds more than she bargained for including a mysterious Aztec treasure.
Other books you might like:
Jeffrey Wilds Deaver, *Mistress of Justice*, 1992
Gini Hartzmark, *Principal Defense*, 1992
Lia Matera, *Prior Convictions*, 1991
Julie Smith, *The Rebecca Schwartz Series*, 1982-
Judith Van Gieson, *The Other Side of Death*, 1991

852
Michael A. Kahn
Due Diligence (New York: Dutton, 1995)
Series: Rachel Gold
Story type: Amateur Detective—Female Lead; Legal
Major character(s): Rachel Gold, Lawyer; Benny Goldberg, Lawyer, Professor
Time period(s): 1990s
Locale(s): St. Louis, Missouri
What the book is about: Rachel is in love and her new man is Rabbi David Marcus. David has recommended her to a member of his congregation, CPA Bruce Rosenthal, who says he needs legal advice. They set up a meeting but Rosenthal never makes it; he is murdered and leaves behind a cryptic list that relates to his earlier investigation of a pharmaceutical company. David feels responsible and starts asking questions. When he too, is brutally murdered, Rachel realizes something is horribly wrong and is determined to find the killer.
Other books you might like:
Jeffrey Wilds Deaver, *Mistress of Justice*, 1992
John Grisham, *The Pelican Brief*, 1992
Gini Hartzmark, *The Katherine Milholland Series*, 1992-
Mercedes Lambert, *Dogtown*, 1991
Lia Matera, *The Laura Di Palma Series*, 1988-

853
Michael A. Kahn
Firm Ambitions (New York: Dutton, 1994)
Series: Rachel Gold
Story type: Amateur Detective—Female Lead; Legal
Major character(s): Rachel Gold, Lawyer; Benny Goldberg, Professor, Lawyer
Time period(s): 1990s
Locale(s): St. Louis, Missouri
What the book is about: Somehow Rachel Gold has ended up specializing in divorce work, which she hates. Her latest client is Eileen Landau, wife of Tommy Landau, a well-known upper class thug. Eileen is having an affair with a handsome aerobics instructor and during one of their liaisons, he dies of poisoning. The police uncover a book of pictures of all the women he had affairs with, including Rachel's sister, Ann. When Ann is charged with the murder, Rachel starts working overtime to find the real killer.
Other books you might like:
Jeffrey Wilds Deaver, *Mistress of Justice*, 1992
Lia Matera, *The Willa Jansson Series*, 1987-
Janet L. Smith, *Practice to Deceive*, 1992
Julie Smith, *The Rebecca Schwartz Series*, 1982-
E.L. Wyrick, *A Strange and Bitter Fruit*, 1994

854
Tom Kakonis
Double Down (New York: Dutton, 1991)
Series: Tim Waverly
Story type: Action/Adventure
Major character(s): Tim Waverly, Businessman, Gambler (ex-professor; ex-con)
Time period(s): 1990s
Locale(s): Miami, Florida
What the book is about: Tim Waverly is on the hook for a quarter of a million dollars to some very heavy drug dealers. A high-stakes poker game offers a chance to make the big score. The other players, Tim's partner and an old love are all working their own games and the stakes may be a lot higher than Tim knows.
Other books you might like:
K. Patrick Conner, *Kingdom Road*, 1991
Robert Ferrigno, *The Horse Latitudes*, 1990
James W. Hall, *Tropical Freeze*, 1988
Carl Hiaasen, *Skin Tight*, 1989
Elmore Leonard, *Stick*, 1983

855
Tom Kakonis
Shadow Counter (New York: Dutton, 1993)
Series: Tim Waverly
Story type: Action/Adventure
Major character(s): Tim Waverly, Gambler (ex-professor; ex-con)
Time period(s): 1990s
Locale(s): Las Vegas, Nevada

What the book is about: Tim Waverly is in Las Vegas trying to build a stake by playing blackjack. Tim is a "counter", a practice frowned upon by the casinos. He then gets involved in a basketball point-shaving scheme and saving his sister from the attentions of a ruthless psychopath. Everyone has a plan to make the big score but some people may die before they can make it.

Other books you might like:
K. Patrick Connor, *Kingdom Road*, 1991
Pete Hautman, *Drawing Dead*, 1993
Elmore Leonard, *Rum Punch*, 1992
Tim Powers, *Last Call*, 1992
Charles Willeford, *Miami Blues*, 1984

856
Stuart M. Kaminsky
Lieberman's Choice (New York: St. Martin's, 1993)
Series: Abe Lieberman
Story type: Police Procedural—Male Lead
Major character(s): Abe Lieberman, Police Officer (60 years old; Jewish); Bill Hanrahan, Police Officer (Lieberman's partner)
Time period(s): 1990s
Locale(s): Chicago, Illinois
What the book is about: Bernie Shepard was a strict by-the-book cop until he found out his wife was unfaithful to him. Now he is a double murderer - his wife and her lover - and has taken refuge on the roof of a building he has rigged with explosives. It's up to "Rabbi" Lieberman to figure out how to take Shepard without blowing up a whole city block.

Other books you might like:
Richard Fliegal, *The Allerton Avenue Precinct Series*, 1987-
Nat Hentoff, *Blues for Charlie Darwin*, 1982
Ed McBain, *The 87th Precinct Series*, 1956-
Donald E. Westlake, *Levine*, 1984
Collin Wilcox, *The Lieutenant Hastings Series*, 1969-

857
Stuart M. Kaminsky
Lieberman's Day (New York: Holt, 1994)
Series: Abe Lieberman
Story type: Police Procedural—Male Lead
Major character(s): Abe Lieberman, Police Officer, Detective—Homicide; Bill Hanrahan, Police Officer (Lieberman's partner)
Time period(s): 1990s
Locale(s): Chicago, Illinois
What the book is about: Homicide detective Abe Lieberman's nephew and pregnant wife are shot in a mugging. The nephew dies and the wife and the baby are barely alive. Lieberman is forced to deal with some evil people to try and catch the killers. His alcoholic partner, Bill Hanrahan, has some serious problems of his own to deal with. As Lieberman gets further into the investigation, he discovers that the nephew's death may not have been just a random mugging.

Other books you might like:
Nat Hentoff, *Blues for Charlie Darwin*, 1982
Ed McBain, *The 87th Precinct Series*, 1956
Carol O'Connell, *Mallory's Oracle*, 1994
Donald E. Westlake, *Levine*, 1984
Collin Wilcox, *The Lieutenant Hastings Series*, 1969-

858
Stuart M. Kaminsky
Lieberman's Folly (New York: St. Martins, 1991)
Story type: Police Procedural—Male Lead
Major character(s): Abe Lieberman, Police Officer (60 years old); Bill Hanrahan, Police Officer (alcoholic, Lieberman's partner)
Time period(s): 1990s (1990)
Locale(s): Chicago, Illinois
What the book is about: A ten year old robbery in Texas turns out to have ramifications for Lieberman and his partner in Chicago.

Other books you might like:
William Bayer, *Switch*, 1984
Jack Early, *Donato and Daughter*, 1987
Vincent McConnor, *The Man Who Knew Hammett*, 1989
Donald E. Westlake, *Levine*, 1984
Collin Wilcox, *The Lieutenant Hastings Series*, 1969-

859
Stuart M. Kaminsky
The Man Who Walked Like a Bear (New York: Scribners, 1990)
Series: Inspector Rostnikov
Story type: Police Procedural—Male Lead
Major character(s): Porfiry Rostnikov, Police Officer (Inspector)
Time period(s): 1980s
Locale(s): Moscow, Russia (then Soviet Union)
What the book is about: The escape of a man from the mental ward at the hospital where Rostnikov's wife is laid up sets the stage for other events, all tieing back to this original episode. Kaminsky won the best novel Edgar for the previous book in this series.

Other books you might like:
Anthony Olcott, *Murder at the Red October*, 1981
Martin Cruz Smith, *Gorky Park*, 1981

860
Stuart M. Kaminsky
The Melting Clock (New York: Mysterious, 1991)
Series: Toby Peters
Story type: Private Detective—Male Lead; Historical
Major character(s): Toby Peters, Detective—Private; Salvador Dali, Historical Figure, Artist
Time period(s): 1940s (1942)

Locale(s): Los Angeles, California

What the book is about: Toby Peters gets involved with Salvador Dali's plot to have two of his paintings stolen as a publicity stunt. But three have disappeared. Peters must find out what happened to the third one. But, of course, it's more complicated than that.

Other books you might like:
Andrew Bergman, *Hollywood and LeVine*, 1975
Andrew J. Fenady, *The Man with Bogart's Face*, 1977
Joe Gores, *Hammett*, 1975
Peter Lovesey, *Keystone*, 1983
L.J. Washburn, *Dead-Stick*, 1989

861
Stuart M. Kaminsky
Rostnikov's Vacation (New York: Scribners, 1991)

Series: Inspector Rostnikov

Story type: Police Procedural—Male Lead

Major character(s): Porfiry Rostnikov, Police Officer (inspector, MVD); Emil Karpo, Police Officer

Time period(s): 1990s

Locale(s): Yalta, Russia; Moscow, Russia

What the book is about: Rostnikov has been ordered to take a vacation at Yalta. While there he meets Georgi Vasilevich, an old colleague. Georgi hints that he is working on a big case but won't say any more. He dies suddenly, supposedly of a heart attack but Rostnikov is sure it is murder. Meanwhile, Karpo, back in Moscow is following a woman in the hope she will lead to a murder suspect. While he is watching she is killed. Both cases may lead to world-shaking events.

Other books you might like:
Len Deighton, *SS-GB*, 1978
David Madsen, *U.S.S.A.*, 1989
Anthony Olcott, *Murder at the Red October*, 1981
Martin Cruz Smith, *Gorky Park*, 1981

862
Rob Kantner
Concrete Hero (New York: HarperCollins, 1994)

Series: Ben Perkins

Story type: Private Detective—Male Lead

Major character(s): Ben Perkins, Detective—Private, Maintenance Worker (part-time supervisor)

Time period(s): 1990s

Locale(s): Detroit, Michigan

What the book is about: Ben Perkins is now trying to be a family man and has promised the mother of his new daughter to no longer take violent cases. When he donates some time to a radio station for an auction, he figures it will be some simple case. When a widow asks him to confirm the police findings of accidental death of her husband, it still sounds routine. When he finds the husband has been involved in high-tech computer pornography, he knows he's in trouble once more.

Other books you might like:
Wayne Dundee, *The Joe Hannibal Series*, 1990-
Loren D. Estleman, *The Amos Walker Series*, 1983-
Arthur Lyons, *The Jacob Asch Series*, 1974-
Benjamin M. Schutz, *The Leo Haggerty Series*, 1984-
Jonathan Valin, *The Harry Stoner Series*, 1980-

863
Rob Kantner
The Quick and the Dead (New York: Harper, 1992)

Series: Ben Perkins

Story type: Private Detective—Male Lead

Major character(s): Ben Perkins, Detective—Private, Maintenance Worker (at an apartment complex)

Time period(s): 1990s

Locale(s): Detroit, Michigan

What the book is about: The Pope is coming to Detroit and St. Angela's Church to beatify their former priest, Father Joe. Unfortunately the body of Father Joe is missing. Ben is hired to find the body but it may have been missing for fifty years and a lot of people don't want the past dug up.

Other books you might like:
Earl Emerson, *The Thomas Black Series*, 1985-
Loren D. Estleman, *The Amos Walker Series*, 1983-
Jeremiah Healy, *The John Francis Cuddy Series*, 1984-
Benjamin M. Schutz, *The Leo Haggerty Series*, 1985-
Jonathan Valin, *The Harry Stoner Series*, 1980

864
Rob Kantner
The Red, White, and Blues (New York: Harper, 1993)

Series: Ben Perkins

Story type: Private Detective—Male Lead

Major character(s): Ben Perkins, Detective—Private, Maintenance Worker (at an apartment complex)

Time period(s): 1990s

Locale(s): Detroit, Michigan

What the book is about: Ben Perkins is hired to investigate the disappearance of a newborn baby. Ben, a new father himself, is sympathetic but has reservations. The mother's story is questionable and why did she wait a year before doing something? Ben takes the case and soon finds himself involved in a conspiracy that may prove lethal.

Other books you might like:
Jerome Doolittle, *The Tom Bethany Series*, 1990-
Jeremiah Healy, *The John Francis Cuddy Series*, 1984-
Zachary Klein, *The Matt Jacob Series*, 1990-
Benjamin M. Schutz, *The Leo Haggerty Series*, 1985
Jonathan Valin, *The Harry Stoner Series*, 1980-

865
Rob Kantner
The Thousand Yard Stare (New York: Bantam, 1991)

866 Karl

Series: Ben Perkins
Story type: Private Detective—Male Lead
Major character(s): Ben Perkins, Detective—Private
Time period(s): 1990s
Locale(s): Detroit, Michigan
What the book is about: It's time for Ben's twenty-fifth high school reunion. Ben doesn't want to go because it brings up painful memories of Sara Gerbstadt and her suicide. A former classmate and girlfriend asks him to go and look into the suicide because she feels it was murder.
Other books you might like:
Earl Emerson, *The Thomas Black Series*, 1985-
Loren D. Estleman, *The Amos Walker Series*, 1983-
William J. Reynolds, *The Nebraska Series*, 1984-
Benjamin M. Schutz, *The Leo Haggerty Series*, 1985-
Jonathan Valin, *The Harry Stoner Series*, 1980-

866
M.S. Karl (Pseudonym of M.K. Shuman)
Death Notice (New York: St. Martin's, 1990)
Series: Peter Brady
Story type: Amateur Detective—Male Lead
Major character(s): Peter Brady, Journalist
Time period(s): 1980s (1989)
Locale(s): Troy, Louisiana
What the book is about: When a man convicted of murdering a local girl years ago returns to Troy, people are less than pleased. Soon, more murder occurs.
Other books you might like:
Lucille Kallen, *Introducing C.B. Greenfield*, 1979
Douglas Kiker, *Murder on Clam Pond*, 1986
Keith Peterson, *The Trapdoor*, 1988
Alice Storey, *Then Hang All the Lawyers*, 1989

867
M.S. Karl (Pseudonym of M.K. Shuman)
Deerslayer (New York: St. Martin's, 1991)
Series: Peter Brady
Story type: Amateur Detective—Male Lead; Action/Adventure
Major character(s): Peter Brady, Journalist, Publisher (of a newspaper)
Time period(s): 1990s
Locale(s): Troy Parrish, Louisiana
What the book is about: Pete has been talked into going on a deer hunt with Sheriff Matt Garritty and his son Scott. When Scott shoots and the men go to find the deer, they are shocked to find a human body, auto dealer Dwayne Elkins. Matt accepts it as a tragic accident but Pete has some questions. Such as, if Dwayne was hunting, why didn't he have a gun?

Other books you might like:
Douglas Kiker, *Murder on Clam Pond*, 1986
Keith Peterson, *The Trapdoor*, 1988
John R. Riggs, *Wolf in Sheep's Clothing*, 1989
Celestine Sibley, *Ah, Sweet Mystery*, 1991
Alice Storey, *Then Hang All the Liars*, 1989

868
Leona Karr
Murder in Bandora (New York: Walker, 1993)
Story type: Amateur Detective—Female Lead
Major character(s): Addie Devore, Journalist (reporter), Publisher (of a newspaper)
Time period(s): 1990s
Locale(s): Bandora, Colorado
What the book is about: Addie Devore is trying to make it as a newspaper publisher with the *Bandora Bulletin*, a small town paper she has inherited. Now is her chance as a local figure has been killed and left in the Wyatt Earp exhibit. With the help of her alcoholic St. Bernard and a strange loner she sets out to solve the murder and get the big story. It may lead to her own obituary. First mystery.
Other books you might like:
Mary Daheim, *The Alpine Advocate*, 1992
Mary Kittredge, *Poison Pen*, 1990
Meg O'Brien, *The Jessica James Series*, 1990-
Nancy Pickard, *Bum Steer*, 1990
Julie Robitaille, *Jinx*, 1991

869
Jon Katz
Death by Station Wagon (New York: Doubleday, 1993)
Series: Suburban Detective
Story type: Private Detective—Male Lead
Major character(s): Kit Deleeuw, Detective—Private (house-husband; ex-broker)
Time period(s): 1990s
Locale(s): Rochambeau, New Jersey
What the book is about: Kit was a successful broker on Wall Street until the SEC closed his firm for insider trading. Now he has fallen back on skills he learned in the Army CID and has opened a private detective agency. He is also the primary care-giver for his children. He spends most of his time on routine skip tracing, repo work, etc. Then he gets his big chance - he is hired by a group of students to prove that the murder - suicide of a young couple was really a double murder. More strange attacks occur and Kit discovers a link to a crime that took place over 100 years before.
Other books you might like:
James Lee Burke, *A Stained White Radiance*, 1992
Earl Emerson, *The Thomas Black Series*, 1985-
Kate Gallison, *The Nick Magaracz Series*, 1988-
Les Roberts, *The Milan Jacovich Series*, 1988-
Michael W. Sherer, *Little Use for Death*, 1992

870
Jon Katz
The Family Stalker (New York: Doubleday, 1994)

Series: Suburban Detective

Story type: Private Detective—Male Lead

Major character(s): Kit Deleeuw, Detective—Private (ex-Wall Street broker)

Time period(s): 1990s

Locale(s): Rochambeau, New Jersey

What the book is about: Thanks to the success of his last case, Kit Deleeuw is finally doing well as a private eye and is no longer taking care of his family while his wife earns the money. He takes the case of lawyer Mariane Dow who says that Andrea Lucca is deliberately trying to destroy her marriage. When Kit investigates, he finds that this may not be the first time Andrea has broken up a family. When Mariane's husband is murdered, she is the prime suspect. But could it be the elusive Andrea who is the killer?

Other books you might like:
Jeff Andrus, *Tracer, Inc.*, 1994
E.C. Ayres, *Hour of the Manatee*, 1993
Rob Kantner, *Concrete Hero*, 1994
Kate Wilhelm, *The Hamlet Trap*, 1987
Steven Womack, *Dead Folks' Blues*, 1992

871
Michael J. Katz
The Big Freeze (New York: Putnam, 1991)

Series: Andy Sussman/Murray Glick

Story type: Private Detective—Male Lead; Amateur Detective—Male Lead

Major character(s): Andy Sussman, Journalist (television sportscaster); Murray Glick, Detective—Private

Time period(s): 1990s

Locale(s): California

What the book is about: Andy receives in the mail a manuscript written by private eye Murray Glick about a missing girl and Colorado business interests versus the environment. But now Murray has disappeared, or so Andy thinks, and why has he sent the manuscript?

Other books you might like:
Jon L. Breen, *Loose Lips*, 1990
Rex Burns, *Suicide Season*, 1987
Crabbe Evers, *Murder in Wrigley Field*, 1990
Michael Geller, *Dead Fix*, 1989
Doug Hornig, *Foul Shot*, 1984

872
Michael J. Katz
Last Dance in Redondo Beach (New York: Putnam, 1989)

Series: Andy Sussman/Murray Glick

Story type: Amateur Detective—Male Lead

Major character(s): Andy Sussman, Journalist (television sportscaster); Murray Glick, Detective—Private

Time period(s): 1980s

Locale(s): Los Angeles, California; Chicago, Illinois

What the book is about: While Sussman is covering a superstars competition, one of the competitors, a wrestler known as Dr. Double-X, dies. Sussman, much to his dismay, is told to stay on the story.

Other books you might like:
William L. DeAndrea, *Killed on the Ice*, 1984
Tucker Halleran, *A Cool Clear Death*, 1985
Doug Hornig, *Foul Shot*, 1984
Dave Klein, *Blind Side*, 1980
Richard Rosen, *Strike Three, You're Dead*, 1984

873
John Katzenbach
Just Cause (New York: Putnam, 1992)

Story type: Action/Adventure

Major character(s): Matthew Cowart, Journalist (reporter and editorial writer); Robert Earl Ferguson, Criminal (convicted killer)

Time period(s): 1990s

Locale(s): Miami, Florida

What the book is about: Bored and lonely reporter Matthew Cowart receives a letter from death-row inmate, Robert Earl Ferguson, claiming his innocence in a rape and murder. Not believing him but intrigued nonetheless Cowart sets out to find the truth. He discovers enough to get Ferguson released from jail and another man condemned. Then he finds out he has been duped. He and homicide detective Tanny Brown set out to find Ferguson.

Other books you might like:
Gary Paulsen, *Night Rituals*, 1989
Keith Peterson, *Rough Justice*, 1990
W.R. Philbrick, *Paint It Black*, 1989
Robert J. Randisi, *Full Contact*, 1987
John Sandford, *Silent Prey*, 1992

874
H.R.F. Keating
Dead on Time (New York: Mysterious, 1989)

Series: Inspector Ghote

Story type: Police Procedural—Male Lead

Major character(s): Ganeesh Ghote, Police Officer (inspector)

Time period(s): 1980s

Locale(s): Bombay, India; Dharbani, India (Small village)

What the book is about: A murder at the Bombay Tick Tock Watch works involves Ghote more than he would wish.

Other books you might like:
Gary Alexander, *Pigeon Blood*, 1988
Tony Hillerman, *The Dark Wind*, 1982
O.K. Joshee, *Mr. Surie*, 1984
B.N. Sidwa, *The Crow Eaters*, 1981
Arthur W. Upfield, *The Inspector Napoleon Bonaparte Series*, (1929-1966)

875
H.R.F. Keating
The Iciest Sin (New York: Mysterious, 1990)

Series: Inspector Ghote

Story type: Police Procedural—Male Lead

Major character(s): Ganeesh Ghote, Police Officer (inspector)

Time period(s): 1980s

Locale(s): Bombay, India

What the book is about: Inspector Ghote is assigned to watch Dolly Daruwala, the "most dangerous woman in Bombay" and an accomplished blackmailer. While he watches, she is killed by a man Ghote knows is good and noble. Should he cover up the crime?

Other books you might like:
Melvin A. Casberg, *Death Stalks the Punjab*, 1980
O.K. Joshee, *Mr. Surie*, 1984
B.N. Sidwa, *The Crow Eaters*, 1981
Arthur W. Upfield, *The Scribner Crime Classic Series*, 1929-1966
Robert Van Gulik, *The Judge Dee Series*, 1949-1968

876
John E. Keegan
Clearwater Summer (New York: Carroll & Graf, 1994)

Story type: Psychological Suspense; Legal

Major character(s): Will Bradford, Teenager (14 years old); Taylor Clark, Teenager; Wellesley Baker, Teenager

Time period(s): 1950s (1959)

Locale(s): Clearwater, Washington

What the book is about: The idyllic summer of three teenage friends comes to an abrupt end when one of them, Wellesley Baker, is accused of killing her father. Will Bradford is convinced of her innocence and gets very involved in trying to prove it. First novel.

Other books you might like:
Harper Lee, *To Kill a Mockingbird*, 1959
Steven Yount, *Wandering Star*, 1994

877
Douglas J. Keeling
A Case of Innocence (New York: Birch Lane, 1989)

Story type: Private Detective—Male Lead

Major character(s): James P. Casey, Lawyer, Detective—Private

Time period(s): 1980s

Locale(s): Midwest

What the book is about: A woman hires Casey to find her six-year-old daughter who has been kidnapped by the girl's father's drug dealer associates. First book.

Other books you might like:
Stephen Greenleaf, *The John Marshall Tanner Series*, 1979
J.P. Hailey, *The Baxter Trust*, 1988
Edward Mathis, *The Dan Roman Series*, (1986-)
William J. Reynolds, *The Nebraska Series*, (1984-)

878
Faye Kellerman
Day of Atonement (New York: Morrow, 1991)

Series: Peter Decker/Rina Lazarus

Story type: Police Procedural—Male Lead; Psychological Suspense

Major character(s): Rina Lazarus, Widow(er) (and mother; orthodox Jew); Peter Decker, Police Officer (lover of Rina)

Time period(s): 1990s

Locale(s): Los Angeles, California; New York, New York

What the book is about: Peter, still trying to come to terms with being Jewish, has accompanied Rina to New York to be with her family for the High Holy Days. While there he is asked to help in looking for a teenager who has rebelled against his orthodox upbringing and has disappeared. While investigating Peter discovers a secret that will turn his life upside down.

Other books you might like:
Mary Anne Kelly, *Park Lane South, Queens*, 1990
Harry Kemelman, *The Rabbi Small Series*, 1965-
Roger L. Simon, *Raising the Dead*, 1988
Joseph Telushkin, *The Unorthodox Murder of Rabbi Wahl*, 1987

879
Faye Kellerman
False Prophet (New York: Morrow, 1992)

Series: Peter Decker/Rina Lazarus

Story type: Police Procedural—Male Lead

Major character(s): Peter Decker, Police Officer (Jewish); Rina Lazarus, Spouse (of Peter; orthodox Jew)

Time period(s): 1990s

Locale(s): Los Angeles, California

What the book is about: Peter is trying to get home to Rina who is five months pregnant with their first child, when he gets a call to investigate the rape and robbery of Lilah Brecht. Lilah is the daughter of famous actress Davida Eversong and the owner of a world famous spa of the stars. Investigating the case involves Peter with the very strange family of Lilah and employees of the spa, all of whom seem to be protecting secrets.

Other books you might like:
Mary Higgins Clark, *Weep No More, My Lady*, 1987
Chris Crutcher, *The Deep End*, 1992
Jonathan Kellerman, *Blood Test*, 1986
Rochelle Majer Krich, *Till Death Do Us Part*, 1992
Marissa Piesman, *Unorthodox Practices*, 1989

880
Faye Kellerman
Grievous Sin (New York: Morrow, 1993)
Series: Peter Decker/Rina Lazarus
Story type: Police Procedural—Male Lead; Amateur Detective
Major character(s): Rina Decker, Spouse (wife of Peter and new mother); Peter Decker, Police Officer (detective sergeant)
Time period(s): 1990s
Locale(s): Los Angeles, California
What the book is about: Rina Decker is in the hospital having her and Peter's first child when another infant disappears. The nurse in charge of the children the night of the disappearance has vanished as well but is she the guilty party or an innocent victim of the kidnapper? LAPD Officer Decker begins to delve into the nurse's past life in search of the truth behind the disappearance of both child and nurse.
Other books you might like:
Wendy Hornsby, *Midnight Baby*, 1993
Susan Kelly, *Out of the Darkness*, 1992
Rochelle Majer Krich, *Till Death Do Us Part*, 1992
Yvonne Montgomery, *Obstacle Course*, 1990
Nancy Pickard, *Confession*, 1994

881
Faye Kellerman
Justice (New York: Morrow, 1995)
Series: Peter Decker/Rina Lazarus
Story type: Police Procedural—Male Lead
Major character(s): Peter Decker, Police Officer (sergeant, homicide); Teresa McLaughlin, Student—High School; Rina Lazarus, Spouse (Peter's)
Time period(s): 1990s
Locale(s): Los Angeles, California
What the book is about: Terry McLaughlin has finally met a boy she can fall in love with, the strange and mysterious Chris Whitman. Just as their relationship is getting started, one of their classmates is murdered. Chris is one of the major suspects as he had been intimate with the victim, but so had most of the males in her class. Peter is not convinced of Chris' guilt and digs deeper. Something is not right with Chris but that doesn't make him a murderer. Or does it?
Other books you might like:
Thomas Adcock, *Thrown Away Child*, 1996
Michael Connelly, *The Last Coyote*, 1994
Wendy Hornsby, *Bad Intent*, 1994
Rochelle Majer Krich, *Angel of Death*, 1994
April Smith, *North of Montana*, 1994

882
Faye Kellerman
Milk and Honey (New York: Morrow, 1990)
Series: Peter Decker/Rina Lazarus
Story type: Police Procedural—Male Lead

Major character(s): Peter Decker, Police Officer (sergeant); Rina Lazarus, Widow(er) (orthodox Jew)
Time period(s): 1980s
Locale(s): Los Angeles, California
What the book is about: After finding a two-year old girl alone in a park, Decker and his partner are drawn to a multiple murder at a honey farm. This case and one that involves a friend accused of rape put extra pressure on Decker while he waits for Rina Lazarus to decide whether she'll marry him.
Other books you might like:
Sophie Belfort, *The Lace Curtain Murders*, 1986
Bob Fenster, *The Last Page*, 1989
Susan Kelly, *The Gemini Man*, 1985

883
Faye Kellerman
The Quality of Mercy (New York: Morrow, 1989)
Story type: Historical
Major character(s): William Shakespeare, Writer, Historical Figure; Rebecca Lopez, Smuggler (of Jews from Inquisition Spain)
Time period(s): 16th century (Reign of Queen Elizabeth I)
What the book is about: A fictionalized Shakespeare searches for the killer of a fellow actor. Meanwhile, his love Rebecca Lopez, daughter of Roderigo Lopez, physician to Queen Elizabeth I, works with English Jews to smuggle Jews out of Spain to escape the Inquisition.
Other books you might like:
P.C. Doherty, *Satan in St. Mary's*, 1987
Margaret Doody, *Aristotle, Detective*, 1980
Ellis Peters, *Dead Man's Ransom*, 1984
Leonard Tourney, *Low Treason*, 1983
Donald Zochert, *Murder in the Hellfire Club*, 1978

884
Faye Kellerman
Sanctuary (New York: Morrow, 1994)
Series: Peter Decker/Rina Lazarus
Story type: Private Detective—Male Lead
Major character(s): Peter Decker, Police Officer, Detective—Homicide; Rina Lazarus, Spouse (Peter's)
Time period(s): 1990s
Locale(s): Los Angeles, California
What the book is about: Peter Decker is investigating the disappearance of a diamond dealer and his family. Everything in their house is normal but they have completely vanished. Peter is sure something is wrong. Meanwhile, an old friend of Rina's, Honey Klein, and her family are visiting, supposedly on a vacation, but actually escaping from her husband, a New York diamond dealer. Soon both dealers are found murdered and Honey and her children disappear. This seems to be more than mere coincidence.

Other books you might like:
Jonathan Kellerman, *The Butcher's Theater*, 1988
Rochelle Majer Krich, *Angel of Death*, 1994
Rochelle Majer Krich, *Till Death Do Us Part*, 1992
Medora Sale, *Short Cut to Santa Fe*, 1994

885
Jonathan Kellerman
Bad Love (New York: Bantam, 1994)

Series: Alex Delaware

Story type: Amateur Detective—Male Lead

Major character(s): Alex Delaware, Psychologist (specializing in children); Milo Sturgis, Police Officer, Homosexual (friend of Alex)

Time period(s): 1990s

Locale(s): Los Angeles, California

What the book is about: Alex Delaware has just received an audio tape with the voice of a child screaming and someone chanting the phrase "bad love." This is just the start of a campaign of harassment and intimidation. The only connection Alex can come up with is a seminar he was involved with years ago with the famous Dr. Andre de Bosch and his daughter. With the help of his cop friend Milo, he tries to find who is responsible and discovers an ominous pattern of death connected with Dr. de Bosch.

Other books you might like:
Chris Crutcher, *The Deep End*, 1992
Andrew Klavan, *Don't Say a Word*, 1991
Donna Levin, *California Street*, 1990
Stephen White, *Private Practices*, 1992

886
Jonathan Kellerman
Private Eyes (New York: Bantam, 1992)

Series: Alex Delaware

Story type: Amateur Detective—Male Lead; Psychological Suspense

Major character(s): Alex Delaware, Psychologist (specializing in children); Milo Sturgis, Police Officer (on suspension), Homosexual

Time period(s): 1990s

Locale(s): Los Angeles, California

What the book is about: Ten years ago Alex successfully treated seven year old Melissa Dickinson who was suffering from a strange home life causing severe problems. Her mother had been attacked with acid and permanently scarred. This had caused her to retreat to her house and never leave. Now Melissa needs Alex's help again. Her mother seems to be getting better, but her attacker is back in Los Angeles. Alex agrees to help but then Mom disappears.

Other books you might like:
Robert Campbell, *Alice in La-La Land*, 1987
Donna Levin, *California Street*, 1990
Joyce Anne Schneider, *Darkness Falls*, 1989
Andrew Vachss, *Strega*, 1988
S.K. Wolf, *Long Chain of Death*, 1989

887
Jonathan Kellerman
Self-Defense (New York: Bantam, 1995)

Series: Alex Delaware

Story type: Amateur Detective—Male Lead; Psychological Suspense

Major character(s): Alex Delaware, Psychologist (specializing in children); Milo Sturgis, Police Officer, Homosexual

Time period(s): 1990s

Locale(s): Los Angeles, California

What the book is about: The experience of being a juror at the trial of a serial killer triggers the return of a bizarre nightmare for Lucy Lowell. Milo Sturgis, Alex's cop friend, has sent Lucy to seek Alex's help. Could Lucy's dream be a repressed memory of a murder she witnessed as a child? Her family certainly has enough secrets. Does the fact that a copy-cat killer is continuing the crime wave of the convicted serial killer have any connection?

Other books you might like:
Chris Crutcher, *The Deep End*, 1992
Leslie Glass, *Burning Time*, 1993
Donna Levin, *California Street*, 1990
Stephen White, *Private Practices*, 1994
R.D. Zimmerman, *Blood Trance*, 1993

888
Jonathan Kellerman
Time Bomb (New York: Bantam, 1990)

Series: Alex Delaware

Story type: Amateur Detective—Male Lead; Psychological Suspense

Major character(s): Alex Delaware, Psychologist (specializing in children)

Time period(s): 1990s

Locale(s): Los Angeles, California

What the book is about: A sniper opens fire, and is killed, at an elementary school where two rival politicians are visiting. Called in to help the children deal with the trauma, Alex is drawn in deeper by the sniper's father who asks him to investigate.

Other books you might like:
Robert Campbell, *Sweet La-La Land*, 1990
Robin Cook, *Coma*, 1977
Donna Levin, *California Street*, 1990
Andrew Vachss, *Flood*, 1985

889
Mary Anne Kelly
Foxglove (New York: St. Martin's, 1992)

Story type: Amateur Detective—Female Lead; Police Procedural

Major character(s): Claire Breslinsky, Photographer, Housewife; Johnny Benedetto, Police Officer (Claire's husband)

Time period(s): 1990s

Locale(s): New York, New York

What the book is about: Claire has married and become a mother, while recovering from the traumatic events of helping to uncover a child killer in her old family neighborhood. Now she is buying a new house and meets her old schoolgirl friend, Theresa, called "Tree." But before Claire can move in, Tree mysteriously dies. Tree's husband seems much too happy and Tree's daughter is troubled by bad dreams while being ignored by her father. Claire tries to help but is having family problems of her own.

Other books you might like:
Jeanne Hart, *Some Die Young*, 1989
Wendy Hornsby, *No Harm*, 1989
Susan Kelly, *And Soon I'll Come to Kill You*, 1991
Eve K. Sandstrom, *Death Down Home*, 1990

890
Mary Anne Kelly
Park Lane South, Queens (New York: St. Martin's, 1990)

Story type: Amateur Detective—Female Lead

Major character(s): Claire Breslinsky, Photographer; Johnny Benedetto, Police Officer

Time period(s): 1980s

Locale(s): New York, New York

What the book is about: Claire joins her sisters at their parent's home and soon after the body of a child is found in the woods nearby. Kelly's first novel.

Other books you might like:
Thomas Boyle, *Only the Dead Know Brooklyn*, 1985
Dorothy Salisbury Davis, *Lullaby of Murder*, 1984
Wendy Hornsby, *No Harm*, 1989
Faye Kellerman, *The Ritual Bath*, 1986
Susan Kelly, *The Gemini Man*, 1985

891
Nora Kelly
Bad Chemistry (New York: St. Martin's, 1994)

Series: Gillian Adams

Story type: Police Procedural; Amateur Detective—Female Lead

Major character(s): Gillian Adams, Professor (of history); Edward Gisborne, Police Officer (detective chief inspector)

Time period(s): 1990s

Locale(s): Cambridge, England

What the book is about: Gillian Adams is back at Cambridge on sabbatical for the summer. She is hoping to renew old acquaintances and to spend some time with her lover, Edward Gisborne. But all does not go as planned. First there is a break-in at the Pregnancy Information Centre, then a young woman chemist is killed. Gillian and Edward, who is visiting at the time, are drawn into the case. Another body is soon discovered.

Other books you might like:
P.M. Carlson, *Murder Is Academic*, 1986
Gillian Linscott, *Unknown Hand*, 1989
Valerie Miner, *Murder in the English Department*, 1982
Janet Neel, *Death Among the Dons*, 1994
Joan Smith, *Why Aren't They Screaming?*, 1988

892
Nora Kelly
My Sister's Keeper (New York: St. Martin's, 1992)

Series: Gillian Adams

Story type: Amateur Detective—Female Lead

Major character(s): Gillian Adams, Professor (of history; department head)

Time period(s): 1990s

Locale(s): Canada (University of the Pacific Northwest)

What the book is about: Gillian is being co-opted by the Feminist Union because she is tired of the subtle (and sometimes not-so-subtle) bias at the university. First a gross display of "slave women"' by the engineering students, then the passing over of one of Gillian's brilliant students, Rita Gordon, who is also the leader of the feminist union, for a prestigious fellowship, angers Gillian. She is now pushing for the establishment of a womens' studies program. Then Rita dies in a tragic accident that may have been murder.

Other books you might like:
J.S. Borthwick, *The Student Body*, 1986
Amanda Cross, *Death in a Tenured Position*, 1981
Susan Kenney, *Garden of Malice*, 1983
Valerie Miner, *Murder in the English Department*, 1982
Joan Smith, *A Masculine Ending*, 1987

893
Susan Kelly
And Soon I'll Come to Kill You (New York: Villard, 1991)

Series: Liz Connors

Story type: Amateur Detective—Female Lead

Major character(s): Liz Connors, Journalist (free-lance); Jack Lingemann, Police Officer (lover of Liz)

Time period(s): 1990s

Locale(s): Cambridge, Massachusetts

What the book is about: Liz Connors doesn't take the first threatening letter too seriously-just a crank she thinks. But as more come and then become more vicious she becomes worried. Jack too is concerned. When a mutilated doll shows up it is time to act. Going over past stories she realizes she might have made someone mad. Then people involved in some of these stories begin to die.

Other books you might like:
Gary Amo, *Silent Night*, 1991
Jo Bannister, *Death and Other Lovers*, 1991
Barbara D'Amato, *Hardball*, 1990
Kathryn Lasky Knight, *Mortal Words*, 1990
D.B. Taylor, *Fatal Obsession*, 1989

894
Susan Kelly
Out of the Darkness (New York: Villard, 1992)
Series: Liz Connors
Story type: Amateur Detective—Female Lead
Major character(s): Liz Connors, Journalist (investigative reporter); Griffen Marcus, Journalist (best-selling crime writer)
Time period(s): 1990s
Locale(s): Cambridge, Massachusetts
What the book is about: Liz is asked by famous writer Griffen Marcus to assist him in writing his latest book - the story of the Merrimack Valley killer who murdered seven young women. The police and Griffen think they know who the killer is - a man already in jail for the murder of two prostitutes. While trying to get proof against him, Liz uncovers facts that cause her to question his guilt.
Other books you might like:
Barbara D'Amato, *Hardball*, 1990
Judith Garwood, *Make Friends with Murder*, 1992
D.F. Mills, *Deadline*, 1991
Annette Roome, *A Second Shot in the Dark*, 1992
Sarah Shankman, *First Kill All the Lawyers*, 1988

895
Susan Kelly
Until Proven Innocent (New York: Villard, 1990)
Series: Liz Connors
Story type: Amateur Detective—Female Lead; Police Procedural
Major character(s): Liz Connors, Journalist (investigative reporter); Jack Lingemann, Police Officer (lieutenant)
Time period(s): 1990s
Locale(s): Cambridge, Massachusetts
What the book is about: Liz Connors' boyfriend, policeman Jack Lingemann, is accused of murder. Liz must use all of her skill as an investigator to help prove his innocence—without much help from his colleagues.
Other books you might like:
Barbara D'Amato, *Hardball*, 1990
Bob Fenster, *The Last Page*, 1989
Nancy Pickard, *Say No to Murder*, 1985
Gillian Roberts, *Caught Dead in Philadelphia*, 1987

896
Susan B. Kelly
Hope Against Hope (New York: Scribners, 1991)
Series: Nick Trevellyan/Alison Hope
Story type: Police Procedural
Major character(s): Nick Trevellyan, Police Officer (detective inspector, CID); Alison Hope, Businesswoman (owner of computer firm)
Time period(s): 1990s
Locale(s): Hopbridge, England

What the book is about: Alison Hope has just moved to the Hop Valley to get away from the hustle and bustle of London. Here she runs into Nick Trevellyan-almost literally. They soon meet professionally, however, when Alison's cousin Aidan is murdered at a party at Alison's-and Alison is a prime suspect. First novel.
Other books you might like:
Alisa Craig, *A Pint of Murder*, 1980
Ann Granger, *Say It with Poison*, 1991
Janet Neel, *Death's Bright Angel*, 1988
Medora Sale, *Murder in Focus*, 1988

897
Susan B. Kelly
Kid's Stuff (New York: Scribners, 1994)
Series: Nick Trevellyan/Alison Hope
Story type: Police Procedural
Major character(s): Nick Trevellyan, Police Officer (detective chief inspector, CID); Alison Hope, Computer Expert (Nick's lover)
Time period(s): 1990s
Locale(s): Hop Valley, England
What the book is about: Nick Trevellyan has just arrested Arturo Bottone for possession and sale of child pornography. He hopes to find out more about Arturo's customers and suppliers, but Arturo is found dead, an apparent suicide. Nick thinks it's awfully convenient for a lot of people but can't prove it was murder. While trying to find an elusive customer list, he becomes involved with Arturo's enigmatic wife and family. There is also an arsonist at work who seems to be taking justice into his own hands.
Other books you might like:
Deborah Crombie, *A Share in Death*, 1993
Ann Granger, *Cold in the Earth*, 1993
Janet Neel, *Death of a Partner*, 1991
Mary Monica Pulver, *Ashes to Ashes*, 1988
Medora Sale, *Sleep of the Innocent*, 1991

898
Susan B. Kelly
Time of Hope (New York: Scribners, 1992)
Series: Nick Trevellyan/Alison Hope
Story type: Police Procedural; Amateur Detective
Major character(s): Nick Trevellyan, Police Officer (detective inspector, CID); Alison Hope, Businesswoman (owner of computer firm)
Time period(s): 1990s
Locale(s): Hopbridge, England (West Country)
What the book is about: Alison's cleaning lady's son, Ben, has become involved with young free spirit, Frisco Carstairs, and the family is not happy. When Nick and Alison return from a holiday in Italy, they learn that Frisco has been killed - strangled and dumped in the woods. When the autopsy shows that she was pregnant, Nick suspects the case may involve secrets and passions that no one wants uncovered.

Other books you might like:
Alisa Craig, *A Pint of Murder*, 1980
Elizabeth George, *Payment in Blood*, 1989
Janet Neel, *Death on Site*, 1989
Mary Monica Pulver, *Original Sin*, 1991
Medora Sale, *Murder in Focus*, 1989

899
Judith Kelman
The House on the Hill (New York: Bantam, 1992)
Story type: Psychological Suspense
Major character(s): Abigail Eakins, Child (11 years old); Quinn Gallagher, Parole Officer; Eldon Weir, Criminal (paroled child molester)
Time period(s): 1990s
Locale(s): Vermont
What the book is about: Runaway Abigail Eakins ends up lost in a house that has been specially designed for surveillance of convicted, blind child molester Eldon Weir. But is Weir the one holding her prisoner? Can or will parole officer Quinn Gallagher be able to effect a rescue of the 11-year-old girl?
Other books you might like:
Michael Allegretto, *Night of Reunion*, 1990
Gary Amo, *Silent Night*, 1991
Mary Higgins Clark, *A Cry in the Night*, 1982
Andrew Klavan, *Don't Say a Word*, 1991

900
Toni L.P. Kelner
Dead Ringer (New York: Zebra, 1994)
Series: Laura Fleming
Story type: Amateur Detective—Female Lead
Major character(s): Laura Fleming, Computer Expert; Richard Fleming, Professor (of English; Laura's husband)
Time period(s): 1990s
Locale(s): Byerly, North Carolina
What the book is about: Laura and Richard Fleming are visiting Byerly once again, this time for the annual family reunion. While trying to help one of her cousin's girlfriends with a computer problem, she discovers a body that looks strangely like the head of the town's leading industry. The sheriff is not thrilled that every time Laura comes to town someone is killed. Then there is another death and Laura is drawn into a web of old family secrets that someone is desperate to keep hidden.
Other books you might like:
Connie Feddersen, *Dead in the Water*, 1993
Muriel Resnick Jackson, *The Garden Club*, 1992
Margaret Maron, *Bootlegger's Daughter*, 1992
Patricia Houck Sprinkle, *A Mystery Bred in Buckhead*, 1994
Elizabeth Daniels Squire, *Kill the Messenger*, 1990

901
Toni L.P. Kelner
Down Home Murder (New York: Zebra, 1993)
Series: Laura Fleming
Story type: Amateur Detective—Female Lead
Major character(s): Laura Fleming, Computer Expert; Richard Fleming, Professor (of English; Laura's husband)
Time period(s): 1990s
Locale(s): Byerly, North Carolina
What the book is about: Laura Fleming has come back home from Boston because her grandfather has been in an accident and may die. As she finds out more, it becomes clear that this was no accident. Did one of her numerous relatives actually try to murder Paw and does it have anything to do with the disappearance of a young girl? Laura tries to find the truth before more people are hurt. First novel.
Other books you might like:
Richard Forrest, *Death on the Mississippi*, 1989
Muriel Resnick Jackson, *The Garden Club*, 1992
Margaret Maron, *Bootlegger's Daughter*, 1992
Patricia Houck Sprinkle, *Somebody's Dead in Snellville*, 1992
Kerry Tucker, *Still Waters*, 1991

902
Toni L.P. Kelner
Trouble Looking for a Place to Happen (New York: Kensington, 1995)
Series: Laura Fleming
Story type: Amateur Detective—Female Lead
Major character(s): Laura Fleming, Computer Expert; Richard Fleming, Professor (of English; Laura's husband)
Time period(s): 1990s
Locale(s): Byerly, North Carolina
What the book is about: Laura is back in Byerly to attend her Aunt Ruby Lee's wedding. Ruby Lee's daughter, Ilene, has started seeing a somewhat disreputable man and has run off to the Rocky Shoals Music Festival against the wishes of her parents. Soon the dead body of the young man is found and members of Laura's family are prime suspects. It's up to Laura to clear them by finding the real killer. But is her family innocent?
Other books you might like:
Kathryn Buckstaff, *No One Dies in Branson*, 1994
Susan Rogers Cooper, *Funny as a Dead Relative*, 1994
Connie Feddersen, *The Amanda Hazard Series*, 1993-
Eve K. Sandstrom, *The Devil Down Home*, 1991
Steven Womack, *Way Past Dead*, 1995

903
Paul Kemprecos
Death in Deep Water (New York: Doubleday, 1992)
Series: Aristotle Socarides
Story type: Private Detective—Male Lead
Major character(s): Aristotle "Soc" Socarides, Detective—Private, Fisherman
Time period(s): 1990s
Locale(s): Cape Cod, Massachusetts

What the book is about: The Oceanus Aquatic Park is for sale to Japanese investors but there are problems. Already under fire by animal rights groups, the publicity generated by the death of trainer Eddy Byron while in the tank of Rocky, the killer whale, may kill the sale. Soc is hired by the park to go undercover and prove that Rocky is not responsible. Soc finds a lot of people who didn't like Eddy but did someone hate him enough to kill him?

Other books you might like:
Rick Boyer, *The Whale's Footprints*, 1988
Philip R. Craig, *A Beautiful Place to Die*, 1990
Carl Hiaasen, *Native Tongue*, 1991
John Walter Putre, *A Small and Incidental Murder*, 1990
Mary Willis Walker, *Zero at the Bone*, 1991

904
Paul Kemprecos
Feeding Frenzy (New York: Doubleday, 1993)
Series: Aristotle Socarides
Story type: Action/Adventure; Police Procedural—Male Lead
Major character(s): Aristotle "Soc" Socarides, Detective—Private, Fisherman
Time period(s): 1990s
Locale(s): Quanset Beach, Massachusetts

What the book is about: A mysterious freighter sinks off the coast after its unknown cargo gets loose. Soon after swimmers are being attacked by something nobody can identify. Soon more bodies are drifting ashore. "Soc" Socarides is trying to help Tillie Talbot save her sailing club for her children. Developers and politicians are circling like sharks waiting for her to be forced to sell. They are up against some powerful forces.

Other books you might like:
Rick Boyer, *The Whale's Footprints*, 1988
Philip R. Craig, *The Woman Who Walked into the Sea*, 1991
Ken Grissom, *Big Fish*, 1991
Douglas Kiker, *Death Below Deck*, 1991
John Walter Putre, *Death Among the Angels*, 1991

905
Paul Kemprecos
Neptune's Eye (New York: Bantam, 1991)
Series: Aristotle Socarides
Story type: Private Detective—Male Lead
Major character(s): Aristotle "Soc" Socarides, Detective—Private, Fisherman (scuba diver)
Time period(s): 1990s
Locale(s): Cape Cod, Massachusetts

What the book is about: Soc is hired by wealthy Frederick Walther to find his daughter Leslie who has been missing for a month. After Soc interviews Leslie's employer, Dr. Drake, Drake is murdered. Does the murder have anything to do with Leslie's disappearance or the search for a fortune in sunken treasure?

Other books you might like:
Philip R. Craig, *A Beautiful Place to Die*, 1989
Ken Grissom, *Drop-Off*,
Doug Hornig, *Deep Dive*, 1988
W.R. Philbrick, *The Crystal Blue Persuasion*, 1988
John Walter Purtre, *Down Among the Angels*, 1991

906
Jerry Kennealy
Beggar's Choice (New York: St. Martin's, 1994)
Series: Nick Polo
Story type: Private Detective—Male Lead
Major character(s): Nick Polo, Detective—Private
Time period(s): 1990s
Locale(s): San Francisco, California

What the book is about: Nick Polo knows Scratchy as a vagrant who is a cut above the usual homeless person, so when he asks Polo to check a few license plates for him, Polo agrees. Soon after, Scratchy is killed in a hit-and-run. Polo is suspicious and is soon involved with a powerful local politician and the Chinese mafia. What was their connection to a man who made a living begging for change?

Other books you might like:
David Berlinski, *A Clean Sweep*, 1993
Bill Crider, *When Old Men Die*, 1994
Stephen Greenleaf, *Blood Type*, 1992
John T. Lescroart, *Dead Irish*, 1990
Bill Pronzini, *The Nameless Detective Series*, 1971-

907
Jerry Kennealy
Special Delivery (New York: St. Martin's, 1992)
Series: Nick Polo
Story type: Private Detective—Male Lead
Major character(s): Nick Polo, Detective—Private
Time period(s): 1990s
Locale(s): San Francisco, California; London, England

What the book is about: An old friend of Polo's, Raymond Singh, asks him to deliver a package - a check, a letter and a tape cassette - to a cousin in London. This sounds easy so Nick agrees, but it becomes difficult when the cousin is nowhere to be found and seems to be actively discouraging anyone who is looking for him. Then Nick becomes a suspect in a murder.

Other books you might like:
William Babula, *The St. John Series*, 1988-
John T. Lescroart, *Dead Irish*, 1990
Bill Pronzini, *The Nameless Detective Series*, 1971-
Shelley Singer, *The Jake Samson Series*, 1983-
Mike Weiss, *The Ben Henry Series*, 1987-

908
Jerry Kennealy
Vintage Polo (New York: St. Martin's, 1993)

Series: Nick Polo

Story type: Private Detective—Male Lead

Major character(s): Nick Polo, Detective—Private; Jane Tobin, Journalist (Nick's sometime lover)

Time period(s): 1990s

Locale(s): Napa Valley, California

What the book is about: Jane asks Nick to accompany her to a party introducing Baroni Sparkling Wine, located in the Napa Valley. The festivities are interrupted by a fire that proves to be arson. Baroni, Sr. hires Polo to find out who is trying to ruin him and his son. Polo finds that a bitter ex-wife, mysterious financiers, and local gangsters all seem to be interested in the winery, and none of them want Polo to find the truth.

Other books you might like:
Linda Barnes, *Bitter Finish*, 1983
Judith Garwood, *Make Friends with Murder*, 1992
John T. Lescroart, *The Dismas Hardy Series*, 1991-
A.E. Maxwell, *Gatsby's Vineyard*, 1987
Bill Pronzini, *The Nameless Detective Series*, 1971-

909

Charles Kenney
Hammurabi's Code (New York: Simon & Schuster, 1995)

Story type: Police Procedural—Male Lead; Psychological Suspense

Major character(s): Frank Cronin, Journalist (investigative reporter); Thomas McCormick, Police Officer; Susan Sloan, Lawyer

Time period(s): 1990s

Locale(s): Boston, Massachusetts

What the book is about: Philip Stewart, beloved local politician, has been murdered in his home. Viewed as a saint by most, obviously someone thought differently. As one of the best crime reporters in the country, Frank Cronin is assigned to the story. An old friend, Thomas McCormick, is in charge of the investigation for the police, and an ex-lover, Susan Sloan, is representing the District Attorney's Office. What these three discover is that many people may have had reason to kill Stewart, who was more devil than saint. First mystery.

Other books you might like:
Michael Connelly, *The Concrete Blonde*, 1993
Ruby Horansky, *Dead Center*, 1994
David L. Lindsey, *An Absence of Light*, 1994
Mary Willis Walker, *The Red Scream*, 1994
Minette Walters, *The Sculptress*, 1993

910

Bill Kent
Down by the Sea (New York: St. Martin's, 1993)

Series: Louis Monroe

Story type: Police Procedural—Male Lead

Major character(s): Louis Monroe, Police Officer (detective, vice)

Time period(s): 1990s

Locale(s): Atlantic City, New Jersey

What the book is about: Louis Monroe has just busted a fellow officer and old enemy, Reuben "Roo" Claymore for drug dealing. When Roo offers to turn informant, a chain reaction of double-crossing, deceit and violence is started involving Louis, his fiancee—a reformed and very pregnant hooker, Fatsie Morgan—a 360 pound madam, Raymond Deegan—the dirtiest cop in America, and the corrupt police brass and city politicians.

Other books you might like:
James Colbert, *Skinny Man*, 1991
Michael Connelly, *The Black Ice*, 1993
Thomas H. Cook, *Streets of Fire*, 1989
Jon A. Jackson, *Grootka*, 1990
Stephen Solomita, *A Piece of the Action*, 1992

911

Michael Kenyon
Kill the Butler! (New York: St. Martin's, 1992)

Series: Inspector Peckover

Story type: Police Procedural—Male Lead

Major character(s): Henry Peckover, Police Officer (detective chief inspector)

Time period(s): 1990s

Locale(s): Dunehampton, New York

What the book is about: Lou Langley has been killed by a hit-and-run driver while mowing his lawn. Since Langley was a multi-millionaire, the police are suspicious and request Scotland Yard to lend them someone to go undercover at the Langley estate as a butler. Who else should be picked but Henry Peckover, the "Bard of the Yard"

Other books you might like:
Catherine Aird, *The Body Politic*, 1991
Ruth Dudley Edwards, *Clubbed to Death*, 1992
Colin Watson, *The Inspector Purbright Series*, 1958-1982
R.D. Wingfield, *The Frost Series*, 1984

912

Michael Kenyon
Peckover Joins the Choir (New York: St. Martin's, 1994)

Series: Inspector Peckover

Story type: Police Procedural—Male Lead

Major character(s): Henry Peckover, Police Officer (detective chief inspector); Jason Twitty, Police Officer (detective constable)

Time period(s): 1990s

Locale(s): Sealeigh, England

What the book is about: Henry Peckover, the "Bard of the Yard," is back undercover again. This time he, and the less than indomitable Constable Twitty, are assigned to join the Sealeigh Choral Society as they go on tour. Everywhere the group tours, it seems, priceless religious artifacts are stolen, Just as Peckover thinks he may die of boredom listening to the choral members rambling, one of them shows up dead.

913 · Kerr

Other books you might like:
Catherine Aird, *The Inspector Sloane Series*, 1966-
M.C. Beaton, *The Hamish MacBeth Series*, 1985-
Leo Bruce, *The Sergeant Beef Series*, 1937-1952
Ruth Dudley Edwards, *Clubbed to Death*, 1992
R.D. Wingfield, *The Frost Series*, 1984-

913
Philip Kerr
Dead Meat (New York: Mysterious, 1994)

Story type: Police Procedural—Male Lead

Major character(s): Yevgeni Ivanovitch Grushko, Police Officer (criminal services department); Anonymous, Lawyer (Moscow investigator; narrator)

Time period(s): 1990s

Locale(s): St. Petersburg, Russia

What the book is about: After the breakup of the Soviet Union, the black market flourished and was the cause of the rise of a criminal organization known as the Russian Mafia. Colonel Grushko is the acknowledged expert on the mafia. He knows that the killing of a famous journalist and a Georgian gangster may cause a gang war between the various factions. Can he solve the crime and control the escalating violence?

Other books you might like:
Robert Cullen, *Soviet Sources*, 1993
Stuart M. Kaminsky, *The Inspector Rostnikov Series*, 1984-
Anthony Olcott, *Murder at the Red October*, 1981
Martin Cruz Smith, *Polar Star*, 1992

914
Philip Kerr
The Pale Criminal (New York: Viking, 1990)

Series: Bernie Gunther

Story type: Private Detective—Male Lead; Historical

Major character(s): Bernie Gunther, Detective—Private

Time period(s): 1930s (1938)

Locale(s): Berlin, Germany

What the book is about: A widow hires Gunther to find out who is blackmailing her. At the same time he gets involved with a serial killer who is stalking the streets of Berlin.

Other books you might like:
Jack Gerson, *Death's Head Berlin*, 1989
Ian McEwan, *The Innocent*, 1989
R.D. Zimmerman, *Deadfall in Berlin*, 1990

915
William X. Kienzle
Chameleon (New York: Andrews and McMeel, 1991)

Series: Father Koesler

Story type: Amateur Detective—Male Lead

Major character(s): Robert Koesler, Religious (priest); Alonzo "Zoo" Tully, Police Officer (lieutenant)

Time period(s): 1990s

Locale(s): Detroit, Michigan

What the book is about: When three people with close ties to the church are targeted for murder, Lt. Tully asks Father Koesler to help him with the cases, which seem to be for revenge tied to canon law.

Other books you might like:
Andrew M. Greeley, *Virgin and Martyr*, 1985
Harry Kemelman, *The Rabbi Small Series*, 1964-
William F. Love, *The Chartreuse Clue*, 1990
Ralph McInerny, *Second Vespers*, 1980
Jack Webb, *The Bad Blonde*, 1956

916
William X. Kienzle
Masquerade (New York: Andrews & McMeel, 1990)

Series: Father Koesler

Story type: Amateur Detective—Male Lead

Major character(s): Robert Koesler, Religious (priest)

Time period(s): 1980s

Locale(s): Detroit, Michigan

What the book is about: Murder at a writer's conference, where all the participants are authors of murder mysteries.

Other books you might like:
Andrew M. Greeley, *Happy Are Those Who Thirst for Justice*, 1987
Isabelle Holland, *A Fatal Advent*, 1989
Leonard Holton, *The Father Bredder Series*, (1959-1977)
Harry Kemelman, *The Rabbi Small Series*, (1964-)
Ralph McInerny, *The Father Dowling Series*, (1977-)

917
Karen Kijewski
Alley Kat Blues (New York: Doubleday, 1995)

Series: Kat Colorado

Story type: Private Detective—Female Lead

Major character(s): Kat Colorado, Detective—Private; Hank Parker, Police Officer (sergeant, homicide)

Time period(s): 1990s

Locale(s): Sacramento, California; Las Vegas, Nevada

What the book is about: Kat is in emotional turmoil. Her latest case has her investigating a young woman whose death in a traffic accident might have been deliberate. Kat is already involved as it was she who first found and reported the accident. She finds that Courtney, the deceased, was raised as a devout Mormon but had recently left the church, making several people very unhappy. Meanwhile Kat's boyfriend, Las Vegas detective Hank Parker, seems to be getting too deeply involved in his hunt for a serial killer and she feels she is losing him.

Other books you might like:
Linda Barnes, *The Carlotta Carlyle Series*, 1987-
Catherine Dain, *The Freddie O'Neal Series*, 1992-
Sue Grafton, *The Kinsey Millhone Series*, 1982-
Marcia Muller, *The Sharon McCone Series*, 1977-
Maxine O'Callaghan, *The Delilah West Series*, 1980-

918
Karen Kijewski
Copy Kat (New York: Doubleday, 1992)
Series: Kat Colorado
Story type: Private Detective—Female Lead
Major character(s): Kat Colorado, Detective—Private
Time period(s): 1990s
Locale(s): Nevada City, California; Sacramento, California
What the book is about: Diedre Durkin was killed in an apparent robbery-homicide. Her godfather hires Kat to find out the truth. The gossip in town says that Diedre's husband may have killed her. Kat jumps at the opportunity to go undercover as Kate Collins because she is trying to escape her own past. As she talks to people she realizes Diedre was many things to many people and they may all have had reason to kill her.
Other books you might like:
Linda Barnes, *The Carlotta Carlyle Series*, 1987-
Sue Grafton, *The Kinsey Millhone Series*, 1982-
Linda Grant, *The Catherine Saylor Series*, 1988-
Marcia Muller, *The Sharon McCone Series*, 1977-
Sara Paretsky, *The V.I. Warshawski Series*, 1982-

919
Karen Kijewski
Katapult (New York: St. Martins, 1990)
Series: Kat Colorado
Story type: Private Detective—Female Lead
Major character(s): Kat Colorado, Detective—Private
Time period(s): 1990s
Locale(s): Sacramento, California
What the book is about: Kat's cousin Johnny is murdered and his sister Michaela has disappeared. Kat investigates and becomes involved with a teenage hooker, Lindy.
Other books you might like:
Linda Barnes, *A Trouble of Fools*, 1987
Sue Grafton, *#A Is for Alibi*, 1982
Linda Grant, *Random Access Murder*, 1988
Marcia Muller, *Edwin of the Iron Shoes*, 1977
Sara Paretsky, *Indemnity Only*, 1982

920
Karen Kijewski
Katwalk (New York: St. Martin's, 1989)
Series: Kat Colorado
Story type: Private Detective—Female Lead
Major character(s): Kat Colorado, Detective—Private; Charity Collins, Journalist (advice columnist)
Time period(s): 1980s
Locale(s): Sacramento, California
What the book is about: Kat Colorado is asked by her friend, Charity Collins, to look into the missing $200,000 that Charity's husband supposedly gambled away. First book.

Other books you might like:
Linda Barnes, *A Trouble of Fools*, 1988
Robert J. Bowman, *The House of Blue Lights*, 1987
Sue Grafton, *The Kinsey Millhone Series*, (1982-)
Marcia Muller, *The Sharon McCone Series*, (1977-)
Sara Paretsky, *The V.I. Warshawski Series*, (1982-)

921
Karen Kijewski
Wild Kat (New York: Doubleday, 1994)
Series: Kat Colorado
Story type: Private Detective—Female Lead
Major character(s): Kat Colorado, Detective—Private
Time period(s): 1990s
Locale(s): Sacramento, California
What the book is about: After Kat Colorado pulls Jude Hudson from a burning car, Jude hires her to protect his wife Amanda, who has been receiving death threats after blowing the whistle on the company for which she works for manufacturing a faulty heart valve. Jude is sure the car wreck was no accident, but a deliberate attempt to silence Amanda. Kat does her best and foils one attempt, but then Amanda dies in another strange "accident."
Other books you might like:
Linda Barnes, *The Carlotta Carlyle Series*, 1987-
Catherine Dain, *The Freddie O'Neal Series*, 1992-
Janet Dawson, *The Jeri Howard Series*, 1990-
Sue Grafton, *The Kinsey Millhone Series*, 1982-
Linda Grant, *The Catherine Saylor Series*, 1988-

922
Douglas Kiker
Death Below Deck (New York: Random, 1991)
Series: Mac MacFarland
Story type: Amateur Detective—Male Lead
Major character(s): Mac MacFarland, Journalist (retired); Bitsy Binford, Businesswoman (TV station/newspaper owner)
Time period(s): 1990s
Locale(s): Cape Cod, Massachusetts
What the book is about: Mac is summoned to the Cape Cod compound of old friend and colleague Bitsy Binford. It seems that her son-in-law is dead, an apparent suicide. She wants Mac to find out the truth behind his death though this may force her family into some painful revelations.
Other books you might like:
Rick Boyer, *The Penny Ferry*, 1984
Philip R. Craig, *A Beautiful Place to Die*, 1990
Jeremiah Healy, *Yesterday's News*, 1989
John R. Riggs, *The Garth Ryland Series*, 1984
William G. Tapply, *Spotted Cats*, 1991

923
D. Kincaid
A Lawyer's Tale (New York: Random House, 1992)

Series: Harry Cain
Story type: Legal
Major character(s): Harry Cain, Lawyer
Time period(s): 1990s
Locale(s): Los Angeles, California
What the book is about: Harry Cain is a very high priced lawyer who never loses and is known as the "Sunset Bomber" for his tactics in and out of court. Now he is involved in a contempt of court charge stemming from the theft of a 40 million dollar film, he is defending a wife accused of murdering her husband and he is trying to protect a woman from being blackmailed over her erotic library.
Other books you might like:
J.P. Hailey, *The Steve Winslow Series*, 1988-
Richard Harris, *Honor Bound*, 1982
Joe L. Hensley, *The Don Roback Series*, 1974-
John Mortimer, *The Rumpole Series*, 1980-
Grif Stockley, *Expert Testimony*, 1991

924
Laurie R. King
The Beekeeper's Apprentice (New York: St. Martin's, 1994)
Series: Mary Russell/Sherlock Holmes
Story type: Historical
Major character(s): Mary Russell, Student; Sherlock Holmes, Detective—Private
Time period(s): 1900s (1915)
Locale(s): England (London, Oxford, and Sussex)
What the book is about: Mary Russell is walking in the Sussex countryside when she almost steps on a middle-aged man studying bees. She soon realizes that it is Sherlock Holmes. Holmes, much to his astonishment, recognizes that this young girl has a mind every bit the equal of his own. She becomes Holmes' apprentice and learns all that he can teach. Eventually they find themselves pitted against a criminal mastermind reminiscent of the evil Moriarty.
Other books you might like:
Abbey Penn Baker, *In the Dead of Winter*, 1994
Carole Nelson Douglas, *The Irene Adler Series*, 1990-
Mark Frost, *The List of 7*, 1993
Marian J.A. Jackson, *The Abigail Danforth Series*, 1990-

925
Laurie R. King
A Grave Talent (New York: St. Martins, 1993)
Series: Kate Martinelli
Story type: Police Procedural—Female Lead
Major character(s): Kate Martinelli, Police Officer, Lesbian; Alonzo Hawkin, Police Officer (Kate's partner)
Time period(s): 1990s
Locale(s): San Francisco, California
What the book is about: Alonzo Hawkins is assigned Casey Martinelli as a partner to investigate three child murders centered around an artist's community outside of San Francisco. Vaun Adams seems the perfect suspect. Once convicted of murdering a child, now secretive and reclusive, she may be the perfect suspect but is she the killer? First mystery. Edgar winner for best first novel.
Other books you might like:
Susan Dunlap, *The Jill Smith Series*, 1981-
Margaret Maron, *The Sigrid Harald Series*, 1981-
Mary Morell, *Final Session*, 1990
Julie Smith, *New Orleans Mourning*, 1990
Charlene Weir, *The Winter Widow*, 1992

926
Laurie R. King
A Monstrous Regiment of Women (New York: St. Martin's, 1995)
Series: Mary Russell/Sherlock Holmes
Story type: Amateur Detective—Female Lead; Historical
Major character(s): Mary Russell, Student; Sherlock Holmes, Aged Person, Detective—Private (former)
Time period(s): 1920s (1920)
Locale(s): London, England
What the book is about: Having just finished her studies at Oxford, Mary is off to London where a chance meeting with a friend involves her with the New Temple of God, a feminist group of theologians and social activists. The leader is Margery Childe, a charismatic sort who seems to attract young, wealthy women to her inner circle. Since Mary is about to come into her inheritance she finds herself in the inner circle and involved in murder. She also gets Holmes involved and finds her feelings toward him becoming confused.
Other books you might like:
Abbey Penn Baker, *In the Dead of Winter*, 1994
Carole Nelson Douglas, *Good Night, Mr. Holmes*, 1990
Mark Frost, *The List of 7*, 1993
William Hjortsberg, *Nevermore*, 1994
Sena Jeter Nasland, *Sherlock in Love*, 1993

927
Laurie R. King
To Play the Fool (New York: St. Martin's, 1995)
Series: Kate Martinelli
Story type: Police Procedural—Female Lead
Major character(s): Kate Martinelli, Police Officer, Lesbian; Alonzo Hawkin, Police Officer (Kate's partner)
Time period(s): 1990s
Locale(s): San Francisco, California

What the book is about: Three weeks ago the homeless folks of Golden Gate Park had a funeral for a beloved stray dog. It was such a success, they decided to repeat it. But this time it's the funeral of a murdered homeless man. Kate and Al are assigned the case, but Kate is still suffering from their last case, which left her lover in a wheelchair. One of the prime suspects is Brother Erasmus, a strange man who speaks only in quotations from the Bible. Is he the killer, a witness, or just a poor fool?

Other books you might like:
Susan Dunlap, *The Jill Smith Series*, 1981-
Katherine V. Forrest, *The Kate Delafield Series*, 1984-
Mary Morel, *The Lucia Ramos Series*, 1991-
Sandra Scoppettone, *The Lauren Laurano Series*, 1991-
Julie Smith, *The Skip Langdon Series*, 1990-

928
Kate Kingsbury
Check-out Time (New York: Berkley, 1995)
Series: Pennyfoot Hotel
Story type: Amateur Detective—Female Lead; Historical
Major character(s): Cecily Sinclair, Hotel Owner
Time period(s): 1900s (1908)
Locale(s): Badger's End, England

What the book is about: A heat wave in London has caused business to boom at the Pennyfoot Hotel. The female help and many of the guests are swooning, not from the heat, but from the handsome new doorman. Then Sir Richard Milton, an aristocratic but thoroughly disagreeable guest plunges to his death from a balcony. It is doubtful that he would commit suicide—how could the world do without him?—so it must have been an accident—or murder.

Other books you might like:
Ann Crowleigh, *Clively Close: Dead as Dead Can Be*, 1993
Gillian Linscott, *The Nell Bray Series*, 1991
Amy Myers, *The August Didier Series*, 1992-
Anne Perry, *The Thomas and Charlotte Pitt Series*, 1979-
Elizabeth Peters, *The Amelia Peabody Series*, 1974-

929
Kate Kingsbury
Eat, Drink and Be Buried (New York: Berkley, 1994)
Series: Pennyfoot Hotel
Story type: Amateur Detective—Female Lead; Historical
Major character(s): Cecily Sinclair, Hotel Owner
Time period(s): 1900s (1908)
Locale(s): Badger's End, England

What the book is about: The Boscombes are having a family gathering at the Pennyfoot Hotel. During the night Lady Sherbourne goes missing and is found dead and tied to a Maypole. The only witness is a drunken colonel who swears he saw a headless horseman in the vicinity. The police are trying to blame the local Gypsies but Cecily thinks not and sets out to find the truth.

Other books you might like:
Emily Brightwell, *The Mrs. Jeffries Series*, 1993-
Ann Crowleigh, *Clively Close: Dead as Dead Can Be*, 1993
Alanna Knight, *The Inspector Faro Series*, 1989-
Peter Lovesey, *The Prince of Wales Series*, 1988-
Anne Perry, *The Thomas and Charlotte Pitt Series*, 1979-

930
Kate Kingsbury
Room with a Clue (New York: Jove, 1993)
Series: Pennyfoot Hotel
Story type: Amateur Detective—Female Lead; Historical
Major character(s): Cecily Sinclair, Hotel Owner
Time period(s): 1900s (1906)
Locale(s): Badger's End, England

What the book is about: Badger's End has become a fashionable place to take a holiday and the Pennyfoot Hotel is quite popular, but there are problems such as jewelry thefts, a missing 18-foot python and the dead body in the courtyard. What seems like an accident is really a carefully planned murder of the universally disliked Lady Danbury. It's up to Cecily Sinclair to solve the murder and restore the reputation of her hotel. First novel.

Other books you might like:
Carole Nelson Douglas, *The Irene Adler Series*, 1990-
Marian J.A. Jackson, *The Abigail Danforth Series*, 1990-
Gillian Linscott, *Sister Beneath the Sheet*, 1991
Anne Perry, *Belgrave Square*, 1992
Elizabeth Peters, *The Amelia Peabody Series*, 1974-

931
Mary Kittredge
Desperate Remedy (New York: St. Martin's, 1993)
Series: Edwina Crusoe
Story type: Private Detective—Female Lead
Major character(s): Edwina Crusoe, Detective—Private, Nurse; Martin McIntyre, Police Officer (retired; husband of Edwina)
Time period(s): 1990s
Locale(s): New Haven, Connecticut

What the book is about: Edwina Crusoe is pregnant and so has temporarily given up investigating, but she still wants to help an old friend as a nurse. While she is at the hospital a doctor and his wife are brought in, both victims of gunshots in separate incidents. The wife dies but the husband is still alive. That night a nurse is killed in another attempt on the doctor's life. Edwina is dragged into the case by nervous hospital administrators.

Other books you might like:
Jo Bailey, *Bagged*, 1992
Eileen Dreyer, *A Man to Die For*, 1991
Christine Green, *Deadly Errand*, 1992
Janet McGiffin, *Prescription for Death*, 1993
C.F. Roe, *A Nasty Bit of Murder*, 1992

932
Mary Kittredge
Kill or Cure (New York: St. Martin's, 1995)
Series: Edwina Crusoe
Story type: Private Detective—Female Lead
Major character(s): Edwina Crusoe, Detective—Private, Nurse
Time period(s): 1990s
Locale(s): New Haven, Connecticut
What the book is about: Young Gerry Bailey is rushed to the hospital by his mother for breathing difficulty due, she thinks, to an allergic reaction. But the doctors discover that he has been shot. When a young doctor at the hospital shoots a security guard and the nurse who is his wife and attempts to shoot Gerry, Edwina is asked to help in the insanity defense her friend, Ed Chernoff, is being pressured into conducting. As she investigates, Edwina learns more than she wants to know.
Other books you might like:
Jo Bailey, *Bagged*, 1992
Eileen Dreyer, *A Man to Die For*, 1991
Christine Green, *The Kate Kinsella Series*, 1991-
Janet McGiffin, *The Maxene St. Clair Series*, 1992-
C.F. Roe, *The Jean Montrose Series*, 1991-

933
Mary Kittredge
Poison Pen (New York: Walker, 1990)
Series: Charlotte Kent
Story type: Amateur Detective—Female Lead
Major character(s): Charlotte Kent, Editor (magazine editor)
Time period(s): 1990s
Locale(s): New Haven, Connecticut
What the book is about: Charlotte arrives at the office of the magazine she edits to find her star contributor sitting dead at her desk. Accused of the murder is Owen Strathmore, a freelance writer friend of Charlotte's. Owen maintains his innocence, even though he was having an affair with the victim's wife.
Other books you might like:
Joan Hess, *Strangled Prose*, 1986
Sharyn McCrumb, *Sick of Shadows*, 1984
Orania Papazoglou, *Wicked, Loving Murder*, 1985
Nancy Pickard, *Generous Death*, 1984
Gillian Roberts, *Caught Dead in Philadelphia*, 1987

934
Mary Kittredge
Walking Dead Man (New York: St. Martin's, 1992)
Series: Edwina Crusoe
Story type: Amateur Detective—Female Lead; Private Detective—Female Lead
Major character(s): Edwina Crusoe, Detective—Private, Nurse; Michael McIntyre, Police Officer (husband of Edwina)
Time period(s): 1990s
Locale(s): New Haven, Connecticut
What the book is about: Theresa Whitlock wants to hire Edwina to help her protect herself against a dead man - a dead man she had killed. Edwina is about to refuse the case when Theresa hands her a check and runs out. Then Theresa's body is found in the lobby of her office. It may be too late to help Theresa but Edwina is determined to find the killer.
Other books you might like:
Jo Bailey, *Bagged*, 1991
Robin Cook, *Vital Signs*, 1991
Eileen Dreyer, *A Man to Die For*, 1991
Christine Green, *Deadly Errand*, 1992
C.F. Roe, *A Nasty Bit of Murder*, 1992

935
Andrew Klavan
The Animal Hour (New York: Pocket, 1993)
Story type: Psychological Suspense; Action/Adventure
Major character(s): Nancy Kincaid, Office Worker; Oliver Perkins, Writer (poet)
Time period(s): 1990s
Locale(s): New York, New York
What the book is about: When Nancy Kincaid arrives for work one morning, her co-workers don't recognize her. She is also hearing voices and finds a gun in her purse. After shooting a panhandler in the park, she is on the run. Parallel to her story is Oliver Perkins, a poet whose book has the title of *The Animal Hour*, which is also one of the things that Nancy is hearing the voices saying. Oliver is looking for his brother Zach, who has disappeared and may be back on drugs. While looking he finds the mutilated corpse of a young woman. Eventually Oliver and Nancy's paths must cross.
Other books you might like:
Neal Barrett Jr., *Pink Vodka Blues*, 1993
D.L. Flusfeder, *Man Kills Woman*, 1993
Richard Harris, *Enemies*, 1979
Dan Simmons, *Summer of Night*, 1992
Thomas Tryon, *The Night of the Moonbow*, 1989

936
Andrew Klavan
Corruption (New York: Morrow, 1994)
Story type: Amateur Detective—Female Lead; Psychological Suspense
Major character(s): Cyrus Dolittle, Police Officer (sheriff); Sally Dawes, Journalist (bureau chief); Sid Merriwether, Journalist (reporter)
Time period(s): 1990s
Locale(s): New York (upstate)

What the book is about: Sally Dawes, bureau chief of the *Daily Champion*, has been out to get Sheriff Cyrus Dolittle for years, ever since she felt he was trying to cover up the guilty party in a rape case early in her reporting career. Now she may finally have the chance with the death of a realtor who had ties to the sheriff. With the help of reporter Sid Merriwether, who really doesn't want to be there, and over the hill reporter Ernie Rumplemeyer, she expects to find the truth. Then the sheriff's daughter's boyfriend is killed in a drug bust and the daughter turns on her father, though her truths may be different than the reality.

Other books you might like:
Mary Logue, *Still Explosion*, 1993
Margaret Maron, *Bootlegger's Daughter*, 1992
Archer Mayor, *Scent of Evil*, 1992
Sharyn McCrumb, *The Hangman's Beautiful Daughter*, 1992
Stuart Woods, *Grass Roots*, 1989

937
Andrew Klavan
Don't Say a Word (New York: Pocket, 1991)

Story type: Psychological Suspense

Major character(s): Nathan Conrad, Doctor (psychiatrist); Lewis "Sport" McIlvaine, Criminal

Time period(s): 1990s

Locale(s): New York, New York

What the book is about: Why are two psychotics terrorizing Dr. Conrad's family? Is it because they enjoy it? Or is it because the doctor, known as psychiatrist to the damned, has some information they want? Conrad must find out without getting the police involved. Edgar nominee for Best Novel of 1991. Klavan also writes as Keith Peterson.

Other books you might like:
Michael Allegretto, *Night of Reunion*, 1990
Gary Amo, *Silent Night*, 1991
Kate Green, *Night Angel*, 1989
Thomas Harris, *The Silence of the Lambs*, 1988
John Katzenbach, *In the Heat of the Summer*, 1982

938
Zachary Klein
Still Among the Living (New York: Harper, 1990)

Story type: Private Detective—Male Lead

Major character(s): Matt Jacob, Detective—Private

Time period(s): 1990s

Locale(s): Boston, Massachusetts

What the book is about: Matt Jacobs' psychiatrist asks him to look into a break-in at her office. Matt, who wants to do nothing more than lie around stoned and watch television, reluctantly agrees. At the same time his best friend asks for his help in discovering the cause of his wife's nightmares. It appears that the two cases may be related when Jacobs sees his friend's wife going into his psychiatrist's building. First novel.

Other books you might like:
Timothy Harris, *Kyd for Hire*, 1978
Gar Anthony Haywood, *Fear of the Dark*, 1988
Jeremiah Healy, *Blunt Darts*, 1984
W.R. Philbrick, *Shadow Kills*, 1985
Charles Willeford, *Sideswipe*, 1987

939
Zachary Klein
Two Way Toll (New York: Harper, 1991)

Series: Matt Jacob

Story type: Private Detective—Male Lead

Major character(s): Matt Jacob, Detective—Private (former social worker)

Time period(s): 1990s

Locale(s): Boston, Massachusetts

What the book is about: Matt is working mall security when he sees a face out of his past, Emil Porter. He keeps Emil from being busted for shoplifting. Emil wants to hire Matt to find out who is threatening him with involvement in the twenty year old death of Peter Knight. This case will drag Matt back to "The End", Boston's dumping ground for losers, where he was a young social worker.

Other books you might like:
Jerome Doolittle, *Body Scissors*, 1990
Jeremiah Healy, *The John Francis Cuddy Series*, 1985-
Benjamin M. Schutz, *The Leo Haggerty Series*, 1985-
David Stout, *Carolina Skeletons*, 1989
Ned White, *The Very Bad Thing*, 1990

940
Joseph T. Klempner
Felony Murder (New York: St Martin's, 1995)

Story type: Amateur Detective—Male Lead; Legal

Major character(s): Dean Abernathy, Lawyer; Joey Spadafino, Streetperson

Time period(s): 1990s

Locale(s): New York, New York

What the book is about: When the police commissioner dies of an apparent heart attack during a mugging, the police think they have a convenient scapegoat in homeless guy Joey Spadafino, who was robbing the body. But Joey claims he's innocent and refuses to accept a plea bargain. His lawyer, gung-ho attorney Dean Abernathy, begins to find that all is not what it seems to be in the commissioner's death and when he presses the case he soon finds himself and his loved ones in serious danger. First novel.

Other books you might like:
William Bernhardt, *Perfect Justice*, 1994
Robert Daley, *Wall of Brass*, 1994
R.A. Forster, *Keeping Counsel*, 1996
James Neal Harvey, *Flesh and Blood*, 1994
Robert K. Tanenbaum, *Material Witness*, 1994

941
Alanna Knight
Blood Line (New York: St. Martin's, 1989)

Series: Inspector Faro

Story type: Historical

Major character(s): Jeremy Faro, Police Officer (detective inspector)

Time period(s): 19th century

Locale(s): Edinburgh, Scotland

What the book is about: While investigating an apparent murder, Faro ties the death to his own father's death 30 years earlier.

Other books you might like:
D.M. Devine, *The Devil at Your Elbow*, 1967
Richard Falkirk, *Blackstone*, 1973
J.G. Jeffreys, *The Thief Taker*, 1972
Anne Perry, *Silence in Hanover Close*, 1988

942
Alanna Knight
Deadly Beloved (New York: St. Martins, 1990)

Series: Inspector Faro

Story type: Historical; Police Procedural—Male Lead

Major character(s): Jeremy Faro, Detective—Police (detective inspector); Vincent Laurie, Doctor (Faro's stepson)

Time period(s): 19th century

Locale(s): Edinburgh, Scotland

What the book is about: Inspector Faro and Vincent attend a dinner party given by police doctor Keller and his wife Mabel. The next day Mabel leaves for Berwick but she never arrives. After two weeks her fur and a carving knife are found, both stained with blood.

Other books you might like:
Richard Grayson, *The Murders at Impasse Louvain*, 1979
Ray Harrison, *Death of an Honourable Member*, 1984
J.G. Jeffreys, *The Thief Taker*, 1972
Peter Lovesey, *Abracadaver*, 1972
Anne Perry, *The Cater Street Hangman*, 1979

943
Alanna Knight
Killing Cousins (New York: St. Martin's, 1992)

Series: Inspector Faro

Story type: Historical; Police Procedural

Major character(s): Jeremy Faro, Police Officer (detective inspector); Vincent Laurie, Doctor (Faro's Stepson)

Time period(s): 1870s (1878)

Locale(s): Orkney Islands, Scotland

What the book is about: Vincent receives a letter from a classmate, Francis Balfray, telling about his wife's illness and asking for help. As Faro's mother is now Balfray's housekeeper they both decide to visit but Faro is detained. He arrives at Balfray's mansion on the Orkney Islands just in time for the wife's funeral. Vincent is convinced it was not a natural death but arsenic poisoning. When another person is killed, Faro knows he is up against a smart and vicious murderer.

Other books you might like:
M.C. Beaton, *The Hamish MacBeth Series*, 1985-
Richard Grayson, *The Inspector Gautier Series*, 1979-
Ray Harrison, *The Bragg and Morton Series*, 1984-
Bill Knox, *The Colin Thane Series*, 1958-
Anne Perry, *The Thomas and Charlotte Pitt Series*, 1979-

944
Kathryn Lasky Knight
Dark Swan (New York: St. Martin's, 1994)

Series: Calista Jacobs

Story type: Amateur Detective—Female Lead

Major character(s): Calista Jacobs, Artist (children's book illustrator); Charley Jacobs, Child (Calista's son)

Time period(s): 1990s

Locale(s): Boston, Massachusetts

What the book is about: Calista Jacobs and her son, Charley, are staying on Beacon Hill while their own house is being remodeled. One of their neighbors, Quintana "Queenie" Kinsley, has a beautiful garden that Calista is using as a model for her illustrations. It is a shock when Calista finds Queenie's dead body. Calista becomes involved with a Boston aristocratic family—a family that has a sense of service to the community, but also seems to have a history of scandal and bizarre behavior.

Other books you might like:
Susan Wittig Albert, *The China Bayles Series*, 1992-
Susan Kelly, *The Liz Connors Series*, 1986-
Marlys Millhiser, *Murder at Moot Point*, 1992
Triss Stein, *Murder at the Class Reunion*, 1993
Kerry Tucker, *The Libby Kincaid Series*, 1991-

945
Kathryn Lasky Knight
Mortal Words (New York: Summit, 1990)

Series: Calista Jacobs

Story type: Amateur Detective—Female Lead

Major character(s): Calista Jacobs, Artist (children's book illustrator), Widow(er); Charley Jacobs, Child (Calista's son)

Time period(s): 1990s

Locale(s): Boston, Massachusetts

What the book is about: After appearing with two others on a panel at a children's literature conference Calista and later the other panelists are the victims of vicious pranks, resulting in one murder. Are the three incidents connected? Do the fundamentalists protesters have anything to do with what is happening? Or are the pranks only a cover for something much more deadly?

Other books you might like:
Rochelle Majer Krich, *Where's Mommy Now?*, 1990
Janet LaPierre, *Children's Games*, 1989
Dick Lochte, *Laughing Dog*, 1986
Nancy Pickard, *Say No to Murder*, 1985
Gillian Roberts, *Caught Dead in Philadelphia*, 1987

946
Phyllis Knight
Shattered Rhythms (New York: St. Martin's, 1994)

Series: Lil Ritchie

Story type: Private Detective—Female Lead

Major character(s): Lillian Ritchie, Detective—Private, Musician (singer and guitarist)

Time period(s): 1990s

Locale(s): Portland, Maine

What the book is about: Lil Ritchie is a musician and jazz lover. She is hired to find Andre Ledoux, the brilliant but haunted jazz guitarist. She quickly finds him but he tells her he disappeared because someone had drugged him after he finally kicked his habit and he was afraid. He seems to know more but doesn't want to discuss it. Soon Andre is dead and Lil wants to know who could silence his great talent.

Other books you might like:
Lauren Wright Douglas, *Ninth Life*, 1990
Laurie R. King, *A Grave Talent*, 1993
Randye Lordon, *Brotherly Love*, 1993
Sandra Scoppettone, *The Lauren Laurano Series*, 1991-
Eve Zaremba, *Work for a Million*, 1986

947
Phyllis Knight
Switching the Odds (New York: St. Martin's, 1992)

Series: Lil Ritchie

Story type: Private Detective—Female Lead

Major character(s): Lillian Ritchie, Detective—Private, Musician (singer and guitarist)

Time period(s): 1990s

Locale(s): Maine (Down East)

What the book is about: Lil is hired by James Cooper, a real estate developer from Richmond, to find his son who may have run off to Maine to find his grandfather. Lil finds the boy, Jesse, but the case is just starting because Jesse was a witness to a murder committed by his father's partner. When he was threatened he ran away. Now Lil vows to protect the boy, but to do this she will have to deal with a vicious killer. First novel.

Other books you might like:
Susan Baker, *My First Murder*, 1989
Elisabeth Bowers, *No Forwarding Address*, 1991
Marcia Muller, *Eye of the Storm*, 1988
Pat Welch, *Murder by the Book*, 1990
Barbara Wilson, *Sisters of the Road*, 1986

948
Bill Knox (Pseudonym of Robert MacLeod and Michael Kirk)
The Interface Man (New York: Doubleday, 1990)

Series: Superintendent Thane

Story type: Police Procedural—Male Lead

Major character(s): Colin Thane, Police Officer (superintendent)

Time period(s): 1980s

Locale(s): Glasgow, Scotland

What the book is about: After a computer thief slips through their fingers, Superintendent Thane and his crime squad must go high-tech to catch him.

Other books you might like:
M.C. Beaton, *Death of a Gossip*, 1985
Alan Hunter, *The Scottish Decision*, 1981
William McIlvanney, *Laidlaw*, 1977
Peter Turnbull, *Dead Knock*, 1983

949
Vince Kohler
Banjo Boy (New York: St. Martin's, 1994)

Series: Eldon Larkin

Story type: Amateur Detective—Male Lead

Major character(s): Eldon Larkin, Journalist (reporter); Melissa Lafky, Lawyer (deputy district attorney)

Time period(s): 1970s (1979)

Locale(s): Oregon (south coast)

What the book is about: Eldon Larkin is covering the murder of Archie Loris, 500 pounds of pimp and pornographer who thought he was an artist. The police aren't trying too hard to solve the case, so D.A. Melissa Lafky bets Eldon that if he solves the case she will sleep with him. Talk about motivation. Eldon finds that Archie was in trouble with the Chicago "bent-nose boys" and was working with local gambling interests. With the help of an odd group of sources Eldon tries to win the bet. But he may not live to collect.

Other books you might like:
Carl Hiaasen, *Double Whammy*, 1987
M.S. Karl, *Deerslayer*, 1991
Douglas Kiker, *Murder on Clam Pond*, 1986
Thomas Perry, *Metzger's Dog*, 1984
Stephen F. Wilcox, *The NIMBY Factor*, 1992

950
Vince Kohler
Rainy North Woods (New York: St. Martin's, 1990)

Story type: Amateur Detective—Male Lead

Major character(s): Eldon Larkin, Journalist (reporter); Shelly Sherwood, Journalist (reporter)

Time period(s): 1980s

Locale(s): Port Jerome, Oregon

951 Kohler

What the book is about: Interest in the story of Hector the elephant crushing a poor immigrant causes both Eldon and Shelly to rush headlong into danger—because there's more to this story then just Hector. First book.

Other books you might like:
Lilian Jackson Braun, *The Cat Who Series*, (1967-)
Sean Hanlon, *The Cold Front*, 1989
Douglas Kiker, *Death at the Cut*, 1988
Keith Peterson, *The Rain*, 1989

951
Vince Kohler
Rising Dog (New York: St. Martin's, 1992)

Series: Eldon Larkin

Story type: Amateur Detective—Male Lead

Major character(s): Eldon Larkin, Journalist (reporter)

Time period(s): 1970s (1979)

Locale(s): Port Jerome, Oregon

What the book is about: Eldon is called to write a story on a faith healer who claims to have resurrected his dog. While talking to the healer, he becomes involved with an environmentalist who chains himself to trees, a beautiful woman who likes riding horses topless (the woman, not the horses), a born-again Finn, and more. Then the dog, while digging in a nearby landfill, discovers a mummified foot.

Other books you might like:
Noreen Gilpatrick, *The Piano Man*, 1991
Carl Hiaasen, *Double Whammy*, 1987
M.S. Karl, *Killer's Ink*, 1988
Douglas Kiker, *Death at the Cut*, 1988
Bernie Lee, *Murder without Reservation*, 1991

952
Todd Komarnicki
Free (New York: Doubleday, 1993)

Story type: Psychological Suspense; Action/Adventure

Major character(s): Jefferson "Free" Freeman, Streetperson; Agatha Li, Police Officer

Locale(s): New Orleans, Louisiana; Hong Kong

What the book is about: Free has heard voices in his head ever since an accident. Now he's a homeless person involved in a series of murders. First he finds the body of a Chinese man with two bullet holes and a cueball in his mouth. Another Chinese man is killed and then his stripper friend. They all have a red fleur-de-lis tattoo. Free tells all to detective Agatha Li and they end up investigating together. But more deaths follow. First novel.

Other books you might like:
George Dawes Green, *The Caveman's Valentine*, 1994
James W. Hall, *Hard Aground*, 1993
Randy Russell, *Hot Wire*, 1988
Sin Soracco, *Edge City*, 1992
Don Winslow, *The Trail to Buddha's Mirror*, 1992

953
Rochelle Majer Krich
Angel of Death (New York: Mysterious, 1994)

Series: Jessica Drake

Story type: Police Procedural—Female Lead

Major character(s): Jessica Drake, Police Officer, Detective—Homicide

Time period(s): 1990s

Locale(s): Los Angeles, California

What the book is about: Although a homicide detective, Jessica Drake is assigned to investigate the threats to Barry Lewis and his family. This is a high profile case and her boss needs Jessie's ability to deal with the media. Lewis is Jewish and is defending the rights of a neo-nazi group to celebrate Hitler's birthday. Many in the Jewish community feel he is a traitor. The case eventually becomes a homicide investigation.

Other books you might like:
Eleanor Taylor Bland, *Dead Time*, 1992
Faye Kellerman, *Sacred and Profane*, 1987
Carol O'Connell, *Mallory's Oracle*, 1994
April Smith, *North of Montana*, 1994
Julie Smith, *New Orleans Mourning*, 1990

954
Rochelle Majer Krich
Fair Game (New York: Mysterious, 1993)

Series: Jessica Drake

Story type: Police Procedural—Female Lead

Major character(s): Jessica Drake, Police Officer, Detective—Homicide

Time period(s): 1990s

Locale(s): Los Angeles, California

What the book is about: Jessie Drake's sister and nephew are visiting, and there seems to be more going on than her sister will admit. Jessie has been assigned a case that has an odd twist—an unknown cause of death and a bank deposit slip pinned to the body. When Jessie asks about other similar cases she finds five deaths in all. First dismissed as the results of natural causes, the deaths are now found to be poisonings.

Other books you might like:
Eleanor Taylor Bland, *Dead Time*, 1992
David L. Lindsey, *Mercy*, 1990
Margaret Maron, *The Sigrid Harald Series*, 1982-
Lillian O'Donnell, *The Kate Mulcahaney Series*, 1979-
James Schermerhorn, *Night of the Cat*, 1993

955
Rochelle Majer Krich
Till Death Do Us Part (New York: Avon, 1992)

Story type: Psychological Suspense

Major character(s): Deena Vogler, Student (law student; Orthodox Jew); Sam Ryker, Police Officer (homicide detective)

Time period(s): 1990s

Locale(s): Los Angeles, California

What the book is about: Deena Vogler wants a "get", a religious divorce, that will allow her to get on with her life, but Alex, her ex-husband (by a civil divorce) refuses to give her one. He is also harassing her with vicious phone calls and threats. When he is killed, Deena and her father, who hated Alex, become prime suspects.

Other books you might like:
Faye Kellerman, *Day of Atonement*, 1991
Faye Kellerman, *The Ritual Bath*, 1986
Harry Kemelman, *The Rabbi Small Series*, 1965-

956
Ken Kuhlken
The Angel Gang (New York: St. Martin's, 1994)

Series: Tom Hickey

Story type: Private Detective—Male Lead

Major character(s): Tom Hickey, Detective—Private (retired), Musician; Wendy Hickey, Spouse (Tom's wife)

Time period(s): 1950s (1951)

Locale(s): Tahoe, California; San Diego, California

What the book is about: Tom Hickey and his wife Wendy are happily living in Tahoe. Tom has given up the P.I. business and is making ends meet playing the clarinet, and is about to become a father. An old and beautiful acquaintance asks for help, saying she has been unjustly accused of arson and murder. Tom leaves for San Diego and quickly becomes involved with Jewish gangsters Charlie Schwartz and Mickey Cohen. When someone kidnaps Wendy in an effort to get him to back off, Tom will do anything to get her back alive—anything but give in.

Other books you might like:
Harold Adams, *The Carl Wilcox Series*, 1981-
Max Allan Collins, *The Nate Heller Series*, 1983-
Stuart M. Kaminsky, *The Toby Peters Series*, 1977-
Walter Mosley, *The Easy Rawlins Series*, 1990-
Robert B. Parker, *Poodle Springs*, 1989

957
Ken Kuhlken
The Loud Adios (New York: St. Martin's, 1991)

Story type: Private Detective—Male Lead; Historical

Major character(s): Tom Hickey, Military Personnel (Military Police border guard), Detective—Private

Time period(s): 1940s (1943)

Locale(s): San Diego, California; Tijuana, Mexico

What the book is about: Tom Hickey, ex-cop and private eye in civilian life, is now a border guard at Tijuana. He meets Clifford, a young G.I. he went through boot camp with. Clifford is shipping out but first he must get his sister Wendy back. A beautiful young woman who lives in a world of her own, she is being held prisoner in a Tijuana night club. When they try to rescue her, they get involved with Mexican gangsters and a mysterious group of Germans. First mystery.

Other books you might like:
Max Allan Collins, *The Million-Dollar Wound*, 1990
Stuart M. Kaminsky, *Poor Butterfly*, 1990
Philip Kerr, *March Violets*, 1989
Kirk Mitchell, *With Siberia Comes a Chill*, 1990

958
Ken Kuhlken
The Venus Deal (New York: St. Martin's, 1993)

Series: Tom Hickey

Story type: Private Detective—Male Lead

Major character(s): Tom Hickey, Detective—Private (part-time), Businessman (nightclub owner)

Time period(s): 1940s (1942)

Locale(s): San Diego, California

What the book is about: Tom Hickey is part owner of a successful nightclub. The success is due to the young singer, Cynthia Moon. Now Cynthia has disappeared and Tom is trying to find her. Tom's personal life is also a mess. His partner seems to be a mobster and his wife and child are threatening to leave him. Cynthia's trail leads Tom to her mother, Venus, the leader of a strange cult.

Other books you might like:
Harold Adams, *The Carl Wilcox Series*, 1981-
Max Allan Collins, *Stolen Away*, 1991
Stuart M. Kaminsky, *The Toby Peters Series*, 1977-
Philip Kerr, *The Pale Criminal*, 1990
Walter Mosley, *Devil in a Blue Dress*, 1990

959
Kathleen Kunz
Murder Once Removed (New York: Walker, 1993)

Story type: Psychological Suspense; Police Procedural—Female Lead

Major character(s): Terry Girard, Businesswoman (genealogist); Dan Kevlehan, Police Officer (sergeant)

Time period(s): 1990s

Locale(s): St. Louis, Missouri

What the book is about: Terry Girard's Aunt Cece's business—The Family Album—is to trace family histories and genealogies. When Cece is found dead of a fall the police conclude accident or suicide and lean toward the latter because of a cryptic note. Terry is not convinced and starts to review their cases. She discovers that many families have secrets that they don't want revealed and someone is willing to kill to keep them hidden. First novel.

Other books you might like:
Susan Wittig Albert, *Thyme of Death*, 1992
Nancy Atherton, *Aunt Dimity's Death*, 1992
K.K. Beck, *A Hopeless Case*, 1992
Denise Dietz, *Throw Darts at a Cheesecake*, 1992
Marjorie Dorner, *Family Closets*, 1988

960
Fern Kupfer
Love Lies (New York: Simon and Schuster, 1994)

Story type: Amateur Detective—Female Lead

Major character(s): Fran Meltzer, Teacher (of English); Julia Markem, Teacher (of English; Fran's best friend); Frank Rhodes, Widow(er), Detective—Homicide

Time period(s): 1990s

Locale(s): Midwest

What the book is about: Fran Meltzer's best friend, Julia Markem, seemed to have an ideal marriage. But Julia discovers he was having an affair—not his first affair, at that. Now Julia's husband is dead in what seems to be a tragic accident. Detective Frank Rhodes isn't convinced the death was accidental and discovers that Julia had a prime motive for murder. Fran, who is smart and smart-mouthed, is determined to clear her friend. The handsome Detective Rhodes, a widower, also catches Fran's interest. First novel.

Other books you might like:
Sophie Belfort, *The Marvell College Murders*, 1991
Nora Kelly, *My Sister's Keeper*, 1992
Susan Kenney, *The Roz Howard Series*, 1983-
M.D. Lake, *Murder by Mail*, 1993
Joan Smith, *What Men Say*, 1994

961
Peter Lacey
The Bag Man (New York: Doubleday, 1990)

Story type: Action/Adventure

Major character(s): Mordecai "Maudie" Morgan, Criminal (retired)

Time period(s): 1990s

Locale(s): England

What the book is about: Retired hood "Maudie" Morgan wants nothing more out of life than the pursuit of an attractive hotel owner. His old associates have other ideas, however, and use said lady to force him into one last bag job.

Other books you might like:
Michael Gilbert, *End-Game*, 1982
James Graham, *The Run to Morning*, 1974
Pete Hamill, *The Guns of Heaven*, 1983

962
Sarah Lacey
File Under: Deceased (New York: St. Martin's, 1993)

Story type: Amateur Detective—Female Lead

Major character(s): Leah Hunter, Businesswoman (tax inspector)

Time period(s): 1990s

Locale(s): York, England

What the book is about: Leah is attending an art show and strikes up a casual conversation with a good-looking man. As they are leaving he suddenly keels over dead. The only other witness, a Chinese with an umbrella, disappears. Leah has no idea what is going on but someone thinks differently as she becomes the victim of an escalating campaign of violence. She better do something herself as the police don't seem to be able to protect her. First novel.

Other books you might like:
Nancy Livingston, *The G.D.H. Pringle Series*, 1986-
Roger Ormerod, *Hung in the Balance*, 1991
Sheila Simonson, *Skylark*, 1992
Joan Smith, *A Masculine Ending*, 1987
Hannah Wakefield, *A Woman's Own Mystery*, 1991

963
Carrol Lachint
Murder in Brief (New York: Berkley, 1995)

Story type: Amateur Detective—Female Lead; Legal

Major character(s): Hannah Barlow, Student (law; ex-police officer)

Time period(s): 1990s

Locale(s): Las Almas, California

What the book is about: Hannah quit the police force when she found she couldn't deal with it anymore. She thought law school would be better. Now in her second year, she and a fellow student, wealthy and good-looking Bradley Gogburn, are involved in a plagarism scandal. Hannah knows she is innocent but things look bad when Bradley kills himself. Hannah's instincts tell her it wasn't a suicide. To save herself she is once more forced to investigate the sordid secrets of people she knows and likes. First mystery.

Other books you might like:
Jeffrey Wilds Deaver, *Mistress of Justice*, 1992
Michael A. Kahn, *Death Benefits*, 1992
Lia Matera, *Where Lawyers Fear to Tread*, 1986
Janet L. Smith, *Practice to Deceive*, 1992
Susan Wolfe, *The Last Billable Hour*, 1989

964
Deidre S. Laiken
Killing Time in Buffalo (New York: Little, 1990)

Story type: Psychological Suspense

Major character(s): Renee, Student; Fran, Student

Time period(s): 1960s (1967)

Locale(s): Buffalo, New York

What the book is about: Renee's husband has disappeared and now Renee is sure someone is trying to kill her.

Other books you might like:
Kate Green, *Night Angel*, 1988
Madison Jones, *Season of the Strangler*, 1982
Keith Peterson, *The Scarred Man*, 1990

965
David Laing
Double Blind (New York: St. Martin's, 1992)

Story type: Action/Adventure; Amateur Detective—Male Lead

Major character(s): David Snow, Doctor, Alcoholic (recovering)

Time period(s): 1990s

Locale(s): Baltimore, Maryland

What the book is about: Recovering alcoholic doctor David Snow is trying to rebuild his life and career in a state hospital in Baltimore when he finds himself involved in something he doesn't understand. Within one weekend at the hospital four of the patients admitted are gay, psychotic and HIV positive. Convinced that this pattern means something he sets out to find out what. But somebody or something doesn't want him doing this. He is beaten and raped and develops schizophrenia but none of this stops him from trying to get at the truth.

Other books you might like:
Robin Cook, *Coma*, 1978
R.D. Zimmerman, *Mindscream*, 1988

966
M.D. Lake (Pseudonym of J.A. Thompson)
Amends for Murder (New York: Avon, 1989)

Story type: Police Procedural—Female Lead

Major character(s): Peggy O'Neill, Police Officer (university campus police)

Time period(s): 1980s

Locale(s): Minneapolis, Minnesota; St. Paul, Minnesota

What the book is about: When Officer O'Neill finds the body of English professor Adam Warren, she is reluctant to hand the investigation over to the regular police department.

Other books you might like:
Susan Dunlap, *The Bohemian Connection*, 1985
Michael T. Hinkemeyer, *A Time to Reap*, 1984
Mary Logue, *Red Lake of the Heart*, 1987
Nancy Pickard, *Generous Death*, 1984
L.A. Taylor, *A Murder Waiting to Happen*, 1989

967
M.D. Lake (Pseudonym of J.A. Simpson)
Cold Comfort (New York: Avon, 1990)

Series: Peggy O'Neill

Story type: Police Procedural—Female Lead

Major character(s): Peggy O'Neill, Police Officer (university campus police)

Time period(s): 1990s

Locale(s): Minneapolis, Minnesota; St. Paul, Minnesota

What the book is about: Was the death of computer whiz Mike Parrish a suicide - or did the sexy Swedish student Ann-Marie Ekdahl have something to do with his death? When Ann-Marie's current boyfriend turns up missing, Peggy's suspicions seem to be confirmed.

Other books you might like:
Susan Dunlap, *The Jill Smith Series*, 1981-
Ellen Hart, *Vital Lies*, 1991
Joan Hess, *The Claire Malloy Series*, 1987
Cathleen Jordan, *Carol in the Dark*, 1984

968
M.D. Lake (Pseudonym of J.A. Simpson)
A Gift for Murder (New York: Avon, 1992)

Series: Peggy O'Neill

Story type: Police Procedural—Female Lead

Major character(s): Peggy O'Neill, Police Officer (university campus police); Buck Hansen, Police Officer (homicide lieutenant)

Time period(s): 1990s

Locale(s): Minneapolis/St. Paul, Minnesota

What the book is about: Peggy has become invovled with one of the writers of "The Tower," a local writers group. Cameron Harris, one of its more famous members who left years ago, has come back but no one in the Tower seems happy about it. When he announces his new book is to be about the other members of the group and their history, he is just inviting trouble. The next day he is killed.

Other books you might like:
Jo Bailey, *Bagged*, 1991
Richard Barth, *The Final Shot*, 1992
Jill Churchill, *A Quiche Before Dying*, 1993
Susan Dunlap, *The Jill Smith Series*, 1981-
Lillian O'Donnell, *The Mici Anhalt Series*, 1979-1983

969
M.D. Lake (Pseudonym of J.A. Simpson)
Murder by Mail (New York: Avon, 1993)

Series: Peggy O'Neill

Story type: Police Procedural—Female Lead

Major character(s): Peggy O'Neill, Police Officer (university campus police); Paula Henderson, Police Officer (university campus police)

Time period(s): 1990s

Locale(s): Minneapolis/St. Paul, Minnesota

What the book is about: Peggy's co-workers are in love, but as an interracial couple have become the victims of a campaign of vicious hate mail. Peggy has an idea who is behind the attacks but before she can do anything, the suspect dies in a mysterious fire - and her co-worker, Paula, is a prime suspect. Somehow this may all lead back to the university and the suicide of a graduate student.

Other books you might like:
Susan Dunlap, *The Jill Smith Series*, 1986-
Ruby Horansky, *Dead Ahead*, 1990
Margaret Maron, *The Sigrid Harald Series*, 1982-
Lee Martin, *The Deb Ralston Series*, 1984-
Julie Smith, *The Skip Langdon Series*, 1990-

970
M.D. Lake (Pseudonym of J.A. Simpson)
Once upon a Crime (New York: Avon, 1995)
Series: Peggy O'Neill
Story type: Police Procedural—Female Lead
Major character(s): Peggy O'Neill, Police Officer (university campus police)
Time period(s): 1990s
Locale(s): Minneapolis/St. Paul, Minnesota
What the book is about: Peggy is on medical leave and looking for something to keep from being bored to death. She becomes friends with Pia Austin, a senior with an interest in Hans Christian Andersen. She falls in with a group of Danophiles and even gets talked into acting in *The Emperor's New Clothes*. Pia's father, a renowned Andersen scholar, is visiting from Denmark. He is rather arrogant but that doesn't seem to be any reason to crush his skull. So much for Peggy's vacation.
Other books you might like:
Jo Bailey, *Bagged*, 1992
P.M. Carlson, *The Marty Hopkins Series*, 1992-
Susan Dunlap, *The Jill Smith Series*, 1981-
Joan Hess, *The Maggody Series*, 1987-
James Schermerhorn, *Night of the Cat*, 1993

971
M.D. Lake (Pseudonym of J.A. Simpson)
Poisoned Ivy (New York: Avon, 1992)
Series: Peggy O'Neill
Story type: Police Procedural—Female Lead
Major character(s): Peggy O'Neill, Police Officer (university campus police)
Time period(s): 1990s
Locale(s): Minnesota
What the book is about: Was the poisoned apple that Donna Trask bit into—and that killed her—meant for Dean Jeremiah Strauss, whose speech she interrupted? It appears so as the dean had been the target of death threats and is universally despised. Things on a college campus, as elsewhere, are not always as they seem and Peggy O'Neill, encouraged to investigate by the arrest of a professor that she likes, is determined to find out the truth.
Other books you might like:
Susan Dunlap, *The Jill Smith Series*, 1981-
Ellen Hart, *Hallowed Murder*, 1989
Joan Hess, *The Maggody Series*, 1989-
Charlotte MacLeod, *The Peter Shandy Series*, 1978-

972
Mercedes Lambert
Dogtown (New York: Viking, 1991)
Story type: Amateur Detective—Female Lead
Major character(s): Whitney Logan, Lawyer
Time period(s): 1990s
Locale(s): Los Angeles, California
What the book is about: Struggling to come up with rent money, attorney Whitney Logan is hired to find a missing Hispanic maid. She doesn't speak Spanish or know anything about illegal aliens, but one thousand dollars is too much to turn down. She hooks up with a tough-talking prostitute for assistance and the case soon turns nasty, involving drugs and murder. First novel.
Other books you might like:
Linda Barnes, *Coyote*, 1990
Robert J. Bowman, *The House of Blue Lights*, 1988
Mary Bowen Hall, *Emma Chizzit and the Sacramento Stalker*, 1991
Lia Matera, *Prior Convictions*, 1991
Judith Van Gieson, *Raptor*, 1989

973
Gunnard Landers
The Deer Killers (New York: Walker, 1990)
Story type: Action/Adventure
Major character(s): Reed Erickson, Government Official (special agent of the U.S. Fish); Doyle Monroe, Businessman, Criminal
Time period(s): 1970s
Locale(s): Magnolia, Louisiana
What the book is about: Reed Erickson goes undercover in Louisiana to try and catch poachers suspected of killing a game warden. But by living with the missing, and probably dead, warden's family, he creates many problems for himself and the investigation. First book.
Other books you might like:
J. Madison Davis, *White Rook*, 1990
James W. Hall, *Tropical Freeze*, 1988
John D. MacDonald, *The Drowner*, 1963
Charles Williams, *Dead Calm*, 1963
Daniel Woodrell, *Under the Bright Lights*, 1988

974
Marsha Landreth
A Clinic for Murder (New York: Walker, 1993)
Series: Samantha Turner
Story type: Amateur Detective—Female Lead; Action/Adventure
Major character(s): Samantha Turner, Doctor (medical examiner), Widow(er); Derek Turner, Journalist, Spy (CIA agent)
Time period(s): 1990s
Locale(s): San Diego, California; Sheridan, Wyoming
What the book is about: Samantha Turner is in San Diego for a medical conference, and at a lecture on criminology a doctor passes out and dies—but not before asking Sam to deliver a letter. Sam is off on the chase gaining entry to his room by less than legal means, and finds the room has already been searched. She gets arrested and it takes Derek to free her. They continue to investigate and find more deaths. Someone is desperate to hide something.

Other books you might like:
Patricia D. Cornwell, *The Kay Scarpetta Series*, 1990-
D.J. Donaldson, *Blood on the Bayou*, 1991
Eileen Dreyer, *A Man to Die For*, 1991
Susan Dunlap, *Rogue Wave*, 1991
Janet McGiffin, *Prescription for Death*, 1992

975

Marsha Landreth
The Holiday Murders (New York: Walker, 1992)

Series: Samantha Turner

Story type: Police Procedural—Female Lead

Major character(s): Samantha Turner, Doctor (medical examiner), Widow(er); Derek Turner, Journalist

Time period(s): 1990s

Locale(s): Sheridan, Wyoming

What the book is about: Sheridan has a serial killer who likes to kill women on the holidays and Samantha is doing her best, but the killer leaves no clues and the local police are uncooperative with a "woman doing a man's job". To further complicate matters, Sam's stepson - four years older than Sam and the spitting image of his father - is in town, supposedly doing research for an article on buffalo ranching but really investigating the murders for Washington - one of the victims was a protected witness. First mystery.

Other books you might like:
Patricia D. Cornwell, *The Kay Scarpetta Series*, 1990-
D.J. Donaldson, *Blood on the Bayou*, 1991
Susan Dunlap, *Rogue Wave*, 1991
David L. Lindsey, *Mercy*, 1990
Joyce Anne Schneider, *Darkness Falls*, 1989

976

Marsha Landreth
Vial Murders (New York: Walker, 1994)

Series: Samantha Turner

Story type: Amateur Detective—Female Lead

Major character(s): Samantha Turner, Doctor (medical examiner); Derek Turner, Spy

Time period(s): 1990s

Locale(s): Sheridan, Wyoming

What the book is about: As part of her duties as medical examiner, Samantha Turner is examining the body of a teenager, David Crider, when she realizes that he may have died of smallpox. She immediately contacts the Centers for Disease Control. Soon after a CDC team arrives, another mysterious disease attacks everyone who had anything to do with the Crider boy's body. This disease causes amnesia. Samantha has to try and piece together the events of the last week. Then one of the CDC team is killed. What is going on and why is the government, including Derek Turner, trying to hush things up?

Other books you might like:
William Appel, *Whisper.He Might Hear You*, 1991
Robin Cook, *Outbreak*, 1987
Patricia D. Cornwell, *The Kay Scarpetta Series*, 1990-
D.J. Donaldson, *The Kit Franklin/Andy Broussard Series*, 1991-
Janice Law, *Infected Be the Air*, 1991

977

Graham Landrum
The Famous DAR Murder Mystery (New York: St. Martin's, 1992)

Story type: Amateur Detective—Female Lead

Major character(s): Helen Delaporte, Musician (choir director); Elizabeth Wheeler, Public Relations

Time period(s): 1990s

Locale(s): Borderville, Virginia

What the book is about: Four members of the Old Orchard Chapter of the Daughters of the American Revolution are looking for the grave of a Revolutionary War soldier when they stumble on a real corpse. The town sheriff is quick to call it an accidental death resulting from a drunken brawl. The ladies think otherwise and set out to prove it. First novel.

Other books you might like:
Richard Barth, *Deathics*, 1993
Virginia Crosby, *The Fast-Death Factor*, 1990
Charlotte MacLeod, *The Grub-and-Stakers Series*, 1981-
Sharyn McCrumb, *The Elizabeth MacPherson Series*, 1984
A.J. Orde, *A Little Neighborhood Murder*, 1989

978

Graham Landrum
The Rotary Club Mystery (New York: St. Martins, 1993)

Series: Borderville Mystery

Story type: Amateur Detective—Female Lead

Major character(s): Harriet Bushrow, Aged Person (88 years old)

Time period(s): 1990s

Locale(s): Borderville, Virginia

What the book is about: The police are having trouble finding out the truth behind the apparent locked-room suicide of an important member of the Rotary Club, so 88 year old Harriet Bushrow decides to take charge. The man had a current wife and a first wife and other women in various relationships and Harriet must decide who, if anyone, was responsible for the death.

Other books you might like:
Richard Barth, *The Margaret Binton Series*, 1978-
B. Comfort, *The Tish McWhinney Series*, 1986-
Hazel Holt, *The Mrs. Malory Series*, 1990-
David Osborn, *The Margaret Barlow Series*, 1990-
Serita Stevens, *Bagels for Tea*, 1993 (Rayanne Moore, co-author)

979
Jane Langton
The Dante Game (New York: Viking, 1991)
Series: Homer Kelly
Story type: Amateur Detective—Male Lead
Major character(s): Homer Kelly, Professor (at Harvard)
Time period(s): 1990s
Locale(s): Florence, Italy
What the book is about: In Florence to study Italian and Dante, Homer Kelly gets involved in kidnapping, murder and the attempted assassination of the Pope.
Other books you might like:
P.M. Carlson, *Murder Misread*, 1990
Sarah Caudwell, *Thus Was Adonis Murdered*, 1981
Amanda Cross, *The Players Come Again*, 1991
Hazel Wynn Jones, *Death and the Trumpets of Tuscany*, 1989
Roy Harley Lewis, *Death in Verona*, 1989

980
Joe R. Lansdale
Act of Love (New York: Zebra, 1991)
Story type: Psychological Suspense
Major character(s): Marvin Hanson, Police Officer (homicide lieutenant); Philip Barlowe, Journalist (serial killer)
Time period(s): 1980s
Locale(s): Houston, Texas
What the book is about: There is a serial killer loose in Houston. Police officer Marvin Hanson takes the case personally—even before the killer begins to stalk his family. Reissue of a 1981 novel.
Other books you might like:
Marc Berrenson, *Perfection*, 1991
Thomas Harris, *Red Dragon*, 1981
David L. Lindsey, *Mercy*, 1990
Gary Paulsen, *Night Rituals*, 1989
Bill Pronzini, *The Running of Beasts*, 1976 (Barry Malzberg, co-author)

981
John Lantigua
Burn Season (New York: Putnam, 1989)
Story type: Action/Adventure
Major character(s): Jack Lacey, Businessman (nightclub owner)
Time period(s): 1980s
Locale(s): San Jose
What the book is about: When a small-time bad guy gets killed in the parking lot of Jack's club, he is drawn into the fray against his will.
Other books you might like:
James Lee Burke, *The Neon Rain*, 1986
James W. Hall, *Under Cover of Daylight*, 1987
Thomas Perry, *The Butcher's Boy*, 1982
Gerald Petievich, *The Quality of the Informant*, 1985
Ross Thomas, *The Cold War Swap*, 1966

982
Janet LaPierre
Children's Games (New York: Scribner's, 1989)
Story type: Police Procedural
Major character(s): Meg Halloran, Teacher (high school); Vince Gutierez, Police Officer (chief of police)
Time period(s): 1980s
Locale(s): California (Northern)
What the book is about: When one of Meg Halloran's students is murdered, she is a prime suspect because of a previous run-in with him.
Other books you might like:
Sophie Belfort, *The Lace Curtain Murders*, 1986
Susan Kelly, *The Gemini Man*, 1985
Marcia Muller, *The Cheshire Cat's Eye*, 1983
Nancy Pickard, *Say No to Murder*, 1985
Gillian Roberts, *Caught Dead in Philadelphia*, 1987

983
Janet LaPierre
Grandmother's House (New York: Scribners, 1991)
Series: Port Silva
Story type: Amateur Detective—Female Lead
Major character(s): Charlotte Birdsong, Businesswoman, Single Parent; Val Kuisma, Police Officer
Time period(s): 1990s
Locale(s): Port Silva, California
What the book is about: Single mother Charlotte Birdsong and her son are living in a house that Cynthia Leino wants to buy as part of a development project. An underground environmental group is opposed to the project and when proponets of the project begin to disappear, Charlotte and police officer Val Kuisma fear that Charlotte's son Petey may be involved. LaPierre's series characters Meg Hallonar and Vince Gutierrez make cameo appearances.
Other books you might like:
Rita Mae Brown, *Wish You Were Here*, 1990
Virginia Crosby, *The Fast-Death Factor*, 1990
Carolyn G. Hart, *The Annie Laurance/Max Darling Series*, 1987-
Joan Hess, *The Maggody Series*, 1988-
B.J. Oliphant, *Dead in the Scrub*, 1990

984
Gaylord Larsen
Dorothy and Agatha (New York: Dutton, 1990)
Story type: Historical; Amateur Detective—Female Lead

Major character(s): Dorothy L. Sayers, Historical Figure, Writer; Agatha Christie, Historical Figure, Writer

Time period(s): 1930s (1937)

Locale(s): Witham, England

What the book is about: When a man is found murdered in Dorothy L. Sayers' dining room, the other members of The Detection Club, particularly Agatha Christie, set out to solve the crime. But could Dorothy be guilty?

Other books you might like:
Brett Halliday, *She Woke to Darkness*, 1954
Edward D. Hoch, *The Shattered Raven*, 1969
Marc Olden, *Poe Must Die*, 1978
William J. Palmer, *The Detective and Mr. Dickens*, 1990

985
William Lashner
Hostile Witness (New York: HarperCollins, 1995)

Story type: Legal

Major character(s): Victor Carl, Lawyer

Time period(s): 1990s

Locale(s): Philadelphia, Pennsylvania

What the book is about: Embittered lawyer Victor Carl is given the opportunity to make the big-time. He is asked to represent the assistant to an indicted councilman. What he soon discovers is that his client is expected to take the fall for the bigger fish. Victor sets out to sabotage the plans. However, this puts him in serious danger as the people in power have no interest in truth and justice and will stop at nothing to get their way. First novel.

Other books you might like:
John Grisham, *The Rainmaker*, 1995
John T. Lescroart, *The 13th Juror*, 1994
Paul Levine, *To Speak for the Dead*, 1990
Susan R. Sloan, *Guilt by Association*, 1995
Walter Sorrells, *Will to Murder*, 1996

986
Emma Lathen
East Is East (New York: Simon & Schuster, 1991)

Series: John Putnam Thatcher

Story type: Amateur Detective—Male Lead

Major character(s): John Putnam Thatcher, Banker

Time period(s): 1990s

Locale(s): United States; England; Japan

What the book is about: In Tokyo to witness the signing of a distribution agreement between two of the bank's clients, Thatcher gets involved in the investigation of a murdered accountant. There appear to be suggestions of bribery involved in setting up the agreement which would help pull one of the companies out of bankruptcy. Political issues collide with business interests and the trail of corruption and murder takes Thatcher from Tokyo to Alaska and England. Lathen also writes as R.B. Dominic.

Other books you might like:
Robert Eversz, *The Bottom Line Is Murder*, 1988
Linda Grant, *Blind Trust*, 1990
Lia Matera, *The Smart Money*, 1988
Annette Meyers, *The Big Killing*, 1988
Haughton Murphy, *Murders and Acquisitions*, 1987

987
Emma Lathen
Right on the Money (New York: Simon & Schuster, 1993)

Series: John Putnam Thatcher

Story type: Amateur Detective—Male Lead

Major character(s): John Putnam Thatcher, Banker

Time period(s): 1990s

Locale(s): New York, New York

What the book is about: Merger negotiations go awry and murder and arson are the result. Thatcher helps the police, who are in over their heads, unravel the various scams so they can find out who stood to profit the most from the breaking off of the merger.

Other books you might like:
Annette Meyers, *The Smith and Wetzon Series*, 1987-
Haughton Murphy, *Murders and Acquisitions*, 1988
S.L. Stebel, *The Boss's Wife*, 1992

988
Janet Laurence
A Deepe Coffyn (New York: Doubleday, 1990)

Series: Darina Lisle

Story type: Amateur Detective—Female Lead

Major character(s): Darina Lisle, Cook, Caterer

Time period(s): 1980s

What the book is about: Darina Lisle is hired to cater the annual weekend for the Society of Historical Gastronomes, but the murder of her cousin and then another person puts quite a damper on the weekend, particularly when Darina is the chief suspect in both deaths. First book.

Other books you might like:
Marion Babson, *Death Warmed Up*, 1982
Michael Bond, *The Monsieur Pamplemousse Series*, (1985-)
Dorothy Cannell, *The Thin Woman*, 1986
Julie Smith, *The Sourdough Wars*, 1984
Rex Stout, *Too Many Cooks*, 1938

989
Janet Laurence
Hotel Morgue (New York: Doubleday, 1992)

Series: Darina Lisle

Story type: Amateur Detective; Police Procedural

Major character(s): Darina Lisle, Caterer; William Pigram, Police Officer

Time period(s): 1990s

Locale(s): Somerset, England

What the book is about: When the opportunity arises for Darina to get involved with a hostelry with the potential for future investment she takes it. Soon, however there is a murder that brings in her boyfriend, Detective Sergeant Pigram, who has been working on a suspicious death at another hotel in the area. Are the two deaths connected? And can Darina help without getting herself killed?

Other books you might like:
Deborah Adams, *All the Great Pretenders*, 1992
Carole Berry, *Island Girl*, 1991
Dorothy Cannell, *The Thin Woman*, 1986
Diane Mott Davidson, *Catering to Nobody*, 1990
Virginia Rich, *The Cooking School Murders*, 1982

990
Janet Laurence
Recipe for Death (New York: Doubleday, 1993)

Series: Darina Lisle

Story type: Amateur Detective—Female Lead

Major character(s): Darina Lisle, Writer (cookbook columnist), Caterer

Time period(s): 1990s

Locale(s): Somerset, England

What the book is about: The winner of a cookery contest that Darina Lisle was judging invites her to visit the farm where they raise organic meat. While there she gets involved in the family and with a local restaurant owner. Her relationship with the restaurant owner starts out well, her relationship with the family less so. Then there is a hit-and-run accident—or was it murder? Another death, supposedly from food poisoning, follows and Darina determines to find out the truth behind the deaths.

Other books you might like:
Dorothy Cannell, *The Thin Woman*, 1984
Jill Churchill, *Grime and Punishment*, 1989
Mary Higgins Clark, *Weep No More, My Lady*, 1987
Jaqueline Girdner, *The Last Resort*, 1991

991
Janice Law
Infected Be the Air (New York: Walker, 1991)

Story type: Amateur Detective—Female Lead; Action/Adventure

Major character(s): Alice Bertram, Farmer

Time period(s): 1990s

Locale(s): Connecticut

What the book is about: Refusing to believe that her ex-husband would kill his girlfriend and her son and then himself Alice sets out to solve the crime. She also gets involved with her plumber who is involved with a Senator, who is involved in dumping toxic waste.

Other books you might like:
Joan Hess, *The Claire Malloy Series*, 1987-
Janet LaPierre, *Children's Games*, 1989
Kathryn Lasky Knight, *The Calista Jacobs Series*, 1987-
Nancy Pickard, *The Jenny Cain Series*, 1986-
Gillian Roberts, *The Amanda Pepper Series*, 1988-

992
Janice Law
Time Lapse (New York: Walker, 1992)

Series: Anna Peters

Story type: Private Detective—Female Lead

Major character(s): Anna Peters, Detective—Private

Time period(s): 1990s

Locale(s): New York, New York

What the book is about: The best selling novel, *The Lazarus Gambit*, was being filmed as a big budget movie until the star died by drowning in a shallow lake. Now Anna has been hired by the insurance company which is on the hook for one million dollars to the widow and forty million dollars to the film company. They want Anna to prove suicide. While investigating Anna finds several people who wanted the movie stopped or the star dead. Could it have been murder?

Other books you might like:
Trella Crespi, *The Trouble with Moonlighting*, 1991
Howard Engel, *Murder on Location*, 1985
Maureen O'Brien, *Close-Up on Death*, 1989
Jim Stinson, *Double Exposure*, 1985
Eric Wright, *Final Cut*, 1991

993
Martha C. Lawrence
Murder in Scorpio (New York: St. Martin's, 1995)

Story type: Private Detective—Female Lead

Major character(s): Elizabeth Chase, Detective—Private (psychic); Tom McGowan, Police Officer

Time period(s): 1990s

Locale(s): San Diego, California

What the book is about: Tom McGowan is having a difficult time agreeing with the official department report on the death of an old high school love. The department says that the two-car accident, which killed both drivers, was in fact, just an accident. Tom has nowhere else to turn so, though doubtful, he comes to Elizabeth Chase, Psychic, who has turned to solving crimes after some experiences in helping people almost by accident. Edgar nominee for best first novel.

Other books you might like:
George Dawes Green, *The Caveman's Valentine*, 1994
Kate Green, *Black Dreams*, 1993
R.D. Zimmerman, *Death Trance*, 1993

994
John Lawton
Black Out (New York: Viking, 1995)

Story type: Historical; Police Procedural—Male Lead

Major character(s): Frederick Troy, Police Officer (sergeant)

Time period(s): 1940s (1945)

Locale(s): London, England

What the book is about: Sergeant Troy is assigned to solve a murder that has no clues except a severed arm. Upon investigation, the arm turns out to belong to a German scientist who has been working for the British. Who killed him and why are the crux of his investigation—but he must investigate with the spectre of war, a war about which he is somewhat ambivalent, hanging over him. First novel.

Other books you might like:
Robert Barnard, *Out of the Blackout*, 1984
Robert Harris, *Enigma*, 1993
Philip Kerr, *The Bernie Gunther Series*, 1989-1991

995
John Le Carre (Pseudonym of David Cornwell)
The Russia House (New York: Knopf, 1989)

Story type: Espionage

Major character(s): Barley Blair, Businessman, Publisher; Horatio DePalrey, Spy

Time period(s): 1980s (1987)

Locale(s): Moscow, Union of Soviet Socialist Republics (Moscow Book Fair)

What the book is about: When a mysterious woman gives a notebook of military secrets to Barley Blair at a publishing trade show, British Intelligence must recruit Barley to find out the truth behind the secrets therein.

Other books you might like:
Ted Allbeury, *Shadow of Shadows*, 1982
Len Deighton, *Catch a Falling Spy*, 1976
Brian Freemantle, *Charlie M*, 1977
Robert Littell, *The Defection of A.J. Lewinter*, 1973
Anthony Price, *The Labyrinth Makers*, 1971

996
James Leasor
Frozen Assets (New York: St. Martin's, 1989)

Series: Jason Love

Story type: Amateur Detective—Male Lead

Major character(s): Jason Love, Doctor (antique car enthusiast)

Time period(s): 1980s

Locale(s): Islamabad, Pakistan

What the book is about: While in Pakistan to appraise a one-of-a-kind 1935 Cord automobile, Dr. Love finds himself drawn into the spy game.

Other books you might like:
Ian Fleming, *The James Bond Series*, (1954-)
Dorothy Gilman, *The Unexpected Mrs. Pollifax*, 1966
Marc Lovell, *Spy on the Run*, 1982

997
Stephen Leather
The Fireman (New York: St. Martin's, 1990)

Story type: Amateur Detective—Male Lead

Time period(s): 1980s

What the book is about: While trying to find the truth about his sister's supposed suicide he finds more than he bargained for.

Other books you might like:
Keith Peterson, *The John Wells Series*, (1988-)

998
Bernie Lee
Murder at Musket Beach (New York: Fine, 1990)

Series: Tony and Pat Pratt

Story type: Amateur Detective

Major character(s): Tony Pratt, Writer (freelance); Pat Pratt, Consultant (financial; Tony's wife)

Time period(s): 1980s

Locale(s): Musket Beach, Oregon

What the book is about: While spending the summer in the small town of Musket Beach, Tony Pratt and his wife Pat stumble upon the body of the mayor. First book.

Other books you might like:
Douglas Kiker, *Death at the Cut*, 1988
M.K. Wren, *The Conan Flagg Series*, (1973-)

999
Bernie Lee
Murder Without Reservation (New York: Fine, 1991)

Series: Tony and Pat Pratt

Story type: Amateur Detective; Humor

Major character(s): Tony Pratt, Writer (mystery novelist, freelance); Pat Pratt, Consultant (financial; Tony's wife)

Time period(s): 1990s

Locale(s): Oregon

What the book is about: Free-lancing between mystery novels as a location manager for a Japanese TV crew shooting an episode of a show in Oregon, Tony's problems start with trying to find a Shinto priest to bless the shoot. The problems quickly escalate to dead horses, dead drug dealers and dead cowboys. Pat puts her business aside to come and help him.

Other books you might like:
Willetta Barber, *The Christopher Storm Series*, 1940-1952 (R.F. Schabelitz, co-author)
Dashiell Hammett, *The Thin Man*, 1934
Frances and Richard Lockridge, *The Mr. and Mrs. North Series*, 1940-1963 (Frances Lockridge, co-author)
B.J. Oliphant, *Dead in the Scrub*, 1990
M.K. Wren, *The Conan Flagg Series*, 1974-

1000
Dennis Lehane
A Drink Before the War (New York: Harcourt, 1994)

Story type: Private Detective

Major character(s): Patrick Kenzie, Detective—Private; Angela Gennaro, Detective—Private

Time period(s): 1990s

Locale(s): Boston, Massachusetts

What the book is about: Patrick Kenzie and Angela Gennaro, partners in a Boston P.I. firm, are hired by some politicians to find a missing cleaning woman who may have taken some important documents. What the documents are, they are not told. They soon find the woman and discern that she has no documents, but does have some incriminating photos involving one of the politicians and her husband, a street gang leader. Then the woman is killed and Angela and Patrick must move quickly before they too are shot down, either by the politicians or the gangs. First novel.

Other books you might like:
Peter Blauner, *Slow Motion Riot*, 1991
James Lee Burke, *A Stained White Radiance*, 1992
Robert Crais, *Stalking the Angel*, 1989
Jerome Doolittle, *Body Scissors*, 1990
Jeremiah Healy, *So Like Sleep*, 1987

1001
Elizabeth Lemarchand
The Glade Manor Murder (New York: Walker, 1989)

Series: Pollard and Toye

Story type: Police Procedural—Male Lead

Major character(s): Tom Pollard, Detective—Police (detective superintendent); Gregory Toye, Detective—Police (detective inspector)

Time period(s): 1980s

What the book is about: When a family's nanny and dog are pushed off a cliff, Pollard and Toye must sort through the family rubble to get at the truth.

Other books you might like:
W.J. Burley, *To Kill a Cat*, 1970
Colin Dexter, *Service of All the Dead*, 1980
Jonathan Ross, *Dark Blue and Dangerous*, 1981
Dorothy Simpson, *Dead by Morning*, 1989
John Wainwright, *All on a Summer's Day*, 1981

1002
Donna Leon
Death and Judgment (New York: HarperCollins, 1995)

Series: Guido Brunetti

Story type: Police Procedural—Male Lead

Major character(s): Guido Brunetti, Police Officer (commissario of police)

Time period(s): 1990s

Locale(s): Venice, Italy

What the book is about: A powerful lawyer has been shot and killed on what the headlines refer to as "The Train of Death". Brunetti is assigned to the case. When an associate of the dead lawyer dies, supposedly of suicide, Brunetti realizes he is involved in something sinister and deadly. What were the lawyers' connections to the mysterious Romanian truck that crashed with eight dead women as part of the cargo?

Other books you might like:
Sarah Caudwell, *Thus Was Adonis Murdered*, 1981
Mickey Friedman, *Venetian Mask*, 1987
Roderic Jeffries, *The Inspector Alvarez Series*, 1974-
Magdalen Nabb, *The Marshall Guarnaccia Series*, 1982-
Edward Sklepowich, *Death in a Serene City*, 1990

1003
Donna Leon
Death at La Fenice (New York: Harper, 1992)

Story type: Police Procedural—Male Lead

Major character(s): Guido Brunetti, Police Officer (commissario of police)

Time period(s): 1990s

Locale(s): Venice, Italy

What the book is about: At the world famous Teatro La Fenice, noted conductor Helmut Wellauer has been found dead during intermission. When the doctor in attendance notices the smell of bitter almonds—indicating cyanide poisoning—it is a job for Commissario Brunetti. Evidence points to the conductor's wife as the prime suspect but Brunetti realizes a lot of people wanted Wellauer dead. First mystery.

Other books you might like:
Sarah Caudwell, *Thus Was Adonis Murdered*, 1981
Mikel Dunham, *Casting for Murder*, 1992
Hazel Wynn Jones, *Death and the Trumpets of Tuscany*, 1989
Magdalen Nabb, *Death of a Dutchman*, 1982
Edward Sklepowich, *Death in a Serene City*, 1990

1004
Donna Leon
Death in a Strange Country (New York: HarperCollins, 1993)

Series: Guido Brunetti

Story type: Police Procedural—Male Lead

Major character(s): Guido Brunetti, Police Officer (commissario of police)

Time period(s): 1990s

Locale(s): Venice, Italy

What the book is about: The body of an American soldier—knifed to death—turns up in a Venice canal, miles from where the soldier was supposed to be. How he got there and who put him there is just one of the problems for police commissario Guido Brunetti. He must also deal with his boss, who is more concerned with tourism than with the truth, and with the possiblity of government involvement in toxic waste dumping. There also appears to be an art theft ring operating right under the boss's nose.

Other books you might like:
Sarah Caudwell, *Thus Was Adonis Murdered*, 1981
Mickey Friedman, *Venetian Mask*, 1987
Jonathan Gash, *The Gondola Scam*, 1984
Reginald Hill, *Another Death in Venice*, 1987
Edward Sklepowich, *Death in a Serene City*, 1990

1005
Elmore Leonard
Get Shorty (New York: Delacorte, 1990)

Story type: Action/Adventure

Major character(s): Chili Palmer, Criminal (loan shark); Harry Zimm, Producer (of bad films); Karen Flores, Actress

Time period(s): 1990s

Locale(s): Los Angeles, California

What the book is about: Chili Palmer, small-time loan shark, follows a skipped client to Los Angeles where he falls in with small-time producer Harry Zimm and small-time actress Karen Flores. Together the three make plans for the big-time. Of course, things never go as planned but it's interesting along the way.

Other books you might like:
J.F. Burke, *Location Shots*, 1974
Tucker Halleran, *A Cool Clear Death*, 1985
Michael Kakonis, *Double-Cross*, 1988
Michael J. Katz, *Last Dance in Redondo Beach*, 1989
Lue Zimmelman, *Honolulu Red*, 1990

1006
Elmore Leonard
Maximum Bob (New York: Delacorte, 1991)

Story type: Action/Adventure

Major character(s): Bob Gibbs, Judge (nickname—Maximum Bob); Kathy Diaz Baker, Probation Officer; Gary Hammond, Police Officer

Time period(s): 1990s

Locale(s): Palm Beach, Florida

What the book is about: Someone is trying to kill Maximum Bob. Maybe. That someone is Kathy Baker's probationer, Elvin Crowe. Maybe. Who brought an alligator to Bob's home? Police officer Gary Hammond and Kathy Baker team up to find out what is going on—and fall in love.

Other books you might like:
Robert Ferrigno, *The Horse Latitudes*, 1990
Carl Hiaasen, *Native Tongue*, 1991
David L. Lindsey, *In the Lake of the Moon*, 1987
John Lutz, *Hot*, 1992
Michael Malone, *Time's Witness*, 1989

1007
Elmore Leonard
Rum Punch (New York: Delacorte, 1992)

Story type: Action/Adventure

Major character(s): Jackie Burke, Flight Attendent; Max Cherry, Businessman (bail bondsman); Ordell Robbie, Criminal (gun dealer)

Time period(s): 1990s

Locale(s): Miami, Florida

What the book is about: After being caught smuggling for gun dealer Ordell Robbie, flight attendant Jackie Burke agrees to work with the Feds to catch Robbie in a criminal act. Max Cherry, who posts Jackie's bail, finds himself falling for her and supporting her when she decides a sting of her own might be a good idea.

Other books you might like:
Bruce Cook, *Rough Cut*, 1990
Bill Crider, *Dead on the Island*, 1991
John Katzenbach, *Just Cause*, 1992
John Leslie, *Killer in Paradise*, 1990
Edward Mathis, *September Song*, 1991

1008
John T. Lescroart
A Certain Justice (New York: Fine, 1995)

Story type: Police Procedural—Male Lead; Psychological Suspense

Major character(s): Kevin Shea, Student, Fugitive; Abe Glitsky, Police Officer

Time period(s): 1990s

Locale(s): San Francisco, California

What the book is about: A black man, in the wrong place at the wrong time, is in the process of being lynched by a drunken mob. Trying to save the man is graduate student Kevin Shea. Unfortunately the hanging is successful and a photograph taken at the scene makes it look like Kevin is trying to stab the man instead of trying to save him. This turns him into a fugitive with everyone in the city out for his blood, except Lieutenant Abe Glitsky who thinks maybe Kevin is the innocent he claims to be. Can he save Kevin before the mobs get him?

Other books you might like:
Michael Connelly, *The Last Coyote*, 1995
Ken Gross, *Hell Bent*, 1992
John Sandford, *The Lucas Davenport Series*, 1989-
Stephen Solomita, *A Piece of the Action*, 1992
Collin Wilcox, *The Lieutenant Hastings Series*, 1968-

1009
John T. Lescroart
Hard Evidence (New York: Fine, 1993)

Series: Dismas Hardy

Story type: Legal; Amateur Detective—Male Lead

Major character(s): Dismas Hardy, Lawyer, Saloon Keeper/Owner

Time period(s): 1990s

Locale(s): San Francisco, California

What the book is about: First hired as part of the prosecution team in the case of a murdered Japanese billionaire, Dismas Hardy soon finds himself fired and then is hired to defend the second person charged in the crime, his ex-father-in-law, who was also the judge in the trial of the first person accused of the crime.

Other books you might like:
Karen Kijewski, *The Kat Colorado Series*, 1988-
Marcia Muller, *The Sharon McCone Series*, 1977-
Bill Pronzini, *The Nameless Detective Series*, 1971-
Ronald Levitsky, *Stone Boy*, 1993
Shelley Singer, *Samson's Deal*, 1983

1010
John T. Lescroart
The Vig (New York: Fine, 1991)

Series: Dismas Hardy

Story type: Private Detective—Male Lead

Major character(s): Dismas Hardy, Detective—Private (unlicensed), Lawyer (district attorney)

Time period(s): 1990s

Locale(s): San Francisco, California

What the book is about: An old lawyer friend drops by to warn Dismas about a recently released criminal who is looking for revenge on the people who put him away. Then the friend disappears - blood but no body. Is he dead and who is responsible?

Other books you might like:
Lawrence Block, *A Ticket to the Boneyard*, 1990
Kenn Davis, *Melting Point*, 1986
James N. Frey, *A Long Way to Die*, 1987
Joe Gores, *Interface*, 1974
Robert Upton, *Fade Out*, 1984

1011
John Leslie
Killer in Paradise (New York: Pocket, 1990)

Story type: Police Procedural—Male Lead; Action/Adventure

Major character(s): Patrick Bowman, Police Officer (lieutenant); Lee Bowman, Spouse (of Patrick Bowman)

Time period(s): 1990s

Locale(s): Key West, Florida

What the book is about: While on medical leave in Key West after a shooting in Chicago, Patrick Bowman is asked to assist local police in tracking a female serial killer. This killer is preying on the young women who hustle on the streets, and because Bowman has the reputation of being a serial killer expert the Key West police think he will be useful.

Other books you might like:
Edna Buchanan, *Nobody Lives Forever*, 1990
Frederic Huber, *Axx Goes South*, 1989
John Katzenbach, *In the Heat of the Summer*, 1982
John Lutz, *Flame*, 1990
Randy Wayne White, *Sanibel Flats*, 1990

1012
John Leslie
Killing Me Softly (New York: Pocket, 1994)

Series: Gideon Lowry

Story type: Private Detective—Male Lead

Major character(s): Gideon Lowry, Detective—Private, Musician (piano player)

Time period(s): 1990s

Locale(s): Key West, Florida

What the book is about: Virginia Murphy asks Gideon Lowry, drunken musician and private eye, to look into the death of her sister. The fact that her sister died nearly 40 years ago seems not be be important to her. She just wants the truth. Then Virginia herself is dead, apparently in an accidental fall. Gideon now has two deaths to investigate.

Other books you might like:
Lawrence Block, *The Matt Scudder Series*, 1976
James W. Hall, *Hard Aground*, 1993
Carl Hiaasen, *Double Whammy*, 1987
Laurence Shames, *Scavenger Reef*, 1993
Les Standiford, *Done Deal*, 1993

1013
Ira Levin
Sliver (New York: Bantam, 1991)

Story type: Psychological Suspense

Major character(s): Kay Norris, Editor (book editor); Sam Yale, Director (retired film director); Peter Henderson, Computer Expert, Landlord (of a "sliver building")

Time period(s): 1990s (1991)

Locale(s): New York, New York

What the book is about: Kay Norris takes an apartment in a building on Manhattan's upper east side, unaware that the former tenant committed suicide and that the landlord has installed hidden observation cameras in every unit.

Other books you might like:
Robert Bloch, *Psycho*, 1959
Roland Topor, *The Tenant*, 1964

1014
Paul Levine
Mortal Sin (New York: Morrow, 1994)

Series: Jake Lassiter

Story type: Legal; Action/Adventure

Major character(s): Jake Lassiter, Lawyer; Nicky Florio, Businessman (real estate developer), Criminal

Time period(s): 1990s

Locale(s): Miami, Florida

What the book is about: As usual, Jake Lassiter is in trouble with the bar association. He's not innocent, but he betrayed his client in a good cause—to save a man's life. His current client however, is another matter. Nicky Florio, erstwhile real estate developer, is probably responsible for the death of an environmentalist who was opposing his plans for development in the Everglades. If he is guilty, Jake has a problem. Actually, even if he's not guilty, Jake has a problem as he's sleeping with Nicky's wife. Then Jake is accused of bribery and murder and is forced to run.

Other books you might like:
William Diehl, *Primal Fear*, 1992
James W. Hall, *Hard Aground*, 1993
Carl Hiaasen, *Native Tongue*, 1991
John Katzenbach, *In the Heat of the Summer*, 1982
D. Kincaid, *A Lawyer's Tale*, 1992

1015
Paul Levine
Night Vision (New York: Bantam, 1991)
Series: Jake Lassiter
Story type: Legal; Action/Adventure
Major character(s): Jake Lassiter, Lawyer; Pamela Metcalf, Doctor (psychiatrist), Writer
Time period(s): 1990s
Locale(s): Miami, Florida
What the book is about: Talked into becoming a special prosecutor on a serial killer case, Lassiter runs up against political corruption. Most, but not all, trails lead to Compumate, a computer service where people talk dirty to each other. Lassiter feels out of his element so he asks for assistance from visiting British psychiatrist Pamela Metcalf. This, of course, leads to further complications and not just in his personal life.

Other books you might like:
Harrison Arnston, *Act of Passion*, 1991
A.W. Gray, *In Defense of Judges*, 1990
John Grisham, *The Firm*, 1990
Carl Hiaasen, *Tourist Season*, 1985
Robert K. Tanenbaum, *Immoral Certainty*, 1991

1016
Paul Levine
To Speak for the Dead (New York: Bantam, 1990)
Story type: Legal; Amateur Detective—Male Lead
Major character(s): Jake Lassiter, Lawyer; Charlie Riggs, Doctor (retired county coroner)
Time period(s): 1990s
Locale(s): Miami, Florida
What the book is about: Jake Lassiter is defending orthopedic surgeon Dr. Roger Salisbury against a charge of medical malpractice in the death of wealthy Philip Corrigan. What appears to be routing turns deadly when the dead man's daughter accuses the doctor and her stepmother of murder. Lassiter doesn't quite believe it but then the stepmother makes a play for him. First novel.

Other books you might like:
Jay Brandon, *Fade the Heat*, 1990
Philip Friedman, *Reasonable Doubt*, 1989
Richard Harris, *Honor Bound*, 1982
Scott Turow, *Presumed Innocent*, 1988
Walter Walker, *Two Dude Defense*, 1985

1017
Ronald Levitsky
Stone Boy (New York: Scribners, 1993)
Series: Nate Rosen
Story type: Legal; Amateur Detective—Male Lead
Major character(s): Nate Rosen, Lawyer
Time period(s): 1990s
Locale(s): Bear Coat, South Dakota
What the book is about: Nate Rosen is a representative of the Committee to Defend the Constitution and as such is sent to South Dakota to defend an elderly Native American, Saul True Sky, against a charge of murder. True Sky is accused of the murder of a wealthy businessman. It appears, however, that True Sky, though he had reason to kill the man, may have been set up. He owns land that other men want for use as a spot for a gambling casino.

Other books you might like:
John Grisham, *A Time to Kill*, 1989
Jake Page, *The Stolen Gods*, 1993
Richard Parrish, *The Dividing Line*, 1993
Sandra West Prowell, *The Killing of Monday Brown*, 1994
J.F. Trainor, *Dynamite Pass*, 1993

1018
J.R. Levitt
Ten of Swords (New York: St. Martins, 1991)
Series: Jason Coulter
Story type: Private Detective—Male Lead
Major character(s): Jason Coulter, Detective—Private (former police officer)
Time period(s): 1990s
Locale(s): Salt Lake City, Utah
What the book is about: Jason Coulter is hired to find a missing daughter, but, of course, it's not that simple. Complications include the Church of the Four-sided Triangle, the apparently racially motivated shooting of two black teenagers, and the Mormon Church.

Other books you might like:
Rex Burns, *The Avenging Angel*, 1983
Thomas H. Cook, *Tabernacle*, 1983
R.R. Irvine, *The Moroni Traveler Series*, 1988-
Cleo Jones, *Prophet Motive*, 1984
Gary Stewart, *The Tenth Virgin*, 1983

1019
Michael Z. Lewin
Called by a Panther (New York: Mysterious, 1991)

Series: Albert Samson
Story type: Private Detective—Male Lead
Major character(s): Albert Samson, Detective—Private
Time period(s): 1990s
Locale(s): Indianapolis, Indiana
What the book is about: Someone is trying to frame an environmental group for a fatal bombing. The group hires Samson to find out who is behind the frame.
Other books you might like:
Wayne D. Dundee, *The Skintight Shroud*, 1989
Loren D. Estleman, *The Amos Walker Series*, 1982-
Stephen Greenleaf, *Death Bed*, 1984
Jonathan Valin, *The Harry Stoner Series*, 1980-

1020
Roy Harley Lewis
Death in Verona (New York: St. Martin's, 1989)
Series: Matthew Coll
Story type: Amateur Detective—Male Lead
Major character(s): Matthew Coll, Businessman (bookseller)
Time period(s): 1980s
Locale(s): Verona, Italy
What the book is about: While researching the historical roots of Romeo and Juliet, Coll finds himself involved with the modern day Capulets and Montagues.
Other books you might like:
S.F.X. Dean, *It Can't Be My Grave*, 1983
James Gollin, *The Verona Passamezzo*, 1985
Will Harriss, *The Bay Psalm Book Murder*, 1983
Wayne Warga, *Hardcover*, 1985
M.K. Wren, *Curiosity Didn't Kill the Cat*, 1973

1021
Sherry Lewis
No Place for Secrets (New York: Berkley, 1995)
Story type: Amateur Detective—Male Lead
Major character(s): Fred Vickery, Aged Person
Time period(s): 1990s
Locale(s): Cutler, Colorado
What the book is about: Fred Vickery has been advised to take it easy because of his heart. Easy to say, but when he finds the body of wealthy socialite Joan Cavanaugh, he is convinced she was murdered. The sheriff wants to call it an accident and the victim's husband wants to call it suicide. Fred talks Joan's estranged sister into asking for an investigation. When more people start to die, Fred realizes he may have started something he may not live to finish. First mystery.
Other books you might like:
Leo Axler, *The Bill Hawley Series*, 1994-
Steven F. Havill, *Bitter Recoil*, 1992
James MacCahery, *The Lavinia London Series*, 1989-
Susanna Hofmann McShea, *The Pumpkin-Shell Wife*, 1992
Karen Hanson Stuyck, *Cry for Help*, 1995

1022
Stephen Lewis
And Baby Makes None (New York: Walker, 1991)
Series: Seymour Lipp
Story type: Legal; Amateur Detective—Male Lead
Major character(s): Seymour Lipp, Lawyer
Time period(s): 1990s
Locale(s): New York, New York
What the book is about: Seymour agrees to help a young woman get back a baby she's given up for adoption. When the young woman's father—who arranged the adoption—turns up dead, Seymour finds himself involved in more than just a legal battle. Was the father murdered or was it suicide—as the police think?
Other books you might like:
William Bernhardt, *Primary Justice*, 1992
Miriam Borgenicht, *No Duress*, 1991
J.P. Hailey, *The Naked Typist*, 1990
Richard Harris, *Honor Bound*, 1982
Ed McBain, *Cinderella*, 1986

1023
Stephen Lewis
The Monkey Rope (New York: Walker, 1990)
Series: Seymour Lipp
Story type: Psychological Suspense; Action/Adventure
Major character(s): Seymour Lipp, Lawyer; Junior Constantino, Criminal
Time period(s): 1990s
Locale(s): New York, New York
What the book is about: Unable to distance himself emotionally from people out of his past, lawyer Lipp gets involved in a murder case. This involves him as well in sexual and emotional obsession. First mystery.
Other books you might like:
Thomas Bunn, *Closing Costs*, 1990
Thomas H. Cook, *Night Secrets*, 1990
Richard Harris, *Honor Bound*, 1982
Paul Levine, *To Speak for the Dead*, 1990
Scott Turow, *Presumed Innocent*, 1988

1024
Jeffry P. Lindsay
Tropical Depression (New York: Fine, 1994)
Story type: Amateur Detective—Male Lead; Action/Adventure
Major character(s): Billy Knight, Police Officer (retired)
Time period(s): 1990s
Locale(s): Key West, Florida; Los Angeles, California

What the book is about: Burnt-out cop Billy Knight has left Los Angeles for Key West to fish and forget. He lost his wife and daughter in a hostage situation gone wrong and just wants to ignore the world. Another Los Angeles cop tracks him to Key West and asks for Billy's help in solving what the cop feels is the murder of his son under cover of the Rodney King riots. Billy refuses to help, but when his friend is killed, the guilt kicks in and Billy is off to L.A. to find some answers. First novel.

Other books you might like:
James Lee Burke, *The Neon Rain*, 1986
James W. Hall, *Hard Aground*, 1992
Joe R. Lansdale, *The Savage Season*, 1990
Laurence Shames, *Florida Straits*, 1992
Stephen Solomita, *The Stanley Moodrow Series*, 1989-

1025
Paul Lindsay
Gentkill: A Novel of the FBI (New York: Villard, 1995)

Series: Mike Devlin

Story type: Police Procedural—Male Lead; Action/Adventure

Major character(s): Mike Devlin, FBI Agent

Time period(s): 1990s

Locale(s): Detroit, Michigan

What the book is about: Someone is killing FBI agents in Detroit and an extortionist is planting bombs at a hospital. Agent Mike Devlin, who may be the final target of the killer, is not allowed on either case. He is on the outs with his boss and has been exiled to cold case files. That, however, doesn't stop him from being very involved.

Other books you might like:
James Lee Burke, *Black Cherry Blues*, 1992
Michael Connelly, *The Concrete Blonde*, 1994
James Ellroy, *L.A. Confidential*, 1990
David L. Lindsey, *An Absence of Light*, 1994
John Sandford, *Sudden Prey*, 1996

1026
David L. Lindsey
An Absence of Light (New York: Doubleday, 1994)

Story type: Police Procedural—Male Lead; Action/Adventure

Major character(s): Marcus Graver, Police Officer

Time period(s): 1990s

Locale(s): Houston, Texas

What the book is about: The apparent suicide of a detective in the CID division begins an investigation that will lead Detective Marcus Graver places he may not want to go. The dead detective appears to have been implicated in CID corruption and may have been murdered to keep him silent. One of Marcus's friends may also be implicated and the plot may extend out of the police department into the shadowy world of espionage. Marcus has only five days to solve the crime or his investigation will be shut down.

Other books you might like:
James Lee Burke, *The Dave Robicheaux Series*, 1986-
Michael Connelly, *The Harry Bosch Series*, 1992-
Joseph Koenig, *Floater*, 1987
John Sandford, *Night Prey*, 1994

1027
David L. Lindsey
Mercy (New York: Doubleday, 1990)

Story type: Psychological Suspense

Major character(s): Carmen Palma, Detective—Police

Time period(s): 1980s

Locale(s): Houston, Texas

What the book is about: Someone is killing and mutilating women in Houston. Policewoman Carmen Palma is trying desperately to find the killer before he strikes again.

Other books you might like:
Patricia D. Cornwell, *Postmortem*, 1990
John Katzenbach, *The Traveler*, 1987
Rex Miller, *Slob*, 1988
Michael Slade, *Headhunter*, 1984
Shane Stevens, *By Reason of Insanity*, 1979

1028
Gillian Linscott
Hanging on the Wire (New York: St. Martins, 1993)

Series: Nell Bray

Story type: Historical; Amateur Detective—Female Lead

Major character(s): Nell Bray, Activist; Jenny Chesney, Nurse

Time period(s): 1910s (1916)

Locale(s): Wales

What the book is about: Asked by her friend Jenny Chesney to come to a small hospital in Wales to help stop war supporter Monica Minter from closing the hospital, Nell soons finds herself involved with what she thinks is murder. The director of the hospital thinks otherwise and wants to stop Nell and Jenny from investigating.

Other books you might like:
K.K. Beck, *Young Mrs. Cavendish and the Kaiser's Men*, 1987
Carole Nelson Douglas, *The Irene Adler Series*, 1990-
Ray Harrison, *Death of a Dancing Lady*, 1986
Michael Hastings, *The Devil's Spy*, 1988
Julian Symons, *Bland Beginning*, 1949

1029
Gillian Linscott
Sister Beneath the Sheet (New York: St. Martin's, 1991)

Story type: Historical; Amateur Detective—Female Lead

Major character(s): Nell Bray, Activist

Time period(s): 1900s (1900)

Locale(s): Biarritz, France

1030

What the book is about: Sent to Biarritz, by Emmeline Pankhurst, to collect a legacy left the Women's social and Political Union by a famous courtesan, Nell Bray soon finds herself involved in trying to discover whether the courtesan did, in fact, commit suicide or was murdered as the maid implies.

Other books you might like:
Carole Nelson Douglas, *Good Morning, Irene*, 1991
Ray Harrison, *Tincture of Death*, 1989
Anne Perry, *Belgrave Square*, 1992
Elizabeth Peters, *The Amelia Peabody Series*, 1974-

1030

Gillian Linscott
Stage Fright (New York: St. Martin's, 1993)

Series: Nell Bray

Story type: Amateur Detective; Historical

Major character(s): Nell Bray, Activist; George Bernard Shaw, Writer (playwright), Historical Figure; Bella Flanagan, Actress

Time period(s): 1900s (1909)

Locale(s): London, England

What the book is about: Nell Bray has established herself as something of a detective and is approached by a playwright to help protect one of his actresses. The playwright is George Bernard Shaw and the actress is Bella Flanagan, wife of powerful Lord Penwardine who is not at all happy with her being in a play. Accidents plague the production but the play goes on - interrupted first by hecklers and then by murder.

Other books you might like:
Carole Nelson Douglas, *The Irene Adler Series*, 1990-
Marian J.A. Jackson, *Diamond Head*, 1992
Kate Kingsbury, *The Pennyfoot Hotel Series*, 1993-
Amy Myers, *Murder in the Limelight*, 1987
William J. Palmer, *The Detective and Mr. Dickens*, 1990

1031

Gillian Linscott
Unknown Hand (New York: St. Martin's, 1989)

Story type: Amateur Detective—Male Lead

Major character(s): Colin Counsel, Teacher (Oxford University researcher)

Time period(s): 1980s

Locale(s): Oxford, England

What the book is about: While doing research in the Bodleian Library, Colin Counsel receives the wrong book. As he reads it he becomes convinced that the murder described therein really took place and determines to find out the truth.

Other books you might like:
Charity Blackstock, *Dewey Death*, 1977
Michael Delving, *The Devil Finds Work*, 1969
Charles A. Goodrum, *Dewey Decimated*, 1977
Will Harriss, *The Bay Psalm Book Murder*, 1983
Michael Innes, *Paper Thunderbolt*, 1951

1032

Thomas Lipinski
The Fall-Down Artist (New York: St. Martin's, 1994)

Story type: Private Detective—Female Lead

Major character(s): Carroll Dorsey, Detective—Private, Insurance Investigator

Time period(s): 1990s

Locale(s): Pittsburgh, Pennsylvania

What the book is about: Carroll Dorsey is an ex-college basketball star, ex-investigator for the District Attorney, and ex-army MP. He is also the son of a local politician who seems to be involved in some shady dealings. While doing some investigating for an insurance company, Carroll stumbles upon some crimes that seem to be connected to his father. Should he continue to investigate? Or is blood thicker than water? First novel.

Other books you might like:
Bill Crider, *The Truman Smith Series*, 1992-
Robert R. Irvine, *The Moroni Traveler Series*, 1986-
Ronald Clair Roat, *A Still and Icy Silence*, 1993
Les Roberts, *The Milan Jacovich Series*, 1989-
Stephen F. Wilcox, *The Elias Hackshaw Series*, 1992-

1033

Jayson Livingston
Point Blank (New York: St. Martins, 1990)

Story type: Police Procedural—Male Lead

Major character(s): Stuart Redlam, Detective—Police (homicide); Robert Hollinger, Detective—Police (robbery)

Time period(s): 1990s

Locale(s): Sacramento, California

What the book is about: A beautiful woman is brutally killed and sexually assaulted. Stu Redlam investigates and finds a mysterious coded book. Another woman is killed and has a similar book. Is this the work of a serial killer or a professional hit man? First novel.

Other books you might like:
David L. Lindsey, *Mercy*, 1990
Ed McBain, *The 87th Precinct Series*, 1956-
Tom Philbin, *Precinct Siberia Series*, 1985-
Joseph Wambaugh, *The Delta Star*, 1983
Collin Wilcox, *The Lieutenant Hastings Series*, 1969-

1034

Nancy Livingston
Death in Close-Up (New York: St. Martins, 1990)

Series: G.D.H. Pringle

Story type: Amateur Detective—Male Lead

Major character(s): G.D.H. Pringle, Accountant (retired tax inspector)

Time period(s): 1980s

Locale(s): England

What the book is about: Pringle, in need of cash, offers his accounting skills to a television producer. Though he doesn't expect it, this gets him involved in the investigation of the stabbing death of an actress virtually on-screen and the hit-and-run death of another member of the show. Are the two deaths connected? Pringle thinks so.

Other books you might like:
Marian Babson, *Murder, Murder, Little Star*, 1980
Lionel Black, *Death by Hoax*, 1978
Tim Heald, *Business Unusual*, 1990
Janet Laurence, *A Deepe Coffyn*, 1990

1035
Nancy Livingston
Mayhem in Parva (New York: St. Martin's, 1991)
Series: G.D.H. Pringle
Story type: Amateur Detective—Male Lead
Major character(s): G.D.H. Pringle, Accountant (retired tax inspector)
Time period(s): 1990s
Locale(s): Wuffinge Parva, England
What the book is about: On a visit to the village where he lived as a child when Pringle discovers things are not as he remembers. There is a murder, then the body disappears and Pringle finds himself drawn into ancient history—in which the causes of the current problems may lie.

Other books you might like:
Tim Heald, *Business Unusual*, 1990
Janet Laurence, *A Deepe Coffyn*, 1990
Anthony Oliver, *The Pew Group*, 1981
Emma Page, *Last Walk Home*, 1983
Sheila Radley, *A Talent for Destruction*, 1982

1036
Nancy Livingston
Unwillingly to Vegas (New York: St. Martin's, 1992)
Series: G.D.H. Pringle
Story type: Amateur Detective—Male Lead
Major character(s): G.D.H. Pringle, Accountant (retired tax inspector); Mavis Bignell, Friend (Pringle's significant other)
Time period(s): 1990s
Locale(s): Las Vegas, Nevada; England
What the book is about: Members of "the Family" - a second rate Mafia - are out to steal 23 million dollars from a Frank Sinatra telethon in Las Vegas. They hire a British film company as a front for the heist but they make one mistake - they hire Pringle as their accountant. When he suspects something is wrong, he takes action that starts a chain reaction of double-crosses and violence across the southwest.

Other books you might like:
Jonathan Gash, *The Very Last Gambado*, 1990
T.G. Gilpin, *Is Anybody There?*, 1992
Tim Heald, *The Simon Bognor Series*, 1979-

1037
Sam Llewellyn
Deadeye (New York: Summit, 1990)
Story type: Action/Adventure
Major character(s): Harry Frazer, Lawyer, Sailor
Time period(s): 1990s
Locale(s): Scotland (at sea)
What the book is about: When his boat is damaged off the coast of Scotland, Harry Frazer puts into a small, seemingly peaceful village. He soon falls in love with the place but discovers an undercurrent of menace that threatens the village. He determines to stop the evil taking place and this determination will take him to London, Rotterdam, Geneva, and Antwerp before the chase is over.

Other books you might like:
Bernard Cornwell, *Killer's Wake*, 1989
George Foy, *Coaster*, 1986
Dick Francis, *Flying Finish*, 1967
Tony Gibbs, *Running Fix*, 1990
Stuart Woods, *Run Before the Wind*, 1986

1038
Dick Lochte
Blue Bayou (New York: Simon & Schuster, 1992)
Series: Terry Manion
Story type: Private Detective—Male Lead
Major character(s): Terry Manion, Detective—Private; Nadia Wells, Detective—Private (runs her own agency)
Time period(s): 1990s
Locale(s): New Orleans, Louisiana
What the book is about: When Terry Manion comes out of his detox program he finds out that his partner has killed himself. Nadia Wells, herself a private detective and friend of both Manion and the dead man, thinks the death was not a suicide. Other deaths follow, all seeming to tie to Reevie Benedetto who is trying to take over his father's business—the mob. And what does New Orleans cop Eben Mann have to do with all of this?

Other books you might like:
Neal Barrett Jr., *Pink Vodka Blues*, 1992
James Lee Burke, *A Morning for Flamingos*, 1990
Jonathan Latimer, *Headed for a Hearse*, 1935
Julie Smith, *New Orleans Mourning*, 1990
Chris Wiltz, *The Emerald Lizard*, 1991

1039
Dick Lochte
The Neon Smile (New York: Simon & Schuster, 1995)
Series: Terry Manion
Story type: Private Detective—Male Lead
Major character(s): Terry Manion, Detective—Private; J.J. Legendre, Detective—Private (dead when the book starts)
Time period(s): 1990s (flashbacks to 1965)
Locale(s): New Orleans, Louisiana

What the book is about: Terry has been hired by a TV producer who wants to do a story on the 30-year-old case of a black militant cult leader. During his investigation Terry discovers that his mentor, J.J. Legendre was involved in the case, which paralleled the supposed capture of a serial killer. Was either case solved correctly? It appears that some of the people earlier involved and still alive are less than pleased with the current investigation.

Other books you might like:
Lawrence Block, *The Matt Scudder Series*, 1976-
James Lee Burke, *The Dave Robicheaux Series*, 1986-
John Clarkson, *And Justice for One*, 1992
John Sandford, *Rules of Prey*, 1989
Julie Smith, *New Orleans Mourning*, 1990

1040
Margaret Logan
A Killing in Venture Capital (New York: Walker, 1989)

Story type: Amateur Detective—Male Lead

Major character(s): Drew Lispenard, Businessman

Time period(s): 1980s

Locale(s): Boston, Massachusetts

What the book is about: When his cousin's lover is killed, investor Drew Lispenard needs to find out the truth for both personal and professional reasons.

Other books you might like:
Bruce Ducker, *Bankroll*, 1989
Emma Lathen, *Murder Against the Grain*, 1967
Annette Meyers, *The Big Killing*, 1988
Frank Orenstein, *The Man in the Gray Flannel Shroud*, 1984
Henry Slesar, *The Gray Flannel Shroud*, 1959

1041
Mary Logue
Still Explosion (New York: Seal, 1993)

Story type: Amateur Detective—Female Lead

Major character(s): Laura Malloy, Journalist (newspaper reporter)

Time period(s): 1990s

Locale(s): Minneapolis/St. Paul, Minnesota

What the book is about: Reporter Laura Malloy is at a Twin Cities family planning clinic when a bomb explodes. It kills the boyfriend of a young woman who is there for an abortion. It is possible that the boyfriend was himself carrying the bomb. Clinic officials blame Lifeline, the anti-abortion group headed by Tom Chasen. Laura isn't so sure and sets out to find the truth.

Other books you might like:
Mary Daheim, *The Alpine Advocate*, 1992
Nancy Baker Jacobs, *The Silver Scapel*, 1993
Susan Kelly, *The Liz Connors Series*, 1984-
Sarah Shankman, *First Kill All the Lawyers*, 1988
Kerry Tucker, *Still Waters*, 1991

1042
Randye Lordon
Sister's Keeper (New York: St. Martin's, 1994)

Series: Sydney Sloane

Story type: Private Detective

Major character(s): Sydney Sloane, Detective—Private, Lesbian; Nora Bradshaw, Housewife (Syd's sister)

Time period(s): 1990s

Locale(s): New York, New York

What the book is about: Sydney and Nora have been asked to attend a charity auction being handled by their old childhood friend, Zoe Freeman. Afterward Zoe is run down by a driver who swears it was an accident. While trying to arrange Zoe's funeral, they discover some odd things. Zoe's apartment has been trashed and she apparently had a second identity, with a secret bank account. She was also the mistress of an African diplomat, whose government may have taken a dim view of his behavior. Then a second person dies.

Other books you might like:
Ellen Hart, *Hallowed Murder*, 1989
Laurie R. King, *A Grave Talent*, 1993
Phyllis Knight, *Switching the Odds*, 1992
Sandra Scoppettone, *I'll Be Leaving You Always*, 1993
Pat Welch, *Murder by the Book*, 1990

1043
M.K. Lorens (Pseudonym of Margaret Fieldstrup)
Deception Island (New York: Bantam, 1991)

Series: Winston Sherman

Story type: Amateur Detective—Male Lead

Major character(s): Winston Sherman, Professor (of English), Writer (of mysteries); Sarah Cromwell, Musician (pianist), Companion

Time period(s): 1990s (1990)

Locale(s): Ainsley, New York

What the book is about: Art dealer Richard Brant is killed while impersonating an art critic. Does this have anything to do with the two paintings that may or not be by a famed artist?

Other books you might like:
V.C. Clinton-Baddeley, *Only a Matter of Time*, 1969
Jocelyn Davey, *A Capitol Offense*, 1956
S.F.X. Dean, *Such Pretty Toys*, 1982
Conrad Haynes, *Bishop's Gambit, Declined*, 1987
Roy Harley Lewis, *Where Agents Fear to Tread*, 1984

1044
M.K. Lorens (Pseudonym of Margaret Fieldstrup)
Dreamland (New York: Doubleday, 1992)

Series: Winston Sherman

Story type: Amateur Detective—Male Lead

Major character(s): Winston Sherman, Professor (of English), Writer (of mysteries); David Cromwell, Adoptee (adopted son of Winston Sherman), Actor

Time period(s): 1990s

Locale(s): New York, New York

What the book is about: Two murders—one at the Mystery Writers of America Edgar Award dinner and one in Central Park—occur within moments of each other. Winston Sherman, professor and mystery writer, is the suspect in one and his adopted son, actor David Cromwell, is the suspect in the other. Working together—sometimes—they try to find the truth and if the murders are connected, what connects them.

Other books you might like:
Brett Halliday, *She Woke to Darkness*, 1954
Edward D. Hoch, *The Shattered Raven*, 1976
M.D. Lake, *A Gift for Murder*, 1992
Robert Richardson, *The Book of the Dead*, 1989
Michael W. Sherer, *Little Use for Death*, 1992

1045
M.K. Lorens (Pseudonym of Margaret Feilstrup)
Sweet Narcissus (New York: Bantam, 1990)

Series: Winston Sherman

Story type: Amateur Detective—Male Lead

Major character(s): Winston Sherman, Professor (of English), Writer (of mysteries); Sarah Cromwell, Musician (Pianist), Companion

Time period(s): 1980s (1983)

Locale(s): New York

What the book is about: Thirty years ago a valuable manuscript was stolen and a servant was found dead during a reception for Dylan Thomas. Now the manuscript has turned up and a murderer strikes again. This is Lorens' first mystery.

Other books you might like:
V.C. Clinton-Baddeley, *To Study a Long Silence*, 1972
Amanda Cross, *The James Joyce Murder*, 1967
Conrad Haynes, *Bishop's Gambit, Declined*, 1987
Charlotte MacLeod, *Rest You Merry*, 1978
Robert Robinson, *Landscape with Dead Dons*, 1956

1046
David Lorne (Pseudonym of David L. Hoof)
Sight Unseen (New York: Signet, 1990)

Story type: Police Procedural

Major character(s): Jack "Spike" Halleck, Handicapped (Blind); Debra Seraphicos, Police Officer

Time period(s): 1980s

Locale(s): Illinois

What the book is about: When someone kidnaps Spike's niece, he and Seraphicos must find her before it's too late. First book.

Other books you might like:
Mary Higgins Clark, *A Stranger Is Watching*, 1977
Susan Kelly, *The Gemini Man*, 1985
Gregory McDonald, *Who Took Toby Rinaldi?*, 1980

1047
William F. Love
Bloody Ten (New York: Fine, 1992)

Series: Bishop Regan/Davey Goldman

Story type: Amateur Detective—Male Lead; Private Detective—Male Lead

Major character(s): Francis Regan, Religious (bishop), Detective—Amateur (frustrated crime-solver); David Goldman, Detective—Private (Regan's assistant)

Time period(s): 1990s

Locale(s): New York, New York; Minnesota

What the book is about: Davey gets involved in a murder off-off Broadway when he agrees to help an actor, Jim Kearney, dig up some information on a recently arrived half-brother. Soon the half-brother, who was in debt to the mob, turns up dead and Jim is the prime suspect. Seems the fellow was shot with Jim's gun. From New York to Minnesota Davey searches out clues to bring back to the Bishop.

Other books you might like:
Lawrence Block, *Make Out with Murder*, 1974
Dale L. Gilbert, *The Black Star Murders*, 1988
Robert Goldsborough, *Fade to Black*, 1991
Herbert Resnicow, *The Gold Solution*, 1983

1048
William F. Love
The Chartreuse Clue (New York: Fine, 1990)

Series: Bishop Regan/Davey Goldman

Story type: Private Detective—Male Lead

Major character(s): David Goldman, Detective—Private; Francis Regan, Religious (priest, bishop in New York)

Time period(s): 1980s

Locale(s): New York, New York

What the book is about: The wheelchair-bound Bishop Regan calls on his assistant, private detective David Goldman, to help in tracking down the killer of a woman who was killed to frame a monk. First book.

Other books you might like:
Dale L. Gilbert, *The Black Star Murders*, 1988
Isabelle Holland, *A Fatal Advent*, 1989
William X. Kienzle, *Deathbed*, 1986
Rex Stout, *The Nero Wolfe Series*, (1934-1975)

1049
Peter Lovesey
Bertie and the Seven Bodies (New York: Mysterious, 1990)

Series: Prince of Wales

Story type: Historical

Major character(s): Edward, Prince of Wales, Historical Figure

Time period(s): 1890s

What the book is about: At a shooting party someone begins to kill the guests and Bertie feels he must investigate.

Other books you might like:
K.K. Beck, *Young Mrs. Cavendish and the Kaiser's Men*, 1987
Richard Grayson, *The Murders at Impasse Louvain*, 1979
Ray Harrison, *Why Kill Arthur Potter?*, 1983
Anne Perry, *Paragon Walk*, 1982
Mark Schorr, *Bully!*, 1985

1050
Peter Lovesey
The Summons (New York: Mysterious, 1995)
Series: Peter Diamond
Story type: Police Procedural—Male Lead
Major character(s): Peter Diamond, Police Officer (resigned); Julie Hargreaves, Police Officer (detective inspector)
Time period(s): 1990s
Locale(s): Bath, England
What the book is about: Peter Diamond has resigned from the police force when a convict that he put away escapes from prison and kidnaps the Chief Constable's daughter demanding that the police reopen his case. Called back to help, Peter begins to think he may have made a mistake in the first case, but needs to find the truth quickly, with the assistance of Detective Inspector Julie Hargreaves. Some other police seem less interested in capturing him than killing him.

Other books you might like:
Robert Barnard, *The Cherry Blossom Corpse*, 1987
John Harvey, *Cold Night*, 1994
Ian Rankin, *The Inspector Rebus Series*, 1987-
Robert Richardson, *The Latimer Mercy*, 1987
Peter Robinson, *The Alan Banks Series*, 1988-

1051
Sarah Lovett
Dangerous Attachments (New York: Villard, 1995)
Story type: Psychological Suspense; Action/Adventure
Major character(s): Sylvia Strange, Doctor (forensic psychologist); Lucas Watson, Criminal
Time period(s): 1990s
Locale(s): New Mexico
What the book is about: Sylvia has been asked to evaluate inmate Lucas Watson for parole. Against the wishes of his father, a powerful politician, she recommends against parole but for transfer to a psych unit at another prison. Before that can happen there is a prison riot in which Lucas is killed—or is he? Someone is harvesting body parts from prisoners, both living and dead. Meanwhile, Lucas' brother has his own plans that may include Sylvia. First novel.

Other books you might like:
Patricia D. Cornwell, *The Kay Scarpetta Series*, 1990-
Eileen Dreyer, *Bad Medicine*, 1995
Susan Dunlap, *The Kiernan O'Shaughnessy Series*, 1990-
Gary Gottesfeld, *White Angel*, 1995
Mary Willis Walker, *Under the Beetle's Cellar*, 1995

1052
Margaret Lucke
A Relative Stranger (New York: St. Martin's, 1991)
Story type: Private Detective—Female Lead
Major character(s): Jessica Randolph, Detective—Private, Artist
Time period(s): 1990s
Locale(s): San Francisco, California
What the book is about: After abandoning her and her mother twenty years ago, Jessica Randolph's father has returned. He needs her help to clear his name in the murder of his business partner's daughter. Jessica rejects him, but when he is jailed and charged, she decides to help him. First novel.

Other books you might like:
Barbara D'Amato, *The Cat Marsala Series*, 1989-
Karen Kijewski, *Katwalk*, 1989
Marcia Muller, *The Joanna Stark Series*, 1987-1989
Marcia Muller, *The Sharon McCone Series*, 1977-
Maxine O'Callaghan, *The Delilah West Series*, 1982-

1053
Mike Lupica
Limited Partner (New York: Villard, 1990)
Series: Peter Finley
Story type: Amateur Detective—Male Lead
Major character(s): Peter Finley, Journalist (investigative reporter)
Time period(s): 1990s
Locale(s): New York, New York
What the book is about: When former drug addict Bobby Wyman is found dead of a heroin overdose, everyone assumes he went back to drugs except his friend Peter Finley. Peter is convinced that Bobby really was clean and was murdered. Now all he has to do is prove it.

Other books you might like:
Don Flynn, *Murder Isn't Enough*, 1983
Alison Gordon, *The Dead Pull Hitter*, 1989
Keith Peterson, *Rough Justice*, 1990
Mike Phillips, *Blood Rights*, 1989
Stephen F. Wilcox, *The Dry White Tear*, 1989

1054
Richard A. Lupoff
The Classic Car Killer (New York: Bantam, 1992)
Series: Hobart Lindsay
Story type: Amateur Detective; Police Procedural
Major character(s): Hobart Lindsay, Insurance Investigator; Marvia Plum, Police Officer (African-American)
Time period(s): 1990s
Locale(s): Oakland, California

What the book is about: Everyone involved in this case lives in the past in some way. Lindsay's mother acknowledges nothing past 1953, an eccentric club pretends it's still 1929 and a group of outwardly normal folks decorate themselves in Nazi regalia. The hook is the disappearance of a 1928 Dusenberg valued at half a million dollars, but everything else mentioned also comes into play as Lindsay and his lady love, female cop Marvia Plum, try to find the car and solve the murder of its supposed owner.

Other books you might like:
Jon L. Breen, *Touch of the Past*, 1988
John Dunning, *Booked to Die*, 1992
Joseph Hansen, *The Dave Brandstetter Series*, 1967-
Robert J. Randisi, *The Steinway Collection*, 1983
Wayne Warga, *Hardcover*, 1985

1055
Richard A. Lupoff
The Comic Book Killer (New York: Bantam, 1989)

Series: Hobart Lindsay

Story type: Amateur Detective—Male Lead

Major character(s): Hobart Lindsay, Insurance Investigator

Time period(s): 1980s

Locale(s): San Francisco, California

What the book is about: Due to the theft of a quarter million dollars worth of comics from a California comics shop, insurance adjuster Bart Lindsay must make himself familiar with the world of comics, something he has tried to avoid for years as his father was a comic artist and left the family when Bart was a child. Lupoff's first mystery, though he has written many science fiction and fantasy books.

Other books you might like:
Jon L. Breen, *Touch of the Past*, 1988
Harry Carmichael, *Naked to the Grave*, 1973
Bill Pronzini, *Hoodwink*, 1981
Robert J. Randisi, *The Steinway Collection*, 1983
Wayne Warga, *Hardcover*, 1985

1056
John Lutz
Diamond Eyes (New York: St. Martins, 1990)

Series: Alo Nudger

Story type: Private Detective—Male Lead

Major character(s): Alo Nudger, Detective—Private

Time period(s): 1990s

Locale(s): St. Louis, Missouri

What the book is about: Alo Nudger is at the airport waiting for a neighbor's flight when an airplane explodes on the runway. There should be diamonds somewhere in the wreakage but they can't be found. A woman Nudger had met at the airport turns up murdered and her dead lover appears to have been involved with the missing diamonds and the explosion.

Other books you might like:
Loren D. Estleman, *The Amos Walker Series*, 1980-
Steve Knickmeyer, *Cranmer*, 1977
Michael Z. Lewin, *Called by a Panther*, 1991
William J. Reynolds, *The Nebraska Quotient*, 1984
Les Roberts, *Pepper Pike*, 1988

1057
John Lutz
Flame (New York: Holt, 1990)

Series: Fred Carver

Story type: Private Detective—Male Lead

Major character(s): Fred Carver, Detective—Private (ex-policeman), Handicapped; Alfonso Desoto, Police Officer (former colleague of Carver)

Time period(s): 1980s

Locale(s): Florida

What the book is about: Carver's client has been hired to impersonate someone and wants Carver to find out why. When a murderer strikes, is the victim Carver's client.or the one being impersonated?

Other books you might like:
John Katzenbach, *In the Heat of the Summer*, 1982
Ed McBain, *The Matthew Hope Series*, (1978-)
John D. MacDonald, *The Travis McGee Series*, (1964-)
Charles Willeford, *Miami Blues*, 1984
Charles Williams, *Dead Calm*, 1963

1058
John Lutz
Spark (New York: Holt, 1993)

Series: Fred Carver

Story type: Private Detective—Male Lead

Major character(s): Fred Carver, Detective—Private (ex-policeman), Handicapped (has full use of only one leg)

Time period(s): 1990s

Locale(s): Florida

What the book is about: The widow of an apparent heart attack victim receives a note suggesting that he was, in fact, murdered. She asks Carver to investigate. While talking to people at the retirement community, Carver discovers evidence of adultery, drug-dealing, and soon, more murder.

Other books you might like:
Alison Drake, *Black Moon*, 1989
James W. Hall, *Tropical Heat*, 1989
Carl Hiaasen, *Double Whammy*, 1989
Elmore Leonard, *Split Images*, 1982
Charles Willeford, *Miami Blues*, 1984

1059
John Lutz
Thicker than Blood (New York: St. Martins, 1993)

Series: Alo Nudger

Story type: Private Detective—Male Lead
Major character(s): Alo Nudger, Detective—Private
Time period(s): 1990s
Locale(s): St. Louis, Missouri
What the book is about: As usual, P.I. Alo Nudger's client has lied to him. Hired by Norvella Beane to investigate securities fraud, Nudger is soon involved with neo-Nazis, drug dealers and maybe a crooked stockbroker. Then dead bodies begin to pile up and Nudger wants to make very sure that one of them isn't his.
Other books you might like:
Loren D. Estleman, *The Amos Walker Series*, 1980-
Michael Geller, *Three Strikes, You're Dead*, 1992
Rob Kantner, *The Ben Perkins Series*, 1986-
Dick Lochte, *Blue Bayou*, 1992
Les Roberts, *The Milan Jacovich Series*, 1988-

1060
John Lutz
Time Exposure (New York: St. Martins, 1989)
Series: Alo Nudger
Story type: Private Detective—Male Lead
Major character(s): Alo Nudger, Detective—Private
Time period(s): 1980s
Locale(s): St. Louis, Missouri
What the book is about: Nudger is asked by a librarian to find her missing sister who supposedly ran off with a city official.
Other books you might like:
Loren D. Estleman, *Amos Walker*, 1980
Steve Knickmeyer, *Straight*, 1976
Michael Z. Lewin, *The Albert Samson Series*, 1971
William J. Reynolds, *Nebraska*, 1984
Les Roberts, *Pepper Pike*, 1988

1061
Nan Lyons
Co-Author: Ivan Lyons
Someone Is Killing the Great Chefs of America (New York: Little, Brown, 1993)
Series: Natasha O'Brien
Story type: Amateur Detective—Female Lead
Major character(s): Natasha O'Brien, Businesswoman, Cook; Alex Gordon, Criminal, Critic (food critic)
Time period(s): 1990s
Locale(s): United States; France
What the book is about: Chef and businesswoman Natasha O'Brien is in the U.S. promoting American regional cooking and preparing to start *American Cuisine* magazine. She is also organizing the upcoming Culinary Olympics to take place in Paris. Her former mentor, murderer Achille van Golk, is supposedly dead and buried but in reality is alive and working in the U.S. at her magazine, under the name Alex Gordon. Someone is also killing American chefs. Is it Achille/Alex?

Other books you might like:
Michael Bond, *The Monsieur Pamplemousse Series*, 1985-
Dorothy Cannell, *Mum's the Word*, 1990
Mary Daheim, *Holy Terrors*, 1992
Diane Mott Davidson, *Catering to Nobody*, 1990
Virginia Rich, *The Cooking School Murders*, 1982

1062
Patricia MacDonald
No Way Home (New York: Delacorte, 1989)
Story type: Psychological Suspense
Major character(s): Lillie Burdette, Housewife; Jordan Hill, Actor
Time period(s): 1980s
Locale(s): Tennessee
What the book is about: Lillie Burdette's daughter, Michelle, is bludgeoned to death. When it seems the killer might be the sheriff's son, Lillie decides to do some investigating on her own, with the encouragement of Jordan Hill, New York actor and Michelle's father.
Other books you might like:
Mary Higgins Clark, *Stillwatch*, 1984
Mary Higgins Clark, *Where Are the Children?*, 1975
Kate Green, *Shattered Moon*, 1986
Ruth Rendell, *A Judgement in Stone*, 1986
Joyce Anne Schneider, *Darkness Falls*, 1989

1063
Charlotte MacLeod
The Gladstone Bag (New York: Mysterious, 1990)
Story type: Amateur Detective—Female Lead
Major character(s): Emma Kelling, Housewife (little old lady); Sarah Kelling, Housewife (niece of Emma)
Time period(s): 1980s
Locale(s): Maine
What the book is about: While staying at a friend's Maine retreat, Emma gets involved in theft, a possible murder, and what-all, which prompts her to ask her niece Sarah and her husband Max Bittersohn to help out.
Other books you might like:
Robert Barnard, *Death by Sheer Torture*, 1981
Richard Barth, *The Rag Bag Clan*, 1978
J.S. Borthwick, *The Down-East Murders*, 1986
Virginia Rich, *The Baked Bean Supper Murders*, 1983
Evelyn Smith, *Miss Melville Regrets*, 1986

1064
Charlotte MacLeod
An Owl Too Many (New York: Mysterious, 1991)
Series: Peter Shandy
Story type: Amateur Detective; Humor
Major character(s): Peter Shandy, Professor (of botany); Helen Shandy, Librarian (wife of Peter)

Time period(s): 1990s

Locale(s): Balaclava Junction, Maine

What the book is about: During Balaclava College's Annual Owl Count, one of the owl counters—who, it appears, wasn't who he claimed to be—turns up dead.

Other books you might like:
Simon Brett, *The Charles Paris Series*, 1975-
Joan Hadley, *The Theo Bloomer Series*, 1986-
Carolyn G. Hart, *The Annie Laurance/Max Darling Series*, 1984-
Bernie Lee, *Murder at Musket Beach*, 1990
Nancy Pickard, *The Jenny Cain Series*, 1984-

1065
Charlotte MacLeod
Something in the Water (New York: Mysterious, 1994)

Series: Peter Shandy

Story type: Amateur Detective—Male Lead

Major character(s): Peter Shandy, Professor (of botany)

Time period(s): 1990s

Locale(s): Maine

What the book is about: Peter Shandy is dining in a coastal Maine inn when one of the other guests dies in his plate of chicken pot pie. It turns out he died by cyanide poisoning. The dead man, Jasper Flodge, was not well-loved but Shandy nonetheless sets out to find his murderer.

Other books you might like:
Lydia Adamson, *A Cat on a Winning Streak*, 1994
Nancy Atherton, *Aunt Dimity's Death*, 1992
D.B. Borton, *Three Is a Crowd*, 1994
Mary Daheim, *The Alpine Decoy*, 1994
Jaqueline Girdner, *Fat-Free and Fatal*, 1994

1066
David Madsen
U.S.S.A. (New York: Morrow, 1989)

Story type: Police Procedural—Male Lead

Major character(s): Dean Joplin, Detective—Private (former C.I.A. agent); Richard Gardner, Detective—Police (homicide)

Time period(s): Indeterminate Future

Locale(s): Moscow, Union of Soviet Socialist Republics

What the book is about: In the world of the future, the Soviet Union has been occupied by the United States. Occupation Forces homicide detective Richard Gardner comes to his former teacher, Dean Joplin, now a Moscow P.I., for help in solving a murder with political implications.

Other books you might like:
Len Deighton, *SS-GB*, 1978
Stuart M. Kaminsky, *Black Knight in Red Square*, 1983
Stuart M. Kaminsky, *Death of a Dissident*, 1981
Anthony Olcott, *Murder at the Red October*, 1989
Martin Cruz Smith, *Gorky Park*, 1981

1067
Don Mahoney
Detective First Grade (New York: St. Martins, 1993)

Story type: Police Procedural—Male Lead; Action/Adventure

Major character(s): Brian McKenna, Police Officer, Detective

Time period(s): 1990s

Locale(s): New York, New York (Brooklyn)

What the book is about: Detective Brian McKenna has just been transferred from Manhattan to Brooklyn because he isn't a team player. He is not happy about it. Promotion seems unlikely until a routine traffic stop turns into a gun battle and uncovers a cocaine cartel and a kidnapping. First novel.

Other books you might like:
Peter Blauner, *Slow Motion Riot*, 1991
Lawrence Block, *A Dance at the Slaughterhouse*, 1992
William J. Caunitz, *Suspects*, 1986
Michael Connelly, *The Concrete Blond*, 1994
Joseph Wambaugh, *The Blue Knight*, 1972

1068
John Malcolm
Sheep, Goats and Soap (New York: Scribners, 1992)

Series: Tim Simpson

Story type: Amateur Detective—Male Lead

Major character(s): Tim Simpson, Banker (art expert)

Time period(s): 1990s

Locale(s): England

What the book is about: Searching for some pre-Raphaelite art for an art investment fund, Tim Simpson finds himself immersed in schemes that may be hazardous to his health. When he arrives at a cliffside cottage just after it has fallen (with help) into the sea, he knows that someone doesn't want him to find the art. Or is there more involved than just paintings?

Other books you might like:
Dick Francis, *Longshot*, 1990
Jonathan Gash, *The Lovejoy Series*, 1977-
Neville Steed, *The Peter Marklin Series*, 1986-
Wayne Warga, *Fatal Impressions*, 1989
David Williams, *The Mark Treasure Series*, 1977-

1069
John Malcolm
The Wrong Impression (New York: Scribners, 1990)

Series: Tim Simpson

Story type: Amateur Detective—Male Lead

Major character(s): Tim Simpson, Banker (art expert)

Time period(s): 1980s

Locale(s): London, England

What the book is about: Tim Simpson is determined to get revenge on the men who have put his friend, Chief Inspector Roberts, in the hospital in critical condition. He is also on the look-out for the perfect painting for the bank he works for. It appears that finding the painting might also lead him to Roberts's assailants. But it may also cost him his life.

Other books you might like:
B. Comfort, *Grave Consequences*, 1990
Jonathan Gash, *The Lovejoy Series*, 1977-
Roy Harley Lewis, *Death in Verona*, 1989
Neville Steed, *Clockwork*, 1990
David Williams, *Holy Treasure!*, 1989

1070
Michael Malone
Time's Witness (New York: Little, Brown, 1989)
Story type: Police Procedural—Male Lead
Major character(s): Cuddy Magnum, Police Officer (chief of police); Justin Savile, Police Officer
Time period(s): 1980s
Locale(s): Hillston, North Carolina (Fictional city)
What the book is about: When the brother of a convicted murderer is murdered on the eve of the execution, Cuddy, as the arresting officer in the original case, finds himself thrust back into the past to solve the current crime.

Other books you might like:
William J. Caunitz, *One Police Plaza*, 1984
K.C. Constantine, *The Rocksburg Railroad Murders*, 1972
Robert Daley, *Hands of a Stranger*, 1985
Joseph McNamara, *The First Directive*, 1984
Stuart Woods, *Chiefs*, 1981

1071
Jessica Mann
Faith, Hope and Homicide (New York: St. Martin's, 1991)
Series: Tamara Hoyland
Story type: Amateur Detective—Female Lead
Major character(s): Tamara Hoyland, Archaeologist (former spy); Alastair Hope, Archaeologist
Time period(s): 1990s
Locale(s): England
What the book is about: Botanist Louise Dench turns up dead, an apparent suicide. But there were some people interested in having her die including Tamara Hoyland's current boyfriend, Alastair Hope, a colleague of the dead woman. A few years earlier Hope and the dead woman's husband had been on an expedition from which only Hope had returned. Has he been responsible for the death of both husband and wife? Tamara hopes not but sets out to find the truth.

Other books you might like:
Aaron Elkins, *The Gideon Oliver Series*, 1982-
Gwen Moffat, *The Miss Pink Series*, 1973-
Anne Morice, *The Tessa Crichton Series*, 1970-
Paul Myers, *The Mark Holland Series*, 1986-
Elizabeth Peters, *The Amelia Peabody Series*, 1976-

1072
D. Keith Mano
Topless (New York: Random, 1991)
Story type: Action/Adventure; Amateur Detective—Male Lead
Major character(s): Mike Wilson, Religious (Episcopal priest)
Time period(s): 1990s
Locale(s): New York, New York (Queens)
What the book is about: Mike Wilson, shy, retiring priest in Nebraska, is called back to his old neighborhood in Queens to help out in his brother's bar. Nothing is as it seems. His brother has disappeared, the bar is a topless joint, drugs may be being sold and nobody believes Mike is as innocent as he appears to be. First crime novel.

Other books you might like:
Ed Gorman, *Night Kills*, 1990
Vince Kohler, *Rainy North Woods*, 1990
Thomas Maxwell, *The Suspense Is Killing Me*, 1990
Geoffrey Norman, *Sweetwater Ranch*, 1991
Stephen Robinett, *Unfinished Business*, 1990

1073
Cynthia Manson, Editor
Women of Mystery (New York: Carroll & Graf, 1992)
Story type: Anthology
Time period(s): 20th century
What the book is about: A collection of stories, all originally from *Ellery Queen's Mystery Magazine* and *Alfred Hitchcock's Mystery Magazine*. Authors include Ruth Rendell, Mary Higgins Clark, Amanda Cross, Anne Perry and Sara Paretsky.

Other books you might like:
Jen Green, *Reader, I Murdered Him*, 1989 (editor)
Sara Paretsky, *A Woman's Eye*, 1991 (editor)
Marie Smith, *Ms. Murder*, 1989 (editor)
Marilyn Wallace, *The Sisters in Crime Series*, 1989- (editor)

1074
Seth Jacob Margolis
False Faces (New York: St. Martin's, 1991)
Series: Joe DiGregorio
Story type: Police Procedural—Male Lead
Major character(s): Joe DeGregorio, Police Officer
Time period(s): 1990s
Locale(s): Fire Island, New York
What the book is about: When the body of party girl Linda Levinson washes up on the beach at Fire Island, Officer Joe DeGregorio is chosen to try and find out what happened. It is difficult as Linda's friends are particularly close-knit but Joe perseveres. First novel.

Other books you might like:
Rick Boyer, *The Penny Ferry*, 1984
Philip R. Craig, *A Beautiful Place to Die*, 1989
Jeremiah Healy, *Yesterday's News*, 1989
Douglas Kiker, *Death on Clam Pond*, 1987

1075
Seth Jacob Margolis
Vanishing Act (New York: St. Martins, 1993)

Series: Joe DiGregorio

Story type: Private Detective—Male Lead

Major character(s): Joe DiGregorio, Detective—Private (former police chief)

Time period(s): 1990s

Locale(s): New York, New York

What the book is about: Reading about the death of clothing king George Samson makes private detective Joe DiGregorio think that Samson is the man who wanted to hire him to stage his phony murder. DiGregorio gets in touch with the man now in charge of the business and gets hired to find the killer. Things, as always, are not as they appear.

Other books you might like:
Lawrence Block, *The Matt Scudder Series*, 1976-
Andrew Klavan, *The Scarred Man*, 1990
George P. Pelecanos, *Nick's Trip*, 1992
Bill Pronzini, *The Nameless Detective Series*, 1971-
Stephen Solomita, *A Twist of the Knife*, 1988

1076
Margaret Maron
Bootlegger's Daughter (New York: Mysterious, 1992)

Series: Deborah Knott

Story type: Amateur Detective—Female Lead

Major character(s): Deborah Knott, Lawyer

Time period(s): 1990s

Locale(s): Cotton Grove, North Carolina

What the book is about: Gayle Whitehead asks lawyer Deborah Knott to investigate the unsolved murder of her mother—18 years ago. Though involved in a campaign for a judgeship, Deb agrees. The trail is very cold, as one would expect, but by making a nuisance of herself, Deborah is able to find out the truth. First in a proposed series. Edgar nominee for Best Novel.

Other books you might like:
Linda Barnes, *Steel Guitar*, 1992
K.K. Beck, *A Hopeless Case*, 1991
Lia Matera, *Prior Convictions*, 1990
Judith Van Gieson, *The Neil Hamel Series*, 1988-
Carolyn Wheat, *Where Nobody Dies*, 1986

1077
Margaret Maron
Past Imperfect (New York: Doubleday, 1991)

Series: Sigrid Harald

Story type: Police Procedural—Female Lead

Major character(s): Sigrid Harald, Police Officer (homicide lieutenant)

Time period(s): 1990s

Locale(s): New York, New York

What the book is about: A cop nearing retirement is shot to death outside of a bar. As this man used to work with her policeman father before her father was killed years earlier, Sigrid Harald takes an uncommon interest in the case. When another investigator is killed, it appears that the deaths are connected and that a cop may be the killer.

Other books you might like:
Susan Dunlap, *The Jill Smith Series*, 1984-
Jack Early, *Donato and Daughter*, 1987
Ed McBain, *The 87th Precinct Series*, 1954-
Lillian O'Donnell, *Casual Affairs*, 1985
Dorothy Uhnak, *The Bait*, 1968

1078
Margaret Maron
Shooting at Loons (New York: Mysterious, 1994)

Series: Deborah Knott

Story type: Amateur Detective

Major character(s): Deborah Knott, Judge

Time period(s): 1990s

Locale(s): Harker's Island, North Carolina

What the book is about: Judge Deborah Knott is on vacation on Harker's Island, off the coast of North Carolina. While there she gets involved in disputes between the locals and people who are interested in development. She also finds a dead body. Someone has murdered Andy Bynum, who had been acting as a peacemaker between the two factions. Who killed him and why? As Deborah investigates she fears that the killer may be someone she knows and likes, and maybe loves.

Other books you might like:
Philip R. Craig, *The Woman Who Walked into the Sea*, 1991
Sally Gunning, *Underwater*, 1992
Carolyn G. Hart, *Dead Man's Island*, 1993
Doug Hornig, *Waterman*, 1987
Sharyn McCrumb, *If Ever I Return, Pretty Peggy-O*, 1990

1079
William Marshall
Faces in the Crowd (New York: Mysterious, 1991)

Series: Tillman and Muldoon

Story type: Historical; Police Procedural—Male Lead

Major character(s): Virgil Tillman, Police Officer; Ned Muldoon, Police Officer

Time period(s): 1880s (1884)

Locale(s): New York, New York

What the book is about: Is the missing prostitute, Rotary Rosie, just missing or is she dead? Is she in hiding? Why were there 187 wedding rings in her room? What is the secret society, The Custers? Tillman and Muldoon, at turns confused and hopeful, try to put everything together.

Other books you might like:
Lawrence Alexander, *The Big Stick*, 1986
William L. DeAndrea, *The Lunatic Fringe*, 1986
Robert J. Randisi, *The Ham Reporter*, 1987
James Sherburne, *Death's Pale Horse*, 1980

1080
William Marshall
The New York Detective (New York: Mysterious, 1989)
Series: Tillman and Muldoon
Story type: Historical
Major character(s): Virgil Tillman, Police Officer; Ned Muldoon, Police Officer
Time period(s): 1880s (1883)
Locale(s): New York, New York
What the book is about: Is there a connection between the murder of a stagehand, a holdup in the men's room and the appearance of a presidential candidate at the same theatre at the same time?
Other books you might like:
Robert J. Randisi, *The Ham Reporter*, 1987
James Sherburne, *Death's Pale Horse*, 1980

1081
Edward Marston
The Mad Courtesan (New York: St. Martin's, 1992)
Series: Nicholas Bracewell
Story type: Historical; Amateur Detective—Male Lead
Major character(s): Nicholas Bracewell, Actor (manager of an acting troupe)
Time period(s): 16th century (1590s)
Locale(s): England
What the book is about: Not only does Nicholas Bracewell have to deal with the future of his troupe—for there are rumors that the Queen is dying and who knows what the new monarch might like in terms of drama—but someone has murdered a potential shareholder. At the funeral Bracewell agrees to try and find the killer for the man's sister. But who is this mystery woman tempting the lead actor? Does this have anything to do with the murder as the lead actor was supporting the dead man?
Other books you might like:
P.C. Doherty, *Satan in St. Mary's*, 1987
Faye Kellerman, *The Quality of Mercy*, 1989
Leonard Tourney, *The Player's Boy Is Dead*, 1980

1082
Edward Marston
The Nine Giants (New York: St. Martin's, 1991)
Series: Nicholas Bracewell
Story type: Historical; Amateur Detective—Male Lead
Major character(s): Nicholas Bracewell, Actor (manager of an acting troupe)
Time period(s): 16th century (1590s)
Locale(s): England
What the book is about: Keeping the various egos of the company happy is a full-time job. When Bracewell and a ferryman discover a corpse, Bracewell feels there may be a link between the corpse and the current travails of the company.
Other books you might like:
P.C. Doherty, *Satan in St. Mary's*, 1987
Faye Kellerman, *The Quality of Mercy*, 1989
Leonard Tourney, *The Player's Boy Is Dead*, 1980

1083
Edward Marston
The Queen's Head (New York: St. Martins, 1989)
Series: Nicholas Bracewell
Story type: Historical
Major character(s): Nicholas Bracewell, Actor
Time period(s): 16th century (1588)
Locale(s): London, England
What the book is about: After the defeat of the Spanish Armada, London theater companies rush to get plays about it on the stage. Murder strikes one of these companies. First book.
Other books you might like:
Richard Falkirk, *Blackstone*, 1973
Keith Heller, *Man's Illegal Life*, 1985
Keith Heller, *Man's Storm*, 1986
Faye Kellerman, *The Quality of Mercy*, 1989
Charlotte Keppel, *The Villains*, 1982

1084
Edward Marston
The Trip to Jerusalem (New York: St. Martins, 1990)
Series: Nicholas Bracewell
Story type: Historical; Amateur Detective—Male Lead
Major character(s): Nicholas Bracewell, Actor (manager of an acting troupe)
Time period(s): 16th century (1590)
Locale(s): England
What the book is about: Beset by disasters to their troupe (intentional and otherwise) and ensnared in a spy network to capture Catholic traitors, Bracewell and company are not having an easy go of it.
Other books you might like:
P.C. Doherty, *Satan in St. Mary's*, 1987
Faye Kellerman, *The Quality of Mercy*, 1989
Leonard Tourney, *Low Treason*, 1983

1085
James E. Martin
The Flip Side of Life (New York: Putnam, 1990)
Story type: Private Detective—Male Lead
Major character(s): Gil Disbro, Detective—Private
Time period(s): 1980s
Locale(s): Cleveland, Ohio; Cincinnati, Ohio; Fort Wayne, Indiana

What the book is about: While searching for a missing professor and his son, Disbro discovers that the supposed suicide of the man's wife was, perhaps, murder.

Other books you might like:
Michael Z. Lewin, *The Albert Samson Series*, (1974-)
Robert Martin, *To Have and to Kill*, 1961
Les Roberts, *Full Cleveland*, 1988
Jonathan Valin, *The Harry Stoner Series*, (1980-)

1086
Lee Martin (Pseudonym of Martha G. Webb)
Bird in a Cage (New York: St. Martin's, 1995)
Series: Deb Ralston
Story type: Police Procedural—Female Lead
Major character(s): Deb Ralston, Police Officer
Time period(s): 1990s
Locale(s): Dallas/Fort Worth, Texas
What the book is about: While Deb and her husband are celebrating their 25th wedding anniversary, a terrible accident happens at the nightclub they're at. At least it is thought to be an accident. A trapeze artist falls to her death when a cable breaks. It appears that the nightclub owner had been getting extortion threats and that this may have had something to do with the fall. But maybe not.

Other books you might like:
Bill Crider, *The Sheriff Dan Rhodes Series*, 1986-
Susan Dunlap, *The Jill Smith Series*, 1986-
Jean Hager, *Ravenmocker*, 1992
Margaret Maron, *The Sigrid Harald Series*, 1982-
D.R. Meredith, *The Sheriff and the Panhandle Murders*, 1988

1087
Lee Martin (Pseudonym of Martha G. Webb)
The Day That Dusty Died (New York: St. Martin's, 1994)
Series: Deb Ralston
Story type: Police Procedural—Female Lead
Major character(s): Deb Ralston, Police Officer (detective)
Time period(s): 1990s
Locale(s): Fort Worth, Texas
What the book is about: Called to help talk 16-year-old Dusty Miller off a ledge—because she and Dusty are both women—Detective Deb Ralston fails when Dusty jumps. Obviously a clear-cut case of suicide—or is it? Deb needs to find out more about the girl's life to understand her death. At the same time she has been reassigned to the Sex Crimes Unit and is unhappy about the change, particularly when she finds herself dealing with a serial rapist. This is bringing back memories from her own past and a visit from her sister with AIDS isn't helping.

Other books you might like:
Bill Crider, *The Sheriff Dan Rhodes Series*, 1986-
Susan Dunlap, *Death and Taxes*, 1992
Jean Hager, *Ravenmocker*, 1992
Margaret Maron, *One Coffee With*, 1982
D.R. Meredith, *The Sheriff Charles Matthews Series*, 1987-

1088
Lee Martin (Pseudonym of Martha G. Webb and Anne Wingate)
Deficit Ending (New York: St. Martin's, 1990)
Series: Deb Ralston
Story type: Police Procedural—Female Lead
Major character(s): Deb Ralston, Police Officer (Just back from maternity leave)
Time period(s): 1980s
Locale(s): Fort Worth, Texas
What the book is about: When Deb witnesses a bank robbery in which a hostage is taken and later killed, she finds herself trying desperately to find the bank robbers before they hit again.

Other books you might like:
Alison Drake, *Tango Key*, 1988
Margaret Maron, *Baby Doll Games*, 1988
Lillian O'Donnell, *No Business Being a Cop*, 1979
L.V. Sims, *Murder Is Only Skin Deep*, 1987
Dorothy Uhnak, *The Ledger*, 1970

1089
Lee Martin (Pseudonym of Martha G. Webb)
The Mensa Murders (New York: St. Martins, 1990)
Series: Deb Ralston
Story type: Police Procedural—Female Lead
Major character(s): Deb Ralston, Police Officer
Time period(s): 1990s
Locale(s): Fort Worth, Texas
What the book is about: Beverly, a friend of Deb Ralston, asks Deb to investigate her sister's death, supposedly by a heart attack, but there are suspicious circumstances. It turns out to be murder, and other victims turn up and the only link is they all belong to MENSA. Martin also writes as Anne Wingate.

Other books you might like:
Susan Dunlap, *As a Favor*, 1984
M.D. Lake, *Cold Comfort*, 1990
Margaret Maron, *One Coffee With*, 1982
Lillian O'Donnell, *No Business Being a Cop*, 1979
L.V. Sims, *Murder Is Only Skin Deep*, 1987

1090
Steve Martini
Compelling Evidence (New York: Putnam, 1992)
Story type: Legal
Major character(s): Paul Madriani, Lawyer
Time period(s): 1990s
Locale(s): California
What the book is about: Philandering lawyer Paul Madriani finds himself defending one of his former lovers who is going on trial for killing her husband, formerly Paul's boss. He is being lied to at every turn and an unfriendly judge doesn't make things any easier. Is she guilty or is she innocent? First novel.

1091 Matera

Other books you might like:
Jay Brandon, *Fade the Heat*, 1990
Philip Friedman, *Reasonable Doubt*, 1989
Richard Harris, *Honor Bound*, 1982
Paul Levine, *To Speak for the Dead*, 1990
Walter Walker, *Two Dude Defense*, 1986

1091
Lia Matera
The Good Fight (New York: Simon & Schuster, 1990)
Series: Laura Di Palma
Story type: Amateur Detective—Female Lead
Major character(s): Laura Di Palma, Lawyer
Time period(s): 1980s
Locale(s): San Francisco, California
What the book is about: While Laura is supposed to be defending a former comrade accused of killing an FBI agent, she gets distracted in searching for her lover who has disappeared.

Other books you might like:
John Katzenbach, *Day of Reckoning*, 1988
Robert R. McCammon, *Mine*, 1990
Sharyn McCrumb, *If Ever I Return, Pretty Peggy-O*, 1990

1092
Lia Matera
A Hard Bargain (New York: Simon & Schuster, 1992)
Series: Laura Di Palma
Story type: Amateur Detective—Female Lead; Psychological Suspense
Major character(s): Laura Di Palma, Lawyer (currently unemployed)
Time period(s): 1990s
Locale(s): California (northern)
What the book is about: Laura is currently unemployed and living the small town life when her former lover asks for her help in finding out the truth behind another friend's death—apparently a suicide. Much familial angst must be sorted through before Laura can get to the truth.

Other books you might like:
Harrison Arnston, *Trade-Off*, 1991
Kate Green, *Night Angel*, 1989
Archer Mayor, *Borderlines*, 1990
Sharyn McCrumb, *If Ever I Return, Pretty Peggy-O*, 1990
Marcia Muller, *Trophies and Dead Things*, 1990

1093
Lia Matera
Prior Convictions (New York: Simon and Schuster, 1991)
Series: Willa Jansson
Story type: Amateur Detective—Female Lead; Legal
Major character(s): Willa Jansson, Lawyer (former radical)

Time period(s): 1990s
Locale(s): San Francisco, California
What the book is about: What appears to be a simple domestic squabble turns out to be something much bigger - involving Willa's radical past and threatening her future.

Other books you might like:
Linda Barnes, *Coyote*, 1990
John Katzenbach, *Day of Reckoning*, 1988
Marcia Muller, *Dark Star*, 1989
Jonathan Valin, *Fire Lake*, 1987
Susan Wolfe, *The Last Billable Hour*, 1989

1094
Linda Mather
Blood of an Aries (New York: St. Martin's, 1994)
Story type: Private Detective—Female Lead
Major character(s): Josephine "Jo" Hughes, Detective—Private (part-time investigator), Astrologer
Time period(s): 1990s
Locale(s): Coventry, England
What the book is about: Jo Hughes needs money—her astrology column doesn't pay enough to pay the rent—so she takes a job as a part-time phone tracer for a private inquiry agent. One of her first cases is that of tracing the activities of Graham Holt. She is led to Warwick University where she meets the young daughter of a professor who has just been found dead of a gunshot. She then learns that Graham has also been killed. Can the stars tell her what is going on? First novel.

Other books you might like:
Liza Cody, *The Anna Lee Series*, 1980-
Sarah Dunant, *Fatlands*, 1994
Christine T. Jorgensen, *A Love to Die For*, 1994
Sarah Lacey, *File Under: Missing*, 1994
Michelle Spring, *Every Breath You Take*, 1994

1095
Edward Mathis
See No Evil (New York: Berkley, 1990)
Story type: Police Procedural—Male Lead
Major character(s): Hamilton Pope, Police Officer (homicide detective)
Time period(s): 1980s
Locale(s): Dallas/Fort Worth, Texas
What the book is about: Twenty years after the death of a student on a class trip, someone is killing off his classmates, following the order of the poem—rich man, poor man, beggar man, thief. Can Pope catch the killer before he or she finishes the verse?

Other books you might like:
David L. Lindsey, *The Stuart Haydon Series*, 1983-
Lee Martin, *Deficit Ending*, 1990
John Sandford, *Eyes of Prey*, 1991
David Stout, *Night of the Ice Storm*, 1991
Rex Stout, *The League of Frightened Men*, 1935

1096
Edward Mathis
September Song (New York: Scribners, 1991)
Series: Dan Roman
Story type: Private Detective—Male Lead
Major character(s): Dan Roman, Detective—Private
Time period(s): 1990s
Locale(s): Texas
What the book is about: Dan's ex-wife comes to him for help when a convict she helped put in prison gets out and starts following her around. Dan is still obsessed with her, so it's not easy for him to be around her but he agrees to help anyway. He thinks it might help their relationship and he doesn't really feel she's in any danger.
Other books you might like:
Bruce Cook, *Rough Cut*, 1990
Bill Crider, *Dead on the Island*, 1991
James Crumley, *The Last Good Kiss*, 1978
Robert J. Ray, *Cage of Mirrors*, 1980
James Reasoner, *Texas Wind*, 1980

1097
Stefanie Matteson
Murder at the Spa (New York: Charter, 1990)
Series: Charlotte Graham
Story type: Amateur Detective—Female Lead
Major character(s): Charlotte Graham, Actress; Paulina Langenberg, Businesswoman (owner of a beauty empire)
Time period(s): 1990s
Locale(s): High Rock Springs, New York (Adirondacks)
What the book is about: Paulina Langenberg thinks someone is trying to sabotage her spa so she sends out a call for help to her old acquaintance Charlotte Graham, who has quite a reputation as an amateur sleuth. Soon murder arrives at the spa as well. First mystery.
Other books you might like:
Dorothy Cannell, *The Thin Woman*, 1984
Agatha Christie, *The Miss Marple Series*, 1930-1976
Joyce Christmas, *Simply to Die For*, 1989
Mary Higgins Clark, *Weep No More, My Lady*, 1987
James McCahery, *Grave Undertaking*, 1990

1098
Stefanie Matteson
Murder on the Cliff (New York: Berkley, 1991)
Series: Charlotte Graham
Story type: Amateur Detective—Female Lead
Major character(s): Charlotte Graham, Actress (aging movie star)
Time period(s): 1990s
Locale(s): Newport, Rhode Island
What the book is about: While in Newport for a festival honoring Commodore Perry's opening of Japan, Charlotte gets herself involved in solving the murder of one of the guests of honor. There are sumo wrestlers, geishas and other less interesting things to learn about as she investigates.
Other books you might like:
Dorothy Cannell, *The Thin Woman*, 1984
Agatha Christie, *The Miss Marple Series*, 1930-1976
Joyce Christmas, *The Lady Margaret Priam Series*, 1987-
Dorothy Gilman, *The Mrs. Pollifax Series*, 1966-
Corinne Holt Sawyer, *The J. Alfred Prufrock Murders*, 1988

1099
Francine Matthews
Death on Rough Water (New York: Morrow, 1995)
Series: Merry Folger
Story type: Police Procedural—Female Lead
Major character(s): Merry Folger, Police Officer, Detective—Police
Time period(s): 1990s
Locale(s): Nantucket, Massachusetts
What the book is about: Del Duarte, Merry's childhood friend, has returned home for the funeral of her father, who died at sea. Del doesn't believe it was an accident and is staying in town to find the truth and to take over her father's fishing business. People are not pleased with this. Then Del turns up dead, stabbed with a harpoon. Merry must investigate Del's past to find out who killed her.
Other books you might like:
Linda Barnes, *The Carlotta Carlyle Series*, 1987-
P.M. Carlson, *The Marty Hopkins Series*, 1993-
Philip R. Craig, *Cliff Hanger*, 1993
Sally Gunning, *Ice Water*, 1993
Paul Kemprecos, *Neptune's Eye*, 1990

1100
A.E. Maxwell (Pseudonym of Ann Maxwell and Evan Maxwell)
Money Burns (New York: Villard, 1991)
Series: Fiddler
Story type: Amateur Detective; Action/Adventure
Major character(s): Fiddler Flynn, Businessman (idependently wealthy); Fiora Flynn, Businesswoman (Fiddler's ex-wife)
Time period(s): 1990s
Locale(s): California
What the book is about: Fiddler and Fiora get involved with a banker in a small California town who is worried about her son. He seems to be involved with drug dealers who have designs on the bank for their money laundering schemes.
Other books you might like:
John Camp, *The Fool's Run*, 1990
Jerome Doolittle, *Body Scissors*,
David Handler, *The Stewart Hoag Series*, 1988-
Ross Thomas, *The Fourth Durango*, 1989

1101
Jan Maxwell
Baptism for Murder (New York: Avon, 1995)

Story type: Amateur Detective—Male Lead

Major character(s): Eldon Littlejohn, Religious (Baptist minister)

Time period(s): 1990s

Locale(s): Austin, Texas

What the book is about: The day following a baptism, the church treasurer's body is found in the Baptistry. The unfortunate Leroy Boyd has been shot. Eldon soon discovers that Leroy had been using the church as a money laundry for some local drug dealers. Eldon, in trying to save his church, is put between the police, who think he may be a murderer, and drug dealers who are sure he knows something he shouldn't. First mystery.

Other books you might like:
Andrew M. Greeley, *The Blackie Ryan Series*, 1986-
Harry Kemelman, *The Rabbi Small Series*, 1965-
William Kienzle, *The Father Koesler Series*, 1979-
Ralph McInerny, *The Father Dowling Series*, 1979-
Charles Merrill Smith, *The Reverend Randollph Series*, 1977-1985

1102
Thomas Maxwell (Pseudonym of Thomas Gifford)
The Suspense Is Killing Me (New York: Mysterious, 1990)

Story type: Action/Adventure; Amateur Detective—Male Lead

Major character(s): Lee Tripper, Heir (brother of a dead rock star), Journalist (retired)

Time period(s): 1990s (with many flashbacks to the 1960s)

Locale(s): United States; England

What the book is about: A reclusive writer hires Lee Triper to investigate whether Lee's brother, rock star J.C. Tripper, really died in Tangiers in the 1960s. It appears someone does not want Lee Tripper to find out the truth about the life - or death - of his brother.

Other books you might like:
Kate Green, *Night Angel*, 1989
Deidre S. Laiken, *Killing Time in Buffalo*, 1990
George R.R. Martin, *The Armageddon Rag*, 1986
David J. Schow, *The Kill Riff*, 1988
Roger L. Simon, *The Big Fix*, 1973

1103
Archer Mayor
Borderlines (New York: Putnam, 1990)

Series: Joe Gunther

Story type: Police Procedural—Male Lead

Major character(s): Joe Gunther, Police Officer

Time period(s): 1990s

Locale(s): Gannett, Vermont

What the book is about: On assignment in Gannett, Vermont, where he spent his childhood summers—he is normally a Brattleboro cop—Joe Gunther gets between a cult and the townspeople and a couple who arrive to rescue their daughter from the cult. Murder soon arrives as well and it appears that an old friend of Joe's is responsible.

Other books you might like:
B. Comfort, *Grave Consequences*, 1989
K.C. Constantine, *Sunshine Enemies*, 1990
Susan Rogers Cooper, *Houston in the Rearview Mirror*, 1990
Joseph Koenig, *Floater*, 1987
Ted Wood, *On the Inside*, 1990

1104
Archer Mayor
Fruits of the Poisonous Tree (New York: Mysterious, 1994)

Series: Joe Gunther

Story type: Police Procedural—Male Lead

Major character(s): Joe Gunther, Police Officer; Gail Zigman, Political Figure (Joe's lover)

Time period(s): 1990s

Locale(s): Brattleboro, Vermont

What the book is about: Joe Gunther's lover, Gail Zigman, has been raped and tortured. Joe is very angry, particularly when it appears that the crime was not a random act, but something done to get his attention. But why?

Other books you might like:
K.C. Constantine, *Bottom-Feeder Blues*, 1993
Joseph Koenig, *Floater*, 1987
Darian North, *Criminal Seduction*, 1994
Benjamin M. Schutz, *A Fistful of Empty*, 1991
Steven Womack, *Way Past Dead*, 1995

1105
Archer Mayor
Scent of Evil (New York: Mysterious, 1992)

Series: Joe Gunther

Story type: Police Procedural—Male Lead

Major character(s): Joe Gunther, Police Officer (lieutenant)

Time period(s): 1990s

Locale(s): Brattleboro, Vermont

What the book is about: Local stockbroker and drug user Charlie Jardine is found buried. He was having an affair with a policeman's wife which makes the cop the prime suspect. Lt. Gunther thinks not however and sets out to prove the cop's innocence. When another dealer is shot and killed Gunther's feelings are even stronger, but he is having a difficult time proving it because there's a leak from inside the police department.

Other books you might like:
B. Comfort, *Grave Consequences*, 1989
K.C. Constantine, *Bottom-Feeder Blues*, 1993
Bill Crider, *Shotgun Saturday Night*, 1987
Joseph Koenig, *Floater*, 1987
Ted Wood, *On the Inside*, 1990

1106
Ed McBain (Pseudonym of Evan Hunter)
Three Blind Mice (New York: Arcade, 1990)
Series: Matthew Hope
Story type: Legal; Amateur Detective—Male Lead
Major character(s): Matthew Hope, Lawyer
Time period(s): 1990s
Locale(s): Calusa, Florida
What the book is about: Three Vietnamese men are acquitted of raping a rich man's wife. After the trial the husband swears he will take justice into his own hands. When the three are found tortured, mutilated and murdered sometime later, the husband is immediately arrested. But is he really guilty or did someone set him up? Or are the deaths totally unrelated to the rape? Matthew Hope is hired to defend the husband and investigate.

Other books you might like:
Jay Brandon, *Predator's Waltz*, 1989
Philip Friedman, *Reasonable Doubt*, 1990
Colin Harrison, *Break and Enter*, 1990
Paul Levine, *To Speak for the Dead*, 1990
T. Jefferson Parker, *Little Saigon*, 1988

1107
Ed McBain (Pseudonym of Evan Hunter)
Vespers (New York: Morrow, 1990)
Series: 87th Precinct
Story type: Police Procedural—Male Lead
Major character(s): Steve Carella, Detective—Police; Cotton Hawes, Detective—Police
Time period(s): 1980s
What the book is about: When a Catholic priest is murdered the prime suspects are satanists who have headquarters near the church. But all is not what it seems.

Other books you might like:
Dell Shannon, *Case Pending*, 1960
Hillary Waugh, *Last Seen Wearing. . .*, 1952
Collin Wilcox, *The Lieutenant Hastings Series*, (1969-)

1108
Douglas McBriarty
Carolina Gold (New York: St. Martins, 1991)
Series: Pete McPhee
Story type: Police Procedural—Male Lead
Major character(s): Pete McPhee, Police Officer (sheriff)
Time period(s): 1990s
Locale(s): North Carolina
What the book is about: A black labrador is shot and a shopowner disappears. Are these two things connected and do they have anything to do with the newly discovered gold mine in the mountains? Sheriff McPhee thinks so and with the assistance of his trusty staff he sets out to find out.

Other books you might like:
Bill Crider, *Shotgun Saturday Night*, 1987
Richard Forrest, *Death on the Mississippi*, 1989
Steven F. Havill, *Heartshot*, 1981
Michael T. Hinkemeyer, *A Time to Reap*, 1985
Frank C. Strunk, *Jordon's Wager*, 1991

1109
Peter McCabe
City of Lies (New York: Morrow, 1993)
Story type: Amateur Detective—Male Lead
Major character(s): Mike Kincaid, Journalist
Time period(s): 1990s
Locale(s): New York, New York
What the book is about: Crime journalist Mike Kincaid is asked by the associate publisher of a New York magazine to help her when she is the suspect in the murder of the magazine's art director. While helping her and following the story, Kincaid gets involved with one of the murdered man's old girlfriends who is also a suspect. First novel.

Other books you might like:
James Grady, *River of Darkness*, 1991
M.S. Karl, *Deerslayer*, 1991
Michael J. Katz, *Last Dance in Redondo Beach*, 1989
Andrew Klavan, *Corruption*, 1994
Keith Peterson, *The John Wells Series*, 1988-

1110
Peter McCabe
Wasteland (New York: Scribners, 1994)
Story type: Amateur Detective—Male Lead; Action/Adventure
Major character(s): Will Dunbar, Public Relations
Time period(s): 1990s
Locale(s): Los Angeles, California
What the book is about: Will Dunbar, head of public relations for a big real estate firm, finds out that one of his co-workers is having an affair with his wife. When the man turns up dead, Will is arrested and charged with the man's murder. He is being set up, all because of a land deal in which the company stands to make millions and which he knows is fraudulent. Can he discover the real killer before he is convicted?

Other books you might like:
Neil Albert, *The February Trouble*, 1992
Michael Allegretto, *Blood Relative*, 1992
Robert Crais, *Lullaby Town*, 1992
John Grisham, *The Firm*, 1991
Richard Nehrbass, *Dark of Night*, 1992

1111
Taylor McCafferty
Pet Peeves (New York: Pocket, 1990)

Story type: Private Detective—Male Lead

Major character(s): Haskell Blevins, Detective—Private (former police officer)

Time period(s): 1990s

Locale(s): Pigeon Fork, Kentucky

What the book is about: Business is slow for new P.I. Haskell Blevins when Cordelia Turley wanders into his office and asks him to find out who killed her grandmother and her grandmother's cat and parakeet. Doesn't seem like much of a problem until someone slashes Haskell's tires and starts sending him threatening letters. First novel.

Other books you might like:
Bill Crider, *The Dan Rhodes Series*, 1987-
Steven F. Havill, *Heartshot*, 1991
Joe L. Hensley, *Fort's Law*, 1987
Joan Hess, *The Arly Hanks Series*, 1987-
Douglas Kiker, *Death at the Cut*, 1988

1112
James McCahery
Grave Undertaking (New York: Knightsbridge, 1990)

Story type: Amateur Detective—Female Lead

Major character(s): Lavina London, Actress (retired radio actress, 71 year)

Time period(s): 1990s

Locale(s): Catskills, New York

What the book is about: When Lavina London discovers the body of the town's funeral director in one of his own caskets, she determines to stay on the case—especially since her theories on the murder differ quite dramatically from the police theories. More death soon follows and the police are glad for her help. First novel.

Other books you might like:
Richard Barth, *Furnished for Murder*, 1990
John Keith Drummond, *The Matilda Worthing Series*, 1985-
Dorothy Gilman, *The Mrs. Pollifax Series*, 1966
Corinne Holt Sawyer, *The J. Alfred Prufrock Murders*, 1988
Remar Sutton, *Long Lines*, 1989

1113
Thomas McCall
A Wide and Capable Revenge (New York: Hyperion, 1993)

Story type: Police Procedural—Female Lead

Major character(s): Nora Callum, Police Officer, Handicapped (has only one leg)

Time period(s): 1990s

Locale(s): Chicago, Illinois

What the book is about: One-legged police officer Nora Callum discovers a link between the shooting of a woman in the Holy Name Cathedral and the body of an old man who had been bothering the police about someone following him. The link seems to be something that happened years ago at the siege of Leningrad. Her daughter's baby-sitter was also a Russian survivor of World War II and knows many of the people that seem to be involved in the cases. First novel.

Other books you might like:
Barbara D'Amato, *Hardball*, 1990
Margaret Maron, *Corpus Christmas*, 1989
Lee Martin, *Hacker*, 1992
Sara Paretsky, *Indemnity Only*, 1982
R.D. Zimmerman, *Deadfall in Berlin*, 1990

1114
James McClure
The Song Dog (New York: Mysterious, 1991)

Series: Kramer and Zondi

Story type: Police Procedural—Male Lead; Historical

Major character(s): Tromp Kramer, Police Officer (CID lieutenant); Mickey Zondi, Police Officer (sergeant; Bantu)

Time period(s): 1960s (1962)

Locale(s): South Africa

What the book is about: The case that brought Kramer and Zondi together involves the murder of a white housewife—not exactly a pure woman—and a respected policeman in a dynamited house. Was the killer the cuckolded husband or was the husband the target. Set against the backdrop of the ANC and Nelson Mandela's imprisonment.

Other books you might like:
June Drummond, *Junta*, 1989
June Drummond, *The Saboteurs*, 1967
Wessel Ebersohn, *Divide the Night*, 1981
Wessel Ebersohn, *A Lonely Place to Die*, 1980
Peter Niesewand, *A Member of the Club*, 1979

1115
Sharyn McCrumb
The Hangman's Beautiful Daughter (New York: Scribners, 1992)

Series: Spencer Arrowood

Story type: Psychological Suspense; Police Procedural—Male Lead

Major character(s): Spencer Arrowood, Police Officer (sheriff); Laura Bruce, Housewife (minister's wife); Nora Bonesteel, Aged Person, Psychic

Time period(s): 1990s

Locale(s): Dark Hollow, Tennessee

What the book is about: The apparent murder/suicide of most of the family of a retired Army officer sets in motion a chain of events that will affect most everyone in Dark Hollow. Why have the surviving children dug up their father? Can old Nora Bonesteel and her "sight" help Sheriff Arrowood and Laura Bruce find the truth behind the deaths?

Other books you might like:
Deborah Adams, *All the Great Pretenders*, 1992
Tony Gibbs, *Shadow Queen*, 1991
Marcia Muller, *Where Echoes Live*, 1991

1116
Sharyn McCrumb
If Ever I Return, Pretty Peggy-O (New York: Scribners, 1990)

Story type: Psychological Suspense

Major character(s): Peggy Muryan, Singer (folksinger); Spencer Arrowood, Police Officer (sheriff)

Time period(s): 1980s

Locale(s): Hamelin, Tennessee

What the book is about: When Peggy Muryan comes to a small town in Tennessee to get away from it all, she finds instead that the 1960s have followed her there to wreak havoc with her life. McCrumb won the best paperback Edgar for her previous novel, *Bimbos of the Death Sun*.

Other books you might like:
Robert J. Bowman, *The House of Blue Lights*, 1987
J.C. Pollack, *Centrifuge*, 1984
Margaret Tracy, *Mrs. White*, 1983
Teri White, *Triangle*, 1982

1117
Sharyn McCrumb
MacPherson's Lament (New York: Ballantine, 1992)

Series: Elizabeth MacPherson

Story type: Amateur Detective—Female Lead

Major character(s): Elizabeth MacPherson, Anthropologist (forensic); Bill MacPherson, Lawyer (Elizabeth's brother)

Time period(s): 1990s; 1860s (1865)

Locale(s): Danville, Virginia

What the book is about: Bill MacPherson has just graduated from law school and opened a law office with his partner A.P. (Amy) Hill. One of his first cases is for a group of old ladies who want to sell their historic home. He manages to sell the home but when the new owner tries to move in, he is told the home is owned by the state. Bill is charged with fraud, and since the old ladies have disappeared, he is suspected of murder. Elizabeth returns from Scotland to help and gets involved in a treasure hunt for Civil War gold. Short chapters follow the exploits of Gabriel Hawks in 1865.

Other books you might like:
P.M. Carlson, *The Maggie Ryan Series*, 1987-
Jaqueline Girdner, *The Kate Jasper Series*, 1991-
Carolyn G. Hart, *The Annie Laurance Series*, 1987-
Nancy Pickard, *The Jenny Cain Series*, 1984-
Gillian Roberts, *The Amanda Pepper Series*, 1987-

1118
Sharyn McCrumb
Missing Susan (New York: Ballantine, 1991)

Series: Elizabeth MacPherson

Story type: Amateur Detective—Female Lead

Major character(s): Elizabeth MacPherson, Anthropologist (forensic); Rowan Rover, Tour Guide (murder tours of England)

Time period(s): 1990s

Locale(s): England (On tour)

What the book is about: Elizabeth MacPherson, on a tour of famous murder sites of England, becomes suspicious when accidents begin to befall others on the tour. She thinks attempted murder may be afoot. She's correct. The guide, Rowan Rover, has contracted to kill Susan, one of the more obnoxious tour members. He is so inept however, that others keep suffering. Will he ever get Susan or will Elizabeth discover the truth before he does?

Other books you might like:
Sarah Caudwell, *Thus Was Adonis Murdered*, 1981
Joan Hess, *A Diet to Die For*, 1989
Elizabeth Peters, *The Amelia Peabody Series*, 1976-
Nancy Pickard, *Generous Death*, 1984
Mary Monica Pulver, *Murder at the War*, 1987

1119
Sharyn McCrumb
She Walks These Hills (New York: Scribners, 1994)

Series: Spencer Arrowood

Story type: Psychological Suspense; Private Detective—Male Lead

Major character(s): Jeremy Cobb, Professor (of history); Spencer Arrowood, Police Officer (sheriff); Martha Ayers, Police Officer (deputy sheriff)

Time period(s): 1990s (1993)

Locale(s): Tennessee (Appalachian Trail)

What the book is about: History professor Jeremy Cobb is determined to retrace the steps of Katie Wyler who was kidnapped on the Appalachian Trail in 1789. At the same time, an escaped convict is on his way back home and Martha Ayers, newly appointed deputy, is trying to prove herself by finding the escapee. All three will converge on the trail and maybe the spirit of Katie Wyler will be there as well.

Other books you might like:
Deborah Adams, *All the Great Pretenders*, 1992
Margaret Maron, *Shooting at Loons*, 1994
Marcia Muller, *Where Echoes Live*, 1991
Sarah Shankman, *She Walks in Beauty*, 1991
Elizabeth Atwood Taylor, *The Northwest Murders*, 1992

1120
Sharyn McCrumb
The Windsor Knot (New York: Ballantine, 1990)

Series: Elizabeth MacPherson

Story type: Amateur Detective—Female Lead

Major character(s): Elizabeth MacPherson, Anthropologist (forensic)

Time period(s): 1990s

1121 McCrumb

Locale(s): Chandler Grove, Virginia

What the book is about: While trying to plan her wedding, on very short notice so she can meet the Queen of England, Elizabeth MacPherson manages to get involved in the mystery of the man who died twice.

Other books you might like:
Carolyn G. Hart, *Honeymoon with Murder*, 1989
Joan Hess, *Strangled Prose*, 1985
Melodie Johnson Howe, *The Mother Shadow*, 1989
Janet LaPierre, *Children's Games*, 1989
Nancy Pickard, *Bum Steer*, 1989

1121
Sharyn McCrumb
Zombies of the Gene Pool (New York: Ballantine, 1992)

Series: Jay Omega

Story type: Amateur Detective—Male Lead

Major character(s): Jay Omega, Writer (science fiction writer), Professor (of engineering); Marion Farley, Professor (of English)

Time period(s): 1990s

Locale(s): Wall Hollow, Tennessee

What the book is about: The reunion of former aspiring SF writers from the fifties leads to murder in the nineties. When the members of a long defunct group - the Lanthanides - get together to open a time capsule they burined years ago, one of the members - thought to be long dead - turns up alive. But not for long.

Other books you might like:
Jacqueline Babbin, *Bloody Soaps: A Tale of Love and Death in the Afternoon*, 1989
Susan Baker, *My First Murder*, 1989
K.K. Beck, *The Body in the Volvo*, 1987
Ed Gorman, *Night Kills*, 1990
L.A. Taylor, *Poetic Justice*, 1986

1122
David Willis McCullough
City Sleuths and Tough Guys (New York: Houghton Mifflin, 1989)

Story type: Anthology

What the book is about: Collection of mostly hard-boiled detective stories by Poe, Vidocq, Simenon, Jim Thompson, Ross Macdonald, Stanley Ellin, Sara Paretsky, Sue Grafton and others. Also prints the screenplay for *Double Indemnity*.

Other books you might like:
Ed Gorman, *The Black Lizard Anthology of Crime Fiction*, 1987 (editor)
William F. Nolan, *The Black Mask Boys*, 1985 (editor)
Bill Pronzini, *A Treasury of Detective and Mystery Stories from the Great Pulps*, 1983

1123
David Willis McCullough
Point No-Point (New York: Viking, 1992)

Series: Ziza Todd

Story type: Amateur Detective—Female Lead

Major character(s): Ziza Todd, Religious (minister)

Time period(s): 1990s

Locale(s): Quarryville-on-Hudson, New York

What the book is about: Arguments about what to do with a development project lead to the murder of a teenage boy scout. What did he know and does his death really have anything to do with the project? Ziza gets herself in danger and takes plenty of heat from her superiors as she tries to solve the murder.

Other books you might like:
Isabelle Holland, *A Fatal Advent*, 1989
William X. Kienzle, *Deathbed*, 1986
Sister Carol Anne O'Marie, *Advent of Dying*, 1986
Monica Quill, *Sine Qua Nun*, 1986

1124
David Willis McCullough
Think on Death (New York: Viking, 1991)

Story type: Amateur Detective—Female Lead

Major character(s): Ziza Todd, Religious (scholar and religious leader)

Time period(s): 1990s

Locale(s): Catskills, New York

What the book is about: In residence at a former utopian community that is now a business and manufacturing community to do some research, the Reverend Ziza Todd decides to do some sleuthing when pieces of a body - from someone who disappeared 20 years earlier - start showing up. Is someone trying to give the community a bad name so they can buy it? First novel.

Other books you might like:
Isabelle Holland, *A Death at St. Anselm's*, 1984
Cleo Jones, *Prophet Motive*, 1984
Sister Carol Anne O'Marie, *Advent of Dying*, 1986
Monica Quill, *Sine Qua Nun*, 1986
Charles Merrill Smith, *Reverend Randollph and the Avenging Angel*, 1977

1125
Val McDermid
Crack Down (New York: Scribners, 1994)

Series: Kate Brannigan

Story type: Private Detective—Female Lead

Major character(s): Kate Brannigan, Detective—Private

Time period(s): 1990s

Locale(s): Manchester, England

What the book is about: Kate Brannigan has asked her lover, Richard, to help with an auto fraud investigation. When he agrees and is then arrested for possession of cocaine, she realizes that the auto fraud scam may just be a cover for some serious misdoings. She can't blow Richard's cover without putting him in danger, so she must track down the people responsible and the evidence to put them away to get Richard out of jail. Of course, this is easier said than done.

Other books you might like:
Liza Cody, *The Anna Lee Series*, 1980-
Liza Cody, *Bucket Nut*, 1993
Sarah Dunant, *Birthmarks*, 1992
P.D. James, *The Cordelia Gray Series*, 1962-
Jennie Melville, *The Charmian Daniels Series*, 1962-

1126

Val McDermid
Report for Murder (New York: St. Martin's, 1990)

Story type: Amateur Detective—Female Lead

Major character(s): Lindsay Gordon, Journalist; Cordelia Brown, Writer (Playwright)

Time period(s): 1980s

What the book is about: There is a murder at the girl's school that Lindsay Gordon has been commissioned to write a story about, and one of her friends is the chief suspect. First book.

Other books you might like:
Katherine V. Forrest, *The Beverly Malibu*, 1989
Lesley Grant-Adamson, *Guilty Knowledge*, 1988
Maria-Antonia Oliver, *Study in Lilac*, 1988
Pat Welch, *Murder by the Book*, 1990

1127

Patricia McFall
Night Butterfly (New York: St. Martin's, 1992)

Story type: Action/Adventure

Major character(s): Nora James, Student, Linguist; Kenaburo Nishi, Journalist

Time period(s): 1990s

Locale(s): Tokyo, Japan; Kyoto, Japan

What the book is about: Nora James is working as a "Night Butterfly," a hostess at a nightclub on the notorious Ginza, hoping to learn the old traditional language that outsiders seldom hear. When she tries to record the conversation of a powerful businessman and war criminal, she is thought to be a spy and is kidnapped. Meanwhile Nishi is also investigating the man for an expose that he may or not live to see published. First novel.

Other books you might like:
Michael Crichton, *Rising Sun*, 1992
Warren Murphy, *The Temple Dogs*, 1989 (Molly Cochran, co-author)
Shizuko Natsuki, *Innocent Journey*, 1989
Akimitsu Takagi, *No Patent on Death*, 1977
Masako Togawa, *The Lady Killer*, 1985

1128

Mark McGarrity (Pseudonym of Bartholomew Gill)
Neon Caesar (New York: Pocket, 1989)

Story type: Action/Adventure

Major character(s): Toni Spina, Criminal; Lucca Furco, Criminal

Time period(s): 1980s

What the book is about: After Spina's husband disappears, she is forced to work as a money runner for gamblers. This gives her a chance to pay off her debts once and for all.

Other books you might like:
Anthony Bruno, *Bad Blood*, 1989
Brian Garfield, *Necessity*, 1984
Eugene Izzi, *The Prime Roll*, 1990
Elmore Leonard, *Get Shorty*, 1990

1129

Janet McGiffin
Elective Murder (New York: Fawcett, 1995)

Series: Maxene St. Clair

Story type: Amateur Detective; Police Procedural

Major character(s): Maxene St. Clair, Doctor (emergency medicine); Joseph Grabowski, Detective—Homicide

Time period(s): 1990s

Locale(s): Madison, Wisconsin

What the book is about: Maxene has been asked by State Senator Irene Wisnewski to testify at a hearing on health care. As Maxene is finishing, Irene mysteriously collapses and dies before anyone can save her. Joseph Grabowski, hotshot detective and Maxene's current boyfriend, is asked to head the investigation. Then another female senator is stricken. Is there a plot against the feminist contingent in the senate? If so Maxene may be in danger, as she has been asked to fill Wisnewski's vacant seat.

Other books you might like:
Christine Green, *The Kate Kinsella Series*, 1993-
Louise Hendricksen, *The Amy Prescott Series*, 1993-
Mary Kittredge, *The Edwina Crusoe Series*, 1990-
Marsha Landreth, *The Samantha Turner Series*, 1992
C.F. Roe, *The Jean Montrose Series*, 1990-

1130

Janet McGiffin
Prescription for Death (New York: Fawcett, 1993)

Series: Maxene St. Clair

Story type: Amateur Detective; Police Procedural

Major character(s): Maxene St. Clair, Doctor (emergency medicine); Joseph Grabowski, Police Officer (Maxene's romantic interest)

Time period(s): 1990s

Locale(s): Milwaukee, Wisconsin

1131 McGown

What the book is about: It hasn't been a good night for Dr. St. Clair. She is talked into a house call by a local pimp where she finds a very sick woman. Before she can help, a man and a woman are gunned down in the street outside. She helps them and goes to find her policeman friend at an art exhibit. There a famous sculptor has one of his exhibits fall on him. When both the young prostitute and the sculptor die - even though neither of them should have - Dr. St. Clair wants to know what is going on and if there is a connection.

Other books you might like:
Jo Bailey, *Bagged*, 1992
Robin Cook, *Fatal Cure*, 1993
Christine Green, *Deadly Errand*, 1992
Mary Kittredge, *The Edwina Crusoe Series*, 1990-
C.F. Roe, *A Nasty Bit of Murder*, 1992

1131
Jill McGown
Murder Movie (New York: St. Martins, 1991)

Story type: Police Procedural—Male Lead

Major character(s): Frank Derwent, Director (film); Hugh Patterson, Detective—Police

Time period(s): 1990s

Locale(s): Ardcraig, Scotland

What the book is about: A movie set, with all its intendent passions, is the perfect setting for murder. And so it happens. But was the wrong person killed? Detective Patterson must wade through the falsehoods, half-truths and publicity-seekers to find the truth.

Other books you might like:
Simon Brett, *The Charles Paris Series*, 1976-
Howard Engel, *Murder on Location*, 1985
Anne Morice, *The Tessa Crichton Series*, 1970-1991
Patricia Moyes, *Falling Star*, 1964

1132
Jill McGown
The Other Woman (New York: St. Martins, 1993)

Series: Chief-Inspector Lloyd and Sergeant Judy Hill

Story type: Police Procedural

Major character(s): Lloyd, Detective—Police; Judy Hill, Detective—Police

Time period(s): 1990s

Locale(s): London, England

What the book is about: A dead mistress, a motorcyclist dressed in black, a reporter working on a story about illicit love affairs and the relationship between police officers Lloyd and Hill are all tied up together. Lloyd and Hill must find the common thread before they and their relationship come to a bad end.

Other books you might like:
Deborah Crombie, *All Shall Be Well*, 1994
Elizabeth George, *A Great Deliverance*, 1988
Reginald Hill, *A Pinch of Snuff*, 1978
Lydia LaPlante, *Prime Suspect*, 1991
Medora Sale, *Murder in Focus*, 1989

1133
Iona McGregor
Death Wore a Diadem (New York: St. Martin's, 1990)

Story type: Historical

Major character(s): Christabel MacKenzie, Student, Lesbian; Eleanor Stewart, Teacher, Lesbian (Christabel's lover)

Time period(s): 1860s (1860)

Locale(s): Edinburgh

What the book is about: When the housemaid is murdered and a tiara is stolen, Christabel and Eleanor set out to find the connection between the two events. This is McGregor's first mystery.

Other books you might like:
Ellen Hart, *Hallowed Murder*, 1989
Valerie Miner, *Murder in the English Department*, 1982

1134
William McIlvanney
Strange Loyalties (New York: Morrow, 1992)

Series: Jack Laidlaw

Story type: Police Procedural—Male Lead; Psychological Suspense

Major character(s): Jack Laidlaw, Police Officer

Time period(s): 1990s

Locale(s): Glasgow, Scotland

What the book is about: Desperately needing to make sense of his brother's death in an auto accident, Laidlaw's search brings him in touch with some thoughts, feelings and facts that might have been better left unearthed.

Other books you might like:
Marten Claridge, *Nobody's Fool*, 1992
Barry Cork, *Unnatural Hazard*, 1989
Bartholomew Gill, *Death of a Joyce Scholar*, 1989
Stephen Leather, *Pay Off*, 1988

1135
Ralph McInerny (Pseudonym of Monica Quill)
Body and Soil (New York: Atheneum, 1989)

Series: Andrew Broom

Story type: Legal

Major character(s): Andrew Broom, Lawyer; Gerald Rowan, Lawyer (nephew of Andrew Broom)

Time period(s): 1980s

Locale(s): Wyler, Indiana (Fictional small town)

What the book is about: The husband of a client that Broom is representing in a divorce is murdered.

Other books you might like:
K.C. Constantine, *A Fix Like This*, 1975
Erle Stanley Gardner, *The Perry Mason Series*, (1933-1973)
Joe L. Hensley, *The Don Robak Series*, (1971-)
Michael T. Hinkemeyer, *The Fields of Eden*, 1977
Martha G. Webb, *White Male Running*, 1985

1136
Ralph McInerny
The Search Committee (New York: Atheneum, 1990)
Series: Matt Rogerson
Story type: Amateur Detective—Male Lead
Major character(s): Matt Rogerson, Professor (of philosophy)
Time period(s): 1990s
Locale(s): Fort Elbow, Ohio
What the book is about: While Rogerson is trying to avoid being named chancellor at the college, someone is killing off the other candidates. For his own protection he must get involved in the investigation.
Other books you might like:
Bill Crider, *One Dead Dean*, 1988
Amanda Cross, *In the Last Analysis*, 1964
Jane Langton, *The Homer Kelly Series*, 1964-
Gillian Roberts, *Caught Dead in Philadelphia*, 1987
Edith Skom, *The Mark Twain Murders*, 1989

1137
Karin McQuillan
The Cheetah Chase (New York: Ballantine, 1994)
Series: Jazz Jasper
Story type: Action/Adventure; Private Detective—Female Lead
Major character(s): Jazz Jasper, Businesswoman (owner of a safari company), Detective—Private
Time period(s): 1990s
Locale(s): Kenya
What the book is about: After she witnesses the death of investigative reporter Nick Hunter, Jazz Jasper, safari company owner and sometime private detective, is determined to find out what he was investigating when he was killed. She discovers that he was looking into the world of illegal poaching and that some wealthy people have much to hide. She also finds out that if she keeps looking into this situation her life may be as endangered as some of the species she wants to protect.
Other books you might like:
Nevada Barr, *Track of the Cat*, 1993
James W. Hall, *Gone Wild*, 1995
Paul Mann, *Season of the Monsoon*, 1992
Linda Mariz, *Snake Dance*, 1992
John Straley, *The Woman Who Married a Bear*, 1992

1138
Susanna Hofmann McShea
The Pumpkin-Shell Wife (New York: St. Martin's, 1992)
Series: Hometown Heroes
Story type: Amateur Detective—Male Lead
Major character(s): Forrest Haggerty, Aged Person, Police Officer (former police chief); Irene Purdy, Aged Person (companion to Forrest); Mildred Bennett, Aged Person, Socialite
Time period(s): 1990s
Locale(s): Connecticut; New York
What the book is about: The 14-year-old son of a woman who died in a New York City hotel asks Forrest Haggerty and his friends to find out why his mother died. Forrest and the gang agree to see what they can do and after they discover that the manner of death - slipping in the shower - was very suspicious they begin to investigate with a vengeance. The first question to be answered is what was the housewife doing in this New York City fleabag hotel registered under a false name.
Other books you might like:
Richard Barth, *The Margaret Binton Series*, 1981-
Bill Crider, *The Sheriff Dan Rhodes Series*, 1988-
Kathryn Lasky Knight, *Mumbo Jumbo*, 1991
A.J. Orde, *A Little Neighborhood Murder*, 1989
David Osborn, *The Margaret Barlow Series*, 1989-

1139
M.R.D. Meek
A Loose Connection (New York: Scribners, 1989)
Series: Lennox Kemp
Story type: Legal
Major character(s): Lennox Kemp, Lawyer
Time period(s): 1980s
What the book is about: When the wife of one of the other lawyers at Kemp's firm gets obsessed with the suicide of one of her friends, Kemp must get involved.
Other books you might like:
Michael Gilbert, *Smallbone Deceased*, 1950
Cyril Hare, *Tragedy at Law*, 1942
P.D. James, *Death of an Expert Witness*, 1977
June Thomson, *The Inspector Rudd Series*, (1971-)

1140
Leslie Meier
Mail-Order Murder (New York: Viking, 1991)
Story type: Amateur Detective—Female Lead
Major character(s): Lucy Stone, Worker; Barney Culpepper, Police Officer
Time period(s): 1990s
Locale(s): Maine
What the book is about: When Lucy Stone finds her popular and wealthy boss, Sam Miller III, dead in his car in the parking lot, the police quickly decide he was murdered. There is no dearth of suspects but one after another they are cleared. Lucy convinces Officer Culpepper to help her spring a trap to catch the killer. Then he is nearly killed in a traffic accident, and she discovers a suicide. Believing that these things are related to Miller's death, she decides to try and catch the killer on her own. First novel.
Other books you might like:
J.S. Borthwick, *The Down-East Murders*, 1985
Susan Kenney, *Graves in Academe*, 1984
B.J. Morison, *Beer and Skittles*, 1985
Virginia Rich, *The Baked Bean Supper Murders*, 1983
Gillian Roberts, *Caught Dead in Philadelphia*, 1987

1141

Jennie Melville
Dead Set (New York: St. Martins, 1993)

Series: Charmian Daniels

Story type: Police Procedural—Female Lead

Major character(s): Charmian Daniels, Police Officer, Widow(er)

Time period(s): 1990s

Locale(s): Windsor, England

What the book is about: Investigating the strangulation death of a teenage girl, Charmian finds herself looking at too many suspects: the married man, now gone missing; the boyfriend, now dead in a hit and run accident; the girl's school headmaster; and an eight-year-old boy.

Other books you might like:
Trevor Barnes, *A Midsummer Night's Killing*, 1992
Liza Cody, *Dupe*, 1984
Deborah Crombie, *A Share in Death*, 1993
Elizabeth George, *For the Sake of Elena*, 1991
P.D. James, *An Unsuitable Job for a Woman*, 1973

1142

Jennie Melville (Pseudonym of Gwendoline Butler)
Murder Has a Pretty Face (New York: St. Martin's, 1989)

Series: Charmian Daniels

Story type: Police Procedural—Female Lead

Major character(s): Charmian Daniels, Police Officer (CID Inspector); Diana King, Businesswoman, Criminal (Leader of a gang of women)

Time period(s): 1980s

What the book is about: When Charmian has to take over the investigations of a murder and several burglaries, she soon suspects the owner of the beauty shop that she patronizes.

Other books you might like:
Antonia Fraser, *Oxford Blood*, 1985
P.D. James, *An Unsuitable Job for a Woman*, 1973

1143

Jennie Melville
Whoever Has the Heart (New York: St. Martin's, 1994)

Series: Charmian Daniels

Story type: Police Procedural—Female Lead

Major character(s): Charmian Daniels, Police Officer

Time period(s): 1990s

Locale(s): Brideswell, England

What the book is about: Charmian Daniels hopes for some rest and relaxation at her new cottage in the village of Brideswell, but murder finds her even there. First she is asked by the lover of a friend for help with a problem. It seems he was seen arguing with a young woman who has since disappeared and the police are suggesting he may have had something to do with her disappearance. When the woman's body is found, it is not just a disappearance in which the fellow may be implicated. While investigating, Charmian finds that this is not the first mysterious death the village has had in the recent past. She also finds herself attracted to the police officer in charge of the case.

Other books you might like:
Liza Cody, *The Anna Lee Series*, 1986-
Deborah Crombie, *A Share in Death*, 1993
Sarah Dunant, *Birthmarks*, 1992
Elizabeth George, *A Great Deliverance*, 1988
P.D. James, *An Unsuitable Job for a Woman*, 1973

1144

Jennie Melville (Pseudonym of Gwendoline Butler)
Witching Murder (New York: St. Martin's, 1991)

Series: Charmian Daniels

Story type: Police Procedural—Female Lead

Major character(s): Charmain Daniels, Police Officer (Superintendent)

Time period(s): 1990s

Locale(s): London, England

What the book is about: While on medical leave, Charmain is interrupted by the murder of beautiful Vivian Charles, a member of a witch's coven. As the murdered woman was pregnant, suspicion falls on the male member of the coven. But then he too is stabbed. Though every clue leads to the coven, Charmain thinks the truth may lie somewhere in Vivian's past.

Other books you might like:
Trevor Barnes, *A Midsummer Night's Killing*, 1992
Liza Cody, *Dupe*, 1984
Antonia Fraser, *The Cavalier Case*, 1990
Susan Moody, *Penny Dreadful*, 1984

1145

Michael Mewshaw
True Crime (New York: Poseidon, 1991)

Story type: Amateur Detective—Male Lead

Major character(s): Tom Heller, Writer (of true crime)

Time period(s): 1990s

Locale(s): Maryland

What the book is about: Brought back to his home in Maryland because his father has been shot, true crime writer Tom Heller soon becomes involved in a true crime case of his own. His father dies and soon there comes the murder of the father and son of his former lover. Are these deaths related? He intends to find out—if he can live that long. First novel.

Other books you might like:
L.L. Enger, *Comeback*, 1990
Lesley Grant-Adamson, *Curse the Darkness*, 1990
Vince Kohler, *Rainy North Woods*, 1988
Sarah Shankman, *Now Let's Talk of Graves*, 1990
Kerry Tucker, *Still Waters*, 1991

1146
Annette Meyers
Blood on the Street (New York: Bantam, 1992)
Series: Smith and Wetzon
Story type: Amateur Detective—Female Lead
Major character(s): Xenia Smith, Businesswoman (executive headhunter); Leslie Wetzon, Businesswoman (executive headhunter)
Time period(s): 1990s
Locale(s): New York, New York
What the book is about: When one of their recent placements turns up dead in Central Park, Smith and Wetzon can't help but get involved. The dead stockbroker was having an affair with the sixteen year old daughter of a woman he'd cheated in the market. Did she kill him or was it an innocent mugging? Then the sixteen year old turns up dead and her diary, which may give the answer to both murders, is missing.
Other books you might like:
Jill Churchill, *Grime and Punishment*, 1989
Jaqueline Girdner, *The Last Resort*, 1991
Susan Isaacs, *Compromising Positions*, 1978
Mary Kittredge, *Poison Pen*, 1990
Valerie Wolzien, *We Wish You a Merry Murder*, 1991

1147
Annette Meyers
The Deadliest Option (New York: Bantam, 1991)
Series: Smith and Wetzen
Story type: Amateur Detective—Female Lead
Major character(s): Xenia Smith, Businesswoman (executive headhunter); Leslie Wetzon, Businesswoman (executive headhunter)
Time period(s): 1990s
Locale(s): New York, New York
What the book is about: A death at a retirement party for a Wall Street biggie plunges Smith and Wetzen into a case that threatens not only their lives but their partnership as well.
Other books you might like:
Joan Hess, *A Diet to Die For*, 1989
Bernie Lee, *Murder at Musket Beach*, 1990
Nancy Pickard, *Bum Steer*, 1990

1148
Maan Meyers (Pseudonym of Annette Meyers and Martin Meyers)
The Kingsbridge Plot (New York: Doubleday, 1993)
Series: Old New York
Story type: Historical; Amateur Detective—Male Lead
Major character(s): John Tonneman, Doctor (city coroner); Mariana Mendoza, Teenager (15 years old)
Time period(s): 1760s
Locale(s): New York, New York, American Colonies
What the book is about: Returning from seven years in England to take over the job of city coroner in old New York, John Tonneman soon finds himself embroiled in the hunt for a killer who is murdering red-headed women. The killer has also been hired to poison George Washington. Tonneman must also decide with whom to side in the coming revolution.
Other books you might like:
Robert Lee Hall, *The Benjamin Franklin Series*, 1991-

1149
Simon Michael
The Cut Throat (New York: St. Martin's, 1990)
Story type: Legal
Major character(s): Charles Howard, Lawyer (accused murderer); Rachel Golding, Friend
Time period(s): 1980s
Locale(s): London
What the book is about: While on the run after being accused of the murder of his wife, Charles Howard runs into an old friend, Rachel Golding, who agrees to shelter him and help him find the real guilty party. First book.
Other books you might like:
Jeffrey Ashford, *Hostage to Death*, 1977
Marion Babson, *Dangerous to Know*, 1980
Richard Neely, *The Plastic Nightmare*, 1969

1150
Grant Michaels
A Body to Dye For (New York: St. Martins, 1990)
Series: Stan Kraychik
Story type: Amateur Detective—Male Lead
Major character(s): Stan Kraychik, Hairdresser, Homosexual; Nikki Albright, Businesswoman (Stan's boss and friend)
Time period(s): 1990s (1990)
Locale(s): Boston, Massachusetts
What the book is about: Stan Kraychik, Vannos to his customers, is frosting Calvin Reddings hair when he meets Calvin's new friend, a visiting park ranger from Yosemite. Invited to their place later that evening, Stan arrives to discover the ranger's dead body wea ring only two bow ties. When Calvin tries to implicate Stan, Stan feels the only way to clear himself is to find the real killer. First novel.
Other books you might like:
Nathan Aldyne, *The Daniel Valentine Series*, 1980-1986
Tony Fennelly, *The Glory Hole Murders*, 1985
Joseph Hansen, *The Dave Brandstetter Series*, 1970-
Michael Nava, *The Little Death*, 1986
Mark Richard Zubro, *The Tom Mason Series*, 1988-

1151

Grant Michaels
Love You to Death (New York: St. Martin's, 1992)
Series: Stan Kraychik
Story type: Amateur Detective—Male Lead
Major character(s): Stan Kraychik, Hairdresser, Homosexual
Time period(s): 1990s
Locale(s): Boston, Massachusetts
What the book is about: At a reception to celebrate the grand opening of a new upscale Chocolatier, murder rears its ugly head. Unfortunately someone has poisoned the chocolate and a guest bites the dust. Stan's friend Lanvett Cole is arrested for the murder. In addition to wanting to get her off because she's innocent, Stan has also become responsible for her five-year-old son, not a child to warm one's heart. Though the police are not encouraging Stan's help, he gives it anyway.

Other books you might like:
Nathan Aldyne, *The Daniel Valentine Series*, 1980-1986
Tony Fennelly, *The Glory Hole Murders*, 1985
Joseph Hansen, *The Dave Brandstetter Series*, 1970-1991
Richard Stevenson, *The Donald Strachey Series*, 1984-
Mark Richard Zubro, *The Tom Mason Series*, 1988-

1152

Monty Mickleson
Purgatory (New York: St. Martins, 1993)
Story type: Action/Adventure
Major character(s): Danny Castellano, Criminal (bag man); Carl Dupree, Criminal (ex-con)
Time period(s): 1990s
Locale(s): Arizona; Alaska; New Orleans, Louisiana
What the book is about: As the bag man for a Hispanic drug mob, Danny Castellano is used to living on the edge. When he is forced by the mob to take a partner, he is not pleased. He is even less pleased when this guy steals the money they are supposed to be laundering and leaves him for dead in the Arizona desert. Unsure whether this is a mob set-up or a single crazy, he sets out to find the answers. Along the way he hooks up with the thief's former cellmate, Carl Dupree, and a new age shaman. They criss-cross the country as they search for the money, though Dupree has his own agenda which may or may not jibe with Danny's. First novel.

Other books you might like:
Peter Blauner, *Slow Motion Riot*, 1991
Robert Campbell, *Juice*, 1988
John Clarkson, *One Man's Law*, 1994
Robert Ferrigno, *The Horse Latitudes*, 1992
Brian Garfield, *Fear in a Handful of Dust*, 1977

1153

John Miles (Pseudonym of Jack Bickham)
A Permanent Retirement (New York: Walker, 1992)
Story type: Amateur Detective—Female Lead
Major character(s): Laura Michaels, Businesswoman (asst. mgr. of a nursing home), Single Parent; Aaron Lassiter, Police Officer (deputy sheriff)
Time period(s): 1990s
Locale(s): Oklahoma
What the book is about: Laura Michaels, assistant manager of the Timberlake Retirement Center, is suspicious of the death of resident Cora Chandler. The presence of cigarette smoke and the odor of Ben-Gay—neither of which were on Cora's list of vices—tell Laura that all is not kosher. The police decide that given only the age of the dead woman the death was by natural causes. Laura investigates on her own and gets threatened. Then another resident is found dead. Perhaps the police will take this one a little more seriously. First novel under this name.

Other books you might like:
Bill Crider, *The Sheriff Dan Rhodes Series*, 1987-
Jean Hager, *The Grandmother Medicine*, 1989
Joan Hess, *The Claire Malloy Series*, 1987-
Joan Hess, *The Maggody Series*, 1987-
D.R. Meredith, *The Sheriff Charles Matthews Series*, 1986-

1154

Rex Miller
Stone Shadow (New York: NAL/Onyx, 1989)
Series: Jake Eichord
Story type: Police Procedural—Male Lead
Major character(s): Jake Eichord, Detective—Police (serial killer specialist); Joseph Hackabee, Murderer (serial killer)
Time period(s): 1980s
Locale(s): Dallas, Texas
What the book is about: When a deviate is caught after keeping a woman prisoner for a month and starts confessing to multiple murders Eichord is called in. It seems impossible for the confessed killer to have committed the crimes. Meanwhile, Eichord becomes involved in an affair with the killer's only survivor.

Other books you might like:
Thomas Harris, *Red Dragon*, 1981
Joe R. Lansdale, *Act of Love*, 1981
David L. Lindsey, *Mercy*, 1990
Shane Stevens, *By Reason of Insanity*, 1979

1155

Marlys Millhiser
Death of the Office Witch (New York: Penzler, 1993)
Series: Charlie Greene
Story type: Amateur Detective—Female Lead
Major character(s): Charlie Greene, Businesswoman (literary agent), Single Parent
Time period(s): 1990s
Locale(s): Los Angeles, California

What the book is about: Charlie Greene is stuck in traffic so she calls Gloria, her receptionist, to explain. When she arrives, Gloria is missing. While looking for her, Charlie hears a voice saying Gloria is in the trash can. Charlie doesn't believe she's psychic, but she can't explain the voice. Gloria's body is discovered, and the police want Charlie to help, but she's too busy trying to do her job. Then another person dies.

Other books you might like:
Susan Wittig Albert, *Thyme of Death*, 1992
Carole Berry, *The Bonnie Indermill Series*, 1988-
Trella Crespi, *The Trouble with a Small Raise*, 1990
Kathleen Kunz, *Murder Once Removed*, 1993
Susan Wolfe, *The Last Billable Hour*, 1989

1156
Marlys Millhiser
Murder at Moot Point (New York: Doubleday, 1992)
Series: Charlie Greene
Story type: Amateur Detective—Female Lead
Major character(s): Charlie Greene, Businesswoman (literary agent); Wes Bennett, Police Officer (sheriff)
Time period(s): 1990s
Locale(s): Moot Point, Oregon
What the book is about: Charlie Greene is in Moot Point to convince a prospective client to let her sell his book. She arrives in fog so thick she can barely find her way. When the body of an old woman and her bicycle are found under her car, she is suspected of vehicular homicide. Then it is discovered that the woman had been shot. Sheriff Bennett seems interested in Charlie as more than a suspect and as the evidence against her mounts, it may be up to her to clear herself.

Other books you might like:
Susan Wittig Albert, *Thyme of Death*, 1992
Mary Daheim, *The Alpine Advocate*, 1992
Katherine Lasky Knight, *Trace Elements*, 1986
Janet LaPierre, *Grandmother's House*, 1991
Ann M. Williams, *Flowers for the Dead*, 1991

1157
D.F. Mills
Deadline (New York: Berkley, 1991)
Story type: Psychological Suspense
Major character(s): Tess Alexander, Writer
Time period(s): 1990s
Locale(s): Texas (west central)
What the book is about: Tess Alexander has been chosen to write a true-crime account of one of the most sensational murder trials of the decade. Little does she know that this assignment will lead her back into the depths of her own family secrets.

Other books you might like:
Mary Higgins Clark, *All Around the Town*, 1992
Marjorie Dorner, *Family Closets*, 1988
Nell Kincaid, *To the Fourth Generation*, 1992
Domoni Taylor, *Praying Mantis*, 1988

1158
John Minahan
The Great Grave Robbery (New York: Norton, 1989)
Series: John Rawlings
Story type: Police Procedural—Male Lead
Major character(s): John Rawlings, Detective—Police
Time period(s): 1980s
Locale(s): New York, New York
What the book is about: Rawlings' current assignment involves the 22-year-old disappearance of a scientist.

Other books you might like:
Nat Hentoff, *Blues for Charlie Darwin*, 1982
Robert L. Pike, *The Lieutenant Reardon Series*, (1972-)
Lawrence Sanders, *The First Deadly Sin*, 1973
Collin Wilcox, *The Lieutenant Hastings Series*, (1969-)

1159
Kay Mitchell
In Stoney Places (New York: St. Martin's, 1992)
Series: Inspector John Morrissey
Story type: Police Procedural—Male Lead
Major character(s): John Morrissey, Police Officer (inspector)
Time period(s): 1990s
Locale(s): England
What the book is about: Three women have been strangled in close proximity, and the police are focusing on the boyfriend of one of the three. When Inspector Morrissey's daughter is attacked and a fourth victim shows up, the case becomes somewhat more personal.

Other books you might like:
Catherine Aird, *The Inspector Sloane Series*, 1966-
Douglas Clark, *The Masters and Green Series*, 1969-
Paula Gosling, *Death Penalties*, 1991
Susannah Stacey, *The Superintendent Bone Series*, 1987-
June Thomson, *The Inspector Rudd Series*, 1971-

1160
Kay Mitchell
A Lively Form of Death (New York: St. Martins, 1991)
Series: Inspector John Morrissey
Story type: Police Procedural—Male Lead
Major character(s): John Morrissey, Police Officer (detective chief inspector); Neil Barrett, Police Officer (partner of Morrissey)
Time period(s): 1990s
Locale(s): Malminster, England
What the book is about: A cleaning lady and notorious gossip is found poisoned from milk laced with cyanide. When Morrissey and Barrett investigate, they find that she took the milk from Marion Walsh who knows an awful lot of secrets and has a town full of enemies - mostly the wives of the men she has seduced. First novel.

1161 Mitchell — What Mystery Do I Read Next?

Other books you might like:
Douglas Clark, *The Masters and Green Series*, 1969-
Reginald Hill, *The Dalziel and Pascoe Series*, 1970-
Dorothy Simpson, *The Inspector Luke Thanet Series*, 1981-
Susannah Stacey, *Goodbye, Nanny Gray*, 1987
June Thomson, *Not One of Us*, 1971

1161
Kirk Mitchell
With Siberia Comes a Chill (New York: St. Martins, 1991)
Story type: Historical; Police Procedural—Male Lead
Major character(s): John Kost, Police Officer (born Ivan Kostoff)
Time period(s): 1940s (1945)
Locale(s): San Francisco, California
What the book is about: While investigating the death of a cop during an apparent domestic dispute, Kost also gets involved with a plot to assassinate a Soviet diplomat during the charter meeting of the United Nations. He must also deal with his alcoholic father, a white Russian interested in revenge on the Bolsheviks. Could his father possibly be involved in the assassination plot?
Other books you might like:
Max Allan Collins, *True Detective*, 1983
Robert Davis, *Kimura*, 1989
James Ellroy, *The Big Nowhere*, 1988
Jack Gerson, *Death Squad London*, 1990
John T. Lescroart, *Dead Irish*, 1989

1162
Gwen Moffat
Rage (New York: St. Martins, 1990)
Series: Miss Pink
Story type: Amateur Detective—Female Lead
Major character(s): Melinda Pink, Writer (mountain climber)
Time period(s): 1990s
Locale(s): California (Southwest; Sierras)
What the book is about: Timothy Argent was following a trail described in a pioneer diary when he disappeared in the Sierras. He was last seen with a beautiful woman who turns up on the other side of the mountain with blood on her shirt. After two months there isn't much trail to follow, but Miss Pink perseveres.
Other books you might like:
Tony Hillerman, *The Ghostway*, 1985
Jessica Mann, *Faith, Hope and Homicide*, 1990
Marcia Muller, *Where Echoes Live*, 1991
Walter Satterthwait, *Wall of Glass*, 1988

1163
Gwen Moffat
The Stone Hawk (New York: St. Martin's, 1989)
Series: Miss Pink
Story type: Amateur Detective—Female Lead
Major character(s): Melinda Pink, Writer (mountain climber)
Time period(s): 1980s
Locale(s): Utah
What the book is about: While in a small Utah community, Miss Pink must investigate the brutal rape-murder of a six-year-old girl.
Other books you might like:
Sylvia Angus, *Dead to Rites*, 1978
Glyn Carr, *Swing Away, Climber*, 1959
Dorothy Gilman, *The Amazing Mrs. Pollifax*, 1970
Patricia Wentworth, *The Miss Silver Series*, 1929

1164
Miriam Grace Monfredo
North Star Conspiracy (New York: St. Martins, 1993)
Series: Glynis Tryon
Story type: Historical; Amateur Detective—Female Lead
Major character(s): Glynis Tryon, Librarian, Activist (feminist and abolitionist)
Time period(s): 1850s (1854)
Locale(s): Seneca Falls, New York; Virginia
What the book is about: Having recently rejected a marriage proposal—and missing the man who proposed—librarian Glynis Tryon throws herself into the social life of Seneca Falls. She gets involved in planning the new theatre and in a political campaign as well. She also begins to investigate the recent deaths of both a freed slave and a slave catcher. They may be connected. There is also her involvement with the Underground Railroad and the trial of her landlady's son for helping an escaped slave.
Other books you might like:
Ron Burns, *The Strange Death of Meriweather Lewis*, 1993
Carole Nelson Douglas, *Good Morning, Irene*, 1991
Edward Marston, *The Mad Courtesan*, 1992
Sharan Newman, *Death Comes as Epiphany*, 1993
Peter Rowland, *The Disappearance of Edwin Drood*, 1992

1165
Joseph Monniger
Incident at Potter's Bridge (New York: Fine, 1992)
Story type: Psychological Suspense
Major character(s): George Denkin, Criminal, Serial Killer
Time period(s): 1990s
Locale(s): New Hampshire
What the book is about: George Denkin, wearing woman's clothing and a wig, is stalking a rural New Hampshire college for victims. All the while he is himself being stalked by two youngsters and the campus police. First genre novel.

Other books you might like:
Thomas Harris, *Red Dragon*, 1981
William Heffernan, *Blood Rose*, 1991
Joe R. Lansdale, *Act of Love*, 1981
Ronald Munson, *Nothing Human*, 1991
Charles Wilson, *Nightwatcher*, 1990

1166
Richard Montanari
Deviant Way (New York: Simon & Schuster, 1995)

Story type: Police Procedural—Male Lead; Psychological Suspense

Major character(s): Jack Paris, Police Officer

Time period(s): 1990s

Locale(s): Cleveland, Ohio

What the book is about: Someone is cruising the yuppie bars of Cleveland picking up young women and killing them after having kinky sex. The forensic evidence suggests that it might be a couple. As Jack closes in on the guilty party or parties, he gets distracted by his partner and by the fact that the killers have changed their tactics. Now they are targeting him and his family. First novel.

Other books you might like:
Thomas Harris, *Red Dragon*, 1981
John Katzenbach, *In the Heat of the Summer*, 1982
Joe R. Lansdale, *Act of Love*, 1981
David L. Lindsey, *Mercy*, 1990
Roderick Thorp, *River*, 1995

1167
Yvonne Montgomery
Obstacle Course (New York: Avon, 1990)

Series: Finny Aletter

Story type: Amateur Detective—Female Lead

Major character(s): Finny Aletter, Carpenter (former stock broker); Chris Barelli, Police Officer (Finny Aletter's lover)

Time period(s): 1990s

Locale(s): Denver, Colorado

What the book is about: At a party to celebrate Finny Aletter's career change from stockbroker to carpenter someone decides an unpopular judge has lived long enough. One of Finny's friends confesses to the murder, but Finny knows she is innocent. Finny feels she must get involved.

Other books you might like:
Lia Matera, *Prior Convictions*, 1991
Meg O'Brien, *The Daphne Decisions*, 1990
A.J. Orde, *A Little Neighborhood Murder*, 1989
Nancy Pickard, *Generous Death*, 1984
Edith Skom, *The Mark Twain Murders*, 1989

1168
Margaret Moore
Dangerous Conceits (New York: Walker, 1989)

Series: Chief Inspector Baxter

Story type: Police Procedural—Male Lead

Major character(s): Richard Baxter, Police Officer (chief inspector)

Time period(s): 1980s

Locale(s): England (Cambridgeshire)

What the book is about: When Michael Giddings, new leader of England's New Radical Right, is murdered and his wife disappears, it falls to Chief Inspector Baxter to sort out motives and truths.

Other books you might like:
Catherine Aird, *Henrietta Who?*, 1968
J.R.L. Anderson, *A Sprig of Sea Lavender*, 1978
Colin Dexter, *The Dead of Jericho*, 1982
Ruth Rendell, *An Unkindness of Ravens*, 1985
Jonathan Ross, *Dropped Dead*, 1984

1169
William Moore
The Last Surprise (New York: St. Martin's, 1990)

Story type: Private Detective—Male Lead

Major character(s): Russ McGarvey, Detective—Private

Time period(s): 1980s

Locale(s): Washington, District of Columbia

What the book is about: Hired by the widow of a Senator to investigate his death in a supposed mugging, McGarvey soon finds that there is much, much more than a mugging involved. First book.

Other books you might like:
R.B. Dominic, *Murder in High Places*, 1970
Lawrence Meyer, *A Capitol Crime*, 1977
Lawrence Sanders, *Capital Crimes*, 1989
Margaret Truman, *Murder at the Kennedy Center*, 1989
Stuart Woods, *Grass Roots*, 1988

1170
Mary Morell
Final Session (Spinsters, 1991)

Story type: Police Procedural—Female Lead

Major character(s): Lucia Ramos, Police Officer, Lesbian; Amy Trager, Doctor (psychotherapist), Lesbian

Time period(s): 1990s

Locale(s): San Antonio, Texas

What the book is about: Someone has murdered a psychotherapist in her office. There are no patient files but that doesn't stop police detective Ramos from coming up with a number of suspects, including the head of the licensing board, a former patient who accused the deceased of sexual misconduct, a mystery writer, and the ex-husband. First novel.

Other books you might like:
Susan Dunlap, *Not Exactly a Brahmin*, 1985
Katherine V. Forrest, *The Kate Delafield Series*, 1984-
Lee Martin, *Too Sane a Murder*, 1984
Claire McNab, *Cop-Out*, 1991
Julie Smith, *New Orleans Mourning*, 1990

1171
Kate Morgan
Home Sweet Homicide (New York: Berkley, 1991)
Series: Dewey James
Story type: Amateur Detective—Female Lead
Major character(s): Dewey James, Librarian (semi-retired)
Time period(s): 1990s
Locale(s): Hamilton, Kentucky
What the book is about: Not everyone is as excited as Dewey James about Hamilton's homecoming celebration for locals who have made good. Someone, in fact, is so displeased that Broadway star Jenny Riley soon turns up dead. The police chief himself is one suspect, but Dewey thinks that others could also be guilty.
Other books you might like:
Richard Barth, *The Margaret Binton Series*, 1978-
Eleanor Boylan, *Working Murder*, 1989
Simon Brett, *Mrs. Pargeter's Package*, 1992
James McCahery, *Grave Undertaking*, 1990
Patricia Wentworth, *The Miss Silver Series*, 1928-1961

1172
Kate Morgan
A Slay at the Races (New York: Berkley, 1990)
Series: Dewey James
Story type: Amateur Detective—Female Lead
Major character(s): Dewey James, Librarian; George Farnham, Lawyer (suitor of Dewey)
Time period(s): 1990s
Locale(s): Hamilton, Kentucky
What the book is about: Planning for The Hamilton Cup, an annual charity race, is not going as planned. One of the entrants has hired a professional jockey, and someone turns up dead in a horse's stall. Did the horse kill him - or was it murder? First novel.
Other books you might like:
Virginia Anderson, *King of the Roses*, 1988
Jon L. Breen, *Listen for the Click*, 1984
Dick Francis, *Longshot*, 1990
James McCahery, *Grave Undertaking*, 1990
Nancy Pickard, *Bum Steer*, 1989

1173
Anne Morice
Fatal Charm (New York: St. Martin's, 1989)
Series: Tessa Crichton
Story type: Amateur Detective—Female Lead
Major character(s): Tessa Crichton, Actress; Robin Price, Police Officer (husband of Tessa), Inspector
Time period(s): 1980s
What the book is about: When the prodigal daughter of a prominent theatrical family is found dead, Tessa and her husband feel that it was murder, not suicide.

Other books you might like:
Simon Brett, *Murder Unprompted*, 1982
Jane Dentinger, *Death Mask*, 1988
Ngaio Marsh, *Night of the Vulcan*, 1951
Patricia Moyes, *Who Is Simon Warwick?*, 1979

1174
David Morrell
The Covenant of the Flame (New York: Warner, 1991)
Story type: Action/Adventure
Major character(s): Tess Drake, Journalist (investigative reporter); William Craig, Police Officer (lieutenant; works for missing)
Time period(s): 1990s
Locale(s): United States
What the book is about: Someone is killing environmental polluters. Are the killers the good guys? How does this tie into the death by fire of the strange man Tess fell in love with on sight? While delving into the history of that man, Tess and Lt. Craig get involved in a plot that reaches back into history and into the highest echelons of government.
Other books you might like:
Peter Abrahams, *Pressure Drop*, 1989
Kathleen Dougherty, *Moth to the Flame*, 1991
Warren Murphy, *Jericho Day*, 1989
Steve Shagan, *Pillars of Fire*, 1989

1175
Ian Morson
Falconer's Crusade (New York: St. Martin's, 1995)
Story type: Historical; Amateur Detective—Male Lead
Major character(s): William Falconer, Teacher (calls himself a deductionist)
Time period(s): 13th century (1264)
Locale(s): Oxford, England
What the book is about: A servant girl is stabbed to death. Soon three students' deaths follow. Are these deaths related, and what connection could they have with the visit of Prince Edward to Oxford? Master William Falconer, who would much rather be trying to fly, sets out to find the truth. First mystery.
Other books you might like:
P.C. Doherty, *Tapestry of Murders*, 1996
Sharan Newman, *The Devil's Door*, 1994
Ellis Peters, *The Brother Cadfael Series*, 1977-1995
Candace M. Robb, *The Lady Chapel*, 1994
Steven Saylor, *Arms of Nemesis*, 1993

1176
Walter Mosley
Devil in a Blue Dress (New York: Norton, 1990)
Series: Easy Rawlins
Story type: Historical; Amateur Detective—Male Lead

Major character(s): Easy Rawlins, Worker (laid-off plant worker), Veteran

Time period(s): 1940s (1948)

Locale(s): Los Angeles, California

What the book is about: Recently laid off from his job at a defense plant, Easy reluctantly agrees to search for the missing Daphne Monet, a singer, for white gangster Dewitt Albright. First novel.

Other books you might like:
Raymond Chandler, *The Philip Marlowe Series*, 1939-1958
Max Allan Collins, *True Detective*, 1984
Gar Anthony Haywood, *The Aaron Gunner Series*, 1988-
Richard Hilary, *The Easy Barnes Series*, 1987-

1177
Walter Mosley
A Red Death (New York: Norton, 1991)

Series: Easy Rawlins

Story type: Amateur Detective—Male Lead; Historical

Major character(s): Easy Rawlins, Businessman (part-time investigator)

Time period(s): 1950s (early)

Locale(s): Los Angeles, California

What the book is about: Easy is being harassed by the IRS, bullied by the FBI and suspected of two murders. All of this is set against the background of the red-baiting McCarthy era, and Easy could easily become a victim if he doesn't cooperate.

Other books you might like:
Raymond Chandler, *The Philip Marlowe Series*, 1939-1958
Max Allan Collins, *The Nate Heller Series*, 1984-
James Ellroy, *The Big Nowhere*, 1989
Gar Anthony Haywood, *The Aaron Gunner Series*, 1988
Chester Himes, *A Rage in Harlem*, 1956

1178
Walter Mosley
White Butterfly (New York: Norton, 1992)

Series: Easy Rawlins

Story type: Private Detective—Male Lead; Historical

Major character(s): Easy Rawlins, Detective—Private (unlicensed; African-American); Raymond "Mouse" Alexander, Criminal

Time period(s): 1950s (1956)

Locale(s): Los Angeles, California

What the book is about: When the police realize they have a serial killer who likes to rape and kill black "party girls," they ask Easy to help. Easy has a new wife and child to think of and refuses. Then a white girl from a powerful family - with a secret life - is killed. The police put the pressure on Easy, and he agrees to look into it. Can he stop the killing and keep his life and family intact?

Other books you might like:
Kenn Davis, *The Carver Bascombe Series*, 1979-
Loren D. Estleman, *Motown*, 1991
Gar Anthony Haywood, *The Aaron Gunner Series*, 1988-
Chester Himes, *A Rage in Harlem*, 1956
Bennie Lee Sinclair, *The Lynching*, 1992

1179
Patricia Moyes
Black Girl, White Girl (New York: Holt, 1989)

Series: Henry and Emmy Tibbet

Story type: Traditional

Major character(s): Henry Tibbet, Police Officer (chief superintendent); Emmy Tibbet, Spouse

Time period(s): 1980s

Locale(s): Caribbean

What the book is about: When Henry and Emmy go to a Caribbean island at the request of a friend, they find that the idyllic place is being ruined by drugs and corrupt officials.

Other books you might like:
Margaret Erskine, *The Septimus Finch Series*, 1939
Anne Morice, *The Tessa Crichton Series*, 1970
Sheila Radley, *Death in the Morning*, 1978
David Williams, *The Mark Treasure Series*, 1977

1180
Marcia Muller
Dark Star (New York: St. Martin's, 1989)

Series: Joanna Stark

Story type: Amateur Detective—Female Lead

Major character(s): Joanna Stark, Art Dealer

Time period(s): 1980s

Locale(s): Sonoma, California; San Francisco, California

What the book is about: Joanna's former husband, art thief Anthony Parducci, although thought dead at the end of the previous book in the series, may still be alive and planning to steal a Van Gogh, soon to be auctioned in San Francisco.

Other books you might like:
Oliver Banks, *The Rembrandt Panel*, 1980
Peter Clothier, *Chiaroscuro*, 1985
Carolyn Coker, *The Other David*, 1984
Susan Dunlap, *Not Exactly a Brahmin*, 1987
Sue Grafton, *F Is for Fugitive*, 1989

1181
Marcia Muller
The Shape of Dread (New York: Mysterious, 1989)

Series: Sharon McCone

Story type: Private Detective—Female Lead

Major character(s): Sharon McCone, Detective—Private

Time period(s): 1980s

Locale(s): San Francisco, California

1182 Muller

What the book is about: Did the man on death row really commit the murder he was convicted of? As Sharon delves into the life of his victim, her own life is threatened.

Other books you might like:
Liza Cody, *Dupe*, 1981
Sue Grafton, *G Is for Gumshoe*, 1990
Sara Paretsky, *Burn Marks*, 1990
Bill Pronzini, *Nameless Detective Series*, 1971

1182
Marcia Muller
Till The Butchers Cut Him Down (New York: Mysterious, 1994)

Series: Sharon McCone
Story type: Private Detective—Female Lead
Major character(s): Sharon McCone, Detective—Private
Time period(s): 1990s
Locale(s): San Francisco, California

What the book is about: Sharon McCone has decided to go out on her own as a private detective, leaving the security of All Soul's Cooperative that she's known for years. Before she can even get set up, she has a client. An old acquaintance, T.J. Gordon, formerly known as Suitcase Gordon, shows up and wants to hire her. He seems to think someone is trying to kill him. She agrees to investigate, but before she can do much, he fires her. Then his wife is killed in an explosion and Gordon disappears, perhaps to seek revenge. Sharon must find him and the killer—that is if it isn't Gordon himself.

Other books you might like:
Linda Barnes, *The Carlotta Carlyle Series*, 1989-
Barbara D'Amato, *The Cat Marsala Series*, 1990-
Janet Dawson, *The Jeri Howard Series*, 1990-
Linda Grant, *The Catherine Saylor Series*, 1989-
Karen Kijewski, *The Kat Colorado Series*, 1989-

1183
Marcia Muller
Trophies and Dead Things (New York: Mysterious, 1990)

Series: Sharon McCone
Story type: Private Detective—Female Lead
Major character(s): Sharon McCone, Detective—Private
Time period(s): 1990s
Locale(s): San Francisco, California

What the book is about: When one of the firm's legal clients is killed by a random serial killer, a holographic will is found that disinherits the victim's children and leaves his money to four apparent strangers. Sharon must try to find these people. As she follows the trail, more violence ensues, and she realizes the random killings may not be so random.

Other books you might like:
Janet Dawson, *Kindred Crimes*, 1990
Sue Grafton, *The Kinsey Millhone Series*, 1982-
Linda Grant, *Random Access Murder*, 1988
Kate Green, *Night Angel*, 1989
Julie Smith, *Death Turns a Trick*, 1982

1184
Marcia Muller
Where Echoes Live (New York: Mysterious, 1991)

Series: Sharon McCone
Story type: Private Detective—Female Lead
Major character(s): Sharon McCone, Detective—Private
Time period(s): 1990s
Locale(s): California

What the book is about: McCone leaves San Francisco for the desert country near the Nevada border. There she is to help an environmental group discover a corporation's plans for a ghost town. Things soon degenerate into murder and kidnapping. Who is behind the two incidents and are they connected? Shamus award nominee for Best Novel.

Other books you might like:
Janet Dawson, *Kindred Crimes*, 1990
Sue Grafton, *The Kinsey Millhone Series*, 1982-
Linda Grant, *The Catherine Saylor Series*, 1988-
Sara Paretsky, *The V.I. Warshawski Series*, 1982-

1185
Marcia Muller
A Wild and Lonely Place (New York: Mysterious, 1995)

Series: Sharon McCone
Story type: Private Detective
Major character(s): Sharon McCone, Detective—Private
Time period(s): 1990s
Locale(s): San Francisco, California; Caribbean

What the book is about: Sharon agrees to help with tracking down someone calling himself the Diplo-bomber, who has been claiming responsiblity for assorted bombings at embassies and consulates all over the country for the last five years. The firm she will be working for is one that her boyfriend is also involved with, but that doesn't necessarily mean the relationships there will go smoothly. The case will take Sharon from San Francisco to the Caribbean and to Miami and involve her in trying to save the life of a nine-year-old girl.

Other books you might like:
Linda Barnes, *The Carlotta Carlyle Series*, 1987-
D.B. Borton, *The Cat Caliban Series*, 1993-
Janet Dawson, *The Jeri Howard Series*, 1990-
Linda Grant, *The Catherine Saylor Series*, 1993-
Sara Paretsky, *The V.I. Warshawski Series*, 1982-

1186
Haughton Murphy
Murder Times Two (New York: Simon, 1990)

Series: Reuben Frost
Story type: Amateur Detective—Male Lead
Major character(s): Reuben Frost, Lawyer (Retired)
Time period(s): 1980s
Locale(s): New York, New York

What the book is about: While at a meeting of a literary club discussing *Vanity Fair*, the host keels over dead. He has been poisoned. It appears that the needlepoint he was working on as well as the novel hold clues to his murder.

Other books you might like:
Charles A. Goodrum, *Carnage of the Realm*, 1979
Emma Lathen, *The John Putnam Thatcher Series*, 1961
Annette Meyers, *The Big Killing*, 1988

1187
Haughton Murphy (Pseudonym of James Duffy)
A Very Venetian Murder (New York: Simon & Schuster, 1992)

Series: Reuben Frost

Story type: Amateur Detective—Male Lead

Major character(s): Reuben Frost, Lawyer (retired)

Time period(s): 1990s

Locale(s): Venice, Italy

What the book is about: On vacation in Venice, retired lawyer Reuben Frost and his wife are invited to dinner with a famous fashion designer. The designer, Gregg Baxter, believes someone is trying to poison him by tampering with his insulin. The next day Baxter is dead, but not from poisoning—he has been stabbed. The police ask for Frost's help. When he investigates, he finds that everyone has a motive.

Other books you might like:
Sarah Caudwell, *Thus Was Adonis Murdered*, 1981
Amanda Cross, *The Players Come Again*, 1991
Jane Langton, *The Dante Game*, 1991
Roy Harley Lewis, *Death in Verona*, 1989
Edward Sklepowich, *Death in a Serene City*, 1990

1188
Warren Murphy
Co-Author: Molly Cochran
The Temple Dogs (New York: NAL, 1989)

Story type: Action/Adventure

Major character(s): Miles Haverford, Lawyer

Time period(s): 1980s

Locale(s): New York, New York; Tokyo, Japan

What the book is about: Miles Haverford's sister and her husband are gunned down on their wedding day by the mob. He screams vengeance and goes to Japan to become a Yakuza, hoping to bring the group to New York to wipe out the mob.

Other books you might like:
Anthony Bruno, *Bad Guys*, 1988
William Goldman, *Marathon Man*, 1974
Joe Gores, *Wolf Time*, 1989
David Morrell, *Testament*, 1975
Stuart Woods, *White Cargo*, 1988

1189
Stephen Murray
The Noose of Time (New York: St. Martin's, 1989)

Series: Inspector Alec Stainton

Story type: Police Procedural—Male Lead

Major character(s): Alec Stainton, Detective—Police (Inspector)

Time period(s): 1980s

What the book is about: Who executed schoolmaster Justin Hamilton? There seems to be no dearth of suspects.

Other books you might like:
Colin Dexter, *The Dead of Jericho*, 1981
Peter Hill, *The Liars*, 1977
Jack S. Scott, *The View from Deacon Hill*, 1981
John Wainwright, *The Man Who Wasn't There*, 1989
Colin Watson, *Hopjoy was Here*, 1963

1190
William Murray
I'm Getting Killed Right Here (New York: Doubleday, 1991)

Series: Shifty Anderson

Story type: Amateur Detective—Male Lead

Major character(s): Shifty Lou Anderson, Magician, Gambler (horseplayer)

Time period(s): 1990s

Locale(s): New York

What the book is about: Shifty has taken on a partner to help support a horse with great potential. Unfortunately he is also sleeping with said partner's wife. This, of course, sets the stage for much conflict.

Other books you might like:
Virginia Anderson, *King of the Roses*, 1983
Jon L. Breen, *The Jerry Brogan Series*, 1983-
Stephen Dobyns, *Saratoga Longshot*, 1984
Dick Francis, *Longshot*, 1990
Michael Geller, *Dead Last*, 1986

1191
Paul Myers
Deadly Crescendo (New York: Doubleday, 1990)

Series: Mark Holland

Story type: Espionage

Major character(s): Mark Holland, Musician (manager of classical musicians)

Time period(s): 1980s

Locale(s): Geneva, Switzerland

What the book is about: At a performance of *Tosca* in Covent Garden, Mark Holland is told that one of the stars of the opera company is a courier passing NATO secrets to the enemy. Mark is asked to assist and is reluctant, but then the man asking for help is killed. So Mark trails along to Geneva, the company's next stop, falling in love along the way.

1192 Myers

Other books you might like:
Robert Barnard, *Death on the High C's*, 1978
James Gollin, *Broken Consort*, 1989
Lucille Kallen, *The Tanglewood Murder*, 1980
Ngaio Marsh, *Overture to Death*, 1939
Audrey Peterson, *The Nocturne Murder*, 1987

1192
Paul Myers
Deadly Sonata (New York: Doubleday, 1990)

Series: Mark Holland

Story type: Action/Adventure

Major character(s): Mark Holland, Businessman (Music promoter), Spy (Former)

Time period(s): 1980s

What the book is about: Holland meets and befriends a Russian pianist and his dancer sister who wish to defect. Holland agrees to help, but the pianist disappears. While searching for him, Holland uncovers a plot to assassinate the president.

Other books you might like:
Robert Barnard, *Death on the High C's*, 1978
James Gollin, *Broken Consort*, 1989
James Gollin, *The Philomel Foundation*, 1981
Audrey Peterson, *The Nocturne Murder*, 1987

1193
Ed Naha
On the Edge (New York: Pocket, 1989)

Story type: Police Procedural—Male Lead

Major character(s): Kevin Broskey, Police Officer (Lieutenant)

Time period(s): 1980s

Locale(s): Los Angeles, California

What the book is about: Someone is torturing and killing beautiful young women. Is there a connection among them?

Other books you might like:
William Bayer, *Switch*, 1984
James Ellroy, *Blood on the Moon*, 1984
Joseph McNamara, *The First Directive*, 1984
Gerald Petievich, *Earth Angels*, 1989

1194
Michael Nava
How Town (New York: Harper, 1990)

Series: Henry Rios

Story type: Legal; Action/Adventure

Major character(s): Henry Rios, Lawyer

Time period(s): 1990s

Locale(s): Los Robles, California

What the book is about: Brought back to his home town to defend convicted child molester Paul Windsor from a charge of murdering a child pornographer, Rios must deal with his past as well as with the actual murderer.

Other books you might like:
Joseph Hansen, *The Dave Brandstetter Series*, 1974-
Ellen Hart, *Hallowed Murder*, 1989
Grant Michaels, *A Body to Dye For*, 1990
Mark Richard Zubro, *A Simple Suburban Murder*, 1987

1195
Martina Navratilova
Co-Author: Liz Nickles
The Total Zone (New York: Villard, 1995)

Story type: Amateur Detective—Female Lead; Private Detective—Female Lead

Major character(s): Jordan Myles, Sports Figure (former tennis star), Doctor (physical therapist); Noel Fisher, Detective—Private

Time period(s): 1990s

Locale(s): Palm Springs, California

What the book is about: Jordan Myles was a rising young tennis star when an accident ended her career. She became a physical therapist working at the Desert Springs Sport Center. Tennis phenom Audrey Armat needs help and checks into the center but soon disappears and is found dead, apparently a suicide. When her father is murdered soon after, Jordan is asked to help solve the case by Noel Fisher, investigator for Global Sport. First novel.

Other books you might like:
Rita Mae Brown, *Sudden Death*, 1985
Harlan Coben, *Dropshot*, 1996
Charlotte Elkins, *Rotten Lies*, 1995 (Aaron Elkins, co-author)
Alison Gordon, *The Kate Henry Series*, 1990-
Ilie Nastase, *Break Point*, 1986

1196
Janet Neel
Death Among the Dons (New York: St. Martin's, 1994)

Series: John McLeish/Francesca Wilson

Story type: Amateur Detective; Police Procedural

Major character(s): Francesca Wilson, Civil Servant; John McLeish, Police Officer (detective superintendent)

Time period(s): 1990s

Locale(s): London, England

What the book is about: Francesca Wilson is suffering from severe depression following the birth of her son. She accepts an offer from Dame Sarah Murchison to become the bursar of Bradstone College. Dame Sarah has become the college's warden following the death of its previous warden, a case that John McLeish had investigated. Francesca finds that all is not well in academia. The college is in desperate financial trouble, and there have been attacks on students. Then a professor is almost killed.

Other books you might like:
Sophie Belfort, *The Marvell College Murders*, 1991
Amanda Cross, *An Imperfect Spy*, 1995
Nora Kelly, *Bad Chemistry*, 1994
Susan Kenney, *Graves in Academe*, 1985
Joan Smith, *What Men Say*, 1994

1197
Janet Neel
Death of a Partner (New York: St. Martins, 1991)

Series: John McLeish/Francesca Wilson

Story type: Police Procedural

Major character(s): John McLeish, Police Officer (detective chief inspector); Francesca Wilson, Government Official (John's lover)

Time period(s): 1990s (1990)

Locale(s): London, England

What the book is about: McLeish is called in when Angela Morgan, fiancee of a cabinet official, is missing. Soon her bludgeoned body is found, and there is no shortage of suspects. To complicate matters, Francesca has left for New York to help one of her brothers, and McLeish finds himself attracted to his beautiful assistant.

Other books you might like:
Elizabeth George, *Payment in Blood*, 1989
Martha Grimes, *The Old Fox Deceiv'd*, 1982
Peter Robinson, *Gallows View*, 1990
Medora Sale, *Murder in a Good Cause*, 1990

1198
Barbara Neely
Blanche on the Lam (New York: St. Martin's, 1992)

Story type: Amateur Detective—Female Lead

Major character(s): Blanche White, Servant (African-American; domestic)

Time period(s): 1990s

Locale(s): Fairleigh, North Carolina

What the book is about: Blanche White, an ironic name for a proud, independent black woman, is on the run. A judge has sentenced her to 30 days in jail for inadvertently writing a bad check, and when the opportunity arises, Blanche skips out. Now she needs a place to hide, so she takes a job as a domestic with a very strange family - a family plagued by mysterious accidents, suicide and finally murder. To save herself, Blanche has to figure out what is going on. First novel.

Other books you might like:
Nikki Baker, *In the Game*, 1991
Eleanor Taylor Bland, *Dead End*, 1992

1199
Arthur F. Nehrbass
Dead Easy (New York: Dutton, 1992)

Story type: Police Procedural—Male Lead; Action/Adventure

Major character(s): Jean Stockton, Housewife (kidnap victim); Donald Stanley, Criminal; Al Lawrence, FBI Agent (agent in charge)

Time period(s): 1990s

Locale(s): Miami, Florida

What the book is about: Psychopath Don Stanley is after the big score and decides the way to this is to kidnap Jean Stockton, wife of a wealthy businessman. The FBI is called in, and Al Lawrence is placed in charge of the investigation. When the ransom payoff goes wrong, the FBI must act quickly. Don Stanley is beginning to like abusing a helpless woman. First novel.

Other books you might like:
Peter Blauner, *Slow Motion Riot*, 1991
Anthony Bruno, *Bad Guys*, 1988
Elmore Leonard, *City Primeval*, 1980
Ridley Pearson, *Hard Fall*, 1992
Brian Tobin, *The Ransom*, 1991

1200
Richard Nehrbass
Dark of Night (New York: Harper, 1992)

Series: Vic Eton

Story type: Private Detective—Male Lead

Major character(s): Vic Eton, Detective—Private (former police officer), Single Parent

Time period(s): 1990s

Locale(s): Los Angeles, California

What the book is about: Famous film producer Mackenzie Gordon's daughter has run away from home, taking with her some crucial papers for his latest film. Vic is hired to find her and the storyboards, while keeping her disappearance from the police, the newspapers and the girl's mother. Gordon seems more concerned about the papers than about his daughter and is acting strangely. When Gordon is killed, Vic realizes there is a lot more to the case than he originally thought.

Other books you might like:
Bruce Cook, *Rough Cut*, 1990
Robert Crais, *Lullaby Town*, 1992
Arthur Lyons, *Fast Fade*, 1987
Les Roberts, *Not Enough Horses*, 1988
Walter Satterthwait, *A Flower in the Desert*, 1992

1201
Ron Nessen
Co-Author: Johanna Neuman
Knight & Day (New York: St. Martin's, 1995)

Story type: Amateur Detective; Action/Adventure

Major character(s): Jerry Knight, Journalist (radio talk show host); Jane Day, Journalist (reporter); A.L. Jones, Police Officer

Time period(s): 1990s

Locale(s): Washington, District of Columbia

What the book is about: Jane Day has just published an expose of environmental wrongdoing by a prominent senator. Jerry Knight has just had a confrontational interview with well-known environmentalist, Curtis Davenport. Davenport is killed after leaving the studio. When Jane's story begins to fall apart, she is asked to confirm her source, which will be difficult as her source was Davenport. Jerry and Jane find themselves joining forces to find who killed Davenport and why. First novel.

Other books you might like:
Michael Bowen, *Fielder's Choice*, 1991
Sparkle Hayter, *What's a Girl Gotta Do?*, 1994
Bernie Lee, *The Toni and Pat Pratt Series*, 1991-
Matt Taylor, *Neon Flamingos*, 1989 (Bonnie Taylor, co-author)
Polly Whitney, *Until the End of Time*, 1995

1202
Christopher Newman
19th Precinct (New York: Fawcett, 1992)

Series: Joe Dante

Story type: Police Procedural—Male Lead; Action/Adventure

Major character(s): Joe Dante, Police Officer (detective lieutenant); Billy Mannion, Criminal, Terrorist

Time period(s): 1990s

Locale(s): New York, New York

What the book is about: After killing a bystander during a chase, Dante turns in his badge; but it's actually a ploy as he goes undercover to find IRA terrorist Billy Mannion. Mannion is suspected of killing an engineer and his lover and stealing information worth billions. Has Mannion tried to resell the information to the widow and daughter or is there more to the murder than Mannion?

Other books you might like:
Anthony Bruno, *Bad Guys*, 1988
William J. Caunitz, *Suspects*, 1986
Daniel Hearn, *Black Light*, 1991
Jack O'Connell, *Box Nine*, 1991
Ridley Pearson, *Hard Fall*, 1992

1203
Sharan Newman
Death Comes as Epiphany (New York: St. Martin's, 1993)

Story type: Amateur Detective—Female Lead; Historical

Major character(s): Catherine LeVender, Student (at a convent)

Time period(s): 12th century (1139)

Locale(s): Paris, France

What the book is about: The Convent of Paraclete under the Abbess Heloise (of Abelard and Heloise fame), is under attack from rumors of heresy and sacrilege. A book has supposedly been altered by the convent. Catherine is asked by Heloise to return home in pretended disgrace so that she can investigate the claims at the Abbey of St. Denis, run by Abbe Sueer, an avowed enemy of Peter Abelard. Can a young woman do anything against such powerful forces of the Church? First novel.

Other books you might like:
Umberto Eco, *The Name of the Rose*, 1986
Margaret Frazer, *The Sister Frevisse Series*, 1992-
C.L. Grace, *A Shrine of Murders*, 1993
Ellis Peters, *The Brother Cadfael Series*, 1977-

1204
David F. Nighbert
Shutout (New York: St. Martin's, 1995)

Series: Bull Cochran

Story type: Amateur Detective—Male Lead

Major character(s): William "Bull" Cochran, Writer (ex-baseball player); Molly Flanagan, Police Officer (Bull's lover)

Time period(s): 1990s

Locale(s): Tennessee

What the book is about: Bull is accompanying Molly back to her family in East Tennessee. It seems her Uncle Dewey has gotten himself in trouble and his brothers are trying to get him declared insane. He did shoot at one of the brothers six times, but Molly knows that if Dewey had been serious, the brother would be dead. When Dewey dies, his death triggers a rash of deaths that threaten to wipe out the entire family, including Molly, unless she and Bull can stop what's happening.

Other books you might like:
Susan Rogers Cooper, *Funny as a Dead Relative*, 1994
L.L. Enger, *Comeback*, 1990
James W. Hall, *Bones of Coral*, 1990
Toni L.P. Kelner, *Trouble Looking for a Place to Happen*, 1995
Patricia Houck Sprinkle, *A Mystery Bred in Buckhead*, 1993

1205
David F. Nighbert
Squeezeplay (New York: St. Martin's, 1992)

Series: Bull Cochran

Story type: Amateur Detective—Male Lead

Major character(s): William "Bull" Cochran, Businessman, Writer (former baseball player)

Time period(s): 1990s

Locale(s): Houston, Texas

What the book is about: Bull gets a call from sure Hall-of-Fame Astro pitcher Joe Ahern, saying he has a story about "bad people." The next day Joe is found dead in a condo with the body of a high-priced escort. The police are ready to label it murder-suicide but Bull and most of the people who really knew "Holy Joe" don't believe it. Can Bull clear his former teammate's reputation?

Other books you might like:
Paul Benjamin, *Squeeze Play*, 1982
L.L. Enger, *Swing*, 1991
Paul Engleman, *Dead in Center Field*, 1983
David Everson, *Suicide Squeeze*, 1991
Michael Geller, *Major League Murder*, 1986

1206
David F. Nighbert
Strikezone (New York: St. Martin's, 1989)

Story type: Amateur Detective—Male Lead

Major character(s): William "Bull" Cochran, Businessman, Sports Figure (former baseball player)

Time period(s): 1980s

Locale(s): Texas

What the book is about: When two masked men kill Cochran's partner, he is the initial suspect. When the police investigation hits a snag, "Bull" decides to investigate on his own.

Other books you might like:
Paul Benjamin, *Squeeze Play*, 1982
Paul Engleman, *The Mark Renzler Series*, 1983
L.L. Enger, *Comeback*, 1990
Richard Rosen, *Strike Three, You're Dead*, 1984

1207
William F. Nolan
The Black Mask Murders (New York: St. Martin's, 1994)

Story type: Historical; Private Detective—Male Lead

Major character(s): Dashiell Hammett, Writer, Historical Figure

Time period(s): 1930s

Locale(s): Hollywood, California

What the book is about: An aging film star asks Dashiell Hammett to help her with her gambling debt and see if everything was straight. He finds out the roulette wheel was crooked and falls afoul of gangster Tony Richett. Murder and mayhem ensue along with a lot of historical and biographical details about the life and times of Dashiell Hammett.

Other books you might like:
Howard Browne, *Pork City*, 1988
Max Allan Collins, *The Nate Heller Series*, 1983-
Loren D. Estleman, *Whiskey River*, 1990
Joe Gores, *Hammett*, 1975
Stuart M. Kaminsky, *The Toby Peters Series*, 1977-

1208
Robert Nordan
Death Beneath the Christmas Tree (New York: Fawcett, 1991)

Series: Mavis Lashley

Story type: Amateur Detective—Female Lead

Major character(s): Mavis Lashley, Widow(er)

Time period(s): 1990s

Locale(s): Georgia (near Atlanta)

What the book is about: Mavis and her nephew are attending the "Living Christmas Tree" pageant at their local church. Suddenly shots are fired and Frances Sedbury falls dead. This may be the first time anyone noticed Frances. Who would want to kill such a harmless person? As Mavis indulges her curiosity, she discovers secrets a lot of people don't want exposed.

Other books you might like:
Jill Churchill, *A Farewell to Yarns*, 1991
John Keith Drummond, *'Tis the Season to Be Dying*, 1988
Charlotte MacLeod, *Rest You Merry*, 1978
Celestine Sibley, *Ah, Sweet Mystery*, 1991
Valerie Wolzien, *We Wish You a Merry Murder*, 1991

1209
Robert Nordan
Death on Wheels (New York: Fawcett, 1993)

Series: Mavis Lashley

Story type: Amateur Detective—Female Lead

Major character(s): Mavis Lashley, Widow(er); Wilton Early, Police Officer (homicide)

Time period(s): 1990s

Locale(s): Markham, Georgia

What the book is about: Mavis is at the Fall Festival Bazaar at the Lakeview Nursing Home when Luna Dixon's wheelchair, with Luna in it, mysteriously ends up in the lake. Her husband was supposedly watching her. Is it an accident or murder? When Lt. Early asks Mavis to go undercover at the nursing home to investigate this and other mysterious accidents, she is more than willing. But she may end up the next victim.

Other books you might like:
Joyce Christmas, *The Lady Margaret Priam Series*, 1987-
Graham Landrum, *The Famous DAR Murder Mystery*, 1992
John Miles, *A Permanent Retirement*, 1992
Corinne Holt Sawyer, *Murder by Owl Light*, 1992
Celestine Sibley, *Ah, Sweet Mystery*, 1991

1210
Geoffrey Norman
Deep End (New York: Morrow, 1994)

Series: Morgan Hunt

Story type: Private Detective—Male Lead; Action/Adventure

Major character(s): Morgan Hunt, Detective—Private (part-time; ex-soldier, ex-con); Nat Semmes, Lawyer (Hunt's friend)

Time period(s): 1990s

Locale(s): Florida (Gulf Coast)

What the book is about: Morgan Hunt is asked by an old friend from his Navy SEAL days to help salvage his diving school from foreclosure. With the help of lawyer Nat Semmes, Morgan seems to be making progress. Then his friend, Phil Garvey, disappears. His boat is found at the site of a sunken plane which holds a treasure and two bodies as well. Does this have anything to do with the sunken treasure that Garvey had talked about? Someone wants what was on the plane and won't hesitate to kidnap of kill anyone who gets in the way.

Other books you might like:
Kenneth Abel, *Bait*, 1994
Harlen Campbell, *Monkey on a Chain*, 1993
Michael Connelly, *The Black Ice*, 1992
Thorton Elliott, *Hard Guy*, 1993
Stephen Hunter, *Point of Impact*, 1993

1211
Darian North (Pseudonym of Daranna Gidel)
Criminal Seduction (New York: Dutton, 1993)
Story type: Psychological Suspense; Amateur Detective—Male Lead
Major character(s): Owen Byrne, Writer (aspiring); Lenore Serian, Widow(er)
Time period(s): 1990s
Locale(s): New York, New York
What the book is about: Wannabe writer Owen Byrne manages to get an assignment to cover the trial of Lenore Serian. She is accused of murdering her famous artist husband, Bram Serian. While trying to maintain his objectivity Owen finds himself drawn to Lenore and soon finds himself living and sleeping with her at the home she shared with her husband. He thinks she is innocent and is determined to find the truth which will be difficult as the artist buried himself under layers of identity. First mystery.
Other books you might like:
Oliver Banks, *The Rembrandt Panel*, 1980
John Clarkson, *And Justice for One*, 1993
Peter Clothier, *Chiaroscuro*, 1985
Carolyn Coker, *The Other David*, 1984

1212
Frank Norwood
The Man in the Moon (New York: St. Martin's, 1989)
Story type: Action/Adventure
Major character(s): Charlie Tone, Businessman (bail bondsman)
Time period(s): 1980s
Locale(s): Los Angeles, California; Washington, District of Columbia
What the book is about: An FBI agent hires Charlie Tone to find the murderer of a friend. This is the tip of the iceberg as Charlie discovers a plot to discredit the FBI at the highest levels. First book.
Other books you might like:
William L. DeAndrea, *Killed in the Ratings*, 1978
Richard Hoyt, *Decoys*, 1980
Elmore Leonard, *La Brava*, 1983

1213
Maureen O'Brien
Close-Up on Death (New York: St. Martin's, 1989)
Story type: Police Procedural—Male Lead
Major character(s): Millie Hale, Actress; John Bright, Police Officer (Detective Inspector)
Time period(s): 1980s
What the book is about: When Millie Hale finds her best friend and fellow actress murdered, Inspector Bright is called in to solve the case.
Other books you might like:
Anne Morice, *The Tessa Crichton Series*, (1970-1989)
Dorothy Simpson, *The Inspector Luke Thanet Series*, 1981

1214
Meg O'Brien
The Daphne Decisions (New York: Bantam, 1990)
Series: Jessica James
Story type: Amateur Detective—Female Lead
Major character(s): Jessica "Jessie" James, Journalist (newspaper reporter)
Time period(s): 1980s
Locale(s): Rochester, New York
What the book is about: When Jessica James wakes up in the hospital with people thinking she's Daphne Malcross, heiress, she decides to let the deception go on for a while. This is O'Brien's first mystery.
Other books you might like:
Dick Belsky, *One for the Money*, 1986
Elaine Raco Chase, *Dangerous Places*, 1987
Susan Kelly, *The Gemini Man*, 1985
Sherryl Woods, *Reckless*, 1989

1215
Meg O'Brien
Eagles Die Too (New York: Doubleday, 1992)
Series: Jessica James
Story type: Amateur Detective—Female Lead
Major character(s): Jessica "Jessie" James, Journalist (freelance); Mac Devlin, Pilot, Veteran (Vietnam)
Time period(s): 1990s
Locale(s): Rochester, New York
What the book is about: Jessie's sometime lover and organized crime boss, Marcus Andrelli, has gotten her involved with writing a story about a school for bodyguards. While there she becomes involved with a handsome (think Gregory Peck) pilot, Mac Devlin. However, Marcus, Mac and her mother's new husband, Charlie (think Paul Newman) seem to be involved in some shady goings on and nobody wants to tell Jessie anything. Then Charlie and her mom disappear. Jessie tries to find out what is happening and doesn't know who to trust.
Other books you might like:
Barbara D'Amato, *The Cat Marsala Series*, 1990-
Susan Kelly, *The Liz Connors Series*, 1985-
Mary Kittredge, *Poison Pen*, 1990
Sarah Shankman, *Now Let's Talk of Graves*, 1990
David Stout, *Night of the Ice Storm*, 1991

1216
Meg O'Brien
Hare Today, Gone Tomorrow (New York: Bantam, 1991)
Series: Jessica James
Story type: Amateur Detective—Female Lead
Major character(s): Jessica "Jessie" James, Journalist (freelance)
Time period(s): 1990s

Locale(s): San Francisco, California; Rochester, New York

What the book is about: Jessie's mother shows up on her doorstep with a new boyfriend, Charlie, and a painting that she has stolen. When Jessie tries to investigate Charlie's background, she finds herself involved with art theft, a forty year-old murder, blackmail and a brand new murder. She also finds that Charlie doesn't seem to have officially existed for the last twenty years.

Other books you might like:
Carolyn Coker, *The Balmoral Nude*, 1990
Fredrick D. Huebner, *Picture Postcard*, 1990
Marcia Muller, *The Joanna Stark Series*, 1986-1989
Sarah Shankman, *Now Let's Talk of Graves*, 1990
Joan Smith, *A Brush with Death*, 1990

1217
Meg O'Brien
The Keeper (New York: Doubleday, 1992)

Story type: Private Detective—Male Lead; Action/Adventure

Major character(s): John Creed, Detective—Private (ex-policeman); Brooke Hayes, Actress (divorced mother), Alcoholic

Time period(s): 1990s

Locale(s): Los Angeles, California; San Francisco, California

What the book is about: Brooke Hayes is a recovering alcoholic trying to put her life in order so she can regain custody of her daughter, Charlie. One night she gets a call from Charlie that leads Brooke to believe her daughter is in trouble. Her ex-husband says everything is all right, but he won't let Charlie talk. When Brooke asks the police to look into it, they can't or won't help. Brooke goes to John Creed for help. Creed, also known as "The Keeper," specializes in finding missing children ever since his own son was lost.

Other books you might like:
Robert Campbell, *Alice in La-La Land*, 1986
Timothy Hallinan, *Everything but the Squeal*, 1990
Walter Satterthwait, *A Flower in the Desert*, 1992
Andrew Vachss, *Sacrifice*, 1991
Marilyn Wallace, *A Single Stone*, 1991

1218
Tim O'Brien
In the Lake of the Woods (Boston: Houghton Mifflin, 1994)

Story type: Psychological Suspense

Major character(s): John Wade, Political Figure

Time period(s): 1990s

Locale(s): Minnesota

What the book is about: John Wade is a candidate for higher office when it is revealed that he was present at the massacre of a village in Vietnam. After this ruins his career, he and his wife try to escape to their cabin in the north woods of Minnesota. Wade awakes one morning to find his wife missing. When a search fails to turn her up, it is thought that he has killed her. Then Wade himself is missing. Not your average mystery, but more a study of what might happen to people under pressure. First book that could be considered in this field.

Other books you might like:
James Lee Burke, *The Dave Robicheaux Series*, 1986-
David Guterson, *Snow Falling on Cedars*, 1994
Craig Holden, *The River Sorrow*, 1994
Dennis Lehane, *A Drink Before the War*, 1994

1219
Maxine O'Callaghan
Hit and Run (New York: St. Martins, 1989)

Series: Delilah West

Story type: Private Detective—Female Lead

Major character(s): Delilah West, Detective—Private

Time period(s): 1980s

Locale(s): California (southern)

What the book is about: Delilah West, down on her luck P.I., is asked to take on the case of a hit and run accident to which she was the only witness. Teenager Mike Morales, arrested for the crime, claims that the victim was already dead.

Other books you might like:
Jane Dentinger, *First Hit of the Season*, 1984
Sue Grafton, *F Is for Fugitive*, 1989
Michael Hendricks, *Money to Burn*, 1989
Marcia Muller, *The Shape of Dread*, 1989
Sara Paretsky, *Bitter Medicine*, 1986

1220
Maxine O'Callaghan
Set-Up (New York: St. Martin's, 1991)

Series: Delilah West

Story type: Private Detective—Female Lead

Major character(s): Delilah West, Detective—Private, Widow(er)

Time period(s): 1990s

Locale(s): Orange County, California

What the book is about: Delilah is finally doing well. She has just finished a case for a councilman, having caught one of the workers with her hands in the till. Now she may have a job from another council member, Bobbi Calder, who has received threatening notes. When Delilah gets a call from the woman she had arrested, she goes to her house and finds the woman dead with Bobbi sitting in the same room. Bobbi swears she is innocent.

1221 O'Connell

Other books you might like:
Linda Barnes, *Coyote*, 1990
Sue Grafton, *The Kinsey Millhone Series*, 1982-
Linda Grant, *Love nor Money*, 1991
Marcia Muller, *The Sharon McCone Series*, 1977-
Gloria White, *Murder on the Run*, 1991

1221
Carol O'Connell
Mallory's Oracle (New York: Putnam, 1994)

Story type: Police Procedural—Female Lead

Major character(s): Kathleen Mallory, Police Officer (sergeant, special crimes); Charles Butler, Businessman

Time period(s): 1990s

Locale(s): New York, New York

What the book is about: A serial killer stalks elderly women in Gramercy Park. At the scene of the killer's latest crime, the body of Louis Markowitz of the Special Crimes section is also found. Kathleen Mallory is determined to find the killer because Markowitz is the person who took her off the streets and gave her a home. Mallory is smart and beautiful, but inexperienced in field work. She has one advantage, however: she will stop at nothing to solve this case. First novel.

Other books you might like:
Rochelle Majer Krich, *Fair Game*, 1993
David L. Lindsey, *Mercy*, 1990
Jack O'Connell, *Box Nine*, 1992
Soledad Santiago, *Undercover*, 1988
April Smith, *North of Montana*, 1994

1222
Catherine O'Connell
Skins (New York: Fine, 1993)

Story type: Police Procedural—Female Lead

Major character(s): Karen Levinson, Police Officer, Detective—Homicide; Tony Perilli, Police Officer, Detective—Homicide

Time period(s): 1990s

Locale(s): New York, New York

What the book is about: Karen Levinson is a rookie detective on her first case. Famous model Jennifer O'Grady has been beaten to death, apparently by someone who objected to her modeling of fur coats. The trail leads to a radical animal rights group. The case is hard enough, but Karen has to fight against the prejudice of her partner who considers her a dilettante princess, not a real cop. First novel.

Other books you might like:
Eleanor Taylor Bland, *Dead Time*, 1992
Susan Dunlap, *The Jill Smith Series*, 1981-
Jack Early, *Donato and Daughter*, 1988
Ruby Horansky, *Dead Ahead*, 1990
Laurie R. King, *A Grave Talent*, 1993

1223
Jack O'Connell
Box Nine (New York: Mysterious, 1992)

Story type: Police Procedural—Female Lead

Major character(s): Lenore Thomas, Police Officer (lieutenant, narcotics), Twin; Ike Thomas, Postal Worker, Twin (Lenore's)

Time period(s): 1990s

Locale(s): New England

What the book is about: Lenore Thomas is a narc with a growing amphetamine habit and a love for heavy metal music, her brother, and especially guns. She is working on bringing down a major druglord and controlling the spread of the new designer drug, Lingo. This drug enhances the speech center of the brain but also induces homicidal rages. Meanwhile her brother and his supervisor at the post office are involved with strange packages with very odd and disgusting contents being sent to Box 9. First novel.

Other books you might like:
Soledad Santiago, *Undercover*, 1988
Kim Wozencraft, *Rush*, 1990
Lue Zimmelman, *Honolulu Red*, 1990

1224
Lillian O'Donnell
Lockout (New York: Putnam, 1994)

Series: Norah Mulcahaney

Story type: Police Procedural—Female Lead

Major character(s): Norah Mulcahaney, Detective—Homicide (lieutenant)

Time period(s): 1990s

Locale(s): New York, New York

What the book is about: Norah Mulcahaney has enough to worry about with the murder of the brother of famous rock musician Bo Russell. Talk about a high profile case. She is additionally concerned about a young woman who killed her abusive brother and is now charged with murder. Norah also wants to adopt a baby. Then she shoots a mugger who she is sure had a gun, but the weapon can't be found, so now she is involved in an internal affairs investigation. Her career may not survive.

Other books you might like:
Jack Early, *Donato and Daughter*, 1988
Ruby Horansky, *Dead Center*, 1994
Margaret Maron, *The Sigrid Harald Series*, 1981-
Lee Martin, *The Deb Ralston Series*, 1984-
Carol O'Connell, *Mallory's Oracle*, 1994

1225
Lillian O'Donnell
A Private Crime (New York: Putnam, 1991)

Series: Norah Mulcahaney

Story type: Police Procedural—Female Lead

Major character(s): Norah Mulcahaney, Detective—Homicide (lieutenant); Randall Tye, Journalist (TV anchorman, loves Norah)

Time period(s): 1990s

Locale(s): New York, New York

What the book is about: Norah, in charge of the fourth homicide division, is given the case of a young woman and baby who were shot down when a gunman opened fire with an assault rifle at a flea market. In the crowd they were the only casualties. Randall thinks the crime was drug related, but Norah disagrees.

Other books you might like:
Susan Dunlap, *The Jill Smith Series*, 1982-
Margaret Maron, *The Sigrid Harald Series*, 1982-
Lee Martin, *The Deb Ralston Series*, 1984-
Julie Smith, *New Orleans Mourning*, 1990
Dorothy Uhnak, *The Ledger*, 1970

1226
Lillian O'Donnell
Pushover (New York: Putnam, 1992)

Series: Norah Mulcahaney

Story type: Police Procedural—Female Lead

Major character(s): Norah Mulcahaney, Detective—Homicide (lieutenant)

Time period(s): 1990s

Locale(s): New York, New York

What the book is about: Elderly movie star Wilma Danay is dead after a severe beating. To complicate matters her grandson is missing and a ransom demand is accompanied by a threat that any police activity will cause his death. Norah has to investigate carefully. She is also assigned to act as liason with the transit authority to look into a series of women falling to their deaths at the same subway station.

Other books you might like:
Susan Dunlap, *The Jill Smith Series*, 1982-
Ruby Horansky, *Dead Ahead*, 1991
Margaret Maron, *The Sigrid Harald Series*, 1982
Lee Martin, *The Deb Ralston Series*, 1984-
Julie Smith, *The Skip Langdon Series*, 1990-

1227
Lillian O'Donnell
The Raggedy Man (New York: Putnam, 1995)

Series: Gwenn Ramadge

Story type: Private Detective—Female Lead

Major character(s): Gwenn Ramadge, Detective—Private; Ray Dixon, Police Officer (Gwenn's lover)

Time period(s): 1990s

Locale(s): New York, New York

What the book is about: Gwenn is asked by her friend Ray Dixon to help Jayne Harrow, one of his former students at the academy. She once blew the whistle on her partner while working narcotics and is now suspended and suspected of dealing drugs herself. Gwenn hires Jayne and assigns her to a case involving a nanny and her young charge whose behavior is notably odd. Then Jayne is killed. Was it the case she was working on or did someone on the police force decide to shut her up permanently? Gwenn wants the truth and justice.

Other books you might like:
Jack Early, *Donato and Daugher*, 1988
Karen Kijewski, *Alley Kat Blues*, 1995
Janice Law, *Backfire*, 1994
Maxine O'Callaghan, *Death Is Forever*, 1981
Sharon Zukowski, *Dancing in the Dark*, 1992

1228
Lillian O'Donnell
Used to Kill (New York: Putnam, 1993)

Series: Gwenn Ramadge

Story type: Private Detective—Female Lead

Major character(s): Gwenn Ramadge, Detective—Private; Ray Dixon, Police Officer (detective sergeant, homicide)

Time period(s): 1990s

Locale(s): New York, New York

What the book is about: Emma Trent's husband has been brutally beaten to death in an apparent robbery of the couple's home. After investigating, the police arrest Emma for hiring two young men to kill her husband. Gwenn Ramadge, whose agency had previously investigated Emma for the husband, is drawn into the case and asked to prove Emma's innocence.

Other books you might like:
Gillian B. Farrell, *Alibi for an Actress*, 1992
Michael Hendricks, *Money to Burn*, 1989
Janice Law, *The Big Payoff*, 1989
Maxine O'Callaghan, *Set-Up*, 1991
Sharon Zukowski, *Dancing in the Dark*, 1992

1229
Lillian O'Donnell
A Wreath for the Bride (New York: Putnam, 1990)

Series: Gwenn Ramadge

Story type: Private Detective—Female Lead

Major character(s): Gwenn Ramadge, Detective—Private

Time period(s): 1980s

Locale(s): New York, New York

What the book is about: Ramadge is hired to investigate the death of a bride on her honeymoon. She is working for the bride's mother, who suspects the new husband. Though Ramadge is able to clear the husband, she hears of the murder of another new bride and soon the murder of a bride-to-be. Is there a connection between these deaths?

1230 Oleksiw

Other books you might like:
Sue Grafton, *G Is for Gumshoe*, 1990
Marcia Muller, *The Shape of Dread*, 1989
Sara Paretsky, *Burn Marks*, 1990

1230
Susan Oleksiw
Family Album (New York: Scribners, 1995)

Series: Mellingham Mystery

Story type: Police Procedural—Male Lead

Major character(s): Joe Silva, Police Officer (chief of police); Gwen McDuffy, Single Mother

Time period(s): 1990s

Locale(s): Mellingham, Massachusetts

What the book is about: Something strange is going on at the Arbella House, home of the Arbella Historical Society. George Frome has asked Joe Silva to conduct a security check, but Joe suspects George has something more in mind. Before he can find out, George dies. When it is discovered that George was poisoned, Joe starts investigating the staff of Arbella House. One volunteer, Gwen McDuffy, seems to be harboring some dark secret. But is she capable of murder?

Other books you might like:
Andrew Coburn, *No Way Home*, 1992
K.C. Constantine, *The Mario Balzac Series*, 1974-
Susan Rogers Cooper, *The Milt Kovak Series*, 1988-
Archer Mayor, *The Joe Gunther Series*, 1988-
Anne Wingate, *The Mark Shigata Series*, 1988-

1231
Susan Oleksiw
Murder in Mellingham (New York: Scribners, 1993)

Series: Mellingham Mystery

Story type: Police Procedural—Male Lead

Major character(s): Joe Silva, Police Officer (chief of police); Ken Dupoulis, Police Officer (sergeant)

Time period(s): 1990s

Locale(s): Mellingham, Massachusetts

What the book is about: There is no dearth of suspects when Beth O'Donnell is found clubbed to death in her brother's guest cottage. There are the relatives that she had harassed over the years, the local publishing mogul she forced out of business some years earlier, and an editor that she had threatened. All in all, she was terribly unlikable, and chief of police Joe Silva is having a difficult time finding anyone who wants to help find her killer. First mystery.

Other books you might like:
K.C. Constantine, *The Man Who Liked Slow Tomatoes*, 1982
Susan Rogers Cooper, *Other People's Houses*, 1990
Douglas Kiker, *Murder on Clam Pond*, 1986
Archer Mayor, *Open Season*, 1988
P.B. Shaw, *The Seraphim Kill*, 1994

1232
B.J. Oliphant (Pseudonym of Sheri S. Tepper)
Dead in the Scrub (New York: Fawcett, 1990)

Series: Shirley McClintock

Story type: Amateur Detective—Female Lead

Major character(s): Shirley McClintock, Rancher

Time period(s): 1990s

Locale(s): Colorado

What the book is about: While tracking a wounded deer, rancher Shirley McClintock runs across a human skeleton. Soon there is another murder. Are the two bodies—and the deer—connected?

Other books you might like:
Jan Adkins, *Cookie*, 1988
Jean Hager, *The Grandfather Medicine*, 1989
Joan Hess, *Strangled Prose*, 1987
Kathryn Lasky Knight, *Trace Elements*, 1986

1233
B.J. Oliphant (Pseudonym of Sheri S. Tepper)
Death and the Delinquent (New York: Fawcett, 1993)

Series: Shirley McClintock

Story type: Amateur Detective—Female Lead

Major character(s): Shirley McClintock, Rancher

Time period(s): 1990s

Locale(s): Los Arboles, New Mexico

What the book is about: Shirley and her family are on a tour of New Mexico and have been talked into taking along a schoolmate of Allison's, April Shaour. While the group is out riding, April is shot and killed and Shirley is injured. Although April was a thief, liar and snoop, Shirley is outraged at her death. April's parents are more concerned with recovering a stolen gold horse, and the police are occupied with a baby kidnapping. Are any or all of these events connected? Oliphant also writes mysteries as A. J. Orde.

Other books you might like:
Christine Andreae, *Trail of Murder*, 1992
J.A. Jance, *Desert Heat*, 1992
Walter Satterthwait, *At Ease with the Dead*, 1990
Judith Van Gieson, *The Wolf Path*, 1992

1234
B.J. Oliphant (Pseudonym of Sheri S. Tepper)
Death Served Up Cold (New York: Fawcett, 1994)

Series: Shirley McClintock

Story type: Amateur Detective—Female Lead

Major character(s): Shirley McClintock, Rancher, Innkeeper

Time period(s): 1990s

Locale(s): Taos, New Mexico

What the book is about: Shirley McClintock, her lover J.Q., and her foster daughter Alison have recently moved to New Mexico and Rancho Del Valle, a ranch and inn. One of her guests complains of a bad headache and is soon dead. The dead woman, Alicia Tremple, strangely seems to have no past, and any clue to who or what she was has mysteriously vanished. The other guests are acting oddly too. Could one of them be a murderer?

Other books you might like:
Christine Andreae, *Trail of Murder*, 1992
Nevada Barr, *Track of the Cat*, 1993
Mary Bowen Hall, *The Emma Chizzit Series*, 1989-1993
Rebecca Rothenberg, *The Bulrush Murders*, 1991
Judith Van Gieson, *Raptor*, 1990

1235
B.J. Oliphant (Pseudonym of Sheri S. Tepper)
The Unexpected Corpse (New York: Fawcett, 1990)

Series: Shirley McClintock

Story type: Amateur Detective—Female Lead

Major character(s): Shirley McClintock, Rancher

Time period(s): 1990s

Locale(s): Ridge County, Colorado

What the book is about: Shirley's uncle and his wife are killed in a traffic accident in London. When their ashes are returned for burial, a third box of ashes arrives too. No sooner are they buried when someone digs them up. After the discovery of a fourth box of ashes, Shirley decides she had better find out what is going on.

Other books you might like:
Mary Bowen Hall, *Emma Chizzit and the Queen Anne Killer*, 1989
Mary Kittredge, *Murder in Mendocino*, 1987
Janet LaPierre, *The Cruel Mother*, 1987
Nancy Pickard, *Bum Steer*, 1990
Judith Van Gieson, *Raptor*, 1990

1236
Maria-Antonia Oliver
Antipodes (Seattle: Seal, 1989)

Series: Lonia Guiu

Story type: Private Detective—Female Lead

Major character(s): Lonia Guiu, Detective—Private; Cristina Segura, Heiress

Time period(s): 1980s

Locale(s): Melbourne, Australia; Majorca, Spain

What the book is about: While on vacation in Australia, Lonia Guiu gets involved in the case of a disappearing heiress.

Other books you might like:
David Serafin, *The Body in Cadiz Bay*, 1985
Manuel Vazquez Montalban, *Murder in the Central Commitee*, 1985
Eve Zaremba, *Work for a Million*, 1987

1237
Sister Carol Anne O'Marie
Death Goes on Retreat (New York: Delacorte, 1995)

Series: Sister Mary Helen

Story type: Amateur Detective—Female Lead

Major character(s): Sister Mary Helen, Religious (nun)

Time period(s): 1990s

Locale(s): California (Santa Cruz Mountains)

What the book is about: Sister Mary Helen is beginning to develop a reputation as someone who attracts murder—but what could happen when she goes on a retreat? She and Sister Eileen are a week early and are stranded during a priests' retreat. First they witness an emotional scene between a young woman named Laura and Sister Felicitas, the head of the retreat center. Then Sister Mary Helen discovers the body of a young man—Laura's anti-establishment boyfriend. She sets out to solve the crime.

Other books you might like:
Lee Harris, *The Christmas Night Murder*, 1995
Veronica Black, *The Sister Joan Series*, 1991-
Gerelyn Hollingsworth, *Murder at St. Adelaide's*, 1995
Monica Quill, *The Sister Mary Teresa Series*, 1981-
Winona Sullivan, *A Sudden Death at the Norfolk Cafe*, 1993

1238
Sister Carol Anne O'Marie
Murder in Ordinary Time (New York: Delacorte, 1991)

Series: Sister Mary Helen

Story type: Amateur Detective—Female Lead

Major character(s): Sister Mary Helen, Religious (nun)

Time period(s): 1990s

Locale(s): San Francisco, California

What the book is about: Sister Mary Helen is going to be interviewed on the noon news by investigative reporter Christina Kelly. Just as they go on the air, Christina takes a bite of a cookie and drops dead of cyanide poisoning. Complicating the case of who killed her is the problem of who was the intended victim, Christina or one of the other people eating the cookies, maybe even Sister Mary Helen herself.

Other books you might like:
Veronica Black, *Vow of Silence*, 1990
Anthony Boucher, *Nine Times Nine*, 1940
Monica Quill, *The Sister Mary Teresa Series*, 1981-

1239
Sister Carol Anne O'Marie
Murder Makes a Pilgrimage (New York: Delacorte, 1993)

Series: Sister Mary Helen

Story type: Amateur Detective—Female Lead

Major character(s): Sister Mary Helen, Religious (nun); Sister Eileen, Religious (nun)

Time period(s): 1990s

Locale(s): Santiago, Spain

1240

What the book is about: Sister Mary Helen has won a trip to Spain; at least that's what the owner of the restaurant sponsoring the contest tells her. She doesn't remember entering any contest, but perhaps it's divine intervention. So she and Sister Eileen end up in a tour group with many interesting people. When one of them is killed, Sister Mary Helen decides to investigate, but now somebody seems to be stalking her.

Other books you might like:
Veronica Black, *The Sister Joan Series*, 1990-
D.M. Greenwood, *The Theodora Braithwaite Series*, 1991-
Lee Harris, *The Christine Bennett Series*, 1992-
Isabelle Holland, *The Claire Aldington Series*, 1984-
Monica Quill, *The Sister Mary Teresa Series*, 1980-

1240

A.J. Orde (Pseudonym of Sheri S. Tepper)
Death and the Dogwalker (New York: Doubleday, 1990)

Series: Jason Lynx

Story type: Amateur Detective—Male Lead

Major character(s): Jason Lynx, Antiques Dealer; Grace Willis, Police Officer (Jason's friend)

Time period(s): 1990s

Locale(s): Denver, Colorado

What the book is about: While walking his dog and a visiting cat, Jason encounters the carefully posed body of sometime acquaintance Freederick Foret. Does this murder have anything to do with a previous murder in the same park? Jason, addicted to puzzles, can't keep from looking into it, but he may be sorry.

Other books you might like:
Richard Barth, *Furnished for Murder*, 1990
Eliza G.C. Collins, *Going, Going, Gone*, 1986
Jonathan Gash, *The Lovejoy Series*, 1977-
Victor Wuamett, *Teardown*, 1990

1241

A.J. Orde (Pseudonym of Sheri S. Tepper)
A Little Neighborhood Murder (New York: Doubleday, 1989)

Story type: Amateur Detective—Male Lead

Major character(s): Jason Lynx, Antiques Dealer; Grace Willis, Police Officer

Time period(s): 1980s

Locale(s): Denver, Colorado

What the book is about: When Jason Lynx's neighbors are killed, he begins to get emotionally involved with one of the officers investigating the case. First book.

Other books you might like:
Jonathan Gash, *The Judas Pair*, 1977
Barbara Moore, *The Doberman Wore Black*, 1983
Lillian O'Donnell, *A Good Night to Kill*, 1988
Julie Smith, *True-Life Adventure*, 1985

1242

A.J. Orde (Pseudonym of Sheri S. Tepper)
A Long Time Dead (New York: Fawcett, 1995)

Series: Jason Lynx

Story type: Amateur Detective—Male Lead

Major character(s): Jason Kynx, Antiques Dealer; Grace Willis, Police Officer (Jason's lover)

Time period(s): 1990s

Locale(s): Denver, Colorado

What the book is about: Grace's brother Ron has come home with bad news—he is dying of AIDS. Although Ron has always been flighty, he seems to take a great interest in Jason's business and his latest projects, restoring some furniture and designing a building. The building is to be built in the mountains and used as the offices for a think tank for environmental issues. When Ron is killed by a booby trap at the site of the proposed building, Grace is devastated. Was Ron the intended victim? Orde also writes as B.J. Oliphant.

Other books you might like:
Jeff Abbott, *The Jordan Poteet Series*, 1994-
Leo Axler, *The Bill Hawley Series*, 1994-
Richard A. Lupoff, *The Hobart Lindsey Series*, 1989-
John Malcolm, *The Tim Simpson Series*, 1983-
Neville Steed, *The Peter Marklin Series*, 1987-

1243

Roger Ormerod
By Death Possessed (New York: Doubleday, Crime Club, 1989)

Story type: Action/Adventure

Major character(s): Tony Hine, Rake; Margaret Dennis, Art Historian

Time period(s): 1980s

What the book is about: Art historian Margaret Dennis is after a cache of paintings that she thinks once belonged to Tony Hine's grandmother, the lover of renowned painter Frederick Ashe.

Other books you might like:
Oliver Banks, *The Rembrandt Panel*, 1980
Sarah Caudwell, *Thus Was Adonis Murdered*, 1982
Carolyn Coker, *The Other David*, 1984
Jonathan Gash, *Jade Woman*, 1989
Isabelle Holland, *The Lost Madonna*, 1981

1244

Roger Ormerod
Hung in the Balance (New York: Doubleday, 1991)

Story type: Amateur Detective; Police Procedural

Major character(s): Philipa Lowe, Businesswoman; Oliver Simpson, Police Officer (Inspector)

Time period(s): 1990s

Locale(s): Birmingham, England

What the book is about: Philipa Lowe is coming back to England for the funeral of her estranged husband. She learns that he committed suicide by driving over a cliff. But she knows that he would never kill himself—especially that way, since he never drove. More revelations follow, making Philipa wonder what kind of secret life her husband was leading.

Other books you might like:
Paula Gosling, *Death Penalties*, 1991
Susan B. Kelly, *Hope Against Hope*, 1991
Sheila Radley, *Death in the Morning*, 1987

1245
David Osborn
Murder in the Napa Valley (New York: Simon & Schuster, 1993)

Series: Margaret Barlow

Story type: Amateur Detective—Female Lead

Major character(s): Margaret Barlow, Photojournalist

Time period(s): 1990s

Locale(s): Napa Valley, California

What the book is about: Margaret Barlow is on assignment to do a story on wine-making and is visiting L'Abbaye Ste. Denise, a small but promising winery owned by former movie star Ellisa Seldridge and her husband John. Margaret learns that someone is sabotaging the winery and that Ellisa and John are being pressured to sell by John's ex-wife and part-owner, who demands that they unload the winery. The next day the ex-wife's body is found cut to pieces. Margaret wants to help, so she starts snooping.

Other books you might like:
Eleanor Boylan, *Working Murder*, 1989
Judith Garwood, *Make Friends with Murder*, 1992
Mary Bowen Hall, *Emma Chizzit and the Napa Nemesis*, 1992
Jerry Kennealy, *Vintage Polo*, 1993
Stephanie Matteson, *The Charlotte Graham Series*, 1990-

1246
David Osborn
Murder on the Chesapeake (New York: Simon & Schuster, 1992)

Series: Margaret Barlow

Story type: Amateur Detective—Female Lead

Major character(s): Margaret Barlow, Photojournalist (freelance), Grandparent

Time period(s): 1990s

Locale(s): Burnham State, Maryland

What the book is about: Mary Hughes, a friend of Martha's granddaughter Nancy—both students at an exclusive girls school—has been found hanging from a bell rope. This was perhaps a tragic accident. When Martha arrives to help Nancy cope, Nancy says it must be suicide. A local policeman, interested in Martha as well as the case, suspects murder. It's up to Margaret, with her inside knowledge of the school, to find the truth.

Other books you might like:
Richard Barth, *The Margaret Binton Series*, 1978-
Simon Brett, *The Mrs. Pargeter Series*, 1988-
B. Comfort, *Grave Consequences*, 1989
Dorothy Gilman, *The Mrs. Pollifax Series*, 1964-
Hazel Holt, *Mrs. Malory Investigates*, 1990

1247
Denise Osborne
Cut To—Murder (New York: Holt, 1995)

Series: Queenie Davilov

Story type: Private Detective—Female Lead

Major character(s): Queenie Davilov, Writer (scriptwriter), Detective—Private

Time period(s): 1990s

Locale(s): Spain

What the book is about: Queenie is called to Spain to complete a script that purports to tell a true story set during the Spanish Civil War. The original scriptwriter has vanished, and Queenie must now find out what happened to the scriptwriter and the real truth behind the script. Does a past death have anything to do with the current disappearance?

Other books you might like:
Trella Crespi, *The Trouble with Moonlighting*, 1991
Gillian B. Farrell, *Alibi for an Actress*, 1992
Kate Green, *Shooting Star*, 1992
Maureen O'Brien, *Close-Up on Death*, 1989
Jim Stinson, *The Stoney Winston Series*, 1985

1248
Denise Osborne
Murder Offscreen (New York: Holt, 1994)

Story type: Private Detective—Female Lead

Major character(s): Queenie Davilov, Detective—Private, Writer (screenwriter)

Time period(s): 1990s

Locale(s): Los Angeles, California

What the book is about: Queenie Davilov was the script supervisor on Lymon Burke's latest picture, *Lucifer's Shadow*, which featured as many strange occurrences and deaths offscreen as on. Now Lymon and his wife are receiving bloody threats. Queenie is asked to help; but before she learns anything, Lymon is horribly murdered at the premiere of the movie. Is this the work of a religious maniac or is someone close to Lymon being clever? First novel.

Other books you might like:
Trella Crespi, *The Trouble with Moonlighting*, 1991
Gillian B. Farrell, *Alibi for an Actress*, 1992
Kate Green, *Shooting Star*, 1992
Maureen O'Brien, *Close-Up on Death*, 1989
Dorian Yeager, *Cancellation by Death*, 1992

1249
Jerry Oster
Fixing to Die (New York: Bantam, 1992)

Story type: Police Procedural—Male Lead; Action/Adventure

Major character(s): Joe Cullen, Police Officer (detective internal affairs)

Time period(s): 1990s

Locale(s): New York

What the book is about: Elvis Polk was a small-time crook who said he wanted to talk about a heist. When two officers are transporting him back to New York, he is friendly and cooperative until he suddenly kills them with a concealed gun. Why? When television reporter Samantha Cox starts asking embarassing questions, Joe Cullen has all that he can handle. Were the two officers set up by other policemen?

Other books you might like:
William Bayer, *Switch*, 1984
Nat Hentoff, *The Man From Internal Affairs*, 1985
Joseph McNamara, *The First Directive*, 1984
Ed Naha, *On the Edge*, 1989
William D. Pease, *Playing the Dozens*, 1990

1250
George Owens
The Judas Pool (New York: Putnam, 1994)

Story type: Psychological Suspense; Amateur Detective—Male Lead

Major character(s): Steven Black, Teacher (high school)

Time period(s): 1990s

Locale(s): Delaware

What the book is about: A student accuses high school teacher Steven Black of seducing her. Privately she tells him that her father forced her to make the accusation and that she is going to sabotage her father's business plans. She does that, but is then found murdered. There is no proof that she told Steven the truth so he is thought to be the murderer. He must find the truth before he is convicted for a crime he didn't commit. First novel.

Other books you might like:
W. Edward Blain, *Passion Play*, 1990
S.F.X. Dean, *By Frequent Anguish*, 1982
Terence Faherty, *The Lost Keats*, 1993
Michael T. Hinkemeyer, *Fourth Down, Death*, 1984
Gillian Roberts, *Caught Dead in Philadelphia*, 1987

1251
Abigail Padgett
Child of Silence (New York: Mysterious, 1993)

Story type: Amateur Detective—Female Lead; Psychological Suspense

Major character(s): Barbara "Bo" Bradley, Social Worker (child protective services), Mentally Ill Person (manic depressive)

Time period(s): 1990s

Locale(s): San Diego, California

What the book is about: Assigned the case of a four-year-old John Doe found in an abandoned house on an Indian reservation, child abuse investigator Bo Bradley must try and keep her equilibrium (she's a manic-depressive) while trying to find the identity of the boy. When someone takes a shot at her, she realizes that this case may be more than a typical child abuse case. First novel.

Other books you might like:
Linda Barnes, *Coyote*, 1992
Jonathan Kellerman, *The Alex Delaware Series*, 1985-
Sara Paretsky, *Guardian Angel*, 1992
Richard Parrish, *The Dividing Line*, 1993
Andrew Vachss, *Strega*, 1987

1252
Abigail Padgett
Strawgirl (New York: Mysterious, 1994)

Series: Bo Bradley

Story type: Amateur Detective—Female Lead; Psychological Suspense

Major character(s): Barbara "Bo" Bradley, Social Worker (child protection services), Mentally Ill Person (manic depressive); Andrew LaMarche, Doctor

Time period(s): 1990s

Locale(s): San Diego, California; Adirondacks, New York

What the book is about: Bo Bradley is called in to investigate the rape of a three-year-old girl. When the girl dies and the mother commits suicide, Bo shifts her attention to the older sister, Hannah, who has apparently been left with the mother's boyfriend, the prime suspect in the rape. The trail leads to New York state and a group of people, all of whom have had contact with the "Silver People." Bo feels that the boyfriend is innocent, and that means a psychopath is still at large.

Other books you might like:
Linda Barnes, *Coyote*, 1992
Jonathan Kellerman, *The Alex Delaware Series*, 1985-
Sara Paretsky, *Guardian Angel*, 1992
Walter Satterthwait, *A Flower in the Desert*, 1992
Andrew Vachss, *Sacrifice*, 1992

1253
Emma Page
A Violent End (New York: Doubleday, 1990)

Series: Inspector Kelsey

Story type: Police Procedural

Major character(s): Kelsey, Detective—Police (chief inspector)

Time period(s): 1980s

What the book is about: When 16 year old Karen Boland is murdered, the police find more complications than they expect.

Other books you might like:
Catherine Aird, *Harm's Way*, 1984
W.J. Burley, *Wycliffe and the Beales*, 1983
Colin Dexter, *The Dead of Jericho*, 1975
Sheila Radley, *The Quiet Road to Death*, 1983
June Thomson, *The Habit of Loving*, 1978

1254
Katherine Hall Page
The Body in the Basement (New York: St. Martin's, 1994)
Series: Faith Fairchild
Story type: Amateur Detective—Female Lead
Major character(s): Faith Fairchild, Caterer; Myrtle "Pix" Rowe Miller, Housewife (mother; caterer's assistant)
Time period(s): 1990s
Locale(s): San Pere, Maine
What the book is about: Faith Fairchild's friend, Pix Miller, is on vacation in Maine, hoping to spend some time with her mother and daughter. She is also supervising the construction of the Fairchild's new summer home. While checking it out with Samantha, they find a dead body buried in the basement. The body, wrapped in a fancy quilt, proves to be that of a local scoundrel who had several people mad at him. But were they mad enough to kill?
Other books you might like:
P.M. Carlson, *The Maggie Ryan Series*, 1987-
Jill Churchill, *The Jane Jeffry Series*, 1990-
Leslie Meier, *Mail-Order Murder*, 1991
Gillian Roberts, *The Amanda Pepper Series*, 1987-
Valerie Wolzien, *The Susan Henshaw Series*, 1989-

1255
Katherine Hall Page
The Body in the Belfry (New York: St. Martins, 1990)
Series: Faith Fairchild
Story type: Amateur Detective—Female Lead
Major character(s): Faith Fairchild, Caterer, Housewife; Tom Fairchild, Religious (minister), Spouse (Faith's)
Time period(s): 1990s
Locale(s): Aleford, Massachusetts
What the book is about: Faith, a businesswoman, is feeling bored, even with a house and a five- month-old son to take care of. While on a walk to Belfrey Hill she discovers the body of Cindy Shepherd, stabbed with a kitchen knife. She alerts the town by ringing the bell. Faith, no longer bored, starts to look into who would want to kill Cindy. Meanwhile the townsfolk are debating fiercely - not about who killed Cindy, but about whether Faith should have rung the bell. First novel. Winner of the Agatha award for best first novel.
Other books you might like:
J.S. Borthwick, *The Down-East Murders*, 1985
Jill Churchill, *Grime and Punishment*, 1989
Jaqueline Girdner, *Adjusted to Death*, 1991
Virginia Rich, *The Cooking School Murders*, 1982
Valerie Wolzien, *Murder at the PTA Luncheon*, 1988

1256
Katherine Hall Page
The Body in the Bouillon (New York: St. Martin's, 1991)
Series: Faith Fairchild
Story type: Amateur Detective—Female Lead
Major character(s): Faith Fairchild, Housewife (former businesswoman); Tom Fairchild, Religious, Spouse (Faith's)
Time period(s): 1990s
Locale(s): Aleford, Massachusetts
What the book is about: Asked to look into the strange happenings at a fancy retirement retreat, Faith uncovers blackmail, illicit sex, drugs, and murder. Hard to believe, given that the place is run by the saintly Dr. Hubbard, his doctor son, and his nurse daughter. But are they innocents, victims, or perpetrators?
Other books you might like:
J.S. Borthwick, *The Student Body*, 1988
Jill Churchill, *A Farewell to Yarns*, 1991
Diane Mott Davidson, *Catering to Nobody*, 1990
Jaqueline Girdner, *The Last Resort*, 1991
Valerie Wolzien, *We Wish You a Merry Murder*, 1991

1257
Katherine Hall Page
The Body in the Cast (New York: St. Martin's, 1993)
Series: Faith Fairchild
Story type: Amateur Detective—Female Lead
Major character(s): Faith Fairchild, Caterer
Time period(s): 1990s
Locale(s): Aleford, Massachusetts
What the book is about: Faith Fairchild has promised her husband not to get involved with any more murder investigations and has re-established her gourmet catering service. She has the job of supplying food to a movie company in town to film *The Scarlett Letter*. When the cast becomes sick from food poisoning and a cast member dies, Faith knows it wasn't her food. Someone is making Faith a scapegoat for murder. So much for her promise, but she must protect her reputation.
Other books you might like:
Dorothy Cannell, *The Thin Woman*, 1984
Diane Mott Davidson, *Dying for Chocolate*, 1992
Jane Dentinger, *Dead Pan*, 1992
Janice Law, *Time Lapse*, 1992
Nancy Pickard, *The 27 Ingredient Chili Con Carne Murders*, 1993

1258
Katherine Hall Page
The Body in the Vestibule (New York: St. Martin's, 1992)
Series: Faith Fairchild
Story type: Amateur Detective—Female Lead
Major character(s): Faith Fairchild, Housewife (former businesswoman); Tom Fairchild, Religious (minister), Spouse (Faith's)

1259 Paige

Time period(s): 1990s
Locale(s): Lyon, France
What the book is about: Faith and Tom are spending a month in France, and Faith is having a wonderful time. The only disturbing aspect is a sometimes violent tramp and his disreputable friends. After a successful party, Faith is cleaning up and discovers the body of the tramp in a dumpster. But when she returns with her husband and the police, the body has disappeared. Knowing the police don't believe her, she decides to find out the truth herself.

Other books you might like:
Jill Churchill, *Grime and Punishment*, 1990
Diane Mott Davidson, *Dying for Chocolate*, 1992
Jaqueline Girdner, *Adjusted to Death*, 1990
Leslie Meier, *Mail-Order Murder*, 1991
Valerie Wolzien, *Murder at the PTA Luncheon*, 1988

1259

Robin Paige (Pseudonym of Susan Wittig Albert and William J. Albert)
Death at Bishop's Keep (New York: Avon, 1994)
Series: Kate Ardleigh
Story type: Historical; Amateur Detective—Female Lead
Major character(s): Kathryn "Kate" Ardleigh, Secretary, Writer (of thrillers)
Time period(s): 1890s (1894)
Locale(s): Colchester, England
What the book is about: Kate Ardleigh is unemployed at the moment and is supporting herself by writing thrillers. She finds herself approached by a man who is a representative of her aunt who is offering her a job as secretary if she will move to England. Kate didn't even know she had an aunt but decides to take the job. She arrives just after a body has been discovered at a local archaeological dig. She becomes involved with her aunt's secret society—whose members include Oscar Wilde and Sir Arthur Conan Doyle—and that may have some connection to the murder. First novel under this name.

Other books you might like:
Abbey Penn Baker, *In the Dead of Winter*, 1994
Carole Nelson Douglas, *The Irene Adler Series*, 1990-
Marian J.A. Jackson, *The Abigail Danforth Series*, 1990-
Laurie R. King, *The Beekeeper's Apprentice*, 1994
Gillian Linscott, *The Nell Bray Series*, 1991-

1260

Robin Paige (Pseudonym of Susan Wittig Albert and William J. Albert)
Death at Gallows Green (New York: Avon, 1995)
Series: Kate Ardleigh
Story type: Historical; Amateur Detective—Female Lead
Major character(s): Kathryn "Kate" Ardleigh, Heiress, Writer; Sir Charles Sheriden, Photographer, Criminologist (amateur)
Time period(s): 1880s
Locale(s): Essex, England

What the book is about: Kate is settling in at Bishop's Keep after inheriting it from her aunts. She is meeting the local gentry including a young woman named Beatrix Potter who writes children's stories. When a local policeman is murdered, she again meets Sir Charles who is using his photographic skills to assist in the investigation. When their mutual friend Detective Edward Laken is removed from the case, they are determined to find out what is happening.

Other books you might like:
Carole Nelson Douglas, *The Irene Adler Series*, 1990-
Marian J.A. Jackson, *The Abigail Danforth Series*, 1990-
Laurie R. King, *The Beekeeper's Apprentice*, 1994
Gillian Linscott, *The Nell Bray Series*, 1991-
Miriam Grace Monfredo, *The Glynis Tryon Series*, 1992-

1261

Daniel Paisner
Obit (New York: Dutton, 1990)
Story type: Amateur Detective—Male Lead; Police Procedural—Male Lead
Major character(s): Axel Pimletz, Journalist; Charles Abigail, Police Officer, Detective
Time period(s): 1990s
Locale(s): Boston, Massachusetts
What the book is about: Two college athletes are dead, one an apparent suicide, one dead in his chili. A sexy young blonde was with them both not long before they died. Coincidence? Or is she more seriously involved? And what was the relationship between the two athletes? Obituary writer Axel Pimletz gets involved to recover his self-esteem, but police detective Charles Abigail is just doing his job. The cases soon become much more for both of them.

Other books you might like:
Don Flynn, *Murder on the Hudson*, 1985
Sean Hanlon, *The Cold Front*, 1989
M.S. Karl, *Death Notice*, 1990
Vince Kohler, *Rainy North Woods*, 1990
Keith Peterson, *The Trapdoor*, 1988

1262

Michael Palmer
Natural Causes (New York: Bantam, 1994)
Story type: Amateur Detective—Female Lead; Action/Adventure
Major character(s): Sarah Baldwin, Doctor (OB/GYN resident)
Time period(s): 1990s
Locale(s): Boston, Massachusetts
What the book is about: After Sarah Baldwin saves the life of one her patients with some unorthodox medicine, she is hailed as a hero, until it is discovered that this patient and two others that have died have been taking a herbal vitamin supplement that she had prescribed. While trying to save her career, she soon finds that it is more than her career that is in danger—it is her life.

Other books you might like:
Robin Cook, *Coma*, 1977
Louise Hendricksen, *Lethal Legacy*, 1995
Stanley Pottinger, *The Fourth Procedure*, 1995
C.F. Roe, *A Torrid Piece of Murder*, 1994
Martha Stearn, *Deadly Diagnosis*, 1995

1263
Orania Papazoglou
Once and Always Murder (New York: Doubleday, 1990)
Series: Patience McKenna
Story type: Amateur Detective—Female Lead
Major character(s): Patience McKenna, Writer (Romance writer)
Time period(s): 1980s
Locale(s): Connecticut
What the book is about: While in her hometown preparing for her wedding, Patience must solve the murders of some her family members.
Other books you might like:
Max Allan Collins, *Kill Your Darlings*, 1984
Carolyn G. Hart, *Death on Demand*, 1987
Joan Hess, *Strangled Prose*, 1986
Elizabeth Peters, *Die for Love*, 1984
Nora Roberts, *Brazen Virtue*, 1988

1264
Sara Paretsky
Burn Marks (New York: Delacorte, 1990)
Series: V.I. Warshawski
Story type: Private Detective—Female Lead
Major character(s): V.I. Warshawski, Detective—Private (female)
Time period(s): 1980s
Locale(s): Chicago, Illinois
What the book is about: How do the murder of a hooker, the political campaign of a Hispanic woman, and the fire at Warshawski's aunt's hotel tie together?
Other books you might like:
Linda Barnes, *A Trouble of Fools*, 1988
Sue Grafton, *G Is for Gumshoe*, 1990
Lee McGraw, *Hatchett*, 1976
Marcia Muller, *The Shape of Dread*, 1989
Maxine O'Callaghan, *Hit and Run*, 1989

1265
Sara Paretsky
Guardian Angel (New York: Delacorte, 1992)
Series: V.I. Warshawski
Story type: Private Detective—Female Lead
Major character(s): V.I. Warshawski, Detective—Private
Time period(s): 1990s
Locale(s): Chicago, Illinois
What the book is about: Two of V.I.'s cases tie together. One involves the guardianship of one of her neighbors by another couple in the neighborhood. And the other involves the murder of an old friend of her landlord's.
Other books you might like:
Linda Barnes, *Coyote*, 1990
Barbara D'Amato, *Hardball*, 1990
Sue Grafton, *F Is for Fugitive*, 1989
Karen Kijewski, *Katwalk*, 1989
Marcia Muller, *Where Echoes Live*, 1991

1266
Sara Paretsky
Tunnel Vision (New York: Delacorte, 1994)
Series: V.I. Warshawski
Story type: Private Detective—Female Lead
Major character(s): V.I. Warshawski, Detective—Private
Time period(s): 1990s
Locale(s): Chicago, Illinois
What the book is about: V.I. discovers a homeless woman and her children living in a decrepit office building. She asks a friend, Deidre Messenger, who is involved in an organization called Home Free, for assistance. Soon after Deidre is found murdered in V.I.'s office. Surely there is no connection between the homeless family and Deidre's death. V.I. sets out to discover the truth. It may be that the dead woman's husband was behind it, or a U.S. senator, or the director of Home Free. Whoever was responsible, V.I. will hunt them down.
Other books you might like:
Linda Barnes, *The Carlotta Carlyle Series*, 1987-
Catherine Dain, *The Freddie O'Neal Series*, 1992-
Barbara D'Amato, *The Cat Marsala Series*, 1988-
Karen Kijewski, *The Kat Colorado Series*, 1989-
Marcia Muller, *The Sharon McCone Series*, 1977-

1267
Sara Paretsky, Editor
A Woman's Eye (New York: Delacorte, 1991)
Story type: Anthology
What the book is about: A collection of short stories, all by women. Includes stories by Marcia Muller, Susan Dunlap, Sue Grafton, Sara Paretsky, Julie Smith, Carolyn G. Gart, Margaret Maron, and Carolyn Wheat.
Other books you might like:
Jen Green, *Reader, I Murdered Him*, 1989 (editor)
Marie Smith, *More Ms. Murder*, 1991 (editor)
Marie Smith, *Ms. Murder*, 1989 (editor)
Marilyn Wallace, *The Sisters in Crime Series*, 1989- (editor)
Irene Zahava, *The Womansleuth Anthology Series*, 1988- (editor)

1268
Barbara Parker
Suspicion of Guilt (New York: Dutton, 1995)

1269 Parker

Series: Gail Connor
Story type: Legal
Major character(s): Gail Connor, Lawyer
Time period(s): 1990s
Locale(s): Miami, Florida

What the book is about: Against the wishes of her law firm, Gail agrees to represent an old friend, Patrick Norris, in the contesting of the will of his dead aunt, Althea Tillet. The will as read leaves most of her million-dollar estate to charity, but Patrick thinks it is a fake. The police think Althea was murdered and Patrick is the prime suspect. Gail needs to find a forger and a killer

Other books you might like:
Nevada Barr, *Track of the Cat*, 1993
Patricia D. Benke, *False Witness*, 1996
Gini Hartzmark, *Final Option*, 1994
Sandra West Prowell, *By Evil Means*, 1993
April Smith, *North of Montana*, 1994

1269
Robert B. Parker
Double Deuce (New York: Putnam, 1992)

Series: Spenser
Story type: Private Detective—Male Lead
Major character(s): Spenser, Detective—Private; Hawk, Sidekick
Time period(s): 1990s
Locale(s): Boston, Massachusetts

What the book is about: At Hawk's request Spenser finds himself involved in trying to find the people responsible for the drive-by shooting of a teenage mother and her baby. This involves spending a lot of time in the "Double Deuce", one of the more notorious projects in Boston. The personal lives of Hawk and Spenser, specifically their relationships with women, also get an airing.

Other books you might like:
Robert Crais, *Free Fall*, 1993
Sue Grafton, *H Is for Homicide*, 1991
Jeremiah Healy, *The John Francis Cuddy Series*, 1982
Arthur Lyons, *The Jacob Asch Series*, 1974
Bill Pronzini, *Epitaphs*, 1992

1270
Robert B. Parker
Perchance to Dream (New York: Putnam, 1991)

Series: Philip Marlowe
Story type: Private Detective—Male Lead
Major character(s): Philip Marlowe, Detective—Private
Time period(s): 1930s (1939)
Locale(s): Los Angeles, California

What the book is about: Marlowe has seen to it that Vivian Regan had her sister Carmen Sternwood committed to a sanitarium. Now their father, General Sternwood, is dead and Carmen has disappeared. The family butler asks Marlowe to help find Carmen and to keep gangster Eddie Mars from once again controlling their lives. Sequel to Raymond Chandler's novel *The Big Sleep*.

Other books you might like:
Andrew Bergman, *The Big Kiss-Off of 1944*, 1971
Howard Browne, *Halo in Blood*, 1946
Joe Gores, *Hammett*, 1975
Timothy Harris, *Kyd for Hire*, 1977

1271
Robert B. Parker
Stardust (New York: Putnam, 1990)

Series: Spenser
Story type: Private Detective—Male Lead
Major character(s): Spenser, Detective—Private; Susan Silverman, Counselor (Spenser's lover)
Time period(s): 1980s
Locale(s): Boston, Massachusetts

What the book is about: Spenser is convinced by his lover, Susan Silverman, to play bodyguard to a television star. When the star's stand-in is killed, Spenser realizes that the star might really be in danger. Parker won the Edgar for best novel for *Promised Land* in 1976.

Other books you might like:
Linda Barnes, *A Trouble of Fools*, 1988
Robert Crais, *The Monkey's Raincoat*, 1987
Jeremiah Healy, *The John Francis Cuddy Series*, 1984
Arthur Lyons, *The Jacob Asch Series*, 1974
Richard Rosen, *Strike Three, You're Dead*, 1984

1272
Robert B. Parker
Walking Shadow (New York: Putnam, 1994)

Series: Spenser
Story type: Private Detective—Male Lead
Major character(s): Spenser, Detective—Private; Susan Silverman, Counselor (Spenser's lover)
Time period(s): 1990s
Locale(s): Port City, Massachusetts

What the book is about: Spenser's lover, Susan Silverman, asks him to discover who is following the artistic director of a small town theatre company on whose board she sits. He agrees reluctantly, until an actor is shot during a performance that he and Susan are attending. Then he takes things a little more seriously. Soon after he begins his investigation, he is warned out of town by an important member of a Boston tong. So there may be more involved here than just a simple stalking and murder.

Other books you might like:
Harlen Campbell, *Monkey on a Chain*, 1993
Robert Crais, *The Elvis Cole Series*, 1987-
Jeremiah Healy, *The John Francis Cuddy Series*, 1984-
Bill Pronzini, *The Nameless Detective Series*, 1971-
Benjamin M. Schutz, *The Leo Haggerty Series*, 1985-

1273
Richard Parrish
The Dividing Line (New York: Dutton, 1993)

Story type: Legal; Historical

Major character(s): Joshua Rabb, Lawyer (wounded war veteran)

Time period(s): 1940s (1946)

Locale(s): Tucson, Arizona

What the book is about: After his wife is killed, lawyer Joshua Rabb has moved with his children to Tucson, Arizona to take a job with the Bureau of Indian Affairs. He soon gets involved in defending one of the natives on a charge of rape and murder. Also involved are blackmail, crooked politicians and a plan to move the Indians off their land. Rabb is not going to get the rest he desires. First mystery.

Other books you might like:
Tony Hillerman, *The Joe Leaphorn Series*, 1970-
Richard Hugo, *Death and the Good Life*, 1981
Jake Page, *The Stolen Gods*, 1993
J.F. Trainor, *Dynamite Pass*, 1993

1274
Jill Paton Walsh
A Piece of Justice (New York: St. Martin's, 1995)

Series: Imogen Quy

Story type: Amateur Detective—Female Lead

Major character(s): Imogen Quy, Nurse (school nurse)

Time period(s): 1990s

Locale(s): Cambridge, England

What the book is about: Imogen's young boarder, Fran Bullion has been asked by her professor to finish the biography of the late mathematician Gideon Summerfield. Needing the money, Fran gladly accepts. Fran and Imogen discover that three previous biographers have failed to finish the work—one died tragically and two have mysteriously disappeared. Imogen is concerned for Fran's safety, especially after having met Gideon's strange disagreeable widow. What could there be about Gideon's rather boring life that might cause so much death?

Other books you might like:
Nora Kelly, *Bad Chemistry*, 1994
Susan Kenney, *Graves in Academe*, 1985
Janet Neel, *Death Among the Dons*, 1994
Joan Smith, *What Men Say*, 1994
Veronica Stallwood, *Death and the Oxford Box*, 1993

1275
Jill Paton Walsh
The Wyndham Case (New York: St. Martin's, 1993)

Story type: Amateur Detective—Female Lead

Major character(s): Imogen Quy, Nurse

Time period(s): 1990s

Locale(s): Cambridge, Massachusetts

What the book is about: Imogen Quy is called to the Wyndham Library when the body of a student is found. Everyone assumes this student fell while attempting to steal a book from the Wyndham Case, a strangely endowed collection of rare books. Imogen is convinced it was murder and that things are much more complicated than they seem. Then a student disappears and another body is found. First mystery.

Other books you might like:
Terrie Curran, *All Booked Up*, 1987
Bill Crider, *A Dangerous Thing*, 1994
Dorothy Fiske, *Bound to Murder*, 1987
Charles A. Goodrum, *The Best Cellar*, 1990
Hazel Holt, *The Cruellest Month*, 1991

1276
James Patterson
Along Came a Spider (New York: Little, Brown, 1993)

Story type: Police Procedural—Male Lead; Psychological Suspense

Major character(s): Alex Cross, Police Officer (African-American), Doctor (psychiatrist); Gary Soneji, Serial Killer

Time period(s): 1990s

Locale(s): Washington, District of Columbia

What the book is about: Someone is killing black ghetto kids and kidnapping children of prominent parents. Is it the same someone? Alex Cross thinks it is and with the assistance of a beautiful Secret Service agent sets out to capture the killer/kidnapper. Once captured, Gary Soneji appears to be a multiple personality. Which one is guilty?

Other books you might like:
Harlan Ellison, *Mefisto in Onyx*, 1993
Ron Handberg, *Cry Vengeance*, 1993
Jonathan Kellerman, *Time Bomb*, 1990
Ridley Pearson, *The Angel Maker*, 1993
Stephen White, *Private Practices*, 1993

1277
Barbara Paul
In-laws and Outlaws (New York: Scribners, 1990)

Story type: Psychological Suspense

Major character(s): Gillian Clifford Decker, Businesswoman (runs a small theater museum)

Time period(s): 1990s

Locale(s): Martha's Vineyard, Massachusetts

1278 Paul

What the book is about: Someone is killing off the Decker family. The widow of the latest victim calls for in-law Gillian Decker to come and help stop the killings. Is it an outsider or is the killer someone from inside the family? And what is the motive in either case?

Other books you might like:
John Fink, *The Leaf Boat*, 1991
Patricia Highsmith, *People Who Knock on the Door*, 1985
Ruth Rendell, *Gallowsglass*, 1990

1278
Celeste Paul
Berlin Covenant (New York: Signet, 1992)

Story type: Action/Adventure

Major character(s): Brie Prescott, Student, Orphan; Isaac Kauffman, Businessman

Time period(s): 1990s

Locale(s): Pennsylvania

What the book is about: The Nazis are on the verge of the discovery of an explosive more powerful than the A-Bomb when a young Jewish researcher steals it and before he is killed, passes the formula on to a convent. 50 years later the Nazis are back and the nun originally involved - now the Mother Superior in an American convent - gives the formula to a young girl raised in the convent and sends her off to give the formula to the family of the original Jewish researcher. The Nazis are in close pursuit. First novel.

Other books you might like:
Ted Allbeury, *The Lantern Network*, 1989
Sean Flannery, *False Prophets*, 1983
Bill Granger, *The British Cross*, 1983
R.D. Zimmerman, *Deadfall in Berlin*, 1991

1279
Gary Paulsen
Night Rituals (New York: Donald I. Fine, 1989)

Story type: Police Procedural—Male Lead

Major character(s): "Push" Tincker, Police Officer (Homicide)

Time period(s): 1980s

Locale(s): Seattle, Washington; Denver, Colorado

What the book is about: A serial killer is on the prowl, mutilating and murdering young women. Homicide detective "Push" Tincker, a middle-aged cop going to seed, is put on the case.

Other books you might like:
Thomas Cook, *Sacrificial Lamb*, 1988
Thomas Harris, *Red Dragon*, 1981
Thomas Harris, *The Silence of the Lambs*, 1988
John Katzenbach, *In the Heat of the Summer*, 1982
Joe R. Lansdale, *Act of Love*, 1981

1280
John A. Peak
Spare Change (New York: St. Martin's, 1994)

Story type: Legal; Amateur Detective—Male Lead

Major character(s): Jeff Talbot, Lawyer, Alcoholic; Peter St. John, Lawyer (retired; horse breeder)

Time period(s): 1980s (1989)

Locale(s): San Francisco, California

What the book is about: Two lawyers, Jeff Talbot, a down-and-out drunk, and Peter St. John, successful, retired, and now breeding horses, will soon find themselves involved together in cases that seem entirely unrelated, at least at the beginning. Talbot awakes in a park to find his female companion murdered and himself wounded and being stalked by people who mean to do him harm. St. John's son, a doctor, is being sued for malpractice, so St. John finds himself drawn back to his former firm to find out what's going on. More people will die before these two men get to the truth. First novel.

Other books you might like:
Bill Blum, *Prejudicial Error*, 1995
A.W. Gray, *Bino*, 1988
Richard Harris, *Honor Bound*, 1982
Paul Levine, *To Speak for the Dead*, 1990
Barbara Parker, *Suspicion of Innocence*, 1994

1281
Gerald Pearce
Orphans (New York: Walker, 1990)

Story type: Legal; Amateur Detective—Male Lead

Major character(s): Jim Keller, Lawyer

Time period(s): 1990s

Locale(s): Dos Cruces, California

What the book is about: Getting ready to leave Dos Cruces for Los Angeles, lawyer Jim Keller finds himself embroiled in a murder which has roots buried deep, twenty years or more. Mostly he just wants to clear it up and get to Los Angeles so he can get custody of his 3-year-old daughter. First novel.

Other books you might like:
Michael Cormany, *Red Winter*, 1989
J. Madison Davis, *White Rook*, 1990
Joe L. Hensley, *The Don Roback Series*, 1971-
Michael Malone, *Time's Witness*, 1989
Geoff Peterson, *Medicine Dog*, 1989

1282
Ridley Pearson
The Angel Maker (New York: Delacorte, 1993)

Series: Lou Boldt

Story type: Police Procedural; Psychological Suspense

Major character(s): Lou Boldt, Police Officer (trying to be retired); Daphne Matthews, Psychologist

Time period(s): 1990s

Locale(s): Seattle, Washington

What the book is about: When police psychologist Daphne Matthews can find no evidence of legal surgery on a runaway—though the runaway it missing a kidney—she calls on her ex-partner and sometime lover, retired police officer Lou Boldt. Boldt, who now spends his days and nights playing piano in bars and taking care of his son, is reluctant to get involved but does anyway. He and Daphne discover an underground black market selling illegally harvested organs. They must try and catch whoever is responsible for this before they strike again.

Other books you might like:
John Katzenbach, *The Traveler*, 1987
Joe R. Lansdale, *Act of Love*, 1981
David L. Lindsey, *Mercy*, 1990
Gary Paulsen, *Night Rituals*, 1989
Stephen Smoke, *Pacific Coast Highway*, 1994

1283
Ridley Pearson
Chain of Evidence (New York: Hyperion, 1995)

Story type: Police Procedural—Male Lead

Major character(s): Joe Dartelli, Police Officer (detective)

Time period(s): 1990s

Locale(s): Hartford, Connecticut

What the book is about: Some current deaths, called suicides, remind Joe of a death, also called a suicide, that he investigated some years earlier. That death was a murder that he covered up to protect his friend, Walter Zeller. Is it possible that Walter is killing again or is it someone else being a vigilante? The fact that Joe cannot find Walter, supposedly retired to the West, gives credence to the thought that he's behind these crimes.

Other books you might like:
William Diehl, *Primal Fear*, 1993
David L. Lindsey, *Mercy*, 1990
Francis Roe, *Dangerous Practices*, 1993
Randall Silvis, *An Occasional Hell*, 1993
David Wiltse, *Into the Fire*, 1994

1284
Ridley Pearson
Hard Fall (New York: Delacorte, 1992)

Story type: Action/Adventure

Major character(s): Cameron Daggett, FBI Agent; Anthony Kort, Terrorist

Time period(s): 1990s

Locale(s): Washington, District of Columbia; Los Angeles, California; Seattle, Washington

What the book is about: Obsessed with capturing the terrorist who blew up the plane that killed his parents and paralyzed his son, FBI agent Cameron Daggett finds himself chasing Anthony Kort, terrorist, who is himself obsessed with killing heads of companies that are responsible for a toxic waste disaster that killed his wife and child. From Seattle to D.C. to L.A., Daggett and Kort play cat and mouse—along with two women they get involved with along the way.

Other books you might like:
Tom Clancy, *Patriot Games*, 1987
James Grady, *Six Days of the Condor*, 1974
R. Lance Hill, *The Evil That Men Do*, 1978
Paul Kavanagh, *The Triumph of Evil*, 1971
John Le Carre, *The Little Drummer Girl*, 1983

1285
Ridley Pearson
Probable Cause (New York: St. Martin's, 1990)

Story type: Police Procedural—Male Lead

Major character(s): James Dewitt, Police Officer (former forensic investigator)

Time period(s): 1980s

Locale(s): Carmel, California

What the book is about: After taking a new job as a police sergeant, Dewitt soon finds himself tracking and being tracked by a serial killer. He is also a suspect.

Other books you might like:
Patricia D. Cornwell, *Postmortem*, 1990
John Katzenbach, *In the Heat of the Summer*, 1982
Joe R. Lansdale, *Act of Love*, 1981
Thomas T. Noguchi, *Unnatural Causes*, 1989 (Arthur Lyons, co-author)

1286
William D. Pease
Playing the Dozens (New York: Viking, 1990)

Story type: Legal; Police Procedural—Male Lead

Major character(s): Michael Holden, Lawyer (district attorney); Eddie Nickles, Police Officer (homicide detective)

Time period(s): 1990s

Locale(s): Washington, District of Columbia

What the book is about: It begins with the seemingly random shooting of a Washington, D.C. patrolman in a seedy bar. The killer, quickly captured, refuses to talk with anyone but D.A. Michael Holden. He begins to tell a story of drug dealing, corruption and blackmail within the police department and involving major D.C. political figures. Before he can tell the whole story he's found dead in his cell, an apparent suicide. First novel.

Other books you might like:
Eugene Izzi, *The Prime Roll*, 1990
John Lutz, *The Shadow Man*, 1982
Lawrence Meyer, *A Capitol Crime*, 1977
Ridley Pearson, *Probable Cause*, 1990
Jerome Sanford, *Miami Heat*, 1991

1287
Allan Pedrazas
The Harry Chronicles (New York: St. Martin's, 1995)

Story type: Private Detective—Male Lead

Major character(s): Harry Rice, Detective—Private, Businessman (bar owner)

1288 Pelecanos

Time period(s): 1990s

Locale(s): Fort Lauderdale, Florida

What the book is about: Eloise Loftus wants Harry to find a gun collection supposedly stolen from her apartment. It appears that the robbery would have been physically impossible, and besides Eloise's husband doesn't want Harry looking and lets him know this in no uncertain terms. When the husband turns up dead, Harry is an obvious suspect and must solve the murder to save himself. First novel. Edgar nominee for best first novel.

Other books you might like:
Joe R. Lansdale, *Cold in July*, 1989
Sam Reaves, *A Long Cold Fall*, 1991
David Stout, *The Dog Hermit*, 1993
Jonathan Valin, *Second Chance*, 1991
Richard Whittingham, *Their Kind of Town*, 1994

1288
George Pelecanos
Shoedog (New York: St. Martin's, 1994)

Story type: Action/Adventure

Major character(s): Constantine, Drifter; Grimes, Businessman (wealthy)

Time period(s): 1990s

Locale(s): Washington, District of Columbia

What the book is about: Constantine is hitchhiking to nowhere in particular when he gets introduced to Grimes, a wealthy old man who organizes robberies as a hobby. He suggests that Constantine and the fellow who picked him up hitching might want to get involved. Things quickly go wrong and Constantine soon finds himself trying to avenge his partners, while he is also falling for Grimes' young girlfriend.

Other books you might like:
Thornton Elliott, *Hard Guy*, 1993
Tom Kakonis, *Criss Cross*, 1990
Joe R. Lansdale, *The Savage Season*, 1990
Elmore Leonard, *Stick*, 1983
Timothy Watts, *Cons*, 1993

1289
Joanne Pence
Cooking Up Trouble (New York: HarperCollins, 1995)

Series: Angie Amalfi

Story type: Amateur Detective—Female Lead

Major character(s): Angie Amalfi, Journalist (food columnist); Paavo Smith, Police Officer (Angie's lover)

Time period(s): 1990s

Locale(s): Hayesville, California

What the book is about: Angie needs a job. She also needs to figure out where her relationship with Paavo is going. When she is asked to help design the menu selection at Hill Haven Inn, a newly renovated Victorian mansion in northern California, she thinks this will provide a chance for her and Paavo to work things out. However, the owner disappears shortly after Angie's arrival. Present are an odd assortment of guests and ghosts. Then the owner is found dead.

Other books you might like:
Claudia Bishop, *A Taste for Murder*, 1994
Mary Daheim, *Murder, My Suite*, 1995
Diane Mott Davidson, *The Goldy Bear Series*, 1989-
Janet Laurence, *A Tasty Way to Die*, 1990
Tamar Myers, *Too Many Cooks Spoil the Broth*, 1994

1290
Joanne Pence
Something's Cooking (New York: Harper, 1993)

Series: Angie Amalfi

Story type: Amateur Detective; Police Procedural

Major character(s): Angie Amalfi, Journalist (food columnist); Paavo Smith, Police Officer (Angie's lover)

Time period(s): 1990s

Locale(s): San Francisco, California

What the book is about: Food columnist Angie Amalfi receives a ticking package that seems suspicious, so she puts it in her dishwasher. When the dishwasher explodes she realizes she has a problem. Several more attacks follow. Do they have anything to do with the death of Sammy Blade, who delivered bizarre recipes to Angie from the even more bizarre Mr. Crane? To complicate things Angie feels a strange attraction to the policeman in charge of her case.

Other books you might like:
Dorothy Cannell, *The Thin Woman*, 1986
Trella Crespi, *The Trouble with Moonlighting*, 1991
Diane Mott Davidson, *Dying for Chocolate*, 1992
Denise Dietz, *Throw Darts at a Cheesecake*, 1992
Janet Laurence, *A Tasty Way to Die*, 1990

1291
Joanne Pence
Too Many Cooks (New York: HarperCollins, 1994)

Series: Angie Amalfi

Story type: Amateur Detective—Female Lead

Major character(s): Angie Amalfi, Journalist (food columnist); Paavo Smith, Police Officer (Angie's lover)

Time period(s): 1990s

Locale(s): San Francisco, California

What the book is about: When the paper she works for folds, Angie Amalfi needs a new job. She bullies her way into being Henry La Tour's assistant on his radio talk show "Chef Henri." A famous local restauranteur is poisoned and the death is made to seem as if it happened in a car crash. Angie is having trouble persuading Paavo Smith, a cop and her lover, to investigate, so she decides to look into it herself. Paavo is not happy about that and neither is the killer.

Other books you might like:
Claudia Bishop, *A Taste for Murder*, 1994
Dorothy Cannell, *The Thin Woman*, 1984
Diane Mott Davidson, *The Goldy Bear Series*, 1990-
Janet Laurence, *A Tasty Way to Die*, 1991
Katherine Hall Page, *The Body in the Cast*, 1993

1292
Anne Perry
Cain His Brother (New York: Fawcett, 1995)
Series: William Monk
Story type: Private Detective—Male Lead; Historical
Major character(s): William Monk, Detective—Private; Hester Latterly, Nurse
Time period(s): 1860s
Locale(s): London, England
What the book is about: Genevieve Stonefield turns to Monk for help in finding her missing husband. She is convinced that he was killed by his twin brother. Is he dead and did the brother kill him? These are the things that Monk must discover. He must also continue to work out things in his own life, including his relationship with Hester and a woman from his past whom he can't remember.

Other books you might like:
Ray Harrison, *Deathwatch*, 1986
John Buxton Hilton, *The Quiet Stranger*, 1985
Kate Kingsbury, *The Pennyfoot Hotel Series*, 1993-
Peter Lovesey, *Waxwork*, 1978
Julian Symons, *The Blackheath Poisonings*, 1978

1293
Anne Perry
A Dangerous Mourning (New York: Fawcett, 1991)
Series: Inspector Monk
Story type: Historical; Police Procedural—Male Lead
Major character(s): William Monk, Police Officer (Inspector); Hester Latterly, Nurse (served w/Florence Nightingale)
Time period(s): 1880s
Locale(s): London, England
What the book is about: The widowed daughter of Sir Basil Moidore is found stabbed in her bedroom. Inspector Monk proves that no outsider could have entered the house, so the family and servants are the only ones who could have done it. To help, Monk introduces his friend Hester Latterly into the household. Political pressure forces him off the police force but that doesn't stop him and Hester from continuing to search for the truth.

Other books you might like:
Ray Harrison, *Deathwatch*, 1986
John Buxton Hilton, *The Quiet Stranger*, 1985
Fergus Hume, *The Mystery of a Hansom Cab*, 1886
Peter Lovesey, *Waxwork*, 1978
Julian Symons, *The Blackheath Poisonings*, 1978

1294
Anne Perry
Farrier's Lane (New York: Fawcett, 1993)
Series: Thomas and Charlotte Pitt
Story type: Historical; Police Procedural
Major character(s): Thomas Pitt, Police Officer (inspector); Charlotte Pitt, Spouse (wife of Thomas)
Time period(s): 1890s
Locale(s): London, England
What the book is about: The Pitts are at the theatre when another member of the audience, Judge Samuel Stafford, keels over dead. The inspector immediately suspects poison and when he begins to investigate finds some connections to a case from some five years earlier which the dead judge wanted to reopen. There is also the judge's adulteress wife and her lover to consider and the spectre of anti-semitism also raises its head.

Other books you might like:
Ray Harrison, *Deathwatch*, 1986
John Buxton Hilton, *The Quiet Stranger*, 1985
Kate Kingsbury, *Room with a Clue*, 1993
Peter Lovesey, *Waxwork*, 1978
Julian Symons, *The Blackheath Poisonings*, 1978

1295
Anne Perry
Highgate Rise (New York: Fawcett, 1991)
Series: Thomas and Charlotte Pitt
Story type: Historical; Police Procedural
Major character(s): Thomas Pitt, Police Officer (inspector); Charlotte Pitt, Housewife
Time period(s): 1880s (1888)
Locale(s): London, England
What the book is about: An arsonist burns down the house of a prominent physician, but it's the doctor's wife who dies. Who was the intended victim—the wife or the doctor? Inspector Pitt, with the assistance of his high-born wife Charlotte, turns up conflicting evidence but eventually they get to the truth.

Other books you might like:
Ray Harrison, *Deathwatch*, 1986
Evelyn Hervey, *The Man of Gold*, 1985
John Buxton Hilton, *The Quiet Stranger*, 1985
Peter Lovesey, *Wobble to Death*, 1970
Leonard Tourney, *The Player's Boy Is Dead*, 1982

1296
Anne Perry
A Sudden, Fearful Death (New York: Fawcett, 1993)
Series: William Monk
Story type: Historical; Private Detective—Male Lead
Major character(s): William Monk, Detective—Private (former police officer); Oliver Rathbone, Lawyer
Time period(s): 1890s
Locale(s): London, England

1297 Perry

What the book is about: William Monk is asked by his benefator, Lady Callandra Daviot, to investigate the strangulation of a nurse in a London hospital. He soon discovers a link between the dead woman and Dr. Herbert Stanhope. Stanhope is arrested for the murder, but his lawyer asks Monk to continue his investigation as the lawyer thinks there is more here than just murder. He is right.

Other books you might like:
Ray Harrison, *Death of a Dancing Lady*, 1986
Peter Lovesey, *Waxwork*, 1978
Julian Symons, *The Blackheath Poisonings*, 1978

1297
Thomas Perry
Sleeping Dogs (New York: Random, 1992)

Series: Butcher's Boy

Story type: Action/Adventure

Major character(s): Michael Schaeffer, Criminal (former hitman); Elizabeth Waring, Lawyer (Justice Department attorney)

Time period(s): 1990s

Locale(s): United States; England

What the book is about: After hiding out in England for 10 years to avoid people trying to kill him, it appears that Michael Schaeffer's cover has been blown. There is an attempt on his life and he realizes he must return to the U.S. to discover who is on his trail. Among those he gets involved with are Elizabeth Waring from the Justice Department. Should he kill her or not is one of the questions that must be answered.

Other books you might like:
Loren D. Estleman, *The Macklin Series*, 1984-1986
John Katzenbach, *In the Heat of the Summer*, 1982
Andrew Klavan, *Don't Say a Word*, 1991
Richard Stark, *Butcher's Moon*, 1974
Stuart Woods, *Santa Fe Rules*, 1992

1298
Elizabeth Peters (Pseudonym of Barbara Mertz)
The Last Camel Died at Noon (New York: Warner, 1991)

Story type: Historical; Action/Adventure

Major character(s): Amelia Peabody Emerson, Archaeologist; Radcliffe Emerson, Archaeologist

Time period(s): 1890s (1897)

Locale(s): Egypt (the Sudan)

What the book is about: Being denied the opportunity for research where they desire, the Emersons take up the search for fellow archaeologist Willoughby Forth, who disappeared 14 years earlier while searching for a lost civilization. When their camels die and their guides disappear the Emersons are in a bad way. The rescue comes from members of a lost civilization. They find themselves among an ancient Egyptian people and in the middle of a blood feud. Also writes as Barbara Michaels.

Other books you might like:
Carole Nelson Douglas, *Good Morning, Irene*, 1991
Dorothy Gilman, *Caravan*, 1992
H. Rider Haggard, *King Solomon's Mines*, 1894
H. Rider Haggard, *She*, 1890
Marian J.A. Jackson, *The Punjat's Ruby*, 1990

1299
Elizabeth Peters, Editor
Malice Domestic #1 (New York: Pocket, 1992)

Story type: Anthology; Amateur Detective

Time period(s): 1990s

What the book is about: A collection of stories, all original, celebrating the "traditional" mystery. No private detectives allowed. Authors include P.M. Carlson, Diane Mott Davidson, and Aaron and Charlotte Elkins.

Other books you might like:
Ed Gorman, *Cat Crimes*, 1990 (Martin Greenberg, co-editor)
Jen Green, *Reader, I Murdered Him*, 1989 (editor)
Edward D. Hoch, *Murder Most Sacred*, 1989 (Martin Greenberg, co-editor)
Sara Paretsky, *A Woman's Eye*, 1991 (editor)

1300
Elizabeth Peters (Pseudonym of Barbara Mertz)
Naked Once More (New York: Warner, 1989)

Series: Jacqueline Kirby

Story type: Romantic Suspense; Amateur Detective—Female Lead

Major character(s): Jacqueline Kirby, Writer (romance), Librarian (former)

Time period(s): 1980s

Locale(s): Pine Grove, West Virginia

What the book is about: Kirby is chosen to write a sequel to a bestselling novel whose author disappeare dseven years earlier. When she goes to the author's hometown she is plagued by accidents and becomes embroiled in murder, mystery and romance.

Other books you might like:
Jon L. Breen, *The Gathering Place*, 1984
Dorothy Salisbury Davis, *A Death in the Life*, 1976
Mickey Friedman, *A Temporary Ghost*, 1989
Melodie Johnson Howe, *The Mother Shadow*, 1989
Helen McCloy, *Two Thirds of a Ghost*, 1956

1301
Ellis Peters (Pseudonym of Edith Pargeter)
Brother Cadfael's Penance (New York: Mysterious, 1994)

Series: Brother Cadfael

Story type: Historical; Amateur Detective—Male Lead

Major character(s): Brother Cadfael, Religious (monk)

Time period(s): 12th century

Locale(s): England

What the book is about: Brother Cadfael's son (who doesn't know he's Cadfael's son) is taken prisoner during one of England's wars. Cadfael is determined to find him, and to do so, must leave the monastery to travel to a peace conference. Once there, he gets involved in trying to find his son's brother-in-law, who has been kidnapped by someone who feels he is responsible for a murder. Now Cadfael has to find two men and the real murderer.

Other books you might like:
Umberto Eco, *The Name of the Rose*, 1986
Margaret Frazer, *The Sister Frevisse Series*, 1992
C.L. Grace, *A Shrine of Murders*, 1993
Sharan Newman, *Death Comes as Epiphany*, 1993

1302
Ellis Peters
The Potter's Field (New York: Mysterious, 1990)

Series: Brother Cadfael

Story type: Historical; Amateur Detective—Male Lead

Major character(s): Brother Cadfael, Religious (monk)

Time period(s): 12th century (1143)

Locale(s): Shrewsbury, England

What the book is about: Shortly after taking possession of a field the monks discover a body dead a year or more. Could it be the wife of the original owner, now a novice monk. Another novice arrives who appears to know more than he is saying about the potter and his wife. Can Brother Cadfael get to the bottom of the mystery?

Other books you might like:
P.C. Doherty, *The Crown in Darkness*, 1988
Umberto Eco, *The Name of the Rose*, 1986

1303
Ellis Peters
The Summer of the Danes (New York: Mysterious, 1991)

Series: Brother Cadfael

Story type: Historical; Amateur Detective—Male Lead

Major character(s): Brother Cadfael, Religious (monk)

Time period(s): 12th century

Locale(s): Wales

What the book is about: On a pilgrimage for the Church to Wales, Cadfael and his compatriots become pawns in a battle between two Welsh princes. There is a murder, but a battle precludes Cadfael from investigating in his usual manner. Nonetheless he gets to the truth.

Other books you might like:
P.C. Doherty, *The Crown in Darkness*, 1988
Umberto Eco, *The Name of the Rose*, 1986
Paul Harding, *The Nightingale Gallery*, 1992

1304
Audrey Peterson
Elegy in a Country Graveyard (New York: Pocket, 1990)

Series: Andrew Quentin/Jane Winfield

Story type: Amateur Detective

Major character(s): Jane Winfield, Journalist (music writer); Andrew Quentin, Professor (of music)

Time period(s): 1990s (1990)

Locale(s): London, England; West Yorkshire, England

What the book is about: Jane's Aunt Carlotta, the former governess of famed pianist Silvio Antonelli, is killed by a hit-and-run driver. Jane inherits most of her aunt's estate, left to her by Silvio, including some journals. Meanwhile Jane's long lost cousin, Donna, arrives in England with a friend, Hazel, and Hazel's boyfriend. The next day Hazel is found dead. Donna turns to Jane and her husband, Andrew, for help.

Other books you might like:
Sara Hoskinson Frommer, *Murder in C Major*, 1988
James Gollin, *Broken Consort*, 1989
Thomas Hauser, *The Beethoven Conspiracy*, 1984
Joan Higgins, *A Little Death Music*, 1987
Lucille Kallen, *The C.B. Greenfield Series*, 1981-1986

1305
Audrey Peterson
Murder in Burgundy (New York: Pocket, 1989)

Series: Andrew Quentin/Jane Winfield

Story type: Amateur Detective

Major character(s): Jane Winfield, Student (Doctorate in music history); Andrew Quentin, Professor (Jane's teacher)

Time period(s): 1980s

What the book is about: While on a cruise with some friends, Andrew and Jane once again get involved with a murder.

Other books you might like:
Alisa Craig, *Trouble in the Brasses*, 1989
Sara Hoskinson Frommer, *Murder in C Major*, 1988
Joan Higgins, *A Little Death Music*, 1987
Lucille Kallen, *C.B. Greenfield: The Tanglewood Murder*, 1981
Joan Smith, *A Masculine Ending*, 1987

1306
Audrey Peterson
Shroud for a Scholar (New York: Pocket, 1995)

Series: Claire Camden

Story type: Amateur Detective—Female Lead

Major character(s): Claire Camden, Professor, Writer

Time period(s): 1990s

Locale(s): London, England

What the book is about: Claire's friend, Iris Franklin, has asked her to spend the night. They don't get much of a chance to talk and Claire leaves early the next morning. When she returns, she finds the body of Iris who has been strangled. Claire is the prime suspect and decides to clear herself. Could there be a connection to the mysterious phone call Iris receives after her death saying, "He knows where you are."

Other books you might like:
Natasha Cooper, *Bitter Herbs*, 1994
Nora Kelly, *Bad Chemistry*, 1994
Gillian Linscott, *Unknown Hand*, 1989
Janet Neel, *Death Among the Dons*, 1994
Joan Smith, *Don't Leave Me This Way*, 1990

1307
Geoff Peterson
Medicine Dog (New York: St. Martin's, 1989)

Story type: Private Detective—Male Lead

Major character(s): Boyd Sherman, Detective—Private, Journalist (Former)

Time period(s): 1980s

Locale(s): Bleak Medicine, Wyoming (Fictional city)

What the book is about: Former sports writer and neophyte P.I. Boyd Sherman is asked by Jennifer Landrus to find her husband, who seems to be involved with a group of modern day rustlers. First book.

Other books you might like:
Cleve F. Adams, *Shady Lady*, 1955
James Lee Burke, *Black Cherry Blues*, 1989
James Crumley, *The Wrong Case*, 1976
A.B. Guthrie Jr., *Playing Catch-Up*, 1985
Donald Zochert, *Another Weeping Woman*, 1980

1308
Keith Peterson (Pseudonym of Andrew Klavan)
Don't Say a Word (New York: Pocket, 1991)

Story type: Psychological Suspense

Major character(s): Lewis "Sport" McIlvaine, Criminal; Nathan Conrad, Doctor (Psychiatrist)

Time period(s): 1990s (1990)

Locale(s): New York, New York

What the book is about: Two psychotics terrorize Nathan Conrad's family and kidnap his young daughter. Maybe just for kicks, maybe because they want something from one of Conrad's patients that only he can get.

Other books you might like:
James Lee Burke, *A Morning for Flamingos*, 1990
Kate Green, *Shattered Moon*, 1987
John Katzenbach, *Day of Reckoning*, 1988
Rex Miller, *Stone Shadow*, 1989
Sam Reaves, *A Long Cold Fall*, 1990

1309
Keith Peterson (Pseudonym of Andrew Klavan)
Rough Justice (New York: Bantam, 1989)

Series: John Wells

Story type: Action/Adventure

Major character(s): John Wells, Journalist; Vicki Lansing, Journalist (In love with Wells)

Time period(s): 1980s

Locale(s): New York, New York

What the book is about: When John Wells thinks he has something dirty on a cop, the cop comes after him with both barrels.

Other books you might like:
Don Flynn, *Ed Fitzgerald Series*, 1983
Geoffrey Homes, *The Man Who Murdered Goliath*, 1938
Lucille Kallen, *Introducing C.B. Greenfield*, 1979
Gregory McDonald, *The Fletch Series*, (1974-1985)
Judson Philips, *The Peter Styles Series*, 1964

1310
Keith Peterson (Pseudonym of Andrew Klavan)
The Scarred Man (New York: Doubleday, 1990)

Story type: Psychological Suspense

Major character(s): Michael North, Journalist (Reporter); Susannah McGill, Student (Daughter of North's boss)

Time period(s): 1980s

Locale(s): New York, New York; Hickman, Indiana

What the book is about: The story that Michael North makes up on Christmas Eve about a scarred man seems to have its roots in truth. He and Susannah McGill may have known each other when they were children and both have buried memories of this same scarred man. Keith Peterson won the best paperback novel Edgar for his previous book.

Other books you might like:
Michael Allegretto, *Night of Reunion*, 1990
John Katzenbach, *Day of Reckoning*, 1988
Barbara Vine, *A Fatal Inversion*, 1987

1311
Gerald Petievich
Earth Angels (New York: NAL, 1989)

Story type: Police Procedural—Male Lead

Major character(s): Jose Stepanovich, Police Officer

Time period(s): 1980s

Locale(s): Los Angeles, California

What the book is about: Stepanovich heads a special Gangs Unit of the LAPD and he and his men find themselves in the middle of a gang war.

Other books you might like:
Eugene Izzi, *King of the Hustlers*, 1989
Elmore Leonard, *City Primeval*, 1980
Mike Lundy, *Raven*, 1985
Roderick Thorp, *Rainbow Drive*, 1986
Joseph Wambaugh, *The Delta Star*, 1983

1312
Gerald Petievich
Paramour (New York: Dutton, 1991)

Story type: Action/Adventure

Major character(s): Jack Powers, Police Officer (Secret Service agent)

Time period(s): 1990s (1996)

Locale(s): Washington, District of Columbia

What the book is about: The murder of a secret service agent in the White House is just the tip of the iceberg in this political thriller. Was the dead agent a spy? Is the president having an affair with a CIA agent? Is the CIA agent a double agent? Why is Jack Powers being set up as the fall guy?

Other books you might like:
Michael Bowen, *Washington Deceased*, 1990
Jerome Doolittle, *Body Scissors*, 1990
Joe Gores, *Wolf Time*, 1989
John Grisham, *The Pelican Brief*, 1992
Ross Thomas, *Briarpatch*, 1984

1313
W.R. Philbrick
Paint It Black (New York: St. Martin's, 1989)

Series: Jack Hawkins

Story type: Amateur Detective—Male Lead

Major character(s): Jack Hawkins, Writer (Ex-Policeman; mystery writer)

Time period(s): 1980s

Locale(s): Boston, Massachusetts

What the book is about: Someone is trying to kill Hawkins' old friend, Homicide Lt. Tim Sullivan, who may be the basis for Jack's fictional homicide detective. The murder attempts come during filming of one of Jack's novels.

Other books you might like:
Robert Crais, *The Monkey's Raincoat*, 1987
Jeremiah Healy, *So Like Sleep*, 1987
John Lutz, *Scorcher*, 1987
Robert B. Parker, *Crimson Joy*, 1988
Robert J. Randisi, *Full Contact*, 1984

1314
Mike Phillips
Blood Rights (New York: St. Martin's, 1989)

Story type: Amateur Detective—Male Lead

Major character(s): Sam Dean, Writer (Black man), Journalist

Time period(s): 1980s

Locale(s): England

What the book is about: Sam Dean is asked to look into the disappearance of wealthy, white Virginia Baker, who was last seen in the company of a black man. This brings him into inevitable conflict between the two communities, one rich and white, the other poor and colored. (N.B.: This is not an editorial comment but the fact that the racial communities in Britain consist not only of black people, but of many people of color.)

Other books you might like:
John Ball, *In the Heat of the Night*, 1965
J.F. Burke, *Death Trick*, 1975
Chester Himes, *Blind Man with a Pistol*, 1969
Ed Lacy, *Room to Swing*, 1957
Percy Spurlark Parker, *Good Girls Don't Get Murdered*, 1974

1315
Nancy Pickard
The 27 Ingredient Chili Con Carne Murders (New York: Delacorte, 1993)

Series: Eugenia Potter

Story type: Amateur Detective—Female Lead

Major character(s): Eugenia Potter, Widow(er), Cook

Time period(s): 1990s

Locale(s): Tucson, Arizona (on a ranch outside of Tucson)

What the book is about: Arriving at her Arizona ranch after receiving a phone call from her manager that hints at trouble, Eugenia Potter discovers that the manager and his granddaughter are missing. While others conduct a search for the missing folks, Mrs. Potter tries to ascertain what caused the initial phone call that hinted at some sort of trouble. Then the manager's body turns up, but his granddaughter is still missing. Others soon start dying, ostensibly from being poisoned by Mrs. Potter's chili. Will Eugenia be the next to die? And where is the granddaughter? This is the continuation of a series started by Virginia Rich.

Other books you might like:
Katherine Hall Page, *The Body in the Belfry*, 1990
Virginia Rich, *The Baked Bean Supper Murders*, 1983
Virginia Rich, *The Cooking School Murders*, 1982
Virginia Rich, *The Nantucket Diet Murders*, 1985
Corinne Holt Sawyer, *The J. Alfred Prufrock Murders*, 1987
Celestine Sibley, *Straight as an Arrow*, 1992
Patricia Houck Sprinkle, *Murder in the Charleston Manner*, 1990
Valerie Wolzien, *We Wish You a Merry Murder*, 1991

1316
Nancy Pickard
Bum Steer (New York: Pocket, 1990)

Series: Jenny Cain

Story type: Amateur Detective—Female Lead

Major character(s): Jenny Cain, Businesswoman (Foundation administrator), Philanthropist

Time period(s): 1980s

Locale(s): Kansas City, Kansas

What the book is about: When a dying Kansas cattle rancher decides to leave his ranch to the foundation, Jenny flies to Kansas to find out why. The rancher is murdered before she can talk with him.

Other books you might like:
Karin Berne, *False Impressions*, 1986
Joan Hess, *Murder at the Mimosa Inn*, 1986
Sharyn McCrumb, *Highland Laddie Gone*, 1986
Gillian Roberts, *Caught Dead in Philadelphia*, 1987
Julie Smith, *Tourist Trap*, 1986

1317
Nancy Pickard
But I Wouldn't Want to Die There (New York: Pocket, 1993)

Series: Jenny Cain

Story type: Amateur Detective—Female Lead

Major character(s): Jenny Cain, Businesswoman (former foundation director)

Time period(s): 1990s

Locale(s): New York, New York

What the book is about: Jenny Cain loves New York City and she jumps at any chance to go there. Unfortunately her current visit is to take on a temporary job that was brought about by the stabbing death of her good friend Carol Margolis. Though the police have decided that her friend's death occurred during a robbery attempt, the friend's parents think that her husband had her killed and ask Jenny to find out the truth. Jenny is not sure herself, and as she gets more involved with her friend's former job, it appears that the husband might not have been the only one who wanted Carol dead.

Other books you might like:
Wendy Hornsby, *Midnight Baby*, 1993
Susan Kelly, *The Liz Connors Series*, 1985-
Janet LaPierre, *Grandmother's House*, 1991
Katherine Hall Page, *The Body in the Bouillon*, 1991
Soledad Santiago, *Room 9*, 1992

1318
Nancy Pickard
I.O.U. (New York: Pocket, 1991)

Series: Jenny Cain

Story type: Amateur Detective—Female Lead

Major character(s): Jenny Cain, Businesswoman (foundation administrator), Philanthropist; Geof Bushfield, Police Officer (husband of Jenny)

Time period(s): 1990s

Locale(s): Port Frederick, Massachusetts

What the book is about: Jenny's mother finally dies after having been in a coma for years. No one has ever been able to explain what was wrong with her. When at the funeral someone whispers "Forgive me, it was an accident", Jenny decides to investigate her mother's past.

Other books you might like:
Wendy Hornsby, *No Harm*, 1989
Susan Kelly, *The Gemini Man*, 1985
Sharyn McCrumb, *The Elizabeth MacPherson Series*, 1984-
Gillian Roberts, *Caught Dead in Philadelphia*, 1988
Alice Storey, *First Kill All the Lawyers*, 1988

1319
Marissa Piesman
Close Quarters (New York: Delacorte, 1994)

Series: Nina Fischman

Story type: Amateur Detective—Female Lead; Legal

Major character(s): Nina Fischman, Lawyer (legal services for the elderly)

Time period(s): 1990s

Locale(s): Fire Island, New York

What the book is about: While spending some time sharing a house on Fire Island, Nina Fischman gets involved with murder. The organizer of the house sharing, one Barry Adleman, has been murdered with a poisoned motion-sickness patch. As Barry was a notorious womanizer, there is no shortage of suspects within the house. Was it another woman scorned, or Nina's new love interest, Jonathan Harris, who had known the victim since high school? Jonathan seems to be the most likely because Barry had slept with his wife, but Nina is convinced otherwise and sets out to prove it.

Other books you might like:
Jeff Abbott, *Do Unto Others*, 1994
Carole Berry, *Good Night, Sweet Prince*, 1991
Judith Viorst, *Murdering Mr. Monti*, 1994
Valerie Wolzien, *A Star-Spangled Murder*, 1993
Sharon Zukowski, *Dancing in the Dark*, 1992

1320
Marissa Piesman
Unorthodox Practices (New York: Pocket, 1989)

Story type: Amateur Detective—Female Lead

Major character(s): Nina Fischman, Lawyer (Legal Services attorney); Ida Fischman, Housewife (Mother of Nina)

Time period(s): 1980s

Locale(s): New York, New York

What the book is about: Would someone actually kill an old lady to free up her rent-controlled apartment? Nina and her mom want to find out. First book.

Other books you might like:
K.K. Beck, *Murder in a Mummy Case*, 1987
Lia Matera, *A Radical Departure*, 1988
Julie Smith, *The Sourdough Wars*, 1984
Judith Van Gieson, *North of the Border*, 1988

1321
Richard Platt
Co-Author: Orah Platt
Letting Blood (New York: St. Martin's, 1989)

Story type: Amateur Detective—Male Lead

Major character(s): Archer Rush Montana, Doctor (Head of infection control); Molly Montana, Doctor

Time period(s): 1980s

Locale(s): Philadelphia, Pennsylvania

What the book is about: When several physicians affiliated with the hospital begin to die, the Montanas are suspicious, and when a wealthy philanthropist also dies, of AIDS, they decide something is really wrong. First book.

Other books you might like:
Anthea Cohen, *Angel of Death*, 1985
Robin Cook, *Outbreak*, 1987
Patricia D. Cornwell, *Postmortem*, 1990
James Kahn, *The Echo Vector*, 1987
Leah Ruth Robinson, *Blood Run*, 1988

1322
Joyce Porter
Dover and the Claret Tappers (Vermont: Foul Play, 1989)

Series: Inspector Dover

Story type: Police Procedural—Male Lead

Major character(s): Wilf Dover, Detective—Police (Detective Chief Inspector)

Time period(s): 1980s

What the book is about: Dover is kidnapped but Scotland Yard doesn't really want him back. That's all right because his kidnapping is just a trial run for the kidnapping of the Prime Minister's grandson.

Other books you might like:
Robert Barnard, *Death by Sheer Torture*, 1981
Reginald Hill, *The Dalziel and Pascoe Series*, 1970
Colin Watson, *Six Nuns and a Shotgun*, 1975

1323
Deborah Powell
Bayou City Secrets (Tallahassee: Naiad, 1991)

Story type: Amateur Detective—Female Lead; Historical

Major character(s): Hollis Carpenter, Journalist (Crime reporter), Lesbian; Lily Delacroix, Lesbian

Time period(s): 1930s

Locale(s): Houston, Texas

What the book is about: After resigning in disgust from the newspaper, Hollis is invited to dinner with the newspaper owner and his wife to discuss the story she was working on—involving disappearing evidence. When she returns home she discovers that her apartment has been burgled. Going for help she discovers the corpse of her friend, cop Joe Mahan. From here the case gets dangerous as does Hollis' relationship with Lily Delacroix. First novel.

Other books you might like:
Nikki Baker, *In the Game*, 1991
Katherine V. Forrest, *The Beverly Malibu*, 1989
Ellen Hart, *Hallowed Murder*, 1989
Diane K. Shah, *As Crime Goes By*, 1990
Barbara Wilson, *The Dog Collar Murders*, 1989

1324
David Poyer
Louisiana Blue (New York: St. Martin's, 1994)

Series: Tiller Galloway

Story type: Action/Adventure

Major character(s): Tiller Galloway, Diver (deep-sea); Shad Aydlett, Diver (deep-sea)

Time period(s): 1990s

Locale(s): Louisiana

What the book is about: Tiller Galloway and his friend Shad Aydlett are on the run from some hired guns when they hook up with Deep Tech, an outfit that is doing some work on the underwater pipelines of Coastal Oil. Of course, all is not as it should be on the oil rigs and when a helicopter appears to have been sabotaged Tiller and Shad again get involved to find out what is going on—and to save their own skins.

Other books you might like:
Rick Boyer, *The Whale's Footprints*, 1988
Ken Grissom, *Big Fish*, 1991
Paul Kemprecos, *Death in Deep Water*, 1992
John Walter Putre, *A Small and Incidental Murder*, 1990

1325
Bill Pronzini
Blue Lonesome (New York: Walker, 1995)

Story type: Psychological Suspense; Action/Adventure

Major character(s): Jim Messenger, Accountant

Time period(s): 1990s

Locale(s): Beulah, Nevada; San Francisco, California

What the book is about: Jim Messenger is a lonely guy, but a woman he sees eating dinner often appears even lonelier. He starts to think about her more than is healthy and when she commits suicide he is determined to find out more about her and what would drive her to that point. His search takes him to the small town of Beulah, Nevada where the townsfolk seem not to appreciate his questions and point it out to him. The dead woman's sister, after an initial coolness, begins to help him.

Other books you might like:
Richard Barre, *The Innocents*, 1995
James W. Hall, *Hard Aground*, 1993
James Sallis, *Moth*, 1994
Randall Silvis, *An Occasional Hell*, 1993
Richard Parrish, *The Dividing Line*, 1993

1326
Bill Pronzini
Breakdown (New York: Delacorte, 1991)

Series: Nameless Detective

Story type: Private Detective—Male Lead

Major character(s): Nameless Detective, Detective—Private

Time period(s): 1990s

Locale(s): San Francisco, California

1327 Bill Pronzini

What the book is about: Nameless is undercover, spending a lot of time in a bar in the process. He has been hired by a businessman accused of killing his partner in a hit and run. But Nameless may actually be being set-up for a fall of his own because someone doesn't want him getting close to the truth about the death.

Other books you might like:
Thomas B. Dewey, *The "Mac" Series*, 1947-1970
Ed Gorman, *The Night Remembers*, 1991
Jeremiah Healy, *Blunt Darts*, 1984
John Lutz, *The Alo Nudger Series*, 1976-
Marcia Muller, *Trophies and Dead Things*, 1990

1327
Bill Pronzini
Epitaphs (New York: Delacorte, 1992)

Series: Nameless Detective

Story type: Private Detective—Male Lead

Major character(s): Nameless Detective, Detective—Private

Time period(s): 1990s

Locale(s): San Francisco, California

What the book is about: An old Italian asks Nameless to help his granddaughter, who has been accused of stealing. When Nameless goes to the girl's apartment she's not around and her roommate shows no inclination to be helpful. Soon the roommate turns up dead and further investigation shows the girls to have been involved in a call girl ring. The grandfather denies this is possible. In Nameless's own life things are also in turmoil. Though his relationship with his lady is still great, his relationship with his partner may be unreconcilable.

Other books you might like:
James Lee Burke, *Black Cherry Blues*, 1988
Thomas B. Dewey, *The "Mac" Series*, 1947-1970
Ed Gorman, *The Night Remembers*, 1991
Jeremiah Healy, *The John Francis Cuddy Series*, 1984-
John Lutz, *The Alo Nudger Series*, 1976-

1328
Bill Pronzini
Jackpot (New York: Delacorte, 1990)

Series: Nameless Detective

Story type: Private Detective—Male Lead

Major character(s): Nameless Detective, Detective—Private

Time period(s): 1980s

Locale(s): San Francisco, California; Reno, Nevada

What the book is about: Why did David Burnett, who had recently won $200,000 in Reno, commit suicide? Or did he?

Other books you might like:
Thomas B. Dewey, *The "Mac" Series*, (1947-1970)
Jeremiah Healy, *Blunt Darts*, 1984
Marcia Muller, *Sharon McCone Series*, 1977

1329
Bill Pronzini
Quarry (New York: Delacorte, 1992)

Series: Nameless Detective

Story type: Private Detective—Male Lead

Major character(s): Nameless Detective, Detective—Private

Time period(s): 1990s

Locale(s): San Francisco, California

What the book is about: Arlo Haas' daughter, Grady, has come home to their ranch in a near-catatonic state. Obviously some traumatic experience happened to her in the city. But she refuses to talk about it, or even acknowledge that anything is wrong. Haas asks Nameless to investigate as Grady is the only thing he has left in the world and he can't stand seeing her this way. Nameless agrees to investigate but what he finds is not just sadness but psychological torture of the worst kind.

Other books you might like:
Thomas B. Dewey, *The "Mac" Series*, 1947-1970
James Lee Burke, *Black Cherry Blues*, 1988
Ed Gorman, *The Night Remembers*, 1991
Jeremiah Healy, *Right to Die*, 1990
John Lutz, *The Alo Nudger Series*, 1976-

1330
Bill Pronzini
Stacked Deck (Eugene, Oregon: Mystery Scene Press, 1991)

Story type: Collection

Locale(s): United States

What the book is about: A collection of seven short stories from all stages of Pronzini's career, including one with his series character the "Nameless Detective".

Other books you might like:
Stuart M. Kaminsky, *Opening Shots*, 1991
Joe R. Lansdale, *Stories by Mama Lansdale's Youngest Boy*, 1990
John Lutz, *Better Mousetraps*, 1988
Marcia Muller, *Deceptions*, 1991

1331
Bill Pronzini
With an Extreme Burning (New York: Carroll & Graf, 1994)

Story type: Amateur Detective; Psychological Suspense

Major character(s): Dix Mallory, Professor; Cecca Bellini, Real Estate Agent

Time period(s): 1990s

Locale(s): Los Alegres, California

What the book is about: Dix Mallory's wife has recently died in a car crash that was thought to be an accident. However, now Dix is getting phone calls suggesting that the caller was his wife's lover and that the accident may have been murder. His close friend Cecca Bellini has also been getting threatening phone calls, these against her daughter. They combine forces to find out who and what is behind these terrors. Pronzini also writes a private detective series featuring the "Nameless Detective."

Other books you might like:
J.F. Freedman, *Against the Wind*, 1991
M.D. Lake, *Murder by Mail*, 1993
Sean McGrady, *Sealed with a Kiss*, 1995
Abigail Padgett, *Child of Silence*, 1993
Richard Parrish, *The Dividing Line*, 1993

1332
Sandra West Prowell
By Evil Means (New York: Walker, 1993)

Story type: Private Detective—Female Lead

Major character(s): Phoebe Siegal, Detective—Private

Time period(s): 1990s

Locale(s): Billings, Montana

What the book is about: Though reluctant to take a case involving a drug-taking daughter and deal with her personality change while being treated, Phoebe finally relents when it appears that the girl and her doctor may have had something to do with the death—purportedly suicide—of Phoebe's brother some years earlier. First novel.

Other books you might like:
Nevada Barr, *Track of the Cat*, 1993
Jan Burke, *Goodnight, Irene*, 1993
Jean Hager, *Ravenmocker*, 1993
Kathryn Lasky Knight, *Trace Elements*, 1986
Marcia Muller, *The Sharon McCone Series*, 1977-

1333
Dianne G. Pugh
Cold Call (New York: Pocket, 1993)

Story type: Amateur Detective—Female Lead

Major character(s): Iris Thorne, Businesswoman (investment counselor); John Somers, Police Officer, Detective—Homicide

Time period(s): 1990s

Locale(s): Los Angeles, California

What the book is about: Iris Thorne has become a success at selling stocks and bonds in spite of not being one of the "good old boys", but there is trouble at work. One of the mailroom workers, a deaf man and also a friend of Iris', is killed by a gang. He has left Iris a key to a safe deposit box where she finds over two hundred thousand dollars and a lot of stock certificates. What is going on? To complicate matters, the policeman assigned to the case is Iris' first love. First novel.

Other books you might like:
Susan Wittig Albert, *Thyme of Death*, 1992
Carole Berry, *The Letter of the Law*, 1988
Michael A. Kahn, *Grave Designs*, 1991
Annette Meyers, *The Smith and Wetzon Series*, 1987-
Yvonne Montgomery, *Scavengers*, 1987

1334
Mary Monica Pulver
Original Sin (New York: Walker, 1991)

Series: Kori and Peter Brichter

Story type: Police Procedural; Amateur Detective

Major character(s): Peter Brichter, Police Officer (sergeant); Kori Brichter, Businesswoman (horse farm owner)

Time period(s): 1990s

Locale(s): Charter, Illinois

What the book is about: Peter and Kori are hosting a Christmas party at their farm. One of the guests is Evelyn Biggins, Kori's second cousin, whom nobody has seen in years. Just after arriving, Evelyn is killed. A snow storm has made roads impassable so the killer must be one of the guests, all of whom seem to have some past connection with the victim.

Other books you might like:
Wendy Hornsby, *Half a Mind*, 1990
Sharyn McCrumb, *If Ever I Return, Pretty Peggy-O*, 1990
Nancy Pickard, *I.O.U.*, 1991
Medora Sale, *Murder in a Good Cause*, 1990
Eve K. Sandstrom, *Death Down Home*, 1990

1335
Mary Monica Pulver
Show Stopper (New York: Walker, 1992)

Series: Kori and Peter Brichter

Story type: Amateur Detective

Major character(s): Kori Brichter, Businesswoman (horse farm owner)

Time period(s): 1990s

Locale(s): Lafite, Illinois

What the book is about: Without husband Peter, Kori Brichter, her trainer and groom take horses to an all-Arabian horse show in Illinois. While there she witnesses horse brutality and when the trainer guilty of this is found dead, Kori decides to investigate. Then her groom, who is relatively new in her employ, is arrested for the murder. To clear her, Kori must find and dig out secrets that a number of people would rather stay buried.

Other books you might like:
Wendy Hornsby, *Half a Mind*, 1990
Sharyn McCrumb, *The Elizabeth MacPherson Series*, 1987-
Nancy Pickard, *The Jenny Cain Series*, 1986-
Eve K. Sandstrom, *Death Down Home*, 1990

1336
John Walter Putre
Death Among the Angels (New York: Scribners, 1991)
Series: D-O-L-L
Story type: Amateur Detective—Male Lead; Action/Adventure
Major character(s): Doll, Veteran (Vietnam, Navy special forces), Detective—Private (not a licensed P.I.)
Time period(s): 1990s
Locale(s): Treasure Coast, Florida
What the book is about: Diana Raney is found in the same room as the body of her murdered lover. Doll, who once loved Diana, is called to Florida to help clear her. Diana, however, doesn't know if she did it, saying she doesn't remember, and won't do anything to help.
Other books you might like:
Ken Grissom, *Drop-Off*, 1988
Doug Hornig, *Deep Dive*, 1988
Paul Kemprecos, *Cool Blue Tomb*, 1991
John D. MacDonald, *The Travis McGee Series*, 1964-1982
W.R. Philbrick, *The T.D. Stash Series*, 1987-

1337
John Walter Putre
A Small and Incidental Murder (New York: Scribners, 1990)
Series: D-O-L-L
Story type: Amateur Detective—Male Lead
Major character(s): Doll, Troubleshooter (Diver), Veteran (Vietnam Vet)
Time period(s): 1980s
Locale(s): Chesapeake Bay, Maryland
What the book is about: Doll is asked by a former partner to find out the truth behind the death of a Chesapeake Bay fisherman. He finds more than that. Putre's first novel.
Other books you might like:
J.H. Hull, *Nicole*, 1985
John D. MacDonald, *The Deep Blue Goodbye*, 1964
Don Matheson, *Stray Cat*, 1984
W.R. Philbrick, *The Crystal Blue Persuasion*, 1988
Stirling Silliphant, *Steel Tiger*, 1983

1338
Erica Quest
Model Murder (New York: Doubleday, 1991)
Series: Kate Maddox
Story type: Police Procedural—Female Lead
Major character(s): Kate Maddox, Police Officer (Chief Detective Inspector); Tim Boulter, Police Officer (Detective Sergeant)
Time period(s): 1990s
Locale(s): South Midlands, England
What the book is about: Ex-model Corinne Saxon has been found raped and strangled. Kate Maddox gets the case but it has personal complications. Her boyfriend, Richard, once had a relationship with Corinne and must be considered a suspect.
Other books you might like:
Liza Cody, *The Anna Lee Series*, 1980-
P.D. James, *The Cordelia Gray Series*, 1973-1982
Jennie Melville, *The Charmian Daniels Series*, 1962-

1339
Monica Quill (Pseudonym of Ralph McInerny)
Nun Plussed (New York: St. Martin's, 1993)
Series: Sister Mary Teresa
Story type: Amateur Detective—Female Lead
Major character(s): Sister Mary Teresa Dempsey, Religious (nun)
Time period(s): 1990s
Locale(s): Chicago, Illinois
What the book is about: Sister Mary Teresa has received an invitation to a wedding - unfortunately the bride has already been married and has left her husband and the church cannot recognize the marriage. The problem is solved when the woman is murdered and the husband, a noted book dealer, confesses. Sister Mary Teresa has doubts and once again turns detective.
Other books you might like:
Veronica Black, *The Sister Joan Series*, 1990-
D.M. Greenwood, *The Theodora Braithwaite Series*, 1991-
Lee Harris, *The Christine Bennett Series*, 1992
Isabelle Holland, *The Claire Aldington Series*, 1984-
Sister Carol Anne O'Marie, *The Sister Mary Helen Series*, 1984-

1340
Elizabeth Quinn
Murder Most Grizzly (New York: Pocket, 1993)
Series: Lauren Maxwell
Story type: Amateur Detective—Female Lead
Major character(s): Lauren Maxwell, Naturalist; Nina Alexeyev, Veterinarian (Lauren's roommate)
Time period(s): 1990s
Locale(s): Anchorage, Alaska (McNeil River Sanctuary)
What the book is about: Roland Taft, Lauren's old friend, has asked her to meet him at the McNeil River Sanctuary but when she arrives she finds Roland's body, apparently killed by a grizzly bear. Lauren, an investigator for the Wild America Society, is suspicious of the circumstances, especially when she finds out that the man in charge of the sanctuary is anti-ecology with ties to the oil industry. First mystery.

Other books you might like:
Nevada Barr, *Track of the Cat*, 1993
B.J. Oliphant, *Dead in the Scrub*, 1990
Dana Stabenow, *The Kate Shugak Series*, 1992-
J.F. Trainor, *Dynamite Pass*, 1993
Judith Van Gieson, *The Wolf Path*, 1992

1341
Elizabeth Quinn
A Wolf in Death's Clothing (New York: Pocket, 1995)
Series: Lauren Maxwell
Story type: Psychological Suspense
Major character(s): Lauren Maxwell, Police Officer, Naturalist (wildlife affairs)
Time period(s): 1990s
Locale(s): Tanana, Alaska
What the book is about: Lauren's friend Belle Doyon, a Native American trapper and activist, opens her door one morning and is shot. Now she lies in a coma and Lauren wants to know who could have done such a thing and why. Lauren and her young son Jake journey to the small, isolated village of Tanana to find some answers and a would-be killer who leaves skinned wolves as warning signs.
Other books you might like:
Christine Andreae, *Grizzly*, 1994
Nevada Barr, *Track of the Cat*, 1993
Dana Stabenow, *A Cold Day for Murder*, 1992
J.F. Trainor, *Dynamite Pass*, 1993
Lee Wallingford, *Clear-Cut Murder*, 1993

1342
Joshua Quittner
Co-Author: Michelle Slatalla
Shoofly Pie to Die (New York: St. Martin's, 1992)
Story type: Amateur Detective
Major character(s): Sam Popkin, Journalist (writer and publisher); Sara Amstel, Journalist (writer and publisher)
Time period(s): 1990s
Locale(s): New York, New York; Pennsylvania (Amish country)
What the book is about: Sam and Sara are in Pennsylvania doing research for their food newsletter, *The Thin Man*, when they buy a chest that turns out to have a body without a head, hands or feet. The body is apparently that of an Amish dwarf. First novel.
Other books you might like:
Diane Mott Davidson, *Catering to Nobody*, 1990
Janet Laurence, *A Deepe Coffyn*, 1990
E.J. McGill, *Immaculate in Black*, 1991
Elizabeth Travis, *Under the Influence*, 1989

1343
Sheila Radley
This Way Out (New York: Scribners, 1989)
Series: Inspector Quantrill
Story type: Psychological Suspense
Major character(s): Douglas Quantrill, Police Officer (Chief Inspector)
Time period(s): 1980s
What the book is about: When Derek Cartwright expresses the wish to be rid of his mother-in-law to another businessman he soon regrets it.
Other books you might like:
Frances Fyfield, *A Question of Guilt*, 1989
Elizabeth George, *A Great Deliverance*, 1988
Martha Grimes, *The Dirty Duck*, 1984
P.D. James, *Cover Her Face*, 1962
Ruth Rendell, *The Inspector Wexford Series*, 1964

1344
Jeff Raines
Unbalanced Acts (New York: Avon, 1990)
Story type: Police Procedural—Male Lead
Major character(s): Michael Kelly, Police Officer (Captain); Thomas Kane, Police Officer (Sergeant)
Time period(s): 1980s
Locale(s): New York, New York
What the book is about: When 12 criminals escape from prison and head for New York, the anti-terrorist team has its work cut out for it.
Other books you might like:
William J. Caunitz, *One Police Plaza*, 1984
Nelson DeMille, *Cathedral*, 1981
William Diehl, *Hooligans*, 1984
Kenneth W. Godard, *Balefire*, 1983
Lawrence Sanders, *The First Deadly Sin*, 1973

1345
Michael Raleigh
Death in Uptown (New York: St. Martin's, 1991)
Story type: Private Detective—Male Lead
Major character(s): Paul Whelan, Detective—Private
Time period(s): 1990s
Locale(s): Chicago, Illinois
What the book is about: Two cases are creating problems for P.I. Paul Whelan. He is having no luck tracking down a missing construction worker, while at the same time he is at wits end trying to discover who killed an old friend, an alcoholic ex-newspaperman, in an alley. First novel.
Other books you might like:
D.C. Brod, *Murder in Store*, 1989
Michael Cormany, *Red Winter*, 1989
Sara Paretsky, *The V.I. Warshawski Series*, 1982-
Sam Reaves, *A Long Cold Fall*, 1990
Les Roberts, *The Milan Jacovich Series*, 1988-

1346
Diana Ramsay
Four Steps to Death (New York: St. Martin's, 1990)
Story type: Amateur Detective—Female Lead
Major character(s): Maggie Tremayne, Dancer (Ballet teacher)
Time period(s): 1980s
Locale(s): New York, New York
What the book is about: The death in her studio of her best friend and rival makes Maggie Tremayne the chief suspect. She soon realizes that she is marked for death as well and must find out why. First book.
Other books you might like:
Linda Barnes, *Blood Will Have Blood*, 1982
Edgar Box, *Death in the Fifth Position*, 1952
Lucy Cores, *Corpse de Ballet*, 1944
Gypsy Rose Lee, *The G-String Murders*, 1941

1347
Robert J. Randisi
The Dead of Brooklyn (New York: St. Martin's, 1991)
Series: Nick Delvecchio
Story type: Private Detective—Male Lead
Major character(s): Nick Delvecchio, Detective—Private
Time period(s): 1990s
Locale(s): Brooklyn, New York
What the book is about: When Nick Delvecchio's brother, a Catholic priest, is accused of murdering a woman after having slept with her, Nick is forced to try and find out the truth all the while not shortchanging his current client. To accomplish this dual task he must ask for help for the Brooklyn "Godfather", Dominick Barracondi.
Other books you might like:
Lawrence Block, *A Ticket to the Boneyard*, 1990
Bill Crider, *Dead on the Island*, 1991
Loren D. Estleman, *The Amos Walker Series*, 1982-
Bill Pronzini, *The Nameless Detective Series*, 1971-
Jonathan Valin, *The Harry Stoner Series*, 1980-

1348
Robert J. Randisi, Editor
Co-Editor: Marilyn Wallace
Deadly Allies (New York: Doubleday, 1992)
Story type: Anthology
Locale(s): United States
What the book is about: A collection of short stories by the combined membership of the Private Eye Writers of America and Sisters in Crime. Some of the authors include Jeremiah Healy, John Lutz, Sue Grafton, Susan Dunlap, Carolyn G. Hart, and Loren D. Estleman.
Other books you might like:
Loren D. Estleman, *P.I. Files*, 1990 (editor)
Ed Gorman, *Invitation to Murder*, 1991 (editor)
Marie Smith, *More Ms. Murder*, 1991 (editor)

1349
Robert J. Randisi
Hard Look (New York: Walker, 1993)
Series: Miles Jacoby
Story type: Private Detective—Male Lead
Major character(s): Miles Jacoby, Detective—Private, Saloon Keeper/Owner
Time period(s): 1990s
Locale(s): Tampa, Florida
What the book is about: New York based private detective Miles Jacoby is asked to go to Florida to track down a missing wife. The woman's husband has no clue to her whereabouts except for a postcard that he says has her picture on it. Specious though Jacoby thinks the story is, Miles takes off for Florida where he soon finds himself involved with the mob, bodybuilders, drugs and a luscious female cop.
Other books you might like:
Elmore Leonard, *Stick*, 1983
Paul Levine, *To Speak for the Dead*, 1990
John Lutz, *The Fred Carver Series*, 1986-
John D. MacDonald, *Pale Gray for Guilt*, 1968
Charles Willeford, *New Hope for the Dead*, 1985

1350
Robert J. Randisi
Separate Cases (New York: Walker, 1990)
Series: Miles Jacoby
Story type: Private Detective—Male Lead
Major character(s): Miles Jacoby, Detective—Private; Caroline McWilliams, Detective—Private
Time period(s): 1990s
Locale(s): New York, New York
What the book is about: Jacoby is asked to track down a missing prostitute who is an alibi for a Mafia client charged with killing his wife. Along the way he runs into and teams up with neophyte P.I. Caroline McWilliams who is searching for her husband's killer.
Other books you might like:
Jack Early, *A Creative Kind of Killer*, 1984
Paul Engleman, *Catch a Fallen Angel*, 1986
Pete Hamill, *Dirty Laundry*, 1978
Richard Hoyt, *Decoys*, 1980
Bill Pronzini, *The Nameless Detective Series*, 1971-

1351
Constance Rauch
A Deep Disturbance (New York: St. Martins, 1990)
Story type: Action/Adventure; Psychological Suspense
Major character(s): Madeline Rafferty, Writer
Time period(s): 1990s
Locale(s): Indian Meadows, New York (Adirondacks)

What the book is about: After discovering that her husband has taken kiddie porn shots of their two young daughters, Madeline Rafferty takes the girls away to a small town in the Adirondacks. But it may be that what she's run to is nearly as bad as what she's run from.

Other books you might like:
Mary Higgins Clark, *Where Are the Children?*, 1975
Brian Garfield, *Necessity*, 1984
Stuart M. Kaminsky, *Exercise in Terror*, 1985
Stuart Kaminsky, *When the Dark Man Calls*, 1983
Stuart Woods, *Palindrome*, 1991

1352
Robert J. Ray
Merry Christmas, Murdock (New York: Delacorte, 1989)

Series: Matt Murdock

Story type: Private Detective—Male Lead

Major character(s): Matt Murdock, Detective—Private, Veteran (Vietnam veteran); Wally St. Moritz, Businessman (Ex-college professor)

Time period(s): 1980s

Locale(s): Newport Beach, California

What the book is about: When the daughter of a Texas senator is nearly killed by a hit and run driver, the senator hires Murdock to track down the culprit.

Other books you might like:
William Babula, *St. John's Baptism*, 1988
Robert Crais, *The Monkey's Raincoat*, 1987
John D. MacDonald, *The Travis McGee Series*, 1964
T. Jefferson Parker, *Laguna Heat*, 1985
Eric Sauter, *Hunter*,

1353
Robert J. Ray
Murdock Cracks Ice (New York: Delacorte, 1992)

Series: Matt Murdock

Story type: Private Detective—Male Lead

Major character(s): Matt Murdock, Detective—Private, Veteran (Vietnam veteran)

Time period(s): 1990s

Locale(s): California (southern); Seattle, Washington

What the book is about: The father of a recently murdered, low level drug dealing college student hires Murdock to find out if drug dealing was the real reason behind his son's death. A teenage girl who may have known something is killed and someone tries to scare Murdock off the case. He is not easy to scare.

Other books you might like:
Jerome Doolittle, *Stranglehold*, 1991
J.A. Jance, *The J.P. Beaumont Series*, 1986-
Paul Kemprecos, *Neptune's Eye*, 1991
Zachary Klein, *Two Way Toll*, 1991
Bill Pronzini, *Jackpot*, 1990

1354
Sam Reaves
Get What's Coming (New York: Putnam, 1995)

Series: Cooper MacLeish

Story type: Amateur Detective—Male Lead; Action/Adventure

Major character(s): Cooper MacLeish, Taxi Driver; Regis Swanson, Businessman (real estate)

Time period(s): 1990s

Locale(s): Chicago, Illinois

What the book is about: Coop has taken a regular job as chauffeur for Regis Swanson, real-estate tycoon. This is not as cushy as it seems. A million dollars seems to be floating around loose and a lot of different people are trying to find it. For self-preservation, and to help Swanson, Cooper must get involved. The bodies begin to fall and the DEA is soon on the scene. They are not necessarily the good guys.

Other books you might like:
Joe Gores, *Dead Man*, 1993
Mitchell Smith, *Karma*, 1994
Scott Smith, *A Simple Plan*, 1993
Les Standiford, *Raw Deal*, 1994
John Straley, *The Woman Who Married a Bear*, 1992

1355
Sam Reaves
A Long Cold Fall (New York: Putnam, 1991)

Series: Cooper MacLeish

Story type: Action/Adventure; Amateur Detective—Male Lead

Major character(s): Cooper MacLeish, Veteran, Taxi Driver

Time period(s): 1990s

Locale(s): Chicago, Illinois

What the book is about: An old love of MacLeish's falls to her death. Her fourteen year old son - who may also be MacLeish's son - has disappeared. Was the woman murdered? Is the son's disappearance connected to her death? First novel.

Other books you might like:
Linda Barnes, *Coyote*, 1990
Ed Gorman, *The Autumn Dead*, 1989
Kate Green, *Night Angel*, 1989
Sara Paretsky, *Blood Shot*, 1988
Robert B. Parker, *Early Autumn*, 1981

1356
J.M. Redmann
The Intersection of Law and Desire (New York: Norton, 1995)

Series: Mickey Knight

Story type: Private Detective—Female Lead

Major character(s): Mickey Knight, Detective—Private, Lesbian

Time period(s): 1990s

Locale(s): New Orleans, Louisiana

What the book is about: Mickey Knight has two new clients—Karen Holloway, who is being blackmailed and nine-year-old Cissy Selby who wants the death of a classmate investigated. The two cases may be related and the problems may center around Joey Robedaux, a supposed investment banker.

Other books you might like:
Karen Allen, *Give My Secrets Back*, 1995
Nikki Baker, *In the Game*, 1991
Lauren Wright Douglas, *The Daughters of Artemis*, 1991
Jaye Maiman, *Someone to Watch*, 1995
Pat Welch, *Murder by the Book*, 1990

1357
Barry Reed
The Choice (New York: Crown, 1991)

Series: Frank Galvin

Story type: Legal

Major character(s): Frank Galvin, Lawyer; Tina Alvarez, Lawyer

Time period(s): 1990s

Locale(s): Massachusetts

What the book is about: Asked by Tina Alvarez to help sue an English drug company for knowingly marketing a drug that causes birth defects, Galvin must decline when he discovers that the big-time firm he is currently working for represents the company in question. Moral questions abound when he is assigned to defend the company.

Other books you might like:
Harrison Arnston, *Trade-Off*, 1992
William Bernhardt, *Primary Justice*, 1992
A.W. Gray, *Bino*, 1988
Colin Harrison, *Break and Enter*, 1989
Lia Matera, *Prior Convictions*, 1991

1358
Robert Reeves
Peeping Thomas (New York: Crown, 1990)

Series: Thomas Theron

Story type: Amateur Detective—Male Lead

Major character(s): Thomas Theron, Professor (of English); Beth Theron, Lawyer (ex-wife of Thomas)

Time period(s): 1990s

Locale(s): Boston, Massachusetts

What the book is about: Summoned by a colleague to a porn shop in Boston's Combat Zone, Thomas Theron wonders why but agrees to meet her. Just as she hands him a videotape and begins to explain, a bomb goes off. The colleague, an eminent feminist and anti-porn protester, is killed and Theron is injured. After his recovery he determines to get to the bottom of things. He is aided by his ex-wife, who was an admirer of the dead woman.

Other books you might like:
David Handler, *The Man Who Would Be F. Scott Fitzgerald*, 1990
Jeremiah Healy, *Yesterday's News*, 1989
Robert B. Parker, *Mortal Stakes*, 1975
Benjamin M. Schutz, *The Things We Do for Love*, 1989
William G. Tapply, *Follow the Sharks*, 1985

1359
Bob Reiss
Flamingo (New York: St. Martin's, 1990)

Story type: Amateur Detective—Male Lead

Major character(s): Raleigh Fixx, Writer (Author of true-crime books)

Time period(s): 1980s

Locale(s): Florida

What the book is about: While planning a book about preserving a bird sanctuary in Florida, Raleigh Fixx is arrested for murder.

Other books you might like:
Douglas Kiker, *Death at the Cut*, 1988
John D. MacDonald, *A Flash of Green*, 1962
L.A. Taylor, *Poetic Justice*, 1988

1360
Ruth Rendell
Going Wrong (New York: Mysterious, 1990)

Story type: Psychological Suspense

Major character(s): Guy Curran, Criminal

Time period(s): 1990s

Locale(s): England

What the book is about: Obsessed by love for his childhood sweetheart and haunted by the death of a man he supplied LSD for, Guy Curran is not entirely sane. He orders the murder of the member of his former sweethearts family that he thinks turned her against him. And then changes the target. And again.

Other books you might like:
Gary Devon, *Bad Desire*, 1990
Patricia Highsmith, *Strangers on a Train*, 1950
D.B. Taylor, *Fatal Obsession*, 1989
Barbara Vine, *The Dark-Adapted Eye*, 1986

1361
Ruth Rendell
Kissing the Gunner's Daughter (New York: Mysterious, 1992)

Series: Inspector Wexford

Story type: Police Procedural—Male Lead; Psychological Suspense

Major character(s): Reginald Wexford, Police Officer (chief inspector)

Time period(s): 1990s

Locale(s): Kingsmarkham, England

What the book is about: Who shot up the family of anthropologist and novelist Davina Flory? Though granddaughter Daisy survives her wounds she is no help in solving the crime. She soon moves into the family estate and as Wexford continues to investigate the crime, he becomes close to her. He may see her as a surrogate daughter as he's currently estranged from his own daughter. More murders follow, including the hanging of a local blackmailer.

Other books you might like:
Elizabeth George, *The Inspector Lynley Series*, 1989-
Martha Grimes, *The Inspector Jury Series*, 1981-
Reginald Hill, *The Dalziel and Pascoe Series*, 1977-
Janet Neel, *The McLeish and Wilson Series*, 1988-
Peter Robinson, *The Inspector Banks Series*, 1990-

1362
John Lawrence Reynolds
And Leave Her Lay Dying (New York: Viking, 1990)

Series: Joe McGuire

Story type: Police Procedural—Male Lead

Major character(s): Joe McGuire, Police Officer; Ollie Schantz, Handicapped (former cop, partner of Joe)

Time period(s): 1990s

Locale(s): Boston, Massachusetts

What the book is about: Having punched an attorney while in court, McGuire is banished to the unsolved murder files. Instead of being punished, he reopens the investigation into the death of a strangely attractive woman. Also, it seems the woman's brother disappeared at the same time. He talks the case over with his former partner, Ollie Schantz, and together they think they can solve the case.

Other books you might like:
Anthony Bruno, *Bad Guys*, 1988
Nat Hentoff, *Internal Affairs*, 1987
Susan Kelly, *Until Proven Innocent*, 1990
John Minahan, *The Great Grave Robbery*, 1989
W.R. Philbrick, *Paint It Black*, 1989

1363
John Lawrence Reynolds
Whisper Death (New York: Viking, 1992)

Series: Joe McGuire

Story type: Police Procedural—Male Lead

Major character(s): Joe McGuire, Police Officer

Time period(s): 1990s

Locale(s): Massachusetts; California

What the book is about: Returning from his unofficial sabbatical, Joe McGuire is immediately assigned the task of extraditing a former post office employee, who has been accused of murder, from California. Before he can finish the task however, his new partner is shot and the former post office employee is assassinated. There would appear to be more to this case than meets the eye.

Other books you might like:
Anthony Bruno, *Bad Blood*, 1989
Nat Hentoff, *Internal Affairs*, 1987
John Minahan, *The Great Hotel Robbery*, 1986
W.R. Philbrick, *Paint It Black*, 1989
John Sandford, *Silent Prey*, 1992

1364
William J. Reynolds
The Naked Eye (New York: Putnam, 1990)

Series: Nebraska Mystery

Story type: Private Detective—Male Lead

Major character(s): Nebraska, Detective—Private

Time period(s): 1980s

Locale(s): Minnesota; Nebraska

What the book is about: After Nebraska has traced a runaway to Minnesota and convinced him to return, the private detective thinks the case is finished, but someone else doesn't.

Other books you might like:
Michael Allegretto, *Dead of Winter*, 1989
Max Allan Collins, *A Nice Weekend for Murder*, 1986
Robert B. Parker, *Early Autumn*, 1981

1365
Robert Richardson
The Book of the Dead (New York: St. Martin's, 1989)

Series: Augustus Maltravers

Story type: Amateur Detective—Male Lead

Major character(s): Augustus Maltravers, Writer

Time period(s): 1980s

What the book is about: While staying with friends in the country, Augustus "Gus" Maltravers gets to know their neighbors, the Carrintons—elderly Charles, his teenaged wife Jennifer and her lover, Duggie Lyden. Charles is murdered and Duggie is accused of the crime. With the help of an unpublished Sherlock Holmes adventure, Gus finds the real answers.

Other books you might like:
Anthony Boucher, *The Case of the Baker Street Irregulars*, 1940
A.A. Milne, *The Red House Mystery*, 1922
Ellery Queen, *A Study in Terror*, 1966
Julian Symons, *The Kentish Manor Murders*, 1988
Julian Symons, *A Three-Pipe Problem*, 1975

1366
Robert Richardson
The Dying of the Light (New York: St. Martins, 1990)

Series: Augustus Maltravers

Story type: Amateur Detective—Male Lead

Major character(s): Augustus Maltravers, Writer (playwright); Tess Davy, Actress (girlfriend of Augustus)

Time period(s): 1990s

Locale(s): Cornwall, England

What the book is about: Tess is in Portennis, home of a well-known artist colony, for a series of plays and Augustus is along for the ride. When Martha Shaw, local sculptor, is crushed to death by the statue she was working on, Mortimer Lacey, a gypsy who has "The Gift", feels her death and knows it is murder. He convinces Tess and Augustus by sensing things only they know, and asks them to investigate.

Other books you might like:
Nicholas Blake, *The Nigel Strangeways Series*, 1935-1968
Leo Bruce, *The Carolus Deene Series*, 1955-1974
Edmund Crispin, *The Gervase Fen Series*, 1944-1978
Jocelyn Davey, *The Ambrose Usher Series*, 1956-
Cyril Hare, *The Wind Blows Death*, 1950

1367
Robert Richardson
Murder in Waiting (New York: St. Martin's, 1991)
Series: Augustus Maltravers
Story type: Amateur Detective—Male Lead
Major character(s): Augustus Maltravers, Writer (playwright), Journalist; Jenni Hilton, Singer
Time period(s): 1990s
Locale(s): England

What the book is about: Pleased to be granted an exclusive interview with singing star Jenni Hilton who is making a comeback, Maltravers, who knows her history well, is unbelieving when she claims no knowledge of a record producer's death in 1968. It appears that the fallout from this death will be coming back to haunt, not only Jenni, but Maltravers as well.

Other books you might like:
Edmund Crispin, *The Gervase Fen Series*, 1944-1978
Michael Gilbert, *The Doors Open*, 1962
Reginald Hill, *A Very Good Hater*, 1974
Sharyn McCrumb, *If Ever I Return, Pretty Peggy-O*, 1990
Barbara Vine, *A Fatal Inversion*, 1987

1368
John R. Riggs
A Dragon Lives Forever (New York: Barricade, 1992)
Series: Garth Ryland
Story type: Amateur Detective—Male Lead; Action/Adventure
Major character(s): Garth Ryland, Journalist
Time period(s): 1990s
Locale(s): Oakalla, Wisconsin

What the book is about: Two crimes two decades apart are linked by the annual visit of a carnival to this small town. The crimes are the disappearance of a teenage boy - the earlier crime - and the death, apparently murder, of an over-the-hill stock-car driver.

Other books you might like:
Don Flynn, *Murder on the Hudson*, 1985
M.S. Karl, *Killer's Ink*, 1988
Douglas Kiker, *Death at the Cut*, 1988
Vince Kohler, *Rainy North Woods*, 1990
Keith Peterson, *The Trapdoor*, 1988

1369
John R. Riggs
Wolf in Sheep's Clothing (New York: Dembner, 1989)
Series: Garth Ryland
Story type: Amateur Detective—Male Lead
Major character(s): Garth Ryland, Journalist (Owner/publisher of a newspaper)
Time period(s): 1980s
Locale(s): Wisconsin; Minnesota

What the book is about: Garth Ryland's former lover has been missing since going on vacation in the North Woods with a college professor. Ryland is determined to find out what happened to her.

Other books you might like:
Don Flynn, *Murder on the Hudson*, 1985
Lesley Grant-Adamson, *Wild Justice*, 1988
M.S. Karl, *Killer's Ink*, 1988
Keith Peterson, *The Trapdoor*, 1988

1370
W.L. Ripley
Dreamsicle (New York: Little, Brown, 1993)
Story type: Action/Adventure
Major character(s): Wyatt Storme, Veteran
Time period(s): 1990s
Locale(s): Missouri

What the book is about: While hunting in Missouri, Wyatt Storme and his friend, Chick Easton run across a fairly extensive marijuana crop. Before they leave the area they report their find to the local sheriff. When he turns up murdered, they decide to stick around and see if they can assist in finding the killer. Then Chick is arrested for the murder and the stakes get much higher. First novel.

Other books you might like:
Harlen Campbell, *Monkey on a Chain*, 1993
John Clarkson, *And Justice for One*, 1992
James Crumley, *The Mexican Tree Duck*, 1993
Sin Soracco, *Edge City*, 1992
Marc Savage, *Flamingos*, 1992

1371
Simon Ritchie
Work for a Dead Man (New York: Scribner's, 1989)
Series: J.K.G. Jantarro
Story type: Private Detective—Male Lead

Major character(s): J.K.G. Jantarro, Detective—Private; Glenda Redway, Lawyer

Time period(s): 1980s

Locale(s): Toronto, Ontario, Canada

What the book is about: Jantarro is hired by film producer Alan Laki to investigate his wife's excessive spending. Soon his client is poisoned and then two other people die.

Other books you might like:
George C. Chesbro, *Shadow of a Broken Man*, 1977
Michael Collins, *Minnesota Strip*, 1987
John Lutz, *Scorcher*, 1987
John Milne, *Dead Birds*, 1987
M.K. Shuman, *The Maya Stone Murders*, 1989

1372
Caryl Rivers
Indecent Behavior (New York: Dutton, 1990)

Story type: Amateur Detective

Major character(s): Sally Ellenberg, Journalist (Reporter); John Forbes Aiken, Journalist (Reporter)

Time period(s): 1980s

Locale(s): Boston, Massachusetts

What the book is about: Ellenberg and Aiken try to get to the bottom of plot to control human behavior by electrode brain implants. First book.

Other books you might like:
James Kahn, *The Echo Vector*, 1987
Shelly Reuben, *Julian Solo*, 1988
Leah Ruth Robinson, *Blood Run*, 1988

1373
Ronald Clair Roat
Close Softly the Doors (Brownsville, OR: Story Line, 1991)

Story type: Private Detective—Male Lead

Major character(s): Stuart Mallory, Detective—Private

Time period(s): 1990s

Locale(s): Lansing, Michigan

What the book is about: Private eye Stuart Mallory is trying to protect a former lover from a criminal who wants her dead before she can testify against him. Just to complicate matters he is also involved with a fortune in stolen coins. First novel.

Other books you might like:
H.C. Branson, *The John Bent Series*, 1941-1953
Loren D. Estleman, *The Amos Walker Series*, 1980-
Rob Kantner, *The Ben Perkins Series*, 1986
John Walter Putre, *Death Among the Angels*, 1991
Jonathan Valin, *The Harry Stoner Series*, 1980-

1374
Ronald Clair Roat
A Still and Icy Silence (Brownsville, OR: Story Line, 1993)

Story type: Private Detective—Male Lead

Major character(s): Stuart Mallory, Detective—Private

Time period(s): 1990s

Locale(s): Lansing, Michigan

What the book is about: The daughter of an old acquaintance asks Mallory to investigate the death of her father. He was a known arsonist and died when his house burned down. She thinks it was murder.

Other books you might like:
Loren D. Estleman, *The Amos Walker Series*, 1980-
Rob Kantner, *The Ben Perkins Series*, 1986-
Elmore Leonard, *City Primeval*, 1980
John Lutz, *The Alo Nudger Series*, 1976-
John Straley, *The Woman Who Married a Bear*, 1992

1375
Candace M. Robb
The Apothecary Rose (New York: St. Martins, 1993)

Series: Owen Archer

Story type: Historical; Amateur Detective—Male Lead

Major character(s): Owen Archer, Military Personnel, Spy (part-time)

Time period(s): 14th century

Locale(s): York, England

What the book is about: Owen Archer is sent to York to find out what killed a pilgrim in the infirmary of St. Mary's Abbey. He goes disguised as an apothecary's apprentice. Then a second, and similar murder occurs. There is no dearth of suspects including the apothecary, his wife, an innkeeper, a prelate, and a high-placed harlot. Owen must find the guilty party before his real identity is discovered. First novel.

Other books you might like:
Michael Clynes, *The White Rose Murders*, 1993
P.C. Doherty, *The Fate of Princes*, 1991
Edward Marston, *The Nicholas Bracewell Series*, 1988-
Sharan Newman, *Death Comes as Epiphany*, 1993
Kate Sedley, *Death and the Chapman*, 1992

1376
Candace M. Robb
The Lady Chapel (New York: St. Martin's, 1994)

Series: Owen Archer

Story type: Historical; Amateur Detective—Male Lead

Major character(s): Owen Archer, Military Personnel (retired); John Thoresby, Religious (archbishop)

Time period(s): 14th century (1365)

Locale(s): York, England

What the book is about: A prominent member of the Mercer's Guild has been murdered and his severed hand found in the room of Gilbert Ridley, a fellow guildsman and rival. Archbishop Thoresby asks Owen Archer to look into the matter and prove Ridley's innocence or guilt. Owen is soon involved in sinister plots and counterplots that threaten him, his wife, and possibly the throne of England.

Other books you might like:
Michael Clynes, *The White Rose Murders*, 1993
P.C. Doherty, *The Death of a King*, 1985
Paul Harding, *The Brother Athelstan Series*, 1991-
Faye Kellerman, *The Quality of Mercy*, 1989
Kate Sedley, *The Roger the Chapman Series*, 1992-

1377
Candace M. Robb
The Nun's Tale (New York: St. Martin's, 1995)

Series: Owen Archer

Story type: Historical; Amateur Detective—Male Lead

Major character(s): Owen Archer, Military Personnel, Spy

Time period(s): 14th century

Locale(s): England

What the book is about: The coming war between England and France is the background as Owen Archer, agent for the Lord Chancellor seeks to determine if there are any links between the alleged resurrection of a nun and the man who helped her, a possible traitor to England. Owen's wife also gets involved, which may put her and their unborn child at risk.

Other books you might like:
P.F. Chisholm, *A Famine of Horses*, 1995
Michael Clynes, *The White Rose Murders*, 1993
Paul Harding, *The Nightingale Gallery*, 1991
Edward Marston, *The Nicholas Bracewell Series*, 1988-
Sharan Newman, *Death Comes as Epiphany*, 1993

1378
Gillian Roberts (Pseudonym of Judith Greber)
I'd Rather Be in Philadelphia (New York: Ballantine, 1992)

Series: Amanda Pepper

Story type: Amateur Detective—Female Lead

Major character(s): Amanda Pepper, Teacher (High School English); C.K. MacKenzie, Police Officer

Time period(s): 1990s

Locale(s): Philadelphia, Pennsylvania

What the book is about: Amanda's showing of *The Taming of the Shrew* to her class starts a chain reaction — her students become interested in women's rights and Amanda starts reading a book about battered women. In the book are notes that indicate that the woman who used to own the book was in fear for her life. Amanda tracks her down, and discovers that the women's husband is dead, murdered in their home. The wife claims she is innocent and Amanda believes her, even though the dead husband was a well-known educator.

Other books you might like:
Susan Kelly, *The Liz Connors Series*, 1985-
Mary Kittredge, *The Charlotte Kent Series*, 1987-
Janet LaPierre, *Children's Games*, 1989
Leslie Meier, *Mail-Order Murder*, 1991
Nancy Pickard, *Marriage Is Murder*, 1987

1379
Gillian Roberts (Pseudonym of Judith Greber)
Philly Stakes (New York: Scribner's, 1989)

Series: Amanda Pepper

Story type: Amateur Detective—Female Lead

Major character(s): Amanda Pepper, Teacher (Prep school English); C.K. MacKenzie, Police Officer

Time period(s): 1980s

Locale(s): Philadelphia, Pennsylvania

What the book is about: When the parent of one of her better students is killed during a banquet for the homeless, Amanda can't help getting involved in the investigation.

Other books you might like:
Robert J. Bowman, *The House of Blue Lights*, 1987
Bob Fenster, *The Last Page*, 1989
Carolyn G. Hart, *A Little Class on Murder*, 1989
Joan Hess, *Strangled Prose*, 1985
Nancy Pickard, *Generous Death*, 1985

1380
Gillian Roberts (Pseudonym of Judith Greber)
With Friends Like These (New York: Ballantine, 1993)

Series: Amanda Pepper

Story type: Amateur Detective—Female Lead

Major character(s): Amanda Pepper, Teacher; C.K. MacKenzie, Police Officer

Time period(s): 1990s

Locale(s): Philadelphia, Pennsylvania

What the book is about: TV producer Lyle Zacharias drops dead at his 50th birthday party. There is no lack of suspects, including his current wife, his ex-wife, hotel personnel and his Aunt Hattie. It turns out, however, that the poison was delivered to him in a tart made by Amanda Pepper's mom, Bea. This, of course, causes Amanda to jump into the investigation with both feet.

Other books you might like:
Wendy Hornsby, *Midnight Baby*, 1993
Susan Kelly, *The Liz Connors Series*, 1985-
M.D. Lake, *The Peggy O'Neill Series*, 1989-
Nancy Pickard, *The Jenny Cain Series*, 1985-
Mary Monica Pulver, *The Kori and Peter Brichter Series*, 1988-

1381
Jan Roberts
A Blood Affair (New York: Simon & Schuster, 1992)

Story type: Action/Adventure

Major character(s): India Grey, Housewife (daughter of a British diplomat)

Time period(s): 1990s

Locale(s): Washington, District of Columbia

What the book is about: After being raped, India Grey is slow to recover but is helped along by two men—Jack Donovan, who wants to marry her and Father Fitzgerald, a young Catholic priest. She marries Donovan and has an affair with Fitzgerald and carries his baby. Neither man is what they appear to be. Her husband is the son of a Mafia don and her priest is an IRA gunman. First crime novel.

Other books you might like:
Brian Garfield, *Necessity*, 1984
Jack Higgins, *Touch the Devil*, 1982
David Morrell, *The Covenant of the Flame*, 1991
Nancy Taylor Rosenberg, *Mitigating Circumstances*, 1992
John Sandford, *Eyes of Prey*, 1990

1382
John Maddox Roberts
SPQR (New York: Avon, 1990)

Story type: Historical; Amateur Detective—Male Lead

Major character(s): Decius Caecilius Metellus the Younger, Government Official

Time period(s): 1st century B.C. (70 B.C.)

Locale(s): Rome, Italy

What the book is about: Decius is determined to investigate the connection between the garroting of an ex-slave and the disembowlment of a foreign merchant - despite apathy, threats, and attempted bribery. First mystery.

Other books you might like:
Lindsey Davis, *The Silver Pigs*, 1989
Margaret Doody, *Aristotle, Detective*, 1980

1383
Les Roberts
The Cleveland Connection (New York: St. Martins, 1993)

Series: Milan Jacovich

Story type: Private Detective—Male Lead

Major character(s): Milan Jacovich, Detective—Private

Time period(s): 1990s

Locale(s): Cleveland, Ohio

What the book is about: Hired by the good-looking granddaughter to find the missing Bogdan Zdrale, Milan Jacovich soon finds himself involved in the hunt for war criminals and global politics.

Other books you might like:
Robert Crais, *The Monkey's Raincoat*, 1987
Michael Z. Lewin, *The Albert Samson Series*, 1974-
James E. Martin, *The Mercy Trap*, 1989
Jonathan Valin, *The Harry Stoner Series*, 1980-

1384
Les Roberts
Deep Shaker (New York: St. Martin's, 1991)

Series: Milan Jacovich

Story type: Private Detective—Male Lead

Major character(s): Milan Jacovich, Detective—Private

Time period(s): 1990s

Locale(s): Cleveland, Ohio

What the book is about: Milan is asked by a friend to look into the friend's son's supposed drug dealing. What Milan finds isn't pretty and to break up the drug ring without sending the friend's son to jail won't be easy. But he is determined to try.

Other books you might like:
Wayne Dundee, *The Burning Season*, 1988
Earl Emerson, *The Thomas Black Series*, 1985-
Loren D. Estleman, *The Amos Walker Series*, 1980-
Rob Kantner, *The Back Door Man*, 1986
Robert B. Parker, *God Save the Child*, 1975

1385
Les Roberts
The Duke of Cleveland (New York: St. Martin's, 1995)

Series: Milan Jacovich

Story type: Private Detective—Male Lead

Major character(s): Milan Jacovich, Detective—Private

Time period(s): 1990s

Locale(s): Cleveland, Ohio

What the book is about: Milan's latest client is a woman trying to find a man, supposedly an art broker, to whom she lent $18,000. Milan soon discovers that his client is not the only woman this fellow has left holding the bag. During his search for the missing man, he gets involved with a gangster, gallery owner, and one pretty artist—who is soon killed.

Other books you might like:
Robert Crais, *The Elvis Cole Series*, 1987-
Rob Kantner, *The Ben Perkins Series*, 1987-
Michael Z. Lewin, *The Albert Samson Series*, 1974-
James E. Martin, *The Gil Disbro Series*, 1989-
Jonathan Valin, *The Harry Stoner Series*, 1980-

1386
Les Roberts
Full Cleveland (New York: St. Martin's, 1989)

Series: Milan Jacovich

Story type: Private Detective—Male Lead

Major character(s): Milan Jacovich, Detective—Private

Time period(s): 1980s

Locale(s): Cleveland, Ohio

What the book is about: Jacovich is hired to find a group of con men who sold ads for a nonexistent magazine. Of course, it gets much more complicated.

Other books you might like:
Wayne Dundee, *The Burning Season*, 1988
Earl Emerson, *The Thomas Black Series*, 1985
Loren D. Estleman, *The Amos Walker Series*, 1980
Rob Kantner, *The Back Door Man*, 1986
Michael Z. Lewin, *The Albert Samson Series*, 1971

1387
Les Roberts
Seeing the Elephant (New York: St. Martin's, 1992)
Series: Saxon
Story type: Private Detective—Male Lead
Major character(s): Saxon, Detective—Private, Actor
Time period(s): 1990s
Locale(s): Chicago, Illinois
What the book is about: Saxon flies to Chicago for the funeral of his mentor in the PI business. When he discovers that the man died from a drug overdose he is immediately suspicious - his friend, though a serious alcoholic, hated drugs. Determined to find the truth - painful though it may be - Saxon sets out to investigate his friend's life.
Other books you might like:
Robert Crais, *The Monkey's Raincoat*, 1987
Parnell Hall, *Actor*, 1993
Richard Stark, *The Grofield Series*, 1969-1974
Wayne Warga, *Hardcover*, 1987
Collin Wilcox, *Except for the Bones*, 1992

1388
Lora Roberts
Murder in a Nice Neighborhood (New York: Fawcett, 1994)
Story type: Amateur Detective—Female Lead
Major character(s): Liz Sullivan, Journalist (free-lance writer), Streetperson; Paul Drake, Police Officer
Time period(s): 1990s
Locale(s): Palo Alto, California
What the book is about: Liz Sullivan is homeless by choice because she doesn't want to be tied down. One night while getting ready to sleep in her VW van, she is hassled by another vagrant, Pigpen Murphy. She fends him off but the next morning he is found dead under her van. Of course she is the obvious suspect. She knows she didn't do it and finding the real killer seems to be the only way to prove it. Along the way she finds friends she didn't know she had including the unfortunately named policeman, Paul Drake.
Other books you might like:
Barbara D'Amato, *The Cat Marsala Series*, 1990-
Jaqueline Girdner, *The Kate Jasper Series*, 1990-
Susan Kelly, *The Liz Connors Series*, 1986-
Kathryn Lasky Knight, *The Calista Jacobs Series*, 1986-
Kerry Tucker, *The Libby Kincaid Series*, 1991-

1389
Stephen Robinett
Final Option (New York: Avon, 1990)
Story type: Amateur Detective—Male Lead
Major character(s): Jerry Jeeter, Journalist (Financial reporter)
Time period(s): 1980s
Locale(s): New York, New York
What the book is about: While writing a story on the disappearance of a Wall Street whiz kid, Jeeter finds that he's not the only one interested in what happened.
Other books you might like:
Lawrence Meyer, *A Capitol Crime*, 1977
Annette Meyers, *The Big Killing*, 1989

1390
Lynda S. Robinson
Murder in the Place of Anubis (New York: Walker, 1994)
Story type: Historical; Amateur Detective—Male Lead
Major character(s): Lord Meren, Nobleman (confidant of the pharaoh); Tutankhamun, Ruler (pharaoh), Historical Figure
Time period(s): 14th century B.C.
Locale(s): Thebes, Egypt
What the book is about: The discovery of an extra body in the sacred Place of Anubis could cause endless problems for the pharaoh if Lord Meren cannot get to the bottom of the mystery. Who killed the scribe Hormin and how did his body end up where it did? First mystery.
Other books you might like:
Ron Burns, *Roman Nights*, 1991
Lindsey Davis, *The Marcus Didius Series*, 1989-
John Maddox Roberts, *The SPQR Series*, 1990-
Steven Saylor, *Catalina's Riddle*, 1993

1391
Patricia Robinson
A Trick of Light (New York: St. Martin's, 1994)
Story type: Amateur Detective—Female Lead
Major character(s): Jervey Parmalee, Actress; Roberta Parmalee, Actress (Jervey's mother)
Time period(s): 1990s
Locale(s): South Carolina
What the book is about: Jervey Parmalee has returned home to direct a play that was originally done by her father. She is trying to collect all the original cast members and locates all but two, Keith Lynch and Elissa Dowell. When she finds some bones in a mummy case that was used in the original production, she is convinced that they are the bones of one of the missing cast members. After she begins to investigate, someone who may have known something is murdered.
Other books you might like:
Lydia Adamson, *The Alice Nestleton Series*, 1991-
P.M. Carlson, *Rehearsal for Murder*, 1988
Jane Dentinger, *The Queen Is Dead*, 1994
Gillian B. Farrell, *Alibi for an Actress*, 1993
Anne Morice, *The Tessa Crichton Series*, 1979-1993

1392
Peter Robinson
A Dedicated Man (New York: Scribners, 1991)
Series: Inspector Alan Banks

Story type: Police Procedural—Male Lead

Major character(s): Alan Banks, Police Officer (detective chief inspector)

Time period(s): 1990s

Locale(s): Helmthorpe, England

What the book is about: The body of wealthy archeologist Henry Steadman is found outside of Helmthorpe. When Inspector Banks begins to investigate he has trouble finding anyone with the motive and opportunity. Then there is another murder—perhaps to stop someone from talking. Banks finds that he must delve deep into Steadman's past to find the truth.

Other books you might like:
Colin Dexter, *The Dead of Jericho*, 1981
Elizabeth George, *A Great Deliverance*, 1988
Reginald Hill, *Ruling Passion*, 1973
Sharyn McCrumb, *If Ever I Return, Pretty Peggy-O*, 1990
Dorothy Simpson, *Six Feet Under*, 1982

1393
Peter Robinson
Gallows View (New York: Scribners, 1990)

Series: Inspector Alan Banks

Story type: Police Procedural—Male Lead

Major character(s): Alan Banks, Police Officer (chief inspector)

Time period(s): 1990s

Locale(s): Eastvale, England (Yorkshire)

What the book is about: The police of Eastvale have problems. There is a peeping tom frightening young women and a gang terrorizing and robbing elderly women. Feminists are up in arms over the failure to catch the peeper and an old woman is found dead in her home. Banks has all he can handle when psychologist Jenny Fuller is assigned to help. Although happily married, Banks is drawn to Jenny too.

Other books you might like:
Elizabeth George, *A Great Deliverance*, 1988
Caroline Graham, *The Killings at Badger's Drift*, 1987
Martha Grimes, *The Man with a Load of Mischief*, 1981
Janet Neel, *Death of a Partner*, 1991
Ruth Rendell, *The Inspector Wexford Series*, 1964-

1394
Peter Robinson
The Hanging Valley (New York: Scribners, 1992)

Series: Inspector Alan Banks

Story type: Police Procedural—Male Lead

Major character(s): Alan Banks, Police Officer (inspector)

Time period(s): 1990s

Locale(s): Swainshead, England (Yorkshire); Canada

What the book is about: The recent murder of a young man visiting from Canada takes Inspector Banks back five years to the murder of a private detective investigating yet an earlier murder of a young girl and a woman's disappearance at the same time. Before finding the truth about the young man's murder, Banks must travel to Canada to try and find the woman gone missing earlier.

Other books you might like:
Colin Dexter, *The Inspector Morse Series*, 1975-
Elizabeth George, *The Inspector Lynley Series*, 1987-
Reginald Hill, *The Dalziel and Pascoe Series*, 1977-
Ruth Rendell, *The Inspector Wexford Series*, 1965-
Dorothy Simpson, *The Inspector Thanet Series*, 1981-

1395
Peter Robinson
A Necessary End (New York: Scribners, 1992)

Series: Inspector Alan Banks

Story type: Police Procedural—Male Lead

Major character(s): Alan Banks, Police Officer (chief inspector); Richard "Dirty Dick" Burgess, Police Officer (special investigator, CID)

Time period(s): 1990s

Locale(s): Eastvale, England

What the book is about: A murderer has struck during an anti-nuclear demonstration. Since the victim is a police officer Dirty Dick Burgess is sent up from London to help with the investigation. He and Chief Inspector Banks are not in agreement as to how to proceed—and that's putting it mildly.

Other books you might like:
Elizabeth George, *A Great Deliverance*, 1988
Caroline Graham, *The Killings at Badger's Drift*, 1987
Martha Grimes, *The Old Silent*, 1990
Janet Neel, *Death of a Partner*, 1991
Ruth Rendell, *The Inspector Wexford Series*, 1964-

1396
Peter Robinson
Past Reason Hated (New York: Scribners, 1993)

Series: Inspector Alan Banks

Story type: Police Procedural—Male Lead

Major character(s): Alan Banks, Police Officer (inspector)

Time period(s): 1990s

Locale(s): Yorkshire, England

What the book is about: Two murders, one of a lesbian, the other of an old lecher, seem to be tied together with the slashing of the costumes for a production of Twelfth Night and the near-fatal strangulation of detective Susan Gay. Inspector Alan Banks must determine what ties these apparently unrelated events together. It's possible that there may be more than one guilty party or that the person responsible may, in fact, be a member of the police force.

Other books you might like:
Colin Dexter, *The Inspector Morse Series*, 1975-
Deborah Crombie, *All Shall Be Well*, 1994
Elizabeth George, *The Inspector Lynley Series*, 1987-
Ruth Rendell, *The Inspector Wexford Series*, 1965-
Medora Sale, *The Inspector Sanders Series*, 1986-

1397
Peter Robinson
Wednesday's Child (New York: Scribners, 1994)
Series: Inspector Alan Banks
Story type: Police Procedural—Male Lead
Major character(s): Alan Banks, Police Officer (inspector); Susan Gray, Police Officer (detective constable)
Time period(s): 1990s
Locale(s): Yorkshire, England
What the book is about: Inspector Alan Banks is investigating the abduction of seven-year-old Gemma Scupham, who was taken from her single mother by a couple posing as social workers. At the same time he is trying to track down the murderer of an ex-con found in an abandoned mine.
Other books you might like:
Deborah Crombie, *The Duncan Kincaid Series*, 1993-
Colin Dexter, *The Inspector Morse Series*, 1975-
Caroline Graham, *The Inspector Barnaby Series*, 1987-
Ruth Rendell, *The Inspector Wexford Series*, 1965-
Medora Sale, *The Inspector Sanders Series*, 1986-

1398
Julie Robitaille
Jinx (Tulsa, Oklahoma: Council Oak, 1991)
Story type: Amateur Detective—Female Lead
Major character(s): Kit Powell, Journalist (TV reporter)
Time period(s): 1990s
Locale(s): San Diego, California
What the book is about: Recently promoted to on camera sports reporter, Kit Powell is present when the general manager of the Sharks football team falls from his skybox. Was he pushed? Kit is determined to discover what, if anything, is behind his death. First novel.
Other books you might like:
Barbara D'Amato, *The Cat Marsala Series*, 1989-
Karen Kijewski, *The Kat Colorado Series*, 1989-
Marcia Muller, *The Joanna Stark Series*, 1987-
Meg O'Brien, *The Jessica James Series*, 1990-
Sara Paretsky, *The V.I. Warshawski Series*, 1982-

1399
Annette Roome
A Second Shot in the Dark (New York: Crown, 1992)
Series: Chris Martin
Story type: Amateur Detective—Female Lead
Major character(s): Chris Martin, Journalist (reporter)
Time period(s): 1990s
Locale(s): England
What the book is about: Assigned to cover the death of a woman thought to be the latest victim of the "Face Murderer," Chris discovers that those closest to the victim have stories that don't add up. As she continues to investigate she becomes a target. While this is going on, her personal life is a shambles as her husband, who she has left, is badgering her to take him back.
Other books you might like:
Antonia Fraser, *The Jemima Shore Series*, 1977-
Anne Morice, *The Tessa Crichton Series*, 1970-
Janet Neel, *Death's Bright Angel*, 1988
Eve K. Sandstrom, *Death Down Home*, 1990
Sarah Shankman, *First Kill All the Lawyers*, 1988

1400
Richard Rosen
World of Hurt (New York: Walker, 1994)
Series: Harvey Blissberg
Story type: Private Detective—Male Lead
Major character(s): Harvey Blissberg, Detective—Private (former baseball player)
Time period(s): 1990s
Locale(s): Portland, Maine; Garden Hills, Illinois (suburb of Chicago)
What the book is about: Harvey Blissberg finds himself travelling between Portland, Maine and the suburbs of Chicago while investigating the life of dead realtor Larry Peplow. Was Peplow's death related to the suicide of a woman in Maine from his past life (he used to be a psychotherapist), or is it something more recent?
Other books you might like:
Robert Crais, *The Elvis Cole Series*, 1987-
David Everson, *Suicide Squeeze*, 1991
Jeremiah Healy, *The John Francis Cuddy Series*, 1984-
Robert B. Parker, *The Spenser Series*, 1974-
Maynard F. Thomson, *Trade Secrets*, 1994

1401
Nancy Taylor Rosenberg
Mitigating Circumstances (New York: Dutton, 1993)
Story type: Legal; Psychological Suspense
Major character(s): Lily Forrester, Lawyer (assistant district attorney)
Time period(s): 1990s
Locale(s): Los Angeles, California
What the book is about: After her daughter is raped while she watches, Lily Forrester must decide whether to turn the man into the police or try to find and punish him herself. When she does decide, what will the repercussions be, both for herself and for her daughter? First novel.

Other books you might like:
Susan Wittig Albert, *Thyme of Death*, 1992
Harrison Arnston, *Trade-Off*, 1993
Susan Kelly, *And Soon I'll Come to Kill You*, 1991
Marlys Millhiser, *Murder at Moot Point*, 1992
Judith Van Gieson, *The Other Side of Death*, 1991

1402
Jonathan Ross (Pseudonym of John Rossiter)
A Time for Dying (New York: St. Martin's, 1989)
Series: Inspector George Rogers
Story type: Police Procedural—Male Lead
Major character(s): George Rogers, Police Officer
Time period(s): 1980s
What the book is about: When a drug dealer is killed by a crossbow, Rogers must find the killer and find the kidnapped woman that the drug dealer lived with.
Other books you might like:
Douglas Clark, *Premedicated Murder*, 1976
Michael Gilbert, *Blood and Judgement*, 1959
June Thomson, *Death Cap*, 1977
John Wainwright, *The Venus Fly Trap*, 1980

1403
Kate Ross
A Broken Vessel (New York: Viking, 1994)
Series: Julian Kestrel
Story type: Historical
Major character(s): Julian Kestrel, Gentleman; Sally Stokes, Criminal, Prostitute
Time period(s): 1820s
Locale(s): London, England
What the book is about: Aristocratic dandy Julian Kestrel gets involved with the sister of his valet, Sally Stokes, a prostitute who likes to steal the handkerchiefs from her customers. One such handkerchief has a letter with it from a young woman who is depressed over her current position. Julian and Sally decide to see if they can find out the identity of both the woman and the owner of the handkerchief. What seems to be a fairly innocent task soon puts Sally and Julian in serious jeopardy.
Other books you might like:
Elizabeth Eyre, *Death of the Duchess*, 1992
Richard Falkirk, *The Blackstone Series*, 1973-1977
John Gardner, *The Moriarty Series*, 1974-1976
Ray Harrison, *Tincture of Death*, 1989
Raymond Paul, *The Thomas Street Horror*, 1982

1404
Kate Ross
Cut to the Quick (New York: Viking, 1993)
Series: Julian Kestrel
Story type: Historical; Amateur Detective—Male Lead
Major character(s): Julian Kestrel, Gentleman

Time period(s): 1820s
Locale(s): England
What the book is about: When Julian Kestrel arrives at the country estate of Sir Robert Fontclair for the wedding of a reluctant bride and groom, he soon finds himself involved in murder and intrigue. First the reluctant bride asks for his help in stopping the wedding, then he finds a dead woman, whom nobody seems to know, in his bed. He and his servant are both suspected of the murder, so he must get to work and solve the crime. First mystery.
Other books you might like:
P.C. Doherty, *The Hugh Corbett Series*, 1985-
Elizabeth Eyre, *Death of the Duchess*, 1992
Richard Falkirk, *Blackstone*, 1973
John Gardner, *The Return of Moriarty*, 1974
Raymond Paul, *The Thomas Street Horror*, 1982

1405
Rebecca Rothenberg
The Bulrush Murders (New York: Carroll & Graf, 1991)
Story type: Amateur Detective
Major character(s): Claire Sharples, Scientist (microbiologist); Sam Cooper, Scientist
Time period(s): 1990s
Locale(s): California (San Joaquin valley)
What the book is about: At an agricultural research center in California scientists Claire Sharples and Sam Cooper work together to try to figure out why a Mexican family's farm crops seem helpless in the face of nature. When the family's young son is killed they realize that more than crops are at stake. While this is happening they are also working on their relationship and learning to trust one another. First novel.
Other books you might like:
Patricia D. Cornwell, *Postmortem*, 1990
Michael Crichton, *Jurassic Park*, 1991
Charlotte Elkins, *A Wicked Slice*, 1989 (Aaron Elkins, co-author)
Kathryn Lasky Knight, *Trace Elements*, 1986

1406
Jennifer Rowe
Death in Store (New York: Doubleday, 1992)
Story type: Amateur Detective—Female Lead; Collection
Major character(s): Verity Birdwood, Businesswoman
Locale(s): Australia
What the book is about: A collection of six short stories and two novellas featuring Verity Birdwood. The title novella takes place in a department store at Christmas when someone takes a pair of scissors to Santa Claus.
Other books you might like:
Eleanor Boylan, *Working Murder*, 1989
Agatha Christie, *The Miss Marple Series*, 1930-1976
Kate Morgan, *The Dewey James Series*, 1990-
David Osborn, *The Margaret Barlow Series*, 1990-
John Sherwood, *The Celia Grant Series*, 1984-

1407
Peter Rowland
The Disappearance of Edwin Drood (New York: St. Martin's, 1992)

Story type: Historical; Private Detective—Male Lead

Major character(s): Sherlock Holmes, Detective—Private

Time period(s): 1890s (1894)

Locale(s): England

What the book is about: At the urging of John Jasper, Sherlock Holmes agrees to look into the disappearance of Edwin Drood. First novel. Another attempt to provide answers to Charles Dickens' unfinished detective novel.

Other books you might like:
Richard M. Baker, *The Drood Murder Case*, 1951
Charles Dickens, *The Mystery of Edwin Drood*, 1870
Loren D. Estleman, *Sherlock Holmes vs. Dracula*, 1978
Nicholas Meyer, *The Seven-Percent Solution*, 1974

1408
Betty Rowlands
Exhaustive Enquiries (New York: Walker, 1994)

Series: Melissa Craig

Story type: Amateur Detective—Female Lead

Major character(s): Melissa Craig, Writer (of mysteries); Ken Harris, Police Officer (detective chief inspector)

Time period(s): 1990s

Locale(s): The Cotswolds, England

What the book is about: Mystery writer Melissa Craig is asked by millionaire Richard Mitchell to write a murder mystery script for his birthday which coincides with Halloween. During rehearsal someone is killed, supposedly in an accidental fall. Mitchell thinks it was murder and asks Melissa to investigate. With the help of her friend Inspector Harris, she succeeds in finding the truth.

Other books you might like:
Deborah Crombie, *A Share in Death*, 1993
Ann Granger, *Cold in the Earth*, 1993
Susan B. Kelly, *Hope Against Hope*, 1991
Janet Neel, *Death's Bright Angel*, 1991
Medora Sale, *Murder in a Good Cause*, 1990

1409
Betty Rowlands
Over the Edge (New York: Walker, 1993)

Series: Melissa Craig

Story type: Amateur Detective—Female Lead

Major character(s): Melissa Craig, Writer (of mysteries)

Time period(s): 1990s

Locale(s): France

What the book is about: Melissa Craig is researching her next novel in the south of France near the Cevannes mountains. Soon after her arrival, two bodies are found at the bottom of the mountains. With nothing but research to keep her occupied, Melissa sets out to find the guilty party or parties. It appears that the deaths may have their roots in the Nazi occupation and perhaps as far back as religious conspiracies of the 17th and 18th centuries.

Other books you might like:
Aaron Elkins, *Old Bones*, 1987
Charlaine Harris, *A Bone to Pick*, 1992
Patricia Moyes, *Death on the Agenda*, 1962
Elizabeth Peters, *Trojan Gold*, 1987
Celestine Sibley, *Ah, Sweet Mystery*, 1991

1410
S.J. Rozan
China Trade (New York: St. Martin's, 1994)

Story type: Private Detective—Female Lead

Major character(s): Lydia Chin, Detective—Private (Asian American)

Time period(s): 1990s

Locale(s): New York, New York

What the book is about: Lydia Chin is hired by the Chinatown Pride Museum to recover some stolen antiques. What she discovers is a theft ring that involves the gangs of Chinatown. She sets herself up for a killer to break the ring. First novel.

Other books you might like:
Nikki Baker, *In the Game*, 1991
Linda Barnes, *Coyote*, 1990
Karen Kijewski, *Katwalk*, 1989
Marcia Muller, *Dark Star*, 1987
Sara Paretsky, *Tunnel Vision*, 1994

1411
Jane Rubino
Death of a DJ (Aurora, Colorado: Write Way, 1995)

Story type: Amateur Detective—Female Lead

Major character(s): Cat Austen, Writer; Vic Cardenas, Police Officer, Widow(er)

Time period(s): 1990s

Locale(s): Ocean City, New Jersey

What the book is about: Cat Austen is on assignment to do a piece on radio shock-jocks. She gets more involved than she wants to be with a pair called Tom and Jerry when Jerry is killed during a stunt called "The Perfect Murder". Instead of pretending to be a corpse, Jerry turns out to be a real one. Since he has offended nearly everyone, finding his killer won't be an easy task. First novel.

Other books you might like:
Natasha Cooper, *Bloody Roses*, 1993
Stan Cutler, *Shot on Location*, 1993
Denise Osborne, *Murder Offscreen*, 1994
Barbara Burnett Smith, *Writers of the Purple Sage*, 1995
Elizabeth Daniels Squire, *The Peaches Dann Series*, 1993-

1412
Patrick Ruell (Pseudonym of Reginald Hill)
Dream of Darkness (Vermont: Foul Play, 1991)

Story type: Psychological Suspense

Major character(s): Sairey Ellis, Student; Nigel Ellis, Political Figure, Parent (Sairey's father, involved in e)

Time period(s): 1980s (1988)

Locale(s): England

What the book is about: Eighteen year old Sairey Ellis is haunted by dreams about her mother's death in Uganda. At the same time, her father is writing his memoirs which some people would just as soon not see finished. When danger threatens, Sairey and her father must face the truth about the past.

Other books you might like:
Michael Dibdin, *The Tryst*, 1990
Julian Symons, *Death's Darkest Face*, 1990
Margaret Yorke, *Admit to Murder*, 1990

1413
Alan Russell
The Hotel Detective (New York: Musterious, 1994)

Story type: Amateur Detective—Male Lead

Major character(s): Am Caulfield, Hotel Worker (assistant general manager)

Time period(s): 1990s

Locale(s): San Diego, California

What the book is about: While the boss is away, assistant general manager Am Caulfield hopes to play. Unfortunately, before he left, the boss insisted that Am be head of security for the hotel as well as doing his regular job. He is quickly confronted with such diverse doings as an apparent suicide, a lingerie thief, and the murders of a local lawyer and the lawyer's mistress. He must get all things under control before his boss gets back. And then there is the Bob Johnsons Society convention. Yes, a convention of hundreds of guys named Bob Johnson.

Other books you might like:
Robert Crais, *Lullaby Town*, 1992
William L. DeAndrea, *The Matt Cobb Series*, 1978-
Janet Evanovich, *One for the Money*, 1994
Arthur Lyons, *The Jacob Asch Series*, 1974-
Dianne G. Pugh, *Slow Squeeze*, 1994

1414
Alan Russell
No Sign of Murder (New York: Walker, 1990)

Story type: Private Detective—Male Lead

Major character(s): Stuart Winter, Detective—Private

Time period(s): 1990s

Locale(s): San Francisco, California

What the book is about: Stuart is hired by Tammy Walters to find her missing daughter, Anita, a beautiful deaf model. As he investigates he discovers Anita was involved with many strange people - a father she hated, an ex-roommate whose boyfriend she stole, a group of avant-garde artists with strange tastes in sex and a scientist who wants to teach sign language to gorillas. First novel.

Other books you might like:
William Babula, *St. John's Baptism*, 1988
H. Edward Hunsburger, *Death Signs*, 1988
Jack Livingston, *The Joe Binney Series*, 1982-
Bill Pronzini, *The Nameless Detective Series*, 1971-
Shelley Singer, *The Jake Samson Series*, 1983-

1415
E.S. Russell
Dead Easy (New York: Walker, 1992)

Series: Ben Louis

Story type: Amateur Detective—Male Lead

Major character(s): Ben Louis, Principal (high school)

Time period(s): 1990s

Locale(s): Manton, Massachusetts

What the book is about: Bizarre murders and other strange happenings are taking place in the small town of Manton. A town councilman is electrocuted, another man is discovered dead in a skin-diving suit and the school board suspends Ben Louis for really silly reasons. Ben and his wife Jane decide that all of these things are related and set out to prove it.

Other books you might like:
Susan Isaacs, *Compromising Positions*, 1978
A.J. Orde, *A Little Neighborhood Murder*, 1989
Gillian Roberts, *Caught Dead in Philadelphia*, 1989
Valerie Wolzien, *Murder at the PTA Luncheon*, 1988
Mark Richard Zubro, *A Simple Suburban Murder*, 1988

1416
Randy Russell
Caught Looking (New York: Doubleday, 1992)

Series: Alton "Rooster" Franklin

Story type: Action/Adventure

Major character(s): Alton "Rooster" Franklin, Criminal (ex-con; gambler)

Time period(s): 1990s

Locale(s): Kansas City, Missouri

What the book is about: Because he served time for car theft Rooster is asked to help the friend of a friend recover a stolen car. Just so happens that the car belongs to a pitcher for the Kansas City Royals and his special glove was in the car. Making contact with the car thief leads Rooster into a hornet's nest of blackmail, adultery and murder.

1417 Sale

Other books you might like:
James Colbert, *Skinny Man*, 1991
Eugene Izzi, *Prowlers*, 1990
Tom Kakonis, *Michigan Roll*, 1989
Elmore Leonard, *Stick*, 1986
Charles Willeford, *Miami Blues*, 1984

1417
Medora Sale
Murder in a Good Cause (New York: Scribners, 1990)
Series: John Sanders/Harriet Jeffries
Story type: Police Procedural; Amateur Detective
Major character(s): John Sanders, Police Officer (inspector); Harriet Jeffries, Photographer (Architectural)
Time period(s): 1990s
Locale(s): Toronto, Ontario, Canada
What the book is about: While at a party Harriet witnesses the death of the hostess. Murder or suicide? As old flame Inspector John Sanders investigates, he and Harriet renew their relationship while she puts herself in danger by insinuating herself into the murdered woman's household. At the same time Sanders is also investigating a series of break-ins at wealthy residences. These may tie into the murder case.

Other books you might like:
Alisa Craig, *Murder Goes Mumming*, 1981
Laurence Gough, *Hot Shots*, 1990
Dorothy L. Sayers, *Strong Poison*, 1930
Ted Wood, *On the Inside*, 1990
Eric Wright, *A Question of Murder*, 1988

1418
Medora Sale
Murder in Focus (New York: Scribner's, 1989)
Series: John Sanders/Harriet Jeffries
Story type: Police Procedural
Major character(s): John Sanders, Police Officer (inspector); Harriet Jeffries, Photographer (Architectural)
Time period(s): 1980s
Locale(s): Ottawa, Ontario, Canada
What the book is about: Harriet Jeffries and Inspector John Sanders are in Ottawa for an international trade show when a picture that Harriet takes gets them involved in assassination and treachery at the highest level of the government.

Other books you might like:
Alisa Craig, *Murder Goes Mumming*, 1981
Tim Heald, *Murder at Moose Jaw*, 1981
Ted Wood, *Dead in the Water*, 1983
Eric Wright, *The Man Who Changed His Name*, 1986
L.R. Wright, *The Suspect*, 1985

1419
Medora Sale
Pursued by Shadows (New York: Scribners, 1992)
Series: John Sanders/Harriet Jeffries
Story type: Police Procedural; Amateur Detective
Major character(s): John Sanders, Police Officer (inspector); Harriet Jeffries, Photographer (Architectural)
Time period(s): 1990s
Locale(s): Toronto, Ontario, Canada
What the book is about: Harriet's old lover, Guy Beaumont, is back in town looking for his girlfriend, Jane Sinclair, who was also Harriet's assistant before she and Guy ran off together. Jane has run off with something of Guy's worth a great deal of money. And he wants it back. Guy tries to question Harriet not so gently and John is outraged. When Jane writes to ask for help they try to find her but she disappears again. When Guy is found dead in Harriet's living room, John is a prime suspect. Now they have to solve the mystery to clear themselves.

Other books you might like:
Alisa Craig, *Murder Goes Mumming*, 1981
David Delman, *The Last Gambit*, 1991
Wendy Hornsby, *No Harm*, 1989
Susan B. Kelly, *Hope Against Hope*, 1991
Janet Neel, *Death's Bright Angel*, 1988

1420
Medora Sale
Short Cut to Santa Fe (New York: Scribners, 1994)
Series: John Sanders/Harriet Jeffries
Story type: Police Procedural; Action/Adventure
Major character(s): John Sanders, Police Officer (inspector); Harriet Jeffries, Photographer (Architectural)
Time period(s): 1990s
Locale(s): Taos, New Mexico
What the book is about: Harriet Jeffries has asked John Sanders to join her in New Mexico for a bit of vacation and romance. John flies to Santa Fe on a charter plan with a tour group. The tour bus leaves without two young children, so John and Harriet offer to catch-up with the bus and return the youngsters. They drive into a bloody bus hijacking and are taken prisoner themselves. They become involved with the group and soon realize that nobody on the tour seems to be who they say they are.

Other books you might like:
Alisa Craig, *Trouble in the Brasses*, 1989
Margaret Duffy, *Who Killed Cock Robin?*, 1990
Wendy Hornsby, *No Harm*, 1989
Susan Kelly, *The Summertime Soldiers*, 1989
Mary Monica Pulver, *The Unforgiving Minutes*, 1988

1421
James Sallis
Black Hornet (New York: Carroll & Graf, 1994)
Series: Lew Griffin
Story type: Private Detective—Male Lead
Major character(s): Lew Griffin, Detective—Private (African American)

Time period(s): 1960s

Locale(s): New Orleans, Louisiana

What the book is about: Lew Griffin is a witness when a white female journalist he has come to know is gunned down by a black man. While trying to track the shooter, he befriends a white cop whose brother was shot by the same person. At the same time, Lew is trying to understand the black power movement.

Other books you might like:
James Lee Burke, *The Neon Rain*, 1986
James Ellroy, *American Tabloid*, 1995
Loren D. Estleman, *Motown*, 1992
Jon A. Jackson, *The Blind Pig*, 1978
Walter Mosley, *White Butterfly*, 1993

1422

James Sallis
Moth (New York: Carroll & Graf, 1993)

Series: Lew Griffin

Story type: Private Detective—Male Lead

Major character(s): Lew Griffin, Detective—Private, Writer (novelist; recovering alcoholic)

Time period(s): 1990s

Locale(s): New Orleans, Louisiana

What the book is about: Lew Griffin is trying to find the runaway daughter of his recently deceased lover, LaVerne Adams. Some of the story is told in flashbacks detailing the history of Lew and LaVerne, but the bulk of the story concerns his search for the missing daughter. Along the way he gets involved with a French teacher, LaVerne's mother, a counselor at a women's shelter and assorted low-lifes, all the while thinking about his son with whom he doesn't have much of a relationship.

Other books you might like:
Lawrence Block, *The Matt Scudder Series*, 1976-
James Lee Burke, *The Dave Robicheaux Series*, 1986-
James Ellroy, *The Black Dahlia*, 1987
John Lutz, *Scorcher*, 1987
Julie Smith, *New Orleans Mourning*, 1990

1423

William Sanders
The Next Victim (New York: St. Martin's, 1993)

Story type: Private Detective—Male Lead; Amateur Detective—Male Lead

Major character(s): Taggert Roper, Writer (of Westerns), Detective—Private (unofficial)

Time period(s): 1990s

Locale(s): Tulsa, Oklahoma

What the book is about: Taggert Roper is not doing well with his writing so what little money he has comes from his unofficial investigating. He is in no position to refuse when Amy Matson asks him to look into the murder of a prostitute who was Amy's mother. She wants to know what her past life was like. The investigation leads to a local famous TV evangelist and his family, and some people don't want Tag investigating.

Other books you might like:
Jerome Doolittle, *The Tom Bethany Series*, 1990-
Kinky Friedman, *The Kinky Friedman Series*, 1987-
Robert J. Randisi, *The Miles Jacoby Series*, 1984-
William J. Reynolds, *The Naked Eye*, 1990
Walter Satterthwait, *A Flower in the Desert*, 1992

1424

John Sandford
Night Prey (New York: Putnam, 1994)

Series: Lucas Davenport

Story type: Police Procedural—Male Lead

Major character(s): Lucas Davenport, Police Officer (deputy police chief)

Time period(s): 1990s

Locale(s): Minneapolis, Minnesota

What the book is about: Lucas Davenport is assigned the task of tracking down the murderer of young women. Much to his dismay, he is to be assisted in this task by Bureau of Criminal Apprehension investigator Meagan Connell, who is dying of cancer. She wants to capture this guy before she dies, which though understandable, doesn't make her easy to work with. Davenport is also assigned a new partner, the husband of the mayor's niece and also the former "Officer Friendly", the grade school cop. He's not a great match with the streetwise Davenport.

Other books you might like:
Michael Connelly, *The Harry Bosch Series*, 1992-
Mark Olshaker, *The Edge*, 1994
James Patterson, *Kiss the Girls*, 1995
Ridley Pearson, *No Witnesses*, 1994
Stan Washburn, *Intent to Harm*, 1994

1425

John Sandford (Pseudonym of John Camp)
Rules of Prey (New York: Putnam, 1989)

Story type: Police Procedural—Male Lead

Major character(s): Lucas Davenport, Police Officer (independently wealthy)

Time period(s): 1980s

Locale(s): Minneapolis, Minnesota; St. Paul, Minnesota

What the book is about: A serial killer is loose in the Twin Cities and independently wealthy cop Lucas Davenport is given the assignment of tracking him down.

1426 Sandford

Other books you might like:
Joe Gash, *The El Murders*, 1986
Thomas Harris, *Red Dragon*, 1981
John Katzenbach, *In the Heat of the Summer*, 1982
David L. Lindsey, *A Cold Mind*, 1983
Rex Miller, *Slob*, 1987

1426
John Sandford (Pseudonym of John Camp)
Shadow Prey (New York: Putnam, 1990)

Series: Lucas Davenport

Story type: Police Procedural—Male Lead; Action/Adventure

Major character(s): Lucas Davenport, Police Officer (homicide detective); Lily Rothenberg, Police Officer (on assignment from New York)

Time period(s): 1990s

Locale(s): Minneapolis/St. Paul, Minnesota

What the book is about: Revolving around the rape of a Native American girl by the head of the FBI, the case also involves the murder of politicians and bureaucrats and the relationship between Minneapolis policeman Lucas Davenport and New York policewoman Lily Rothenberg, who has been sent to the Twin Cities to find the link between killings in New York and Minnesota.

Other books you might like:
David L. Lindsey, *Heat From Another Sun*, 1984
Rex Miller, *Stone Shadow*, 1989
Gerald Petievich, *Earth Angels*, 1989
Whitley Strieber, *The Wolfen*, 1978
Joseph Wambaugh, *The Glitter Dome*, 1981

1427
John Sandford (Pseudonym of John Camp)
Silent Prey (New York: Putnam, 1992)

Series: Lucas Davenport

Story type: Police Procedural—Male Lead; Action/Adventure

Major character(s): Lucas Davenport, Police Officer; Michael Bekker, Criminal (psychotic pathologist)

Time period(s): 1990s

Locale(s): New York, New York

What the book is about: Because Lucas Davenport was responsible for the original capture of serial killer Michael Bekker, when Bekker escapes Davenport is asked to come to New York to help find him again. A parallel plot involves police vigilantes who may also have killed a fellow cop. Complicating matters is Davenport's past relationship with New York cop Loty Rothenberg and his current relationship with New York cop Barbara Fell.

Other books you might like:
Thomas Harris, *Red Dragon*, 1981
John Katzenbach, *In the Heat of the Summer*, 1982
David L. Lindsey, *A Cold Mind*, 1983
Ridley Pearson, *Probable Cause*, 1989
Eric Sauter, *Skeletons*, 1990

1428
John Sandford (Pseudonym of John Camp)
Winter Prey (New York: Putnam, 1993)

Series: Lucas Davenport

Story type: Action/Adventure; Police Procedural—Male Lead

Major character(s): Lucas Davenport, Police Officer (on leave); Weather Karkinnen, Doctor (medical examiner)

Time period(s): 1990s

Locale(s): Grant, Wisconsin (north woods)

What the book is about: A family of three is brutally murdered in northern Wisconsin and their house is burned down. Minneapolis policeman Lucas Davenport is living in the area to change his life and is asked by the local cops to get involved, as they have very little experience with this kind of killer. Davenport agrees and finds himself quickly immersed in another serial killer case. He also finds himself getting seriously involved with the local medical examiner, Weather Karkinnen. She is in danger from the killer as well.

Other books you might like:
Nevada Barr, *A Superior Death*, 1994
Thomas Gifford, *Wind Chill Factor*, 1975
Ron Handberg, *Savage Justice*, 1992
Orania Papazoglou, *Charisma*, 1991

1429
J.G. Sandom
Gospel Truths (New York: Doubleday, 1992)

Story type: Police Procedural—Male Lead

Major character(s): Nigel Lyman, Police Officer (Scotland Yard inspector); Kazimierz Grabowski, Religious (Vatican Archbishop)

Time period(s): 1980s (1983)

Locale(s): England; France

What the book is about: Nigel Lyman's life is falling apart. His son has died, his wife has left him and he blames himself for the death of a co-worker. He is given one last chance—the case of a banker who has apparently hanged himself. The banker was an embezzler who was involved with drugs and gun-running with a notorious criminal and an archbishop of the Vatican. Was it murder and do his bosses want him to succeed or fail? First novel.

Other books you might like:
Michael David Anthony, *The Becket Factor*, 1991
Thomas Gifford, *The Assassini*, 1990
Ralph McInerny, *The Noonday Devil*, 1984
Sara Paretsky, *Killing Orders*, 1985
Robert Rosenblum, *The Good Thief*,

1430
Eve K. Sandstrom
Death Down Home (New York: Scribners, 1990)

Series: Nicky and Sam Titus

Story type: Amateur Detective

Major character(s): Nicky Titus, Photographer (bride of Sam); Sam Titus, Military Personnel (Criminal Investigation divisio)

Time period(s): 1990s

Locale(s): Holton, Oklahoma

What the book is about: While stationed in Germany, Sam and Nicky have just been married when Sam is called back to Oklahoma. An accident has left Sam's father in a coma. When they arrive, Sam realizes this couldn't have been an accident. Meanwhile Sam's brother has disappeared. Someone may want the whole family dead. First novel.

Other books you might like:
Al Guthrie, *Grave Murder*, 1990
Jean Hager, *The Grandfather Medicine*, 1989
Bernie Lee, *Murder at Musket Beach*, 1990
Charlotte MacLeod, *The Bilbao Looking Glass*, 1983
E.J. McGill, *Immaculate in Black*, 1991

1431
Eve K. Sandstrom
The Devil Down Home (New York: Scribners, 1991)

Series: Nicky and Sam Titus

Story type: Police Procedural; Amateur Detective

Major character(s): Nicky Titus, Photograhper, Police Officer (sheriff of Catlin County); Sam Titus, Photographer

Time period(s): 1990s

Locale(s): Holton, Oklahoma

What the book is about: Sam and Nicky are out driving when they meet hitchhiker Damon Revels. Damon is decidedly odd but seems relatively harmless so Sam offers to put him up at the jail for the night. Damon leaves to get a meal and that is the last time he is seen alive. His body is found the next day in a prop coffin that was for the Halloween haunted house. There are rumors of Satanic cults at work.

Other books you might like:
Bill Crider, *The Sheriff Dan Rhodes Series*, 1989-
Al Guthrie, *Murder by Tarot*, 1992
Jean Hager, *Night Walker*, 1991
Joan Hess, *Malice in Maggody*, 1987
Anne Wingate, *Death by Deception*, 1988

1432
Eve K. Sandstrom
The Down Home Heifer Heist (New York: Walker, 1993)

Series: Nicky and Sam Titus

Story type: Police Procedural; Amateur Detective

Major character(s): Nicky Titus, Photographer; Sam Titus, Police Officer (sheriff)

Time period(s): 1990s

Locale(s): Holton, Oklahoma (Catlin County)

What the book is about: Sam Titus is involved in investigating the death of local rancher Joe Pilkington. Joe was run down when he apparently came across a gang of modern day cattle rustlers. Nicky is helping as a police photographer but is also involved in more domestic concerns like helping her nephew get his heifer ready for the livestock fair. The case may put them all in danger.

Other books you might like:
Joan Hess, *The Maggody Series*, 1987-
Nancy Pickard, *Bum Steer*, 1990
Mary Monica Pulver, *Original Sin*, 1991
Sheila Simonson, *Mudlark*, 1993
Charlene Weir, *Consider the Crows*, 1993

1433
Jerome Sanford
Miami Heat (New York: St. Martins, 1991)

Story type: Action/Adventure

Major character(s): David Knight, Lawyer (former FBI agent); Jennifer Ferrer, Secretary (former cop)

Time period(s): 1990s

Locale(s): United States; Mexico

What the book is about: David Knight has been cashiered from the FBI and he still doesn't know why when a news item about the death a Cuban emigre starts him on the path toward the truth. But it's a path strewn with obstacles and death. First novel.

Other books you might like:
Anthony Bruno, *Bad Guys*, 1988
James Ellroy, *Blood on the Moon*, 1984
Elmore Leonard, *City Primeval*, 1980
Gerald Petievich, *To Live and Die in L.A.*, 1984
John Westermann, *High Crimes*, 1988

1434
Soledad Santiago
Nightside (New York: Doubleday, 1994)

Story type: Police Procedural; Amateur Detective

Major character(s): Anna Eltern, Social Worker (ex-nun); Jesus O'Shaugnessy, Police Officer (community affairs officer)

Time period(s): 1990s

Locale(s): New York, New York (Hell's Kitchen)

What the book is about: Anna Eltern has enough trouble just running a shelter for street kids, getting funding, and keeping the kids alive. Now there is a serial killer who is murdering young girls. One of her kids is killed, another is charged with the murder, and the pimps and junkies who prey on the children will do anything to get rid of Anna. Officer O'Shaugnessy tries to help but he may not be able to save her.

Other books you might like:
Jeffrey Wilds Deaver, *Manhattan Is My Beat*, 1989
Lee Harris, *The Good Friday Murder*, 1992
James Patterson, *Along Came a Spider*, 1993
Shelley Singer, *Searching for Sara*, 1994
Winona Sullivan, *A Sudden Death at the Norfolk Cafe*, 1993

1435
Soledad Santiago
Room 9 (New York: Doubleday, 1992)

Story type: Amateur Detective—Female Lead

Major character(s): Marie Terranova, Administrator (assistant to the mayor), Single Parent (widow)

Time period(s): 1990s

Locale(s): New York, New York

What the book is about: Marie Terranova is becoming disillusioned with city hall. Trying to balance her job with her responsiblities as a parent is hard enough. Now, after the death of a deputy mayor and the mysterious fires around the city, people are running scared. When a handsome, ambitious reporter begins romancing her, Marie finds herself dragged into a net of conflict of interest and political intrigue that may destroy her.

Other books you might like:
Bill Crider, *The Texas Capitol Murders*, 1991
John Grisham, *The Pelican Brief*, 1992
Mercedes Lambert, *Dogtown*, 1991
Anna Porter, *Hidden Agenda*, 1987
Jean Warmbold, *June Mail*, 1986

1436
Al Sarrantonio
Summer Cool (New York: Walker, 1993)

Story type: Private Detective—Male Lead

Major character(s): Jack Paine, Detective—Private (ex-police officer)

Time period(s): 1990s

Locale(s): Yonkers, New York

What the book is about: Jack Paine is called by Terry Petty, wife of Bobby Petty, and is asked to find Bobby who has quit the police force and disappeared. Bobby was the only cop to stand by Jack when he was set up and busted off the force and Jack wants to help. What Jack finds, however, is a trail of dead bodies and the obvious killer is his friend Bobby.

Other books you might like:
Thomas Bunn, *Closing Costs*, 1990
Harlen Campbell, *Monkey on a Chain*, 1993
Michael Connelly, *The Black Echo*, 1992
Archer Mayor, *Borderlines*, 1990
J.W. Rider, *Jersey Tomatoes*, 1986

1437
Walter Satterthwait
At Ease with the Dead (New York: St. Martins, 1990)

Series: Joshua Croft

Story type: Private Detective—Male Lead

Major character(s): Joshua Croft, Detective—Private (in love with Rita); Rita Mondragon, Businesswoman (owns the Mondragon Detective A), Handicapped (paraplegic)

Time period(s): 1990s

Locale(s): Santa Fe, New Mexico

What the book is about: While camping, Joshua saves Navajo Daniel Begay from three bullies. Later Daniel hires Joshua to find out what happened to the body of a Navajo leader that disappeared 65 years ago when its discoverer was murdered.

Other books you might like:
Jean Hager, *The Grandfather Medicine*, 1989
Tony Hillerman, *The Joe Leaphorn Series*, 1970-
Bernard Schopen, *The Big Silence*, 1989
Richard Martin Stern, *The Johnny Ortiz Series*, 1973-
Judith Van Gieson, *The Other Side of Death*, 1991

1438
Walter Satterthwait
Escapade (New York: St. Martin's, 1995)

Story type: Amateur Detective—Male Lead; Historical

Major character(s): Arthur Conan Doyle, Historical Figure, Writer; Harry Houdini, Historical Figure, Magician

Time period(s): 1920s (1921)

Locale(s): England

What the book is about: Houdini and Doyle are invited to attend a seance at the home of Lord Purleigh. While there they get involved with ghosts, attempted murder, nymphomaniacs, untrustworthy aristocrats, and death.

Other books you might like:
Mark Frost, *The List of 7*, 1993
William Hjortsberg, *Nevermore*, 1994
John T. Lescroart, *Rasputin's Revenge*, 1987

1439
Walter Satterthwait
A Flower in the Desert (New York: St. Martin's, 1992)

Series: Joshua Croft

Story type: Private Detective—Male Lead

Major character(s): Joshua Croft, Detective—Private; Rita Mondragon, Businesswoman (head of detective agency)

Time period(s): 1990s

Locale(s): Sante Fe, New Mexico; Los Angeles, California

What the book is about: Joshua is approached by Roy Alozo to find his wife, Melissa and his daughter, Wynona. Melissa has accused Roy of sexually abusing their daughter and when the courts disagreed, Melissa disappeared with Wynona. Roy wants his daughter back. Joshua doesn't like Roy and refuses the case but the local head of the Mexican mafia, Roy's uncle, makes Joshua an offer he can't refuse. Why is Melissa so frightened and why is the FBI involved?

Other books you might like:
Rex Burns, *Parts Unknown*, 1990
Tony Hillerman, *The Joe Leaphorn Series*, 1970-
Alan Russell, *No Sign of Murder*, 1990
Bernard Schopen, *The Big Silence*, 1989
Judith Van Gieson, *North of the Border*, 1988

1440
Walter Satterthwait
The Hanged Man (New York: St. Martin's, 1993)

Series: Joshua Croft

Story type: Private Detective—Male Lead

Major character(s): Joshua Croft, Detective—Private; Rita Mondragon, Detective—Private (Croft's lover and boss)

Time period(s): 1990s

Locale(s): Santa Fe, New Mexico

What the book is about: At a convention of New Age healers, psychics and other believers, the much detested Quentin Bouvier is found hanged. The police determine it was murder and that a valuable tarot card has been stolen. A tarot reader is arrested and Joshua is hired to prove his innocence. The investigation involves Joshua with as strange a group of folks as he has ever met, but is one of them a murderer?

Other books you might like:
Robert Crais, *The Elvis Cole Series*, 1987-
Loren D. Estleman, *The Amos Walker Series*, 1975-
Jeremiah Healy, *The John Francis Cuddy Series*, 1984-
Arthur Lyons, *The Jacob Asch Series*, 1975-
Judith Van Gieson, *The Other Side of Death*, 1990

1441
Walter Satterthwait
Miss Lizzie (New York: St. Martin's, 1989)

Story type: Amateur Detective—Female Lead

Major character(s): Lizzie Borden, Spinster, Historical Figure (former accused murderer); Amanda Burton, Teenager (13 year old girl)

Time period(s): 1920s (1921)

Locale(s): Massachusetts

What the book is about: When Amanda's stepmother is murdered with an ax the neighbor lady, who is none other than Lizzie Borden is suspected. She and Amanda set out to find the real killer.

Other books you might like:
Ed McBain, *Lizzie*, 1987

1442
Karen Saum
Murder Is Germane (Tallahassee, Florida: Naiad, 1992)

Series: Brigid Donovan

Story type: Amateur Detective—Female Lead

Major character(s): Brigid Donovan, Religious (ex-nun), Lesbian

Time period(s): 1990s

Locale(s): Panama

What the book is about: While visiting Panama, where she was born, Brigid gets involved with drugs, parentage issues and murder. Her trials start with the disappearance of an INS agent who was last seen in Maine and get much more complicated than a simple disappearance.

Other books you might like:
Isabelle Holland, *A Fatal Advent*, 1989
James McCahery, *Grave Undertaking*, 1990
Sister Carol Anne O'Marie, *Advent of Dying*, 1986
Sandra Scoppettone, *Everything You Have Is Mine*, 1991
Pat Welch, *Murder by the Book*, 1990

1443
Eric Sauter
Skeletons (New York: Dutton, 1990)

Story type: Police Procedural—Male Lead

Major character(s): Patrick Paige, Police Officer; Edward Grant, Criminal

Time period(s): 1980s

Locale(s): Philadelphia, Pennsylvania

What the book is about: Patrick Paige has been trying to catch Edward Grant for years, for burglary. Now he wants to catch him for murder.

Other books you might like:
William J. Caunitz, *One Police Plaza*, 1984
Jack Early, *Donato and Daughter*, 1987
Jay Robert Nash, *A Crime Story*, 1981
Richard North Patterson, *The Lasko Tangent*, 1979

1444
Marc Savage
Flamingos (New York: Doubleday, 1992)

Story type: Action/Adventure

Major character(s): Elvis Mahoney, Criminal (African-American), Convict (ex-convict); Joseph Scorcese, Organized Crime Figure (crime boss)

Time period(s): 1990s

Locale(s): Phoenix, Arizona; New York, New York

What the book is about: Elvis Mahoney, small-time crook, is just out of jail teaming up with his old partner and they come to Phoenix looking for the big score. This will involve them with the Scorcese family and organized crime. Joseph Scorcese is in Phoenix recuperating from an attempted assassination attempt. Elvis' big score may be his last as he get involved in a Mafia power struggle.

Other books you might like:
Eugene Izzi, *King of the Hustlers*, 1989
Tom Kakonis, *Michigan Roll*, 1988
Elmore Leonard, *Stick*, 1983
Randy Russell, *Hot Wire*, 1988
Sin Soracco, *Edge City*, 1992

1445
Corinne Holt Sawyer
Murder by Owl Light (New York: Fine, 1992)

Series: Angela Benbow and Caledonia Wingate

Story type: Amateur Detective—Female Lead

Major character(s): Caledonia Wingate, Aged Person; Angela Benbow, Aged Person

Time period(s): 1990s

Locale(s): San Diego, California

What the book is about: Two people have been killed at the retirement home — a repairman and a gardener. Caledonia and Angela try to help the police but their friend Lt. Martinez is not in charge and the new man doesn't want their help. When a new resident, Lena Gardener, is killed, they are determined to solve the crime, especially since Angela is a suspect — accused of theft by Mrs. Gardener right before she died.

Other books you might like:
Richard Barth, *The Margaret Binton Series*, 1978-
B. Comfort, *Grave Consequences*, 1989
Hazel Holt, *Mrs. Malory Investigates*, 1990
David Osborn, *Murder on Martha's Vineyard*, 1990
Virginia Rich, *The Mrs. Potter Series*, 1982-

1446
Corinne Holt Sawyer
Murder Has No Calories (New York: Fine, 1994)

Series: Angela Benbow and Caledonia Wingate

Story type: Amateur Detective—Female Lead

Major character(s): Angela Benbow, Aged Person; Caledonia Wingate, Aged Person

Time period(s): 1990s

Locale(s): San Diego, California

What the book is about: Dorothy McGraw has had a lot of adversity in her life but this may be the last straw. She is the owner of the health spa/fat farm called The Time Out Inn and her chief chef has been murdered—broiled to death in a steam room. She is afraid she may have to close the inn, so she asks her friend, Angela Benbow, to help. Angela talks her friend, Caledonia Wingate, into going to the farm undercover. Can they solve the crime before they discover that losing weight can be murder?

Other books you might like:
Richard Barth, *The Margaret Binton Series*, 1978-
B. Comfort, *The Tish McWhinney Series*, 1986-
Mary Bowen Hall, *The Emma Chizzit Series*, 1989-1994
Hazel Holt, *The Mavis Lashley Series*, 1989-
Susanna Hofmann McShea, *The Pumpkin-Shell Wife*, 1992

1447
Corinne Holt Sawyer
Murder in Gray and White (New York: Fine, 1989)

Series: Angela Benbow and Caledonia Wingate

Story type: Amateur Detective—Female Lead

Major character(s): Angela Benbow, Aged Person; Caledonia Wingate, Aged Person

Time period(s): 1980s

What the book is about: After the murder of an unpopular retirement home resident, Angela and Caledonia can't help trying to assist Lieutenant Martinez in his investigation.

Other books you might like:
Richard Barth, *The Margaret Binton Series*, 1978
Arthur D. Goldstein, *Nobody's Sorry He Got Killed*, 1976
Charlotte MacLeod, *The Family Vault*, 1979

1448
Steven Saylor
Catalina's Riddle (New York: St. Martin's, 1993)

Series: Gordianus the Finder

Story type: Historical; Amateur Detective—Male Lead

Major character(s): Gordianus the Finder, Farmer

Time period(s): 1st century B.C. (63 B.C.)

Locale(s): Etruria, Roman Empire; Rome, Roman Empire

What the book is about: Gordianus has left Rome and is living on a farm in Etruria. His major problem is when to harvest the crop but he finds himself sometimes missing the intrigue of Rome. The intrigue finds him when a messenger from his patron Cicero asks him to entertain the scheming senator, Catalina, and report on anything he learns. Then a headless corpse shows up.

Other books you might like:
Ron Burns, *Roman Nights*, 1991
Lindsey Davis, *The Marcus Didius Series*, 1989-
John Maddox Roberts, *The SPQR Series*, 1990-

1449
Steven Saylor
Roman Blood (New York: St. Martin's, 1991)

Story type: Historical; Private Detective—Male Lead

Major character(s): Gordianus the Finder, Detective—Private; Marcus Tullius Cicero, Historical Figure, Lawyer

Time period(s): 1st century B.C. (80 B.C.)

Locale(s): Rome, Italy

What the book is about: A local P.I. is hired by a lawyer to help his client who has been accused of murdering his father. The P.I. investigates and finds the murder has political implications. Sounds familiar, but all this takes place in ancient Rome, complete with slaves, gladiators and a young Marcus Cicero. First novel.

Other books you might like:
Lindsey Davis, *The Silver Pigs*, 1989
Margaret Doody, *Aristotle, Detective*, 1980
John Maddox Roberts, *SPQR*, 1990

1450
Steven Saylor
The Venus Throw (New York: St. Martin's, 1995)

Series: Gordianus the Finder

Story type: Historical; Private Detective—Male Lead

Major character(s): Gordianus the Finder, Detective—Private

Time period(s): 6th century B.C. (56 B.C.)

Locale(s): Rome, Roman Empire

What the book is about: Rome is expanding it's territory. Currently it is looking to conquer Egypt. King Ptolemy of Egypt has been deposed and seeks sanctuary in Rome. Egyptian.

Other books you might like:
Ron Burns, *The Livinius Severus Series*, 1991-
Lindsey Davis, *The Marcus Didius Series*, 1989-
John Maddox Roberts, *The SPQR Series*, 1990-
Lynda S. Robinson, *Murder in the Place of Anubis*, 1994

1451
S.E. Schenkel
In Blacker Moments (Seattle: AKA/Seattle, 1994)

Story type: Police Procedural; Amateur Detective

Major character(s): Ray Fredrick, Police Officer (chief of detectives); Kay Fredrick, Spouse (Ray's wife)

Time period(s): 1990s

Locale(s): Tanglewood, Michigan; Washington

What the book is about: Ray Fredrick witnesses a hit-and-run that almost kills his and his wife's friend, Sister Theresa Loomis. He doesn't think it was an accident, particularly when he feels that Sister Theresa is holding information back from him. He is not able to trace the car and then gets distracted with his dying uncle and conflicts at work. When Sister Theresa is shot and killed at his uncle's memorial service, Ray takes time off work to fly, with his wife Kate, to the state of Washington to investigate the sister's past and see if anything there has any bearing on her murder now. First novel.

Other books you might like:
Lee Harris, *The Christening Day Murder*, 1993
Will Harriss, *Noble Rot*, 1993
Carolyn G. Hart, *Southern Ghost*, 1992
Wendy Hornsby, *Midnight Baby*, 1993
Nancy Pickard, *But I Wouldn't Want to Die There*, 1993

1452
James Schermerhorn
Night of the Cat (New York: St. Martin's, 1993)

Story type: Police Procedural—Female Lead

Major character(s): Caroline "Carrie" Lubick, Police Officer; Ian MacKenzie, Police Officer (acting lieutenant)

Time period(s): 1990s

Locale(s): San Francisco, California

What the book is about: Carrie Lubick is a dedicated police officer and she considers her beat as her home. She tries to help the victims and treats crime as a personal affront. The police are after a serial rapist who preys on the elderly. When the rapist attacks a young girl the hunt intensifies. Carrie is determined to stop this man and also finds herself attracted to the man in charge of the case. First novel.

Other books you might like:
Eleanor Taylor Bland, *Dead Time*, 1992
Susan Dunlap, *The Jill Smith Series*, 1981-
Ruby Horansky, *Dead Ahead*, 1991
Laurie R. King, *A Grave Talent*, 1993
Lee Martin, *The Deb Ralston Series*, 1984-

1453
Joyce Anne Schneider
Darkness Falls (New York: Pocket Books, 1989)

Story type: Psychological Suspense

Major character(s): Amanda Hammond, Doctor (Psychiatrist); Peter Barron, Doctor (Medical Examiner)

Time period(s): 1980s

Locale(s): Connecticut; Long Island, New York

What the book is about: Thrown together by the drowning death (labeled a murder by Medical Examiner Peter Barron) of her patient Kelly Payne, Amanda and Peter work to solve the mystery. A renewed romantic relationship, threats to Amanda, and a fascinating cast of supporting characters are part of this first novel which effectively combines the elements of both mystery and romance.

Other books you might like:
Mary Higgins Clark, *A Cry in the Night*, 1982
Kate Green, *Night Angel*, 1989
Barbara Michaels, *Search the Shadows*, 1987
Ruth Rendell, *Live Flesh*, 1986
Phyllis Whitney, *Rainbow in the Mist*, 1989

1454
Alan Scholefield
Thieftaker (New York: St. Martin's, 1992)

Series: George Macrae/Leopold Silver

Story type: Police Procedural—Male Lead

Major character(s): George Macrae, Police Officer (Detective Superintendent); Leopold Silver, Police Officer (Detective Sergeant)

Time period(s): 1990s

Locale(s): London, England

What the book is about: Robson Healey, shipping magnate, was cruel and ruthless. Now he is dead. A lot of people are glad including his estranged wife and his daughter. Macrae and Silver have their work cut out for them. To complicate matters, Silver and his girlfriend are being stalked by a man they helped send to prison.

Other books you might like:
Douglas Clark, *The Masters and Green Series*, 1969-
Elizabeth George, *The Inspector Lynley Series*, 1988-
Reginald Hill, *The Dalziel and Pascoe Series*, 1970-
Kay Mitchell, *A Lively Form of Death*, 1991
Janet Neel, *Death of a Partner*, 1991

1455
Bernard Schopen
The Desert Look (New York: Mysterious, 1990)

Series: Jack Ross

Story type: Private Detective—Male Lead

Major character(s): Jack Ross, Detective—Private (Trying to be retired); Miranda Santee, Journalist (Television reporter)

Time period(s): 1980s

Locale(s): Nevada

What the book is about: Jack Ross is lured out of retirement to learn more about his mother, who has been dead for years. Before she died she appears to have stolen a lot of cash from a casino and her partner never was found, alive or dead.

Other books you might like:
Lawrence Block, *Out on the Cutting Edge*, 1989
Max Byrd, *California Thriller*, 1981
James Crumley, *The Last Good Kiss*, 1978
Teri White, *Fault Lines*, 1988

1456
Mark Schorr
Gunpower (New York: Pocket, 1990)

Story type: Action/Adventure

Major character(s): Robert Stark, Businessman (anti-terrorist/rescue service), Spy (Ex-CIA)

Time period(s): 1980s

What the book is about: While working on the rescue of an American publisher's daughter, Stark hears rumblings of a terrorist conspiracy.

Other books you might like:
Clive Cussler, *Night Probe*, 1981
Colin Dunne, *Retrieval*, 1984
Paul Geddes, *Codename Hangman*, 1977
William Goldman, *Marathon Man*, 1974
William H. Hallahan, *The Trade*, 1981

1457
Benjamin M. Schutz
A Fistful of Empty (New York: Viking, 1991)

Series: Leo Haggerty

Story type: Private Detective—Male Lead

Major character(s): Leo Haggerty, Detective—Private

Time period(s): 1990s

Locale(s): Washington, District of Columbia

What the book is about: Leo gets a call from his bounty hunter friend, Arnie Kendall. Arnie needs a back-up so Leo leaves against the wishes of his girlfriend, Samantha. A day after the job, Samatha is beaten and raped. When Leo calls Arnie for help he discovers Arnie has been murdered. Leo wants revenge.

Other books you might like:
Joe Gores, *A Time of Predators*, 1969
Ed Gorman, *The Autumn Dead*, 1987
Faye Kellerman, *The Ritual Bath*, 1986
Jonathan Kellerman, *Silent Partner*, 1989
Philip Lee Williams, *Slow Dance in Autumn*, 1988

1458
Benjamin M. Schutz
Mexico Is Forever (New York: St. Martin's, 1994)

Series: Leo Haggerty

Story type: Private Detective—Male Lead

Major character(s): Leo Haggerty, Detective—Private

Time period(s): 1990s

Locale(s): Washington, District of Columbia

What the book is about: Leo Haggerty's firm has been hired to investigate Sarabeth Timmons. She claims to be the daughter of Edmund Timmons and wants her share of his estate. Leo proves that she is not who she claims to be, but becomes involved in finding out who she really is. A lot of other people seem to be interested as well.

Other books you might like:
Lawrence Block, *The Matt Scudder Series*, 1976-
Rob Kantner, *The Ben Perkins Series*, 1986-
Arthur Lyons, *The Jacob Asch Series*, 1974-
Walter Satterthwait, *The Joshua Croft Series*, 1988
Jonathan Valin, *The Harry Stoner Series*, 1980-

1459
Richard B. Schwartz
Frozen Stare (New York: St. Martin's, 1989)

Story type: Private Detective—Male Lead

Major character(s): Jack Grant, Detective—Private

Time period(s): 1980s

Locale(s): Los Angeles, California

What the book is about: Someone kills Grant's client shortly after he is hired to find a "friend." Soon after, two more people are killed in the same manner, drowned in a tub of ice water. Things seem to point to an organized crime figure. First book.

Other books you might like:
Robert Crais, *The Monkey's Raincoat*, 1987
Geoffrey Miller, *The Black Glove*, 1981

1460
Sandra Scoppettone
Everything You Have Is Mine (New York: Little, Brown, 1991)

Series: Lauren Laurano

Story type: Private Detective—Female Lead

Major character(s): Lauren Laurano, Detective—Private, Lesbian; Kip Adams, Doctor (psychotherapist), Lesbian (Lauren's lover)

Time period(s): 1990s

Locale(s): New York, New York

What the book is about: Lauren is hired by Ursula Huron to find the rapist of her sister, the improbably named Lake Huron. Just as the investigation starts, Lake is found dead. At first the police assume suicide but quickly determine it was murder. Lauren wants to find the killer but the only way may be for her to use herself as bait.

Other books you might like:
Agnes Bushnell, *Shadow Dance*, 1989
Diana McRae, *All the Muscle You Need*, 1988
Pat Welch, *Murder by the Book*, 1990
Mary Wings, *She Came Too Late*, 1987
Eve Zaremba, *Beyond Hope*, 1987

1461
Sandra Scoppettone
I'll Be Leaving You Always (New York: Little, Brown, 1993)

Series: Lauren Laurano

Story type: Private Detective—Female Lead

Major character(s): Lauren Laurano, Detective—Private, Lesbian; Kip Adams, Doctor (psychotherapist), Lesbian (Lauren's lover)

Time period(s): 1990s

Locale(s): New York, New York

What the book is about: Lauren's best friend, jewelry store owner Megan Harbaugh, has been the victim of a robbery. When Lauren calls to ask about Megan she is informed that Megan has been killed. Did the robbers return or is there something more complicated and sinister happening? As Lauren investigates she finds her straight friend had several secrets in her life that may have led to her death. Scoppettone has also written as Jack Early.

Other books you might like:
Lauren Wright Douglas, *Ninth Life*, 1990
Ellen Hart, *Hallowed Murder*, 1989
Laurie R. King, *A Grave Talent*, 1993
Pat Welch, *Murder by the Book*, 1990
Mary Wings, *She Came Too Late*, 1987

1462
Sandra Scoppettone
My Sweet Untraceable You (New York: Little, Brown, 1994)

Series: Lauren Laurano

Story type: Private Detective—Female Lead

Major character(s): Lauren Laurano, Detective—Private, Lesbian; Kip Adams, Doctor, Lesbian (Lauren's lover)

Time period(s): 1990s

Locale(s): New York, New York; Ulster County, New York (upstate New York)

What the book is about: The improbably named Boston Blackie has hired Lauren Laurano to investigate the death of his mother in a car accident. He thinks it was a murder and that his father is the killer. The one small difficulty is that this all happened 40 years ago. While investigating, Lauren runs into many people who seem to think that the mother is alive and well, and living in Hollywood making movies. Coincidentally, a movie is being made of Lauren's life and one of the actresses is killed. Or is it coincidence? Scoppettone has also written as Jack Early.

Other books you might like:
Lauren Wright Douglas, *Ninth Life*, 1990
Laurie R. King, *A Grave Talent*, 1993
Phyllis Knight, *Switching the Odds*, 1992
Randye Lordon, *Brotherly Love*, 1993
Mary Wings, *She Came Too Late*, 1987

1463
Justin Scott
Hardscape (New York: Viking, 1993)

Story type: Amateur Detective—Male Lead

Major character(s): Ben Abbott, Real Estate Agent (ex-con); Rita Long, Artist

Time period(s): 1990s

Locale(s): Newbury, Connecticut

What the book is about: Ben Abbott is back in his home town after serving time for insider trading. He is approached by a New York private detective wanting him to do some snooping on a recent arrival, artist Rita Long. Rita's husband suspects she is having an affair. Ben soon finds out this is true but then the boyfriend is killed. Ben finds himself attracted to the beautiful Rita and gets involved more than he wants.

Other books you might like:
Richard Barth, *Furnished for Murder*, 1990
Alan Dennis Burke, *Dead Wrong*, 1990
Philip R. Craig, *A Beautiful Place to Die*, 1990
Jon Katz, *Death by Station Wagon*, 1993
Victor Wuamett, *Artichoke Hearts*, 1991

1464
Justin Scott
StoneDust (New York: Viking, 1995)

Story type: Amateur Detective—Male Lead

Major character(s): Ben Abbott, Real Estate Agent

Time period(s): 1990s

Locale(s): Newbury, Connecticut

What the book is about: Ben gets involved in trying to prove that a friend did not die from an accidental heroin overdose. It's the accidental part that Ben doesn't believe. He has to investigate the rich and powerful of Newbury, most of whom do not wish to be investigated, particularly by a former convict. But will one of them kill to stop him?

Other books you might like:
Jeff Abbott, *The Jordan Poteet Series*, 1994-
Deborah Adams, *The Jesus Creek Series*, 1992-
Leo Axler, *The Bill Hawley Series*, 1994-
Sally Gunning, *The Peter Bartholomew Series*, 1990-
David Handler, *The Stewart Hoag Series*, 1988-

1465
Lisa Scottoline
Running From the Law (New York: HarperCollins, 1995)

Story type: Psychological Suspense; Legal

Major character(s): Rita Morrone, Lawyer

Time period(s): 1990s

Locale(s): Philadelphia, Pennsylvania

What the book is about: Rita Morrone is defending federal judge Fiske Hamilton against a charge of sexual harassment. The judge is also the father of her boyfriend. When the woman accuser is found dead, Fiske is the obvious suspect, but things may not be what they seem. Trying to find the truth will force Rita to reevaluate her life and her relationships.

1466 Sebastian

Other books you might like:
Patricia D. Benke, *Guilty by Choice*, 1995
Gillian B. Farrell, *Murder and a Muse*, 1995
R.A. Forster, *Keeping Counsel*, 1996
Barbara Parker, *Suspicion of Guilt*, 1995
Nancy Taylor Rosenberg, *Mitigating Circumstances*, 1994

1466
Tim Sebastian
Spy Shadow (New York: Delacorte, 1990)

Story type: Espionage

Major character(s): James Tristram, Spy (British)

Time period(s): 1990s

Locale(s): Europe

What the book is about: It appears that there is a plot to overthrow the Polish government and Tristram must try to unravel it.

Other books you might like:
Ted Allbeury, *The Other Side of Silence*, 1981
Len Deighton, *XPD*, 1981
Michael Delahaye, *Stalking-Horse*, 1988
Will Perry, *The Kremlin Watcher*, 1978

1467
Kate Sedley
Death and the Chapman (New York: St. Martin's, 1992)

Series: Roger the Chapman

Story type: Historical; Amateur Detective—Male Lead

Major character(s): Roger the Chapman, Peddler (former member of monastery)

Time period(s): 15th century (1471 The War of the Roses)

Locale(s): England

What the book is about: Roger has left the monastery to seek fame and fortune as a solver of puzzles. He is engaged by Laderman Weaver and his daughter to find the Weaver's son who was last seen near the Crossed Hands Inn. Roger soon discovers that he is not the first to disappear from this inn. First novel.

Other books you might like:
P.C. Doherty, *The Death of a King*, 1985
Umberto Eco, *The Name of the Rose*, 1986
Edward Marston, *The Queen's Head*, 1988
Ellis Peters, *The Brother Cadfael Series*, 1977-
Leonard Tourney, *The Matthew Stock Series*, 1980-

1468
Kate Sedley
The Holy Innocents (New York: St. Martin's, 1995)

Series: Roger the Chapman

Story type: Historical; Amateur Detective—Male Lead

Major character(s): Roger the Chapman, Peddler

Time period(s): 15th century (1475)

Locale(s): England

What the book is about: Roger is on the road again, having lost his wife in childbirth. He escapes being robbed by an outlaw band, but is set upon by a band of women celebrating "Hick Monday" by holding him for ransom. He pays the ransom—some trinkets and a kiss—and is then asked for his help by the charming Grizelda Harbourne. Grizelda was the nurse for two young children who have disappeared. The villagers blame the outlaws, but Grizelda thinks there may be more to it. Roger agrees to help.

Other books you might like:
P.F. Chisholm, *A Famine of Horses*, 1995
Michael Clynes, *The Roger Shallot Series*, 1993-
Edward Marston, *The Nicholas Bracewell Series*, 1988-
Ian Morson, *Falconer's Crusade*, 1994
Leonard Tourney, *The Matthew Stock Series*, 1980-

1469
Kate Sedley
The Plymouth Cloak (New York: St. Martin's, 1993)

Series: Roger the Chapman

Story type: Historical

Major character(s): Roger the Chapman, Peddler

Time period(s): 15th century (1473)

Locale(s): Plymouth, England

What the book is about: In the aftermath of the War of the Roses, Roger the Chapman is asked by Richard, Duke of Glouster and brother of King Edward to accompany Philip Underdown on a mission to try and forstall an invasion from Brittany. Philip is not happy about this mission, whether from arrogance, treachery or stupidity. Philip has many enemies, both personal and political and his manner is quite capable of creating many more. Can Roger keep him alive and ensure the success of the mission?

Other books you might like:
Michael Clynes, *The White Rose Murders*, 1993
P.C. Doherty, *The Fate of Princes*, 1991
Edward Marston, *The Nicholas Bracewell Series*, 1988-
Candace M. Robb, *The Apothecary Rose*, 1993
Leonard Tourney, *The Matthew Stock Series*, 1980-

1470
Kate Sedley
The Weaver's Tale (New York: St. Martin's, 1994)

Series: Roger the Chapman

Story type: Historical; Amateur Detective—Male Lead

Major character(s): Roger the Chapman, Peddler

Time period(s): 15th century (1474)

Locale(s): Bristol, England

What the book is about: While in Bristol, Roger the Chapman becomes ill and is taken in and cared for by Lillis Walker and her mother. When he recovers he realizes that the Walker family has a cloud over it. It seems the town rake had been hanged for robbery and the murder of Lillis' grandfather. Two months after the hanging, the grandfather had come home with a strange tale of kidnapping and torture. The townspeople blame the family for their guilt in hanging an innocent man. Roger is asked to find the truth.

Other books you might like:
Umberto Eco, *The Name of the Rose*, 1986
Paul Harding, *The Brother Athelstan Series*, 1991-
Edward Marston, *The Nicholas Bracewell Series*, 1988-
Ellis Peters, *The Brother Cadfael Series*, 1977-
Leonard Tourney, *The Matthew Stock Series*, 1980-

1471
Kathrin King Segal
Wild Again (New York: Dutton, 1991)

Story type: Psychological Suspense

Major character(s): Art Glenn, Musician (piano player); Margo Magill, Social Worker

Time period(s): 1990s

Locale(s): New York, New York

What the book is about: Another woman's obsession threatens the love of Art and Margo. Art isn't strong enough to deal with what needs to be done, until he believes that he has killed the obsessed woman. First novel.

Other books you might like:
Alexi Brix, *Blood Ties*, 1992
Gary Devon, *Bad Desire*, 1991
Marjorie Dorner, *Freeze Frame*, 1990

1472
Tom Sehler (Pseudonym of Rex Burns)
When Reason Sleeps (New York: Viking, 1991)

Story type: Action/Adventure; Private Detective—Male Lead

Major character(s): Jack Steele, Military Personnel, Widow(er) (Colonel, USMC)

Time period(s): 1990s

Locale(s): San Diego, California; Denver, Colorado

What the book is about: Jack Steele has been separated from the Marine Corps for turning in a crooked Representative to Congress. He's now working for the Osiris Corporation, a civilian intelligence consulting firm. An old friend, a retired admiral, asks him to look for his granddaughter who has disappeared. What Jack finds is a link to a mysterious satanic cult. First novel as Sehler. Also writes as Rex Burns.

Other books you might like:
Jack Barnao, *Hammerlocke*, 1986
Bill Crider, *Dead on the Island*, 1991
Deforest Day, *August Ice*, 1990
Jerome Doolittle, *Body Scissors*, 1990
J.R. Levitt, *Ten of Swords*, 1991

1473
Steve Shagan
Pillars of Fire (New York: Pocket, 1989)

Story type: Techno-Thriller

Major character(s): Tom Lawford, Spy (CIA, acting as a journalist)

Time period(s): 1990s (1992)

Locale(s): Middle East

What the book is about: When the Israelis want to destroy both a Pakistani nuclear facility and a Libyan launch site, their success depends on CIA agent Tom Lawford.

Other books you might like:
David Aaron, *State Scarlet*, 1987
Nelson DeMille, *By the Waters of Babylon*, 1978
Simon Harvester, *Assassins Road*, 1965
A.J. Quinnell, *The Mahdi*, 1982

1474
Sarah Shankman
He Was Her Man (New York: Pocket, 1993)

Series: Samantha Adams

Story type: Action/Adventure; Amateur Detective—Female Lead

Major character(s): Samantha Adams, Journalist (reporter)

Time period(s): 1990s

Locale(s): Hot Springs, Arkansas

What the book is about: Samantha Adams is headed for Hot Springs to be consoled by her best friend Kitty because her boyfriend has left her. She becomes involved with Olive Adair, owner of Gas 'N' Grub; Jinx Watson, lottery winner and bride-to-be; and many more strange and possibly dangerous people—all of whom are involved in kidnapping, mayhem, and murder.

Other books you might like:
Carl Hiaasen, *Native Tongue*, 1991
Carl Hiaasen, *Skin Tight*, 1990
Vince Kohler, *Rising Dog*, 1992
Meg O'Brien, *Hare Today, Gone Tomorrow*, 1991
Steven Womack, *Torch Town Boogie*, 1993

1475
Sarah Shankman
The King Is Dead (New York: Pocket, 1992)

Series: Samantha Adams

Story type: Action/Adventure; Amateur Detective—Female Lead

Major character(s): Samantha Adams, Journalist (reporter); Harry Zack, Musician (Sam's boyfriend)

Time period(s): 1990s

Locale(s): Tupelo, Mississippi

1476 Shankman

What the book is about: Sam and Harry are driving to Tupelo — birthplace of Elvis — for the third annual international barbecue cookoff. They're driving a pink Cadillac. Also headed for Tupelo is Mary Ann McClanahan, who has just sort-of killed her husband for the insurance and has found out he already had a wife. She has hooked up with a truck driver and Elvis impersonator (and self-proclaimed murderer) on an Elvis pilgrimmage. All of them are on a collision course.

Other books you might like:
Carl Hiaasen, *Double Whammy*, 1987
Carl Hiaasen, *Tourist Season*, 1985
Vince Kohler, *Rising Dog*, 1992
Meg O'Brien, *Hare Today, Gone Tomorrow*, 1991
John Bartholomew Tucker, *He's Dead-She's Dead: Details at Eleven*, 1990

1476
Sarah Shankman
Now Let's Talk of Graves (New York: Pocket, 1990)

Series: Samantha Adams

Story type: Amateur Detective—Female Lead

Major character(s): Samantha Adams, Journalist; Harry Zack, Insurance Investigator (part-time musician)

Time period(s): 1990s

Locale(s): New Orleans, Louisiana

What the book is about: Sam is in New Orleans for Mardi Gras at the invitation of her college friend, Kitty Lee. She becomes involved with the rest of the high society Lee family when Church Lee is killed by a masked figure driving an old car. An accident? Harry Zack doesn't think so and he and Sam team up to solve the case with a mixture of sex, drugs, rock and roll and a little voodoo. The two earlier books in this series were written under the name Alice Story.

Other books you might like:
Barbara D'Amato, *Hardball*, 1990
Mickey Friedman, *A Temporary Ghost*, 1989
Susan Kelly, *The Gemini Man*, 1985
Meg O'Brien, *The Daphne Decisions*, 1990
Julie Smith, *New Orleans Mourning*, 1990

1477
Sarah Shankman
She Walks in Beauty (New York: Pocket, 1991)

Series: Samantha Adams

Story type: Amateur Detective—Female Lead

Major character(s): Samantha Adams, Journalist (reporter); Harry Zack, Musician (Sam's boyfriend), Insurance Investigator (part-time)

Time period(s): 1990s

Locale(s): Atlantic City, New Jersey

What the book is about: Sam is forced into covering the Miss America Pageant. The disappearance of a sleazy judge sets Sam to investigating. The first two books in this series initially appeared under the pseudonym of Alice Storey.

Other books you might like:
Joan Hess, *A Really Cute Corpse*, 1988
Vince Kohler, *Rainy North Woods*, 1990
Meg O'Brien, *Salmon in the Soup*, 1991
Orania Papazoglou, *The Patience McKenna Series*, 1984-
John Bartholomew Tucker, *He's Dead-She's Dead: Details at Eleven*, 1990

1478
Simon Shaw
Killer Cinderella (New York: Doubleday, 1992)

Story type: Psychological Suspense

Major character(s): Mark Harvey, Banker; Maddie Harvey, Housewife

Time period(s): 1990s

Locale(s): Fareham, England

What the book is about: Mark Harvey is a quiet, unassuming banker with an overweight, unfaithful, nagging wife—who swears she is not fat but pregnant—for the last four years. Now she wants a divorce. Mark takes all this but when she breaks his precious trophies he is enraged. He decides to hide the body and pretend she is still alive.

Other books you might like:
Patricia Highsmith, *People Who Knock on the Door*, 1985
Anthony Oliver, *The Pew Group*, 1980
Conall Ryan, *Black Gravity*, 1985
Evelyn E. Smith, *Miss Melville Regrets*, 1986

1479
Stella Shepherd
Nurse Dawes Is Dead (New York: St. Martin's, 1995)

Series: Inspector Richard Montgomery

Story type: Police Procedural—Male Lead

Major character(s): Richard Montgomery, Police Officer (detective inspector); William Bird, Police Officer (detective sergeant)

Time period(s): 1990s

Locale(s): Nottingham, England

What the book is about: Beautiful nurse, Loretta Dawes, wants to announce some great news at one of several parties being held on the same night. Before she can find the right time, though, she mysteriously dies. An autopsy reveals she was poisoned and was three months pregnant. When Montgomery and Bird investigate, they find a closed group of doctors, nurses and their spouses in which both professional and personal jealousies flourish. Did Loretta's secret lover kill her or was it someone else?

Other books you might like:
Douglas Clark, *The Masters and Green Series*, 1969-1988
Marjorie Eccles, *The Gil Mayo Series*, 1988-
Reginald Hill, *The Dalziel and Pascoe Series*, 1977-
P.D. James, *Shroud for a Nightingale*, 1971
Kay Mitchell, *In Stoney Places*, 1991

1480
Stella Shepherd
Thinner than Blood (New York: Doubleday, 1992)
Series: Inspector Richard Montgomery
Story type: Police Procedural—Male Lead
Major character(s): Richard Montgomery, Police Officer (Inspector, CID); William Bird, Police Officer (Sergeant, CID)
Time period(s): 1990s
Locale(s): Nottingham, England
What the book is about: Maud Witherspoon, tyrannical matriarch of the Witherspoon family, dies after changing her will. Everyone assumes natural causes until a note to the police claims she was murdered. As Montgomery starts to investigate, another death in the family occurs and Maud's granddaughter and her cat disappear.
Other books you might like:
Paula Gosling, *Death Penalties*, 1991
Caroline Graham, *The Inspector Barnaby Series*, 1988
Peter Robinson, *The Alan Banks Series*, 1990
Dorothy Simpson, *The Inspector Thanet Series*, 1981-
Susannah Stacey, *The Superintendent Bone Series*, 1988-

1481
Michael W. Sherer
Death Came Dressed in White (New York: Harper, 1992)
Series: Emerson Ward
Story type: Amateur Detective—Male Lead
Major character(s): Emerson Ward, Writer (freelance)
Time period(s): 1990s
Locale(s): Chicago, Illinois
What the book is about: It's a bad time for Emerson. Unsure of his life, he is slowly becoming an alcoholic. One day he learns one of his friends is missing, another has been seriously injured in a mugging, his girlfriend is leaving him and his phone is tapped. Emerson tries to put his life together and find his missing friend. Then another shocking death occurs. He wants to know what is going on. When he finds out, someone will pay.
Other books you might like:
Gar Anthony Haywood, *Fear of the Dark*, 1988
Zachary Klein, *Still Among the Living*, 1990
Mike Lupica, *Limited Partner*, 1990
Benjamin M. Schutz, *A Fistful of Empty*, 1991
Philip Lee Williams, *Slow Dance in Autumn*, 1988

1482
Michael W. Sherer
Little Use for Death (New York: Harper, 1992)
Series: Emerson Ward
Story type: Amateur Detective—Male Lead
Major character(s): Emerson Ward, Writer (freelance; lecturer)
Time period(s): 1990s
Locale(s): New York (upstate)
What the book is about: Emerson is serving a semester as a guest lecturer on creative writing at his alma mater. When a student asks his help on a personal matter, Emerson pays little attention and when the student changes his mind, Emerson is relieved. Then the student is dead, an apparent suicide. Emerson feels guilty and investigates to find out why.
Other books you might like:
Bill Crider, *One Dead Dean*, 1988
Marshall Jevons, *The Fatal Equilibrium*, 1985
M.D. Lake, *Poisoned Ivy*, 1992
Ralph McInerny, *The Search Committee*, 1990
William L. Story, *Final Thesis*, 1989

1483
John Sherwood
Bones Gather No Moss (New York: Scribners, 1994)
Series: Celia Grant
Story type: Amateur Detective—Female Lead
Major character(s): Celia Grant, Businesswoman (owner of a plant nursery)
Time period(s): 1990s
Locale(s): Orleans, France
What the book is about: Adrienne De Fleury, an old friend of Celia Grant's uncle, wants her to travel to France and put her late son's notes on plant species in order and publish them. Celia doesn't want to go and suggests a friend for the job, botanist Jane Greenwood. Then Jane disappears mysteriously. Celia feels obligated to find out what happened. She finds the De Fleury household to be filled with hate and suspicion that seems to center on a series of murders and the son's suicide 11 years earlier.
Other books you might like:
Simon Brett, *The Mrs. Pargeter Series*, 1988-
B. Comfort, *The Tish McWhinney Series*, 1986-
B.J. Oliphant, *The Shirley McClintock Series*, 1990-
David Osborn, *The Margaret Barlow Series*, 1990-
Celestine Sibley, *The Kate Mulcay Series*, 1991-

1484
John Sherwood
A Bouquet of Thorns (New York: Scribners, 1989)
Series: Celia Grant
Story type: Amateur Detective—Female Lead
Major character(s): Celia Grant, Businesswoman (owner of a plant nursery)
Time period(s): 1980s
Locale(s): Melbury (Fictional village)
What the book is about: When Celia's head gardener is arrested for a murder, she is sure he is innocent and that others are lying to make sure he gets convicted.

1485 Sherwood

Other books you might like:
Agatha Christie, *The Miss Marple Series*, (1930-1976)
Joan Hadley, *The Night-Blooming Cereus*, 1987
H.R.F. Keating, *Mrs. Craggs: Crimes Cleaned Up*, 1986
Gladys Mitchell, *The Saltmarsh Murders*, 1933
Ellis Peters, *The Grass-Widow's Tale*, 1968

1485
John Sherwood
The Hanging Garden (New York: Scribners, 1992)
Series: Celia Grant
Story type: Amateur Detective—Female Lead
Major character(s): Celia Grant, Businesswoman (owner of a plant nursery)
Time period(s): 1990s
Locale(s): Funchal, Portugal (island)
What the book is about: Celia's niece, Antonia Hanbury, has been found dead, presumably after getting drunk and falling down stairs. Celia is asked to be executor of the will and so goes to Portugal. Upon her arrival she finds a number of strange circumstances - an ex-con husband who is acting suspiciously, a nurse who is not what she pretends to be, and a group of tourists who act more like thugs.
Other books you might like:
Richard Barth, *The Margaret Binton Series*, 1978-
Trella Crespi, *The Trouble with Too Much Sun*, 1992
Joan Hadley, *The Night-Blooming Cereus*, 1987
Hazel Holt, *Mrs. Malory Investigates*, 1990
David Osborn, *Murder on Martha's Vineyard*, 1990

1486
Bill Shoemaker
Fire Horse (New York: Fawcett, 1995)
Series: Coley Killebrew
Story type: Private Detective—Male Lead
Major character(s): Coley Killebrew, Detective—Private (former jockey)
Time period(s): 1990s
Locale(s): Los Angeles, California
What the book is about: Coley's partner has gotten himself involved with a femme fatale, or so Coley thinks. He is proved right when he finds that she has gotten them mixed up with smuggled horses, hoodlums, and murder.
Other books you might like:
Mark Daniel, *The Devil to Pay*, 1992
Dick Francis, *Flying Finish*, 1966
John Francome, *Outsider*, 1993
William Murray, *The Shifty Anderson Series*, 1974-
Robert Reeves, *Doubting Thomas*, 1985

1487
Bill Shoemaker
Stalking Horse (New York: Fawcett, 1994)
Story type: Amateur Detective—Male Lead; Action/Adventure
Major character(s): Coley Killebrew, Restauranteur (former jockey); Raymond Starbuck, Businessman
Time period(s): 1990s
Locale(s): New Orleans, Louisiana
What the book is about: Coley Killebrew has been banned from the sport he loves—horse racing—for seven years. He is now the co-owner of a Los Angeles restaurant. He is asked by Raymond Starbuck, the man responsible for his being banned, to investigate a Louisiana race track that Starbuck fears may have been taken over by unnamed bad guys, who appear to have their eyes on a California track. First novel.
Other books you might like:
Carolyn Banks, *Death by Dressage*, 1994
Mark Daniel, *The Devil to Pay*, 1993
Dick Francis, *Whip Hand*, 1980
John Francome, *Stone Cold*, 1994
Robert J. Randisi, *The Disappearance of Penny*, 1980

1488
Anna Shone
Mr. Donaghue Investigates (New York: St. Martin's, 1995)
Story type: Private Detective—Male Lead
Major character(s): Ulysses Donaghue, Detective—Private (Shakespearean scholar)
Time period(s): 1990s
Locale(s): St. Pierre La Croix, France
What the book is about: Ulysses is asked by a woman to keep her daughter, the famous singer/actress Salome, safe while she's in London. The woman is suspicious of her daughter's new husband, director Thelonius Kapp, who is forty years older than his bride. Ulysses says he will help when he gets back from vacation. Coincidentally, while in the south of France, he learns that Kapp is also nearby at a retreat. Then Kapp dies, allegedly by his own hand, with a Shakespearean quote as his last words. Ulysses suspects murder and investigates. First mystery.
Other books you might like:
Marvin Albert, *The Stone Angel Series*, 1986-
Desmond Cory, *The Mask of Zeus*, 1993
John Milne, *Dead Birds*, 1986
Denise Osborne, *Cut To—Murder*, 1995
Miles Tripp, *The John Samson Series*, 1973-

1489
Sharon Gwyn Short
Angel's Bidding (New York: Fawcett, 1994)
Series: Patricia Delaney
Story type: Private Detective—Female Lead
Major character(s): Patricia Delaney, Detective—Private
Time period(s): 1990s
Locale(s): Cincinnati, Ohio

What the book is about: Elsa Kauffman has asked Patricia Delaney to try and find out who is sending her father threatening letters attached to antique hat pins that once belonged to Elsa's grandmother. Does it have anything to do with a missing employee or a missing $100,000? Patricia is an expert at computer searching but this is going to take more than that, especially when family skeletons start to fall out of closets and dead bodies begin to show up. First mystery.

Other books you might like:
Linda Barnes, *The Carlotta Carlyle Series*, 1987-
D.B. Borton, *The Cat Caliban Series*, 1993-
Sally Chapman, *Love Bytes*, 1994
Linda Grant, *The Catherine Saylor Series*, 1988-

1490
Sharon Gwyn Short
The Death We Share (New York: Fawcett, 1995)

Series: Patricia Delaney

Story type: Private Detective—Female Lead

Major character(s): Patricia Delaney, Detective—Private

Time period(s): 1990s

Locale(s): Cincinnati, Ohio

What the book is about: Pat Delaney is one of the new wave of private detectives, preferring to use her computer and data bases to solve her cases. Her new assignment seems perfect, find out who is telling a scandal magazine that famed opera star Carlotta Moses abandoned a child years ago. Pat's father is in town and wants to help. However, the investigation uncovers some secrets that somebody doesn't want revealed. They will do anything to keep them quiet.

Other books you might like:
Linda Barnes, *The Carlotta Carlyle Series*, 1987-
Janet Dawson, *The Jeri Howard Series*, 1990-
Susan Dunlap, *The Kiernan O'Shaughnessy Series*, 1989-
Linda Grant, *The Catherine Saylor Series*, 1988-
Nancy Baker Jacobs, *The Devon MacDonald Series*, 1991-

1491
M.K. Shuman
The Caesar Clue (New York: St. Martins, 1990)

Series: Micah Dunn

Story type: Private Detective—Male Lead

Major character(s): Micah Dunn, Detective—Private, Veteran (Vietnam vet with paralyzed arm)

Time period(s): 1990s (1990)

Locale(s): New Orleans, Louisiana

What the book is about: Micah receives a message to meet Julia Morvant at the airport because she needs help. When her plane blows up just before landing, Micah is haunted by the feeling somebody killed an entire planeload of people to keep Julia quiet. Then an old Vietnam War buddy shows up and asks for his help in finding the assassin. Also writes as M.S. Karl.

Other books you might like:
James Lee Burke, *The Neon Rain*, 1986
Michael Collins, *The Dan Fortune Series*, 1967-
Simon Ritchie, *The Hollow Woman*, 1986
Julie Smith, *New Orleans Mourning*, 1990
Chris Wiltz, *The Killing Circle*, 1981

1492
M.K. Shuman
Deep Kill (New York: St. Martin's, 1991)

Series: Micah Dunn

Story type: Private Detective—Male Lead

Major character(s): Micah Dunn, Detective—Private, Veteran (Vietnam vet with paralyzed arm)

Time period(s): 1990s

Locale(s): New Orleans, Louisiana

What the book is about: Micah's mechanic, Cal, is accused of molesting a young black boy. He claims he is being framed. When Micah investigates he finds a lot of people who would benefit from Cal's conviction. But he also discovers some disturbing secrets of his client's. Then the boy is found murdered in the swamp. This case may destroy Micah and the people he loves. Shuman also writes as M.S. Karl.

Other books you might like:
James Lee Burke, *A Morning for Flamingos*, 1990
Michael Collins, *The Dan Fortune Series*, 1967-
John Lutz, *The Fred Carver Series*, 1986-
Simon Ritchie, *Work for a Dead Man*, 1989
Chris Wiltz, *The Emerald Lizard*, 1991

1493
M.K. Shuman (Pseudonym of M.S. Karl)
The Last Man to Die (New York: St. Martin's, 1992)

Series: Micah Dunn

Story type: Private Detective—Male Lead

Major character(s): Micah Dunn, Detective—Private, Veteran (Vietnam vet with paralyzed arm)

Time period(s): 1990s

Locale(s): New Orleans, Louisiana

What the book is about: Micah is present at an archeological dig when a human skeleton is uncovered. The bones prove to be those of Max Chantry, a reform politician of the late 1940s who disappeared after an attempt on his life resulted in the death of his best friend. Micah is drawn into the case but looking into the old crime leads to new murder.

Other books you might like:
James Lee Burke, *A Stained White Radiance*, 1992
Michael Collins, *The Dan Fortune Series*, 1967-
D.J. Donaldson, *No Mardi Gras for the Dead*, 1992
Aaron Elkins, *Old Bones*, 1992
Chris Wiltz, *The Killing Circle*, 1981

1494
M.K. Shuman (Pseudonym of M.S. Karl)
The Maya Stone Murders (New York: St. Martin's, 1989)

Story type: Private Detective—Male Lead

Major character(s): Micah Dunn, Detective—Private, Veteran (Vietnam vet with paralyzed arm)

Time period(s): 1980s

Locale(s): New Orleans, Louisiana

What the book is about: P.I. Micah Dunn is hired to find out why someone is smuggling artifacts into a Mayan exhibit. What seems harmless at first soon turns deadly.

Other books you might like:
James Lee Burke, *The Neon Rain*, 1986
Michael Collins, *Freak*, 1983
Jack Livingston, *A Piece of the Silence*, 1982
Simon Ritchie, *Work for a Dead Man*, 1989
Chris Wiltz, *The Killing Circle*, 1981

1495
Celestine Sibley
Ah, Sweet Mystery (New York: Harper, 1991)

Series: Kate Mulcay

Story type: Amateur Detective—Female Lead

Major character(s): Kate Mulcay, Journalist (columnist; ex-police reporter), Widow(er)

Time period(s): 1990s

Locale(s): Atlanta, Georgia

What the book is about: Miss Willie Wilcox, a feisty octegenerian, has confessed to killing her son Garney. Kate, who has liked and respected Willie for years, knows that almost everyone who knew Garney hated him except for his mother who loved him. Why then would she confess? First mystery.

Other books you might like:
M.S. Karl, *Killer's Ink*, 1988
Mary Kittredge, *Murder in Mendocino*, 1987
B.J. Oliphant, *Dead in the Scrub*, 1990
Sarah Shankman, *She Walks in Beauty*, 1991

1496
Celestine Sibley
Dire Happenings at Scratch Ankle (New York: HarperCollins, 1993)

Series: Kate Mulcay

Story type: Amateur Detective—Female Lead

Major character(s): Kate Mulcay, Journalist (columnist; ex-police reporter), Widow(er)

Time period(s): 1990s

Locale(s): Georgia

What the book is about: Kate Mulcay is on assignment at the state house of representatives and is there when Return Pickett demands that Georgia reannex the disputed area of Plum Nelly, the land between Georgia and Tennessee, for the sake of his Cherokee ancestors. Kate is intrigued and promises to meet him there for a tour but when she arrives in the company of two young neighbor girls they find an empty trailer and a trail of blood. Is Pickett dead or is this just a publicity stunt?

Other books you might like:
Nat Brandt, *A Death in Bulloch Parish*, 1993 (Yanna Brandt, co-author)
Susan Kelly, *Out of the Darkness*, 1992
B.J. Oliphant, *Death and the Delinquent*, 1993
Sarah Shankman, *Then Hang All the Liars*, 1989
Patricia Houck Sprinkle, *Somebody's Dead in Snellville*, 1993

1497
Celestine Sibley
A Plague of Kinfolks (New York: HarperCollins, 1995)

Series: Kate Mulcay

Story type: Amateur Detective—Female Lead

Major character(s): Kate Mulcay, Journalist (columnist, ex-police reporter)

Time period(s): 1990s

Locale(s): Atlanta, Georgia

What the book is about: Kate's days of peaceful gardening seem to be at an end. She is being visited by relatives of her late husband (relatives she didn't even know existed) and they are showing no signs of leaving. Then a strange old man who owns a large parcel of land is beaten and killed, and the body of Bet Dunn, a neighbor is found floating in a fountain. To restore order, Kate has to find a killer and figure out a way to get rid of the kinfolk from hell.

Other books you might like:
Mary Daheim, *The Alpine Series*, 1992-
Carolyn G. Hart, *The Henrietta O'Dwyer Series*, 1993-
B.J. Oliphant, *The Shirley McClintock Series*, 1990-
Patricia Houck Sprinkle, *The Sheila Travis Series*, 1988-
Kerry Tucker, *Death Echo*, 1993

1498
Celestine Sibley
Straight as an Arrow (New York: Harper, 1992)

Series: Kate Mulcay

Story type: Amateur Detective—Female Lead

Major character(s): Kate Mulcay, Journalist (columnist, ex-police reporter), Widow(er)

Time period(s): 1990s

Locale(s): Ila Island, Florida

What the book is about: Kate and her husband had spent many wonderful summers on Ila Island. Now Benjy is dead and Kate doesn't feel like returning. Her friend Nora Noble asks for her help because Nora feels someone is killing off the residents of the island. Three people are mysteriously dead and someone has tried to frighten Nora's husband, Phil, to death. Kate is determined to help no matter how hard it is to return.

Other books you might like:
Susan Kelly, *The Summertime Soldiers*, 1986
Mary Kittredge, *Murder in Mendocino*, 1987
B.J. Oliphant, *Dead in the Scrub*, 1990
Sarah Shankman, *First Kill All the Lawyers*, 1988
Kerry Tucker, *Still Waters*, 1991

1499
Leonard Simon
Disassociated States (New York: Bantam, 1994)

Story type: Psychological Suspense

Major character(s): Jake Silver, Doctor (psychiatrist; Claire's husband); Claire Baxter, Doctor (psychiatrist; Jake's wife); Felix Kiehl, Stock Broker, Mentally Ill Person (multiple personality)

Time period(s): 1990s

Locale(s): New York, New York

What the book is about: Husband and wife psychiatrists Jake Silver and Claire Baxter are having marital problems. But that's not all. They have discovered that they are treating the same patient. At least they think he's the same patient, Felix Kiehl, a man with multiple personalities. In addition to being a stock broker he may also be an artist, and perhaps, a murderer. When he is put on trial for insider trading, Jake and Claire must determine his guilt or innocence—and not just of the current crime of which he is accused.

Other books you might like:
Jeffrey Wilds Deaver, *Praying for Sleep*, 1994
D.J. Donaldson, *Blood on the Bayou*, 1991
Jonathan Kellerman, *The Alex Delaware Series*, 1984-
Ridley Pearson, *Hard Fall*, 1993
Stephen White, *The Alan Gregory Series*, 1992-

1500
Sheila Simonson
Larkspur (New York: St. Martin's, 1990)

Story type: Amateur Detective—Female Lead

Major character(s): Lark Daily, Businesswoman (Bookstore owner); Jay Dodge, Police Officer (Lover of Lark Daily)

Time period(s): 1980s

Locale(s): Monte, California

What the book is about: Someone has murdered a rich, homosexual poet during one of his parties and his houseboy/lover is the main suspect, particularly after he disappears. Daily and Dodge, however, believe differently. This is Simonson's first mystery, though she has written a number of romances.

Other books you might like:
Jon L. Breen, *Touch of the Past*, 1988
Carolyn G. Hart, *Something Wicked*, 1988
Joan Hess, *Strangled Prose*, 1986
Orania Papazoulou, *Sweet, Savage Death*, 1985
Wayne Warga, *Hardcover*, 1985

1501
Sheila Simonson
Skylark (New York: St. Martin's, 1992)

Series: Lark Dodge

Story type: Amateur Detective—Female Lead

Major character(s): Lark Dodge, Businesswoman (bookstore owner); Jay Dodge, Police Officer (husband of Lark); Ann Veryan, Teacher

Time period(s): 1990s

Locale(s): London, England

What the book is about: Lark is in London for a bookseller's convention and some sightseeing. She shares a room with Ann Veryan. While out with Milos Vlacek, a waiter they have befriended, they see Milos receive a package of papers. When Milos is stabbed and almost killed, their room searched and their landlady killed, they realize something sinister is happening - something very dangerous.

Other books you might like:
Toni Brill, *Date with a Dead Doctor*, 1991
Sarah Caudwell, *Thus Was Adonis Murdered*, 1981
Joan Smith, *A Masculine Ending*, 1987
Elizabeth Travis, *Finders Keepers*, 1990
Hannah Wakefield, *A Woman's Own Mystery*, 1991

1502
Dorothy Simpson
Dead by Morning (New York: Scribners, 1989)

Series: Luke Thanet

Story type: Police Procedural—Male Lead

Major character(s): Luke Thanet, Detective—Police (Inspector); Michael Lineham, Police Officer (Sergeant)

Time period(s): 1980s

What the book is about: The heir to an estate is killed shortly after returning to his family to claim his inheritance. Thanet and company must sort out the killer from all the likely suspects.

Other books you might like:
Douglas Clark, *Death After Evensong*, 1970
Colin Dexter, *Service of All the Dead*, 1980
Michael Gilbert, *Blood and Judgement*, 1959
Reginald Hill, *Ruling Passion*, 1977
John Buxton Hilton, *Some Run Crooked*, 1978

1503
Bennie Lee Sinclair
The Lynching (New York: Walker, 1992)

Story type: Amateur Detective

1504 Singer

Major character(s): Justyn Jones, Administrator (political aide); Thomas More Levity, Teacher

Time period(s): 1970s (1978)

Locale(s): Green Hills, South Carolina

What the book is about: Thomas Levity has come to Green Hills to find out the truth about his father who was lynched before Thomas was born. On the way he meets Justyn Jones who did not know about the lynching. When she finds out her father tried to prosecute the mob and failed and that this was what drove him to suicide she joins forces with Thomas to find out what really happened thirty years ago. First novel.

Other books you might like:
Thomas H. Cook, *Streets of Fire*, 1989
Robert Davis, *Kimura*, 1989
Robert Specht, *The Soul of Betty Fairchild*, 1991
Elizabeth Daniels Squire, *Kill the Messenger*, 1990
David Stout, *Carolina Skeletons*, 1989

1504
Shelley Singer
Interview with Mattie (New York: Signet, 1995)

Series: Barrett Lake

Story type: Private Detective—Female Lead

Major character(s): Barrett Lake, Detective—Private (part-time), Teacher (high school); Tito Broz, Detective—Private (Barrett's boss)

Time period(s): 1990s

Locale(s): Berkeley, California

What the book is about: Barrett Lake specializes in finding missing children. This time, Mattie isn't missing, he is dead, killed on the streets of Berkeley after giving a revealing interview to a reporter for the local newspaper. Now the editor of the paper is being threatened. Barrett is hired to find the killer and stop the threats.

Other books you might like:
Linda Barnes, *Coyote*, 1990
Susan Dunlap, *The Jill Smith Series*, 1981-
Nancy Baker Jacobs, *The Turquoise Tattoo*, 1991
Abigail Padgett, *Strawgirl*, 1994
Sara Paretsky, *Guardian Angel*, 1992

1505
Shelley Singer
Picture of David (New York: Signet, 1993)

Series: Barrett Lake

Story type: Private Detective—Female Lead

Major character(s): Barrett Lake, Detective—Private, Teacher; Tito Broz, Detective—Private (Barrett's boss)

Time period(s): 1990s

Locale(s): San Francisco, California

What the book is about: Part-time private detective Barrett Lake has a new case. 14 year old David Minsky has been kidnapped and his parents are receiving threatening letters and a burned photo of David. The kidnapping seems to be part of a plot against the Minskys, newly immigrated from Russia. They seem to have secrets from the old country, but who would want to harm David? Barrett knows she's on to something when her car is bombed.

Other books you might like:
Linda Barnes, *Coyote*, 1990
Janet Dawson, *Kindred Crimes*, 1989
Nancy Baker Jacobs, *The Turquoise Tattoo*, 1991
J.R. Levitt, *Ten of Swords*, 1991
Walter Satterthwait, *A Flower in the Desert*, 1992

1506
Shelley Singer
Searching for Sara (New York: Signet, 1994)

Series: Barrett Lake

Story type: Private Detective—Female Lead

Major character(s): Barrett Lake, Teacher, Detective—Private (part-time); Tito Broz, Detective—Private (Barrett's boss)

Time period(s): 1990s

Locale(s): San Francisco, California; Berkeley, California

What the book is about: Barrett Lake, a part-time private detective specializing in missing children, has been hired to find Sara Henry. An uncle has done the hiring as Sara's parents have given up and think she would be better off dead. Barrett quickly finds Sara at a shelter in San Francisco along with her friends, a strange group of lost kids who have nowhere to go but the streets. Then a shelter volunteer is murdered and Barrett literally becomes a target. What has she stumbled into?

Other books you might like:
D.B. Borton, *The Cat Caliban Series*, 1993-
Janet Dawson, *The Jeri Howard Series*, 1990-
Linda Grant, *The Catherine Saylor Series*, 1988-
Karen Kijewski, *The Kat Colorado Series*, 1989-
Marcia Muller, *The Sharon McCone Series*, 1977-

1507
Douglas Skeggs
The Estuary Pilgrim (New York: St. Martin's, 1989)

Story type: Action/Adventure

Major character(s): John Napier, Art Historian (Impressionist expert)

Time period(s): 1980s

Locale(s): Honfleur, France

What the book is about: After Napier authenticates a Monet painting thought to have been destroyed by the Nazis, a stranger shows up who claims he can prove the painting is a forgery. Said stranger soon turns up dead. First book.

Other books you might like:
Peter Clothier, *Chiaroscuro*, 1985
Michael Gilbert, *Paint, Gold and Blood*, 1989
John Malcolm, *Whistler in the Dark*, 1987
Marcia Muller, *There Hangs the Knife*, 1988
Wayne Warga, *Fatal Impressions*, 1989

1508
Douglas Skeggs
The Talinin Madonna (New York: St. Martin's, 1992)

Story type: Action/Adventure

Major character(s): Philip "Pip" Spencer, Lawyer; Katya Leskova, Linguist (translator)

Time period(s): 1980s (1989)

Locale(s): Russia; England

What the book is about: Pip Spencer is approached by an old Russian immigrant who claims to have seen a painting, supposedly stored away in Russia, for sale in a London gallery. When the old man dies hours later, Pip looks into matters. He writes a letter to the Russian Ministry of Culture setting in motion a series of events that may cause many more deaths.

Other books you might like:
Aaron Elkins, *A Glancing Light*, 1991
Isabelle Holland, *The Lost Madonna*, 1981
John Le Carre, *The Russia House*, 1987
John Malcolm, *Whistler in the Dark*, 1987
Wayne Warga, *Fatal Impressions*, 1989

1509
Douglas Skeggs
The Triumph of Bacchus (New York: St. Martin's, 1993)

Story type: Action/Adventure

Major character(s): Tom Shaugnessy, Criminal (forger); Patricia Drew, Journalist (TV reporter); James Trevelyn, Insurance Investigator

Time period(s): 1990s

Locale(s): London, England

What the book is about: The painting *The Triumph of Bacchus* by Titian has just been stolen and is being held for a ransom of 5 million pounds. James Trevelyn is responsible for recovering the painting. Meanwhile Tom Shaugnessy is working on creating a perfect forgery and Patricia Drew is on the story of the theft and the gang of art thieves. They are all on a collision course.

Other books you might like:
Peter Clothier, *Dirty-Down*, 1987
Aaron Elkins, *A Glancing Light*, 1991
John Malcolm, *The Wrong Impression*, 1990
Don Matheson, *Ninth Life*, 1989
Joan Smith, *A Brush with Death*, 1990

1510
Edward Sklepowich
Death in a Serene City (New York: Morrow, 1990)

Story type: Amateur Detective

Major character(s): Urbino McIntyre, Writer (American, now lives in Venice); Barbara Capo-Zendrini, Noblewoman (contessa)

Time period(s): 1990s

Locale(s): Venice, Italy

What the book is about: When the mummified body of Santa Teodora is stolen and a woman is found dead nearby, the police blame the woman's hunchback son. Urbino and Barbara are not so sure and set out to find the real culprits. First novel.

Other books you might like:
Sarah Caudwell, *Thus Was Adonis Murdered*, 1981
Jonathan Gash, *The Gondola Scam*, 1984
Hazel Wynn Jones, *Death and the Trumpets of Tuscany*, 1989
Helen MacInnes, *The Venetian Affair*, 1963

1511
Edith Skom
The George Eliot Murders (New York: Delacorte, 1995)

Series: Beth Austin

Story type: Amateur Detective—Female Lead

Major character(s): Beth Austin, Professor (of English literature)

Time period(s): 1990s

Locale(s): Hawaii

What the book is about: Professor Beth Austin is tired of snow and ice so she decides to take a soothing vacation in Hawaii. When she arrives at the Royal Aloha, she finds most of the other guests are regulars. One of the guests, a famous designer, plunges to her death, soon after, Beth overhears a cryptic conversation. Accident or suicide? The question becomes academic as two more murders occur. Beth, with the help of a retired lawyer and a good looking writer, begins to snoop.

Other books you might like:
Amanda Cross, *The Kate Fansler Series*, 1964-
Nora Kelly, *The Gillian Adams Series*, 1992-
Fran Kupfer, *Love Lies*, 1994
Susan Kenney, *The Roz Howard Series*, 1983-
Joan Smith, *The Loretta Lawson Series*, 1987-

1512
Edith Skom
The Mark Twain Murders (Tulsa: Council Oak, 1989)

Story type: Amateur Detective—Female Lead

Major character(s): Beth Austin, Professor (College English); Gil Bailey, Police Officer (F.B.I. agent)

Time period(s): 1980s

Locale(s): Midwest

What the book is about: There seems to be a connection between a plagiarized paper on Mark Twain and the thefts of rare books from the university library. Then there's the murder of the alleged plagiarist. First book.

1513 Slater

Other books you might like:
Marcia Biederman, *Post No Bonds*, 1988
Bill Crider, *Dying Voices*, 1989
Amanda Cross, *The James Joyce Murder*, 1967
Julie Smith, *Huckleberry Fiend*, 1986

1513
Ian Slater
Deep Chill (New York: Worldwide, 1989)

Story type: Techno-Thriller

Major character(s): Frank Hall, Scientist (Oceanographer); Alexander Kornon, Military Personnel (Soviet General)

Time period(s): 1980s

Locale(s): Bering Sea, Pacific Ocean (Underwater)

What the book is about: When an American submarine becomes entangled in drift nets in the Bering Sea and goes down, it's a race to see who will salvage her (and perhaps her still alive crew)—the Soviets or the U.S.

Other books you might like:
Dale Brown, *Day of the Cheetah*, 1989
Tom Clancy, *The Hunt for Red October*, 1984
Clive Cussler, *Raise the Titanic!*, 1976
Payne Harrison, *Storming Intrepid*, 1989
Dean Ing, *The Ransom of Black Stealth One*, 1989

1514
Susan R. Sloan
Guilt by Association (New York: Warner, 1995)

Story type: Psychological Suspense

Major character(s): Karen Kern, Lawyer; Robert Willmont, Political Figure

Time period(s): 1990s

Locale(s): New York, New York; California

What the book is about: Karen Kern is raped in 1962 and nobody believes her. It is thought that she provoked the rape. Now, 30 years later, her rapist is a respected politician and she is determined to bring him down. First novel.

Other books you might like:
Kenneth Abel, *Bait*, 1994
Carol Brennan, *In the Dark*, 1994
Kate Green, *Shooting Star*, 1992
Susan Kelly, *Out of the Darkness*, 1994
John Lutz, *S.W.F. Seeks Same*, 1991

1515
April Smith
North of Montana (New York: Knopf, 1994)

Story type: Police Procedural—Female Lead

Major character(s): Ana Grey, FBI Agent

Time period(s): 1990s

Locale(s): Los Angeles, California

What the book is about: Ana Grey expects to be rewarded for making a high-profile arrest, but instead she is reprimanded and assigned to a case she feels is beneath her—dealing with drugs among the jetset, including a respected actress and a high-society doctor. She also finds that a young woman who has been murdered in an alleged street crime may be involved and that the woman may have been Ana's cousin. She may learn more than she wanted to know about her past and the people involved there. First novel.

Other books you might like:
Susan Dunlap, *The Jill Smith Series*, 1981-
Laurie R. King, *A Grave Talent*, 1993
Rochelle Majer Krich, *Angel of Death*, 1994
Carol O'Connell, *Mallory's Oracle*, 1994
Julie Smith, *The Axeman's Jazz*, 1991

1516
Barbara Burnett Smith
Dust Devils of the Purple Sage (New York: St. Martin's, 1995)

Series: Jolie Wyatt

Story type: Amateur Detective—Female Lead

Major character(s): Jolie Wyatt, Writer

Time period(s): 1990s

Locale(s): Purple Sage, Texas

What the book is about: Jolie Wyatt has recently taken a job with a local radio station as a newswriter and broadcaster. One of her first stories is about the prison break of a local young man, James Jorgenson. James and his sister are apparently on their way back to Purple Sage. Everyone thought James was wild but not dangerous, then another nice teenage boy is killed. James seems the perfect supsect, but Jolie thinks he may be the perfect scapegoat.

Other books you might like:
Deborah Adams, *The Jesus Creek Series*, 1992-
Susan Wittig Albert, *The China Bayles Series*, 1992-
Connie Fedderson, *Dead in the Cellar*, 1994
Earlene Fowler, *The Benni Harper Series*, 1994-
Charlaine Harris, *The Aurora Teagarden Series*, 1990-

1517
Barbara Burnett Smith
Writers of the Purple Sage (New York: St. Martin's, 1994)

Story type: Amateur Detective—Female Lead

Major character(s): Jolie Wyatt, Writer (unpublished); Diane Atwood, Writer (unpublished)

Time period(s): 1990s

Locale(s): Purple Sage, Texas

What the book is about: Jolie Wyatt wants to be a writer of mysteries, but so far hasn't had any luck. Recently divorced and trying to support herself and her teenage son, she needs a job and may have to leave town. Her latest mystery has a good chance to be accepted though. Then Judge Osler, "the patron saint of Purple Sage," is killed, murdered by the same method as in Jolie's latest book. The only ones who knew the method were members of Jolie's writing group and the investigating officer, all of whom had reason to dislike the judge. First novel.

Other books you might like:
Deborah Adams, *The Jesus Creek Series*, 1992-
Susan Rogers Cooper, *Funny as a Dead Relative*, 1994
Connie Fedderson, *Dead in the Water*, 1993
Muriel Resnick Jackson, *The Garden Club*, 1992
Toni L.P. Kelner, *Down Home Murder*, 1993

1518
Evelyn E. Smith
Miss Melville Rides a Tiger (New York: Fine, 1991)
Series: Miss Melville
Story type: Action/Adventure
Major character(s): Susan Melville, Criminal (contract killer), Artist (society matron)
Time period(s): 1990s
Locale(s): New York, New York

What the book is about: Susan Melville is a successful painter, a leading member of New York's High Society, the head of a large foundation and a highly proficient assassin. The government wants her to kill the Begum of Gandistan, the mother and ruthless power behind the throne of the Sultan. She refuses, but soon circumstances may force her to change her mind.

Other books you might like:
Margaret Duffy, *A Murder of Crows*, 1987
Robert L. Fish, *The Murder League*, 1968
Dorothy Gilman, *Mrs. Pollifax and the Whirling Dervish*, 1990

1519
Joan Smith
A Brush with Death (New York: Berkley, 1990)
Story type: Amateur Detective—Female Lead
Major character(s): Cassie Newman, Student; John Weiss, Insurance Investigator (Fiance of Cassie)
Time period(s): 1980s
Locale(s): Montreal, Quebec, Canada

What the book is about: Cassie Newman gets involved in finding out who is behind a Van Gogh forgery ring, which happens to be the case her fiance is also investigating. This is Smith's first mystery, though she has written a number of romance novels.

Other books you might like:
K.K. Beck, *Death in a Deck Chair*, 1984
Dorothy Salisbury Davis, *Scarlet Night*, 1980
Howard Engel, *Murder on Location*, 1984
Victoria Silver, *Death of a Harvard Freshman*, 1984

1520
Joan Smith
Don't Leave Me This Way (New York: Scribners, 1990)
Series: Loretta Lawson
Story type: Amateur Detective—Female Lead
Major character(s): Loretta Lawson, Professor (English)
Time period(s): 1990s
Locale(s): London, England

What the book is about: It's Christmas Eve when an old acquaintance, Sandra Neil, asks to stay with Loretta for a few days because of a flooded apartment. On New Years Eve, Sandra is still there but when Loretta returns from a night out, Sandra is gone leaving all her clothes. Several days later Loretta finds out Sandra was killed in a car crash. Loretta is uneasy about this - and why did Sandra have a large amount of money hidden in her luggage?

Other books you might like:
J.S. Borthwick, *The Student Body*, 1986
Amanda Cross, *Death in a Tenured Position*, 1981
Susan Kenney, *Garden of Malice*, 1983
Valerie Miner, *Murder in the English Department*, 1982
Theodora Wender, *Knight Must Fall*, 1985

1521
Joan Smith
Follow That Blonde (New York: Berkley, 1990)
Story type: Amateur Detective—Female Lead
Major character(s): Lana Morton, Teacher (English); Nick Hansen, Artist (painter)
Time period(s): 1990s
Locale(s): Rome, Italy

What the book is about: Lana Morton and her friend Nancy are on vacation touring Europe. In Rome they meet an old high school acquaintance who happens to be the agent for famous artist Nick Hansen. They quickly become involved in an art scam that concerns Nick's former agent. The only way to prevent the fraud is to kill Nick.

Other books you might like:
Oliver Banks, *The Rembrandt Panel*, 1980
Peter Clothier, *Chiaroscuro*, 1985
Carolyn Coker, *The Balmoral Nude*, 1990
Caroline Llewellyn, *The Masks of Rome*, 1988
Marcia Muller, *The Cavalier in White*, 1986

1522
Joan Smith
What Men Say (New York: Fawcett, 1994)
Series: Loretta Lawson
Story type: Amateur Detective—Female Lead
Major character(s): Loretta Lawson, Professor (of English); Bridget Bennet, Professor (of English)
Time period(s): 1990s
Locale(s): Oxford, England

What the book is about: Loretta Lawson is attending a housewarming for her old friend Bridget Bennet and her husband at a farm they have bought in the country. The festivities are interrupted when the body of a woman is discovered in the old barn. She has been dead for two weeks and no one seems to know who she was. The tabloids call it the "death farm" and hint that Bridget is the murderer. Loretta thinks differently—but Bridget has been acting strangely and may know more than she says.

Other books you might like:
Amanda Cross, *Death in a Tenured Position*, 1981
Nora Kelly, *My Sister's Keeper*, 1992
Susan Kenney, *Garden of Malice*, 1983
Valerie Miner, *Murder in the English Department*, 1982
Janet Neel, *Death Among the Dons*, 1994

1523
Julie Smith
The Axeman's Jazz (New York: St. Martin's, 1991)
Series: Skip Langdon
Story type: Police Procedural—Female Lead
Major character(s): Skip Langdon, Police Officer (female), Detective—Homicide
Time period(s): 1990s
Locale(s): New Orleans, Louisiana
What the book is about: In 1919 a serial killer known as the Axeman terrorized New Orleans. Now after two people are killed, the Axeman claims he is back. Skip Langdon finds that the only connection between the two victims is they both belonged to various twelve-step programs. Skip's problem is how to investigate a group of suspects when anonymity is the mainstay of the groups.

Other books you might like:
Susan Dunlap, *The Jill Smith Series*, 1984-
Ruby Horansky, *Dead Ahead*, 1990
Margaret Maron, *The Sigrid Harald Series*, 1982-
Lee Martin, *The Deb Ralston Series*, 1984-
Lillian O'Donnell, *The Norah Mulcahaney Series*, 1972-

1524
Julie Smith
Dead in the Water (New York: Ballantine, 1991)
Series: Rebecca Schwartz
Story type: Amateur Detective—Female Lead
Major character(s): Rebecca Schwartz, Lawyer
Time period(s): 1990s
Locale(s): Monterey, California
What the book is about: Rebecca's acquaintance, Marty Whitehead, has asked her down to see the Monterey Bay Aquarium where Marty works. While Marty is showing her the kelp tank, they notice a floating body. The body turns out to be Marty's boss, Sadie, and she is wearing Marty's coat. Further Sadie was having an affair with Marty's husband. Marty retains Rebecca to prove her innocence.

Other books you might like:
Mercedes Lambert, *Dogtown*, 1991
Lia Matera, *The Smart Money*, 1988
Judith Van Gieson, *Raptor*, 1990
Carolyn Wheat, *Dead Man's Thoughts*, 1983
Susan Wolfe, *The Last Billable Hour*, 1989

1525
Julie Smith
House of Blues (New York: Fawcett, 1995)
Series: Skip Langdon
Story type: Police Procedural—Female Lead
Major character(s): Skip Langdon, Police Officer (homicide)
Time period(s): 1990s
Locale(s): New Orleans, Louisiana
What the book is about: The Herbert family are famous for owning and running a world-famous restaurant bearing their name. One night at a family meeting, gunfire erupts. When the police arrive, the head of the family, Arthur Herbert, is dead and his daughter, son-in-law and granddaughter have disappeared. A kidnapping gone wrong? A family argument ending in violence? Skip tries to find the truth and discovers a link to organized crime, among other family secrets.

Other books you might like:
Susan Dunlap, *The Jill Smith Series*, 1981-
Laurie R. King, *The Kate Martinelli Series*, 1993-
Rochelle Majer Krich, *The Jessica Drake Series*, 1993-
Lee Martin, *The Deb Ralston Series*, 1984-
April Smith, *North of Montana*, 1994

1526
Julie Smith
Jazz Funeral (New York: Ballantine, 1993)
Series: Skip Langdon
Story type: Police Procedural—Female Lead
Major character(s): Skip Langdon, Police Officer, Detective—Homicide; Melody Brocato, Student
Time period(s): 1990s
Locale(s): New Orleans, Louisiana
What the book is about: It's the start of the New Orleans Jazz and Heritage Festival and its producer, Ham Brocato, scion of the Poor Boy Restaurant chain, is cooking for the party. One of the knives ends up in his chest and Skip Langdon must now find the killer. She becomes involved in the New Orleans music scene and with old family secrets. She must also find Melody Brocato, the victim's 16 year old sister, who has disappeared. Is she a killer, a witness, or the next victim?

Other books you might like:
Susan Dunlap, *The Jill Smith Series*, 1981-
Laurie R. King, *A Grave Talent*, 1993
Rochelle Majer Krich, *Fair Game*, 1993
Catherine O'Connell, *Skins*, 1993
James Schermerhorn, *Night of the Cat*, 1993

1527
Julie Smith
New Orleans Beat (New York: Fawcett, 1994)
Series: Skip Langdon
Story type: Police Procedural—Female Lead
Major character(s): Skip Langdon, Police Officer, Detective—Homicide
Time period(s): 1990s
Locale(s): New Orleans, Louisiana
What the book is about: A routine accident investigation—a fall from a ladder—becomes a possible murder when the autopsy results come in. Now four days later Skip Langdon is assigned to find out what happened to Geoff Cavanaugh. He was bright, reclusive and socially inept—a typical "computer nerd." But Geoff was also involved with a network of computer users and may have mentioned that he witnessed a murder when he was a child. Skip becomes involved with the new electronic magic and a group that believes in a much more ancient type of magic.
Other books you might like:
Noreen Ayres, *A World the Color of Salt*, 1992
Ruby Horansky, *Dead Ahead*, 1992
Laurie R. King, *A Grave Talent*, 1993
John Lutz, *Nightlines*, 1984
April Smith, *North of Montana*, 1994

1528
Julie Smith
New Orleans Mourning (New York: St. Martin's, 1990)
Series: Skip Langdon
Story type: Police Procedural—Female Lead
Major character(s): Skip Langdon, Police Officer (Female, rookie)
Time period(s): 1980s
Locale(s): New Orleans, Louisiana
What the book is about: Who killed Chauncey St. Amant just as he was about to be crowned King of Carnival?
Other books you might like:
Susan Dunlap, *As a Favor*, 1986
M.D. Lake, *Amends for Murder*, 1990
Claire McNab, *Death Down Under*, 1990
Lillian O'Donnell, *A Good Night to Kill*, 1988

1529
Julie Smith
Other People's Skeletons (New York: Ballantine, 1993)
Series: Rebecca Schwartz
Story type: Amateur Detective—Female Lead; Legal
Major character(s): Rebecca Schwartz, Lawyer; Chris Nicholson, Lawyer (Rebecca's partner)
Time period(s): 1990s
Locale(s): San Francisco, California
What the book is about: Rebecca Schwartz's partner Chris Nicholson is a prime suspect in the hit and run murder of noted critic Jason McKendrick. Chris' car has been identified as the vehicle involved and although Chris says she has an alibi, she won't say who or what it is. Not only does Rebecca have to look into Jason's secret life to discover who wanted him dead, she must find out her friend's secrets too.
Other books you might like:
Michael A. Kahn, *Death Benefits*, 1992
Mercedes Lambert, *Dogtown*, 1991
Lia Matera, *A Hard Bargain*, 1992
Judith Van Gieson, *The Other Side of Death*, 1991
Hannah Wakefield, *The Price You Pay*, 1989

1530
Martin Cruz Smith
Polar Star (New York: Random House, 1989)
Series: Arkady Renko
Story type: Action/Adventure
Major character(s): Arkady Renko, Police Officer (Former)
Time period(s): 1980s
Locale(s): Poland (The Arctic)
What the book is about: Renko, a former Moscow police officer, is charged with finding out who killed a worker on a Russian trawler.
Other books you might like:
Tom Clancy, *The Hunt for Red October*, 1984
Colin Forbes, *Target Five*, 1972
David Madsen, *U.S.S.A.*, 1989
Alistair MacLean, *Ice Station Zebra*, 1963
Edward Topol, *Red Snow*, 1987

1531
Mitchell Smith
Karma (New York: Dutton, 1994)
Story type: Action/Adventure
Major character(s): Evan Scott, Architect
Time period(s): 1990s
Locale(s): New York, New York
What the book is about: When he witnesses a woman falling to her death from a skyscraper, architect Evan Scott has no idea that this will lead to him and his family being put in mortal danger from the Raos family. Can he find enough evidence to get the police to put the family out of business before they find and kill Scott and his loved ones?
Other books you might like:
Jeffrey Wilds Deaver, *The Lesson of Her Death*, 1993
John Grisham, *The Firm*, 1991
Evan Hunter, *Criminal Conversation*, 1994
Elmore Leonard, *Killshot*, 1989
David Morrell, *Blood Oath*, 1982

1532
Stephen Solomita
Bad to the Bone (New York: Putnam, 1991)
Series: Stanley Moodrow
Story type: Private Detective—Male Lead
Major character(s): Stanley Moodrow, Detective—Private (former police officer); Davis Craddock, Criminal (leader of a sex cult)
Time period(s): 1990s
Locale(s): New York, New York
What the book is about: Investigating a woman in a coma and searching for her missing son leads Moodrow into involvement with the Jim Jones-like cult of Davis Craddock.
Other books you might like:
Lawrence Block, *Out on the Cutting Edge*, 1989
Tucker Coe, *The Mitch Tobin Series*, 1966-1972
Stephen Paul Cohen, *Island of Steel*, 1988
Thomas H. Cook, *Flesh and Blood*, 1989
Robert J. Randisi, *No Exit From Brooklyn*, 1987

1533
Stephen Solomita
Force of Nature (New York: Putnam, 1989)
Series: Stanley Moodrow
Story type: Police Procedural—Male Lead
Major character(s): Stanley Moodrow, Detective—Police; Jim Tilley, Detective—Police (Ex-boxer)
Time period(s): 1980s
Locale(s): New York, New York
What the book is about: Moodrow and Tilley search for a drug dealer and cop-killer as Stanley prepares to retire.
Other books you might like:
William Bayer, *Switch*, 1984
William J. Caunitz, *One Police Plaza*, 1984
Thomas H. Cook, *Sacrificial Ground*, 1988
David L. Lindsey, *Spiral*, 1986
Lawrence Sanders, *The First Deadly Sin*, 1973

1534
Stephen Solomita
A Good Day to Die (New York: Penzler, 1993)
Story type: Police Procedural; Action/Adventure
Major character(s): Roland Means, Police Officer (Vietnam Vet), Indian; Vanessa Bouton, Police Officer (African-American)
Time period(s): 1990s
Locale(s): New York, New York
What the book is about: Captain Bouton approaches Roland Means with an offer, she will get him out of ballistics where he has been buried and back on the streets if he will help her prove "King Thong", a serial killer of male prostitutes, is really a clever murderer disguising one killing as a series. Meanwhile a young Asian woman has been kidnapped by a strange family. Are these cases related?

Other books you might like:
William J. Caunitz, *Exceptional Clearance*, 1991
Michael Connelly, *The Black Ice*, 1993
David L. Lindsey, *Mercy*, 1990
John Lawrence Reynolds, *And Leave Her Lay Dying*, 1990
John Sandford, *Shadow Prey*, 1990

1535
Stephen Solomita
A Piece of the Action (New York: Putnam, 1992)
Series: Stanley Moodrow
Story type: Police Procedural—Male Lead; Action/Adventure
Major character(s): Stanley Moodrow, Detective—Police
Time period(s): 1950s (1958)
Locale(s): New York, New York
What the book is about: Previous books have followed the career of Stanley Moodrow as senior detective and private detective. This book goes back to 1958 when Stanley first receives his gold detective shield, partly because he is engaged to the daughter of Pat Cohen, a high ranking inspector on the force. Stanley is young and eager to solve cases and make arrests, but he finds that in the world of the "pad", some of the bad guys are his co-workers.
Other books you might like:
William J. Caunitz, *Exceptional Clearance*, 1991
Thomas H. Cook, *Streets of Fire*, 1989
Nat Hentoff, *The Man From Internal Affairs*, 1985
Joseph Trigoboff, *The Bone Orchard*, 1990
John Westermann, *Exit Wounds*, 1990

1536
Troy Soos
Murder at Fenway Park (New York: Kensington, 1994)
Story type: Historical; Amateur Detective—Male Lead
Major character(s): Mickey Rawlings, Sports Figure (baseball player)
Time period(s): 1910s (1912)
Locale(s): Boston, Massachusetts; New York, New York
What the book is about: Mickey Rawlings is a utility infielder who has just been told to report to the Boston Red Sox. Upon reporting he immediately trips over the body of Red Corriden whose head has been bashed in by a baseball bat. Mickey is questioned by the local cops and team officials and is then released to play ball. When he realizes that the crime is being covered up he is determined to investigate. It seems that Corriden had been part of a group that tried to cheat Ty Cobb out of a batting championship. Could Cobb be the killer? First novel.
Other books you might like:
Loren D. Estleman, *Whiskey River*, 1990
Crabbe Evers, *Fear in Fenway*, 1993
Jack Finney, *Time and Again*, 1970
Richard Rosen, *Strike Three, You're Dead*, 1987

1537
Sin Soracco
Edge City (New York: Dutton, 1992)

Story type: Psychological Suspense; Action/Adventure

Major character(s): Reno, Thief, Convict (ex-convict); Susanna, Dancer (exotic dancer)

Time period(s): 1990s

Locale(s): United States

What the book is about: Reno is just out of prison and she is trying to decide whether to go straight or go for the big score. She is drawn to the Club Istanbul, a nightclub of exotic dancers, where she meets an old roomate, who is not the featured dancer. She also meets a strange collection of dancers, junkies and criminals — all looking for the big time.

Other books you might like:
Eugene Izzi, *King of the Hustlers*, 1989
Mark McGarrity, *Neon Caesar*, 1989
Randy Russell, *Hot Wire*, 1988
Marc Savage, *Flamingos*, 1992

1538
Robert Specht
The Soul of Betty Fairchild (New York: St. Martin's, 1991)

Story type: Psychological Suspense

Major character(s): Drew Summers, Advertising (copywriter for an ad agency)

Time period(s): 1990s

Locale(s): Greenview, South Carolina; New York, New York

What the book is about: In 1967, beautiful, wealthy Betty Fairchild was brutally murdered. Now successful and young businesswoman Drew Summers has a problem. She is undergoing spells where she talks in a southern accent. As more episodes occur she is drawn to Greenview where she discovers she looks exactly like Betty Fairchild. Has Betty come back to take over Drew and find her own killer?

Other books you might like:
John Camp, *The Empress File*, 1991
Bennie Lee Sinclair, *The Lynching*, 1992
David Stout, *Carolina Skeletons*, 1989
Charles Wilson, *Silent Witness*, 1992

1539
Michael Spicer
Cotswold Moles (New York: St. Martin's, 1993)

Series: Lady Jane Hildreth

Story type: Espionage

Major character(s): Lady Jane Hildreth, Spy (counter-espionage, MI5); Patricia Huntington, Spy (retired)

Time period(s): 1990s

Locale(s): The Cotswolds, England; Broome, Australia

What the book is about: Lady Jane Hildreth is asked by her chief to look into the death of an elderly recluse, Veronica Langhorn. When she arrives she finds the body of the caretaker hanging from a tree, an obvious suicide. However, in Lady Jane's opinion things are not as they seem. When some old photos point to Broome, Australia many years ago, her chief takes her off the case. Jane and Patricia investigate on their own and find more than they want to know.

Other books you might like:
Margaret Duffy, *The Lanley and Gillard Series*, 1987-
Katherine Neville, *The Eight*, 1988
Evelyn E. Smith, *The Miss Melville Series*, 1987-
Janice Weber, *Frost the Fiddler*, 1992

1540
Mickey Spillane
The Killing Man (New York: Dutton, 1989)

Series: Mike Hammer

Story type: Private Detective—Male Lead

Major character(s): Mike Hammer, Detective—Private

Time period(s): 1980s

Locale(s): New York, New York

What the book is about: A man turns up dead in Hammer's office and Hammer's secretary, Velda, has been roughed up. Why was the dead man left for Hammer to find and who is "Penta"?

Other books you might like:
Jonathan Latimer, *Solomon's Vineyard*, 1950
L.A. Morse, *The Big Enchilada*, 1982
Jonathan Valin, *Day of Wrath*, 1982

1541
Michelle Spring
Every Breath You Take (New York: Pocket, 1994)

Story type: Private Detective—Female Lead

Major character(s): Laura Principal, Detective—Private; Helen Cochrane, Librarian, Single Parent (friend of Laura)

Time period(s): 1990s

Locale(s): London, England; Norfolk, England

What the book is about: Laura Principal and Helen Cochrane are old friends who share a weekend retreat in Norfolk. When they decide to include a third person to share expenses they meet Monica Harcourt, an artist and teacher at Cambridge. Just as they are getting to know Monica she is brutally tortured and murdered. Then the killer phones Laura and Helen to play them a tape of Monica's last moments. Who hated her so much and why does he now seem to be after them? First novel.

Other books you might like:
Liza Cody, *The Anna Lee Series*, 1980-
Sarah Dunant, *Birthmarks*, 1992
Gillian Slovo, *The Kate Baeier Series*, 1984-
Joan Smith, *The Loretta Lawson Series*, 1988-
Hannah Wakefield, *A Woman's Own Mystery*, 1991

1542
Patricia Houck Sprinkle
Deadly Secrets on the St. Johns (New York: Bantam, 1995)
Series: Sheila Travis
Story type: Amateur Detective—Female Lead
Major character(s): Sheila Travis, Businesswoman, Widow(er)
Time period(s): 1990s
Locale(s): Jacksonville, Florida
What the book is about: Crispin Montgomery, Sheila's lover, is taking her off to Jacksonville to meet his relatives, a strange mix of southern aristocracy. At the dinner party, Daphne Larkens, wife of Crispin's cousin, dies mysteriously. The police call it a tragic accident. Sheila is relieved as she has had her fill of murder. But then more bodies start showing up.
Other books you might like:
Toni L.P. Kelner, *The Laura Fleming Series*, 1993-
Sarah Shankman, *The Samantha Adams Series*, 1989-
Celestine Sibley, *Dire Happenings at Scratch Ankle*, 1993
Elizabeth Daniels Squire, *The Peaches Dann Series*, 1994-
Kathy Hogan Trocheck, *The Callahan Garrity Series*, 1993-

1543
Patricia Houck Sprinkle
Murder on Peachtree Street (New York: St. Martins, 1991)
Series: Sheila Travis
Story type: Amateur Detective—Female Lead
Major character(s): Sheila Travis, Businesswoman (director of international rela); Mary Beaufort, Businesswoman (Sheila's aunt)
Time period(s): 1990s
Locale(s): Atlanta, Georgia
What the book is about: When Dean Anderson, head of Galaxia's video program is found dead, Sheila is pressured by her boss and her Aunt Mary into discreetly assisting in the investigation. The police believe it was suicide but Sheila knows her friend had no reason to kill himself and finds several people who wished Dean dead.
Other books you might like:
Liza Bennett, *Madison Avenue Murder*, 1989
Carole Berry, *The Year of the Monkey*, 1988
Jaqueline Girdner, *Adjusted to Death*, 1991
Yvonne Montgomery, *Scavengers*, 1988
Nancy Pickard, *Say No to Murder*, 1984

1544
Patricia Houck Sprinkle
A Mystery Bred in Buckhead (New York: Bantam, 1994)
Series: Sheila Travis
Story type: Amateur Detective—Female Lead
Major character(s): Sheila Travis, Businesswoman; Mary Beaufort, Businesswoman (Sheila's aunt)
Time period(s): 1990s
Locale(s): Buckhead, Georgia (Atlanta suburb)
What the book is about: Fifty years ago at a high society party, a soldier died. Now Rippen Delacourt is throwing his annual Christmas party with many of the same people present. It is announced that a manuscript written by Margaret Mitchell has been discovered and seems to be based on the secrets she discovered at the long ago party. Sheila Travis and her aunt, Mary Beaufort, get involved when people start to die. Sheila wants to know the truth, but Mary wants to protect her friends and family.
Other books you might like:
Muriel Resnick Jackson, *The Garden Club*, 1992
Toni L.P. Kelner, *Dead Ringer*, 1994
Sarah Shankman, *The Samantha Adams Series*, 1989-
Celestine Sibley, *Dire Happenings at Scratch Ankle*, 1993
Kathy Hogan Trocheck, *To Live and Die in Dixie*, 1993

1545
Patricia Houck Sprinkle
Somebody's Dead in Snellville (New York: St. Martin's, 1992)
Series: Sheila Travis
Story type: Amateur Detective—Female Lead
Major character(s): Sheila Travis, Businesswoman; Mary Beaufort, Businesswoman (Sheila's aunt)
Time period(s): 1990s
Locale(s): Atlanta, Georgia; Snellville, Georgia
What the book is about: Sheila is trying to be a good neighbor and accompanies Sara Sims Tait to a Sims family dinner to lend moral support. There it is disclosed that an offer of ten million dollars has been made for the family land but Grandma Sims won't sell. This would be a perfect motive for murder but other people begin to die. Once again, the irrepressible Aunt Mary urges Sheila to investigate.
Other books you might like:
Carole Berry, *The Year of the Monkey*, 1988
Yvonne Montgomery, *Scavengers*, 1988
Katherine Hall Page, *The Body in the Belfry*, 1990
Sarah Shankman, *First Kill All the Lawyers*, 1988
Celestine Sibley, *Ah, Sweet Mystery*, 1991

1546
Elizabeth Daniels Squire
Kill the Messenger (New York: St. Martin's, 1990)
Story type: Amateur Detective—Male Lead
Major character(s): Howard Justice, Heir (son of the murdered man)
Time period(s): 1980s
Locale(s): South
What the book is about: Who killed Howard Justice's father? Was it the sinister corporation? Was it some one hurt by the rough reporting in his newspaper? Or was it one of his children? First book.

Other books you might like:
Alexander Law, *To an Easy Grave*, 1986
Dave Pedneau, *D.O.A.*, 1988
Keith Peterson, *The Trapdoor*, 1988
John R. Riggs, *Wolf in Sheep's Clothing*, 1989
Stuart Woods, *Chiefs*, 1981

1547
Elizabeth Daniels Squire
Memory Can Be Murder (New York: Berkley, 1995)
Series: Peaches Dann
Story type: Amateur Detective—Female Lead
Major character(s): Peaches Dann, Writer
Time period(s): 1990s
Locale(s): Bloodroot Creek, North Carolina
What the book is about: Peaches is gaining a reputation as a sleuth, albeit an absent-minded one. She is asked by her cousin Anne to look into the disappearance of the son of a client to Anne and her husband, Sam. Sam is painting a portrait of Revonda Roland, a well-known actress who has returned home after giving up her career. The son finally reappears, but is then found suffocated by a plastic bag and stuffed in a laundry chute. He is only the first in a series of victims killed in the same bizarre fashion.
Other books you might like:
Carolyn G. Hart, *The Henrietta O'Dwyer Series*, 1993-
Toni L.P. Kelner, *The Laura Fleming Series*, 1993-
Kate Morgan, *The Dewey James Series*, 1990-
Celestine Sibley, *Straight as an Arrow*, 1992
Patricia Houck Sprinkle, *Murder in the Charleston Manner*, 1990

1548
Elizabeth Daniels Squire
Who Killed What's-Her-Name? (New York: Berkley, 1994)
Series: Peaches Dann
Story type: Amateur Detective—Female Lead
Major character(s): Peaches Dann, Writer, Widow(er)
Time period(s): 1990s
Locale(s): North Carolina
What the book is about: Peaches Dann is notorious for her memory-she doesn't have one. She is writing a book *How to Survive Without a Memory* filled with tricks she learned in order to survive while taking care of her elderly father. She is interrupted when she finds the body of her aunt in the family pond. It is clear she was murdered and Peaches realizes that her aunt was dressed almost exactly like Peaches that day. Was somebody trying to kill her? She decides to investigate to protect herself.
Other books you might like:
B. Comfort, *The Tish McWhinney Series*, 1989-
Muriel Resnick Jackson, *The Garden Club*, 1992
Celestine Sibley, *The Kate Mulcay Series*, 1991-
Patricia Houck Sprinkle, *The Sheila Travis Series*, 1988-
Kathy Hogan Trocheck, *The Callahan Garrity Series*, 1992

1549
Dana Stabenow
A Cold Day for Murder (New York: Berkley, 1992)
Series: Kate Shugak
Story type: Private Detective—Female Lead
Major character(s): Kate Shugak, Detective—Private (ex-investigator for the D.A.), Indian; Jack Morgan, Police Officer
Time period(s): 1990s
Locale(s): Niniltna, Alaska
What the book is about: Kate has become a recluse in the wilds of Alaska after killing a child molester in self-defense - her only companion a half-wolf dog named Mutt. Now her former boss and the FBI want to hire her to investigate the disappearances of a park ranger and the investigator sent to find him. Kate, with intimate knowledge of the area and the people, seems perfect to solve the mystery. First novel.
Other books you might like:
Sean Hanlon, *The Cold Front*, 1989
Sue Henry, *Murder on the Iditarod Trail*, 1991
Gwen Moffat, *Rage*, 1990
John Straley, *The Woman Who Married a Bear*, 1992
Ted Wood, *The Reid Bennett Series*, 1986-

1550
Dana Stabenow
A Cold-Blooded Business (New York: Berkley, 1994)
Series: Kate Shugak
Story type: Private Detective—Female Lead
Major character(s): Kate Shugak, Detective—Private, Indian (Aleut); Jack Morgan, Police Officer (Kate's lover)
Time period(s): 1990s
Locale(s): Prudhoe, Alaska
What the book is about: Kate Shugak is asked by an oil company executive to investigate the death by drug overdose of an oil worker, to discover how the drugs are being transported, and to put a stop to it. What Kate finds is an isolated and intimate community in the wilds of Alaska where nobody wants the drug trade stopped and some will do whatever it takes to keep the oil and the cocaine flowing.
Other books you might like:
Jean Hager, *Ravenmocker*, 1992
Sue Henry, *Murder on the Iditarod Trail*, 1991
John Straley, *The Woman Who Married a Bear*, 1992
J.F. Trainor, *The Angela Biwaban Series*, 1993-
Scott Young, *Murder in a Cold Climate*, 1988

1551
Dana Stabenow
Dead in the Water (New York: Berkley, 1993)
Series: Kate Shugak
Story type: Private Detective—Female Lead
Major character(s): Kate Shugak, Detective—Private, Indian (Aleut); Jack Morgan, Police Officer (Kate's lover)
Time period(s): 1990s

Locale(s): Aleutian Islands, Alaska

What the book is about: Jack Morgan has hired Kate to look into the disappearance of two fisherman, part of the crew of the fishing boat *Avilda*. The *Avilda* has had some trouble before. Now Kate has hired on to do some undercover investigating. She finds the crew covering up something, but what? If the harsh Aleutian sea doesn't kill her, a determined murderer might.

Other books you might like:
Sue Henry, *Murder on the Iditarod Trail*, 1991
B.J. Oliphant, *The Shirley McClintock Series*, 1990-
Elizabeth Quinn, *Murder Most Grizzly*, 1993
John Straley, *The Woman Who Married a Bear*, 1992
J.F. Trainor, *The Angela Biwaban Series*, 1993-

1552
Dana Stabenow
Play with Fire (New York: Berkley, 1995)

Series: Kate Shugak

Story type: Private Detective—Female Lead

Major character(s): Kate Shugak, Detective—Private, Indian (Aleut)

Time period(s): 1990s

Locale(s): Tanada, Alaska

What the book is about: A huge forest fire has devastated a forest in Alaska, but the good news is that morel mushrooms thrive after such a fire. Kate has joined her friend Bobby to make some money gathering the mushrooms. Unfortunately she also discovers the remains of a body, killed at the time of the fire. She is in town to report the find when she is approached by a young boy asking for help in finding his father who has disappeared. She agrees to help but is afraid she already knows where the father is. How did he die, and why?

Other books you might like:
Nevada Barr, *Firestorm*, 1996
Sue Henry, *Termination Dust*, 1995
Elizabeth Quinn, *A Wolf in Death's Clothing*, 1995
John Straley, *The Woman Who Married a Bear*, 1992
Scott Young, *Murder in a Cold Climate*, 1988

1553
Susannah Stacey (Pseudonym of Jill Staynes and Margaret Storey)
Bone Idle (New York: Pocket, 1995)

Series: Superintendent Bone

Story type: Police Procedural—Male Lead

Major character(s): Robert Bone, Police Officer (superintendent, CID); Grizel Bone, Teacher (Bone's wife)

Time period(s): 1990s

Locale(s): Winterford, England

What the book is about: Superintendent Bone and his wife, Grizel, have decided to take a belated honeymoon. They plan on staying with Grizel's friend, Jane, and her husband, who just happens to be Lord Roke, owner of Roke Castle. The castle is also part of a stately homes tour. When the tour arrives, one of the party falls to his death. Shortly thereafter Lord Roke is also killed. Bone finds himself a suspect rather than an investigator. Naturally he resents this and, with the help of Grizel, begins to question the tour group and the house guests to find the killer.

Other books you might like:
Deborah Crombie, *Leave the Grave Green*, 1995
Ann Granger, *Murder Among Us*, 1994
Susan B. Kelly, *Time of Hope*, 1992
Janet Neel, *Death on Site*, 1989

1554
Susannah Stacey (Pseudonym of Jill Staynes and Margaret Storey)
Grave Responsibility (New York: Simon & Schuster, 1991)

Series: Superintendent Bone

Story type: Police Procedural—Male Lead

Major character(s): Robert Bone, Police Officer (superintendent), Widow(er)

Time period(s): 1990s

Locale(s): London, England

What the book is about: Dr. Lionel Clare has been found dead with his throat slit in a car wash. The police are leaning toward suicide but when his mother and uncle are also discovered dead they may have to reconsider. Prime suspects are Clovis Clare, Lionel's brother, and Edwin Clare, Lionel's father. As Bone digs deeper he finds the whole Clare family is odd, to say the least.

Other books you might like:
Elizabeth George, *A Great Deliverance*, 1988
Martha Grimes, *The Old Fox Deceiv'd*, 1982
P.D. James, *A Taste for Death*, 1986
Dorothy Simpson, *Puppet for a Corpse*, 1983
June Thomson, *The Habit of Loving*, 1979

1555
Susannah Stacey (Pseudonym of Jill Staynes and Margaret Storey)
A Knife at the Opera (New York: Summit, 1989)

Series: Superintendent Bone

Story type: Police Procedural—Male Lead

Major character(s): Peter Bone, Police Officer (superintendent); Charlotte Bone, Student (Peter Bone's daughter)

Time period(s): 1980s

Locale(s): Tunbridge Wells

What the book is about: During a performance of *The Beggar's Opera* at Charlotte's school, one of the teachers is stabbed to death. Was she the intended victim?

Other books you might like:
Martha Grimes, *The Old Fox Deceiv'd*, 1982
Roy Hart, *A Pretty Place for a Murder*, 1988
P.D. James, *Cover Her Face*, 1962
Stephen Murray, *The Noose of Time*, 1989
Dorothy Simpson, *Element of Doubt*, 1988

1556
Susannah Stacey (Pseudonym of Jill Staynes and Margaret Storey)
The Late Lady (New York: Pocket, 1993)
Series: Superintendent Bone
Story type: Police Procedural—Male Lead
Major character(s): Robert Bone, Police Officer (superintendent)
Time period(s): 1990s
Locale(s): Beneden, England (Kent)
What the book is about: Superintendent Bone gives a ride to seventeen year old Ravenna Marsh, who somehow reminds Bone of his own daughter. Just after Ravenna enters her house there is a scream. When Bone enters the house he finds the housekeeper dead of a broken neck and Ravenna's grandmother suffering a heart attack. This involves Bone with the strange household of writer Jake Marsh. Soon there is another death and Bone finds himself drawn into finding the truth.

Other books you might like:
Deborah Crombie, *A Share in Death*, 1993
Elizabeth George, *A Great Deliverance*, 1988
Caroline Graham, *The Killings at Badger's Drift*, 1987
Peter Robinson, *A Dedicated Man*, 1991
Stella Shepherd, *Thinner than Blood*, 1992

1557
Veronica Stallwood
Death and the Oxford Box (New York: Scribners, 1994)
Series: Kate Ivory
Story type: Amateur Detective—Female Lead
Major character(s): Kate Ivory, Writer
Time period(s): 1990s
Locale(s): Oxford, England
What the book is about: Kate Ivory is a member of the Fridesley runners, a group of joggers that have become friends. Another member, Rose, has a problem. Her husband has left her and taken half of her ornamental boxes including the Oxford Box, worth a fortune. The group decides to help by stealing the boxes back. Thanks to Kate the plan works except that the Oxford Box is missing. Then one of the other ringleaders of the plot is found murdered. Kate is convinced one of the runners is a murderer and is determined to find out who.

Other books you might like:
Dorothy Cannell, *Femmes Fatal*, 1992
Janet Laurence, *Hotel Morgue*, 1992
Annette Roome, *A Second Shot in the Dark*, 1992
Betty Rowlands, *Finishing Touch*, 1991
Joan Smith, *A Masculine Ending*, 1987

1558
Veronica Stallwood
Deathspell (New York: Scribners, 1992)
Story type: Psychological Suspense
Major character(s): Tess Farrell, Child (10 years old)
Time period(s): 1990s
Locale(s): Oxford, England
What the book is about: Tess is a very strange young girl with yellow eyes like a cat and a belief in witchcraft. She lives with her mother, stepfather, sister and three stepbrothers. Joe, the oldest brother, likes to kill small animals and is threatening to torture the girls. But Tess and her father have a plan, even though her father died three years ago. And Tess also carries a very sharp knife. First mystery.

Other books you might like:
Barry Berg, *Hide and Seek*, 1989
Dick Lochte, *Sleeping Dog*, 1985
Lin Summerfield, *Never Walk Behind Me*, 1992
Susan Zannos, *Trust the Liar*, 1988

1559
Veronica Stallwood
Oxford Exit (New York: Scribners, 1995)
Series: Kate Ivory
Story type: Amateur Detective—Female Lead
Major character(s): Kate Ivory, Writer (novelist)
Time period(s): 1990s
Locale(s): Oxford, England
What the book is about: A friend of Kate's, knowing her penchant for snooping, has asked her to look into the disappearance of several rare books from the various Oxford libraries, including the Bodleian. Going undercover as a computer book cataloguer, she finds that the scope of the thefts may be larger than anyone suspected and that there seems to be a connection to the year-old murder of another young woman cataloguer. If Kate gets too close to the truth she may meet the same fate.

Other books you might like:
Charity Blackstock, *Dewey Death*, 1977
Terrie Curran, *All Booked Up*, 1989
Dorothy Fiske, *Bound to Murder*, 1987
Charles A. Goodrum, *A Slip of the Tong*, 1992
Jill Paton Walsh, *The Wyndham Case*, 1993

1560
Les Standiford
Deal to Die For (New York: HarperCollins, 1995)
Series: John Deal
Story type: Amateur Detective—Male Lead; Action/Adventure
Major character(s): John Deal, Businessman (building contractor)
Time period(s): 1990s
Locale(s): Miami, Florida

1561 Standiford

What the book is about: Deal finds himself involved with Chinese gangsters who are trying to horn in on some local pornographers. A friend has also committed suicide soon after telling her sister she was adopted. Was it really suicide and what does the death have to do with the pornography racket? Deal and his friend John Driscoll may be in over their heads.

Other books you might like:
James W. Hall, *Bones of Coral*, 1991
Vicki Hendricks, *Miami Purity*, 1995
Carl Hiaasen, *Double Whammy*, 1987
John Lutz, *The Fred Carver Series*, 1989-
Laurence Shames, *Florida Straits*, 1992

1561
Les Standiford
Done Deal (New York: HarperCollins, 1993)

Series: John Deal

Story type: Action/Adventure

Major character(s): John Deal, Businessman (owns a construction company); Leon Straight, Criminal

Time period(s): 1990s

Locale(s): Florida

What the book is about: Someone doesn't want John Deal to finish an apartment complex he's trying to build. If he doesn't finish it he may go out of business. When his wife is forced off a bridge and apparently killed, he realizes that these people, whoever they are, are deadly serious. He sets out to avenge his wife and bollix up the plans for a professional baseball franchise.

Other books you might like:
Robert Ferrigno, *The Cheshire Moon*, 1993
James W. Hall, *Hard Aground*, 1993
Carl Hiaasen, *Native Tongue*, 1991
Elmore Leonard, *Maximum Bob*, 1991
Arthur F. Nehrbass, *Dead Easy*, 1992

1562
S.L. Stebel
The Boss's Wife (New York: Walker, 1992)

Story type: Action/Adventure

Major character(s): Jack Noble, Computer Expert (head of data management)

Time period(s): 1990s

Locale(s): Los Angeles, California; Reno, Nevada

What the book is about: Jack Noble is head of computers for a large bank and has just finished transferring a lot of their money into a secret account. He's planning on returning the money but before he can an investigation is started by his new boss. When Jack meets his boss's wife he is intrigued by her beauty and her bag filled with money. She slowly leads him into a network of lies, greed and murder.

Other books you might like:
William Bayer, *Blind Side*, 1989
Alan Dennis Burke, *Dead Wrong*, 1990
James M. Cain, *The Postman Always Rings Twice*, 1934
K. Patrick Conner, *Kingdom Road*, 1991
Charles Wilson, *Silent Witness*, 1992

1563
Neville Steed
Black Eye (New York: St. Martin's, 1990)

Story type: Private Detective

Major character(s): Johnny Black, Detective—Private, Pilot (ex-pilot)

Time period(s): 1930s

Locale(s): England (West Country)

What the book is about: A woman wants Black to investigate the death of her sister who she believes was murdered.

Other books you might like:
Jonathan Gash, *The Judas Pair*, 1977
John Malcolm, *A Back Room in Somers Town*, 1984
Martin Sylvester, *A Lethal Vintage*, 1988

1564
Neville Steed
Boxed In (New York: St. Martin's, 1992)

Series: Peter Marklin

Story type: Amateur Detective—Male Lead

Major character(s): Peter Marklin, Antiques Dealer (of toys); Arabella Trench, Journalist (TV reporter)

Time period(s): 1990s

Locale(s): Bournemouth, England

What the book is about: Peter is at an auto jumble, a flea market for cars, trying to sell some of his car models when he runs into Desmond Granger. Desmond wants Peter to look at a car he is selling but when they open the trunk, they find the body of a local boy. Desmond asks Peter to help as he is sure he will be arrested since he is a homosexual and the police wil make unwarranted assumptions.

Other books you might like:
Jonathan Gash, *The Lovejoy Series*, 1977-
James Leasor, *Frozen Assets*, 1989
Richard A. Lupoff, *The Classic Car Killer*, 1992
John Malcolm, *The Tim Simpson Series*, 1984-
Martin Sylvester, *The William Warner Series*, 1988-

1565
Neville Steed
Clockwork (New York: St. Martin's, 1989)

Series: Peter Marklin

Story type: Amateur Detective—Male Lead

Major character(s): Peter Marklin, Antiques Dealer

Time period(s): 1980s

Locale(s): Studland, England (Dorset)

What the book is about: A burglary and a murder at a friend's school cause Marklin to get involved in the investigation.

Other books you might like:
Eliza G.C. Collins, *Going, Going, Gone*, 1986
Jonathan Gash, *The Lovejoy Series*, (1977-)
Carolyn G. Hart, *A Settling of Accounts*, 1976
John Malcolm, *The Godwin Sideboard*, 1985

1566
Neville Steed
Wind-Up (New York: St. Martins, 1991)
Series: Peter Marklin
Story type: Amateur Detective—Male Lead
Major character(s): Peter Marklin, Antiques Dealer (specializing in toys); Arabella Trench, Journalist
Time period(s): 1990s
Locale(s): Bournemouth, England (Dorset)

What the book is about: Peter Marklin is called upon by the police to value some toys stolen from a murdered man's secret collection. He manages to keep out of it but his friend Gus asks him to investigate because his current lady friend's son is the prime suspect.

Other books you might like:
Jonathan Gash, *The Lovejoy Series*, 1977-
John Malcolm, *The Tim Simpson Series*, 1984-
Martin Sylvester, *A Lethal Vintage*, 1988

1567
Triss Stein
Murder at the Class Reunion (New York: Walker, 1993)
Story type: Amateur Detective—Female Lead
Major character(s): Kay Engels, Journalist
Time period(s): 1990s
Locale(s): Falls City, New York

What the book is about: Kay Engels isn't sure she wants to go to her 20th high school reunion—she doesn't have many memories she wants to relive. She finally decides to go and do a story on the changes her small town has undergone. Then the class tease, who is up to her old tricks, is murdered. Now Kay has a real story if she can survive to write it. First novel.

Other books you might like:
Susan Wittig Albert, *Thyme of Death*, 1992
Leslie Meier, *Mail-Order Murder*, 1991
Marlys Millhiser, *Murder at Moot Point*, 1992
Orania Papazoglou, *The Patience McKenna Series*, 1984-
Gillian Roberts, *The Amanda Pepper Series*, 1987-

1568
Janice Steinberg
Death of a Postmodernist (New York: Berkley, 1995)
Story type: Amateur Detective—Female Lead
Major character(s): Margo Simon, Journalist (public radio)
Time period(s): 1990s
Locale(s): San Diego, California

What the book is about: The Capelli Foundation for Postmodern Art is hosting the opening of a new show and Margo is assigned to interview the participants for KSDR, the local public radio station. She finds tensions are running high among the artists. One gruesome exhibit's "fake" blood is discovered to be real and the artist murdered. Margo wants to find the killer but may end up the next exhibit. First novel.

Other books you might like:
Dick Belsky, *The Jenny McKay Series*, 1992-
Aaron Elkins, *A Deceptive Clarity*, 1987
Janice Law, *A Safe Place to Die*, 1995
Julie Robitaille, *Jinx*, 1991
Dorian Yeager, *Murder Will Out*, 1994

1569
Susan Steiner
Library: No Murder Aloud (New York: Fawcett, 1993)
Series: Alex Winter
Story type: Private Detective—Female Lead
Major character(s): Alex Winter, Detective—Private
Time period(s): 1990s
Locale(s): Santa Linda, California

What the book is about: Alex Winter is hired to investigate a gigolo who is taking advantage of a rich widow. Her investigation involves her with the local library, where she stops an attempted stabbing. Soon an enemy of the library is found murdered and the chief librarian is the main suspect. Alex believes he is innocent and decides to help and gets involved in drugs, rare books and old family secrets.

Other books you might like:
Sue Grafton, *The Kinsey Millhone Series*, 1982-
Charlaine Harris, *A Bone to Pick*, 1992
Marcia Muller, *The Elena Oliverez Series*, 1983-1986
Marcia Muller, *The Sharon McCone Series*, 1977-
Maxine O'Callaghan, *The Delilah West Series*, 1982-

1570
Richard Martin Stern
Missing Man (New York: Pocket, 1990)
Series: Johnny Ortiz
Story type: Police Procedural—Male Lead
Major character(s): Johnny Ortiz, Police Officer, Indian (half Apache)
Time period(s): 1980s
Locale(s): Santo Cristo, New Mexico

What the book is about: Did the college professor kill the bird-watcher by setting off an avalanche?

Other books you might like:
Rex Burns, *The Alvarez Journal*, 1975
Warwick Downing, *The Mountains West of Town*, 1975
Tony Hillerman, *The Blessing Way*, 1970
Judith Van Gieson, *Raptor*, 1990

1571
Serita Stevens
Co-Author: Rayanne Moore
Bagels for Tea (New York: St. Martins, 1993)
Series: Fanny Zindel
Story type: Amateur Detective—Female Lead
Major character(s): Fanny Zindel, Aged Person (grandparent)
Time period(s): 1990s
Locale(s): York, England
What the book is about: Fanny Zindel has gone to England to visit her granddaughter at her boarding school in York. Soon after her arrival, her granddaughter is expelled because of a frame-up by another student. Fanny and her boyfriend, an ex-Mossad agent, try to find out what's behind the expulsion, but before they can get very far, the accusing student is murdered and the police think Fanny's granddaughter is the guilty party.
Other books you might like:
Richard Barth, *The Margaret Binton Series*, 1978-
B. Comfort, *Grave Consequences*, 1989
Dorothy Gilman, *The Mrs. Pollifax Series*, 1966-
Hazel Holt, *The Mrs. Malory Series*, 1990-
Virginia Rich, *The Mrs. Potter Series*, 1982-

1572
Richard Stevenson
Third Man Out (New York: St. Martin's, 1992)
Series: Donald Strachey
Story type: Private Detective—Male Lead
Major character(s): Donald Strachey, Detective—Private, Homosexual
Time period(s): 1990s
Locale(s): Albany, New York
What the book is about: John Rutka, gay activist of Queer Nation and publisher of *Queerscreed* is engaged in "outing" some of Albany's high placed gays. When he is shot, he hires Strachey to protect him and find out who is after him.
Other books you might like:
Nathan Aldyne, *The Daniel Valentine Series*, 1980-1986
Tony Fennelly, *The Glory Hole Murders*, 1985
Joseph Hansen, *The Dave Brandstetter Series*, 1970-1991
Grant Michaels, *A Body to Dye For*, 1990
Mark Richard Zubro, *The Tom Mason Series*, 1988-

1573
Samuel M. Steward
The Caravaggio Shawl (Boston: Alyson, 1989)
Story type: Amateur Detective—Female Lead
Major character(s): Gertrude Stein, Writer, Historical Figure; Alice B. Toklas, Writer, Historical Figure
Time period(s): 1930s (1937)
Locale(s): Paris, France
What the book is about: Toklas and Stein attempt to discover who stole the Louvre's Caravaggio and replaced it with a forgery.
Other books you might like:
Oliver Banks, *The Caravaggio Obsession*, 1984
Dan Kavanagh, *Duffy*, 1986
Stephen Lewis, *Cowboy Blues*, 1985
Shelley Singer, *Free Draw*, 1984
Eve Zaremba, *Work for a Million*, 1987

1574
Jim Stinson
Truck Shot (New York: Scribner's, 1989)
Series: Stoney Winston
Story type: Amateur Detective—Male Lead
Major character(s): Stoney Winston, Filmmaker, Teacher (film)
Time period(s): 1980s
Locale(s): Los Angeles, California
What the book is about: When the president of a design college where Winston is teaching a filmmaking class is killed, the acting president, a friend of Stoney's, asks that he investigate.
Other books you might like:
Michael Avallone, *Shoot It Again, Sam*, 1972
R. Wright Campbell, *Killer of Kings*, 1979
Pamela Chais, *Final Cut*, 1981
Thomas Gifford, *Hollywood Gothic*, 1979
R.R. Irvine, *Ratings Are Murder*, 1985

1575
Jim Stinson
TV Safe (New York: Scribners, 1991)
Series: Stoney Winston
Story type: Amateur Detective—Male Lead
Major character(s): Stoney Winston, Filmmaker
Time period(s): 1990s
Locale(s): Los Angeles, California
What the book is about: A contestant on the super-hit game show "Oh-Pun Sesame" is doing too well. The producers think she must be cheating, but the only person who could be giving the answers is beautiful air-head Kelli Dengham. Stoney is hired to look into the situation. He discovers Kelli is receiving threats and may also be being blackmailed over some pornographic photos. With millions of dollars at stake on the success of the show, tensions are running high, enough for murder.

Other books you might like:
Bruce Cook, *Rough Cut*, 1990
Robert Crais, *The Monkey's Raincoat*, 1987
Arthur Lyons, *Fast Fade*, 1987
Les Roberts, *Not Enough Horses*, 1988
Robert Upton, *Fade Out*, 1984

1576
Grif Stockley
Illegal Motion (New York: Simon & Schuster, 1995)

Series: Gideon Page

Story type: Legal

Major character(s): Gideon Page, Lawyer

Time period(s): 1990s

Locale(s): Fayetteville, Arkansas

What the book is about: Gideon has been hired to defend a star football player for the Arkansas Razorbacks against a charge of rape. Making the case more volatile is the fact that the athlete is black and the woman is white. It doesn't help that Gideon's daughter also attends the universtiy and is becoming involved with women's rights groups. His personal life is also undergoing considerable change. Gideon is sure that his client is innocent, but then again. . .

Other books you might like:
A.W. Gray, *The Bino Phillips Series*, 1988-
Joe L. Hensley, *Color Him Guilty*, 1988
John T. Lescroart, *The 13th Juror*, 1994
Ronald Levitsky, *The Love That Kills*, 1991
Richard North Patterson, *Degree of Guilt*, 1992

1577
Griff Stockley
Probable Cause (New York: Simon & Schuster, 1992)

Series: Gideon Page

Story type: Legal; Amateur Detective—Male Lead

Major character(s): Gideon Page, Lawyer, Single Parent; Andrew Chapman, Psychologist

Time period(s): 1990s

Locale(s): Blackwell County, Arkansas

What the book is about: Gideon Page has just been fired from his law firm and is trying to make it on his own. His first case involves Dr. Andrew Chapman who is accused of causing the death of a young retarded girl during electro-therapy. Gideon is up against an ambitious prosecutor who has made her name in child abuse cases. Gideon knows he's in trouble when evidence of a relationship between Chapman and the girl's mother causes the charges to be upgraded to first degree murder.

Other books you might like:
J.F. Freedman, *Against the Wind*, 1991
Philip Friedman, *Reasonable Doubt*, 1989
Joe L. Hensley, *Color Him Guilty*, 1988
Paul Levine, *To Speak for the Dead*, 1990
Steve Martini, *Compelling Evidence*, 1992

1578
David Stout
The Dog Hermit (New York: Mysterious, 1993)

Story type: Amateur Detective—Male Lead; Psychological Suspense

Major character(s): Will Schafer, Journalist (newspaper editor)

Time period(s): 1990s

Locale(s): New York (upstate)

What the book is about: An old friend of Will Schafer's, reporter Fran Spicer, is killed in what the police say is an alcohol-related car crash. Fran was covering the abduction of five year old Jamie Brokaw and Will believes that Fran's death is related to that story. Though ransom demands have been made and met, the child has not been returned. Will sets out to find the boy and the truth behind the death of his friend.

Other books you might like:
George Dawes Green, *The Caveman's Valentine*, 1993
Andrew Klavan, *Corruption*, 1994
Todd Komarnicki, *Free*, 1993
Archer Mayor, *Open Season*, 1988
Keith Peterson, *The John Wells Series*, 1988-

1579
David Stout
Night of the Ice Storm (New York: Mysterious, 1991)

Story type: Psychological Suspense

Major character(s): Marlee West, Journalist (columnist); Ed Delaney, Police Officer (detective)

Time period(s): 1990s (1991)

Locale(s): Bessemer, New York (Upstate)

What the book is about: In 1971, during a massive ice storm, someone beat a young priest to death. Twenty years later, as the town newspaper is throwing a party to celebrate its ninetieth birthday, murder has returned. Someone wants the truth to stay buried.

Other books you might like:
Robert J. Bowman, *The House of Blue Lights*, 1988
Aaron Elkins, *The Gideon Oliver Series*, 1982-
Ed Gorman, *The Autumn Dead*, 1987
Kate Green, *Night Angel*, 1989
Marcia Muller, *Trophies and Dead Things*, 1990

1580
John Straley
The Curious Eat Themselves (New York: Soho, 1993)

Series: Cecil Younger

Story type: Private Detective

Major character(s): Cecil Younger, Detective—Private

Time period(s): 1990s

Locale(s): Alaska

1581
John Straley
The Woman Who Married a Bear (New York: Soho, 1992)

Series: Cecil Younger

Story type: Private Detective

Major character(s): Cecil Younger, Detective—Private

Time period(s): 1990s

Locale(s): Sitka, Alaska

What the book is about: The investigation of a rape and then the murder of a woman and the investigation of an environmentalist seem to be coming together to make life dangerous for Alaskan private detective Cecil Younger. It seems that the environmentalist had a previous relationship with the dead woman and may have wanted to keep it hidden. Or is someone just using the woman to set the environmentalist up for a fall?

Other books you might like:
James Crumley, *The Last Good Kiss*, 1976
Sean Hanlon, *The Cold Front*, 1989
Sue Henry, *Murder on the Iditarod Trail*, 1991
Dana Stabenow, *A Cold Day for Murder*, 1992
Ted Wood, *The Reid Bennett Series*, 1986-

1581
John Straley
The Woman Who Married a Bear (New York: Soho, 1992)

Series: Cecil Younger

Story type: Private Detective

Major character(s): Cecil Younger, Detective—Private

Time period(s): 1990s

Locale(s): Sitka, Alaska

What the book is about: Cecil Younger is hired by the mother of Lewis Victor, an Indian hunting guide who was killed two years before. Although a man is in jail for the murder, Mrs. Victor wants to know why he killed her son - if he did - and if he didn't, who really did. Young takes the case but somebody doesn't want it reopened and decides the best way to insure this is to kill Young. First novel.

Other books you might like:
Sean Hanlon, *The Prestor John Riordan Series*, 1989-
Sue Henry, *Murder on the Iditarod Trail*, 1991
Walter Satterthwait, *A Flower in the Desert*, 1992
Dana Stabenow, *A Cold Day for Murder*, 1992

1582
Carsten Stroud
Lizardskin (New York: Bantam, 1992)

Story type: Police Procedural—Male Lead; Action/Adventure

Major character(s): Beau McAllister, Police Officer (Montana Highway Patrol)

Time period(s): 1990s

Locale(s): Montana

What the book is about: The investigation of a truck-stop shoot-out takes Sergeant Beau McAllister onto the reservation and into extortion and more murder.

Other books you might like:
Warwick Downing, *The Water Cure*, 1992
Carl Hiaasen, *Tourist Season*, 1986
Joseph Koenig, *Floater*, 1987
Ronald Levitsky, *The Love That Kills*, 1990
S.K. Wolf, *Long Chain of Death*, 1991

1583
Frank C. Strunk
Jordon's Showdown (New York: Walker, 1993)

Series: Berkley Jordan

Story type: Historical; Action/Adventure

Major character(s): Berkley Jordan, Saloon Keeper/Owner (ex-police officer)

Time period(s): 1930s (1934)

Locale(s): Buxton, Kentucky

What the book is about: Berkley Jordan is making do running a roadhouse and casino after his unsuccessful campaign for sheriff. Tensions are high in the coal-mining town between the mine owners and the union that wants to organize the miners. The mine owner asks Jordan to help keep the lid on but his loyalties are more on the side of the miners. Now there is an assassin on the loose.

Other books you might like:
Harold Adams, *The Carl Wilcox Series*, 1985-
Howard Browne, *Scotch on the Rocks*, 1991
Gordon DeMarco, *October Heat*, 1989
David Stout, *Carolina Skeletons*, 1988

1584
Frank C. Strunk
Jordon's Wager (New York: Walker, 1991)

Series: Berkley Jordan

Story type: Historical; Police Procedural—Male Lead

Major character(s): Berkley Jordan, Police Officer (deputy sheriff)

Time period(s): 1930s (1933)

Locale(s): Kentucky (eastern mountain country)

What the book is about: Determined to get to the bottom of the murder of Bitsy Trotter, Jordon doesn't care where the trail leads or if it costs him the election for county sheriff. First mystery.

Other books you might like:
Harold Adams, *The Carl Wilcox Series*, 1981-
James Lee Burke, *To the Bright and Shining Sun*, 1976
A.B. Guthrie Jr., *The Chick Charleston Series*, 1973-
Michael T. Hinkemeyer, *The Fields of Eden*, 1977

1585
Dev Stryker (Pseudonym of Molly Cochran and Warren Murphy)
End Game (New York: Forge, 1994)

Story type: Police Procedural—Male Lead; Action/Adventure

Major character(s): Paul Regal, Police Officer (head of an elite drug unit)

Time period(s): 1990s

Locale(s): New York, New York

What the book is about: One of Paul Regal's officers is murdered and he finds himself attracted to the dead man's wife. Regal is also involved in a hunt for a serial killer who leaves his victims with a chess move carved into their foreheads. His wife is having an affair with a billionaire and he doesn't have anybody to trust. All in all he is having a bad year at the office.

Other books you might like:
Lawrence Block, *The Matt Scudder Series*, 1976-
Thomas Chastain, *Vital Statistics*, 1979
John Clarkson, *And Justice for One*, 1992
Michael Connelly, *The Harry Bosch Series*, 1992-
Michael Jahn, *City of God*, 1992

1586
Karen Hanson Stuyck
Cry for Help (New York: Berkley, 1995)

Story type: Amateur Detective—Female Lead

Major character(s): Liz James, Administrator, Divorced Person; Nick Finley, Journalist (investigative reporter)

Time period(s): 1990s

Locale(s): Texas

What the book is about: Liz is recently divorced and not up to comforting her friend, Caroline Marshall, about her problems. As far as Liz can tell, Caroline's life is perfect. She regrets her attitude when she learns Caroline has committed suicide. Jonathan, Caroline's son and Liz's godson, seems to think it was murder. It seems unlikely, but Caroline and her partner, Nick Finley, were investigating a sensitive story about doctors taking advantage of their patients and there may be a connection to Caroline's death. First novel.

Other books you might like:
Carol Cail, *Private Lies*, 1993
Sherry Lewis, *No Place for Secrets*, 1995
Audrey Peterson, *Shroud for a Scholar*, 1995
Barbara Burnett Smith, *Dust Devils of the Purple Sage*, 1995
Joan Smith, *Don't Leave Me This Way*, 1990

1587
Jesse Sublett
Boiled in Concrete (New York: Viking, 1992)

Series: Martin Fender

Story type: Amateur Detective—Male Lead; Private Detective—Male Lead

Major character(s): Martin Fender, Musician (part-time skip tracer)

Time period(s): 1990s

Locale(s): Los Angeles, California; Austin, Texas

What the book is about: Cyclone Davis hires Martin to play at a session to record one of the late, sometime great, Richard James' songs. Davis swears James is still alive. Later that night Davis is shot and killed. When a record company executive hires Martin to help, he gets dragged into murder, deadly secrets, sex, drugs and rock-and-roll.

Other books you might like:
Dick Clark, *Murder on Tour*, 1991
Bruce Cook, *Death as a Career Move*, 1992
Kinky Friedman, *The Kinky Friedman Series*, 1980-
Thomas Maxwell, *The Suspense Is Killing Me*, 1990
Benjamin M. Schutz, *The Things We Do for Love*, 1989

1588
Dorothy Sucher
Dead Men Don't Marry (New York: St. Martin's, 1989)

Story type: Amateur Detective

Major character(s): Victor Newman, Social Worker; Sabrina Swift, Social Worker

Time period(s): 1980s

Locale(s): Maryland

What the book is about: A serial killer is targeting social workers. Sucher's previous book, *Dead Men Don't Give Seminars*, was a nominee for the Agatha Award.

Other books you might like:
Nathan Aldyne, *Cobalt*, 1982
J.S. Borthwick, *The Down-East Murders*, 1985
Virginia Rich, *The Cooking School Murders*, 1982
Dorothy & Sidney Rosen, *Death and Blintzes*, 1985
L.A. Taylor, *Poetic Justice*, 1988

1589
Mark T. Sullivan
The Fall Line (New York: Kensington, 1994)

Story type: Action/Adventure

Major character(s): Jack Farrell, Sports Figure (skier); Inez Didier, Filmmaker

Time period(s): 1990s

Locale(s): Utah (the Grand Tetons)

What the book is about: Former bank executive Jack Farrell is on the run with a new identity, required after he got involved in a money laundering scheme for South American drug dealers. He ends up at the Utah ski area where he learned the sport many years ago. With the plastic surgery, no one there recognizes him, but he soon finds himself falling under the spell of French filmmaker Inez Didier, who entices him into becoming involved in her film about daredevil skiers. She may not be exactly who she purports to be either, so he is still in danger. First novel.

Other books you might like:
Thornton Elliott, *Hard Guy*, 1992
Ron Faust, *In the Forest of the Night*, 1993
Tom Kakonis, *Criss Cross*, 1990
Joe R. Lansdale, *The Savage Season*, 1990
Timothy Watts, *Cons*, 1993

1590
Mark T. Sullivan
Hard News (New York: Kensington, 1995)

1591
Sullivan

Story type: Amateur Detective—Male Lead; Action/Adventure

Major character(s): Gideon McCarthy, Journalist (reporter); Prentice LaFontaine, Journalist (reporter)

Time period(s): 1990s

Locale(s): California (southern)

What the book is about: Reporters Gideon McCarthy and Prentice LaFontaine think they have made it when they stumble on what promises to be the biggest story of their careers. A high-priced prostitute has been found murdered shortly after her testimony about police corruption. Why was she murdered after her testimony? During their investigation they begin to uncover much more than just police corruption and put themselves at considerable risk while doing so.

Other books you might like:
Gerry Boyle, *Deadline*, 1994
James Preston Girard, *The Late Man*, 1993
Richard Harris, *Honor Bound*, 1982
Andrew Klavan, *Corruption*, 1994
Mary Logue, *Still Explosion*, 1993

1591
Winona Sullivan
A Sudden Death at the Norfolk Cafe (New York: St. Martin's, 1993)

Story type: Private Detective—Female Lead

Major character(s): Sister Cecile, Religious (nun), Detective—Private

Time period(s): 1990s

Locale(s): Boston, Massachusetts

What the book is about: Sister Cecile is left a fortune as long as she doesn't use it for the church. Sister Cecile is also a licensed private detective. So she uses her money for investigating and donates her fees to the church. She has a new client, political hopeful Abe Hersy, who wants her to protect his daughter, Jane. Eighteen year old Jane is pregnant and on the run from Martin Moon, a blackmailer and the father-to-be. Jane has taken Moon's files and he wants them back. First novel.

Other books you might like:
Veronica Black, *A Vow of Chastity*, 1992
Lee Harris, *The Good Friday Murder*, 1992
Frank McConnell, *Liar's Poker*, 1993
Sister Carol Anne O'Marie, *The Missing Madonna*, 1989
Monica Quill, *Sister Hood*, 1990

1592
Lin Summerfield
Count the Days (New York: Walker, 1991)

Story type: Amateur Detective—Female Lead

Major character(s): Cassie Wade, Child (11 years old)

Time period(s): 1980s

Locale(s): Upper Grisham, England

What the book is about: Cassie Wade's classmate, pretty, blond Margie Thoroughgood, has disappeared. She was last seen getting into a car with an unidentified man. As time goes on Margie's mom is frantic. Cassie with her insatiable curiosity may be the only one who can put all the pieces together. First novel.

Other books you might like:
Barry Berg, *Hide and Seek*, 1989
Gwendoline Butler, *The Dull Dead*, 1958
Dick Lochte, *Sleeping Dog*, 1985
Emma Page, *A Violent End*, 1990

1593
Lin Summerfield
Never Walk Behind Me (New York: Walker, 1992)

Story type: Psychological Suspense

Major character(s): Rowena Farrady, Teenager

Time period(s): 1990s

Locale(s): Micklefield, England

What the book is about: Rowena and her sister Margaret are the adopted daughters of the Farraday family. Now Rowena is ecstatic. She has turned eighteen and her beloved stepbrother Simon is returning from a year in Germany. She is sure Simon will declare his love for her and they will be married. But Simon returns with a new girlfriend upsetting all Rowena's plans. Then strange accidents start to happen.

Other books you might like:
Barry Berg, *Hide and Seek*, 1989
W. Edward Blain, *Passion Play*, 1990
Patrick Ruell, *Dream of Darkness*, 1991
Veronica Stallwood, *Deathspell*, 1992

1594
Remar Sutton
Boiling Rock (New York: British American, 1991)

Series: Evelyn Wade

Story type: Amateur Detective

Major character(s): Evelyn Wade, Aged Person (73 years old); August Clevenger, Journalist (free-lance)

Time period(s): 1990s

Locale(s): Bahamas

What the book is about: On her way to teach English to Haitians, Evelyn Wade hooks up with freelance journalist August Clevenger. Upon their arrival in the Bahamas they get involved in voodoo, body-snatching, drug-trafficking, and biomedical research. Any one of these could be hazardous to their well-being; together they put the two in definite danger.

Other books you might like:
Simon Brett, *Mrs., Presumed Dead*, 1989
Dorothy Gilman, *The Mrs. Pollifax Series*, 1966-
Gwen Moffat, *The Miss Pink Series*, 1973-
Patricia Moyes, *Angel Death*, 1981
Virginia Rich, *The Cooking School Murders*, 1982

1595
James Swain
The Man Who Walked Through Walls (New York: St. Martin's, 1989)

Story type: Action/Adventure

Major character(s): Vincent Hardare, Magician (supposed nephew of Houdini); Frank Kincaid, Mercenary

Time period(s): 1980s

Locale(s): Mexico

What the book is about: While performing in London, magician Vincent Hardare learns that his daughter has been falsely accused of drug-dealing and imprisoned in Mexico. Though her cell mate is a CIA agent, the U.S. government is reluctant to help in getting the women out. Hardare must use his skill to break into the prison to rescue his daughter. First book.

Other books you might like:
Patrick Kelley, *Sleight of Hand*, 1984
Warren B. Murphy, *The Red Moon*, 1982

1596
Doug J. Swanson
Dreamboat (New York: HarperCollins, 1995)

Series: Jack Flippo

Story type: Private Detective—Male Lead

Major character(s): Jack Flippo, Detective—Private; Sally Danvers, Saloon Keeper/Owner (bartender)

Time period(s): 1990s

Locale(s): Bagget County, Texas

What the book is about: Sent to East Baggett by an insurance company to check out an accidental drowning, Jack soon finds himself at odds with the sheriff and other assorted no-goods who don't want him looking too deeply into the "accident." He forms a relationship, of sorts, with Sally Danvers, a local bartender, and the only one in town who seems to be interested in the truth.

Other books you might like:
E.C. Ayres, *Hour of the Manatee*, 1994
Robert Crais, *Voodoo River*, 1995
A.W. Gray, *The Man Offside*, 1992
Joe R. Lansdale, *Cold in July*, 1989
David L. Lindsey, *Black Gold, Red Death*, 1983

1597
Paco Ignacio Taibo II
An Easy Thing (New York: Viking, 1990)

Story type: Private Detective—Male Lead

Major character(s): Hector Belascoran Shayne, Detective—Private

Time period(s): 1980s (1989)

Locale(s): Mexico City, Mexico

What the book is about: Shayne is involved in three cases at once. One involves the kidnapping of an ex-porn star's daughter; another is two murders at a steel plant; and the third is following up the rumors that Emiliano Zapata is still alive. First book.

Other books you might like:
Manuel Vazquez Montalban, *Murder in the Central Committee*, 1985

1598
Paco Ignacio Taibo II
The Shadow of the Shadow (New York: Viking, 1991)

Story type: Historical

Major character(s): Pioquinto Manterola, Journalist (crime reporter); Alberto Verdugo, Lawyer (disreputable); Fermin Valencia, Writer (poet)

Time period(s): 1920s (1922)

Locale(s): Mexico

What the book is about: Four domino playing "friends" are drawn into a plot to overthrow the government. Not the usual type of crime novel.

Other books you might like:
Derek Raymond, *I Was Dora Suarez*, 1990
Earl Thompson, *Caldo Largo*, 1976

1599
Robert K. Tanenbaum
Justice Denied (New York: Dutton, 1994)

Series: Butch Karp

Story type: Legal; Police Procedural—Male Lead

Major character(s): Butch Karp, Lawyer (chief homicide prosecutor); Marlene Ciampi, Lawyer (Karp's wife)

Time period(s): 1970s

Locale(s): New York, New York

What the book is about: A political assassination starts Butch Karp on a trail that will lead him to a centuries old political conflict, part of which may center on a stolen antique icon with echoes of the fictional Maltese Falcon. The man arrested in the assassination appears to be innocent, but before Butch can prove it he must find out why everyone who seems to be involved is after the icon.

Other books you might like:
Steve Martini, *Undue Influence*, 1994
Lia Matera, *Prior Convictions*, 1991
Richard Parrish, *The Dividing Line*, 1993
Robert Robin, *Above the Law*, 1992
Gallatin Warfield, *Silent Son*, 1994

1600
Robert K. Tanenbaum
Reversible Error (New York: Dutton, 1992)

Series: Butch Karp

Story type: Legal

1601 Tanner

Major character(s): Butch Karp, Lawyer (assistant district attorney); Marlene Ciampi, Lawyer (prosecutor; Karp's lover)

Time period(s): 1990s

Locale(s): New York, New York

What the book is about: Someone is murdering drug dealers. Is it a cop? More importantly, is it Karp's cop friend, Clay Fulton? At the same time prosecutor Marlene Ciampi, Karp's lover who is carrying his baby, is unhappy. She doesn't want to leave her job and she thinks there is a serial rapist at work. No one believes her so she sets out to trap him herself.

Other books you might like:
Ronald Levitsky, *The Love That Kills*, 1991
Steve Martini, *Compelling Evidence*, 1992
Barry Reed, *The Choice*, 1991
John Sandford, *Silent Prey*, 1992
Scott Turow, *Presumed Innocent*, 1987

1601
Jake Tanner
Saint Louie Blues (New York: Crown, 1992)

Series: B.F. Hooper

Story type: Private Detective

Major character(s): B.F. Hooper, Detective—Private, Veteran

Time period(s): 1990s

Locale(s): Richmond, Missouri

What the book is about: Undercover in a small Missouri town to try and find out who is behind a drug manufacturing and distribution ring, B.F. and his pal Cochise get in a world of trouble. Outlaw bikers, hookers and some of the town powers may be working together and the death of a DEA agent may already be on their hands.

Other books you might like:
James Crumley, *Dancing Bear*, 1983
Walter Satterthwait, *Wall of Glass*, 1988
Benjamin M. Schutz, *A Tax in the Blood*,
Jonathan Valin, *Extenuating Circumstances*, 1991
Ted Wood, *On the Inside*, 1990

1602
William G. Tapply
Dead Winter (New York: Delacorte, 1989)

Series: Brady Coyne

Story type: Amateur Detective—Male Lead

Major character(s): Brady Coyne, Lawyer

Time period(s): 1980s

Locale(s): Boston, Massachusetts

What the book is about: When a long-time client's son is accused of murder, Coyne tries to ferret out the truth, which may lie in the disappearance of the man's wife many years before.

Other books you might like:
Rick Boyer, *Billingsgate Shoal*, 1982
Stephen Paul Cohen, *Heartless*, 1986
Jeremiah Healy, *Blunt Darts*, 1984
Joe L. Hensley, *Song of Corpus Juris*, 1974
Robert B. Parker, *The Godwulf Manuscript*, 1974

1603
William G. Tapply
Spotted Cats (New York: Delacorte, 1991)

Series: Brady Coyne

Story type: Amateur Detective—Male Lead

Major character(s): Brady Coyne, Lawyer

Time period(s): 1990s

Locale(s): Cape Cod, Massachusetts; West Yellowstone, Montana

What the book is about: Brady is asked to drop by Jeff Newton's house to discuss a new will. Newton is an invalid, having been mauled by a leopard when he was a professional hunter. During the night, Brady is tied up and beaten by two unknown men. When he wakes up he finds Newton near death and seven gold Mayan jaguars valued at over a million dollars missing. Brady wants to get the statues back and to get even.

Other books you might like:
James Lee Burke, *Black Cherry Blues*, 1989
Frederick D. Huebner, *The Joshua Sequence*, 1986
Ed McBain, *The Matthew Hope Series*, 1978
Ralph McInerny, *Body and Soul*, 1989
Judith Van Gieson, *Raptor*, 1990

1604
William G. Tapply
Tight Lines (New York: Delacorte, 1992)

Series: Brady Coyne

Story type: Amateur Detective—Male Lead

Major character(s): Brady Coyne, Lawyer

Time period(s): 1990s

Locale(s): Boston, Massachusetts

What the book is about: At the request of an old friend, now dying, Brady Coyne takes up the search for the woman's daughter, who disappeared while at college 11 years ago. Setting off on the quest soon involves Brady with murder, murder, and more murder.

Other books you might like:
Rick Boyer, *The Doc Adams Series*, 1984-
Earl Emerson, *The Thomas Black Series*, 1987-
Frederick D. Huebner, *The Matt Riordan Series*, 1986-
Ed McBain, *The Matthew Hope Series*, 1978-
Judith Van Gieson, *Raptor*, 1990

1605
Kelly A. Tate
Co-Author: Jack Hanna
The Lion's Share (New York: Viking, 1992)

Story type: Amateur Detective—Male Lead

Major character(s): Carlson "Mac" MacIntire, Veterinarian, Widow(er); Claire Burke, Secretary

Time period(s): 1990s

Locale(s): Rockland, Massachusetts

What the book is about: Hired by the Rockland Zoo to help create a survival plan for the red wolf, Mac MacIntire soon finds himself embroiled in a controversy. When one of the zookeepers is found dead, with the wolves, the zoo director seems in quite a hurry to condemn the wolves to death. Since this death follows on the heels of death by snake bite (and the apparent manipulation of the antivenom) this makes Mac suspect that a human is behind the deaths. First novel.

Other books you might like:
Nevada Barr, *Track of the Cat*, 1993
Carter Dickson, *He Wouldn't Kill Patience*, 1944
B.J. Oliphant, *Dead in the Scrub*, 1990
Mary Willis Walker, *Zero at the Bone*, 1991

1606
D.B. Taylor
Fatal Obsession (New York: Bantam, 1989)

Story type: Police Procedural—Male Lead

Major character(s): Lorelei Carmody, Student; James Kramer, Police Officer

Time period(s): 1980s

Locale(s): Illinois

What the book is about: Someone has been killing off all the men in Lorelei Carmody's life. Can Kramer catch him before it happens again?

Other books you might like:
Robert Bloch, *Psycho*, 1959
Peter Fox, *The Trail of the Reaper*, 1983
Cornell Woolrich, *The Bride Wore Black*, 1940

1607
Elizabeth Atwood Taylor
The Northwest Murders (New York: St. Martin's, 1992)

Series: Maggie Elliott

Story type: Private Detective—Female Lead

Major character(s): Maggie Elliott, Detective—Private

Time period(s): 1990s

Locale(s): California (near the Oregon border)

What the book is about: Maggie is suffering from Chronic Fatigue Syndome so she decides to move to her partner's cabin near the Oregon border for an extended vacation. She arrives just after a vicious attack on two hikers leaves one dead and the other in a coma. She is drawn into the investigation when she realizes she knew one of the victims. She also tries to protect a young girl, who may have been a witness to the attack.

Other books you might like:
Christine Andreae, *Trail of Murder*, 1992
Jean Hager, *Ravenmocker*, 1992
Karen Kijewski, *Copy Kat*, 1992
Marcia Muller, *Where Echoes Live*, 1991
Dana Stabenow, *A Cold Day for Murder*, 1992

1608
Matt Taylor
Co-Author: Bonnie Taylor
Neon Dancers (New York: Walker, 1991)

Series: Palmer Kingston/A.J. Egan

Story type: Amateur Detective

Major character(s): Palmer Kingston, Journalist (reporter); Alice Jane "A.J." Egan, Journalist (reporter)

Time period(s): 1990s

Locale(s): Marlinsport, Florida

What the book is about: Since they work for competing papers, A.J. and Palmer are in competition to find the truth in the alleged real estate scam that has resulted in the jailing of the mayor by the U.S. Attorney—and longtime Palmer nemesis—Ken Trewaster. Though they are lovers and housemates the competition for the story between Palmer and A.J. makes for some testy times. Not to mention that the real estate scam may not be as it seems. Suicide—or was it?—and murder, complicate things further.

Other books you might like:
Susan Crosland, *Dangerous Games*, 1992
Bernie Lee, *Murder Without Reservation*, 1991
John Leslie, *Killer in Paradise*, 1991
John D. MacDonald, *Barrier Island*, 1984
Thomas Perry, *Island*, 1987

1609
Steve Thayer
Saint Mudd (New York: Viking, 1992)

Story type: Historical; Action/Adventure

Major character(s): Grover Mudd, Journalist (columnist/reporter)

Time period(s): 1930s

Locale(s): St. Paul, Minnesota

What the book is about: Set in Saint Paul, Minnesota in the 1930s, this novel uses the fictional character of Grover Mudd, newspaperman, and the real life activities of Dillinger, Karpis, the Barkers and other underworld denizens to tell the history of a few short years in this wide open town. First novel, originally self-published. Edgar nominee, since disqualified, for MWA Best First Novel.

Other books you might like:
Howard Browne, *Pork City*, 1988
Max Allan Collins, *The Nate Heller Series*, 1983
James Ellroy, *The Black Dahlia*, 1988
Loren D. Estleman, *Whiskey River*, 1990
Walter Mosley, *Devil in a Blue Dress*, 1990

1610
Donald Thomas
The Ripper's Apprentice (New York: St. Martin's, 1989)

Story type: Historical

Major character(s): Alfred Swain, Police Officer (Scotland Yard)

Time period(s): 1890s

Locale(s): London

What the book is about: Scotland Yard veteran Alfred Swain tries to find a killer who is murdering prostitutes with poison.

Other books you might like:
Peter Lovesey, *Waxwork*, 1978
Anne Perry, *Silence in Hanover Close*, 1988
Francis Selwyn, *Cracksman on Velvet*, 1974
Terrence Lore Smith, *Yours Truly, From Hell*, 1987

1611
Ross Thomas
Ah, Treachery (New York: Mysterious, 1994)

Story type: Action/Adventure

Major character(s): Edd "Twodees" Partain, Military Personnel (former soldier)

Time period(s): 1990s (1993)

Locale(s): Los Angeles, California; Washington, District of Columbia

What the book is about: Edd "Twodees" Partain was an Army major who was involved in covert operations in El Salvador. It appears that information is coming to light that some people want to keep hidden. Partain doesn't really care if his role becomes public but he is not pleased when people decide he would be better off dead. He is hired to bodyguard political money person Millicent Altford and her daughter, Jessica, and find a missing million. What to do and who to trust is Partain's difficulty.

Other books you might like:
William Diehl, *Hooligans*, 1984
Carl Hiaasen, *Native Tongue*, 1992
Thomas Perry, *Metzger's Dog*, 1983

1612
Ross Thomas
The Fourth Durango (New York: Mysterious, 1989)

Story type: Action/Adventure

Major character(s): B.D. Huckins, Political Figure (mayor); Sid Fork, Police Officer (chief)

Time period(s): 1980s

Locale(s): Durango, California

What the book is about: Chief Fork and Mayor Huckins have turned Durango into a hideout for criminals. Their current clients are a former supreme court justice and his son-in-law.

Other books you might like:
William Diehl, *Hooligans*, 1984
Stanley Ellin, *The Bind*, 1970
Carl Hiaasen, *Tourist Season*, 1986
Thomas Perry, *Metzger's Dog*, 1983

1613
Ross Thomas
Twilight at Mac's Place (New York: Mysterious, 1990)

Series: McCorkle and Padillo

Story type: Action/Adventure

Major character(s): Cyril "Mac" McCorkle, Businessman (formerly a spy); Michael Padillo, Businessman (formerly a spy)

Time period(s): 1980s (1989)

Locale(s): Washington, District of Columbia

What the book is about: Veteran CIA man Steadfast Haynes has died unexpectedly. He appears to have left his memoirs. Their existence is making any number of people—and governments—nervous. Steadfast's son, Granville, comes to McCorkle and Padillo for advice and assistance in deciding how to handle things and in the process gets involved with McCorkle's beautiful daughter.

Other books you might like:
Michael Bowen, *Washington Deceased*, 1990
William Diehl, *Hooligans*, 1984
Jerome Dolittle, *Body Scissors*, 1990
Carl Hiaasen, *Tourist Season*, 1986
Thomas Perry, *Metzger's Dog*, 1983

1614
June Thomson
The Spoils of Time (New York: Doubleday, 1989)

Series: Inspector Rudd

Story type: Police Procedural—Male Lead

Major character(s): Rudd, Police Officer (inspector)

Time period(s): 1980s

What the book is about: Former music hall performer Kitty Laud asks Inspector Rudd to find her missing brother, but another case intervenes. However, a sudden death in the new case also provides the answer to the brother's disappearance.

Other books you might like:
John Buxton Hilton, *Passion in the Peak*, 1985
S.B. Hough, *Dear Daughter Dead*, 1966
Jonathan Ross, *A Rattling of Old Bones*, 1982
Simon Troy, *Swift to Its Close*, 1969

1615
Maynard F. Thomson
Trade Secrets (New York: Pocket, 1994)

Story type: Private Detective—Male Lead

Major character(s): Nason Nichols, Detective—Private

Time period(s): 1990s

Locale(s): Boston, Massachusetts

What the book is about: Nason Nichols takes a case of industrial espionage and soon finds himself a thief and suspected murderer. The theft, or more accurately re-theft, of a computer chip is designed to make a company's stock safe for the inventor and her lover, but, as expected, they haven't told Nason the whole truth, so he finds himself in serious trouble. First novel.

Other books you might like:
Rick Boyer, *The Doc Adams Series*, 1984-
Michael Crichton, *Disclosure*, 1994
Jeremiah Healy, *The John Francis Cuddy Series*, 1984-
Robert B. Parker, *The Spenser Series*, 1974-
William G. Tapply, *The Brady Coyne Series*, 1984-

1616
David Thoreau
The Book of Numbers (New York: Pocket, 1990)

Series: Jimmy Lujack

Story type: Private Detective—Male Lead

Major character(s): Jimmy Lujack, Detective—Private (former vice cop)

Time period(s): 1980s

Locale(s): Los Angeles, California

What the book is about: Luack helps to track down the killer of a teenaged Chinese-American model, who has turned up headless in an L.A. cocaine dealer's bed.

Other books you might like:
Robert Crais, *The Monkey's Raincoat*, 1987
W. Glenn Duncan, *Rafferty's Rules*, 1987
Parnell Hall, *Murder*, 1986
Jack Lynch, *Bragg's Hunch*, 1981

1617
Newton Thornburg
The Lion at the Door (New York: Morrow, 1990)

Story type: Action/Adventure

Major character(s): Tom Kohl, Farmer (lost the family farm)

Time period(s): 1980s

Locale(s): Seattle, Washington

What the book is about: Trying to put his life back together, Tom Kohl is staying with his cousin in Seattle. When the cousin is involved in a hit and run and Tom tries to help him cover it up, things go from bad to worse.

Other books you might like:
Richard Bachman, *Roadwork*, 1981
Ross Thomas, *Briarpatch*, 1984

1618
L.L. Thrasher (Pseudonym of Linda Thrasher Baty)
Cat's Paw, Inc. (Tulsa: Council Oak, 1991)

Story type: Private Detective—Male Lead

Major character(s): Zack Smith, Detective—Private

Time period(s): 1990s

Locale(s): Portland, Oregon (and on the road)

What the book is about: Hired by Lilly and Jason Finney to find their runaway daughter, Zack is on his way to Portland—where he thinks the daughter has run to—when he picks up a beautiful young woman walking along the highway. As they drive along the news comes over the radio of a murder in Zack's home base. Does the enigmatic young woman, with whom Zack has fallen in love, know anything about it? And does the missing daughter fit in anywhere? First novel.

Other books you might like:
James Crumley, *The Last Good Kiss*, 1978
Richard Hugo, *Death and the Good Life*, 1981
Jonathan Valin, *The Lime Pit*, 1980
M.K. Wren, *Curiosity Didn't Kill the Cat*, 1973
Fred Zackel, *Cocaine and Blue Eyes*, 1978

1619
Ronald Tierney
The Iron Glove (New York: St. Martin's, 1992)

Series: Deets Shanahan

Story type: Private Detective—Male Lead

Major character(s): Dietrich "Deets" Shanahan, Detective—Private (70 years old)

Time period(s): 1990s

Locale(s): Indianapolis, Indiana

What the book is about: Senator Holland, in the midst of a campaign, manages to lose his wife who turns up naked and dead in the river. The son-in-law of one of Deets's friends finds the body and is a suspect. Deets agrees to investigate and in doing so turns up 1-900 numbers, simulated S & M and a husband who seems not real concerned about who killed his wife.

Other books you might like:
Ed Gorman, *The Night Remembers*, 1991
Vincent McConnor, *The Man Who Knew Hammett*, 1988
L.A. Morse, *The Old Dick*, 1981
Jonathan Valin, *The Lime Pit*, 1978

1620
Ronald Tierney
The Steel Web (New York: St. Martin's, 1991)

Series: Deets Shanahan

Story type: Private Detective—Male Lead

Major character(s): Dietrich "Deets" Shanahan, Detective—Private (70 years old)

Time period(s): 1990s

Locale(s): Indianapolis, Indiana

What the book is about: Two 16-year old boys are arrested for the murder of an undercover police officer. Though they were on the scene and had money taken from the dead men, Deets doesn't believe they are guilty. The prosecutor in the case, however, wants to hear nothing of their innocence because he is soon up for reelection and wants this case closed quickly to impress the voters. Deets does not let this deter him and crosses swords with many different people in his search for the truth.

Other books you might like:
Ed Gorman, *The Night Remembers*, 1991
Vincent McConnor, *The Man Who Knew Hammett*, 1988
L.A. Morse, *The Old Dick*, 1981

1621
Ronald Tierney
The Stone Veil (New York: St. Martin's, 1990)

Series: Deets Shanahan

Story type: Private Detective—Male Lead

Major character(s): Dietrich "Deets" Shanahan, Detective—Private (70 years old)

Time period(s): 1980s

Locale(s): Indianapolis, Indiana

What the book is about: A rich woman wants Dietrich (Deets) Shanahan to find her missing husband. Though he doesn't want to take the case (he wants to retire), he does and soon finds the husband's body on his client's estate. First book.

Other books you might like:
Arthur D. Goldstein, *Nobody's Sorry He Got Killed*, 1976
Vincent McConnor, *The Man Who Knew Hammett*, 1988
L.A. Morse, *The Old Dick*, 1981

1622
Brian Tobin
The Ransom (New York: St. Martin's, 1991)

Story type: Action/Adventure

Major character(s): Baker Wyatt, Criminal (just out of prison); Mark Lahey, Police Officer (FBI agent)

Time period(s): 1990s

Locale(s): New York, New York

What the book is about: Just out of prison Baker Wyatt has a plan to get wealthy quickly with little risk from the police. He intends to kidnap a drug lord and hold him for ransom. What he and his gang fail to realize is that FBI agent Mark Lahey, working with the drug lord's wife, will try to capture both kidnappers and kidnapped in one fell swoop. First novel.

Other books you might like:
Anthony Bruno, *Bad Guys*, 1988
Eugene Izzi, *The Take*, 1988
Andrew Klavan, *Don't Say a Word*, 1991
Elmore Leonard, *City Primeval*, 1980

1623
Tom Topor
The Codicil (New York: Hyperion, 1995)

Story type: Private Detective—Male Lead; Action/Adventure

Major character(s): Adam Bruno, Detective—Private, Lawyer

Time period(s): 1990s

Locale(s): United States

What the book is about: Adam Bruno is hired to fulfill the codicil of the will of Matthew Marshall, millionaire. His family is stunned to discover that their father added the codicil, which leaves half his estate to a child he fathered in Vietnam. Needless to say the family will be just as happy if Adam is unable to find this child—and it appears that someone is not content to see if he fails, but to help him fail. Murder is just one of the things that Adam must contend with.

Other books you might like:
Thomas Adcock, *Dark Maze*, 1991
Peter Blauner, *Slow Motion Riot*, 1991
Michael Connelly, *The Black Echo*, 1992
George Dawes Green, *The Juror*, 1995
James Patterson, *The Thomas Berryman Number*, 1976

1624
Leonard Tourney
Frobisher's Savage (New York: St. Martin's, 1994)

Series: Matthew Stock

Story type: Historical; Amateur Detective—Male Lead

Major character(s): Matthew Stock, Businessman (clothier); Adam Nemo, Servant; Joan Stock, Spouse (Matthew's wife)

Time period(s): 16th century (1596)

Locale(s): England

What the book is about: Imported servant Adam Nemo and his friend, Nicholas Crookbank, are the main suspects when Nicholas' father, mother, and siblings are found stabbed one morning. Matthew Stock and his wife Joan don't think they are guilty and take on the task of proving their innocence. The discovery of a letter from a London goldsmith makes Matthew and Joan think they may be on the right track, but the investigation may also cost them their lives.

Other books you might like:
P.F. Chisholm, *A Famine of Horses*, 1995
P.C. Doherty, *The Prince of Darkness*, 1993
Faye Kellerman, *The Quality of Mercy*, 1989
Sharan Newman, *Death Comes as Epiphany*, 1993
Kate Sedley, *The Weaver's Tale*, 1994

1625
J.F. Trainor
Corona Blue (New York: Kensington, 1994)

Series: Angela Biwaban

Story type: Private Detective—Female Lead; Amateur Detective—Female Lead

Major character(s): Angela Biwaban, Detective—Private (unlicensed; ex-con), Indian

Time period(s): 1990s

Locale(s): South Dakota

What the book is about: While working on a South Dakota farm, Native American Angela Biwaban discovers a still-warm corpse. By the time she gets the police to the spot, the body has vanished. Given her track record as an ex-con, nobody believes her and she's tossed in jail. While in jail she meets some power line activists and thinks their protests might be connected to the dead man. But there is also the 30-year-old abduction of a little girl and the recent death of an old lady said to have information about the abduction. Can Angela tie all the loose ends together?

Other books you might like:
Harold Adams, *The Carl Wilcox Series*, 1980-
Christine Andreae, *Grizzly*, 1994
Jean Hager, *Ravenmocker*, 1993
Dana Stabenow, *The Kate Shugak Series*, 1992-
Judith Van Gieson, *The Neil Hamel Series*, 1988-

1626
J.F. Trainor
Dynamite Pass (New York: Zebra, 1993)

Series: Angela Biwaban

Story type: Amateur Detective—Female Lead

Major character(s): Angela Biwaban, Criminal (accountant; ex-con), Indian

Time period(s): 1990s

Locale(s): Utah; South Dakota

What the book is about: Angela Biwaban, a real Anishinabe princess, is out on parole after serving time for embezzlement. She is trying to keep one step ahead of her parole officer while skirting the law running various scams. Then her cousin Billy dies in a mysterious accident that Angela feels was staged. Billy was trying to prevent the clear-cutting of land and created several powerful enemies. Now Angela is determined to uncover the truth. First novel.

Other books you might like:
Christine Andreae, *Trail of Murder*, 1992
Jean Hager, *Ravenmocker*, 1993
Elizabeth Quinn, *Murder Most Grizzly*, 1993
Dana Stabenow, *The Kate Shugak Series*, 1992-
Judith Van Gieson, *Raptor*, 1990

1627
Elizabeth Travis
Finders Keepers (New York: St. Martins, 1990)

Series: Ben and Carrie Porter

Story type: Amateur Detective

Major character(s): Ben Porter, Publisher; Carrie Porter, Publisher

Time period(s): 1990s (1990)

Locale(s): Nice, France (Cote D'Azur)

What the book is about: When famous author Charles Melton dies, he leaves his last work, a novel, in sections to six different heirs. The copyright will go to the person who can collect all six sections together. Ben and Carrie interrupt their vacation to see if they can acquire the rights to this sure best seller. Then the heirs begin to die.

Other books you might like:
Charles A. Goodrum, *Dewey Decimated*, 1977
Will Harriss, *The Bay Psalm Book Murder*, 1983
E.J. McGill, *Immaculate in Black*, 1991
Eve K. Sandstrom, *Death Down Home*, 1990
Edith Skom, *The Mark Twain Murders*, 1989

1628
Joseph Trigoboff
The Bone Orchard (New York: Walker, 1990)

Story type: Police Procedural—Male Lead

Major character(s): Alvin Yablonsky, Detective—Police

Time period(s): 1980s

Locale(s): New York, New York

What the book is about: While being investigated by Internal Affairs, detective Yablonsky must himself investigate the murder of a male stripper. First book.

Other books you might like:
Thomas Boyle, *Only the Dead Know Brooklyn*, 1985
Bill Granger, *Public Murders*, 1980
Nat Hentoff, *The Man From Internal Affairs*, 1985
David Wiltse, *The Serpent*, 1983

1629
Miles Tripp
The Cords of Vanity (New York: St. Martin's, 1990)

Series: John Samson

Story type: Private Detective—Male Lead

Major character(s): John Samson, Detective—Private

Time period(s): 1980s

What the book is about: Mrs. Huntingdon-Winstanley wants Samson to find out why her much younger husband keeps going to France with his chauffeur-valet.

Other books you might like:
Peter Cheyney, *Lady Beware*, 1950
John Milne, *The Moody Man*, 1988
Hugh Munro, *Who Told Clutha?*, 1958
Peter Whalley, *Robbers*, 1987

1630
Miles Tripp
Video Vengeance (New York: St. Martins, 1991)

Series: John Samson

Story type: Private Detective—Male Lead

Major character(s): John Samson, Detective—Private

Time period(s): 1990s

Locale(s): London, England

What the book is about: Frank Ruddick is engaged to the widow Coomber. Her aunt has died and left her a large inheritance, and now her presumed dead husband has reappeared, pleading amnesia. Frank hires Samson to find out what really happened to the husband and why he is back.

Other books you might like:
John Bowen, *The McGuffin*, 1984
Liza Cody, *Dupe*, 1981
Jonathan Gash, *The Judas Pair*, 1977
John Milne, *Dead Birds*, 1986
Peter Whalley, *Robbers*, 1987

1631
Kathy Hogan Trocheck
Every Crooked Nanny (New York: Harper, 1992)

Series: Callahan Garrity

Story type: Private Detective—Female Lead

Major character(s): Callahan Garrity, Detective—Private, Businesswoman (head of a cleaning service); Edna Mae Garrity, Parent

Time period(s): 1990s

Locale(s): Atlanta, Georgia

What the book is about: Callahan Garrity, owner of a cleaning service and part-time P.I., is asked to find the missing nanny of one of her cleaning clients who is also an ex-sorority sister. The nanny stole some valuable jewelry and some business papers. Callahan finds the nanny was not who she claimed to be. When the nanny's body is discovered, the police are quick to blame her lesbian lover but Callahan is not so sure. First novel.

Other books you might like:
Michael Hendricks, *Money to Burn*, 1989
Kay Hooper, *Crime of Passion*, 1991
Sarah Shankman, *Then Hang All the Liars*, 1989
Celestine Sibley, *Ah, Sweet Mystery*, 1991
Patricia Houck Sprinkle, *Murder on Peachtree Street*, 1991

1632
Kathy Hogan Trocheck
To Live and Die in Dixie (New York: HarperCollins, 1993)

Series: Callahan Garrity

Story type: Private Detective—Female Lead

Major character(s): Callahan Garrity, Detective—Private, Businesswoman (owner of a cleaning service)

Time period(s): 1990s

Locale(s): Atlanta, Georgia

What the book is about: While cleaning the mansion of Civil War buff and racist Elliott Littlefield Callahan Garrity's cleaning crew find the corpse of a seventeen year old girl. This is much like the murder that took place in Littlefield's home twenty years ago, but he claims innocence and says the killer also took a valuable Civil War diary, that of a madam. Callahan is hired by Littlefield to find the diary and incidentally clear his name. She thinks he's guilty, but sets out to find the truth no matter where it leads.

Other books you might like:
Meg O'Brien, *The Jessica James Series*, 1989-
Sarah Shankman, *The Samantha Adams Series*, 1989-
Celestine Sibley, *Ah, Sweet Mystery*, 1991
Julie Smith, *Jazz Funeral*, 1993
Patricia Houck Sprinkle, *Murder on Peachtree Street*, 1991

1633
Jack Trolley (Pseudonym of Tom Ardies)
Balboa Firefly (New York: Carrol & Graf, 1994)

Story type: Action/Adventure; Police Procedural—Male Lead

Major character(s): Joseph Foley, Businessman (realtor), Criminal; Grayson Grenier, Businessman (executive), Criminal; Tommy Donahoo, Police Officer (sergeant)

Time period(s): 1990s

Locale(s): San Diego, California

What the book is about: Not one, but two people, are planning to blow up an airplane as it lands at the San Diego airport. Because of the location of the airport, both men stand to make a fortune in real estate if the plane goes down. Though they know each other slightly, their plans are separate and one of them plans to frame the other for the crime. Can Sergeant Tommy Donahoo stop them both in time? First novel under this name.

Other books you might like:
Stanley Ellin, *The Dark Fantastic*, 1983
Mark Graham, *The Harbinger*, 1988
Lee Gruenfeld, *All Fall Down*, 1994
Drew Mallory, *Target Manhattan*, 1975
Ridley Pearson, *Hard Fall*, 1992

1634
Margaret Truman
Murder at the Kennedy Center (New York: Random House, 1989)

Series: Murder in Washington, D.C.

Story type: Amateur Detective—Male Lead

Major character(s): MacKenzie "Mac" Smith, Professor (law); Tony Buffolino, Detective—Private

Time period(s): 1980s

Locale(s): Washington, District of Columbia

What the book is about: When Mac Smith finds the body of a campaign worker from his friend Senator Ewald's presidential campaign, he gets himself involved in more than the discovery of the body. The senator's son is arrested for the murder and Mac has to use his skills to find out the truth.

Other books you might like:
R.B. Dominic, *Epitaph for a Lobbyist*, 1971
Richard Forrest, *A Child's Garden of Death*, 1975
David Linzee, *Death in Connecticutt*, 1980
John Lutz, *The Shadow Man*, 1981
Elliott Roosevelt, *Murder and the First Lady*, 1984

1635
John Bartholomew Tucker
He's Dead-She's Dead: Details at Eleven (New York: St. Martins, 1990)

Story type: Amateur Detective—Male Lead

Major character(s): Jim Sasser, Writer (former TV newsman)

Time period(s): 1990s

Locale(s): New York, New York

What the book is about: While visiting New York, Jim stops to see some old colleagues at the network, recently bought by a conglomerate. In the midst of massive lay-offs there are crank letters, bomb threats, arson and finally murder. Jim's friends ask him to look into this from the inside.

Other books you might like:
Steve Allen, *The Talk Show Murders*, 1982
William L. DeAndrea, *Killed in the Ratings*, 1978
Mike Lupica, *Dead Air*, 1986
Patricia Houck Sprinkle, *Murder on Peachtree Street*, 1991

1636
Kerry Tucker
Cold Feet (New York: Harper, 1992)

Series: Libby Kincaid

Story type: Amateur Detective—Female Lead

Major character(s): Libby Kincaid, Photojournalist

Time period(s): 1990s

Locale(s): New York, New York

What the book is about: Libby is involved in a project—photographing the nonpariels, a tap dancing group of many years. After their first performance the group's leader, businessman and social reformer Hank Monsell, is killed, apparently by a snake bite. Another group member, Silver Gaines, who works at the snake house in the Bronx Zoo, is arrested for the murder and Libby, who visited him the day before and also found the body, is arrested as an accomplice. Out on bail, she must find the real killer to clear herself.

Other books you might like:
Dick Belsky, *One for the Money*, 1986
Barbara D'Amato, *Hardball*, 1990
Susan Kelly, *The Liz Connors Series*, 1986-
Mary Kittredge, *Poison Pen*, 1990
Kathryn Lasky Knight, *Mortal Words*, 1990

1637
Kerry Tucker
Death Echo (New York: HarperCollins, 1993)

Series: Libby Kincaid

Story type: Amateur Detective—Female Lead

Major character(s): Libby Kincaid, Photojournalist

Time period(s): 1990s

Locale(s): Echo, Ohio

What the book is about: Libby Kincaid is back home in Ohio visiting her old boyfriend when she learns that an old acquaintance, Pam Bates, is the foster niece of Mavis Rihiser, a famous and mysteriously reclusive author. Back in New York Pam calls and asks Libby to help her mother who may be being blackmailed. In exchange Libby can have an interview with Mavis. Then Pam's mother is found dead, shot with an arrow.

Other books you might like:
Marjorie Dorner, *Blood Kin*, 1992
Wendy Hornsby, *Telling Lies*, 1992
Susan Kelly, *The Liz Connors Series*, 1986-
Margaret Maron, *Bootlegger's Daughter*, 1992
Eve K. Sandstrom, *Death Down Home*, 1990

1638
Kerry Tucker
Still Waters (New York: Harper, 1991)

Series: Libby Kincaid

Story type: Amateur Detective—Female Lead; Psychological Suspense

Major character(s): Libby Kincaid, Photojournalist

Time period(s): 1990s

Locale(s): Darby, Ohio

What the book is about: Returning from New York to her hometown of Darby, Ohio for the funeral of her brother, photojournalist Libby Kincaid finds that things are not as they seem. Her brother, supposedly a suicide, had a secret that may have brought about his murder. Though Libby has no idea what that secret might be, someone is still trying to kill her. First novel.

Other books you might like:
Dorothy Salisbury Davis, *A Death in the Life*, 1976
Michael Hendricks, *Money to Burn*, 1989
Michael Mewshaw, *True Crime*, 1991
Meg O'Brien, *The Daphne Decisions*, 1990
Sara Paretsky, *Deadlock*, 1984

1639
Peter Turnbull
Condition Purple (New York: St. Martin's, 1989)

Story type: Police Procedural—Male Lead

Major character(s): Ray Sussock, Police Officer (Scottish)

Time period(s): 1980s

Locale(s): Glasgow, Scotland

What the book is about: Prostitute and dope addict, Stephanie Craigellachie, is found stabbed to death in an alley. Detective Sergeant Ray Sussock thinks it's more than just a mugging gone wrong.

Other books you might like:
M.C. Beaton, *Death of a Gossip*, 1985
Michael Gilbert, *Blood and Judgement*, 1959
William McIlvanney, *Laidlaw*, 1977
Jonathan Ross, *Burial Deferred*, 1986
John Wainwright, *All Through the Night*, 1985

1640
Scott Turow
Pleading Guilty (New York: Farrar, Strauss & Giroux, 1993)

Story type: Legal; Action/Adventure

Major character(s): Mack Malloy, Lawyer (ex-cop), Alcoholic (recovering)

Time period(s): 1990s

Locale(s): Kindle County

What the book is about: One of the members of the law firm that Mack Malloy works for has vanished with over five million dollars of a client's money. As low man on the totem pole in the law offices, Mack is assigned the task of tracking him down. Needless to say things are not what they seem to be at the beginning and what seems to be a simple scam turns out to be much, much more.

Other books you might like:
Harrison Arnston, *Trade-Off*, 1992
Lawrence Block, *The Matt Scudder Series*, 1976-
J.F. Freedman, *Against the Wind*, 1991
Philip Friedman, *Reasonable Doubt*, 1990
Robert K. Tanenbaum, *Immoral Certainty*, 1992

1641
Peg Tyre
Strangers in the Night (New York: Crown, 1994)

Story type: Action/Adventure; Amateur Detective—Female Lead

Major character(s): Kate Murray, Journalist (crime reporter); John Finn, Detective—Police; Dominick Donatti, Criminal, Addict

Time period(s): 1990s

Locale(s): New York, New York

What the book is about: Kate Murray is a rookie crime reporter and needs a story, so she decides to investigate the murder of a black nurse who was shot in front of her apartment building, apparently in a drug-related killing. Two people involved in her investigation are New York city police detective John Finn and drug addict Dominick Donatti. Both men soon fall for Kate and she is in danger from one of them as well as from the people who don't want her looking into the murder. First novel.

Other books you might like:
Edna Buchanan, *Contents under Pressure*, 1992
Alison Glen, *Showcase*, 1992
Ron Handberg, *Cry Vengeance*, 1993
Meg O'Brien, *Eagles Die Too*, 1993
Steve Thayer, *The Weatherman*, 1994

1642
Michael Underwood (Pseudonym of John Michael Evelyn)
Seeds of Murder (New York: St. Martin's, 1992)

Series: Rosa Epton

Story type: Legal

Major character(s): Rosa Epton, Lawyer

Time period(s): 1990s

Locale(s): Greenborough, England

What the book is about: Rosa Epton takes on the defence of her godmother's younger husband who has been arrested for murder. What does this case have to do with the disappearance of an eleven-year-old boy in 1932? Seems a lot of the people involved in the earlier case are still alive and involved in some manner with the current murder.

Other books you might like:
Sarah Caudwell, *Thus Was Adonis Murdered*, 1981
Lesley Grant-Adamson, *Curse the Darkness*, 1990
Hannah Wakefield, *The Price You Pay*, 1989
Sara Woods, *Nor Live So Long*, 1986

1643
Andrew Vachss
Blossom (New York: Knopf, 1990)

Series: Burke

Story type: Action/Adventure

Major character(s): Burke, Criminal (ex-convict)

Time period(s): 1990s

Locale(s): New York, New York; Merrillville, Indiana

What the book is about: Burke, New York City's self-appointed protector of abused children, is called to Indiana by his ex-cellmate, Virgil. A lover's lane sniper is killing people and the prime suspect is Virgil's teen-age nephew.

Other books you might like:
Robert Campbell, *The Whistler Series*, 1986-
Jonathan Kellerman, *When the Bough Breaks*, 1985
Judith Kelman, *Hush Little Darlings*, 1989
Robert B. Parker, *God Save the Child*, 1974

1644
Andrew Vachss
Footsteps of the Hawk (New York: Knopf, 1995)

Series: Burke

Story type: Action/Adventure; Psychological Suspense

Major character(s): Burke, Avenger

Time period(s): 1990s

Locale(s): New York, New York

What the book is about: There is a serial killer on the loose and the next target may be Burke. He must delve into his past to discover the true stalker—and for a man with no past, that isn't easy.

Other books you might like:
James Ellroy, *White Jazz*, 1993
David L. Lindsey, *Heat From Another Sun*, 1984
Ridley Pearson, *Undercurrents*, 1988
Sam Reaves, *A Long Cold Fall*, 1991
Stephen Solomita, *A Twist of the Knife*, 1988

1645
Deborah Valentine
A Collector of Photographs (New York: Bantam, 1989)

Story type: Amateur Detective—Male Lead

Major character(s): Kevin Bryce, Writer, Police Officer (former policeman); Roxanne Gautier, Artist (painter)

Time period(s): 1980s

Locale(s): San Francisco, California

What the book is about: When Roxanne Gautier's paintings take a decided turn toward the bizarre and one of her models turns up dead, her husband asks Kevin Bryce to investigate further. This is Deborah Valentine's first mystery to be published in the U.S. Nominated for both an Edgar and a Shamus.

Other books you might like:
Jo Bannister, *Gilgamesh*, 1989
John Brett, *Who'd Hire Brett?*, 1980
Peter Clothier, *Chiaroscuro*, 1985
Marcia Muller, *The Cavalier in White*, 1986

1646
Jonathan Valin
Missing (New York: Doubleday, 1995)

Series: Harry Stoner

Story type: Private Detective—Male Lead

Major character(s): Harry Stoner, Detective—Private

Time period(s): 1990s

Locale(s): Cincinnati, Ohio

What the book is about: Cindy Dorn hires Harry to find her missing boyfriend. Before he can do much, the boyfriend is found dead in a seedy hotel, an apparent suicide. Cindy doesn't believe he killed himself and the information Harry turns up also suggests otherwise. The trail leads him deep into the gay community and puts him at odds with a police force not known for its liberal attitude towards homosexuals.

Other books you might like:
Robert Crais, *The Elvis Cole Series*, 1987-
Lawrence Block, *The Matt Scudder Series*, 1976-
Loren D. Estleman, *The Amos Walker Series*, 1979-
Jeremiah Healy, *The John Francis Cuddy Series*, 1984-
Les Roberts, *The Milan Jacovich Series*, 1990-

1647
Jonathan Valin
The Music Lovers (New York: Delacorte, 1993)

Series: Harry Stoner

Story type: Private Detective—Male Lead

Major character(s): Harry Stoner, Detective—Private

Time period(s): 1990s

Locale(s): Cincinnati, Ohio

What the book is about: Hired by stereophile Leon Tubin to find some missing and valuable records, Harry Stoner soon finds himself in much deeper waters than he initially expected. When Leon is beaten and Harry finds a cache of cash in his freezer he thinks there may be more to this stereo thing than first thought.

Other books you might like:
Barbara D'Amato, *Hard Tack*, 1992
Loren D. Estleman, *Downriver*, 1988
James E. Martin, *The Flip Side of Life*, 1990
Bill Pronzini, *Quarry*, 1992
Les Roberts, *Pepper Pike*, 1988

1648
Jonathan Valin
Second Chance (New York: Delacorte, 1991)

Series: Harry Stoner

Story type: Private Detective—Male Lead

Major character(s): Harry Stoner, Detective—Private

Time period(s): 1990s

Locale(s): Cincinnati, Ohio

What the book is about: Stoner is hired by prominent psychiatrist Phil Pearson to find his daughter Kirsten, who has disappeared. As Harry investigates he keeps turning up links between the disappearance and the death of the girl's mother fifteen years earlier. Shamus nominee for Best Novel.

Other books you might like:
Wayne D. Dundee, *The Skintight Shroud*, 1990
Loren D. Estleman, *The Amos Walker Series*, 1980-
Stephen Greenleaf, *The John Marshall Tanner Series*, 1979-
Les Roberts, *The Milan Jacovich Series*, 1989-
Benjamin M. Schutz, *The Leo Haggerty Series*, 1985-

1649
Judith Van Gieson
The Lies That Bind (New York: HarperCollins, 1993)

Series: Neil Hamel

Story type: Amateur Detective—Female Lead; Legal

Major character(s): Neil Hamel, Lawyer

Time period(s): 1990s

Locale(s): Albuquerque, New Mexico

What the book is about: Neil Hamel finds herself defending the defendant in a hit-and-run. The woman is the mother of her childhood friend, Cindy Reid. The woman that Cindy's mother is accused of killing is the woman who was driving a car that was involved in an accident three years earlier that killed Cindy's son and her mother's only grandson. The dead woman was also an Argentine terrorist and there is also some suggestion that she may have stepped in front of the car on purpose. Then there are the pursuing bad guys from Argentina.

1650 Van Gieson

Other books you might like:
Nevada Barr, *The Anna Pigeon Series*, 1993-
J.F. Freedman, *Against the Wind*, 1992
Tony Hillerman, *The Joe Leaphorn and Jim Chee Series*, 1970-
J.A. Jance, *Desert Heat*, 1992
Richard Parrish, *The Dividing Line*, 1993

1650
Judith Van Gieson
The Other Side of Death (New York: Harper, 1991)
Series: Neil Hamel
Story type: Amateur Detective—Female Lead
Major character(s): Neil Hamel, Lawyer
Time period(s): 1990s
Locale(s): Santa Fe, New Mexico; Albuquerque, New Mexico

What the book is about: Neil Hamel attends a party that reunites her with old friends from her counter-culture days in Mexico. She ends up driving Lonnie Dormer home and staying overnight with her. In the morning Lonnie is gone and is later discovered dead in some Indian ruins. The official verdict is suicide but Neil thinks it's murder and sets out to prove it.

Other books you might like:
Karin Berne, *False Impressions*, 1986
Lia Matera, *The Good Fight*, 1990
B.J. Oliphant, *Dead in the Scrub*, 1990
Walter Satterthwait, *Wall of Glass*, 1988
Carolyn Wheat, *Where Nobody Dies*, 1986

1651
Judith Van Gieson
Raptor (New York: Harper, 1990)
Series: Neil Hamel
Story type: Amateur Detective—Female Lead
Major character(s): Neil Hamel, Lawyer (bird-watcher)
Time period(s): 1980s
Locale(s): Montana

What the book is about: While bird-watching in Montana, Neil Hamel witnesses the death of a poacher. When one of her fellow birders is arrested for the poacher's murder, Neil decides the birder isn't guilty and sets out to prove the man's innocence.

Other books you might like:
Lia Matera, *The Good Fight*, 1990
Gwen Moffat, *Grizzly Trail*, 1984
Julie Smith, *Death Turns a Trick*, 1982
Michael Underwood, *Double Jeopardy*, 1981

1652
Judith Van Gieson
The Wolf Path (New York: HarperCollins, 1992)
Series: Neil Hamel
Story type: Legal; Amateur Detective—Female Lead
Major character(s): Neil Hamel, Lawyer, Activist
Time period(s): 1990s
Locale(s): New Mexico (southern)

What the book is about: Neil Hamel is asked to help activist Juan Sololobo as he tours the country with a timber wolf. While in southern New Mexico the wolf is set free under suspicious circumstances. The ranchers fear that it will attack their cattle and this leads to conflict with Sololobo. When a government worker who had quarrelled with Sololobo is found murdered, the activist is arrested.

Other books you might like:
Nevada Barr, *Track of the Cat*, 1993
B.J. Oliphant, *Dead in the Scrub*, 1990
Mary Willis Walker, *Zero at the Bone*, 1991
Lee Wallingford, *Cold Tracks*, 1992

1653
David A. Van Meter
Body of Evidence (New York: Berkley, 1990)
Story type: Private Detective
Major character(s): Gardner Wells, Detective—Private
Time period(s): 1980s
Locale(s): Mexico City

What the book is about: Wells offers to help a friend whose daughter has run away to Mexico, taking her four-year-old son. When Wells finds her she says that she has given the boy up for adoption. But then she disappears and her live-in boyfriend is killed. First book.

Other books you might like:
Ed Gorman, *The Autumn Dead*, 1987
John D. MacDonald, *Dress Her in Indigo*, 1969
Glendon Swarthout, *Skeletons*, 1979

1654
Daniel D. Victor
The Seventh Bullet (New York: St. Martin's, 1992)
Story type: Private Detective—Male Lead; Historical
Major character(s): Sherlock Holmes, Detective—Private
Time period(s): 1910s (1911)
Locale(s): New York, New York

What the book is about: The killing of a muckraking reporter brings Sherlock Holmes and Dr. Watson across the ocean to New York in 1911. Was it really a crazy man who killed David Graham Phillips or was it some sort of plot? And how did the killer put six bullets from a six shot revolver into Phillips and still have one left for himself? What did the killer's belief in vampires have to do with Phillips? Can Teddy Roosevelt and William Randolph Hearst shed any light on the subject?

Other books you might like:
William L. DeAndrea, *The Lunatic Fringe*, 1986
Loren D. Estleman, *Sherlock Holmes vs. Dracula*, 1978
L.B. Greenwood, *Sherlock Holmes and the Thistle of Scotland*, 1989
H. Paul Jeffers, *The Adventure of the Stalwart Companions*, 1978
Robert J. Randisi, *The Ham Reporter*, 1987

1655
L.M. Vincent
Final Dictation (New York: St. Martin's, 1989)
Series: Townsend Reeves
Story type: Amateur Detective—Male Lead
Major character(s): Townsend Reeves, Doctor (radiologist), Sports Figure (former basketball star)
Time period(s): 1980s
Locale(s): Kansas City, Kansas
What the book is about: Reeves, a bored radiologist and former basketball star, gets a call from his former college coach. Soon he finds a colleague murdered and tries to find out what happened. Vincent's first novel.
Other books you might like:
Michael J. Katz, *Murder Off the Glass*, 1987
Robert B. Parker, *Playmates*, 1989
Richard Rosen, *Fadeaway*, 1986

1656
L.M. Vincent
Pas De Death (New York: St. Martin's, 1994)
Series: Townsend Reeves
Story type: Amateur Detective—Male Lead
Major character(s): Townsend Reeves, Doctor (radiologist), Sports Figure (former basketball star)
Time period(s): 1990s
Locale(s): Kansas City, Missouri
What the book is about: Townsend Reeves has been separated from his wife. She dances with a New York City company but now the troupe is in Kansas City for a dance festival and he looks at this as a chance for reconciliation. While attending a rehearsal he thinks he glimpses someone with a gun. When a dancer nearly dies from a drug overdose, Townsend thinks that there may have been something to his feeling of foreboding and sets out to discover the truth.
Other books you might like:
Jo Bailey, *Bagged*, 1992
Robin Cook, *Fatal Cure*, 1993
Christine Green, *Deadly Errand*, 1992
Janet McGiffin, *Emergency Murder*, 1992
C.F. Roe, *A Nasty Bit of Murder*, 1992

1657
Bill Waggoner
Sweet Death (New York: Walker, 1992)
Story type: Amateur Detective—Male Lead
Major character(s): Fowler McFarland, Professor (ex-FBI agent), Writer; Beth Bush, Student (law student)
Time period(s): 1990s
Locale(s): Nacogdoches, Texas
What the book is about: Fowler has quit the FBI and is back in his home town teaching at the local university. When his old friend and poker buddy, Sheriff Case Bayhill asks for help, he can't refuse. Maureen Wilson has been found brutally raped and strangled. The sheriff thinks it was a sex killing but Fowler thinks it was a professional hit. First novel.
Other books you might like:
Bill Crider, *Dying Voices*, 1989
S.F.X. Dean, *By Frequent Anguish*, 1982
Conrad Haynes, *Bishop's Gambit, Declined*, 1987
Robert Reeves, *Doubting Thomas*, 1985

1658
Hannah Wakefield
A Woman's Own Mystery (New York: St. Martins, 1991)
Series: Dee Street
Story type: Amateur Detective—Female Lead; Psychological Suspense
Major character(s): Dee Street, Lawyer (U.S. citizen living in England)
Time period(s): 1990s
Locale(s): London, England
What the book is about: Dee Street wakes up drugged and tied-up in a dark room. The last thing she remembers is defending Gillian Shiraz in a child custody case and that their key witness had been found dead of a broken neck. As she slowly remembers more, she realizes she is in great danger.
Other books you might like:
Sarah Caudwell, *Thus Was Adonis Murdered*, 1981
E.X. Giroux, *A Death for Adonis*, 1984
Lesley Grant-Adamson, *Curse the Darkness*, 1990
Michael Underwood, *Rosa's Dilemma*, 1990
Sara Woods, *Nor Live So Long*, 1986

1659
Mary Willis Walker
The Red Scream (New York: Doubleday, 1994)
Series: Molly Cates
Story type: Amateur Detective—Female Lead
Major character(s): Molly Cates, Journalist (crime writer)
Time period(s): 1990s
Locale(s): Austin, Texas

1660 Mary Willis Walker

What the book is about: Ten years ago Louie Bronk was convicted of killing a local society woman Tiny McFarland. Molly Cates covered the trial and later interviewed the killer for a best-selling book. Now the appeals have run out and Louie is about to be executed. Molly wants to do an article on the execution but is discouraged from continuing. Then the second wife of Charles McFarland is killed in an identical manner to the first murder. Was Bronk, a self-confessed serial killer, really innocent of the one killing he was convicted for?

Other books you might like:
Jan Burke, *Goodnight, Irene*, 1993
Barbara D'Amato, *Hard Women*, 1993
John Katzenbach, *Just Cause*, 1992
Susan Kelly, *Out of the Darkness*, 1992
John Lutz, *Ride the Lightning*, 1987

1660
Mary Willis Walker
Under the Beetle's Cellar (New York: Doubleday, 1995)

Series: Molly Cates

Story type: Psychological Suspense

Major character(s): Molly Cates, Journalist (crime writer); Walter Demming, Driver (bus driver), Veteran (Vietnam)

Time period(s): 1990s

Locale(s): Austin, Texas

What the book is about: Molly Cates has been asked to write the story of a lifetime. Samuel Mordecai, leader of a strange cult, has kidnapped a busload of children and kept them entombed in the bus, underground, for 45 days of negotiations with the FBI. Molly begins to investigate Mordecai's strange past to find what brought him to this final stand. Meanwhile, Walter Demming, the children's bus driver, is fighting his own demons while trying to care for the children who have come to rely on him.

Other books you might like:
Susan Kelly, *Out of the Darkness*, 1992
Charles Kenney, *Hammurabi's Code*, 1995
Carol O'Connell, *The Man Who Cast Two Shadows*, 1995
April Smith, *North of Montana*, 1994
Minette Walters, *The Scold's Bridle*, 1993

1661
Mary Willis Walker
Zero at the Bone (New York: St. Martin's, 1991)

Story type: Amateur Detective—Female Lead

Major character(s): Katherine Driscoll, Animal Trainer (dog trainer)

Time period(s): 1990s

Locale(s): Austin, Texas

What the book is about: Katherine is in deep financial trouble. Before her mother died she amassed huge hospital bills and now the bank is threatening to foreclose on her dog-training business. When she gets a letter from her father, whom she hasn't seen in thirty years, offering help, she goes to Austin to see him. When she arrives, she finds he has been killed, mauled by a tiger at the zoo where he worked. The police suspect human assistance and Katherine decides to help. First novel. Edgar nominee for Best First Novel - 1991.

Other books you might like:
Mary Bowen Hall, *Emma Chizzit and the Queen Anne Killer*, 1989
Carolyn G. Hart, *The Annie Laurance Series*, 1987-
Joan Hess, *The Claire Malloy Series*, 1985-
B.J. Oliphant, *Dead in the Scrub*, 1990
Nancy Pickard, *I.O.U.*, 1991

1662
Walter Walker
The Immediate Prospect of Being Hanged (New York: Viking, 1989)

Story type: Legal

Major character(s): Patterson Starbuck, Lawyer; John Michael Keough, Lawyer (District Attorney)

Time period(s): 1980s

Locale(s): Exeter County, Massachusetts

What the book is about: When D.A. John Michael Keough decides to make political hay out of the murder of a wealthy young woman, he assigns Patt Starbuck to dig up all the dirt he can find on the murdered woman and her husband. All the easier to try the case in the press.

Other books you might like:
Stephen Greenleaf, *State's Evidence*, 1982
Richard Harris, *Honor Bound*, 1982
Joe L. Hensley, *Fort's Law*, 1987
Thomas Thompson, *Celebrity*, 1982
Scott Turow, *Presumed Innocent*, 1988

1663
David Cooper Wall
One Cried Murder (New York: Dembner, 1990)

Story type: Private Detective—Male Lead

Major character(s): David Hamilton, Detective—Private; Marc Florio, Police Officer (Captain)

Time period(s): 1980s

Locale(s): New York, New York

What the book is about: P.I. David Hamilton is asked to look into the death of an actor. First book.

Other books you might like:
Jerome Charyn, *The Good Policeman*, 1990
Jack Early, *A Creative Kind of Killer*, 1984
Jack Early, *Razzamatazz*, 1985

1664
Marilyn Wallace
A Single Stone (New York: Doubleday, 1991)

Series: Goldstein and Cruz

Story type: Police Procedural—Male Lead; Psychological Suspense

Major character(s): Carlos Cruz, Police Officer; Jay Goldstein, Police Officer; Linda Orett, Housewife

Time period(s): 1990s

Locale(s): Oakland, California

What the book is about: Three years ago, a young girl was murdered and a mutilated doll left at the scene. Linda Orett, the girl's mother, was arrested and tried, but acquitted. Now a similar crime has occurred. The book follows both Linda hearing the news bringing the horror back and the police who still aren't sure Linda was innocent.

Other books you might like:
Mary Higgins Clark, *Where Are the Children?*, 1975
Jeanne Hart, *Some Die Young*, 1990
Mary Anne Kelly, *Park Lane South, Queens*, 1990
Patricia MacDonald, *No Way Home*, 1989
Teri White, *Tightrope*, 1986

1665
Marilyn Wallace
So Shall You Reap (New York: Doubleday, 1992)

Story type: Psychological Suspense

Major character(s): Sarah Hoving, Businesswoman, Beekeeper

Time period(s): 1990s

Locale(s): Taconic Hills, New York

What the book is about: Sarah Hoving has a loving husband and a successful business and should be happy but she is still haunted by her mother leaving her family twenty-five years ago. Now Sarah has been asked to play the role of Emily Schiller, an important figure in the town's history, in the annual pageant. There are strange parallels between Sarah, her mother, and Emily. Then past tragedies in Emily's life begin to be repeated.

Other books you might like:
Kate Green, *Night Angel*, 1989
C.A. Haddad, *Caught in the Shadows*, 1992
Sharyn McCrumb, *The Hangman's Beautiful Daughter*, 1992
Nancy Pickard, *I.O.U.*, 1991
David Stout, *Night of the Ice Storm*, 1991

1666
Robert Wallace
To Catch a Forger (New York: St. Martin's, 1989)

Story type: Amateur Detective—Male Lead

Major character(s): Essington Holt, Art Dealer

Time period(s): 1980s

What the book is about: Art dealer Essington Holt is asked to go to France by his elderly Aunt Eloise. She wants him to recover some Degas works from a thief. First book published in the U.S.

Other books you might like:
Oliver Banks, *The Rembrandt Panel*, 1980
Peter Clothier, *Chiaroscuro*, 1985
Marcia Muller, *There Hangs the Knife*, 1988
Wayne Warga, *Fatal Impressions*, 1989
Clarissa Watson, *The Fourth Stage of Gainsborough Brown*, 1979

1667
Lee Wallingford
Clear-Cut Murder (New York: Walker, 1993)

Series: Frank Carver/Ginny Trask

Story type: Police Procedural

Major character(s): Frank Carver, Police Officer (forest service); Ginny Trask, Ranger (forest)

Time period(s): 1990s

Locale(s): Coffee Creek, Washington (Neskanie National Forest)

What the book is about: Loggers want to clear-cut Burnt Meadow and environmentalists don't want it to happen. Tempers are running hot and when hometown boy Ward Tomasovic returns to help settle things he is threatened. Frank Carver and Ginny Trask are assigned to protect him and keep the peace. When Ward is killed, they have to decide if it was the loggers, the environmentalists or someone out of his very stormy past.

Other books you might like:
Christine Andreae, *Trail of Murder*, 1992
B.J. Oliphant, *Death and the Delinquent*, 1993
Elizabeth Atwood Taylor, *The Northwest Murders*, 1992
J.F. Trainor, *Dynamite Pass*, 1993
Judith Van Gieson, *The Wolf Path*, 1992

1668
Lee Wallingford
Cold Tracks (New York: Walker, 1992)

Series: Frank Carver/Ginny Trask

Story type: Police Procedural

Major character(s): Frank Carver, Police Officer (forest service); Ginny Trask, Ranger (forest ranger), Widow(er) (single parent)

Time period(s): 1990s

Locale(s): Neskanie National Forest, Washington

What the book is about: Ginny Trask is concerned when Nino Alvarez disappears - he didn't seem the type to leave his wife and family. A month later Ginny finds his dismembered corpse in the forest. Enter Frank Carver, who took this job with the Forest Service to get away from violent crime. First novel.

Other books you might like:
Richard Hugo, *Death and the Good Life*, 1978
Janet LaPierre, *Children's Games*, 1989
B.J. Oliphant, *Dead in the Scrub*, 1990
Judith Van Gieson, *Raptor*, 1990
Ann M. Williams, *Flowers for the Dead*, 1991

1669
Minette Walters
The Ice House (New York: St. Martin's, 1992)

Story type: Psychological Suspense; Police Procedural—Male Lead

Major character(s): Andy McLoughlin, Police Officer; Ann Cattrell, Journalist (freelance)

Time period(s): 1990s

Locale(s): Streech Grange, England

What the book is about: Ten years ago David Maybury disappeared and the police are convinced that his wife Phoebe killed him and disposed of the body. Since that time Phoebe has lived in her house with two other women, Diana and Ann, and her children, while shutting herself off from any contact with the village. Now a body has been discovered in the icehouse on the property and the police are back trying to prove this is the missing husband. Forensic evidence cannot prove his identity but does show this man has been dead less than a year. First mystery.

Other books you might like:
Paula Gosling, *Death Penalties*, 1991
Martha Grimes, *The Man with a Load of Mischief*, 1981
Janet Neel, *Death's Bright Angel*, 1988
Sheila Radley, *The Chief Inspector's Daughter*, 1980
Peter Robinson, *Gallows View*, 1990

1670
Minette Walters
The Scold's Bridle (New York: St. Martin's, 1994)

Story type: Psychological Suspense; Amateur Detective—Female Lead

Major character(s): Sarah Blakeney, Doctor

Time period(s): 1990s

Locale(s): Fontwell, England

What the book is about: Nobody much liked Mathilda Gillespie, so when she is found dead in her bath nobody much cares except her doctor, Sarah Blakeney, who actually liked the old curmudgeon. She decides to look into Mathilda's death and this search becomes more important when it is discovered that she is the main beneficiary of Mathilda's will and the police think she might be guilty of murder.

Other books you might like:
Elizabeth George, *The Inspector Lynley Series*, 1989-
Paula Gosling, *Death Penalties*, 1991
Jill McGown, *The Other Woman*, 1993
Jennie Melville, *Dead Set*, 1993
Kay Mitchell, *In Stoney Places*, 1992

1671
Minette Walters
The Sculptress (New York: St. Martin's, 1993)

Story type: Amateur Detective—Female Lead; Psychological Suspense

Major character(s): Rosalind Leigh, Journalist; Hal Hawksley, Saloon Keeper/Owner (former police officer)

Time period(s): 1990s

Locale(s): Dawlington, England (Southampton)

What the book is about: Rosalind Leigh is cajoled into writing the story of Olive Martin, the woman who killed her mother and sister and carved them into pieces. Now known as The Sculptress for the bizarre figures she makes, Olive is not what Rosalind expects. Although Olive confessed to the murders, it appears that she may be innocent. As Roz investigates she finds herself drawn to Olive's arresting officer, now retired.

Other books you might like:
Jeffrey Wilds Deaver, *Hard News*, 1991
Mickey Friedman, *A Temporary Ghost*, 1989
Susan Kelly, *Out of the Darkness*, 1992
Janet Neel, *Death's Bright Angel*, 1988
Annette Roome, *A Second Shot in the Dark*, 1992

1672
Robert Ward
The Cactus Garden (New York: Pocket, 1995)

Story type: Action/Adventure; Police Procedural—Male Lead

Major character(s): Jack Walker, Police Officer (DEA agent); Buddy Wingate, Criminal (drug dealer); Charlotte Rae Wingate, Criminal (Buddy's wife)

Time period(s): 1990s

Locale(s): California; New Mexico; Mexico

What the book is about: Jack Walker finds himself undercover working for serious drug dealer Buddy Walker. He also finds himself having an affair with Buddy's wife, Charlotte. This is definitely not healthy, but it may be that Charlotte is trying to set Buddy up for a fall. Or is she trying to set Jack up? Can he discover who is double-crossing whom before it's too late? First crime novel.

Other books you might like:
Kenneth Abel, *Bait*, 1994
Anthony Bruno, *Bad Guys*, 1988
James Lee Burke, *Heaven's Prisoners*, 1987
Michael Connelly, *The Black Echo*, 1992
Pete Hautman, *Drawing Dead*, 1993

1673
Wayne Warga
Singapore Transfer (New York: Viking, 1991)

Series: Jeffrey Dean

Story type: Amateur Detective—Male Lead; Action/Adventure

Major character(s): Jeffrey Dean, Businessman (rare book dealer); Leilani Martin, Police Officer (U.S. customs agent)

Time period(s): 1990s

Locale(s): Singapore

What the book is about: Jeffrey is tired of the book business so when he is offered the chance to ghostwrite a book on the economics of Singapore, he quickly takes it. When he gets to Singapore he is quickly and accidently involved in an undercover operation to track down and stop the jade smuggling trade.

Other books you might like:
Michael Delving, *Smiling, the Boy Fell Dead*, 1973
S.F.X. Dean, *The Neil Kelly Series*, 1982-
Will Harris, *Timor Mortis*, 1986
Stephen Leather, *The Fireman*, 1990
Roy Harley Lewis, *The Matthew Coll Series*, 1982-

1674
L.J. Washburn (Pseudonym of Livia Reasoner)
Dead-Stick (New York: Tor, 1989)

Series: Lucas Hallam

Story type: Private Detective—Male Lead

Major character(s): Lucas Hallam, Detective—Private (former Texas Ranger), Stuntman (movies)

Time period(s): 1920s

Locale(s): Hollywood, California

What the book is about: Someone is trying to sabotage the film that Lucas is doing stunt-work on and the studio hires him to ferret out the guilty party.

Other books you might like:
Harold Adams, *The Carl Wilcox Series*, (1981-)
Max Allan Collins, *The Nate Heller Series*, (1983-)
Joe Gores, *Hammett*, 1975
Peter Lovesey, *Keystone*, 1983
Jeff Rovin, *Hollywood Detective: Garrison*, 1975

1675
L.J. Washburn (Pseudonym of Livia Reasoner)
Dog Heavies (New York: Tor, 1990)

Series: Lucas Hallam

Story type: Private Detective—Male Lead; Historical

Major character(s): Lucas Hallam, Detective—Private (former Texas Ranger), Stuntman

Time period(s): 1920s

Locale(s): Hollywood, California; Fort Worth, Texas

What the book is about: Lucas is hired to turn a stuck-up New York actor into a real cowboy star. Taking him to a ranch in Texas and keeping him sober and away from women are the least of Hallam's troubles. At the ranch there are real rustlers, cowboys, Indians and a dead body.

Other books you might like:
Joe Gores, *Hammett*, 1975
Stuart M. Kaminsky, *The Man Who Shot Lewis Vance*, 1987
Peter Lovesey, *Keystone*, 1983
Bill Pronzini, *Quincannon*, 1984

1676
Peter Watson
Landscape of Lies (New York: Atheneum, 1990)

Story type: Action/Adventure

Major character(s): Isobel Sadler, Heiress (impoverished); Michael Whiting, Art Dealer

Time period(s): 1980s

What the book is about: After stopping a burglar from stealing what appears to be a worthless 16th-century painting, Isobel Sadler consults with art dealer Whiting for advice. They are soon involved in a search for a long-lost treasure.

Other books you might like:
L.L. Blackmur, *Love Lies Slain*, 1987
Peter Clothier, *Dirty-Down*, 1987
Carolyn Coker, *The Hand of the Lion*, 1987
Wayne Warga, *Fatal Impressions*, 1989

1677
Timothy Watts
Cons (New York: Soho, 1993)

Story type: Action/Adventure

Major character(s): Frank "Cully" Cullen, Criminal (ex-con); Benny Marsh, Criminal (bank robber)

Time period(s): 1990s

Locale(s): Beaufort, South Carolina

What the book is about: Ex-con Frank Cullen is "rescued" from a jail term by wealthy farmer Herb Dorrance. He is hired as a chauffeur for Dorrance's seductive wife. Cullen thinks this may not be all for the good and he is proven right when the woman's bank-robbing ex-husband gets out of jail and comes to visit. Then there is the wife's lookalike sister and the missing bank-robber's partner. It gets more dangerous and confusing day by day for Cully, who would really rather go straight. First novel.

Other books you might like:
James Crumley, *Dancing Bear*, 1984
Thornton Elliott, *Hard Guy*, 1993
Joe R. Lansdale, *Mucho Mojo*, 1994
Elmore Leonard, *The Big Bounce*, 1969
Paul Levine, *To Speak for the Dead*, 1990

1678
Hillary Waugh
A Death in a Town (New York: Carroll & Graf, 1989)

Story type: Psychological Suspense

Major character(s): Sally Anders, Teenager

Time period(s): 1980s

Locale(s): Crockford, Connecticut (fictional town)

What the book is about: When 16-year-old Sally Anders is found raped and murdered, everyone hopes that it was an intruder from out of town who did it. But was it?

Other books you might like:
K.C. Constantine, *The Blank Page*, 1974
Richard Forrest, *A Child's Garden of Death*, 1975
R.R. Irvine, *The Angel's Share*, 1988

1679
W.J. Weatherby
Coronation (New York: Pocket, 1990)

Story type: Action/Adventure

Major character(s): Moses Blake, Police Officer (from Jamaica); Belinda Stone, Writer (of historical romances)

Time period(s): 1950s (1953)

Locale(s): London, England

What the book is about: Someone is going to try to assassinate Princess Elizabeth during her coronation as Queen of England.

Other books you might like:
Ken Follett, *Eye of the Needle*, 1978
Frederick Forsyth, *The Day of the Jackal*, 1971
Jack Higgins, *The Eagle Has Landed*, 1975

1680
Lise McClendon Webb
The Bluejay Shaman (New York: Walker, 1994)

Story type: Amateur Detective—Female Lead

Major character(s): Alix Thorssen, Art Dealer (gallery owner; FBI consultant)

Time period(s): 1990s

Locale(s): Wyoming; Montana

What the book is about: Alix Thorssen is an art dealer who occasionally lends her expertise to the FBI and other law enforcement agencies. She has been asked to examine the contents of an abandoned trailer when she gets word that her brother-in-law has been charged with the murder of the head of a New Age women's group involved with Indian lore. Alix, in trying to clear him, becomes intimately involved with the Salish tribe, stolen Indian artifacts, and the mysterious Bluejay Pictograph. First mystery.

Other books you might like:
James D. Doss, *The Shaman Sings*, 1994
Jean Hager, *The Molly Bearpaw Series*, 1992-
Sandra West Prowell, *By Evil Means*, 1993
J.F. Trainor, *The Angela Biwaban Series*, 1993-
Scott Young, *The Shaman's Knife*, 1993

1681
Janice Weber
Frost the Fiddler (New York: St. Martin's, 1992)

Story type: Espionage

Major character(s): Leslie Frost, Spy, Musician (concert violinist)

Time period(s): 1990s

Locale(s): Leipzig, Germany

What the book is about: After a concert rehearsal, Leslie Frost is out on the town when she witnesses the murder of a policeman and some mysterious activity at the church where Bach is buried. Professional curiosity - not of the musical type - leads her to find an ultra powerful computer in the church and to identify the killer as Emil Flick, an ex-East German agent. Flick seems as interested in her as she is in him. This leads her into love and an international plot of intrigue and murder.

Other books you might like:
Margaret Duffy, *A Murder of Crows*, 1987
Paul Myers, *Deadly Crescendo*, 1990
Katherine Neville, *The Eight*, 1988
Evelyn E. Smith, *Miss Melville's Revenge*, 1989

1682
Noah Webster
The Spanish Maze Game (New York: Doubleday, 1991)

Series: Jonathan Gaunt

Story type: Action/Adventure

Major character(s): Jonathan Gaunt, Police Officer (Remembrancer; ex-paratrooper)

Time period(s): 1990s

Locale(s): Scotland; Bavaria, Germany; Majorca, Spain

What the book is about: Gaunt is to give Florian Beck an inheritance of 400,000 pounds. When he arrives he finds several suspicious circumstances. Florian is being hounded by mysterious tax collectors, who shouldn't know about the money. Gaunt's room is broken into and he is temporarily blinded. Then Florian is killed. Webster also writes as Bill Knox, Robert MacLeod and Michael Kirk.

Other books you might like:
Jack Barnao, *Timelocke*, 1990
Clare Curzon, *Three-Core Lead*, 1990

1683
Jim Weikart
Casualty Loss (New York: Walker, 1991)

Story type: Amateur Detective—Male Lead

Major character(s): Jay Jasen, Accountant (tax accountant); Bruce Scarf, Police Officer, Detective—Homicide

Time period(s): 1990s

Locale(s): New York, New York

What the book is about: Jay has just returned from a weekend with his brother, Donald, and sister-in-law, Joan, and their friends. They were celebrating the sixties when they all lived in a commune. Suddenly a phone call informs Jay that Donald and Joan have been killed in a car crash. When he arrives at the scene, he finds a partially burned briefcase filled with money. Where did the money come from? And why is a filmed record of the get-together stolen? First novel.

Other books you might like:
Martin Blank, *Shadowchase*, 1989
Alan Dennis Burke, *Dead Wrong*, 1990
Kate Green, *Night Angel*, 1991
A.J. Orde, *A Little Neighborhood Murder*, 1989
David Stout, *Carolina Skeletons*, 1989

1684
Irving Weinman
Virgil's Ghost (New York: Fawcett, 1990)

Series: Lenny Schwartz

Story type: Private Detective—Male Lead

Major character(s): Lenny Schwartz, Detective—Private (ex-police officer)

Time period(s): 1980s

Locale(s): New York, New York

What the book is about: Hired to investigate the death of a young mathematician by the young man's parents, Lenny finds that no one but the boy's parents have any interest in the truth.

Other books you might like:
Thomas Chastain, *Pandora's Box*, 1974
Michael Collins, *The Dan Fortune Series*, (1967-)
Jack Early, *A Creative Kind of Killer*, 1984
Howard Engel, *Murder on Location*, 1983
Paul Engleman, *The Mark Renzler Series*, (1983-)

1685
Charlene Weir
Consider the Crows (New York: St. Martin's, 1993)

Series: Susan Wren

Story type: Police Procedural—Female Lead

Major character(s): Susan Wren, Police Officer (chief of police), Widow(er)

Time period(s): 1990s

Locale(s): Hampstead, Kansas

What the book is about: Susan Wren has an uneasy relationship with the mayor. Now he wants her to get rid of a "hippie girl" who has moved into town. That problem is solved for Susan when the girl is murdered. Now she has to find who would want to kill her. Then the vice-chancellor of the university where she worked disappears. Is there a connection?

Other books you might like:
P.M. Carlson, *Gravestone*, 1993
Joan Hess, *The Maggody Series*, 1987-
Margaret Maron, *Bootlegger's Daughter*, 1992
Lee Martin, *The Deb Ralston Series*, 1984-
Eve K. Sandstrom, *The Devil Down Home*, 1991

1686
Charlene Weir
Family Practice (New York: St. Martin's, 1994)

Series: Susan Wren

Story type: Police Procedural—Female Lead

Major character(s): Susan Wren, Police Officer (chief of police)

Time period(s): 1990s

Locale(s): Hampstead, Kansas

What the book is about: Dorothy Barrington, head of the Barrington family of doctors, calls a family meeting to discuss something important but she never makes it. She is shot and killed in her office. Susan Wren is determined to find the killer. It must be one of the family and suspicion soon centers on Ellen, the failure, who shunned medicine, is now trying to be a farmer, and who desperately needs money. Other members of the family seem to be hiding things as well.

Other books you might like:
P.M. Carlson, *Bloodstream*, 1995
Jean Hager, *The Molly Bearpaw Series*, 1993-
Lee Martin, *The Deb Ralston Series*, 1984-
Carol O'Connell, *Mallory's Oracle*, 1994
Julie Smith, *The Skip Langdon Series*, 1990-

1687
Charlene Weir
The Winter Widow (New York: St. Martin's, 1992)

Series: Susan Wren

Story type: Police Procedural—Female Lead

Major character(s): Susan Wren, Police Officer

Time period(s): 1990s

Locale(s): Hampstead, Kansas

What the book is about: Susan was a police officer in San Francisco. But now, after a whirlwind romance, she is the wife of Daniel Wren, police chief of Hampstead, Kansas. Trying to adjust to small town life, Susan is suddenly a widow. Daniel has been shot and killed. Susan asks the mayor to appoint her chief so she can bring the killer to justice. First novel.

Other books you might like:
Susan Dunlap, *As a Favor*, 1984
Joan Hess, *The Maggody Series*, 1987-
Margaret Maron, *Bloody Kin*, 1985
Lee Martin, *Too Sane a Murder*, 1984
Lillian O'Donnell, *Cop Without a Shield*, 1983

1688
Mike Weiss
A Dry and Thirsty Ground (New York: St. Martin's, 1992)

Series: Ben Henry

Story type: Private Detective—Male Lead

Major character(s): Ben Henry, Detective—Private

Time period(s): 1990s

Locale(s): Big Sur, California

What the book is about: Ben has given up driving a taxi and is now a full-time private detective. When his best friend from the old days calls and asks for help, how can he refuse? Paul Richards is accused of killing the local bully with an ax. Paulie has the classic motive, means and opportunity, plus the man's blood on him when he was arrested. To clear him Ben will have to find the real killer while everyone in the area is fighting a raging wildfire.

Other books you might like:
Michael Allegretto, *Blood Relative*, 1992
Stephen Greenleaf, *State's Evidence*, 1982
Jerry Kennealy, *The Nick Polo Series*, 1987-
John Lutz, *The Alo Nudger Series*, 1976-
Walter Satterthwait, *Wall of Glass*, 1988

1689
Pat Welch
Murder by the Book (Tallahassee: Naiad, 1990)
Story type: Private Detective—Female Lead
Major character(s): Helen Black, Detective—Private (former cop), Lesbian
Time period(s): 1980s
Locale(s): San Francisco, California
What the book is about: Helen Black is asked to investigate a bank robbery that appears to have been an inside job. First book.
Other books you might like:
Agnes Bushnell, *Shadow Dance*,
Dolores Klaich, *Heavy Gilt*, 1988
Diana McRae, *All the Muscle You Need*, 1988
Eve Zaremba, *Beyond Hope*, 1987

1690
Edward Wellen
An Hour to Kill (New York: St. Martin's, 1993)
Story type: Action/Adventure
Major character(s): Mal, Criminal (professional hit-man); Carol Shanley, Police Officer; Marita Garcia, Abuse Victim
Time period(s): 1990s
Locale(s): Miami, Florida; Las Vegas, Nevada; Los Angeles, California
What the book is about: Mal is in Miami after successfully fulfilling his latest contract, the killing of a potential informer. At a coffee shop he sees a woman being abused by her boyfriend. He is attracted to the woman and since he has an hour to kill, he decides to eliminate the problem. Unfortunately the boyfriend was the brother of a powerful drug dealer. Now Mal is being hunted by the police and his former employers.
Other books you might like:
Tom Kakonis, *Michigan Roll*, 1989
Ridley Pearson, *Hard Fall*, 1992
Randy Russell, *Hot Wire*, 1992
Marc Savage, *Flamingos*, 1992
Richard Stark, *The Parker Series*, 1963-1974

1691
Valerie Wilson Wesley
Devil's Gonna Get Him (New York: Putnam, 1995)
Series: Tamara Hayle
Story type: Private Detective—Female Lead
Major character(s): Tamara Hayle, Detective—Private, Single Parent (African American)
Time period(s): 1990s
Locale(s): Newark, New Jersey
What the book is about: Wealthy and influential Lincoln Story has hired Tamara to investigate Brandon Pike, the boyfriend of his stepdaughter. Although Pike once broke Tamara's heart, she agrees to follow him. Soon, however, Story is dead of a lethal dose of peanut butter and the police suspect the sister of Tamara's friend, Wyvetta Green. Now Tamara has a new client whom she can only clear by finding the real killer.
Other books you might like:
Nikki Baker, *The Virginia Kelly Series*, 1991-
Eleanor Taylor Bland, *The Marti MacAlister Series*, 1992-
Gar Anthony Haywood, *The Aaron Gunner Series*, 1988-
Barbara Neely, *Blanche Among the Talented Tenth*, 1994
James Sallis, *The Lew Griffin Series*, 1992-

1692
Valerie Wilson Wesley
When Death Comes Stealing (New York: Putnam, 1994)
Series: Tamara Hayle
Story type: Private Detective—Female Lead
Major character(s): Tamara Hayle, Detective—Private (African American), Single Parent
Time period(s): 1990s
Locale(s): Newark, New Jersey
What the book is about: Tamara Hayle, formerly a cop, is now a private detective who is tough, smart, and reasonably satisfied with her life. Her biggest mistake was marrying DeWayne Curtis, but it resulted in her greatest joy, her son Jamal. Now DeWayne wants to hire her and she can't say no. Someone is systematically killing his sons and soon it will be Jamal's turn unless Tamara can stop it. First novel.
Other books you might like:
Nikki Baker, *The Virginia Kelly Series*, 1991-
Eleanor Taylor Bland, *The Marti MacAlister Series*, 1992-
Michael Jahn, *City of God*, 1992
Barbara Neely, *Blanche on the Lam*, 1993

1693
Charles West
Funnelweb (New York: Walker, 1989)
Story type: Amateur Detective—Male Lead
Major character(s): Tom Grant, Actor (former detective); Alison Easterbrook, Heiress (love interest of Grant)
Time period(s): 1980s
Locale(s): Australia (Queensland Outback)
What the book is about: While filming a movie Grant finds a decayed corpse. Is there a connection between this body and the recent death of an elderly woman supposedly killed by wild dogs? First book.

Other books you might like:
J.F. Burke, *Location Shots*, 1974
Peter Corris, *The Green Apartments*, 1988
A.E. Martin, *Death in the Limelight*, 1946

1694
Charles West
Rat's Nest (New York: Walker, 1990)

Story type: Amateur Detective—Male Lead; Action/Adventure

Major character(s): John Tallis, Student (graduate student), Writer (poet)

Time period(s): 1990s

Locale(s): Sydney, Australia

What the book is about: John Tallis has just asked Helen Simons to marry him when she is brutally gunned down in front of him. When evidence suggests that Helen was really Heidi Saxon, a prostitute and pornographer, John can't believe it. Furthermore, several people are trying to kill him, including a policeman. This is the revised edition of *The Destruction Man*, first published in 1976.

Other books you might like:
Alan Dennis Burke, *Dead Wrong*, 1990
Peter Corris, *The Cliff Hardy Series*, 1980-
S.F.X. Dean, *By Frequent Anguish*, 1982
M.K. Shuman, *The Caesar Clue*, 1990

1695
Charles West
Stonefish (New York: Walker, 1991)

Story type: Private Detective—Male Lead

Major character(s): Paul Crook, Detective—Private, Cowboy

Time period(s): 1990s

Locale(s): Sydney, Australia

What the book is about: Paul's father, a night club comic, has inherited a private investigation firm from Mike Sthenios who died in a car crash. He hands over the running of the firm to Paul until it can be sold. An awful lot of sinister people are interested in the agency and the dead owner including Stonefish, the head of the Sydney drug traffic. Paul might not live long enough to sell out.

Other books you might like:
Jon Cleary, *The Scobie Malone Series*, 1966-
Peter Corris, *The Cliff Hardy Series*, 1980-
Laurence Meynell, *The Hooky Heffernan Series*, 1975-
Neville Steed, *Black Eye*, 1990
Arthur W. Upfield, *The Inspector Napoleon Bonaparte Series*, 1929-1966

1696
John Westermann
Exit Wounds (New York: Soho, 1990)

Story type: Action/Adventure

Major character(s): Orin Boyd, Police Officer, Veteran (burned-out Vietnam veteran)

Time period(s): 1980s

Locale(s): Long Island, New York

What the book is about: Orin Boyd, burned-out, depressed cop, is sent to spy on his fellow cops in another precinct. Trying to drink his troubles away, he discovers how the bagman cometh and must make the decision whether to snitch or steal.

Other books you might like:
William Diehl, *Sharky's Machine*, 1978
Nat Hentoff, *The Man From Internal Affairs*, 1985
Stephen Solomita, *A Twist of the Knife*, 1988
Joseph Wambaugh, *The Glitter Dome*, 1981
Robert Westbrook, *Nostalgia Kills*, 1988

1697
Donald E. Westlake
Don't Ask (New York: Mysterious, 1993)

Series: John Dortmunder

Story type: Action/Adventure; Humor

Major character(s): John Dortmunder, Thief (inept)

Time period(s): 1990s

Locale(s): New York, New York

What the book is about: John Dortmunder and his gang are talked into helping a group of Tsergovians recover (steal) a bone—a religious relic—so that Tsergovia can get a seat in the United Nations, rather than the rival country of Votskojek. Things do not go as planned—which is usual with Dortmunder's gang. Dortmunder himself ends up in a dungeon and must escape to finalize the rescue of the bone.

Other books you might like:
K.K. Beck, *A Hopeless Case*, 1992
Lawrence Block, *The Burglar Who Traded Ted Williams*, 1994
Lawrence Block, *The Thief Who Couldn't Sleep*, 1966
Peter Dickinson, *King & Joker*, 1976
Loren D. Estleman, *Peeper*, 1989

1698
Donald E. Westlake
Drowned Hopes (New York: Mysterious, 1990)

Series: John Dortmunder

Story type: Action/Adventure; Humor

Major character(s): John Dortmunder, Thief (inept)

Time period(s): 1980s

Locale(s): New York

What the book is about: An ex-cellmate of Dortmunder's wants him to help get a $700,000 stash from a previous robbery. The only catch is that the money is buried under an upstate New York reservoir.

1699 Wheat

Other books you might like:
Lawrence Block, *Burglars Can't Be Choosers*, 1977
Marvin Kaye, *My Brother, the Druggist*, 1979
Gregory McDonald, *Fletch*, 1974
Thomas Perry, *Metzger's Dog*, 1983

1699
Carolyn Wheat
Fresh Kills (New York: Berkley, 1995)

Series: Cass Jameson

Story type: Legal

Major character(s): Cass Jameson, Lawyer

Time period(s): 1990s

Locale(s): New York, New York

What the book is about: A kill on Staten Island is a term for a narrow inlet, but it takes on a more sinister meaning when the body of a teenager is found in one. The body is Amber, a client of Cass'. He represented her when she put her baby up for adoption. Things went smoothly until Amber got married and wanted her baby back. Now she is dead. Did the adoptive parents kill Amber to keep her from reclaiming the child or did Amber have other secrets that led to her death?

Other books you might like:
Leslie Glass, *To Do No Harm*, 1992
Lia Matera, *The Laura Di Palma Series*, 1988-
Joyce Anne Schneider, *Darkness Falls*, 1989
Judith Van Gieson, *The Neil Hamel Series*, 1988-
E.L. Wyrick, *A Strange and Bitter Crop*, 1994

1700
Gloria White
Charged with Guilt (New York: Dell, 1995)

Series: Ronnie Ventana

Story type: Private Detective—Female Lead

Major character(s): Ronnie Ventana, Detective—Private; Blackie Coogan, Detective—Private (Ronnie's mentor and friend)

Time period(s): 1990s

Locale(s): San Francisco, California

What the book is about: Ronnie Ventana specializes in security. One of the ways she evaluates possible problems is to stage a break-in, something she is very good at thanks to her cat-burglar parents, now deceased. This time when she breaks in, however, she finds the dead body of a former senator. The woman who hired her has disappeared, leaving Ronnie as the prime suspect in a murder. The more she tries to clear herself, the deeper into trouble she gets.

Other books you might like:
Catherine Dain, *The Freddie O'Neal Series*, 1992-
Janet Dawson, *The Jeri Howard Series*, 1990-
Linda Grant, *The Catherine Saylor Series*, 1988-
Karen Kijewski, *The Kat Colorado Series*, 1989-
Marcia Muller, *The Sharon McCone Series*, 1977-

1701
Gloria White
Money to Burn (New York: Dell, 1993)

Series: Ronnie Ventana

Story type: Private Detective—Female Lead

Major character(s): Ronnie Ventana, Detective—Private; Blackie Coogan, Detective—Private

Time period(s): 1990s

Locale(s): San Francisco, California

What the book is about: Ronnie is spending a quiet evening at home when a friend of her husband, Bunk Hanover, shows up asking for help. Soon after his departure four Uzi-toting thugs show up. They work for a "Black Widow", a woman whose lovers die mysteriously. Bunk has dumped this woman for a rich debutante and she doesn't like it. Ronnie reluctantly agrees to help, but she may be sorry.

Other books you might like:
Janet Dawson, *Kindred Crimes*, 1990
Linda Grant, *Blind Trust*, 1990
Karen Kijewski, *Katwalk*, 1989
Marcia Muller, *The Sharon McCone Series*, 1977-
Shelley Singer, *Following Jane*, 1993

1702
Gloria White
Murder on the Run (New York: Dell, 1991)

Series: Ronnie Ventana

Story type: Private Detective—Female Lead

Major character(s): Ronnie Ventana, Detective—Private (security specialist); Blackie Coogan, Detective—Private

Time period(s): 1990s

Locale(s): San Francisco, California

What the book is about: Ronnie Ventana is the daughter of *the* Ventanas, two of the most successful cat-burglars. Not surprisingly she is an expert at security systems. When she is out jogging she sees a man beating a woman. She runs to get help but when the police arrive, nobody is there. She later identifies the man as a local politico with clout. Now she may really be on the run - for her life. First novel.

Other books you might like:
Linda Barnes, *The Snake Tattoo*, 1989
Janet Dawson, *Kindred Crimes*, 1990
Linda Grant, *Love nor Money*, 1991
Marcia Muller, *The Sharon McCone Series*, 1977-
Sara Paretsky, *The V.I. Warshawski Series*, 1982

1703
Ned White
The Very Bad Thing (New York: Viking, 1990)

Story type: Private Detective—Male Lead

Major character(s): Dred Balcazar, Detective—Private

Time period(s): 1990s

Locale(s): Boston, Massachusetts

What the book is about: Dred is hired to find out who "infected" a computer network with a virus that threatens to destroy years of work. He is also becoming involved with a beautiful and mysterious woman who may also be involved with the threat to the computer but is certainly not who she says she is. First novel.

Other books you might like:
Linda Grant, *Random Access Murder*, 1988
Jeremiah Healy, *The John Francis Cuddy Series*, 1985-
Roger L. Simon, *California Roll*, 1985
Richard C. Smith, *A Secret Singing*, 1988

1704
Randy Wayne White
Sanibel Flats (New York: St. Martin's, 1990)

Story type: Action/Adventure

Major character(s): Doc Ford, Scientist (Marine biologist; former spy)

Time period(s): 1980s

Locale(s): Florida; Central America

What the book is about: Trying to forget his previous life as a spy, "Doc" Ford is working as a marine biologist in Florida when a friend from his childhood shows up to ask for help in finding his child. First book.

Other books you might like:
James Lee Burke, *The Neon Rain*, 1986
Carl Hiaasen, *Double Whammy*, 1987
R. Lance Hill, *The Evil That Men Do*, 1978
Paul Kavanaugh, *Such Men are Dangerous*, 1969
John Walter Putre, *A Small and Incidental Murder*, 1990

1705
Teri White
Thursday's Child (New York: Mysterious, 1991)

Story type: Action/Adventure; Private Detective

Major character(s): Robert Turchek, Criminal (contract killer); Gar Sinclair, Detective—Private (former cop; disabled); Beau Epstein, Runaway (orphan)

Time period(s): 1990s

Locale(s): Los Angeles, California; New York, New York

What the book is about: 15-year-old Beau Epstein runs away from his wealthy, elderly uncle and hooks up with contract killer Robert Turchek whose brother is in a coma. Meanwhile bitter ex-cop Gar Sinclair, who is now a P.I., is hired to track Beau down and bring him home. The relationship between these three disparate characters form the heart of this book.

Other books you might like:
Dick Lochte, *Laughing Dog*, 1986
John Lutz, *The Carver Series*, 1986-
W.R. Philbrick, *Paint It Black*, 1989
John Lawrence Reynolds, *The Man Who Murdered God*, 1990

1706
Barbara Whitehead
The Dean It Was That Died (New York: St. Martin's, 1991)

Story type: Amateur Detective—Male Lead; Police Procedural—Male Lead

Major character(s): George Grindal, Religious (canon, Church of England); David Smart, Police Officer (detective inspector)

Time period(s): 1990s

Locale(s): York, England

What the book is about: Henry Parsifal, the new Dean of York Minster Cathedral was not a nice man. A lot of people wished him gone. Wasn't it fortunate that a falling stone killed him?

Other books you might like:
Michael David Anthony, *The Becket Factor*, 1991
D.M. Greenwood, *Clerical Errors*, 1992
Robert Richardson, *The Latimer Mercy*, 1985
Charles Merrill Smith, *The Reverend Randollph Series*, 1977-1980
David Williams, *Treasure by Post*, 1992

1707
Barbara Whitehead
Playing God (New York: St. Martin's, 1989)

Story type: Amateur Detective—Male Lead

Major character(s): Tom Churchyard, Engineer (works for British Telcom); Robert Southwell, Police Officer (chief inspector)

Time period(s): 1980s

Locale(s): York, England

What the book is about: When a rock artist is cast as Christ in the production of a medieval play, his presence causes more than just talk. This is Whitehead's first mystery.

Other books you might like:
Simon Brett, *So Much Blood*, 1977
P.M. Carlson, *Audition for Murder*, 1985
Jane Dentinger, *Murder on Cue*, 1983
Caroline Graham, *Death of a Hollow Man*, 1989
Anne Morice, *Sleep of Death*, 1982

1708
Barbara Whitehead
Sweet Death, Come Softly (New York: St. Martin's, 1993)

Series: York Mysteries

Story type: Police Procedural—Male Lead

Major character(s): Robert Southwell, Police Officer (detective chief inspector); Hannah Benn, Businesswoman

Time period(s): 1990s

Locale(s): York, England

1709 Whitney

What the book is about: York is home to Benn Chocolate, famous for Benn Bars. Pierre Fontaine is their genius chocolatier and he is perfecting a new recipe. Before he can get it finished, he disappears. Hannah Benn goes to the police and they start investigating but they have little to work on. Did Pierre leave voluntarily or has he been kidnapped or murdered?

Other books you might like:
Marjorie Eccles, *More Deaths than One*, 1991
Paula Gosling, *Death Penalties*, 1991
Roger Ormerod, *Hung in the Balance*, 1986
Alan Scholefield, *Never Die in January*, 1993
Susannah Stacey, *Grave Responsibility*, 1990

1709
Polly Whitney
Until Death (New York: St. Martin's, 1994)
Series: Ike and Abby
Story type: Amateur Detective
Major character(s): Abby Abagnard, Television (news director); Mary "Ike" Tygart, Television (news producer)
Time period(s): 1990s
Locale(s): New York, New York

What the book is about: Abby Abagnard and Ike Tygart are recently divorced, but they still work together on the network news show "Morning Watch." The show has recently changed its anchorwoman, getting rid of the aging Hannah Van Stone and replacing her with the young and pretty Connie Candela. Then Connie is found dead on the set. She was ready for the show in full makeup but the autopsy reveals the cause of death as drowning. First novel.

Other books you might like:
William L. DeAndrea, *Killed in the Ratings*, 1978
Sparkle Hayter, *What's a Girl Gotta Do?*, 1994
Mike Lupica, *Dead Air*, 1987
Richard Rosen, *Saturday Night Dead*, 1988
John Bartholomew Tucker, *He's Dead-She's Dead: Details at Eleven*, 1990

1710
Polly Whitney
Until the End of Time (New York: St. Martin's, 1995)
Series: Ike and Abby
Story type: Action/Adventure
Major character(s): Abby Abagnaro, Television (news director); Mary "Ike" Tygart, Television (news producer)
Time period(s): 1990s
Locale(s): New York, New York

What the book is about: Abby is mugged by a homeless man who seems to know him and wants to talk about death. Later Abby realizes the man may have known something about the "Yellow-Man Killer," a serial killer who preys on the homeless and paints his victims' faces yellow. Meanwhile Ike is busy producing a show that features a doctor critical of the FDA and their procedures for releasing new drugs. The doctor is killed after leaving the studio—and his face is painted yellow. Abby and Ike have the inside track, but to what?

Other books you might like:
Ron Goulart, *Now He Thinks He's Dead*, 1992
Sparkle Hayter, *What's a Girl Gotta Do?*, 1994
Ron Nessen, *Knight & Day*, 1995 (Johanna Neuman, co-author)
Joshua Quittner, *Shoofly Pie to Die*, 1992 (Michelle Slatella, co-author)
Matt Taylor, *Neon Dancers*, 1991 (Bonnie Taylor, co-author)

1711
Collin Wilcox
Dead Center (New York: Henry Holt, 1992)
Series: Frank Hastings
Story type: Police Procedural—Male Lead
Major character(s): Frank Hastings, Police Officer (homicide lieutenant)
Time period(s): 1990s
Locale(s): San Francisco, California

What the book is about: A high society playboy has been shot and killed while walking home, apparently by a street person. After investigation, however, it appears this may have been a professional hit. Then more wealthy and powerful people are killed with the same weapon. Lt. Hastings is under pressure to stop the killings. Is this the work of someone who hates rich people or is there some other connection among the victims?

Other books you might like:
Rex Burns, *The Gabe Wager Series*, 1976-
J.A. Jance, *The J.P. Beaumont Series*, 1985-
David L. Lindsey, *The Stuart Haydon Series*, 1983-
Jerry Oster, *The Joe Cullen Series*, 1990-
Irving Weinman, *The Lenny Schwartz Series*, 1986-

1712
Collin Wilcox
A Death Before Dying (New York: Holt, 1990)
Series: Frank Hastings
Story type: Police Procedural—Male Lead
Major character(s): Frank Hastings, Police Officer (lieutenant-homicide)
Time period(s): 1980s
Locale(s): San Francisco, California

What the book is about: Meredith Powell's murder means more to Lt. Frank Hastings than the average homicide. He's known her all his life.

Other books you might like:
John Ball, *Chief Tallon and the S.O.R.*, 1984
K.C. Constantine, *Always a Body to Trade*, 1983
E.V. Cunningham, *The Case of the Kidnapped Angel*, 1982
Bill Granger, *Public Murders*, 1980
Joseph McNamara, *The First Directive*, 1984

1713
Collin Wilcox
Except for the Bones (New York: Tor, 1991)
Series: Alan Bernhardt
Story type: Private Detective—Male Lead
Major character(s): Alan Bernhardt, Detective—Private, Actor (writer)
Time period(s): 1990s
Locale(s): San Francisco, California
What the book is about: Diane Cutler and her boyfriend witness her stepfather burying the body of his mistress. Diane decides to keep quiet knowing how ruthless her stepfather can be. The boyfriend is not so discrete and tries his hand at blackmail. When the boyfriend is killed, Diane runs to San Francisco. Alan Bernhardt is hired by Diane's friend to find out what is bothering her.
Other books you might like:
Linda Barnes, *Bitter Finish*, 1983
Jerry Kennealy, *Polo Solo*, 1987
John T. Lescroart, *Dead Irish*, 1990
Bill Pronzini, *The Nameless Detective Series*, 1971-
Bruce Zimmerman, *Blood under the Bridge*, 1990

1714
Collin Wilcox
Full Circle (New York: Forge, 1994)
Series: Alan Bernhardt
Story type: Private Detective—Male Lead
Major character(s): Alan Bernhardt, Actor, Detective—Private
Time period(s): 1990s
Locale(s): San Francisco, California
What the book is about: The past is coming back to haunt actor and part-time private detective Alan Bernhardt. He is asked by millionaire Raymond DuBois to help him return some stolen art to its rightful owners. At the same time, the FBI is after Bernhardt to reveal the whereabouts of Betty Giles, the woman who stole the art in the first place. What he gets involved with is not as simple as it appears at first glance.
Other books you might like:
Aaron Elkins, *A Glancing Light*, 1991
Parnell Hall, *Actor*, 1993
Jerry Kennealy, *The Nick Polo Series*, 1987-
John Leslie, *Killing Me Softly*, 1994
Bill Pronzini, *The Nameless Detective Series*, 1971-

1715
Collin Wilcox
Hire a Hangman (New York: Tor, 1991)
Series: Frank Hastings
Story type: Police Procedural—Male Lead
Major character(s): Frank Hastings, Police Officer (lieutenant, homicide)
Time period(s): 1990s
Locale(s): San Francisco, California
What the book is about: The head of a medical center's transplant team is shot as he's getting into his car. Disgruntled former patient (or family member), drug deal gone sour, or just a robbery? Hastings must find the truth.
Other books you might like:
Rex Burns, *The Gabe Wager Series*, 1976-
J.A. Jance, *The J.P. Beaumont Series*, 1985-
David L. Lindsey, *The Stuart Haydon Series*, 1983-
Jayson Livingston, *Point Blank*, 1990
Joseph McNamara, *The First Directive*, 1984

1716
Collin Wilcox
Silent Witness (New York: Tor, 1990)
Series: Alan Bernhardt
Story type: Private Detective—Male Lead
Major character(s): Alan Bernhardt, Detective—Private, Actor (playwright, director)
Time period(s): 1990s
Locale(s): San Francisco, California
What the book is about: Janice Hale's sister has been beaten to death in her home while her husband and son were asleep. Now the husband will not let Janice see her seven-year-old nephew. Fortunately, her best friend is in love with Bernhardt who she hires to investigate. But some very important people are bringing pressure to bear to keep any one from talking to the boy.
Other books you might like:
William Babula, *According to St. John*, 1989
Jerry Kennealy, *Polo Solo*, 1987
John T. Lescroart, *Dead Irish*, 1989
Bill Pronzini, *The Nameless Detective Series*, 1971-
Julie Smith, *Tourist Trap*, 1986

1717
Collin Wilcox
Switchback (New York: Holt, 1993)
Series: Frank Hastings
Story type: Police Procedural—Male Lead
Major character(s): Frank Hastings, Police Officer (lieutenant); Janet Collier, Police Officer
Time period(s): 1990s
Locale(s): San Francisco, California
What the book is about: A self-described high level hooker, or as she called herself, a courtesan, is found dead in a park. The killing of Lisa Franklin leads Lt. Frank Hastings and fellow police officer Janet Collier to investigate some wealthy city businessmen who might have had reason to kill this woman. In addition there seems to be a relationship developing between Hastings and Collier and neither is quite sure what to do about it.

1718 Wilcox

Other books you might like:
Rex Burns, *The Gabe Wager Series*, 1976-
James Neal Harvey, *Painted Ladies*, 1992
Archer Mayor, *The Joe Gunther Series*, 1988-
James Schermerhorn, *Night of the Cat*, 1993
Irving Weinman, *The Lenny Schwartz Series*, 1986-

1718
Stephen F. Wilcox
All the Dead Heroes (New York: St. Martin's, 1992)
Series: T.S.W. Sheridan
Story type: Amateur Detective—Male Lead
Major character(s): T.S.W. Sheridan, Journalist (freelance crime reporter)
Time period(s): 1990s
Locale(s): New York
What the book is about: One of Sheridan's boyhood heroes, Hall of Fame second baseman Frank Wooley - now banned from baseball for consorting with gamblers - is back in the news. He is the perpetrator of an apparent murder/suicide, with a sleazy sportswriter as his victim. T.S. doesn't believe it and attempts to right the wrong and save Wooley's reputation for the ages.
Other books you might like:
L.L. Enger, *Swing*, 1991
Crabbe Evers, *Murderer's Row*, 1992
Alison Gordon, *The Dead Pull Hitter*, 1989
Mike Lupica, *Limited Partner*, 1990
Robert B. Parker, *Mortal Stakes*, 1976

1719
Stephen F. Wilcox
The Dry White Tear (New York: St. Martins, 1989)
Series: T.S.W. Sheridan
Story type: Amateur Detective—Male Lead
Major character(s): T.S.W. Sheridan, Journalist; J.D. Staub, Police Officer (deputy sheriff)
Time period(s): 1980s
Locale(s): Mohaca Springs, New York (New York wine country)
What the book is about: Journalist Sheridan decides to investigate the death of his uncle, Charlie Dugan. First book.
Other books you might like:
Don Flynn, *Murder Isn't Enough*, 1983
Douglas Kiker, *Murder on Clam Pond*, 1987
Douglas Kiker, *Murder on the Cut*, 1988
Geoff Peterson, *Medicine Dog*, 1989
Keith Peterson, *There Fell a Shadow*, 1988

1720
Stephen F. Wilcox
The Green Mosaic (New York: St. Martin's, 1994)
Series: T.S.W. Sheridan
Story type: Amateur Detective—Male Lead
Major character(s): T.S.W. Sheridan, Journalist (free-lance crime reporter)
Time period(s): 1990s
Locale(s): Adirondacks, New York
What the book is about: T.S.W. Sheridan is spending some time with his current lady in the Adirondacks. She is helping with a camp and he is looking for crime. What he finds is the death, three years ago, of Glenny Oldham. Glenny, an environmentalist, was the ex-wife of a radical activist who was on the run from the feds. He disappeared and then Glenny was found dead, supposedly from a fall. The locals think that Larry Podolak killed her, but there is no proof. Rumor says Glenny's ghost is still around. Then Podolak is killed with Glenny's old gun.
Other books you might like:
Nat Brandt, *Land Kills*, 1991 (Yanna Brandt, co-author)
M.S. Karl, *Deerslayer*, 1991
Douglas Kiker, *Death at the Cut*, 1988
John R. Riggs, *The Garth Ryland Series*, 1985-
David Stout, *The Dog Hermit*, 1993

1721
Stephen F. Wilcox
The NIMBY Factor (New York: St. Martin's, 1992)
Series: Hackshaw
Story type: Amateur Detective—Male Lead
Major character(s): Elias "Hack" Hackshaw, Journalist (part-time house restorer)
Time period(s): 1990s
Locale(s): Kirkville, New York
What the book is about: For ten years the state has been trying to put a landfill in Kirkville, and for ten years the residents have been fighting it. Hackshaw was part of the NIMBY (Not In My Back Yard) group but has recently had a change of opinion and written an editorial in favor of the landfill. Now the head of the opposition, Elton Venable, is livid. When Hack tries to interview him, he finds Elton's dead body. Then the body disappears. Can Hack find out what is going on and, incidentally, stay out of jail?
Other books you might like:
Nat Brandt, *Land Kills*, 1991 (Yanna Brandt, co-author)
M.S. Karl, *Death Notice*, 1990
Douglas Kiker, *Murder on Clam Pond*, 1986
Vince Kohler, *Rainy North Woods*, 1990
John R. Riggs, *Wolf in Sheep's Clothing*, 1989

1722
Stephen F. Wilcox
The Painted Lady (New York: St. Martin's, 1994)
Series: Hackshaw
Story type: Amateur Detective—Male Lead
Major character(s): Elias "Hack" Hackshaw, Journalist (also restores houses)
Time period(s): 1990s

Locale(s): Kirkville-Port Erie, New York

What the book is about: Hester Del Gado has bought the old Mott house, a grand old Victorian "painted lady." It needs some restoration however, so she asks Hackshaw to help out. He is willing as the money is good and Hester is beautiful, but Hester's plans include turning the house into a home for troubled teens. The rest of the neighborhood doesn't want any part of it, blaming the girls for a recent outbreak of vandalism. Then one of the girls is killed.

Other books you might like:
Jonathan Gash, *The Lies of Fair Ladies*, 1992
Sally Gunning, *Hot Water*, 1990
M.S. Karl, *Death Notice*, 1990
Vince Kohler, *Rising Dog*, 1992
John R. Riggs, *Hunting Ground*, 1987

1723
Kate Wilhelm
Death Qualified: A Mystery of Chaos (New York: St. Martin's, 1991)

Story type: Legal; Psychological Suspense

Major character(s): Barbara "Bobby" Holloway, Lawyer; Mike Dinesen, Computer Expert, Scientist (mathematician); Lucas Kendricks, Student, Researcher

Time period(s): 1990s

Locale(s): Turner's Point, Oregon; Denver, Colorado

What the book is about: Having given up law, Barbara Holloway is less than thrilled to be asked by her father to help defend a woman who has been indicted for the murder of her estranged husband. She agrees to do it anyway—and may regret it. Though outwardly a courtroom drama, this book is absolutely unique to the field. There has never been another one like it.

Other books you might like:
Harrison Arnston, *Trade-Off*, 1992
Kerry Tucker, *Still Waters*, 1991
Scott Turow, *The Burden of Proof*, 1990

1724
Kate Wilhelm
Justice for Some (New York: St. Martins, 1993)

Story type: Legal; Amateur Detective—Female Lead

Major character(s): Sarah Drexler, Judge, Widow(er); Arthur Fernandez, Police Officer

Time period(s): 1990s

Locale(s): East Shasta, California

What the book is about: What was supposed to be a pleasant family gathering turns into much more for Oregon judge Sarah Drexler. First her father shows up with a strange woman whose presence he does not explain. Then her father and the strange woman turn up dead the next day. The dead woman turns out to have been a private detective—but what was Fran's father doing with her? The P.I.'s office has also been ransacked, but does any of this have anything to do with Fran's family and the death of her father? The police certainly think so.

Other books you might like:
Harrison Arnston, *Trade-Off*, 1992
Marjorie Dorner, *Blood Kin*, 1992
John Grisham, *The Client*, 1993
Carolyn Hougan, *Blood Relative*, 1992
John T. Lescroart, *The 13th Juror*, 1994

1725
Kate Wilhelm
Seven Kinds of Death (New York: St. Martin's, 1992)

Series: Charlie Meiklejohn/Constance Leidl

Story type: Private Detective

Major character(s): Constance Leidl, Detective—Private, Psychologist; Charlie Meiklejohn, Detective—Private (ex-firefighter)

Time period(s): 1990s

Locale(s): Maryville, Maryland

What the book is about: Constance receives a letter from her friend Marion Olsen asking her to attend a party celebrating the start of a tour of her sculptures. Marion also indicates she has trouble and needs help at the artist's colony she helps run. When Constance arrives, a well-known editor is missing and some of the sculptures have been vandalized. Then the editor is found dead.

Other books you might like:
Richard Forrest, *Death on the Mississippi*, 1989
Al Guthrie, *Grave Murder*, 1990
Bernie Lee, *Murder at Musket Beach*, 1990
E.J. McGill, *Immaculate in Black*, 1991
Elizabeth Travis, *Under the Influence*, 1989

1726
Gordon Randolph Willey
Selena (New York: Walker, 1993)

Story type: Amateur Detective—Male Lead

Major character(s): Colin Edwards, Professor (retired), Anthropologist

Time period(s): 1980s (1985)

Locale(s): St. Christopher, Florida

What the book is about: Colin Edwards hasn't been back to his home town in 50 years—since his parents moved to Boston. He is called back by his cousin Charles who wants to excavate some Indian mounds that supposedly hide a family treasure. Charles is opposed by the rest of the family and says people are trying to kill him to stop him. Colin becomes involved with old family secrets and a woman he wants to forget—Selena Crawford. Then one of the cousins is killed. First novel.

Other books you might like:
Thomas H. Cook, *Evidence of Blood*, 1991
D.J. Donaldson, *No Mardi Gras for the Dead*, 1992
Aaron Elkins, *Make No Bones*, 1991
Roy Lewis, *Bloodeagle*,
Michael Mewshaw, *True Crime*, 1991

1727
Amanda Kyle Williams
A Singular Spy (Tallahassee, Florida: Naiad, 1992)
Series: Madison McGuire
Story type: Espionage
Major character(s): Madison McGuire, Spy, Lesbian
Time period(s): 1990s
Locale(s): United States; Switzerland
What the book is about: A murder in Geneva starts CIA agent Madison McGuire on the search for a mole inside U.S. intelligence. The search will lead her from Geneva to D.C. and finally back to her own home in North Carolina, where her lover Terry is in serious danger.
Other books you might like:
David Morrell, *The Covenant of the Flame*, 1991
Peter O'Donnell, *The Modesty Blaise Series*, 1966-
S.K. Wolf, *The Harbinger Effect*, 1990

1728
Ann M. Williams
Flowers for the Dead (New York: St. Martin's, 1991)
Story type: Police Procedural—Male Lead
Major character(s): Brian Kayne, Detective (investigator for the DA); Joanna Starrett, Artist (painter)
Time period(s): 1990s
Locale(s): California
What the book is about: Brian is visiting his mother when he attends a showing of Joanna's paintings. The paintings are of flowers that illustrate a series of poems by Sam Fox. The poems seem to relate to an unsolved crime, but no one seems to know who Sam Fox is. First novel.
Other books you might like:
Wendy Hornsby, *No Harm*, 1987
Susan B. Kelly, *Hope Against Hope*, 1991
Janet LaPierre, *Unquiet Grave*, 1988
Lee Wallingford, *Cold Tracks*, 1992

1729
David Williams
Holy Treasure! (New York: St. Martin's, 1989)
Series: Mark Treasure
Story type: Amateur Detective—Male Lead
Major character(s): Mark Treasure, Businessman (chief executive officer); Molly Forbes, Actress (wife of Mark)
Time period(s): 1980s
Locale(s): London, England
What the book is about: Treasure is dragooned into trying to help a group save an old church from being razed in the name of progress. One of the supporters of the church is then murdered.
Other books you might like:
W.J. Burley, *Death in the Willow Pattern*, 1969
Emma Lathen, *John Putnam Thatcher Series*, (1961-)
Herbert Resnicow, *The Gold Deadline*, 1984
Sara Woods, *The Case Is Altered*, 1967

1730
David Williams
Treasure by Post (New York: St. Martin's, 1992)
Series: Mark Treasure
Story type: Amateur Detective—Male Lead
Major character(s): Mark Treasure, Banker (investment banker); Molly Forbes, Actress, Spouse (of Mark)
Time period(s): 1990s
Locale(s): England (West Country)
What the book is about: St. Timothy's Convent has only three elderly nuns left, but despite that, it has a fund of 11 million pounds. When one of the three members of the financial advisory board dies of a heart attack while being beaten by robbers, Mark is asked to take his place. When he arrives he soon encounters a mysterious fire, a counterfeit stamp ring and the strange death of another board member.
Other books you might like:
Lesley Grant-Adamson, *Threatening Eye*, 1988
D.M. Greenwood, *Clerical Errors*, 1992
Tim Heald, *Business Unusual*, 1990
Emma Lathen, *The John Putnam Thatcher Series*, 1961-
Barbara Whitehead, *The Dean It Was That Died*, 1991

1731
Barbara Wilson
Gaudi Afternoon (Seattle: Seal, 1990)
Series: Cassandra Reilly
Story type: Amateur Detective—Female Lead
Major character(s): Cassandra Reilly, Writer, Linguist
Time period(s): 1990s
Locale(s): Barcelona, Spain
What the book is about: Cassandra Reilly is asked to track down femme fatale Frankie Stevens' husband. Frankie thinks he is in Spain and so Cassandra is off, all the while trying to finish this translation she's working on.
Other books you might like:
Joyce Maiman, *Left My Heart*, 1991
Maria-Antonia Oliver, *Antipodes*, 1989
Rosie Scott, *Glory Days*, 1988
David Serafin, *The Body in Cadiz Bay*, 1985
Eve Zaremba, *Beyond Hope*, 1988

1732
Charles Wilson
Silent Witness (New York: Carroll & Graf, 1992)
Story type: Amateur Detective—Male Lead

Major character(s): Mark Ramsey, Businessman (oil executive); Ray Hopkins, Police Officer (Mark's older half-brother)

Time period(s): 1990s

Locale(s): Davis County, Mississippi

What the book is about: A young woman is brutally raped and stabbed. Leigh Ann Mueller goes to Mark for help. She is afraid her husband will be accused of the murder and because of an incident in his past will be unable to pass a lie detector test. Mark, who once loved Leigh Ann, agrees to help. He finds several people who might have killed the not-so-innocent girl with a strange past.

Other books you might like:
William Bayer, *Blind Side*, 1989
Alan Dennis Burke, *Dead Wrong*, 1990
Noreen Gilpatrick, *The Piano Man*, 1991
Victor Wuamett, *Artichoke Hearts*, 1991

1733
Karen Ann Wilson
Copy Cat Crimes (New York: Berkley, 1995)

Series: Samantha Holt

Story type: Amateur Detective

Major character(s): Samantha Holt, Veterinarian (assistant); Louis Augustin, Veterinarian

Time period(s): 1990s

Locale(s): Brightwater Beach, Florida

What the book is about: Three deformed kittens and $300 for their care have been left on the doorstep of the clinic. Samantha's boss, Dr. Augustin, is dedicated to animals, but would sometimes rather be a detective. When the money turns out to be counterfeit and the kittens' owner turns up as a mutilated corpse in the canal, he has his chance. Why then is Samantha doing most of the work and taking the risks?

Other books you might like:
Lydia Adamson, *The Dr. Nightingale Series*, 1993-
Lilian Jackson Braun, *The Cat Who Series*, 1966-
Laura Crum, *The Gail McCarthy Series*, 1994-
Carole Nelson Douglas, *Catnap*, 1992
Mary Willis Walker, *Zero at the Bone*, 1991

1734
Karen Ann Wilson
Eight Dogs Flying (New York: Berkley, 1994)

Series: Samantha Holt

Story type: Amateur Detective

Major character(s): Samantha Holt, Veterinarian (assistant); Louis Augustin, Veterinarian

Time period(s): 1990s

Locale(s): Paradise Cay, Florida

What the book is about: Samantha Holt works for the handsome and temperamental Dr. Louis Augustin, who drives her crazy—sometimes charming and sometimes an ogre—but always dedicated to the animals they treat. Now strange things are happening to the doctor's ex-wife's greyhounds. When one of the dogs attacks a young girl and then another dog dies, they investigate and find a systematic series of drugging and intimidation. Then the murders start. First novel.

Other books you might like:
Lydia Adamson, *The Dr. Nightingale Series*, 1994-
Melissa Cleary, *The Jackie Walsh Series*, 1990-
Susan Conant, *The Holly Winter Series*, 1990-
Barbara Moore, *The Doberman Wore Black*, 1984
Mary Willis Walker, *Zero at the Bone*, 1990

1735
Robin Wilson
Death by Degrees (New York: St. Martin's, 1995)

Story type: Action/Adventure

Major character(s): Peter Haas, Police Officer (ex-CIA); Harold Piggott, Administrator (university president; ex-CIA); Hildy Barnes, Police Officer (campus security officer)

Time period(s): 1990s

Locale(s): Monterey, California

What the book is about: Harold Piggott was Peter's old boss at the agency. Now he has hired him to be a general troubleshooter at Monterey University. Peter has his work cut out for him. One of the university staff has been found dead of asphyxiation while in a very compromising situation. While Peter and Hildy investigate they find that someone seems to be planting evidence and covering up something. Then another death is connected to the university. First novel.

Other books you might like:
Bill Crider, *Dying Voices*, 1989
Robert Reeves, *Doubting Thomas*, 1985
Michael W. Sherer, *Little Use for Death*, 1992
William L. Story, *Final Thesis*, 1989
Bill Waggoner, *Sweet Death*, 1992

1736
David Wiltse
The Edge of Sleep (New York: Putnam, 1993)

Series: John Becker

Story type: Action/Adventure; Police Procedural—Male Lead

Major character(s): John Becker, FBI Agent (semi-retired); Karen Crist, FBI Agent

Time period(s): 1990s

Locale(s): New York (suburbs of New York City)

What the book is about: Someone is kidnapping and torturing young boys outside of New York City. Semi-retired FBI agent John Becker teams up with former lover and head of the FBI's kidnapping unit, Karen Crist. Then Crist's own son is abducted and Crist and Becker must race against time to find the miscreants.

1737 Wiltse

Other books you might like:
Patricia D. Cornwell, *All That Remains*, 1992
Thomas Harris, *The Silence of the Lambs*, 1988
Richard LaPlante, *Mantis*, 1993
David L. Lindsey, *Mercy*, 1984
John Sandford, *Silent Prey*, 1992

1737
David Wiltse
Into the Fire (New York: Putnam, 1994)

Series: John Becker

Story type: Police Procedural—Male Lead; Psychological Suspense

Major character(s): John Becker, FBI Agent (retired); Cooper, Serial Killer

Time period(s): 1990s

Locale(s): Virginia

What the book is about: John Becker, the FBI's best agent at finding serial killers, is burned out. He has quit because he realized he was becoming more and more like the people he tracked. But now letters are arriving from Springfield Prison with coded messages describing more killings and Becker is drawn back into the hunt despite himself.

Other books you might like:
Patricia D. Cornwell, *Cruel and Unusual*, 1993
Thomas Harris, *Red Dragon*, 1981
David L. Lindsey, *Mercy*, 1984
Ridley Pearson, *The Angel Maker*, 1993
John Sandford, *Silent Prey*, 1992

1738
Chris Wiltz
The Emerald Lizard (New York: Dutton, 1991)

Series: Neal Rafferty

Story type: Private Detective—Female Lead

Major character(s): Neal Rafferty, Detective—Private; Bubba Brevna, Criminal (loan shark)

Time period(s): 1990s

Locale(s): New Orleans, Louisiana

What the book is about: Rafferty is asked to intercede between a former lover who owns a bar and the loan shark who helped her start her business. Though assured by the loan shark that he is not planning anything, the lover is killed and the bar burned down. Since both the police and the shark think Rafferty is involved he must find the guilty party.

Other books you might like:
James Lee Burke, *A Morning for Flamingos*, 1990
J. Madison Davis, *White Rook*, 1990
M.K. Shuman, *The Maya Stone Murders*, 1989
Daniel Woodrell, *Under the Bright Lights*, 1986
Steven Womack, *Murphy's Fault*, 1990

1739
Anne Wingate (Pseudonym of Martha G. Webb and Lee Martin)
The Buzzards Must Also Be Fed (New York: Walker, 1991)

Series: Mark Shigata

Story type: Police Procedural—Male Lead

Major character(s): Mark Shigata, Police Officer (chief of police); Al Quinn, Police Officer (deputy)

Time period(s): 1990s

Locale(s): Bayport, Texas

What the book is about: Former Bayport police sergeant Steve Hansen, in jail for murdering his wife and step-daughter, escapes and returns to Bayport to kill Dale Shipp, former police chief. Instead he meets Shigata and interests him in the case. Mark decides to reopen the investigation.

Other books you might like:
Susan Rogers Cooper, *The Man in the Green Chevy*, 1988
Bill Crider, *Shotgun Saturday Night*, 1987
Jean Hager, *Night Walker*, 1990
D.R. Meredith, *The Sheriff and the Panhandle Murders*, 1984
Ted Wood, *Live Bait*, 1985

1740
Anne Wingate (Pseudonym of Martha G. Webb)
Exception to Murder (New York: Walker, 1992)

Series: Mark Shigata

Story type: Police Procedural—Male Lead

Major character(s): Mark Shigata, Police Officer (chief; former FBI agent); Al Quinn, Police Officer (second in command to Shigata)

Time period(s): 1990s

Locale(s): Bayport, Texas

What the book is about: Councilwoman Margaret Ruskin has just been found half-eaten in an alligator pit at Ark Park, a combination zoo and religious theme park. It isn't an accident because she had been shot before being thrown in the pit. Wingate also writes as Lee Martin.

Other books you might like:
K.C. Constantine, *The Rocksburg Railroad Murders*, 1972
Susan Rogers Cooper, *The Man in the Green Chevy*, 1988
Bill Crider, *Too Late to Die*, 1986
D.R. Meredith, *The Sheriff and the Panhandle Murders*, 1984
Eve K. Sandstrom, *The Devil Down Home*, 1991

1741
Anne Wingate (Pseudonym of Martha G. Webb and Lee Martin)
The Eye of Anna (New York: Walker, 1990)

Series: Mark Shigata

Story type: Police Procedural—Male Lead

Major character(s): Mark Shigata, Police Officer (chief)

Time period(s): 1980s

Locale(s): Bayport, Texas

What the book is about: A serial killer and a hurricane strike the town together.

Other books you might like:
K.C. Constantine, *The Rocksburg Railroad Murders*, 1972
Bill Crider, *Shotgun Saturday Night*, 1987
Joan Hess, *Malice in Maggody*, 1987
Edward Mathis, *From a High Place*, 1985
D.R. Meredith, *Murder by Impulse*, 1987

1742

Anne Wingate (Pseudonym of Martha G. Webb and Lee Martin)
Yakuza, Go Home (New York: Walker, 1993)

Series: Mark Shigata

Story type: Police Procedural—Male Lead

Major character(s): Mark Shigata, Police Officer (former FBI agent)

Time period(s): 1990s

Locale(s): Bayport, Texas

What the book is about: During the worst storm in years with a flooding town to deal with, Mark Shigata's cousin Rocky and his wife appear and ask Mark to take care of their son if anything should happen to them. They are on the run from Rocky's father-in-law, a leader of the Yakuza—the Japanese Mafia. They soon turn up dead and Mark must protect not only the son but his family as well.

Other books you might like:
Susan Rogers Cooper, *Chasing Away the Devil*, 1992
Michael Crichton, *Rising Sun*, 1992
Jean Hager, *Night Walker*, 1990
Sharyn McCrumb, *If Ever I Return, Pretty Peggy-O*, 1990
Ted Wood, *When the Killing Starts*, 1989

1743

Don Winslow
A Cool Breeze on the Underground (New York: St. Martin's, 1991)

Series: Neal Carey

Story type: Amateur Detective—Male Lead; Action/Adventure

Major character(s): Neal Carey, Student, Troubleshooter (for "The Bank")

Time period(s): 1990s

Locale(s): United States

What the book is about: As penance for being rescued from dire straits when younger by "The Bank," Neal must, much to his dismay, take on the occassional task, usually involving another ne'er-do-well. Such is the case here. First novel. Edgar nominee for Best First Novel-1991.

Other books you might like:
K.K. Beck, *A Hopeless Case*, 1992
Charlotte Epstein, *Murder at the Friendship Hotel*, 1991
Jonathan Gash, *Jade Woman*, 1988
Stephen Leather, *The Fireman*, 1990

1744

Don Winslow
The Trail to Buddha's Mirror (New York: St. Martin's, 1992)

Series: Neal Carey

Story type: Amateur Detective—Male Lead; Action/Adventure

Major character(s): Neal Carey, Student, Troubleshooter; Li Lan, Artist (painter; Chinese national)

Time period(s): 1990s

Locale(s): San Francisco, California; Hong Kong

What the book is about: Neal has been asked by "the Bank" to fly to San Francisco and convince an important biologist to give up his "china doll" lover and return to work. What Neal expects to find is a cheap Chinese hooker - what he actually finds is the beautiful and talented Li Lan and her exquisite paintings. From here Neal gets invovled in a plot of international intrigue.

Other books you might like:
Edward Cline, *Whisper the Guns*, 1992
Jonathan Gash, *Jade Woman*, 1988
Stephen Leather, *The Fireman*, 1990
Douglas Skeggs, *The Talinin Madonna*, 1992
Wayne Warga, *Singapore Transfer*, 1991

1745

H. Fred Wiser (Pseudonym of Harry Friedman and Linda Friedman)
Deadly Stakes (New York: Walker, 1989)

Story type: Private Detective

Major character(s): Jason Reddy, Detective—Private; Jessica Monroe, Detective—Private

Time period(s): 1980s

Locale(s): New York, New York

What the book is about: Investigating the blackmailing of a conservative politician, Jessica and Jason are forced to use their skills as martial arts expert and computer hacker, respectively. First book.

Other books you might like:
Lawrence Block, *The Burglar Who Studied Spinoza*, 1981
Frank McConnell, *Murder Among Friends*, 1983
Robert B. Parker, *The Widening Gyre*, 1983
Brad Solomon, *The Open Shadow*, 1978
Richard Werry, *Casket for a Lying Lady*, 1985

1746

S.K. Wolf
The Harbinger Effect (New York: Simon and Schuster, 1989)

Story type: Espionage

Major character(s): Molly Davison, Social Worker (relief agency worker); Yuri Klebanoff, Photojournalist

Time period(s): 1980s

1747

What the book is about: When the grandson of Pravda's editor decides to defect, the C.I.A. asks Molly Davison to help. Things quickly go to pieces and Molly and Yuri are left pretty much on their own.

Other books you might like:
Ken Follett, *Eye of the Needle*, 1978
Brian Garfield, *Necessity*, 1984
David Gurr, *A Woman Called Scylla*, 1981
Michael Hastings, *The Devil's Spy*, 1988

1747
S.K. Wolf
Long Chain of Death (New York: Ballantine, 1991)

Story type: Action/Adventure; Psychological Suspense

Major character(s): David Brett, Teacher (high school); Phillip Decker, Police Officer

Time period(s): 1980s

Locale(s): Fairfield, Indiana

What the book is about: Soon after David Brett's wife is killed by a car bomb, someone kills two of his students. The police think the deaths are connected and that Brett is involved. Originally published in 1987.

Other books you might like:
Joe Gores, *A Time of Predators*, 1969
James W. Hall, *Under Cover of Daylight*, 1987
Jonathan Kellerman, *The Alex Delaware Series*, 1985-
Keith Peterson, *The Scarred Man*, 1989
R.D. Zimmerman, *Deadfall in Berlin*, 1990

1748
Valerie Wolzien
All Hallows Evil (New York: Fawcett, 1992)

Series: Susan Henshaw

Story type: Amateur Detective—Female Lead

Major character(s): Susan Henshaw, Housewife; Kathleen Gordon, Police Officer (former)

Time period(s): 1990s

Locale(s): Hancock, Connecticut

What the book is about: It's Halloween and Susan finds a body in the town library. She thinks it's a joke until the man dies as she watches. A second body is found almost immediately thereafter. Someone has killed Jason Armstrong, famous host of a network morning show. His wife and co-host of the show feels she will be the prime suspect and, aware of Susan's reputation as a detective, asks her to investigate. Susan will have to solve the murders just to get rid of Rebecca Armstrong and the network executives who threaten to become permanent house guests.

Other books you might like:
Jill Churchill, *Grime and Punishment*, 1989
Jaqueline Girdner, *Adjusted to Death*, 1991
Susan Isaacs, *Compromising Positions*, 1978
Katherine Hall Page, *The Body in the Belfry*, 1990
Gillian Roberts, *Caught Dead in Philadelphia*, 1987

1749
Valerie Wolzien
A Good Year for a Corpse (New York: Fawcett, 1994)

Series: Susan Henshaw

Story type: Amateur Detective—Female Lead

Major character(s): Susan Henshaw, Housewife; Kathleen Gordon, Police Officer (retired)

Time period(s): 1990s

Locale(s): Hancock, Connecticut

What the book is about: Horace Harvey has lots of money and wants to give it away to a local group. All the groups certainly want his money and are courting Horace to get the inside track. Then Horace's body is dicovered with money stuffed in his mouth. The prime suspect is the head of FOPP (Friends of Potted Plants). Kathleen Gordon is sure that she is innocent and enlists the help of her friend, Susan Henshaw, to help prove it.

Other books you might like:
Mary Cahill, *Carpool*, 1991
Jill Churchill, *The Jane Jeffry Series*, 1989-
Jaqueline Girdner, *The Kate Jasper Series*, 1990-
Katherine Hall Page, *The Faith Fairchild Series*, 1990-
Gillian Roberts, *The Amanda Pepper Series*, 1987-

1750
Valerie Wolzien
We Wish You a Merry Murder (New York: Fawcett, 1991)

Series: Susan Henshaw

Story type: Amateur Detective—Female Lead

Major character(s): Susan Henshaw, Housewife; Kathleen Gordon, Businesswoman (security consultant)

Time period(s): 1990s

Locale(s): Hancock, Connecticut

What the book is about: Kelly Knowlson is recently divorced but her ex and his new wife still live almost next door. At a Christmas get-together, Kelly confides to Susan and Kathleen that he will be coming back to her any day now. And he does, calmly sitting in her house by the fire, with a glass of eggnog in his hand and a bullet in his head. Susan tries to cope with Christmas, a visiting mother-in-law, her new boyfriend and now murder.

Other books you might like:
Jill Churchill, *A Farewell to Yarns*, 1991
Susan Isaacs, *Compromising Positions*, 1978
Robert Nordan, *Death Beneath the Christmas Tree*, 1991
Katherine Hall Page, *The Body in the Belfry*, 1990
Gillian Roberts, *Caught Dead in Philadelphia*, 1989

1751
Steven Womack
Dead Folks' Blues (New York: Ballantine, 1992)

Series: Harry Denton

Story type: Private Detective—Male Lead

Major character(s): Harry James Denton, Detective—Private (former newspaper reporter)

Time period(s): 1990s

Locale(s): Nashville, Tennessee

What the book is about: After being fired from his job as a reporter, Harry Denton thinks it would be a good idea to become a private investigator. After six months of scraping by doing repo work and skip-tracing he's not so sure. Then an old lover asks him to help her husband who is being threatened by a bookie. Before he can get started, the husband is murdered.

Other books you might like:
Richard Hoyt, *The John Denson Series*, 1980-
Michael Z. Lewin, *The Albert Samson Series*, 1974-
James E. Martin, *The Flip Side of Life*, 1990
Taylor McCafferty, *Ruffled Feathers*, 1992
Geoff Peterson, *Medicine Dog*, 1989

1752
Steven Womack
Murphy's Fault (St. Martin's, 1990)

Series: Jack Lynch

Story type: Amateur Detective—Male Lead

Major character(s): Jack Lynch, Public Relations (for a bank)

Time period(s): 1980s

Locale(s): New Orleans, Louisiana

What the book is about: Lynch is assigned to dig up some dirt on a political foe of his boss. He finds more than he bargained for. Womack's first novel.

Other books you might like:
David Everson, *Recount*, 1987
Ross Thomas, *The Fools in Town Are on Our Side*, 1971
Chris Wiltz, *A Diamond Before You Die*, 1987

1753
Steven Womack
The Software Bomb (New York: St. Martin's, 1993)

Series: Jack Lynch

Story type: Private Detective—Male Lead

Major character(s): Jack Lynch, Detective—Private

Time period(s): 1990s

Locale(s): New Orleans, Louisiana

What the book is about: Jack Lynch is back from Los Angeles after burying his mother. He's almost broke, has been asked to vacate his apartment and has been evicted from his office. Fortunately a friend has a job for him. A bank is being threatened with a computer virus that will destroy all their records unless they pay five million dollars. As Jack goes to work on the case he finds that computer hackers are not as non-violent as he thought.

Other books you might like:
Richard Abshire, *The Dallas Deception*, 1992
Denise Danks, *User Deadly*, 1992
Jerome Doolittle, *Bear Hug*, 1992
Roger L. Simon, *California Roll*, 1985
Ned White, *The Very Bad Thing*, 1990

1754
Steven Womack
Torch Town Boogie (New York: Ballantine, 1993)

Series: Harry Denton

Story type: Private Detective—Male Lead

Major character(s): Harry James Denton, Detective—Private (former reporter)

Time period(s): 1990s

Locale(s): Nashville, Tennessee

What the book is about: Harry Denton is still scraping together a living when a fire in the mansion across the street from his home is set afire, supposedly by the East Nashville arsonist. But this time there is a dead body. The body proves to be the fiance of Harry's ex-wife, and because she now inherits his money, she is the chief suspect in his death. Harry sets out to prove her innocent.

Other books you might like:
Earl Emerson, *The Thomas Black Series*, 1985-
Richard Hoyt, *The John Denson Series*, 1980-
Michael Z. Lewin, *The Albert Samson Series*, 1974-
John Lutz, *The Alo Nudger Series*, 1976-
William J. Reynolds, *The Nebraska Series*, 1984-

1755
Steven Womack
Way Past Dead (New York: Ballantine, 1995)

Series: Harry Denton

Story type: Private Detective—Male Lead

Major character(s): Harry James Denton, Detective—Private; Marsha Helms, Doctor (medical examiner)

Time period(s): 1990s

Locale(s): Nashville, Tennessee

What the book is about: Harry is feeling good. He has just finished a case that may actually pay off big. When he gets back to town, he finds that members of a religious cult have surrounded the morgue and won't let anyone leave, including Harry's lover, Dr. Marsha Helms. Next, Slim Gibson—one of the songwriters that shares Harry's building, and Harry's friend—is accused of beating his ex-wife to death. Finally, someone is threatening Harry. When he tries to help, things get even worse.

Other books you might like:
John Birkett, *The Last Private Eye*, 1988
Steve Brewer, *Lonely Street*, 1994
Kathryn Buckstaff, *No One Dies in Branson*, 1994
Jesse Sublett, *The Martin Fender Series*, 1989-
Donald E. Westlake, *Baby Would I Lie*, 1994

1756
Ted Wood
Flashback (New York: Scribners, 1992)

Series: Reid Bennett

Story type: Police Procedural—Male Lead

Major character(s): Reid Bennett, Police Officer (chief of police)

Time period(s): 1990s

Locale(s): Murphy's Harbor, Ontario, Canada

What the book is about: Reid has enough worries as his wife is just about ready to deliver their first child. Then in one day a young gang "swarms" the town, an escaped prisoner threatens Reid, and the body of a woman is discovered in the trunk of a car that has been driven into the lake. Then things start to get complicated. Wood also writes as Jack Barnao.

Other books you might like:
Susan Rogers Cooper, *The Milt Kovak Series*, 1988
Jean Hager, *Night Walker*, 1990
D.R. Meredith, *The Sheriff Charles Matthews Series*, 1984-
Anne Wingate, *The Mark Shigata Series*, 1988-
L.R. Wright, *The Karl Alberg Series*, 1985-

1757
Ted Wood
On the Inside (New York: Scribners, 1990)

Series: Reid Bennett

Story type: Police Procedural—Male Lead

Major character(s): Reid Bennett, Police Officer (chief)

Time period(s): 1980s

Locale(s): Elliot, Ontario, Canada (Fictional, small Northern mining town)

What the book is about: Reid Bennett takes his new wife and goes undercover as a police officer to ferret out corruption on the police force of a small Northern mining town.

Other books you might like:
Howard Engel, *A City Called July*, 1986
Doug Hornig, *Waterman*, 1987
Joseph Koenig, *Smuggler's Notch*, 1989
Alexander Law, *To an Easy Grave*, 1986

1758
Ted Wood
Snow Job (New York: Scribners, 1993)

Series: Reid Bennett

Story type: Police Procedural—Male Lead

Major character(s): Reid Bennett, Police Officer (chief of police); Sam, Animal (German Shepherd)

Time period(s): 1990s

Locale(s): Chambers, Vermont

What the book is about: Reid Bennett's old Marine friend, Doug Ford, has asked for help. He is suspected of murdering a woman with whom he was supposedly having an affair. The woman was a bookkeeper and some missing money is found in Doug's car. Doug says he is innocent but seems to be keeping something secret. It doesn't help that Doug is the only black policeman in town and that the woman was white.

Other books you might like:
Andrew Coburn, *No Way Home*, 1992
Susan Rogers Cooper, *The Milt Kovak Series*, 1988-
D.R. Meredith, *The Sheriff Charles Matthews Series*, 1984-
Susan Oleksiw, *Murder in Mellingham*, 1992
L.R. Wright, *The Karl Alberg Series*, 1985-

1759
Sherryl Woods
Ties That Bind (New York: Warner, 1991)

Series: Amanda Roberts/Joe Donelli

Story type: Amateur Detective

Major character(s): Amanda Roberts, Journalist; Joe Donelli, Boyfriend (ex-policeman)

Time period(s): 1990s

Locale(s): Atlanta, Georgia

What the book is about: Amanda and Joe are finally getting married. Joe is late for the wedding - with good reason. His car has been blown up. At first it is thought that Joe has been killed but the body in the car is that of the best man. But where is Joe?

Other books you might like:
Elaine Raco Chase, *Dangerous Places*, 1987
Barbara D'Amato, *Hardball*, 1990
Susan Kelly, *Until Proven Innocent*, 1989
Dave Pedneau, *A.P.B.*, 1987

1760
Stuart Woods
Heat (New York: HarperCollins, 1994)

Story type: Action/Adventure

Major character(s): Jesse Warden, Police Officer (ex-DEA agent); Jack Gene Coldwater, Religious (head of religious cult)

Time period(s): 1990s

Locale(s): St. Clair, Idaho

What the book is about: Jesse Warden, former DEA agent, is in prison for a murder he didn't commit. He is offered a pardon if he will go undercover to get the goods on a religious cult that has taken over the town of St. Clair, Idaho. Though he doesn't trust the man who is offering the pardon—his former boss—and the last two agents who have gone there have been killed, he agrees to give it a try. In reality he is planning to escape from the clutches of his former boss, but he finds himself in love and seriously concerned about the plans of the cult. Can he foil their plans, escape from his ex-boss, and stay alive to raise a family with his new love?

Other books you might like:
Anthony Bruno, *The Tozzi and Gibbons Series*, 1988-
Joe Gores, *Dead Man*, 1993
James Graham, *The Run to Morning*, 1974
Ross Thomas, *The Fools in Town Are on Our Side*, 1970
Timothy Watts, *Cons*, 1993

1761
Stuart Woods
Imperfect Strangers (New York: HarperCollins, 1995)

Story type: Action/Adventure; Psychological Suspense

Major character(s): Sandy Kinsolving, Businessman (wine merchant); Peter Martindale, Art Dealer

Time period(s): 1990s

Locale(s): London, England; New York, New York

What the book is about: On a flight from London to New York, Peter Martindale and Sandy Kinsolving get to talking (after seeing *Strangers on a Train*) and discover that they would both like to be rid of their wives. So why not take a frame from Hitchcock? After one of the wives ends up dead things quickly spiral out of control. Who did the killing and who else will end up dead?

Other books you might like:
Mary Higgins Clark, *Loves Music, Loves to Dance*, 1993
Patricia Highsmith, *Strangers on a Train*, 1950
John Lutz, *S.W.F. Seeks Same*, 1990
Joyce Anne Schneider, *Darkness Falls*, 1989

1762
Stuart Woods
Palindrome (New York: Harper, 1991)

Story type: Action/Adventure; Psychological Suspense

Major character(s): Liz Barwick, Photographer; Lee Williams, Police Officer

Time period(s): 1990s

Locale(s): Cumberland Island, Georgia

What the book is about: After being beaten nearly to death by her steriod-crazed football player husband, Liz Barwick takes refuge on a private island off the coast of Georgia. There she gets very involved with the family that owns the island. Meanwhile her husband is killing people while trying to discover her whereabouts and policeman Williams is on his trail.

Other books you might like:
Michael Allegretto, *Night of Reunion*, 1990
Brian Garfield, *Necessity*, 1984
Richard North Patterson, *Escape the Night*, 1983
Thomas Perry, *Island*, 1988
Ross Thomas, *Briarpatch*, 1984

1763
Stuart Woods
Santa Fe Rules (New York: HarperCollins, 1992)

Story type: Action/Adventure

Major character(s): Wolf Willett, Filmmaker (producer/director)

Time period(s): 1990s

Locale(s): Santa Fe, New Mexico

What the book is about: Wolf Willett wakes up one morning with no memory of yesterday, not an uncommon occurrence for this heavy drinker. He leaves for Los Angeles but is forced down in a small town by engine trouble on his plane. When he finally reads a newspaper he discovers that three people—his partner, his wife, and him—have been found dead in his house. He decides to stay dead for a bit, mostly to finish his current film without interference, but also because he thinks he may have been the target of the killer or killers. After finishing the film he hires a top-notch attorney and resurfaces.

Other books you might like:
Neal Barrett Jr., *Pink Vodka Blues*, 1992
Lawrence Block, *After the First Death*, 1969
Kate Green, *Shooting Star*, 1992
James W. Hall, *Bones of Coral*, 1991

1764
M.K. Wren (Pseudonym of Martha Kay Renfroe)
Dead Matter (New York: Ballantine, 1993)

Series: Conan Flagg

Story type: Private Detective—Male Lead

Major character(s): Conan Flagg, Detective—Private, Store Owner (of a bookstore)

Time period(s): 1990s

Locale(s): Holiday Beach, Oregon

What the book is about: Ravin Gould, famous author, is in town to sign books and finish his latest book, supposedly a roman a clef. The book signing is interrupted by an irate husband, armed with a chain-saw, accusing Ravin of having an affair with his wife. Later, when Gould is found dead with his throat cut by a chain-saw, there is an obvious suspect. Conan doesn't think the guy is guilty and decides to investigate. He finds an awful lot of people who hated Gould.

Other books you might like:
Jon L. Breen, *Touch of the Past*, 1988
John Dunning, *Booked to Die*, 1992
M.D. Lake, *A Gift for Murder*, 1992
Sheila Simonson, *Larkspur*, 1990
Wayne Warga, *Hardcover*, 1985

1765
M.K. Wren (Pseudonym of Martha Kay Renfroe)
King of the Mountain (New York: Ballantine, 1995)

Series: Conan Flagg

Story type: Private Detective—Male Lead

Major character(s): Conan Flagg, Detective—Private, Store Owner (of a bookstore)

Time period(s): 1990s

Locale(s): Mount Hood, Oregon

What the book is about: Conan has been asked by his old friend, Lise King, to attend the annual family reunion of the King family. The family patriarch, A.C. King, has remarried after the death of his first wife and Lise hopes Conan's presence will help keep things calm between A.C. and his sons. However, on the ritual pilgrimage to Mount Hood, tragedy strikes and three are killed. Conan barely survives and realizes that someone is trying to kill off the King family.

Other books you might like:
Earl Emerson, *The Thomas Black Series*, 1985-
Richard Hoyt, *The John Denson Series*, 1980-
Frederick D. Huebner, *Methods of Execution*, 1994
Benjamin M. Schutz, *A Fistful of Empty*, 1991
Jonathan Valin, *The Harry Stoner Series*, 1980-

1766
Eric Wright
Buried in Stone (New York: Scribners, 1995)
Story type: Police Procedural—Male Lead
Major character(s): Mel Pickett, Police Officer (retired), Widow(er); Lyman Caxton, Police Officer (chief)
Time period(s): 1990s
Locale(s): Larch River, Ontario, Canada

What the book is about: Mel has retired and bought land in Larch River to see if he can build a log cabin. A body is found near his land. Although the body is mutilated, it is soon identified as the brother of the local police chief's girlfriend. The chief, Lyman Caxton, asks Mel to help out as Lyman is inexperienced in serious crime investigation and may have a personal involvement. Soon Mel is personally involved too.

Other books you might like:
Susan Rogers Cooper, *Dead Moon on the Rise*, 1994
Howard Engel, *The Benny Cooperman Series*, 1980
Medora Sale, *Short Cut to Santa Fe*, 1994
Ted Wood, *The Reid Bennett Series*, 1983-
L.R. Wright, *Mother Love*, 1995

1767
Eric Wright
Death by Degrees (New York: Scribners, 1993)
Series: Inspector Charlie Salter
Story type: Police Procedural—Male Lead
Major character(s): Charlie Salter, Police Officer (Special Affairs unit)
Time period(s): 1990s
Locale(s): Toronto, Ontario, Canada

What the book is about: Charlie Salter's father is ill and may be dying. To take his mind off feelings of guilt and mortality, Charlie volunteers to investigate the death of Professor Lyall, dismissed as a killing during a robbery. Some anonymous notes have raised some questions about his death—it seems that several people at Bathurst College may have wanted him dead. Charlie finds the notes may be true; the politics and professional jealousy at the college could have resulted in murder.

Other books you might like:
J.S. Borthwick, *The Student Body*, 1986
Bill Crider, *One Dead Dean*, 1988
Nora Kelly, *My Sister's Keeper*, 1992
Peter Robinson, *The Hanging Valley*, 1992
Medora Sale, *Sleep of the Innocent*, 1991

1768
Eric Wright
Final Cut (New York: Scribners, 1991)
Series: Inspector Charlie Salter
Story type: Police Procedural—Male Lead
Major character(s): Charlie Salter, Police Officer (head of Special Affairs)
Time period(s): 1990s
Locale(s): Toronto, Ontario, Canada

What the book is about: Charlie is assigned to a movie set, supposedly as an advisor on police procedure, but he is actually investigating a series of incidents and practical jokes that are delaying production. The jokes start escalating and it seems that someone wants this movie halted and won't stop until somebody is dead.

Other books you might like:
Simon Brett, *Star Trap*, 1977
Howard Engel, *Murder on Location*, 1985
Caroline Graham, *Death of a Hollow Man*, 1990
Patricia Moyes, *Falling Star*, 1964
Medora Sale, *Murder in a Good Cause*, 1990

1769
Eric Wright
A Fine Italian Hand (New York: Scribners, 1992)
Series: Inspector Charlie Salter
Story type: Police Procedural—Male Lead
Major character(s): Charlie Salter, Police Officer (Special Affairs Section)
Time period(s): 1990s
Locale(s): Toronto, Ontario, Canada

What the book is about: Actor Alec Hunter has been found dead in a disreputable motel - stabbed and strangled. The first investigators assume a mob hit for non-payment of gambling debts but ruffle the feathers of the Italian community with some injudicious comments. Charlie is assigned to the case with orders to avoid any more publicity. To complicate his life, his wife Annie is on an extended visit to her family and Charlie's first love, of thirty years ago, is in town.

Other books you might like:
Alisa Craig, *Trouble in the Brasses*, 1989
Caroline Graham, *Death of a Hollow Man*, 1990
Mary Monica Pulver, *Ashes to Ashes*, 1988
Peter Robinson, *Gallows View*, 1990
Medora Sale, *Sleep of the Innocent*, 1991

1770
Eric Wright
A Sensitive Case (New York: Scribners, 1990)

Series: Inspector Charlie Salter

Story type: Police Procedural—Male Lead

Major character(s): Charlie Salter, Police Officer (inspector); Mel Pickett, Police Officer (sergeant, nearing retirement)

Time period(s): 1980s

Locale(s): Toronto, Ontario

What the book is about: Salter and Pickett investigate the murder of Linda Thomas, a massage therapist with a number of influential clients, most of whom are very nervous.

Other books you might like:
Alisa Craig, *Murder Goes Mumming*, 1981
Howard Engel, *Murder on Location*, 1985
Tim Heald, *Murder at Moose Jaw*, 1981
Ted Wood, *On the Inside*, 1990

1771
Jim Wright
The Last Man Standing (New York: Carroll & Graf, 1991)

Story type: Amateur Detective—Male Lead; Action/Adventure

Major character(s): Stuart Reed, Journalist (newspaper reporter)

Time period(s): 1990s

Locale(s): New York

What the book is about: Having landed on his head and been reduced to writing obituaries on a small paper, Stuart Reed finds himself being framed for a murder. He sets out to clear himself and to kill the man he suspects of the crime.

Other books you might like:
William L. DeAndrea, *Killed on the Rocks*, 1990
Michael J. Katz, *The Big Freeze*, 1991
Susan Kelly, *Until Proven Innocent*, 1990
Mike Lupica, *Limited Partner*, 1990
Keith Peterson, *The John Wells Series*, 1988-

1772
L.R. Wright
A Chill Wind in January (New York: Viking, 1990)

Series: Karl Alberg

Story type: Psychological Suspense

Major character(s): Zoe Strachan, Heiress; Karl Alberg, Police Officer (mountie)

Time period(s): 1980s

Locale(s): British Columbia

What the book is about: Karl Alberg is suspicious of the circumstances surrounding the death of Zoe Strachan's brother. Zoe challenges him to find out the truth. Wright won the Edgar for Best Novel for *The Suspect*, 1985.

Other books you might like:
Susan Rogers Cooper, *The Man in the Green Chevy*, 1988
Medora Sale, *Murder in Focus*, 1989
Eric Wright, *A Body Surrounded by Water*, 1987

1773
L.R. Wright
Fall From Grace (New York: Viking, 1991)

Series: Karl Alberg

Story type: Police Procedural—Male Lead

Major character(s): Karl Alberg, Police Officer (mountie)

Time period(s): 1990s

Locale(s): Sechelt, British Columbia, Canada

What the book is about: While on vacation with his lover, Cassandra, Karl Alberg sees a body fall from a cliff. The victim, Steven Grayson, has recently returned to the small village at the same time that Booby Ransome has been released from prison. Are the two events connected?

Other books you might like:
Elizabeth George, *The Inspector Lynley Series*, 1989-
P.D. James, *The Inspector Adam Dalgliesh Series*, 1962-
Ruth Rendell, *The Inspector Wexford Series*, 1964-
Ted Wood, *The Reid Bennett Series*, 1983-
Eric Wright, *The Charlie Salter Series*, 1983-

1774
L.R. Wright
Mother Love (New York: Scribners, 1995)

Series: Karl Alberg

Story type: Police Procedural—Male Lead

Major character(s): Karl Alberg, Police Officer (sergeant, Canadian mountie); Cassandra Mitchell, Teacher (Karl's lover)

Time period(s): 1990s

Locale(s): British Columbia, Canada

What the book is about: Marie Buscombe abandoned her husband and teenage daughter seven years ago. Now she wants to see her daughter again. Before she can do so she is murdered. Karl is assigned the case and must discover the family secrets that lead to Maria's death. Meanwhile Cassandra is trying to recover from a traumatic kidnapping and Maria's daughter is searching for some answers as to why her mother deserted her. All of these author's other books are under the name L.R. Wright.

Other books you might like:
Andrew Coburn, *Voices in the Dark*, 1994
Susan Rogers Cooper, *The Milt Kovak Series*, 1988-
Sharyn McCrumb, *The Spencer Arrowood Series*, 1990-
Ted Wood, *The Reid Bennett Series*, 1983-
Eric Wright, *Buried in Stone*, 1995

1775
L.R. Wright
Prized Possessions (New York: Viking, 1993)

1776 Wright

Series: Karl Alberg

Story type: Police Procedural—Male Lead; Psychological Suspense

Major character(s): Karl Alberg, Police Officer; Eddie Addison, Criminal (psychopath); Emma O'Brea, Housewife

Time period(s): 1990s

Locale(s): Vancouver, British Columbia, Canada

What the book is about: Karl Alberg is taking some time off and is introduced to Charlie and Emma O'Brea. When Charlie disappears Emma asks Karl to look for him and Karl reluctantly agrees. At the same time Eddie Addison is on the road to ruin. What started as an infatuation with a young student leads to assault and murder. Soon the lives of all these people will intersect in more violence.

Other books you might like:
Susan Rogers Cooper, *Houston in the Rearview Mirror*, 1989
Anne Wingate, *Death by Deception*, 1988
Ted Wood, *When the Killing Starts*, 1989
Scott Young, *Murder in a Cold Climate*, 1988

1776
L.R. Wright
A Touch of Panic (New York: Scribners, 1994)

Series: Karl Alberg

Story type: Police Procedural—Male Lead

Major character(s): Karl Alberg, Police Officer (staff sergeant, RCMP); Cassandra Mitchell, Librarian (Karl's lover); Gordon Murphy, Teacher (library science)

Time period(s): 1990s

Locale(s): Vancouver Island, British Columbia, Canada

What the book is about: Karl Alberg is very busy these days, what with a missing drug dealer and an outbreak of very strange burglaries. Meanwhile, his lover, Cassandra Mitchell, has attracted the attention of the sophisticated and wealthy lottery winner, Gordon Murphy. Gordon, looking for the perfect woman to love, thinks he may have found her in Cassandra. Of course, he has been disappointed before—four times before—and then he had to kill the women who let him down.

Other books you might like:
Andrew Coburn, *Voices in the Dark*, 1994
K.C. Constantine, *The Mario Balzac Series*, 1972-
Susan Rogers Cooper, *The Milt Kovack Series*, 1989-
Archer Mayor, *Scent of Evil*, 1992
Ted Wood, *The Reid Bennett Series*, 1988-

1777
Victor Wuamett
Artichoke Hearts (New York: St. Martin's, 1991)

Series: Chase Randel

Story type: Amateur Detective—Male Lead

Major character(s): Chase Randel, Businessman (real estate broker); Molly Gish, Journalist

Time period(s): 1990s

Locale(s): Mar Vista, California

What the book is about: Chase is trying to help an old friend, Joe Pacheco, and his family by selling his artichoke farm to a development company. The deal is about to be signed when it is threatened by the supposed discovery of an endangered species of mouse. Joe is enraged and when the biologist who was to confirm the discovery is found dead, Joe is the prime suspect.

Other books you might like:
Richard Barth, *Furnished for Murder*, 1990
Margaret Logan, *Deathampton Summer*, 1988
A.J. Orde, *A Little Neighborhood Murder*, 1989
E.C. Ward, *A Nice Little Beach Town*, 1989
Steven Womack, *Murphy's Fault*, 1990

1778
Victor Wuamett
Deeds of Trust (New York: St. Martins, 1991)

Series: Chase Randel

Story type: Amateur Detective—Male Lead

Major character(s): Chase Randel, Businessman (real estate broker); Molly Gish, Journalist

Time period(s): 1990s

Locale(s): California (Silicon Valley)

What the book is about: Frank Baker hires Chase to look into an investment group that sold him some condos that are now going broke. Was it bad luck or fraud? Before Chase can get started, Frank falls to his death while talking to the man who sold him the condos. When the police determine that Frank was dead of cyanide poisoning before he fell, Chase gets involved in trying to recover the money for Frank's family.

Other books you might like:
Richard Barth, *Furnished for Murder*, 1990
Haughton Murphy, *The Reuben Frost Series*, 1986
Margaret Logan, *A Killing in Venture Capital*, 1989
A.J. Orde, *A Little Neighborhood Murder*, 1989
Steven Womack, *Murphy's Fault*, 1990

1779
Victor Wuamett
Teardown (New York: St. Martin's, 1990)

Series: Chase Randel

Story type: Amateur Detective—Male Lead

Major character(s): Chase Randel, Agent (Real estate agent)

Time period(s): 1980s

Locale(s): San Jose, California

What the book is about: Randel's friend Ed falls down an elevator shaft while working on renovations to a building. Randel inherits part interest in the building and wonders if Ed was, perhaps, "helped" down the shaft. This is Wuamett's first novel.

Other books you might like:
Rick Boyer, *Billingsgate Shoal*, 1982
John T. Lescroart, *Dead Irish*, 1989
Art Spikol, *The Physalia Incident*, 1988
Bruce Zimmerman, *Blood under the Bridge*, 1989

1780
E.L. Wyrick
A Strange and Bitter Crop (New York: St. Martin's, 1994)
Story type: Legal; Amateur Detective—Female Lead
Major character(s): Tammi Randall, Lawyer (legal aid); Dan Bushnell, Counselor (high school)
Time period(s): 1990s
Locale(s): Patsboro, California
What the book is about: Tammi Randall is asked to represent 15-year-old James Cleveland, who is charged with the brutal murders of a respectable doctor and his wife. James admits to being there, but indicates that he was set up to take the fall. He mentions a name out of Tammi's past—Buddy Crowe—a sociopath who wants revenge. As Tammi tries to help and find out what is going on, she is in grave danger from Buddy. And there may be more sinister forces at work directing Buddy.
Other books you might like:
Harrison Arnston, *Trade-Off*, 1992
Gini Hartzmark, *Principal Defense*, 1992
Michael A. Kahn, *Firm Ambitions*, 1994
Lia Matera, *The Laura Di Palma Series*, 1988-
Nancy Taylor Rosenberg, *Mitigating Circumstances*, 1993

1781
Chelsea Quinn Yarbro
Poison Fruit (New York: Jove, 1991)
Series: Charlie Moon
Story type: Legal
Major character(s): Charlie Moon, Lawyer, Indian (Ojibwa); Morgan Studevant, Judge (Charlie's wife)
Time period(s): 1990s
Locale(s): San Francisco, California
What the book is about: Charlie is hired to represent Frank Girouard who has been accused of sexually abusing five female students. He swears he is innocent but if he is, why would so many students lie about a serious crime? Then one of the students is murdered.
Other books you might like:
William Babula, *St. John's Baptism*, 1988
Jean Hager, *The Grandfather Medicine*, 1989
Tony Hillerman, *The Joe Leaphorn Series*, 1970-
Walter Satterthwait, *At Ease with the Dead*, 1990
Richard Martin Stern, *The Johnny Ortiz Series*, 1973-

1782
Dorian Yeager
Cancellation by Death (New York: St. Martin's, 1992)
Series: Victoria Bowering
Story type: Amateur Detective—Female Lead
Major character(s): Victoria Bowering, Actress, Psychic
Time period(s): 1990s
Locale(s): New York, New York
What the book is about: Vic Bowering is in the middle of a divorce and trying to make a living as an actress. She is happy to get a job as an extra on the soap opera "Raging Passions." The hot lead actor, an old friend of Vic's and a client of her ex-husband, is leaving the show. This is the week he is to be killed off. Someone take this literally. With her ex as the prime suspect, Vic is drawn into the investigation. First novel.
Other books you might like:
Lydia Adamson, *A Cat of a Different Color*, 1991
Trella Crespi, *The Trouble with Moonlighting*, 1991
Jeffrey Wilds Deaver, *Death of a Blue Movie Star*, 1990
Jane Dentinger, *The Jocelyn O'Roarke Series*, 1983-
Gillian B. Farrell, *Alibi for an Actress*, 1992

1783
Dorian Yeager
Eviction by Death (New York: St. Martin's, 1993)
Series: Victoria Bowering
Story type: Amateur Detective—Female Lead
Major character(s): Victoria Bowering, Actress
Time period(s): 1990s
Locale(s): New York, New York
What the book is about: Vic Bowering is having trouble with her elderly upstairs neighbor so she is not terribly upset when he dies. She's too concerned with getting the lead in a new production of *Auntie Mame*. She also has a few run-ins with her new landlord. When the death of the neighbor is determined to be murder and more tenants start to die mysteriously, Vic becomes a prime suspect and decides to clear herself.
Other books you might like:
Lydia Adamson, *The Alice Nestleton Series*, 1990-
Trella Crespi, *The Trouble with Moonlighting*, 1991
Jane Dentinger, *Death Mask*, 1988
Gillian B. Farrell, *Alibi for an Actress*, 1992
Marissa Piesman, *Unorthodox Practices*, 1989

1784
Dorian Yeager
Murder Will Out (New York: St. Martin's, 1994)
Story type: Amateur Detective—Female Lead
Major character(s): Elizabeth Will, Artist, Art Dealer (art gallery owner); Ginny Philbrick, Police Officer (chief of police)
Time period(s): 1990s
Locale(s): Dovekey, New Hampshire

1785 Young

What the book is about: Elizabeth Will and her father have spent their lives taking the opposite sides of any issue. The latest point of contention is the legalization of gambling and prostitution and the establishment of casinos and resorts on town land. Elizabeth is all for it, along with town councilman Al Jennes. Dad is against it, as he makes clear in a public argument with Jennes. When Jennes shows up dead with his head stuck in one of Dad's lobster traps, Dad is the prime suspect. Elizabeth knows her father couldn't be a murderer—could he?

Other books you might like:
Christine Andreae, *Grizzly*, 1994
Nevada Barr, *Track of the Cat*, 1993
B.J. Oliphant, *The Unexpected Corpse*, 1990
Dana Stabenow, *A Cold Day for Murder*, 1992
Lee Wallingford, *Clear-Cut Murder*, 1993

1785
Scott Young
Murder in a Cold Climate (New York: Viking, 1989)

Series: Inspector Matthew Kitologitak

Story type: Police Procedural—Male Lead

Major character(s): Matthew "Matteesie" Kitologitak, Police Officer (Royal Canadian Police)

Time period(s): 1980s

Locale(s): Northwest Territories, Canada

What the book is about: The search for a missing plane overlaps with the search for a cold-blooded killer. First book.

Other books you might like:
Alisa Craig, *The Madoc Rhys Series*, 1980
James B. Hendryx, *All Titles*, 1919
Ted Wood, *The Reid Bennett Series*, 1984 (1984-)
L.R. Wright, *The Suspect*, 1985

1786
Scott Young
The Shaman's Knife (New York: Viking, 1993)

Series: Inspector Matthew Kitologitak

Story type: Police Procedural—Male Lead

Major character(s): Matthew "Matteesie" Kitologitak, Police Officer (RCMP inspector)

Time period(s): 1990s

Locale(s): Victoria Island, British Columbia, Canada

What the book is about: Inspector Kitologitak is to investigate the double murder of an Inuit couple on Victoria Island. The case holds special interest for the inspector as it appears that his 90 year old mother may have been the only witness to the crime. Therefore her life may be in danger. There appears to be some involvement by the local shaman whose knife seems to be missing and there also seems to be some past history to dig up.

Other books you might like:
Sue Henry, *Murder on the Iditarod Trail*, 1991
Dana Stabenow, *A Cold Day for Murder*, 1992
John Straley, *The Woman Who Married a Bear*, 1992
Ted Wood, *The Reid Bennett Series*, 1984-

1787
Eric Zencey
Panama (New York: Farrar, Straus & Giroux, 1995)

Story type: Amateur Detective—Male Lead; Historical

Major character(s): Henry Adams, Historical Figure, Historian

Time period(s): 1890s (1892)

Locale(s): Paris, France; Panama

What the book is about: Henry Adams is in Paris and involved in the scandal about the collapse of the Panama Canel plan. He is also involved with a couple of women, one of whom, a young American painter named Miriam, disappears. Adams sets out to find her, becoming involved with murder, political intrigue, and Paris. First novel.

Other books you might like:
Caleb Carr, *The Alienist*, 1994
William L. DeAndrea, *The Lunatic Fringe*, 1980
Mark Frost, *The List of 7*, 1993
William Hjortsberg, *Nevermore*, 1994
Robert J. Randisi, *The Ham Reporter*, 1986

1788
Thomas Zigal
Into Thin Air (New York: Delcorte, 1995)

Story type: Police Procedural—Male Lead; Action/Adventure

Major character(s): Kurt Muller, Police Officer (sheriff)

Time period(s): 1990s

Locale(s): Aspen, Colorado

What the book is about: FBI agents quickly become involved when the body of a famous Argentinean journalist turns up. Sheriff Kurt Muller is not on good terms with the FBI and when another Argentinean disappears while with Kurt, he finds himself even further on the outs. In fact, he finds himself on the run accused of murder and drug smuggling. First novel.

Other books you might like:
Gregory Bean, *No Comfort in Victory*, 1995
Jameson Cole, *A Killing in Quail County*, 1996
Bill Crider, *The Sheriff Dan Rhodes Series*, 1986-
Craig Holden, *The Last Sanctuary*, 1996
B.J. Oliphant, *A Ceremonial Death*, 1995

1789
Lue Zimmelman
Honolulu Red (New York: St. Martin's, 1990)

Story type: Action/Adventure

Major character(s): Rachel Starr, Detective—Police; Nicholas Snow, Criminal (connoisseur, art thief), Professor

Time period(s): 1980s

Locale(s): Los Angeles, California; Honolulu, Hawaii

What the book is about: Catching Nicholas Snow in the act of robbing a museum, Starr offers him immunity if he will help her trap a killer. First book.

Other books you might like:
Marcia Muller, *Dark Star*, 1989
Lillian O'Donnell, *Cop Without a Shield*, 1983
Dorothy Uhnak, *The Bait*, 1968

1790
Bruce Zimmerman
Full-Bodied Red (New York: HarperCollins, 1993)

Series: Quinn Parker

Story type: Amateur Detective—Male Lead

Major character(s): Quinn Parker, Health Care Professional (therapist)

Time period(s): 1990s

Locale(s): Napa Valley, California

What the book is about: A patient of therapist Quinn Parker has disappeared. When Quinn arrives at the missing patient's house in the Napa Valley, he is attacked by the patient's stepfather who seems to blame Quinn for the disappearance. When the stepfather turns up dead in a wine vat, the police think the missing man is the prime suspect in the death. Quinn sets out to find his patient and the patient's girlfriend who is also missing. It appears that these crimes have their roots in Southeast Asia.

Other books you might like:
Harlen Campbell, *Monkey on a Chain*, 1993
Mary Bowen Hall, *Emma Chizzit and the Napa Nemesis*, 1992
Will Harriss, *Noble Rot*, 1993
Martin Sylvester, *A Lethal Vintage*, 1988

1791
R.D. Zimmerman
Blood Trance (New York: Morrow, 1993)

Series: Maddy and Alex Phillips

Story type: Amateur Detective; Psychological Suspense

Major character(s): Maddy Phillips, Psychologist, Handicapped (blind, paraplegic); Alex Phillips, Assistant (Maddy's brother)

Time period(s): 1990s

Locale(s): Chicago, Illinois; Michigan (an island off the coast)

What the book is about: Alex Phillips serves as his blind, paraplegic sister Maddy's eyes and legs. He has just returned from Chicago where he had gone to see an ex-patient of hers. While there he walks in on what appears to be the patient murdering her stepmother. Certainly the police think so. Maddy goes bail and brings the woman to the island, where much buried family secrets will eventually come to light.

Other books you might like:
Mary Higgins Clark, *Remember Me*, 1994
Chris Crutcher, *The Deep End*, 1992
Jonathan Kellerman, *Private Eyes*, 1992
John Lutz, *Single White Female*, 1990
S.K. Wolf, *Long Chain of Death*, 1989

1792
R.D. Zimmerman
Deadfall in Berlin (New York: Fine, 1990)

Story type: Historical; Psychological Suspense

Major character(s): Will Walker, Actor; Alecia Brenner, Doctor (psychiatrist)

Time period(s): 1970s (1975); 1940s (flashbacks to 1945)

Locale(s): Chicago, Illinois; Berlin, Germany

What the book is about: Will Walker, who was orphaned in the war, goes to a psychiatrist to help him remember his mother's death—or was it murder? And why is someone trying to kill him today in Chicago? Nominee for MWA Best Novel.

Other books you might like:
Jack Gerson, *Deathwatch '39*, 1991
Philip Kerr, *March Violets*, 1989
Keith Peterson, *The Scarred Man*, 1990

1793
R.D. Zimmerman
Red Trance (New York: Morrow, 1994)

Series: Maddy and Alex Phillips

Story type: Amateur Detective; Psychological Suspense

Major character(s): Maddy Phillips, Psychologist, Handicapped (blind, paraplegic); Alex Phillips, Assistant (Maddy's brother)

Time period(s): 1990s

Locale(s): Moscow, Russia; Michigan (island off the coast)

What the book is about: While in Moscow, Alex Phillips witnesses some murders. His sister, Maddy, hypnotizes him to try to help him make sense of things, but nothing can replace a trip back to Moscow to visit some of the people involved. The change in the system creates problems for Alex that he hasn't foreseen, including causing changes in his relationships with some friends, who may have been involved with the murders.

Other books you might like:
Stuart M. Kaminsky, *The Man Who Walked Like a Bear*, 1990
Bob Leuci, *Odessa Beach*, 1985
Anthony Olcott, *Murder at the Red October*, 1981
Martin Cruz Smith, *Gorky Park*, 1981

1794
Norman Zollinger
Lautrec (New York: Dutton, 1990)

Story type: Legal

Major character(s): Jack Lautrec, Lawyer; Martine Lautrec, Lawyer (daughter and partner of Jack)

Time period(s): 1980s

Locale(s): Southwest

What the book is about: Jack Lautrec gets involved in the case of a Hispanic artist accused of killing his model. First book.

1795 Zubro

Other books you might like:
Edwin Gage, *Phoenix No More*, 1978
Joe L. Hensley, *Color Him Guilty*, 1987
Walter Satterthwait, *Wall of Glass*, 1988

1795
Mark Richard Zubro
The Only Good Priest (New York: St. Martins, 1991)
Series: Tom Mason
Story type: Amateur Detective—Male Lead
Major character(s): Tom Mason, Teacher (high school), Homosexual; Scott Carpenter, Sports Figure, Homosexual (Tom's lover)
Time period(s): 1990s
Locale(s): Chicago, Illinois
What the book is about: Father Sabastian, a priest involved with a gay Catholic activist group, is found poisoned. Other members of the group ask Tom to look into the case because church officials have pressured the police not to investigate.
Other books you might like:
Nathan Aldyne, *The Daniel Valentine Series*, 1980-1986
Susan Dunlap, *Pious Deception*, 1990
Joseph Hansen, *The Dave Brandstetter Series*, 1970-1991
Grant Michaels, *A Body to Dye For*, 1990
Sara Paretsky, *Killing Orders*, 1985

1796
Mark Richard Zubro
Sorry Now? (New York: St. Martin's, 1991)
Story type: Police Procedural—Male Lead
Major character(s): Paul Turner, Police Officer, Homosexual
Time period(s): 1990s
Locale(s): Chicago, Illinois
What the book is about: Is a radical gay organization behind the murders of homophobes? Paul Turner, Chicago police officer, doesn't think so. But when an AIDS infected informant is killed after suggesting he knows who is behind the crimes, Paul may have to re-think his attitude. Between threats toward his sons and pressure from his superiors he feels that he may never get to the truth.
Other books you might like:
Nathan Aldyne, *The Daniel Valentine Series*, 1980-1986
Katherine V. Forrest, *The Beverly Malibu*, 1989
Joseph Hansen, *The Dave Brandstetter Series*, 1970-1991
Grant Michaels, *A Body to Dye For*, 1990
Richard Stevenson, *Ice Blues*, 1986

1797
Mark Richard Zubro
Why Isn't Becky Twitchell Dead? (New York: St. Martin's, 1990)
Series: Tom Mason
Story type: Amateur Detective—Male Lead
Major character(s): Tom Mason, Teacher (High school), Homosexual
Time period(s): 1980s
Locale(s): Maryland
What the book is about: When one of his students is arrested for the murder of his girlfriend, teacher Tom Mason allows himself to get involved in trying to prove the boy's innocence.
Other books you might like:
J.S. Borthwick, *The Student Body*, 1986
P.M. Carlson, *Murder Is Academic*, 1985
Bill Crider, *Dying Voices*, 1989
Ellen Hart, *Hallowed Murder*, 1989
Michael Nava, *The Little Death*, 1986

1798
Sharon Zukowski
Dancing in the Dark (New York: St. Martin's, 1992)
Series: Blaine Stewart
Story type: Private Detective—Female Lead
Major character(s): Blaine Stewart, Detective—Private, Widow(er)
Time period(s): 1990s
Locale(s): New York, New York
What the book is about: Blaine is hired to infiltrate an extremely militant animal rights group which is threatening a large cattle ranch with violence. She is also involved with a local store owner who is being hassled by the police. The store owner is killed in a fire and Blaine's sister is left in critical condition by a bomb meant for Blaine. Which case has caused them to be targets?
Other books you might like:
Sue Grafton, *H Is for Homicide*, 1991
Linda Grant, *The Catherine Saylor Series*, 1988-
Maxine O'Callaghan, *The Delilah West Series*, 1980-
Lillian O'Donnell, *The Gwen Ramadge Series*, 1990
Gloria White, *Murder on the Run*, 1991

1799
Sharon Zukowski
Leap of Faith (New York: Dutton, 1994)
Series: Blaine Stewart
Story type: Private Detective—Female Lead
Major character(s): Blaine Stewart, Detective—Private, Widow(er); Eileen Aldridge, Lawyer (Blaine's sister and partner)
Time period(s): 1990s
Locale(s): New York, New York

What the book is about: Blaine Stewart is hired by Judith Marsden to find her missing son; except he hasn't been born yet! The surrogate mother who was carrying the baby has disappeared. The surrogate, Hannah Wyrick, is the sister of Blaine's housekeeper, Nikki. The doctor at the fertility clinic is no help. When Blaine contacts the Wyrick family, she learns that Hannah and Nikki have been dead for years. Then people start showing up dead.

Other books you might like:
Robin Cook, *Vital Signs*, 1990
Leslie Glass, *To Do No Harm*, 1992
Michael Hendricks, *Friends in High Places*, 1991
Janice Law, *The Anna Peters Series*, 1976-
Lillian O'Donnell, *The Gwen Ramadge Series*, 1990-[/gs]

Series Index

This index alphabetically lists series to which books featured in the entries belong. Beneath each series name, book titles are listed alphabetically with author names. Numbers refer to the entries that feature each title.

62 New Square Lawyers
The Sirens Sang of Murder - Sarah Caudwell 228

87th Precinct
Vespers - Ed McBain 1107

Aaron Gunner
Not Long for This World - Gar Anthony Haywood 762

Abby & Mac McKenzie
Murder by Tarot - Al Guthrie 693

Abe Lieberman
Lieberman's Choice - Stuart M. Kaminsky 856
Lieberman's Day - Stuart M. Kaminsky 857

Abigail Danforth
Diamond Head - Marian J.A. Jackson 834
The Sunken Treasure - Marian J.A. Jackson 835

Adam Dalgliesh
Devices and Desires - P.D. James 841

Adam McCleet
Mortal Remains - Rick Hanson 728

Agatha Raisin
Agatha Raisin and the Quiche of Death - M.C. Beaton 107
Agatha Raisin and the Vicious Vet - M.C. Beaton 108

Alan Bernhardt
Except for the Bones - Collin Wilcox 1713
Full Circle - Collin Wilcox 1714
Silent Witness - Collin Wilcox 1716

Albert Samson
Called by a Panther - Michael Z. Lewin 1019

Albert Tretheway
Murder on the Thirteenth - A.E. Eddenden 471

Alex Delaware
Bad Love - Jonathan Kellerman 885
Private Eyes - Jonathan Kellerman 886
Self-Defense - Jonathan Kellerman 887
Time Bomb - Jonathan Kellerman 888

Alex Glauberman
Obligations of the Bone - Dick Cluster 263

Alex Tanner
The Glass Ceiling - Anabel Donald 428

Alex Winter
Library: No Murder Aloud - Susan Steiner 1569

Alice Nestleton
A Cat in a Glass House - Lydia Adamson 15
A Cat in Fine Style - Lydia Adamson 16
A Cat in the Manger - Lydia Adamson 17
A Cat in the Wings - Lydia Adamson 18
A Cat in Wolf's Clothing - Lydia Adamson 19
A Cat on the Cutting Edge - Lydia Adamson 20

Alo Nudger
Diamond Eyes - John Lutz 1056
Thicker than Blood - John Lutz 1059
Time Exposure - John Lutz 1060

Alternate Royal Family
Skeleton-in-Waiting - Peter Dickinson 419

Alton "Rooster" Franklin
Caught Looking - Randy Russell 1416

Amanda Hazard
Dead in the Cellar - Connie Fedderson 520

Amanda Pepper
I'd Rather Be in Philadelphia - Gillian Roberts 1378
Philly Stakes - Gillian Roberts 1379
With Friends Like These - Gillian Roberts 1380

Amanda Roberts/Joe Donelli
Ties That Bind - Sherryl Woods 1759

Amos Walker
Sweet Women Lie - Loren D. Estleman 500

Amy Prescott
Grave Secrets - Louise Hendricksen 774

Andrew Broom
Body and Soil - Ralph McInerny 1135

Andrew Quentin/Jane Winfield
Elegy in a Country Graveyard - Audrey Peterson 1304
Murder in Burgundy - Audrey Peterson 1305

Andy Broussard/Kit Franklyn
Blood on the Bayou - D.J. Donaldson 429
New Orleans Requiem - D.J. Donaldson 430
No Mardi Gras for the Dead - D.J. Donaldson 431

Andy Sussman/Murray Glick
The Big Freeze - Michael J. Katz 871
Last Dance in Redondo Beach - Michael J. Katz 872

Angela Benbow and Caledonia Wingate
Murder by Owl Light - Corinne Holt Sawyer 1445
Murder Has No Calories - Corinne Holt Sawyer 1446
Murder in Gray and White - Corinne Holt Sawyer 1447

Angela Biwaban
Corona Blue - J.F. Trainor 1625
Dynamite Pass - J.F. Trainor 1626

Angie Amalfi
Cooking Up Trouble - Joanne Pence 1289
Something's Cooking - Joanne Pence 1290
Too Many Cooks - Joanne Pence 1291

Angus Straun
Unnatural Hazard - Barry Cork 317
Winter Rules - Barry Cork 318

Anna Lee
Backhand - Liza Cody 269

Anna Peters
Time Lapse - Janice Law 992

Anna Pigeon
A Superior Death - Nevada Barr 96
Track of the Cat - Nevada Barr 97

Anneke Haagen
Curly Smoke - Susan Holtzer 803

Annie Laurance/Max Darling
The Christie Caper - Carolyn G. Hart 741
A Little Class on Murder - Carolyn G. Hart 743
Mint Julep Murder - Carolyn G. Hart 744

Annie McGrogan
Alibi for an Actress - Gillian B. Farrell 516
Murder and a Muse - Gillian B. Farrell 517

Antiqua Players
Broken Consort - James Gollin 609

Aristotle Socarides
Death in Deep Water - Paul Kemprecos 903
Feeding Frenzy - Paul Kemprecos 904
Neptune's Eye - Paul Kemprecos 905

Arkady Renko
Polar Star - Martin Cruz Smith 1530

Arly Hanks
Madness in Maggody - Joan Hess 777
Miracles in Maggody - Joan Hess 778
Mortal Remains in Maggody - Joan Hess 779
O Little Town of Maggody - Joan Hess 780

Augustus Maltravers
The Book of the Dead - Robert Richardson 1365
The Dying of the Light - Robert Richardson 1366
Murder in Waiting - Robert Richardson 1367

Aunt Dimity
Aunt Dimity and the Duke - Nancy Atherton 68
Aunt Dimity's Death - Nancy Atherton 69

Aurora Teagarden
A Bone to Pick - Charlaine Harris 731
The Julius House - Charlaine Harris 732

B.F. Hooper
Saint Louie Blues - Jake Tanner 1601

Bamsan Kiet
Kiet Goes West - Gary Alexander 34
Unfunny Money - Gary Alexander 35

Barrett Lake
Interview with Mattie - Shelley Singer 1504
Picture of David - Shelley Singer 1505
Searching for Sara - Shelley Singer 1506

Bea and Lyon Wentworth
Death on the Mississippi - Richard Forrest 535

Bed-and-Breakfast Mystery
Bantam of the Opera - Mary Daheim 374
A Fit of Tempera - Mary Daheim 375
Holy Terrors - Mary Daheim 376
Murder, My Suite - Mary Daheim 377

Ben and Carrie Porter

Ben and Carrie Porter
Finders Keepers - Elizabeth Travis 1627

Ben Henry
A Dry and Thirsty Ground - Mike Weiss 1688

Ben Louis
Dead Easy - E.S. Russell 1415

Ben Perkins
Concrete Hero - Rob Kantner 862
The Quick and the Dead - Rob Kantner 863
The Red, White, and Blues - Rob Kantner 864
The Thousand Yard Stare - Rob Kantner 865

Ben Tolliver
Painted Ladies - James Neal Harvey 750

Benni Harper
Fool's Puzzle - Earlene Fowler 536
Irish Chain - Earlene Fowler 537

Berkley Jordan
Jordon's Showdown - Frank C. Strunk 1583
Jordon's Wager - Frank C. Strunk 1584

Bernie Gunther
The Pale Criminal - Philip Kerr 914

Bernie Rhodenbarr Mystery
The Burglar Who Traded Ted Williams - Lawrence Block 145

Beth Austin
The George Eliot Murders - Edith Skom 1511

Bill Donovan
City of God - Michael Jahn 840

Bill Gastner
Bitter Recoil - Steven F. Havill 757
Heartshot - Steven F. Havill 758

Bill Hawley
Double Plot - Leo Axler 70
Grave Matters - Leo Axler 71

Bino Phillips
Bino's Blues - A.W. Gray 650
Killings - A.W. Gray 651

Bishop Regan/Davey Goldman
Bloody Ten - William F. Love 1047
The Chartreuse Clue - William F. Love 1048

Blackford Oakes
Tucker's Last Stand - William F. Buckley Jr. 188

Blackie Ryan
Happy Are the Merciful - Andrew M. Greeley 656

Blackwater Bay Mystery
A Few Dying Words - Paula Gosling 626

Blaine Stewart
Dancing in the Dark - Sharon Zukowski 1798
Leap of Faith - Sharon Zukowski 1799

Blanche Hampton
A Pound of Flesh - Trevor Barnes 95

Bo Bradley
Strawgirl - Abigail Padgett 1252

Bonnie Indermill
Death of a Dancing Fool - Carole Berry 124
The Death of a Difficult Woman - Carole Berry 125
Good Night, Sweet Prince - Carole Berry 126
Island Girl - Carole Berry 127

Borderville Mystery
The Rotary Club Mystery - Graham Landrum 978

Brad Smith
Dropshot: A Brad Smith Novel - Jack Bickham 129

Brady Coyne
Dead Winter - William G. Tapply 1602
Spotted Cats - William G. Tapply 1603
Tight Lines - William G. Tapply 1604

Bragg/Morton
Patently Murder - Ray Harrison 737
Tincture of Death - Ray Harrison 738

Brian Donodio
Forty Whacks - Sheila MacGill Callahan 207

Brigid Donovan
Murder Is Germane - Karen Saum 1442

Brother Cadfael
Brother Cadfael's Penance - Ellis Peters 1301
The Potter's Field - Ellis Peters 1302
The Summer of the Danes - Ellis Peters 1303

Bull Cochran
Shutout - David F. Nighbert 1204
Squeezeplay - David F. Nighbert 1205

Burke
Blossom - Andrew Vachss 1643
Footsteps of the Hawk - Andrew Vachss 1644

Butch Karp
Justice Denied - Robert K. Tanenbaum 1599
Reversible Error - Robert K. Tanenbaum 1600

Butcher's Boy
Sleeping Dogs - Thomas Perry 1297

C.D. Sloan
The Body Politic - Catherine Aird 25

C.W. Sughrue
The Mexican Tree Duck - James Crumley 363

Caitlin Reece
Ninth Life - Lauren Wright Douglas 444

Calista Jacobs
Dark Swan - Kathryn Lasky Knight 944
Mortal Words - Kathryn Lasky Knight 945

Callahan Garrity
Every Crooked Nanny - Kathy Hogan Trocheck 1631
To Live and Die in Dixie - Kathy Hogan Trocheck 1632

Carl Burns
Dying Voices - Bill Crider 351

Carl Pedersen
Threnody for Two - Jeanne Hart 747

Carl Wilcox
The Ditched Blonde - Harold Adams 12
The Man Who Missed the Party - Harold Adams 13
A Perfectly Proper Murder - Harold Adams 14

Carlotta Carlyle
Coyote - Linda Barnes 92
Snapshot - Linda Barnes 93
Steel Guitar - Linda Barnes 94

Carver Bascombe
Blood of Poets - Kenn Davis 393

Cass Jameson
Fresh Kills - Carolyn Wheat 1699

Cassandra Reilly
Gaudi Afternoon - Barbara Wilson 1731

Cat Caliban
Four Elements of Murder - D.B. Borton 155
Three Is a Crowd - D.B. Borton 156
Two Points for Murder - D.B. Borton 157

Cat Crimes
Cat Crimes II - Ed Gorman 620

Cat Marsala
Hard Tack - Barbara D'Amato 382
Hard Women - Barbara D'Amato 383
Hardball - Barbara D'Amato 384

What Mystery Do I Read Next?

Cat Who.
The Cat Who Moved a Mountain - Lilian Jackson Braun 167
The Cat Who Talked to Ghosts - Lilian Jackson Braun 168
The Cat Who Went into the Closet - Lilian Jackson Braun 169

Catherine Sayler
Love nor Money - Linda Grant 648
A Woman's Place - Linda Grant 649

Cecil Younger
The Curious Eat Themselves - John Straley 1580
The Woman Who Married a Bear - John Straley 1581

Celia Grant
Bones Gather No Moss - John Sherwood 1483
A Bouquet of Thorns - John Sherwood 1484
The Hanging Garden - John Sherwood 1485

Charles Paris
Corporate Bodies - Simon Brett 174
A Series of Murders - Simon Brett 176

Charlie Greene
Death of the Office Witch - Marlys Millhiser 1155
Murder at Moot Point - Marlys Millhiser 1156

Charlie Meiklejohn/Constance Leidl
Seven Kinds of Death - Kate Wilhelm 1725

Charlie Moon
Poison Fruit - Chelsea Quinn Yarbro 1781

Charlie Muffin
The Run Around - Brian Freemantle 550

Charlie Resnick
Cold Light - John Harvey 751
Cutting Edge - John Harvey 752
Off Minor - John Harvey 753
The Wasted Years - John Harvey 754

Charlotte Graham
Murder at the Spa - Stefanie Matteson 1097
Murder on the Cliff - Stefanie Matteson 1098

Charlotte Kent
Poison Pen - Mary Kittredge 933

Charlotte Sams
Trunk Show - Alison Glen 604

Charmian Daniels
Dead Set - Jennie Melville 1141
Murder Has a Pretty Face - Jennie Melville 1142
Whoever Has the Heart - Jennie Melville 1143
Witching Murder - Jennie Melville 1144

Chase Randel
Artichoke Hearts - Victor Wuamett 1777
Deeds of Trust - Victor Wuamett 1778
Teardown - Victor Wuamett 1779

Chico Cervantes
Death as a Career Move - Bruce Cook 299
Rough Cut - Bruce Cook 300
The Sidewalk Hilton - Bruce Cook 301

Chief Inspector Baxter
Dangerous Conceits - Margaret Moore 1168

Chief-Inspector Lloyd and Sergeant Judy Hill
The Other Woman - Jill McGown 1132

China Bayles
Hangman's Root - Susan Wittig Albert 32

Chris Martin
A Second Shot in the Dark - Annette Roome 1399

Chris Norgren
A Glancing Light - Aaron Elkins 477
Old Scores - Aaron Elkins 479

Series Index

Christine Bennett
The Christening Day Murder - Lee Harris 733
The Christmas Night Murder - Lee Harris 734

Claire Aldington
A Fatal Advent - Isabelle Holland 797

Claire Camden
Shroud for a Scholar - Audrey Peterson 1306

Claire Conrad/Maggie Hill
Beauty Dies - Melodie Johnson Howe 813
The Mother Shadow - Melodie Johnson Howe 814

Claire Malloy
A Diet to Die For - Joan Hess 776
Roll Over and Play Dead - Joan Hess 781

Cliff Hardy
Matrimonial Causes - Peter Corris 327
O'Fear - Peter Corris 328
Wet Graves - Peter Corris 329

Cliff Janeway
Booked to Die - John Dunning 466
The Bookman's Wake - John Dunning 467

Clio and Harry Marsh
The Going Down of the Sun - Jo Bannister 87

Coley Killebrew
Fire Horse - Bill Shoemaker 1486

Colin Burke
Cover Story - Robert Cullen 365

Conan Flagg
Dead Matter - M.K. Wren 1764
King of the Mountain - M.K. Wren 1765

Cooper MacLeish
Get What's Coming - Sam Reaves 1354
A Long Cold Fall - Sam Reaves 1355

D.L. Blacker
Party Till You Die - David Charnee 236
To Kill a Clown - David Charnee 237

D-O-L-L
Death Among the Angels - John Walter Putre 1336
A Small and Incidental Murder - John Walter Putre 1337

Daisy Dalrymple
The Winter Garden Mystery - Carola Dunn 465

Dalziel and Pascoe
Bones and Silence - Reginald Hill 789
Recalled to Life - Reginald Hill 790

Dan Fortune
Cassandra in Red - Michael Collins 281
Chasing Eights - Michael Collins 282
Crime, Punishment and Resurrection - Michael Collins 283

Dan Kruger
Red Winter - Michael Cormany 319
Skin Deep Is Fatal - Michael Cormany 320

Dan Roman
September Song - Edward Mathis 1096

Darina Lisle
A Deepe Coffyn - Janet Laurence 988
Hotel Morgue - Janet Laurence 989
Recipe for Death - Janet Laurence 990

Dave Brandstetter
The Boy Who Was Buried This Morning - Joseph Hansen 726
A Country of Old Men - Joseph Hansen 727

Dave Garrett
Burning March - Neil Albert 28
Cruel April - Neil Albert 29
The February Trouble - Neil Albert 30
The January Corpse - Neil Albert 31

Dave Robicheaux
Black Cherry Blues - James Lee Burke 193
Burning Angel - James Lee Burke 194
Dixie City Jam - James Lee Burke 195
In the Electric Mist with Confederate Dead - James Lee Burke 196
A Morning for Flamingos - James Lee Burke 197

Deb Ralston
Bird in a Cage - Lee Martin 1086
The Day That Dusty Died - Lee Martin 1087
Deficit Ending - Lee Martin 1088
The Mensa Murders - Lee Martin 1089

Deborah Knott
Bootlegger's Daughter - Margaret Maron 1076
Shooting at Loons - Margaret Maron 1078

Dee Street
A Woman's Own Mystery - Hannah Wakefield 1658

Deets Shanahan
The Iron Glove - Ronald Tierney 1619
The Steel Web - Ronald Tierney 1620
The Stone Veil - Ronald Tierney 1621

Delilah West
Hit and Run - Maxine O'Callaghan 1219
Set-Up - Maxine O'Callaghan 1220

Detroit Trilogy
King of the Corner - Loren D. Estleman 497

Devlin Kirk
Body Guard - Rex Burns 199
Parts Unknown - Rex Burns 200

Devon MacDonald
The Silver Scapel - Nancy Baker Jacobs 837
The Turquoise Tattoo - Nancy Baker Jacobs 838

Dewey James
Home Sweet Homicide - Kate Morgan 1171
A Slay at the Races - Kate Morgan 1172

Dismas Hardy
Hard Evidence - John T. Lescroart 1009
The Vig - John T. Lescroart 1010

DKA
32 Cadillacs - Joe Gores 616

Doc Adams
Yellow Bird - Rick Boyer 162

Dr. Nightingale
Dr. Nightingale Goes the Distance - Lydia Adamson 21
Dr. Nightingale Rides the Elephant - Lydia Adamson 22

Donald Strachey
Third Man Out - Richard Stevenson 1572

Doran Fairweather
The Bandersnatch - Mollie Hardwick 729

Dottie and Joe Loudermilk
Bad News Travels Fast - Gar Anthony Haywood 761

Dub Greenert
Red Knight - J. Madison Davis 391

Duffy House
Bleeding Dodger Blue - Crabbe Evers 505
Fear in Fenway - Crabbe Evers 506
Murder in Wrigley Field - Crabbe Evers 507
Tigers Burning - Crabbe Evers 508

Duncan Kincaid/Gemma James
All Shall Be Well - Deborah Crombie 356
Leave the Grave Green - Deborah Crombie 357
A Share in Death - Deborah Crombie 358

"Easy" Barnes
Behind the Fact - Richard Hilary 788

Easy Rawlins
Devil in a Blue Dress - Walter Mosley 1176
A Red Death - Walter Mosley 1177
White Butterfly - Walter Mosley 1178

Ed Fitzgerald
A Suitcase in Berlin - Don Flynn 532

Edwina Crusoe
Desperate Remedy - Mary Kittredge 931
Kill or Cure - Mary Kittredge 932
Walking Dead Man - Mary Kittredge 934

Eldon Larkin
Banjo Boy - Vince Kohler 949
Rising Dog - Vince Kohler 951

Eliot Ness
Murder by the Numbers - Max Allan Collins 278

Elizabeth Elliot
Quaker Silence - Irene Allen 45
Quaker Witness - Irene Allen 46

Elizabeth MacPherson
MacPherson's Lament - Sharyn McCrumb 1117
Missing Susan - Sharyn McCrumb 1118
The Windsor Knot - Sharyn McCrumb 1120

Ellie Bernstein
Beat Up a Cookie - Denise Dietz 422

Ellie Haskell
Femmes Fatal - Dorothy Cannell 214
How to Murder Your Mother-in-Law - Dorothy Cannell 215

Elvis Cole
Free Fall - Robert Crais 341
Lullaby Town - Robert Crais 342
Stalking the Angel - Robert Crais 343
Voodoo River - Robert Crais 344

Em Hansen
A Fall in Denver - Sarah Andrews 56
Tensleep - Sarah Andrews 57

Emerson Ward
Death Came Dressed in White - Michael W. Sherer 1481
Little Use for Death - Michael W. Sherer 1482

Emma Chizzit
Emma Chizzit and the Mother Lode Marauder - Mary Bowen Hall 711
Emma Chizzit and the Napa Nemesis - Mary Bowen Hall 712
Emma Chizzit and the Queen Anne Killer - Mary Bowen Hall 713

Emma Lord
The Alpine Advocate - Mary Daheim 370
The Alpine Christmas - Mary Daheim 371
The Alpine Decoy - Mary Daheim 372
The Alpine Fury - Mary Daheim 373

Ernst Lohmann
Death Squad London - Jack Gerson 579

Eugenia Potter
The 27 Ingredient Chili Con Carne Murders - Nancy Pickard 1315

Eva Wylie
Bucket Nut - Liza Cody 270
Monkey Wrench - Liza Cody 271

Evangeline Sinclair/Trixie Dolan
Encore Murder - Marian Babson 76

Evelyn Wade
Boiling Rock - Remar Sutton 1594

Faith Fairchild

Faith Fairchild
The Body in the Basement - Katherine Hall Page 1254
The Body in the Belfry - Katherine Hall Page 1255
The Body in the Bouillon - Katherine Hall Page 1256
The Body in the Cast - Katherine Hall Page 1257
The Body in the Vestibule - Katherine Hall Page 1258

"Fang" Mulheisen
Grootka - Jon A. Jackson 832
Hit on the House - Jon A. Jackson 833

Fanny Zindel
Bagels for Tea - Serita Stevens 1571

Father Koesler
Chameleon - William X. Kienzle 915
Masquerade - William X. Kienzle 916

Fiddler
Money Burns - A.E. Maxwell 1100

Finny Aletter
Obstacle Course - Yvonne Montgomery 1167

Frank Carver/Ginny Trask
Clear-Cut Murder - Lee Wallingford 1667
Cold Tracks - Lee Wallingford 1668

Frank Galvin
The Choice - Barry Reed 1357

Frank Hastings
Dead Center - Collin Wilcox 1711
A Death Before Dying - Collin Wilcox 1712
Hire a Hangman - Collin Wilcox 1715
Switchback - Collin Wilcox 1717

Fred Carver
Flame - John Lutz 1057
Spark - John Lutz 1058

Freddie O'Neal
Bet Against the House - Catherine Dain 378
Lay It on the Line - Catherine Dain 379
Sing a Song of Death - Catherine Dain 380
Walk a Crooked Mile - Catherine Dain 381

G.D.H. Pringle
Death in Close-Up - Nancy Livingston 1034
Mayhem in Parva - Nancy Livingston 1035
Unwillingly to Vegas - Nancy Livingston 1036

Gail Connor
Suspicion of Guilt - Barbara Parker 1268

Garth Ryland
A Dragon Lives Forever - John R. Riggs 1368
Wolf in Sheep's Clothing - John R. Riggs 1369

General Jack Hospital
Recycled - Jo Bailey 80

George Macrae/Leopold Silver
Thieftaker - Alan Scholefield 1454

Georgia Lee Maxwell
A Temporary Ghost - Mickey Friedman 556

Gibbons and Tozzi
Bad Apple - Anthony Bruno 184
Bad Blood - Anthony Bruno 185
Bad Moon - Anthony Bruno 186

Gideon Lowry
Killing Me Softly - John Leslie 1012

Gideon Oliver
Dead Men's Hearts - Aaron Elkins 476
Make No Bones - Aaron Elkins 478

Gideon Page
Illegal Motion - Grif Stockley 1576
Probable Cause - Griff Stockley 1577

Gillian Adams
Bad Chemistry - Nora Kelly 891
My Sister's Keeper - Nora Kelly 892

Glynis Tryon
North Star Conspiracy - Miriam Grace Monfredo 1164

Goldstein and Cruz
A Single Stone - Marilyn Wallace 1664

Goldy Bear
The Cereal Murders - Diane Mott Davidson 389
Dying for Chocolate - Diane Mott Davidson 390

Goodman/Bradley
Shot on Location - Stan Cutler 369

Gordianus the Finder
Catalina's Riddle - Steven Saylor 1448
The Venus Throw - Steven Saylor 1450

Gregor Demarkian
Not a Creature Was Stirring - Jane Haddam 695
Quoth the Raven - Jane Haddam 696
A Stillness in Bethlehem - Jane Haddam 697

Grover Bramlet
A Homecoming for Murder - John Armistead 65

Guido Brunetti
Death and Judgment - Donna Leon 1002
Death in a Strange Country - Donna Leon 1004

Gun Pedersen
Strike - L.L. Enger 492
Swing - L.L. Enger 493

Gwenn Ramadge
The Raggedy Man - Lillian O'Donnell 1227
Used to Kill - Lillian O'Donnell 1228
A Wreath for the Bride - Lillian O'Donnell 1229

Hackshaw
The NIMBY Factor - Stephen F. Wilcox 1721
The Painted Lady - Stephen F. Wilcox 1722

Hamish MacBeth
Death of a Charming Man - M.C. Beaton 109
Death of a Hussy - M.C. Beaton 110
Death of a Nag - M.C. Beaton 111
Death of a Perfect Wife - M.C. Beaton 112
Death of a Traveling Man - M.C. Beaton 113

Harry Bosch
The Black Echo - Michael Connelly 292
The Black Ice - Michael Connelly 293
The Concrete Blonde - Michael Connelly 294

Harry Cain
A Lawyer's Tale - D. Kincaid 923

Harry Denton
Dead Folks' Blues - Steven Womack 1751
Torch Town Boogie - Steven Womack 1754
Way Past Dead - Steven Womack 1755

Harry Stoner
Missing - Jonathan Valin 1646
The Music Lovers - Jonathan Valin 1647
Second Chance - Jonathan Valin 1648

Harvey Blissberg
World of Hurt - Richard Rosen 1400

Helen West
Deep Sleep - Frances Fyfield 561

Henri Castang
Not as Far as Velma - Nicholas Freeling 548

Henry and Emmy Tibbet
Black Girl, White Girl - Patricia Moyes 1179

Henry Lightstone
Wildfire - Kenneth W. Goddard 605

Henry Rios
How Town - Michael Nava 1194

What Mystery Do I Read Next?

History of Detroit
Motown - Loren D. Estleman 498
Whiskey River - Loren D. Estleman 501

Hobart Lindsay
The Classic Car Killer - Richard A. Lupoff 1054
The Comic Book Killer - Richard A. Lupoff 1055

Holly Winter
A Bite of Death - Susan Conant 287
Black Ribbon - Susan Conant 288
Bloodlines - Susan Conant 289
Paws Before Dying - Susan Conant 290
Ruffly Speaking - Susan Conant 291

Homer Kelly
The Dante Game - Jane Langton 979

Hometown Heroes
The Pumpkin-Shell Wife - Susanna Hofmann McShea 1138

Hugh Corbett
Murder Wears a Cowl - P.C. Doherty 426
The Prince of Darkness - P.C. Doherty 427

Ike and Abby
Until Death - Polly Whitney 1709
Until the End of Time - Polly Whitney 1710

Imogen Quy
A Piece of Justice - Jill Paton Walsh 1274

Inspector Alan Banks
A Dedicated Man - Peter Robinson 1392
Gallows View - Peter Robinson 1393
The Hanging Valley - Peter Robinson 1394
A Necessary End - Peter Robinson 1395
Past Reason Hated - Peter Robinson 1396
Wednesday's Child - Peter Robinson 1397

Inspector Alec Stainton
The Noose of Time - Stephen Murray 1189

Inspector Alvarez
Too Clever by Half - Roderic Jeffries 845

Inspector Barnaby
Death in Disguise - Caroline Graham 640
Death of a Hollow Man - Caroline Graham 641

Inspector Bill Slider
Death Watch - Cynthia Harrod-Eagles 740

Inspector Charlie Salter
Death by Degrees - Eric Wright 1767
Final Cut - Eric Wright 1768
A Fine Italian Hand - Eric Wright 1769
A Sensitive Case - Eric Wright 1770

Inspector Coffin
Coffin on Murder Street - Gwendoline Butler 203
Coffin Underground - Gwendoline Butler 204

Inspector Dover
Dover and the Claret Tappers - Joyce Porter 1322

Inspector Faro
Blood Line - Alanna Knight 941
Deadly Beloved - Alanna Knight 942
Killing Cousins - Alanna Knight 943

Inspector Gautier
Death Off Stage - Richard Grayson 655

Inspector George Rogers
A Time for Dying - Jonathan Ross 1402

Inspector Ghote
Dead on Time - H.R.F. Keating 874
The Iciest Sin - H.R.F. Keating 875

Inspector John Morrissey
In Stoney Places - Kay Mitchell 1159
A Lively Form of Death - Kay Mitchell 1160

Inspector Jurnet
A Very Particular Murder - S.T. Haymon 759

Series Index

Inspector Kelsey
A Violent End - Emma Page 1253

Inspector Lynley
Missing Joseph - Elizabeth George 575
Payment in Blood - Elizabeth George 576
Playing for the Ashes - Elizabeth George 577
A Suitable Vengeance - Elizabeth George 578

Inspector Matthew Kitologitak
Murder in a Cold Climate - Scott Young 1785
The Shaman's Knife - Scott Young 1786

Inspector Maybridge
The Fifth Rapunzel - B.M. Gill 586

Inspector Monk
A Dangerous Mourning - Anne Perry 1293

Inspector Morse
The Wench Is Dead - Colin Dexter 418

Inspector Peckover
Kill the Butler! - Michael Kenyon 911
Peckover Joins the Choir - Michael Kenyon 912

Inspector Pel
Pel and the Missing Persons - Mark Hebden 768

Inspector Quantrill
This Way Out - Sheila Radley 1343

Inspector Richard Montgomery
Nurse Dawes Is Dead - Stella Shepherd 1479
Thinner than Blood - Stella Shepherd 1480

Inspector Roper
Breach of Promise - Roy Hart 748

Inspector Ross
The Killing of Ellis Martin - Lucretia Grindle 677
So Little to Die For - Lucretia Grindle 678

Inspector Rostnikov
The Man Who Walked Like a Bear - Stuart M. Kaminsky 859
Rostnikov's Vacation - Stuart M. Kaminsky 861

Inspector Rudd
The Spoils of Time - June Thomson 1614

Inspector Stephen Ramsey
A Day in the Death of Dorothea Cassidy - Ann Cleeves 260

Inspector Van Der Valk
Sand Castles - Nicholas Freeling 549

Inspector Wexford
Kissing the Gunner's Daughter - Ruth Rendell 1361

Irene Adler
Good Morning, Irene - Carole Nelson Douglas 440
Irene at Large - Carole Nelson Douglas 442

Iris Cooper
Peril under the Palms - K.K. Beck 117

Iris House Mystery
Blooming Murder - Jean Hager 698
Dead and Buried - Jean Hager 699

J.K.G. Jantarro
Work for a Dead Man - Simon Ritchie 1371

J.P. Beaumont
Minor in Possession - J.A. Jance 844

Jack Bodine
Closing Costs - Thomas Bunn 189
Worse than Death - Thomas Bunn 190

Jack Flippo
Dreamboat - Doug J. Swanson 1596

Jack Hawkins
Paint It Black - W.R. Philbrick 1313

Jack Kyle
The Dallas Deception - Richard Abshire 7
Turnaround Jack - Richard Abshire 8

Jack Laidlaw
Strange Loyalties - William McIlvanney 1134

Jack Lynch
Murphy's Fault - Steven Womack 1752
The Software Bomb - Steven Womack 1753

Jack Ross
The Desert Look - Bernard Schopen 1455

Jack Ryan
The Sum of All Fears - Tom Clancy 248

Jack Sparks
The 6 Messiahs - Mark Frost 560

Jack Stryker
The Body in Blackwater Bay - Paula Gosling 624

Jack Willows/Claire Parker
Hot Shots - Laurence Gough 627

Jackie Walsh
First Pedigree Murder - Melissa Cleary 257
The Maltese Puppy - Melissa Cleary 258
A Tail of Two Murders - Melissa Cleary 259

Jacob & Helen Horowitz
The Last Gambit - David Delman 411

Jacob Lomax
Blood Relative - Michael Allegretto 39
The Dead of Winter - Michael Allegretto 40
Grave Doubt - Michael Allegretto 41

Jacqueline Kirby
Naked Once More - Elizabeth Peters 1300

Jake Eichord
Stone Shadow - Rex Miller 1154

Jake Lassiter
Mortal Sin - Paul Levine 1014
Night Vision - Paul Levine 1015

Jake Sands
East Beach - Ron Ely 485
Night Shadows - Ron Ely 486

James Bond
Win, Lose or Die - John Gardner 567

James Morgan
No Way Home - Andrew Coburn 267
Voices in the Dark - Andrew Coburn 268

James Shaw
Bad Neighbors - Isidore Haiblum 703

Jane Da Silva
Amateur Night - K.K. Beck 114
Electric City - K.K. Beck 115
A Hopeless Case - K.K. Beck 116

Jane Jeffry
The Class Menagerie - Jill Churchill 244
A Farewell to Yarns - Jill Churchill 245
From Here to Paternity - Jill Churchill 246
A Quiche Before Dying - Jill Churchill 247

Jane Lawless/Cordelia Thorn
Vital Lies - Ellen Hart 746

Jason Coulter
Ten of Swords - J.R. Levitt 1018

Jason Love
Frozen Assets - James Leasor 996

Jason Lynx
Death and the Dogwalker - A.J. Orde 1240
A Long Time Dead - A.J. Orde 1242

Jay Omega
Zombies of the Gene Pool - Sharyn McCrumb 1121

Joe Leaphorn and Jim Chee

Jazz Jasper
The Cheetah Chase - Karin McQuillan 1137

Jeff Jackson/Martha's Vineyard Mystery
A Beautiful Place to Die - Philip R. Craig 335
A Case of Vineyard Poisoning - Philip R. Craig 336
Cliff Hanger - Philip R. Craig 337
The Double Minded Men - Philip R. Craig 338
Off Season - Philip R. Craig 339
The Woman Who Walked into the Sea - Philip R. Craig 340

Jeffrey Dean
Singapore Transfer - Wayne Warga 1673

Jemima Shore
The Cavalier Case - Antonia Fraser 543

Jenny Cain
Bum Steer - Nancy Pickard 1316
But I Wouldn't Want to Die There - Nancy Pickard 1317
I.O.U. - Nancy Pickard 1318

Jeremiah St. John
According to St. John - William Babula 77

Jeri Howard
Kindred Crimes - Janet Dawson 397
Nobody's Child - Janet Dawson 398

Jerry Brogan
Hot Air - Jon L. Breen 170
Loose Lips - Jon L. Breen 171

Jessica Drake
Angel of Death - Rochelle Majer Krich 953
Fair Game - Rochelle Majer Krich 954

Jessica James
The Daphne Decisions - Meg O'Brien 1214
Eagles Die Too - Meg O'Brien 1215
Hare Today, Gone Tomorrow - Meg O'Brien 1216

Jill Smith
Death and Taxes - Susan Dunlap 460
Diamond in the Buff - Susan Dunlap 461
Time Expired - Susan Dunlap 464

Jimmy Drover
Drover and the Zebras - Bill Granger 646

Jimmy Flannery
The Gift Horse's Mouth - Robert Campbell 212
Nibbled to Death by Ducks - Robert Campbell 213

Jimmy Lujack
The Book of Numbers - David Thoreau 1616

Joan Spencer
Buried in Quilts - Sara Hoskinson Frommer 559

Joanna Stark
Dark Star - Marcia Muller 1180

Jocelyn O'Roarke
Dead Pan - Jane Dentinger 413
The Queen Is Dead - Jane Dentinger 414

Joe Dante
19th Precinct - Christopher Newman 1202

Joe DiGregorio
False Faces - Seth Jacob Margolis 1074
Vanishing Act - Seth Jacob Margolis 1075

Joe Gunther
Borderlines - Archer Mayor 1103
Fruits of the Poisonous Tree - Archer Mayor 1104
Scent of Evil - Archer Mayor 1105

Joe Hannibal
The Skintight Shroud - Wayne Dundee 459

Joe Leaphorn and Jim Chee
Sacred Clowns - Tony Hillerman 792
Talking God - Tony Hillerman 793

Joe McGuire

Joe McGuire
And Leave Her Lay Dying - John Lawrence Reynolds 1362
Whisper Death - John Lawrence Reynolds 1363

Joe Noonan
Black Light - Daniel Hearn 767

John Becker
The Edge of Sleep - David Wiltse 1736
Into the Fire - David Wiltse 1737

John Deal
Deal to Die For - Les Standiford 1560
Done Deal - Les Standiford 1561

John Denson
Bigfoot - Richard Hoyt 815
Whoo? - Richard Hoyt 816

John Dobie
The Catalyst - Desmond Cory 330
The Dobie Paradox - Desmond Cory 331

John Dortmunder
Don't Ask - Donald E. Westlake 1697
Drowned Hopes - Donald E. Westlake 1698

John Francis Cuddy
Act of God - Jeremiah Healy 764
Foursome - Jeremiah Healy 765
Yesterday's News - Jeremiah Healy 766

John Marshall Tanner
Blood Type - Stephen Greenleaf 667
Book Case - Stephen Greenleaf 668
Southern Cross - Stephen Greenleaf 669

John McLeish/Francesca Wilson
Death Among the Dons - Janet Neel 1196
Death of a Partner - Janet Neel 1197

John Putnam Thatcher
East Is East - Emma Lathen 986
Right on the Money - Emma Lathen 987

John Rawlings
The Great Grave Robbery - John Minahan 1158

John Rodrigue
Drowned Man's Key - Ken Grissom 683

John Rodrique
Big Fish - Ken Grissom 682

John Samson
The Cords of Vanity - Miles Tripp 1629
Video Vengeance - Miles Tripp 1630

John Sanders/Harriet Jeffries
Murder in a Good Cause - Medora Sale 1417
Murder in Focus - Medora Sale 1418
Pursued by Shadows - Medora Sale 1419
Short Cut to Santa Fe - Medora Sale 1420

John Wells
Rough Justice - Keith Peterson 1309

Johnny Ortiz
Missing Man - Richard Martin Stern 1570

Jolie Wyatt
Dust Devils of the Purple Sage - Barbara Burnett Smith 1516

Jonathan Gaunt
The Spanish Maze Game - Noah Webster 1682

Jordon Poteet
The Only Good Yankee - Jeff Abbott 2

Joshua Croft
At Ease with the Dead - Walter Satterthwait 1437
A Flower in the Desert - Walter Satterthwait 1439
The Hanged Man - Walter Satterthwait 1440

Julian Kestrel
A Broken Vessel - Kate Ross 1403
Cut to the Quick - Kate Ross 1404

Karl Alberg
A Chill Wind in January - L.R. Wright 1772
Fall From Grace - L.R. Wright 1773
Mother Love - L.R. Wright 1774
Prized Possessions - L.R. Wright 1775
A Touch of Panic - L.R. Wright 1776

Kat Colorado
Alley Kat Blues - Karen Kijewski 917
Copy Kat - Karen Kijewski 918
Katapult - Karen Kijewski 919
Katwalk - Karen Kijewski 920
Wild Kat - Karen Kijewski 921

Kate and Josh Berman
Whisper.He Might Hear You - William Appel 62
Widowmaker - William Appel 63

Kate Ardleigh
Death at Bishop's Keep - Robin Paige 1259
Death at Gallows Green - Robin Paige 1260

Kate Brannigan
Crack Down - Val McDermid 1125

Kate Delafield
The Beverly Malibu - Katherine V. Forrest 533
Murder by Tradition - Katherine V. Forrest 534

Kate Fansler
An Imperfect Spy - Amanda Cross 360

Kate Henry
The Dead Pull Hitter - Alison Gordon 612
Night Game - Alison Gordon 613
Safe at Home - Alison Gordon 614
Striking Out - Alison Gordon 615

Kate Ivory
Death and the Oxford Box - Veronica Stallwood 1557
Oxford Exit - Veronica Stallwood 1559

Kate Jasper
Adjusted to Death - Jaqueline Girdner 593
The Last Resort - Jaqueline Girdner 594
A Stiff Critique - Jaqueline Girdner 595
Tea-Totally Dead - Jaqueline Girdner 596

Kate Kinsella
Deadly Admirer - Christine Green 658
Deadly Practice - Christine Green 660

Kate Maddox
Model Murder - Erica Quest 1338

Kate Martinelli
A Grave Talent - Laurie R. King 925
To Play the Fool - Laurie R. King 927

Kate Mulcay
Ah, Sweet Mystery - Celestine Sibley 1495
Dire Happenings at Scratch Ankle - Celestine Sibley 1496
A Plague of Kinfolks - Celestine Sibley 1497
Straight as an Arrow - Celestine Sibley 1498

Kate Shugak
A Cold-Blooded Business - Dana Stabenow 1550
A Cold Day for Murder - Dana Stabenow 1549
Dead in the Water - Dana Stabenow 1551
Play with Fire - Dana Stabenow 1552

Kate Yancy
All the Great Pretenders - Deborah Adams 10

Kathryn Swinbrooke/Colum Murtagh
The Eye of God - C.L. Grace 631

Kay Scarpetta
All That Remains - Patricia D. Cornwell 321
The Body Farm - Patricia D. Cornwell 322
Body of Evidence - Patricia D. Cornwell 323
Cruel and Unusual - Patricia D. Cornwell 324
From Potter's Field - Patricia D. Cornwell 325
Postmortem - Patricia D. Cornwell 326

Keith Calder
A Brace of Skeet - Gerald Hammond 719
Home to Roost - Gerald Hammond 720

Kidd
The Empress File - John Camp 210

Kiernan O'Shaughnessy
Pious Deception - Susan Dunlap 462

Kiernan O'Shaugnessy
Rogue Wave - Susan Dunlap 463

Kimmey Kruse
Funny as a Dead Comic - Susan Rogers Cooper 312
Funny as a Dead Relative - Susan Rogers Cooper 313

Kinky Friedman
God Bless John Wayne - Kinky Friedman 554
Musical Chairs - Kinky Friedman 555

Kinsey Millhone
F Is for Fugitive - Sue Grafton 634
G Is for Gumshoe - Sue Grafton 635
H Is for Homicide - Sue Grafton 636
I Is for Innocent - Sue Grafton 637
K Is for Killer - Sue Grafton 638
L Is for Lawless - Sue Grafton 639

Kori and Peter Brichter
Original Sin - Mary Monica Pulver 1334
Show Stopper - Mary Monica Pulver 1335

Kramer and Zondi
The Song Dog - James McClure 1114

L.A. Quartet
L.A. Confidential - James Ellroy 483

Lady Jane Hildreth
Cotswold Moles - Michael Spicer 1539

Langley and Gillard
Rook-Shoot - Margaret Duffy 452
Who Killed Cock Robin? - Margaret Duffy 453

Lark Dodge
Skylark - Sheila Simonson 1501

Laura Di Palma
The Good Fight - Lia Matera 1091
A Hard Bargain - Lia Matera 1092

Laura Fleming
Dead Ringer - Toni L.P. Kelner 900
Down Home Murder - Toni L.P. Kelner 901
Trouble Looking for a Place to Happen - Toni L.P. Kelner 902

Lauren Laurano
Everything You Have Is Mine - Sandra Scoppettone 1460
I'll Be Leaving You Always - Sandra Scoppettone 1461
My Sweet Untraceable You - Sandra Scoppettone 1462

Lauren Maxwell
Murder Most Grizzly - Elizabeth Quinn 1340
A Wolf in Death's Clothing - Elizabeth Quinn 1341

Lee Ofsted
Rotten Lies - Charlotte Elkins 481

Lee Squires
Grizzly - Christine Andreae 54
Trail of Murder - Christine Andreae 55

Lennox Kemp
A Loose Connection - M.R.D. Meek 1139

Lenny Schwartz
Virgil's Ghost - Irving Weinman 1684

Leo Haggerty
A Fistful of Empty - Benjamin M. Schutz 1457
Mexico Is Forever - Benjamin M. Schutz 1458

Lew Griffin
Black Hornet - James Sallis 1421
Moth - James Sallis 1422

Liam Devlin
The Eagle Has Flown - Jack Higgins 787

Libby Kincaid
Cold Feet - Kerry Tucker 1636
Death Echo - Kerry Tucker 1637
Still Waters - Kerry Tucker 1638

Lil Ritchie
Shattered Rhythms - Phyllis Knight 946
Switching the Odds - Phyllis Knight 947

Liz Connors
And Soon I'll Come to Kill You - Susan Kelly 893
Out of the Darkness - Susan Kelly 894
Until Proven Innocent - Susan Kelly 895

Liz Wareham
Full Commission - Carol Brennan 172

Lonia Guiu
Antipodes - Maria-Antonia Oliver 1236

Loretta Lawson
Don't Leave Me This Way - Joan Smith 1520
What Men Say - Joan Smith 1522

Lou Boldt
The Angel Maker - Ridley Pearson 1282

Louis Monroe
Down by the Sea - Bill Kent 910

Lovejoy
The Great California Game - Jonathan Gash 570
The Lies of Fair Ladies - Jonathan Gash 571
The Sin Within Her Smile - Jonathan Gash 572

Lucas Davenport
Night Prey - John Sandford 1424
Shadow Prey - John Sandford 1426
Silent Prey - John Sandford 1427
Winter Prey - John Sandford 1428

Lucas Hallam
Dead-Stick - L.J. Washburn 1674
Dog Heavies - L.J. Washburn 1675

Luke Abbot
Death Penalties - Paula Gosling 625

Luke Thanet
Dead by Morning - Dorothy Simpson 1502

Mac Fontana
Help Wanted: Orphans Preferred - Earl Emerson 487
Morons and Madmen - Earl Emerson 488

Mac MacFarland
Death Below Deck - Douglas Kiker 922

Maddy and Alex Phillips
Blood Trance - R.D. Zimmerman 1791
Red Trance - R.D. Zimmerman 1793

Madison McGuire
A Singular Spy - Amanda Kyle Williams 1727

Madoc Rhys
The Wrong Rite - Alisa Craig 334

Maggie Elliott
The Northwest Murders - Elizabeth Atwood Taylor 1607

Maggie MacGowen
Midnight Baby - Wendy Hornsby 808
Telling Lies - Wendy Hornsby 809

Maggie Ryan
Bad Blood - P.M. Carlson 218

Margaret Barlow
Murder in the Napa Valley - David Osborn 1245
Murder on the Chesapeake - David Osborn 1246

Margaret Binton
Deathics - Richard Barth 100

Mario Balzic
Sunshine Enemies - K.C. Constantine 298

Mark Holland
Deadly Crescendo - Paul Myers 1191
Deadly Sonata - Paul Myers 1192

Mark Renzler
Who Shot Longshot Sam? - Paul Engleman 495

Mark Shigata
The Buzzards Must Also Be Fed - Anne Wingate 1739
Exception to Murder - Anne Wingate 1740
The Eye of Anna - Anne Wingate 1741
Yakuza, Go Home - Anne Wingate 1742

Mark Treasure
Holy Treasure! - David Williams 1729
Treasure by Post - David Williams 1730

Marston/Cantini Mystery
False Profit - Robert Eversz 511

Marti MacAlister
Dead Time - Eleanor Taylor Bland 141
Slow Burn - Eleanor Taylor Bland 142

Martin Fender
Boiled in Concrete - Jesse Sublett 1587

Mary Russell/Sherlock Holmes
The Beekeeper's Apprentice - Laurie R. King 924
A Monstrous Regiment of Women - Laurie R. King 926

Matilda Worthing
Mass Murder - John Keith Drummond 449

Matt Cobb
Killed on the Rocks - William L. DeAndrea 401

Matt Doyle/Carter Winfield
Murder Begins at Home - Dale L. Gilbert 585

Matt Jacob
Two Way Toll - Zachary Klein 939

Matt Murdock
Merry Christmas, Murdock - Robert J. Ray 1352
Murdock Cracks Ice - Robert J. Ray 1353

Matt Riordan
Methods of Execution - Frederick D. Huebner 818
Picture Postcard - Fredrick D. Huebner 819

Matt Rogerson
The Search Committee - Ralph McInerny 1136

Matt Scudder
A Dance at the Slaughterhouse - Lawrence Block 146
The Devil Knows You're Dead - Lawrence Block 147
Out on the Cutting Edge - Lawrence Block 148
A Ticket to the Boneyard - Lawrence Block 149
A Walk Among the Tombstones - Lawrence Block 150

Matthew Coll
Death in Verona - Roy Harley Lewis 1020

Matthew Hope
Three Blind Mice - Ed McBain 1106

Matthew Stock
Frobisher's Savage - Leonard Tourney 1624

Mavis Lashley
Death Beneath the Christmas Tree - Robert Nordan 1208
Death on Wheels - Robert Nordan 1209

Mavity and Spanner
Even the Butler Was Poor - Ron Goulart 628
Now He Thinks He's Dead - Ron Goulart 629

Maxene St. Clair
Elective Murder - Janet McGiffin 1129
Prescription for Death - Janet McGiffin 1130

Maxey Burnell
Unsafe Keeping - Carol Cail 206

McCorkle and Padillo
Twilight at Mac's Place - Ross Thomas 1613

Meg Lacey
No Forwarding Address - Elisabeth Bowers 161

Melissa Craig
Exhaustive Enquiries - Betty Rowlands 1408
Over the Edge - Betty Rowlands 1409

Mellingham Mystery
Family Album - Susan Oleksiw 1230
Murder in Mellingham - Susan Oleksiw 1231

Merry Folger
Death on Rough Water - Francine Matthews 1099

Micah Dunn
The Caesar Clue - M.K. Shuman 1491
Deep Kill - M.K. Shuman 1492
The Last Man to Die - M.K. Shuman 1493

Michael Ohayon
Murder on a Kibbutz - Batya Gur 690
The Saturday Morning Murder - Batya Gur 691

Michael Rhinehart
The Queen's Mare - John Birkett 133

Mickey Knight
The Intersection of Law and Desire - J.M. Redmann 1356

Midnight Louie
Cat on a Blue Monday - Carole Nelson Douglas 438
Pussyfoot - Carole Nelson Douglas 443

Mike Devlin
Gentkill: A Novel of the FBI - Paul Lindsay 1025

Mike Hammer
The Killing Man - Mickey Spillane 1540

Milan Jacovich
The Cleveland Connection - Les Roberts 1383
Deep Shaker - Les Roberts 1384
The Duke of Cleveland - Les Roberts 1385
Full Cleveland - Les Roberts 1386

Miles Jacoby
Hard Look - Robert J. Randisi 1349
Separate Cases - Robert J. Randisi 1350

Milt Kovack
Houston in the Rearview Mirror - Susan Rogers Cooper 314

Milt Kovak
Dead Moon on the Rise - Susan Rogers Cooper 310
Doctors, Lawyers and Such - Susan Rogers Cooper 311
Other People's Houses - Susan Rogers Cooper 316

Miss Melville
Miss Melville Rides a Tiger - Evelyn E. Smith 1518

Miss Pink
Rage - Gwen Moffat 1162
The Stone Hawk - Gwen Moffat 1163

Miss Zukas
Miss Zukas and the Island Murders - Jo Dereske 415

Mitchell and Markby

Mitchell and Markby
Cold in the Earth - Ann Granger 642
A Fine Place for Death - Ann Granger 643
Murder Among Us - Ann Granger 644
A Season for Murder - Ann Granger 645

Mitchell Bushyhead
Ghostland - Jean Hager 700

Molly Bearpaw
Ravenmocker - Jean Hager 701
The Redbird's Cry - Jean Hager 702

Molly Cates
The Red Scream - Mary Willis Walker 1659
Under the Beetle's Cellar - Mary Willis Walker 1660

Molly Rafferty/Nick Hannibal
The Marvell College Murders - Sophie Belfort 119

Mongo
In the House of Secret Enemies - George C. Chesbro 241
The Language of Cannibals - George C. Chesbro 242

Monsieur Pamplemousse
Monsieur Pamplemousse Investigates - Michael Bond 151
Pamplemousse Rests His Case - Michael Bond 152

Morgan Hunt
Deep End - Geoffrey Norman 1210

Moroni Traveler
The Angel's Share - R.R. Irvine 826
Called Home - R.R. Irvine 828
The Great Reminder - R.R. Irvine 829
Pillar of Fire - R.R. Irvine 830

Mrs. Murphy
Murder at Monticello - Rita Mae Brown 180
Rest in Pieces - Rita Mae Brown 181
Wish You Were Here - Rita Mae Brown 182

Mrs. Pargeter
Mrs. Pargeter's Package - Simon Brett 175

Mrs. Pollifax
Mrs. Pollifax and the Whirling Dervish - Dorothy Gilman 588

Murder in Washington, D.C.
Murder at the Kennedy Center - Margaret Truman 1634

Nameless Detective
Breakdown - Bill Pronzini 1326
Epitaphs - Bill Pronzini 1327
Jackpot - Bill Pronzini 1328
Quarry - Bill Pronzini 1329

Natasha O'Brien
Someone Is Killing the Great Chefs of America - Nan Lyons 1061

Nate Heller
Carnal Hours - Max Allan Collins 277
Murder in the Post-War World - Max Allan Collins 279
Stolen Away - Max Allan Collins 280

Nate Rosen
Stone Boy - Ronald Levitsky 1017

Neal Carey
A Cool Breeze on the Underground - Don Winslow 1743
The Trail to Buddha's Mirror - Don Winslow 1744

Neal Rafferty
The Emerald Lizard - Chris Wiltz 1738

Nebraska Mystery
The Naked Eye - William J. Reynolds 1364

Neil Hamel
The Lies That Bind - Judith Van Gieson 1649
The Other Side of Death - Judith Van Gieson 1650
Raptor - Judith Van Gieson 1651
The Wolf Path - Judith Van Gieson 1652

Neil Hockaday
Drown All the Dogs - Thomas Adcock 23

Nell Bray
Hanging on the Wire - Gillian Linscott 1028
Stage Fright - Gillian Linscott 1030

Nero Wolfe
Fade to Black - Robert Goldsborough 607
Silver Spire - Robert Goldsborough 608

Niccolo Benedetti
The Manx Murders - William L. DeAndrea 402

Nicholas Barlow
Casual Slaughters - Robert A. Carter 223
Final Edit - Robert A. Carter 224

Nicholas Bracewell
The Mad Courtesan - Edward Marston 1081
The Nine Giants - Edward Marston 1082
The Queen's Head - Edward Marston 1083
The Trip to Jerusalem - Edward Marston 1084

Nick Delvecchio
The Dead of Brooklyn - Robert J. Randisi 1347

Nick Magaracz
Jersey Monkey - Kate Gallison 565

Nick Polo
Beggar's Choice - Jerry Kennealy 906
Special Delivery - Jerry Kennealy 907
Vintage Polo - Jerry Kennealy 908

Nick Trevellyan/Alison Hope
Hope Against Hope - Susan B. Kelly 896
Kid's Stuff - Susan B. Kelly 897
Time of Hope - Susan B. Kelly 898

Nicky and Sam Titus
Death Down Home - Eve K. Sandstrom 1430
The Devil Down Home - Eve K. Sandstrom 1431
The Down Home Heifer Heist - Eve K. Sandstrom 1432

Nikki Trakos
Dead Ahead - Ruby Horansky 804
Dead Center - Ruby Horansky 805

Nina Fischman
Close Quarters - Marissa Piesman 1319

Norah Mulcahaney
Lockout - Lillian O'Donnell 1224
A Private Crime - Lillian O'Donnell 1225
Pushover - Lillian O'Donnell 1226

November Man
The Last Good German - Bill Granger 647

Old New York
The Kingsbridge Plot - Maan Meyers 1148

Owen Archer
The Apothecary Rose - Candace M. Robb 1375
The Lady Chapel - Candace M. Robb 1376
The Nun's Tale - Candace M. Robb 1377

Owen Keane
Deadstick - Terence Faherty 513
Die Dreaming - Terence Faherty 514
The Lost Keats - Terence Faherty 515

Palmer Kingston/A.J. Egan
Neon Dancers - Matt Taylor 1608

Patience McKenna
Once and Always Murder - Orania Papazoglou 1263

What Mystery Do I Read Next?

Patricia Delaney
Angel's Bidding - Sharon Gwyn Short 1489
The Death We Share - Sharon Gwyn Short 1490

Peaches Dann
Memory Can Be Murder - Elizabeth Daniels Squire 1547
Who Killed What's-Her-Name? - Elizabeth Daniels Squire 1548

Peggy O'Neill
Cold Comfort - M.D. Lake 967
A Gift for Murder - M.D. Lake 968
Murder by Mail - M.D. Lake 969
Once upon a Crime - M.D. Lake 970
Poisoned Ivy - M.D. Lake 971

Pennyfoot Hotel
Check-out Time - Kate Kingsbury 928
Eat, Drink and Be Buried - Kate Kingsbury 929
Room with a Clue - Kate Kingsbury 930

Perry Mason
Perry Mason in The Case of Too Many Murders - Thomas Chastain 239

Pete McPhee
Carolina Gold - Douglas McBriarty 1108

Peter Bartholomew
Hot Water - Sally Gunning 686
Rough Water - Sally Gunning 687
Still Water - Sally Gunning 688
Troubled Water - Sally Gunning 689

Peter Brady
Death Notice - M.S. Karl 866
Deerslayer - M.S. Karl 867

Peter Decker/Rina Lazarus
Day of Atonement - Faye Kellerman 878
False Prophet - Faye Kellerman 879
Grievous Sin - Faye Kellerman 880
Justice - Faye Kellerman 881
Milk and Honey - Faye Kellerman 882
Sanctuary - Faye Kellerman 884

Peter Diamond
The Summons - Peter Lovesey 1050

Peter Finley
Limited Partner - Mike Lupica 1053

Peter Marklin
Boxed In - Neville Steed 1564
Clockwork - Neville Steed 1565
Wind-Up - Neville Steed 1566

Peter Shandy
An Owl Too Many - Charlotte MacLeod 1064
Something in the Water - Charlotte MacLeod 1065

Philip Marlowe
Perchance to Dream - Robert B. Parker 1270

Pollard and Toye
The Glade Manor Murder - Elizabeth Lemarchand 1001

Port Silva
Grandmother's House - Janet LaPierre 983

Prester John Riordan
The Frozen Franklin - Sean Hanlon 725

Prince of Wales
Bertie and the Seven Bodies - Peter Lovesey 1049

Queenie Davilov
Cut To—Murder - Denise Osborne 1247

Quiller
Quiller KGB - Adam Hall 706

Quinn Parker
Full-Bodied Red - Bruce Zimmerman 1790

Rachel Gold
Death Benefits - Michael A. Kahn 851
Due Diligence - Michael A. Kahn 852
Firm Ambitions - Michael A. Kahn 853

Rafferty
Rafferty: Fatal Sisters - W. Glenn Duncan 458

Randall Sierra
Shoot the Piper - Richard Hill 791

Rebecca Schwartz
Dead in the Water - Julie Smith 1524
Other People's Skeletons - Julie Smith 1529

Regan Reilly
Decked - Carol Higgins Clark 250
Snagged - Carol Higgins Clark 251

Reid Bennett
Flashback - Ted Wood 1756
On the Inside - Ted Wood 1757
Snow Job - Ted Wood 1758

Reuben Frost
Murder Times Two - Haughton Murphy 1186
A Very Venetian Murder - Haughton Murphy 1187

Richard Harrison
Dark Provenance - Michael David Anthony 61

Richard Jury
The Old Contemptibles - Martha Grimes 675
The Old Silent - Martha Grimes 676

Richard Michaelson
Faithfully Executed - Michael Bowen 159

Rick Decker
Hidden City - Jim DeBrosse 407
Southern Cross - Jim DeBrosse 408

Rita Noonan
Friends in High Places - Michael Hendricks 771
Money to Burn - Michael Hendricks 772

Robert Amiss
Clubbed to Death - Ruth Dudley Edwards 472

Robert Forsythe
A Death for a Dancing Doll - E.X. Giroux 597
A Death for a Dodo - E.X. Giroux 598

Robert Miles
False Profits - David Everson 509
Suicide Squeeze - David Everson 510

Roger Shallot
The Poisoned Chalice - Michael Clynes 264
The White Rose Murders - Michael Clynes 265

Roger Tejeda and Kate Teague
Half a Mind - Wendy Hornsby 807

Roger the Chapman
Death and the Chapman - Kate Sedley 1467
The Holy Innocents - Kate Sedley 1468
The Plymouth Cloak - Kate Sedley 1469
The Weaver's Tale - Kate Sedley 1470

Ronnie Ventana
Charged with Guilt - Gloria White 1700
Money to Burn - Gloria White 1701
Murder on the Run - Gloria White 1702

Rosa Epton
Seeds of Murder - Michael Underwood 1642

Rune
Hard News - Jeffrey Wilds Deaver 403
Manhattan Is My Beat - Jeffrey Wilds Deaver 404

Samantha Adams
He Was Her Man - Sarah Shankman 1474
The King Is Dead - Sarah Shankman 1475
Now Let's Talk of Graves - Sarah Shankman 1476
She Walks in Beauty - Sarah Shankman 1477

Samantha Holt
Copy Cat Crimes - Karen Ann Wilson 1733
Eight Dogs Flying - Karen Ann Wilson 1734

Samantha Turner
A Clinic for Murder - Marsha Landreth 974
The Holiday Murders - Marsha Landreth 975
Vial Murders - Marsha Landreth 976

Sarah Deane & Alex McKenzie
The Bridled Groom - J.S. Borthwick 154

Sarah Quilliam
A Dash of Death - Claudia Bishop 134
A Taste for Murder - Claudia Bishop 135

Saxon
Seeing the Elephant - Les Roberts 1387

Scobie Malone
Babylon South - Jon Cleary 255
Murder Song - Jon Cleary 256

Seymour Lipp
And Baby Makes None - Stephen Lewis 1022
The Monkey Rope - Stephen Lewis 1023

Sharon McCone
The Shape of Dread - Marcia Muller 1181
Till The Butchers Cut Him Down - Marcia Muller 1182
Trophies and Dead Things - Marcia Muller 1183
Where Echoes Live - Marcia Muller 1184
A Wild and Lonely Place - Marcia Muller 1185

Sheila Malory
The Cruelest Month - Hazel Holt 800
Mrs. Malory and the Festival Murders - Hazel Holt 801
Mrs. Malory Investigates - Hazel Holt 802

Sheila Travis
Deadly Secrets on the St. Johns - Patricia Houck Sprinkle 1542
Murder on Peachtree Street - Patricia Houck Sprinkle 1543
A Mystery Bred in Buckhead - Patricia Houck Sprinkle 1544
Somebody's Dead in Snellville - Patricia Houck Sprinkle 1545

Sherlock Holmes and Edward Porter Jones
The Glendower Conspiracy - Lloyd Biggle Jr. 131

Shifty Anderson
I'm Getting Killed Right Here - William Murray 1190

Shirley McClintock
Dead in the Scrub - B.J. Oliphant 1232
Death and the Delinquent - B.J. Oliphant 1233
Death Served Up Cold - B.J. Oliphant 1234
The Unexpected Corpse - B.J. Oliphant 1235

Sid Halley
Come to Grief - Dick Francis 538

Sidney Holden
Elsinore - Jerome Charyn 238

Sigrid Harald
Past Imperfect - Margaret Maron 1077

Simeon Grist
Everything but the Squeal - Timothy Hallinan 716
Incinerator - Timothy Hallinan 717
Skin Deep - Timothy Hallinan 718

Simon Bogner
Business Unusual - Tim Heald 763

Simona Griffo
The Trouble with Going Home - Camilla T. Crespi 345
The Trouble with Moonlighting - Trella Crespi 346
The Trouble with Too Much Sun - Trella Crespi 347

Sister Frevisse
The Bishop's Tale - Margaret Frazer 544
The Boy's Tale - Margaret Frazer 545

Sister Joan
A Vow of Chastity - Veronica Black 136
A Vow of Obedience - Veronica Black 137
A Vow of Sanctity - Veronica Black 138

Sister Mary Helen
Death Goes on Retreat - SisterCarol Anne O'Marie 1237
Murder in Ordinary Time - SisterCarol Anne O'Marie 1238
Murder Makes a Pilgrimage - SisterCarol Anne O'Marie 1239

Sister Mary Teresa
Nun Plussed - Monica Quill 1339

Skinny
All I Have Is Blue - James Colbert 272
Skinny Man - James Colbert 273

Skip Langdon
The Axeman's Jazz - Julie Smith 1523
House of Blues - Julie Smith 1525
Jazz Funeral - Julie Smith 1526
New Orleans Beat - Julie Smith 1527
New Orleans Mourning - Julie Smith 1528

Slots Resnick
Three Strikes, You're Dead - Michael Geller 574

Smith and Wetzen
The Deadliest Option - Annette Meyers 1147

Smith and Wetzon
Blood on the Street - Annette Meyers 1146

Smithsonian
The India Exhibition - Richard Timothy Conroy 296
Mr. Smithson's Bones - Richard Timothy Conroy 297

Smokey Brandon
Carcass Trade - Noreen Ayres 74

Spencer Arrowood
The Hangman's Beautiful Daughter - Sharyn McCrumb 1115
She Walks These Hills - Sharyn McCrumb 1119

Spenser
Double Deuce - Robert B. Parker 1269
Stardust - Robert B. Parker 1271
Walking Shadow - Robert B. Parker 1272

Stan Kraychik
A Body to Dye For - Grant Michaels 1150
Love You to Death - Grant Michaels 1151

Stanley Hastings
Juror - Parnell Hall 714
Strangler - Parnell Hall 715

Stanley Moodrow
Bad to the Bone - Stephen Solomita 1532
Force of Nature - Stephen Solomita 1533
A Piece of the Action - Stephen Solomita 1535

Steve Winslow
The Naked Typist - J.P. Hailey 704
The Underground Man - J.P. Hailey 705

Stewart Hoag
The Man Who Cancelled Himself - David Handler 722
The Man Who Would Be F. Scott Fitzgerald - David Handler 723
The Woman Who Fell From Grace - David Handler 724

Stone Angel
The Riviera Contract - Marvin Albert 26
The Zig-Zag Man - Marvin Albert 27

Stoney Winston
Truck Shot - Jim Stinson 1574
TV Safe - Jim Stinson 1575

Suburban Detective
Death by Station Wagon - Jon Katz 869
The Family Stalker - Jon Katz 870

Superintendent Bone
Bone Idle - Susannah Stacey 1553
Grave Responsibility - Susannah Stacey 1554
A Knife at the Opera - Susannah Stacey 1555
The Late Lady - Susannah Stacey 1556

Superintendent Thane
The Interface Man - Bill Knox 948

Susan Henshaw
All Hallows Evil - Valerie Wolzien 1748
A Good Year for a Corpse - Valerie Wolzien 1749
We Wish You a Merry Murder - Valerie Wolzien 1750

Susan Wren
Consider the Crows - Charlene Weir 1685
Family Practice - Charlene Weir 1686
The Winter Widow - Charlene Weir 1687

Sydney Sloane
Sister's Keeper - Randye Lordon 1042

T.S.W. Sheridan
All the Dead Heroes - Stephen F. Wilcox 1718
The Dry White Tear - Stephen F. Wilcox 1719
The Green Mosaic - Stephen F. Wilcox 1720

Tamara Hayle
Devil's Gonna Get Him - Valerie Wilson Wesley 1691
When Death Comes Stealing - Valerie Wilson Wesley 1692

Tamara Hoyland
Faith, Hope and Homicide - Jessica Mann 1071

Tango Key
High Strangeness - Alison Drake 447

Terry Manion
Blue Bayou - Dick Lochte 1038
The Neon Smile - Dick Lochte 1039

Tessa Crichton
Fatal Charm - Anne Morice 1173

Thea Kozak
Death in a Funhouse Mirror - Kate Clark Flora 531

Theodora Braithwaite
Idol Bones - D.M. Greenwood 671
Unholy Ghosts - D.M. Greenwood 672

Theodore Roosevelt
The Strenuous Life - Lawrence Alexander 36

Thomas and Charlotte Pitt
Farrier's Lane - Anne Perry 1294
Highgate Rise - Anne Perry 1295

Thomas Black
The Portland Laugher - Earl Emerson 489
The Vanishing Smile - Earl Emerson 490
Yellow Dog Party - Earl Emerson 491

Thomas Curry and Sandine Cadette
Act of Faith - Michael Bowen 158
Fielder's Choice - Michael Bowen 160

Thomas Theron
Peeping Thomas - Robert Reeves 1358

Thorn
Gone Wild - James W. Hall 708
Mean High Tide - James W. Hall 710

Tiller Galloway
Louisiana Blue - David Poyer 1324

Tillman and Muldoon
Faces in the Crowd - William Marshall 1079
The New York Detective - William Marshall 1080

Tim Simpson
Sheep, Goats and Soap - John Malcolm 1068
The Wrong Impression - John Malcolm 1069

Tim Waverly
Double Down - Tom Kakonis 854
Shadow Counter - Tom Kakonis 855

Tish McWhinny
The Cashmere Kid - B. Comfort 284
Elusive Quarry - B. Comfort 285
Grave Consequences - B. Comfort 286

Toby Peters
The Melting Clock - Stuart M. Kaminsky 860

Tom Bethany
Bear Hug - Jerome Doolittle 432
Body Scissors - Jerome Doolittle 433
Kill Story - Jerome Doolittle 434
Stranglehold - Jerome Doolittle 435

Tom Hickey
The Angel Gang - Ken Kuhlken 956
The Venus Deal - Ken Kuhlken 958

Tom Mason
The Only Good Priest - Mark Richard Zubro 1795
Why Isn't Becky Twitchell Dead? - Mark Richard Zubro 1797

Tony and Pat Pratt
Murder at Musket Beach - Bernie Lee 998
Murder Without Reservation - Bernie Lee 999

Tony Lowell
Eye of the Gator - E.C. Ayres 72
Hour of the Manatee - E.C. Ayres 73

Townsend Reeves
Final Dictation - L.M. Vincent 1655
Pas De Death - L.M. Vincent 1656

Truman Smith
Dead on the Island - Bill Crider 350
Gator Kill - Bill Crider 352
When Old Men Die - Bill Crider 354

V.I. Warshawski
Burn Marks - Sara Paretsky 1264
Guardian Angel - Sara Paretsky 1265
Tunnel Vision - Sara Paretsky 1266

Vic Eton
Dark of Night - Richard Nehrbass 1200

Victoria Bowering
Cancellation by Death - Dorian Yeager 1782
Eviction by Death - Dorian Yeager 1783

Virginia Kelly
In the Game - Nikki Baker 82
The Lavender House Murder - Nikki Baker 83

Wanda Mallory
Prime Time for Murder - Valerie Frankel 542

Werner-Bok Library
A Slip of the Tong - Charles A. Goodrum 611

Willa Jansson
Prior Convictions - Lia Matera 1093

William Monk
Cain His Brother - Anne Perry 1292
A Sudden, Fearful Death - Anne Perry 1296

Willow King
Bitter Herbs - Natasha Cooper 307
Bloody Roses - Natasha Cooper 308
Rotten Apples - Natasha Cooper 309

Wilson and O'Neill
Die in My Dreams - Christine Green 661

Winston Sherman
Deception Island - M.K. Lorens 1043
Dreamland - M.K. Lorens 1044
Sweet Narcissus - M.K. Lorens 1045

Yeadings and Mott
Cat's Cradle - Clare Curzon 366
Death Prone - Clare Curzon 367
Three-Core Lead - Clare Curzon 368

York Mysteries
Sweet Death, Come Softly - Barbara Whitehead 1708

Ziza Todd
Point No-Point - David Willis McCullough 1123

Time Period Index

This index chronologically lists the time settings in which the featured books take place. Main headings refer to a century; where no specific time is given, the headings INDETERMINATE PAST, INDETERMINATE FUTURE, and INDETERMINATE are used. The 18th through 21st centuries are broken down into decades when possible. (Note: 1800s, for example, refers to the first decade of the 19th century.) Featured titles are listed alphabetically beneath time headings, with author names and entry numbers also provided.

14th CENTURY B.C.

Murder in the Place of Anubis - Lynda S. Robinson 1390

6th CENTURY B.C.

The Venus Throw - Steven Saylor 1450

1st CENTURY B.C.

Catalina's Riddle - Steven Saylor 1448
Roman Blood - Steven Saylor 1449
SPQR - John Maddox Roberts 1382

1st CENTURY

The Silver Pigs - Lindsey Davis 394

2nd CENTURY

Roman Nights - Ron Burns 201

4th CENTURY

Thyme of Death - Susan Wittig Albert 33

12th CENTURY

Brother Cadfael's Penance - Ellis Peters 1301
Death Comes as Epiphany - Sharan Newman 1203
The Potter's Field - Ellis Peters 1302
The Summer of the Danes - Ellis Peters 1303

13th CENTURY

Falconer's Crusade - Ian Morson 1175

14th CENTURY

The Apothecary Rose - Candace M. Robb 1375
The Lady Chapel - Candace M. Robb 1376
Murder Wears a Cowl - P.C. Doherty 426
The Nun's Tale - Candace M. Robb 1377
The Prince of Darkness - P.C. Doherty 427

15th CENTURY

The Bishop's Tale - Margaret Frazer 544
The Boy's Tale - Margaret Frazer 545
Death and the Chapman - Kate Sedley 1467
The Eye of God - C.L. Grace 631
The Fate of Princes - P.C. Doherty 424
The Holy Innocents - Kate Sedley 1468
The Masked Man - P.C. Doherty 425
The Plymouth Cloak - Kate Sedley 1469
The Weaver's Tale - Kate Sedley 1470

16th CENTURY

Death of the Duchess - Elizabeth Eyre 512
A Famine of Horses - P.F. Chisholm 243
Frobisher's Savage - Leonard Tourney 1624
The Mad Courtesan - Edward Marston 1081
The Nine Giants - Edward Marston 1082
The Poisoned Chalice - Michael Clynes 264
The Quality of Mercy - Faye Kellerman 883
The Queen's Head - Edward Marston 1083
The Trip to Jerusalem - Edward Marston 1084
The White Rose Murders - Michael Clynes 265

17th CENTURY

A Bone to Pick - Charlaine Harris 731

18th CENTURY

1760s
The Kingsbridge Plot - Maan Meyers 1148

19th CENTURY

Blood Line - Alanna Knight 941
Deadly Beloved - Alanna Knight 942

1800s
Napoleon Must Die - Quinn Fawcett 519

1820s
A Broken Vessel - Kate Ross 1403
Cut to the Quick - Kate Ross 1404

1840s
To Die Like a Gentleman - Bernard Bastable 103

1850s
North Star Conspiracy - Miriam Grace Monfredo 1164

1860s
Cain His Brother - Anne Perry 1292
Death Wore a Diadem - Iona McGregor 1133
MacPherson's Lament - Sharyn McCrumb 1117

1870s
Clively Close: Dead as Dead Can Be - Ann Crowleigh 361
Killing Cousins - Alanna Knight 943

1880s
A Dangerous Mourning - Anne Perry 1293
Death at Gallows Green - Robin Paige 1260
Faces in the Crowd - William Marshall 1079
Good Morning, Irene - Carole Nelson Douglas 440
Highgate Rise - Anne Perry 1295
The New York Detective - William Marshall 1080

1890s
Bertie and the Seven Bodies - Peter Lovesey 1049
Death at Bishop's Keep - Robin Paige 1259
The Disappearance of Edwin Drood - Peter Rowland 1407
Farrier's Lane - Anne Perry 1294

Good Night, Mr. Holmes - Carole Nelson Douglas 441
Irene at Large - Carole Nelson Douglas 442
The Last Camel Died at Noon - Elizabeth Peters 1298
Panama - Eric Zencey 1787
Patently Murder - Ray Harrison 737
The Ripper's Apprentice - Donald Thomas 1610
The Strenuous Life - Lawrence Alexander 36
A Sudden, Fearful Death - Anne Perry 1296
Tincture of Death - Ray Harrison 738

20th CENTURY

Crime, Punishment and Resurrection - Michael Collins 283
In the House of Secret Enemies - George C. Chesbro 241
Whiskey River - Loren D. Estleman 501
Women of Mystery - Cynthia Manson 1073
The Yellow Room Conspiracy - Peter Dickinson 420

1900s
The Beekeeper's Apprentice - Laurie R. King 924
Check-out Time - Kate Kingsbury 928
Death Off Stage - Richard Grayson 655
Diamond Head - Marian J.A. Jackson 834
Eat, Drink and Be Buried - Kate Kingsbury 929
The Glendower Conspiracy - Lloyd Biggle Jr. 131
Room with a Clue - Kate Kingsbury 930
Sister Beneath the Sheet - Gillian Linscott 1029
Stage Fright - Gillian Linscott 1030
The Strange Files of Fremont Jones - Dianne Day 400
The Sunken Treasure - Marian J.A. Jackson 835

1910s
Hanging on the Wire - Gillian Linscott 1028
In the Dead of Winter - Abbey Penn Baker 81
Murder at Fenway Park - Troy Soos 1536
The Seventh Bullet - Daniel D. Victor 1654

1920s
Dead-Stick - L.J. Washburn 1674
Dog Heavies - L.J. Washburn 1675
Escapade - Walter Satterthwait 1438
Miss Lizzie - Walter Satterthwait 1441
A Monstrous Regiment of Women - Laurie R. King 926
Peril under the Palms - K.K. Beck 117
The Shadow of the Shadow - Paco Ignacio Taibo II 1598
The Winter Garden Mystery - Carola Dunn 465

1930s
Bayou City Secrets - Deborah Powell 1323
Black Eye - Neville Steed 1563
The Black Mask Murders - William F. Nolan 1207
Blood and Thunder - Max Allan Collins 276
The Caravaggio Shawl - Samuel R. Steward 1573
Death Squad London - Jack Gerson 579
The Ditched Blonde - Harold Adams 12
Dorothy and Agatha - Gaylord Larsen 984
Fell and Foul Play - John Dickson Carr 221

385

20th Century

Jordon's Showdown - Frank C. Strunk   1583
Jordon's Wager - Frank C. Strunk   1584
The Man Who Missed the Party - Harold Adams   13
Murder by the Numbers - Max Allan Collins   278
Murder, Mystery and Mayhem - Jennifer Carnell   220
The Pale Criminal - Philip Kerr   914
Perchance to Dream - Robert B. Parker   1270
A Perfectly Proper Murder - Harold Adams   14
Saint Mudd - Steve Thayer   1609
Scotch on the Rocks - Howard Browne   183
Stolen Away - Max Allan Collins   280

1940s
Black Out - John Lawton   994
Carnal Hours - Max Allan Collins   277
City of Gold - Len Deighton   410
Deadfall in Berlin - R.D. Zimmerman   1792
Devil in a Blue Dress - Walter Mosley   1176
The Dividing Line - Richard Parrish   1273
The Eagle Has Flown - Jack Higgins   787
The Faust Conspiracy - James Baddock   78
Fell and Foul Play - John Dickson Carr   221
The Lantern Network - Ted Allbeury   37
The Loud Adios - Ken Kuhlken   957
The Melting Clock - Stuart M. Kaminsky   860
Murder in the Post-War World - Max Allan Collins   279
Murder on the Thirteenth - A.E. Eddenden   471
Praetorian - Thomas Gifford   584
Spandau Phoenix - Greg Iles   824
A Time Without Shadows - Ted Allbeury   38
The Venus Deal - Ken Kuhlken   958
With Siberia Comes a Chill - Kirk Mitchell   1161

1950s
The Angel Gang - Ken Kuhlken   956
Clearwater Summer - John E. Keegan   876
Coronation - W.J. Weatherby   1679
Death and the Trumpets of Tuscany - Hazel Wynn Jones   847
L.A. Confidential - James Ellroy   483
A Piece of the Action - Stephen Solomita   1535
A Red Death - Walter Mosley   1177
A Scandal in Belgravia - Robert Barnard   91
Snow Falling on Cedars - David Guterson   692
White Butterfly - Walter Mosley   1178

1960s
Act of Faith - Michael Bowen   158
Black Hornet - James Sallis   1421
Brideprice - J.N. Catanach   226
Fielder's Choice - Michael Bowen   160
Killing Time in Buffalo - Deidre S. Laiken   964
Matrimonial Causes - Peter Corris   327
Motown - Loren D. Estleman   498
The Song Dog - James McClure   1114
Streets of Fire - Thomas H. Cook   306
Tucker's Last Stand - William F. Buckley Jr.   188

1970s
August Ice - Deforest Day   399
Bad Blood - P.M. Carlson   218
Banjo Boy - Vince Kohler   949
Coffin Underground - Gwendoline Butler   204
Deadfall in Berlin - R.D. Zimmerman   1792
The Deer Killers - Gunnard Landers   973
Die Dreaming - Terence Faherty   514
The Gombeen Man - Randy Lee Eickoff   474
The India Exhibition - Richard Timothy Conroy   296
Justice Denied - Robert K. Tanenbaum   1599
Kimura - Robert Davis   395
The Last Good German - Bill Granger   647
The Lost Keats - Terence Faherty   515
The Lynching - Bennie Lee Sinclair   1503
The Masters of the House - Robert Barnard   90
Mr. Smithson's Bones - Richard Timothy Conroy   297
Rising Dog - Vince Kohler   951
Who Shot Longshot Sam? - Paul Engleman   495

1980s
According to St. John - William Babula   77
Act of Love - Joe R. Lansdale   980
Amends for Murder - M.D. Lake   966
The Angel's Share - R.R. Irvine   826
Antipodes - Maria-Antonia Oliver   1236
Axx Goes South - Frederic Huber   817
Babylon South - Jon Cleary   255
Bad Blood - Anthony Bruno   185
Bad Neighbors - Isidore Haiblum   703
The Bandersnatch - Mollie Hardwick   729
Bankroll - Bruce Ducker   450
A Beautiful Place to Die - Philip R. Craig   335
Behind the Fact - Richard Hilary   788
The Beverly Malibu - Katherine V. Forrest   533
Black Cherry Blues - James Lee Burke   193
Black Girl, White Girl - Patricia Moyes   1179
A Black Legend - John Horton   810
Blind Side - William Bayer   105
Blood Lies - Virginia Anderson   52
Blood Rights - Mike Phillips   1314
Bloody Soaps: A Tale of Love and Death in the Afternoon - Jacqueline Babbin   75
Body and Soil - Ralph McInerny   1135
Body of Evidence - David A. Van Meter   1653
The Bone Orchard - Joseph Trigoboff   1628
The Book of Numbers - David Thoreau   1616
The Book of the Dead - Robert Richardson   1365
A Bouquet of Thorns - John Sherwood   1484
The Boy Who Was Buried This Morning - Joseph Hansen   726
Break and Enter - Colin Harrison   735
Bright Shark - Robert Ballard   85
Broken Consort - James Gollin   609
A Brush with Death - Joan Smith   1519
Bum Steer - Nancy Pickard   1316
Burn Marks - Sara Paretsky   1264
Burn Season - John Lantigua   981
Business Unusual - Tim Heald   763
By Death Possessed - Roger Ormerod   1243
By Reason of Insanity - James Neal Harvey   749
The Cambridge Theorem - Tony Cape   217
A Case of Innocence - Douglas J. Keeling   877
The Cat Who Talked to Ghosts - Lilian Jackson Braun   168
The Chartreuse Clue - William F. Love   1048
Chasing Eights - Michael Collins   282
The Cheerio Killings - Douglas Allyn   47
Children's Games - Janet LaPierre   982
A Chill Wind in January - L.R. Wright   1772
Clockwork - Neville Steed   1565
Close-Up on Death - Maureen O'Brien   1213
Closing Costs - Thomas Bunn   189
A Collector of Photographs - Deborah Valentine   1645
The Comic Book Killer - Richard A. Lupoff   1055
Condition Purple - Peter Turnbull   1639
The Cords of Vanity - Miles Tripp   1149
Count the Days - Lin Summerfield   1592
Crossed Swords - Sean Flannery   528
The Cut Throat - Simon Michael   1149
Dangerous Conceits - Margaret Moore   1168
The Daphne Decisions - Meg O'Brien   1214
Dark Star - Marcia Muller   1180
Darkness Falls - Joyce Anne Schneider   1453
Dead by Morning - Dorothy Simpson   1502
Dead Fix - Michael Geller   573
Dead Men Don't Marry - Dorothy Sucher   1588
The Dead of Winter - Michael Allegretto   40
Dead on Time - H.R.F. Keating   874
The Dead Pull Hitter - Alison Gordon   612
Dead Winter - William G. Tapply   1602
Deadly Crescendo - Paul Myers   1191
Deadly Resolutions - Anna Ashwood Collins   274
Deadly Sonata - Paul Myers   1192
Deadly Stakes - H. Fred Wiser   1745
Death and the Chaste Apprentice - Robert Barnard   89
A Death Before Dying - Collin Wilcox   1712
A Death in a Town - Hillary Waugh   1678
Death in Close-Up - Nancy Livingston   1034
Death in Verona - Roy Harley Lewis   1020
Death Notice - M.S. Karl   866
Death of a Fantasy Life - T.G. Gilpin   590
Death of a Hollow Man - Caroline Graham   641
Death of a Perfect Wife - M.C. Beaton   112
Death on the Mississippi - Richard Forrest   535
Deep Chill - Ian Slater   1513
A Deepe Coffyn - Janet Laurence   988
Deficit Ending - Lee Martin   1088
The Desert Look - Bernard Schopen   1455
Devices and Desires - P.D. James   841
Diamond in the Buff - Susan Dunlap   461
Die Dreaming - Terence Faherty   514
A Diet to Die For - Joan Hess   776
Dover and the Claret Tappers - Joyce Porter   1322
Dream of Darkness - Patrick Ruell   1412
Dropshot: A Brad Smith Novel - Jack Bickham   129
Drowned Hopes - Donald E. Westlake   1698
The Dry White Tear - Stephen F. Wilcox   1719
Dying Voices - Bill Crider   351
Earth Angels - Gerald Petievich   1311
An Easy Thing - Paco Ignacio Taibo II   1597
Emma Chizzit and the Queen Anne Killer - Mary Bowen Hall   713
The Estuary Pilgrim - Douglas Skeggs   1507
Everything but the Squeal - Timothy Hallinan   716
Exit Wounds - John Westermann   1696
The Eye of Anna - Anne Wingate   1741
F Is for Fugitive - Sue Grafton   634
False Profit - Robert Eversz   511
A Fatal Advent - Isabelle Holland   797
Fatal Charm - Anne Morice   1173
Fatal Obsession - D.B. Taylor   1606
Final Dictation - L.M. Vincent   1655
Final Option - Stephen Robinett   1389
The Fireman - Stephen Leather   997
Flame - John Lutz   1057
Flamingo - Bob Reiss   1359
The Flip Side of Life - James E. Martin   1085
Force of Nature - Stephen Solomita   1533
Four Steps to Death - Diana Ramsay   1346
The Fourth Durango - Ross Thomas   1612
Friends till the End - Gloria Dank   387
Frozen Assets - James Leasor   996
Frozen Stare - Richard B. Schwartz   1459
Full Cleveland - Les Roberts   1386
Funnelweb - Charles West   1693
G Is for Gumshoe - Sue Grafton   635
The Glade Manor Murder - Elizabeth Lemarchand   1001
The Gladstone Bag - Charlotte MacLeod   1063
The Going Down of the Sun - Jo Bannister   87
The Gold Coast - Nelson DeMille   412
The Good Fight - Lia Matera   1091
Good Night, Sweet Prince - Carole Berry   126
Gospel Truths - J.G. Sandom   1429
Grave Consequences - B. Comfort   286
The Great Grave Robbery - John Minahan   1158
Gunpower - Mark Schorr   1456
Half a Mind - Wendy Hornsby   807
Hallowed Murder - Ellen Hart   745
The Harbinger Effect - S.K. Wolf   1746
Hardball - Barbara D'Amato   384
Help Wanted: Orphans Preferred - Earl Emerson   487
Hide and Seek - Barry Berg   122
Hit and Run - Maxine O'Callaghan   1219
Holy Treasure! - David Williams   1729
Honolulu Red - Lue Zimmelman   1789
The Honourable Detective - Jeffrey Ashford   67
The Horse Latitudes - Robert Ferrigno   526
Hot Shots - Laurence Gough   627
Houston in the Rearview Mirror - Susan Rogers Cooper   314
Hush, Money - Jean Femling   523
The Iciest Sin - H.R.F. Keating   875
If Ever I Return, Pretty Peggy-O - Sharyn McCrumb   1116
The Immediate Prospect of Being Hanged - Walter Walker   1662
Indecent Behavior - Caryl Rivers   1372

Time Period Index — 20th Century

The Interface Man - Bill Knox 948
Jackpot - Bill Pronzini 1328
Katwalk - Karen Kijewski 920
Kill the Messenger - Elizabeth Daniels Squire 1546
A Killing in Venture Capital - Margaret Logan 1040
The Killing Man - Mickey Spillane 1540
King of the Hustlers - Eugene Izzi 831
A Knife at the Opera - Susannah Stacey 1555
Landscape of Lies - Peter Watson 1676
The Language of Cannibals - George C. Chesbro 242
The Lantern Network - Ted Allbeury 37
Larkspur - Sheila Simonson 1500
Last Dance in Redondo Beach - Michael J. Katz 872
The Last Page - Bob Fenster 524
The Last Surprise - William Moore 1169
Lautrec - Norman Zollinger 1794
Letting Blood - Richard Platt 1321
The Lion at the Door - Newton Thornburg 1617
A Little Class on Murder - Carolyn G. Hart 743
A Little Neighborhood Murder - A.J. Orde 1241
Long Chain of Death - S.K. Wolf 1747
A Loose Connection - M.R.D. Meek 1139
Loose Lips - Jon L. Breen 171
Love Lies Slain - L.L. Blackmur 139
The Man in the Moon - Frank Norwood 1212
The Man Who Walked Like a Bear - Stuart M. Kaminsky 859
The Man Who Walked Through Walls - James Swain 1595
Manhattan Is My Beat - Jeffrey Wilds Deaver 404
The Mark Twain Murders - Edith Skom 1512
Masquerade - William X. Kienzle 916
The Maya Stone Murders - M.K. Shuman 1494
Medicine Dog - Geoff Peterson 1307
Mercy - David L. Lindsey 1027
Merry Christmas, Murdock - Robert J. Ray 1352
Milk and Honey - Faye Kellerman 882
Minor in Possession - J.A. Jance 844
Missing Man - Richard Martin Stern 1570
Money to Burn - Michael Hendricks 772
Monsieur Pamplemousse Investigates - Michael Bond 151
The Mooncalf Murders - Noel Vreeland Carter 222
The Mother Shadow - Melodie Johnson Howe 814
Mrs. Malory Investigates - Hazel Holt 802
Mrs. Pollifax and the Whirling Dervish - Dorothy Gilman 588
Murder at Musket Beach - Bernie Lee 998
Murder at the Kennedy Center - Margaret Truman 1634
Murder Begins at Home - Dale L. Gilbert 585
Murder by the Book - Pat Welch 1689
Murder Has a Pretty Face - Jennie Melville 1142
Murder in a Cold Climate - Scott Young 1785
Murder in Burgundy - Audrey Peterson 1305
Murder in Focus - Medora Sale 1418
Murder in Gray and White - Corinne Holt Sawyer 1447
Murder in Store - D.C. Brod 178
Murder Times Two - Haughton Murphy 1186
Murphy's Fault - Steven Womack 1752
Musical Chairs - Kinky Friedman 555
My First Murder - Susan Baker 84
The Naked Eye - William J. Reynolds 1364
Naked Once More - Elizabeth Peters 1300
Neon Caesar - Mark McGarrity 1128
New Orleans Mourning - Julie Smith 1528
Nibbled to Death by Ducks - Robert Campbell 213
Night Angel - Kate Green 664
Night of Reunion - Michael Allegretto 42
Night Rituals - Gary Paulsen 1279
Nightwalker - Sidney Filson 527
No Way Home - Patricia MacDonald 1062
Nobody Lives Forever - Edna Buchanan 187
The Noose of Time - Stephen Murray 1189
Not as Far as Velma - Nicholas Freeling 548
Not Long for This World - Gar Anthony Haywood 762

The Old Silent - Martha Grimes 676
On the Edge - Ed Naha 1193
On the Inside - Ted Wood 1757
Once and Always Murder - Orania Papazoglou 1263
One Cried Murder - David Cooper Wall 1663
Out on the Cutting Edge - Lawrence Block 148
Paint It Black - W.R. Philbrick 1313
Park Lane South, Queens - Mary Anne Kelly 890
Passion Play - W. Edward Blain 140
Payment in Blood - Elizabeth George 576
Peeper - Loren D. Estleman 499
Personal - C.K. Cambray 208
Philly Stakes - Gillian Roberts 1379
Picture Postcard - Fredrick D. Huebner 819
Pious Deception - Susan Dunlap 462
Play Dead - Harlan Coben 266
Playing God - Barbara Whitehead 1707
Polar Star - Martin Cruz Smith 1530
Postmortem - Patricia D. Cornwell 326
Predator's Waltz - Jay Brandon 165
Pressure Drop - Peter Abrahams 5
Probable Cause - Ridley Pearson 1285
A Question of Guilt - Frances Fyfield 562
Quiller KGB - Adam Hall 706
Rainy North Woods - Vince Kohler 950
The Ransom of Black Stealth One - Dean Ing 825
Raptor - Judith Van Gieson 1651
Reasonable Doubt - Philip Friedman 558
Red Winter - Michael Cormany 319
Report for Murder - Val McDermid 1126
Rough Justice - Keith Peterson 1309
Rules of Prey - John Sandford 1425
The Run Around - Brian Freemantle 550
Running Fix - Tony Gibbs 582
The Russia House - John Le Carre 995
Sanibel Flats - Randy Wayne White 1704
The Scarred Man - Keith Peterson 1310
Screaming Bones - Pat Burden 191
See No Evil - Edward Mathis 1095
Selena - Gordon Randolph Willey 1726
A Sensitive Case - Eric Wright 1770
A Series of Murders - Simon Brett 176
Shadow Dance - Agnes Bushnell 202
Shadowchase - Martin Blank 143
The Shape of Dread - Marcia Muller 1181
Sight Unseen - David Lorne 1046
The Sirens Sang of Murder - Sarah Caudwell 228
Skeleton-in-Waiting - Peter Dickinson 419
Skeletons - Eric Sauter 1443
Skin Tight - Carl Hiaasen 783
The Skintight Shroud - Wayne Dundee 459
A Small and Incidental Murder - John Walter Putre 1337
South Street Confidential - Dick Belsky 120
Spandau Phoenix - Greg Iles 824
Spare Change - John A. Peak 1280
The Spoils of Time - June Thomson 1614
Stalking the Angel - Robert Crais 343
Stardust - Robert B. Parker 1271
The Stone Hawk - Gwen Moffat 1163
Stone Shadow - Rex Miller 1154
The Stone Veil - Ronald Tierney 1621
Straight - Dick Francis 541
Strangler - Parnell Hall 715
Strikezone - David F. Nighbert 1206
Suicide Squeeze - David Everson 510
A Suitable Vengeance - Elizabeth George 578
A Suitcase in Berlin - Don Flynn 532
Sunshine Enemies - K.C. Constantine 298
Sweet Narcissus - M.K. Lorens 1045
Swindle - George Adams 11
The Talinin Madonna - Douglas Skeggs 1508
Talking God - Tony Hillerman 793
Teardown - Victor Wuamett 1779
The Temple Dogs - Warren Murphy 1188
A Temporary Ghost - Mickey Friedman 556
This Way Out - Sheila Radley 1343
Three-Core Lead - Clare Curzon 368
A Ticket to the Boneyard - Lawrence Block 149
The Tijuana Bible - Ron Goulart 630

Time and Time Again - B.M. Gill 587
Time Exposure - John Lutz 1060
A Time for Dying - Jonathan Ross 1402
A Time Without Shadows - Ted Allbeury 38
Time's Witness - Michael Malone 1070
To Catch a Forger - Robert Wallace 1666
To Killashea - Norman Flood 530
The Toy Cupboard - Lee Jordan 848
Truck Shot - Jim Stinson 1574
Twilight at Mac's Place - Ross Thomas 1613
Unbalanced Acts - Jeff Raines 1344
The Underground Man - J.P. Hailey 705
Undue Influence - Miriam Borgenicht 153
Unfunny Money - Gary Alexander 35
Unknown Hand - Gillian Linscott 1031
Unnatural Hazard - Barry Cork 317
Unorthodox Practices - Marissa Piesman 1320
User Deadly - Denise Danks 388
A Very Particular Murder - S.T. Haymon 759
Vespers - Ed McBain 1107
A Violent End - Emma Page 1253
Virgil's Ghost - Irving Weinman 1684
The Wench Is Dead - Colin Dexter 418
White Rook - J. Madison Davis 392
Why Isn't Becky Twitchell Dead? - Mark Richard Zubro 1797
A Wicked Slice - Aaron Elkins 480
Win, Lose or Die - John Gardner 567
With Extreme Prejudice - Frederick Barton 102
Wolf in Sheep's Clothing - John R. Riggs 1369
Work for a Dead Man - Simon Ritchie 1371
Worse than Death - Thomas Bunn 190
A Wreath for the Bride - Lillian O'Donnell 1229
The Wrong Impression - John Malcolm 1069
Yesterday's News - Jeremiah Healy 766

1990s

The 6 Messiahs - Mark Frost 560
19th Precinct - Christopher Newman 1202
The 27 Ingredient Chili Con Carne Murders - Nancy Pickard 1315
32 Cadillacs - Joe Gores 616
An Absence of Light - David L. Lindsey 1026
Act of God - Jeremiah Healy 764
Adjusted to Death - Jaqueline Girdner 593
Against the Wind - J.F. Freedman 547
Agatha Raisin and the Quiche of Death - M.C. Beaton 107
Agatha Raisin and the Vicious Vet - M.C. Beaton 108
Ah, Sweet Mystery - Celestine Sibley 1495
Ah, Treachery - Ross Thomas 1611
Alibi for an Actress - Gillian B. Farrell 516
All Around the Town - Mary Higgins Clark 252
All Hallows Evil - Valerie Wolzien 1748
All I Have Is Blue - James Colbert 272
All Shall Be Well - Deborah Crombie 356
All That Remains - Patricia D. Cornwell 321
All the Dead Heroes - Stephen F. Wilcox 1718
All the Great Pretenders - Deborah Adams 10
Alley Kat Blues - Karen Kijewski 917
Along Came a Spider - James Patterson 1276
The Alpine Advocate - Mary Daheim 370
The Alpine Christmas - Mary Daheim 371
The Alpine Decoy - Mary Daheim 372
The Alpine Fury - Mary Daheim 373
Amateur Night - K.K. Beck 114
And Baby Makes None - Stephen Lewis 1022
And Justice for One - John Clarkson 254
And Leave Her Lay Dying - John Lawrence Reynolds 1362
And Soon I'll Come to Kill You - Susan Kelly 893
The Angel Maker - Ridley Pearson 1282
Angel of Death - Jack Higgins 786
Angel of Death - Rochelle Majer Krich 953
Angel's Bidding - Sharon Gwyn Short 1489
The Animal Hour - Andrew Klavan 935
Artichoke Hearts - Victor Wuamett 1777
At Ease with the Dead - Walter Satterthwait 1437
Aunt Dimity and the Duke - Nancy Atherton 68
Aunt Dimity's Death - Nancy Atherton 69

20th Century — What Mystery Do I Read Next?

Avenging Angel - Anthony Appiah 64
The Axeman's Jazz - Julie Smith 1523
Backhand - Liza Cody 269
Bad Apple - Anthony Bruno 184
Bad Chemistry - Nora Kelly 891
Bad Desire - Gary Devon 417
Bad Love - Jonathan Kellerman 885
Bad Moon - Anthony Bruno 186
Bad News Travels Fast - Gar Anthony Haywood 761
Bad to the Bone - Stephen Solomita 1532
The Bag Man - Peter Lacey 961
Bagels for Tea - Serita Stevens 1571
Bagged - Jo Bailey 79
Bait - Kenneth Abel 3
Balboa Firefly - Jack Trolley 1633
Bantam of the Opera - Mary Daheim 374
Baptism for Murder - Jan Maxwell 1101
Barking Dogs - R.R. Irvine 827
Bear Hug - Jerome Doolittle 432
Beat Up a Cookie - Denise Dietz 422
Beauty Dies - Melodie Johnson Howe 813
The Becket Factor - Michael David Anthony 60
Beggar's Choice - Jerry Kennealy 906
Behind Eclaire's Doors - Sophie Dunbar 457
Berlin Covenant - Celeste Paul 1278
Bet Against the House - Catherine Dain 378
Big Fish - Ken Grissom 682
The Big Freeze - Michael J. Katz 871
Bigfoot - Richard Hoyt 815
Bino's Blues - A.W. Gray 650
Bird in a Cage - Lee Martin 1086
Birthmarks - Sarah Dunant 455
A Bite of Death - Susan Conant 287
Bitter Herbs - Natasha Cooper 307
Bitter Recoil - Steven F. Havill 757
The Black Echo - Michael Connelly 292
The Black Ice - Michael Connelly 293
Black Light - Daniel Hearn 767
Black Ribbon - Susan Conant 288
Blanche on the Lam - Barbara Neely 1198
Bleeding Dodger Blue - Crabbe Evers 505
Blindsight - Robin Cook 302
A Blood Affair - Jan Roberts 1381
Blood Kin - Marjorie Dorner 436
Blood Marks - Bill Crider 349
Blood Music - Jessie Prichard Hunter 821
Blood of an Aries - Linda Mather 1094
Blood of Poets - Kenn Davis 393
Blood on the Bayou - D.J. Donaldson 429
Blood on the Street - Annette Meyers 1146
Blood Relative - Michael Allegretto 39
Blood Relative - Carolyn Hougan 811
Blood Trance - R.D. Zimmerman 1791
Blood Type - Stephen Greenleaf 667
Bloodlines - Susan Conant 289
Bloody Roses - Natasha Cooper 308
Bloody Ten - William F. Love 1047
Blooming Murder - Jean Hager 698
Blossom - Andrew Vachss 1643
Blue Bayou - Dick Lochte 1038
Blue Lonesome - Bill Pronzini 1325
The Bluejay Shaman - Lise McClendon Webb 1680
The Body Farm - Patricia D. Cornwell 322
Body Guard - Rex Burns 199
The Body in Blackwater Bay - Paula Gosling 624
The Body in the Basement - Katherine Hall Page 1254
The Body in the Belfry - Katherine Hall Page 1255
The Body in the Bouillon - Katherine Hall Page 1256
The Body in the Cast - Katherine Hall Page 1257
The Body in the Transept - Jeanne M. Dams 385
The Body in the Vestibule - Katherine Hall Page 1258
Body of Evidence - Patricia D. Cornwell 323
The Body Politic - Catherine Aird 25
Body Scissors - Jerome Doolittle 433
A Body to Dye For - Grant Michaels 1150
Boiled in Concrete - Jesse Sublett 1587

Boiling Rock - Remar Sutton 1594
Bone Idle - Susannah Stacey 1553
A Bone to Pick - Charlaine Harris 731
Bones and Silence - Reginald Hill 789
Bones Gather No Moss - John Sherwood 1483
Bones of Coral - James W. Hall 707
Book Case - Stephen Greenleaf 668
Booked to Die - John Dunning 466
The Bookman's Wake - John Dunning 467
Bootlegger's Daughter - Margaret Maron 1076
Borderlines - Archer Mayor 1103
The Boss's Wife - S.L. Stebel 1562
Box Nine - Jack O'Connell 1223
Boxed In - Neville Steed 1564
A Brace of Skeet - Gerald Hammond 719
Breach of Promise - Roy Hart 748
Breakdown - Bill Pronzini 1326
The Bridled Groom - J.S. Borthwick 154
Bucket Nut - Liza Cody 270
The Bulrush Murders - Rebecca Rothenberg 1405
The Burglar Who Traded Ted Williams - Lawrence Block 145
Buried in Quilts - Sara Hoskinson Frommer 559
Buried in Stone - Eric Wright 1766
Burning Angel - James Lee Burke 194
Burning March - Neil Albert 28
Bury the Bishop - Kate Gallison 564
But I Wouldn't Want to Die There - Nancy Pickard 1317
The Buzzards Must Also Be Fed - Anne Wingate 1739
By Evil Means - Sandra West Prowell 1332
The Cactus Garden - Robert Ward 1672
The Caesar Clue - M.K. Shuman 1491
Called by a Panther - Michael Z. Lewin 1019
Called Home - R.R. Irvine 828
Came a Dead Cat - James N. Frey 551
Cancellation by Death - Dorian Yeager 1782
Capitol Offense - Tony Gibbs 580
Carcass Trade - Noreen Ayres 74
Carolina Gold - Douglas McBriarty 1108
A Case of Vineyard Poisoning - Philip R. Craig 336
The Cashmere Kid - B. Comfort 284
Cassandra in Red - Michael Collins 281
Casual Slaughters - Robert A. Carter 223
Casualty Loss - Jim Weikart 1683
Cat Crimes - Ed Gorman 619
Cat Crimes II - Ed Gorman 620
A Cat in a Glass House - Lydia Adamson 15
A Cat in Fine Style - Lydia Adamson 16
A Cat in the Manger - Lydia Adamson 17
A Cat in the Wings - Lydia Adamson 18
A Cat in Wolf's Clothing - Lydia Adamson 19
Cat on a Blue Monday - Carole Nelson Douglas 438
A Cat on the Cutting Edge - Lydia Adamson 20
The Cat Who Moved a Mountain - Lilian Jackson Braun 167
The Cat Who Went into the Closet - Lilian Jackson Braun 169
The Catalyst - Desmond Cory 330
Catnap - Carole Nelson Douglas 439
Cat's Cradle - Clare Curzon 366
Cat's Paw, Inc. - L.L. Thrasher 1618
Caught in the Shadows - C.A. Haddad 694
Caught Looking - Randy Russell 1416
The Cavalier Case - Antonia Fraser 543
The Caveman's Valentine - George Dawes Green 662
The Cereal Murders - Diane Mott Davidson 389
A Certain Justice - John T. Lescroart 1008
Chain of Evidence - Ridley Pearson 1283
The Chamber - John Grisham 679
Chameleon - William X. Kienzle 915
Charged with Guilt - Gloria White 1700
The Cheetah Chase - Karin McQuillan 1137
The Chesapeake Project - Phyllis Horn 806
The Cheshire Moon - Robert Ferrigno 525
Child of Silence - Abigail Padgett 1251
China Lake - Anthony Hyde 823

China Trade - S.J. Rozan 1410
The Choice - Barry Reed 1357
The Christening Day Murder - Lee Harris 733
The Christie Caper - Carolyn G. Hart 741
The Christmas Night Murder - Lee Harris 734
Circumstances Unknown - Jonellen Heckler 769
City of God - Michael Jahn 840
City of Lies - Peter McCabe 1109
A City of Strangers - Robert Barnard 88
The City When It Rains - Thomas H. Cook 305
The Class Menagerie - Jill Churchill 244
The Classic Car Killer - Richard A. Lupoff 1054
A Clean Sweep - David Berlinski 123
A Clear Case of Murder - Warwick Downing 445
Clear-Cut Murder - Lee Wallingford 1667
Clerical Errors - D.M. Greenwood 670
The Cleveland Connection - Les Roberts 1383
The Client - John Grisham 680
Cliff Hanger - Philip R. Craig 337
A Clinic for Murder - Marsha Landreth 974
Close Quarters - Marissa Piesman 1319
Close Softly the Doors - Ronald Clair Roat 1373
Clubbed to Death - Ruth Dudley Edwards 472
The Codicil - Tom Topor 1623
Coffin on Murder Street - Gwendoline Butler 203
A Cold-Blooded Business - Dana Stabenow 1550
Cold Call - Dianne G. Pugh 1333
Cold Comfort - M.D. Lake 967
A Cold Day for Murder - Dana Stabenow 1549
Cold Feet - Kerry Tucker 1636
Cold in the Earth - Ann Granger 642
Cold Light - John Harvey 751
Cold Tracks - Lee Wallingford 1668
Come to Grief - Dick Francis 538
Comeback - Dick Francis 539
Compelling Evidence - Steve Martini 1090
The Concrete Blonde - Michael Connelly 294
Concrete Hero - Rob Kantner 862
Cons - Timothy Watts 1677
Consider the Crows - Charlene Weir 1685
Cooking Up Trouble - Joanne Pence 1289
A Cool Breeze on the Underground - Don Winslow 1743
Copy Cat Crimes - Karen Ann Wilson 1733
Copy Kat - Karen Kijewski 918
Corona Blue - J.F. Trainor 1625
Corporate Bodies - Simon Brett 174
Corruption - Andrew Klavan 936
Cotswold Moles - Michael Spicer 1539
A Country of Old Men - Joseph Hansen 727
The Covenant of the Flame - David Morrell 1174
Cover Story - Robert Cullen 365
Coyote - Linda Barnes 92
Crack Down - Val McDermid 1125
Criminal Conversation - Evan Hunter 820
Criminal Seduction - Darian North 1211
Crossover - Judith Eubank 502
Cruel and Unusual - Patricia D. Cornwell 324
Cruel April - Neil Albert 29
The Cruellest Month - Hazel Holt 800
Cry for Help - Karen Hanson Stuyck 1586
The Curious Eat Themselves - John Straley 1580
Curly Smoke - Susan Holtzer 803
Cut To—Murder - Denise Osborne 1247
Cutter - Laura Crum 362
Cutting Edge - John Harvey 752
The Cutting Hours - Julia Grice 673
The Dallas Deception - Richard Abshire 7
A Dance at the Slaughterhouse - Lawrence Block 146
Dancing in the Dark - Sharon Zukowski 1798
Dangerous Attachments - Sarah Lovett 1051
Dangerous Waters - Bill Eidson 475
The Dante Game - Jane Langton 979
Dark of Night - Richard Nehrbass 1200
Dark Provenance - Michael David Anthony 61
Dark Swan - Kathryn Lasky Knight 944
A Dash of Death - Claudia Bishop 134
Date with a Dead Doctor - Toni Brill 177
A Day in the Death of Dorothea Cassidy - Ann Cleeves 260

Time Period Index — 20th Century

Day of Atonement - Faye Kellerman 878
Day of the Cheetah - Dale Brown 179
The Day That Dusty Died - Lee Martin 1087
Dead Ahead - Ruby Horansky 804
Dead and Buried - Jean Hager 699
Dead Before Morning - Geraldine Evans 504
Dead Center - Ruby Horansky 805
Dead Center - Collin Wilcox 1711
Dead Easy - Arthur F. Nehrbass 1199
Dead Easy - E.S. Russell 1415
Dead Fit - Stephen Cook 304
Dead Folks' Blues - Steven Womack 1751
Dead in the Cellar - Connie Fedderson 520
Dead in the Scrub - B.J. Oliphant 1232
Dead in the Water - W.J. Chaput 233
Dead in the Water - Julie Smith 1524
Dead in the Water - Dana Stabenow 1551
Dead Man - Joe Gores 617
Dead Man's Island - Carolyn G. Hart 742
Dead Matter - M.K. Wren 1764
Dead Meat - Philip Kerr 913
Dead Men's Hearts - Aaron Elkins 476
Dead Moon on the Rise - Susan Rogers Cooper 310
The Dead of Brooklyn - Robert J. Randisi 1347
Dead on the Island - Bill Crider 350
Dead Pan - Jane Dentinger 413
Dead Ringer - Toni L.P. Kelner 900
Dead Set - Jennie Melville 1141
Dead Time - Eleanor Taylor Bland 141
Dead Wrong - Alan Dennis Burke 192
Deadeye - Sam Llewellyn 1037
The Deadliest Option - Annette Meyers 1147
Deadline - Gerry Boyle 163
Deadline - D.F. Mills 1157
Deadly Admirer - Christine Green 658
Deadly Errand - Christine Green 659
Deadly Practice - Christine Green 660
Deadly Secrets on the St. Johns - Patricia Houck Sprinkle 1542
Deadstick - Terence Faherty 513
Deal to Die For - Les Standiford 1560
The Dean It Was That Died - Barbara Whitehead 1706
Death Among the Angels - John Walter Putre 1336
Death Among the Dons - Janet Neel 1196
Death and Judgment - Donna Leon 1002
Death and Other Lovers - Jo Bannister 86
Death and Taxes - Susan Dunlap 460
Death and the Delinquent - B.J. Oliphant 1233
Death and the Dogwalker - A.J. Orde 1240
Death and the Oxford Box - Veronica Stallwood 1557
Death as a Career Move - Bruce Cook 299
Death at La Fenice - Donna Leon 1003
Death Below Deck - Douglas Kiker 922
Death Beneath the Christmas Tree - Robert Nordan 1208
Death Benefits - Michael A. Kahn 851
Death by Degrees - Robin Wilson 1735
Death by Degrees - Eric Wright 1767
Death by Station Wagon - Jon Katz 869
Death Came Dressed in White - Michael W. Sherer 1481
Death Down Home - Eve K. Sandstrom 1430
Death Echo - Kerry Tucker 1637
A Death for a Dancing Doll - E.X. Giroux 597
A Death for a Dodo - E.X. Giroux 598
Death Goes on Retreat - Sister Carol Anne O'Marie 1237
Death in a Funhouse Mirror - Kate Clark Flora 531
Death in a Serene City - Edward Sklepowich 1510
Death in a Strange Country - Donna Leon 1004
Death in Deep Water - Paul Kemprecos 903
Death in Disguise - Caroline Graham 640
Death in Uptown - Michael Raleigh 1345
Death of a Charming Man - M.C. Beaton 109
Death of a Dancing Fool - Carole Berry 124
The Death of a Difficult Woman - Carole Berry 125
Death of a DJ - Jane Rubino 1411

Death of a Hussy - M.C. Beaton 110
Death of a Nag - M.C. Beaton 111
Death of a Partner - Janet Neel 1197
Death of a Postmodernist - Janice Steinberg 1568
Death of a Traveling Man - M.C. Beaton 113
Death of the Office Witch - Marlys Millhiser 1155
Death on Rough Water - Francine Matthews 1099
Death on Wheels - Robert Nordan 1209
Death Penalties - Paula Gosling 625
Death Prone - Clare Curzon 367
Death Qualified: A Mystery of Chaos - Kate Wilhelm 1723
Death Served Up Cold - B.J. Oliphant 1234
Death Underfoot - Dennis Casley 225
Death Watch - Cynthia Harrod-Eagles 740
The Death We Share - Sharon Gwyn Short 1490
Deathics - Richard Barth 100
Deathspell - Veronica Stallwood 1558
Deception Island - M.K. Lorens 1043
Decked - Carol Higgins Clark 250
A Dedicated Man - Peter Robinson 1392
Deeds of Trust - Victor Wuamett 1778
A Deep Disturbance - Constance Rauch 1351
The Deep End - Chris Crutcher 364
Deep End - Geoffrey Norman 1210
Deep Kill - M.K. Shuman 1492
Deep Shaker - Les Roberts 1384
Deep Sleep - Frances Fyfield 561
Deerslayer - M.S. Karl 867
Desert Heat - J.A. Jance 842
Desperate Remedy - Mary Kittredge 931
Detective First Grade - Don Mahoney 1067
Deviant Way - Richard Montanari 1166
The Devil Down Home - Eve K. Sandstrom 1431
The Devil Knows You're Dead - Lawrence Block 147
Devil's Gonna Get Him - Valerie Wilson Wesley 1691
Diamond Eyes - John Lutz 1056
Die in My Dreams - Christine Green 661
Dire Happenings at Scratch Ankle - Celestine Sibley 1496
Disassociated States - Leonard Simon 1499
Divorcing Jack - Colin Bateman 104
Dixie City Jam - James Lee Burke 195
Do Unto Others - Jeff Abbott 1
The Dobie Paradox - Desmond Cory 331
Dr. Nightingale Goes the Distance - Lydia Adamson 21
Dr. Nightingale Rides the Elephant - Lydia Adamson 22
Doctors, Lawyers and Such - Susan Rogers Cooper 311
The Dog Hermit - David Stout 1578
Dogtown - Mercedes Lambert 972
Done Deal - Les Standiford 1561
Don't Ask - Donald E. Westlake 1697
Don't Leave Me This Way - Joan Smith 1520
Don't Say a Word - Andrew Klavan 937
Don't Say a Word - Keith Peterson 1308
Double Blind - David Laing 965
Double Deuce - Robert B. Parker 1269
Double Down - Tom Kakonis 854
The Double Minded Men - Philip R. Craig 338
Double Plot - Leo Axler 70
Down by the Sea - Bill Kent 910
The Down Home Heifer Heist - Eve K. Sandstrom 1432
Down Home Murder - Toni L.P. Kelner 901
A Dragon Lives Forever - John R. Riggs 1368
Dreamboat - Doug J. Swanson 1596
Dreamland - M.K. Lorens 1044
Dreamsicle - W.L. Ripley 1370
A Drink Before the War - Dennis Lehane 1000
A Drink of Deadly Wine - Kate Charles 235
Drover and the Zebras - Bill Granger 646
Drown All the Dogs - Thomas Adcock 23
Drowned Man's Key - Ken Grissom 683
A Dry and Thirsty Ground - Mike Weiss 1688
Due Diligence - Michael A. Kahn 852
The Duke of Cleveland - Les Roberts 1385

Dust Devils of the Purple Sage - Barbara Burnett Smith 1516
Dying for Chocolate - Diane Mott Davidson 390
The Dying of the Light - Robert Richardson 1366
The Dying Room - E.X. Giroux 599
Dynamite Pass - J.F. Trainor 1626
Eagles Die Too - Meg O'Brien 1215
East Beach - Ron Ely 485
East Is East - Emma Lathen 986
Edge City - Sin Soracco 1537
The Edge of Sleep - David Wiltse 1736
The Edge of the Crazies - Jamie Harrison 736
Eight Dogs Flying - Karen Ann Wilson 1734
Elective Murder - Janet McGiffin 1129
Electric City - K.K. Beck 115
Elegy in a Country Graveyard - Audrey Peterson 1304
Elsinore - Jerome Charyn 238
Elusive Quarry - B. Comfort 285
The Emerald Lizard - Chris Wiltz 1738
Emma Chizzit and the Mother Lode Marauder - Mary Bowen Hall 711
Emma Chizzit and the Napa Nemesis - Mary Bowen Hall 712
The Empress File - John Camp 210
Encore Murder - Marian Babson 76
End Game - Dev Stryker 1585
The End of the Pier - Martha Grimes 674
Enemy's Enemy - Jan Guillou 685
Epitaphs - Bill Pronzini 1327
Even the Butler Was Poor - Ron Goulart 628
Every Breath You Take - Michelle Spring 1541
Every Crooked Nanny - Kathy Hogan Trocheck 1631
Everything You Have Is Mine - Sandra Scoppettone 1460
Eviction by Death - Dorian Yeager 1783
Except for the Bones - Collin Wilcox 1713
Exception to Murder - Anne Wingate 1740
Exceptional Clearance - William J. Caunitz 229
Exhaustive Enquiries - Betty Rowlands 1408
Eye of the Gator - E.C. Ayres 72
Fade to Black - Robert Goldsborough 607
Fair Game - Rochelle Majer Krich 954
Faith, Hope and Homicide - Jessica Mann 1071
Faithfully Executed - Michael Bowen 159
The Fall-Down Artist - Thomas Lipinski 1032
Fall From Grace - L.R. Wright 1773
A Fall in Denver - Sarah Andrews 56
The Fall Line - Mark T. Sullivan 1589
False Faces - Seth Jacob Margolis 1074
False Profits - David Everson 509
False Prophet - Faye Kellerman 879
Family Album - Susan Oleksiw 1230
Family Practice - Charlene Weir 1686
The Family Stalker - Jon Katz 870
The Famous DAR Murder Mystery - Graham Landrum 977
A Farewell to Yarns - Jill Churchill 245
The Fast-Death Factor - Virginia Crosby 359
Fear in Fenway - Crabbe Evers 506
The February Trouble - Neil Albert 30
Feeding Frenzy - Paul Kemprecos 904
Felony Murder - Joseph T. Klempner 940
Femmes Fatal - Dorothy Cannell 214
A Few Dying Words - Paula Gosling 626
The Fifth Rapunzel - B.M. Gill 586
File Under: Deceased - Sarah Lacey 962
Final Cut - Eric Wright 1768
Final Edit - Robert A. Carter 224
Final Session - Mary Morell 1170
Final Tour - Jonellen Heckler 770
Finders Keepers - Elizabeth Travis 1627
A Fine Italian Hand - Eric Wright 1769
A Fine Place for Death - Ann Granger 643
Fire Horse - Bill Shoemaker 1486
Firm Ambitions - Michael A. Kahn 853
First and Ten - Douglas Anderson 50
First Pedigree Murder - Melissa Cleary 257
A Fistful of Empty - Benjamin M. Schutz 1457
A Fit of Tempera - Mary Daheim 375

20th Century

Fixing to Die - Jerry Oster   1249
Flamingos - Marc Savage   1444
Flashback - Ted Wood   1756
Flawless - Adam Barrow   99
A Flower in the Desert - Walter Satterthwait   1439
Flowers for the Dead - Ann M. Williams   1728
Follow That Blonde - Joan Smith   1521
Fool's Puzzle - Earlene Fowler   536
Footsteps of the Hawk - Andrew Vachss   1644
The Forever Beat - John Cline   262
Forty Whacks - Sheila MacGill Callahan   207
Four Elements of Murder - D.B. Borton   155
Foursome - Jeremiah Healy   765
Foxglove - Mary Anne Kelly   889
Free Fall - Robert Crais   341
Fresh Kills - Carolyn Wheat   1699
Friends in High Places - Michael Hendricks   771
From Here to Paternity - Jill Churchill   246
From Potter's Field - Patricia D. Cornwell   325
Frost the Fiddler - Janice Weber   1681
The Frozen Franklin - Sean Hanlon   725
Fruits of the Poisonous Tree - Archer Mayor   1104
Full-Bodied Red - Bruce Zimmerman   1790
Full Circle - Collin Wilcox   1714
Full Commission - Carol Brennan   172
Funny as a Dead Comic - Susan Rogers Cooper   312
Funny as a Dead Relative - Susan Rogers Cooper   313
Furnished for Murder - Richard Barth   101
Fuse Time - Max Byrd   205
Gallows View - Peter Robinson   1393
The Garden Club - Muriel Resnick Jackson   836
Gator Kill - Bill Crider   352
Gaudi Afternoon - Barbara Wilson   1731
The Genesis Files - Bob Biderman   130
Gentkill: A Novel of the FBI - Paul Lindsay   1025
The George Eliot Murders - Edith Skom   1511
Get Shorty - Elmore Leonard   1005
Get What's Coming - Sam Reaves   1354
Ghostland - Jean Hager   700
A Gift for Murder - M.D. Lake   968
The Gift Horse's Mouth - Robert Campbell   212
A Glancing Light - Aaron Elkins   477
The Glass Ceiling - Anabel Donald   428
God Bless John Wayne - Kinky Friedman   554
Going Wrong - Ruth Rendell   1360
Golden Fleece - Jack Becklund   118
Gone Wild - James W. Hall   708
A Good Day to Die - Stephen Solomita   1534
A Good Year for a Corpse - Valerie Wolzien   1749
Goodnight, Irene - Jan Burke   198
Grandmother's House - Janet LaPierre   983
Grave Doubt - Michael Allegretto   41
Grave Matters - Leo Axler   71
Grave Responsibility - Susannah Stacey   1554
Grave Secrets - Louise Hendricksen   774
A Grave Talent - Laurie R. King   925
Grave Undertaking - James McCahery   1112
Gravestone - P.M. Carlson   219
The Great California Game - Jonathan Gash   570
The Great Reminder - R.R. Irvine   829
The Green Mosaic - Stephen F. Wilcox   1720
Grievous Sin - Faye Kellerman   880
Grizzly - Christine Andreae   54
Grootka - Jon A. Jackson   832
Guardian Angel - Sara Paretsky   1265
Guilt by Association - Susan R. Sloan   1514
Gun Men - Gary Friedman   553
A Gypsy Good Time - Gustav Hasford   755
H Is for Homicide - Sue Grafton   636
Hammurabi's Code - Charles Kenney   909
The Hanged Man - Walter Satterthwait   1440
The Hanging Garden - John Sherwood   1485
Hanging Time - Leslie Glass   601
The Hanging Valley - Peter Robinson   1394
The Hangman's Beautiful Daughter - Sharyn McCrumb   1115
Hangman's Root - Susan Wittig Albert   32
Happy Are the Merciful - Andrew M. Greeley   656

Hard Aground - James W. Hall   709
A Hard Bargain - Lia Matera   1092
Hard Evidence - John T. Lescroart   1009
Hard Fall - Ridley Pearson   1284
Hard Guy - Thorton Elliott   482
Hard Look - Robert J. Randisi   1349
Hard News - Jeffrey Wilds Deaver   403
Hard News - Mark T. Sullivan   1590
Hard Tack - Barbara D'Amato   382
Hard Women - Barbara D'Amato   383
Hardscape - Justin Scott   1463
Hare Today, Gone Tomorrow - Meg O'Brien   1216
The Harry Chronicles - Allan Pedrazas   1287
The Hawthorne Group - Thomas Hauser   756
A Hazard of Losers - Lloyd Biggle Jr.   132
He Was Her Man - Sarah Shankman   1474
Heartshot - Steven F. Havill   758
Heat - Stuart Woods   1760
The Heaven Stone - David Daniel   386
Hell Bent - Ken Gross   684
He's Dead-She's Dead: Details at Eleven - John Bartholomew Tucker   1635
Hidden City - Jim DeBrosse   407
High Strangeness - Alison Drake   447
Hire a Hangman - Collin Wilcox   1715
Hit on the House - Jon A. Jackson   833
The Holiday Murders - Marsha Landreth   975
Hollywood Requiem - Peter Freeborn   546
Holy Terrors - Mary Daheim   376
Home Sweet Homicide - Kate Morgan   1171
Home to Roost - Gerald Hammond   720
A Homecoming for Murder - John Armistead   65
Hope Against Hope - Susan B. Kelly   896
A Hopeless Case - K.K. Beck   116
Horse of a Different Killer - Jody Jaffe   839
Hostile Witness - William Lashner   985
Hot Air - Jon L. Breen   170
Hot Water - Sally Gunning   686
The Hotel Detective - Alan Russell   1413
Hotel Morgue - Janet Laurence   989
Hour of the Hunter - J.A. Jance   843
Hour of the Manatee - E.C. Ayres   73
An Hour to Kill - Edward Wellen   1690
House of Blues - Julie Smith   1525
The House on the Hill - Judith Kelman   899
How to Murder Your Mother-in-Law - Dorothy Cannell   215
How Town - Michael Nava   1194
Hubbert and Lil: Partners in Crime - Gallagher Gray   654
Hung in the Balance - Roger Ormerod   1244
I Is for Innocent - Sue Grafton   637
I.O.U. - Nancy Pickard   1318
The Ice - Louis Charbonneau   234
The Ice House - Minette Walters   1669
Icewater Mansions - Douglas Allyn   48
I'd Rather Be in Philadelphia - Gillian Roberts   1378
Idol Bones - D.M. Greenwood   671
I'll Be Leaving You Always - Sandra Scoppettone   1461
Illegal Motion - Grif Stockley   1576
I'm Getting Killed Right Here - William Murray   1190
An Imperfect Spy - Amanda Cross   360
Imperfect Strangers - Stuart Woods   1761
In Blacker Moments - S.E. Schenkel   1451
In Deep - Bruce Jones   846
In-laws and Outlaws - Barbara Paul   1277
In Stoney Places - Kay Mitchell   1159
In the Dark - Carol Brennan   173
In the Electric Mist with Confederate Dead - James Lee Burke   196
In the Game - Nikki Baker   82
In the Lake of the Woods - Tim O'Brien   1218
Inadmissible Evidence - Philip Friedman   557
Incident at Potter's Bridge - Joseph Monniger   1165
Incinerator - Timothy Hallinan   751
Infected Be the Air - Janice Law   991
Inherit the Mob - Zev Chafets   231

The Intersection of Law and Desire - J.M. Redmann   1356
Interview with Mattie - Shelley Singer   1504
Into the Fire - David Wiltse   1737
Into Thin Air - Thomas Zigal   1788
Irish Chain - Earlene Fowler   537
Irish Gold - Andrew M. Greeley   657
The Iron Glove - Ronald Tierney   1619
Is Anybody There? - T.G. Gilpin   591
Island Girl - Carole Berry   127
The January Corpse - Neil Albert   31
Jazz Funeral - Julie Smith   1526
Jersey Monkey - Kate Gallison   565
Jinx - Julie Robitaille   1398
The Judas Pool - George Owens   1250
The Julius House - Charlaine Harris   732
Juror - Parnell Hall   714
Just Cause - John Katzenbach   873
Justice - Faye Kellerman   881
Justice for Some - Kate Wilhelm   1724
K Is for Killer - Sue Grafton   638
Karma - Mitchell Smith   1531
Katapult - Karen Kijewski   919
The Keeper - Meg O'Brien   1217
Kid's Stuff - Susan B. Kelly   897
Kiet Goes West - Gary Alexander   34
Kill or Cure - Mary Kittredge   932
Kill Story - Jerome Doolittle   434
Kill the Butler! - Michael Kenyon   911
Killed on the Rocks - William L. DeAndrea   401
Killer Cinderella - Simon Shaw   1478
Killer in Paradise - John Leslie   1011
Killing Me Softly - John Leslie   1012
The Killing of Ellis Martin - Lucretia Grindle   677
Killings - A.W. Gray   651
Kindred Crimes - Janet Dawson   397
The King Is Dead - Sarah Shankman   1475
King of the Corner - Loren D. Estleman   497
King of the Mountain - M.K. Wren   1765
Kingdom Road - K. Patrick Conner   295
Kiss Them Goodbye - Joseph Eastburn   468
Kissing the Gunner's Daughter - Ruth Rendell   1361
Knight & Day - Ron Nessen   1201
L Is for Lawless - Sue Grafton   639
Land Kills - Nat Brandt   166
Landfall - Tony Gibbs   581
The Last Gambit - David Delman   411
The Last Good German - Bill Granger   647
The Last Man Standing - Jim Wright   1771
The Last Man to Die - M.K. Shuman   1493
The Last Resort - Jaqueline Girdner   594
The Last Rite of Hugo T - J.N. Catanach   227
The Late Lady - Susannah Stacey   1556
The Late Man - James Preston Girard   592
Late of This Parish - Marjorie Eccles   469
The Lavender House Murder - Nikki Baker   83
A Lawyer's Tale - D. Kincaid   923
Lay It on the Line - Catherine Dain   379
Leap of Faith - Sharon Zukowski   1799
Leave the Grave Green - Deborah Crombie   357
Library: No Murder Aloud - Susan Steiner   1569
Lieberman's Choice - Stuart M. Kaminsky   856
Lieberman's Day - Stuart M. Kaminsky   857
Lieberman's Folly - Stuart M. Kaminsky   858
The Lies of Fair Ladies - Jonathan Gash   571
The Lies That Bind - Judith Van Gieson   1649
Lights Out - Peter Abrahams   4
Limited Partner - Mike Lupica   1053
The Lion's Share - Kelly A. Tate   1605
Little Use for Death - Michael W. Sherer   1482
A Lively Form of Death - Kay Mitchell   1160
Lizardskin - Carsten Stroud   1582
Lockout - Lillian O'Donnell   1224
A Long Cold Fall - Sam Reaves   1355
The Long Search - Isabelle Holland   798
A Long Time Dead - A.J. Orde   1242
Longshot - Dick Francis   540
Louisiana Blue - David Poyer   1324
Love Bytes - Sally Chapman   232
Love Lies - Fern Kupfer   960
Love nor Money - Linda Grant   648

Time Period Index — 20th Century

A Love to Die For - Christine T. Jorgensen 849
Love You to Death - Grant Michaels 1151
Loves Music, Loves to Dance - Mary Higgins Clark 253
Lullaby Town - Robert Crais 342
MacPherson's Lament - Sharyn McCrumb 1117
Madness in Maggody - Joan Hess 777
Mail-Order Murder - Leslie Meier 1140
Make Friends with Murder - Judith Garwood 569
Make No Bones - Aaron Elkins 478
Malice Domestic #1 - Elizabeth Peters 1299
Mallory's Oracle - Carol O'Connell 1221
The Maltese Puppy - Melissa Cleary 258
Man of Blood - Margaret Duffy 451
The Man Offside - A.W. Gray 652
A Man to Die For - Eileen Dreyer 448
The Man Who Cancelled Himself - David Handler 722
The Man Who Would Be F. Scott Fitzgerald - David Handler 723
The Man with My Name - Paul Engleman 494
The Manx Murders - William L. DeAndrea 402
Margin for Murder - Bronte Adams 9
The Marvell College Murders - Sophie Belfort 119
Mass Murder - John Keith Drummond 449
Maximum Bob - Elmore Leonard 1006
Mayhem in Parva - Nancy Livingston 1035
Mean High Tide - James W. Hall 710
Memory Can Be Murder - Elizabeth Daniels Squire 1547
Menaced Assassin - Joe Gores 618
The Mensa Murders - Lee Martin 1089
Methods of Execution - Frederick D. Huebner 818
The Mexican Tree Duck - James Crumley 363
Mexico Is Forever - Benjamin M. Schutz 1458
Miami Heat - Jerome Sanford 1433
Miami Purity - Vicki Hendricks 773
Midnight Baby - Wendy Hornsby 808
Mint Julep Murder - Carolyn G. Hart 744
Miracles in Maggody - Joan Hess 778
Miss Melville Rides a Tiger - Evelyn E. Smith 1518
Miss Zukas and the Island Murders - Jo Dereske 415
Miss Zukas and the Library Murders - Jo Dereske 416
Missing - Jonathan Valin 1646
Missing Joseph - Elizabeth George 575
Missing Susan - Sharyn McCrumb 1118
Mistress of Justice - Jeffrey Wilds Deaver 405
Mitigating Circumstances - Nancy Taylor Rosenberg 1401
Model Murder - Erica Quest 1338
Mommy and the Murder - Nancy Gladstone 600
Monday's Child Is Dead - James Elward 484
Money Burns - A.E. Maxwell 1100
Money to Burn - Gloria White 1701
Monkey on a Chain - Harlen Campbell 211
The Monkey Rope - Stephen Lewis 1023
Monkey Wrench - Liza Cody 271
The Monster Squad - John Angus 59
More Deaths than One - Marjorie Eccles 470
A Morning for Flamingos - James Lee Burke 197
Morons and Madmen - Earl Emerson 488
Mortal Remains - Rick Hanson 728
Mortal Remains in Maggody - Joan Hess 779
Mortal Sin - Paul Levine 1014
Mortal Words - Kathryn Lasky Knight 945
Moth - James Sallis 1422
Moth to the Flame - Kathleen Dougherty 437
Mother Love - L.R. Wright 1774
Moving Targets - Sean Flannery 529
Mr. Donaghue Investigates - Anna Shone 1488
Mrs. Malory and the Festival Murders - Hazel Holt 801
Mrs. Pargeter's Package - Simon Brett 175
Murder Among Us - Ann Granger 644
Murder and a Muse - Gillian B. Farrell 517
Murder at Monticello - Rita Mae Brown 180
Murder at Moot Point - Marlys Millhiser 1156
Murder at St. Adelaide's - Gerelyn Hollingsworth 799

Murder at the Class Reunion - Triss Stein 1567
Murder at the Friendship Hotel - Charlotte Epstein 496
Murder at the Spa - Stefanie Matteson 1097
Murder by Mail - M.D. Lake 969
Murder by Owl Light - Corinne Holt Sawyer 1445
Murder by Tarot - Al Guthrie 693
Murder by Tradition - Katherine V. Forrest 534
Murder Can Kill Your Social Life - Selma Eichler 473
Murder Has No Calories - Corinne Holt Sawyer 1446
Murder in a Good Cause - Medora Sale 1417
Murder in a Nice Neighborhood - Lora Roberts 1388
Murder in a Quiet Place - Tony Caxton 230
Murder in Bandora - Leona Karr 868
Murder in Brief - Carrol Lachint 963
Murder in Mellingham - Susan Oleksiw 1231
Murder in Ordinary Time - Sister Carol Anne O'Marie 1238
Murder in Scorpio - Martha C. Lawrence 993
Murder in the Napa Valley - David Osborn 1245
Murder in Waiting - Robert Richardson 1367
Murder in Wrigley Field - Crabbe Evers 507
Murder Is Germane - Karen Saum 1442
Murder Makes a Pilgrimage - Sister Carol Anne O'Marie 1239
Murder Most Grizzly - Elizabeth Quinn 1340
Murder Movie - Jill McGown 1131
Murder, My Suite - Mary Daheim 377
Murder Offscreen - Denise Osborne 1248
Murder on a Kibbutz - Batya Gur 690
Murder on Peachtree Street - Patricia Houck Sprinkle 1543
Murder on the Chesapeake - David Osborn 1246
Murder on the Cliff - Stefanie Matteson 1098
Murder on the Iditarod Trail - Sue Henry 775
Murder on the Run - Gloria White 1702
Murder Once Removed - Kathleen Kunz 959
Murder Song - Jon Cleary 256
Murder Will Out - Dorian Yeager 1784
Murder Without Reservation - Bernie Lee 999
Murdock Cracks Ice - Robert J. Ray 1353
The Music Lovers - Jonathan Valin 1647
My Gun Has Bullets - Lee Goldberg 606
My Sister's Keeper - Nora Kelly 892
My Sweet Untraceable You - Sandra Scoppettone 1462
A Mystery Bred in Buckhead - Patricia Houck Sprinkle 1544
The Naked Typist - J.P. Hailey 704
Native Tongue - Carl Hiaasen 782
Natural Causes - Michael Palmer 1262
Natural Enemies - Sara Cameron 209
A Necessary End - Peter Robinson 1395
Neon Dancers - Matt Taylor 1608
The Neon Smile - Dick Lochte 1039
Neptune's Eye - Paul Kemprecos 905
Never Walk Behind Me - Lin Summerfield 1593
New Orleans Beat - Julie Smith 1527
New Orleans Requiem - D.J. Donaldson 430
The Next Victim - William Sanders 1423
Nice Guys Finish Dead - David Debin 406
Night Butterfly - Patricia McFall 1127
Night Game - Alison Gordon 613
Night Kills - Ed Gorman 622
Night of the Cat - James Schermerhorn 1452
Night of the Ice Storm - David Stout 1579
Night Prey - John Sandford 1424
The Night Remembers - Ed Gorman 623
Night Shadows - Ron Ely 486
Night Sins - Tami Hoag 794
Night Vision - Paul Levine 1015
Nightmare Point - Carole Berry 128
Nightside - Soledad Santiago 1434
Ninth Life - Lauren Wright Douglas 444
No Comfort in Victory - Gregory Bean 106
No Forwarding Address - Elisabeth Bowers 161
No Mardi Gras for the Dead - D.J. Donaldson 431

No Place for Secrets - Sherry Lewis 1021
No Sign of Murder - Alan Russell 1414
No Way Home - Andrew Coburn 267
Noble Rot - Will Harriss 739
Nobody's Child - Janet Dawson 398
Nobody's Fool - Marten Claridge 249
North of Montana - April Smith 1515
The Northwest Murders - Elizabeth Atwood Taylor 1607
Not a Creature Was Stirring - Jane Haddam 695
Now He Thinks He's Dead - Ron Goulart 629
Now Let's Talk of Graves - Sarah Shankman 1476
Nun Plussed - Monica Quill 1339
Nurse Dawes Is Dead - Stella Shepherd 1479
O Little Town of Maggody - Joan Hess 780
Obit - Daniel Paisner 1261
Obligations of the Bone - Dick Cluster 263
Obstacle Course - Yvonne Montgomery 1167
O'Fear - Peter Corris 328
Off Minor - John Harvey 753
Off Season - Philip R. Craig 339
The Old Contemptibles - Martha Grimes 675
Old Scores - Aaron Elkins 479
Once upon a Crime - M.D. Lake 970
One for the Money - Janet Evanovich 503
One Kiss Led to Another - Harris Dulaney 454
One, Two, What Did Daddy Do? - Susan Rogers Cooper 315
The Only Good Priest - Mark Richard Zubro 1795
The Only Good Yankee - Jeff Abbott 2
Original Sin - Mary Monica Pulver 1334
Orphans - Gerald Pearce 1281
Other People's Houses - Susan Rogers Cooper 316
Other People's Skeletons - Julie Smith 1529
The Other Side of Death - Judith Van Gieson 1650
The Other Woman - Jill McGown 1132
Out of the Darkness - Susan Kelly 894
Over the Edge - Betty Rowlands 1409
An Owl Too Many - Charlotte MacLeod 1064
Oxford Exit - Veronica Stallwood 1559
Painted Ladies - James Neal Harvey 750
The Painted Lady - Stephen F. Wilcox 1722
Palindrome - Stuart Woods 1762
Pamplemousse Rests His Case - Michael Bond 152
Paramour - Gerald Petievich 1312
Parts Unknown - Rex Burns 200
Party Till You Die - David Charnee 236
Pas De Death - L.M. Vincent 1656
Past Imperfect - Margaret Maron 1077
Past Reason Hated - Peter Robinson 1396
Paws Before Dying - Susan Conant 290
Peckover Joins the Choir - Michael Kenyon 912
A Pedigree to Die For - Laurien Berenson 121
Peeping Thomas - Robert Reeves 1358
Pel and the Missing Persons - Mark Hebden 768
The Pelican Brief - John Grisham 681
Penance - David Housewright 812
A Permanent Retirement - John Miles 1153
Pet Peeves - Taylor McCafferty 1111
The Piano Man - Noreen Gilpatrick 589
Picture of David - Shelley Singer 1505
A Piece of Justice - Jill Paton Walsh 1274
Pillar of Fire - R.R. Irvine 830
Pillars of Fire - Steve Shagan 1473
Pink Vodka Blues - Neal Barrett Jr. 98
A Plague of Kinfolks - Celestine Sibley 1497
Play with Fire - Dana Stabenow 1552
Playing for the Ashes - Elizabeth George 577
Playing the Dozens - William D. Pease 1286
Pleading Guilty - Scott Turow 1640
A Pocketful of Karma - Taffy Cannon 216
Point Blank - Jayson Livingston 1033
Point No-Point - David Willis McCullough 1123
Point of Impact - Stephen Hunter 822
Poison Fruit - Chelsea Quinn Yarbro 1781
Poison Pen - Mary Kittredge 933
Poisoned Ivy - M.D. Lake 971
The Portland Laugher - Earl Emerson 489
A Pound of Flesh - Trevor Barnes 95
Prescription for Death - Janet McGiffin 1130
The Price of Victory - Vincent Green 666

20th Century

Primal Fear - William Diehl 421
Prime Suspect - A.W. Gray 653
Prime Time for Murder - Valerie Frankel 542
Prior Convictions - Lia Matera 1093
A Private Crime - Lillian O'Donnell 1225
Private Eyes - Jonathan Kellerman 886
Prized Possessions - L.R. Wright 1775
Probable Cause - Griff Stockley 1577
The Prosecutor - Thomas Chastain 240
The Pumpkin-Shell Wife - Susanna Hofmann McShea 1138
Purgatory - Monty Mickleson 1152
Pursued by Shadows - Medora Sale 1419
Pushover - Lillian O'Donnell 1226
Pussyfoot - Carole Nelson Douglas 443
Quaker Silence - Irene Allen 45
Quaker Witness - Irene Allen 46
Quarry - Bill Pronzini 1329
The Queen Is Dead - Jane Dentinger 414
The Queen's Mare - John Birkett 133
A Quiche Before Dying - Jill Churchill 247
The Quick and the Dead - Rob Kantner 863
Quoth the Raven - Jane Haddam 696
Rafferty: Fatal Sisters - W. Glenn Duncan 458
Rage - Gwen Moffat 1162
The Raggedy Man - Lillian O'Donnell 1227
The Ransom - Brian Tobin 1622
Rat's Nest - Charles West 1694
Ravenmocker - Jean Hager 701
Recalled to Life - Reginald Hill 790
Recipe for Death - Janet Laurence 990
Recycled - Jo Bailey 80
Red Knight - J. Madison Davis 391
The Red Scream - Mary Willis Walker 1659
Red Trance - R.D. Zimmerman 1793
The Red, White, and Blues - Rob Kantner 864
The Redbird's Cry - Jean Hager 702
A Relative Stranger - Margaret Lucke 1052
Rest in Pieces - Rita Mae Brown 181
Reversible Error - Robert K. Tanenbaum 1600
Revolution #9 - Peter Abrahams 6
Right on the Money - Emma Lathen 987
Rising Sun - Michael Crichton 348
River of Darkness - James Grady 632
The Riviera Contract - Marvin Albert 26
Rogue Wave - Susan Dunlap 463
Roll Over and Play Dead - Joan Hess 781
Rook-Shoot - Margaret Duffy 452
Room 9 - Soledad Santiago 1435
Rostnikov's Vacation - Stuart M. Kaminsky 861
The Rotary Club Mystery - Graham Landrum 978
Rotten Apples - Natasha Cooper 309
Rotten Lies - Charlotte Elkins 481
Rough Cut - Bruce Cook 300
Rough Water - Sally Gunning 687
Ruffly Speaking - Susan Conant 291
Rum Punch - Elmore Leonard 1007
Running From the Law - Lisa Scottoline 1465
Running Mates - John Feinstein 521
Sacred Clowns - Tony Hillerman 792
Safe at Home - Alison Gordon 614
Saint Louie Blues - Jake Tanner 1601
Sanctuary - Faye Kellerman 884
Santa Fe Rules - Stuart Woods 1763
The Saturday Morning Murder - Batya Gur 691
Savage Justice - Ron Handberg 721
A Scandal in Belgravia - Robert Barnard 91
Scent of Evil - Archer Mayor 1105
The Scold's Bridle - Minette Walters 1670
The Sculptress - Minette Walters 1671
The Search Committee - Ralph McInerny 1136
Searching for Sara - Shelley Singer 1506
A Season for Murder - Ann Granger 645
Second Chance - Jonathan Valin 1648
A Second Shot in the Dark - Annette Roome 1399
Seeds of Murder - Michael Underwood 1642
Seeing the Elephant - Les Roberts 1387
Self-Defense - Jonathan Kellerman 887
Separate Cases - Robert J. Randisi 1350
September Song - Edward Mathis 1096
Set-Up - Maxine O'Callaghan 1220

Seven Kinds of Death - Kate Wilhelm 1725
Shadow Counter - Tom Kakonis 855
Shadow of a Doubt - William J. Coughlin 333
Shadow Prey - John Sandford 1426
Shadow Queen - Tony Gibbs 583
Shadows on the Mirror - Frances Fyfield 563
The Shaman's Knife - Scott Young 1786
Shameless - Judy Collins 275
A Share in Death - Deborah Crombie 358
Shattered Rhythms - Phyllis Knight 946
She Walks in Beauty - Sarah Shankman 1477
She Walks These Hills - Sharyn McCrumb 1119
Sheep, Goats and Soap - John Malcolm 1068
Shoedog - George Pelecanos 1288
Shoofly Pie to Die - Joshua Quittner 1342
Shoot the Piper - Richard Hill 791
Shooting at Loons - Margaret Maron 1078
Shooting Script - Gordon Cotler 332
Shooting Star - Kate Green 665
Short Cut to Santa Fe - Medora Sale 1420
Shot on Location - Stan Cutler 369
Show Stopper - Mary Monica Pulver 1335
Showcase - Alison Glen 603
Shroud for a Scholar - Audrey Peterson 1306
Shutout - David F. Nighbert 1204
The Sidewalk Hilton - Bruce Cook 301
Silent Night - Gary Amo 49
Silent Prey - John Sandford 1427
Silent Witness - Collin Wilcox 1716
Silent Witness - Charles Wilson 1732
The Silver Scapel - Nancy Baker Jacobs 837
Silver Spire - Robert Goldsborough 608
The Sin Within Her Smile - Jonathan Gash 572
Sing a Song of Death - Catherine Dain 380
Singapore Transfer - Wayne Warga 1673
A Single Stone - Marilyn Wallace 1664
A Singular Spy - Amanda Kyle Williams 1727
Sister's Keeper - Randye Lordon 1042
Skin Deep - Timothy Hallinan 718
Skin Deep Is Fatal - Michael Cormany 320
Skinny Man - James Colbert 273
Skins - Catherine O'Connell 1222
Skylark - Sheila Simonson 1501
A Slay at the Races - Kate Morgan 1172
Sleeping Dogs - Thomas Perry 1297
A Slip of the Tong - Charles A. Goodrum 611
Sliver - Ira Levin 1013
Slow Burn - Eleanor Taylor Bland 142
Slow Motion Riot - Peter Blauner 144
Snagged - Carol Higgins Clark 251
Snapshot - Linda Barnes 93
Snow Job - Ted Wood 1758
So Little to Die For - Lucretia Grindle 678
So Shall You Reap - Marilyn Wallace 1665
The Society Ball Murders - Jack Albin Anderson 51
The Software Bomb - Steven Womack 1753
Somebody's Dead in Snellville - Patricia Houck Sprinkle 1545
Someone Is Killing the Great Chefs of America - Nan Lyons 1061
Something in the Water - Charlotte MacLeod 1065
Something's Cooking - Joanne Pence 1290
Sorry Now? - Mark Richard Zubro 1796
The Soul of Betty Fairchild - Robert Specht 1538
Southern Cross - Jim DeBrosse 408
Southern Cross - Stephen Greenleaf 669
The Spanish Maze Game - Noah Webster 1682
Spark - John Lutz 1058
Special Delivery - Jerry Kennealy 907
Spotted Cats - William G. Tapply 1603
Spy Shadow - Tim Sebastian 1466
Squeezeplay - David F. Nighbert 1205
Stalking Horse - Bill Shoemaker 1487
Stand-In for Murder - Lynn Bradley 164
The Standoff - Chuck Hogan 796
Steel Guitar - Linda Barnes 94
The Steel Web - Ronald Tierney 1620
A Stiff Critique - Jaqueline Girdner 595
Still Among the Living - Zachary Klein 938
A Still and Icy Silence - Ronald Clair Roat 1374
Still Explosion - Mary Logue 1041

Still Water - Sally Gunning 688
Still Waters - Kerry Tucker 1638
A Stillness in Bethlehem - Jane Haddam 697
Stone Boy - Ronald Levitsky 1017
StoneDust - Justin Scott 1464
Stonefish - Charles West 1695
Storm Front - Virginia Anderson 53
Stormy Weather - Carl Hiaasen 784
Straight as an Arrow - Celestine Sibley 1498
A Strange and Bitter Crop - E.L. Wyrick 1780
Strange Loyalties - William McIlvanney 1134
Strangers in the Night - Peg Tyre 1641
Stranglehold - Jerome Doolittle 435
Strawgirl - Abigail Padgett 1252
Strike - L.L. Enger 492
Striking Out - Alison Gordon 615
Strip Tease - Carl Hiaasen 785
A Sudden Death at the Norfolk Cafe - Winona Sullivan 1591
Suffer Little Children - Thomas D. Davis 396
The Suitor - Michael Allegretto 43
The Sum of All Fears - Tom Clancy 248
Summer Cool - Al Sarrantonio 1436
The Summons - Peter Lovesey 1050
A Superior Death - Nevada Barr 96
The Suspense Is Killing Me - Thomas Maxwell 1102
Suspicion of Guilt - Barbara Parker 1268
Sweet Death - Bill Waggoner 1657
Sweet Death, Come Softly - Barbara Whitehead 1708
Sweet Women Lie - Loren D. Estleman 500
Swing - L.L. Enger 493
Switchback - Collin Wilcox 1717
Switching the Odds - Phyllis Knight 947
A Tail of Two Murders - Melissa Cleary 259
A Taste for Murder - Claudia Bishop 135
Tea-Totally Dead - Jaqueline Girdner 596
Telling Lies - Wendy Hornsby 809
Ten of Swords - J.R. Levitt 1018
Tensleep - Sarah Andrews 57
The Texas Capitol Murders - Bill Crider 353
Thicker than Blood - John Lutz 1059
Thieftaker - Alan Scholefield 1454
Think on Death - David Willis McCullough 1124
Thinner than Blood - Stella Shepherd 1480
Third Man Out - Richard Stevenson 1572
The Thirteenth Apostle - Gloria Gonzalez 610
The Thousand Yard Stare - Rob Kantner 865
Three Blind Mice - Ed McBain 1106
Three Is a Crowd - D.B. Borton 156
Three Strikes, You're Dead - Michael Geller 574
Threnody for Two - Jeanne Hart 747
Throw Darts at a Cheesecake - Denise Dietz 423
Thunder - James Grady 633
Thursday's Child - Teri White 1705
Thyme of Death - Susan Wittig Albert 33
Ties That Bind - Sherryl Woods 1759
Tigers Burning - Crabbe Evers 508
Tight Lines - William G. Tapply 1604
Till Death Do Us Part - Rochelle Majer Krich 955
Till The Butchers Cut Him Down - Marcia Muller 1182
Time Bomb - Jonathan Kellerman 888
Time Expired - Susan Dunlap 464
Time Lapse - Janice Law 992
Time of Hope - Susan B. Kelly 898
To Do No Harm - Leslie Glass 602
To Kill a Clown - David Charnee 237
To Live and Die in Dixie - Kathy Hogan Trocheck 1632
To Play the Fool - Laurie R. King 927
To Speak for the Dead - Paul Levine 1016
Too Clever by Half - Roderic Jeffries 845
Too Many Cooks - Joanne Pence 1291
Topless - D. Keith Mano 1072
Torch Town Boogie - Steven Womack 1754
The Total Zone - Martina Navratilova 1195
A Touch of Panic - L.R. Wright 1776
Town on Trial - William Harrington 730
Tracer, Inc. - Jeff Andrus 58

Track of the Cat - Nevada Barr 97
Trade-Off - Harrison Arnston 66
Trade Secrets - Ray Garton 568
Trade Secrets - Maynard F. Thomson 1615
Trail of Murder - Christine Andreae 55
The Trail to Buddha's Mirror - Don Winslow 1744
Treasure by Post - David Williams 1730
A Trick of Light - Patricia Robinson 1391
The Triumph of Bacchus - Douglas Skeggs 1509
Trophies and Dead Things - Marcia Muller 1183
Tropical Depression - Jeffry P. Lindsay 1024
Trouble Looking for a Place to Happen - Toni L.P. Kelner 902
The Trouble with Going Home - Camilla T. Crespi 345
The Trouble with Moonlighting - Trella Crespi 346
The Trouble with Too Much Sun - Trella Crespi 347
Troubled Water - Sally Gunning 689
True Crime - Michael Mewshaw 1145
Trunk Show - Alison Glen 604
Tunnel Vision - Sara Paretsky 1266
Turnaround Jack - Richard Abshire 8
The Turquoise Tattoo - Nancy Baker Jacobs 838
Turtle Moon - Alice Hoffman 795
TV Safe - Jim Stinson 1575
Two Points for Murder - D.B. Borton 157
Two Way Toll - Zachary Klein 939
Under My Skin - Sarah Dunant 456
Under the Beetle's Cellar - Mary Willis Walker 1660
The Unexpected Corpse - B.J. Oliphant 1235
Unholy Ghosts - D.M. Greenwood 672
Unsafe Keeping - Carol Cail 206
Until Death - Polly Whitney 1709
Until Proven Innocent - Susan Kelly 895
Until the End of Time - Polly Whitney 1710
Unwillingly to Vegas - Nancy Livingston 1036
Used to Kill - Lillian O'Donnell 1228
Vanishing Act - Seth Jacob Margolis 1075
The Vanishing Smile - Earl Emerson 490
Vertical Run - Joseph R. Garber 566
The Very Bad Thing - Ned White 1703
A Very Proper Death - Alex Juniper 850
A Very Venetian Murder - Haughton Murphy 1187

Vial Murders - Marsha Landreth 976
Video Vengeance - Miles Tripp 1630
The Vig - John T. Lescroart 1010
Vintage Polo - Jerry Kennealy 908
Viper Quarry - Dean Feldmeyer 522
Vital Lies - Ellen Hart 746
Vital Signs - Robin Cook 303
Voices in the Dark - Andrew Coburn 268
Voodoo River - Robert Crais 344
A Vow of Chastity - Veronica Black 136
A Vow of Obedience - Veronica Black 137
A Vow of Sanctity - Veronica Black 138
Walk a Crooked Mile - Catherine Dain 381
A Walk Among the Tombstones - Lawrence Block 150
Walking Dead Man - Mary Kittredge 934
Walking Shadow - Robert B. Parker 1272
The Wasted Years - John Harvey 754
Wasteland - Peter McCabe 1110
The Watchman - Michael Allegretto 44
The Water Cure - Warwick Downing 446
Way Past Dead - Steven Womack 1755
We Wish You a Merry Murder - Valerie Wolzien 1750
Wednesday's Child - Peter Robinson 1397
Wet Graves - Peter Corris 329
What Men Say - Joan Smith 1522
What's a Girl Gotta Do? - Sparkle Hayter 760
When Death Comes Stealing - Valerie Wilson Wesley 1692
When Old Men Die - Bill Crider 354
When Reason Sleeps - Tom Sehler 1472
When She Was Bad - Ron Faust 518
Where Echoes Live - Marcia Muller 1184
Whisper Death - John Lawrence Reynolds 1363
Whisper.He Might Hear You - William Appel 62
Whisper the Guns - Edward Cline 261
Who Killed What's-Her-Name? - Elizabeth Daniels Squire 1548
Whoever Has the Heart - Jennie Melville 1143
Whoo? - Richard Hoyt 816
A Wide and Capable Revenge - Thomas McCall 1113
Widowmaker - William Appel 63

Wild Again - Kathrin King Segal 1471
A Wild and Lonely Place - Marcia Muller 1185
Wild Kat - Karen Kijewski 921
Wildfire - Kenneth W. Goddard 605
Wind-Up - Neville Steed 1566
The Windsor Knot - Sharyn McCrumb 1120
Winter of the Wolves - James N. Frey 552
Winter Prey - John Sandford 1428
Winter Rules - Barry Cork 318
The Winter Widow - Charlene Weir 1687
Wiseguys in Love - C. Clark Criscuolo 355
Wish You Were Here - Rita Mae Brown 182
Witching Murder - Jennie Melville 1144
With an Extreme Burning - Bill Pronzini 1331
With Friends Like These - Gillian Roberts 1380
A Wolf in Death's Clothing - Elizabeth Quinn 1341
The Wolf Path - Judith Van Gieson 1652
The Woman Who Fell From Grace - David Handler 724
The Woman Who Married a Bear - John Straley 1581
The Woman Who Walked into the Sea - Philip R. Craig 340
A Woman's Own Mystery - Hannah Wakefield 1658
A Woman's Place - Linda Grant 649
World of Hurt - Richard Rosen 1400
Writers of the Purple Sage - Barbara Burnett Smith 1517
The Wrong Rite - Alisa Craig 334
The Wyndham Case - Jill Paton Walsh 1275
Yakuza, Go Home - Anne Wingate 1742
Yellow Bird - Rick Boyer 162
Yellow Dog Party - Earl Emerson 491
Zero at the Bone - Mary Willis Walker 1661
The Zig-Zag Man - Marvin Albert 27
Zombies of the Gene Pool - Sharyn McCrumb 1121

INDETERMINATE FUTURE

Coyote Bird - Jim DeFelice 409
U.S.S.A. - David Madsen 1066

Geographic Index

This index provides access to all featured books by geographic settings—such as countries, continents, oceans, and planets. States and provinces are indicated for the United States and Canada. Also interfiled are headings for fictional place names (Spaceships, Imaginary Planets, etc.). Sections are further broken down by city or the specific name of the imaginary locale. Book titles are listed alphabetically under headings, and author names and entry numbers are also provided.

AMERICAN COLONIES

NEW YORK

New York
The Kingsbridge Plot - Maan Meyers 1148

AT SEA

Bright Shark - Robert Ballard 85
Broken Consort - James Gollin 609
Decked - Carol Higgins Clark 250
Running Fix - Tony Gibbs 582
The Sunken Treasure - Marian J.A. Jackson 835
When She Was Bad - Ron Faust 518
Win, Lose or Die - John Gardner 567

AUSTRALIA

Death in Store - Jennifer Rowe 1406
Funnelweb - Charles West 1693

Broome
Cotswold Moles - Michael Spicer 1539

Melbourne
Antipodes - Maria-Antonia Oliver 1236

New South Wales
Babylon South - Jon Cleary 255

Sydney
Matrimonial Causes - Peter Corris 327
Murder Song - Jon Cleary 256
O'Fear - Peter Corris 328
Rat's Nest - Charles West 1694
Stonefish - Charles West 1695
Wet Graves - Peter Corris 329

BAHAMAS

Boiling Rock - Remar Sutton 1594
Carnal Hours - Max Allan Collins 277
Island Girl - Carole Berry 127

BRITISH VIRGIN ISLANDS

Southern Cross - Jim DeBrosse 408

BURUNDI

Act of Faith - Michael Bowen 158

CANADA

The Hanging Valley - Peter Robinson 1394
Murder, My Suite - Mary Daheim 377
My Sister's Keeper - Nora Kelly 892

BRITISH COLUMBIA

Mother Love - L.R. Wright 1774

Sechelt
Fall From Grace - L.R. Wright 1773

Vancouver
Amateur Night - K.K. Beck 114
A Death for a Dancing Doll - E.X. Giroux 597
Hot Shots - Laurence Gough 627
Ninth Life - Lauren Wright Douglas 444
No Forwarding Address - Elisabeth Bowers 161
Prized Possessions - L.R. Wright 1775

Vancouver Island
A Touch of Panic - L.R. Wright 1776

Victoria Island
The Shaman's Knife - Scott Young 1786

NORTHWEST TERRITORIES

Murder in a Cold Climate - Scott Young 1785

ONTARIO

Elliot
On the Inside - Ted Wood 1757

Fort York
Murder on the Thirteenth - A.E. Eddenden 471

Hampton
The Dying Room - E.X. Giroux 599

Larch River
Buried in Stone - Eric Wright 1766

Murphy's Harbor
Flashback - Ted Wood 1756

Ottawa
Murder in Focus - Medora Sale 1418

Toronto
The Dead Pull Hitter - Alison Gordon 612
Death by Degrees - Eric Wright 1767
Final Cut - Eric Wright 1768
A Fine Italian Hand - Eric Wright 1769
Murder in a Good Cause - Medora Sale 1417
Pursued by Shadows - Medora Sale 1419
Safe at Home - Alison Gordon 614
Striking Out - Alison Gordon 615
Work for a Dead Man - Simon Ritchie 1371

QUEBEC

Montreal
A Brush with Death - Joan Smith 1519

CARIBBEAN

Black Girl, White Girl - Patricia Moyes 1179
Broken Consort - James Gollin 609
Landfall - Tony Gibbs 581
A Wild and Lonely Place - Marcia Muller 1185

CENTRAL AMERICA

Sanibel Flats - Randy Wayne White 1704

CHINA

Beijing
Murder at the Friendship Hotel - Charlotte Epstein 496

CZECHOSLOVAKIA

Prague
Three-Core Lead - Clare Curzon 368

EGYPT

City of Gold - Len Deighton 410
The Last Camel Died at Noon - Elizabeth Peters 1298
Napoleon Must Die - Quinn Fawcett 519

Thebes
Murder in the Place of Anubis - Lynda S. Robinson 1390

Valley of the Nile
Dead Men's Hearts - Aaron Elkins 476

ENGLAND

Angel of Death - Jack Higgins 786
The Bag Man - Peter Lacey 961
The Beekeeper's Apprentice - Laurie R. King 924
Black Eye - Neville Steed 1563
Blood Rights - Mike Phillips 1314
The Boy's Tale - Margaret Frazer 545
Brother Cadfael's Penance - Ellis Peters 1301
The Cavalier Case - Antonia Fraser 543
Come to Grief - Dick Francis 538
Comeback - Dick Francis 539
Corporate Bodies - Simon Brett 174
Cut to the Quick - Kate Ross 1404
Dangerous Conceits - Margaret Moore 1168
Death and the Chapman - Kate Sedley 1467
Death and the Chaste Apprentice - Robert Barnard 89
Death in Close-Up - Nancy Livingston 1034
The Disappearance of Edwin Drood - Peter Rowland 1407
Dream of Darkness - Patrick Ruell 1412
The Eagle Has Flown - Jack Higgins 787
East Is East - Emma Lathen 986
Escapade - Walter Satterthwait 1438
Faith, Hope and Homicide - Jessica Mann 1071
The Fate of Princes - P.C. Doherty 424
Fell and Foul Play - John Dickson Carr 221
The Fifth Rapunzel - B.M. Gill 586
Frobisher's Savage - Leonard Tourney 1624
Going Wrong - Ruth Rendell 1360
The Gombeen Man - Randy Lee Eickoff 474
Gospel Truths - J.G. Sandom 1429

England

The Holy Innocents - Kate Sedley 1468
In Stoney Places - Kay Mitchell 1159
Is Anybody There? - T.G. Gilpin 591
The Mad Courtesan - Edward Marston 1081
Missing Susan - Sharyn McCrumb 1118
Murder in Waiting - Robert Richardson 1367
The Nine Giants - Edward Marston 1082
The Nun's Tale - Candace M. Robb 1377
Off Minor - John Harvey 753
Recalled to Life - Reginald Hill 790
A Scandal in Belgravia - Robert Barnard 91
A Second Shot in the Dark - Annette Roome 1399
Sheep, Goats and Soap - John Malcolm 1068
Shoot the Piper - Richard Hill 791
Skeleton-in-Waiting - Peter Dickinson 419
Sleeping Dogs - Thomas Perry 1297
The Suspense Is Killing Me - Thomas Maxwell 1102
The Talinin Madonna - Douglas Skeggs 1508
A Time Without Shadows - Ted Allbeury 38
Tincture of Death - Ray Harrison 738
To Die Like a Gentleman - Bernard Bastable 103
The Toy Cupboard - Lee Jordan 848
Treasure by Post - David Williams 1730
The Trip to Jerusalem - Edward Marston 1084
Unwillingly to Vegas - Nancy Livingston 1036
User Deadly - Denise Danks 388
A Vow of Chastity - Veronica Black 136
The Yellow Room Conspiracy - Peter Dickinson 420

Badger's End
Check-out Time - Kate Kingsbury 928
Eat, Drink and Be Buried - Kate Kingsbury 929
Room with a Clue - Kate Kingsbury 930

Bamford
Cold in the Earth - Ann Granger 642
A Fine Place for Death - Ann Granger 643
A Season for Murder - Ann Granger 645

Bath
The Summons - Peter Lovesey 1050

Beneden
The Late Lady - Susannah Stacey 1556

Berkshire
Cat's Cradle - Clare Curzon 366
Under My Skin - Sarah Dunant 456

Birmingham
Hung in the Balance - Roger Ormerod 1244

Bournemouth
Boxed In - Neville Steed 1564
Wind-Up - Neville Steed 1566

Bramford
Murder Among Us - Ann Granger 644

Brideswell
Whoever Has the Heart - Jennie Melville 1143

Bristol
The Weaver's Tale - Kate Sedley 1470

Burtle
A City of Strangers - Robert Barnard 88

Cambridge
Avenging Angel - Anthony Appiah 64
Bad Chemistry - Nora Kelly 891
The Cambridge Theorem - Tony Cape 217
A Piece of Justice - Jill Paton Walsh 1274

Canterbury
The Becket Factor - Michael David Anthony 60
Dark Provenance - Michael David Anthony 61
The Eye of God - C.L. Grace 631

Carlisle
A Famine of Horses - P.F. Chisholm 243

Carsley
Agatha Raisin and the Quiche of Death - M.C. Beaton 107
Agatha Raisin and the Vicious Vet - M.C. Beaton 108

Channel Islands
The Sirens Sang of Murder - Sarah Caudwell 228

Chiltern Hills
Leave the Grave Green - Deborah Crombie 357

Chitterton Falls
Femmes Fatal - Dorothy Cannell 214
How to Murder Your Mother-in-Law - Dorothy Cannell 215

Colchester
Death at Bishop's Keep - Robin Paige 1259

Compton Dando
Death in Disguise - Caroline Graham 640

Cornwall
Aunt Dimity and the Duke - Nancy Atherton 68
The Dying of the Light - Robert Richardson 1366
A Vow of Obedience - Veronica Black 137

The Cotswolds
Aunt Dimity's Death - Nancy Atherton 69
Cotswold Moles - Michael Spicer 1539
Exhaustive Enquiries - Betty Rowlands 1408
Screaming Bones - Pat Burden 191

Coventry
Blood of an Aries - Linda Mather 1094
More Deaths than One - Marjorie Eccles 470

Dawlington
The Sculptress - Minette Walters 1671

East Anglia
The Lies of Fair Ladies - Jonathan Gash 571
The Sin Within Her Smile - Jonathan Gash 572

East Berebury, Calleshire
The Body Politic - Catherine Aird 25

Eastvale
Gallows View - Peter Robinson 1393
A Necessary End - Peter Robinson 1395

Elmhurst
Dead Before Morning - Geraldine Evans 504

Essex
Death at Gallows Green - Robin Paige 1260

Ewelme Manor
The Bishop's Tale - Margaret Frazer 544

Exeter
Crossover - Judith Eubank 502

Fareham
Killer Cinderella - Simon Shaw 1478

Fontwell
The Scold's Bridle - Minette Walters 1670

Fowchester
Die in My Dreams - Christine Green 661

Greater Springburn
Playing for the Ashes - Elizabeth George 577

Greenborough
Seeds of Murder - Michael Underwood 1642

Hampstead
All Shall Be Well - Deborah Crombie 356

Helmthorpe
A Dedicated Man - Peter Robinson 1392

Hop Valley
Kid's Stuff - Susan B. Kelly 897

Hopbridge
Hope Against Hope - Susan B. Kelly 896
Time of Hope - Susan B. Kelly 898

Kingsmarkham
Kissing the Gunner's Daughter - Ruth Rendell 1361

Lake District
The Old Contemptibles - Martha Grimes 675

Larsoken
Devices and Desires - P.D. James 841

Lavenstock
Late of This Parish - Marjorie Eccles 469

Leeds
The Masters of the House - Robert Barnard 90

London
Backhand - Liza Cody 269
Birthmarks - Sarah Dunant 455
Bitter Herbs - Natasha Cooper 307
Black Out - John Lawton 994
Bloody Roses - Natasha Cooper 308
A Broken Vessel - Kate Ross 1403
Bucket Nut - Liza Cody 270
Cain His Brother - Anne Perry 1292
Clively Close: Dead as Dead Can Be - Ann Crowleigh 361
Clubbed to Death - Ruth Dudley Edwards 472
Coffin on Murder Street - Gwendoline Butler 203
Coronation - W.J. Weatherby 1679
A Dangerous Mourning - Anne Perry 1293
Dead Fit - Stephen Cook 304
Death Among the Dons - Janet Neel 1196
Death and Other Lovers - Jo Bannister 86
A Death for a Dodo - E.X. Giroux 598
Death of a Fantasy Life - T.G. Gilpin 590
Death of a Partner - Janet Neel 1197
Death Penalties - Paula Gosling 625
Death Squad London - Jack Gerson 579
Death Watch - Cynthia Harrod-Eagles 740
Deep Sleep - Frances Fyfield 561
Don't Leave Me This Way - Joan Smith 1520
A Drink of Deadly Wine - Kate Charles 235
Elegy in a Country Graveyard - Audrey Peterson 1304
Encore Murder - Marian Babson 76
Every Breath You Take - Michelle Spring 1541
Farrier's Lane - Anne Perry 1294
The Glass Ceiling - Anabel Donald 428
Good Night, Mr. Holmes - Carole Nelson Douglas 441
Grave Responsibility - Susannah Stacey 1554
Highgate Rise - Anne Perry 1295
Holy Treasure! - David Williams 1729
Idol Bones - D.M. Greenwood 671
Imperfect Strangers - Stuart Woods 1761
Man of Blood - Margaret Duffy 451
Margin for Murder - Bronte Adams 9
Monkey Wrench - Liza Cody 271
A Monstrous Regiment of Women - Laurie R. King 926
Murder Wears a Cowl - P.C. Doherty 426
The Old Silent - Martha Grimes 676
The Other Woman - Jill McGown 1132
Patently Murder - Ray Harrison 737
A Pound of Flesh - Trevor Barnes 95
The Queen's Head - Edward Marston 1083
Rotten Apples - Natasha Cooper 309
Shadows on the Mirror - Frances Fyfield 563
A Share in Death - Deborah Crombie 358
Shroud for a Scholar - Audrey Peterson 1306
The Sirens Sang of Murder - Sarah Caudwell 228
Skylark - Sheila Simonson 1501
Special Delivery - Jerry Kennealy 907
Stage Fright - Gillian Linscott 1030
A Sudden, Fearful Death - Anne Perry 1296
Thieftaker - Alan Scholefield 1454
The Triumph of Bacchus - Douglas Skeggs 1509
Video Vengeance - Miles Tripp 1630
The White Rose Murders - Michael Clynes 265
Who Killed Cock Robin? - Margaret Duffy 453
Winter Rules - Barry Cork 318
Witching Murder - Jennie Melville 1144

Geographic Index

A Woman's Own Mystery - Hannah Wakefield 1658
The Wrong Impression - John Malcolm 1069

Long Slaughter
Murder in a Quiet Place - Tony Caxton 230

Longborough
Deadly Admirer - Christine Green 658
Deadly Errand - Christine Green 659
Deadly Practice - Christine Green 660

Malminster
A Lively Form of Death - Kay Mitchell 1160

Manchester
Crack Down - Val McDermid 1125

Medewich
Clerical Errors - D.M. Greenwood 670

Micklefield
Never Walk Behind Me - Lin Summerfield 1593

Nanrunnet
A Suitable Vengeance - Elizabeth George 578

Norfolk
Every Breath You Take - Michelle Spring 1541
Unholy Ghosts - D.M. Greenwood 672

Northumberland
A Day in the Death of Dorothea Cassidy - Ann Cleeves 260

Nottingham
Cold Light - John Harvey 751
Cutting Edge - John Harvey 752
Nurse Dawes Is Dead - Stella Shepherd 1479
Thinner than Blood - Stella Shepherd 1480
The Wasted Years - John Harvey 754

Occleswich
The Winter Garden Mystery - Carola Dunn 465

Oxford
The Cruellest Month - Hazel Holt 800
Death and the Oxford Box - Veronica Stallwood 1557
Deathspell - Veronica Stallwood 1558
Decked - Carol Higgins Clark 250
Falconer's Crusade - Ian Morson 1175
Oxford Exit - Veronica Stallwood 1559
Unknown Hand - Gillian Linscott 1031
The Wench Is Dead - Colin Dexter 418
What Men Say - Joan Smith 1522

Oxfordshire
The Prince of Darkness - P.C. Doherty 427

Plymouth
The Plymouth Cloak - Kate Sedley 1469

Scarpinton
Business Unusual - Tim Heald 763

Sealeigh
Peckover Joins the Choir - Michael Kenyon 912

Shellerton, Berkshire
Longshot - Dick Francis 540

Sherebury
The Body in the Transept - Jeanne M. Dams 385

Shrewsbury
The Potter's Field - Ellis Peters 1302

Somerset
Hotel Morgue - Janet Laurence 989
Recipe for Death - Janet Laurence 990

South Midlands
Model Murder - Erica Quest 1338

Streech Grange
The Ice House - Minette Walters 1669

Studland
Clockwork - Neville Steed 1565

Swainshead
The Hanging Valley - Peter Robinson 1394

Taviscombe
Mrs. Malory and the Festival Murders - Hazel Holt 801

Thames River Valley
Death Prone - Clare Curzon 367
Three-Core Lead - Clare Curzon 368

Upper Gorton
Breach of Promise - Roy Hart 748

Upper Grisham
Count the Days - Lin Summerfield 1592

West Yorkshire
Elegy in a Country Graveyard - Audrey Peterson 1304

Wildesham
The Killing of Ellis Martin - Lucretia Grindle 677

Windsor
Dead Set - Jennie Melville 1141

Winslough
Missing Joseph - Elizabeth George 575

Winterford
Bone Idle - Susannah Stacey 1553

Witham
Dorothy and Agatha - Gaylord Larsen 984

Woolsey-under-Bank
A Share in Death - Deborah Crombie 358

Wuffinge Parva
Mayhem in Parva - Nancy Livingston 1035

York
The Apothecary Rose - Candace M. Robb 1375
Bagels for Tea - Serita Stevens 1571
The Dean It Was That Died - Barbara Whitehead 1706
File Under: Deceased - Sarah Lacey 962
The Lady Chapel - Candace M. Robb 1376
Playing God - Barbara Whitehead 1707
Sweet Death, Come Softly - Barbara Whitehead 1708

Yorkshire
Bones and Silence - Reginald Hill 789
The Old Silent - Martha Grimes 676
Past Reason Hated - Peter Robinson 1396
Wednesday's Child - Peter Robinson 1397

EUROPE

Praetorian - Thomas Gifford 584
The Price of Victory - Vincent Green 666
Spy Shadow - Tim Sebastian 1466

FICTIONAL COUNTRY

Luong
Unfunny Money - Gary Alexander 35

FRANCE

Gospel Truths - J.G. Sandom 1429
Irene at Large - Carole Nelson Douglas 442
The Masked Man - P.C. Doherty 425
Old Scores - Aaron Elkins 479
Over the Edge - Betty Rowlands 1409
Pel and the Missing Persons - Mark Hebden 768
Someone Is Killing the Great Chefs of America - Nan Lyons 1061
A Time Without Shadows - Ted Allbeury 38
The Toy Cupboard - Lee Jordan 848

Biarritz
Sister Beneath the Sheet - Gillian Linscott 1029

Cote D'Azur
The Zig-Zag Man - Marvin Albert 27

Honfleur
The Estuary Pilgrim - Douglas Skeggs 1507

Lyon
The Body in the Vestibule - Katherine Hall Page 1258

Nice
Finders Keepers - Elizabeth Travis 1627

Orleans
Bones Gather No Moss - John Sherwood 1483

Paris
The Caravaggio Shawl - Samuel M. Steward 1573
Death Comes as Epiphany - Sharan Newman 1203
Death Off Stage - Richard Grayson 655
False Profit - Robert Eversz 511
Good Morning, Irene - Carole Nelson Douglas 440
The Last Rite of Hugo T - J.N. Catanach 227
Monsieur Pamplemousse Investigates - Michael Bond 151
Panama - Eric Zencey 1787
The Poisoned Chalice - Michael Clynes 264

The Riviera
The Riviera Contract - Marvin Albert 26

St. Pierre La Croix
Mr. Donaghue Investigates - Anna Shone 1488

Vichy
Pamplemousse Rests His Case - Michael Bond 152

GERMANY

The Eagle Has Flown - Jack Higgins 787

Bavaria
The Spanish Maze Game - Noah Webster 1682

Berlin
Deadfall in Berlin - R.D. Zimmerman 1792
The Pale Criminal - Philip Kerr 914
Spandau Phoenix - Greg Iles 824
A Suitcase in Berlin - Don Flynn 532

Leipzig
Frost the Fiddler - Janice Weber 1681

GREECE

Mrs. Pargeter's Package - Simon Brett 175

GUADELOUPE

Pointe-a-Pitre
The Trouble with Too Much Sun - Trella Crespi 347

HONG KONG

Free - Todd Komarnicki 952
The Trail to Buddha's Mirror - Don Winslow 1744
Whisper the Guns - Edward Cline 261

INDIA

The India Exhibition - Richard Timothy Conroy 296

Bombay
Dead on Time - H.R.F. Keating 874
The Iciest Sin - H.R.F. Keating 875

Dharbani
Dead on Time - H.R.F. Keating 874

IRELAND

The Gombeen Man - Randy Lee Eickoff 474

Dublin
Drown All the Dogs - Thomas Adcock 23
Irish Gold - Andrew M. Greeley 657

Galway
Hell Bent - Ken Gross 684

ISRAEL

Murder on a Kibbutz - Batya Gur 690

Jerusalem
The Saturday Morning Murder - Batya Gur 691

ITALY

Death of the Duchess - Elizabeth Eyre 512

Bologna
A Glancing Light - Aaron Elkins 477

Florence
The Dante Game - Jane Langton 979

Rome
Follow That Blonde - Joan Smith 1521
Roman Blood - Steven Saylor 1449
Roman Nights - Ron Burns 201
The Silver Pigs - Lindsey Davis 394
SPQR - John Maddox Roberts 1382
The Trouble with Going Home - Camilla T. Crespi 345

Venice
Death and Judgment - Donna Leon 1002
Death at La Fenice - Donna Leon 1003
Death in a Serene City - Edward Sklepowich 1510
Death in a Strange Country - Donna Leon 1004
A Very Venetian Murder - Haughton Murphy 1187

Verona
Death in Verona - Roy Harley Lewis 1020

JAPAN

East Is East - Emma Lathen 986

Kyoto
Night Butterfly - Patricia McFall 1127

Tokyo
Night Butterfly - Patricia McFall 1127
The Temple Dogs - Warren Murphy 1188

KENYA

Brideprice - J.N. Catanach 226
The Cheetah Chase - Karin McQuillan 1137
Natural Enemies - Sara Cameron 209

Nairobi
Death Underfoot - Dennis Casley 225

MALAYSIA

Gone Wild - James W. Hall 708

MEXICO

The Cactus Garden - Robert Ward 1672
The Man Who Walked Through Walls - James Swain 1595
The Mexican Tree Duck - James Crumley 363
Miami Heat - Jerome Sanford 1433
The Shadow of the Shadow - Paco Ignacio Taibo II 1598

Mexico City
A Black Legend - John Horton 810
An Easy Thing - Paco Ignacio Taibo II 1597

Tijuana
The Loud Adios - Ken Kuhlken 957

MIDDLE EAST

Pillars of Fire - Steve Shagan 1473
The Sum of All Fears - Tom Clancy 248

NORTHERN IRELAND

Belfast
Divorcing Jack - Colin Bateman 104

PACIFIC OCEAN

Bering Sea
Deep Chill - Ian Slater 1513

PAKISTAN

Islamabad
Frozen Assets - James Leasor 996

PANAMA

Murder Is Germane - Karen Saum 1442
Panama - Eric Zencey 1787

POLAND

Polar Star - Martin Cruz Smith 1530

Antarctica
The Ice - Louis Charbonneau 234

PORTUGAL

Funchal
The Hanging Garden - John Sherwood 1485

ROMAN EMPIRE

Etruria
Catalina's Riddle - Steven Saylor 1448

Rome
Catalina's Riddle - Steven Saylor 1448
The Venus Throw - Steven Saylor 1450

RUSSIA

Enemy's Enemy - Jan Guillou 685
The Talinin Madonna - Douglas Skeggs 1508

Moscow
Cover Story - Robert Cullen 365
The Man Who Walked Like a Bear - Stuart M. Kaminsky 859
Red Trance - R.D. Zimmerman 1793
Rostnikov's Vacation - Stuart M. Kaminsky 861

St. Petersburg
Dead Meat - Philip Kerr 913

Yalta
Rostnikov's Vacation - Stuart M. Kaminsky 861

SCOTLAND

Deadeye - Sam Llewellyn 1037
The Spanish Maze Game - Noah Webster 1682
A Vow of Sanctity - Veronica Black 138

Ardcraig
Murder Movie - Jill McGown 1131

Edinburgh
Blood Line - Alanna Knight 941
Deadly Beloved - Alanna Knight 942
Nobody's Fool - Marten Claridge 249

Glasgow
Condition Purple - Peter Turnbull 1639
The Interface Man - Bill Knox 948
Strange Loyalties - William McIlvanney 1134

Gleneagles
So Little to Die For - Lucretia Grindle 678

Lochdubh
Death of a Charming Man - M.C. Beaton 109
Death of a Hussy - M.C. Beaton 110
Death of a Traveling Man - M.C. Beaton 113

Newton Lauder
A Brace of Skeet - Gerald Hammond 719
Home to Roost - Gerald Hammond 720

Orkney Islands
Killing Cousins - Alanna Knight 943

Skag
Death of a Nag - M.C. Beaton 111

SINGAPORE

Singapore Transfer - Wayne Warga 1673

SOUTH AFRICA

The Song Dog - James McClure 1114
Spandau Phoenix - Greg Iles 824

SPAIN

Cut To—Murder - Denise Osborne 1247

Barcelona
Gaudi Afternoon - Barbara Wilson 1731

Majorca
Antipodes - Maria-Antonia Oliver 1236
The Spanish Maze Game - Noah Webster 1682
Too Clever by Half - Roderic Jeffries 845

Santiago
Murder Makes a Pilgrimage - Sister Carol Anne O'Marie 1239

SWEDEN

Enemy's Enemy - Jan Guillou 685

SWITZERLAND

A Singular Spy - Amanda Kyle Williams 1727

Geneva
Deadly Crescendo - Paul Myers 1191
The Run Around - Brian Freemantle 550

UNION OF SOVIET SOCIALIST REPUBLICS

Moving Targets - Sean Flannery 529

Moscow
The Russia House - John Le Carre 995
U.S.S.A. - David Madsen 1066

UNITED STATES

The 6 Messiahs - Mark Frost 560
The Black Echo - Michael Connelly 292

Geographic Index

United States—California

The Codicil - Tom Topor 1623
A Cool Breeze on the Underground - Don Winslow 1743
The Covenant of the Flame - David Morrell 1174
Deadly Allies - Robert J. Randisi 1348
East Is East - Emma Lathen 986
Edge City - Sin Soracco 1537
The End of the Pier - Martha Grimes 674
Flawless - Adam Barrow 99
In the House of Secret Enemies - George C. Chesbro 241
Inadmissible Evidence - Philip Friedman 557
Miami Heat - Jerome Sanford 1433
Moving Targets - Sean Flannery 529
Nice Guys Finish Dead - David Debin 406
Pink Vodka Blues - Neal Barrett Jr. 98
Point of Impact - Stephen Hunter 822
Recalled to Life - Reginald Hill 790
River of Darkness - James Grady 632
A Scandal in Belgravia - Robert Barnard 91
Scotch on the Rocks - Howard Browne 183
A Singular Spy - Amanda Kyle Williams 1727
Sleeping Dogs - Thomas Perry 1297
Someone Is Killing the Great Chefs of America - Nan Lyons 1061
Stacked Deck - Bill Pronzini 1330
The Suspense Is Killing Me - Thomas Maxwell 1102
Thunder - James Grady 633
Vital Signs - Robin Cook 303
Winter of the Wolves - James N. Frey 552
The Woman Who Fell From Grace - David Handler 724

Blackwater Bay
A Few Dying Words - Paula Gosling 626

Kindle County
Pleading Guilty - Scott Turow 1640

Victoria Springs
Blooming Murder - Jean Hager 698

ALASKA

The Curious Eat Themselves - John Straley 1580
The Frozen Franklin - Sean Hanlon 725
Murder on the Iditarod Trail - Sue Henry 775
Purgatory - Monty Mickleson 1152

Aleutian Islands
Dead in the Water - Dana Stabenow 1551

Anchorage
Murder Most Grizzly - Elizabeth Quinn 1340

Niniltna
A Cold Day for Murder - Dana Stabenow 1549

Prudhoe
A Cold-Blooded Business - Dana Stabenow 1550

Sitka
The Woman Who Married a Bear - John Straley 1581

Tanada
Play with Fire - Dana Stabenow 1552

Tanana
A Wolf in Death's Clothing - Elizabeth Quinn 1341

ARIZONA

Minor in Possession - J.A. Jance 844
Purgatory - Monty Mickleson 1152

Bisbee
Desert Heat - J.A. Jance 842

Navajo Reservation
Sacred Clowns - Tony Hillerman 792

Phoenix
Flamingos - Marc Savage 1444
Pious Deception - Susan Dunlap 462
Silent Night - Gary Amo 49

Tucson
The 27 Ingredient Chili Con Carne Murders - Nancy Pickard 1315
The Dividing Line - Richard Parrish 1273

ARKANSAS

Blackwell County
Probable Cause - Griff Stockley 1577

Farberville
Roll Over and Play Dead - Joan Hess 781

Fayetteville
Illegal Motion - Grif Stockley 1576

Hot Springs
He Was Her Man - Sarah Shankman 1474

Lawrenceton
A Bone to Pick - Charlaine Harris 731

Maggody
Madness in Maggody - Joan Hess 777
Miracles in Maggody - Joan Hess 778
Mortal Remains in Maggody - Joan Hess 779
O Little Town of Maggody - Joan Hess 780

CALIFORNIA

The Big Freeze - Michael J. Katz 871
The Boy Who Was Buried This Morning - Joseph Hansen 726
The Bulrush Murders - Rebecca Rothenberg 1405
The Cactus Garden - Robert Ward 1672
China Lake - Anthony Hyde 823
Compelling Evidence - Steve Martini 1090
Crime, Punishment and Resurrection - Michael Collins 283
Death Goes on Retreat - Sister Carol Anne O'Marie 1237
Deeds of Trust - Victor Wuamett 1778
F Is for Fugitive - Sue Grafton 634
False Profit - Robert Eversz 511
The Fast-Death Factor - Virginia Crosby 359
Flowers for the Dead - Ann M. Williams 1728
Guilt by Association - Susan R. Sloan 1514
Gun Men - Gary Friedman 553
A Hard Bargain - Lia Matera 1092
Hard News - Mark T. Sullivan 1590
Hit and Run - Maxine O'Callaghan 1219
The Horse Latitudes - Robert Ferrigno 526
Hush, Money - Jean Femling 523
In Deep - Bruce Jones 846
In the Dark - Carol Brennan 173
Kingdom Road - K. Patrick Conner 295
Money Burns - A.E. Maxwell 1100
Murdock Cracks Ice - Robert J. Ray 1353
The Northwest Murders - Elizabeth Atwood Taylor 1607
Rage - Gwen Moffat 1162
The Tijuana Bible - Ron Goulart 630
Where Echoes Live - Marcia Muller 1184
Whisper Death - John Lawrence Reynolds 1363

Azalea
Suffer Little Children - Thomas D. Davis 396

Bay Cove
Threnody for Two - Jeanne Hart 747

Berkeley
Death and Taxes - Susan Dunlap 460
Diamond in the Buff - Susan Dunlap 461
Interview with Mattie - Shelley Singer 1504
Searching for Sara - Shelley Singer 1506
Time Expired - Susan Dunlap 464

Big Sur
A Dry and Thirsty Ground - Mike Weiss 1688

Buckeye
Emma Chizzit and the Mother Lode Marauder - Mary Bowen Hall 711

Carmel
Probable Cause - Ridley Pearson 1285
A Wicked Slice - Aaron Elkins 480

Delores
The Last Resort - Jaqueline Girdner 594

Dos Cruces
Orphans - Gerald Pearce 1281

Durango
The Fourth Durango - Ross Thomas 1612

East Shasta
Justice for Some - Kate Wilhelm 1724

Hayesville
Cooking Up Trouble - Joanne Pence 1289

Hollywood
The Black Mask Murders - William F. Nolan 1207
Dead-Stick - L.J. Washburn 1674
Dog Heavies - L.J. Washburn 1675

Jolliston
Mass Murder - John Keith Drummond 449

La Jolla
Pious Deception - Susan Dunlap 462

Las Almas
Murder in Brief - Carrol Lachint 963

Las Piernas
Goodnight, Irene - Jan Burke 198

Long Beach
Midnight Baby - Wendy Hornsby 808

Los Alegres
With an Extreme Burning - Bill Pronzini 1331

Los Angeles
Ah, Treachery - Ross Thomas 1611
Angel of Death - Rochelle Majer Krich 953
Bad Love - Jonathan Kellerman 885
The Beverly Malibu - Katherine V. Forrest 533
The Black Ice - Michael Connelly 293
Bleeding Dodger Blue - Crabbe Evers 505
Boiled in Concrete - Jesse Sublett 1587
The Book of Numbers - David Thoreau 1616
The Boss's Wife - S.L. Stebel 1562
Carcass Trade - Noreen Ayres 74
The Cheshire Moon - Robert Ferrigno 525
Cold Call - Dianne G. Pugh 1333
The Concrete Blonde - Michael Connelly 294
A Country of Old Men - Joseph Hansen 727
Dark of Night - Richard Nehrbass 1200
Day of Atonement - Faye Kellerman 878
Dead Pan - Jane Dentinger 413
Death as a Career Move - Bruce Cook 299
Death of the Office Witch - Marlys Millhiser 1155
Devil in a Blue Dress - Walter Mosley 1176
Dogtown - Mercedes Lambert 972
Earth Angels - Gerald Petievich 1311
Everything but the Squeal - Timothy Hallinan 716
Fair Game - Rochelle Majer Krich 954
False Prophet - Faye Kellerman 879
Fire Horse - Bill Shoemaker 1486
A Flower in the Desert - Walter Satterthwait 1439
The Forever Beat - John Cline 262
Free Fall - Robert Crais 341
Frozen Stare - Richard B. Schwartz 1459
Fuse Time - Max Byrd 205
Get Shorty - Elmore Leonard 1005
Grievous Sin - Faye Kellerman 880
A Gypsy Good Time - Gustav Hasford 755
H Is for Homicide - Sue Grafton 636
Hard Fall - Ridley Pearson 1284

United States—California

Hollywood Requiem - Peter Freeborn 546
Honolulu Red - Lue Zimmelman 1789
Hot Air - Jon L. Breen 170
An Hour to Kill - Edward Wellen 1690
Incinerator - Timothy Hallinan 717
Justice - Faye Kellerman 881
The Keeper - Meg O'Brien 1217
L.A. Confidential - James Ellroy 483
Last Dance in Redondo Beach - Michael J. Katz 872
A Lawyer's Tale - D. Kincaid 923
Loose Lips - Jon L. Breen 171
Lullaby Town - Robert Crais 342
The Man in the Moon - Frank Norwood 1212
The Melting Clock - Stuart M. Kaminsky 860
Midnight Baby - Wendy Hornsby 808
Milk and Honey - Faye Kellerman 882
Mitigating Circumstances - Nancy Taylor Rosenberg 1401
The Mother Shadow - Melodie Johnson Howe 814
Murder by Tradition - Katherine V. Forrest 534
Murder Offscreen - Denise Osborne 1248
My Gun Has Bullets - Lee Goldberg 606
North of Montana - April Smith 1515
Not Long for This World - Gar Anthony Haywood 762
On the Edge - Ed Naha 1193
Perchance to Dream - Robert B. Parker 1270
Perry Mason in The Case of Too Many Murders - Thomas Chastain 239
A Pocketful of Karma - Taffy Cannon 216
Private Eyes - Jonathan Kellerman 886
A Red Death - Walter Mosley 1177
Rising Sun - Michael Crichton 348
Rough Cut - Bruce Cook 300
Sanctuary - Faye Kellerman 884
Self-Defense - Jonathan Kellerman 887
Shooting Script - Gordon Cotler 332
Shot on Location - Stan Cutler 369
The Sidewalk Hilton - Bruce Cook 301
Skin Deep - Timothy Hallinan 718
Stalking the Angel - Robert Crais 343
Telling Lies - Wendy Hornsby 809
Thursday's Child - Teri White 1705
Till Death Do Us Part - Rochelle Majer Krich 955
Time Bomb - Jonathan Kellerman 888
Tropical Depression - Jeffry P. Lindsay 1024
Truck Shot - Jim Stinson 1574
TV Safe - Jim Stinson 1575
Voodoo River - Robert Crais 344
Wasteland - Peter McCabe 1110
White Butterfly - Walter Mosley 1178

Los Robles
How Town - Michael Nava 1194

Malibu
The Great California Game - Jonathan Gash 570

Mar Vista
Artichoke Hearts - Victor Wuamett 1777

Marin County
A Stiff Critique - Jaqueline Girdner 595
Tea-Totally Dead - Jaqueline Girdner 596

Meridan
Bad Desire - Gary Devon 417

Mill Valley
Adjusted to Death - Jaqueline Girdner 593

Monte
Larkspur - Sheila Simonson 1500

Monterey
Dead in the Water - Julie Smith 1524
Death by Degrees - Robin Wilson 1735

Napa Valley
Emma Chizzit and the Napa Nemesis - Mary Bowen Hall 712
Full-Bodied Red - Bruce Zimmerman 1790
Murder in the Napa Valley - David Osborn 1245

Noble Rot - Will Harriss 739
Vintage Polo - Jerry Kennealy 908

Nevada City
Copy Kat - Karen Kijewski 918

Newport Beach
Merry Christmas, Murdock - Robert J. Ray 1352

Oakland
The Classic Car Killer - Richard A. Lupoff 1054
Nobody's Child - Janet Dawson 398
A Single Stone - Marilyn Wallace 1664

Orange County
Set-Up - Maxine O'Callaghan 1220

Palm Springs
The Total Zone - Martina Navratilova 1195

Palo Alto
Murder in a Nice Neighborhood - Lora Roberts 1388

Patsboro
A Strange and Bitter Crop - E.L. Wyrick 1780

Port Silva
Grandmother's House - Janet LaPierre 983

Sacramento
Alley Kat Blues - Karen Kijewski 917
Copy Kat - Karen Kijewski 918
Katapult - Karen Kijewski 919
Katwalk - Karen Kijewski 920
Point Blank - Jayson Livingston 1033
Wild Kat - Karen Kijewski 921

Salinas
Cutter - Laura Crum 362
Tracer, Inc. - Jeff Andrus 58

San Celina
Fool's Puzzle - Earlene Fowler 536
Irish Chain - Earlene Fowler 537

San Diego
The Angel Gang - Ken Kuhlken 956
Balboa Firefly - Jack Trolley 1633
Child of Silence - Abigail Padgett 1251
A Clinic for Murder - Marsha Landreth 974
Death of a Postmodernist - Janice Steinberg 1568
The Hotel Detective - Alan Russell 1413
Jinx - Julie Robitaille 1398
The Loud Adios - Ken Kuhlken 957
Murder Begins at Home - Dale L. Gilbert 585
Murder by Owl Light - Corinne Holt Sawyer 1445
Murder Has No Calories - Corinne Holt Sawyer 1446
Murder in Scorpio - Martha C. Lawrence 993
Strawgirl - Abigail Padgett 1252
The Venus Deal - Ken Kuhlken 958
When Reason Sleeps - Tom Sehler 1472

San Francisco
32 Cadillacs - Joe Gores 616
According to St. John - William Babula 77
Beggar's Choice - Jerry Kennealy 906
Blood of Poets - Kenn Davis 393
Blood Type - Stephen Greenleaf 667
Blue Lonesome - Bill Pronzini 1325
Book Case - Stephen Greenleaf 668
Breakdown - Bill Pronzini 1326
Came a Dead Cat - James N. Frey 551
A Certain Justice - John T. Lescroart 1008
Charged with Guilt - Gloria White 1700
A Clean Sweep - David Berlinski 123
The Comic Book Killer - Richard A. Lupoff 1055
Dark Star - Marcia Muller 1180
Dead Center - Collin Wilcox 1711
Dead Man - Joe Gores 617
Epitaphs - Bill Pronzini 1327
Except for the Bones - Collin Wilcox 1713
Full Circle - Collin Wilcox 1714
The Genesis Files - Bob Biderman 130

What Mystery Do I Read Next?

The Good Fight - Lia Matera 1091
A Grave Talent - Laurie R. King 925
Hard Evidence - John T. Lescroart 1009
Hare Today, Gone Tomorrow - Meg O'Brien 1216
Hire a Hangman - Collin Wilcox 1715
Jackpot - Bill Pronzini 1328
The Keeper - Meg O'Brien 1217
Kimura - Robert Davis 395
Kindred Crimes - Janet Dawson 397
Love nor Money - Linda Grant 648
Menaced Assassin - Joe Gores 618
Money to Burn - Gloria White 1701
Murder by the Book - Pat Welch 1689
Murder in Ordinary Time - Sister Carol Anne O'Marie 1238
Murder on the Run - Gloria White 1702
Night of the Cat - James Schermerhorn 1452
No Sign of Murder - Alan Russell 1414
Nobody's Child - Janet Dawson 398
Other People's Skeletons - Julie Smith 1529
Picture of David - Shelley Singer 1505
Poison Fruit - Chelsea Quinn Yarbro 1781
Prior Convictions - Lia Matera 1093
Quarry - Bill Pronzini 1329
A Relative Stranger - Margaret Lucke 1052
Rogue Wave - Susan Dunlap 463
Searching for Sara - Shelley Singer 1506
The Shape of Dread - Marcia Muller 1181
Silent Witness - Collin Wilcox 1716
The Society Ball Murders - Jack Albin Anderson 51
Something's Cooking - Joanne Pence 1290
Spare Change - John A. Peak 1280
Special Delivery - Jerry Kennealy 907
The Strange Files of Fremont Jones - Dianne Day 400
Switchback - Collin Wilcox 1717
Till The Butchers Cut Him Down - Marcia Muller 1182
To Play the Fool - Laurie R. King 927
Too Many Cooks - Joanne Pence 1291
The Trail to Buddha's Mirror - Don Winslow 1744
Trophies and Dead Things - Marcia Muller 1183
The Vig - John T. Lescroart 1010
A Wild and Lonely Place - Marcia Muller 1185
With Siberia Comes a Chill - Kirk Mitchell 1161
A Woman's Place - Linda Grant 649

San Miguel
The Watchman - Michael Allegretto 44

Santa Angelica
Half a Mind - Wendy Hornsby 807

Santa Barbara
Cassandra in Red - Michael Collins 281
Chasing Eights - Michael Collins 282
East Beach - Ron Ely 485
Night Shadows - Ron Ely 486

Santa Clarissa
Make Friends with Murder - Judith Garwood 569

Santa Linda
Library: No Murder Aloud - Susan Steiner 1569

Santa Teresa
G Is for Gumshoe - Sue Grafton 635
I Is for Innocent - Sue Grafton 637
K Is for Killer - Sue Grafton 638
L Is for Lawless - Sue Grafton 639

Sequoia National Park
Wildfire - Kenneth W. Goddard 605

Silicon Valley
Love Bytes - Sally Chapman 232

Sonoma
Dark Star - Marcia Muller 1180

Tahoe
The Angel Gang - Ken Kuhlken 956

Geographic Index

United States—Georgia

COLORADO

Dead in the Scrub - B.J. Oliphant 1232
From Here to Paternity - Jill Churchill 246
Night of Reunion - Michael Allegretto 42

Aspen
Into Thin Air - Thomas Zigal 1788
When She Was Bad - Ron Faust 518

Aspen Meadow
The Cereal Murders - Diane Mott Davidson 389
Dying for Chocolate - Diane Mott Davidson 390

Bandora
Murder in Bandora - Leona Karr 868

Boulder
Unsafe Keeping - Carol Cail 206

Colorado Springs
Beat Up a Cookie - Denise Dietz 422
Throw Darts at a Cheesecake - Denise Dietz 423

Cutler
No Place for Secrets - Sherry Lewis 1021

Denver
Blood Relative - Michael Allegretto 39
Body Guard - Rex Burns 199
Booked to Die - John Dunning 466
Death and the Dogwalker - A.J. Orde 1240
Death Qualified: A Mystery of Chaos - Kate Wilhelm 1723
A Fall in Denver - Sarah Andrews 56
Grave Doubt - Michael Allegretto 41
A Little Neighborhood Murder - A.J. Orde 1241
A Long Time Dead - A.J. Orde 1242
A Love to Die For - Christine T. Jorgensen 849
Night Rituals - Gary Paulsen 1279
Obstacle Course - Yvonne Montgomery 1167
Parts Unknown - Rex Burns 200
The Suitor - Michael Allegretto 43
The Water Cure - Warwick Downing 446
When Reason Sleeps - Tom Sehler 1472

Norville
Three Strikes, You're Dead - Michael Geller 574

Ridge County
The Unexpected Corpse - B.J. Oliphant 1235

Sopris County
A Clear Case of Murder - Warwick Downing 445

CONNECTICUT

Darkness Falls - Joyce Anne Schneider 1453
Infected Be the Air - Janice Law 991
Once and Always Murder - Orania Papazoglou 1263
Personal - C.K. Cambray 208
The Pumpkin-Shell Wife - Susanna Hofmann McShea 1138
The Tijuana Bible - Ron Goulart 630

Brimstone
Even the Butler Was Poor - Ron Goulart 628
Now He Thinks He's Dead - Ron Goulart 629

Hancock
All Hallows Evil - Valerie Wolzien 1748
A Good Year for a Corpse - Valerie Wolzien 1749
We Wish You a Merry Murder - Valerie Wolzien 1750

Hartford
Chain of Evidence - Ridley Pearson 1283

Murphysville
Death on the Mississippi - Richard Forrest 535

New Haven
Desperate Remedy - Mary Kittredge 931
Kill or Cure - Mary Kittredge 932
Poison Pen - Mary Kittredge 933
Walking Dead Man - Mary Kittredge 934

Newbury
Hardscape - Justin Scott 1463
StoneDust - Justin Scott 1464

Ridgewood
Friends till the End - Gloria Dank 387

Stamford
A Pedigree to Die For - Laurien Berenson 121

DELAWARE

The Judas Pool - George Owens 1250

DISTRICT OF COLUMBIA

Washington
Ah, Treachery - Ross Thomas 1611
Along Came a Spider - James Patterson 1276
Bad News Travels Fast - Gar Anthony Haywood 761
A Blood Affair - Jan Roberts 1381
Closing Costs - Thomas Bunn 189
Faithfully Executed - Michael Bowen 159
A Fistful of Empty - Benjamin M. Schutz 1457
Hard Fall - Ridley Pearson 1284
The India Exhibition - Richard Timothy Conroy 296
Knight & Day - Ron Nessen 1201
The Last Good German - Bill Granger 647
The Last Surprise - William Moore 1169
The Man in the Moon - Frank Norwood 1212
Mexico Is Forever - Benjamin M. Schutz 1458
Mr. Smithson's Bones - Richard Timothy Conroy 297
Murder at the Kennedy Center - Margaret Truman 1634
Paramour - Gerald Petievich 1312
The Pelican Brief - John Grisham 681
Playing the Dozens - William D. Pease 1286
Shoedog - George Pelecanos 1288
A Slip of the Tong - Charles A. Goodrum 611
The Sum of All Fears - Tom Clancy 248
Talking God - Tony Hillerman 793
Tucker's Last Stand - William F. Buckley Jr. 188
Twilight at Mac's Place - Ross Thomas 1613

FLORIDA

Backhand - Liza Cody 269
Deep End - Geoffrey Norman 1210
Done Deal - Les Standiford 1561
Flame - John Lutz 1057
Flamingo - Bob Reiss 1359
God Bless John Wayne - Kinky Friedman 554
Gone Wild - James W. Hall 708
Hour of the Manatee - E.C. Ayres 73
In the Dark - Carol Brennan 173
Mean High Tide - James W. Hall 710
Native Tongue - Carl Hiaasen 782
Sanibel Flats - Randy Wayne White 1704
Skin Tight - Carl Hiaasen 783
Spark - John Lutz 1058
Storm Front - Virginia Anderson 53
Stormy Weather - Carl Hiaasen 784

Brightwater Beach
Copy Cat Crimes - Karen Ann Wilson 1733

Calusa
Three Blind Mice - Ed McBain 1106

Fort Lauderdale
The Harry Chronicles - Allan Pedrazas 1287
Strip Tease - Carl Hiaasen 785

Gulf Shores
Axx Goes South - Frederic Huber 817

Ila Island
Straight as an Arrow - Celestine Sibley 1498

Jacksonville
Deadly Secrets on the St. Johns - Patricia Houck Sprinkle 1542

Key West
Bones of Coral - James W. Hall 707
Killer in Paradise - John Leslie 1011
Killing Me Softly - John Leslie 1012
The Thirteenth Apostle - Gloria Gonzalez 610
Tropical Depression - Jeffry P. Lindsay 1024

Manatee City
Eye of the Gator - E.C. Ayres 72

Marlinsport
Neon Dancers - Matt Taylor 1608

Miami
Dead Easy - Arthur F. Nehrbass 1199
Deal to Die For - Les Standiford 1560
Double Down - Tom Kakonis 854
Hard Aground - James W. Hall 709
An Hour to Kill - Edward Wellen 1690
Just Cause - John Katzenbach 873
Miami Purity - Vicki Hendricks 773
Mortal Sin - Paul Levine 1014
Night Vision - Paul Levine 1015
Nobody Lives Forever - Edna Buchanan 187
Rum Punch - Elmore Leonard 1007
Suspicion of Guilt - Barbara Parker 1268
To Speak for the Dead - Paul Levine 1016

Miami Beach
Snagged - Carol Higgins Clark 251

Orlando
Trade-Off - Harrison Arnston 66

Palm Beach
Maximum Bob - Elmore Leonard 1006

Paradise Cay
Eight Dogs Flying - Karen Ann Wilson 1734

St. Christopher
Selena - Gordon Randolph Willey 1726

Sunland
Night Game - Alison Gordon 613

Tampa
Hard Look - Robert J. Randisi 1349

Tango Key
High Strangeness - Alison Drake 447

Treasure Coast
Death Among the Angels - John Walter Putre 1336

Verity
Turtle Moon - Alice Hoffman 795

West Palm Beach
Swing - L.L. Enger 493

GEORGIA

Death Beneath the Christmas Tree - Robert Nordan 1208
Dire Happenings at Scratch Ankle - Celestine Sibley 1496

Atlanta
Ah, Sweet Mystery - Celestine Sibley 1495
Every Crooked Nanny - Kathy Hogan Trocheck 1631
Murder on Peachtree Street - Patricia Houck Sprinkle 1543
A Plague of Kinfolks - Celestine Sibley 1497
Somebody's Dead in Snellville - Patricia Houck Sprinkle 1545
Ties That Bind - Sherryl Woods 1759
To Live and Die in Dixie - Kathy Hogan Trocheck 1632
The Water Cure - Warwick Downing 446

United States—Great Lakes

Buckhead
A Mystery Bred in Buckhead - Patricia Houck Sprinkle   1544

Cumberland Island
Palindrome - Stuart Woods   1762

Lawrenceton
The Julius House - Charlaine Harris   732

Markham
Death on Wheels - Robert Nordan   1209

Snellville
Somebody's Dead in Snellville - Patricia Houck Sprinkle   1545

GREAT LAKES

The Body in Blackwater Bay - Paula Gosling   624
Hard Tack - Barbara D'Amato   382

HAWAII

The George Eliot Murders - Edith Skom   1511
Peril under the Palms - K.K. Beck   117

Honolulu
Honolulu Red - Lue Zimmelman   1789

Oahu
Diamond Head - Marian J.A. Jackson   834

IDAHO

Barking Dogs - R.R. Irvine   827

Rock Springs
Grave Secrets - Louise Hendricksen   774

St. Clair
Heat - Stuart Woods   1760

ILLINOIS

Fatal Obsession - D.B. Taylor   1606
Sight Unseen - David Lorne   1046

Charter
Original Sin - Mary Monica Pulver   1334

Chicago
Blood Trance - R.D. Zimmerman   1791
Burn Marks - Sara Paretsky   1264
Caught in the Shadows - C.A. Haddad   694
The Class Menagerie - Jill Churchill   244
Dead Man - Joe Gores   617
Deadfall in Berlin - R.D. Zimmerman   1792
Death Came Dressed in White - Michael W. Sherer   1481
Death in Uptown - Michael Raleigh   1345
Drover and the Zebras - Bill Granger   646
A Farewell to Yarns - Jill Churchill   245
Funny as a Dead Comic - Susan Rogers Cooper   312
Get What's Coming - Sam Reaves   1354
The Gift Horse's Mouth - Robert Campbell   212
Guardian Angel - Sara Paretsky   1265
Happy Are the Merciful - Andrew M. Greeley   656
Hard Tack - Barbara D'Amato   382
Hard Women - Barbara D'Amato   383
In the Game - Nikki Baker   82
King of the Hustlers - Eugene Izzi   831
Last Dance in Redondo Beach - Michael J. Katz   872
The Last Gambit - David Delman   411
Lieberman's Choice - Stuart M. Kaminsky   856
Lieberman's Day - Stuart M. Kaminsky   857
Lieberman's Folly - Stuart M. Kaminsky   858
A Long Cold Fall - Sam Reaves   1355
The Man with My Name - Paul Engleman   494
Murder in Store - D.C. Brod   178

Murder in the Post-War World - Max Allan Collins   279
Murder in Wrigley Field - Crabbe Evers   507
Nibbled to Death by Ducks - Robert Campbell   213
Nun Plussed - Monica Quill   1339
The Only Good Priest - Mark Richard Zubro   1795
Primal Fear - William Diehl   421
A Quiche Before Dying - Jill Churchill   247
Seeing the Elephant - Les Roberts   1387
Shadowchase - Martin Blank   143
The Sidewalk Hilton - Bruce Cook   301
Skin Deep Is Fatal - Michael Cormany   320
Sorry Now? - Mark Richard Zubro   1796
Suicide Squeeze - David Everson   510
Tunnel Vision - Sara Paretsky   1266
A Wide and Capable Revenge - Thomas McCall   1113

Garden Hills
World of Hurt - Richard Rosen   1400

Lafite
Show Stopper - Mary Monica Pulver   1335

Lincoln Prairie
Dead Time - Eleanor Taylor Bland   141
Slow Burn - Eleanor Taylor Bland   142

Rockford
The Skintight Shroud - Wayne Dundee   459

Sarahville
Murder by Tarot - Al Guthrie   693

Springfield
False Profits - David Everson   509

INDIANA

The Lost Keats - Terence Faherty   515

Dunning
Gravestone - P.M. Carlson   219

Fairfield
Long Chain of Death - S.K. Wolf   1747

Fort Wayne
The Flip Side of Life - James E. Martin   1085

Indianapolis
Called by a Panther - Michael Z. Lewin   1019
The Iron Glove - Ronald Tierney   1619
The Steel Web - Ronald Tierney   1620
The Stone Veil - Ronald Tierney   1621

Merrillville
Blossom - Andrew Vachss   1643

Oliver
Buried in Quilts - Sara Hoskinson Frommer   559

Wyler
Body and Soil - Ralph McInerny   1135

IOWA

Cedar Rapids
The Night Remembers - Ed Gorman   623

Steubenville
32 Cadillacs - Joe Gores   616

KANSAS

Braddock
Murder at St. Adelaide's - Gerelyn Hollingsworth   799

Hampstead
Consider the Crows - Charlene Weir   1685
Family Practice - Charlene Weir   1686
The Winter Widow - Charlene Weir   1687

Kansas City
Bum Steer - Nancy Pickard   1316

What Mystery Do I Read Next?

Final Dictation - L.M. Vincent   1655

Wichita
The Late Man - James Preston Girard   592

KENTUCKY

Blood Lies - Virginia Anderson   52
Jordon's Wager - Frank C. Strunk   1584

Baird
Viper Quarry - Dean Feldmeyer   522

Buxton
Jordon's Showdown - Frank C. Strunk   1583

Hamilton
Home Sweet Homicide - Kate Morgan   1171
A Slay at the Races - Kate Morgan   1172

Louisville
The Queen's Mare - John Birkett   133

Pigeon Fork
Pet Peeves - Taylor McCafferty   1111

Portland
L Is for Lawless - Sue Grafton   639

LOUISIANA

Black Cherry Blues - James Lee Burke   193
Blood and Thunder - Max Allan Collins   276
Louisiana Blue - David Poyer   1324
Voodoo River - Robert Crais   344

Magnolia
The Deer Killers - Gunnard Landers   973

New Orleans
All I Have Is Blue - James Colbert   272
The Axeman's Jazz - Julie Smith   1523
Behind Eclaire's Doors - Sophie Dunbar   457
Black Hornet - James Sallis   1421
Blood on the Bayou - D.J. Donaldson   429
Blue Bayou - Dick Lochte   1038
Burning Angel - James Lee Burke   194
The Caesar Clue - M.K. Shuman   1491
Dead Man - Joe Gores   617
Deep Kill - M.K. Shuman   1492
Dixie City Jam - James Lee Burke   195
The Emerald Lizard - Chris Wiltz   1738
Free - Todd Komarnicki   952
House of Blues - Julie Smith   1525
In the Electric Mist with Confederate Dead - James Lee Burke   196
The Intersection of Law and Desire - J.M. Redmann   1356
Jazz Funeral - Julie Smith   1526
The Last Man to Die - M.K. Shuman   1493
The Maya Stone Murders - M.K. Shuman   1494
A Morning for Flamingos - James Lee Burke   197
Moth - James Sallis   1422
The Neon Smile - Dick Lochte   1039
New Orleans Beat - Julie Smith   1527
New Orleans Mourning - Julie Smith   1528
New Orleans Requiem - D.J. Donaldson   430
No Mardi Gras for the Dead - D.J. Donaldson   431
Now Let's Talk of Graves - Sarah Shankman   1476
Purgatory - Monty Mickleson   1152
Red Knight - J. Madison Davis   391
Skinny Man - James Colbert   273
The Software Bomb - Steven Womack   1753
Stalking Horse - Bill Shoemaker   1487
White Rook - J. Madison Davis   392
With Extreme Prejudice - Frederick Barton   102

Troy
Death Notice - M.S. Karl   866

Troy Parrish
Deerslayer - M.S. Karl   867

Geographic Index

MAINE

Black Ribbon - Susan Conant   288
The Bridled Groom - J.S. Borthwick   154
Foursome - Jeremiah Healy   765
The Gladstone Bag - Charlotte MacLeod   1063
Mail-Order Murder - Leslie Meier   1140
Something in the Water - Charlotte MacLeod   1065
Switching the Odds - Phyllis Knight   947

Androscoggin
Deadline - Gerry Boyle   163

Balaclava Junction
An Owl Too Many - Charlotte MacLeod   1064

Portland
Shadow Dance - Agnes Bushnell   202
Shattered Rhythms - Phyllis Knight   946
World of Hurt - Richard Rosen   1400

San Pere
The Body in the Basement - Katherine Hall Page   1254

MARYLAND

The Chesapeake Project - Phyllis Horn   806
Running Mates - John Feinstein   521
True Crime - Michael Mewshaw   1145
Why Isn't Becky Twitchell Dead? - Mark Richard Zubro   1797

Annapolis
Trade Secrets - Ray Garton   568

Baltimore
Double Blind - David Laing   965
Moth to the Flame - Kathleen Dougherty   437

Burnham State
Murder on the Chesapeake - David Osborn   1246

Chesapeake Bay
A Small and Incidental Murder - John Walter Putre   1337

Maryville
Seven Kinds of Death - Kate Wilhelm   1725

MASSACHUSETTS

The Choice - Barry Reed   1357
Death in a Funhouse Mirror - Kate Clark Flora   531
Love Lies Slain - L.L. Blackmur   139
Miss Lizzie - Walter Satterthwait   1441
Whisper Death - John Lawrence Reynolds   1363
Yellow Bird - Rick Boyer   162

Aleford
The Body in the Belfry - Katherine Hall Page   1255
The Body in the Bouillon - Katherine Hall Page   1256
The Body in the Cast - Katherine Hall Page   1257

Althol
Bait - Kenneth Abel   3

Bensington
No Way Home - Andrew Coburn   267
Voices in the Dark - Andrew Coburn   268

The Berkshires
Mommy and the Murder - Nancy Gladstone   600

Boston
Act of God - Jeremiah Healy   764
And Leave Her Lay Dying - John Lawrence Reynolds   1362
Aunt Dimity's Death - Nancy Atherton   69
Bear Hug - Jerome Doolittle   432
Body Scissors - Jerome Doolittle   433
A Body to Dye For - Grant Michaels   1150
Coyote - Linda Barnes   92
Dangerous Waters - Bill Eidson   475
Dark Swan - Kathryn Lasky Knight   944
Dead Winter - William G. Tapply   1602
Die Dreaming - Terence Faherty   514
Double Deuce - Robert B. Parker   1269
A Drink Before the War - Dennis Lehane   1000
Fear in Fenway - Crabbe Evers   506
Hammurabi's Code - Charles Kenney   909
Indecent Behavior - Caryl Rivers   1372
Kill Story - Jerome Doolittle   434
A Killing in Venture Capital - Margaret Logan   1040
Love You to Death - Grant Michaels   1151
The Marvell College Murders - Sophie Belfort   119
Mortal Words - Kathryn Lasky Knight   945
Murder at Fenway Park - Troy Soos   1536
Natural Causes - Michael Palmer   1262
Obit - Daniel Paisner   1261
Obligations of the Bone - Dick Cluster   263
Paint It Black - W.R. Philbrick   1313
Peeping Thomas - Robert Reeves   1358
Snapshot - Linda Barnes   93
Stardust - Robert B. Parker   1271
Steel Guitar - Linda Barnes   94
Still Among the Living - Zachary Klein   938
Stranglehold - Jerome Doolittle   435
A Sudden Death at the Norfolk Cafe - Winona Sullivan   1591
Tight Lines - William G. Tapply   1604
Trade Secrets - Maynard F. Thomson   1615
Two Way Toll - Zachary Klein   939
The Very Bad Thing - Ned White   1703
A Very Proper Death - Alex Juniper   850

Cambridge
And Soon I'll Come to Kill You - Susan Kelly   893
A Bite of Death - Susan Conant   287
Bloodlines - Susan Conant   289
Out of the Darkness - Susan Kelly   894
Paws Before Dying - Susan Conant   290
Quaker Silence - Irene Allen   45
Quaker Witness - Irene Allen   46
Ruffly Speaking - Susan Conant   291
Until Proven Innocent - Susan Kelly   895
The Wyndham Case - Jill Paton Walsh   1275

Cape Cod
Death Below Deck - Douglas Kiker   922
Death in Deep Water - Paul Kemprecos   903
Neptune's Eye - Paul Kemprecos   905
Nightmare Point - Carole Berry   128
Revolution #9 - Peter Abrahams   6
Spotted Cats - William G. Tapply   1603

Close Harbor
Rough Water - Sally Gunning   687

Exeter County
The Immediate Prospect of Being Hanged - Walter Walker   1662

Fall River
Forty Whacks - Sheila MacGill Callahan   207

Lowell
The Heaven Stone - David Daniel   386

Manton
Dead Easy - E.S. Russell   1415

Martha's Vineyard
A Beautiful Place to Die - Philip R. Craig   335
A Case of Vineyard Poisoning - Philip R. Craig   336
Cliff Hanger - Philip R. Craig   337
The Double Minded Men - Philip R. Craig   338
In-laws and Outlaws - Barbara Paul   1277
Off Season - Philip R. Craig   339
The Woman Who Walked into the Sea - Philip R. Craig   340

Mellingham
Family Album - Susan Oleksiw   1230
Murder in Mellingham - Susan Oleksiw   1231

Nantucket
Death on Rough Water - Francine Matthews   1099

Nasharbor
Yesterday's News - Jeremiah Healy   766

Nashtoba
Hot Water - Sally Gunning   686
Still Water - Sally Gunning   688
Troubled Water - Sally Gunning   689

Norham
Dead Wrong - Alan Dennis Burke   192

Northampton
In the Dead of Winter - Abbey Penn Baker   81

Palmer
First Pedigree Murder - Melissa Cleary   257
A Tail of Two Murders - Melissa Cleary   259

Port City
Walking Shadow - Robert B. Parker   1272

Port Frederick
I.O.U. - Nancy Pickard   1318

Provincetown
The Lavender House Murder - Nikki Baker   83

Quanset Beach
Feeding Frenzy - Paul Kemprecos   904

Rockland
The Lion's Share - Kelly A. Tate   1605

Strike's Landing
Dead in the Water - W.J. Chaput   233

MICHIGAN

Blood Trance - R.D. Zimmerman   1791
The Cutting Hours - Julia Grice   673
Hardball - Barbara D'Amato   384
Red Trance - R.D. Zimmerman   1793
Worse than Death - Thomas Bunn   190

Ann Arbor
Curly Smoke - Susan Holtzer   803

Detroit
Chameleon - William X. Kienzle   915
The Cheerio Killings - Douglas Allyn   47
Concrete Hero - Rob Kantner   862
Gentkill: A Novel of the FBI - Paul Lindsay   1025
Grootka - Jon A. Jackson   832
Hit on the House - Jon A. Jackson   833
King of the Corner - Loren D. Estleman   497
Masquerade - William X. Kienzle   916
Motown - Loren D. Estleman   498
Peeper - Loren D. Estleman   499
The Quick and the Dead - Rob Kantner   863
The Red, White, and Blues - Rob Kantner   864
Shadow of a Doubt - William J. Coughlin   333
Sweet Women Lie - Loren D. Estleman   500
The Thousand Yard Stare - Rob Kantner   865
Tigers Burning - Crabbe Evers   508
Whiskey River - Loren D. Estleman   501

Huron Harbor
Icewater Mansions - Douglas Allyn   48

Isle Royale National Park
A Superior Death - Nevada Barr   96

Lansing
Close Softly the Doors - Ronald Clair Roat   1373
A Still and Icy Silence - Ronald Clair Roat   1374

Pickax City
The Cat Who Went into the Closet - Lilian Jackson Braun   169

Tanglewood
In Blacker Moments - S.E. Schenkel   1451

United States—Midwest

MIDWEST
The Cat Who Talked to Ghosts - Lilian Jackson Braun 168
Love Lies - Fern Kupfer 960
The Mark Twain Murders - Edith Skom 1512

MINNESOTA
Bloody Ten - William F. Love 1047
Golden Fleece - Jack Becklund 118
In the Lake of the Woods - Tim O'Brien 1218
The Naked Eye - William J. Reynolds 1364
Poisoned Ivy - M.D. Lake 971
Recycled - Jo Bailey 80
Wolf in Sheep's Clothing - John R. Riggs 1369

Deer Lake
Night Sins - Tami Hoag 794

Minneapolis
Amends for Murder - M.D. Lake 966
Cold Comfort - M.D. Lake 967
Hallowed Murder - Ellen Hart 745
Night Prey - John Sandford 1424
Rules of Prey - John Sandford 1425
The Turquoise Tattoo - Nancy Baker Jacobs 838

Minneapolis/St. Paul
A Gift for Murder - M.D. Lake 968
Murder by Mail - M.D. Lake 969
Night Kills - Ed Gorman 622
Once upon a Crime - M.D. Lake 970
Penance - David Housewright 812
Savage Justice - Ron Handberg 721
Shadow Prey - John Sandford 1426
The Silver Scapel - Nancy Baker Jacobs 837
Still Explosion - Mary Logue 1041

Repentance River
Vital Lies - Ellen Hart 746

St. Paul
Amends for Murder - M.D. Lake 966
Cold Comfort - M.D. Lake 967
Hallowed Murder - Ellen Hart 745
Rules of Prey - John Sandford 1425
Saint Mudd - Steve Thayer 1609
Swing - L.L. Enger 493
The Turquoise Tattoo - Nancy Baker Jacobs 838

San Francisco
Night Angel - Kate Green 664

Stony Lake
Strike - L.L. Enger 492

Woodard
Blood Kin - Marjorie Dorner 436

MISSISSIPPI
The Chamber - John Grisham 679

Davis County
Silent Witness - Charles Wilson 1732

Longstreet
The Empress File - John Camp 210

Sheffield
A Homecoming for Murder - John Armistead 65

Tupelo
The King Is Dead - Sarah Shankman 1475

MISSOURI
Dreamsicle - W.L. Ripley 1370

Kansas City
Caught Looking - Randy Russell 1416
Pas De Death - L.M. Vincent 1656

Richmond
Saint Louie Blues - Jake Tanner 1601

St. Louis
Death Benefits - Michael A. Kahn 851
Diamond Eyes - John Lutz 1056
Due Diligence - Michael A. Kahn 852
Firm Ambitions - Michael A. Kahn 853
A Man to Die For - Eileen Dreyer 448
Murder Once Removed - Kathleen Kunz 959
Thicker than Blood - John Lutz 1059
Time Exposure - John Lutz 1060

Victoria Springs
Dead and Buried - Jean Hager 699

MONTANA
Black Cherry Blues - James Lee Burke 193
The Bluejay Shaman - Lise McClendon Webb 1680
Lizardskin - Carsten Stroud 1582
The Mexican Tree Duck - James Crumley 363
The Standoff - Chuck Hogan 796
Trail of Murder - Christine Andreae 55

Billings
By Evil Means - Sandra West Prowell 1332

Blue Deer
The Edge of the Crazies - Jamie Harrison 736

Choteau
Grizzly - Christine Andreae 54

West Yellowstone
Spotted Cats - William G. Tapply 1603

NEBRASKA
The Naked Eye - William J. Reynolds 1364

NEVADA
The Desert Look - Bernard Schopen 1455

Beulah
Blue Lonesome - Bill Pronzini 1325

Lake Tahoe
Sing a Song of Death - Catherine Dain 380

Las Vegas
Alley Kat Blues - Karen Kijewski 917
Cat on a Blue Monday - Carole Nelson Douglas 438
Catnap - Carole Nelson Douglas 439
A Hazard of Losers - Lloyd Biggle Jr. 132
An Hour to Kill - Edward Wellen 1690
Pussyfoot - Carole Nelson Douglas 443
Shadow Counter - Tom Kakonis 855
Unwillingly to Vegas - Nancy Livingston 1036

Reno
Bet Against the House - Catherine Dain 378
The Boss's Wife - S.L. Stebel 1562
Jackpot - Bill Pronzini 1328
Lay It on the Line - Catherine Dain 379
Sing a Song of Death - Catherine Dain 380
Walk a Crooked Mile - Catherine Dain 381

NEW ENGLAND
Box Nine - Jack O'Connell 1223

NEW HAMPSHIRE
Incident at Potter's Bridge - Joseph Monniger 1165

Dovekey
Murder Will Out - Dorian Yeager 1784

What Mystery Do I Read Next?

NEW JERSEY
Bad Moon - Anthony Bruno 186
Blood Music - Jessie Prichard Hunter 821
Deadstick - Terence Faherty 513
Stolen Away - Max Allan Collins 280

Atlantic City
Die Dreaming - Terence Faherty 514
Down by the Sea - Bill Kent 910
One Kiss Led to Another - Harris Dulaney 454
She Walks in Beauty - Sarah Shankman 1477

Chester
To Do No Harm - Leslie Glass 602

Fisherville
Bury the Bishop - Kate Gallison 564

Newark
Behind the Fact - Richard Hilary 788
Devil's Gonna Get Him - Valerie Wilson Wesley 1691
When Death Comes Stealing - Valerie Wilson Wesley 1692

Ocean City
Death of a DJ - Jane Rubino 1411

Ridgewood
All Around the Town - Mary Higgins Clark 252

Rochambeau
Death by Station Wagon - Jon Katz 869
The Family Stalker - Jon Katz 870

Trenton
Jersey Monkey - Kate Gallison 565
One for the Money - Janet Evanovich 503

NEW MEXICO
Bitter Recoil - Steven F. Havill 757
The Cactus Garden - Robert Ward 1672
Dangerous Attachments - Sarah Lovett 1051
Talking God - Tony Hillerman 793
The Wolf Path - Judith Van Gieson 1652

Albuquerque
The Lies That Bind - Judith Van Gieson 1649
The Other Side of Death - Judith Van Gieson 1650

Los Alamos
Rotten Lies - Charlotte Elkins 481

Los Arboles
Death and the Delinquent - B.J. Oliphant 1233

Posadas County
Heartshot - Steven F. Havill 758

Santa Fe
Against the Wind - J.F. Freedman 547
At Ease with the Dead - Walter Satterthwait 1437
The Hanged Man - Walter Satterthwait 1440
The Other Side of Death - Judith Van Gieson 1650
Santa Fe Rules - Stuart Woods 1763
Shooting Star - Kate Green 665

Sante Fe
A Flower in the Desert - Walter Satterthwait 1439

Taos
Death Served Up Cold - B.J. Oliphant 1234
Short Cut to Santa Fe - Medora Sale 1420

NEW YORK
All the Dead Heroes - Stephen F. Wilcox 1718
Bad Moon - Anthony Bruno 186
Circumstances Unknown - Jonellen Heckler 769
Corruption - Andrew Klavan 936
Crime, Punishment and Resurrection - Michael Collins 283
The Dog Hermit - David Stout 1578
Drowned Hopes - Donald E. Westlake 1698

Geographic Index

The Edge of Sleep - David Wiltse   1736
Fixing to Die - Jerry Oster   1249
I'm Getting Killed Right Here - William Murray   1190
In the Dark - Carol Brennan   173
Killed on the Rocks - William L. DeAndrea   401
The Last Man Standing - Jim Wright   1771
Little Use for Death - Michael W. Sherer   1482
Passion Play - W. Edward Blain   140
The Pumpkin-Shell Wife - Susanna Hofmann McShea   1138
Sweet Narcissus - M.K. Lorens   1045

Adirondacks
The Green Mosaic - Stephen F. Wilcox   1720
Strawgirl - Abigail Padgett   1252

Ainsley
Deception Island - M.K. Lorens   1043

Albany
Third Man Out - Richard Stevenson   1572

Bessemer
Night of the Ice Storm - David Stout   1579

Brooklyn
The Dead of Brooklyn - Robert J. Randisi   1347

Buffalo
First and Ten - Douglas Anderson   50

Cairn
The Language of Cannibals - George C. Chesbro   242

Catskills
Grave Undertaking - James McCahery   1112
Think on Death - David Willis McCullough   1124

Corinth
The Queen Is Dead - Jane Dentinger   414

Dunehampton
Kill the Butler! - Michael Kenyon   911

Falls City
Murder at the Class Reunion - Triss Stein   1567

Fire Island
Close Quarters - Marissa Piesman   1319
False Faces - Seth Jacob Margolis   1074

Hemlock Falls
A Dash of Death - Claudia Bishop   134
A Taste for Murder - Claudia Bishop   135

High Rock Springs
Murder at the Spa - Stefanie Matteson   1097

Hillsbrook
Dr. Nightingale Goes the Distance - Lydia Adamson   21
Dr. Nightingale Rides the Elephant - Lydia Adamson   22

Indian Meadows
A Deep Disturbance - Constance Rauch   1351

Kirkville
The NIMBY Factor - Stephen F. Wilcox   1721

Kirkville-Port Erie
The Painted Lady - Stephen F. Wilcox   1722

Long Island
A Cat in the Manger - Lydia Adamson   17
Darkness Falls - Joyce Anne Schneider   1453
Exit Wounds - John Westermann   1696
The Gold Coast - Nelson DeMille   412

New York
19th Precinct - Christopher Newman   1202
Alibi for an Actress - Gillian B. Farrell   516
And Baby Makes None - Stephen Lewis   1022
And Justice for One - John Clarkson   254
The Animal Hour - Andrew Klavan   935
Bad Apple - Anthony Bruno   184

Bad Blood - Anthony Bruno   185
Bad Blood - P.M. Carlson   218
Bad Neighbors - Isidore Haiblum   703
Bad to the Bone - Stephen Solomita   1532
Beauty Dies - Melodie Johnson Howe   813
Black Light - Daniel Hearn   767
Blind Side - William Bayer   105
Blindsight - Robin Cook   302
Blood Music - Jessie Prichard Hunter   821
Blood on the Street - Annette Meyers   1146
Bloody Soaps: A Tale of Love and Death in the Afternoon - Jacqueline Babbin   75
Bloody Ten - William F. Love   1047
Blossom - Andrew Vachss   1643
The Bone Orchard - Joseph Trigoboff   1628
The Burglar Who Traded Ted Williams - Lawrence Block   145
But I Wouldn't Want to Die There - Nancy Pickard   1317
By Reason of Insanity - James Neal Harvey   749
Cancellation by Death - Dorian Yeager   1782
Capitol Offense - Tony Gibbs   580
Casual Slaughters - Robert A. Carter   223
Casualty Loss - Jim Weikart   1683
A Cat in a Glass House - Lydia Adamson   15
A Cat in Fine Style - Lydia Adamson   16
A Cat in the Wings - Lydia Adamson   18
A Cat in Wolf's Clothing - Lydia Adamson   19
A Cat on the Cutting Edge - Lydia Adamson   20
The Caveman's Valentine - George Dawes Green   662
The Chartreuse Clue - William F. Love   1048
China Trade - S.J. Rozan   1410
City of God - Michael Jahn   840
City of Lies - Peter McCabe   1109
The City When It Rains - Thomas H. Cook   305
Cold Feet - Kerry Tucker   1636
Criminal Conversation - Evan Hunter   820
Criminal Seduction - Darian North   1211
A Dance at the Slaughterhouse - Lawrence Block   146
Dancing in the Dark - Sharon Zukowski   1798
Date with a Dead Doctor - Toni Brill   177
Day of Atonement - Faye Kellerman   878
Dead Ahead - Ruby Horansky   804
Dead Center - Ruby Horansky   805
The Deadliest Option - Annette Meyers   1147
Deadly Resolutions - Anna Ashwood Collins   274
Death of a Dancing Fool - Carole Berry   124
The Death of a Difficult Woman - Carole Berry   125
Deathics - Richard Barth   100
Detective First Grade - Don Mahoney   1067
The Devil Knows You're Dead - Lawrence Block   147
Disassociated States - Leonard Simon   1499
Don't Ask - Donald E. Westlake   1697
Don't Say a Word - Andrew Klavan   937
Don't Say a Word - Keith Peterson   1308
Dreamland - M.K. Lorens   1044
Drown All the Dogs - Thomas Adcock   23
Elsinore - Jerome Charyn   238
End Game - Dev Stryker   1585
Everything You Have Is Mine - Sandra Scoppettone   1460
Eviction by Death - Dorian Yeager   1783
Exceptional Clearance - William J. Caunitz   229
Faces in the Crowd - William Marshall   1079
Fade to Black - Robert Goldsborough   607
A Fatal Advent - Isabelle Holland   797
Felony Murder - Joseph T. Klempner   940
Fielder's Choice - Michael Bowen   160
Final Edit - Robert A. Carter   224
Final Option - Stephen Robinett   1389
Final Tour - Jonellen Heckler   770
Flamingos - Marc Savage   1444
Footsteps of the Hawk - Andrew Vachss   1644
Force of Nature - Stephen Solomita   1533
The Forever Beat - John Cline   262
Four Steps to Death - Diana Ramsay   1346
Foxglove - Mary Anne Kelly   889

United States—New York

Fresh Kills - Carolyn Wheat   1699
Friends in High Places - Michael Hendricks   771
From Potter's Field - Patricia D. Cornwell   325
Full Commission - Carol Brennan   172
God Bless John Wayne - Kinky Friedman   554
The Gold Coast - Nelson DeMille   412
A Good Day to Die - Stephen Solomita   1534
Good Night, Sweet Prince - Carole Berry   126
The Great California Game - Jonathan Gash   570
The Great Grave Robbery - John Minahan   1158
Guilt by Association - Susan R. Sloan   1514
Hanging Time - Leslie Glass   601
Hard News - Jeffrey Wilds Deaver   403
The Hawthorne Group - Thomas Hauser   756
Hell Bent - Ken Gross   684
He's Dead-She's Dead: Details at Eleven - John Bartholomew Tucker   1635
Hide and Seek - Barry Berg   122
Hubbert and Lil: Partners in Crime - Gallagher Gray   654
I'll Be Leaving You Always - Sandra Scoppettone   1461
An Imperfect Spy - Amanda Cross   360
Imperfect Strangers - Stuart Woods   1761
Inherit the Mob - Zev Chafets   231
Juror - Parnell Hall   714
Justice Denied - Robert K. Tanenbaum   1599
Karma - Mitchell Smith   1531
The Killing Man - Mickey Spillane   1540
The Last Good German - Bill Granger   647
The Last Rite of Hugo T - J.N. Catanach   227
Leap of Faith - Sharon Zukowski   1799
Lights Out - Peter Abrahams   4
Limited Partner - Mike Lupica   1053
Lockout - Lillian O'Donnell   1224
The Long Search - Isabelle Holland   798
Loves Music, Loves to Dance - Mary Higgins Clark   253
Mallory's Oracle - Carol O'Connell   1221
The Man Who Cancelled Himself - David Handler   722
The Man Who Would Be F. Scott Fitzgerald - David Handler   723
Manhattan Is My Beat - Jeffrey Wilds Deaver   404
Miss Melville Rides a Tiger - Evelyn E. Smith   1518
Mistress of Justice - Jeffrey Wilds Deaver   405
Monday's Child Is Dead - James Elward   484
Money to Burn - Michael Hendricks   772
The Monkey Rope - Stephen Lewis   1023
Murder and a Muse - Gillian B. Farrell   517
Murder at Fenway Park - Troy Soos   1536
Murder Can Kill Your Social Life - Selma Eichler   473
Murder Times Two - Haughton Murphy   1186
Musical Chairs - Kinky Friedman   555
My Sweet Untraceable You - Sandra Scoppettone   1462
The Naked Typist - J.P. Hailey   704
The New York Detective - William Marshall   1080
Nightside - Soledad Santiago   1434
One Kiss Led to Another - Harris Dulaney   454
Out on the Cutting Edge - Lawrence Block   148
Painted Ladies - James Neal Harvey   750
Park Lane South, Queens - Mary Anne Kelly   890
Party Till You Die - David Charnee   236
Past Imperfect - Margaret Maron   1077
A Piece of the Action - Stephen Solomita   1535
Pressure Drop - Peter Abrahams   5
Prime Time for Murder - Valerie Frankel   542
A Private Crime - Lillian O'Donnell   1225
The Prosecutor - Thomas Chastain   240
Pushover - Lillian O'Donnell   1226
The Raggedy Man - Lillian O'Donnell   1227
The Ransom - Brian Tobin   1622
Reasonable Doubt - Philip Friedman   558
Reversible Error - Robert K. Tanenbaum   1600
Right on the Money - Emma Lathen   987
Room 9 - Soledad Santiago   1435
Rough Justice - Keith Peterson   1309
Separate Cases - Robert J. Randisi   1350
The Seventh Bullet - Daniel D. Victor   1654

United States—North Carolina

Shadow Dance - Agnes Bushnell 202
Shadow Queen - Tony Gibbs 583
Shameless - Judy Collins 275
Shoofly Pie to Die - Joshua Quittner 1342
Shooting Script - Gordon Cotler 332
Silent Prey - John Sandford 1427
Silver Spire - Robert Goldsborough 608
Sister's Keeper - Randye Lordon 1042
Skins - Catherine O'Connell 1222
Sliver - Ira Levin 1013
Slow Motion Riot - Peter Blauner 144
The Soul of Betty Fairchild - Robert Specht 1538
South Street Confidential - Dick Belsky 120
Strangers in the Night - Peg Tyre 1641
Strangler - Parnell Hall 715
The Strenuous Life - Lawrence Alexander 36
Swindle - George Adams 11
The Temple Dogs - Warren Murphy 1188
The Thirteenth Apostle - Gloria Gonzalez 610
Thursday's Child - Teri White 1705
A Ticket to the Boneyard - Lawrence Block 149
Time Lapse - Janice Law 992
To Kill a Clown - David Charnee 237
Topless - D. Keith Mano 1072
The Trouble with Moonlighting - Trella Crespi 346
Unbalanced Acts - Jeff Raines 1344
The Underground Man - J.P. Hailey 705
Undue Influence - Miriam Borgenicht 153
Unorthodox Practices - Marissa Piesman 1320
Until Death - Polly Whitney 1709
Until the End of Time - Polly Whitney 1710
Used to Kill - Lillian O'Donnell 1228
Vanishing Act - Seth Jacob Margolis 1075
Vertical Run - Joseph R. Garber 566
Virgil's Ghost - Irving Weinman 1684
A Walk Among the Tombstones - Lawrence Block 150
What's a Girl Gotta Do? - Sparkle Hayter 760
Whisper.He Might Hear You - William Appel 62
Who Shot Longshot Sam? - Paul Engleman 495
Widowmaker - William Appel 63
Wild Again - Kathrin King Segal 1471
Wiseguys in Love - C. Clark Criscuolo 355
A Wreath for the Bride - Lillian O'Donnell 1229

Oakwood
The Christmas Night Murder - Lee Harris 734

Quarryville-on-Hudson
Point No-Point - David Willis McCullough 1123

Ravenstown
Kiss Them Goodbye - Joseph Eastburn 468

Rochester
The Daphne Decisions - Meg O'Brien 1214
Eagles Die Too - Meg O'Brien 1215
Hare Today, Gone Tomorrow - Meg O'Brien 1216

Seneca Falls
North Star Conspiracy - Miriam Grace Monfredo 1164

Studberg
The Christening Day Murder - Lee Harris 733

Taconic Hills
So Shall You Reap - Marilyn Wallace 1665

Ulster County
My Sweet Untraceable You - Sandra Scoppettone 1462

Westchester
Furnished for Murder - Richard Barth 101

Yonkers
Summer Cool - Al Sarrantonio 1436

NORTH CAROLINA

Carolina Gold - Douglas McBriarty 1108
Who Killed What's-Her-Name? - Elizabeth Daniels Squire 1548

Black Mountain
The Body Farm - Patricia D. Cornwell 322

Bloodroot Creek
Memory Can Be Murder - Elizabeth Daniels Squire 1547

Byerly
Dead Ringer - Toni L.P. Kelner 900
Down Home Murder - Toni L.P. Kelner 901
Trouble Looking for a Place to Happen - Toni L.P. Kelner 902

Charlotte
Horse of a Different Killer - Jody Jaffe 839

Cotton Grove
Bootlegger's Daughter - Margaret Maron 1076

Davis Landing
The Garden Club - Muriel Resnick Jackson 836

Fairleigh
Blanche on the Lam - Barbara Neely 1198

Harker's Island
Shooting at Loons - Margaret Maron 1078

Hillston
Time's Witness - Michael Malone 1070

Spudsboro
The Cat Who Moved a Mountain - Lilian Jackson Braun 167

OHIO

Town on Trial - William Harrington 730

Cincinnati
Angel's Bidding - Sharon Gwyn Short 1489
The Death We Share - Sharon Gwyn Short 1490
The Flip Side of Life - James E. Martin 1085
Four Elements of Murder - D.B. Borton 155
Hidden City - Jim DeBrosse 407
Missing - Jonathan Valin 1646
The Music Lovers - Jonathan Valin 1647
Second Chance - Jonathan Valin 1648
Three Is a Crowd - D.B. Borton 156
Two Points for Murder - D.B. Borton 157

Cleveland
The Cleveland Connection - Les Roberts 1383
Deep Shaker - Les Roberts 1384
Deviant Way - Richard Montanari 1166
Double Plot - Leo Axler 70
The Duke of Cleveland - Les Roberts 1385
The Flip Side of Life - James E. Martin 1085
Full Cleveland - Les Roberts 1386
Grave Matters - Leo Axler 71
Murder by the Numbers - Max Allan Collins 278
Murder in the Post-War World - Max Allan Collins 279
The Thirteenth Apostle - Gloria Gonzalez 610

Columbus
Showcase - Alison Glen 603
Trunk Show - Alison Glen 604

Darby
Still Waters - Kerry Tucker 1638

Echo
Death Echo - Kerry Tucker 1637

Fort Elbow
The Search Committee - Ralph McInerny 1136

Palmer
The Maltese Puppy - Melissa Cleary 258

OKLAHOMA

A Permanent Retirement - John Miles 1153

What Mystery Do I Read Next?

Buckskin
Ghostland - Jean Hager 700

Fort Sill
The Strenuous Life - Lawrence Alexander 36

Holton
Death Down Home - Eve K. Sandstrom 1430
The Devil Down Home - Eve K. Sandstrom 1431
The Down Home Heifer Heist - Eve K. Sandstrom 1432

Prophesy County
Dead Moon on the Rise - Susan Rogers Cooper 310
Doctors, Lawyers and Such - Susan Rogers Cooper 311
Other People's Houses - Susan Rogers Cooper 316

Tahlequah
Ravenmocker - Jean Hager 701
The Redbird's Cry - Jean Hager 702

Tulsa
The Next Victim - William Sanders 1423

Vamoose
Dead in the Cellar - Connie Fedderson 520

OREGON

Banjo Boy - Vince Kohler 949
Murder Without Reservation - Bernie Lee 999

Bend
Make No Bones - Aaron Elkins 478

Holiday Beach
Dead Matter - M.K. Wren 1764

Madison
The Monster Squad - John Angus 59

Moot Point
Murder at Moot Point - Marlys Millhiser 1156

Mount Hood
King of the Mountain - M.K. Wren 1765

Musket Beach
Murder at Musket Beach - Bernie Lee 998

Port Jerome
Rainy North Woods - Vince Kohler 950
Rising Dog - Vince Kohler 951

Portland
Cat's Paw, Inc. - L.L. Thrasher 1618
Mortal Remains - Rick Hanson 728

Turner's Point
Death Qualified: A Mystery of Chaos - Kate Wilhelm 1723

PACIFIC NORTHWEST

Holy Terrors - Mary Daheim 376

PENNSYLVANIA

August Ice - Deforest Day 399
Berlin Covenant - Celeste Paul 1278
The Manx Murders - William L. DeAndrea 402
Quoth the Raven - Jane Haddam 696
Shoofly Pie to Die - Joshua Quittner 1342

Lancaster
The February Trouble - Neil Albert 30

Philadelphia
Break and Enter - Colin Harrison 735
Burning March - Neil Albert 28
Cruel April - Neil Albert 29
Hostile Witness - William Lashner 985
I'd Rather Be in Philadelphia - Gillian Roberts 1378

Geographic Index

The January Corpse - Neil Albert 31
The Last Gambit - David Delman 411
Letting Blood - Richard Platt 1321
Not a Creature Was Stirring - Jane Haddam 695
Philly Stakes - Gillian Roberts 1379
Running From the Law - Lisa Scottoline 1465
Skeletons - Eric Sauter 1443
With Friends Like These - Gillian Roberts 1380

Pittsburgh
The Fall-Down Artist - Thomas Lipinski 1032

Rocksburg
Sunshine Enemies - K.C. Constantine 298

RHODE ISLAND

Newport
Murder on the Cliff - Stefanie Matteson 1098

SOUTH
Kill the Messenger - Elizabeth Daniels Squire 1546

SOUTH CAROLINA
Dead Man's Island - Carolyn G. Hart 742
A Trick of Light - Patricia Robinson 1391

Beaufort
Cons - Timothy Watts 1677

Broward Rock
The Christie Caper - Carolyn G. Hart 741
A Little Class on Murder - Carolyn G. Hart 743

Charleston
Southern Cross - Stephen Greenleaf 669

Green Hills
The Lynching - Bennie Lee Sinclair 1503

Greenview
The Soul of Betty Fairchild - Robert Specht 1538

Hilton Head
Mint Julep Murder - Carolyn G. Hart 744

SOUTH DAKOTA
Corona Blue - J.F. Trainor 1625
Dynamite Pass - J.F. Trainor 1626

Bear Coat
Stone Boy - Ronald Levitsky 1017

Corden
The Man Who Missed the Party - Harold Adams 13

Greenhill
The Ditched Blonde - Harold Adams 12

Podunkville
A Perfectly Proper Murder - Harold Adams 14

SOUTHWEST
Hour of the Hunter - J.A. Jance 843
Lautrec - Norman Zollinger 1794
Monkey on a Chain - Harlen Campbell 211

TENNESSEE
Hard Guy - Thorton Elliott 482
No Way Home - Patricia MacDonald 1062
She Walks These Hills - Sharyn McCrumb 1119
Shutout - David F. Nighbert 1204

Cayter
Four Elements of Murder - D.B. Borton 155

Dark Hollow
The Hangman's Beautiful Daughter - Sharyn McCrumb 1115

Hamelin
If Ever I Return, Pretty Peggy-O - Sharyn McCrumb 1116

Jesus Creek
All the Great Pretenders - Deborah Adams 10

Memphis
The Client - John Grisham 680

Nashville
Dead Folks' Blues - Steven Womack 1751
Torch Town Boogie - Steven Womack 1754
Way Past Dead - Steven Womack 1755

Wall Hollow
Zombies of the Gene Pool - Sharyn McCrumb 1121

TEXAS
Cry for Help - Karen Hanson Stuyck 1586
Deadline - D.F. Mills 1157
Drowned Man's Key - Ken Grissom 683
The Man Offside - A.W. Gray 652
The Mexican Tree Duck - James Crumley 363
September Song - Edward Mathis 1096
Strikezone - David F. Nighbert 1206
Track of the Cat - Nevada Barr 97

Abilene
Bagged - Jo Bailey 79

Austin
Baptism for Murder - Jan Maxwell 1101
Boiled in Concrete - Jesse Sublett 1587
The Red Scream - Mary Willis Walker 1659
The Texas Capitol Murders - Bill Crider 353
Under the Beetle's Cellar - Mary Willis Walker 1660
Zero at the Bone - Mary Willis Walker 1661

Bagget County
Dreamboat - Doug J. Swanson 1596

Bayport
The Buzzards Must Also Be Fed - Anne Wingate 1739
Exception to Murder - Anne Wingate 1740
The Eye of Anna - Anne Wingate 1741
Yakuza, Go Home - Anne Wingate 1742

Black Cat Ridge
One, Two, What Did Daddy Do? - Susan Rogers Cooper 315

Dallas
Bino's Blues - A.W. Gray 650
The Dallas Deception - Richard Abshire 7
Killings - A.W. Gray 651
Rafferty: Fatal Sisters - W. Glenn Duncan 458
Turnaround Jack - Richard Abshire 8

Dallas/Fort Worth
Bird in a Cage - Lee Martin 1086
See No Evil - Edward Mathis 1095

Eagle Lake
Gator Kill - Bill Crider 352

Fort Worth
The Day That Dusty Died - Lee Martin 1087
Deficit Ending - Lee Martin 1088
Dog Heavies - L.J. Washburn 1675
The Mensa Murders - Lee Martin 1089
Prime Suspect - A.W. Gray 653

Galveston
Big Fish - Ken Grissom 682
Dead on the Island - Bill Crider 350
When Old Men Die - Bill Crider 354

Houston
An Absence of Light - David L. Lindsey 1026
Act of Love - Joe R. Lansdale 980
Bayou City Secrets - Deborah Powell 1323
Bear Hug - Jerome Doolittle 432
Blood Marks - Bill Crider 349
Houston in the Rearview Mirror - Susan Rogers Cooper 314
My First Murder - Susan Baker 84
Predator's Waltz - Jay Brandon 165
Squeezeplay - David F. Nighbert 1205
Stand-In for Murder - Lynn Bradley 164

Mirabeau
Do Unto Others - Jeff Abbott 1
The Only Good Yankee - Jeff Abbott 2

Nacogdoches
Sweet Death - Bill Waggoner 1657

Pecan Springs
Hangman's Root - Susan Wittig Albert 32
Thyme of Death - Susan Wittig Albert 33

Port Arthur
Funny as a Dead Relative - Susan Rogers Cooper 313

Purple Sage
Dust Devils of the Purple Sage - Barbara Burnett Smith 1516
Writers of the Purple Sage - Barbara Burnett Smith 1517

San Antonio
Final Session - Mary Morell 1170

UTAH
Dynamite Pass - J.F. Trainor 1626
The Fall Line - Mark T. Sullivan 1589
Pillar of Fire - R.R. Irvine 830
The Stone Hawk - Gwen Moffat 1163

Salt Lake City
The Angel's Share - R.R. Irvine 826
Called Home - R.R. Irvine 828
The Great Reminder - R.R. Irvine 829
Ten of Swords - J.R. Levitt 1018

VERMONT
The House on the Hill - Judith Kelman 899

Bethlehem
A Stillness in Bethlehem - Jane Haddam 697

Brattleboro
Fruits of the Poisonous Tree - Archer Mayor 1104
Scent of Evil - Archer Mayor 1105

Chambers
Snow Job - Ted Wood 1758

Gannett
Borderlines - Archer Mayor 1103

Lofton
The Cashmere Kid - B. Comfort 284
Elusive Quarry - B. Comfort 285

Southborough
Land Kills - Nat Brandt 166

VIRGINIA
Into the Fire - David Wiltse 1737
North Star Conspiracy - Miriam Grace Monfredo 1164
Passion Play - W. Edward Blain 140

Alexandria
Blood Relative - Carolyn Hougan 811

United States—Washington

Borderville
The Famous DAR Murder Mystery - Graham Landrum 977
The Rotary Club Mystery - Graham Landrum 978

Chandler Grove
The Windsor Knot - Sharyn McCrumb 1120

Crozet
Murder at Monticello - Rita Mae Brown 180
Rest in Pieces - Rita Mae Brown 181
Wish You Were Here - Rita Mae Brown 182

Danville
MacPherson's Lament - Sharyn McCrumb 1117

Quantico
The Body Farm - Patricia D. Cornwell 322

Richmond
All That Remains - Patricia D. Cornwell 321
Body of Evidence - Patricia D. Cornwell 323
Cruel and Unusual - Patricia D. Cornwell 324
From Potter's Field - Patricia D. Cornwell 325
Postmortem - Patricia D. Cornwell 326

WASHINGTON
Bantam of the Opera - Mary Daheim 374
Help Wanted: Orphans Preferred - Earl Emerson 487
In Blacker Moments - S.E. Schenkel 1451
The Piano Man - Noreen Gilpatrick 589
Whoo? - Richard Hoyt 816

Alpine
The Alpine Advocate - Mary Daheim 370
The Alpine Christmas - Mary Daheim 371
The Alpine Decoy - Mary Daheim 372
The Alpine Fury - Mary Daheim 373

Bellehaven
Miss Zukas and the Island Murders - Jo Dereske 415
Miss Zukas and the Library Murders - Jo Dereske 416

Clearwater
Clearwater Summer - John E. Keegan 876

Coffee Creek
Clear-Cut Murder - Lee Wallingford 1667

Glacier Falls
A Fit of Tempera - Mary Daheim 375

Heraldsgate Hill
Murder, My Suite - Mary Daheim 377

Mt. St. Helens
Bigfoot - Richard Hoyt 815

Neskanie National Forest
Cold Tracks - Lee Wallingford 1668

San Piedro Island
Snow Falling on Cedars - David Guterson 692

Seattle
The Angel Maker - Ridley Pearson 1282
The Bookman's Wake - John Dunning 467
Electric City - K.K. Beck 115
Hard Fall - Ridley Pearson 1284
A Hopeless Case - K.K. Beck 116
Kiet Goes West - Gary Alexander 34
Methods of Execution - Frederick D. Huebner 818
Morons and Madmen - Earl Emerson 488
Murdock Cracks Ice - Robert J. Ray 1353
Night Rituals - Gary Paulsen 1279
Picture Postcard - Fredrick D. Huebner 819
The Portland Laugher - Earl Emerson 489
The Vanishing Smile - Earl Emerson 490
Yellow Dog Party - Earl Emerson 491

Three Forks
The Deep End - Chris Crutcher 364

WEST VIRGINIA

Pine Grove
Naked Once More - Elizabeth Peters 1300

WISCONSIN

Wolf in Sheep's Clothing - John R. Riggs 1369

Grant
Winter Prey - John Sandford 1428

Madison
Elective Murder - Janet McGiffin 1129

Milwaukee
Prescription for Death - Janet McGiffin 1130

Oakalla
A Dragon Lives Forever - John R. Riggs 1368

WYOMING

The Bluejay Shaman - Lise McClendon Webb 1680

Meeteetse
Tensleep - Sarah Andrews 57

Sheridan
A Clinic for Murder - Marsha Landreth 974
The Holiday Murders - Marsha Landreth 975
Vial Murders - Marsha Landreth 976

Victory
No Comfort in Victory - Gregory Bean 106

Yellowstone National Park
Wildfire - Kenneth W. Goddard 605

VIETNAM

Tucker's Last Stand - William F. Buckley Jr. 188

WALES

The Glendower Conspiracy - Lloyd Biggle Jr. 131
Hanging on the Wire - Gillian Linscott 1028
Rook-Shoot - Margaret Duffy 452
The Sin Within Her Smile - Jonathan Gash 572
The Summer of the Danes - Ellis Peters 1303
The Wrong Rite - Alisa Craig 334

Cardiff
The Catalyst - Desmond Cory 330
The Dobie Paradox - Desmond Cory 331

WEST INDIES

St. Maarten
Dropshot: A Brad Smith Novel - Jack Bickham 129

Story Type Index

This index is a listing of the story types arranged in alphabetical order. An alphabetical listing of the featured book titles that fall under the story type is provided, along with author names and entry numbers. (For definitions of the story types, see the "Key to Story Types" following the Introduction.)

MYSTERY

Action/Adventure

The 6 Messiahs - Mark Frost 560
19th Precinct - Christopher Newman 1202
32 Cadillacs - Joe Gores 616
An Absence of Light - David L. Lindsey 1026
Against the Wind - J.F. Freedman 547
Ah, Treachery - Ross Thomas 1611
All I Have Is Blue - James Colbert 272
And Justice for One - John Clarkson 254
Angel of Death - Jack Higgins 786
The Animal Hour - Andrew Klavan 935
August Ice - Deforest Day 399
Bad Apple - Anthony Bruno 184
Bad Blood - Anthony Bruno 185
Bad Moon - Anthony Bruno 186
The Bag Man - Peter Lacey 961
Bait - Kenneth Abel 3
Balboa Firefly - Jack Trolley 1633
Barking Dogs - R.R. Irvine 827
Berlin Covenant - Celeste Paul 1278
Big Fish - Ken Grissom 682
Bigfoot - Richard Hoyt 815
The Black Echo - Michael Connelly 292
A Blood Affair - Jan Roberts 1381
Blood Relative - Carolyn Hougan 811
Blossom - Andrew Vachss 1643
Blue Lonesome - Bill Pronzini 1325
Body Scissors - Jerome Doolittle 433
Bones of Coral - James W. Hall 707
The Boss's Wife - S.L. Stebel 1562
Bucket Nut - Liza Cody 270
Burn Season - John Lantigua 981
Burning Angel - James Lee Burke 194
By Death Possessed - Roger Ormerod 1243
The Cactus Garden - Robert Ward 1672
Capitol Offense - Tony Gibbs 580
Caught Looking - Randy Russell 1416
The Cheetah Chase - Karin McQuillan 1137
The Chesapeake Project - Phyllis Horn 806
The Cheshire Moon - Robert Ferrigno 525
China Lake - Anthony Hyde 823
City of God - Michael Jahn 840
The Client - John Grisham 680
A Clinic for Murder - Marsha Landreth 974
The Codicil - Tom Topor 1623
Comeback - Dick Francis 539
Cons - Timothy Watts 1677
A Cool Breeze on the Underground - Don Winslow 1743
Coronation - W.J. Weatherby 1679
The Covenant of the Flame - David Morrell 1174
Cover Story - Robert Cullen 365
Criminal Conversation - Evan Hunter 820
Crossover - Judith Eubank 502
Dangerous Attachments - Sarah Lovett 1051
Dangerous Waters - Bill Eidson 475
Dark Provenance - Michael David Anthony 61
Dead Easy - Arthur F. Nehrbass 1199
Dead Man - Joe Gores 617
Dead Wrong - Alan Dennis Burke 192

Deadeye - Sam Llewellyn 1037
Deadly Sonata - Paul Myers 1192
Deal to Die For - Les Standiford 1560
Death Among the Angels - John Walter Putre 1336
Death and Other Lovers - Jo Bannister 86
Death by Degrees - Robin Wilson 1735
A Deep Disturbance - Constance Rauch 1351
Deep End - Geoffrey Norman 1210
The Deer Killers - Gunnard Landers 973
Deerslayer - M.S. Karl 867
Desert Heat - J.A. Jance 842
Detective First Grade - Don Mahoney 1067
Divorcing Jack - Colin Bateman 104
Done Deal - Les Standiford 1561
Don't Ask - Donald E. Westlake 1697
Double Blind - David Laing 965
Double Down - Tom Kakonis 854
A Dragon Lives Forever - John R. Riggs 1368
Dreamsicle - W.L. Ripley 1370
Dropshot: A Brad Smith Novel - Jack Bickham 129
Drover and the Zebras - Bill Granger 646
Drown All the Dogs - Thomas Adcock 23
Drowned Hopes - Donald E. Westlake 1698
Drowned Man's Key - Ken Grissom 683
East Beach - Ron Ely 485
Edge City - Sin Soracco 1537
The Edge of Sleep - David Wiltse 1736
The Edge of the Crazies - Jamie Harrison 736
The Empress File - John Camp 210
End Game - Dev Stryker 1585
The Estuary Pilgrim - Douglas Skeggs 1507
Even the Butler Was Poor - Ron Goulart 628
Exit Wounds - John Westermann 1696
The Fall Line - Mark T. Sullivan 1589
Feeding Frenzy - Paul Kemprecos 904
First and Ten - Douglas Anderson 50
Fixing to Die - Jerry Oster 1249
Flamingos - Marc Savage 1444
Flawless - Adam Barrow 99
Footsteps of the Hawk - Andrew Vachss 1644
The Forever Beat - John Cline 262
The Fourth Durango - Ross Thomas 1612
Free - Todd Komarnicki 952
Fuse Time - Max Byrd 205
The Genesis Files - Bob Biderman 130
Gentkill: A Novel of the FBI - Paul Lindsay 1025
Get Shorty - Elmore Leonard 1005
Get What's Coming - Sam Reaves 1354
The Gold Coast - Nelson DeMille 412
Golden Fleece - Jack Becklund 118
The Gombeen Man - Randy Lee Eickoff 474
Gone Wild - James W. Hall 708
A Good Day to Die - Stephen Solomita 1534
The Great California Game - Jonathan Gash 570
Gun Men - Gary Friedman 553
Gunpower - Mark Schorr 1456
A Gypsy Good Time - Gustav Hasford 755
Hard Aground - James W. Hall 709
Hard Fall - Ridley Pearson 1284
Hard Guy - Thorton Elliott 482
Hard News - Mark T. Sullivan 1590
The Hawthorne Group - Thomas Hauser 756
He Was Her Man - Sarah Shankman 1474

Heat - Stuart Woods 1760
Hell Bent - Ken Gross 684
Hidden City - Jim DeBrosse 407
Hide and Seek - Barry Berg 122
Honolulu Red - Lue Zimmelman 1789
A Hopeless Case - K.K. Beck 116
The Horse Latitudes - Robert Ferrigno 526
Hour of the Hunter - J.A. Jance 843
An Hour to Kill - Edward Wellen 1690
How Town - Michael Nava 1194
The Ice - Louis Charbonneau 234
Icewater Mansions - Douglas Allyn 48
Imperfect Strangers - Stuart Woods 1761
The India Exhibition - Richard Timothy Conroy 296
Infected Be the Air - Janice Law 991
Inherit the Mob - Zev Chafets 231
Into Thin Air - Thomas Zigal 1788
Irish Gold - Andrew M. Greeley 657
Jordon's Showdown - Frank C. Strunk 1583
Just Cause - John Katzenbach 873
Karma - Mitchell Smith 1531
The Keeper - Meg O'Brien 1217
Kill Story - Jerome Doolittle 434
Killer in Paradise - John Leslie 1011
Killings - A.W. Gray 651
Kimura - Robert Davis 395
The King Is Dead - Sarah Shankman 1475
King of the Corner - Loren D. Estleman 497
King of the Hustlers - Eugene Izzi 831
Kingdom Road - K. Patrick Conner 295
Kiss Them Goodbye - Joseph Eastburn 468
Knight & Day - Ron Nessen 1201
L.A. Confidential - James Ellroy 483
Landfall - Tony Gibbs 581
Landscape of Lies - Peter Watson 1676
The Last Camel Died at Noon - Elizabeth Peters 1298
The Last Man Standing - Jim Wright 1771
The Last Rite of Hugo T - J.N. Catanach 227
Lights Out - Peter Abrahams 4
The Lion at the Door - Newton Thornburg 1617
Lizardskin - Carsten Stroud 1582
Long Chain of Death - S.K. Wolf 1747
A Long Cold Fall - Sam Reaves 1355
Longshot - Dick Francis 540
Louisiana Blue - David Poyer 1324
The Man in the Moon - Frank Norwood 1212
Man of Blood - Margaret Duffy 451
The Man Offside - A.W. Gray 652
The Man Who Walked Through Walls - James Swain 1595
Maximum Bob - Elmore Leonard 1006
Mean High Tide - James W. Hall 710
The Mexican Tree Duck - James Crumley 363
Miami Heat - Jerome Sanford 1433
Miami Purity - Vicki Hendricks 773
Miss Melville Rides a Tiger - Evelyn E. Smith 1518
Money Burns - A.E. Maxwell 1100
Monkey on a Chain - Harlen Campbell 211
The Monkey Rope - Stephen Lewis 1023
Monkey Wrench - Liza Cody 271
A Morning for Flamingos - James Lee Burke 197
Mortal Sin - Paul Levine 1014

Alternate History

Moth to the Flame - Kathleen Dougherty 437
Murder on the Iditarod Trail - Sue Henry 775
Murder Song - Jon Cleary 256
My Gun Has Bullets - Lee Goldberg 606
Native Tongue - Carl Hiaasen 782
Natural Causes - Michael Palmer 1262
Natural Enemies - Sara Cameron 209
Neon Caesar - Mark McGarrity 1128
Nice Guys Finish Dead - David Debin 406
Night Butterfly - Patricia McFall 1127
Night Kills - Ed Gorman 622
Night Vision - Paul Levine 1015
Nightwalker - Sidney Filson 527
Now He Thinks He's Dead - Ron Goulart 629
Painted Ladies - James Neal Harvey 750
Palindrome - Stuart Woods 1762
Paramour - Gerald Petievich 1312
The Pelican Brief - John Grisham 681
A Piece of the Action - Stephen Solomita 1535
Pink Vodka Blues - Neal Barrett Jr. 98
Play Dead - Harlan Coben 266
Pleading Guilty - Scott Turow 1640
Point of Impact - Stephen Hunter 822
Polar Star - Martin Cruz Smith 1530
Praetorian - Thomas Gifford 584
Predator's Waltz - Jay Brandon 165
Pressure Drop - Peter Abrahams 5
Prime Suspect - A.W. Gray 653
Purgatory - Monty Mickleson 1152
The Ransom - Brian Tobin 1622
Rat's Nest - Charles West 1694
Recycled - Jo Bailey 80
Revolution #9 - Peter Abrahams 6
River of Darkness - James Grady 632
Rook-Shoot - Margaret Duffy 452
Rough Justice - Keith Peterson 1309
Rum Punch - Elmore Leonard 1007
Running Fix - Tony Gibbs 582
Running Mates - John Feinstein 521
Saint Mudd - Steve Thayer 1609
Sanibel Flats - Randy Wayne White 1704
Santa Fe Rules - Stuart Woods 1763
Savage Justice - Ron Handberg 721
Shadow Counter - Tom Kakonis 855
Shadow of a Doubt - William J. Coughlin 333
Shadow Prey - John Sandford 1426
Shoedog - George Pelecanos 1288
Short Cut to Santa Fe - Medora Sale 1420
Silent Prey - John Sandford 1427
Singapore Transfer - Wayne Warga 1673
Skin Tight - Carl Hiaasen 783
Skinny Man - James Colbert 273
Sleeping Dogs - Thomas Perry 1297
Slow Motion Riot - Peter Blauner 144
Southern Cross - Jim DeBrosse 408
Spandau Phoenix - Greg Iles 824
The Spanish Maze Game - Noah Webster 1682
Stalking Horse - Bill Shoemaker 1487
The Standoff - Chuck Hogan 796
Stormy Weather - Carl Hiaasen 784
Straight - Dick Francis 541
Strangers in the Night - Peg Tyre 1641
Stranglehold - Jerome Doolittle 435
Strip Tease - Carl Hiaasen 785
The Sum of All Fears - Tom Clancy 248
The Suspense Is Killing Me - Thomas Maxwell 1102
The Talinin Madonna - Douglas Skeggs 1508
The Temple Dogs - Warren Murphy 1188
The Thirteenth Apostle - Gloria Gonzalez 610
Thunder - James Grady 633
Thursday's Child - Teri White 1705
To Do No Harm - Leslie Glass 602
Topless - D. Keith Mano 1072
The Toy Cupboard - Lee Jordan 848
Trade Secrets - Ray Garton 568
The Trail to Buddha's Mirror - Don Winslow 1744
The Triumph of Bacchus - Douglas Skeggs 1509
Tropical Depression - Jeffry P. Lindsay 1024
Twilight at Mac's Place - Ross Thomas 1613
Unnatural Hazard - Barry Cork 317

Until the End of Time - Polly Whitney 1710
Vertical Run - Joseph R. Garber 566
A Very Proper Death - Alex Juniper 850
Vital Signs - Robin Cook 303
Wasteland - Peter McCabe 1110
The Watchman - Michael Allegretto 44
The Water Cure - Warwick Downing 446
When Reason Sleeps - Tom Sehler 1472
When She Was Bad - Ron Faust 518
Whisper the Guns - Edward Cline 261
Wildfire - Kenneth W. Goddard 605
Winter of the Wolves - James N. Frey 552
Winter Prey - John Sandford 1428
Winter Rules - Barry Cork 318
Wiseguys in Love - C. Clark Criscuolo 355
With Extreme Prejudice - Frederick Barton 102

Alternate History

Skeleton-in-Waiting - Peter Dickinson 419

Amateur Detective

Act of Faith - Michael Bowen 158
Bad News Travels Fast - Gar Anthony Haywood 761
Barking Dogs - R.R. Irvine 827
Behind Eclaire's Doors - Sophie Dunbar 457
Blood on the Bayou - D.J. Donaldson 429
Blood Trance - R.D. Zimmerman 1791
Boiling Rock - Remar Sutton 1594
The Bridled Groom - J.S. Borthwick 154
Broken Consort - James Gollin 609
The Bulrush Murders - Rebecca Rothenberg 1405
Cat on a Blue Monday - Carole Nelson Douglas 438
Catnap - Carole Nelson Douglas 439
The Classic Car Killer - Richard A. Lupoff 1054
Copy Cat Crimes - Karen Ann Wilson 1733
Dead Men Don't Marry - Dorothy Sucher 1588
Death Among the Dons - Janet Neel 1196
Death Down Home - Eve K. Sandstrom 1430
Death in a Serene City - Edward Sklepowich 1510
Death on the Mississippi - Richard Forrest 535
The Devil Down Home - Eve K. Sandstrom 1431
The Down Home Heifer Heist - Eve K. Sandstrom 1432
Eight Dogs Flying - Karen Ann Wilson 1734
Elective Murder - Janet McGiffin 1129
Elegy in a Country Graveyard - Audrey Peterson 1304
Fielder's Choice - Michael Bowen 160
Finders Keepers - Elizabeth Travis 1627
The Going Down of the Sun - Jo Bannister 87
Grievous Sin - Faye Kellerman 880
Home to Roost - Gerald Hammond 720
Hotel Morgue - Janet Laurence 989
Hubbert and Lil: Partners in Crime - Gallagher Gray 654
Hung in the Balance - Roger Ormerod 1244
Icewater Mansions - Douglas Allyn 48
In Blacker Moments - S.E. Schenkel 1451
Indecent Behavior - Caryl Rivers 1372
Knight & Day - Ron Nessen 1201
Landfall - Tony Gibbs 581
The Lynching - Bennie Lee Sinclair 1503
Malice Domestic #1 - Elizabeth Peters 1299
The Manx Murders - William L. DeAndrea 402
The Marvell College Murders - Sophie Belfort 119
Money Burns - A.E. Maxwell 1100
Murder at Musket Beach - Bernie Lee 998
Murder in a Good Cause - Medora Sale 1417
Murder in Burgundy - Audrey Peterson 1305
Murder Without Reservation - Bernie Lee 999
Neon Dancers - Matt Taylor 1608
New Orleans Requiem - D.J. Donaldson 430
Nightside - Soledad Santiago 1434
No Mardi Gras for the Dead - D.J. Donaldson 431
Noble Rot - Will Harriss 739
Original Sin - Mary Monica Pulver 1334
An Owl Too Many - Charlotte MacLeod 1064
Prescription for Death - Janet McGiffin 1130
Pursued by Shadows - Medora Sale 1419

What Mystery Do I Read Next?

Pussyfoot - Carole Nelson Douglas 443
Red Trance - R.D. Zimmerman 1793
A Season for Murder - Ann Granger 645
Shoofly Pie to Die - Joshua Quittner 1342
Shooting at Loons - Margaret Maron 1078
Show Stopper - Mary Monica Pulver 1335
The Sirens Sang of Murder - Sarah Caudwell 228
Something's Cooking - Joanne Pence 1290
Stage Fright - Gillian Linscott 1030
The Texas Capitol Murders - Bill Crider 353
Ties That Bind - Sherryl Woods 1759
Time of Hope - Susan B. Kelly 898
Until Death - Polly Whitney 1709
A Wicked Slice - Aaron Elkins 480
With an Extreme Burning - Bill Pronzini 1331

Amateur Detective—Female Lead

The 27 Ingredient Chili Con Carne Murders - Nancy Pickard 1315
Adjusted to Death - Jaqueline Girdner 593
Agatha Raisin and the Quiche of Death - M.C. Beaton 107
Agatha Raisin and the Vicious Vet - M.C. Beaton 108
Ah, Sweet Mystery - Celestine Sibley 1495
All Hallows Evil - Valerie Wolzien 1748
All That Remains - Patricia D. Cornwell 321
All the Great Pretenders - Deborah Adams 10
The Alpine Advocate - Mary Daheim 370
The Alpine Christmas - Mary Daheim 371
The Alpine Decoy - Mary Daheim 372
The Alpine Fury - Mary Daheim 373
Amateur Night - K.K. Beck 114
And Soon I'll Come to Kill You - Susan Kelly 893
Aunt Dimity and the Duke - Nancy Atherton 68
Aunt Dimity's Death - Nancy Atherton 69
Bad Blood - P.M. Carlson 218
Bad Chemistry - Nora Kelly 891
Bagels for Tea - Serita Stevens 1571
Bagged - Jo Bailey 79
The Bandersnatch - Mollie Hardwick 729
Bantam of the Opera - Mary Daheim 374
Bayou City Secrets - Deborah Powell 1323
Beat Up a Cookie - Denise Dietz 422
The Bishop's Tale - Margaret Frazer 544
A Bite of Death - Susan Conant 287
Bitter Herbs - Natasha Cooper 307
Black Ribbon - Susan Conant 288
Blanche on the Lam - Barbara Neely 1198
Blindsight - Robin Cook 302
Blood Kin - Marjorie Dorner 436
Blood on the Street - Annette Meyers 1146
Bloodlines - Susan Conant 289
Bloody Roses - Natasha Cooper 308
Blooming Murder - Jean Hager 698
The Bluejay Shaman - Lise McClendon Webb 1680
The Body in the Basement - Katherine Hall Page 1254
The Body in the Belfry - Katherine Hall Page 1255
The Body in the Bouillon - Katherine Hall Page 1256
The Body in the Cast - Katherine Hall Page 1257
The Body in the Transept - Jeanne M. Dams 385
The Body in the Vestibule - Katherine Hall Page 1258
Body of Evidence - Patricia D. Cornwell 323
A Bone to Pick - Charlaine Harris 731
Bones Gather No Moss - John Sherwood 1483
Bootlegger's Daughter - Margaret Maron 1076
A Bouquet of Thorns - John Sherwood 1484
The Boy's Tale - Margaret Frazer 545
Brideprice - J.N. Catanach 226
A Brush with Death - Joan Smith 1519
Bucket Nut - Liza Cody 270
Bum Steer - Nancy Pickard 1316
Buried in Quilts - Sara Hoskinson Frommer 559
Bury the Bishop - Kate Gallison 564
But I Wouldn't Want to Die There - Nancy Pickard 1317
Cancellation by Death - Dorian Yeager 1782

Story Type Index

Amateur Detective—Female Lead

Capitol Offense - Tony Gibbs 580
The Caravaggio Shawl - Samuel M. Steward 1573
The Cashmere Kid - B. Comfort 284
A Cat in a Glass House - Lydia Adamson 15
A Cat in Fine Style - Lydia Adamson 16
A Cat in the Manger - Lydia Adamson 17
A Cat in the Wings - Lydia Adamson 18
A Cat in Wolf's Clothing - Lydia Adamson 19
A Cat on the Cutting Edge - Lydia Adamson 20
The Cavalier Case - Antonia Fraser 543
The Cereal Murders - Diane Mott Davidson 389
Check-out Time - Kate Kingsbury 928
Child of Silence - Abigail Padgett 1251
The Christening Day Murder - Lee Harris 733
The Christie Caper - Carolyn G. Hart 741
The Christmas Night Murder - Lee Harris 734
The Class Menagerie - Jill Churchill 244
Clerical Errors - D.M. Greenwood 670
A Clinic for Murder - Marsha Landreth 974
Clively Close: Dead as Dead Can Be - Ann Crowleigh 361
Close Quarters - Marissa Piesman 1319
Cold Call - Dianne G. Pugh 1333
Cold Feet - Kerry Tucker 1636
Cooking Up Trouble - Joanne Pence 1289
Corona Blue - J.F. Trainor 1625
Corruption - Andrew Klavan 936
Count the Days - Lin Summerfield 1592
Cruel and Unusual - Patricia D. Cornwell 324
The Cruellest Month - Hazel Holt 800
Cry for Help - Karen Hanson Stuyck 1586
Curly Smoke - Susan Holtzer 803
Cutter - Laura Crum 362
The Daphne Decisions - Meg O'Brien 1214
Dark Star - Marcia Muller 1180
Dark Swan - Kathryn Lasky Knight 944
A Dash of Death - Claudia Bishop 134
Date with a Dead Doctor - Toni Brill 177
Dead and Buried - Jean Hager 699
Dead in the Cellar - Connie Feddersen 520
Dead in the Scrub - B.J. Oliphant 1232
Dead in the Water - Julie Smith 1524
Dead Man's Island - Carolyn G. Hart 742
Dead Pan - Jane Dentinger 413
The Dead Pull Hitter - Alison Gordon 612
Dead Ringer - Toni L.P. Kelner 900
The Deadliest Option - Annette Meyers 1147
Deadly Secrets on the St. Johns - Patricia Houck Sprinkle 1542
Death and the Delinquent - B.J. Oliphant 1233
Death and the Oxford Box - Veronica Stallwood 1557
Death and the Trumpets of Tuscany - Hazel Wynn Jones 847
Death at Bishop's Keep - Robin Paige 1259
Death at Gallows Green - Robin Paige 1260
Death Beneath the Christmas Tree - Robert Nordan 1208
Death Benefits - Michael A. Kahn 851
Death Comes as Epiphany - Sharan Newman 1203
Death Echo - Kerry Tucker 1637
Death Goes on Retreat - Sister Carol Anne O'Marie 1237
Death in a Funhouse Mirror - Kate Clark Flora 531
Death in Store - Jennifer Rowe 1406
Death of a Dancing Fool - Carole Berry 124
The Death of a Difficult Woman - Carole Berry 125
Death of a DJ - Jane Rubino 1411
Death of a Postmodernist - Janice Steinberg 1568
Death of the Office Witch - Marlys Millhiser 1155
Death on Wheels - Robert Nordan 1209
Death Served Up Cold - B.J. Oliphant 1234
Deathics - Richard Barth 100
A Deepe Coffyn - Janet Laurence 988
Desert Heat - J.A. Jance 842
A Diet to Die For - Joan Hess 776
Dire Happenings at Scratch Ankle - Celestine Sibley 1496

Dr. Nightingale Goes the Distance - Lydia Adamson 21
Dr. Nightingale Rides the Elephant - Lydia Adamson 22
Dogtown - Mercedes Lambert 972
Don't Leave Me This Way - Joan Smith 1520
Dorothy and Agatha - Gaylord Larsen 984
Down Home Murder - Toni L.P. Kelner 901
Due Diligence - Michael A. Kahn 852
Dust Devils of the Purple Sage - Barbara Burnett Smith 1516
Dying for Chocolate - Diane Mott Davidson 390
Dynamite Pass - J.F. Trainor 1626
Eagles Die Too - Meg O'Brien 1215
Eat, Drink and Be Buried - Kate Kingsbury 929
Electric City - K.K. Beck 115
Elusive Quarry - B. Comfort 285
Emma Chizzit and the Mother Lode Marauder - Mary Bowen Hall 711
Emma Chizzit and the Napa Nemesis - Mary Bowen Hall 712
Emma Chizzit and the Queen Anne Killer - Mary Bowen Hall 713
Encore Murder - Marian Babson 76
Eviction by Death - Dorian Yeager 1783
Exhaustive Enquiries - Betty Rowlands 1408
Faith, Hope and Homicide - Jessica Mann 1071
A Fall in Denver - Sarah Andrews 56
The Famous DAR Murder Mystery - Graham Landrum 977
A Farewell to Yarns - Jill Churchill 245
The Fast-Death Factor - Virginia Crosby 359
A Fatal Advent - Isabelle Holland 797
Fatal Charm - Anne Morice 1173
Femmes Fatal - Dorothy Cannell 214
File Under: Deceased - Sarah Lacey 962
Final Tour - Jonellen Heckler 770
Firm Ambitions - Michael A. Kahn 853
First Pedigree Murder - Melissa Cleary 257
A Fit of Tempera - Mary Daheim 375
Follow That Blonde - Joan Smith 1521
Fool's Puzzle - Earlene Fowler 536
Four Steps to Death - Diana Ramsay 1346
Foxglove - Mary Anne Kelly 889
From Here to Paternity - Jill Churchill 246
Full Commission - Carol Brennan 172
Funny as a Dead Comic - Susan Rogers Cooper 312
Funny as a Dead Relative - Susan Rogers Cooper 313
The Garden Club - Muriel Resnick Jackson 836
Gaudi Afternoon - Barbara Wilson 1731
The George Eliot Murders - Edith Skom 1511
The Gladstone Bag - Charlotte MacLeod 1063
The Good Fight - Lia Matera 1091
Good Morning, Irene - Carole Nelson Douglas 440
Good Night, Mr. Holmes - Carole Nelson Douglas 441
Good Night, Sweet Prince - Carole Berry 126
A Good Year for a Corpse - Valerie Wolzien 1749
Goodnight, Irene - Jan Burke 198
Grandmother's House - Janet LaPierre 983
Grave Consequences - B. Comfort 286
Grave Undertaking - James McCahery 1112
Grizzly - Christine Andreae 54
Hallowed Murder - Ellen Hart 745
The Hanging Garden - John Sherwood 1485
Hanging on the Wire - Gillian Linscott 1028
Hangman's Root - Susan Wittig Albert 32
A Hard Bargain - Lia Matera 1092
Hard News - Jeffrey Wilds Deaver 403
Hard Tack - Barbara D'Amato 382
Hard Women - Barbara D'Amato 383
Hardball - Barbara D'Amato 384
Hare Today, Gone Tomorrow - Meg O'Brien 1216
He Was Her Man - Sarah Shankman 1474
Holy Terrors - Mary Daheim 376
Home Sweet Homicide - Kate Morgan 1171
A Hopeless Case - K.K. Beck 116

Horse of a Different Killer - Jody Jaffe 839
How to Murder Your Mother-in-Law - Dorothy Cannell 215
Hush, Money - Jean Femling 523
I.O.U. - Nancy Pickard 1318
I'd Rather Be in Philadelphia - Gillian Roberts 1378
Idol Bones - D.M. Greenwood 671
An Imperfect Spy - Amanda Cross 360
In the Dark - Carol Brennan 173
In the Dead of Winter - Abbey Penn Baker 81
In the Game - Nikki Baker 82
Infected Be the Air - Janice Law 991
Irene at Large - Carole Nelson Douglas 442
Irish Chain - Earlene Fowler 537
Island Girl - Carole Berry 127
Jinx - Julie Robitaille 1398
The Julius House - Charlaine Harris 732
Justice for Some - Kate Wilhelm 1724
The King Is Dead - Sarah Shankman 1475
Larkspur - Sheila Simonson 1500
The Last Resort - Jaqueline Girdner 594
The Lavender House Murder - Nikki Baker 83
The Lies That Bind - Judith Van Gieson 1649
A Little Class on Murder - Carolyn G. Hart 743
Love Lies - Fern Kupfer 960
A Love to Die For - Christine T. Jorgensen 849
MacPherson's Lament - Sharyn McCrumb 1117
Mail-Order Murder - Leslie Meier 1140
Make Friends with Murder - Judith Garwood 569
The Maltese Puppy - Melissa Cleary 258
A Man to Die For - Eileen Dreyer 448
Manhattan Is My Beat - Jeffrey Wilds Deaver 404
Margin for Murder - Bronte Adams 9
The Mark Twain Murders - Edith Skom 1512
Mass Murder - John Keith Drummond 449
Memory Can Be Murder - Elizabeth Daniels Squire 1547
Midnight Baby - Wendy Hornsby 808
Mint Julep Murder - Carolyn G. Hart 744
Miss Lizzie - Walter Satterthwait 1441
Miss Zukas and the Island Murders - Jo Dereske 415
Miss Zukas and the Library Murders - Jo Dereske 416
Missing Susan - Sharyn McCrumb 1118
Mistress of Justice - Jeffrey Wilds Deaver 405
Mommy and the Murder - Nancy Gladstone 600
Monkey Wrench - Liza Cody 271
A Monstrous Regiment of Women - Laurie R. King 926
The Mooncalf Murders - Noel Vreeland Carter 222
Mortal Words - Kathryn Lasky Knight 945
Mrs. Malory and the Festival Murders - Hazel Holt 801
Mrs. Malory Investigates - Hazel Holt 802
Mrs. Pargeter's Package - Simon Brett 175
Murder at Monticello - Rita Mae Brown 180
Murder at Moot Point - Marlys Millhiser 1156
Murder at the Class Reunion - Triss Stein 1567
Murder at the Friendship Hotel - Charlotte Epstein 496
Murder at the Spa - Stefanie Matteson 1097
Murder by Owl Light - Corinne Holt Sawyer 1445
Murder Has No Calories - Corinne Holt Sawyer 1446
Murder in a Nice Neighborhood - Lora Roberts 1388
Murder in Bandora - Leona Karr 868
Murder in Brief - Carrol Lachint 963
Murder in Gray and White - Corinne Holt Sawyer 1447
Murder in Ordinary Time - Sister Carol Anne O'Marie 1238
Murder in the Napa Valley - David Osborn 1245
Murder Is Germane - Karen Saum 1442
Murder Makes a Pilgrimage - Sister Carol Anne O'Marie 1239
Murder Most Grizzly - Elizabeth Quinn 1340
Murder, My Suite - Mary Daheim 377

Amateur Detective—Male Lead

Murder, Mystery and Mayhem - Jennifer Carnell 220
Murder on Peachtree Street - Patricia Houck Sprinkle 1543
Murder on the Chesapeake - David Osborn 1246
Murder on the Cliff - Stefanie Matteson 1098
Murder Will Out - Dorian Yeager 1784
My Sister's Keeper - Nora Kelly 892
A Mystery Bred in Buckhead - Patricia Houck Sprinkle 1544
Naked Once More - Elizabeth Peters 1300
Napoleon Must Die - Quinn Fawcett 519
Natural Causes - Michael Palmer 1262
Night Game - Alison Gordon 613
North Star Conspiracy - Miriam Grace Monfredo 1164
Now Let's Talk of Graves - Sarah Shankman 1476
Nun Plussed - Monica Quill 1339
Obstacle Course - Yvonne Montgomery 1167
Once and Always Murder - Orania Papazoglou 1263
One for the Money - Janet Evanovich 503
One, Two, What Did Daddy Do? - Susan Rogers Cooper 315
Other People's Skeletons - Julie Smith 1529
The Other Side of Death - Judith Van Gieson 1650
Out of the Darkness - Susan Kelly 894
Over the Edge - Betty Rowlands 1409
Oxford Exit - Veronica Stallwood 1559
Park Lane South, Queens - Mary Anne Kelly 890
Paws Before Dying - Susan Conant 290
A Pedigree to Die For - Laurien Berenson 121
Peril under the Palms - K.K. Beck 117
A Permanent Retirement - John Miles 1153
Philly Stakes - Gillian Roberts 1379
A Piece of Justice - Jill Paton Walsh 1274
A Plague of Kinfolks - Celestine Sibley 1497
A Pocketful of Karma - Taffy Cannon 216
Point No-Point - David Willis McCullough 1123
Poison Pen - Mary Kittredge 933
Postmortem - Patricia D. Cornwell 326
Prior Convictions - Lia Matera 1093
Quaker Silence - Irene Allen 45
Quaker Witness - Irene Allen 46
The Queen Is Dead - Jane Dentinger 414
A Quiche Before Dying - Jill Churchill 247
Rage - Gwen Moffat 1162
Raptor - Judith Van Gieson 1651
Recipe for Death - Janet Laurence 990
The Red Scream - Mary Willis Walker 1659
Report for Murder - Val McDermid 1126
Rest in Pieces - Rita Mae Brown 181
Roll Over and Play Dead - Joan Hess 781
Room 9 - Soledad Santiago 1435
Room with a Clue - Kate Kingsbury 930
The Rotary Club Mystery - Graham Landrum 978
Rotten Apples - Natasha Cooper 309
Rotten Lies - Charlotte Elkins 481
Ruffly Speaking - Susan Conant 291
Safe at Home - Alison Gordon 614
The Scold's Bridle - Minette Walters 1670
The Sculptress - Minette Walters 1671
A Second Shot in the Dark - Annette Roome 1399
Shadow Queen - Tony Gibbs 583
She Walks in Beauty - Sarah Shankman 1477
Showcase - Alison Glen 603
Shroud for a Scholar - Audrey Peterson 1306
Sister Beneath the Sheet - Gillian Linscott 1029
Skeleton-in-Waiting - Peter Dickinson 419
Skylark - Sheila Simonson 1501
A Slay at the Races - Kate Morgan 1172
The Society Ball Murders - Jack Albin Anderson 51
Somebody's Dead in Snellville - Patricia Houck Sprinkle 1545
Someone Is Killing the Great Chefs of America - Nan Lyons 1061
South Street Confidential - Dick Belsky 120
A Stiff Critique - Jaqueline Girdner 595
Still Explosion - Mary Logue 1041
Still Waters - Kerry Tucker 1638
The Stone Hawk - Gwen Moffat 1163

Straight as an Arrow - Celestine Sibley 1498
A Strange and Bitter Crop - E.L. Wyrick 1780
The Strange Files of Fremont Jones - Dianne Day 400
Strangers in the Night - Peg Tyre 1641
Strawgirl - Abigail Padgett 1252
Striking Out - Alison Gordon 615
A Superior Death - Nevada Barr 96
A Tail of Two Murders - Melissa Cleary 259
A Taste for Murder - Claudia Bishop 135
Tea-Totally Dead - Jaqueline Girdner 596
Telling Lies - Wendy Hornsby 809
A Temporary Ghost - Mickey Friedman 556
Tensleep - Sarah Andrews 57
Think on Death - David Willis McCullough 1124
The Thirteenth Apostle - Gloria Gonzalez 610
Throw Darts at a Cheesecake - Denise Dietz 423
Thyme of Death - Susan Wittig Albert 33
Too Many Cooks - Joanne Pence 1291
The Total Zone - Martina Navratilova 1195
Track of the Cat - Nevada Barr 97
Trail of Murder - Christine Andreae 55
A Trick of Light - Patricia Robinson 1391
Trouble Looking for a Place to Happen - Toni L.P. Kelner 902
The Trouble with Going Home - Camilla T. Crespi 345
The Trouble with Moonlighting - Trella Crespi 346
The Trouble with Too Much Sun - Trella Crespi 347
Trunk Show - Alison Glen 604
The Unexpected Corpse - B.J. Oliphant 1235
Unholy Ghosts - D.M. Greenwood 672
Unorthodox Practices - Marissa Piesman 1320
Unsafe Keeping - Carol Cail 206
Until Proven Innocent - Susan Kelly 895
User Deadly - Denise Danks 388
Vial Murders - Marsha Landreth 976
Viper Quarry - Dean Feldmeyer 522
Vital Lies - Ellen Hart 746
A Vow of Chastity - Veronica Black 136
A Vow of Obedience - Veronica Black 137
A Vow of Sanctity - Veronica Black 138
Walking Dead Man - Mary Kittredge 934
We Wish You a Merry Murder - Valerie Wolzien 1750
What Men Say - Joan Smith 1522
What's a Girl Gotta Do? - Sparkle Hayter 760
Who Killed What's-Her-Name? - Elizabeth Daniels Squire 1548
The Windsor Knot - Sharyn McCrumb 1120
The Winter Garden Mystery - Carola Dunn 465
Wish You Were Here - Rita Mae Brown 182
With Friends Like These - Gillian Roberts 1380
The Wolf Path - Judith Van Gieson 1652
A Woman's Own Mystery - Hannah Wakefield 1658
Writers of the Purple Sage - Barbara Burnett Smith 1517
The Wyndham Case - Jill Paton Walsh 1275
Zero at the Bone - Mary Willis Walker 1661

Amateur Detective—Male Lead

All the Dead Heroes - Stephen F. Wilcox 1718
And Baby Makes None - Stephen Lewis 1022
The Apothecary Rose - Candace M. Robb 1375
Artichoke Hearts - Victor Wuamett 1777
Avenging Angel - Anthony Appiah 64
Bad Love - Jonathan Kellerman 885
Banjo Boy - Vince Kohler 949
Baptism for Murder - Jan Maxwell 1101
The Becket Factor - Michael David Anthony 60
The Big Freeze - Michael J. Katz 871
Bino's Blues - A.W. Gray 650
Black Cherry Blues - James Lee Burke 193
Bleeding Dodger Blue - Crabbe Evers 505
Blood Lies - Virginia Anderson 52
Blood Rights - Mike Phillips 1314
Bloody Ten - William F. Love 1047
A Body to Dye For - Grant Michaels 1150
Boiled in Concrete - Jesse Sublett 1587
The Book of the Dead - Robert Richardson 1365

What Mystery Do I Read Next?

Booked to Die - John Dunning 466
Boxed In - Neville Steed 1564
The Boy Who Was Buried This Morning - Joseph Hansen 726
A Brace of Skeet - Gerald Hammond 719
Brother Cadfael's Penance - Ellis Peters 1301
The Burglar Who Traded Ted Williams - Lawrence Block 145
Business Unusual - Tim Heald 763
Casual Slaughters - Robert A. Carter 223
Casualty Loss - Jim Weikart 1683
The Cat Who Moved a Mountain - Lilian Jackson Braun 167
The Cat Who Talked to Ghosts - Lilian Jackson Braun 168
The Cat Who Went into the Closet - Lilian Jackson Braun 169
Catalina's Riddle - Steven Saylor 1448
The Catalyst - Desmond Cory 330
The Caveman's Valentine - George Dawes Green 662
The Chamber - John Grisham 679
Chameleon - William X. Kienzle 915
City of Lies - Peter McCabe 1109
The City When It Rains - Thomas H. Cook 305
A Clear Case of Murder - Warwick Downing 445
Clockwork - Neville Steed 1565
A Collector of Photographs - Deborah Valentine 1645
Comeback - Dick Francis 539
The Comic Book Killer - Richard A. Lupoff 1055
A Cool Breeze on the Underground - Don Winslow 1743
Corporate Bodies - Simon Brett 174
A Country of Old Men - Joseph Hansen 727
Criminal Seduction - Darian North 1211
Cut to the Quick - Kate Ross 1404
Dangerous Waters - Bill Eidson 475
The Dante Game - Jane Langton 979
Dark Provenance - Michael David Anthony 61
Dead Easy - E.S. Russell 1415
Dead Fix - Michael Geller 573
Dead in the Water - W.J. Chaput 233
Dead Men's Hearts - Aaron Elkins 476
Dead Winter - William G. Tapply 1602
Dead Wrong - Alan Dennis Burke 192
Deadline - Gerry Boyle 163
Deadstick - Terence Faherty 513
Deal to Die For - Les Standiford 1560
The Dean It Was That Died - Barbara Whitehead 1706
Death Among the Angels - John Walter Putre 1336
Death and the Chapman - Kate Sedley 1467
Death and the Dogwalker - A.J. Orde 1240
Death Below Deck - Douglas Kiker 922
Death Came Dressed in White - Michael W. Sherer 1481
A Death for a Dancing Doll - E.X. Giroux 597
A Death for a Dodo - E.X. Giroux 598
Death in Close-Up - Nancy Livingston 1034
Death in Verona - Roy Harley Lewis 1020
Death Notice - M.S. Karl 866
Death of a Fantasy Life - T.G. Gilpin 590
Death of the Duchess - Elizabeth Eyre 512
Death Squad London - Jack Gerson 579
Deception Island - M.K. Lorens 1043
Deeds of Trust - Victor Wuamett 1778
The Deep End - Chris Crutcher 364
Deerslayer - M.S. Karl 867
Devil in a Blue Dress - Walter Mosley 1176
Die Dreaming - Terence Faherty 514
The Ditched Blonde - Harold Adams 12
Do Unto Others - Jeff Abbott 1
The Dobie Paradox - Desmond Cory 331
The Dog Hermit - David Stout 1578
Double Blind - David Laing 965
Double Plot - Leo Axler 70
A Dragon Lives Forever - John R. Riggs 1368
Dreamland - M.K. Lorens 1044
A Drink of Deadly Wine - Kate Charles 235
Drover and the Zebras - Bill Granger 646

The Dry White Tear - Stephen F. Wilcox 1719
The Dying of the Light - Robert Richardson 1366
Dying Voices - Bill Crider 351
East Is East - Emma Lathen 986
Escapade - Walter Satterthwait 1438
Faithfully Executed - Michael Bowen 159
Falconer's Crusade - Ian Morson 1175
A Famine of Horses - P.F. Chisholm 243
Fear in Fenway - Crabbe Evers 506
Fell and Foul Play - John Dickson Carr 221
Felony Murder - Joseph T. Klempner 940
Final Dictation - L.M. Vincent 1655
Final Edit - Robert A. Carter 224
Final Option - Stephen Robinett 1389
The Fireman - Stephen Leather 997
First and Ten - Douglas Anderson 50
Flamingo - Bob Reiss 1359
Forty Whacks - Sheila MacGill Callahan 207
Friends till the End - Gloria Dank 387
Frobisher's Savage - Leonard Tourney 1624
Frozen Assets - James Leasor 996
The Frozen Franklin - Sean Hanlon 725
Full-Bodied Red - Bruce Zimmerman 1790
Funnelweb - Charles West 1693
Furnished for Murder - Richard Barth 101
The Genesis Files - Bob Biderman 130
Get What's Coming - Sam Reaves 1354
The Gift Horse's Mouth - Robert Campbell 212
A Glancing Light - Aaron Elkins 477
Grave Matters - Leo Axler 71
The Green Mosaic - Stephen F. Wilcox 1720
Happy Are the Merciful - Andrew M. Greeley 656
Hard Evidence - John T. Lescroart 1009
Hard News - Mark T. Sullivan 1590
Hardscape - Justin Scott 1463
He's Dead-She's Dead: Details at Eleven - John Bartholomew Tucker 1635
Hidden City - Jim DeBrosse 407
The Holy Innocents - Kate Sedley 1468
Holy Treasure! - David Williams 1729
Hot Air - Jon L. Breen 170
Hot Water - Sally Gunning 686
The Hotel Detective - Alan Russell 1413
I'm Getting Killed Right Here - William Murray 1190
Irish Gold - Andrew M. Greeley 657
Is Anybody There? - T.G. Gilpin 591
The Judas Pool - George Owens 1250
Kill the Messenger - Elizabeth Daniels Squire 1546
Killed on the Rocks - William L. DeAndrea 401
A Killing in Venture Capital - Margaret Logan 1040
The Kingsbridge Plot - Maan Meyers 1148
The Lady Chapel - Candace M. Robb 1376
Land Kills - Nat Brandt 166
Last Dance in Redondo Beach - Michael J. Katz 872
The Last Man Standing - Jim Wright 1771
Letting Blood - Richard Platt 1321
The Lies of Fair Ladies - Jonathan Gash 571
Limited Partner - Mike Lupica 1053
The Lion's Share - Kelly A. Tate 1605
A Little Neighborhood Murder - A.J. Orde 1241
Little Use for Death - Michael W. Sherer 1482
A Long Cold Fall - Sam Reaves 1355
A Long Time Dead - A.J. Orde 1242
Loose Lips - Jon L. Breen 171
The Lost Keats - Terence Faherty 515
Love You to Death - Grant Michaels 1151
The Mad Courtesan - Edward Marston 1081
Make No Bones - Aaron Elkins 478
The Man Offside - A.W. Gray 652
The Man Who Cancelled Himself - David Handler 722
The Man Who Missed the Party - Harold Adams 13
The Man Who Would Be F. Scott Fitzgerald - David Handler 723
The Masked Man - P.C. Doherty 425
Masquerade - William X. Kienzle 916
Mayhem in Parva - Nancy Livingston 1035

Methods of Execution - Frederick D. Huebner 818
Monday's Child Is Dead - James Elward 484
Monsieur Pamplemousse Investigates - Michael Bond 151
Mortal Remains - Rick Hanson 728
Mr. Smithson's Bones - Richard Timothy Conroy 297
Murder at Fenway Park - Troy Soos 1536
Murder at the Kennedy Center - Margaret Truman 1634
Murder in Store - D.C. Brod 178
Murder in the Place of Anubis - Lynda S. Robinson 1390
Murder in Waiting - Robert Richardson 1367
Murder in Wrigley Field - Crabbe Evers 507
Murder Times Two - Haughton Murphy 1186
Murder Wears a Cowl - P.C. Doherty 426
Murphy's Fault - Steven Womack 1752
The Naked Typist - J.P. Hailey 704
The Next Victim - William Sanders 1423
Nibbled to Death by Ducks - Robert Campbell 213
Nice Guys Finish Dead - David Debin 406
Night Kills - Ed Gorman 622
The NIMBY Factor - Stephen F. Wilcox 1721
The Nine Giants - Edward Marston 1082
No Place for Secrets - Sherry Lewis 1021
Not a Creature Was Stirring - Jane Haddam 695
The Nun's Tale - Candace M. Robb 1377
Obit - Daniel Paisner 1261
The Old Contemptibles - Martha Grimes 675
Old Scores - Aaron Elkins 479
The Only Good Priest - Mark Richard Zubro 1795
The Only Good Yankee - Jeff Abbott 2
Orphans - Gerald Pearce 1281
Paint It Black - W.R. Philbrick 1313
The Painted Lady - Stephen F. Wilcox 1722
Pamplemousse Rests His Case - Michael Bond 152
Panama - Eric Zencey 1787
Party Till You Die - David Charnee 236
Pas De Death - L.M. Vincent 1656
Peeping Thomas - Robert Reeves 1358
A Perfectly Proper Murder - Harold Adams 14
The Piano Man - Noreen Gilpatrick 589
Picture Postcard - Fredrick D. Huebner 819
Pink Vodka Blues - Neal Barrett Jr. 98
Playing God - Barbara Whitehead 1707
The Poisoned Chalice - Michael Clynes 264
The Potter's Field - Ellis Peters 1302
The Prince of Darkness - P.C. Doherty 427
Private Eyes - Jonathan Kellerman 886
Probable Cause - Griff Stockley 1577
The Pumpkin-Shell Wife - Susanna Hofmann McShea 1138
Quoth the Raven - Jane Haddam 696
Rainy North Woods - Vince Kohler 950
Rat's Nest - Charles West 1694
A Red Death - Walter Mosley 1177
Right on the Money - Emma Lathen 987
Rising Dog - Vince Kohler 951
Roman Nights - Ron Burns 201
Rough Water - Sally Gunning 687
Running Mates - John Feinstein 521
Savage Justice - Ron Handberg 721
A Scandal in Belgravia - Robert Barnard 91
Screaming Bones - Pat Burden 191
The Search Committee - Ralph McInerny 1136
Selena - Gordon Randolph Willey 1726
Self-Defense - Jonathan Kellerman 887
A Series of Murders - Simon Brett 176
Sheep, Goats and Soap - John Malcolm 1068
Shooting Script - Gordon Cotler 332
Shutout - David F. Nighbert 1204
Silent Witness - Charles Wilson 1732
The Sin Within Her Smile - Jonathan Gash 572
Singapore Transfer - Wayne Warga 1673
A Slip of the Tong - Charles A. Goodrum 611
A Small and Incidental Murder - John Walter Putre 1337
Something in the Water - Charlotte MacLeod 1065
Southern Cross - Jim DeBrosse 408
Spare Change - John A. Peak 1280

Spotted Cats - William G. Tapply 1603
SPQR - John Maddox Roberts 1382
Squeezeplay - David F. Nighbert 1205
Stalking Horse - Bill Shoemaker 1487
Still Water - Sally Gunning 688
A Stillness in Bethlehem - Jane Haddam 697
Stone Boy - Ronald Levitsky 1017
StoneDust - Justin Scott 1464
Strangler - Parnell Hall 715
Strike - L.L. Enger 492
Strikezone - David F. Nighbert 1206
A Suitcase in Berlin - Don Flynn 532
The Summer of the Danes - Ellis Peters 1303
The Suspense Is Killing Me - Thomas Maxwell 1102
Sweet Death - Bill Waggoner 1657
Sweet Narcissus - M.K. Lorens 1045
Swindle - George Adams 11
Swing - L.L. Enger 493
Teardown - Victor Wuamett 1779
Three Blind Mice - Ed McBain 1106
Tigers Burning - Crabbe Evers 508
Tight Lines - William G. Tapply 1604
The Tijuana Bible - Ron Goulart 630
Time Bomb - Jonathan Kellerman 888
To Catch a Forger - Robert Wallace 1666
To Kill a Clown - David Charnee 237
To Speak for the Dead - Paul Levine 1016
Topless - D. Keith Mano 1072
The Trail to Buddha's Mirror - Don Winslow 1744
Treasure by Post - David Williams 1730
The Trip to Jerusalem - Edward Marston 1084
Tropical Depression - Jeffry P. Lindsay 1024
Troubled Water - Sally Gunning 689
Truck Shot - Jim Stinson 1574
True Crime - Michael Mewshaw 1145
TV Safe - Jim Stinson 1575
Unknown Hand - Gillian Linscott 1031
Unwillingly to Vegas - Nancy Livingston 1036
A Very Venetian Murder - Haughton Murphy 1187
Wasteland - Peter McCabe 1110
The Weaver's Tale - Kate Sedley 1470
The White Rose Murders - Michael Clynes 265
Why Isn't Becky Twitchell Dead? - Mark Richard Zubro 1797
Wind-Up - Neville Steed 1566
With Extreme Prejudice - Frederick Barton 102
Wolf in Sheep's Clothing - John R. Riggs 1369
The Woman Who Fell From Grace - David Handler 724
The Woman Who Walked into the Sea - Philip R. Craig 340
The Wrong Impression - John Malcolm 1069
Yellow Bird - Rick Boyer 162
Zombies of the Gene Pool - Sharyn McCrumb 1121

Anthology
Cat Crimes - Ed Gorman 619
Cat Crimes II - Ed Gorman 620
City Sleuths and Tough Guys - David Willis McCullough 1122
Dark Crimes: Great Noir Fiction From the '50's to the '90's - Ed Gorman 621
Deadly Allies - Robert J. Randisi 1348
Detective Stories from the Strand - Jack Adrian 24
Malice Domestic #1 - Elizabeth Peters 1299
Reader, I Murdered Him - Jen Green 663
A Woman's Eye - Sara Paretsky 1267
Women of Mystery - Cynthia Manson 1073

Collection
Crime, Punishment and Resurrection - Michael Collins 283
Death in Store - Jennifer Rowe 1406
Stacked Deck - Bill Pronzini 1330

Espionage
A Black Legend - John Horton 810
Bright Shark - Robert Ballard 85
China Lake - Anthony Hyde 823
City of Gold - Len Deighton 410

Historical

Cotswold Moles - Michael Spicer 1539
Cover Story - Robert Cullen 365
Coyote Bird - Jim DeFelice 409
Crossed Swords - Sean Flannery 528
Deadly Crescendo - Paul Myers 1191
The Eagle Has Flown - Jack Higgins 787
Enemy's Enemy - Jan Guillou 685
The Faust Conspiracy - James Baddock 78
Frost the Fiddler - Janice Weber 1681
The Harbinger Effect - S.K. Wolf 1746
The Hawthorne Group - Thomas Hauser 756
The Lantern Network - Ted Allbeury 37
The Last Good German - Bill Granger 647
Moving Targets - Sean Flannery 529
Mrs. Pollifax and the Whirling Dervish - Dorothy Gilman 588
Quiller KGB - Adam Hall 706
River of Darkness - James Grady 632
Rook-Shoot - Margaret Duffy 452
The Run Around - Brian Freemantle 550
The Russia House - John Le Carre 995
A Singular Spy - Amanda Kyle Williams 1727
Spy Shadow - Tim Sebastian 1466
A Time Without Shadows - Ted Allbeury 38
Tucker's Last Stand - William F. Buckley Jr. 188
Who Killed Cock Robin? - Margaret Duffy 453
Win, Lose or Die - John Gardner 567
Winter of the Wolves - James N. Frey 552

Historical

The 6 Messiahs - Mark Frost 560
Act of Faith - Michael Bowen 158
The Apothecary Rose - Candace M. Robb 1375
Bayou City Secrets - Deborah Powell 1323
The Beekeeper's Apprentice - Laurie R. King 924
Bertie and the Seven Bodies - Peter Lovesey 1049
The Bishop's Tale - Margaret Frazer 544
The Black Mask Murders - William F. Nolan 1207
Black Out - John Lawton 994
Blood and Thunder - Max Allan Collins 276
Blood Line - Alanna Knight 941
The Boy's Tale - Margaret Frazer 545
A Broken Vessel - Kate Ross 1403
Brother Cadfael's Penance - Ellis Peters 1301
Cain His Brother - Anne Perry 1292
Carnal Hours - Max Allan Collins 277
Catalina's Riddle - Steven Saylor 1448
Check-out Time - Kate Kingsbury 928
City of Gold - Len Deighton 410
Clively Close: Dead as Dead Can Be - Ann Crowleigh 361
Cut to the Quick - Kate Ross 1404
A Dangerous Mourning - Anne Perry 1293
Deadfall in Berlin - R.D. Zimmerman 1792
Deadly Beloved - Alanna Knight 942
Death and the Chapman - Kate Sedley 1467
Death at Bishop's Keep - Robin Paige 1259
Death at Gallows Green - Robin Paige 1260
Death Comes as Epiphany - Sharan Newman 1203
Death of the Duchess - Elizabeth Eyre 512
Death Off Stage - Richard Grayson 655
Death Wore a Diadem - Iona McGregor 1133
Devil in a Blue Dress - Walter Mosley 1176
Diamond Head - Marian J.A. Jackson 834
The Disappearance of Edwin Drood - Peter Rowland 1407
The Ditched Blonde - Harold Adams 12
The Dividing Line - Richard Parrish 1273
Dog Heavies - L.J. Washburn 1675
Dorothy and Agatha - Gaylord Larsen 984
The Eagle Has Flown - Jack Higgins 787
Eat, Drink and Be Buried - Kate Kingsbury 929
Escapade - Walter Satterthwait 1438
The Eye of God - C.L. Grace 631
Faces in the Crowd - William Marshall 1079
Falconer's Crusade - Ian Morson 1175
A Famine of Horses - P.F. Chisholm 243
Farrier's Lane - Anne Perry 1294
The Fate of Princes - P.C. Doherty 424
Fielder's Choice - Michael Bowen 160
Frobisher's Savage - Leonard Tourney 1624
The Glendower Conspiracy - Lloyd Biggle Jr. 131
Good Morning, Irene - Carole Nelson Douglas 440
Good Night, Mr. Holmes - Carole Nelson Douglas 441
Hanging on the Wire - Gillian Linscott 1028
Highgate Rise - Anne Perry 1295
The Holy Innocents - Kate Sedley 1468
In the Dead of Winter - Abbey Penn Baker 81
Irene at Large - Carole Nelson Douglas 442
Jordon's Showdown - Frank C. Strunk 1583
Jordon's Wager - Frank C. Strunk 1584
Killing Cousins - Alanna Knight 943
The Kingsbridge Plot - Maan Meyers 1148
The Lady Chapel - Candace M. Robb 1376
The Last Camel Died at Noon - Elizabeth Peters 1298
The Lost Keats - Terence Faherty 515
The Loud Adios - Ken Kuhlken 957
The Mad Courtesan - Edward Marston 1081
The Masked Man - P.C. Doherty 425
The Melting Clock - Stuart M. Kaminsky 860
A Monstrous Regiment of Women - Laurie R. King 926
Motown - Loren D. Estleman 498
Murder at Fenway Park - Troy Soos 1536
Murder by the Numbers - Max Allan Collins 278
Murder in the Place of Anubis - Lynda S. Robinson 1390
Murder in the Post-War World - Max Allan Collins 279
Murder Wears a Cowl - P.C. Doherty 426
Napoleon Must Die - Quinn Fawcett 519
The New York Detective - William Marshall 1080
The Nine Giants - Edward Marston 1082
North Star Conspiracy - Miriam Grace Monfredo 1164
The Nun's Tale - Candace M. Robb 1377
The Pale Criminal - Philip Kerr 914
Panama - Eric Zencey 1787
Patently Murder - Ray Harrison 737
A Perfectly Proper Murder - Harold Adams 14
The Plymouth Cloak - Kate Sedley 1469
The Poisoned Chalice - Michael Clynes 264
The Potter's Field - Ellis Peters 1302
Praetorian - Thomas Gifford 584
The Prince of Darkness - P.C. Doherty 427
The Quality of Mercy - Faye Kellerman 883
The Queen's Head - Edward Marston 1083
A Red Death - Walter Mosley 1177
The Ripper's Apprentice - Donald Thomas 1610
Roman Blood - Steven Saylor 1449
Roman Nights - Ron Burns 201
Room with a Clue - Kate Kingsbury 930
Saint Mudd - Steve Thayer 1609
A Scandal in Belgravia - Robert Barnard 91
Scotch on the Rocks - Howard Browne 183
The Seventh Bullet - Daniel D. Victor 1654
The Shadow of the Shadow - Paco Ignacio Taibo II 1598
The Silver Pigs - Lindsey Davis 394
Sister Beneath the Sheet - Gillian Linscott 1029
Snow Falling on Cedars - David Guterson 692
The Song Dog - James McClure 1114
Spandau Phoenix - Greg Iles 824
SPQR - John Maddox Roberts 1382
Stage Fright - Gillian Linscott 1030
Stolen Away - Max Allan Collins 280
The Strange Files of Fremont Jones - Dianne Day 400
The Strenuous Life - Lawrence Alexander 36
A Sudden, Fearful Death - Anne Perry 1296
The Summer of the Danes - Ellis Peters 1303
The Sunken Treasure - Marian J.A. Jackson 835
A Time Without Shadows - Ted Allbeury 38
Tincture of Death - Ray Harrison 738
To Die Like a Gentleman - Bernard Bastable 103
The Trip to Jerusalem - Edward Marston 1084
Tucker's Last Stand - William F. Buckley Jr. 188
The Venus Throw - Steven Saylor 1450
The Weaver's Tale - Kate Sedley 1470
The Wench Is Dead - Colin Dexter 418
Whiskey River - Loren D. Estleman 501
White Butterfly - Walter Mosley 1178
The White Rose Murders - Michael Clynes 265
The Winter Garden Mystery - Carola Dunn 465
With Siberia Comes a Chill - Kirk Mitchell 1161

Humor

Business Unusual - Tim Heald 763
Clubbed to Death - Ruth Dudley Edwards 472
Don't Ask - Donald E. Westlake 1697
Drowned Hopes - Donald E. Westlake 1698
Even the Butler Was Poor - Ron Goulart 628
Femmes Fatal - Dorothy Cannell 214
Juror - Parnell Hall 714
Monsieur Pamplemousse Investigates - Michael Bond 151
Murder Without Reservation - Bernie Lee 999
Now He Thinks He's Dead - Ron Goulart 629
An Owl Too Many - Charlotte MacLeod 1064
Wish You Were Here - Rita Mae Brown 182

Legal

Against the Wind - J.F. Freedman 547
And Baby Makes None - Stephen Lewis 1022
Bino's Blues - A.W. Gray 650
Body and Soil - Ralph McInerny 1135
Break and Enter - Colin Harrison 735
The Chamber - John Grisham 679
The Choice - Barry Reed 1357
A Clear Case of Murder - Warwick Downing 445
Clearwater Summer - John E. Keegan 876
The Client - John Grisham 680
Close Quarters - Marissa Piesman 1319
Compelling Evidence - Steve Martini 1090
The Cut Throat - Simon Michael 1149
Death Benefits - Michael A. Kahn 851
A Death for a Dancing Doll - E.X. Giroux 597
A Death for a Dodo - E.X. Giroux 598
Death Qualified: A Mystery of Chaos - Kate Wilhelm 1723
Deep Sleep - Frances Fyfield 561
The Dividing Line - Richard Parrish 1273
Due Diligence - Michael A. Kahn 852
Felony Murder - Joseph T. Klempner 940
Firm Ambitions - Michael A. Kahn 853
Fresh Kills - Carolyn Wheat 1699
Hard Evidence - John T. Lescroart 1009
Hostile Witness - William Lashner 985
How Town - Michael Nava 1194
Illegal Motion - Grif Stockley 1576
The Immediate Prospect of Being Hanged - Walter Walker 1662
Inadmissible Evidence - Philip Friedman 557
Justice Denied - Robert K. Tanenbaum 1599
Justice for Some - Kate Wilhelm 1724
Killings - A.W. Gray 651
Lautrec - Norman Zollinger 1794
A Lawyer's Tale - D. Kincaid 923
The Lies That Bind - Judith Van Gieson 1649
A Loose Connection - M.R.D. Meek 1139
Methods of Execution - Frederick D. Huebner 818
Mistress of Justice - Jeffrey Wilds Deaver 405
Mitigating Circumstances - Nancy Taylor Rosenberg 1401
Mortal Sin - Paul Levine 1014
Murder in Brief - Carrol Lachint 963
The Naked Typist - J.P. Hailey 704
Night Vision - Paul Levine 1015
Orphans - Gerald Pearce 1281
Other People's Skeletons - Julie Smith 1529
Party Till You Die - David Charnee 236
The Pelican Brief - John Grisham 681
Perry Mason in The Case of Too Many Murders - Thomas Chastain 239
Playing the Dozens - William D. Pease 1286
Pleading Guilty - Scott Turow 1640
A Pocketful of Karma - Taffy Cannon 216
Poison Fruit - Chelsea Quinn Yarbro 1781
The Price of Victory - Vincent Green 666

Story Type Index

Primal Fear - William Diehl 421
Prior Convictions - Lia Matera 1093
Probable Cause - Griff Stockley 1577
The Prosecutor - Thomas Chastain 240
Reasonable Doubt - Philip Friedman 558
Reversible Error - Robert K. Tanenbaum 1600
Running From the Law - Lisa Scottoline 1465
Seeds of Murder - Michael Underwood 1642
Shadow of a Doubt - William J. Coughlin 333
Snow Falling on Cedars - David Guterson 692
Spare Change - John A. Peak 1280
Stone Boy - Ronald Levitsky 1017
A Strange and Bitter Crop - E.L. Wyrick 1780
Suspicion of Guilt - Barbara Parker 1268
Three Blind Mice - Ed McBain 1106
To Kill a Clown - David Charnee 237
To Speak for the Dead - Paul Levine 1016
Town on Trial - William Harrington 730
Trade-Off - Harrison Arnston 66
The Underground Man - J.P. Hailey 705
The Wolf Path - Judith Van Gieson 1652

Police Procedural

All Shall Be Well - Deborah Crombie 356
The Angel Maker - Ridley Pearson 1282
Bad Chemistry - Nora Kelly 891
Children's Games - Janet LaPierre 982
The Classic Car Killer - Richard A. Lupoff 1054
Clear-Cut Murder - Lee Wallingford 1667
Cold in the Earth - Ann Granger 642
Cold Tracks - Lee Wallingford 1668
Death Among the Dons - Janet Neel 1196
Death of a Partner - Janet Neel 1197
Deep Sleep - Frances Fyfield 561
The Devil Down Home - Eve K. Sandstrom 1431
Die in My Dreams - Christine Green 661
The Down Home Heifer Heist - Eve K. Sandstrom 1432
Elective Murder - Janet McGiffin 1129
Farrier's Lane - Anne Perry 1294
A Fine Place for Death - Ann Granger 643
Foxglove - Mary Anne Kelly 889
A Good Day to Die - Stephen Solomita 1534
Half a Mind - Wendy Hornsby 807
High Strangeness - Alison Drake 447
Highgate Rise - Anne Perry 1295
Home to Roost - Gerald Hammond 720
Hope Against Hope - Susan B. Kelly 896
Hot Shots - Laurence Gough 627
Hotel Morgue - Janet Laurence 989
Hung in the Balance - Roger Ormerod 1244
In Blacker Moments - S.E. Schenkel 1451
Irish Chain - Earlene Fowler 537
Kid's Stuff - Susan B. Kelly 897
Killing Cousins - Alanna Knight 943
The Last Gambit - David Delman 411
Leave the Grave Green - Deborah Crombie 357
The Marvell College Murders - Sophie Belfort 119
Midnight Baby - Wendy Hornsby 808
Murder Among Us - Ann Granger 644
Murder in a Good Cause - Medora Sale 1417
Murder in Focus - Medora Sale 1418
New Orleans Requiem - D.J. Donaldson 430
Night Sins - Tami Hoag 794
Nightside - Soledad Santiago 1434
No Mardi Gras for the Dead - D.J. Donaldson 431
Noble Rot - Will Harriss 739
Original Sin - Mary Monica Pulver 1334
The Other Woman - Jill McGown 1132
Prescription for Death - Janet McGiffin 1130
Pursued by Shadows - Medora Sale 1419
Ravenmocker - Jean Hager 701
A Season for Murder - Ann Granger 645
A Share in Death - Deborah Crombie 358
Short Cut to Santa Fe - Medora Sale 1420
Sight Unseen - David Lorne 1046
Something's Cooking - Joanne Pence 1290
Throw Darts at a Cheesecake - Denise Dietz 423
Time of Hope - Susan B. Kelly 898
Until Proven Innocent - Susan Kelly 895
A Violent End - Emma Page 1253

The Water Cure - Warwick Downing 446
A Wicked Slice - Aaron Elkins 480
Widowmaker - William Appel 63

Police Procedural—Female Lead

All That Remains - Patricia D. Cornwell 321
Amends for Murder - M.D. Lake 966
Angel of Death - Rochelle Majer Krich 953
The Axeman's Jazz - Julie Smith 1523
The Beverly Malibu - Katherine V. Forrest 533
Bird in a Cage - Lee Martin 1086
The Body Farm - Patricia D. Cornwell 322
Box Nine - Jack O'Connell 1223
Carcass Trade - Noreen Ayres 74
The Cheerio Killings - Douglas Allyn 47
Cold Comfort - M.D. Lake 967
Consider the Crows - Charlene Weir 1685
Cruel and Unusual - Patricia D. Cornwell 324
The Day That Dusty Died - Lee Martin 1087
Dead Ahead - Ruby Horansky 804
Dead Center - Ruby Horansky 805
Dead Fit - Stephen Cook 304
Dead Set - Jennie Melville 1141
Dead Time - Eleanor Taylor Bland 141
Death and Taxes - Susan Dunlap 460
Death on Rough Water - Francine Matthews 1099
Deficit Ending - Lee Martin 1088
Diamond in the Buff - Susan Dunlap 461
Fair Game - Rochelle Majer Krich 954
Family Practice - Charlene Weir 1686
Final Session - Mary Morell 1170
From Potter's Field - Patricia D. Cornwell 325
A Gift for Murder - M.D. Lake 968
A Grave Talent - Laurie R. King 925
Gravestone - P.M. Carlson 219
Hanging Time - Leslie Glass 601
The Holiday Murders - Marsha Landreth 975
House of Blues - Julie Smith 1525
Jazz Funeral - Julie Smith 1526
Lockout - Lillian O'Donnell 1224
Madness in Maggody - Joan Hess 777
Mallory's Oracle - Carol O'Connell 1221
The Mensa Murders - Lee Martin 1089
Miracles in Maggody - Joan Hess 778
Model Murder - Erica Quest 1338
The Monster Squad - John Angus 59
Mortal Remains in Maggody - Joan Hess 779
Murder by Mail - M.D. Lake 969
Murder by Tradition - Katherine V. Forrest 534
Murder Has a Pretty Face - Jennie Melville 1142
Murder Once Removed - Kathleen Kunz 959
New Orleans Beat - Julie Smith 1527
New Orleans Mourning - Julie Smith 1528
Night of the Cat - James Schermerhorn 1452
North of Montana - April Smith 1515
O Little Town of Maggody - Joan Hess 780
Once upon a Crime - M.D. Lake 970
Past Imperfect - Margaret Maron 1077
Poisoned Ivy - M.D. Lake 971
A Pound of Flesh - Trevor Barnes 95
A Private Crime - Lillian O'Donnell 1225
Pushover - Lillian O'Donnell 1226
Skins - Catherine O'Connell 1222
Slow Burn - Eleanor Taylor Bland 142
Time Expired - Susan Dunlap 464
To Play the Fool - Laurie R. King 927
Whoever Has the Heart - Jennie Melville 1143
A Wide and Capable Revenge - Thomas McCall 1113
The Winter Widow - Charlene Weir 1687
Witching Murder - Jennie Melville 1144

Police Procedural—Male Lead

19th Precinct - Christopher Newman 1202
An Absence of Light - David L. Lindsey 1026
All I Have Is Blue - James Colbert 272
Along Came a Spider - James Patterson 1276
And Leave Her Lay Dying - John Lawrence Reynolds 1362
Axx Goes South - Frederic Huber 817
Babylon South - Jon Cleary 255

Bad Apple - Anthony Bruno 184
Bad Moon - Anthony Bruno 186
Bait - Kenneth Abel 3
Balboa Firefly - Jack Trolley 1633
Bitter Recoil - Steven F. Havill 757
The Black Echo - Michael Connelly 292
The Black Ice - Michael Connelly 293
Black Out - John Lawton 994
Bloody Soaps: A Tale of Love and Death in the Afternoon - Jacqueline Babbin 75
The Body in Blackwater Bay - Paula Gosling 624
The Body Politic - Catherine Aird 25
Bone Idle - Susannah Stacey 1553
The Bone Orchard - Joseph Trigoboff 1628
Bones and Silence - Reginald Hill 789
Borderlines - Archer Mayor 1103
Breach of Promise - Roy Hart 748
Buried in Stone - Eric Wright 1766
Burning Angel - James Lee Burke 194
The Buzzards Must Also Be Fed - Anne Wingate 1739
By Reason of Insanity - James Neal Harvey 749
The Cactus Garden - Robert Ward 1672
The Cambridge Theorem - Tony Cape 217
Carolina Gold - Douglas McBriarty 1108
Cat's Cradle - Clare Curzon 366
A Certain Justice - John T. Lescroart 1008
Chain of Evidence - Ridley Pearson 1283
City of God - Michael Jahn 840
Close-Up on Death - Maureen O'Brien 1213
Clubbed to Death - Ruth Dudley Edwards 472
Coffin on Murder Street - Gwendoline Butler 203
Coffin Underground - Gwendoline Butler 204
Cold Light - John Harvey 751
The Concrete Blonde - Michael Connelly 294
Condition Purple - Peter Turnbull 1639
Cutting Edge - John Harvey 752
Dangerous Conceits - Margaret Moore 1168
A Dangerous Mourning - Anne Perry 1293
A Day in the Death of Dorothea Cassidy - Ann Cleeves 260
Day of Atonement - Faye Kellerman 878
Dead Before Morning - Geraldine Evans 504
Dead by Morning - Dorothy Simpson 1502
Dead Center - Collin Wilcox 1711
Dead Easy - Arthur F. Nehrbass 1199
Dead Meat - Philip Kerr 913
Dead Moon on the Rise - Susan Rogers Cooper 310
Dead on Time - H.R.F. Keating 874
Deadly Beloved - Alanna Knight 942
The Dean It Was That Died - Barbara Whitehead 1706
Death and Judgment - Donna Leon 1002
Death and the Chaste Apprentice - Robert Barnard 89
Death at La Fenice - Donna Leon 1003
A Death Before Dying - Collin Wilcox 1712
Death by Degrees - Eric Wright 1767
Death in a Strange Country - Donna Leon 1004
Death in Disguise - Caroline Graham 640
Death of a Charming Man - M.C. Beaton 109
Death of a Hollow Man - Caroline Graham 641
Death of a Hussy - M.C. Beaton 110
Death of a Nag - M.C. Beaton 111
Death of a Perfect Wife - M.C. Beaton 112
Death of a Traveling Man - M.C. Beaton 113
Death Off Stage - Richard Grayson 655
Death Penalties - Paula Gosling 625
Death Prone - Clare Curzon 367
Death Underfoot - Dennis Casley 225
Death Watch - Cynthia Harrod-Eagles 740
A Dedicated Man - Peter Robinson 1392
Detective First Grade - Don Mahoney 1067
Deviant Way - Richard Montanari 1166
Dixie City Jam - James Lee Burke 195
Doctors, Lawyers and Such - Susan Rogers Cooper 311
Dover and the Claret Tappers - Joyce Porter 1322
Down by the Sea - Bill Kent 910
Earth Angels - Gerald Petievich 1311

Private Detective — What Mystery Do I Read Next?

The Edge of Sleep - David Wiltse 1736
The Edge of the Crazies - Jamie Harrison 736
End Game - Dev Stryker 1585
Exception to Murder - Anne Wingate 1740
Exceptional Clearance - William J. Caunitz 229
The Eye of Anna - Anne Wingate 1741
Faces in the Crowd - William Marshall 1079
Fall From Grace - L.R. Wright 1773
False Faces - Seth Jacob Margolis 1074
False Prophet - Faye Kellerman 879
Family Album - Susan Oleksiw 1230
Fatal Obsession - D.B. Taylor 1606
Feeding Frenzy - Paul Kemprecos 904
A Few Dying Words - Paula Gosling 626
The Fifth Rapunzel - B.M. Gill 586
Final Cut - Eric Wright 1768
A Fine Italian Hand - Eric Wright 1769
Fixing to Die - Jerry Oster 1249
Flashback - Ted Wood 1756
Flowers for the Dead - Ann M. Williams 1728
Force of Nature - Stephen Solomita 1533
Fruits of the Poisonous Tree - Archer Mayor 1104
Fuse Time - Max Byrd 205
Gallows View - Peter Robinson 1393
Gentkill: A Novel of the FBI - Paul Lindsay 1025
Ghostland - Jean Hager 700
The Glade Manor Murder - Elizabeth Lemarchand 1001
Golden Fleece - Jack Becklund 118
Gospel Truths - J.G. Sandom 1429
Grave Responsibility - Susannah Stacey 1554
The Great Grave Robbery - John Minahan 1158
Grievous Sin - Faye Kellerman 880
Grootka - Jon A. Jackson 832
Hammurabi's Code - Charles Kenney 909
The Hanging Valley - Peter Robinson 1394
The Hangman's Beautiful Daughter - Sharyn McCrumb 1115
Heartshot - Steven F. Havill 758
Help Wanted: Orphans Preferred - Earl Emerson 487
Hire a Hangman - Collin Wilcox 1715
Hit on the House - Jon A. Jackson 833
A Homecoming for Murder - John Armistead 65
The Honourable Detective - Jeffrey Ashford 67
Houston in the Rearview Mirror - Susan Rogers Cooper 314
The Ice House - Minette Walters 1669
The Iciest Sin - H.R.F. Keating 875
In Deep - Bruce Jones 846
In Stoney Places - Kay Mitchell 1159
In the Electric Mist with Confederate Dead - James Lee Burke 196
The Interface Man - Bill Knox 948
Into the Fire - David Wiltse 1737
Into Thin Air - Thomas Zigal 1788
Jordon's Wager - Frank C. Strunk 1584
Justice - Faye Kellerman 881
Justice Denied - Robert K. Tanenbaum 1599
Kiet Goes West - Gary Alexander 34
Kill the Butler! - Michael Kenyon 911
Killer in Paradise - John Leslie 1011
The Killing of Ellis Martin - Lucretia Grindle 677
Kiss Them Goodbye - Joseph Eastburn 468
Kissing the Gunner's Daughter - Ruth Rendell 1361
A Knife at the Opera - Susannah Stacey 1555
The Last Page - Bob Fenster 524
The Late Lady - Susannah Stacey 1556
The Late Man - James Preston Girard 592
Late of This Parish - Marjorie Eccles 469
Lieberman's Choice - Stuart M. Kaminsky 856
Lieberman's Day - Stuart M. Kaminsky 857
Lieberman's Folly - Stuart M. Kaminsky 858
A Lively Form of Death - Kay Mitchell 1160
Lizardskin - Carsten Stroud 1582
Man of Blood - Margaret Duffy 451
The Man Who Walked Like a Bear - Stuart M. Kaminsky 859
Menaced Assassin - Joe Gores 618
Milk and Honey - Faye Kellerman 882
Minor in Possession - J.A. Jance 844

Missing Joseph - Elizabeth George 575
Missing Man - Richard Martin Stern 1570
More Deaths than One - Marjorie Eccles 470
A Morning for Flamingos - James Lee Burke 197
Morons and Madmen - Earl Emerson 488
Mother Love - L.R. Wright 1774
Murder by the Numbers - Max Allan Collins 278
Murder in a Cold Climate - Scott Young 1785
Murder in a Quiet Place - Tony Caxton 230
Murder in Mellingham - Susan Oleksiw 1231
Murder Movie - Jill McGown 1131
Murder on a Kibbutz - Batya Gur 690
Murder on the Iditarod Trail - Sue Henry 775
Murder on the Thirteenth - A.E. Eddenden 471
Murder Song - Jon Cleary 256
A Necessary End - Peter Robinson 1395
Night Prey - John Sandford 1424
Night Rituals - Gary Paulsen 1279
No Comfort in Victory - Gregory Bean 106
No Way Home - Andrew Coburn 267
Nobody Lives Forever - Edna Buchanan 187
Nobody's Fool - Marten Claridge 249
The Noose of Time - Stephen Murray 1189
Not as Far as Velma - Nicholas Freeling 548
Nurse Dawes Is Dead - Stella Shepherd 1479
Obit - Daniel Paisner 1261
Off Minor - John Harvey 753
The Old Contemptibles - Martha Grimes 675
The Old Silent - Martha Grimes 676
On the Edge - Ed Naha 1193
On the Inside - Ted Wood 1757
Other People's Houses - Susan Rogers Cooper 316
Painted Ladies - James Neal Harvey 750
Past Reason Hated - Peter Robinson 1396
Patently Murder - Ray Harrison 737
Payment in Blood - Elizabeth George 576
Peckover Joins the Choir - Michael Kenyon 912
Pel and the Missing Persons - Mark Hebden 768
A Piece of the Action - Stephen Solomita 1535
Playing for the Ashes - Elizabeth George 577
Playing the Dozens - William D. Pease 1286
Point Blank - Jayson Livingston 1033
Prized Possessions - L.R. Wright 1775
Probable Cause - Ridley Pearson 1285
Recalled to Life - Reginald Hill 790
Rising Sun - Michael Crichton 348
Rostnikov's Vacation - Stuart M. Kaminsky 861
Rules of Prey - John Sandford 1425
Sacred Clowns - Tony Hillerman 792
Sand Castles - Nicholas Freeling 549
The Saturday Morning Murder - Batya Gur 691
Scent of Evil - Archer Mayor 1105
See No Evil - Edward Mathis 1095
A Sensitive Case - Eric Wright 1770
Shadow Prey - John Sandford 1426
The Shaman's Knife - Scott Young 1786
Shooting Script - Gordon Cotler 332
Silent Prey - John Sandford 1427
A Single Stone - Marilyn Wallace 1664
Skeletons - Eric Sauter 1443
Skinny Man - James Colbert 273
Snow Job - Ted Wood 1758
So Little to Die For - Lucretia Grindle 678
The Song Dog - James McClure 1114
Sorry Now? - Mark Richard Zubro 1796
The Spoils of Time - June Thomson 1614
The Standoff - Chuck Hogan 796
Stone Shadow - Rex Miller 1154
Storm Front - Virginia Anderson 53
Strange Loyalties - William McIlvanney 1134
Streets of Fire - Thomas H. Cook 306
A Suitable Vengeance - Elizabeth George 578
The Summons - Peter Lovesey 1050
Sunshine Enemies - K.C. Constantine 298
Sweet Death, Come Softly - Barbara Whitehead 1708
Switchback - Collin Wilcox 1717
Talking God - Tony Hillerman 793
The Texas Capitol Murders - Bill Crider 353
Thieftaker - Alan Scholefield 1454
Thinner than Blood - Stella Shepherd 1480

Three-Core Lead - Clare Curzon 368
Threnody for Two - Jeanne Hart 747
A Time for Dying - Jonathan Ross 1402
Time's Witness - Michael Malone 1070
To Killashea - Norman Flood 530
Too Clever by Half - Roderic Jeffries 845
A Touch of Panic - L.R. Wright 1776
U.S.S.A. - David Madsen 1066
Unbalanced Acts - Jeff Raines 1344
Unfunny Money - Gary Alexander 35
A Very Particular Murder - S.T. Haymon 759
A Very Proper Death - Alex Juniper 850
Vespers - Ed McBain 1107
Voices in the Dark - Andrew Coburn 268
The Wasted Years - John Harvey 754
Wednesday's Child - Peter Robinson 1397
Whisper Death - John Lawrence Reynolds 1363
Winter Prey - John Sandford 1428
Winter Rules - Barry Cork 318
With Siberia Comes a Chill - Kirk Mitchell 1161
The Wrong Rite - Alisa Craig 334
Yakuza, Go Home - Anne Wingate 1742

Private Detective

Beauty Dies - Melodie Johnson Howe 813
Black Eye - Neville Steed 1563
Body of Evidence - David A. Van Meter 1653
Catnap - Carole Nelson Douglas 439
The Curious Eat Themselves - John Straley 1580
Deadly Stakes - H. Fred Wiser 1745
A Drink Before the War - Dennis Lehane 1000
False Profit - Robert Eversz 511
The Heaven Stone - David Daniel 386
High Strangeness - Alison Drake 447
The Last Gambit - David Delman 411
Love Bytes - Sally Chapman 232
The Mexican Tree Duck - James Crumley 363
The Mother Shadow - Melodie Johnson Howe 814
Rafferty: Fatal Sisters - W. Glenn Duncan 458
Red Knight - J. Madison Davis 391
Saint Louie Blues - Jake Tanner 1601
Seven Kinds of Death - Kate Wilhelm 1725
Sister's Keeper - Randye Lordon 1042
Thursday's Child - Teri White 1705
White Rook - J. Madison Davis 392
A Wild and Lonely Place - Marcia Muller 1185
The Woman Who Married a Bear - John Straley 1581

Private Detective—Female Lead

Alibi for an Actress - Gillian B. Farrell 516
Alley Kat Blues - Karen Kijewski 917
Angel's Bidding - Sharon Gwyn Short 1489
Antipodes - Maria-Antonia Oliver 1236
Backhand - Liza Cody 269
Bet Against the House - Catherine Dain 378
Birthmarks - Sarah Dunant 455
Blood of an Aries - Linda Mather 1094
Burn Marks - Sara Paretsky 1264
By Evil Means - Sandra West Prowell 1332
Came a Dead Cat - James N. Frey 551
Caught in the Shadows - C.A. Haddad 694
Charged with Guilt - Gloria White 1700
The Cheetah Chase - Karin McQuillan 1137
China Trade - S.J. Rozan 1410
A Cold-Blooded Business - Dana Stabenow 1550
A Cold Day for Murder - Dana Stabenow 1549
Copy Kat - Karen Kijewski 918
Corona Blue - J.F. Trainor 1625
Coyote - Linda Barnes 92
Crack Down - Val McDermid 1125
Cut To—Murder - Denise Osborne 1247
Dancing in the Dark - Sharon Zukowski 1798
Dead in the Water - Dana Stabenow 1551
Deadly Admirer - Christine Green 658
Deadly Errand - Christine Green 659
Deadly Practice - Christine Green 660
Deadly Resolutions - Anna Ashwood Collins 274
The Death We Share - Sharon Gwyn Short 1490
Decked - Carol Higgins Clark 250
Desperate Remedy - Mary Kittredge 931

Story Type Index

Devil's Gonna Get Him - Valerie Wilson Wesley 1691
Diamond Head - Marian J.A. Jackson 834
The Emerald Lizard - Chris Wiltz 1738
Every Breath You Take - Michelle Spring 1541
Every Crooked Nanny - Kathy Hogan Trocheck 1631
Everything You Have Is Mine - Sandra Scoppettone 1460
F Is for Fugitive - Sue Grafton 634
The Fall-Down Artist - Thomas Lipinski 1032
Four Elements of Murder - D.B. Borton 155
Friends in High Places - Michael Hendricks 771
G Is for Gumshoe - Sue Grafton 635
The Glass Ceiling - Anabel Donald 428
Grave Secrets - Louise Hendricksen 774
Guardian Angel - Sara Paretsky 1265
H Is for Homicide - Sue Grafton 636
Hit and Run - Maxine O'Callaghan 1219
I Is for Innocent - Sue Grafton 637
I'll Be Leaving You Always - Sandra Scoppettone 1461
The Intersection of Law and Desire - J.M. Redmann 1356
Interview with Mattie - Shelley Singer 1504
K Is for Killer - Sue Grafton 638
Katapult - Karen Kijewski 919
Katwalk - Karen Kijewski 920
Kill or Cure - Mary Kittredge 932
Kindred Crimes - Janet Dawson 397
L Is for Lawless - Sue Grafton 639
Lay It on the Line - Catherine Dain 379
Leap of Faith - Sharon Zukowski 1799
Library: No Murder Aloud - Susan Steiner 1569
Love nor Money - Linda Grant 648
Money to Burn - Michael Hendricks 772
Money to Burn - Gloria White 1701
Murder and a Muse - Gillian B. Farrell 517
Murder at St. Adelaide's - Gerelyn Hollingsworth 799
Murder by the Book - Pat Welch 1689
Murder Can Kill Your Social Life - Selma Eichler 473
Murder in Scorpio - Martha C. Lawrence 993
Murder Offscreen - Denise Osborne 1248
Murder on the Run - Gloria White 1702
My First Murder - Susan Baker 84
My Sweet Untraceable You - Sandra Scoppettone 1462
Ninth Life - Lauren Wright Douglas 444
No Forwarding Address - Elisabeth Bowers 161
Nobody's Child - Janet Dawson 398
The Northwest Murders - Elizabeth Atwood Taylor 1607
One for the Money - Janet Evanovich 503
Picture of David - Shelley Singer 1505
Pious Deception - Susan Dunlap 462
Play with Fire - Dana Stabenow 1552
Prime Time for Murder - Valerie Frankel 542
The Raggedy Man - Lillian O'Donnell 1227
Ravenmocker - Jean Hager 701
The Redbird's Cry - Jean Hager 702
A Relative Stranger - Margaret Lucke 1052
Rogue Wave - Susan Dunlap 463
Searching for Sara - Shelley Singer 1506
Set-Up - Maxine O'Callaghan 1220
Shadow Dance - Agnes Bushnell 202
The Shape of Dread - Marcia Muller 1181
Shattered Rhythms - Phyllis Knight 946
The Silver Scapel - Nancy Baker Jacobs 837
Sing a Song of Death - Catherine Dain 380
Snagged - Carol Higgins Clark 251
Snapshot - Linda Barnes 93
Steel Guitar - Linda Barnes 94
A Sudden Death at the Norfolk Cafe - Winona Sullivan 1591
The Sunken Treasure - Marian J.A. Jackson 835
Switching the Odds - Phyllis Knight 947
Three Is a Crowd - D.B. Borton 156
Till The Butchers Cut Him Down - Marcia Muller 1182

Time Lapse - Janice Law 992
To Live and Die in Dixie - Kathy Hogan Trocheck 1632
The Total Zone - Martina Navratilova 1195
Trophies and Dead Things - Marcia Muller 1183
Tunnel Vision - Sara Paretsky 1266
The Turquoise Tattoo - Nancy Baker Jacobs 838
Two Points for Murder - D.B. Borton 157
Under My Skin - Sarah Dunant 456
Used to Kill - Lillian O'Donnell 1228
Walk a Crooked Mile - Catherine Dain 381
Walking Dead Man - Mary Kittredge 934
When Death Comes Stealing - Valerie Wilson Wesley 1692
Where Echoes Live - Marcia Muller 1184
Wild Kat - Karen Kijewski 921
A Woman's Place - Linda Grant 649
A Wreath for the Bride - Lillian O'Donnell 1229

Private Detective—Male Lead

32 Cadillacs - Joe Gores 616
According to St. John - William Babula 77
Act of God - Jeremiah Healy 764
And Justice for One - John Clarkson 254
The Angel Gang - Ken Kuhlken 956
The Angel's Share - R.R. Irvine 826
At Ease with the Dead - Walter Satterthwait 1437
Bad Neighbors - Isidore Haiblum 703
Bad to the Bone - Stephen Solomita 1532
Bear Hug - Jerome Doolittle 432
A Beautiful Place to Die - Philip R. Craig 335
Beggar's Choice - Jerry Kennealy 906
Behind the Fact - Richard Hilary 788
The Big Freeze - Michael J. Katz 871
Bigfoot - Richard Hoyt 815
Black Hornet - James Sallis 1421
Black Light - Daniel Hearn 767
The Black Mask Murders - William F. Nolan 1207
Blood and Thunder - Max Allan Collins 276
Blood of Poets - Kenn Davis 393
Blood Relative - Michael Allegretto 39
Blood Type - Stephen Greenleaf 667
Bloody Ten - William F. Love 1047
Blue Bayou - Dick Lochte 1038
Body Guard - Rex Burns 199
Body Scissors - Jerome Doolittle 433
Boiled in Concrete - Jesse Sublett 1587
Book Case - Stephen Greenleaf 668
The Book of Numbers - David Thoreau 1616
The Bookman's Wake - John Dunning 467
Breakdown - Bill Pronzini 1326
Burning March - Neil Albert 28
The Caesar Clue - M.K. Shuman 1491
Cain His Brother - Anne Perry 1292
Called by a Panther - Michael Z. Lewin 1019
Called Home - R.R. Irvine 828
Carnal Hours - Max Allan Collins 277
A Case of Innocence - Douglas J. Keeling 877
A Case of Vineyard Poisoning - Philip R. Craig 336
Cassandra in Red - Michael Collins 281
Cat's Paw, Inc. - L.L. Thrasher 1618
The Chartreuse Clue - William F. Love 1048
Chasing Eights - Michael Collins 282
A Clean Sweep - David Berlinski 123
The Cleveland Connection - Les Roberts 1383
Cliff Hanger - Philip R. Craig 337
Close Softly the Doors - Ronald Clair Roat 1373
Closing Costs - Thomas Bunn 189
The Codicil - Tom Topor 1623
Come to Grief - Dick Francis 538
Concrete Hero - Rob Kantner 862
The Cords of Vanity - Miles Tripp 1629
Crime, Punishment and Resurrection - Michael Collins 283
Cruel April - Neil Albert 29
The Dallas Deception - Richard Abshire 7
A Dance at the Slaughterhouse - Lawrence Block 146
Dark of Night - Richard Nehrbass 1200
Dead Folks' Blues - Steven Womack 1751

Private Detective—Male Lead

Dead Man - Joe Gores 617
Dead Matter - M.K. Wren 1764
The Dead of Brooklyn - Robert J. Randisi 1347
The Dead of Winter - Michael Allegretto 40
Dead on the Island - Bill Crider 350
Dead-Stick - L.J. Washburn 1674
Death as a Career Move - Bruce Cook 299
Death by Station Wagon - Jon Katz 869
Death in Deep Water - Paul Kemprecos 903
Death in Uptown - Michael Raleigh 1345
Deep End - Geoffrey Norman 1210
Deep Kill - M.K. Shuman 1492
Deep Shaker - Les Roberts 1384
The Desert Look - Bernard Schopen 1455
The Devil Knows You're Dead - Lawrence Block 147
Diamond Eyes - John Lutz 1056
The Disappearance of Edwin Drood - Peter Rowland 1407
Dog Heavies - L.J. Washburn 1675
Double Deuce - Robert B. Parker 1269
The Double Minded Men - Philip R. Craig 338
Dreamboat - Doug J. Swanson 1596
A Dry and Thirsty Ground - Mike Weiss 1688
The Duke of Cleveland - Les Roberts 1385
East Beach - Ron Ely 485
An Easy Thing - Paco Ignacio Taibo II 1597
Epitaphs - Bill Pronzini 1327
Everything but the Squeal - Timothy Hallinan 716
Except for the Bones - Collin Wilcox 1713
Eye of the Gator - E.C. Ayres 72
Fade to Black - Robert Goldsborough 607
False Profits - David Everson 509
The Family Stalker - Jon Katz 870
The February Trouble - Neil Albert 30
Fire Horse - Bill Shoemaker 1486
A Fistful of Empty - Benjamin M. Schutz 1457
Flame - John Lutz 1057
The Flip Side of Life - James E. Martin 1085
A Flower in the Desert - Walter Satterthwait 1439
Foursome - Jeremiah Healy 765
Free Fall - Robert Crais 341
Frozen Stare - Richard B. Schwartz 1459
Full Circle - Collin Wilcox 1714
Full Cleveland - Les Roberts 1386
Gator Kill - Bill Crider 352
The Glendower Conspiracy - Lloyd Biggle Jr. 131
God Bless John Wayne - Kinky Friedman 554
Gone Wild - James W. Hall 708
Grave Doubt - Michael Allegretto 41
Grave Matters - Leo Axler 71
The Great Reminder - R.R. Irvine 829
The Hanged Man - Walter Satterthwait 1440
Hard Look - Robert J. Randisi 1349
The Harry Chronicles - Allan Pedrazas 1287
A Hazard of Losers - Lloyd Biggle Jr. 132
Hour of the Manatee - E.C. Ayres 73
In the House of Secret Enemies - George C. Chesbro 241
Incinerator - Timothy Hallinan 717
The Iron Glove - Ronald Tierney 1619
Jackpot - Bill Pronzini 1328
The January Corpse - Neil Albert 31
Jersey Monkey - Kate Gallison 565
Juror - Parnell Hall 714
The Keeper - Meg O'Brien 1217
Kill Story - Jerome Doolittle 434
The Killing Man - Mickey Spillane 1540
Killing Me Softly - John Leslie 1012
King of the Mountain - M.K. Wren 1765
The Language of Cannibals - George C. Chesbro 242
The Last Man to Die - M.K. Shuman 1493
The Last Surprise - William Moore 1169
The Loud Adios - Ken Kuhlken 957
Lullaby Town - Robert Crais 342
The Man with My Name - Paul Engleman 494
The Manx Murders - William L. DeAndrea 402
Matrimonial Causes - Peter Corris 327
The Maya Stone Murders - M.K. Shuman 1494
Mean High Tide - James W. Hall 710

Psychological Suspense

Medicine Dog - Geoff Peterson 1307
The Melting Clock - Stuart M. Kaminsky 860
Merry Christmas, Murdock - Robert J. Ray 1352
Mexico Is Forever - Benjamin M. Schutz 1458
Missing - Jonathan Valin 1646
Moth - James Sallis 1422
Mr. Donaghue Investigates - Anna Shone 1488
Murder Begins at Home - Dale L. Gilbert 585
Murder by Tarot - Al Guthrie 693
Murder in the Post-War World - Max Allan Collins 279
Murdock Cracks Ice - Robert J. Ray 1353
The Music Lovers - Jonathan Valin 1647
Musical Chairs - Kinky Friedman 555
The Naked Eye - William J. Reynolds 1364
The Neon Smile - Dick Lochte 1039
Neptune's Eye - Paul Kemprecos 905
The Next Victim - William Sanders 1423
The Night Remembers - Ed Gorman 623
Night Shadows - Ron Ely 486
No Sign of Murder - Alan Russell 1414
Not Long for This World - Gar Anthony Haywood 762
Obligations of the Bone - Dick Cluster 263
O'Fear - Peter Corris 328
Off Season - Philip R. Craig 339
One Cried Murder - David Cooper Wall 1663
One Kiss Led to Another - Harris Dulaney 454
Out on the Cutting Edge - Lawrence Block 148
The Pale Criminal - Philip Kerr 914
Parts Unknown - Rex Burns 200
Peeper - Loren D. Estleman 499
Penance - David Housewright 812
Perchance to Dream - Robert B. Parker 1270
Pet Peeves - Taylor McCafferty 1111
Pillar of Fire - R.R. Irvine 830
The Portland Laugher - Earl Emerson 489
Quarry - Bill Pronzini 1329
The Queen's Mare - John Birkett 133
The Quick and the Dead - Rob Kantner 863
The Red, White, and Blues - Rob Kantner 864
Red Winter - Michael Cormany 319
The Riviera Contract - Marvin Albert 26
Roman Blood - Steven Saylor 1449
Rough Cut - Bruce Cook 300
Sanctuary - Faye Kellerman 884
Second Chance - Jonathan Valin 1648
Seeing the Elephant - Les Roberts 1387
Separate Cases - Robert J. Randisi 1350
September Song - Edward Mathis 1096
The Seventh Bullet - Daniel D. Victor 1654
She Walks These Hills - Sharyn McCrumb 1119
Shoot the Piper - Richard Hill 791
Shooting Star - Kate Green 665
Shot on Location - Stan Cutler 369
The Sidewalk Hilton - Bruce Cook 301
Silent Witness - Collin Wilcox 1716
Silver Spire - Robert Goldsborough 608
Skin Deep - Timothy Hallinan 718
Skin Deep Is Fatal - Michael Cormany 320
The Skintight Shroud - Wayne Dundee 459
The Software Bomb - Steven Womack 1753
Southern Cross - Stephen Greenleaf 669
Spark - John Lutz 1058
Special Delivery - Jerry Kenneally 907
Stalking the Angel - Robert Crais 343
Stand-In for Murder - Lynn Bradley 164
Stardust - Robert B. Parker 1271
The Steel Web - Ronald Tierney 1620
Still Among the Living - Zachary Klein 938
A Still and Icy Silence - Ronald Clair Roat 1374
Stolen Away - Max Allan Collins 361
The Stone Veil - Ronald Tierney 1621
Stonefish - Charles West 1695
Stranglehold - Jerome Doolittle 435
A Sudden, Fearful Death - Anne Perry 1296
Suffer Little Children - Thomas D. Davis 396
Suicide Squeeze - David Everson 510
Summer Cool - Al Sarrantonio 1436
Sweet Women Lie - Loren D. Estleman 500
Ten of Swords - J.R. Levitt 1018

Thicker than Blood - John Lutz 1059
Third Man Out - Richard Stevenson 1572
The Thousand Yard Stare - Rob Kantner 865
Three Strikes, You're Dead - Michael Geller 574
A Ticket to the Boneyard - Lawrence Block 149
Time Exposure - John Lutz 1060
Torch Town Boogie - Steven Womack 1754
Tracer, Inc. - Jeff Andrus 58
Trade Secrets - Maynard F. Thomson 1615
Turnaround Jack - Richard Abshire 8
Two Way Toll - Zachary Klein 939
Vanishing Act - Seth Jacob Margolis 1075
The Vanishing Smile - Earl Emerson 490
The Venus Deal - Ken Kuhlken 958
The Venus Throw - Steven Saylor 1450
The Very Bad Thing - Ned White 1703
Video Vengeance - Miles Tripp 1630
The Vig - John T. Lescroart 1010
Vintage Polo - Jerry Kenneally 908
Virgil's Ghost - Irving Weinman 1684
Voodoo River - Robert Crais 344
A Walk Among the Tombstones - Lawrence Block 150
Walking Shadow - Robert B. Parker 1272
Way Past Dead - Steven Womack 1755
Wet Graves - Peter Corris 329
When Old Men Die - Bill Crider 354
When Reason Sleeps - Tom Sehler 1472
White Butterfly - Walter Mosley 1178
Who Shot Longshot Sam? - Paul Engleman 495
Whoo? - Richard Hoyt 816
Work for a Dead Man - Simon Ritchie 1371
World of Hurt - Richard Rosen 1400
Worse than Death - Thomas Bunn 190
Yellow Dog Party - Earl Emerson 491
Yesterday's News - Jeremiah Healy 766
The Zig-Zag Man - Marvin Albert 27

Psychological Suspense

Act of Love - Joe R. Lansdale 980
All Around the Town - Mary Higgins Clark 252
Along Came a Spider - James Patterson 1276
The Angel Maker - Ridley Pearson 1282
The Animal Hour - Andrew Klavan 935
Bad Desire - Gary Devon 417
Bankroll - Bruce Ducker 450
Blind Side - William Bayer 105
Blood Kin - Marjorie Dorner 436
Blood Marks - Bill Crider 349
Blood Music - Jessie Prichard Hunter 821
Blood Relative - Carolyn Hougan 811
Blood Trance - R.D. Zimmerman 1791
Blue Lonesome - Bill Pronzini 1325
The Body Farm - Patricia D. Cornwell 322
The Caveman's Valentine - George Dawes Green 662
A Certain Justice - John T. Lescroart 1008
Child of Silence - Abigail Padgett 1251
A Chill Wind in January - L.R. Wright 1772
Circumstances Unknown - Jonellen Heckler 769
The City When It Rains - Thomas H. Cook 305
Clearwater Summer - John E. Keegan 876
Corruption - Andrew Klavan 936
Criminal Seduction - Darian North 1211
Crossover - Judith Eubank 502
The Cutting Hours - Julia Grice 673
Dangerous Attachments - Sarah Lovett 1051
Darkness Falls - Joyce Anne Schneider 1453
Day of Atonement - Faye Kellerman 878
Deadfall in Berlin - R.D. Zimmerman 1792
Deadline - D.F. Mills 1157
A Death in a Town - Hillary Waugh 1678
Death Qualified: A Mystery of Chaos - Kate Wilhelm 1723
Deathspell - Veronica Stallwood 1558
A Deep Disturbance - Constance Rauch 1351
Deviant Way - Richard Montanari 1166
Devices and Desires - P.D. James 841
Disassociated States - Leonard Simon 1499
The Dog Hermit - David Stout 1578
Don't Say a Word - Andrew Klavan 937

Don't Say a Word - Keith Peterson 1308
Dream of Darkness - Patrick Ruell 1412
The Dying Room - E.X. Giroux 599
Edge City - Sin Soracco 1537
Elsinore - Jerome Charyn 238
The End of the Pier - Martha Grimes 674
Final Tour - Jonellen Heckler 770
Flawless - Adam Barrow 99
Footsteps of the Hawk - Andrew Vachss 1644
Free - Todd Komarnicki 952
From Potter's Field - Patricia D. Cornwell 325
Going Wrong - Ruth Rendell 1360
Guilt by Association - Susan R. Sloan 1514
Hammurabi's Code - Charles Kenney 909
The Hangman's Beautiful Daughter - Sharyn McCrumb 1115
A Hard Bargain - Lia Matera 1092
Hollywood Requiem - Peter Freeborn 546
The House on the Hill - Judith Kelman 899
The Ice House - Minette Walters 1669
If Ever I Return, Pretty Peggy-O - Sharyn McCrumb 1116
Imperfect Strangers - Stuart Woods 1761
In Deep - Bruce Jones 846
In-laws and Outlaws - Barbara Paul 1277
In the Dark - Carol Brennan 173
In the Electric Mist with Confederate Dead - James Lee Burke 196
In the Lake of the Woods - Tim O'Brien 1218
Incident at Potter's Bridge - Joseph Monniger 1165
Into the Fire - David Wiltse 1737
Is Anybody There? - T.G. Gilpin 591
The Judas Pool - George Owens 1250
Killer Cinderella - Simon Shaw 1478
Killing Time in Buffalo - Deidre S. Laiken 964
Kissing the Gunner's Daughter - Ruth Rendell 1361
The Last Rite of Hugo T - J.N. Catanach 227
The Late Man - James Preston Girard 592
Long Chain of Death - S.K. Wolf 1747
The Long Search - Isabelle Holland 798
Love Lies Slain - L.L. Blackmur 139
Loves Music, Loves to Dance - Mary Higgins Clark 253
The Masters of the House - Robert Barnard 90
Menaced Assassin - Joe Gores 618
Mercy - David L. Lindsey 1027
Miami Purity - Vicki Hendricks 773
Missing Joseph - Elizabeth George 575
Mitigating Circumstances - Nancy Taylor Rosenberg 1401
The Monkey Rope - Stephen Lewis 1023
Moth to the Flame - Kathleen Dougherty 437
Murder Once Removed - Kathleen Kunz 959
Never Walk Behind Me - Lin Summerfield 1593
Night Angel - Kate Green 664
Night of Reunion - Michael Allegretto 42
Night of the Ice Storm - David Stout 1579
Night Sins - Tami Hoag 794
Nightmare Point - Carole Berry 128
No Way Home - Patricia MacDonald 1062
Nobody's Fool - Marten Claridge 249
Palindrome - Stuart Woods 1762
Passion Play - W. Edward Blain 140
Personal - C.K. Cambray 208
Primal Fear - William Diehl 421
Private Eyes - Jonathan Kellerman 886
Prized Possessions - L.R. Wright 1775
Red Trance - R.D. Zimmerman 1793
Running From the Law - Lisa Scottoline 1465
The Saturday Morning Murder - Batya Gur 691
The Scarred Man - Keith Peterson 1310
The Scold's Bridle - Minette Walters 1670
The Sculptress - Minette Walters 1671
Self-Defense - Jonathan Kellerman 887
Shadow Queen - Tony Gibbs 583
Shadowchase - Martin Blank 143
Shadows on the Mirror - Frances Fyfield 563
Shameless - Judy Collins 275
She Walks These Hills - Sharyn McCrumb 1119
Shooting Star - Kate Green 665
Silent Night - Gary Amo 49

Story Type Index

A Single Stone - Marilyn Wallace 1664
Sliver - Ira Levin 1013
So Shall You Reap - Marilyn Wallace 1665
The Soul of Betty Fairchild - Robert Specht 1538
Still Waters - Kerry Tucker 1638
Storm Front - Virginia Anderson 53
Strange Loyalties - William McIlvanney 1134
Strawgirl - Abigail Padgett 1252
A Suitable Vengeance - Elizabeth George 578
The Suitor - Michael Allegretto 43
This Way Out - Sheila Radley 1343
A Ticket to the Boneyard - Lawrence Block 149
Till Death Do Us Part - Rochelle Majer Krich 955
Time and Time Again - B.M. Gill 587
Time Bomb - Jonathan Kellerman 888
To Die Like a Gentleman - Bernard Bastable 103
The Toy Cupboard - Lee Jordan 848
Trade-Off - Harrison Arnston 66
Turtle Moon - Alice Hoffman 795
Under the Beetle's Cellar - Mary Willis Walker 1660
Undue Influence - Miriam Borgenicht 153
Voices in the Dark - Andrew Coburn 268
The Watchman - Michael Allegretto 44
Whisper.He Might Hear You - William Appel 62
Wild Again - Kathrin King Segal 1471
With an Extreme Burning - Bill Pronzini 1331
A Wolf in Death's Clothing - Elizabeth Quinn 1341
A Woman's Own Mystery - Hannah Wakefield 1658
The Yellow Room Conspiracy - Peter Dickinson 420

Romantic Suspense
Naked Once More - Elizabeth Peters 1300

Serial Killer
Whisper.He Might Hear You - William Appel 62

Techno-Thriller
Bright Shark - Robert Ballard 85
Coyote Bird - Jim DeFelice 409
Day of the Cheetah - Dale Brown 179
Deep Chill - Ian Slater 1513
Pillars of Fire - Steve Shagan 1473
The Ransom of Black Stealth One - Dean Ing 825
The Sum of All Fears - Tom Clancy 248

Traditional
Black Girl, White Girl - Patricia Moyes 1179
A City of Strangers - Robert Barnard 88
A Question of Guilt - Frances Fyfield 562

Character Name Index

This index alphabetically lists the major characters in each featured title. Each character name is followed by a description of the character. Citations also provide titles of the books featuring the character, listed alphabetically if there is more than one title; author names; and entry numbers.

A

Aandahl, Trish (Journalist)
The Bookman's Wake - John Dunning   467

Abagnard, Abby (Television)
Until Death - Polly Whitney   1709

Abagnaro, Abby (Television)
Until the End of Time - Polly Whitney   1710

Abbot, Luke (Police Officer)
Death Penalties - Paula Gosling   625

Abbott, Ben (Real Estate Agent)
Hardscape - Justin Scott   1463
StoneDust - Justin Scott   1464

Abernathy, Dean (Lawyer)
Felony Murder - Joseph T. Klempner   940

Abigail, Charles (Police Officer; Detective)
Obit - Daniel Paisner   1261

Ables, Glenn (Criminal)
The Standoff - Chuck Hogan   796

Ackerly, Paul (Businessman)
The Yellow Room Conspiracy - Peter Dickinson   420

Adams, Charlie "Doc" (Dentist)
Yellow Bird - Rick Boyer   162

Adams, Deacon "Deke" (Guard; Friend)
Lay It on the Line - Catherine Dain   379

Adams, Gillian (Professor)
Bad Chemistry - Nora Kelly   891
My Sister's Keeper - Nora Kelly   892

Adams, Henry (Historical Figure; Historian)
Panama - Eric Zencey   1787

Adams, Kip (Doctor; Lesbian)
Everything You Have Is Mine - Sandra Scoppettone   1460
I'll Be Leaving You Always - Sandra Scoppettone   1461
My Sweet Untraceable You - Sandra Scoppettone   1462

Adams, Samantha (Journalist)
He Was Her Man - Sarah Shankman   1474
The King Is Dead - Sarah Shankman   1475
Now Let's Talk of Graves - Sarah Shankman   1476
She Walks in Beauty - Sarah Shankman   1477

Addison, Eddie (Criminal)
Prized Possessions - L.R. Wright   1775

Adler, Irene (Singer)
Good Morning, Irene - Carole Nelson Douglas   440

Adler, Irene (Singer; Adventurer)
Good Night, Mr. Holmes - Carole Nelson Douglas   441

Adler, Irene (Singer)
Irene at Large - Carole Nelson Douglas   442

Aiken, John Forbes (Journalist)
Indecent Behavior - Caryl Rivers   1372

Alberg, Karl (Police Officer)
A Chill Wind in January - L.R. Wright   1772
Fall From Grace - L.R. Wright   1773
Mother Love - L.R. Wright   1774
Prized Possessions - L.R. Wright   1775
A Touch of Panic - L.R. Wright   1776

Albright, Nikki (Businesswoman)
A Body to Dye For - Grant Michaels   1150

Aldington, Claire (Religious)
A Fatal Advent - Isabelle Holland   797

Aldridge, Eileen (Lawyer)
Leap of Faith - Sharon Zukowski   1799

Alessi, George (Police Officer)
King of the Hustlers - Eugene Izzi   831

Aletter, Finny (Carpenter)
Obstacle Course - Yvonne Montgomery   1167

Alexander, Grayson (Nobleman)
Aunt Dimity and the Duke - Nancy Atherton   68

Alexander, Raymond "Mouse" (Criminal)
White Butterfly - Walter Mosley   1178

Alexander, Tess (Writer)
Deadline - D.F. Mills   1157

Alexander, Will (Lawyer)
Against the Wind - J.F. Freedman   547

Alexeyev, Gennadi (Spy)
A Black Legend - John Horton   810

Alexeyev, Nina (Veterinarian)
Murder Most Grizzly - Elizabeth Quinn   1340

Alvarez, Enrique (Police Officer)
Too Clever by Half - Roderic Jeffries   845

Alvarez, Tina (Lawyer)
The Choice - Barry Reed   1357

Amalfi, Angie (Journalist)
Cooking Up Trouble - Joanne Pence   1289
Something's Cooking - Joanne Pence   1290
Too Many Cooks - Joanne Pence   1291

Amery, Rick (Police Officer)
Motown - Loren D. Estleman   498

Amiss, Robert (Unemployed)
Clubbed to Death - Ruth Dudley Edwards   472

Amstel, Sara (Journalist)
Shoofly Pie to Die - Joshua Quittner   1342

Ance, Maynard (Businessman)
King of the Corner - Loren D. Estleman   497

Anders, Sally (Teenager)
A Death in a Town - Hillary Waugh   1678

Anderson, Owen (Doctor)
Shadowchase - Martin Blank   143

Anderson, Shifty Lou (Magician; Gambler)
I'm Getting Killed Right Here - William Murray   1190

Andrews, Jessie (Worker; Lesbian)
The Chesapeake Project - Phyllis Horn   806

Anonymous (Lawyer)
Dead Meat - Philip Kerr   913

Apfel, Hans (Police Officer)
Spandau Phoenix - Greg Iles   824

Archer, Owen (Military Personnel; Spy)
The Apothecary Rose - Candace M. Robb   1375

Archer, Owen (Military Personnel)
The Lady Chapel - Candace M. Robb   1376

Archer, Owen (Military Personnel; Spy)
The Nun's Tale - Candace M. Robb   1377

Ardleigh, Kathryn "Kate" (Secretary; Writer)
Death at Bishop's Keep - Robin Paige   1259

Ardleigh, Kathryn "Kate" (Heiress; Writer)
Death at Gallows Green - Robin Paige   1260

Arkwright, Santa (Sports Figure)
First and Ten - Douglas Anderson   50

Arnold, Jessie (Sports Figure)
Murder on the Iditarod Trail - Sue Henry   775

Arnold, Pat (Entertainer)
Party Till You Die - David Charnee   236
To Kill a Clown - David Charnee   237

Arrington, Molly (Doctor)
Primal Fear - William Diehl   421

Arrowood, Spencer (Police Officer)
The Hangman's Beautiful Daughter - Sharyn McCrumb   1115
If Ever I Return, Pretty Peggy-O - Sharyn McCrumb   1116
She Walks These Hills - Sharyn McCrumb   1119

Asherfeld, Aaron (Detective—Private)
A Clean Sweep - David Berlinski   123

Ashley, Piers (Police Officer)
Man of Blood - Margaret Duffy   451

Atwood, Diane (Writer)
Writers of the Purple Sage - Barbara Burnett Smith   1517

Augustin, Louis (Veterinarian)
Copy Cat Crimes - Karen Ann Wilson   1733
Eight Dogs Flying - Karen Ann Wilson   1734

Austen, Cat (Writer)
Death of a DJ - Jane Rubino   1411

Austin, Beth (Professor)
The George Eliot Murders - Edith Skom   1511

Axx, Brad

The Mark Twain Murders - Edith Skom   1512

Axx, Brad (Police Officer)
Axx Goes South - Frederic Huber   817

Ayars, Laura (Model)
Play Dead - Harlan Coben   266

Aydlett, Shad (Diver)
Louisiana Blue - David Poyer   1324

Ayers, Martha (Police Officer)
She Walks These Hills - Sharyn McCrumb   1119

B

Babicki, Stosh (Journalist)
The Late Man - James Preston Girard   592

Bailey, Geoffrey (Police Officer)
Deep Sleep - Frances Fyfield   561
A Question of Guilt - Frances Fyfield   562

Bailey, Gil (Police Officer)
The Mark Twain Murders - Edith Skom   1512

Bailey, Nick (Spy)
The Lantern Network - Ted Allbeury   37

Bain, Dominic (Criminal)
Nobody's Fool - Marten Claridge   249

Baker, Anne (Writer; Editor)
The Last Page - Bob Fenster   524

Baker, Kathy Diaz (Probation Officer)
Maximum Bob - Elmore Leonard   1006

Baker, Wellesley (Teenager)
Clearwater Summer - John E. Keegan   876

Balcazar, Dred (Detective—Private)
The Very Bad Thing - Ned White   1703

Baldwin, Sarah (Doctor)
Natural Causes - Michael Palmer   1262

Balkan, Peter (Lawyer)
To Do No Harm - Leslie Glass   602

Ballou, Mick (Criminal)
A Dance at the Slaughterhouse - Lawrence Block   146

Balzic, Mario (Police Officer)
Sunshine Enemies - K.C. Constantine   298

Banish, John (FBI Agent)
The Standoff - Chuck Hogan   796

Banks, Alan (Police Officer)
A Dedicated Man - Peter Robinson   1392
Gallows View - Peter Robinson   1393
The Hanging Valley - Peter Robinson   1394
A Necessary End - Peter Robinson   1395
Past Reason Hated - Peter Robinson   1396
Wednesday's Child - Peter Robinson   1397

Bannion, Rick (Sports Figure; Convict)
The Man Offside - A.W. Gray   652

Barclay, Maeve (Housewife; Activist)
Time and Time Again - B.M. Gill   587

Barelli, Chris (Police Officer)
Obstacle Course - Yvonne Montgomery   1167

Barlow, Hannah (Student)
Murder in Brief - Carrol Lachint   963

Barlow, Margaret (Photojournalist)
Murder in the Napa Valley - David Osborn   1245

Barlow, Margaret (Photojournalist; Grandparent)
Murder on the Chesapeake - David Osborn   1246

Barlow, Nicholas (Publisher)
Casual Slaughters - Robert A. Carter   223
Final Edit - Robert A. Carter   224

Barlow, Timothy (Handicapped)
Final Edit - Robert A. Carter   224

Barlowe, Philip (Journalist)
Act of Love - Joe R. Lansdale   980

Barnaby, Thomas (Police Officer)
Death in Disguise - Caroline Graham   640
Death of a Hollow Man - Caroline Graham   641

Barnes, Douglas (Criminal)
Bones of Coral - James W. Hall   707

Barnes, Ezell "Easy" (Detective—Private)
Behind the Fact - Richard Hilary   788

Barnes, Hildy (Police Officer)
Death by Degrees - Robin Wilson   1735

Barnes, Marcie (Police Officer)
City of God - Michael Jahn   840

Barnett, Geoffrey (Photographer)
Blind Side - William Bayer   105

Barnett, Michael (Critic)
With Extreme Prejudice - Frederick Barton   102

Barr, Jeremy (Sailor)
Landfall - Tony Gibbs   581

Barr, Temple (Public Relations)
Cat on a Blue Monday - Carole Nelson Douglas   438

Barr, Temple (Businesswoman; Public Relations)
Catnap - Carole Nelson Douglas   439

Barr, Temple (Public Relations)
Pussyfoot - Carole Nelson Douglas   443

Barrett, Neil (Police Officer)
A Lively Form of Death - Kay Mitchell   1160

Barrett, Ozzie (Fisherman)
Dead in the Water - W.J. Chaput   233

Barrish, Rick (Detective—Police)
Nobody Lives Forever - Edna Buchanan   187

Barron, Peter (Doctor)
Darkness Falls - Joyce Anne Schneider   1453

Barrows, Peter (Businessman; Murderer)
By Reason of Insanity - James Neal Harvey   749

Bartell, Martin (Businessman)
The Julius House - Charlaine Harris   732

Bartholomew, Connie (Spouse)
Rough Water - Sally Gunning   687

Bartholomew, Peter (Businessman)
Hot Water - Sally Gunning   686
Rough Water - Sally Gunning   687
Still Water - Sally Gunning   688
Troubled Water - Sally Gunning   689

Bartlett, Simon (Criminal)
Silent Night - Gary Amo   49

Barwick, Liz (Photographer)
Palindrome - Stuart Woods   1762

Barzeny, Jakob (Sports Figure)
Furnished for Murder - Richard Barth   101

Bascombe, Carver (Detective—Private)
Blood of Poets - Kenn Davis   393

Baskin, David (Sports Figure)
Play Dead - Harlan Coben   266

Bassett, Henry (Farmer)
Screaming Bones - Pat Burden   191

Baugh, Henry (Artist)
Love Lies Slain - L.L. Blackmur   139

Baum, Steven (Probation Officer)
Slow Motion Riot - Peter Blauner   144

Baxter, Claire (Doctor)
Disassociated States - Leonard Simon   1499

Baxter, Richard (Police Officer)
Dangerous Conceits - Margaret Moore   1168

Bayles, China (Businesswoman)
Hangman's Root - Susan Wittig Albert   32
Thyme of Death - Susan Wittig Albert   33

Bear, Goldy (Caterer; Divorced Person)
The Cereal Murders - Diane Mott Davidson   389
Dying for Chocolate - Diane Mott Davidson   390

Bearpaw, Molly (Detective—Private; Indian)
Ravenmocker - Jean Hager   701
The Redbird's Cry - Jean Hager   702

Beaudine, Alex (Detective—Private)
Prime Time for Murder - Valerie Frankel   542

Beaufort, Henry (Religious)
The Bishop's Tale - Margaret Frazer   544

Beaufort, Mary (Businesswoman)
Murder on Peachtree Street - Patricia Houck Sprinkle   1543
A Mystery Bred in Buckhead - Patricia Houck Sprinkle   1544
Somebody's Dead in Snellville - Patricia Houck Sprinkle   1545

Beaumont, J.P. (Detective—Police)
Minor in Possession - J.A. Jance   844

Beaumont, Sophie (Photographer)
The Cashmere Kid - B. Comfort   284

Beaumont, Sophie (Businesswoman)
Elusive Quarry - B. Comfort   285

Beaumont, Sophie (Photographer)
Grave Consequences - B. Comfort   286

Becker, John (FBI Agent)
The Edge of Sleep - David Wiltse   1736
Into the Fire - David Wiltse   1737

Bedrosian, Lena (Police Officer)
Eye of the Gator - E.C. Ayres   72
Hour of the Manatee - E.C. Ayres   73

Bekker, Michael (Criminal)
Silent Prey - John Sandford   1427

Bellini, Cecca (Real Estate Agent)
With an Extreme Burning - Bill Pronzini   1331

Belski, Becky (Computer Expert; Divorced Person)
Caught in the Shadows - C.A. Haddad   694

Benanti, Nina (Serial Killer; Mentally Ill Person)
Widowmaker - William Appel   63

Benbow, Angela (Aged Person)
Murder by Owl Light - Corinne Holt Sawyer   1445
Murder Has No Calories - Corinne Holt Sawyer   1446
Murder in Gray and White - Corinne Holt Sawyer   1447

Benedetti, Niccolo (Professor)
The Manx Murders - William L. DeAndrea   402

Benedetto, Johnny (Police Officer)
Foxglove - Mary Anne Kelly   889
Park Lane South, Queens - Mary Anne Kelly   890

Benn, Hannah (Businesswoman)
Sweet Death, Come Softly - Barbara Whitehead   1708

Bennet, Bridget (Professor)
What Men Say - Joan Smith 1522

Bennett, Christine (Religious)
The Christening Day Murder - Lee Harris 733

Bennett, Christine (Housewife)
The Christmas Night Murder - Lee Harris 734

Bennett, Mildred (Aged Person; Socialite)
The Pumpkin-Shell Wife - Susanna Hofmann McShea 1138

Bennett, Reid (Police Officer)
Flashback - Ted Wood 1756
On the Inside - Ted Wood 1757
Snow Job - Ted Wood 1758

Bennett, Wes (Police Officer)
Murder at Moot Point - Marlys Millhiser 1156

Benno (Servant)
Death of the Duchess - Elizabeth Eyre 512

Berman, Josh (Doctor)
Widowmaker - William Appel 63

Berman, Kate (Doctor)
Whisper.He Might Hear You - William Appel 62

Berman, Kate (Criminologist)
Widowmaker - William Appel 63

Bernhardt, Alan (Detective—Private; Actor)
Except for the Bones - Collin Wilcox 1713

Bernhardt, Alan (Actor; Detective—Private)
Full Circle - Collin Wilcox 1714

Bernhardt, Alan (Detective—Private; Actor)
Silent Witness - Collin Wilcox 1716

Bernstein, Ellie (Businesswoman)
Beat Up a Cookie - Denise Dietz 422
Throw Darts at a Cheesecake - Denise Dietz 423

Bertram, Alice (Farmer)
Infected Be the Air - Janice Law 991

Best, Judy (Police Officer)
Dead Fit - Stephen Cook 304

Bethany, Tom (Detective—Private)
Bear Hug - Jerome Doolittle 432
Body Scissors - Jerome Doolittle 433
Kill Story - Jerome Doolittle 434
Stranglehold - Jerome Doolittle 435

Biggers, Petrinella (Student)
Murder in Wrigley Field - Crabbe Evers 507

Bignell, Mavis (Friend)
Unwillingly to Vegas - Nancy Livingston 1036

Bihn (Police Officer)
Kiet Goes West - Gary Alexander 34

Binford, Bitsy (Businesswoman)
Death Below Deck - Douglas Kiker 922

Binton, Margaret (Aged Person)
Deathics - Richard Barth 100

Birchfield, Kathy (Lawyer)
The Portland Laugher - Earl Emerson 489
The Vanishing Smile - Earl Emerson 490
Yellow Dog Party - Earl Emerson 491

Bird, William (Police Officer)
Nurse Dawes Is Dead - Stella Shepherd 1479
Thinner than Blood - Stella Shepherd 1480

Birdsong, Charlotte (Businesswoman; Single Parent)
Grandmother's House - Janet LaPierre 983

Birdwood, Verity (Businesswoman)
Death in Store - Jennifer Rowe 1406

Bishop, Sabrina (Actress)
My Gun Has Bullets - Lee Goldberg 606

Biwaban, Angela (Detective—Private; Indian)
Corona Blue - J.F. Trainor 1625

Biwaban, Angela (Criminal; Indian)
Dynamite Pass - J.F. Trainor 1626

Black, Helen (Detective—Private; Lesbian)
Murder by the Book - Pat Welch 1689

Black, Johnny (Detective—Private; Pilot)
Black Eye - Neville Steed 1563

Black, Steven (Teacher)
The Judas Pool - George Owens 1250

Black, Thomas (Detective—Private)
The Portland Laugher - Earl Emerson 489
The Vanishing Smile - Earl Emerson 490
Yellow Dog Party - Earl Emerson 491

Blacker, D.L. (Lawyer; Entertainer)
Party Till You Die - David Charnee 236
To Kill a Clown - David Charnee 237

Blackthorne, Nathan (Detective—Private; Indian)
Grave Secrets - Louise Hendricksen 774

Blair, Barley (Businessman; Publisher)
The Russia House - John Le Carre 995

Blake, Julie (Detective—Private; Computer Expert)
Love Bytes - Sally Chapman 232

Blake, Meredith (Student)
Crossover - Judith Eubank 502

Blake, Moses (Police Officer)
Coronation - W.J. Weatherby 1679

Blakeney, Sarah (Doctor)
The Scold's Bridle - Minette Walters 1670

Blevins, Haskell (Detective—Private)
Pet Peeves - Taylor McCafferty 1111

Blissberg, Harvey (Detective—Private)
World of Hurt - Richard Rosen 1400

Blossom, Richie (Inventor)
Snagged - Carol Higgins Clark 251

Blue, Royal (Writer)
Blood of Poets - Kenn Davis 393

Blumenthal, Marissa (Doctor)
Vital Signs - Robin Cook 303

Boatwright, Thomas (Student)
Passion Play - W. Edward Blain 140

Bodine, Jack (Detective—Private)
Closing Costs - Thomas Bunn 189
Worse than Death - Thomas Bunn 190

Bogner, Simon (Insurance Investigator)
Business Unusual - Tim Heald 763

Bohland, Harmon (Detective—Private; Bodyguard)
Shooting Star - Kate Green 665

Boldt, Lou (Police Officer)
The Angel Maker - Ridley Pearson 1282

Bond, James (Spy)
Win, Lose or Die - John Gardner 567

Bone, Charlotte (Student)
A Knife at the Opera - Susannah Stacey 1555

Bone, Grizel (Teacher)
Bone Idle - Susannah Stacey 1553

Bone, Peter (Police Officer)
A Knife at the Opera - Susannah Stacey 1555

Bone, Robert (Police Officer)
Bone Idle - Susannah Stacey 1553

Bone, Robert (Police Officer; Widow(er))
Grave Responsibility - Susannah Stacey 1554

Bone, Robert (Police Officer)
The Late Lady - Susannah Stacey 1556

Bonello, Michael (Criminal)
Wiseguys in Love - C. Clark Criscuolo 355

Bonesteel, Nora (Aged Person; Psychic)
The Hangman's Beautiful Daughter - Sharyn McCrumb 1115

Borden, Liza (Veterinarian)
Forty Whacks - Sheila MacGill Callahan 207

Borden, Lizzie (Spinster; Historical Figure)
Miss Lizzie - Walter Satterthwait 1441

Bosch, Harry (Police Officer; Veteran)
The Black Echo - Michael Connelly 292
The Black Ice - Michael Connelly 293
The Concrete Blonde - Michael Connelly 294

Boucher, Thurman (Publisher)
Kill Story - Jerome Doolittle 434

Boulter, Tim (Police Officer)
Model Murder - Erica Quest 1338

Bourque, Kevin (Businessman)
Dead Wrong - Alan Dennis Burke 192

Bouton, Vanessa (Police Officer)
A Good Day to Die - Stephen Solomita 1534

Bow, April (Student)
Monkey on a Chain - Harlen Campbell 211

Bowering, Victoria (Actress; Psychic)
Cancellation by Death - Dorian Yeager 1782

Bowering, Victoria (Actress)
Eviction by Death - Dorian Yeager 1783

Bowker, Denis (Police Officer)
Murder in a Quiet Place - Tony Caxton 230

Bowman, Lee (Spouse)
Killer in Paradise - John Leslie 1011

Bowman, Patrick (Police Officer)
Killer in Paradise - John Leslie 1011

Boyd, Orin (Police Officer; Veteran)
Exit Wounds - John Westermann 1696

Bracewell, Nicholas (Actor)
The Mad Courtesan - Edward Marston 1081
The Nine Giants - Edward Marston 1082
The Queen's Head - Edward Marston 1083
The Trip to Jerusalem - Edward Marston 1084

Bradford, Will (Teenager)
Clearwater Summer - John E. Keegan 876

Bradley, Barbara "Bo" (Social Worker; Mentally Ill Person)
Child of Silence - Abigail Padgett 1251
Strawgirl - Abigail Padgett 1252

Bradley, Mark (Writer; Homosexual)
Shot on Location - Stan Cutler 369

Bradshaw, Nora (Housewife)
Sister's Keeper - Randye Lordon 1042

Brady, Gerard (Businessman)
Trade Secrets - Ray Garton 568

Brady, Joanna (Office Worker)
Desert Heat - J.A. Jance 842

Brady, Peter (Journalist)
Death Notice - M.S. Karl 866

Brady, Peter (Journalist; Publisher)
Deerslayer - M.S. Karl 867

Bragg, Joseph (Police Officer)
Patently Murder - Ray Harrison 737
Tincture of Death - Ray Harrison 738

Braithwaite, Theodora (Religious)
Clerical Errors - D.M. Greenwood 670
Idol Bones - D.M. Greenwood 671
Unholy Ghosts - D.M. Greenwood 672

Bramlet, Grover (Police Officer)
A Homecoming for Murder - John Armistead 65

Brandon, Samantha "Smokey" (Police Officer)
Carcass Trade - Noreen Ayres 74

Brandstetter, Dave (Insurance Investigator; Homosexual)
The Boy Who Was Buried This Morning - Joseph Hansen 726
A Country of Old Men - Joseph Hansen 727

Brannigan, Kate (Detective—Private)
Crack Down - Val McDermid 1125

Brant, Martha "Moz" (Insurance Investigator)
Hush, Money - Jean Femling 523

Bray, Nell (Activist)
Hanging on the Wire - Gillian Linscott 1028
Sister Beneath the Sheet - Gillian Linscott 1029
Stage Fright - Gillian Linscott 1030

Breedlove, Jack (Hairdresser)
Dead Pan - Jane Dentinger 413

Brenner, Alecia (Doctor)
Deadfall in Berlin - R.D. Zimmerman 1792

Breslinsky, Claire (Photographer; Housewife)
Foxglove - Mary Anne Kelly 889

Breslinsky, Claire (Photographer)
Park Lane South, Queens - Mary Anne Kelly 890

Brett, David (Teacher)
Long Chain of Death - S.K. Wolf 1747

Brevna, Bubba (Criminal)
The Emerald Lizard - Chris Wiltz 1738

Brice, Frederick (Detective—Police)
The Honourable Detective - Jeffrey Ashford 67

Brichter, Kori (Businesswoman)
Original Sin - Mary Monica Pulver 1334
Show Stopper - Mary Monica Pulver 1335

Brichter, Peter (Police Officer)
Original Sin - Mary Monica Pulver 1334

Bright, John (Police Officer)
Close-Up on Death - Maureen O'Brien 1213

Brocato, Melody (Student)
Jazz Funeral - Julie Smith 1526

Brod, Elliot (Criminal)
Gun Men - Gary Friedman 553

Brogan, Jerry (Sports Figure)
Hot Air - Jon L. Breen 170
Loose Lips - Jon L. Breen 171

Brolan, Frank (Advertising)
Night Kills - Ed Gorman 622

Brooks, Jack (Police Officer)
The Christening Day Murder - Lee Harris 733
The Christmas Night Murder - Lee Harris 734

Broom, Andrew (Lawyer)
Body and Soil - Ralph McInerny 1135

Broskey, Kevin (Police Officer)
On the Edge - Ed Naha 1193

Broussard, Andy (Doctor)
Blood on the Bayou - D.J. Donaldson 429
New Orleans Requiem - D.J. Donaldson 430
No Mardi Gras for the Dead - D.J. Donaldson 431

Brown, Cordelia (Writer)
Report for Murder - Val McDermid 1126

Browning, Grace (Actress; Criminal)
Angel of Death - Jack Higgins 786

Broz, Tito (Detective—Private)
Interview with Mattie - Shelley Singer 1504
Picture of David - Shelley Singer 1505
Searching for Sara - Shelley Singer 1506

Bruce, Laura (Housewife)
The Hangman's Beautiful Daughter - Sharyn McCrumb 1115

Brunetti, Guido (Police Officer)
Death and Judgment - Donna Leon 1002
Death at La Fenice - Donna Leon 1003
Death in a Strange Country - Donna Leon 1004

Bruno, Adam (Detective—Private; Lawyer)
The Codicil - Tom Topor 1623

Bryce, Kevin (Writer; Police Officer)
A Collector of Photographs - Deborah Valentine 1645

Buckland, Casey (Teacher; Single Parent)
Blood Marks - Bill Crider 349

Buffolino, Tony (Detective—Private)
Murder at the Kennedy Center - Margaret Truman 1634

Burdette, Lillie (Housewife)
No Way Home - Patricia MacDonald 1062

Burgess, Richard "Dirty Dick" (Police Officer)
A Necessary End - Peter Robinson 1395

Burke (Criminal)
Blossom - Andrew Vachss 1643

Burke (Avenger)
Footsteps of the Hawk - Andrew Vachss 1644

Burke, Claire (Secretary)
The Lion's Share - Kelly A. Tate 1605

Burke, Colin (Journalist)
Cover Story - Robert Cullen 365

Burke, Jackie (Flight Attendant)
Rum Punch - Elmore Leonard 1007

Burke, Riley (Advertising)
Dangerous Waters - Bill Eidson 475

Burnell, Maxey (Journalist)
Unsafe Keeping - Carol Cail 206

Burns, Carl (Professor)
Dying Voices - Bill Crider 351

Burns, Nora (Companion)
Hell Bent - Ken Gross 684

Burton, Amanda (Teenager)
Miss Lizzie - Walter Satterthwait 1441

Bush, Beth (Student)
Sweet Death - Bill Waggoner 1657

Bushfield, Geof (Police Officer)
I.O.U. - Nancy Pickard 1318

Bushnell, Dan (Counselor)
A Strange and Bitter Crop - E.L. Wyrick 1780

Bushrow, Harriet (Aged Person)
The Rotary Club Mystery - Graham Landrum 978

Bushyhead, Mitchell (Police Officer)
Ghostland - Jean Hager 700

Butler, Charles (Businessman)
Mallory's Oracle - Carol O'Connell 1221

Byman, Luke (Writer)
The Forever Beat - John Cline 262

Byrne, Charlie (Photographer)
Swindle - George Adams 11

Byrne, Owen (Writer)
Criminal Seduction - Darian North 1211

C

Cadette, Sandy (Spouse)
Act of Faith - Michael Bowen 158
Fielder's Choice - Michael Bowen 160

Cadfael (Religious)
Brother Cadfael's Penance - Ellis Peters 1301
The Potter's Field - Ellis Peters 1302
The Summer of the Danes - Ellis Peters 1303

Cahill, Winn (Musician)
Kingdom Road - K. Patrick Conner 295

Cain, Harry (Lawyer)
A Lawyer's Tale - D. Kincaid 923

Cain, Jenny (Businesswoman; Philanthropist)
Bum Steer - Nancy Pickard 1316

Cain, Jenny (Businesswoman)
But I Wouldn't Want to Die There - Nancy Pickard 1317

Cain, Jenny (Businesswoman; Philanthropist)
I.O.U. - Nancy Pickard 1318

Calabrese, Dub (Detective—Private)
White Rook - J. Madison Davis 392

Calder, Deborah (Businesswoman)
A Brace of Skeet - Gerald Hammond 719
Home to Roost - Gerald Hammond 720

Calder, Keith (Businessman)
A Brace of Skeet - Gerald Hammond 719

Caliban, Catherine "Cat" (Widow(er); Detective—Private)
Four Elements of Murder - D.B. Borton 155

Caliban, Catherine "Cat" (Detective—Private Widow(er))
Three Is a Crowd - D.B. Borton 156

Caliban, Catherine "Cat" (Detective—Private; Single Parent)
Two Points for Murder - D.B. Borton 157

Callum, Nora (Police Officer; Handicapped)
A Wide and Capable Revenge - Thomas McCall 1113

Camden, Claire (Professor; Writer)
Shroud for a Scholar - Audrey Peterson 1306

Cameron, Justin (Lawyer)
The Strange Files of Fremont Jones - Dianne Day 400

Canada, Lew (Police Officer)
Motown - Loren D. Estleman 498

Cantini, Angel (Detective—Private; Companion)
False Profit - Robert Eversz 511

Cantrip, Michael (Lawyer)
The Sirens Sang of Murder - Sarah Caudwell 228

Capo-Zendrini, Barbara (Noblewoman)
Death in a Serene City - Edward Sklepowich 1510

Cardenas, Vic (Police Officer; Widow(er))
Death of a DJ - Jane Rubino 1411

Carella, Steve (Detective—Police)
Vespers - Ed McBain 1107

Character Name Index

Carey, Neal (Student; Troubleshooter)
A Cool Breeze on the Underground - Don Winslow 1743
The Trail to Buddha's Mirror - Don Winslow 1744

Carey, Robert (Nobleman)
A Famine of Horses - P.F. Chisholm 243

Carl, Victor (Lawyer)
Hostile Witness - William Lashner 985

Carlisle, Andrew (Criminal)
Hour of the Hunter - J.A. Jance 843

Carlyle, Carlotta (Detective—Private; Taxi Driver)
Coyote - Linda Barnes 92

Carlyle, Carlotta (Detective—Private)
Snapshot - Linda Barnes 93

Carlyle, Carlotta (Detective—Private; Taxi Driver)
Steel Guitar - Linda Barnes 94

Carmody, Lorelei (Student)
Fatal Obsession - D.B. Taylor 1606

Carpenter, Hollis (Journalist; Lesbian)
Bayou City Secrets - Deborah Powell 1323

Carpenter, Scott (Sports Figure; Homosexual)
The Only Good Priest - Mark Richard Zubro 1795

Carrera, Rolando (Criminal)
Blood Relative - Carolyn Hougan 811

Carter, Jack "the Poacher" (Writer)
Screaming Bones - Pat Burden 191

Caruso, Wayne (Bodyguard)
Adjusted to Death - Jaqueline Girdner 593

Caruso, Wayne (Boyfriend)
The Last Resort - Jaqueline Girdner 594

Caruso, Wayne (Restauranteur)
Tea-Totally Dead - Jaqueline Girdner 596

Carver, Frank (Police Officer)
Clear-Cut Murder - Lee Wallingford 1667
Cold Tracks - Lee Wallingford 1668

Carver, Fred (Detective—Private; Handicapped)
Flame - John Lutz 1057
Spark - John Lutz 1058

Casey, James P. (Lawyer; Detective—Private)
A Case of Innocence - Douglas J. Keeling 877

Cash, Julian (Police Officer)
Turtle Moon - Alice Hoffman 795

Castang, Henri (Police Officer)
Not as Far as Velma - Nicholas Freeling 548

Castellano, Danny (Criminal)
Purgatory - Monty Mickleson 1152

Cates, Molly (Journalist)
The Red Scream - Mary Willis Walker 1659
Under the Beetle's Cellar - Mary Willis Walker 1660

Cattrell, Ann (Journalist)
The Ice House - Minette Walters 1669

Caulfield, Am (Hotel Worker)
The Hotel Detective - Alan Russell 1413

Caute, Simon (Criminal)
Fuse Time - Max Byrd 205

Caxton, Lyman (Police Officer)
Buried in Stone - Eric Wright 1766

Caylor, Lauren (Architect)
The Watchman - Michael Allegretto 44

Caylor, Richard (Businessman)
The Watchman - Michael Allegretto 44

Cecile (Religious; Detective—Private)
A Sudden Death at the Norfolk Cafe - Winona Sullivan 1591

Cervantes, Antonio "Chico" (Detective—Private)
Death as a Career Move - Bruce Cook 299
Rough Cut - Bruce Cook 300
The Sidewalk Hilton - Bruce Cook 301

Chadwick, Alix (Scientist)
Tensleep - Sarah Andrews 57

Chadwick, Maud (Waiter/Waitress)
The End of the Pier - Martha Grimes 674

Chambers, Ishmael (Journalist; Veteran)
Snow Falling on Cedars - David Guterson 692

Chandler, Shaw (Health Care Professional)
Bones of Coral - James W. Hall 707

Chandler, Wes (Military Personnel)
River of Darkness - James Grady 632

Chapman, Andrew (Psychologist)
Probable Cause - Griff Stockley 1577

Chapman, Harry (Spy)
A Time Without Shadows - Ted Allbeury 38

Chase, Elizabeth (Detective—Private)
Murder in Scorpio - Martha C. Lawrence 993

Chee, Jim (Police Officer; Indian)
Sacred Clowns - Tony Hillerman 792
Talking God - Tony Hillerman 793

Chenier, Lucille (Lawyer; Single Parent)
Voodoo River - Robert Crais 344

Chernov, Yuri (Spy)
Crossed Swords - Sean Flannery 528

Cherry, Max (Businessman)
Rum Punch - Elmore Leonard 1007

Chesney, Jenny (Nurse)
Hanging on the Wire - Gillian Linscott 1028

Chin, Lydia (Detective—Private)
China Trade - S.J. Rozan 1410

Chizzit, Emma (Businesswoman)
Emma Chizzit and the Mother Lode Marauder - Mary Bowen Hall 711
Emma Chizzit and the Napa Nemesis - Mary Bowen Hall 712
Emma Chizzit and the Queen Anne Killer - Mary Bowen Hall 713

Christie, Agatha (Historical Figure; Writer)
Dorothy and Agatha - Gaylord Larsen 984

Churchyard, Tom (Engineer)
Playing God - Barbara Whitehead 1707

Ciampi, Marlene (Lawyer)
Justice Denied - Robert K. Tanenbaum 1599
Reversible Error - Robert K. Tanenbaum 1600

Cicero, Marcus Tullius (Historical Figure; Lawyer)
Roman Blood - Steven Saylor 1449

Claiborne, Claire (Hairdresser)
Behind Eclaire's Doors - Sophie Dunbar 457

Claiborne, Dan (Lawyer)
Behind Eclaire's Doors - Sophie Dunbar 457

Clancey, Jack (Journalist)
Peril under the Palms - K.K. Beck 117

Clark, Taylor (Teenager)
Clearwater Summer - John E. Keegan 876

Clement, Jules (Police Officer)
The Edge of the Crazies - Jamie Harrison 736

Clevenger, August (Journalist)
Boiling Rock - Remar Sutton 1594

Clively, Miranda (Spinster)
Clively Close: Dead as Dead Can Be - Ann Crowleigh 361

Clively-Murdoch, Clare (Widow(er))
Clively Close: Dead as Dead Can Be - Ann Crowleigh 361

Cobb, Jeremy (Professor)
She Walks These Hills - Sharyn McCrumb 1119

Cobb, Matt (Journalist)
Killed on the Rocks - William L. DeAndrea 401

Cochran, William "Bull" (Writer)
Shutout - David F. Nighbert 1204

Cochran, William "Bull" (Businessman; Writer)
Squeezeplay - David F. Nighbert 1205

Cochran, William "Bull" (Businessman; Sports Figure)
Strikezone - David F. Nighbert 1206

Cochrane, Helen (Librarian; Single Parent)
Every Breath You Take - Michelle Spring 1541

Coffin, John (Police Officer)
Coffin on Murder Street - Gwendoline Butler 203
Coffin Underground - Gwendoline Butler 204

Cohen, Magaret Midge (Writer)
Date with a Dead Doctor - Toni Brill 177

Coldwater, Jack Gene (Religious)
Heat - Stuart Woods 1760

Cole, Elvis (Detective—Private)
Free Fall - Robert Crais 341
Lullaby Town - Robert Crais 342
Stalking the Angel - Robert Crais 343
Voodoo River - Robert Crais 344

Cole, Hardy (Detective)
Killings - A.W. Gray 651

Coll, Matthew (Businessman)
Death in Verona - Roy Harley Lewis 1020

Collier, Alex (Journalist; Television Personality)
Savage Justice - Ron Handberg 721

Collier, Janet (Police Officer)
Switchback - Collin Wilcox 1717

Collins, Charity (Journalist)
Katwalk - Karen Kijewski 920

Collins, Henrietta O'Dwyer (Journalist; Widow(er))
Dead Man's Island - Carolyn G. Hart 742

Colorado, Kat (Detective—Private)
Alley Kat Blues - Karen Kijewski 917
Copy Kat - Karen Kijewski 918
Katapult - Karen Kijewski 919
Katwalk - Karen Kijewski 920
Wild Kat - Karen Kijewski 921

Colquhoun, Aphra (Editor)
Margin for Murder - Bronte Adams 9

Coltrane, Grey (Heiress; Martial Arts Expert)
Nightwalker - Sidney Filson 527

Connor, Gail (Lawyer)
Suspicion of Guilt - Barbara Parker 1268

Connor, John (Police Officer)
Rising Sun - Michael Crichton 348

Connor, Ned (Spy)
The Hawthorne Group - Thomas Hauser 756

Connors, Jamison (Security Officer)
Gun Men - Gary Friedman 553

Connors, Liz (Journalist)
And Soon I'll Come to Kill You - Susan Kelly 893
Out of the Darkness - Susan Kelly 894
Until Proven Innocent - Susan Kelly 895

Conrad, Claire (Detective—Private; Wealthy)
Beauty Dies - Melodie Johnson Howe 813

Conrad, Claire (Detective—Private)
The Mother Shadow - Melodie Johnson Howe 814

Conrad, Nathan (Doctor)
Don't Say a Word - Keith Peterson 1308
Don't Say a Word - Andrew Klavan 937

Constantine (Drifter)
Shoedog - George Pelecanos 1288

Constantino, Junior (Criminal)
The Monkey Rope - Stephen Lewis 1023

Coogan, Blackie (Detective—Private)
Charged with Guilt - Gloria White 1700
Money to Burn - Gloria White 1701
Murder on the Run - Gloria White 1702

Cook, Malcolm (Lawyer)
Shadows on the Mirror - Frances Fyfield 563

Cooper (Serial Killer)
Into the Fire - David Wiltse 1737

Cooper, Iris (Student)
Peril under the Palms - K.K. Beck 117

Cooper, Sam (Scientist)
The Bulrush Murders - Rebecca Rothenberg 1405

Corbett, Hugh (Secretary)
Murder Wears a Cowl - P.C. Doherty 426
The Prince of Darkness - P.C. Doherty 427

Corbett, Kyle (Pilot)
The Ransom of Black Stealth One - Dean Ing 825

Corder, Wilson (Psychologist; Single Parent)
The Deep End - Chris Crutcher 364

Corman, David (Photographer)
The City When It Rains - Thomas H. Cook 305

Coulter, Jason (Detective—Private)
Ten of Swords - J.R. Levitt 1018

Counsel, Colin (Teacher)
Unknown Hand - Gillian Linscott 1031

Covington, Janet (Businesswoman; Editor)
The Long Search - Isabelle Holland 798

Cowart, Matthew (Journalist)
Just Cause - John Katzenbach 873

Coyle, Kate (Doctor)
The Catalyst - Desmond Cory 330
The Dobie Paradox - Desmond Cory 331

Coyne, Brady (Lawyer)
Dead Winter - William G. Tapply 1602
Spotted Cats - William G. Tapply 1603
Tight Lines - William G. Tapply 1604

Coyne, Dermot (Businessman)
Irish Gold - Andrew M. Greeley 657

Craddock, Davis (Criminal)
Bad to the Bone - Stephen Solomita 1532

Craig, Melissa (Writer)
Exhaustive Enquiries - Betty Rowlands 1408
Over the Edge - Betty Rowlands 1409

Craig, William (Police Officer)
The Covenant of the Flame - David Morrell 1174

Crayhall, Sam (Convict)
The Chamber - John Grisham 679

Creed, John (Detective—Private)
The Keeper - Meg O'Brien 1217

Crichton, Tessa (Actress)
Fatal Charm - Anne Morice 1173

Crist, Karen (FBI Agent)
The Edge of Sleep - David Wiltse 1736

Croft, Joshua (Detective—Private)
At Ease with the Dead - Walter Satterthwait 1437
A Flower in the Desert - Walter Satterthwait 1439
The Hanged Man - Walter Satterthwait 1440

Croft, Ralph (Criminal)
The Masked Man - P.C. Doherty 425

Croft, Tom (Spy)
Winter of the Wolves - James N. Frey 552

Cromwell, David (Adoptee; Actor)
Dreamland - M.K. Lorens 1044

Cromwell, Sarah (Musician; Companion)
Deception Island - M.K. Lorens 1043
Sweet Narcissus - M.K. Lorens 1045

Cronin, Frank (Journalist)
Hammurabi's Code - Charles Kenney 909

Crook, Paul (Detective—Private; Cowboy)
Stonefish - Charles West 1695

Cross, Alex (Police Officer; Doctor)
Along Came a Spider - James Patterson 1276

Crusoe, Edwina (Detective—Private; Nurse)
Desperate Remedy - Mary Kittredge 931
Kill or Cure - Mary Kittredge 932
Walking Dead Man - Mary Kittredge 934

Cruz, Carlos (Police Officer)
A Single Stone - Marilyn Wallace 1664

Cuddy, John Francis (Detective—Private)
Act of God - Jeremiah Healy 764
Foursome - Jeremiah Healy 765
Yesterday's News - Jeremiah Healy 766

Cullen, Frank "Cully" (Criminal)
Cons - Timothy Watts 1677

Cullen, Joe (Police Officer)
Fixing to Die - Jerry Oster 1249

Culpepper, Barney (Police Officer)
Mail-Order Murder - Leslie Meier 1140

Cunningham, Maude (Companion)
Diamond Head - Marian J.A. Jackson 834
The Sunken Treasure - Marian J.A. Jackson 835

Curran, Guy (Criminal)
Going Wrong - Ruth Rendell 1360

Curry, Thomas (Businessman)
Act of Faith - Michael Bowen 158
Fielder's Choice - Michael Bowen 160

Cussone, Stanley (Police Officer)
The Forever Beat - John Cline 262

D

Da Silva, Jane (Singer)
Amateur Night - K.K. Beck 114

Da Silva, Jane (Singer; Detective—Private)
Electric City - K.K. Beck 115

Da Silva, Jane (Singer)
A Hopeless Case - K.K. Beck 116

Daggett, Cameron (FBI Agent)
Hard Fall - Ridley Pearson 1284

Dahlstrom, Nels (Businessman)
Golden Fleece - Jack Becklund 118

Daily, Lark (Businesswoman)
Larkspur - Sheila Simonson 1500

Dain, Eddie (Detective—Private)
Dead Man - Joe Gores 617

Dalgliesh, Adam (Police Officer)
Devices and Desires - P.D. James 841

Dali, Salvador (Historical Figure; Artist)
The Melting Clock - Stuart M. Kaminsky 860

Dalrymple, Daisy (Writer)
The Winter Garden Mystery - Carola Dunn 465

Dalton, Will (Anthropologist)
Menaced Assassin - Joe Gores 618

Dalziel, Andrew (Police Officer)
Bones and Silence - Reginald Hill 789
Recalled to Life - Reginald Hill 790

Dancer, Karen (Advertising; Single Parent)
The Dying Room - E.X. Giroux 599

Danforth, Abigail (Detective—Private)
Diamond Head - Marian J.A. Jackson 834
The Sunken Treasure - Marian J.A. Jackson 835

D'Angelo, Johnny (Criminal)
Bait - Kenneth Abel 3

Daniels, Charmain (Police Officer)
Witching Murder - Jennie Melville 1144

Daniels, Charmian (Police Officer; Widow(er))
Dead Set - Jennie Melville 1141

Daniels, Charmian (Police Officer)
Murder Has a Pretty Face - Jennie Melville 1142
Whoever Has the Heart - Jennie Melville 1143

Dann, Peaches (Writer)
Memory Can Be Murder - Elizabeth Daniels Squire 1547

Dann, Peaches (Writer; Widow(er))
Who Killed What's-Her-Name? - Elizabeth Daniels Squire 1548

Danno, Joe (Police Officer)
Nice Guys Finish Dead - David Debin 406

Dante, Joe (Police Officer)
19th Precinct - Christopher Newman 1202

Danvers, Sally (Saloon Keeper/Owner)
Dreamboat - Doug J. Swanson 1596

Danzig, John "Jack Dance" (Criminal)
Whiskey River - Loren D. Estleman 501

Darcy, Tess (Innkeeper)
Blooming Murder - Jean Hager 698
Dead and Buried - Jean Hager 699

Darling, Annie Laurance (Store Owner)
The Christie Caper - Carolyn G. Hart 741
Mint Julep Murder - Carolyn G. Hart 744

Darling, Max (Lawyer)
A Little Class on Murder - Carolyn G. Hart 743

Dartelli, Joe (Police Officer)
Chain of Evidence - Ridley Pearson 1283

Darwin, Peter (Diplomat)
Comeback - Dick Francis 539

Daunbey, Benjamin (Nobleman)
The Poisoned Chalice - Michael Clynes 264

Davenport, Lucas (Police Officer)
Night Prey - John Sandford 1424
Rules of Prey - John Sandford 1425
Shadow Prey - John Sandford 1426
Silent Prey - John Sandford 1427
Winter Prey - John Sandford 1428

Davies, Owen (Police Officer)
The Killing of Ellis Martin - Lucretia Grindle 677
So Little to Die For - Lucretia Grindle 678

Davilov, Queenie (Writer; Detective—Private)
Cut To—Murder - Denise Osborne 1247

Davilov, Queenie (Detective—Private; Writer)
Murder Offscreen - Denise Osborne 1248

Davis, Mavis (Detective—Private)
My First Murder - Susan Baker 84

Davison, Molly (Social Worker)
The Harbinger Effect - S.K. Wolf 1746

Davy, Tess (Actress)
The Dying of the Light - Robert Richardson 1366

Dawes, Sally (Journalist)
Corruption - Andrew Klavan 936

Day, Jane (Journalist)
Knight & Day - Ron Nessen 1201

De Gheyn, Sam (Police Officer)
The End of the Pier - Martha Grimes 674

Deacon, Jack (Artist)
The Tijuana Bible - Ron Goulart 630

Deal, John (Businessman)
Deal to Die For - Les Standiford 1560
Done Deal - Les Standiford 1561

Dean, Jeffrey (Businessman)
Singapore Transfer - Wayne Warga 1673

Dean, Sam (Writer; Journalist)
Blood Rights - Mike Phillips 1314

Deane, Sarah (Teacher)
The Bridled Groom - J.S. Borthwick 154

Decker, Gillian Clifford (Businesswoman)
In-laws and Outlaws - Barbara Paul 1277

Decker, Peter (Police Officer)
Day of Atonement - Faye Kellerman 878
False Prophet - Faye Kellerman 879
Grievous Sin - Faye Kellerman 880
Justice - Faye Kellerman 881
Milk and Honey - Faye Kellerman 882

Decker, Peter (Police Officer; Detective—Homicide)
Sanctuary - Faye Kellerman 884

Decker, Phillip (Police Officer)
Long Chain of Death - S.K. Wolf 1747

Decker, Rick (Journalist)
Hidden City - Jim DeBrosse 407
Southern Cross - Jim DeBrosse 408

Decker, Rina (Spouse)
Grievous Sin - Faye Kellerman 880

Defoe, Chase (Spy)
August Ice - Deforest Day 399

DeGregorio, Joe (Police Officer)
False Faces - Seth Jacob Margolis 1074

Delacroix, Lily (Lesbian)
Bayou City Secrets - Deborah Powell 1323

Delafield, Kate (Police Officer; Lesbian)
The Beverly Malibu - Katherine V. Forrest 533
Murder by Tradition - Katherine V. Forrest 534

Delaney, Ed (Police Officer)
Night of the Ice Storm - David Stout 1579

Delaney, Patricia (Detective—Private)
Angel's Bidding - Sharon Gwyn Short 1489
The Death We Share - Sharon Gwyn Short 1490

Delaporte, Helen (Musician)
The Famous DAR Murder Mystery - Graham Landrum 977

Delaware, Alex (Psychologist)
Bad Love - Jonathan Kellerman 885
Private Eyes - Jonathan Kellerman 886
Self-Defense - Jonathan Kellerman 887
Time Bomb - Jonathan Kellerman 888

Deleeuw, Kit (Detective—Private)
Death by Station Wagon - Jon Katz 869
The Family Stalker - Jon Katz 870

Delvecchio, Nick (Detective—Private)
The Dead of Brooklyn - Robert J. Randisi 1347

Demarkian, Gregor (Troubleshooter)
Not a Creature Was Stirring - Jane Haddam 695
Quoth the Raven - Jane Haddam 696

Demarkian, Gregor (Police Officer)
A Stillness in Bethlehem - Jane Haddam 697

DeMedici, Danny (Drug Dealer)
The Horse Latitudes - Robert Ferrigno 526

Demming, Walter (Driver; Veteran)
Under the Beetle's Cellar - Mary Willis Walker 1660

Dempsey, Mary Teresa (Religious)
Nun Plussed - Monica Quill 1339

Denkin, George (Criminal; Serial Killer)
Incident at Potter's Bridge - Joseph Monniger 1165

Dennis, Margaret (Art Historian)
By Death Possessed - Roger Ormerod 1243

DeNobili, Duke (Detective—Private)
Alibi for an Actress - Gillian B. Farrell 516

Denson, John (Detective—Private)
Bigfoot - Richard Hoyt 815
Whoo? - Richard Hoyt 816

Dent, Evan (Criminal)
Personal - C.K. Cambray 208

Denton, Harry James (Detective—Private)
Dead Folks' Blues - Steven Womack 1751
Torch Town Boogie - Steven Womack 1754
Way Past Dead - Steven Womack 1755

DePalrey, Horatio (Spy)
The Russia House - John Le Carre 995

Derwent, Frank (Director)
Murder Movie - Jill McGown 1131

Desoto, Alfonso (Police Officer)
Flame - John Lutz 1057

Detective, Nameless (Detective—Private)
Breakdown - Bill Pronzini 1326
Epitaphs - Bill Pronzini 1327
Jackpot - Bill Pronzini 1328
Quarry - Bill Pronzini 1329

Devereaux (Spy)
The Last Good German - Bill Granger 647

Devine, Matt (Counselor)
Cat on a Blue Monday - Carole Nelson Douglas 438

Devlin, Jack (Detective—Private)
And Justice for One - John Clarkson 254

Devlin, Liam (Criminal)
The Eagle Has Flown - Jack Higgins 787

Devlin, Mac (Pilot; Veteran)
Eagles Die Too - Meg O'Brien 1215

Devlin, Mike (FBI Agent)
Gentkill: A Novel of the FBI - Paul Lindsay 1025

Devore, Addie (Journalist; Publisher)
Murder in Bandora - Leona Karr 868

Dewitt, James (Police Officer)
Probable Cause - Ridley Pearson 1285

Di Palma, Laura (Lawyer)
The Good Fight - Lia Matera 1091
A Hard Bargain - Lia Matera 1092

Diamond, Peter (Police Officer)
The Summons - Peter Lovesey 1050

Didier, Inez (Filmmaker)
The Fall Line - Mark T. Sullivan 1589

DiGregorio, Joe (Detective—Private)
Vanishing Act - Seth Jacob Margolis 1075

Dillon, Sean (Spy)
Angel of Death - Jack Higgins 786

Dinesen, Mike (Computer Expert; Scientist)
Death Qualified: A Mystery of Chaos - Kate Wilhelm 1723

Disbro, Gil (Detective—Private)
The Flip Side of Life - James E. Martin 1085

Dixon, Ray (Police Officer)
The Raggedy Man - Lillian O'Donnell 1227
Used to Kill - Lillian O'Donnell 1228

Dobie, John (Professor)
The Catalyst - Desmond Cory 330
The Dobie Paradox - Desmond Cory 331

Dodge, Jay (Police Officer)
Larkspur - Sheila Simonson 1500
Skylark - Sheila Simonson 1501

Dodge, Lark (Businesswoman)
Skylark - Sheila Simonson 1501

Dogg, David (Police Officer; Detective—Homicide)
Bury the Bishop - Kate Gallison 564

Dolan, Trixie (Actress)
Encore Murder - Marian Babson 76

Dolittle, Cyrus (Police Officer)
Corruption - Andrew Klavan 936

Doll (Veteran; Detective—Private)
Death Among the Angels - John Walter Putre 1336

Doll (Troubleshooter; Veteran)
A Small and Incidental Murder - John Walter Putre 1337

Donaghue, Ulysses (Detective—Private)
Mr. Donaghue Investigates - Anna Shone 1488

Donahoo, Tommy (Police Officer)
Balboa Firefly - Jack Trolley 1633

Donatti, Dominick (Criminal; Addict)
Strangers in the Night - Peg Tyre 1641

Donelli, Joe (Boyfriend)
Ties That Bind - Sherryl Woods 1759

Donodio, Brian (Professor)
Forty Whacks - Sheila MacGill Callahan 207

Donovan, Bill (Police Officer)
City of God - Michael Jahn 840

Donovan, Brigid (Religious; Lesbian)
Murder Is Germane - Karen Saum 1442

Dorsey, Carroll (Detective—Private; Insurance Investigator)
The Fall-Down Artist - Thomas Lipinski 1032

Dortmunder, John (Thief)
Don't Ask - Donald E. Westlake 1697
Drowned Hopes - Donald E. Westlake 1698

Dover, Wilf (Detective—Police)
Dover and the Claret Tappers - Joyce Porter   1322

Doyle, Abigail (Detective—Private)
Deadly Resolutions - Anna Ashwood Collins   274

Doyle, Arthur Conan (Historical Figure)
The 6 Messiahs - Mark Frost   560

Doyle, Arthur Conan (Historical Figure; Writer)
Escapade - Walter Satterthwait   1438

Doyle, Matt (Detective—Private)
Murder Begins at Home - Dale L. Gilbert   585

Drake, Jessica (Police Officer; Detective—Homicide)
Angel of Death - Rochelle Majer Krich   953
Fair Game - Rochelle Majer Krich   954

Drake, Paul (Police Officer)
Murder in a Nice Neighborhood - Lora Roberts   1388

Drake, Tess (Journalist)
The Covenant of the Flame - David Morrell   1174

Drew, Patricia (Journalist)
The Triumph of Bacchus - Douglas Skeggs   1509

Drexler, Sarah (Judge; Widow(er))
Justice for Some - Kate Wilhelm   1724

Driscoll, Katherine (Animal Trainer)
Zero at the Bone - Mary Willis Walker   1661

Driver, Sam (Businessman)
A Pedigree to Die For - Laurien Berenson   121

Drover, Jimmy (Journalist)
Drover and the Zebras - Bill Granger   646

Du Bois, Pierre (Businessman)
Murder, Mystery and Mayhem - Jennifer Carnell   220

Dudgeon, Rene (Criminal)
Time and Time Again - B.M. Gill   587

Dunbar, Will (Public Relations)
Wasteland - Peter McCabe   1110

Duncan, Stephanie (Detective—Amateur)
Brideprice - J.N. Catanach   226

Dundy (Police Officer)
Death and the Chaste Apprentice - Robert Barnard   89

Dunn, Micah (Detective—Private; Veteran)
The Caesar Clue - M.K. Shuman   1491
Deep Kill - M.K. Shuman   1492
The Last Man to Die - M.K. Shuman   1493
The Maya Stone Murders - M.K. Shuman   1494

Dunne, Bettina (Artist)
To Do No Harm - Leslie Glass   602

Dupoulis, Ken (Police Officer)
Murder in Mellingham - Susan Oleksiw   1231

Dupree, Carl (Criminal)
Purgatory - Monty Mickleson   1152

E

Eagle, Ken (Sports Figure)
Dead Fix - Michael Geller   573

Eakins, Abigail (Child)
The House on the Hill - Judith Kelman   899

Early, Wilton (Police Officer)
Death on Wheels - Robert Nordan   1209

Easterbrook, Alison (Heiress)
Funnelweb - Charles West   1693

Ebinger, Mariah (Teenager)
Blood Relative - Carolyn Hougan   811

Edward, Prince of Wales (Historical Figure)
Bertie and the Seven Bodies - Peter Lovesey   1049

Edwards, Colin (Professor; Anthropologist)
Selena - Gordon Randolph Willey   1726

Edwards, Con (Journalist)
The Gombeen Man - Randy Lee Eickoff   474

Edwards, Harry (Police Officer)
Kimura - Robert Davis   395

Egan, Alice Jane "A.J." (Journalist)
Neon Dancers - Matt Taylor   1608

Eichord, Jake (Detective—Police)
Stone Shadow - Rex Miller   1154

Eileen (Religious)
Murder Makes a Pilgrimage - Sister Carol Anne O'Marie   1239

Eldine, Janet (Professor)
Murder at the Friendship Hotel - Charlotte Epstein   496

Ellenberg, Sally (Journalist)
Indecent Behavior - Caryl Rivers   1372

Elliot, David (Businessman; Veteran)
Vertical Run - Joseph R. Garber   566

Elliot, Elizabeth (Widow(er))
Quaker Silence - Irene Allen   45

Elliot, Elizabeth (Religious; Widow(er))
Quaker Witness - Irene Allen   46

Elliott, Maggie (Detective—Private)
The Northwest Murders - Elizabeth Atwood Taylor   1607

Ellis, Nigel (Political Figure; Parent)
Dream of Darkness - Patrick Ruell   1412

Ellis, Sairey (Student)
Dream of Darkness - Patrick Ruell   1412

Eltern, Anna (Social Worker)
Nightside - Soledad Santiago   1434

Emerson, Amelia Peabody (Archaeologist)
The Last Camel Died at Noon - Elizabeth Peters   1298

Emerson, Radcliffe (Archaeologist)
The Last Camel Died at Noon - Elizabeth Peters   1298

Engels, Kay (Journalist)
Murder at the Class Reunion - Triss Stein   1567

Epstein, Beau (Runaway)
Thursday's Child - Teri White   1705

Epton, Rosa (Lawyer)
Seeds of Murder - Michael Underwood   1642

Erickson, Reed (Government Official)
The Deer Killers - Gunnard Landers   973

Estrada, Joe (Lawyer)
Inadmissible Evidence - Philip Friedman   557

Eton, Vic (Detective—Private; Single Parent)
Dark of Night - Richard Nehrbass   1200

Evron, Ronit (Teacher)
Cover Story - Robert Cullen   365

Exley, Ed (Police Officer)
L.A. Confidential - James Ellroy   483

F

Fairchild, Faith (Caterer)
The Body in the Basement - Katherine Hall Page   1254

Fairchild, Faith (Caterer; Housewife)
The Body in the Belfry - Katherine Hall Page   1255

Fairchild, Faith (Housewife)
The Body in the Bouillon - Katherine Hall Page   1256

Fairchild, Faith (Caterer)
The Body in the Cast - Katherine Hall Page   1257

Fairchild, Faith (Housewife)
The Body in the Vestibule - Katherine Hall Page   1258

Fairchild, Tom (Religious; Spouse)
The Body in the Belfry - Katherine Hall Page   1255
The Body in the Bouillon - Katherine Hall Page   1256
The Body in the Vestibule - Katherine Hall Page   1258

Fairweather, Doran (Businesswoman)
The Bandersnatch - Mollie Hardwick   729

Fairweather, Theodore (Spy)
Winter of the Wolves - James N. Frey   552

Falco, M. Didius (Detective—Amateur)
The Silver Pigs - Lindsey Davis   394

Falconer, William (Teacher)
Falconer's Crusade - Ian Morson   1175

Fansler, Kate (Professor)
An Imperfect Spy - Amanda Cross   360

Farabaugh, Mickey (Detective—Private)
According to St. John - William Babula   77

Farleigh, Allison (Businesswoman)
Gone Wild - James W. Hall   708

Farley, Marion (Professor)
Zombies of the Gene Pool - Sharyn McCrumb   1121

Farnham, George (Lawyer)
A Slay at the Races - Kate Morgan   1172

Faro, Jeremy (Police Officer)
Blood Line - Alanna Knight   941

Faro, Jeremy (Detective—Police)
Deadly Beloved - Alanna Knight   942

Faro, Jeremy (Police Officer)
Killing Cousins - Alanna Knight   943

Farrady, Rowena (Teenager)
Never Walk Behind Me - Lin Summerfield   1593

Farrell, Andrew (Criminal)
Criminal Conversation - Evan Hunter   820

Farrell, Jack (Sports Figure)
The Fall Line - Mark T. Sullivan   1589

Farrell, Tess (Child)
Deathspell - Veronica Stallwood   1558

Fay, Miranda (Journalist)
The Mooncalf Murders - Noel Vreeland Carter   222

Fell, Gideon (Doctor)
Fell and Foul Play - John Dickson Carr   221

Fellowes, Ian (Police Officer)
Home to Roost - Gerald Hammond   720

Fender, Martin (Musician)
Boiled in Concrete - Jesse Sublett   1587

Ferguson, Lackey (Businessman)
Prime Suspect - A.W. Gray 653

Ferguson, Robert Earl (Criminal)
Just Cause - John Katzenbach 873

Fernandez, Arthur (Police Officer)
Justice for Some - Kate Wilhelm 1724

Ferrer, Jennifer (Secretary)
Miami Heat - Jerome Sanford 1433

Finley, Nick (Journalist)
Cry for Help - Karen Hanson Stuyck 1586

Finley, Peter (Journalist)
Limited Partner - Mike Lupica 1053

Finn, Frances (Detective—Private)
Murder at St. Adelaide's - Gerelyn Hollingsworth 799

Finn, John (Detective—Police)
Strangers in the Night - Peg Tyre 1641

Fischman, Ida (Housewife)
Unorthodox Practices - Marissa Piesman 1320

Fischman, Nina (Lawyer)
Close Quarters - Marissa Piesman 1319
Unorthodox Practices - Marissa Piesman 1320

Fisher, Noel (Detective—Private)
The Total Zone - Martina Navratilova 1195

Fitzgerald, Ed "Fitz" (Journalist)
A Suitcase in Berlin - Don Flynn 532

Fitzgerald, Jennifer (Scientist; Computer Expert)
Coyote Bird - Jim DeFelice 409

Fixx, Raleigh (Writer)
Flamingo - Bob Reiss 1359

Flagg, Conan (Detective—Private; Store Owner)
Dead Matter - M.K. Wren 1764
King of the Mountain - M.K. Wren 1765

Flagg, Ruby (Actress)
Drown All the Dogs - Thomas Adcock 23

Flam, Victor (Detective—Private)
Flawless - Adam Barrow 99

Flanagan, Bella (Actress)
Stage Fright - Gillian Linscott 1030

Flanagan, John (Journalist)
Inherit the Mob - Zev Chafets 231

Flanagan, Molly (Police Officer)
Shutout - David F. Nighbert 1204

Flannery, Jimmy (Worker; Political Figure)
The Gift Horse's Mouth - Robert Campbell 212

Flannery, Jimmy (Maintenance Worker)
Nibbled to Death by Ducks - Robert Campbell 213

Flaschner, Max (Scientist)
A Very Particular Murder - S.T. Haymon 759

Fleming, Laura (Computer Expert)
Dead Ringer - Toni L.P. Kelner 900
Down Home Murder - Toni L.P. Kelner 901
Trouble Looking for a Place to Happen - Toni L.P. Kelner 902

Fleming, Richard (Professor)
Dead Ringer - Toni L.P. Kelner 900
Down Home Murder - Toni L.P. Kelner 901
Trouble Looking for a Place to Happen - Toni L.P. Kelner 902

Fletcher, Alec (Police Officer)
The Winter Garden Mystery - Carola Dunn 465

Fletcher, J. (Detective—Private)
A Hazard of Losers - Lloyd Biggle Jr. 132

Flint, Mike (Police Officer; Detective—Homicide)
Midnight Baby - Wendy Hornsby 808

Flippo, Jack (Detective—Private)
Dreamboat - Doug J. Swanson 1596

Flores, Karen (Actress)
Get Shorty - Elmore Leonard 1005

Florio, Marc (Police Officer)
One Cried Murder - David Cooper Wall 1663

Florio, Nicky (Businessman; Criminal)
Mortal Sin - Paul Levine 1014

Flynn, Fiddler (Businessman)
Money Burns - A.E. Maxwell 1100

Flynn, Fiora (Businesswoman)
Money Burns - A.E. Maxwell 1100

Flynn, Joe (Police Officer)
Bantam of the Opera - Mary Daheim 374

Flynn, Mickey (Photojournalist)
Death and Other Lovers - Jo Bannister 86

Foley, Joseph (Businessman; Criminal)
Balboa Firefly - Jack Trolley 1633

Folger, Merry (Police Officer; Detective—Police)
Death on Rough Water - Francine Matthews 1099

Fontana, Mac (Fire Fighter)
Help Wanted: Orphans Preferred - Earl Emerson 487
Morons and Madmen - Earl Emerson 488

Forbes, Molly (Actress)
Holy Treasure! - David Williams 1729

Forbes, Molly (Actress; Spouse)
Treasure by Post - David Williams 1730

Ford, Doc (Scientist)
Sanibel Flats - Randy Wayne White 1704

Fork, Sid (Police Officer)
The Fourth Durango - Ross Thomas 1612

Forrester, Lily (Lawyer)
Mitigating Circumstances - Nancy Taylor Rosenberg 1401

Forsythe, Robert (Lawyer)
A Death for a Dancing Doll - E.X. Giroux 597
A Death for a Dodo - E.X. Giroux 598

Fortune, Dan (Detective—Private; Handicapped)
Cassandra in Red - Michael Collins 281
Chasing Eights - Michael Collins 282
Crime, Punishment and Resurrection - Michael Collins 283

Fortune, Sarah (Lawyer)
Shadows on the Mirror - Frances Fyfield 563

Fowler, Nick (Police Officer)
Kiss Them Goodbye - Joseph Eastburn 468

Fran (Student)
Killing Time in Buffalo - Deidre S. Laiken 964

Frank, Jason (Doctor)
Hanging Time - Leslie Glass 601

Frank, Lisa (Prostitute; Teenager)
Hide and Seek - Barry Berg 122

Franklin, Alton "Rooster" (Criminal)
Caught Looking - Randy Russell 1416

Franklin, Derek (Sports Figure)
Straight - Dick Francis 541

Franklyn, Kit (Psychologist)
Blood on the Bayou - D.J. Donaldson 429
New Orleans Requiem - D.J. Donaldson 430
No Mardi Gras for the Dead - D.J. Donaldson 431

Frazer, Harry (Lawyer; Sailor)
Deadeye - Sam Llewellyn 1037

Frazier, Billy (Military Personnel)
The Price of Victory - Vincent Green 666

Frederickson, Garth (Police Officer)
In the House of Secret Enemies - George C. Chesbro 241

Frederickson, Robert "Mongo" (Detective—Private; Professor)
In the House of Secret Enemies - George C. Chesbro 241
The Language of Cannibals - George C. Chesbro 242

Fredrick, Kay (Spouse)
In Blacker Moments - S.E. Schenkel 1451

Fredrick, Ray (Police Officer)
In Blacker Moments - S.E. Schenkel 1451

Freeman, Jefferson "Free" (Streetperson)
Free - Todd Komarnicki 952

French, Alan (Musician)
Broken Consort - James Gollin 609

French, Jackie (Musician)
Broken Consort - James Gollin 609

Frevisse (Religious)
The Bishop's Tale - Margaret Frazer 544
The Boy's Tale - Margaret Frazer 545

Friedman, Kinky (Detective—Private)
God Bless John Wayne - Kinky Friedman 554

Friedman, Kinky (Detective—Private; Musician)
Musical Chairs - Kinky Friedman 555

Frost, Leslie (Spy; Musician)
Frost the Fiddler - Janice Weber 1681

Frost, Reuben (Lawyer)
Murder Times Two - Haughton Murphy 1186
A Very Venetian Murder - Haughton Murphy 1187

Fry, Esmerelda (Spinster)
Murder, Mystery and Mayhem - Jennifer Carnell 220

Furco, Lucca (Criminal)
Neon Caesar - Mark McGarrity 1128

Fury, Merritt (Businessman)
Whisper the Guns - Edward Cline 261

G

Gabriel, Matt (Police Officer)
A Few Dying Words - Paula Gosling 626

Gallagher, Jan (Security Officer)
Bagged - Jo Bailey 79

Gallagher, Jan (Security Officer; Single Parent)
Recycled - Jo Bailey 80

Gallagher, Odyssey (Detective—Private)
Came a Dead Cat - James N. Frey 551

Gallagher, Quinn (Parole Officer)
The House on the Hill - Judith Kelman 899

Gallant, Wayne (Police Officer)
Miss Zukas and the Library Murders - Jo Dereske 416

Galloway, Tiller (Diver)
Louisiana Blue - David Poyer 1324

Galvin, Frank (Lawyer)
The Choice - Barry Reed 1357

Garcia, Lupe (Detective—Police)
The Cheerio Killings - Douglas Allyn   47

Garcia, Marita (Abuse Victim)
An Hour to Kill - Edward Wellen   1690

Garcia, Vicki (Journalist)
Barking Dogs - R.R. Irvine   827

Gardner, Hilda (Businesswoman)
Rafferty: Fatal Sisters - W. Glenn Duncan   458

Gardner, Richard (Detective—Police)
U.S.S.A. - David Madsen   1066

Garrett, Dave (Detective—Private)
Burning March - Neil Albert   28

Garrett, Dave (Detective—Private; Lawyer)
Cruel April - Neil Albert   29

Garrett, Dave (Detective—Private)
The February Trouble - Neil Albert   30
The January Corpse - Neil Albert   31

Garrity, Callahan (Detective—Private; Businesswoman)
Every Crooked Nanny - Kathy Hogan Trocheck   1631
To Live and Die in Dixie - Kathy Hogan Trocheck   1632

Garrity, Edna Mae (Parent)
Every Crooked Nanny - Kathy Hogan Trocheck   1631

Gastner, Bill (Police Officer)
Bitter Recoil - Steven F. Havill   757

Gastner, Bill (Police Officer; Widow(er))
Heartshot - Steven F. Havill   758

Gaunt, Jonathan (Police Officer)
The Spanish Maze Game - Noah Webster   1682

Gautier, Jean-Paul (Police Officer)
Death Off Stage - Richard Grayson   655

Gautier, Roxanne (Artist)
A Collector of Photographs - Deborah Valentine   1645

Gennaro, Angela (Detective—Private)
A Drink Before the War - Dennis Lehane   1000

Gennesko, Karl (Police Officer)
Curly Smoke - Susan Holtzer   803

Gentry, Janice (Psychologist)
The Manx Murders - William L. DeAndrea   402

Gentry, Ron (Detective—Private)
The Manx Murders - William L. DeAndrea   402

George, Edward (Librarian)
A Slip of the Tong - Charles A. Goodrum   611

Gerrard, Phillip (Police Officer)
The Queen Is Dead - Jane Dentinger   414

Ghote, Ganeesh (Police Officer)
Dead on Time - H.R.F. Keating   874
The Iciest Sin - H.R.F. Keating   875

Gibbons, Bert (FBI Agent)
Bad Apple - Anthony Bruno   184

Gibbons, Cuthbert (Police Officer)
Bad Blood - Anthony Bruno   185
Bad Moon - Anthony Bruno   186

Gibbs, Bob (Judge)
Maximum Bob - Elmore Leonard   1006

Gillard, Patrick (Spy)
Rook-Shoot - Margaret Duffy   452
Who Killed Cock Robin? - Margaret Duffy   453

Gilman, Ann (Lawyer)
The Prosecutor - Thomas Chastain   240

Girard, Terry (Businesswoman)
Murder Once Removed - Kathleen Kunz   959

Gisborne, Edward (Police Officer)
Bad Chemistry - Nora Kelly   891

Gish, Molly (Journalist)
Artichoke Hearts - Victor Wuamett   1777
Deeds of Trust - Victor Wuamett   1778

Glauberman, Alex (Detective—Private; Mechanic)
Obligations of the Bone - Dick Cluster   263

Glenn, Art (Musician)
Wild Again - Kathrin King Segal   1471

Glick, Murray (Detective—Private)
The Big Freeze - Michael J. Katz   871
Last Dance in Redondo Beach - Michael J. Katz   872

Glitsky, Abe (Police Officer)
A Certain Justice - John T. Lescroart   1008

Godwin, Rodger (Journalist)
Praetorian - Thomas Gifford   584

Gold, Natalie (Journalist; Equestrian)
Horse of a Different Killer - Jody Jaffe   839

Gold, Rachel (Lawyer)
Death Benefits - Michael A. Kahn   851
Due Diligence - Michael A. Kahn   852
Firm Ambitions - Michael A. Kahn   853

Goldberg, Benny (Lawyer; Professor)
Death Benefits - Michael A. Kahn   851
Due Diligence - Michael A. Kahn   852

Goldberg, Benny (Professor; Lawyer)
Firm Ambitions - Michael A. Kahn   853

Golding, Rachel (Friend)
The Cut Throat - Simon Michael   1149

Goldman, David (Detective—Private)
Bloody Ten - William F. Love   1047
The Chartreuse Clue - William F. Love   1048

Goldstein, Jay (Police Officer)
A Single Stone - Marilyn Wallace   1664

Gondolfo, Sonny (Detective—Private)
Murder and a Muse - Gillian B. Farrell   517

Goode, Henry (Journalist)
Horse of a Different Killer - Jody Jaffe   839

Goodman, Rayford (Detective—Private)
Shot on Location - Stan Cutler   369

Goodwin, Archie (Detective—Private; Sidekick)
Fade to Black - Robert Goldsborough   607
Silver Spire - Robert Goldsborough   608

Gordianus the Finder (Farmer)
Catalina's Riddle - Steven Saylor   1448

Gordianus the Finder (Detective—Private)
Roman Blood - Steven Saylor   1449
The Venus Throw - Steven Saylor   1450

Gordon, Alex (Criminal; Critic)
Someone Is Killing the Great Chefs of America - Nan Lyons   1061

Gordon, Kathleen (Police Officer)
All Hallows Evil - Valerie Wolzien   1748
A Good Year for a Corpse - Valerie Wolzien   1749

Gordon, Kathleen (Businesswoman)
We Wish You a Merry Murder - Valerie Wolzien   1750

Gordon, Lindsay (Journalist)
Report for Murder - Val McDermid   1126

Gordon, William (Journalist)
Inherit the Mob - Zev Chafets   231

Grabowski, Joseph (Detective—Homicide)
Elective Murder - Janet McGiffin   1129

Grabowski, Joseph (Police Officer)
Prescription for Death - Janet McGiffin   1130

Grabowski, Kazimierz (Religious)
Gospel Truths - J.G. Sandom   1429

Graham, Charlotte (Actress)
Murder at the Spa - Stefanie Matteson   1097
Murder on the Cliff - Stefanie Matteson   1098

Graham, Peter (Professor)
Crossover - Judith Eubank   502

Graham, Warren (Computer Expert)
User Deadly - Denise Danks   388

Grant, Celia (Businesswoman)
Bones Gather No Moss - John Sherwood   1483
A Bouquet of Thorns - John Sherwood   1484
The Hanging Garden - John Sherwood   1485

Grant, Edward (Criminal)
Skeletons - Eric Sauter   1443

Grant, Erin (Stripper)
Strip Tease - Carl Hiaasen   785

Grant, Jack (Detective—Private)
Frozen Stare - Richard B. Schwartz   1459

Grant, Paula (Actress)
The Beverly Malibu - Katherine V. Forrest   533

Grant, Tom (Actor)
Funnelweb - Charles West   1693

Grantham, Gray (Journalist)
The Pelican Brief - John Grisham   681

Graveline, Rudy (Doctor)
Skin Tight - Carl Hiaasen   783

Graver, Marcus (Police Officer)
An Absence of Light - David L. Lindsey   1026

Gray, Susan (Police Officer)
Wednesday's Child - Peter Robinson   1397

Greene, Charlie (Businesswoman; Single Parent)
Death of the Office Witch - Marlys Millhiser   1155

Greene, Charlie (Businesswoman)
Murder at Moot Point - Marlys Millhiser   1156

Greenert, Dub (Detective—Private)
Red Knight - J. Madison Davis   391

Greer, Daniel (Businessman)
Predator's Waltz - Jay Brandon   165

Grenier, Grayson (Businessman; Criminal)
Balboa Firefly - Jack Trolley   1633

Grey, Ana (FBI Agent)
North of Montana - April Smith   1515

Grey, India (Housewife)
A Blood Affair - Jan Roberts   1381

Grey, Lavinia (Religious)
Bury the Bishop - Kate Gallison   564

Griffin, Lew (Detective—Private)
Black Hornet - James Sallis   1421

Griffin, Lew (Detective—Private; Writer)
Moth - James Sallis   1422

Griffo, Simona (Advertising)
The Trouble with Going Home - Camilla T. Crespi   345
The Trouble with Moonlighting - Trella Crespi   346
The Trouble with Too Much Sun - Trella Crespi   347

Grimes (Businessman)
Shoedog - George Pelecanos 1288

Grindal, George (Religious)
The Dean It Was That Died - Barbara Whitehead 1706

Grist, Simeon (Detective—Private)
Everything but the Squeal - Timothy Hallinan 716
Incinerator - Timothy Hallinan 717
Skin Deep - Timothy Hallinan 718

Grootka (Police Officer)
Grootka - Jon A. Jackson 832

Grover, Serena "Renie" (Designer)
A Fit of Tempera - Mary Daheim 375

Grushko, Yevgeni Ivanovitch (Police Officer)
Dead Meat - Philip Kerr 913

Guiu, Lonia (Detective—Private)
Antipodes - Maria-Antonia Oliver 1236

Gunner, Aaron (Detective—Private)
Not Long for This World - Gar Anthony Haywood 762

Gunther, Bernie (Detective—Private)
The Pale Criminal - Philip Kerr 914

Gunther, Joe (Police Officer)
Borderlines - Archer Mayor 1103
Fruits of the Poisonous Tree - Archer Mayor 1104
Scent of Evil - Archer Mayor 1105

Gutierez, Vince (Police Officer)
Children's Games - Janet LaPierre 982

Guzman, Estelle (Police Officer)
Bitter Recoil - Steven F. Havill 757

H

Haagen, Anneke (Businesswoman)
Curly Smoke - Susan Holtzer 803

Haas, Peter (Police Officer)
Death by Degrees - Robin Wilson 1735

Hackabee, Joseph (Murderer)
Stone Shadow - Rex Miller 1154

Hackshaw, Elias "Hack" (Journalist)
The NIMBY Factor - Stephen F. Wilcox 1721
The Painted Lady - Stephen F. Wilcox 1722

Haddix, Edna (Military Personnel)
Bright Shark - Robert Ballard 85

Haddon, Ronnie (Criminal)
Nightmare Point - Carole Berry 128

Haggerty, Forrest (Aged Person; Police Officer)
The Pumpkin-Shell Wife - Susanna Hofmann McShea 1138

Haggerty, Leo (Detective—Private)
A Fistful of Empty - Benjamin M. Schutz 1457
Mexico Is Forever - Benjamin M. Schutz 1458

Hairsteen, Mary Miner "Harry" (Postal Worker)
Wish You Were Here - Rita Mae Brown 182

Hairsteen, Mary Minor "Harry" (Postal Worker)
Murder at Monticello - Rita Mae Brown 180
Rest in Pieces - Rita Mae Brown 181

Halburton-Smythe, Priscilla (Hotel Worker)
Death of a Charming Man - M.C. Beaton 109

Hale, Millie (Actress)
Close-Up on Death - Maureen O'Brien 1213

Hall, Adam (Lawyer)
The Chamber - John Grisham 679

Hall, Frank (Scientist)
Deep Chill - Ian Slater 1513

Hall, Ray (Police Officer)
Viper Quarry - Dean Feldmeyer 522

Hallam, Lucas (Detective—Private; Stuntman)
Dead-Stick - L.J. Washburn 1674
Dog Heavies - L.J. Washburn 1675

Halleck, Jack "Spike" (Handicapped)
Sight Unseen - David Lorne 1046

Halley, Sid (Detective—Private; Handicapped)
Come to Grief - Dick Francis 538

Halliwell, Hal (Director)
Death and the Trumpets of Tuscany - Hazel Wynn Jones 847

Halloran, Meg (Teacher)
Children's Games - Janet LaPierre 982

Halperin, Elizabeth (Businesswoman; Single Parent)
Mommy and the Murder - Nancy Gladstone 600

Hamel, Neil (Lawyer)
The Lies That Bind - Judith Van Gieson 1649
The Other Side of Death - Judith Van Gieson 1650
Raptor - Judith Van Gieson 1651

Hamel, Neil (Lawyer; Activist)
The Wolf Path - Judith Van Gieson 1652

Hamilton, Carl (Spy)
Enemy's Enemy - Jan Guillou 685

Hamilton, David (Detective—Private)
One Cried Murder - David Cooper Wall 1663

Hammer, Mike (Detective—Private)
The Killing Man - Mickey Spillane 1540

Hammett, Dashiell (Writer; Historical Figure)
The Black Mask Murders - William F. Nolan 1207

Hammond, Amanda (Doctor)
Darkness Falls - Joyce Anne Schneider 1453

Hammond, Gary (Police Officer)
Maximum Bob - Elmore Leonard 1006

Hampton, Blanche (Police Officer)
A Pound of Flesh - Trevor Barnes 95

Hanks, Arly (Police Officer)
Madness in Maggody - Joan Hess 777
Miracles in Maggody - Joan Hess 778
Mortal Remains in Maggody - Joan Hess 779
O Little Town of Maggody - Joan Hess 780

Hannaford, Bennis (Writer)
Not a Creature Was Stirring - Jane Haddam 695

Hannibal, Joe (Detective—Private)
The Skintight Shroud - Wayne Dundee 459

Hannibal, Nick (Police Officer)
The Marvell College Murders - Sophie Belfort 119

Hannigan, Dev (Writer)
In the Dark - Carol Brennan 173

Hanrahan, Bill (Police Officer)
Lieberman's Choice - Stuart M. Kaminsky 856
Lieberman's Day - Stuart M. Kaminsky 857
Lieberman's Folly - Stuart M. Kaminsky 858

Hansen, Buck (Police Officer)
A Gift for Murder - M.D. Lake 968

Hansen, Emily "Em" (Scientist)
A Fall in Denver - Sarah Andrews 56

Hansen, Emily "Em" (Oil Industry Worker)
Tensleep - Sarah Andrews 57

Hansen, Nick (Artist)
Follow That Blonde - Joan Smith 1521

Hanson, Marvin (Police Officer)
Act of Love - Joe R. Lansdale 980

Harald, Sigrid (Police Officer)
Past Imperfect - Margaret Maron 1077

Hardare, Vincent (Magician)
The Man Who Walked Through Walls - James Swain 1595

Hardy, Cliff (Detective—Private)
Matrimonial Causes - Peter Corris 327
O'Fear - Peter Corris 328
Wet Graves - Peter Corris 329

Hardy, Dismas (Lawyer; Saloon Keeper/Owner)
Hard Evidence - John T. Lescroart 1009

Hardy, Dismas (Detective—Private; Lawyer)
The Vig - John T. Lescroart 1010

Hardy, Nina (Actress)
Hollywood Requiem - Peter Freeborn 546

Hargreaves, Julie (Police Officer)
The Summons - Peter Lovesey 1050

Harper, Benni (Widow(er); Museum Curator)
Fool's Puzzle - Earlene Fowler 536
Irish Chain - Earlene Fowler 537

Harriman, Frank (Police Officer)
Goodnight, Irene - Jan Burke 198

Harris, Ken (Police Officer)
Exhaustive Enquiries - Betty Rowlands 1408

Harris, Liana (Widow(er))
Kingdom Road - K. Patrick Conner 295

Harrison, Richard (Businessman)
The Becket Factor - Michael David Anthony 60

Harrison, Richard (Aged Person)
Dark Provenance - Michael David Anthony 61

Hartman, Seth (Lawyer)
Southern Cross - Stephen Greenleaf 669

Hartnett, Ray (Police Officer)
The Texas Capitol Murders - Bill Crider 353

Harvey, Maddie (Housewife)
Killer Cinderella - Simon Shaw 1478

Harvey, Mark (Banker)
Killer Cinderella - Simon Shaw 1478

Haskell, Ellie (Housewife)
Femmes Fatal - Dorothy Cannell 214
How to Murder Your Mother-in-Law - Dorothy Cannell 215

Hastings, Frank (Police Officer)
Dead Center - Collin Wilcox 1711
A Death Before Dying - Collin Wilcox 1712
Hire a Hangman - Collin Wilcox 1715
Switchback - Collin Wilcox 1717

Hastings, Stanley (Detective—Private)
Juror - Parnell Hall 714

Hastings, Stanley (Writer)
Strangler - Parnell Hall 715

Haun, Sam (Journalist)
The Late Man - James Preston Girard 592

Haverford, Miles (Lawyer)
The Temple Dogs - Warren Murphy 1188

Havers, Barbara (Police Officer)
Payment in Blood - Elizabeth George 576
Playing for the Ashes - Elizabeth George 577

Hawes, Cotton (Detective—Police)
Vespers - Ed McBain 1107

Hawk (Sidekick)
Double Deuce - Robert B. Parker 1269

Hawkin, Alonzo (Police Officer)
A Grave Talent - Laurie R. King 925
To Play the Fool - Laurie R. King 927

Hawkins, Jack (Writer)
Paint It Black - W.R. Philbrick 1313

Hawksley, Hal (Saloon Keeper/Owner)
The Sculptress - Minette Walters 1671

Hawley, Bill (Undertaker)
Double Plot - Leo Axler 70

Hawley, Bill (Undertaker; Detective—Private)
Grave Matters - Leo Axler 71

Hawthorne, Sam (Journalist)
Natural Enemies - Sara Cameron 209

Hayes, Brooke (Actress; Alcoholic)
The Keeper - Meg O'Brien 1217

Hayes, Jack (Lawyer; Military Personnel)
The Price of Victory - Vincent Green 666

Hayle, Tamara (Detective—Private; Single Parent)
Devil's Gonna Get Him - Valerie Wilson Wesley 1691
When Death Comes Stealing - Valerie Wilson Wesley 1692

Hazard, Amanda (Accountant)
Dead in the Cellar - Connie Fedderson 520

Heenan, Annie (Teenager)
The Masters of the House - Robert Barnard 90

Heenan, Matthew (Teenager)
The Masters of the House - Robert Barnard 90

Heinemann, Kurt (Spy)
The Last Good German - Bill Granger 647

Heller, Nate (Detective—Private)
Blood and Thunder - Max Allan Collins 276
Carnal Hours - Max Allan Collins 277
Murder in the Post-War World - Max Allan Collins 279
Stolen Away - Max Allan Collins 280

Heller, Tom (Writer)
True Crime - Michael Mewshaw 1145

Helmers, Jack (Writer)
A Country of Old Men - Joseph Hansen 727

Helms, Marsha (Doctor)
Way Past Dead - Steven Womack 1755

Helstrum, Christine (Criminal)
Night of Reunion - Michael Allegretto 42

Henderson, Paula (Police Officer)
Murder by Mail - M.D. Lake 969

Henderson, Peter (Computer Expert; Landlord)
Sliver - Ira Levin 1013

Henry, Ben (Detective—Private)
A Dry and Thirsty Ground - Mike Weiss 1688

Henry, Kate (Journalist)
The Dead Pull Hitter - Alison Gordon 612
Night Game - Alison Gordon 613
Safe at Home - Alison Gordon 614
Striking Out - Alison Gordon 615

Henshaw, Susan (Housewife)
All Hallows Evil - Valerie Wolzien 1748
A Good Year for a Corpse - Valerie Wolzien 1749
We Wish You a Merry Murder - Valerie Wolzien 1750

Hickey, Tom (Detective—Private; Musician)
The Angel Gang - Ken Kuhlken 956

Hickey, Tom (Military Personnel; Detective—Private)
The Loud Adios - Ken Kuhlken 957

Hickey, Tom (Detective—Private; Businessman)
The Venus Deal - Ken Kuhlken 958

Hickey, Wendy (Spouse)
The Angel Gang - Ken Kuhlken 956

Hildreth, Jane (Spy)
Cotswold Moles - Michael Spicer 1539

Hill, Jordan (Actor)
No Way Home - Patricia MacDonald 1062

Hill, Judy (Detective—Police)
The Other Woman - Jill McGown 1132

Hill, Maggie (Detective—Private)
Beauty Dies - Melodie Johnson Howe 813

Hill, Maggie (Writer)
The Mother Shadow - Melodie Johnson Howe 814

Hilton, Jenni (Singer)
Murder in Waiting - Robert Richardson 1367

Hine, Tony (Rake)
By Death Possessed - Roger Ormerod 1243

Hitchcock, Martha (Young Woman)
Hot Water - Sally Gunning 686

Hoag, Lulu (Animal)
The Man Who Would Be F. Scott Fitzgerald - David Handler 723
The Woman Who Fell From Grace - David Handler 724

Hoag, Stewart (Writer)
The Man Who Cancelled Himself - David Handler 722
The Man Who Would Be F. Scott Fitzgerald - David Handler 723
The Woman Who Fell From Grace - David Handler 724

Hockaday, Neil (Police Officer)
Drown All the Dogs - Thomas Adcock 23

Hodges, Karen (Criminal)
Skinny Man - James Colbert 273

Hodges, Pat (Housewife)
Savage Justice - Ron Handberg 721

Holden, Michael (Lawyer)
Playing the Dozens - William D. Pease 1286

Holden, Sidney (Criminal)
Elsinore - Jerome Charyn 238

Holland, John (Police Officer)
The Prosecutor - Thomas Chastain 240

Holland, Mark (Musician)
Deadly Crescendo - Paul Myers 1191

Holland, Mark (Businessman; Spy)
Deadly Sonata - Paul Myers 1192

Hollinger, Robert (Detective—Police)
Point Blank - Jayson Livingston 1033

Holloway, Barbara "Bobby" (Lawyer)
Death Qualified: A Mystery of Chaos - Kate Wilhelm 1723

Holmes, Sherlock (Detective—Private)
The Beekeeper's Apprentice - Laurie R. King 924
The Disappearance of Edwin Drood - Peter Rowland 1407
The Glendower Conspiracy - Lloyd Biggle Jr. 131

Holmes, Sherlock (Aged Person; Detective—Private)
A Monstrous Regiment of Women - Laurie R. King 926

Holmes, Sherlock (Detective—Private)
The Seventh Bullet - Daniel D. Victor 1654

Holt, Essington (Art Dealer)
To Catch a Forger - Robert Wallace 1666

Holt, Mitch (Police Officer)
Night Sins - Tami Hoag 794

Holt, Samantha (Veterinarian)
Copy Cat Crimes - Karen Ann Wilson 1733
Eight Dogs Flying - Karen Ann Wilson 1734

Hooper, B.F. (Detective—Private; Veteran)
Saint Louie Blues - Jake Tanner 1601

Hope, Alastair (Archaeologist)
Faith, Hope and Homicide - Jessica Mann 1071

Hope, Alison (Businesswoman)
Hope Against Hope - Susan B. Kelly 896

Hope, Alison (Computer Expert)
Kid's Stuff - Susan B. Kelly 897

Hope, Alison (Businesswoman)
Time of Hope - Susan B. Kelly 898

Hope, Joe (Police Officer)
Storm Front - Virginia Anderson 53

Hope, Malachi (Religious)
Miracles in Maggody - Joan Hess 778

Hope, Matthew (Lawyer)
Three Blind Mice - Ed McBain 1106

Hopkins, Marty (Police Officer)
Gravestone - P.M. Carlson 219

Hopkins, Ray (Police Officer)
Silent Witness - Charles Wilson 1732

Horowitz, Helen (Detective—Private)
The Last Gambit - David Delman 411

Horowitz, Jacob (Police Officer)
The Last Gambit - David Delman 411

Houdini, Harry (Historical Figure; Magician)
Escapade - Walter Satterthwait 1438

House, Duffy (Journalist)
Bleeding Dodger Blue - Crabbe Evers 505
Fear in Fenway - Crabbe Evers 506
Murder in Wrigley Field - Crabbe Evers 507
Tigers Burning - Crabbe Evers 508

Hoving, Sarah (Businesswoman; Beekeeper)
So Shall You Reap - Marilyn Wallace 1665

Howard, Charles (Lawyer)
The Cut Throat - Simon Michael 1149

Howard, Jeri (Detective—Private)
Kindred Crimes - Janet Dawson 397
Nobody's Child - Janet Dawson 398

Howard, Vivien (Widow(er))
A Temporary Ghost - Mickey Friedman 556

Hoyland, Tamara (Archaeologist)
Faith, Hope and Homicide - Jessica Mann 1071

Hubbert, Lil (Aged Person)
Hubbert and Lil: Partners in Crime - Gallagher Gray 654

Hubbert, T.S. (Businessman)
Hubbert and Lil: Partners in Crime - Gallagher Gray 654

Huckins, B.D. (Political Figure)
The Fourth Durango - Ross Thomas 1612

Hudnut, Lyle (Actor)
The Man Who Cancelled Himself - David Handler 722

Character Name Index

Hudson, Jane (Teenager)
To Die Like a Gentleman - Bernard Bastable   103

Hudson, Richard (Landowner)
To Die Like a Gentleman - Bernard Bastable   103

Hudson, Robin (Journalist)
What's a Girl Gotta Do? - Sparkle Hayter   760

Hughes, Josephine "Jo" (Detective—Private; Astrologer)
Blood of an Aries - Linda Mather   1094

Humberstone, Hubert (Undertaker)
Deadly Errand - Christine Green   659

Hunsacker, Dale (Doctor)
A Man to Die For - Eileen Dreyer   448

Hunt, Morgan (Detective—Private)
Deep End - Geoffrey Norman   1210

Hunter, Gordon (Police Officer)
A Day in the Death of Dorothea Cassidy - Ann Cleeves   260

Hunter, Leah (Businesswoman)
File Under: Deceased - Sarah Lacey   962

Huntington, Patricia (Spy)
Cotswold Moles - Michael Spicer   1539

Hurley, Brian (Explorer)
The Ice - Louis Charbonneau   234

Huxleigh, Penelope (Nell) (Companion)
Good Morning, Irene - Carole Nelson Douglas   440

Huxleigh, Penelope (Nell) (Servant)
Good Night, Mr. Holmes - Carole Nelson Douglas   441

Huxleigh, Penelope (Nell) (Companion)
Irene at Large - Carole Nelson Douglas   442

I

Indermill, Bonnie (Businesswoman; Detective—Amateur)
Death of a Dancing Fool - Carole Berry   124

Indermill, Bonnie (Office Worker)
The Death of a Difficult Woman - Carole Berry   125

Indermill, Bonnie (Dancer)
Good Night, Sweet Prince - Carole Berry   126

Indermill, Bonnie (Worker)
Island Girl - Carole Berry   127

Ivory, Kate (Writer)
Death and the Oxford Box - Veronica Stallwood   1557
Oxford Exit - Veronica Stallwood   1559

J

Jackson, Graham (Businessman)
Golden Fleece - Jack Becklund   118

Jackson, Jeff (Detective—Private; Fisherman)
A Beautiful Place to Die - Philip R. Craig   335

Jackson, Jeff (Detective—Private)
A Case of Vineyard Poisoning - Philip R. Craig   336
Cliff Hanger - Philip R. Craig   337

Jackson, Jeff (Detective—Private; Fisherman)
The Double Minded Men - Philip R. Craig   338
Off Season - Philip R. Craig   339
The Woman Who Walked into the Sea - Philip R. Craig   340

Jacob, Matt (Detective—Private)
Still Among the Living - Zachary Klein   938
Two Way Toll - Zachary Klein   939

Jacobs, Calista (Artist)
Dark Swan - Kathryn Lasky Knight   944

Jacobs, Calista (Artist; Widow(er))
Mortal Words - Kathryn Lasky Knight   945

Jacobs, Charley (Child)
Dark Swan - Kathryn Lasky Knight   944
Mortal Words - Kathryn Lasky Knight   945

Jacoby, Miles (Detective—Private; Saloon Keeper/Owner)
Hard Look - Robert J. Randisi   1349

Jacoby, Miles (Detective—Private)
Separate Cases - Robert J. Randisi   1350

Jacovich, Milan (Detective—Private)
The Cleveland Connection - Les Roberts   1383
Deep Shaker - Les Roberts   1384
The Duke of Cleveland - Les Roberts   1385
Full Cleveland - Les Roberts   1386

James, Dewey (Librarian)
Home Sweet Homicide - Kate Morgan   1171
A Slay at the Races - Kate Morgan   1172

James, Gemma (Police Officer)
All Shall Be Well - Deborah Crombie   356
Leave the Grave Green - Deborah Crombie   357

James, Gemma (Police Officer; Single Parent)
A Share in Death - Deborah Crombie   358

James, Jessica "Jessie" (Journalist)
The Daphne Decisions - Meg O'Brien   1214
Eagles Die Too - Meg O'Brien   1215
Hare Today, Gone Tomorrow - Meg O'Brien   1216

James, Ken (Pilot; Spy)
Day of the Cheetah - Dale Brown   179

James, Liz (Administrator; Divorced Person)
Cry for Help - Karen Hanson Stuyck   1586

James, Nora (Student; Linguist)
Night Butterfly - Patricia McFall   1127

Jameson, Cass (Lawyer)
Fresh Kills - Carolyn Wheat   1699

Janeway, Cliff (Store Owner)
Booked to Die - John Dunning   466

Janeway, Cliff (Detective—Private; Businessman)
The Bookman's Wake - John Dunning   467

Jansson, Willa (Lawyer)
Prior Convictions - Lia Matera   1093

Jantarro, J.K.G. (Detective—Private)
Work for a Dead Man - Simon Ritchie   1371

January, Cole (Detective—Private)
Stand-In for Murder - Lynn Bradley   164

Jasen, Jay (Accountant)
Casualty Loss - Jim Weikart   1683

Jasper, Jazz (Businesswoman; Detective—Private)
The Cheetah Chase - Karin McQuillan   1137

Jasper, Kate (Store Owner)
Adjusted to Death - Jaqueline Girdner   593
The Last Resort - Jaqueline Girdner   594
A Stiff Critique - Jaqueline Girdner   595
Tea-Totally Dead - Jaqueline Girdner   596

Jeeter, Jerry (Journalist)
Final Option - Stephen Robinett   1389

Jeffries, Harriet (Photographer)
Murder in a Good Cause - Medora Sale   1417
Murder in Focus - Medora Sale   1418
Pursued by Shadows - Medora Sale   1419
Short Cut to Santa Fe - Medora Sale   1420

Jeffry, Jane (Widow(er); Housewife)
The Class Menagerie - Jill Churchill   244

Jeffry, Jane (Housewife; Widow(er))
A Farewell to Yarns - Jill Churchill   245

Jeffry, Jane (Widow(er); Single Parent)
From Here to Paternity - Jill Churchill   246

Jeffry, Jane (Housewife; Widow(er))
A Quiche Before Dying - Jill Churchill   247

Jensen, Alex (Police Officer)
Murder on the Iditarod Trail - Sue Henry   775

Jerome (Religious)
The Lost Keats - Terence Faherty   515

Joan (Religious; Teacher)
A Vow of Chastity - Veronica Black   136

Joan (Religious)
A Vow of Obedience - Veronica Black   137
A Vow of Sanctity - Veronica Black   138

Johnson, Lisa (Secretary)
Wiseguys in Love - C. Clark Criscuolo   355

Johnson, Rebo (Photojournalist)
Southern Cross - Jim DeBrosse   408

Johnson, Toussaint (Police Officer)
Murder by the Numbers - Max Allan Collins   278

Jones, A.L. (Police Officer)
Knight & Day - Ron Nessen   1201

Jones, Caroline Fremont (Businesswoman)
The Strange Files of Fremont Jones - Dianne Day   400

Jones, Crighton (Librarian)
A Slip of the Tong - Charles A. Goodrum   611

Jones, Edward Porter (Detective—Private)
The Glendower Conspiracy - Lloyd Biggle Jr.   131

Jones, Justyn (Administrator)
The Lynching - Bennie Lee Sinclair   1503

Joplin, Dean (Detective—Private)
U.S.S.A. - David Madsen   1066

Jordan, Berkley (Saloon Keeper/Owner)
Jordon's Showdown - Frank C. Strunk   1583

Jordon, Berkley (Police Officer)
Jordon's Wager - Frank C. Strunk   1584

Jurnet, Benjamin (Detective—Police)
A Very Particular Murder - S.T. Haymon   759

Jury, Richard (Police Officer)
The Old Contemptibles - Martha Grimes   675
The Old Silent - Martha Grimes   676

Justice, Howard (Heir)
Kill the Messenger - Elizabeth Daniels Squire   1546

K

Kane, Thomas (Police Officer)
Unbalanced Acts - Jeff Raines   1344

Kaplin, Anatoli (Spy)
Moving Targets - Sean Flannery   529

Karkinnen, Weather (Doctor)
Winter Prey - John Sandford   1428

Karp, Butch (Lawyer)
Justice Denied - Robert K. Tanenbaum 1599
Reversible Error - Robert K. Tanenbaum 1600

Karpo, Emil (Police Officer)
Rostnikov's Vacation - Stuart M. Kaminsky 861

Karr, Ginny (Student)
Monday's Child Is Dead - James Elward 484

Kauffman, Isaac (Businessman)
Berlin Covenant - Celeste Paul 1278

Kayne, Brian (Detective)
Flowers for the Dead - Ann M. Williams 1728

Keane, Owen (Researcher)
Deadstick - Terence Faherty 513

Keane, Owen (Saloon Keeper/Owner; Student)
Die Dreaming - Terence Faherty 514

Keane, Owen (Student)
The Lost Keats - Terence Faherty 515

Kearny, Dan (Detective—Private)
32 Cadillacs - Joe Gores 616

Kelleher, Bobby (Journalist)
Running Mates - John Feinstein 521

Keller, Jim (Lawyer)
Orphans - Gerald Pearce 1281

Kelley, Clovis (Police Officer)
Bloody Soaps: A Tale of Love and Death in the Afternoon - Jacqueline Babbin 75

Kelling, Emma (Housewife)
The Gladstone Bag - Charlotte MacLeod 1063

Kelling, Sarah (Housewife)
The Gladstone Bag - Charlotte MacLeod 1063

Kelly, Homer (Professor)
The Dante Game - Jane Langton 979

Kelly, Irene (Journalist)
Goodnight, Irene - Jan Burke 198

Kelly, Michael (Police Officer)
Unbalanced Acts - Jeff Raines 1344

Kelly, Nick (Journalist; Writer)
River of Darkness - James Grady 632

Kelly, Virginia (Stock Broker; Lesbian)
In the Game - Nikki Baker 82
The Lavender House Murder - Nikki Baker 83

Kelsey (Detective—Police)
A Violent End - Emma Page 1253

Kemp, Lennox (Lawyer)
A Loose Connection - M.R.D. Meek 1139

Kendall, John (Writer)
Longshot - Dick Francis 540

Kendricks, Lucas (Student; Researcher)
Death Qualified: A Mystery of Chaos - Kate Wilhelm 1723

Kennedy, D.J. (Police Officer)
Ravenmocker - Jean Hager 701

Kent, Charlotte (Editor)
Poison Pen - Mary Kittredge 933

Kenyon, Laurie (Student)
All Around the Town - Mary Higgins Clark 252

Kenyon, Sarah (Lawyer)
All Around the Town - Mary Higgins Clark 252

Kenzie, Patrick (Detective—Private)
A Drink Before the War - Dennis Lehane 1000

Keough, John Michael (Lawyer)
The Immediate Prospect of Being Hanged - Walter Walker 1662

Kern, Karen (Lawyer)
Guilt by Association - Susan R. Sloan 1514

Kestrel, Julian (Gentleman)
A Broken Vessel - Kate Ross 1403
Cut to the Quick - Kate Ross 1404

Kettler, Jane (Administrator; Widow(er))
The Texas Capitol Murders - Bill Crider 353

Kevlehan, Dan (Police Officer)
Murder Once Removed - Kathleen Kunz 959

Khai, Tranh Van (Criminal)
Predator's Waltz - Jay Brandon 165

Kidd (Artist; Computer Expert)
The Empress File - John Camp 210

Kiehl, Felix (Stock Broker; Mentally Ill Person)
Disassociated States - Leonard Simon 1499

Kiet, Bamsan (Police Officer)
Kiet Goes West - Gary Alexander 34
Unfunny Money - Gary Alexander 35

Killebrew, Coley (Detective—Private)
Fire Horse - Bill Shoemaker 1486

Killebrew, Coley (Restauranteur)
Stalking Horse - Bill Shoemaker 1487

Kimi (Animal)
A Bite of Death - Susan Conant 287

Kimura, Patti (Student; Activist)
Kimura - Robert Davis 395

Kincaid, Duncan (Police Officer)
All Shall Be Well - Deborah Crombie 356
Leave the Grave Green - Deborah Crombie 357
A Share in Death - Deborah Crombie 358

Kincaid, Frank (Mercenary)
The Man Who Walked Through Walls - James Swain 1595

Kincaid, Libby (Photojournalist)
Cold Feet - Kerry Tucker 1636
Death Echo - Kerry Tucker 1637
Still Waters - Kerry Tucker 1638

Kincaid, Mike (Journalist)
City of Lies - Peter McCabe 1109

Kincaid, Nancy (Office Worker)
The Animal Hour - Andrew Klavan 935

Kincaid, Paul (Artisan)
Circumstances Unknown - Jonellen Heckler 769

Kincaid, Ryan (Detective—Private)
High Strangeness - Alison Drake 447

King, Darryl (Drug Dealer; Murderer)
Slow Motion Riot - Peter Blauner 144

King, Diana (Businesswoman; Criminal)
Murder Has a Pretty Face - Jennie Melville 1142

King, Willow (Writer; Civil Servant)
Bitter Herbs - Natasha Cooper 307

King, Willow (Writer)
Bloody Roses - Natasha Cooper 308

King, Willow (Writer; Civil Servant)
Rotten Apples - Natasha Cooper 309

Kingston, Palmer (Journalist)
Neon Dancers - Matt Taylor 1608

Kinsella, Kate (Detective—Private; Nurse)
Deadly Admirer - Christine Green 658
Deadly Errand - Christine Green 659

Kinsella, Kate (Nurse; Detective—Private)
Deadly Practice - Christine Green 660

Kinsolving, Sandy (Businessman)
Imperfect Strangers - Stuart Woods 1761

Kirby, Jacqueline (Writer; Librarian)
Naked Once More - Elizabeth Peters 1300

Kirk, Devlin (Detective—Private)
Body Guard - Rex Burns 199
Parts Unknown - Rex Burns 200

Kitchener, Nina (Public Relations)
Pressure Drop - Peter Abrahams 5

Kite, Martin (Police Officer)
Late of This Parish - Marjorie Eccles 469
More Deaths than One - Marjorie Eccles 470

Kitologitak, Matthew "Matteesie" (Police Officer)
Murder in a Cold Climate - Scott Young 1785
The Shaman's Knife - Scott Young 1786

Klebanoff, Yuri (Photojournalist)
The Harbinger Effect - S.K. Wolf 1746

Kleinfeldt, Liz (Lawyer)
Methods of Execution - Frederick D. Huebner 818

Knight, Billy (Police Officer)
Tropical Depression - Jeffry P. Lindsay 1024

Knight, David (Lawyer)
Miami Heat - Jerome Sanford 1433

Knight, Jack (Police Officer)
Murder in a Quiet Place - Tony Caxton 230

Knight, Jerry (Journalist)
Knight & Day - Ron Nessen 1201

Knight, Mickey (Detective—Private; Lesbian)
The Intersection of Law and Desire - J.M. Redmann 1356

Knott, Deborah (Lawyer)
Bootlegger's Daughter - Margaret Maron 1076

Knott, Deborah (Judge)
Shooting at Loons - Margaret Maron 1078

Knowles, Richard (Student; Teenager)
Hide and Seek - Barry Berg 122

Koenig, Paul (Spy)
The Faust Conspiracy - James Baddock 78

Koesler, Robert (Religious)
Chameleon - William X. Kienzle 915
Masquerade - William X. Kienzle 916

Kohl, Tom (Farmer)
The Lion at the Door - Newton Thornburg 1617

Koko (Animal)
The Cat Who Moved a Mountain - Lilian Jackson Braun 167
The Cat Who Talked to Ghosts - Lilian Jackson Braun 168
The Cat Who Went into the Closet - Lilian Jackson Braun 169

Komelecki, Owen (Photographer)
All the Great Pretenders - Deborah Adams 10

Kornon, Alexander (Military Personnel)
Deep Chill - Ian Slater 1513

Kort, Anthony (Terrorist)
Hard Fall - Ridley Pearson 1284

Kost, John (Police Officer)
With Siberia Comes a Chill - Kirk Mitchell 1161

Kovak, Milt (Police Officer)
Dead Moon on the Rise - Susan Rogers Cooper 310
Doctors, Lawyers and Such - Susan Rogers Cooper 311

Character Name Index

Houston in the Rearview Mirror - Susan Rogers Cooper 314
Other People's Houses - Susan Rogers Cooper 316

Kozak, Thea (Businesswoman)
Death in a Funhouse Mirror - Kate Clark Flora 531

Kramer, Jack (Businessman)
Blood Kin - Marjorie Dorner 436

Kramer, James (Police Officer)
Fatal Obsession - D.B. Taylor 1606

Kramer, Tromp (Police Officer)
The Song Dog - James McClure 1114

Kraychik, Stan (Hairdresser; Homosexual)
A Body to Dye For - Grant Michaels 1150
Love You to Death - Grant Michaels 1151

Kruger, Dan (Detective—Private)
Red Winter - Michael Cormany 319

Kruger, Dan (Detective—Private; Musician)
Skin Deep Is Fatal - Michael Cormany 320

Kruse, Kimmey (Entertainer)
Funny as a Dead Comic - Susan Rogers Cooper 312
Funny as a Dead Relative - Susan Rogers Cooper 313

Kuisma, Val (Police Officer)
Grandmother's House - Janet LaPierre 983

Kyle, Jack (Detective—Private)
The Dallas Deception - Richard Abshire 7
Turnaround Jack - Richard Abshire 8

Kynx, Jason (Antiques Dealer)
A Long Time Dead - A.J. Orde 1242

L

Lacey, Jack (Businessman)
Burn Season - John Lantigua 981

Lacey, James (Writer)
Agatha Raisin and the Vicious Vet - M.C. Beaton 108

Lacey, Meg (Detective—Private; Single Parent)
No Forwarding Address - Elisabeth Bowers 161

Ladd, Diana (Widow(er))
Hour of the Hunter - J.A. Jance 843

Lafky, Melissa (Lawyer)
Banjo Boy - Vince Kohler 949

LaFontaine, Prentice (Journalist)
Hard News - Mark T. Sullivan 1590

Lahey, Mark (Police Officer)
The Ransom - Brian Tobin 1622

Laidlaw, Jack (Police Officer)
Strange Loyalties - William McIlvanney 1134

Lake, Barrett (Detective—Private; Teacher)
Interview with Mattie - Shelley Singer 1504
Picture of David - Shelley Singer 1505

Lake, Barrett (Teacher; Detective—Private)
Searching for Sara - Shelley Singer 1506

LaMarche, Andrew (Doctor)
Strawgirl - Abigail Padgett 1252

Lan, Li (Artist)
The Trail to Buddha's Mirror - Don Winslow 1744

Lang, John (Spy)
Thunder - James Grady 633

Langdon, Skip (Police Officer; Detective—Homicide)
The Axeman's Jazz - Julie Smith 1523

Langdon, Skip (Police Officer)
House of Blues - Julie Smith 1525

Langdon, Skip (Police Officer; Detective—Homicide)
Jazz Funeral - Julie Smith 1526
New Orleans Beat - Julie Smith 1527

Langdon, Skip (Police Officer)
New Orleans Mourning - Julie Smith 1528

Langenberg, Paulina (Businesswoman)
Murder at the Spa - Stefanie Matteson 1097

Langley, Ingrid (Spy; Writer)
Rook-Shoot - Margaret Duffy 452
Who Killed Cock Robin? - Margaret Duffy 453

Lansing, Vicki (Journalist)
Rough Justice - Keith Peterson 1309

Lapham, Lydia (Nurse)
No Way Home - Andrew Coburn 267

Larkin, Eldon (Journalist)
Banjo Boy - Vince Kohler 949
Rainy North Woods - Vince Kohler 950
Rising Dog - Vince Kohler 951

Lashley, Mavis (Widow(er))
Death Beneath the Christmas Tree - Robert Nordan 1208
Death on Wheels - Robert Nordan 1209

Lassiter, Aaron (Police Officer)
A Permanent Retirement - John Miles 1153

Lassiter, Jake (Lawyer)
Mortal Sin - Paul Levine 1014
Night Vision - Paul Levine 1015
To Speak for the Dead - Paul Levine 1016

Latterly, Hester (Nurse)
Cain His Brother - Anne Perry 1292
A Dangerous Mourning - Anne Perry 1293

Lau, John (Police Officer)
Make No Bones - Aaron Elkins 478

Laurance, Annie (Businesswoman)
A Little Class on Murder - Carolyn G. Hart 743

Laurano, Lauren (Detective—Private; Lesbian)
Everything You Have Is Mine - Sandra Scoppettone 1460
I'll Be Leaving You Always - Sandra Scoppettone 1461
My Sweet Untraceable You - Sandra Scoppettone 1462

Laurie, Vincent (Doctor)
Deadly Beloved - Alanna Knight 942
Killing Cousins - Alanna Knight 943

Lautrec, Jack (Lawyer)
Lautrec - Norman Zollinger 1794

Lautrec, Martine (Lawyer)
Lautrec - Norman Zollinger 1794

Lawford, Tom (Spy)
Pillars of Fire - Steve Shagan 1473

Lawless, Jane (Restaurateur; Lesbian)
Hallowed Murder - Ellen Hart 745
Vital Lies - Ellen Hart 746

Lawrence, Al (FBI Agent)
Dead Easy - Arthur F. Nehrbass 1199

Lawson, Loretta (Professor)
Don't Leave Me This Way - Joan Smith 1520
What Men Say - Joan Smith 1522

Lawton, Dave (Detective—Homicide)
Dead Ahead - Ruby Horansky 804

Lawton, Dave (Police Officer; Detective—Homicide)
Dead Center - Ruby Horansky 805

Lazarus, Rina (Widow(er))
Day of Atonement - Faye Kellerman 878

Lazarus, Rina (Spouse)
False Prophet - Faye Kellerman 879
Justice - Faye Kellerman 881

Lazarus, Rina (Widow(er))
Milk and Honey - Faye Kellerman 882

Lazarus, Rina (Spouse)
Sanctuary - Faye Kellerman 884

Lazzeri, Paul (Recluse)
Shadowchase - Martin Blank 143

Leaphorn, Joe (Police Officer; Indian)
Sacred Clowns - Tony Hillerman 792
Talking God - Tony Hillerman 793

Ledbetter, Romulus (Streetperson)
The Caveman's Valentine - George Dawes Green 662

Lee, Amber (Economist)
Whisper the Guns - Edward Cline 261

Lee, Anna (Detective—Private)
Backhand - Liza Cody 269

Leeds, Cornelius (Detective—Private)
One Kiss Led to Another - Harris Dulaney 454

Legendre, J.J. (Detective—Private)
The Neon Smile - Dick Lochte 1039

Leidl, Constance (Detective—Private; Psychologist)
Seven Kinds of Death - Kate Wilhelm 1725

Leigh, Petra (Student)
The Ransom of Black Stealth One - Dean Ing 825

Leigh, Rosalind (Journalist)
The Sculptress - Minette Walters 1671

Lemieux, Andre (Police Officer)
Death in a Funhouse Mirror - Kate Clark Flora 531

Leskova, Katya (Linguist)
The Talinin Madonna - Douglas Skeggs 1508

Letessier, Vinnie (Businessman)
Noble Rot - Will Harriss 739

LeVender, Catherine (Student)
Death Comes as Epiphany - Sharan Newman 1203

Levinson, Karen (Police Officer; Detective—Homicide)
Skins - Catherine O'Connell 1222

Levity, Thomas More (Teacher)
The Lynching - Bennie Lee Sinclair 1503

Lewis, Dowdy Jr. (Businessman; Veteran)
A Gypsy Good Time - Gustav Hasford 755

Li, Agatha (Police Officer)
Free - Todd Komarnicki 952

Lieberman, Abe (Police Officer)
Lieberman's Choice - Stuart M. Kaminsky 856

Lieberman, Abe (Police Officer; Detective—Homicide)
Lieberman's Day - Stuart M. Kaminsky 857

Lieberman, Abe (Police Officer)
Lieberman's Folly - Stuart M. Kaminsky 858

Lightstone, Henry (Police Officer; Government Official)
Wildfire - Kenneth W. Goddard 605

Lindbergh, Charles (Historical Figure; Pilot)
Stolen Away - Max Allan Collins 280

Lindsay, Hobart (Insurance Investigator)
The Classic Car Killer - Richard A. Lupoff 1054
The Comic Book Killer - Richard A. Lupoff 1055

Lindsey, Sass (Singer)
Final Tour - Jonellen Heckler 770

Lineham, Michael (Police Officer)
Dead by Morning - Dorothy Simpson 1502

Lingemann, Jack (Police Officer)
And Soon I'll Come to Kill You - Susan Kelly 893
Until Proven Innocent - Susan Kelly 895

Lipp, Seymour (Lawyer)
And Baby Makes None - Stephen Lewis 1022
The Monkey Rope - Stephen Lewis 1023

Lisle, Darina (Cook; Caterer)
A Deepe Coffyn - Janet Laurence 988

Lisle, Darina (Caterer)
Hotel Morgue - Janet Laurence 989

Lisle, Darina (Writer; Caterer)
Recipe for Death - Janet Laurence 990

Lispenard, Drew (Businessman)
A Killing in Venture Capital - Margaret Logan 1040

Littlejohn, Eldon (Religious)
Baptism for Murder - Jan Maxwell 1101

Livsey, Horace (Professor)
Monday's Child Is Dead - James Elward 484

Llewellyn, Dafyd (Police Officer)
Dead Before Morning - Geraldine Evans 504

Lloyd (Detective—Police)
The Other Woman - Jill McGown 1132

Lockwood, Taylor (Paraprofessional; Musician)
Mistress of Justice - Jeffrey Wilds Deaver 405

Logan, Whitney (Lawyer)
Dogtown - Mercedes Lambert 972

Lohmann, Ernst (Refugee)
Death Squad London - Jack Gerson 579

Lomax, Jacob (Detective—Private)
Blood Relative - Michael Allegretto 39
The Dead of Winter - Michael Allegretto 40
Grave Doubt - Michael Allegretto 41

London, Lavina (Actress)
Grave Undertaking - James McCahery 1112

Long, Carol (Journalist)
Strike - L.L. Enger 492

Long, Huey (Historical Figure)
Blood and Thunder - Max Allan Collins 276

Long, Rita (Artist)
Hardscape - Justin Scott 1463

Loomis, L.J. (Police Officer)
The Late Man - James Preston Girard 592

Lopez, Rebecca (Smuggler)
The Quality of Mercy - Faye Kellerman 883

Lord, Emma (Journalist; Single Parent)
The Alpine Advocate - Mary Daheim 370

Lord, Emma (Journalist)
The Alpine Christmas - Mary Daheim 371
The Alpine Decoy - Mary Daheim 372
The Alpine Fury - Mary Daheim 373

Loudermilk, Dottie (Aged Person)
Bad News Travels Fast - Gar Anthony Haywood 761

Loudermilk, Joe (Aged Person)
Bad News Travels Fast - Gar Anthony Haywood 761

Louis, Ben (Principal)
Dead Easy - E.S. Russell 1415

Louise (Royalty; Administrator)
Skeleton-in-Waiting - Peter Dickinson 419

Love, Jason (Doctor)
Frozen Assets - James Leasor 996

Love, Reggie (Lawyer)
The Client - John Grisham 680

Lovejoy (Antiques Dealer)
The Great California Game - Jonathan Gash 570
The Lies of Fair Ladies - Jonathan Gash 571
The Sin Within Her Smile - Jonathan Gash 572

Lovell, Francis (Nobleman)
The Fate of Princes - P.C. Doherty 424

Lowe, Philipa (Businesswoman)
Hung in the Balance - Roger Ormerod 1244

Lowell, Tony M.C. (Detective—Private; Photojournalist)
Eye of the Gator - E.C. Ayres 72

Lowell, Tony M.C. (Detective—Private; Photographer)
Hour of the Manatee - E.C. Ayres 73

Lowry, Gideon (Detective—Private; Musician)
Killing Me Softly - John Leslie 1012

Lubick, Caroline "Carrie" (Police Officer)
Night of the Cat - James Schermerhorn 1452

LuEllen (Criminal)
The Empress File - John Camp 210

Lujack, Jimmy (Detective—Private)
The Book of Numbers - David Thoreau 1616

Lundgren, Kate (Adoptee)
Blood Kin - Marjorie Dorner 436

Lundquist, Fred (Police Officer)
Buried in Quilts - Sara Hoskinson Frommer 559

Lyman, Nigel (Police Officer)
Gospel Truths - J.G. Sandom 1429

Lynch, Jack (Public Relations)
Murphy's Fault - Steven Womack 1752

Lynch, Jack (Detective—Private)
The Software Bomb - Steven Womack 1753

Lynley, Thomas (Police Officer)
Missing Joseph - Elizabeth George 575

Lynley, Thomas (Detective—Police)
Payment in Blood - Elizabeth George 576

Lynley, Thomas (Police Officer)
Playing for the Ashes - Elizabeth George 577
A Suitable Vengeance - Elizabeth George 578

Lynx, Jason (Antiques Dealer)
Death and the Dogwalker - A.J. Orde 1240
A Little Neighborhood Murder - A.J. Orde 1241

M

MacAlister, Marti (Police Officer; Widow(er))
Dead Time - Eleanor Taylor Bland 141

MacAlister, Marti (Police Officer)
Slow Burn - Eleanor Taylor Bland 142

MacBeth, Hamish (Police Officer)
Death of a Charming Man - M.C. Beaton 109
Death of a Hussy - M.C. Beaton 110
Death of a Nag - M.C. Beaton 111

Macbeth, Hamish (Police Officer)
Death of a Perfect Wife - M.C. Beaton 112
Death of a Traveling Man - M.C. Beaton 113

MacDonald, Devon (Detective—Private)
The Silver Scapel - Nancy Baker Jacobs 837
The Turquoise Tattoo - Nancy Baker Jacobs 838

MacFarland, Mac (Journalist)
Death Below Deck - Douglas Kiker 922

MacGowen, Maggie (Journalist; Filmmaker)
Midnight Baby - Wendy Hornsby 808

MacGowen, Maggie (Filmmaker; Single Parent)
Telling Lies - Wendy Hornsby 809

MacIntire, Carlson "Mac" (Veterinarian; Widow(er))
The Lion's Share - Kelly A. Tate 1605

MacKenzie, C.K. (Police Officer)
I'd Rather Be in Philadelphia - Gillian Roberts 1378
Philly Stakes - Gillian Roberts 1379
With Friends Like These - Gillian Roberts 1380

MacKenzie, Christabel (Student; Lesbian)
Death Wore a Diadem - Iona McGregor 1133

MacKenzie, Ian (Police Officer)
Night of the Cat - James Schermerhorn 1452

Maclean, Philip (Military Personnel)
A Time Without Shadows - Ted Allbeury 38

MacLeish, Cooper (Taxi Driver)
Get What's Coming - Sam Reaves 1354

MacLeish, Cooper (Veteran; Taxi Driver)
A Long Cold Fall - Sam Reaves 1355

MacNulty, Ray (Police Officer)
Golden Fleece - Jack Becklund 118

MacPherson, Bill (Lawyer)
MacPherson's Lament - Sharyn McCrumb 1117

MacPherson, Elizabeth (Anthropologist)
MacPherson's Lament - Sharyn McCrumb 1117
Missing Susan - Sharyn McCrumb 1118
The Windsor Knot - Sharyn McCrumb 1120

Macrae, George (Police Officer)
Thieftaker - Alan Scholefield 1454

Maddox, Kate (Police Officer)
Model Murder - Erica Quest 1338

Madieras, Zee (Nurse)
A Beautiful Place to Die - Philip R. Craig 335
A Case of Vineyard Poisoning - Philip R. Craig 336
Cliff Hanger - Philip R. Craig 337
The Double Minded Men - Philip R. Craig 338
Off Season - Philip R. Craig 339

Madriani, Paul (Lawyer)
Compelling Evidence - Steve Martini 1090

Magaracz, Nick (Detective—Private)
Jersey Monkey - Kate Gallison 565

Magill, Margo (Social Worker)
Wild Again - Kathrin King Segal 1471

Magnum, Cuddy (Police Officer)
Time's Witness - Michael Malone 1070

Mahoney, Elvis (Criminal; Convict)
Flamingos - Marc Savage 1444

Mahoney, Payne (Businessman)
Miami Purity - Vicki Hendricks 773

Mahoney, Wallace (Spy)
Crossed Swords - Sean Flannery 528

Mal (Criminal)
An Hour to Kill - Edward Wellen 1690

Mallory, Dix (Professor)
With an Extreme Burning - Bill Pronzini 1331

Mallory, Kathleen (Police Officer)
Mallory's Oracle - Carol O'Connell 1221

Mallory, Stuart (Detective—Private)
Close Softly the Doors - Ronald Clair Roat 1373
A Still and Icy Silence - Ronald Clair Roat 1374

Mallory, Wanda (Detective—Private)
Prime Time for Murder - Valerie Frankel 542

Malloy, Claire (Businesswoman)
A Diet to Die For - Joan Hess 776
Roll Over and Play Dead - Joan Hess 781

Malloy, Laura (Journalist)
Still Explosion - Mary Logue 1041

Malloy, Mack (Lawyer; Alcoholic)
Pleading Guilty - Scott Turow 1640

Malloy, Roxie (Servant)
Femmes Fatal - Dorothy Cannell 214
How to Murder Your Mother-in-Law - Dorothy Cannell 215

Malone, Scobie (Detective—Police)
Babylon South - Jon Cleary 255

Malone, Scobie (Police Officer)
Murder Song - Jon Cleary 256

Malone, Wilson (Professor; Friend)
Dead in the Water - W.J. Chaput 233

Malory, Sheila (Writer; Widow(er))
The Cruellest Month - Hazel Holt 800

Malory, Sheila (Writer)
Mrs. Malory and the Festival Murders - Hazel Holt 801

Malory, Sheila (Widow(er))
Mrs. Malory Investigates - Hazel Holt 802

Maltravers, Augustus (Writer)
The Book of the Dead - Robert Richardson 1365
The Dying of the Light - Robert Richardson 1366

Maltravers, Augustus (Writer; Journalist)
Murder in Waiting - Robert Richardson 1367

Manion, Terry (Detective—Private)
Blue Bayou - Dick Lochte 1038
The Neon Smile - Dick Lochte 1039

Mann, Jack (Police Officer)
Hell Bent - Ken Gross 684

Mannion, Billy (Criminal; Terrorist)
19th Precinct - Christopher Newman 1202

Manterola, Pioquinto (Journalist)
The Shadow of the Shadow - Paco Ignacio Taibo II 1598

Manwaring, Kevin (Television)
Barking Dogs - R.R. Irvine 827

March, Edie (Criminal)
Stormy Weather - Carl Hiaasen 784

Marcus, Griffen (Journalist)
Out of the Darkness - Susan Kelly 894

Marino, Pete (Police Officer)
All That Remains - Patricia D. Cornwell 321
The Body Farm - Patricia D. Cornwell 322
Cruel and Unusual - Patricia D. Cornwell 324

Markby, Alan (Police Officer)
Cold in the Earth - Ann Granger 642
A Fine Place for Death - Ann Granger 643
Murder Among Us - Ann Granger 644
A Season for Murder - Ann Granger 645

Markem, Julia (Teacher)
Love Lies - Fern Kupfer 960

Marklake, Robert (Artist)
Not as Far as Velma - Nicholas Freeling 548

Marklin, Peter (Antiques Dealer)
Boxed In - Neville Steed 1564
Clockwork - Neville Steed 1565
Wind-Up - Neville Steed 1566

Marlow, Felicity (Actress)
Three-Core Lead - Clare Curzon 368

Marlowe, Philip (Detective—Private)
Perchance to Dream - Robert B. Parker 1270

Marsala, Cat (Journalist)
Hard Tack - Barbara D'Amato 382
Hard Women - Barbara D'Amato 383
Hardball - Barbara D'Amato 384

Marsh, Benny (Criminal)
Cons - Timothy Watts 1677

Marsh, Clio (Doctor)
The Going Down of the Sun - Jo Bannister 87

Marsh, Harry (Police Officer)
The Going Down of the Sun - Jo Bannister 87

Marston, Paul (Detective—Private)
False Profit - Robert Eversz 511

Martin, Chris (Journalist)
A Second Shot in the Dark - Annette Roome 1399

Martin, Dorothy (Widow(er); Aged Person)
The Body in the Transept - Jeanne M. Dams 385

Martin, Frankie (Journalist)
The Man with My Name - Paul Engleman 494

Martin, Leilani (Police Officer)
Singapore Transfer - Wayne Warga 1673

Martin, Tricia (Sports Figure)
Dead Fix - Michael Geller 573

Martindale, Peter (Art Dealer)
Imperfect Strangers - Stuart Woods 1761

Martinelli, Kate (Police Officer; Lesbian)
A Grave Talent - Laurie R. King 925
To Play the Fool - Laurie R. King 927

Marx, Albie (Businessman)
Nice Guys Finish Dead - David Debin 406

Mary Helen (Religious)
Death Goes on Retreat - Sister Carol Anne O'Marie 1237
Murder in Ordinary Time - Sister Carol Anne O'Marie 1238
Murder Makes a Pilgrimage - Sister Carol Anne O'Marie 1239

Mason, Perry (Lawyer)
Perry Mason in The Case of Too Many Murders - Thomas Chastain 239

Mason, Tom (Teacher; Homosexual)
The Only Good Priest - Mark Richard Zubro 1795
Why Isn't Becky Twitchell Dead? - Mark Richard Zubro 1797

Matthews, Daphne (Psychologist)
The Angel Maker - Ridley Pearson 1282

Mattias, N.H. (Businessman)
Pressure Drop - Peter Abrahams 5

Maury (Animal)
The Maltese Puppy - Melissa Cleary 258

Mavity, H.J. (Artist)
Even the Butler Was Poor - Ron Goulart 628
Now He Thinks He's Dead - Ron Goulart 629

Maxwell, Georgia Lee (Writer; Journalist)
A Temporary Ghost - Mickey Friedman 556

Maxwell, Lauren (Naturalist)
Murder Most Grizzly - Elizabeth Quinn 1340

Maxwell, Lauren (Police Officer; Naturalist)
A Wolf in Death's Clothing - Elizabeth Quinn 1341

Maybridge, Tom (Police Officer)
The Fifth Rapunzel - B.M. Gill 586

Mayo, Gil (Police Officer)
Late of This Parish - Marjorie Eccles 469
More Deaths than One - Marjorie Eccles 470

McAllister, Beau (Police Officer)
Lizardskin - Carsten Stroud 1582

McCarthy, Gail (Veterinarian)
Cutter - Laura Crum 362

McCarthy, Gideon (Journalist)
Hard News - Mark T. Sullivan 1590

McCauley, Maureen (Journalist)
Kiss Them Goodbye - Joseph Eastburn 468

McCauley, Quint (Security Officer)
Murder in Store - D.C. Brod 178

McCleet, Adam (Artist; Veteran)
Mortal Remains - Rick Hanson 728

McClintock, Shirley (Rancher)
Dead in the Scrub - B.J. Oliphant 1232
Death and the Delinquent - B.J. Oliphant 1233

McClintock, Shirley (Rancher; Innkeeper)
Death Served Up Cold - B.J. Oliphant 1234

McClintock, Shirley (Rancher)
The Unexpected Corpse - B.J. Oliphant 1235

McCone, Sharon (Detective—Private)
The Shape of Dread - Marcia Muller 1181
Till The Butchers Cut Him Down - Marcia Muller 1182
Trophies and Dead Things - Marcia Muller 1183
Where Echoes Live - Marcia Muller 1184
A Wild and Lonely Place - Marcia Muller 1185

McCoo, Harold (Police Officer)
Hardball - Barbara D'Amato 384

McCorkle, Cyril "Mac" (Businessman)
Twilight at Mac's Place - Ross Thomas 1613

McCormick, Thomas (Police Officer)
Hammurabi's Code - Charles Kenney 909

McDonnell, Jean (Doctor)
Dead Moon on the Rise - Susan Rogers Cooper 310

McDonough, Casey (Nurse)
A Man to Die For - Eileen Dreyer 448

McDuffy, Gwen (Single Mother)
Family Album - Susan Oleksiw 1230

McFarland, Fowler (Professor; Writer)
Sweet Death - Bill Waggoner 1657

McGarvey, Russ (Detective—Private)
The Last Surprise - William Moore 1169

McGee, Mickey (Criminal)
The Cutting Hours - Julia Grice 673

McGill, Susannah (Student)
The Scarred Man - Keith Peterson 1310

McGowan, Michael (Police Officer)
A Tail of Two Murders - Melissa Cleary 259

McGowan, Tom (Police Officer)
Murder in Scorpio - Martha C. Lawrence 993

McGrail, Nuala (Student; Entertainer)
Irish Gold - Andrew M. Greeley 657

McGrogan, Annie (Actress)
Alibi for an Actress - Gillian B. Farrell 516

McGrogan, Annie (Detective—Private; Actress)
Murder and a Muse - Gillian B. Farrell 517

McGuire, Joe (Police Officer)
And Leave Her Lay Dying - John Lawrence Reynolds 1362
Whisper Death - John Lawrence Reynolds 1363

McGuire, Madison (Spy; Lesbian)
A Singular Spy - Amanda Kyle Williams 1727

McGuire, Maureen (Journalist)
Running Mates - John Feinstein 521

McIlvaine, Lewis "Sport" (Criminal)
Don't Say a Word - Keith Peterson 1308
Don't Say a Word - Andrew Klavan 937

McIntyre, Bill (Judge)
Town on Trial - William Harrington 730

McIntyre, Marie (Young Woman)
Shadow Queen - Tony Gibbs 583

McIntyre, Martin (Police Officer)
Desperate Remedy - Mary Kittredge 931

McIntyre, Michael (Police Officer)
Walking Dead Man - Mary Kittredge 934

McIntyre, Urbino (Writer)
Death in a Serene City - Edward Sklepowich 1510

McKay, Jenny (Journalist)
South Street Confidential - Dick Belsky 120

McKenna, Brian (Police Officer; Detective)
Detective First Grade - Don Mahoney 1067

McKenna, Patience (Writer)
Once and Always Murder - Orania Papazoglou 1263

McKenna, Vincent (Computer Expert; Criminal)
Moth to the Flame - Kathleen Dougherty 437

McKenzie, Abby (Businesswoman; Artist)
Murder by Tarot - Al Guthrie 693

McKenzie, Alex (Doctor)
The Bridled Groom - J.S. Borthwick 154

McKenzie, Cramer (Art Dealer)
First and Ten - Douglas Anderson 50

McKenzie, Mac (Detective—Private)
Murder by Tarot - Al Guthrie 693

McLanahan, Patrick (Pilot)
Day of the Cheetah - Dale Brown 179

McLaughlin, Teresa (Student—High School)
Justice - Faye Kellerman 881

McLeish, John (Police Officer)
Death Among the Dons - Janet Neel 1196
Death of a Partner - Janet Neel 1197

McLoughlin, Andy (Police Officer)
The Ice House - Minette Walters 1669

McMonigle, Judith (Innkeeper)
Bantam of the Opera - Mary Daheim 374
A Fit of Tempera - Mary Daheim 375
Holy Terrors - Mary Daheim 376
Murder, My Suite - Mary Daheim 377

McMorran, Frank (Detective)
Nobody's Fool - Marten Claridge 249

McMorrow, Jack (Journalist)
Deadline - Gerry Boyle 163

McNeely, Kathy (Scientist)
The Ice - Louis Charbonneau 234

McPhee, Pete (Police Officer)
Carolina Gold - Douglas McBriarty 1108

McQuaid, Mike (Teacher)
Hangman's Root - Susan Wittig Albert 32

McWhinny, Tish (Artist)
The Cashmere Kid - B. Comfort 284

McWhinny, Tish (Artist; Aged Person)
Elusive Quarry - B. Comfort 285

McWhinny, Tish (Artist)
Grave Consequences - B. Comfort 286

McWilliams, Caroline (Detective—Private)
Separate Cases - Robert J. Randisi 1350

Means, Roland (Police Officer; Indian)
A Good Day to Die - Stephen Solomita 1534

Meiklejohn, Charlie (Detective—Private)
Seven Kinds of Death - Kate Wilhelm 1725

Meltzer, Fran (Teacher)
Love Lies - Fern Kupfer 960

Melville, Susan (Criminal; Artist)
Miss Melville Rides a Tiger - Evelyn E. Smith 1518

Memphis, Nick (FBI Agent)
Point of Impact - Stephen Hunter 822

Mendoza, Mariana (Teenager)
The Kingsbridge Plot - Maan Meyers 1148

Meren (Nobleman)
Murder in the Place of Anubis - Lynda S. Robinson 1390

Merriwether, Sid (Journalist)
Corruption - Andrew Klavan 936

Messenger, Jim (Accountant)
Blue Lonesome - Bill Pronzini 1325

Metcalf, Pamela (Doctor; Writer)
Night Vision - Paul Levine 1015

Metellus the Younger, Decius Caecilius (Government Official)
SPQR - John Maddox Roberts 1382

Michaels, Laura (Businesswoman; Single Parent)
A Permanent Retirement - John Miles 1153

Michaelson, Richard (Diplomat)
Faithfully Executed - Michael Bowen 159

Middleton-Brown, David (Lawyer)
A Drink of Deadly Wine - Kate Charles 235

Midnight Louie (Animal; Detective—Private)
Cat on a Blue Monday - Carole Nelson Douglas 438
Catnap - Carole Nelson Douglas 439
Pussyfoot - Carole Nelson Douglas 443

Miles, Robert (Detective—Private)
False Profits - David Everson 509
Suicide Squeeze - David Everson 510

Miller, Doc (Criminal)
King of the Corner - Loren D. Estleman 497

Miller, Kassia (Lawyer)
Reasonable Doubt - Philip Friedman 558

Miller, Myrtle "Pix" Rowe (Housewife)
The Body in the Basement - Katherine Hall Page 1254

Miller, Peter (Police Officer; Detective—Homicide)
Beat Up a Cookie - Denise Dietz 422
Throw Darts at a Cheesecake - Denise Dietz 423

Millhone, Kinsey (Detective—Private)
F Is for Fugitive - Sue Grafton 634
G Is for Gumshoe - Sue Grafton 635
H Is for Homicide - Sue Grafton 636
I Is for Innocent - Sue Grafton 637
K Is for Killer - Sue Grafton 638
L Is for Lawless - Sue Grafton 639

Minor, Constantine (Journalist)
Whiskey River - Loren D. Estleman 501

Mitchell, Cassandra (Teacher)
Mother Love - L.R. Wright 1774

Mitchell, Cassandra (Librarian)
A Touch of Panic - L.R. Wright 1776

Mitchell, Meredith (Diplomat)
Cold in the Earth - Ann Granger 642
A Fine Place for Death - Ann Granger 643
Murder Among Us - Ann Granger 644
A Season for Murder - Ann Granger 645

Mitchell, Michelle "Mitch" (Worker; Single Parent)
Icewater Mansions - Douglas Allyn 48

Miyomoto, Hatsue (Spouse)
Snow Falling on Cedars - David Guterson 692

Mondragon, Rita (Businesswoman; Handicapped)
At Ease with the Dead - Walter Satterthwait 1437

Mondragon, Rita (Businesswoman)
A Flower in the Desert - Walter Satterthwait 1439

Mondragon, Rita (Detective—Private)
The Hanged Man - Walter Satterthwait 1440

Monk, William (Detective—Private)
Cain His Brother - Anne Perry 1292

Monk, William (Police Officer)
A Dangerous Mourning - Anne Perry 1293

Monk, William (Detective—Private)
A Sudden, Fearful Death - Anne Perry 1296

Monroe, Andy (Police Officer; Detective—Homicide)
Safe at Home - Alison Gordon 614

Monroe, Doyle (Businessman; Criminal)
The Deer Killers - Gunnard Landers 973

Monroe, Jessica (Detective—Private)
Deadly Stakes - H. Fred Wiser 1745

Monroe, Louis (Police Officer)
Down by the Sea - Bill Kent 910

Montana, Archer Rush (Doctor)
Letting Blood - Richard Platt 1321

Montana, Molly (Doctor)
Letting Blood - Richard Platt 1321

Montana, Tucker (Spy)
Tucker's Last Stand - William F. Buckley Jr. 188

Montgomery, Laurie (Doctor)
Blindsight - Robin Cook 302

Montgomery, Richard (Police Officer)
Nurse Dawes Is Dead - Stella Shepherd 1479
Thinner than Blood - Stella Shepherd 1480

Moodrow, Stanley (Detective—Private)
Bad to the Bone - Stephen Solomita 1532

Moodrow, Stanley (Detective—Police)
Force of Nature - Stephen Solomita 1533
A Piece of the Action - Stephen Solomita 1535

Moon, Charlie (Lawyer; Indian)
Poison Fruit - Chelsea Quinn Yarbro 1781

Moony, Phil (Detective—Private)
The Man with My Name - Paul Engleman 494

Morelli, Joe (Police Officer)
One for the Money - Janet Evanovich 503

Morgan, Cassandra (Journalist)
Silent Night - Gary Amo 49

Morgan, Jack (Police Officer)
A Cold-Blooded Business - Dana Stabenow 1550
A Cold Day for Murder - Dana Stabenow 1549
Dead in the Water - Dana Stabenow 1551

Morgan, James (Police Officer)
No Way Home - Andrew Coburn 267
Voices in the Dark - Andrew Coburn 268

Morgan, Mordecai "Maudie" (Criminal)
The Bag Man - Peter Lacey 961

Morrissey, John (Police Officer)
In Stoney Places - Kay Mitchell 1159
A Lively Form of Death - Kay Mitchell 1160

Morrone, Rita (Lawyer)
Running From the Law - Lisa Scottoline 1465

Morse (Police Officer)
The Wench Is Dead - Colin Dexter 418

Morton, James (Police Officer)
Patently Murder - Ray Harrison 737
Tincture of Death - Ray Harrison 738

Morton, Lana (Teacher)
Follow That Blonde - Joan Smith 1521

Mothersill, Sylvia (Stripper)
Death of a Fantasy Life - T.G. Gilpin 590

Motley, James Leo (Criminal)
A Ticket to the Boneyard - Lawrence Block 149

Mott, Angus (Police Officer)
Cat's Cradle - Clare Curzon 366
Death Prone - Clare Curzon 367

Mrs. Murphy (Animal)
Murder at Monticello - Rita Mae Brown 180
Rest in Pieces - Rita Mae Brown 181
Wish You Were Here - Rita Mae Brown 182

Mudd, Grover (Journalist)
Saint Mudd - Steve Thayer 1609

Muffin, Charlie (Spy)
The Run Around - Brian Freemantle 550

Mulcahaney, Norah (Detective—Homicide)
Lockout - Lillian O'Donnell 1224
A Private Crime - Lillian O'Donnell 1225
Pushover - Lillian O'Donnell 1226

Mulcay, Kate (Journalist; Widow(er))
Ah, Sweet Mystery - Celestine Sibley 1495
Dire Happenings at Scratch Ankle - Celestine Sibley 1496

Mulcay, Kate (Journalist)
A Plague of Kinfolks - Celestine Sibley 1497

Mulcay, Kate (Journalist; Widow(er))
Straight as an Arrow - Celestine Sibley 1498

Muldoon, Ned (Police Officer)
Faces in the Crowd - William Marshall 1079
The New York Detective - William Marshall 1080

Mulheisen, "Fang" (Police Officer)
Grootka - Jon A. Jackson 832
Hit on the House - Jon A. Jackson 833

Muller, Kurt (Police Officer)
Into Thin Air - Thomas Zigal 1788

Munro, Andy (Detective—Homicide)
Striking Out - Alison Gordon 615

Murdock, Matt (Detective—Private; Veteran)
Merry Christmas, Murdock - Robert J. Ray 1352
Murdock Cracks Ice - Robert J. Ray 1353

Murphy, Gordon (Teacher)
A Touch of Panic - L.R. Wright 1776

Murphy, Jake (Police Officer)
A Very Proper Death - Alex Juniper 850

Murphy, Rex (Musician; Boyfriend)
The Society Ball Murders - Jack Albin Anderson 51

Murray, Kate (Journalist)
Strangers in the Night - Peg Tyre 1641

Murray, Russell (Editor; Alcoholic)
Pink Vodka Blues - Neal Barrett Jr. 98

Murtagh, Colum (Military Personnel)
The Eye of God - C.L. Grace 631

Muryan, Peggy (Singer)
If Ever I Return, Pretty Peggy-O - Sharyn McCrumb 1116

Myles, Jordan (Sports Figure; Doctor)
The Total Zone - Martina Navratilova 1195

N

Napier, "Boss" (Police Officer)
Dying Voices - Bill Crider 351

Napier, John (Art Historian)
The Estuary Pilgrim - Douglas Skeggs 1507

Nasson, Carl (Serial Killer)
Whisper.He Might Hear You - William Appel 62

Nebraska (Detective—Private)
The Naked Eye - William J. Reynolds 1364

Nello, Tony (Criminal)
King of the Hustlers - Eugene Izzi 831

Nemo, Adam (Servant)
Frobisher's Savage - Leonard Tourney 1624

Nesbitt, Alan (Police Officer; Widow(er))
The Body in the Transept - Jeanne M. Dams 385

Ness, Eliot (FBI Agent; Historical Figure)
Murder by the Numbers - Max Allan Collins 278

Ness, Lydia (Lawyer; Single Parent)
Undue Influence - Miriam Borgenicht 153

Nestleton, Alice (Actress)
A Cat in a Glass House - Lydia Adamson 15
A Cat in Fine Style - Lydia Adamson 16
A Cat in the Manger - Lydia Adamson 17
A Cat in the Wings - Lydia Adamson 18
A Cat in Wolf's Clothing - Lydia Adamson 19
A Cat on the Cutting Edge - Lydia Adamson 20

Neuhauser, Joyce (Housewife; Mentally Ill Person)
Nightmare Point - Carole Berry 128

Neville, Gabriel (Religious)
A Drink of Deadly Wine - Kate Charles 235

Newman, Cassie (Student)
A Brush with Death - Joan Smith 1519

Newman, Victor (Social Worker)
Dead Men Don't Marry - Dorothy Sucher 1588

Nichols, Nason (Detective—Private)
Trade Secrets - Maynard F. Thomson 1615

Nicholson, Chris (Lawyer)
Other People's Skeletons - Julie Smith 1529

Nickles, Eddie (Police Officer)
Playing the Dozens - William D. Pease 1286

Nightingale, Deirdre "Didi" Quinn (Veterinarian)
Dr. Nightingale Goes the Distance - Lydia Adamson 21
Dr. Nightingale Rides the Elephant - Lydia Adamson 22

Nightingale, Tim (Police Officer)
Death Penalties - Paula Gosling 625

Nishi, Kenaburo (Journalist)
Night Butterfly - Patricia McFall 1127

Noble, Jack (Computer Expert)
The Boss's Wife - S.L. Stebel 1562

Nolan, Maeve (Widow(er))
The Gombeen Man - Randy Lee Eickoff 474

Noonan, Joe (Detective—Private)
Black Light - Daniel Hearn 767

Noonan, Rita (Detective—Private)
Friends in High Places - Michael Hendricks 771
Money to Burn - Michael Hendricks 772

Norgren, Chris (Museum Curator)
A Glancing Light - Aaron Elkins 477
Old Scores - Aaron Elkins 479

Norris, Kay (Editor)
Sliver - Ira Levin 1013

North, Michael (Journalist)
The Scarred Man - Keith Peterson 1310

Norton, Myrl Adler (Professor)
In the Dead of Winter - Abbey Penn Baker 81

Nottingham, Patty (Journalist)
The Society Ball Murders - Jack Albin Anderson 51

Nowack, Shelley (Friend; Housewife)
The Class Menagerie - Jill Churchill 244

Nudger, Alo (Detective—Private)
Diamond Eyes - John Lutz 1056
Thicker than Blood - John Lutz 1059
Time Exposure - John Lutz 1060

Nye, Eddie "Nails" (Criminal; Convict)
Lights Out - Peter Abrahams 4

Nye, Jack (Businessman)
Lights Out - Peter Abrahams 4

O

Oakes, Blackford (Spy)
Tucker's Last Stand - William F. Buckley Jr. 188

O'Brea, Emma (Housewife)
Prized Possessions - L.R. Wright 1775

O'Brien, Brian (Businessman; Criminal)
Murder Song - Jon Cleary 256

O'Brien, Natasha (Businesswoman; Cook)
Someone Is Killing the Great Chefs of America - Nan Lyons 1061

Ochs, Charlie (Fisherman)
Revolution #9 - Peter Abrahams 6

O'Connor, Nick (Actor)
Bad Blood - P.M. Carlson 218

Odhiambo, James (Police Officer)
Death Underfoot - Dennis Casley 225

Odum, Glenn (Veteran; Criminal)
Hard Guy - Thorton Elliott 482

Ofsted, Lee (Sports Figure)
Rotten Lies - Charlotte Elkins 481
A Wicked Slice - Aaron Elkins 480

O'Hanlon, Ike (Police Officer; Detective—Homicide)
Full Commission - Carol Brennan 172

Ohayon, Michael (Police Officer)
Murder on a Kibbutz - Batya Gur 690
The Saturday Morning Murder - Batya Gur 691

Oliver, Gideon (Anthropologist)
Dead Men's Hearts - Aaron Elkins 476
Make No Bones - Aaron Elkins 478

Oliver, Ted (Spy)
A Black Legend - John Horton 810

Oloo, Wellington Waki (Detective—Private)
Brideprice - J.N. Catanach 226

O'Malley, Megan (Police Officer)
Night Sins - Tami Hoag 794

Omega, Jay (Writer; Professor)
Zombies of the Gene Pool - Sharyn McCrumb 1121

O'Neal, Freddie (Detective—Private)
Bet Against the House - Catherine Dain 378
Lay It on the Line - Catherine Dain 379
Sing a Song of Death - Catherine Dain 380
Walk a Crooked Mile - Catherine Dain 381

O'Neil, Caitlin (Police Officer)
The Monster Squad - John Angus 59

O'Neill (Police Officer)
A Fatal Advent - Isabelle Holland 797

O'Neill, Connor (Police Officer)
Die in My Dreams - Christine Green 661

O'Neill, Peggy (Police Officer)
Amends for Murder - M.D. Lake 966
Cold Comfort - M.D. Lake 967
A Gift for Murder - M.D. Lake 968
Murder by Mail - M.D. Lake 969
Once upon a Crime - M.D. Lake 970
Poisoned Ivy - M.D. Lake 971

Orett, Linda (Housewife)
A Single Stone - Marilyn Wallace 1664

O'Roarke, Jocelyn (Actress)
Dead Pan - Jane Dentinger 413
The Queen Is Dead - Jane Dentinger 414

Ortiz, Gabe (Police Officer)
Fool's Puzzle - Earlene Fowler 536

Ortiz, Johnny (Police Officer; Indian)
Missing Man - Richard Martin Stern 1570

O'Shaughnessy, Kiernan (Detective—Private; Doctor)
Pious Deception - Susan Dunlap 462
Rogue Wave - Susan Dunlap 463

O'Shaugnessy, Jesus (Police Officer)
Nightside - Soledad Santiago 1434

Otiz, Gabriel (Police Officer)
Irish Chain - Earlene Fowler 537

P

Padillo, Michael (Businessman)
Twilight at Mac's Place - Ross Thomas 1613

Page, Gideon (Lawyer)
Illegal Motion - Grif Stockley 1576

Page, Gideon (Lawyer; Single Parent)
Probable Cause - Griff Stockley 1577

Paige, Patrick (Police Officer)
Skeletons - Eric Sauter 1443

Paine, Jack (Detective—Private)
Summer Cool - Al Sarrantonio 1436

Palma, Carmen (Detective—Police)
Mercy - David L. Lindsey 1027

Palmer, Chili (Criminal)
Get Shorty - Elmore Leonard 1005

Pamplemousse (Writer; Critic)
Monsieur Pamplemousse Investigates - Michael Bond 151

Pamplemousse (Writer)
Pamplemousse Rests His Case - Michael Bond 152

Paoli, Vic (Detective—Private; Computer Expert)
Love Bytes - Sally Chapman 232

Pargeter, Melita (Widow(er))
Mrs. Pargeter's Package - Simon Brett 175

Paris, Charles (Actor)
Corporate Bodies - Simon Brett 174

Paris, Charles (Actor; Alcoholic)
A Series of Murders - Simon Brett 176

Paris, Jack (Police Officer)
Deviant Way - Richard Montanari 1166

Parker, Charles (Spy)
The Lantern Network - Ted Allbeury 37

Parker, Claire (Detective—Police)
Hot Shots - Laurence Gough 627

Parker, David (Accountant; Serial Killer)
A Pound of Flesh - Trevor Barnes 95

Parker, Hank (Police Officer)
Alley Kat Blues - Karen Kijewski 917

Parker, Quinn (Health Care Professional)
Full-Bodied Red - Bruce Zimmerman 1790

Parley, Sherry (Criminal)
Miami Purity - Vicki Hendricks 773

Parmalee, Jervey (Actress)
A Trick of Light - Patricia Robinson 1391

Parmalee, Roberta (Actress)
A Trick of Light - Patricia Robinson 1391

Partain, Edd "Twodees" (Military Personnel)
Ah, Treachery - Ross Thomas 1611

Pascoe, Peter (Police Officer)
Bones and Silence - Reginald Hill 789
Recalled to Life - Reginald Hill 790

Patterson, Hugh (Detective—Police)
Murder Movie - Jill McGown 1131

Peace, Charlie (Police Officer)
Death and the Chaste Apprentice - Robert Barnard 89

Peckover, Henry (Police Officer)
Kill the Butler! - Michael Kenyon 911
Peckover Joins the Choir - Michael Kenyon 912

Pedersen, Carl (Police Officer)
Threnody for Two - Jeanne Hart 747

Pedersen, Freda (Housewife)
Threnody for Two - Jeanne Hart 747

Pedersen, Gun (Sports Figure)
Strike - L.L. Enger 492
Swing - L.L. Enger 493

Pel, Evariste (Police Officer)
Pel and the Missing Persons - Mark Hebden 768

Pepper, Amanda (Teacher)
I'd Rather Be in Philadelphia - Gillian Roberts 1378
Philly Stakes - Gillian Roberts 1379
With Friends Like These - Gillian Roberts 1380

Perilli, Tony (Police Officer; Detective—Homicide)
Skins - Catherine O'Connell 1222

Perkins, Ben (Detective—Private; Maintenance Worker)
Concrete Hero - Rob Kantner 862
The Quick and the Dead - Rob Kantner 863
The Red, White, and Blues - Rob Kantner 864

Perkins, Ben (Detective—Private)
The Thousand Yard Stare - Rob Kantner 865

Perkins, Leo (Businessman)
Furnished for Murder - Richard Barth 101

Perkins, Oliver (Writer)
The Animal Hour - Andrew Klavan 935

Peters, Anna (Detective—Private)
Time Lapse - Janice Law 992

Peters, Toby (Detective—Private)
The Melting Clock - Stuart M. Kaminsky 860

Phelan, Jack (Unemployed)
A City of Strangers - Robert Barnard 88

Philbrick, Ginny (Police Officer)
Murder Will Out - Dorian Yeager 1784

Phillips, Alex (Assistant)
Blood Trance - R.D. Zimmerman 1791
Red Trance - R.D. Zimmerman 1793

Phillips, Bino (Lawyer)
Bino's Blues - A.W. Gray 650
Killings - A.W. Gray 651

Phillips, Maddy (Psychologist; Handicapped)
Blood Trance - R.D. Zimmerman 1791
Red Trance - R.D. Zimmerman 1793

Phipps, Howard (Businessman; Wealthy)
Elsinore - Jerome Charyn 238

Pickett, Mel (Police Officer; Widow(er))
Buried in Stone - Eric Wright 1766

Pickett, Mel (Police Officer)
A Sensitive Case - Eric Wright 1770

Pigeon, Anna (Ranger)
A Superior Death - Nevada Barr 96
Track of the Cat - Nevada Barr 97

Piggott, Harold (Administrator)
Death by Degrees - Robin Wilson 1735

Pigram, William (Police Officer)
Hotel Morgue - Janet Laurence 989

Pike, Joe (Detective—Private)
Free Fall - Robert Crais 341
Lullaby Town - Robert Crais 342
Stalking the Angel - Robert Crais 343

Pimletz, Axel (Journalist)
Obit - Daniel Paisner 1261

Pink, Melinda (Writer)
Rage - Gwen Moffat 1162
The Stone Hawk - Gwen Moffat 1163

Pitt, Charlotte (Spouse)
Farrier's Lane - Anne Perry 1294

Pitt, Charlotte (Housewife)
Highgate Rise - Anne Perry 1295

Character Name Index

Pitt, Thomas (Police Officer)
Farrier's Lane - Anne Perry 1294
Highgate Rise - Anne Perry 1295

Plant, Melrose (Nobleman)
The Old Contemptibles - Martha Grimes 675

Plum, Marvia (Police Officer)
The Classic Car Killer - Richard A. Lupoff 1054

Plum, Stephanie (Businesswoman; Divorced Person)
One for the Money - Janet Evanovich 503

Pollard, Tom (Detective—Police)
The Glade Manor Murder - Elizabeth Lemarchand 1001

Pollifax, Emily (Spy)
Mrs. Pollifax and the Whirling Dervish - Dorothy Gilman 588

Polo, Nick (Detective—Private)
Beggar's Choice - Jerry Kennealy 906
Special Delivery - Jerry Kennealy 907
Vintage Polo - Jerry Kennealy 908

Ponton, Anthony (Professor)
Death of a Fantasy Life - T.G. Gilpin 590

Pooley, Ellis (Police Officer)
Clubbed to Death - Ruth Dudley Edwards 472

Pope, Hamilton (Police Officer)
See No Evil - Edward Mathis 1095

Popkin, Sam (Journalist)
Shoofly Pie to Die - Joshua Quittner 1342

Porter, Ben (Publisher)
Finders Keepers - Elizabeth Travis 1627

Porter, Carrie (Publisher)
Finders Keepers - Elizabeth Travis 1627

Porter, Emma (Computer Expert; Gardener)
Aunt Dimity and the Duke - Nancy Atherton 68

Porter, Rainbow (Veteran)
Monkey on a Chain - Harlen Campbell 211

Poteet, Jordan (Librarian)
Do Unto Others - Jeff Abbott 1
The Only Good Yankee - Jeff Abbott 2

Poteet, Ralph (Detective—Private)
Peeper - Loren D. Estleman 499

Potter, Eugenia (Widow(er); Cook)
The 27 Ingredient Chili Con Carne Murders - Nancy Pickard 1315

Powell, Kit (Journalist)
Jinx - Julie Robitaille 1398

Powers, Georgina (Journalist)
User Deadly - Denise Danks 388

Powers, Jack (Police Officer)
Paramour - Gerald Petievich 1312

Pratt, Pat (Consultant)
Murder at Musket Beach - Bernie Lee 998
Murder Without Reservation - Bernie Lee 999

Pratt, Tony (Writer)
Murder at Musket Beach - Bernie Lee 998
Murder Without Reservation - Bernie Lee 999

Prescott, Amy (Doctor; Detective—Private)
Grave Secrets - Louise Hendricksen 774

Prescott, Brie (Student; Orphan)
Berlin Covenant - Celeste Paul 1278

Prettybird, Willie (Detective—Private; Indian)
Bigfoot - Richard Hoyt 815

Price, Robin (Police Officer; Inspector)
Fatal Charm - Anne Morice 1173

Principal, Laura (Detective—Private)
Every Breath You Take - Michelle Spring 1541

Pringle, G.D.H. (Accountant)
Death in Close-Up - Nancy Livingston 1034
Mayhem in Parva - Nancy Livingston 1035
Unwillingly to Vegas - Nancy Livingston 1036

Pritchard, Dominic (Lawyer)
A Few Dying Words - Paula Gosling 626

Proctor, Peter (Political Figure)
A Scandal in Belgravia - Robert Barnard 91

Pucci, Sal (Police Officer; Detective—Homicide)
Funny as a Dead Comic - Susan Rogers Cooper 312
Funny as a Dead Relative - Susan Rogers Cooper 313

Pugh, E.J. (Housewife)
One, Two, What Did Daddy Do? - Susan Rogers Cooper 315

Pugh, Willis (Businessman)
One, Two, What Did Daddy Do? - Susan Rogers Cooper 315

Purdy, Irene (Aged Person)
The Pumpkin-Shell Wife - Susanna Hofmann McShea 1138

Q

Quaid, Dermot (Detective—Police)
To Killashea - Norman Flood 530

Quantrill, Douglas (Police Officer)
This Way Out - Sheila Radley 1343

Quentin, Andrew (Professor)
Elegy in a Country Graveyard - Audrey Peterson 1304
Murder in Burgundy - Audrey Peterson 1305

Quiller (Spy)
Quiller KGB - Adam Hall 706

Quilliam, Meg (Cook)
A Dash of Death - Claudia Bishop 134
A Taste for Murder - Claudia Bishop 135

Quilliam, Sarah "Quill" (Artist; Hotel Owner)
A Dash of Death - Claudia Bishop 134

Quilliam, Sarah "Quill" (Innkeeper)
A Taste for Murder - Claudia Bishop 135

Quinn (Journalist)
The Cheshire Moon - Robert Ferrigno 525

Quinn, Al (Police Officer)
The Buzzards Must Also Be Fed - Anne Wingate 1739
Exception to Murder - Anne Wingate 1740

Quy, Imogen (Nurse)
A Piece of Justice - Jill Paton Walsh 1274
The Wyndham Case - Jill Paton Walsh 1275

Qwilleran, Jim (Journalist)
The Cat Who Moved a Mountain - Lilian Jackson Braun 167
The Cat Who Talked to Ghosts - Lilian Jackson Braun 168
The Cat Who Went into the Closet - Lilian Jackson Braun 169

R

Rabb, Joshua (Lawyer)
The Dividing Line - Richard Parrish 1273

Radkin, Joseph (Journalist; Unemployed)
The Genesis Files - Bob Biderman 130

Rafferty (Detective—Private)
Rafferty: Fatal Sisters - W. Glenn Duncan 458

Rafferty, Joseph (Police Officer)
Dead Before Morning - Geraldine Evans 504

Rafferty, Madeline (Writer)
A Deep Disturbance - Constance Rauch 1351

Rafferty, Molly (Professor)
The Marvell College Murders - Sophie Belfort 119

Rafferty, Neal (Detective—Private)
The Emerald Lizard - Chris Wiltz 1738

Raisin, Agatha (Advertising)
Agatha Raisin and the Quiche of Death - M.C. Beaton 107
Agatha Raisin and the Vicious Vet - M.C. Beaton 108

Ralston, Deb (Police Officer)
Bird in a Cage - Lee Martin 1086
The Day That Dusty Died - Lee Martin 1087
Deficit Ending - Lee Martin 1088
The Mensa Murders - Lee Martin 1089

Ramadge, Gwenn (Detective—Private)
The Raggedy Man - Lillian O'Donnell 1227
Used to Kill - Lillian O'Donnell 1228
A Wreath for the Bride - Lillian O'Donnell 1229

Ramos, Lucia (Police Officer; Lesbian)
Final Session - Mary Morell 1170

Ramsey, Mark (Businessman)
Silent Witness - Charles Wilson 1732

Ramsey, Stephen (Police Officer)
A Day in the Death of Dorothea Cassidy - Ann Cleeves 260

Randall, Tammi (Lawyer)
A Strange and Bitter Crop - E.L. Wyrick 1780

Randel, Chase (Businessman)
Artichoke Hearts - Victor Wuamett 1777
Deeds of Trust - Victor Wuamett 1778

Randel, Chase (Agent)
Teardown - Victor Wuamett 1779

Randolph, Arthur B. "Snooky" (Heir)
Friends till the End - Gloria Dank 387

Randolph, Jessica (Detective—Private; Artist)
A Relative Stranger - Margaret Lucke 1052

Raptor (Criminal)
Menaced Assassin - Joe Gores 618

Rasmussen, Alex (Detective—Private)
The Heaven Stone - David Daniel 386

Rathbone, Oliver (Lawyer)
A Sudden, Fearful Death - Anne Perry 1296

Rawlings, John (Detective—Police)
The Great Grave Robbery - John Minahan 1158

Rawlings, Marguerite (Journalist)
Hard Aground - James W. Hall 709

Rawlings, Mickey (Sports Figure)
Murder at Fenway Park - Troy Soos 1536

Rawlins, Easy (Worker; Veteran)
Devil in a Blue Dress - Walter Mosley 1176

Rawlins, Easy (Businessman)
A Red Death - Walter Mosley 1177

Rawlins, Easy (Detective—Private)
White Butterfly - Walter Mosley 1178

Reddman, David (Lawyer)
A Clear Case of Murder - Warwick Downing 445

Reddy, Jason (Detective—Private)
Deadly Stakes - H. Fred Wiser 1745

Redlam, Stuart (Detective—Police)
Point Blank - Jayson Livingston 1033

Redway, Glenda (Lawyer)
Work for a Dead Man - Simon Ritchie 1371

Reece, Caitlin (Detective—Private; Lesbian)
Ninth Life - Lauren Wright Douglas 444

Reece, Mitchell (Lawyer)
Mistress of Justice - Jeffrey Wilds Deaver 405

Reed, Stuart (Journalist)
The Last Man Standing - Jim Wright 1771

Reeves, Morgan (Journalist)
Make Friends with Murder - Judith Garwood 569

Reeves, Townsend (Doctor; Sports Figure)
Final Dictation - L.M. Vincent 1655
Pas De Death - L.M. Vincent 1656

Regal, Paul (Police Officer)
End Game - Dev Stryker 1585

Regan, Francis (Religious; Detective—Amateur)
Bloody Ten - William F. Love 1047

Regan, Francis (Religious)
The Chartreuse Clue - William F. Love 1048

Reilly, Cassandra (Writer; Linguist)
Gaudi Afternoon - Barbara Wilson 1731

Reilly, Regan (Detective—Private)
Decked - Carol Higgins Clark 250
Snagged - Carol Higgins Clark 251

Renee (Student)
Killing Time in Buffalo - Deidre S. Laiken 964

Renko, Arkady (Police Officer)
Polar Star - Martin Cruz Smith 1530

Renner, David (Police Officer)
Fuse Time - Max Byrd 205

Reno (Thief; Convict)
Edge City - Sin Soracco 1537

Renzler, Mark (Detective—Private)
Who Shot Longshot Sam? - Paul Engleman 495

Resnick, Charlie (Police Officer)
Cold Light - John Harvey 751
Cutting Edge - John Harvey 752
Off Minor - John Harvey 753
The Wasted Years - John Harvey 754

Resnick, Slots (Detective—Private)
Three Strikes, You're Dead - Michael Geller 574

Rhinehart, Michael (Detective—Private)
The Queen's Mare - John Birkett 133

Rhodenbarr, Bernie (Store Owner; Criminal)
The Burglar Who Traded Ted Williams - Lawrence Block 145

Rhodes, Anne (Actress; Administrator)
The Hawthorne Group - Thomas Hauser 756

Rhodes, Frank (Widow(er); Detective—Homicide)
Love Lies - Fern Kupfer 960

Rhys, Jenny (Spouse)
The Wrong Rite - Alisa Craig 334

Rhys, Madoc (Police Officer)
The Wrong Rite - Alisa Craig 334

Rice, Harry (Detective—Private; Businessman)
The Harry Chronicles - Allan Pedrazas 1287

Richard III (Ruler)
The Fate of Princes - P.C. Doherty 424

Riggs, Charlie (Doctor)
To Speak for the Dead - Paul Levine 1016

Riordan, Matt (Lawyer)
Methods of Execution - Frederick D. Huebner 818
Picture Postcard - Fredrick D. Huebner 819

Riordan, Prester John (Journalist; Radio Personality)
The Frozen Franklin - Sean Hanlon 725

Rios, Henry (Lawyer)
How Town - Michael Nava 1194

Ritchie, Lillian (Detective—Private; Musician)
Shattered Rhythms - Phyllis Knight 946
Switching the Odds - Phyllis Knight 947

Robbie, Ordell (Criminal)
Rum Punch - Elmore Leonard 1007

Roberts, Amanda (Journalist)
Ties That Bind - Sherryl Woods 1759

Robicheaux, Dave (Detective—Amateur; Veteran)
Black Cherry Blues - James Lee Burke 193

Robicheaux, Dave (Police Officer)
Burning Angel - James Lee Burke 194
Dixie City Jam - James Lee Burke 195
In the Electric Mist with Confederate Dead - James Lee Burke 196
A Morning for Flamingos - James Lee Burke 197

Robinson, Nan (Lawyer)
A Pocketful of Karma - Taffy Cannon 216

Rodrigue, John (Veteran)
Big Fish - Ken Grissom 682
Drowned Man's Key - Ken Grissom 683

Roger the Chapman (Peddler)
Death and the Chapman - Kate Sedley 1467
The Holy Innocents - Kate Sedley 1468
The Plymouth Cloak - Kate Sedley 1469
The Weaver's Tale - Kate Sedley 1470

Rogers, George (Police Officer)
A Time for Dying - Jonathan Ross 1402

Rogerson, Matt (Professor)
The Search Committee - Ralph McInerny 1136

Romain, Dan (Police Officer)
Blood Marks - Bill Crider 349

Roman, Dan (Detective—Private)
September Song - Edward Mathis 1096

Rommel, Frances "Frankie" (Lawyer)
The Water Cure - Warwick Downing 446

Roosevelt, Theodore (Historical Figure)
The Strenuous Life - Lawrence Alexander 36

Roper, Douglas (Police Officer)
Breach of Promise - Roy Hart 748

Roper, Taggert (Writer; Detective—Private)
The Next Victim - William Sanders 1423

Rosen, Lucy (Single Parent)
Turtle Moon - Alice Hoffman 795

Rosen, Michael (Lawyer)
Caught in the Shadows - C.A. Haddad 694

Rosen, Nate (Lawyer)
Stone Boy - Ronald Levitsky 1017

Rosen, Peter (Police Officer)
A Diet to Die For - Joan Hess 776

Ross, Hubert (Police Officer; Widow(er))
The Killing of Ellis Martin - Lucretia Grindle 677
So Little to Die For - Lucretia Grindle 678

Ross, Jack (Detective—Private)
The Desert Look - Bernard Schopen 1455

Ross, Jimmy (Military Personnel)
City of Gold - Len Deighton 410

Rostnikov, Porfiry (Police Officer)
The Man Who Walked Like a Bear - Stuart M. Kaminsky 859
Rostnikov's Vacation - Stuart M. Kaminsky 861

Rothenberg, Lily (Police Officer)
Shadow Prey - John Sandford 1426

Rover, Rowan (Tour Guide)
Missing Susan - Sharyn McCrumb 1118

Rowan, Gerald (Lawyer)
Body and Soil - Ralph McInerny 1135

Rowdy (Animal)
Black Ribbon - Susan Conant 288

Rowe, Valerie (Artist; Single Parent)
The Suitor - Michael Allegretto 43

Rudd (Police Officer)
The Spoils of Time - June Thomson 1614

Rune (Television)
Hard News - Jeffrey Wilds Deaver 403

Rune (Clerk)
Manhattan Is My Beat - Jeffrey Wilds Deaver 404

Runkel, Vida (Secretary)
The Alpine Advocate - Mary Daheim 370

Runkel, Vida (Journalist)
The Alpine Decoy - Mary Daheim 372
The Alpine Fury - Mary Daheim 373

Russell, Mary (Student)
The Beekeeper's Apprentice - Laurie R. King 924
A Monstrous Regiment of Women - Laurie R. King 926

Russo (Police Officer)
Date with a Dead Doctor - Toni Brill 177

Ruth (Secretary)
All I Have Is Blue - James Colbert 272

Ryan (Police Officer)
Shadows on the Mirror - Frances Fyfield 563

Ryan, Blackie (Religious)
Happy Are the Merciful - Andrew M. Greeley 656

Ryan, Jack (Spy)
The Sum of All Fears - Tom Clancy 248

Ryan, Maggie (Businesswoman)
Bad Blood - P.M. Carlson 218

Ryan, Michael (Lawyer)
Reasonable Doubt - Philip Friedman 558

Ryder, Owen (Businessman)
The Thirteenth Apostle - Gloria Gonzalez 610

Ryker, Sam (Police Officer)
Till Death Do Us Part - Rochelle Majer Krich 955

Ryland, Garth (Journalist)
A Dragon Lives Forever - John R. Riggs 1368
Wolf in Sheep's Clothing - John R. Riggs 1369

S

Sadler, Isobel (Heiress)
Landscape of Lies - Peter Watson 1676

Saint, Catherine (Photojournalist)
Shameless - Judy Collins 275

St. Clair, Maxene (Doctor)
Elective Murder - Janet McGiffin 1129
Prescription for Death - Janet McGiffin 1130

St. Claire, Geraldine (Journalist)
The Thirteenth Apostle - Gloria Gonzalez 610

St. James, Deborah (Spouse)
Missing Joseph - Elizabeth George 575

St. James, Simon (Doctor)
Missing Joseph - Elizabeth George 575

St. John, Jeremiah (Detective—Private)
According to St. John - William Babula 77

St. John, Peter (Lawyer)
Spare Change - John A. Peak 1280

St. Moritz, Wally (Businessman)
Merry Christmas, Murdock - Robert J. Ray 1352

Saldinger, Byron (Writer; Divorced Person)
Shooting Script - Gordon Cotler 332

Salter, Charlie (Police Officer)
Death by Degrees - Eric Wright 1767
Final Cut - Eric Wright 1768
A Fine Italian Hand - Eric Wright 1769
A Sensitive Case - Eric Wright 1770

Sam (Animal)
Snow Job - Ted Wood 1758

Sams, Charlotte (Journalist)
Showcase - Alison Glen 603
Trunk Show - Alison Glen 604

Samson, Albert (Detective—Private)
Called by a Panther - Michael Z. Lewin 1019

Samson, John (Detective—Private)
The Cords of Vanity - Miles Tripp 1629
Video Vengeance - Miles Tripp 1630

Sanders, John (Police Officer)
Murder in a Good Cause - Medora Sale 1417
Murder in Focus - Medora Sale 1418
Pursued by Shadows - Medora Sale 1419
Short Cut to Santa Fe - Medora Sale 1420

Sanderson, Laura (Journalist)
Morons and Madmen - Earl Emerson 488

Sanderson, Sandy (Secretary)
A Death for a Dancing Doll - E.X. Giroux 597
A Death for a Dodo - E.X. Giroux 598

Sands, Jake (Detective—Private)
East Beach - Ron Ely 485
Night Shadows - Ron Ely 486

Santee, Miranda (Journalist)
The Desert Look - Bernard Schopen 1455

Sasser, Jim (Writer)
He's Dead-She's Dead: Details at Eleven - John Bartholomew Tucker 1635

Saucier, Vonna (Detective—Private)
White Rook - J. Madison Davis 392

Savile, Justin (Police Officer)
Time's Witness - Michael Malone 1070

Sawyer, Pete (Detective—Private)
The Riviera Contract - Marvin Albert 26
The Zig-Zag Man - Marvin Albert 27

Saxon (Detective—Private; Actor)
Seeing the Elephant - Les Roberts 1387

Sayers, Dorothy L. (Historical Figure; Writer)
Dorothy and Agatha - Gaylord Larsen 984

Sayler, Catherine (Detective—Private)
Love nor Money - Linda Grant 648
A Woman's Place - Linda Grant 649

Scanlon, Joseph (Police Officer)
Casual Slaughters - Robert A. Carter 223

Scarf, Bruce (Police Officer; Detective—Homicide)
Casualty Loss - Jim Weikart 1683

Scarpetta, Kay (Doctor)
All That Remains - Patricia D. Cornwell 321
The Body Farm - Patricia D. Cornwell 322
Body of Evidence - Patricia D. Cornwell 323
Cruel and Unusual - Patricia D. Cornwell 324
From Potter's Field - Patricia D. Cornwell 325
Postmortem - Patricia D. Cornwell 326

Scattergood, Peter (Lawyer)
Break and Enter - Colin Harrison 735

Schaeffer, Michael (Criminal)
Sleeping Dogs - Thomas Perry 1297

Schafer, Will (Journalist)
The Dog Hermit - David Stout 1578

Schantz, Ollie (Handicapped)
And Leave Her Lay Dying - John Lawrence Reynolds 1362

Schulz, Tom (Police Officer; Detective—Homicide)
The Cereal Murders - Diane Mott Davidson 389

Schwartz, Lenny (Detective—Private)
Virgil's Ghost - Irving Weinman 1684

Schwartz, Rebecca (Lawyer)
Dead in the Water - Julie Smith 1524
Other People's Skeletons - Julie Smith 1529

Scorcese, Joseph (Organized Crime Figure)
Flamingos - Marc Savage 1444

Scott, Aline (Police Officer)
High Strangeness - Alison Drake 447

Scott, Davey (Interior Decorator)
Loves Music, Loves to Dance - Mary Higgins Clark 253

Scott, Evan (Architect)
Karma - Mitchell Smith 1531

Scott, Laura (Lawyer)
Trade-Off - Harrison Arnston 66

Scott, Patrick (Lawyer)
Avenging Angel - Anthony Appiah 64

Scruggs, Henry (Diplomat)
The India Exhibition - Richard Timothy Conroy 296
Mr. Smithson's Bones - Richard Timothy Conroy 297

Scudder, Matt (Detective—Private; Alcoholic)
A Dance at the Slaughterhouse - Lawrence Block 146

Scudder, Matt (Detective—Private)
The Devil Knows You're Dead - Lawrence Block 147

Scudder, Matt (Detective—Private; Alcoholic)
Out on the Cutting Edge - Lawrence Block 148
A Ticket to the Boneyard - Lawrence Block 149

Scudder, Matt (Detective—Private)
A Walk Among the Tombstones - Lawrence Block 150

Segura, Cristina (Heiress)
Antipodes - Maria-Antonia Oliver 1236

Semmes, Nat (Lawyer)
Deep End - Geoffrey Norman 1210

Seraphicos, Debra (Police Officer)
Sight Unseen - David Lorne 1046

Serian, Lenore (Widow(er))
Criminal Seduction - Darian North 1211

Severus, Livinius (Lawyer)
Roman Nights - Ron Burns 201

Shaddick, Gerald L. "Shad" (Bouncer)
Strip Tease - Carl Hiaasen 785

Shakespeare, William (Writer; Historical Figure)
The Quality of Mercy - Faye Kellerman 883

Shallot, Roger (Secretary)
The Poisoned Chalice - Michael Clynes 264
The White Rose Murders - Michael Clynes 265

Shanahan, Dietrich "Deets" (Detective—Private)
The Iron Glove - Ronald Tierney 1619
The Steel Web - Ronald Tierney 1620
The Stone Veil - Ronald Tierney 1621

Shandy, Helen (Librarian)
An Owl Too Many - Charlotte MacLeod 1064

Shandy, Peter (Professor)
An Owl Too Many - Charlotte MacLeod 1064
Something in the Water - Charlotte MacLeod 1065

Shanley, Carol (Police Officer)
An Hour to Kill - Edward Wellen 1690

Shapiro, Desiree (Detective—Private; Widow(er))
Murder Can Kill Your Social Life - Selma Eichler 473

Sharples, Claire (Scientist)
The Bulrush Murders - Rebecca Rothenberg 1405

Shaugnessy, Tom (Criminal)
The Triumph of Bacchus - Douglas Skeggs 1509

Shaw, Darby (Student)
The Pelican Brief - John Grisham 681

Shaw, Emma (Writer)
Death and the Trumpets of Tuscany - Hazel Wynn Jones 847

Shaw, Galen (Writer; Journalist)
Love Lies Slain - L.L. Blackmur 139

Shaw, George Bernard (Writer; Historical Figure)
Stage Fright - Gillian Linscott 1030

Shaw, James (Detective—Private)
Bad Neighbors - Isidore Haiblum 703

Shaw, Martha (Businesswoman)
Mass Murder - John Keith Drummond 449

Shayne, Hector Belascoran (Detective—Private)
An Easy Thing - Paco Ignacio Taibo II 1597

Shea, Kevin (Student; Fugitive)
A Certain Justice - John T. Lescroart 1008

Shea, Maggie (Counselor)
Night Angel - Kate Green 664

Sheldon, Graham (Police Officer)
Rotten Lies - Charlotte Elkins 481
A Wicked Slice - Aaron Elkins 480

Shelton, Holly (Police Officer)
Noble Rot - Will Harriss 739

Shepherd, Lori (Office Worker)
Aunt Dimity's Death - Nancy Atherton 69

Sheridan, Chris (Antiques Dealer)
Loves Music, Loves to Dance - Mary Higgins Clark 253

Sheridan, T.S.W. (Journalist)
All the Dead Heroes - Stephen F. Wilcox   1718
The Dry White Tear - Stephen F. Wilcox   1719
The Green Mosaic - Stephen F. Wilcox   1720

Sheriden, Charles (Photographer; Criminologist)
Death at Gallows Green - Robin Paige   1260

Sherman, Boyd (Detective—Private; Journalist)
Medicine Dog - Geoff Peterson   1307

Sherman, Sam (Detective—Private)
The Turquoise Tattoo - Nancy Baker Jacobs   838

Sherman, Winston (Professor; Writer)
Deception Island - M.K. Lorens   1043
Dreamland - M.K. Lorens   1044
Sweet Narcissus - M.K. Lorens   1045

Sherwood, Shelly (Journalist)
Rainy North Woods - Vince Kohler   950

Shigata, Mark (Police Officer)
The Buzzards Must Also Be Fed - Anne Wingate   1739
Exception to Murder - Anne Wingate   1740
The Eye of Anna - Anne Wingate   1741
Yakuza, Go Home - Anne Wingate   1742

Shore, Jemima (Journalist)
The Cavalier Case - Antonia Fraser   543

Shugak, Kate (Detective—Private; Indian)
A Cold-Blooded Business - Dana Stabenow   1550
A Cold Day for Murder - Dana Stabenow   1549
Dead in the Water - Dana Stabenow   1551
Play with Fire - Dana Stabenow   1552

Siegal, Phoebe (Detective—Private)
By Evil Means - Sandra West Prowell   1332

Sierra, Randall (Detective—Private)
Shoot the Piper - Richard Hill   791

Sigismondo (Mercenary)
Death of the Duchess - Elizabeth Eyre   512

Silva, Joe (Police Officer)
Family Album - Susan Oleksiw   1230
Murder in Mellingham - Susan Oleksiw   1231

Silver, Emily (Actress)
In the Dark - Carol Brennan   173

Silver, Jake (Doctor)
Disassociated States - Leonard Simon   1499

Silver, Leopold (Police Officer)
Thieftaker - Alan Scholefield   1454

Silverman, Susan (Counselor)
Stardust - Robert B. Parker   1271
Walking Shadow - Robert B. Parker   1272

Silverthorne, Charlie (Computer Expert)
Moth to the Flame - Kathleen Dougherty   437

Simmons, Louella (Real Estate Agent)
Four Elements of Murder - D.B. Borton   155

Simon, Aaron (Doctor)
To Do No Harm - Leslie Glass   602

Simon, Margo (Journalist)
Death of a Postmodernist - Janice Steinberg   1568

Simpson, Oliver (Police Officer)
Hung in the Balance - Roger Ormerod   1244

Simpson, Tim (Banker)
Sheep, Goats and Soap - John Malcolm   1068
The Wrong Impression - John Malcolm   1069

Sinclair, Cecily (Hotel Owner)
Check-out Time - Kate Kingsbury   928
Eat, Drink and Be Buried - Kate Kingsbury   929
Room with a Clue - Kate Kingsbury   930

Sinclair, Evangeline (Actress)
Encore Murder - Marian Babson   76

Sinclair, Gar (Detective—Private)
Thursday's Child - Teri White   1705

Singer, Kendra (Runaway)
Trade Secrets - Ray Garton   568

Skiles, Brian (Detective—Police)
The Last Page - Bob Fenster   524

Skink (Streetperson)
Stormy Weather - Carl Hiaasen   784

Skinny (Police Officer)
All I Have Is Blue - James Colbert   272
Skinny Man - James Colbert   273

Slater, Faith (Spouse)
Bad Desire - Gary Devon   417

Slater, Henry Lee (Political Figure)
Bad Desire - Gary Devon   417

Slezak, Elmer "Snake" (Detective—Private)
The Portland Laugher - Earl Emerson   489

Slider, Bill (Police Officer)
Death Watch - Cynthia Harrod-Eagles   740

Sloan, C.D. (Police Officer)
The Body Politic - Catherine Aird   25

Sloan, Charley (Lawyer)
Shadow of a Doubt - William J. Coughlin   333

Sloan, Susan (Lawyer)
Hammurabi's Code - Charles Kenney   909

Sloane, Sydney (Detective—Private; Lesbian)
Sister's Keeper - Randye Lordon   1042

Slocum, John (Defendant; Serial Killer)
Trade-Off - Harrison Arnston   66

Smailes, Derek (Police Officer)
The Cambridge Theorem - Tony Cape   217

Smart, David (Police Officer)
The Dean It Was That Died - Barbara Whitehead   1706

Smith, Brad (Sports Figure)
Dropshot: A Brad Smith Novel - Jack Bickham   129

Smith, Jane (Accountant; Psychic)
A Love to Die For - Christine T. Jorgensen   849

Smith, Jill (Detective—Homicide)
Death and Taxes - Susan Dunlap   460
Diamond in the Buff - Susan Dunlap   461
Time Expired - Susan Dunlap   464

Smith, Julia (Secretary)
Clerical Errors - D.M. Greenwood   670

Smith, MacKenzie "Mac" (Professor)
Murder at the Kennedy Center - Margaret Truman   1634

Smith, Paavo (Police Officer)
Cooking Up Trouble - Joanne Pence   1289
Something's Cooking - Joanne Pence   1290
Too Many Cooks - Joanne Pence   1291

Smith, Peter (Police Officer)
Rising Sun - Michael Crichton   348

Smith, Truman (Detective—Private)
Dead on the Island - Bill Crider   350
Gator Kill - Bill Crider   352
When Old Men Die - Bill Crider   354

Smith, Xenia (Businesswoman)
Blood on the Street - Annette Meyers   1146
The Deadliest Option - Annette Meyers   1147

Smith, Zack (Detective—Private)
Cat's Paw, Inc. - L.L. Thrasher   1618

Snow, David (Doctor; Alcoholic)
Double Blind - David Laing   965

Snow, Nicholas (Criminal; Professor)
Honolulu Red - Lue Zimmelman   1789

Socarides, Aristotle "Soc" (Detective—Private; Fisherman)
Death in Deep Water - Paul Kemprecos   903
Feeding Frenzy - Paul Kemprecos   904
Neptune's Eye - Paul Kemprecos   905

Soldano, Lou (Police Officer)
Blindsight - Robin Cook   302

Somers, John (Police Officer; Detective—Homicide)
Cold Call - Dianne G. Pugh   1333

Soneji, Gary (Serial Killer)
Along Came a Spider - James Patterson   1276

Southgate, Carol (Teacher)
A City of Strangers - Robert Barnard   88

Southwell, Robert (Police Officer)
Playing God - Barbara Whitehead   1707
Sweet Death, Come Softly - Barbara Whitehead   1708

Spadafino, Joey (Streetperson)
Felony Murder - Joseph T. Klempner   940

Spanner, Ben (Actor)
Even the Butler Was Poor - Ron Goulart   628
Now He Thinks He's Dead - Ron Goulart   629

Sparks, Jack (Spy)
The 6 Messiahs - Mark Frost   560

Spector (Businessman)
Bankroll - Bruce Ducker   450

Speed, Diana (Businesswoman)
Capitol Offense - Tony Gibbs   580
Shadow Queen - Tony Gibbs   583

Spencer, Joan (Musician)
Buried in Quilts - Sara Hoskinson Frommer   559

Spencer, Merrie Lee (Housewife)
The Garden Club - Muriel Resnick Jackson   836

Spencer, Mitch (Insurance Investigator)
In Deep - Bruce Jones   846

Spencer, Philip "Pip" (Lawyer)
The Talinin Madonna - Douglas Skeggs   1508

Spencer, Warren (Writer; Stock Broker)
The Garden Club - Muriel Resnick Jackson   836

Spenser (Detective—Private)
Double Deuce - Robert B. Parker   1269
Stardust - Robert B. Parker   1271
Walking Shadow - Robert B. Parker   1272

Spina, Toni (Criminal)
Neon Caesar - Mark McGarrity   1128

Springer, Dan (Writer)
Hollywood Requiem - Peter Freeborn   546

Springfield, Quincy (Criminal)
Motown - Loren D. Estleman   498

Squires, Lee (Professor)
Grizzly - Christine Andreae   54
Trail of Murder - Christine Andreae   55

Stagnaro, Dante (Police Officer)
Menaced Assassin - Joe Gores   618

Stainton, Alec (Detective—Police)
The Noose of Time - Stephen Murray   1189

Standish, Margaret (Detective—Police)
Deadly Resolutions - Anna Ashwood Collins   274

Stanley, Donald (Criminal)
Dead Easy - Arthur F. Nehrbass 1199

Starbranch, Harry (Police Officer)
No Comfort in Victory - Gregory Bean 106

Starbuck, Patterson (Lawyer)
The Immediate Prospect of Being Hanged - Walter Walker 1662

Starbuck, Raymond (Businessman)
Stalking Horse - Bill Shoemaker 1487

Stark, Dan (Journalist)
When She Was Bad - Ron Faust 518

Stark, Joanna (Art Dealer)
Dark Star - Marcia Muller 1180

Stark, Robert (Businessman; Spy)
Gunpower - Mark Schorr 1456

Starkey, Dan (Writer)
Divorcing Jack - Colin Bateman 104

Starr, Rachel (Detective—Police)
Honolulu Red - Lue Zimmelman 1789

Starrett, Joanna (Artist)
Flowers for the Dead - Ann M. Williams 1728

Staub, J.D. (Police Officer)
The Dry White Tear - Stephen F. Wilcox 1719

Steele, Jack (Military Personnel; Widow(er))
When Reason Sleeps - Tom Sehler 1472

Stein, Gertrude (Writer; Historical Figure)
The Caravaggio Shawl - Samuel M. Steward 1573

Stein, Henry (Con Artist)
Swindle - George Adams 11

Steiner, Kurt (Military Personnel)
The Eagle Has Flown - Jack Higgins 787

Stepanovich, Jose (Police Officer)
Earth Angels - Gerald Petievich 1311

Stern, Jonas (Spy)
Spandau Phoenix - Greg Iles 824

Stevens, Janet (Student)
Quaker Witness - Irene Allen 46

Stevens, Mitch (Journalist)
Land Kills - Nat Brandt 166

Stewart, Ada Chan (Social Worker)
The Heaven Stone - David Daniel 386

Stewart, Blaine (Detective—Private; Widow(er))
Dancing in the Dark - Sharon Zukowski 1798
Leap of Faith - Sharon Zukowski 1799

Stewart, Eleanor (Teacher; Lesbian)
Death Wore a Diadem - Iona McGregor 1133

Stock, Joan (Spouse)
Frobisher's Savage - Leonard Tourney 1624

Stock, Matthew (Businessman)
Frobisher's Savage - Leonard Tourney 1624

Stockton, Jean (Housewife)
Dead Easy - Arthur F. Nehrbass 1199

Stokes, Sally (Criminal; Prostitute)
A Broken Vessel - Kate Ross 1403

Stone, Belinda (Writer)
Coronation - W.J. Weatherby 1679

Stone, Lucy (Worker)
Mail-Order Murder - Leslie Meier 1140

Stoner, Harry (Detective—Private)
Missing - Jonathan Valin 1646
The Music Lovers - Jonathan Valin 1647
Second Chance - Jonathan Valin 1648

Storme, Wyatt (Veteran)
Dreamsicle - W.L. Ripley 1370

Strachan, Zoe (Heiress)
A Chill Wind in January - L.R. Wright 1772

Strachey, Donald (Detective—Private; Homosexual)
Third Man Out - Richard Stevenson 1572

Straight, Leon (Criminal)
Done Deal - Les Standiford 1561

Stranahan, Mick (Detective)
Skin Tight - Carl Hiaasen 783

Strange, Sylvia (Doctor)
Dangerous Attachments - Sarah Lovett 1051

Straun, Angus (Police Officer; Sports Figure)
Unnatural Hazard - Barry Cork 317
Winter Rules - Barry Cork 318

Strauss, Violet (Designer)
The India Exhibition - Richard Timothy Conroy 296

Street, Dee (Lawyer)
A Woman's Own Mystery - Hannah Wakefield 1658

Strickland, Dave (Detective—Private)
Suffer Little Children - Thomas D. Davis 396

Stryker, Jack (Police Officer)
The Body in Blackwater Bay - Paula Gosling 624

Stuart, Jud (Spy)
River of Darkness - James Grady 632

Studevant, Morgan (Judge)
Poison Fruit - Chelsea Quinn Yarbro 1781

Sturgis, Milo (Police Officer; Homosexual)
Bad Love - Jonathan Kellerman 885
Private Eyes - Jonathan Kellerman 886
Self-Defense - Jonathan Kellerman 887

Sughrue, C.W. (Detective—Private; Veteran)
The Mexican Tree Duck - James Crumley 363

Sullivan, Liz (Journalist; Streetperson)
Murder in a Nice Neighborhood - Lora Roberts 1388

Summers, Drew (Advertising)
The Soul of Betty Fairchild - Robert Specht 1538

Susanna (Dancer)
Edge City - Sin Soracco 1537

Sussman, Andy (Journalist)
The Big Freeze - Michael J. Katz 871
Last Dance in Redondo Beach - Michael J. Katz 872

Sussock, Ray (Police Officer)
Condition Purple - Peter Turnbull 1639

Sutter, John (Lawyer)
The Gold Coast - Nelson DeMille 412

Swagger, Bob Lee (Veteran)
Point of Impact - Stephen Hunter 822

Swain, Alfred (Police Officer)
The Ripper's Apprentice - Donald Thomas 1610

Swanson, Regis (Businessman)
Get What's Coming - Sam Reaves 1354

Sway, Mark (Child)
The Client - John Grisham 680

Swift, Doug (Police Officer; Detective—Homicide)
The Water Cure - Warwick Downing 446

Swift, Sabrina (Social Worker)
Dead Men Don't Marry - Dorothy Sucher 1588

Swinbrooke, Kathryn (Doctor)
The Eye of God - C.L. Grace 631

Szabo, Eric (Security Officer; Alcoholic)
Capitol Offense - Tony Gibbs 580

T

T, Hugo (Aged Person)
The Last Rite of Hugo T - J.N. Catanach 227

Takamura, Jen (Photojournalist)
The Cheshire Moon - Robert Ferrigno 525

Talbot, Jeff (Lawyer; Alcoholic)
Spare Change - John A. Peak 1280

Tallis, John (Student; Writer)
Rat's Nest - Charles West 1694

Tamar, Hilary (Lawyer)
The Sirens Sang of Murder - Sarah Caudwell 228

Tanner, Alex (Detective—Private)
The Glass Ceiling - Anabel Donald 428

Tanner, John Marshall (Detective—Private)
Blood Type - Stephen Greenleaf 667
Book Case - Stephen Greenleaf 668
Southern Cross - Stephen Greenleaf 669

Tannis, Jack (Military Personnel)
China Lake - Anthony Hyde 823

Taylor, Holland (Detective—Private)
Penance - David Housewright 812

Teagarden, Aurora (Librarian)
A Bone to Pick - Charlaine Harris 731

Teagarden, Aurora (Aged Person)
The Julius House - Charlaine Harris 732

Teague, Kate (Professor)
Half a Mind - Wendy Hornsby 807

Tejeda, Roger (Police Officer)
Half a Mind - Wendy Hornsby 807

Terranova, Marie (Administrator; Single Parent)
Room 9 - Soledad Santiago 1435

Terry, Christine (Criminal)
When She Was Bad - Ron Faust 518

Thane, Colin (Police Officer)
The Interface Man - Bill Knox 948

Thanet, Luke (Detective—Police)
Dead by Morning - Dorothy Simpson 1502

Thatcher, John Putnam (Banker)
East Is East - Emma Lathen 986
Right on the Money - Emma Lathen 987

Theron, Beth (Lawyer)
Peeping Thomas - Robert Reeves 1358

Theron, Thomas (Professor)
Peeping Thomas - Robert Reeves 1358

Thomas, Ike (Postal Worker; Twin)
Box Nine - Jack O'Connell 1223

Thomas, Lenore (Police Officer; Twin)
Box Nine - Jack O'Connell 1223

Thompson, Daniel (Religious)
Viper Quarry - Dean Feldmeyer 522

Thoresby, John (Religious)
The Lady Chapel - Candace M. Robb 1376

Thorn (Detective—Private)
Gone Wild - James W. Hall 708
Mean High Tide - James W. Hall 710

Thorn, Cordelia (Actress)
Hallowed Murder - Ellen Hart 745

Thorn, Cordelia (Lesbian; Actress)
Vital Lies - Ellen Hart 746

Thorn, Nick (Police Officer)
Dead in the Cellar - Connie Fedderson 520

Thorne, Iris (Businesswoman)
Cold Call - Dianne G. Pugh 1333

Thorssen, Alix (Art Dealer)
The Bluejay Shaman - Lise McClendon Webb 1680

Tibbet, Emmy (Spouse)
Black Girl, White Girl - Patricia Moyes 1179

Tibbet, Henry (Police Officer)
Black Girl, White Girl - Patricia Moyes 1179

Tilley, Jim (Detective—Police)
Force of Nature - Stephen Solomita 1533

Tillman, Virgil (Police Officer)
Faces in the Crowd - William Marshall 1079
The New York Detective - William Marshall 1080

Tincker, "Push" (Police Officer)
Night Rituals - Gary Paulsen 1279

Titus, Nicky (Photographer)
Death Down Home - Eve K. Sandstrom 1430

Titus, Nicky (Photograhper; Police Officer)
The Devil Down Home - Eve K. Sandstrom 1431

Titus, Nicky (Photographer)
The Down Home Heifer Heist - Eve K. Sandstrom 1432

Titus, Sam (Military Personnel)
Death Down Home - Eve K. Sandstrom 1430

Titus, Sam (Photographer)
The Devil Down Home - Eve K. Sandstrom 1431

Titus, Sam (Police Officer)
The Down Home Heifer Heist - Eve K. Sandstrom 1432

Tobin, Jane (Journalist)
Vintage Polo - Jerry Kennealy 908

Todd, Ziza (Religious)
Point No-Point - David Willis McCullough 1123
Think on Death - David Willis McCullough 1124

Toklas, Alice B. (Writer; Historical Figure)
The Caravaggio Shawl - Samuel M. Steward 1573

Tolliver, Ben (Police Officer)
By Reason of Insanity - James Neal Harvey 749
Painted Ladies - James Neal Harvey 750

Tompkins, Meredith (Lesbian)
The Chesapeake Project - Phyllis Horn 806

Tone, Charlie (Businessman)
The Man in the Moon - Frank Norwood 1212

Tonneman, John (Doctor)
The Kingsbridge Plot - Maan Meyers 1148

Torenson, Lou (Psychologist)
Showcase - Alison Glen 603

Toreson, Lou (Psychologist)
Trunk Show - Alison Glen 604

Townsend, Joanna (Businesswoman)
The Toy Cupboard - Lee Jordan 848

Toye, Gregory (Detective—Police)
The Glade Manor Murder - Elizabeth Lemarchand 1001

Tozzi, Mike (FBI Agent)
Bad Apple - Anthony Bruno 184

Tozzi, Mike (Police Officer)
Bad Blood - Anthony Bruno 185
Bad Moon - Anthony Bruno 186

Tracer, Chris (Secretary; Spouse)
Tracer, Inc. - Jeff Andrus 58

Tracer, John (Detective—Private)
Tracer, Inc. - Jeff Andrus 58

Tracer, Shorty (Student)
Tracer, Inc. - Jeff Andrus 58

Trager, Amy (Doctor; Lesbian)
Final Session - Mary Morell 1170

Trakos, Nikki (Detective—Homicide)
Dead Ahead - Ruby Horansky 804

Trakos, Nikki (Police Officer; Detective—Homicide)
Dead Center - Ruby Horansky 805

Trask, Ginny (Ranger)
Clear-Cut Murder - Lee Wallingford 1667

Trask, Ginny (Ranger; Widow(er))
Cold Tracks - Lee Wallingford 1668

Traveler, Martin (Detective—Private)
Called Home - R.R. Irvine 828
The Great Reminder - R.R. Irvine 829
Pillar of Fire - R.R. Irvine 830

Traveler, Moroni (Detective—Private)
The Angel's Share - R.R. Irvine 826
Called Home - R.R. Irvine 828
The Great Reminder - R.R. Irvine 829
Pillar of Fire - R.R. Irvine 830

Travis, Melanie (Teacher; Single Parent)
A Pedigree to Die For - Laurien Berenson 121

Travis, Sheila (Businesswoman; Widow(er))
Deadly Secrets on the St. Johns - Patricia Houck Sprinkle 1542

Travis, Sheila (Businesswoman)
Murder on Peachtree Street - Patricia Houck Sprinkle 1543
A Mystery Bred in Buckhead - Patricia Houck Sprinkle 1544
Somebody's Dead in Snellville - Patricia Houck Sprinkle 1545

Trayne, Martin (Artist)
Circumstances Unknown - Jonellen Heckler 769

Treasure, Mark (Businessman)
Holy Treasure! - David Williams 1729

Treasure, Mark (Banker)
Treasure by Post - David Williams 1730

Tremayne, Maggie (Dancer)
Four Steps to Death - Diana Ramsay 1346

Trench, Arabella (Journalist)
Boxed In - Neville Steed 1564
Wind-Up - Neville Steed 1566

Trent, Wendell (Government Official; Troubleshooter)
Bright Shark - Robert Ballard 85

Tretheway, Albert (Police Officer)
Murder on the Thirteenth - A.E. Eddenden 471

Trevellyan, Nick (Police Officer)
Hope Against Hope - Susan B. Kelly 896
Kid's Stuff - Susan B. Kelly 897
Time of Hope - Susan B. Kelly 898

Trevelyn, James (Insurance Investigator)
The Triumph of Bacchus - Douglas Skeggs 1509

Trevlyn, Laurel (Criminal)
Nobody Lives Forever - Edna Buchanan 187

Trevorne, Kate (Professor)
The Body in Blackwater Bay - Paula Gosling 624

Tripper, Lee (Heir; Journalist)
The Suspense Is Killing Me - Thomas Maxwell 1102

Tristram, James (Spy)
Spy Shadow - Tim Sebastian 1466

Troy, Frederick (Police Officer)
Black Out - John Lawton 994

Tryon, Glynis (Librarian; Activist)
North Star Conspiracy - Miriam Grace Monfredo 1164

Tullis, Faye (Student)
In the Dead of Winter - Abbey Penn Baker 81

Tully, Alonzo "Zoo" (Police Officer)
Chameleon - William X. Kienzle 915

Tully, Eustes (Detective—Homicide)
In Deep - Bruce Jones 846

Tully, Leonard (Antiques Dealer)
The Suitor - Michael Allegretto 43

Turchek, Robert (Criminal)
Thursday's Child - Teri White 1705

Turner, Derek (Journalist; Spy)
A Clinic for Murder - Marsha Landreth 974

Turner, Derek (Journalist)
The Holiday Murders - Marsha Landreth 975

Turner, Derek (Spy)
Vial Murders - Marsha Landreth 976

Turner, Paul (Police Officer; Homosexual)
Sorry Now? - Mark Richard Zubro 1796

Turner, Samantha (Doctor; Widow(er))
A Clinic for Murder - Marsha Landreth 974
The Holiday Murders - Marsha Landreth 975

Turner, Samantha (Doctor)
Vial Murders - Marsha Landreth 976

Tutankhamun (Ruler; Historical Figure)
Murder in the Place of Anubis - Lynda S. Robinson 1390

Twitty, Jason (Police Officer)
Peckover Joins the Choir - Michael Kenyon 912

Tye, Randall (Journalist)
A Private Crime - Lillian O'Donnell 1225

Tygart, Mary "Ike" (Television)
Until Death - Polly Whitney 1709
Until the End of Time - Polly Whitney 1710

Tyler, Hap (Veteran)
Hard Aground - James W. Hall 709

Tyson, Albert (Government Official)
Moving Targets - Sean Flannery 529

V

Vail, Martin (Lawyer)
Primal Fear - William Diehl 421

Valencia, Fermin (Writer)
The Shadow of the Shadow - Paco Ignacio Taibo II 1598

Van Der Valk, Arlette (Spouse)
Sand Castles - Nicholas Freeling 549

Van Der Valk, Piet (Police Officer)
Sand Castles - Nicholas Freeling 549

Van Dyne, Mel (Police Officer; Detective—Homicide)
A Farewell to Yarns - Jill Churchill 245
From Here to Paternity - Jill Churchill 246

Vance, Lee (Criminal)
Scotch on the Rocks - Howard Browne 183

Vargas, Tony (Criminal)
Desert Heat - J.A. Jance 842

Vecchi, Al (Police Officer)
Shooting Script - Gordon Cotler 332

Ventana, Ronnie (Detective—Private)
Charged with Guilt - Gloria White 1700
Money to Burn - Gloria White 1701
Murder on the Run - Gloria White 1702

Verdean, Gillian (Businesswoman; Sailor)
Landfall - Tony Gibbs 581

Verdean, Gillian (Sailor)
Running Fix - Tony Gibbs 582

Verdugo, Alberto (Lawyer)
The Shadow of the Shadow - Paco Ignacio Taibo II 1598

Vereker, Lucy (Young Woman)
The Yellow Room Conspiracy - Peter Dickinson 420

Vernet, Lucien (Military Personnel)
Napoleon Must Die - Quinn Fawcett 519

Vernet, Victoire (Spouse)
Napoleon Must Die - Quinn Fawcett 519

Verstak, Marni (Real Estate Agent)
A Very Proper Death - Alex Juniper 850

Veryan, Ann (Teacher)
Skylark - Sheila Simonson 1501

Vickers, Tremayne (Businessman; Horse Trainer)
Longshot - Dick Francis 540

Vickery, Fred (Aged Person)
No Place for Secrets - Sherry Lewis 1021

Victor II (Ruler; Doctor)
Skeleton-in-Waiting - Peter Dickinson 419

Vinda, John (Detective—Police)
Exceptional Clearance - William J. Caunitz 229

Voegler, Allie (Police Officer)
Dr. Nightingale Goes the Distance - Lydia Adamson 21
Dr. Nightingale Rides the Elephant - Lydia Adamson 22

Vogel, Karl (Military Personnel)
The Faust Conspiracy - James Baddock 78

Vogler, Deena (Student)
Till Death Do Us Part - Rochelle Majer Krich 955

W

Wade, Cassie (Child)
Count the Days - Lin Summerfield 1592

Wade, Evelyn (Aged Person)
Boiling Rock - Remar Sutton 1594

Wade, John (Political Figure)
In the Lake of the Woods - Tim O'Brien 1218

Wade, Laura (Girlfriend)
Death and Other Lovers - Jo Bannister 86

Wagner, Greg (Handicapped; Computer Expert)
Night Kills - Ed Gorman 622

Walker, Amanda (Businesswoman)
Personal - C.K. Cambray 208

Walker, Amos (Detective—Private)
Sweet Women Lie - Loren D. Estleman 500

Walker, Jack (Police Officer)
The Cactus Garden - Robert Ward 1672

Walker, Mary (Artist)
The Fast-Death Factor - Virginia Crosby 359

Walker, Thad (Police Officer)
The Fast-Death Factor - Virginia Crosby 359

Walker, Will (Actor)
Deadfall in Berlin - R.D. Zimmerman 1792

Walsh, Jack (Police Officer)
Bait - Kenneth Abel 3

Walsh, Jack (Detective—Private)
The Night Remembers - Ed Gorman 623

Walsh, Jackie (Teacher; Actress)
First Pedigree Murder - Melissa Cleary 257

Walsh, Jackie (Teacher)
The Maltese Puppy - Melissa Cleary 258

Walsh, Jackie (Professor; Single Parent)
A Tail of Two Murders - Melissa Cleary 259

Ward, Emerson (Writer)
Death Came Dressed in White - Michael W. Sherer 1481
Little Use for Death - Michael W. Sherer 1482

Warden, Jesse (Police Officer)
Heat - Stuart Woods 1760

Wareham, Liz (Public Relations)
Full Commission - Carol Brennan 172

Waring, Elizabeth (Lawyer)
Sleeping Dogs - Thomas Perry 1297

Warshawski, V.I. (Detective—Private)
Burn Marks - Sara Paretsky 1264
Guardian Angel - Sara Paretsky 1265
Tunnel Vision - Sara Paretsky 1266

Watson, Lucas (Criminal)
Dangerous Attachments - Sarah Lovett 1051

Waverly, Tim (Businessman; Gambler)
Double Down - Tom Kakonis 854

Waverly, Tim (Gambler)
Shadow Counter - Tom Kakonis 855

Weir, Eldon (Criminal)
The House on the Hill - Judith Kelman 899

Weiss, John (Insurance Investigator)
A Brush with Death - Joan Smith 1519

Welles, Sarah (Teacher)
Criminal Conversation - Evan Hunter 820

Wellman, Ben (Detective—Police)
Streets of Fire - Thomas H. Cook 306

Wells, Gardner (Detective—Private)
Body of Evidence - David A. Van Meter 1653

Wells, John (Journalist)
Rough Justice - Keith Peterson 1309

Wells, Nadia (Detective—Private)
Blue Bayou - Dick Lochte 1038

Wentworth, Bea (Political Figure)
Death on the Mississippi - Richard Forrest 535

Wentworth, Lyon (Writer)
Death on the Mississippi - Richard Forrest 535

Wesley, Benton (FBI Agent)
From Potter's Field - Patricia D. Cornwell 325

West, Delilah (Detective—Private)
Hit and Run - Maxine O'Callaghan 1219

West, Delilah (Detective—Private; Widow(er))
Set-Up - Maxine O'Callaghan 1220

West, Helen (Lawyer)
Deep Sleep - Frances Fyfield 561
A Question of Guilt - Frances Fyfield 562

West, Marlee (Journalist)
Night of the Ice Storm - David Stout 1579

Westerland, Sally (Young Woman)
The Tijuana Bible - Ron Goulart 630

Weston, Aleda (Activist)
Telling Lies - Wendy Hornsby 809

Wetzon, Leslie (Businesswoman)
Blood on the Street - Annette Meyers 1146
The Deadliest Option - Annette Meyers 1147

Wexford, Reginald (Police Officer)
Kissing the Gunner's Daughter - Ruth Rendell 1361

Wheeler, Elizabeth (Public Relations)
The Famous DAR Murder Mystery - Graham Landrum 977

Whelan, Paul (Detective—Private)
Death in Uptown - Michael Raleigh 1345

Whitaker, Sarah (Businesswoman)
Night of Reunion - Michael Allegretto 42

Whitcomb, Leah (Student)
Paws Before Dying - Susan Conant 290

White, Blanche (Servant)
Blanche on the Lam - Barbara Neely 1198

White, Bud (Police Officer)
L.A. Confidential - James Ellroy 483

White, Frank (Police Officer)
Bagged - Jo Bailey 79

Whiting, Michael (Art Dealer)
Landscape of Lies - Peter Watson 1676

Whitman, Paul (Musician)
The Piano Man - Noreen Gilpatrick 589

Whitson, Blair (Professor)
An Imperfect Spy - Amanda Cross 360

Whysse, Ted (Heir; Horse Trainer)
Blood Lies - Virginia Anderson 52

Wiggins, Thomas (Police Officer)
Is Anybody There? - T.G. Gilpin 591

Wilcox, Carl (Businessman)
The Ditched Blonde - Harold Adams 12

Wilcox, Carl (Hotel Worker)
The Man Who Missed the Party - Harold Adams 13

Wilcox, Carl (Businessman)
A Perfectly Proper Murder - Harold Adams 14

Wilcox, Ruby (Businesswoman)
Thyme of Death - Susan Wittig Albert 33

Wilder, Johannah (Detective—Private; Lesbian)
Shadow Dance - Agnes Bushnell 202

Will, Elizabeth (Artist; Art Dealer)
Murder Will Out - Dorian Yeager 1784

Willett, Wolf (Filmmaker)
Santa Fe Rules - Stuart Woods 1763

Williams, Lee (Police Officer)
Palindrome - Stuart Woods 1762

Willis, Bill (Lawyer)
Aunt Dimity's Death - Nancy Atherton 69

Willis, Charles (Police Officer; Actor)
My Gun Has Bullets - Lee Goldberg   606

Willis, Dee (Singer)
Steel Guitar - Linda Barnes   94

Willis, Grace (Police Officer)
Death and the Dogwalker - A.J. Orde   1240
A Little Neighborhood Murder - A.J. Orde   1241
A Long Time Dead - A.J. Orde   1242

Willmont, Robert (Political Figure)
Guilt by Association - Susan R. Sloan   1514

Willows, Jack (Detective—Police)
Hot Shots - Laurence Gough   627

Wilson, Everett (Criminal)
Prime Suspect - A.W. Gray   653

Wilson, Fran (Police Officer)
Die in My Dreams - Christine Green   661

Wilson, Francesca (Civil Servant)
Death Among the Dons - Janet Neel   1196

Wilson, Francesca (Government Official)
Death of a Partner - Janet Neel   1197

Wilson, Laurie (Businesswoman)
Winter Rules - Barry Cork   318

Wilson, Mike (Religious)
Topless - D. Keith Mano   1072

Wilson, Ruth (Detective—Private)
Shadow Dance - Agnes Bushnell   202

Winder, Joe (Journalist; Public Relations)
Native Tongue - Carl Hiaasen   782

Winfield, Carter (Detective—Private)
Murder Begins at Home - Dale L. Gilbert   585

Winfield, Jane (Journalist)
Elegy in a Country Graveyard - Audrey Peterson   1304

Winfield, Jane (Student)
Murder in Burgundy - Audrey Peterson   1305

Wingate, Buddy (Criminal)
The Cactus Garden - Robert Ward   1672

Wingate, Caledonia (Aged Person)
Murder by Owl Light - Corinne Holt Sawyer   1445
Murder Has No Calories - Corinne Holt Sawyer   1446
Murder in Gray and White - Corinne Holt Sawyer   1447

Wingate, Charlotte Rae (Criminal)
The Cactus Garden - Robert Ward   1672

Winn, Sherry Lou (Heiress)
Pink Vodka Blues - Neal Barrett Jr.   98

Winslow, Steve (Lawyer)
The Naked Typist - J.P. Hailey   704
The Underground Man - J.P. Hailey   705

Winston, Stoney (Filmmaker; Teacher)
Truck Shot - Jim Stinson   1574

Winston, Stoney (Filmmaker)
TV Safe - Jim Stinson   1575

Winter, Alex (Detective—Private)
Library: No Murder Aloud - Susan Steiner   1569

Winter, Holly (Journalist)
A Bite of Death - Susan Conant   287
Black Ribbon - Susan Conant   288
Bloodlines - Susan Conant   289

Winter, Holly (Animal Trainer)
Paws Before Dying - Susan Conant   290

Winter, Holly (Journalist)
Ruffly Speaking - Susan Conant   291

Winter, Stuart (Detective—Private)
No Sign of Murder - Alan Russell   1414

Winthrop, Ruth (Artist)
Miss Zukas and the Library Murders - Jo Dereske   416

Wolfe, Hannah (Detective—Private)
Birthmarks - Sarah Dunant   455
Under My Skin - Sarah Dunant   456

Wolfe, Nero (Detective—Private)
Fade to Black - Robert Goldsborough   607
Silver Spire - Robert Goldsborough   608

Woo, April (Police Officer)
Hanging Time - Leslie Glass   601

Woodrow, Michael (Businessman; Criminal)
Flawless - Adam Barrow   99

Woodruff, Bernard (Writer)
Friends till the End - Gloria Dank   387

Worth, Tom (Police Officer)
Bitter Herbs - Natasha Cooper   307
Bloody Roses - Natasha Cooper   308
Rotten Apples - Natasha Cooper   309

Worthing, Matilda (Businesswoman)
Mass Murder - John Keith Drummond   449

Wren, Susan (Police Officer; Widow(er))
Consider the Crows - Charlene Weir   1685

Wren, Susan (Police Officer)
Family Practice - Charlene Weir   1686
The Winter Widow - Charlene Weir   1687

Wright, Tom (Military Personnel; Pilot)
Coyote Bird - Jim DeFelice   409

Wyatt, Baker (Criminal)
The Ransom - Brian Tobin   1622

Wyatt, Jolie (Writer)
Dust Devils of the Purple Sage - Barbara Burnett Smith   1516
Writers of the Purple Sage - Barbara Burnett Smith   1517

Wyatt, Nyia (Actress)
Shooting Star - Kate Green   665

Wyche, Pat (Businessman)
Blood Music - Jessie Prichard Hunter   821

Wyche, Zelly (Housewife)
Blood Music - Jessie Prichard Hunter   821

Wylie, Eva (Sports Figure)
Bucket Nut - Liza Cody   270

Monkey Wrench - Liza Cody   271

Wyoming, Shay (Artist)
The Cutting Hours - Julia Grice   673

Y

Yablonsky, Alvin (Detective—Police)
The Bone Orchard - Joseph Trigoboff   1628

Yale, Sam (Director)
Sliver - Ira Levin   1013

Yancy, Kate (Innkeeper)
All the Great Pretenders - Deborah Adams   10

Yarborough, Lamont (Musician)
The Cheerio Killings - Douglas Allyn   47

Yates, Carrie (Lawyer)
A Stiff Critique - Jaqueline Girdner   595

Yates, Kimberly (Model)
Blind Side - William Bayer   105

Yeadings, Mike (Police Officer)
Cat's Cradle - Clare Curzon   366
Death Prone - Clare Curzon   367
Three-Core Lead - Clare Curzon   368

Younger, Cecil (Detective—Private)
The Curious Eat Themselves - John Straley   1580
The Woman Who Married a Bear - John Straley   1581

Yum Yum (Animal)
The Cat Who Went into the Closet - Lilian Jackson Braun   169

Z

Zack, Harry (Musician)
The King Is Dead - Sarah Shankman   1475

Zack, Harry (Insurance Investigator)
Now Let's Talk of Graves - Sarah Shankman   1476

Zack, Harry (Musician; Insurance Investigator)
She Walks in Beauty - Sarah Shankman   1477

Zigman, Gail (Political Figure)
Fruits of the Poisonous Tree - Archer Mayor   1104

Zimm, Harry (Producer)
Get Shorty - Elmore Leonard   1005

Zindel, Fanny (Aged Person)
Bagels for Tea - Serita Stevens   1571

Zondi, Mickey (Police Officer)
The Song Dog - James McClure   1114

Zukas, Helma (Librarian)
Miss Zukas and the Island Murders - Jo Dereske   415
Miss Zukas and the Library Murders - Jo Dereske   416

Character Description Index

This index alphabetically lists descriptions of the major characters in featured titles. The descriptions may be occupations (astronaut, lawyer, etc.) or may describe persona (amnesiac, runaway, teenager, etc.). For each description, character names are listed alphabetically. Also provided are book titles, author names, and entry numbers.

ABUSE VICTIM

Garcia, Marita
An Hour to Kill - Edward Wellen 1690

ACCOUNTANT

Hazard, Amanda
Dead in the Cellar - Connie Feddersen 520

Jasen, Jay
Casualty Loss - Jim Weikart 1683

Messenger, Jim
Blue Lonesome - Bill Pronzini 1325

Parker, David
A Pound of Flesh - Trevor Barnes 95

Pringle, G.D.H.
Death in Close-Up - Nancy Livingston 1034
Mayhem in Parva - Nancy Livingston 1035
Unwillingly to Vegas - Nancy Livingston 1036

Smith, Jane
A Love to Die For - Christine T. Jorgensen 849

ACTIVIST

Barclay, Maeve
Time and Time Again - B.M. Gill 587

Bray, Nell
Hanging on the Wire - Gillian Linscott 1028
Sister Beneath the Sheet - Gillian Linscott 1029
Stage Fright - Gillian Linscott 1030

Hamel, Neil
The Wolf Path - Judith Van Gieson 1652

Kimura, Patti
Kimura - Robert Davis 395

Tryon, Glynis
North Star Conspiracy - Miriam Grace Monfredo 1164

Weston, Aleda
Telling Lies - Wendy Hornsby 809

ACTOR

Bernhardt, Alan
Except for the Bones - Collin Wilcox 1713
Full Circle - Collin Wilcox 1714
Silent Witness - Collin Wilcox 1716

Bracewell, Nicholas
The Mad Courtesan - Edward Marston 1081
The Nine Giants - Edward Marston 1082
The Queen's Head - Edward Marston 1083
The Trip to Jerusalem - Edward Marston 1084

Cromwell, David
Dreamland - M.K. Lorens 1044

Grant, Tom
Funnelweb - Charles West 1693

Hill, Jordan
No Way Home - Patricia MacDonald 1062

Hudnut, Lyle
The Man Who Cancelled Himself - David Handler 722

O'Connor, Nick
Bad Blood - P.M. Carlson 218

Paris, Charles
Corporate Bodies - Simon Brett 174
A Series of Murders - Simon Brett 176

Saxon
Seeing the Elephant - Les Roberts 1387

Spanner, Ben
Even the Butler Was Poor - Ron Goulart 628
Now He Thinks He's Dead - Ron Goulart 629

Walker, Will
Deadfall in Berlin - R.D. Zimmerman 1792

Willis, Charles
My Gun Has Bullets - Lee Goldberg 606

ACTRESS

Bishop, Sabrina
My Gun Has Bullets - Lee Goldberg 606

Bowering, Victoria
Cancellation by Death - Dorian Yeager 1782
Eviction by Death - Dorian Yeager 1783

Browning, Grace
Angel of Death - Jack Higgins 786

Crichton, Tessa
Fatal Charm - Anne Morice 1173

Davy, Tess
The Dying of the Light - Robert Richardson 1366

Dolan, Trixie
Encore Murder - Marian Babson 76

Flagg, Ruby
Drown All the Dogs - Thomas Adcock 23

Flanagan, Bella
Stage Fright - Gillian Linscott 1030

Flores, Karen
Get Shorty - Elmore Leonard 1005

Forbes, Molly
Holy Treasure! - David Williams 1729
Treasure by Post - David Williams 1730

Graham, Charlotte
Murder at the Spa - Stefanie Matteson 1097
Murder on the Cliff - Stefanie Matteson 1098

Grant, Paula
The Beverly Malibu - Katherine V. Forrest 533

Hale, Millie
Close-Up on Death - Maureen O'Brien 1213

Hardy, Nina
Hollywood Requiem - Peter Freeborn 546

Hayes, Brooke
The Keeper - Meg O'Brien 1217

London, Lavina
Grave Undertaking - James McCahery 1112

Marlow, Felicity
Three-Core Lead - Clare Curzon 368

McGrogan, Annie
Alibi for an Actress - Gillian B. Farrell 516
Murder and a Muse - Gillian B. Farrell 517

Nestleton, Alice
A Cat in a Glass House - Lydia Adamson 15
A Cat in Fine Style - Lydia Adamson 16
A Cat in the Manger - Lydia Adamson 17
A Cat in the Wings - Lydia Adamson 18
A Cat in Wolf's Clothing - Lydia Adamson 19
A Cat on the Cutting Edge - Lydia Adamson 20

O'Roarke, Jocelyn
Dead Pan - Jane Dentinger 413
The Queen Is Dead - Jane Dentinger 414

Parmalee, Jervey
A Trick of Light - Patricia Robinson 1391

Parmalee, Roberta
A Trick of Light - Patricia Robinson 1391

Rhodes, Anne
The Hawthorne Group - Thomas Hauser 756

Silver, Emily
In the Dark - Carol Brennan 173

Sinclair, Evangeline
Encore Murder - Marian Babson 76

Thorn, Cordelia
Hallowed Murder - Ellen Hart 745
Vital Lies - Ellen Hart 746

Walsh, Jackie
First Pedigree Murder - Melissa Cleary 257

Wyatt, Nyia
Shooting Star - Kate Green 665

ADDICT

Donatti, Dominick
Strangers in the Night - Peg Tyre 1641

ADMINISTRATOR

James, Liz
Cry for Help - Karen Hanson Stuyck 1586

Jones, Justyn
The Lynching - Bennie Lee Sinclair 1503

Kettler, Jane
The Texas Capitol Murders - Bill Crider 353

Louise
Skeleton-in-Waiting - Peter Dickinson 419

Piggott, Harold
Death by Degrees - Robin Wilson 1735

Adoptee

Rhodes, Anne
The Hawthorne Group - Thomas Hauser 756
Terranova, Marie
Room 9 - Soledad Santiago 1435

ADOPTEE

Cromwell, David
Dreamland - M.K. Lorens 1044
Lundgren, Kate
Blood Kin - Marjorie Dorner 436

ADVENTURER

Adler, Irene
Good Night, Mr. Holmes - Carole Nelson Douglas 441

ADVERTISING

Brolan, Frank
Night Kills - Ed Gorman 622
Burke, Riley
Dangerous Waters - Bill Eidson 475
Dancer, Karen
The Dying Room - E.X. Giroux 599
Griffo, Simona
The Trouble with Going Home - Camilla T. Crespi 345
The Trouble with Moonlighting - Trella Crespi 346
The Trouble with Too Much Sun - Trella Crespi 347
Raisin, Agatha
Agatha Raisin and the Quiche of Death - M.C. Beaton 107
Agatha Raisin and the Vicious Vet - M.C. Beaton 108
Summers, Drew
The Soul of Betty Fairchild - Robert Specht 1538

AGED PERSON

Benbow, Angela
Murder by Owl Light - Corinne Holt Sawyer 1445
Murder Has No Calories - Corinne Holt Sawyer 1446
Murder in Gray and White - Corinne Holt Sawyer 1447
Bennett, Mildred
The Pumpkin-Shell Wife - Susanna Hofmann McShea 1138
Binton, Margaret
Deathics - Richard Barth 100
Bonesteel, Nora
The Hangman's Beautiful Daughter - Sharyn McCrumb 1115
Bushrow, Harriet
The Rotary Club Mystery - Graham Landrum 978
Haggerty, Forrest
The Pumpkin-Shell Wife - Susanna Hofmann McShea 1138
Harrison, Richard
Dark Provenance - Michael David Anthony 61
Holmes, Sherlock
A Monstrous Regiment of Women - Laurie R. King 926
Hubbert, Lil
Hubbert and Lil: Partners in Crime - Gallagher Gray 654
Loudermilk, Dottie
Bad News Travels Fast - Gar Anthony Haywood 761

Loudermilk, Joe
Bad News Travels Fast - Gar Anthony Haywood 761
Martin, Dorothy
The Body in the Transept - Jeanne M. Dams 385
McWhinny, Tish
Elusive Quarry - B. Comfort 285
Purdy, Irene
The Pumpkin-Shell Wife - Susanna Hofmann McShea 1138
T, Hugo
The Last Rite of Hugo T - J.N. Catanach 227
Teagarden, Aurora
The Julius House - Charlaine Harris 732
Vickery, Fred
No Place for Secrets - Sherry Lewis 1021
Wade, Evelyn
Boiling Rock - Remar Sutton 1594
Wingate, Caledonia
Murder by Owl Light - Corinne Holt Sawyer 1445
Murder Has No Calories - Corinne Holt Sawyer 1446
Murder in Gray and White - Corinne Holt Sawyer 1447
Zindel, Fanny
Bagels for Tea - Serita Stevens 1571

AGENT

Randel, Chase
Teardown - Victor Wuamett 1779

ALCOHOLIC

Hayes, Brooke
The Keeper - Meg O'Brien 1217
Malloy, Mack
Pleading Guilty - Scott Turow 1640
Murray, Russell
Pink Vodka Blues - Neal Barrett Jr. 98
Paris, Charles
A Series of Murders - Simon Brett 176
Scudder, Matt
A Dance at the Slaughterhouse - Lawrence Block 146
Out on the Cutting Edge - Lawrence Block 148
A Ticket to the Boneyard - Lawrence Block 149
Snow, David
Double Blind - David Laing 965
Szabo, Eric
Capitol Offense - Tony Gibbs 580
Talbot, Jeff
Spare Change - John A. Peak 1280

ANIMAL

Hoag, Lulu
The Man Who Would Be F. Scott Fitzgerald - David Handler 723
The Woman Who Fell From Grace - David Handler 724
Kimi
A Bite of Death - Susan Conant 287
Koko
The Cat Who Moved a Mountain - Lilian Jackson Braun 167
The Cat Who Talked to Ghosts - Lilian Jackson Braun 168
The Cat Who Went into the Closet - Lilian Jackson Braun 169

Maury
The Maltese Puppy - Melissa Cleary 258
Midnight Louie
Cat on a Blue Monday - Carole Nelson Douglas 438
Catnap - Carole Nelson Douglas 439
Pussyfoot - Carole Nelson Douglas 443
Mrs. Murphy
Murder at Monticello - Rita Mae Brown 180
Rest in Pieces - Rita Mae Brown 181
Wish You Were Here - Rita Mae Brown 182
Rowdy
Black Ribbon - Susan Conant 288
Sam
Snow Job - Ted Wood 1758
Yum Yum
The Cat Who Went into the Closet - Lilian Jackson Braun 169

ANIMAL TRAINER

Driscoll, Katherine
Zero at the Bone - Mary Willis Walker 1661
Winter, Holly
Paws Before Dying - Susan Conant 290

ANTHROPOLOGIST

Dalton, Will
Menaced Assassin - Joe Gores 618
Edwards, Colin
Selena - Gordon Randolph Willey 1726
MacPherson, Elizabeth
MacPherson's Lament - Sharyn McCrumb 1117
Missing Susan - Sharyn McCrumb 1118
The Windsor Knot - Sharyn McCrumb 1120
Oliver, Gideon
Dead Men's Hearts - Aaron Elkins 476
Make No Bones - Aaron Elkins 478

ANTIQUES DEALER

Kynx, Jason
A Long Time Dead - A.J. Orde 1242
Lovejoy
The Great California Game - Jonathan Gash 570
The Lies of Fair Ladies - Jonathan Gash 571
The Sin Within Her Smile - Jonathan Gash 572
Lynx, Jason
Death and the Dogwalker - A.J. Orde 1240
A Little Neighborhood Murder - A.J. Orde 1241
Marklin, Peter
Boxed In - Neville Steed 1564
Clockwork - Neville Steed 1565
Wind-Up - Neville Steed 1566
Sheridan, Chris
Loves Music, Loves to Dance - Mary Higgins Clark 253
Tully, Leonard
The Suitor - Michael Allegretto 43

ARCHAEOLOGIST

Emerson, Amelia Peabody
The Last Camel Died at Noon - Elizabeth Peters 1298
Emerson, Radcliffe
The Last Camel Died at Noon - Elizabeth Peters 1298
Hope, Alastair
Faith, Hope and Homicide - Jessica Mann 1071

Hoyland, Tamara
Faith, Hope and Homicide - Jessica Mann 1071

ARCHITECT

Caylor, Lauren
The Watchman - Michael Allegretto 44

Scott, Evan
Karma - Mitchell Smith 1531

ART DEALER

Holt, Essington
To Catch a Forger - Robert Wallace 1666

Martindale, Peter
Imperfect Strangers - Stuart Woods 1761

McKenzie, Cramer
First and Ten - Douglas Anderson 50

Stark, Joanna
Dark Star - Marcia Muller 1180

Thorssen, Alix
The Bluejay Shaman - Lise McClendon Webb 1680

Whiting, Michael
Landscape of Lies - Peter Watson 1676

Will, Elizabeth
Murder Will Out - Dorian Yeager 1784

ART HISTORIAN

Dennis, Margaret
By Death Possessed - Roger Ormerod 1243

Napier, John
The Estuary Pilgrim - Douglas Skeggs 1507

ARTISAN

Kincaid, Paul
Circumstances Unknown - Jonellen Heckler 769

ARTIST

Baugh, Henry
Love Lies Slain - L.L. Blackmur 139

Dali, Salvador
The Melting Clock - Stuart M. Kaminsky 860

Deacon, Jack
The Tijuana Bible - Ron Goulart 630

Dunne, Bettina
To Do No Harm - Leslie Glass 602

Gautier, Roxanne
A Collector of Photographs - Deborah Valentine 1645

Hansen, Nick
Follow That Blonde - Joan Smith 1521

Jacobs, Calista
Dark Swan - Kathryn Lasky Knight 944
Mortal Words - Kathryn Lasky Knight 945

Kidd
The Empress File - John Camp 210

Lan, Li
The Trail to Buddha's Mirror - Don Winslow 1744

Long, Rita
Hardscape - Justin Scott 1463

Marklake, Robert
Not as Far as Velma - Nicholas Freeling 548

Mavity, H.J.
Even the Butler Was Poor - Ron Goulart 628
Now He Thinks He's Dead - Ron Goulart 629

McCleet, Adam
Mortal Remains - Rick Hanson 728

McKenzie, Abby
Murder by Tarot - Al Guthrie 693

McWhinny, Tish
The Cashmere Kid - B. Comfort 284
Elusive Quarry - B. Comfort 285
Grave Consequences - B. Comfort 286

Melville, Susan
Miss Melville Rides a Tiger - Evelyn E. Smith 1518

Quilliam, Sarah "Quill"
A Dash of Death - Claudia Bishop 134

Randolph, Jessica
A Relative Stranger - Margaret Lucke 1052

Rowe, Valerie
The Suitor - Michael Allegretto 43

Starrett, Joanna
Flowers for the Dead - Ann M. Williams 1728

Trayne, Martin
Circumstances Unknown - Jonellen Heckler 769

Walker, Mary
The Fast-Death Factor - Virginia Crosby 359

Will, Elizabeth
Murder Will Out - Dorian Yeager 1784

Winthrop, Ruth
Miss Zukas and the Library Murders - Jo Dereske 416

Wyoming, Shay
The Cutting Hours - Julia Grice 673

ASSISTANT

Phillips, Alex
Blood Trance - R.D. Zimmerman 1791
Red Trance - R.D. Zimmerman 1793

ASTROLOGER

Hughes, Josephine "Jo"
Blood of an Aries - Linda Mather 1094

AVENGER

Burke
Footsteps of the Hawk - Andrew Vachss 1644

BANKER

Harvey, Mark
Killer Cinderella - Simon Shaw 1478

Simpson, Tim
Sheep, Goats and Soap - John Malcolm 1068
The Wrong Impression - John Malcolm 1069

Thatcher, John Putnam
East Is East - Emma Lathen 986
Right on the Money - Emma Lathen 987

Treasure, Mark
Treasure by Post - David Williams 1730

BEEKEEPER

Hoving, Sarah
So Shall You Reap - Marilyn Wallace 1665

BODYGUARD

Bohland, Harmon
Shooting Star - Kate Green 665

Caruso, Wayne
Adjusted to Death - Jaqueline Girdner 593

BOUNCER

Shaddick, Gerald L. "Shad"
Strip Tease - Carl Hiaasen 785

BOYFRIEND

Caruso, Wayne
The Last Resort - Jaqueline Girdner 594

Donelli, Joe
Ties That Bind - Sherryl Woods 1759

Murphy, Rex
The Society Ball Murders - Jack Albin Anderson 51

BUSINESSMAN

Ackerly, Paul
The Yellow Room Conspiracy - Peter Dickinson 420

Ance, Maynard
King of the Corner - Loren D. Estleman 497

Barrows, Peter
By Reason of Insanity - James Neal Harvey 749

Bartell, Martin
The Julius House - Charlaine Harris 732

Bartholomew, Peter
Hot Water - Sally Gunning 686
Rough Water - Sally Gunning 687
Still Water - Sally Gunning 688
Troubled Water - Sally Gunning 689

Blair, Barley
The Russia House - John Le Carre 995

Bourque, Kevin
Dead Wrong - Alan Dennis Burke 192

Brady, Gerard
Trade Secrets - Ray Garton 568

Butler, Charles
Mallory's Oracle - Carol O'Connell 1221

Calder, Keith
A Brace of Skeet - Gerald Hammond 719

Caylor, Richard
The Watchman - Michael Allegretto 44

Cherry, Max
Rum Punch - Elmore Leonard 1007

Cochran, William "Bull"
Squeezeplay - David F. Nighbert 1205
Strikezone - David F. Nighbert 1206

Coll, Matthew
Death in Verona - Roy Harley Lewis 1020

Coyne, Dermot
Irish Gold - Andrew M. Greeley 657

Curry, Thomas
Act of Faith - Michael Bowen 158
Fielder's Choice - Michael Bowen 160

Dahlstrom, Nels
Golden Fleece - Jack Becklund 118

Deal, John
Deal to Die For - Les Standiford 1560
Done Deal - Les Standiford 1561

Dean, Jeffrey
Singapore Transfer - Wayne Warga 1673

Driver, Sam
A Pedigree to Die For - Laurien Berenson 121

Du Bois, Pierre
Murder, Mystery and Mayhem - Jennifer Carnell 220

Businesswoman

Elliot, David
Vertical Run - Joseph R. Garber 566

Ferguson, Lackey
Prime Suspect - A.W. Gray 653

Florio, Nicky
Mortal Sin - Paul Levine 1014

Flynn, Fiddler
Money Burns - A.E. Maxwell 1100

Foley, Joseph
Balboa Firefly - Jack Trolley 1633

Fury, Merritt
Whisper the Guns - Edward Cline 261

Greer, Daniel
Predator's Waltz - Jay Brandon 165

Grenier, Grayson
Balboa Firefly - Jack Trolley 1633

Grimes
Shoedog - George Pelecanos 1288

Harrison, Richard
The Becket Factor - Michael David Anthony 60

Hickey, Tom
The Venus Deal - Ken Kuhlken 958

Holland, Mark
Deadly Sonata - Paul Myers 1192

Hubbert, T.S.
Hubbert and Lil: Partners in Crime - Gallagher Gray 654

Jackson, Graham
Golden Fleece - Jack Becklund 118

Janeway, Cliff
The Bookman's Wake - John Dunning 467

Kauffman, Isaac
Berlin Covenant - Celeste Paul 1278

Kinsolving, Sandy
Imperfect Strangers - Stuart Woods 1761

Kramer, Jack
Blood Kin - Marjorie Dorner 436

Lacey, Jack
Burn Season - John Lantigua 981

Letessier, Vinnie
Noble Rot - Will Harriss 739

Lewis, Dowdy Jr.
A Gypsy Good Time - Gustav Hasford 755

Lispenard, Drew
A Killing in Venture Capital - Margaret Logan 1040

Mahoney, Payne
Miami Purity - Vicki Hendricks 773

Marx, Albie
Nice Guys Finish Dead - David Debin 406

Mattias, N.H.
Pressure Drop - Peter Abrahams 5

McCorkle, Cyril "Mac"
Twilight at Mac's Place - Ross Thomas 1613

Monroe, Doyle
The Deer Killers - Gunnard Landers 973

Nye, Jack
Lights Out - Peter Abrahams 4

O'Brien, Brian
Murder Song - Jon Cleary 256

Padillo, Michael
Twilight at Mac's Place - Ross Thomas 1613

Perkins, Leo
Furnished for Murder - Richard Barth 101

Phipps, Howard
Elsinore - Jerome Charyn 238

Pugh, Willis
One, Two, What Did Daddy Do? - Susan Rogers Cooper 315

Ramsey, Mark
Silent Witness - Charles Wilson 1732

Randel, Chase
Artichoke Hearts - Victor Wuamett 1777
Deeds of Trust - Victor Wuamett 1778

Rawlins, Easy
A Red Death - Walter Mosley 1177

Rice, Harry
The Harry Chronicles - Allan Pedrazas 1287

Ryder, Owen
The Thirteenth Apostle - Gloria Gonzalez 610

St. Moritz, Wally
Merry Christmas, Murdock - Robert J. Ray 1352

Spector
Bankroll - Bruce Ducker 450

Starbuck, Raymond
Stalking Horse - Bill Shoemaker 1487

Stark, Robert
Gunpower - Mark Schorr 1456

Stock, Matthew
Frobisher's Savage - Leonard Tourney 1624

Swanson, Regis
Get What's Coming - Sam Reaves 1354

Tone, Charlie
The Man in the Moon - Frank Norwood 1212

Treasure, Mark
Holy Treasure! - David Williams 1729

Vickers, Tremayne
Longshot - Dick Francis 540

Waverly, Tim
Double Down - Tom Kakonis 854

Wilcox, Carl
The Ditched Blonde - Harold Adams 12
A Perfectly Proper Murder - Harold Adams 14

Woodrow, Michael
Flawless - Adam Barrow 99

Wyche, Pat
Blood Music - Jessie Prichard Hunter 821

BUSINESSWOMAN

Albright, Nikki
A Body to Dye For - Grant Michaels 1150

Barr, Temple
Catnap - Carole Nelson Douglas 439

Bayles, China
Hangman's Root - Susan Wittig Albert 32
Thyme of Death - Susan Wittig Albert 33

Beaufort, Mary
Murder on Peachtree Street - Patricia Houck Sprinkle 1543
A Mystery Bred in Buckhead - Patricia Houck Sprinkle 1544
Somebody's Dead in Snellville - Patricia Houck Sprinkle 1545

Beaumont, Sophie
Elusive Quarry - B. Comfort 285

Benn, Hannah
Sweet Death, Come Softly - Barbara Whitehead 1708

Bernstein, Ellie
Beat Up a Cookie - Denise Dietz 422
Throw Darts at a Cheesecake - Denise Dietz 423

Binford, Bitsy
Death Below Deck - Douglas Kiker 922

What Mystery Do I Read Next?

Birdsong, Charlotte
Grandmother's House - Janet LaPierre 983

Birdwood, Verity
Death in Store - Jennifer Rowe 1406

Brichter, Kori
Original Sin - Mary Monica Pulver 1334
Show Stopper - Mary Monica Pulver 1335

Cain, Jenny
Bum Steer - Nancy Pickard 1316
But I Wouldn't Want to Die There - Nancy Pickard 1317
I.O.U. - Nancy Pickard 1318

Calder, Deborah
A Brace of Skeet - Gerald Hammond 719
Home to Roost - Gerald Hammond 720

Chizzit, Emma
Emma Chizzit and the Mother Lode Marauder - Mary Bowen Hall 711
Emma Chizzit and the Napa Nemesis - Mary Bowen Hall 712
Emma Chizzit and the Queen Anne Killer - Mary Bowen Hall 713

Covington, Janet
The Long Search - Isabelle Holland 798

Daily, Lark
Larkspur - Sheila Simonson 1500

Decker, Gillian Clifford
In-laws and Outlaws - Barbara Paul 1277

Dodge, Lark
Skylark - Sheila Simonson 1501

Fairweather, Doran
The Bandersnatch - Mollie Hardwick 729

Farleigh, Allison
Gone Wild - James W. Hall 708

Flynn, Fiora
Money Burns - A.E. Maxwell 1100

Gardner, Hilda
Rafferty: Fatal Sisters - W. Glenn Duncan 458

Garrity, Callahan
Every Crooked Nanny - Kathy Hogan Trocheck 1631
To Live and Die in Dixie - Kathy Hogan Trocheck 1632

Girard, Terry
Murder Once Removed - Kathleen Kunz 959

Gordon, Kathleen
We Wish You a Merry Murder - Valerie Wolzien 1750

Grant, Celia
Bones Gather No Moss - John Sherwood 1483
A Bouquet of Thorns - John Sherwood 1484
The Hanging Garden - John Sherwood 1485

Greene, Charlie
Death of the Office Witch - Marlys Millhiser 1155
Murder at Moot Point - Marlys Millhiser 1156

Haagen, Anneke
Curly Smoke - Susan Holtzer 803

Halperin, Elizabeth
Mommy and the Murder - Nancy Gladstone 600

Hope, Alison
Hope Against Hope - Susan B. Kelly 896
Time of Hope - Susan B. Kelly 898

Hoving, Sarah
So Shall You Reap - Marilyn Wallace 1665

Hunter, Leah
File Under: Deceased - Sarah Lacey 962

Indermill, Bonnie
Death of a Dancing Fool - Carole Berry 124

Jasper, Jazz
The Cheetah Chase - Karin McQuillan 1137

Character Description Index

Jones, Caroline Fremont
The Strange Files of Fremont Jones - Dianne Day 400

King, Diana
Murder Has a Pretty Face - Jennie Melville 1142

Kozak, Thea
Death in a Funhouse Mirror - Kate Clark Flora 531

Langenberg, Paulina
Murder at the Spa - Stefanie Matteson 1097

Laurance, Annie
A Little Class on Murder - Carolyn G. Hart 743

Lowe, Philipa
Hung in the Balance - Roger Ormerod 1244

Malloy, Claire
A Diet to Die For - Joan Hess 776
Roll Over and Play Dead - Joan Hess 781

McKenzie, Abby
Murder by Tarot - Al Guthrie 693

Michaels, Laura
A Permanent Retirement - John Miles 1153

Mondragon, Rita
At Ease with the Dead - Walter Satterthwait 1437
A Flower in the Desert - Walter Satterthwait 1439

O'Brien, Natasha
Someone Is Killing the Great Chefs of America - Nan Lyons 1061

Plum, Stephanie
One for the Money - Janet Evanovich 503

Ryan, Maggie
Bad Blood - P.M. Carlson 218

Shaw, Martha
Mass Murder - John Keith Drummond 449

Smith, Xenia
Blood on the Street - Annette Meyers 1146
The Deadliest Option - Annette Meyers 1147

Speed, Diana
Capitol Offense - Tony Gibbs 580
Shadow Queen - Tony Gibbs 583

Thorne, Iris
Cold Call - Dianne G. Pugh 1333

Townsend, Joanna
The Toy Cupboard - Lee Jordan 848

Travis, Sheila
Deadly Secrets on the St. Johns - Patricia Houck Sprinkle 1542
Murder on Peachtree Street - Patricia Houck Sprinkle 1543
A Mystery Bred in Buckhead - Patricia Houck Sprinkle 1544
Somebody's Dead in Snellville - Patricia Houck Sprinkle 1545

Verdean, Gillian
Landfall - Tony Gibbs 581

Walker, Amanda
Personal - C.K. Cambray 208

Wetzon, Leslie
Blood on the Street - Annette Meyers 1146
The Deadliest Option - Annette Meyers 1147

Whitaker, Sarah
Night of Reunion - Michael Allegretto 42

Wilcox, Ruby
Thyme of Death - Susan Wittig Albert 33

Wilson, Laurie
Winter Rules - Barry Cork 318

Worthing, Matilda
Mass Murder - John Keith Drummond 449

CARPENTER

Aletter, Finny
Obstacle Course - Yvonne Montgomery 1167

CATERER

Bear, Goldy
The Cereal Murders - Diane Mott Davidson 389
Dying for Chocolate - Diane Mott Davidson 390

Fairchild, Faith
The Body in the Basement - Katherine Hall Page 1254
The Body in the Belfry - Katherine Hall Page 1255
The Body in the Cast - Katherine Hall Page 1257

Lisle, Darina
A Deepe Coffyn - Janet Laurence 988
Hotel Morgue - Janet Laurence 989
Recipe for Death - Janet Laurence 990

CHILD

Eakins, Abigail
The House on the Hill - Judith Kelman 899

Farrell, Tess
Deathspell - Veronica Stallwood 1558

Jacobs, Charley
Dark Swan - Kathryn Lasky Knight 944
Mortal Words - Kathryn Lasky Knight 945

Sway, Mark
The Client - John Grisham 680

Wade, Cassie
Count the Days - Lin Summerfield 1592

CIVIL SERVANT

King, Willow
Bitter Herbs - Natasha Cooper 307
Rotten Apples - Natasha Cooper 309

Wilson, Francesca
Death Among the Dons - Janet Neel 1196

CLERK

Rune
Manhattan Is My Beat - Jeffrey Wilds Deaver 404

COMPANION

Burns, Nora
Hell Bent - Ken Gross 684

Cantini, Angel
False Profit - Robert Eversz 511

Cromwell, Sarah
Deception Island - M.K. Lorens 1043
Sweet Narcissus - M.K. Lorens 1045

Cunningham, Maude
Diamond Head - Marian J.A. Jackson 834
The Sunken Treasure - Marian J.A. Jackson 835

Huxleigh, Penelope (Nell)
Good Morning, Irene - Carole Nelson Douglas 440
Irene at Large - Carole Nelson Douglas 442

COMPUTER EXPERT

Belski, Becky
Caught in the Shadows - C.A. Haddad 694

Blake, Julie
Love Bytes - Sally Chapman 232

Dinesen, Mike
Death Qualified: A Mystery of Chaos - Kate Wilhelm 1723

Fitzgerald, Jennifer
Coyote Bird - Jim DeFelice 409

Fleming, Laura
Dead Ringer - Toni L.P. Kelner 900
Down Home Murder - Toni L.P. Kelner 901
Trouble Looking for a Place to Happen - Toni L.P. Kelner 902

Graham, Warren
User Deadly - Denise Danks 388

Henderson, Peter
Sliver - Ira Levin 1013

Hope, Alison
Kid's Stuff - Susan B. Kelly 897

Kidd
The Empress File - John Camp 210

McKenna, Vincent
Moth to the Flame - Kathleen Dougherty 437

Noble, Jack
The Boss's Wife - S.L. Stebel 1562

Paoli, Vic
Love Bytes - Sally Chapman 232

Porter, Emma
Aunt Dimity and the Duke - Nancy Atherton 68

Silverthorne, Charlie
Moth to the Flame - Kathleen Dougherty 437

Wagner, Greg
Night Kills - Ed Gorman 622

CON ARTIST

Stein, Henry
Swindle - George Adams 11

CONSULTANT

Pratt, Pat
Murder at Musket Beach - Bernie Lee 998
Murder Without Reservation - Bernie Lee 999

CONVICT

Bannion, Rick
The Man Offside - A.W. Gray 652

Crayhall, Sam
The Chamber - John Grisham 679

Mahoney, Elvis
Flamingos - Marc Savage 1444

Nye, Eddie "Nails"
Lights Out - Peter Abrahams 4

Reno
Edge City - Sin Soracco 1537

COOK

Lisle, Darina
A Deepe Coffyn - Janet Laurence 988

O'Brien, Natasha
Someone Is Killing the Great Chefs of America - Nan Lyons 1061

Potter, Eugenia
The 27 Ingredient Chili Con Carne Murders - Nancy Pickard 1315

Quilliam, Meg
A Dash of Death - Claudia Bishop 134
A Taste for Murder - Claudia Bishop 135

COUNSELOR

Bushnell, Dan
A Strange and Bitter Crop - E.L. Wyrick 1780

Devine, Matt
Cat on a Blue Monday - Carole Nelson Douglas 438

Shea, Maggie
Night Angel - Kate Green 664

Silverman, Susan
Stardust - Robert B. Parker 1271
Walking Shadow - Robert B. Parker 1272

COWBOY

Crook, Paul
Stonefish - Charles West 1695

CRIMINAL

Ables, Glenn
The Standoff - Chuck Hogan 796

Addison, Eddie
Prized Possessions - L.R. Wright 1775

Alexander, Raymond "Mouse"
White Butterfly - Walter Mosley 1178

Bain, Dominic
Nobody's Fool - Marten Claridge 249

Ballou, Mick
A Dance at the Slaughterhouse - Lawrence Block 146

Barnes, Douglas
Bones of Coral - James W. Hall 707

Bartlett, Simon
Silent Night - Gary Amo 49

Bekker, Michael
Silent Prey - John Sandford 1427

Biwaban, Angela
Dynamite Pass - J.F. Trainor 1626

Bonello, Michael
Wiseguys in Love - C. Clark Criscuolo 355

Brevna, Bubba
The Emerald Lizard - Chris Wiltz 1738

Brod, Elliot
Gun Men - Gary Friedman 553

Browning, Grace
Angel of Death - Jack Higgins 786

Burke
Blossom - Andrew Vachss 1643

Carlisle, Andrew
Hour of the Hunter - J.A. Jance 843

Carrera, Rolando
Blood Relative - Carolyn Hougan 811

Castellano, Danny
Purgatory - Monty Mickleson 1152

Caute, Simon
Fuse Time - Max Byrd 205

Constantino, Junior
The Monkey Rope - Stephen Lewis 1023

Craddock, Davis
Bad to the Bone - Stephen Solomita 1532

Croft, Ralph
The Masked Man - P.C. Doherty 425

Cullen, Frank "Cully"
Cons - Timothy Watts 1677

Curran, Guy
Going Wrong - Ruth Rendell 1360

D'Angelo, Johnny
Bait - Kenneth Abel 3

Danzig, John "Jack Dance"
Whiskey River - Loren D. Estleman 501

Denkin, George
Incident at Potter's Bridge - Joseph Monninger 1165

Dent, Evan
Personal - C.K. Cambray 208

Devlin, Liam
The Eagle Has Flown - Jack Higgins 787

Donatti, Dominick
Strangers in the Night - Peg Tyre 1641

Dudgeon, Rene
Time and Time Again - B.M. Gill 587

Dupree, Carl
Purgatory - Monty Mickleson 1152

Farrell, Andrew
Criminal Conversation - Evan Hunter 820

Ferguson, Robert Earl
Just Cause - John Katzenbach 873

Florio, Nicky
Mortal Sin - Paul Levine 1014

Foley, Joseph
Balboa Firefly - Jack Trolley 1633

Franklin, Alton "Rooster"
Caught Looking - Randy Russell 1416

Furco, Lucca
Neon Caesar - Mark McGarrity 1128

Gordon, Alex
Someone Is Killing the Great Chefs of America - Nan Lyons 1061

Grant, Edward
Skeletons - Eric Sauter 1443

Grenier, Grayson
Balboa Firefly - Jack Trolley 1633

Haddon, Ronnie
Nightmare Point - Carole Berry 128

Helstrum, Christine
Night of Reunion - Michael Allegretto 42

Hodges, Karen
Skinny Man - James Colbert 273

Holden, Sidney
Elsinore - Jerome Charyn 238

Khai, Tranh Van
Predator's Waltz - Jay Brandon 165

King, Diana
Murder Has a Pretty Face - Jennie Melville 1142

LuEllen
The Empress File - John Camp 210

Mahoney, Elvis
Flamingos - Marc Savage 1444

Mal
An Hour to Kill - Edward Wellen 1690

Mannion, Billy
19th Precinct - Christopher Newman 1202

March, Edie
Stormy Weather - Carl Hiaasen 784

Marsh, Benny
Cons - Timothy Watts 1677

McGee, Mickey
The Cutting Hours - Julia Grice 673

McIlvaine, Lewis "Sport"
Don't Say a Word - Keith Peterson 1308
Don't Say a Word - Andrew Klavan 937

McKenna, Vincent
Moth to the Flame - Kathleen Dougherty 437

Melville, Susan
Miss Melville Rides a Tiger - Evelyn E. Smith 1518

Miller, Doc
King of the Corner - Loren D. Estleman 497

Monroe, Doyle
The Deer Killers - Gunnard Landers 973

Morgan, Mordecai "Maudie"
The Bag Man - Peter Lacey 961

Motley, James Leo
A Ticket to the Boneyard - Lawrence Block 149

Nello, Tony
King of the Hustlers - Eugene Izzi 831

Nye, Eddie "Nails"
Lights Out - Peter Abrahams 4

O'Brien, Brian
Murder Song - Jon Cleary 256

Odum, Glenn
Hard Guy - Thorton Elliott 482

Palmer, Chili
Get Shorty - Elmore Leonard 1005

Parley, Sherry
Miami Purity - Vicki Hendricks 773

Raptor
Menaced Assassin - Joe Gores 618

Rhodenbarr, Bernie
The Burglar Who Traded Ted Williams - Lawrence Block 145

Robbie, Ordell
Rum Punch - Elmore Leonard 1007

Schaeffer, Michael
Sleeping Dogs - Thomas Perry 1297

Shaugnessy, Tom
The Triumph of Bacchus - Douglas Skeggs 1509

Snow, Nicholas
Honolulu Red - Lue Zimmelman 1789

Spina, Toni
Neon Caesar - Mark McGarrity 1128

Springfield, Quincy
Motown - Loren D. Estleman 498

Stanley, Donald
Dead Easy - Arthur F. Nehrbass 1199

Stokes, Sally
A Broken Vessel - Kate Ross 1403

Straight, Leon
Done Deal - Les Standiford 1561

Terry, Christine
When She Was Bad - Ron Faust 518

Trevlyn, Laurel
Nobody Lives Forever - Edna Buchanan 187

Turchek, Robert
Thursday's Child - Teri White 1705

Vance, Lee
Scotch on the Rocks - Howard Browne 183

Vargas, Tony
Desert Heat - J.A. Jance 842

Watson, Lucas
Dangerous Attachments - Sarah Lovett 1051

Weir, Eldon
The House on the Hill - Judith Kelman 899

Wilson, Everett
Prime Suspect - A.W. Gray 653

Wingate, Buddy
The Cactus Garden - Robert Ward 1672

Wingate, Charlotte Rae
The Cactus Garden - Robert Ward 1672

Woodrow, Michael
Flawless - Adam Barrow 99

Character Description Index

Wyatt, Baker
The Ransom - Brian Tobin 1622

CRIMINOLOGIST

Berman, Kate
Widowmaker - William Appel 63

Sheriden, Charles
Death at Gallows Green - Robin Paige 1260

CRITIC

Barnett, Michael
With Extreme Prejudice - Frederick Barton 102

Gordon, Alex
Someone Is Killing the Great Chefs of America - Nan Lyons 1061

Pamplemousse
Monsieur Pamplemousse Investigates - Michael Bond 151

DANCER

Indermill, Bonnie
Good Night, Sweet Prince - Carole Berry 126

Susanna
Edge City - Sin Soracco 1537

Tremayne, Maggie
Four Steps to Death - Diana Ramsay 1346

DEFENDANT

Slocum, John
Trade-Off - Harrison Arnston 66

DENTIST

Adams, Charlie "Doc"
Yellow Bird - Rick Boyer 162

DESIGNER

Grover, Serena "Renie"
A Fit of Tempera - Mary Daheim 375

Strauss, Violet
The India Exhibition - Richard Timothy Conroy 296

DETECTIVE

Abigail, Charles
Obit - Daniel Paisner 1261

Cole, Hardy
Killings - A.W. Gray 651

Kayne, Brian
Flowers for the Dead - Ann M. Williams 1728

McKenna, Brian
Detective First Grade - Don Mahoney 1067

McMorran, Frank
Nobody's Fool - Marten Claridge 249

Stranahan, Mick
Skin Tight - Carl Hiaasen 783

DETECTIVE—AMATEUR

Duncan, Stephanie
Brideprice - J.N. Catanach 226

Falco, M. Didius
The Silver Pigs - Lindsey Davis 394

Indermill, Bonnie
Death of a Dancing Fool - Carole Berry 124

Regan, Francis
Bloody Ten - William F. Love 1047

Robicheaux, Dave
Black Cherry Blues - James Lee Burke 193

DETECTIVE—HOMICIDE

Decker, Peter
Sanctuary - Faye Kellerman 884

Dogg, David
Bury the Bishop - Kate Gallison 564

Drake, Jessica
Angel of Death - Rochelle Majer Krich 953
Fair Game - Rochelle Majer Krich 954

Flint, Mike
Midnight Baby - Wendy Hornsby 808

Grabowski, Joseph
Elective Murder - Janet McGiffin 1129

Langdon, Skip
The Axeman's Jazz - Julie Smith 1523
Jazz Funeral - Julie Smith 1526
New Orleans Beat - Julie Smith 1527

Lawton, Dave
Dead Ahead - Ruby Horansky 804
Dead Center - Ruby Horansky 805

Levinson, Karen
Skins - Catherine O'Connell 1222

Lieberman, Abe
Lieberman's Day - Stuart M. Kaminsky 857

Miller, Peter
Beat Up a Cookie - Denise Dietz 422
Throw Darts at a Cheesecake - Denise Dietz 423

Monroe, Andy
Safe at Home - Alison Gordon 614

Mulcahaney, Norah
Lockout - Lillian O'Donnell 1224
A Private Crime - Lillian O'Donnell 1225
Pushover - Lillian O'Donnell 1226

Munro, Andy
Striking Out - Alison Gordon 615

O'Hanlon, Ike
Full Commission - Carol Brennan 172

Perilli, Tony
Skins - Catherine O'Connell 1222

Pucci, Sal
Funny as a Dead Comic - Susan Rogers Cooper 312
Funny as a Dead Relative - Susan Rogers Cooper 313

Rhodes, Frank
Love Lies - Fern Kupfer 960

Scarf, Bruce
Casualty Loss - Jim Weikart 1683

Schulz, Tom
The Cereal Murders - Diane Mott Davidson 389

Smith, Jill
Death and Taxes - Susan Dunlap 460
Diamond in the Buff - Susan Dunlap 461
Time Expired - Susan Dunlap 464

Somers, John
Cold Call - Dianne G. Pugh 1333

Swift, Doug
The Water Cure - Warwick Downing 446

Trakos, Nikki
Dead Ahead - Ruby Horansky 804
Dead Center - Ruby Horansky 805

Tully, Eustes
In Deep - Bruce Jones 846

Detective—Police

Van Dyne, Mel
A Farewell to Yarns - Jill Churchill 245
From Here to Paternity - Jill Churchill 246

DETECTIVE—POLICE

Barrish, Rick
Nobody Lives Forever - Edna Buchanan 187

Beaumont, J.P.
Minor in Possession - J.A. Jance 844

Brice, Frederick
The Honourable Detective - Jeffrey Ashford 67

Carella, Steve
Vespers - Ed McBain 1107

Dover, Wilf
Dover and the Claret Tappers - Joyce Porter 1322

Eichord, Jake
Stone Shadow - Rex Miller 1154

Faro, Jeremy
Deadly Beloved - Alanna Knight 942

Finn, John
Strangers in the Night - Peg Tyre 1641

Folger, Merry
Death on Rough Water - Francine Matthews 1099

Garcia, Lupe
The Cheerio Killings - Douglas Allyn 47

Gardner, Richard
U.S.S.A. - David Madsen 1066

Hawes, Cotton
Vespers - Ed McBain 1107

Hill, Judy
The Other Woman - Jill McGown 1132

Hollinger, Robert
Point Blank - Jayson Livingston 1033

Jurnet, Benjamin
A Very Particular Murder - S.T. Haymon 759

Kelsey
A Violent End - Emma Page 1253

Lloyd
The Other Woman - Jill McGown 1132

Lynley, Thomas
Payment in Blood - Elizabeth George 576

Malone, Scobie
Babylon South - Jon Cleary 255

Moodrow, Stanley
Force of Nature - Stephen Solomita 1533
A Piece of the Action - Stephen Solomita 1535

Palma, Carmen
Mercy - David L. Lindsey 1027

Parker, Claire
Hot Shots - Laurence Gough 627

Patterson, Hugh
Murder Movie - Jill McGown 1131

Pollard, Tom
The Glade Manor Murder - Elizabeth Lemarchand 1001

Quaid, Dermot
To Killashea - Norman Flood 530

Rawlings, John
The Great Grave Robbery - John Minahan 1158

Redlam, Stuart
Point Blank - Jayson Livingston 1033

Skiles, Brian
The Last Page - Bob Fenster 524

Stainton, Alec
The Noose of Time - Stephen Murray 1189

Standish, Margaret
Deadly Resolutions - Anna Ashwood Collins 274

Detective—Private

Starr, Rachel
Honolulu Red - Lue Zimmelman 1789
Thanet, Luke
Dead by Morning - Dorothy Simpson 1502
Tilley, Jim
Force of Nature - Stephen Solomita 1533
Toye, Gregory
The Glade Manor Murder - Elizabeth Lemarchand 1001
Vinda, John
Exceptional Clearance - William J. Caunitz 229
Wellman, Ben
Streets of Fire - Thomas H. Cook 306
Willows, Jack
Hot Shots - Laurence Gough 627
Yablonsky, Alvin
The Bone Orchard - Joseph Trigoboff 1628

DETECTIVE—PRIVATE

Asherfeld, Aaron
A Clean Sweep - David Berlinski 123
Balcazar, Dred
The Very Bad Thing - Ned White 1703
Barnes, Ezell "Easy"
Behind the Fact - Richard Hilary 788
Bascombe, Carver
Blood of Poets - Kenn Davis 393
Bearpaw, Molly
Ravenmocker - Jean Hager 701
The Redbird's Cry - Jean Hager 702
Beaudine, Alex
Prime Time for Murder - Valerie Frankel 542
Bernhardt, Alan
Except for the Bones - Collin Wilcox 1713
Full Circle - Collin Wilcox 1714
Silent Witness - Collin Wilcox 1716
Bethany, Tom
Bear Hug - Jerome Doolittle 432
Body Scissors - Jerome Doolittle 433
Kill Story - Jerome Doolittle 434
Stranglehold - Jerome Doolittle 435
Biwaban, Angela
Corona Blue - J.F. Trainor 1625
Black, Helen
Murder by the Book - Pat Welch 1689
Black, Johnny
Black Eye - Neville Steed 1563
Black, Thomas
The Portland Laugher - Earl Emerson 489
The Vanishing Smile - Earl Emerson 490
Yellow Dog Party - Earl Emerson 491
Blackthorne, Nathan
Grave Secrets - Louise Hendricksen 774
Blake, Julie
Love Bytes - Sally Chapman 232
Blevins, Haskell
Pet Peeves - Taylor McCafferty 1111
Blissberg, Harvey
World of Hurt - Richard Rosen 1400
Bodine, Jack
Closing Costs - Thomas Bunn 189
Worse than Death - Thomas Bunn 190
Bohland, Harmon
Shooting Star - Kate Green 665
Brannigan, Kate
Crack Down - Val McDermid 1125
Broz, Tito
Interview with Mattie - Shelley Singer 1504

Picture of David - Shelley Singer 1505
Searching for Sara - Shelley Singer 1506
Bruno, Adam
The Codicil - Tom Topor 1623
Buffolino, Tony
Murder at the Kennedy Center - Margaret Truman 1634
Calabrese, Dub
White Rook - J. Madison Davis 392
Caliban, Catherine "Cat"
Four Elements of Murder - D.B. Borton 155
Three Is a Crowd - D.B. Borton 156
Two Points for Murder - D.B. Borton 157
Cantini, Angel
False Profit - Robert Eversz 511
Carlyle, Carlotta
Coyote - Linda Barnes 92
Snapshot - Linda Barnes 93
Steel Guitar - Linda Barnes 94
Carver, Fred
Flame - John Lutz 1057
Spark - John Lutz 1058
Casey, James P.
A Case of Innocence - Douglas J. Keeling 877
Cecile
A Sudden Death at the Norfolk Cafe - Winona Sullivan 1591
Cervantes, Antonio "Chico"
Death as a Career Move - Bruce Cook 299
Rough Cut - Bruce Cook 300
The Sidewalk Hilton - Bruce Cook 301
Chase, Elizabeth
Murder in Scorpio - Martha C. Lawrence 993
Chin, Lydia
China Trade - S.J. Rozan 1410
Cole, Elvis
Free Fall - Robert Crais 341
Lullaby Town - Robert Crais 342
Stalking the Angel - Robert Crais 343
Voodoo River - Robert Crais 344
Colorado, Kat
Alley Kat Blues - Karen Kijewski 917
Copy Kat - Karen Kijewski 918
Katapult - Karen Kijewski 919
Katwalk - Karen Kijewski 920
Wild Kat - Karen Kijewski 921
Conrad, Claire
Beauty Dies - Melodie Johnson Howe 813
The Mother Shadow - Melodie Johnson Howe 814
Coogan, Blackie
Charged with Guilt - Gloria White 1700
Money to Burn - Gloria White 1701
Murder on the Run - Gloria White 1702
Coulter, Jason
Ten of Swords - J.R. Levitt 1018
Creed, John
The Keeper - Meg O'Brien 1217
Croft, Joshua
At Ease with the Dead - Walter Satterthwait 1437
A Flower in the Desert - Walter Satterthwait 1439
The Hanged Man - Walter Satterthwait 1440
Crook, Paul
Stonefish - Charles West 1695
Crusoe, Edwina
Desperate Remedy - Mary Kittredge 931
Kill or Cure - Mary Kittredge 932
Walking Dead Man - Mary Kittredge 934
Cuddy, John Francis
Act of God - Jeremiah Healy 764
Foursome - Jeremiah Healy 765
Yesterday's News - Jeremiah Healy 766

Da Silva, Jane
Electric City - K.K. Beck 115
Dain, Eddie
Dead Man - Joe Gores 617
Danforth, Abigail
Diamond Head - Marian J.A. Jackson 834
The Sunken Treasure - Marian J.A. Jackson 835
Davilov, Queenie
Cut To—Murder - Denise Osborne 1247
Murder Offscreen - Denise Osborne 1248
Davis, Mavis
My First Murder - Susan Baker 84
Delaney, Patricia
Angel's Bidding - Sharon Gwyn Short 1489
The Death We Share - Sharon Gwyn Short 1490
Deleeuw, Kit
Death by Station Wagon - Jon Katz 869
The Family Stalker - Jon Katz 870
Delvecchio, Nick
The Dead of Brooklyn - Robert J. Randisi 1347
DeNobili, Duke
Alibi for an Actress - Gillian B. Farrell 516
Denson, John
Bigfoot - Richard Hoyt 815
Whoo? - Richard Hoyt 816
Denton, Harry James
Dead Folks' Blues - Steven Womack 1751
Torch Town Boogie - Steven Womack 1754
Way Past Dead - Steven Womack 1755
Detective, Nameless
Breakdown - Bill Pronzini 1326
Epitaphs - Bill Pronzini 1327
Jackpot - Bill Pronzini 1328
Quarry - Bill Pronzini 1329
Devlin, Jack
And Justice for One - John Clarkson 254
DiGregorio, Joe
Vanishing Act - Seth Jacob Margolis 1075
Disbro, Gil
The Flip Side of Life - James E. Martin 1085
Doll
Death Among the Angels - John Walter Putre 1336
Donaghue, Ulysses
Mr. Donaghue Investigates - Anna Shone 1488
Dorsey, Carroll
The Fall-Down Artist - Thomas Lipinski 1032
Doyle, Abigail
Deadly Resolutions - Anna Ashwood Collins 274
Doyle, Matt
Murder Begins at Home - Dale L. Gilbert 585
Dunn, Micah
The Caesar Clue - M.K. Shuman 1491
Deep Kill - M.K. Shuman 1492
The Last Man to Die - M.K. Shuman 1493
The Maya Stone Murders - M.K. Shuman 1494
Elliott, Maggie
The Northwest Murders - Elizabeth Atwood Taylor 1607
Eton, Vic
Dark of Night - Richard Nehrbass 1200
Farabaugh, Mickey
According to St. John - William Babula 77
Finn, Frances
Murder at St. Adelaide's - Gerelyn Hollingsworth 799
Fisher, Noel
The Total Zone - Martina Navratilova 1195
Flagg, Conan
Dead Matter - M.K. Wren 1764
King of the Mountain - M.K. Wren 1765

Flam, Victor
Flawless - Adam Barrow 99

Fletcher, J.
A Hazard of Losers - Lloyd Biggle Jr. 132

Flippo, Jack
Dreamboat - Doug J. Swanson 1596

Fortune, Dan
Cassandra in Red - Michael Collins 281
Chasing Eights - Michael Collins 282
Crime, Punishment and Resurrection - Michael Collins 283

Frederickson, Robert "Mongo"
In the House of Secret Enemies - George C. Chesbro 241
The Language of Cannibals - George C. Chesbro 242

Friedman, Kinky
God Bless John Wayne - Kinky Friedman 554
Musical Chairs - Kinky Friedman 555

Gallagher, Odyssey
Came a Dead Cat - James N. Frey 551

Garrett, Dave
Burning March - Neil Albert 28
Cruel April - Neil Albert 29
The February Trouble - Neil Albert 30
The January Corpse - Neil Albert 31

Garrity, Callahan
Every Crooked Nanny - Kathy Hogan Trocheck 1631
To Live and Die in Dixie - Kathy Hogan Trocheck 1632

Gennaro, Angela
A Drink Before the War - Dennis Lehane 1000

Gentry, Ron
The Manx Murders - William L. DeAndrea 402

Glauberman, Alex
Obligations of the Bone - Dick Cluster 263

Glick, Murray
The Big Freeze - Michael J. Katz 871
Last Dance in Redondo Beach - Michael J. Katz 872

Goldman, David
Bloody Ten - William F. Love 1047
The Chartreuse Clue - William F. Love 1048

Gondolfo, Sonny
Murder and a Muse - Gillian B. Farrell 517

Goodman, Rayford
Shot on Location - Stan Cutler 369

Goodwin, Archie
Fade to Black - Robert Goldsborough 607
Silver Spire - Robert Goldsborough 608

Gordianus the Finder
Roman Blood - Steven Saylor 1449
The Venus Throw - Steven Saylor 1450

Grant, Jack
Frozen Stare - Richard B. Schwartz 1459

Greenert, Dub
Red Knight - J. Madison Davis 391

Griffin, Lew
Black Hornet - James Sallis 1421
Moth - James Sallis 1422

Grist, Simeon
Everything but the Squeal - Timothy Hallinan 716
Incinerator - Timothy Hallinan 717
Skin Deep - Timothy Hallinan 718

Guiu, Lonia
Antipodes - Maria-Antonia Oliver 1236

Gunner, Aaron
Not Long for This World - Gar Anthony Haywood 762

Gunther, Bernie
The Pale Criminal - Philip Kerr 914

Haggerty, Leo
A Fistful of Empty - Benjamin M. Schutz 1457
Mexico Is Forever - Benjamin M. Schutz 1458

Hallam, Lucas
Dead-Stick - L.J. Washburn 1674
Dog Heavies - L.J. Washburn 1675

Halley, Sid
Come to Grief - Dick Francis 538

Hamilton, David
One Cried Murder - David Cooper Wall 1663

Hammer, Mike
The Killing Man - Mickey Spillane 1540

Hannibal, Joe
The Skintight Shroud - Wayne Dundee 459

Hardy, Cliff
Matrimonial Causes - Peter Corris 327
O'Fear - Peter Corris 328
Wet Graves - Peter Corris 329

Hardy, Dismas
The Vig - John T. Lescroart 1010

Hastings, Stanley
Juror - Parnell Hall 714

Hawley, Bill
Grave Matters - Leo Axler 71

Hayle, Tamara
Devil's Gonna Get Him - Valerie Wilson Wesley 1691
When Death Comes Stealing - Valerie Wilson Wesley 1692

Heller, Nate
Blood and Thunder - Max Allan Collins 276
Carnal Hours - Max Allan Collins 277
Murder in the Post-War World - Max Allan Collins 279
Stolen Away - Max Allan Collins 280

Henry, Ben
A Dry and Thirsty Ground - Mike Weiss 1688

Hickey, Tom
The Angel Gang - Ken Kuhlken 956
The Loud Adios - Ken Kuhlken 957
The Venus Deal - Ken Kuhlken 958

Hill, Maggie
Beauty Dies - Melodie Johnson Howe 813

Holmes, Sherlock
The Beekeeper's Apprentice - Laurie R. King 924
The Disappearance of Edwin Drood - Peter Rowland 1407
The Glendower Conspiracy - Lloyd Biggle Jr. 131
A Monstrous Regiment of Women - Laurie R. King 926
The Seventh Bullet - Daniel D. Victor 1654

Hooper, B.F.
Saint Louie Blues - Jake Tanner 1601

Horowitz, Helen
The Last Gambit - David Delman 411

Howard, Jeri
Kindred Crimes - Janet Dawson 397
Nobody's Child - Janet Dawson 398

Hughes, Josephine "Jo"
Blood of an Aries - Linda Mather 1094

Hunt, Morgan
Deep End - Geoffrey Norman 1210

Jackson, Jeff
A Beautiful Place to Die - Philip R. Craig 335
A Case of Vineyard Poisoning - Philip R. Craig 336
Cliff Hanger - Philip R. Craig 337
The Double Minded Men - Philip R. Craig 338
Off Season - Philip R. Craig 339
The Woman Who Walked into the Sea - Philip R. Craig 340

Jacob, Matt
Still Among the Living - Zachary Klein 938
Two Way Toll - Zachary Klein 939

Jacoby, Miles
Hard Look - Robert J. Randisi 1349
Separate Cases - Robert J. Randisi 1350

Jacovich, Milan
The Cleveland Connection - Les Roberts 1383
Deep Shaker - Les Roberts 1384
The Duke of Cleveland - Les Roberts 1385
Full Cleveland - Les Roberts 1386

Janeway, Cliff
The Bookman's Wake - John Dunning 467

Jantarro, J.K.G.
Work for a Dead Man - Simon Ritchie 1371

January, Cole
Stand-In for Murder - Lynn Bradley 164

Jasper, Jazz
The Cheetah Chase - Karin McQuillan 1137

Jones, Edward Porter
The Glendower Conspiracy - Lloyd Biggle Jr. 131

Joplin, Dean
U.S.S.A. - David Madsen 1066

Kearny, Dan
32 Cadillacs - Joe Gores 616

Kenzie, Patrick
A Drink Before the War - Dennis Lehane 1000

Killebrew, Coley
Fire Horse - Bill Shoemaker 1486

Kincaid, Ryan
High Strangeness - Alison Drake 447

Kinsella, Kate
Deadly Admirer - Christine Green 658
Deadly Errand - Christine Green 659
Deadly Practice - Christine Green 660

Kirk, Devlin
Body Guard - Rex Burns 199
Parts Unknown - Rex Burns 200

Knight, Mickey
The Intersection of Law and Desire - J.M. Redmann 1356

Kruger, Dan
Red Winter - Michael Cormany 319
Skin Deep Is Fatal - Michael Cormany 320

Kyle, Jack
The Dallas Deception - Richard Abshire 7
Turnaround Jack - Richard Abshire 8

Lacey, Meg
No Forwarding Address - Elisabeth Bowers 161

Lake, Barrett
Interview with Mattie - Shelley Singer 1504
Picture of David - Shelley Singer 1505
Searching for Sara - Shelley Singer 1506

Laurano, Lauren
Everything You Have Is Mine - Sandra Scoppettone 1460
I'll Be Leaving You Always - Sandra Scoppettone 1461
My Sweet Untraceable You - Sandra Scoppettone 1462

Lee, Anna
Backhand - Liza Cody 269

Leeds, Cornelius
One Kiss Led to Another - Harris Dulaney 454

Legendre, J.J.
The Neon Smile - Dick Lochte 1039

Leidl, Constance
Seven Kinds of Death - Kate Wilhelm 1725

Detective—Private

Lomax, Jacob
Blood Relative - Michael Allegretto 39
The Dead of Winter - Michael Allegretto 40
Grave Doubt - Michael Allegretto 41

Lowell, Tony M.C.
Eye of the Gator - E.C. Ayres 72
Hour of the Manatee - E.C. Ayres 73

Lowry, Gideon
Killing Me Softly - John Leslie 1012

Lujack, Jimmy
The Book of Numbers - David Thoreau 1616

Lynch, Jack
The Software Bomb - Steven Womack 1753

MacDonald, Devon
The Silver Scapel - Nancy Baker Jacobs 837
The Turquoise Tattoo - Nancy Baker Jacobs 838

Magaracz, Nick
Jersey Monkey - Kate Gallison 565

Mallory, Stuart
Close Softly the Doors - Ronald Clair Roat 1373
A Still and Icy Silence - Ronald Clair Roat 1374

Mallory, Wanda
Prime Time for Murder - Valerie Frankel 542

Manion, Terry
Blue Bayou - Dick Lochte 1038
The Neon Smile - Dick Lochte 1039

Marlowe, Philip
Perchance to Dream - Robert B. Parker 1270

Marston, Paul
False Profit - Robert Eversz 511

McCone, Sharon
The Shape of Dread - Marcia Muller 1181
Till The Butchers Cut Him Down - Marcia Muller 1182
Trophies and Dead Things - Marcia Muller 1183
Where Echoes Live - Marcia Muller 1184
A Wild and Lonely Place - Marcia Muller 1185

McGarvey, Russ
The Last Surprise - William Moore 1169

McGrogan, Annie
Murder and a Muse - Gillian B. Farrell 517

McKenzie, Mac
Murder by Tarot - Al Guthrie 693

McWilliams, Caroline
Separate Cases - Robert J. Randisi 1350

Meiklejohn, Charlie
Seven Kinds of Death - Kate Wilhelm 1725

Midnight Louie
Cat on a Blue Monday - Carole Nelson Douglas 438
Catnap - Carole Nelson Douglas 439
Pussyfoot - Carole Nelson Douglas 443

Miles, Robert
False Profits - David Everson 509
Suicide Squeeze - David Everson 510

Millhone, Kinsey
F Is for Fugitive - Sue Grafton 634
G Is for Gumshoe - Sue Grafton 635
H Is for Homicide - Sue Grafton 636
I Is for Innocent - Sue Grafton 637
K Is for Killer - Sue Grafton 638
L Is for Lawless - Sue Grafton 639

Mondragon, Rita
The Hanged Man - Walter Satterthwait 1440

Monk, William
Cain His Brother - Anne Perry 1292
A Sudden, Fearful Death - Anne Perry 1296

Monroe, Jessica
Deadly Stakes - H. Fred Wiser 1745

Moodrow, Stanley
Bad to the Bone - Stephen Solomita 1532

Moony, Phil
The Man with My Name - Paul Engleman 494

Murdock, Matt
Merry Christmas, Murdock - Robert J. Ray 1352
Murdock Cracks Ice - Robert J. Ray 1353

Nebraska
The Naked Eye - William J. Reynolds 1364

Nichols, Nason
Trade Secrets - Maynard F. Thomson 1615

Noonan, Joe
Black Light - Daniel Hearn 767

Noonan, Rita
Friends in High Places - Michael Hendricks 771
Money to Burn - Michael Hendricks 772

Nudger, Alo
Diamond Eyes - John Lutz 1056
Thicker than Blood - John Lutz 1059
Time Exposure - John Lutz 1060

Oloo, Wellington Waki
Brideprice - J.N. Catanach 226

O'Neal, Freddie
Bet Against the House - Catherine Dain 378
Lay It on the Line - Catherine Dain 379
Sing a Song of Death - Catherine Dain 380
Walk a Crooked Mile - Catherine Dain 381

O'Shaughnessy, Kiernan
Pious Deception - Susan Dunlap 462
Rogue Wave - Susan Dunlap 463

Paine, Jack
Summer Cool - Al Sarrantonio 1436

Paoli, Vic
Love Bytes - Sally Chapman 232

Perkins, Ben
Concrete Hero - Rob Kantner 862
The Quick and the Dead - Rob Kantner 863
The Red, White, and Blues - Rob Kantner 864
The Thousand Yard Stare - Rob Kantner 865

Peters, Anna
Time Lapse - Janice Law 992

Peters, Toby
The Melting Clock - Stuart M. Kaminsky 860

Pike, Joe
Free Fall - Robert Crais 341
Lullaby Town - Robert Crais 342
Stalking the Angel - Robert Crais 343

Polo, Nick
Beggar's Choice - Jerry Kennealy 906
Special Delivery - Jerry Kennealy 907
Vintage Polo - Jerry Kennealy 908

Poteet, Ralph
Peeper - Loren D. Estleman 499

Prescott, Amy
Grave Secrets - Louise Hendricksen 774

Prettybird, Willie
Bigfoot - Richard Hoyt 815

Principal, Laura
Every Breath You Take - Michelle Spring 1541

Rafferty
Rafferty: Fatal Sisters - W. Glenn Duncan 458

Rafferty, Neal
The Emerald Lizard - Chris Wiltz 1738

Ramadge, Gwenn
The Raggedy Man - Lillian O'Donnell 1227
Used to Kill - Lillian O'Donnell 1228
A Wreath for the Bride - Lillian O'Donnell 1229

Randolph, Jessica
A Relative Stranger - Margaret Lucke 1052

Rasmussen, Alex
The Heaven Stone - David Daniel 386

Rawlins, Easy
White Butterfly - Walter Mosley 1178

Reddy, Jason
Deadly Stakes - H. Fred Wiser 1745

Reece, Caitlin
Ninth Life - Lauren Wright Douglas 444

Reilly, Regan
Decked - Carol Higgins Clark 250
Snagged - Carol Higgins Clark 251

Renzler, Mark
Who Shot Longshot Sam? - Paul Engleman 495

Resnick, Slots
Three Strikes, You're Dead - Michael Geller 574

Rhinehart, Michael
The Queen's Mare - John Birkett 133

Rice, Harry
The Harry Chronicles - Allan Pedrazas 1287

Ritchie, Lillian
Shattered Rhythms - Phyllis Knight 946
Switching the Odds - Phyllis Knight 947

Roman, Dan
September Song - Edward Mathis 1096

Roper, Taggert
The Next Victim - William Sanders 1423

Ross, Jack
The Desert Look - Bernard Schopen 1455

St. John, Jeremiah
According to St. John - William Babula 77

Samson, Albert
Called by a Panther - Michael Z. Lewin 1019

Samson, John
The Cords of Vanity - Miles Tripp 1629
Video Vengeance - Miles Tripp 1630

Sands, Jake
East Beach - Ron Ely 485
Night Shadows - Ron Ely 486

Saucier, Vonna
White Rook - J. Madison Davis 392

Sawyer, Pete
The Riviera Contract - Marvin Albert 26
The Zig-Zag Man - Marvin Albert 27

Saxon
Seeing the Elephant - Les Roberts 1387

Sayler, Catherine
Love nor Money - Linda Grant 648
A Woman's Place - Linda Grant 649

Schwartz, Lenny
Virgil's Ghost - Irving Weinman 1684

Scudder, Matt
A Dance at the Slaughterhouse - Lawrence Block 146
The Devil Knows You're Dead - Lawrence Block 147
Out on the Cutting Edge - Lawrence Block 148
A Ticket to the Boneyard - Lawrence Block 149
A Walk Among the Tombstones - Lawrence Block 150

Shanahan, Dietrich "Deets"
The Iron Glove - Ronald Tierney 1619
The Steel Web - Ronald Tierney 1620
The Stone Veil - Ronald Tierney 1621

Shapiro, Desiree
Murder Can Kill Your Social Life - Selma Eichler 473

Shaw, James
Bad Neighbors - Isidore Haiblum 703

Shayne, Hector Belascoran
An Easy Thing - Paco Ignacio Taibo II 1597

Sherman, Boyd
Medicine Dog - Geoff Peterson 1307

Sherman, Sam
The Turquoise Tattoo - Nancy Baker Jacobs 838

Shugak, Kate
A Cold-Blooded Business - Dana Stabenow 1550
A Cold Day for Murder - Dana Stabenow 1549
Dead in the Water - Dana Stabenow 1551
Play with Fire - Dana Stabenow 1552

Siegal, Phoebe
By Evil Means - Sandra West Prowell 1332

Sierra, Randall
Shoot the Piper - Richard Hill 791

Sinclair, Gar
Thursday's Child - Teri White 1705

Slezak, Elmer "Snake"
The Portland Laugher - Earl Emerson 489

Sloane, Sydney
Sister's Keeper - Randye Lordon 1042

Smith, Truman
Dead on the Island - Bill Crider 350
Gator Kill - Bill Crider 352
When Old Men Die - Bill Crider 354

Smith, Zack
Cat's Paw, Inc. - L.L. Thrasher 1618

Socarides, Aristotle "Soc"
Death in Deep Water - Paul Kemprecos 903
Feeding Frenzy - Paul Kemprecos 904
Neptune's Eye - Paul Kemprecos 905

Spenser
Double Deuce - Robert B. Parker 1269
Stardust - Robert B. Parker 1271
Walking Shadow - Robert B. Parker 1272

Stewart, Blaine
Dancing in the Dark - Sharon Zukowski 1798
Leap of Faith - Sharon Zukowski 1799

Stoner, Harry
Missing - Jonathan Valin 1646
The Music Lovers - Jonathan Valin 1647
Second Chance - Jonathan Valin 1648

Strachey, Donald
Third Man Out - Richard Stevenson 1572

Strickland, Dave
Suffer Little Children - Thomas D. Davis 396

Sughrue, C.W.
The Mexican Tree Duck - James Crumley 363

Tanner, Alex
The Glass Ceiling - Anabel Donald 428

Tanner, John Marshall
Blood Type - Stephen Greenleaf 667
Book Case - Stephen Greenleaf 668
Southern Cross - Stephen Greenleaf 669

Taylor, Holland
Penance - David Housewright 812

Thorn
Gone Wild - James W. Hall 708
Mean High Tide - James W. Hall 710

Tracer, John
Tracer, Inc. - Jeff Andrus 58

Traveler, Martin
Called Home - R.R. Irvine 828
The Great Reminder - R.R. Irvine 829
Pillar of Fire - R.R. Irvine 830

Traveler, Moroni
The Angel's Share - R.R. Irvine 826
Called Home - R.R. Irvine 828
The Great Reminder - R.R. Irvine 829
Pillar of Fire - R.R. Irvine 830

Ventana, Ronnie
Charged with Guilt - Gloria White 1700
Money to Burn - Gloria White 1701
Murder on the Run - Gloria White 1702

Walker, Amos
Sweet Women Lie - Loren D. Estleman 500

Walsh, Jack
The Night Remembers - Ed Gorman 623

Warshawski, V.I.
Burn Marks - Sara Paretsky 1264
Guardian Angel - Sara Paretsky 1265
Tunnel Vision - Sara Paretsky 1266

Wells, Gardner
Body of Evidence - David A. Van Meter 1653

Wells, Nadia
Blue Bayou - Dick Lochte 1038

West, Delilah
Hit and Run - Maxine O'Callaghan 1219
Set-Up - Maxine O'Callaghan 1220

Whelan, Paul
Death in Uptown - Michael Raleigh 1345

Wilder, Johannah
Shadow Dance - Agnes Bushnell 202

Wilson, Ruth
Shadow Dance - Agnes Bushnell 202

Winfield, Carter
Murder Begins at Home - Dale L. Gilbert 585

Winter, Alex
Library: No Murder Aloud - Susan Steiner 1569

Winter, Stuart
No Sign of Murder - Alan Russell 1414

Wolfe, Hannah
Birthmarks - Sarah Dunant 455
Under My Skin - Sarah Dunant 456

Wolfe, Nero
Fade to Black - Robert Goldsborough 607
Silver Spire - Robert Goldsborough 608

Younger, Cecil
The Curious Eat Themselves - John Straley 1580
The Woman Who Married a Bear - John Straley 1581

DIPLOMAT

Darwin, Peter
Comeback - Dick Francis 539

Michaelson, Richard
Faithfully Executed - Michael Bowen 159

Mitchell, Meredith
Cold in the Earth - Ann Granger 642
A Fine Place for Death - Ann Granger 643
Murder Among Us - Ann Granger 644
A Season for Murder - Ann Granger 645

Scruggs, Henry
The India Exhibition - Richard Timothy Conroy 296
Mr. Smithson's Bones - Richard Timothy Conroy 297

DIRECTOR

Derwent, Frank
Murder Movie - Jill McGown 1131

Halliwell, Hal
Death and the Trumpets of Tuscany - Hazel Wynn Jones 847

Yale, Sam
Sliver - Ira Levin 1013

DIVER

Aydlett, Shad
Louisiana Blue - David Poyer 1324

Galloway, Tiller
Louisiana Blue - David Poyer 1324

DIVORCED PERSON

Bear, Goldy
The Cereal Murders - Diane Mott Davidson 389
Dying for Chocolate - Diane Mott Davidson 390

Belski, Becky
Caught in the Shadows - C.A. Haddad 694

James, Liz
Cry for Help - Karen Hanson Stuyck 1586

Plum, Stephanie
One for the Money - Janet Evanovich 503

Saldinger, Byron
Shooting Script - Gordon Cotler 332

DOCTOR

Adams, Kip
Everything You Have Is Mine - Sandra Scoppettone 1460
I'll Be Leaving You Always - Sandra Scoppettone 1461
My Sweet Untraceable You - Sandra Scoppettone 1462

Anderson, Owen
Shadowchase - Martin Blank 143

Arrington, Molly
Primal Fear - William Diehl 421

Baldwin, Sarah
Natural Causes - Michael Palmer 1262

Barron, Peter
Darkness Falls - Joyce Anne Schneider 1453

Baxter, Claire
Disassociated States - Leonard Simon 1499

Berman, Josh
Widowmaker - William Appel 63

Berman, Kate
Whisper.He Might Hear You - William Appel 62

Blakeney, Sarah
The Scold's Bridle - Minette Walters 1670

Blumenthal, Marissa
Vital Signs - Robin Cook 303

Brenner, Alecia
Deadfall in Berlin - R.D. Zimmerman 1792

Broussard, Andy
Blood on the Bayou - D.J. Donaldson 429
New Orleans Requiem - D.J. Donaldson 430
No Mardi Gras for the Dead - D.J. Donaldson 431

Conrad, Nathan
Don't Say a Word - Keith Peterson 1308
Don't Say a Word - Andrew Klavan 937

Coyle, Kate
The Catalyst - Desmond Cory 330
The Dobie Paradox - Desmond Cory 331

Cross, Alex
Along Came a Spider - James Patterson 1276

Fell, Gideon
Fell and Foul Play - John Dickson Carr 221

Frank, Jason
Hanging Time - Leslie Glass 601

Graveline, Rudy
Skin Tight - Carl Hiaasen 783

Hammond, Amanda
Darkness Falls - Joyce Anne Schneider 1453

Helms, Marsha
Way Past Dead - Steven Womack 1755

Hunsacker, Dale
A Man to Die For - Eileen Dreyer 448

Karkinnen, Weather
Winter Prey - John Sandford 1428

LaMarche, Andrew
Strawgirl - Abigail Padgett 1252

Laurie, Vincent
Deadly Beloved - Alanna Knight 942
Killing Cousins - Alanna Knight 943

Love, Jason
Frozen Assets - James Leasor 996

Marsh, Clio
The Going Down of the Sun - Jo Bannister 87

McDonnell, Jean
Dead Moon on the Rise - Susan Rogers Cooper 310

McKenzie, Alex
The Bridled Groom - J.S. Borthwick 154

Metcalf, Pamela
Night Vision - Paul Levine 1015

Montana, Archer Rush
Letting Blood - Richard Platt 1321

Montana, Molly
Letting Blood - Richard Platt 1321

Montgomery, Laurie
Blindsight - Robin Cook 302

Myles, Jordan
The Total Zone - Martina Navratilova 1195

O'Shaughnessy, Kiernan
Pious Deception - Susan Dunlap 462
Rogue Wave - Susan Dunlap 463

Prescott, Amy
Grave Secrets - Louise Hendricksen 774

Reeves, Townsend
Final Dictation - L.M. Vincent 1655
Pas De Death - L.M. Vincent 1656

Riggs, Charlie
To Speak for the Dead - Paul Levine 1016

St. Clair, Maxene
Elective Murder - Janet McGiffin 1129
Prescription for Death - Janet McGiffin 1130

St. James, Simon
Missing Joseph - Elizabeth George 575

Scarpetta, Kay
All That Remains - Patricia D. Cornwell 321
The Body Farm - Patricia D. Cornwell 322
Body of Evidence - Patricia D. Cornwell 323
Cruel and Unusual - Patricia D. Cornwell 324
From Potter's Field - Patricia D. Cornwell 325
Postmortem - Patricia D. Cornwell 326

Silver, Jake
Disassociated States - Leonard Simon 1499

Simon, Aaron
To Do No Harm - Leslie Glass 602

Snow, David
Double Blind - David Laing 965

Strange, Sylvia
Dangerous Attachments - Sarah Lovett 1051

Swinbrooke, Kathryn
The Eye of God - C.L. Grace 631

Tonneman, John
The Kingsbridge Plot - Maan Meyers 1148

Trager, Amy
Final Session - Mary Morell 1170

Turner, Samantha
A Clinic for Murder - Marsha Landreth 974
The Holiday Murders - Marsha Landreth 975
Vial Murders - Marsha Landreth 976

Victor II
Skeleton-in-Waiting - Peter Dickinson 419

DRIFTER

Constantine
Shoedog - George Pelecanos 1288

DRIVER

Demming, Walter
Under the Beetle's Cellar - Mary Willis Walker 1660

DRUG DEALER

DeMedici, Danny
The Horse Latitudes - Robert Ferrigno 526

King, Darryl
Slow Motion Riot - Peter Blauner 144

ECONOMIST

Lee, Amber
Whisper the Guns - Edward Cline 261

EDITOR

Baker, Anne
The Last Page - Bob Fenster 524

Colquhoun, Aphra
Margin for Murder - Bronte Adams 9

Covington, Janet
The Long Search - Isabelle Holland 798

Kent, Charlotte
Poison Pen - Mary Kittredge 933

Murray, Russell
Pink Vodka Blues - Neal Barrett Jr. 98

Norris, Kay
Sliver - Ira Levin 1013

ENGINEER

Churchyard, Tom
Playing God - Barbara Whitehead 1707

ENTERTAINER

Arnold, Pat
Party Till You Die - David Charnee 236
To Kill a Clown - David Charnee 237

Blacker, D.L.
Party Till You Die - David Charnee 236
To Kill a Clown - David Charnee 237

Kruse, Kimmey
Funny as a Dead Comic - Susan Rogers Cooper 312
Funny as a Dead Relative - Susan Rogers Cooper 313

McGrail, Nuala
Irish Gold - Andrew M. Greeley 657

EQUESTRIAN

Gold, Natalie
Horse of a Different Killer - Jody Jaffe 839

EXPLORER

Hurley, Brian
The Ice - Louis Charbonneau 234

FARMER

Bassett, Henry
Screaming Bones - Pat Burden 191

Bertram, Alice
Infected Be the Air - Janice Law 991

Gordianus the Finder
Catalina's Riddle - Steven Saylor 1448

Kohl, Tom
The Lion at the Door - Newton Thornburg 1617

FBI AGENT

Banish, John
The Standoff - Chuck Hogan 796

Becker, John
The Edge of Sleep - David Wiltse 1736
Into the Fire - David Wiltse 1737

Crist, Karen
The Edge of Sleep - David Wiltse 1736

Daggett, Cameron
Hard Fall - Ridley Pearson 1284

Devlin, Mike
Gentkill: A Novel of the FBI - Paul Lindsay 1025

Gibbons, Bert
Bad Apple - Anthony Bruno 184

Grey, Ana
North of Montana - April Smith 1515

Lawrence, Al
Dead Easy - Arthur F. Nehrbass 1199

Memphis, Nick
Point of Impact - Stephen Hunter 822

Ness, Eliot
Murder by the Numbers - Max Allan Collins 278

Tozzi, Mike
Bad Apple - Anthony Bruno 184

Wesley, Benton
From Potter's Field - Patricia D. Cornwell 325

FILMMAKER

Didier, Inez
The Fall Line - Mark T. Sullivan 1589

MacGowen, Maggie
Midnight Baby - Wendy Hornsby 808
Telling Lies - Wendy Hornsby 809

Willett, Wolf
Santa Fe Rules - Stuart Woods 1763

Winston, Stoney
Truck Shot - Jim Stinson 1574
TV Safe - Jim Stinson 1575

FIRE FIGHTER

Fontana, Mac
Help Wanted: Orphans Preferred - Earl Emerson 487
Morons and Madmen - Earl Emerson 488

FISHERMAN

Barrett, Ozzie
Dead in the Water - W.J. Chaput 233

Jackson, Jeff
A Beautiful Place to Die - Philip R. Craig 335
The Double Minded Men - Philip R. Craig 338
Off Season - Philip R. Craig 339
The Woman Who Walked into the Sea - Philip R. Craig 340

Character Description Index

Ochs, Charlie
Revolution #9 - Peter Abrahams 6

Socarides, Aristotle "Soc"
Death in Deep Water - Paul Kemprecos 903
Feeding Frenzy - Paul Kemprecos 904
Neptune's Eye - Paul Kemprecos 905

FLIGHT ATTENDENT

Burke, Jackie
Rum Punch - Elmore Leonard 1007

FRIEND

Adams, Deacon "Deke"
Lay It on the Line - Catherine Dain 379

Bignell, Mavis
Unwillingly to Vegas - Nancy Livingston 1036

Golding, Rachel
The Cut Throat - Simon Michael 1149

Malone, Wilson
Dead in the Water - W.J. Chaput 233

Nowack, Shelley
The Class Menagerie - Jill Churchill 244

FUGITIVE

Shea, Kevin
A Certain Justice - John T. Lescroart 1008

GAMBLER

Anderson, Shifty Lou
I'm Getting Killed Right Here - William Murray 1190

Waverly, Tim
Double Down - Tom Kakonis 854
Shadow Counter - Tom Kakonis 855

GARDENER

Porter, Emma
Aunt Dimity and the Duke - Nancy Atherton 68

GENTLEMAN

Kestrel, Julian
A Broken Vessel - Kate Ross 1403
Cut to the Quick - Kate Ross 1404

GIRLFRIEND

Wade, Laura
Death and Other Lovers - Jo Bannister 86

GOVERNMENT OFFICIAL

Erickson, Reed
The Deer Killers - Gunnard Landers 973

Lightstone, Henry
Wildfire - Kenneth W. Goddard 605

Metellus the Younger, Decius Caecilius
SPQR - John Maddox Roberts 1382

Trent, Wendell
Bright Shark - Robert Ballard 85

Tyson, Albert
Moving Targets - Sean Flannery 529

Wilson, Francesca
Death of a Partner - Janet Neel 1197

GRANDPARENT

Barlow, Margaret
Murder on the Chesapeake - David Osborn 1246

GUARD

Adams, Deacon "Deke"
Lay It on the Line - Catherine Dain 379

HAIRDRESSER

Breedlove, Jack
Dead Pan - Jane Dentinger 413

Claiborne, Claire
Behind Eclaire's Doors - Sophie Dunbar 457

Kraychik, Stan
A Body to Dye For - Grant Michaels 1150
Love You to Death - Grant Michaels 1151

HANDICAPPED

Barlow, Timothy
Final Edit - Robert A. Carter 224

Callum, Nora
A Wide and Capable Revenge - Thomas McCall 1113

Carver, Fred
Flame - John Lutz 1057
Spark - John Lutz 1058

Fortune, Dan
Cassandra in Red - Michael Collins 281
Chasing Eights - Michael Collins 282
Crime, Punishment and Resurrection - Michael Collins 283

Halleck, Jack "Spike"
Sight Unseen - David Lorne 1046

Halley, Sid
Come to Grief - Dick Francis 538

Mondragon, Rita
At Ease with the Dead - Walter Satterthwait 1437

Phillips, Maddy
Blood Trance - R.D. Zimmerman 1791
Red Trance - R.D. Zimmerman 1793

Schantz, Ollie
And Leave Her Lay Dying - John Lawrence Reynolds 1362

Wagner, Greg
Night Kills - Ed Gorman 622

HEALTH CARE PROFESSIONAL

Chandler, Shaw
Bones of Coral - James W. Hall 707

Parker, Quinn
Full-Bodied Red - Bruce Zimmerman 1790

HEIR

Justice, Howard
Kill the Messenger - Elizabeth Daniels Squire 1546

Randolph, Arthur B. "Snooky"
Friends till the End - Gloria Dank 387

Tripper, Lee
The Suspense Is Killing Me - Thomas Maxwell 1102

Whysse, Ted
Blood Lies - Virginia Anderson 52

HEIRESS

Ardleigh, Kathryn "Kate"
Death at Gallows Green - Robin Paige 1260

Coltrane, Grey
Nightwalker - Sidney Filson 527

Easterbrook, Alison
Funnelweb - Charles West 1693

Sadler, Isobel
Landscape of Lies - Peter Watson 1676

Segura, Cristina
Antipodes - Maria-Antonia Oliver 1236

Strachan, Zoe
A Chill Wind in January - L.R. Wright 1772

Winn, Sherry Lou
Pink Vodka Blues - Neal Barrett Jr. 98

HISTORIAN

Adams, Henry
Panama - Eric Zencey 1787

HISTORICAL FIGURE

Adams, Henry
Panama - Eric Zencey 1787

Borden, Lizzie
Miss Lizzie - Walter Satterthwait 1441

Christie, Agatha
Dorothy and Agatha - Gaylord Larsen 984

Cicero, Marcus Tullius
Roman Blood - Steven Saylor 1449

Dali, Salvador
The Melting Clock - Stuart M. Kaminsky 860

Doyle, Arthur Conan
The 6 Messiahs - Mark Frost 560
Escapade - Walter Satterthwait 1438

Edward, Prince of Wales
Bertie and the Seven Bodies - Peter Lovesey 1049

Hammett, Dashiell
The Black Mask Murders - William F. Nolan 1207

Houdini, Harry
Escapade - Walter Satterthwait 1438

Lindbergh, Charles
Stolen Away - Max Allan Collins 280

Long, Huey
Blood and Thunder - Max Allan Collins 276

Ness, Eliot
Murder by the Numbers - Max Allan Collins 278

Roosevelt, Theodore
The Strenuous Life - Lawrence Alexander 36

Sayers, Dorothy L.
Dorothy and Agatha - Gaylord Larsen 984

Shakespeare, William
The Quality of Mercy - Faye Kellerman 883

Shaw, George Bernard
Stage Fright - Gillian Linscott 1030

Stein, Gertrude
The Caravaggio Shawl - Samuel M. Steward 1573

Toklas, Alice B.
The Caravaggio Shawl - Samuel M. Steward 1573

Tutankhamun
Murder in the Place of Anubis - Lynda S. Robinson 1390

HOMOSEXUAL

Bradley, Mark
Shot on Location - Stan Cutler 369

Brandstetter, Dave
The Boy Who Was Buried This Morning - Joseph Hansen 726
A Country of Old Men - Joseph Hansen 727

Carpenter, Scott
The Only Good Priest - Mark Richard Zubro 1795

Kraychik, Stan
A Body to Dye For - Grant Michaels 1150
Love You to Death - Grant Michaels 1151

Mason, Tom
The Only Good Priest - Mark Richard Zubro 1795
Why Isn't Becky Twitchell Dead? - Mark Richard Zubro 1797

Strachey, Donald
Third Man Out - Richard Stevenson 1572

Sturgis, Milo
Bad Love - Jonathan Kellerman 885
Private Eyes - Jonathan Kellerman 886
Self-Defense - Jonathan Kellerman 887

Turner, Paul
Sorry Now? - Mark Richard Zubro 1796

HORSE TRAINER

Vickers, Tremayne
Longshot - Dick Francis 540

Whysse, Ted
Blood Lies - Virginia Anderson 52

HOTEL OWNER

Quilliam, Sarah "Quill"
A Dash of Death - Claudia Bishop 134

Sinclair, Cecily
Check-out Time - Kate Kingsbury 928
Eat, Drink and Be Buried - Kate Kingsbury 929
Room with a Clue - Kate Kingsbury 930

HOTEL WORKER

Caulfield, Am
The Hotel Detective - Alan Russell 1413

Halburton-Smythe, Priscilla
Death of a Charming Man - M.C. Beaton 109

Wilcox, Carl
The Man Who Missed the Party - Harold Adams 13

HOUSEWIFE

Barclay, Maeve
Time and Time Again - B.M. Gill 587

Bennett, Christine
The Christmas Night Murder - Lee Harris 734

Bradshaw, Nora
Sister's Keeper - Randye Lordon 1042

Breslinsky, Claire
Foxglove - Mary Anne Kelly 889

Bruce, Laura
The Hangman's Beautiful Daughter - Sharyn McCrumb 1115

Burdette, Lillie
No Way Home - Patricia MacDonald 1062

Fairchild, Faith
The Body in the Belfry - Katherine Hall Page 1255
The Body in the Bouillon - Katherine Hall Page 1256
The Body in the Vestibule - Katherine Hall Page 1258

Fischman, Ida
Unorthodox Practices - Marissa Piesman 1320

Grey, India
A Blood Affair - Jan Roberts 1381

Harvey, Maddie
Killer Cinderella - Simon Shaw 1478

Haskell, Ellie
Femmes Fatal - Dorothy Cannell 214
How to Murder Your Mother-in-Law - Dorothy Cannell 215

Henshaw, Susan
All Hallows Evil - Valerie Wolzien 1748
A Good Year for a Corpse - Valerie Wolzien 1749
We Wish You a Merry Murder - Valerie Wolzien 1750

Hodges, Pat
Savage Justice - Ron Handberg 721

Jeffry, Jane
The Class Menagerie - Jill Churchill 244
A Farewell to Yarns - Jill Churchill 245
A Quiche Before Dying - Jill Churchill 247

Kelling, Emma
The Gladstone Bag - Charlotte MacLeod 1063

Kelling, Sarah
The Gladstone Bag - Charlotte MacLeod 1063

Miller, Myrtle "Pix" Rowe
The Body in the Basement - Katherine Hall Page 1254

Neuhauser, Joyce
Nightmare Point - Carole Berry 128

Nowack, Shelley
The Class Menagerie - Jill Churchill 244

O'Brea, Emma
Prized Possessions - L.R. Wright 1775

Orett, Linda
A Single Stone - Marilyn Wallace 1664

Pedersen, Freda
Threnody for Two - Jeanne Hart 747

Pitt, Charlotte
Highgate Rise - Anne Perry 1295

Pugh, E.J.
One, Two, What Did Daddy Do? - Susan Rogers Cooper 315

Spencer, Merrie Lee
The Garden Club - Muriel Resnick Jackson 836

Stockton, Jean
Dead Easy - Arthur F. Nehrbass 1199

Wyche, Zelly
Blood Music - Jessie Prichard Hunter 821

INDIAN

Bearpaw, Molly
Ravenmocker - Jean Hager 701
The Redbird's Cry - Jean Hager 702

Biwaban, Angela
Corona Blue - J.F. Trainor 1625
Dynamite Pass - J.F. Trainor 1626

Blackthorne, Nathan
Grave Secrets - Louise Hendricksen 774

Chee, Jim
Sacred Clowns - Tony Hillerman 792
Talking God - Tony Hillerman 793

Leaphorn, Joe
Sacred Clowns - Tony Hillerman 792
Talking God - Tony Hillerman 793

Means, Roland
A Good Day to Die - Stephen Solomita 1534

Moon, Charlie
Poison Fruit - Chelsea Quinn Yarbro 1781

Ortiz, Johnny
Missing Man - Richard Martin Stern 1570

Prettybird, Willie
Bigfoot - Richard Hoyt 815

Shugak, Kate
A Cold-Blooded Business - Dana Stabenow 1550
A Cold Day for Murder - Dana Stabenow 1549
Dead in the Water - Dana Stabenow 1551
Play with Fire - Dana Stabenow 1552

INNKEEPER

Darcy, Tess
Blooming Murder - Jean Hager 698
Dead and Buried - Jean Hager 699

McClintock, Shirley
Death Served Up Cold - B.J. Oliphant 1234

McMonigle, Judith
Bantam of the Opera - Mary Daheim 374
A Fit of Tempera - Mary Daheim 375
Holy Terrors - Mary Daheim 376
Murder, My Suite - Mary Daheim 377

Quilliam, Sarah "Quill"
A Taste for Murder - Claudia Bishop 135

Yancy, Kate
All the Great Pretenders - Deborah Adams 10

INSPECTOR

Price, Robin
Fatal Charm - Anne Morice 1173

INSURANCE INVESTIGATOR

Bogner, Simon
Business Unusual - Tim Heald 763

Brandstetter, Dave
The Boy Who Was Buried This Morning - Joseph Hansen 726
A Country of Old Men - Joseph Hansen 727

Brant, Martha "Moz"
Hush, Money - Jean Femling 523

Dorsey, Carroll
The Fall-Down Artist - Thomas Lipinski 1032

Lindsay, Hobart
The Classic Car Killer - Richard A. Lupoff 1054
The Comic Book Killer - Richard A. Lupoff 1055

Spencer, Mitch
In Deep - Bruce Jones 846

Trevelyn, James
The Triumph of Bacchus - Douglas Skeggs 1509

Weiss, John
A Brush with Death - Joan Smith 1519

Zack, Harry
Now Let's Talk of Graves - Sarah Shankman 1476
She Walks in Beauty - Sarah Shankman 1477

INTERIOR DECORATOR

Scott, Davey
Loves Music, Loves to Dance - Mary Higgins Clark 253

INVENTOR

Blossom, Richie
Snagged - Carol Higgins Clark   251

JOURNALIST

Aandahl, Trish
The Bookman's Wake - John Dunning   467

Adams, Samantha
He Was Her Man - Sarah Shankman   1474
The King Is Dead - Sarah Shankman   1475
Now Let's Talk of Graves - Sarah Shankman   1476
She Walks in Beauty - Sarah Shankman   1477

Aiken, John Forbes
Indecent Behavior - Caryl Rivers   1372

Amalfi, Angie
Cooking Up Trouble - Joanne Pence   1289
Something's Cooking - Joanne Pence   1290
Too Many Cooks - Joanne Pence   1291

Amstel, Sara
Shoofly Pie to Die - Joshua Quittner   1342

Babicki, Stosh
The Late Man - James Preston Girard   592

Barlowe, Philip
Act of Love - Joe R. Lansdale   980

Brady, Peter
Death Notice - M.S. Karl   866
Deerslayer - M.S. Karl   867

Burke, Colin
Cover Story - Robert Cullen   365

Burnell, Maxey
Unsafe Keeping - Carol Cail   206

Carpenter, Hollis
Bayou City Secrets - Deborah Powell   1323

Cates, Molly
The Red Scream - Mary Willis Walker   1659
Under the Beetle's Cellar - Mary Willis Walker   1660

Cattrell, Ann
The Ice House - Minette Walters   1669

Chambers, Ishmael
Snow Falling on Cedars - David Guterson   692

Clancey, Jack
Peril under the Palms - K.K. Beck   117

Clevenger, August
Boiling Rock - Remar Sutton   1594

Cobb, Matt
Killed on the Rocks - William L. DeAndrea   401

Collier, Alex
Savage Justice - Ron Handberg   721

Collins, Charity
Katwalk - Karen Kijewski   920

Collins, Henrietta O'Dwyer
Dead Man's Island - Carolyn G. Hart   742

Connors, Liz
And Soon I'll Come to Kill You - Susan Kelly   893
Out of the Darkness - Susan Kelly   894
Until Proven Innocent - Susan Kelly   895

Cowart, Matthew
Just Cause - John Katzenbach   873

Cronin, Frank
Hammurabi's Code - Charles Kenney   909

Dawes, Sally
Corruption - Andrew Klavan   936

Day, Jane
Knight & Day - Ron Nessen   1201

Dean, Sam
Blood Rights - Mike Phillips   1314

Decker, Rick
Hidden City - Jim DeBrosse   407
Southern Cross - Jim DeBrosse   408

Devore, Addie
Murder in Bandora - Leona Karr   868

Drake, Tess
The Covenant of the Flame - David Morrell   1174

Drew, Patricia
The Triumph of Bacchus - Douglas Skeggs   1509

Drover, Jimmy
Drover and the Zebras - Bill Granger   646

Edwards, Con
The Gombeen Man - Randy Lee Eickoff   474

Egan, Alice Jane "A.J."
Neon Dancers - Matt Taylor   1608

Ellenberg, Sally
Indecent Behavior - Caryl Rivers   1372

Engels, Kay
Murder at the Class Reunion - Triss Stein   1567

Fay, Miranda
The Mooncalf Murders - Noel Vreeland Carter   222

Finley, Nick
Cry for Help - Karen Hanson Stuyck   1586

Finley, Peter
Limited Partner - Mike Lupica   1053

Fitzgerald, Ed "Fitz"
A Suitcase in Berlin - Don Flynn   532

Flanagan, John
Inherit the Mob - Zev Chafets   231

Garcia, Vicki
Barking Dogs - R.R. Irvine   827

Gish, Molly
Artichoke Hearts - Victor Wuamett   1777
Deeds of Trust - Victor Wuamett   1778

Godwin, Rodger
Praetorian - Thomas Gifford   584

Gold, Natalie
Horse of a Different Killer - Jody Jaffe   839

Goode, Henry
Horse of a Different Killer - Jody Jaffe   839

Gordon, Lindsay
Report for Murder - Val McDermid   1126

Gordon, William
Inherit the Mob - Zev Chafets   231

Grantham, Gray
The Pelican Brief - John Grisham   681

Hackshaw, Elias "Hack"
The NIMBY Factor - Stephen F. Wilcox   1721
The Painted Lady - Stephen F. Wilcox   1722

Haun, Sam
The Late Man - James Preston Girard   592

Hawthorne, Sam
Natural Enemies - Sara Cameron   209

Henry, Kate
The Dead Pull Hitter - Alison Gordon   612
Night Game - Alison Gordon   613
Safe at Home - Alison Gordon   614
Striking Out - Alison Gordon   615

House, Duffy
Bleeding Dodger Blue - Crabbe Evers   505
Fear in Fenway - Crabbe Evers   506
Murder in Wrigley Field - Crabbe Evers   507
Tigers Burning - Crabbe Evers   508

Hudson, Robin
What's a Girl Gotta Do? - Sparkle Hayter   760

James, Jessica "Jessie"
The Daphne Decisions - Meg O'Brien   1214
Eagles Die Too - Meg O'Brien   1215
Hare Today, Gone Tomorrow - Meg O'Brien   1216

Jeeter, Jerry
Final Option - Stephen Robinett   1389

Kelleher, Bobby
Running Mates - John Feinstein   521

Kelly, Irene
Goodnight, Irene - Jan Burke   198

Kelly, Nick
River of Darkness - James Grady   632

Kincaid, Mike
City of Lies - Peter McCabe   1109

Kingston, Palmer
Neon Dancers - Matt Taylor   1608

Knight, Jerry
Knight & Day - Ron Nessen   1201

LaFontaine, Prentice
Hard News - Mark T. Sullivan   1590

Lansing, Vicki
Rough Justice - Keith Peterson   1309

Larkin, Eldon
Banjo Boy - Vince Kohler   949
Rainy North Woods - Vince Kohler   950
Rising Dog - Vince Kohler   951

Leigh, Rosalind
The Sculptress - Minette Walters   1671

Long, Carol
Strike - L.L. Enger   492

Lord, Emma
The Alpine Advocate - Mary Daheim   370
The Alpine Christmas - Mary Daheim   371
The Alpine Decoy - Mary Daheim   372
The Alpine Fury - Mary Daheim   373

MacFarland, Mac
Death Below Deck - Douglas Kiker   922

MacGowen, Maggie
Midnight Baby - Wendy Hornsby   808

Malloy, Laura
Still Explosion - Mary Logue   1041

Maltravers, Augustus
Murder in Waiting - Robert Richardson   1367

Manterola, Pioquinto
The Shadow of the Shadow - Paco Ignacio Taibo II   1598

Marcus, Griffen
Out of the Darkness - Susan Kelly   894

Marsala, Cat
Hard Tack - Barbara D'Amato   382
Hard Women - Barbara D'Amato   383
Hardball - Barbara D'Amato   384

Martin, Chris
A Second Shot in the Dark - Annette Roome   1399

Martin, Frankie
The Man with My Name - Paul Engleman   494

Maxwell, Georgia Lee
A Temporary Ghost - Mickey Friedman   556

McCarthy, Gideon
Hard News - Mark T. Sullivan   1590

McCauley, Maureen
Kiss Them Goodbye - Joseph Eastburn   468

McGuire, Maureen
Running Mates - John Feinstein   521

McKay, Jenny
South Street Confidential - Dick Belsky   120

McMorrow, Jack
Deadline - Gerry Boyle   163

Merriwether, Sid
Corruption - Andrew Klavan   936

Minor, Constantine
Whiskey River - Loren D. Estleman   501

Judge

Morgan, Cassandra
Silent Night - Gary Amo 49

Mudd, Grover
Saint Mudd - Steve Thayer 1609

Mulcay, Kate
Ah, Sweet Mystery - Celestine Sibley 1495
Dire Happenings at Scratch Ankle - Celestine Sibley 1496
A Plague of Kinfolks - Celestine Sibley 1497
Straight as an Arrow - Celestine Sibley 1498

Murray, Kate
Strangers in the Night - Peg Tyre 1641

Nishi, Kenaburo
Night Butterfly - Patricia McFall 1127

North, Michael
The Scarred Man - Keith Peterson 1310

Nottingham, Patty
The Society Ball Murders - Jack Albin Anderson 51

Pimletz, Axel
Obit - Daniel Paisner 1261

Popkin, Sam
Shoofly Pie to Die - Joshua Quittner 1342

Powell, Kit
Jinx - Julie Robitaille 1398

Powers, Georgina
User Deadly - Denise Danks 388

Quinn
The Cheshire Moon - Robert Ferrigno 525

Qwilleran, Jim
The Cat Who Moved a Mountain - Lilian Jackson Braun 167
The Cat Who Talked to Ghosts - Lilian Jackson Braun 168
The Cat Who Went into the Closet - Lilian Jackson Braun 169

Radkin, Joseph
The Genesis Files - Bob Biderman 130

Rawlings, Marguerite
Hard Aground - James W. Hall 709

Reed, Stuart
The Last Man Standing - Jim Wright 1771

Reeves, Morgan
Make Friends with Murder - Judith Garwood 569

Riordan, Prester John
The Frozen Franklin - Sean Hanlon 725

Roberts, Amanda
Ties That Bind - Sherryl Woods 1759

Runkel, Vida
The Alpine Decoy - Mary Daheim 372
The Alpine Fury - Mary Daheim 373

Ryland, Garth
A Dragon Lives Forever - John R. Riggs 1368
Wolf in Sheep's Clothing - John R. Riggs 1369

St. Claire, Geraldine
The Thirteenth Apostle - Gloria Gonzalez 610

Sams, Charlotte
Showcase - Alison Glen 603
Trunk Show - Alison Glen 604

Sanderson, Laura
Morons and Madmen - Earl Emerson 488

Santee, Miranda
The Desert Look - Bernard Schopen 1455

Schafer, Will
The Dog Hermit - David Stout 1578

Shaw, Galen
Love Lies Slain - L.L. Blackmur 139

Sheridan, T.S.W.
All the Dead Heroes - Stephen F. Wilcox 1718
The Dry White Tear - Stephen F. Wilcox 1719
The Green Mosaic - Stephen F. Wilcox 1720

Sherman, Boyd
Medicine Dog - Geoff Peterson 1307

Sherwood, Shelly
Rainy North Woods - Vince Kohler 950

Shore, Jemima
The Cavalier Case - Antonia Fraser 543

Simon, Margo
Death of a Postmodernist - Janice Steinberg 1568

Stark, Dan
When She Was Bad - Ron Faust 518

Stevens, Mitch
Land Kills - Nat Brandt 166

Sullivan, Liz
Murder in a Nice Neighborhood - Lora Roberts 1388

Sussman, Andy
The Big Freeze - Michael J. Katz 871
Last Dance in Redondo Beach - Michael J. Katz 872

Tobin, Jane
Vintage Polo - Jerry Kennealy 908

Trench, Arabella
Boxed In - Neville Steed 1564
Wind-Up - Neville Steed 1566

Tripper, Lee
The Suspense Is Killing Me - Thomas Maxwell 1102

Turner, Derek
A Clinic for Murder - Marsha Landreth 974
The Holiday Murders - Marsha Landreth 975

Tye, Randall
A Private Crime - Lillian O'Donnell 1225

Wells, John
Rough Justice - Keith Peterson 1309

West, Marlee
Night of the Ice Storm - David Stout 1579

Winder, Joe
Native Tongue - Carl Hiaasen 782

Winfield, Jane
Elegy in a Country Graveyard - Audrey Peterson 1304

Winter, Holly
A Bite of Death - Susan Conant 287
Black Ribbon - Susan Conant 288
Bloodlines - Susan Conant 289
Ruffly Speaking - Susan Conant 291

JUDGE

Drexler, Sarah
Justice for Some - Kate Wilhelm 1724

Gibbs, Bob
Maximum Bob - Elmore Leonard 1006

Knott, Deborah
Shooting at Loons - Margaret Maron 1078

McIntyre, Bill
Town on Trial - William Harrington 730

Studevant, Morgan
Poison Fruit - Chelsea Quinn Yarbro 1781

LANDLORD

Henderson, Peter
Sliver - Ira Levin 1013

LANDOWNER

Hudson, Richard
To Die Like a Gentleman - Bernard Bastable 103

LAWYER

Abernathy, Dean
Felony Murder - Joseph T. Klempner 940

Aldridge, Eileen
Leap of Faith - Sharon Zukowski 1799

Alexander, Will
Against the Wind - J.F. Freedman 547

Alvarez, Tina
The Choice - Barry Reed 1357

Anonymous
Dead Meat - Philip Kerr 913

Balkan, Peter
To Do No Harm - Leslie Glass 602

Birchfield, Kathy
The Portland Laugher - Earl Emerson 489
The Vanishing Smile - Earl Emerson 490
Yellow Dog Party - Earl Emerson 491

Blacker, D.L.
Party Till You Die - David Charnee 236
To Kill a Clown - David Charnee 237

Broom, Andrew
Body and Soil - Ralph McInerny 1135

Bruno, Adam
The Codicil - Tom Topor 1623

Cain, Harry
A Lawyer's Tale - D. Kincaid 923

Cameron, Justin
The Strange Files of Fremont Jones - Dianne Day 400

Cantrip, Michael
The Sirens Sang of Murder - Sarah Caudwell 228

Carl, Victor
Hostile Witness - William Lashner 985

Casey, James P.
A Case of Innocence - Douglas J. Keeling 877

Chenier, Lucille
Voodoo River - Robert Crais 344

Ciampi, Marlene
Justice Denied - Robert K. Tanenbaum 1599
Reversible Error - Robert K. Tanenbaum 1600

Cicero, Marcus Tullius
Roman Blood - Steven Saylor 1449

Claiborne, Dan
Behind Eclaire's Doors - Sophie Dunbar 457

Connor, Gail
Suspicion of Guilt - Barbara Parker 1268

Cook, Malcolm
Shadows on the Mirror - Frances Fyfield 563

Coyne, Brady
Dead Winter - William G. Tapply 1602
Spotted Cats - William G. Tapply 1603
Tight Lines - William G. Tapply 1604

Darling, Max
A Little Class on Murder - Carolyn G. Hart 743

Di Palma, Laura
The Good Fight - Lia Matera 1091
A Hard Bargain - Lia Matera 1092

Epton, Rosa
Seeds of Murder - Michael Underwood 1642

Estrada, Joe
Inadmissible Evidence - Philip Friedman 557

Farnham, George
A Slay at the Races - Kate Morgan 1172

Fischman, Nina
Close Quarters - Marissa Piesman 1319
Unorthodox Practices - Marissa Piesman 1320

Character Description Index — Lawyer

Forrester, Lily
Mitigating Circumstances - Nancy Taylor Rosenberg 1401

Forsythe, Robert
A Death for a Dancing Doll - E.X. Giroux 597
A Death for a Dodo - E.X. Giroux 598

Fortune, Sarah
Shadows on the Mirror - Frances Fyfield 563

Frazer, Harry
Deadeye - Sam Llewellyn 1037

Frost, Reuben
Murder Times Two - Haughton Murphy 1186
A Very Venetian Murder - Haughton Murphy 1187

Galvin, Frank
The Choice - Barry Reed 1357

Garrett, Dave
Cruel April - Neil Albert 29

Gilman, Ann
The Prosecutor - Thomas Chastain 240

Gold, Rachel
Death Benefits - Michael A. Kahn 851
Due Diligence - Michael A. Kahn 852
Firm Ambitions - Michael A. Kahn 853

Goldberg, Benny
Death Benefits - Michael A. Kahn 851
Due Diligence - Michael A. Kahn 852
Firm Ambitions - Michael A. Kahn 853

Hall, Adam
The Chamber - John Grisham 679

Hamel, Neil
The Lies That Bind - Judith Van Gieson 1649
The Other Side of Death - Judith Van Gieson 1650
Raptor - Judith Van Gieson 1651
The Wolf Path - Judith Van Gieson 1652

Hardy, Dismas
Hard Evidence - John T. Lescroart 1009
The Vig - John T. Lescroart 1010

Hartman, Seth
Southern Cross - Stephen Greenleaf 669

Haverford, Miles
The Temple Dogs - Warren Murphy 1188

Hayes, Jack
The Price of Victory - Vincent Green 666

Holden, Michael
Playing the Dozens - William D. Pease 1286

Holloway, Barbara "Bobby"
Death Qualified: A Mystery of Chaos - Kate Wilhelm 1723

Hope, Matthew
Three Blind Mice - Ed McBain 1106

Howard, Charles
The Cut Throat - Simon Michael 1149

Jameson, Cass
Fresh Kills - Carolyn Wheat 1699

Jansson, Willa
Prior Convictions - Lia Matera 1093

Karp, Butch
Justice Denied - Robert K. Tanenbaum 1599
Reversible Error - Robert K. Tanenbaum 1600

Keller, Jim
Orphans - Gerald Pearce 1281

Kemp, Lennox
A Loose Connection - M.R.D. Meek 1139

Kenyon, Sarah
All Around the Town - Mary Higgins Clark 252

Keough, John Michael
The Immediate Prospect of Being Hanged - Walter Walker 1662

Kern, Karen
Guilt by Association - Susan R. Sloan 1514

Kleinfeldt, Liz
Methods of Execution - Frederick D. Huebner 818

Knight, David
Miami Heat - Jerome Sanford 1433

Knott, Deborah
Bootlegger's Daughter - Margaret Maron 1076

Lafky, Melissa
Banjo Boy - Vince Kohler 949

Lassiter, Jake
Mortal Sin - Paul Levine 1014
Night Vision - Paul Levine 1015
To Speak for the Dead - Paul Levine 1016

Lautrec, Jack
Lautrec - Norman Zollinger 1794

Lautrec, Martine
Lautrec - Norman Zollinger 1794

Lipp, Seymour
And Baby Makes None - Stephen Lewis 1022
The Monkey Rope - Stephen Lewis 1023

Logan, Whitney
Dogtown - Mercedes Lambert 972

Love, Reggie
The Client - John Grisham 680

MacPherson, Bill
MacPherson's Lament - Sharyn McCrumb 1117

Madriani, Paul
Compelling Evidence - Steve Martini 1090

Malloy, Mack
Pleading Guilty - Scott Turow 1640

Mason, Perry
Perry Mason in The Case of Too Many Murders - Thomas Chastain 239

Middleton-Brown, David
A Drink of Deadly Wine - Kate Charles 235

Miller, Kassia
Reasonable Doubt - Philip Friedman 558

Moon, Charlie
Poison Fruit - Chelsea Quinn Yarbro 1781

Morrone, Rita
Running From the Law - Lisa Scottoline 1465

Ness, Lydia
Undue Influence - Miriam Borgenicht 153

Nicholson, Chris
Other People's Skeletons - Julie Smith 1529

Page, Gideon
Illegal Motion - Grif Stockley 1576
Probable Cause - Griff Stockley 1577

Phillips, Bino
Bino's Blues - A.W. Gray 650
Killings - A.W. Gray 651

Pritchard, Dominic
A Few Dying Words - Paula Gosling 626

Rabb, Joshua
The Dividing Line - Richard Parrish 1273

Randall, Tammi
A Strange and Bitter Crop - E.L. Wyrick 1780

Rathbone, Oliver
A Sudden, Fearful Death - Anne Perry 1296

Reddman, David
A Clear Case of Murder - Warwick Downing 445

Redway, Glenda
Work for a Dead Man - Simon Ritchie 1371

Reece, Mitchell
Mistress of Justice - Jeffrey Wilds Deaver 405

Riordan, Matt
Methods of Execution - Frederick D. Huebner 818
Picture Postcard - Fredrick D. Huebner 819

Rios, Henry
How Town - Michael Nava 1194

Robinson, Nan
A Pocketful of Karma - Taffy Cannon 216

Rommel, Frances "Frankie"
The Water Cure - Warwick Downing 446

Rosen, Michael
Caught in the Shadows - C.A. Haddad 694

Rosen, Nate
Stone Boy - Ronald Levitsky 1017

Rowan, Gerald
Body and Soul - Ralph McInerny 1135

Ryan, Michael
Reasonable Doubt - Philip Friedman 558

St. John, Peter
Spare Change - John A. Peak 1280

Scattergood, Peter
Break and Enter - Colin Harrison 735

Schwartz, Rebecca
Dead in the Water - Julie Smith 1524
Other People's Skeletons - Julie Smith 1529

Scott, Laura
Trade-Off - Harrison Arnston 66

Scott, Patrick
Avenging Angel - Anthony Appiah 64

Semmes, Nat
Deep End - Geoffrey Norman 1210

Severus, Livinius
Roman Nights - Ron Burns 201

Sloan, Charley
Shadow of a Doubt - William J. Coughlin 333

Sloan, Susan
Hammurabi's Code - Charles Kenney 909

Spencer, Philip "Pip"
The Talinin Madonna - Douglas Skeggs 1508

Starbuck, Patterson
The Immediate Prospect of Being Hanged - Walter Walker 1662

Street, Dee
A Woman's Own Mystery - Hannah Wakefield 1658

Sutter, John
The Gold Coast - Nelson DeMille 412

Talbot, Jeff
Spare Change - John A. Peak 1280

Tamar, Hilary
The Sirens Sang of Murder - Sarah Caudwell 228

Theron, Beth
Peeping Thomas - Robert Reeves 1358

Vail, Martin
Primal Fear - William Diehl 421

Verdugo, Alberto
The Shadow of the Shadow - Paco Ignacio Taibo II 1598

Waring, Elizabeth
Sleeping Dogs - Thomas Perry 1297

West, Helen
Deep Sleep - Frances Fyfield 561
A Question of Guilt - Frances Fyfield 562

Willis, Bill
Aunt Dimity's Death - Nancy Atherton 69

Winslow, Steve
The Naked Typist - J.P. Hailey 704
The Underground Man - J.P. Hailey 705

Yates, Carrie
A Stiff Critique - Jaqueline Girdner 595

LESBIAN

Adams, Kip
Everything You Have Is Mine - Sandra Scoppettone 1460
I'll Be Leaving You Always - Sandra Scoppettone 1461
My Sweet Untraceable You - Sandra Scoppettone 1462

Andrews, Jessie
The Chesapeake Project - Phyllis Horn 806

Black, Helen
Murder by the Book - Pat Welch 1689

Carpenter, Hollis
Bayou City Secrets - Deborah Powell 1323

Delacroix, Lily
Bayou City Secrets - Deborah Powell 1323

Delafield, Kate
The Beverly Malibu - Katherine V. Forrest 533
Murder by Tradition - Katherine V. Forrest 534

Donovan, Brigid
Murder Is Germane - Karen Saum 1442

Kelly, Virginia
In the Game - Nikki Baker 82
The Lavender House Murder - Nikki Baker 83

Knight, Mickey
The Intersection of Law and Desire - J.M. Redmann 1356

Laurano, Lauren
Everything You Have Is Mine - Sandra Scoppettone 1460
I'll Be Leaving You Always - Sandra Scoppettone 1461
My Sweet Untraceable You - Sandra Scoppettone 1462

Lawless, Jane
Hallowed Murder - Ellen Hart 745
Vital Lies - Ellen Hart 746

MacKenzie, Christabel
Death Wore a Diadem - Iona McGregor 1133

Martinelli, Kate
A Grave Talent - Laurie R. King 925
To Play the Fool - Laurie R. King 927

McGuire, Madison
A Singular Spy - Amanda Kyle Williams 1727

Ramos, Lucia
Final Session - Mary Morell 1170

Reece, Caitlin
Ninth Life - Lauren Wright Douglas 444

Sloane, Sydney
Sister's Keeper - Randye Lordon 1042

Stewart, Eleanor
Death Wore a Diadem - Iona McGregor 1133

Thorn, Cordelia
Vital Lies - Ellen Hart 746

Tompkins, Meredith
The Chesapeake Project - Phyllis Horn 806

Trager, Amy
Final Session - Mary Morell 1170

Wilder, Johannah
Shadow Dance - Agnes Bushnell 202

LIBRARIAN

Cochrane, Helen
Every Breath You Take - Michelle Spring 1541

George, Edward
A Slip of the Tong - Charles A. Goodrum 611

James, Dewey
Home Sweet Homicide - Kate Morgan 1171

A Slay at the Races - Kate Morgan 1172

Jones, Crighton
A Slip of the Tong - Charles A. Goodrum 611

Kirby, Jacqueline
Naked Once More - Elizabeth Peters 1300

Mitchell, Cassandra
A Touch of Panic - L.R. Wright 1776

Poteet, Jordan
Do Unto Others - Jeff Abbott 1
The Only Good Yankee - Jeff Abbott 2

Shandy, Helen
An Owl Too Many - Charlotte MacLeod 1064

Teagarden, Aurora
A Bone to Pick - Charlaine Harris 731

Tryon, Glynis
North Star Conspiracy - Miriam Grace Monfredo 1164

Zukas, Helma
Miss Zukas and the Island Murders - Jo Dereske 415
Miss Zukas and the Library Murders - Jo Dereske 416

LINGUIST

James, Nora
Night Butterfly - Patricia McFall 1127

Leskova, Katya
The Talinin Madonna - Douglas Skeggs 1508

Reilly, Cassandra
Gaudi Afternoon - Barbara Wilson 1731

MAGICIAN

Anderson, Shifty Lou
I'm Getting Killed Right Here - William Murray 1190

Hardare, Vincent
The Man Who Walked Through Walls - James Swain 1595

Houdini, Harry
Escapade - Walter Satterthwait 1438

MAINTENANCE WORKER

Flannery, Jimmy
Nibbled to Death by Ducks - Robert Campbell 213

Perkins, Ben
Concrete Hero - Rob Kantner 862
The Quick and the Dead - Rob Kantner 863
The Red, White, and Blues - Rob Kantner 864

MARTIAL ARTS EXPERT

Coltrane, Grey
Nightwalker - Sidney Filson 527

MECHANIC

Glauberman, Alex
Obligations of the Bone - Dick Cluster 263

MENTALLY ILL PERSON

Benanti, Nina
Widowmaker - William Appel 63

Bradley, Barbara "Bo"
Child of Silence - Abigail Padgett 1251
Strawgirl - Abigail Padgett 1252

Kiehl, Felix
Disassociated States - Leonard Simon 1499

Neuhauser, Joyce
Nightmare Point - Carole Berry 128

MERCENARY

Kincaid, Frank
The Man Who Walked Through Walls - James Swain 1595

Sigismondo
Death of the Duchess - Elizabeth Eyre 512

MILITARY PERSONNEL

Archer, Owen
The Apothecary Rose - Candace M. Robb 1375
The Lady Chapel - Candace M. Robb 1376
The Nun's Tale - Candace M. Robb 1377

Chandler, Wes
River of Darkness - James Grady 632

Frazier, Billy
The Price of Victory - Vincent Green 666

Haddix, Edna
Bright Shark - Robert Ballard 85

Hayes, Jack
The Price of Victory - Vincent Green 666

Hickey, Tom
The Loud Adios - Ken Kuhlken 957

Kornon, Alexander
Deep Chill - Ian Slater 1513

Maclean, Philip
A Time Without Shadows - Ted Allbeury 38

Murtagh, Colum
The Eye of God - C.L. Grace 631

Partain, Edd "Twodees"
Ah, Treachery - Ross Thomas 1611

Ross, Jimmy
City of Gold - Len Deighton 410

Steele, Jack
When Reason Sleeps - Tom Sehler 1472

Steiner, Kurt
The Eagle Has Flown - Jack Higgins 787

Tannis, Jack
China Lake - Anthony Hyde 823

Titus, Sam
Death Down Home - Eve K. Sandstrom 1430

Vernet, Lucien
Napoleon Must Die - Quinn Fawcett 519

Vogel, Karl
The Faust Conspiracy - James Baddock 78

Wright, Tom
Coyote Bird - Jim DeFelice 409

MODEL

Ayars, Laura
Play Dead - Harlan Coben 266

Yates, Kimberly
Blind Side - William Bayer 105

MURDERER

Barrows, Peter
By Reason of Insanity - James Neal Harvey 749

Hackabee, Joseph
Stone Shadow - Rex Miller 1154

Character Description Index

King, Darryl
Slow Motion Riot - Peter Blauner 144

MUSEUM CURATOR

Harper, Benni
Fool's Puzzle - Earlene Fowler 536
Irish Chain - Earlene Fowler 537

Norgren, Chris
A Glancing Light - Aaron Elkins 477
Old Scores - Aaron Elkins 479

MUSICIAN

Cahill, Winn
Kingdom Road - K. Patrick Conner 295

Cromwell, Sarah
Deception Island - M.K. Lorens 1043
Sweet Narcissus - M.K. Lorens 1045

Delaporte, Helen
The Famous DAR Murder Mystery - Graham Landrum 977

Fender, Martin
Boiled in Concrete - Jesse Sublett 1587

French, Alan
Broken Consort - James Gollin 609

French, Jackie
Broken Consort - James Gollin 609

Friedman, Kinky
Musical Chairs - Kinky Friedman 555

Frost, Leslie
Frost the Fiddler - Janice Weber 1681

Glenn, Art
Wild Again - Kathrin King Segal 1471

Hickey, Tom
The Angel Gang - Ken Kuhlken 956

Holland, Mark
Deadly Crescendo - Paul Myers 1191

Kruger, Dan
Skin Deep Is Fatal - Michael Cormany 320

Lockwood, Taylor
Mistress of Justice - Jeffrey Wilds Deaver 405

Lowry, Gideon
Killing Me Softly - John Leslie 1012

Murphy, Rex
The Society Ball Murders - Jack Albin Anderson 51

Ritchie, Lillian
Shattered Rhythms - Phyllis Knight 946
Switching the Odds - Phyllis Knight 947

Spencer, Joan
Buried in Quilts - Sara Hoskinson Frommer 559

Whitman, Paul
The Piano Man - Noreen Gilpatrick 589

Yarborough, Lamont
The Cheerio Killings - Douglas Allyn 47

Zack, Harry
The King Is Dead - Sarah Shankman 1475
She Walks in Beauty - Sarah Shankman 1477

NATURALIST

Maxwell, Lauren
Murder Most Grizzly - Elizabeth Quinn 1340
A Wolf in Death's Clothing - Elizabeth Quinn 1341

NOBLEMAN

Alexander, Grayson
Aunt Dimity and the Duke - Nancy Atherton 68

Carey, Robert
A Famine of Horses - P.F. Chisholm 243

Daunbey, Benjamin
The Poisoned Chalice - Michael Clynes 264

Lovell, Francis
The Fate of Princes - P.C. Doherty 424

Meren
Murder in the Place of Anubis - Lynda S. Robinson 1390

Plant, Melrose
The Old Contemptibles - Martha Grimes 675

NOBLEWOMAN

Capo-Zendrini, Barbara
Death in a Serene City - Edward Sklepowich 1510

NURSE

Chesney, Jenny
Hanging on the Wire - Gillian Linscott 1028

Crusoe, Edwina
Desperate Remedy - Mary Kittredge 931
Kill or Cure - Mary Kittredge 932
Walking Dead Man - Mary Kittredge 934

Kinsella, Kate
Deadly Admirer - Christine Green 658
Deadly Errand - Christine Green 659
Deadly Practice - Christine Green 660

Lapham, Lydia
No Way Home - Andrew Coburn 267

Latterly, Hester
Cain His Brother - Anne Perry 1292
A Dangerous Mourning - Anne Perry 1293

Madieras, Zee
A Beautiful Place to Die - Philip R. Craig 335
A Case of Vineyard Poisoning - Philip R. Craig 336
Cliff Hanger - Philip R. Craig 337
The Double Minded Men - Philip R. Craig 338
Off Season - Philip R. Craig 339

McDonough, Casey
A Man to Die For - Eileen Dreyer 448

Quy, Imogen
A Piece of Justice - Jill Paton Walsh 1274
The Wyndham Case - Jill Paton Walsh 1275

OFFICE WORKER

Brady, Joanna
Desert Heat - J.A. Jance 842

Indermill, Bonnie
The Death of a Difficult Woman - Carole Berry 125

Kincaid, Nancy
The Animal Hour - Andrew Klavan 935

Shepherd, Lori
Aunt Dimity's Death - Nancy Atherton 69

OIL INDUSTRY WORKER

Hansen, Emily "Em"
Tensleep - Sarah Andrews 57

ORGANIZED CRIME FIGURE

Scorcese, Joseph
Flamingos - Marc Savage 1444

ORPHAN

Prescott, Brie
Berlin Covenant - Celeste Paul 1278

PARAPROFESSIONAL

Lockwood, Taylor
Mistress of Justice - Jeffrey Wilds Deaver 405

PARENT

Ellis, Nigel
Dream of Darkness - Patrick Ruell 1412

Garrity, Edna Mae
Every Crooked Nanny - Kathy Hogan Trocheck 1631

PAROLE OFFICER

Gallagher, Quinn
The House on the Hill - Judith Kelman 899

PEDDLER

Roger the Chapman
Death and the Chapman - Kate Sedley 1467
The Holy Innocents - Kate Sedley 1468
The Plymouth Cloak - Kate Sedley 1469
The Weaver's Tale - Kate Sedley 1470

PHILANTHROPIST

Cain, Jenny
Bum Steer - Nancy Pickard 1316
I.O.U. - Nancy Pickard 1318

PHOTOGRAHPER

Titus, Nicky
The Devil Down Home - Eve K. Sandstrom 1431

PHOTOGRAPHER

Barnett, Geoffrey
Blind Side - William Bayer 105

Barwick, Liz
Palindrome - Stuart Woods 1762

Beaumont, Sophie
The Cashmere Kid - B. Comfort 284
Grave Consequences - B. Comfort 286

Breslinsky, Claire
Foxglove - Mary Anne Kelly 889
Park Lane South, Queens - Mary Anne Kelly 890

Byrne, Charlie
Swindle - George Adams 11

Corman, David
The City When It Rains - Thomas H. Cook 305

Jeffries, Harriet
Murder in a Good Cause - Medora Sale 1417
Murder in Focus - Medora Sale 1418
Pursued by Shadows - Medora Sale 1419
Short Cut to Santa Fe - Medora Sale 1420

Komelecki, Owen
All the Great Pretenders - Deborah Adams 10

Photojournalist

Lowell, Tony M.C.
Hour of the Manatee - E.C. Ayres   73

Sheriden, Charles
Death at Gallows Green - Robin Paige   1260

Titus, Nicky
Death Down Home - Eve K. Sandstrom   1430
The Down Home Heifer Heist - Eve K. Sandstrom   1432

Titus, Sam
The Devil Down Home - Eve K. Sandstrom   1431

PHOTOJOURNALIST

Barlow, Margaret
Murder in the Napa Valley - David Osborn   1245
Murder on the Chesapeake - David Osborn   1246

Flynn, Mickey
Death and Other Lovers - Jo Bannister   86

Johnson, Rebo
Southern Cross - Jim DeBrosse   408

Kincaid, Libby
Cold Feet - Kerry Tucker   1636
Death Echo - Kerry Tucker   1637
Still Waters - Kerry Tucker   1638

Klebanoff, Yuri
The Harbinger Effect - S.K. Wolf   1746

Lowell, Tony M.C.
Eye of the Gator - E.C. Ayres   72

Saint, Catherine
Shameless - Judy Collins   275

Takamura, Jen
The Cheshire Moon - Robert Ferrigno   525

PILOT

Black, Johnny
Black Eye - Neville Steed   1563

Corbett, Kyle
The Ransom of Black Stealth One - Dean Ing   825

Devlin, Mac
Eagles Die Too - Meg O'Brien   1215

James, Ken
Day of the Cheetah - Dale Brown   179

Lindbergh, Charles
Stolen Away - Max Allan Collins   280

McLanahan, Patrick
Day of the Cheetah - Dale Brown   179

Wright, Tom
Coyote Bird - Jim DeFelice   409

POLICE OFFICER

Abbot, Luke
Death Penalties - Paula Gosling   625

Abigail, Charles
Obit - Daniel Paisner   1261

Alberg, Karl
A Chill Wind in January - L.R. Wright   1772
Fall From Grace - L.R. Wright   1773
Mother Love - L.R. Wright   1774
Prized Possessions - L.R. Wright   1775
A Touch of Panic - L.R. Wright   1776

Alessi, George
King of the Hustlers - Eugene Izzi   831

Alvarez, Enrique
Too Clever by Half - Roderic Jeffries   845

Amery, Rick
Motown - Loren D. Estleman   498

Apfel, Hans
Spandau Phoenix - Greg Iles   824

Arrowood, Spencer
The Hangman's Beautiful Daughter - Sharyn McCrumb   1115
If Ever I Return, Pretty Peggy-O - Sharyn McCrumb   1116
She Walks These Hills - Sharyn McCrumb   1119

Ashley, Piers
Man of Blood - Margaret Duffy   451

Axx, Brad
Axx Goes South - Frederic Huber   817

Ayers, Martha
She Walks These Hills - Sharyn McCrumb   1119

Bailey, Geoffrey
Deep Sleep - Frances Fyfield   561
A Question of Guilt - Frances Fyfield   562

Bailey, Gil
The Mark Twain Murders - Edith Skom   1512

Balzic, Mario
Sunshine Enemies - K.C. Constantine   298

Banks, Alan
A Dedicated Man - Peter Robinson   1392
Gallows View - Peter Robinson   1393
The Hanging Valley - Peter Robinson   1394
A Necessary End - Peter Robinson   1395
Past Reason Hated - Peter Robinson   1396
Wednesday's Child - Peter Robinson   1397

Barelli, Chris
Obstacle Course - Yvonne Montgomery   1167

Barnaby, Thomas
Death in Disguise - Caroline Graham   640
Death of a Hollow Man - Caroline Graham   641

Barnes, Hildy
Death by Degrees - Robin Wilson   1735

Barnes, Marcie
City of God - Michael Jahn   840

Barrett, Neil
A Lively Form of Death - Kay Mitchell   1160

Baxter, Richard
Dangerous Conceits - Margaret Moore   1168

Bedrosian, Lena
Eye of the Gator - E.C. Ayres   72
Hour of the Manatee - E.C. Ayres   73

Benedetto, Johnny
Foxglove - Mary Anne Kelly   889
Park Lane South, Queens - Mary Anne Kelly   890

Bennett, Reid
Flashback - Ted Wood   1756
On the Inside - Ted Wood   1757
Snow Job - Ted Wood   1758

Bennett, Wes
Murder at Moot Point - Marlys Millhiser   1156

Best, Judy
Dead Fit - Stephen Cook   304

Bihn
Kiet Goes West - Gary Alexander   34

Bird, William
Nurse Dawes Is Dead - Stella Shepherd   1479
Thinner than Blood - Stella Shepherd   1480

Blake, Moses
Coronation - W.J. Weatherby   1679

Boldt, Lou
The Angel Maker - Ridley Pearson   1282

Bone, Peter
A Knife at the Opera - Susannah Stacey   1555

Bone, Robert
Bone Idle - Susannah Stacey   1553
Grave Responsibility - Susannah Stacey   1554
The Late Lady - Susannah Stacey   1556

What Mystery Do I Read Next?

Bosch, Harry
The Black Echo - Michael Connelly   292
The Black Ice - Michael Connelly   293
The Concrete Blonde - Michael Connelly   294

Boulter, Tim
Model Murder - Erica Quest   1338

Bouton, Vanessa
A Good Day to Die - Stephen Solomita   1534

Bowker, Denis
Murder in a Quiet Place - Tony Caxton   230

Bowman, Patrick
Killer in Paradise - John Leslie   1011

Boyd, Orin
Exit Wounds - John Westermann   1696

Bragg, Joseph
Patently Murder - Ray Harrison   737
Tincture of Death - Ray Harrison   738

Bramlet, Grover
A Homecoming for Murder - John Armistead   65

Brandon, Samantha "Smokey"
Carcass Trade - Noreen Ayres   74

Brichter, Peter
Original Sin - Mary Monica Pulver   1334

Bright, John
Close-Up on Death - Maureen O'Brien   1213

Brooks, Jack
The Christening Day Murder - Lee Harris   733
The Christmas Night Murder - Lee Harris   734

Broskey, Kevin
On the Edge - Ed Naha   1193

Brunetti, Guido
Death and Judgment - Donna Leon   1002
Death at La Fenice - Donna Leon   1003
Death in a Strange Country - Donna Leon   1004

Bryce, Kevin
A Collector of Photographs - Deborah Valentine   1645

Burgess, Richard "Dirty Dick"
A Necessary End - Peter Robinson   1395

Bushfield, Geof
I.O.U. - Nancy Pickard   1318

Bushyhead, Mitchell
Ghostland - Jean Hager   700

Callum, Nora
A Wide and Capable Revenge - Thomas McCall   1113

Canada, Lew
Motown - Loren D. Estleman   498

Cardenas, Vic
Death of a DJ - Jane Rubino   1411

Carver, Frank
Clear-Cut Murder - Lee Wallingford   1667
Cold Tracks - Lee Wallingford   1668

Cash, Julian
Turtle Moon - Alice Hoffman   795

Castang, Henri
Not as Far as Velma - Nicholas Freeling   548

Caxton, Lyman
Buried in Stone - Eric Wright   1766

Chee, Jim
Sacred Clowns - Tony Hillerman   792
Talking God - Tony Hillerman   793

Clement, Jules
The Edge of the Crazies - Jamie Harrison   736

Coffin, John
Coffin on Murder Street - Gwendoline Butler   203
Coffin Underground - Gwendoline Butler   204

Collier, Janet
Switchback - Collin Wilcox   1717

Connor, John
Rising Sun - Michael Crichton   348

Craig, William
The Covenant of the Flame - David Morrell   1174

Cross, Alex
Along Came a Spider - James Patterson   1276

Cruz, Carlos
A Single Stone - Marilyn Wallace   1664

Cullen, Joe
Fixing to Die - Jerry Oster   1249

Culpepper, Barney
Mail-Order Murder - Leslie Meier   1140

Cussone, Stanley
The Forever Beat - John Cline   262

Dalgliesh, Adam
Devices and Desires - P.D. James   841

Dalziel, Andrew
Bones and Silence - Reginald Hill   789
Recalled to Life - Reginald Hill   790

Daniels, Charmain
Witching Murder - Jennie Melville   1144

Daniels, Charmian
Dead Set - Jennie Melville   1141
Murder Has a Pretty Face - Jennie Melville   1142
Whoever Has the Heart - Jennie Melville   1143

Danno, Joe
Nice Guys Finish Dead - David Debin   406

Dante, Joe
19th Precinct - Christopher Newman   1202

Dartelli, Joe
Chain of Evidence - Ridley Pearson   1283

Davenport, Lucas
Night Prey - John Sandford   1424
Rules of Prey - John Sandford   1425
Shadow Prey - John Sandford   1426
Silent Prey - John Sandford   1427
Winter Prey - John Sandford   1428

Davies, Owen
The Killing of Ellis Martin - Lucretia Grindle   677
So Little to Die For - Lucretia Grindle   678

De Gheyn, Sam
The End of the Pier - Martha Grimes   674

Decker, Peter
Day of Atonement - Faye Kellerman   878
False Prophet - Faye Kellerman   879
Grievous Sin - Faye Kellerman   880
Justice - Faye Kellerman   881
Milk and Honey - Faye Kellerman   882
Sanctuary - Faye Kellerman   884

Decker, Phillip
Long Chain of Death - S.K. Wolf   1747

DeGregorio, Joe
False Faces - Seth Jacob Margolis   1074

Delafield, Kate
The Beverly Malibu - Katherine V. Forrest   533
Murder by Tradition - Katherine V. Forrest   534

Delaney, Ed
Night of the Ice Storm - David Stout   1579

Demarkian, Gregor
A Stillness in Bethlehem - Jane Haddam   697

Desoto, Alfonso
Flame - John Lutz   1057

Dewitt, James
Probable Cause - Ridley Pearson   1285

Diamond, Peter
The Summons - Peter Lovesey   1050

Dixon, Ray
The Raggedy Man - Lillian O'Donnell   1227
Used to Kill - Lillian O'Donnell   1228

Dodge, Jay
Larkspur - Sheila Simonson   1500
Skylark - Sheila Simonson   1501

Dogg, David
Bury the Bishop - Kate Gallison   564

Dolittle, Cyrus
Corruption - Andrew Klavan   936

Donahoo, Tommy
Balboa Firefly - Jack Trolley   1633

Donovan, Bill
City of God - Michael Jahn   840

Drake, Jessica
Angel of Death - Rochelle Majer Krich   953
Fair Game - Rochelle Majer Krich   954

Drake, Paul
Murder in a Nice Neighborhood - Lora Roberts   1388

Dundy
Death and the Chaste Apprentice - Robert Barnard   89

Dupoulis, Ken
Murder in Mellingham - Susan Oleksiw   1231

Early, Wilton
Death on Wheels - Robert Nordan   1209

Edwards, Harry
Kimura - Robert Davis   395

Exley, Ed
L.A. Confidential - James Ellroy   483

Faro, Jeremy
Blood Line - Alanna Knight   941
Killing Cousins - Alanna Knight   943

Fellowes, Ian
Home to Roost - Gerald Hammond   720

Fernandez, Arthur
Justice for Some - Kate Wilhelm   1724

Flanagan, Molly
Shutout - David F. Nighbert   1204

Fletcher, Alec
The Winter Garden Mystery - Carola Dunn   465

Flint, Mike
Midnight Baby - Wendy Hornsby   808

Florio, Marc
One Cried Murder - David Cooper Wall   1663

Flynn, Joe
Bantam of the Opera - Mary Daheim   374

Folger, Merry
Death on Rough Water - Francine Matthews   1099

Fork, Sid
The Fourth Durango - Ross Thomas   1612

Fowler, Nick
Kiss Them Goodbye - Joseph Eastburn   468

Frederickson, Garth
In the House of Secret Enemies - George C. Chesbro   241

Fredrick, Ray
In Blacker Moments - S.E. Schenkel   1451

Gabriel, Matt
A Few Dying Words - Paula Gosling   626

Gallant, Wayne
Miss Zukas and the Library Murders - Jo Dereske   416

Gastner, Bill
Bitter Recoil - Steven F. Havill   757
Heartshot - Steven F. Havill   758

Gaunt, Jonathan
The Spanish Maze Game - Noah Webster   1682

Gautier, Jean-Paul
Death Off Stage - Richard Grayson   655

Gennesko, Karl
Curly Smoke - Susan Holtzer   803

Gerrard, Phillip
The Queen Is Dead - Jane Dentinger   414

Ghote, Ganeesh
Dead on Time - H.R.F. Keating   874
The Iciest Sin - H.R.F. Keating   875

Gibbons, Cuthbert
Bad Blood - Anthony Bruno   185
Bad Moon - Anthony Bruno   186

Gisborne, Edward
Bad Chemistry - Nora Kelly   891

Glitsky, Abe
A Certain Justice - John T. Lescroart   1008

Goldstein, Jay
A Single Stone - Marilyn Wallace   1664

Gordon, Kathleen
All Hallows Evil - Valerie Wolzien   1748
A Good Year for a Corpse - Valerie Wolzien   1749

Grabowski, Joseph
Prescription for Death - Janet McGiffin   1130

Graver, Marcus
An Absence of Light - David L. Lindsey   1026

Gray, Susan
Wednesday's Child - Peter Robinson   1397

Grootka
Grootka - Jon A. Jackson   832

Grushko, Yevgeni Ivanovitch
Dead Meat - Philip Kerr   913

Gunther, Joe
Borderlines - Archer Mayor   1103
Fruits of the Poisonous Tree - Archer Mayor   1104
Scent of Evil - Archer Mayor   1105

Gutierez, Vince
Children's Games - Janet LaPierre   982

Guzman, Estelle
Bitter Recoil - Steven F. Havill   757

Haas, Peter
Death by Degrees - Robin Wilson   1735

Haggerty, Forrest
The Pumpkin-Shell Wife - Susanna Hofmann McShea   1138

Hall, Ray
Viper Quarry - Dean Feldmeyer   522

Hammond, Gary
Maximum Bob - Elmore Leonard   1006

Hampton, Blanche
A Pound of Flesh - Trevor Barnes   95

Hanks, Arly
Madness in Maggody - Joan Hess   777
Miracles in Maggody - Joan Hess   778
Mortal Remains in Maggody - Joan Hess   779
O Little Town of Maggody - Joan Hess   780

Hannibal, Nick
The Marvell College Murders - Sophie Belfort   119

Hanrahan, Bill
Lieberman's Choice - Stuart M. Kaminsky   856
Lieberman's Day - Stuart M. Kaminsky   857
Lieberman's Folly - Stuart M. Kaminsky   858

Hansen, Buck
A Gift for Murder - M.D. Lake   968

Hanson, Marvin
Act of Love - Joe R. Lansdale   980

Harald, Sigrid
Past Imperfect - Margaret Maron   1077

Hargreaves, Julie
The Summons - Peter Lovesey   1050

Police Officer

Harriman, Frank
Goodnight, Irene - Jan Burke 198

Harris, Ken
Exhaustive Enquiries - Betty Rowlands 1408

Hartnett, Ray
The Texas Capitol Murders - Bill Crider 353

Hastings, Frank
Dead Center - Collin Wilcox 1711
A Death Before Dying - Collin Wilcox 1712
Hire a Hangman - Collin Wilcox 1715
Switchback - Collin Wilcox 1717

Havers, Barbara
Payment in Blood - Elizabeth George 576
Playing for the Ashes - Elizabeth George 577

Hawkin, Alonzo
A Grave Talent - Laurie R. King 925
To Play the Fool - Laurie R. King 927

Henderson, Paula
Murder by Mail - M.D. Lake 969

Hockaday, Neil
Drown All the Dogs - Thomas Adcock 23

Holland, John
The Prosecutor - Thomas Chastain 240

Holt, Mitch
Night Sins - Tami Hoag 794

Hope, Joe
Storm Front - Virginia Anderson 53

Hopkins, Marty
Gravestone - P.M. Carlson 219

Hopkins, Ray
Silent Witness - Charles Wilson 1732

Horowitz, Jacob
The Last Gambit - David Delman 411

Hunter, Gordon
A Day in the Death of Dorothea Cassidy - Ann Cleeves 260

James, Gemma
All Shall Be Well - Deborah Crombie 356
Leave the Grave Green - Deborah Crombie 357
A Share in Death - Deborah Crombie 358

Jensen, Alex
Murder on the Iditarod Trail - Sue Henry 775

Johnson, Toussaint
Murder by the Numbers - Max Allan Collins 278

Jones, A.L.
Knight & Day - Ron Nessen 1201

Jordon, Berkley
Jordon's Wager - Frank C. Strunk 1584

Jury, Richard
The Old Contemptibles - Martha Grimes 675
The Old Silent - Martha Grimes 676

Kane, Thomas
Unbalanced Acts - Jeff Raines 1344

Karpo, Emil
Rostnikov's Vacation - Stuart M. Kaminsky 861

Kelley, Clovis
Bloody Soaps: A Tale of Love and Death in the Afternoon - Jacqueline Babbin 75

Kelly, Michael
Unbalanced Acts - Jeff Raines 1344

Kennedy, D.J.
Ravenmocker - Jean Hager 701

Kevlehan, Dan
Murder Once Removed - Kathleen Kunz 959

Kiet, Bamsan
Kiet Goes West - Gary Alexander 34
Unfunny Money - Gary Alexander 35

Kincaid, Duncan
All Shall Be Well - Deborah Crombie 356

Leave the Grave Green - Deborah Crombie 357
A Share in Death - Deborah Crombie 358

Kite, Martin
Late of This Parish - Marjorie Eccles 469
More Deaths than One - Marjorie Eccles 470

Kitologitak, Matthew "Matteesie"
Murder in a Cold Climate - Scott Young 1785
The Shaman's Knife - Scott Young 1786

Knight, Billy
Tropical Depression - Jeffry P. Lindsay 1024

Knight, Jack
Murder in a Quiet Place - Tony Caxton 230

Kost, John
With Siberia Comes a Chill - Kirk Mitchell 1161

Kovak, Milt
Dead Moon on the Rise - Susan Rogers Cooper 310
Doctors, Lawyers and Such - Susan Rogers Cooper 311
Houston in the Rearview Mirror - Susan Rogers Cooper 314
Other People's Houses - Susan Rogers Cooper 316

Kramer, James
Fatal Obsession - D.B. Taylor 1606

Kramer, Tromp
The Song Dog - James McClure 1114

Kuisma, Val
Grandmother's House - Janet LaPierre 983

Lahey, Mark
The Ransom - Brian Tobin 1622

Laidlaw, Jack
Strange Loyalties - William McIlvanney 1134

Langdon, Skip
The Axeman's Jazz - Julie Smith 1523
House of Blues - Julie Smith 1525
Jazz Funeral - Julie Smith 1526
New Orleans Beat - Julie Smith 1527
New Orleans Mourning - Julie Smith 1528

Lassiter, Aaron
A Permanent Retirement - John Miles 1153

Lau, John
Make No Bones - Aaron Elkins 478

Lawton, Dave
Dead Center - Ruby Horansky 805

Leaphorn, Joe
Sacred Clowns - Tony Hillerman 792
Talking God - Tony Hillerman 793

Lemieux, Andre
Death in a Funhouse Mirror - Kate Clark Flora 531

Levinson, Karen
Skins - Catherine O'Connell 1222

Li, Agatha
Free - Todd Komarnicki 952

Lieberman, Abe
Lieberman's Choice - Stuart M. Kaminsky 856
Lieberman's Day - Stuart M. Kaminsky 857
Lieberman's Folly - Stuart M. Kaminsky 858

Lightstone, Henry
Wildfire - Kenneth W. Goddard 605

Lineham, Michael
Dead by Morning - Dorothy Simpson 1502

Lingemann, Jack
And Soon I'll Come to Kill You - Susan Kelly 893
Until Proven Innocent - Susan Kelly 895

Llewellyn, Dafyd
Dead Before Morning - Geraldine Evans 504

Loomis, L.J.
The Late Man - James Preston Girard 592

Lubick, Caroline "Carrie"
Night of the Cat - James Schermerhorn 1452

What Mystery Do I Read Next?

Lundquist, Fred
Buried in Quilts - Sara Hoskinson Frommer 559

Lyman, Nigel
Gospel Truths - J.G. Sandom 1429

Lynley, Thomas
Missing Joseph - Elizabeth George 575
Playing for the Ashes - Elizabeth George 577
A Suitable Vengeance - Elizabeth George 578

MacAlister, Marti
Dead Time - Eleanor Taylor Bland 141
Slow Burn - Eleanor Taylor Bland 142

MacBeth, Hamish
Death of a Charming Man - M.C. Beaton 109
Death of a Hussy - M.C. Beaton 110
Death of a Nag - M.C. Beaton 111

Macbeth, Hamish
Death of a Perfect Wife - M.C. Beaton 112
Death of a Traveling Man - M.C. Beaton 113

MacKenzie, C.K.
I'd Rather Be in Philadelphia - Gillian Roberts 1378
Philly Stakes - Gillian Roberts 1379
With Friends Like These - Gillian Roberts 1380

MacKenzie, Ian
Night of the Cat - James Schermerhorn 1452

MacNulty, Ray
Golden Fleece - Jack Becklund 118

Macrae, George
Thieftaker - Alan Scholefield 1454

Maddox, Kate
Model Murder - Erica Quest 1338

Magnum, Cuddy
Time's Witness - Michael Malone 1070

Mallory, Kathleen
Mallory's Oracle - Carol O'Connell 1221

Malone, Scobie
Murder Song - Jon Cleary 256

Mann, Jack
Hell Bent - Ken Gross 684

Marino, Pete
All That Remains - Patricia D. Cornwell 321
The Body Farm - Patricia D. Cornwell 322
Cruel and Unusual - Patricia D. Cornwell 324

Markby, Alan
Cold in the Earth - Ann Granger 642
A Fine Place for Death - Ann Granger 643
Murder Among Us - Ann Granger 644
A Season for Murder - Ann Granger 645

Marsh, Harry
The Going Down of the Sun - Jo Bannister 87

Martin, Leilani
Singapore Transfer - Wayne Warga 1673

Martinelli, Kate
A Grave Talent - Laurie R. King 925
To Play the Fool - Laurie R. King 927

Maxwell, Lauren
A Wolf in Death's Clothing - Elizabeth Quinn 1341

Maybridge, Tom
The Fifth Rapunzel - B.M. Gill 586

Mayo, Gil
Late of This Parish - Marjorie Eccles 469
More Deaths than One - Marjorie Eccles 470

McAllister, Beau
Lizardskin - Carsten Stroud 1582

McCoo, Harold
Hardball - Barbara D'Amato 384

McCormick, Thomas
Hammurabi's Code - Charles Kenney 909

Character Description Index

McGowan, Michael
A Tail of Two Murders - Melissa Cleary 259

McGowan, Tom
Murder in Scorpio - Martha C. Lawrence 993

McGuire, Joe
And Leave Her Lay Dying - John Lawrence Reynolds 1362
Whisper Death - John Lawrence Reynolds 1363

McIntyre, Martin
Desperate Remedy - Mary Kittredge 931

McIntyre, Michael
Walking Dead Man - Mary Kittredge 934

McKenna, Brian
Detective First Grade - Don Mahoney 1067

McLeish, John
Death Among the Dons - Janet Neel 1196
Death of a Partner - Janet Neel 1197

McLoughlin, Andy
The Ice House - Minette Walters 1669

McPhee, Pete
Carolina Gold - Douglas McBriarty 1108

Means, Roland
A Good Day to Die - Stephen Solomita 1534

Miller, Peter
Beat Up a Cookie - Denise Dietz 422
Throw Darts at a Cheesecake - Denise Dietz 423

Monk, William
A Dangerous Mourning - Anne Perry 1293

Monroe, Andy
Safe at Home - Alison Gordon 614

Monroe, Louis
Down by the Sea - Bill Kent 910

Montgomery, Richard
Nurse Dawes Is Dead - Stella Shepherd 1479
Thinner than Blood - Stella Shepherd 1480

Morelli, Joe
One for the Money - Janet Evanovich 503

Morgan, Jack
A Cold-Blooded Business - Dana Stabenow 1550
A Cold Day for Murder - Dana Stabenow 1549
Dead in the Water - Dana Stabenow 1551

Morgan, James
No Way Home - Andrew Coburn 267
Voices in the Dark - Andrew Coburn 268

Morrissey, John
In Stoney Places - Kay Mitchell 1159
A Lively Form of Death - Kay Mitchell 1160

Morse
The Wench Is Dead - Colin Dexter 418

Morton, James
Patently Murder - Ray Harrison 737
Tincture of Death - Ray Harrison 738

Mott, Angus
Cat's Cradle - Clare Curzon 366
Death Prone - Clare Curzon 367

Muldoon, Ned
Faces in the Crowd - William Marshall 1079
The New York Detective - William Marshall 1080

Mulheisen, "Fang"
Grootka - Jon A. Jackson 832
Hit on the House - Jon A. Jackson 833

Muller, Kurt
Into Thin Air - Thomas Zigal 1788

Murphy, Jake
A Very Proper Death - Alex Juniper 850

Napier, "Boss"
Dying Voices - Bill Crider 351

Nesbitt, Alan
The Body in the Transept - Jeanne M. Dams 385

Nickles, Eddie
Playing the Dozens - William D. Pease 1286

Nightingale, Tim
Death Penalties - Paula Gosling 625

Odhiambo, James
Death Underfoot - Dennis Casley 225

O'Hanlon, Ike
Full Commission - Carol Brennan 172

Ohayon, Michael
Murder on a Kibbutz - Batya Gur 690
The Saturday Morning Murder - Batya Gur 691

O'Malley, Megan
Night Sins - Tami Hoag 794

O'Neil, Caitlin
The Monster Squad - John Angus 59

O'Neill
A Fatal Advent - Isabelle Holland 797

O'Neill, Connor
Die in My Dreams - Christine Green 661

O'Neill, Peggy
Amends for Murder - M.D. Lake 966
Cold Comfort - M.D. Lake 967
A Gift for Murder - M.D. Lake 968
Murder by Mail - M.D. Lake 969
Once upon a Crime - M.D. Lake 970
Poisoned Ivy - M.D. Lake 971

Ortiz, Gabe
Fool's Puzzle - Earlene Fowler 536

Ortiz, Johnny
Missing Man - Richard Martin Stern 1570

O'Shaugnessy, Jesus
Nightside - Soledad Santiago 1434

Otiz, Gabriel
Irish Chain - Earlene Fowler 537

Paige, Patrick
Skeletons - Eric Sauter 1443

Paris, Jack
Deviant Way - Richard Montanari 1166

Parker, Hank
Alley Kat Blues - Karen Kijewski 917

Pascoe, Peter
Bones and Silence - Reginald Hill 789
Recalled to Life - Reginald Hill 790

Peace, Charlie
Death and the Chaste Apprentice - Robert Barnard 89

Peckover, Henry
Kill the Butler! - Michael Kenyon 911
Peckover Joins the Choir - Michael Kenyon 912

Pedersen, Carl
Threnody for Two - Jeanne Hart 747

Pel, Evariste
Pel and the Missing Persons - Mark Hebden 768

Perilli, Tony
Skins - Catherine O'Connell 1222

Philbrick, Ginny
Murder Will Out - Dorian Yeager 1784

Pickett, Mel
Buried in Stone - Eric Wright 1766
A Sensitive Case - Eric Wright 1770

Pigram, William
Hotel Morgue - Janet Laurence 989

Pitt, Thomas
Farrier's Lane - Anne Perry 1294
Highgate Rise - Anne Perry 1295

Plum, Marvia
The Classic Car Killer - Richard A. Lupoff 1054

Pooley, Ellis
Clubbed to Death - Ruth Dudley Edwards 472

Pope, Hamilton
See No Evil - Edward Mathis 1095

Powers, Jack
Paramour - Gerald Petievich 1312

Price, Robin
Fatal Charm - Anne Morice 1173

Pucci, Sal
Funny as a Dead Comic - Susan Rogers Cooper 312
Funny as a Dead Relative - Susan Rogers Cooper 313

Quantrill, Douglas
This Way Out - Sheila Radley 1343

Quinn, Al
The Buzzards Must Also Be Fed - Anne Wingate 1739
Exception to Murder - Anne Wingate 1740

Rafferty, Joseph
Dead Before Morning - Geraldine Evans 504

Ralston, Deb
Bird in a Cage - Lee Martin 1086
The Day That Dusty Died - Lee Martin 1087
Deficit Ending - Lee Martin 1088
The Mensa Murders - Lee Martin 1089

Ramos, Lucia
Final Session - Mary Morell 1170

Ramsey, Stephen
A Day in the Death of Dorothea Cassidy - Ann Cleeves 260

Regal, Paul
End Game - Dev Stryker 1585

Renko, Arkady
Polar Star - Martin Cruz Smith 1530

Renner, David
Fuse Time - Max Byrd 205

Resnick, Charlie
Cold Light - John Harvey 751
Cutting Edge - John Harvey 752
Off Minor - John Harvey 753
The Wasted Years - John Harvey 754

Rhys, Madoc
The Wrong Rite - Alisa Craig 334

Robicheaux, Dave
Burning Angel - James Lee Burke 194
Dixie City Jam - James Lee Burke 195
In the Electric Mist with Confederate Dead - James Lee Burke 196
A Morning for Flamingos - James Lee Burke 197

Rogers, George
A Time for Dying - Jonathan Ross 1402

Romain, Dan
Blood Marks - Bill Crider 349

Roper, Douglas
Breach of Promise - Roy Hart 748

Rosen, Peter
A Diet to Die For - Joan Hess 776

Ross, Hubert
The Killing of Ellis Martin - Lucretia Grindle 677
So Little to Die For - Lucretia Grindle 678

Rostnikov, Porfiry
The Man Who Walked Like a Bear - Stuart M. Kaminsky 859
Rostnikov's Vacation - Stuart M. Kaminsky 861

Rothenberg, Lily
Shadow Prey - John Sandford 1426

Rudd
The Spoils of Time - June Thomson 1614

Russo
Date with a Dead Doctor - Toni Brill 177

Political Figure

Ryan
Shadows on the Mirror - Frances Fyfield 563
Ryker, Sam
Till Death Do Us Part - Rochelle Majer Krich 955
Salter, Charlie
Death by Degrees - Eric Wright 1767
Final Cut - Eric Wright 1768
A Fine Italian Hand - Eric Wright 1769
A Sensitive Case - Eric Wright 1770
Sanders, John
Murder in a Good Cause - Medora Sale 1417
Murder in Focus - Medora Sale 1418
Pursued by Shadows - Medora Sale 1419
Short Cut to Santa Fe - Medora Sale 1420
Savile, Justin
Time's Witness - Michael Malone 1070
Scanlon, Joseph
Casual Slaughters - Robert A. Carter 223
Scarf, Bruce
Casualty Loss - Jim Weikart 1683
Schulz, Tom
The Cereal Murders - Diane Mott Davidson 389
Scott, Aline
High Strangeness - Alison Drake 447
Seraphicos, Debra
Sight Unseen - David Lorne 1046
Shanley, Carol
An Hour to Kill - Edward Wellen 1690
Sheldon, Graham
Rotten Lies - Charlotte Elkins 481
A Wicked Slice - Aaron Elkins 480
Shelton, Holly
Noble Rot - Will Harriss 739
Shigata, Mark
The Buzzards Must Also Be Fed - Anne Wingate 1739
Exception to Murder - Anne Wingate 1740
The Eye of Anna - Anne Wingate 1741
Yakuza, Go Home - Anne Wingate 1742
Silva, Joe
Family Album - Susan Oleksiw 1230
Murder in Mellingham - Susan Oleksiw 1231
Silver, Leopold
Thieftaker - Alan Scholefield 1454
Simpson, Oliver
Hung in the Balance - Roger Ormerod 1244
Skinny
All I Have Is Blue - James Colbert 272
Skinny Man - James Colbert 273
Slider, Bill
Death Watch - Cynthia Harrod-Eagles 740
Sloan, C.D.
The Body Politic - Catherine Aird 25
Smailes, Derek
The Cambridge Theorem - Tony Cape 217
Smart, David
The Dean It Was That Died - Barbara Whitehead 1706
Smith, Paavo
Cooking Up Trouble - Joanne Pence 1289
Something's Cooking - Joanne Pence 1290
Too Many Cooks - Joanne Pence 1291
Smith, Peter
Rising Sun - Michael Crichton 348
Soldano, Lou
Blindsight - Robin Cook 302
Somers, John
Cold Call - Dianne G. Pugh 1333
Southwell, Robert
Playing God - Barbara Whitehead 1707
Sweet Death, Come Softly - Barbara Whitehead 1708
Stagnaro, Dante
Menaced Assassin - Joe Gores 618
Starbranch, Harry
No Comfort in Victory - Gregory Bean 106
Staub, J.D.
The Dry White Tear - Stephen F. Wilcox 1719
Stepanovich, Jose
Earth Angels - Gerald Petievich 1311
Straun, Angus
Unnatural Hazard - Barry Cork 317
Winter Rules - Barry Cork 318
Stryker, Jack
The Body in Blackwater Bay - Paula Gosling 624
Sturgis, Milo
Bad Love - Jonathan Kellerman 885
Private Eyes - Jonathan Kellerman 886
Self-Defense - Jonathan Kellerman 887
Sussock, Ray
Condition Purple - Peter Turnbull 1639
Swain, Alfred
The Ripper's Apprentice - Donald Thomas 1610
Swift, Doug
The Water Cure - Warwick Downing 446
Tejeda, Roger
Half a Mind - Wendy Hornsby 807
Thane, Colin
The Interface Man - Bill Knox 948
Thomas, Lenore
Box Nine - Jack O'Connell 1223
Thorn, Nick
Dead in the Cellar - Connie Fedderson 520
Tibbet, Henry
Black Girl, White Girl - Patricia Moyes 1179
Tillman, Virgil
Faces in the Crowd - William Marshall 1079
The New York Detective - William Marshall 1080
Tincker, "Push"
Night Rituals - Gary Paulsen 1279
Titus, Nicky
The Devil Down Home - Eve K. Sandstrom 1431
Titus, Sam
The Down Home Heifer Heist - Eve K. Sandstrom 1432
Tolliver, Ben
By Reason of Insanity - James Neal Harvey 749
Painted Ladies - James Neal Harvey 750
Tozzi, Mike
Bad Blood - Anthony Bruno 185
Bad Moon - Anthony Bruno 186
Trakos, Nikki
Dead Center - Ruby Horansky 805
Tretheway, Albert
Murder on the Thirteenth - A.E. Eddenden 471
Trevellyan, Nick
Hope Against Hope - Susan B. Kelly 896
Kid's Stuff - Susan B. Kelly 897
Time of Hope - Susan B. Kelly 898
Troy, Frederick
Black Out - John Lawton 994
Tully, Alonzo "Zoo"
Chameleon - William X. Kienzle 915
Turner, Paul
Sorry Now? - Mark Richard Zubro 1796
Twitty, Jason
Peckover Joins the Choir - Michael Kenyon 912
Van Der Valk, Piet
Sand Castles - Nicholas Freeling 549

What Mystery Do I Read Next?

Van Dyne, Mel
A Farewell to Yarns - Jill Churchill 245
From Here to Paternity - Jill Churchill 246
Vecchi, Al
Shooting Script - Gordon Cotler 332
Voegler, Allie
Dr. Nightingale Goes the Distance - Lydia Adamson 21
Dr. Nightingale Rides the Elephant - Lydia Adamson 22
Walker, Jack
The Cactus Garden - Robert Ward 1672
Walker, Thad
The Fast-Death Factor - Virginia Crosby 359
Walsh, Jack
Bait - Kenneth Abel 3
Warden, Jesse
Heat - Stuart Woods 1760
Wexford, Reginald
Kissing the Gunner's Daughter - Ruth Rendell 1361
White, Bud
L.A. Confidential - James Ellroy 483
White, Frank
Bagged - Jo Bailey 79
Wiggins, Thomas
Is Anybody There? - T.G. Gilpin 591
Williams, Lee
Palindrome - Stuart Woods 1762
Willis, Charles
My Gun Has Bullets - Lee Goldberg 606
Willis, Grace
Death and the Dogwalker - A.J. Orde 1240
A Little Neighborhood Murder - A.J. Orde 1241
A Long Time Dead - A.J. Orde 1242
Wilson, Fran
Die in My Dreams - Christine Green 661
Woo, April
Hanging Time - Leslie Glass 601
Worth, Tom
Bitter Herbs - Natasha Cooper 307
Bloody Roses - Natasha Cooper 308
Rotten Apples - Natasha Cooper 309
Wren, Susan
Consider the Crows - Charlene Weir 1685
Family Practice - Charlene Weir 1686
The Winter Widow - Charlene Weir 1687
Yeadings, Mike
Cat's Cradle - Clare Curzon 366
Death Prone - Clare Curzon 367
Three-Core Lead - Clare Curzon 368
Zondi, Mickey
The Song Dog - James McClure 1114

POLITICAL FIGURE

Ellis, Nigel
Dream of Darkness - Patrick Ruell 1412
Flannery, Jimmy
The Gift Horse's Mouth - Robert Campbell 212
Huckins, B.D.
The Fourth Durango - Ross Thomas 1612
Proctor, Peter
A Scandal in Belgravia - Robert Barnard 91
Slater, Henry Lee
Bad Desire - Gary Devon 417
Wade, John
In the Lake of the Woods - Tim O'Brien 1218
Wentworth, Bea
Death on the Mississippi - Richard Forrest 535

Character Description Index

Willmont, Robert
Guilt by Association - Susan R. Sloan   1514

Zigman, Gail
Fruits of the Poisoned Tree - Archer Mayor   1104

POSTAL WORKER

Hairsteen, Mary Miner "Harry"
Wish You Were Here - Rita Mae Brown   182

Hairsteen, Mary Minor "Harry"
Murder at Monticello - Rita Mae Brown   180
Rest in Pieces - Rita Mae Brown   181

Thomas, Ike
Box Nine - Jack O'Connell   1223

PRINCIPAL

Louis, Ben
Dead Easy - E.S. Russell   1415

PROBATION OFFICER

Baker, Kathy Diaz
Maximum Bob - Elmore Leonard   1006

Baum, Steven
Slow Motion Riot - Peter Blauner   144

PRODUCER

Zimm, Harry
Get Shorty - Elmore Leonard   1005

PROFESSOR

Adams, Gillian
Bad Chemistry - Nora Kelly   891
My Sister's Keeper - Nora Kelly   892

Austin, Beth
The George Eliot Murders - Edith Skom   1511
The Mark Twain Murders - Edith Skom   1512

Benedetti, Niccolo
The Manx Murders - William L. DeAndrea   402

Bennet, Bridget
What Men Say - Joan Smith   1522

Burns, Carl
Dying Voices - Bill Crider   351

Camden, Claire
Shroud for a Scholar - Audrey Peterson   1306

Cobb, Jeremy
She Walks These Hills - Sharyn McCrumb   1119

Dobie, John
The Catalyst - Desmond Cory   330
The Dobie Paradox - Desmond Cory   331

Donodio, Brian
Forty Whacks - Sheila MacGill Callahan   207

Edwards, Colin
Selena - Gordon Randolph Willey   1726

Eldine, Janet
Murder at the Friendship Hotel - Charlotte Epstein   496

Fansler, Kate
An Imperfect Spy - Amanda Cross   360

Farley, Marion
Zombies of the Gene Pool - Sharyn McCrumb   1121

Fleming, Richard
Dead Ringer - Toni L.P. Kelner   900
Down Home Murder - Toni L.P. Kelner   901
Trouble Looking for a Place to Happen - Toni L.P. Kelner   902

Frederickson, Robert "Mongo"
In the House of Secret Enemies - George C. Chesbro   241
The Language of Cannibals - George C. Chesbro   242

Goldberg, Benny
Death Benefits - Michael A. Kahn   851
Due Diligence - Michael A. Kahn   852
Firm Ambitions - Michael A. Kahn   853

Graham, Peter
Crossover - Judith Eubank   502

Kelly, Homer
The Dante Game - Jane Langton   979

Lawson, Loretta
Don't Leave Me This Way - Joan Smith   1520
What Men Say - Joan Smith   1522

Livsey, Horace
Monday's Child Is Dead - James Elward   484

Mallory, Dix
With an Extreme Burning - Bill Pronzini   1331

Malone, Wilson
Dead in the Water - W.J. Chaput   233

McFarland, Fowler
Sweet Death - Bill Waggoner   1657

Norton, Myrl Adler
In the Dead of Winter - Abbey Penn Baker   81

Omega, Jay
Zombies of the Gene Pool - Sharyn McCrumb   1121

Ponton, Anthony
Death of a Fantasy Life - T.G. Gilpin   590

Quentin, Andrew
Elegy in a Country Graveyard - Audrey Peterson   1304
Murder in Burgundy - Audrey Peterson   1305

Rafferty, Molly
The Marvell College Murders - Sophie Belfort   119

Rogerson, Matt
The Search Committee - Ralph McInerny   1136

Shandy, Peter
An Owl Too Many - Charlotte MacLeod   1064
Something in the Water - Charlotte MacLeod   1065

Sherman, Winston
Deception Island - M.K. Lorens   1043
Dreamland - M.K. Lorens   1044
Sweet Narcissus - M.K. Lorens   1045

Smith, MacKenzie "Mac"
Murder at the Kennedy Center - Margaret Truman   1634

Snow, Nicholas
Honolulu Red - Lue Zimmelman   1789

Squires, Lee
Grizzly - Christine Andreae   54
Trail of Murder - Christine Andreae   55

Teague, Kate
Half a Mind - Wendy Hornsby   807

Theron, Thomas
Peeping Thomas - Robert Reeves   1358

Trevorne, Kate
The Body in Blackwater Bay - Paula Gosling   624

Walsh, Jackie
A Tail of Two Murders - Melissa Cleary   259

Whitson, Blair
An Imperfect Spy - Amanda Cross   360

PROSTITUTE

Frank, Lisa
Hide and Seek - Barry Berg   122

Stokes, Sally
A Broken Vessel - Kate Ross   1403

PSYCHIC

Bonesteel, Nora
The Hangman's Beautiful Daughter - Sharyn McCrumb   1115

Bowering, Victoria
Cancellation by Death - Dorian Yeager   1782

Smith, Jane
A Love to Die For - Christine T. Jorgensen   849

PSYCHOLOGIST

Chapman, Andrew
Probable Cause - Griff Stockley   1577

Corder, Wilson
The Deep End - Chris Crutcher   364

Delaware, Alex
Bad Love - Jonathan Kellerman   885
Private Eyes - Jonathan Kellerman   886
Self-Defense - Jonathan Kellerman   887
Time Bomb - Jonathan Kellerman   888

Franklyn, Kit
Blood on the Bayou - D.J. Donaldson   429
New Orleans Requiem - D.J. Donaldson   430
No Mardi Gras for the Dead - D.J. Donaldson   431

Gentry, Janice
The Manx Murders - William L. DeAndrea   402

Leidl, Constance
Seven Kinds of Death - Kate Wilhelm   1725

Matthews, Daphne
The Angel Maker - Ridley Pearson   1282

Phillips, Maddy
Blood Trance - R.D. Zimmerman   1791
Red Trance - R.D. Zimmerman   1793

Torenson, Lou
Showcase - Alison Glen   603

Toreson, Lou
Trunk Show - Alison Glen   604

PUBLIC RELATIONS

Barr, Temple
Cat on a Blue Monday - Carole Nelson Douglas   438
Catnap - Carole Nelson Douglas   439
Pussyfoot - Carole Nelson Douglas   443

Dunbar, Will
Wasteland - Peter McCabe   1110

Kitchener, Nina
Pressure Drop - Peter Abrahams   5

Lynch, Jack
Murphy's Fault - Steven Womack   1752

Wareham, Liz
Full Commission - Carol Brennan   172

Wheeler, Elizabeth
The Famous DAR Murder Mystery - Graham Landrum   977

Winder, Joe
Native Tongue - Carl Hiaasen   782

PUBLISHER

Barlow, Nicholas
Casual Slaughters - Robert A. Carter   223
Final Edit - Robert A. Carter   224

Blair, Barley
The Russia House - John Le Carre   995

Radio Personality

Boucher, Thurman
Kill Story - Jerome Doolittle 434

Brady, Peter
Deerslayer - M.S. Karl 867

Devore, Addie
Murder in Bandora - Leona Karr 868

Porter, Ben
Finders Keepers - Elizabeth Travis 1627

Porter, Carrie
Finders Keepers - Elizabeth Travis 1627

RADIO PERSONALITY

Riordan, Prester John
The Frozen Franklin - Sean Hanlon 725

RAKE

Hine, Tony
By Death Possessed - Roger Ormerod 1243

RANCHER

McClintock, Shirley
Dead in the Scrub - B.J. Oliphant 1232
Death and the Delinquent - B.J. Oliphant 1233
Death Served Up Cold - B.J. Oliphant 1234
The Unexpected Corpse - B.J. Oliphant 1235

RANGER

Pigeon, Anna
A Superior Death - Nevada Barr 96
Track of the Cat - Nevada Barr 97

Trask, Ginny
Clear-Cut Murder - Lee Wallingford 1667
Cold Tracks - Lee Wallingford 1668

REAL ESTATE AGENT

Abbott, Ben
Hardscape - Justin Scott 1463
StoneDust - Justin Scott 1464

Bellini, Cecca
With an Extreme Burning - Bill Pronzini 1331

Simmons, Louella
Four Elements of Murder - D.B. Borton 155

Verstak, Marni
A Very Proper Death - Alex Juniper 850

RECLUSE

Lazzeri, Paul
Shadowchase - Martin Blank 143

REFUGEE

Lohmann, Ernst
Death Squad London - Jack Gerson 579

RELIGIOUS

Aldington, Claire
A Fatal Advent - Isabelle Holland 797

Beaufort, Henry
The Bishop's Tale - Margaret Frazer 544

Bennett, Christine
The Christening Day Murder - Lee Harris 733

Braithwaite, Theodora
Clerical Errors - D.M. Greenwood 670

Idol Bones - D.M. Greenwood 671
Unholy Ghosts - D.M. Greenwood 672

Cadfael
Brother Cadfael's Penance - Ellis Peters 1301
The Potter's Field - Ellis Peters 1302
The Summer of the Danes - Ellis Peters 1303

Cecile
A Sudden Death at the Norfolk Cafe - Winona Sullivan 1591

Coldwater, Jack Gene
Heat - Stuart Woods 1760

Dempsey, Mary Teresa
Nun Plussed - Monica Quill 1339

Donovan, Brigid
Murder Is Germane - Karen Saum 1442

Eileen
Murder Makes a Pilgrimage - Sister Carol Anne O'Marie 1239

Elliot, Elizabeth
Quaker Witness - Irene Allen 46

Fairchild, Tom
The Body in the Belfry - Katherine Hall Page 1255
The Body in the Bouillon - Katherine Hall Page 1256
The Body in the Vestibule - Katherine Hall Page 1258

Frevisse
The Bishop's Tale - Margaret Frazer 544
The Boy's Tale - Margaret Frazer 545

Grabowski, Kazimierz
Gospel Truths - J.G. Sandom 1429

Grey, Lavinia
Bury the Bishop - Kate Gallison 564

Grindal, George
The Dean It Was That Died - Barbara Whitehead 1706

Hope, Malachi
Miracles in Maggody - Joan Hess 778

Jerome
The Lost Keats - Terence Faherty 515

Joan
A Vow of Chastity - Veronica Black 136
A Vow of Obedience - Veronica Black 137
A Vow of Sanctity - Veronica Black 138

Koesler, Robert
Chameleon - William X. Kienzle 915
Masquerade - William X. Kienzle 916

Littlejohn, Eldon
Baptism for Murder - Jan Maxwell 1101

Mary Helen
Death Goes on Retreat - Sister Carol Anne O'Marie 1237
Murder in Ordinary Time - Sister Carol Anne O'Marie 1238
Murder Makes a Pilgrimage - Sister Carol Anne O'Marie 1239

Neville, Gabriel
A Drink of Deadly Wine - Kate Charles 235

Regan, Francis
Bloody Ten - William F. Love 1047
The Chartreuse Clue - William F. Love 1048

Ryan, Blackie
Happy Are the Merciful - Andrew M. Greeley 656

Thompson, Daniel
Viper Quarry - Dean Feldmeyer 522

Thoresby, John
The Lady Chapel - Candace M. Robb 1376

Todd, Ziza
Point No-Point - David Willis McCullough 1123
Think on Death - David Willis McCullough 1124

What Mystery Do I Read Next?

Wilson, Mike
Topless - D. Keith Mano 1072

RESEARCHER

Keane, Owen
Deadstick - Terence Faherty 513

Kendricks, Lucas
Death Qualified: A Mystery of Chaos - Kate Wilhelm 1723

RESTAURANTEUR

Caruso, Wayne
Tea-Totally Dead - Jaqueline Girdner 596

Killebrew, Coley
Stalking Horse - Bill Shoemaker 1487

Lawless, Jane
Hallowed Murder - Ellen Hart 745
Vital Lies - Ellen Hart 746

ROYALTY

Louise
Skeleton-in-Waiting - Peter Dickinson 419

RULER

Richard III
The Fate of Princes - P.C. Doherty 424

Tutankhamun
Murder in the Place of Anubis - Lynda S. Robinson 1390

Victor II
Skeleton-in-Waiting - Peter Dickinson 419

RUNAWAY

Epstein, Beau
Thursday's Child - Teri White 1705

Singer, Kendra
Trade Secrets - Ray Garton 568

SAILOR

Barr, Jeremy
Landfall - Tony Gibbs 581

Frazer, Harry
Deadeye - Sam Llewellyn 1037

Verdean, Gillian
Landfall - Tony Gibbs 581
Running Fix - Tony Gibbs 582

SALOON KEEPER/OWNER

Danvers, Sally
Dreamboat - Doug J. Swanson 1596

Hardy, Dismas
Hard Evidence - John T. Lescroart 1009

Hawksley, Hal
The Sculptress - Minette Walters 1671

Jacoby, Miles
Hard Look - Robert J. Randisi 1349

Jordan, Berkley
Jordon's Showdown - Frank C. Strunk 1583

Keane, Owen
Die Dreaming - Terence Faherty 514

SCIENTIST

Chadwick, Alix
Tensleep - Sarah Andrews 57

Cooper, Sam
The Bulrush Murders - Rebecca Rothenberg 1405

Dinesen, Mike
Death Qualified: A Mystery of Chaos - Kate Wilhelm 1723

Fitzgerald, Jennifer
Coyote Bird - Jim DeFelice 409

Flaschner, Max
A Very Particular Murder - S.T. Haymon 759

Ford, Doc
Sanibel Flats - Randy Wayne White 1704

Hall, Frank
Deep Chill - Ian Slater 1513

Hansen, Emily "Em"
A Fall in Denver - Sarah Andrews 56

McNeely, Kathy
The Ice - Louis Charbonneau 234

Sharples, Claire
The Bulrush Murders - Rebecca Rothenberg 1405

SECRETARY

Ardleigh, Kathryn "Kate"
Death at Bishop's Keep - Robin Paige 1259

Burke, Claire
The Lion's Share - Kelly A. Tate 1605

Corbett, Hugh
Murder Wears a Cowl - P.C. Doherty 426
The Prince of Darkness - P.C. Doherty 427

Ferrer, Jennifer
Miami Heat - Jerome Sanford 1433

Johnson, Lisa
Wiseguys in Love - C. Clark Criscuolo 355

Runkel, Vida
The Alpine Advocate - Mary Daheim 370

Ruth
All I Have Is Blue - James Colbert 272

Sanderson, Sandy
A Death for a Dancing Doll - E.X. Giroux 597
A Death for a Dodo - E.X. Giroux 598

Shallot, Roger
The Poisoned Chalice - Michael Clynes 264
The White Rose Murders - Michael Clynes 265

Smith, Julia
Clerical Errors - D.M. Greenwood 670

Tracer, Chris
Tracer, Inc. - Jeff Andrus 58

SECURITY OFFICER

Connors, Jamison
Gun Men - Gary Friedman 553

Gallagher, Jan
Bagged - Jo Bailey 79
Recycled - Jo Bailey 80

McCauley, Quint
Murder in Store - D.C. Brod 178

Szabo, Eric
Capitol Offense - Tony Gibbs 580

SERIAL KILLER

Benanti, Nina
Widowmaker - William Appel 63

Cooper
Into the Fire - David Wiltse 1737

Denkin, George
Incident at Potter's Bridge - Joseph Monniger 1165

Nasson, Carl
Whisper.He Might Hear You - William Appel 62

Parker, David
A Pound of Flesh - Trevor Barnes 95

Slocum, John
Trade-Off - Harrison Arnston 66

Soneji, Gary
Along Came a Spider - James Patterson 1276

SERVANT

Benno
Death of the Duchess - Elizabeth Eyre 512

Huxleigh, Penelope (Nell)
Good Night, Mr. Holmes - Carole Nelson Douglas 441

Malloy, Roxie
Femmes Fatal - Dorothy Cannell 214
How to Murder Your Mother-in-Law - Dorothy Cannell 215

Nemo, Adam
Frobisher's Savage - Leonard Tourney 1624

White, Blanche
Blanche on the Lam - Barbara Neely 1198

SIDEKICK

Goodwin, Archie
Fade to Black - Robert Goldsborough 607
Silver Spire - Robert Goldsborough 608

Hawk
Double Deuce - Robert B. Parker 1269

SINGER

Adler, Irene
Good Morning, Irene - Carole Nelson Douglas 440
Good Night, Mr. Holmes - Carole Nelson Douglas 441
Irene at Large - Carole Nelson Douglas 442

Da Silva, Jane
Amateur Night - K.K. Beck 114
Electric City - K.K. Beck 115
A Hopeless Case - K.K. Beck 116

Hilton, Jenni
Murder in Waiting - Robert Richardson 1367

Lindsey, Sass
Final Tour - Jonellen Heckler 770

Muryan, Peggy
If Ever I Return, Pretty Peggy-O - Sharyn McCrumb 1116

Willis, Dee
Steel Guitar - Linda Barnes 94

SINGLE MOTHER

McDuffy, Gwen
Family Album - Susan Oleksiw 1230

SINGLE PARENT

Birdsong, Charlotte
Grandmother's House - Janet LaPierre 983

Buckland, Casey
Blood Marks - Bill Crider 349

SOCIAL WORKER

Caliban, Catherine "Cat"
Two Points for Murder - D.B. Borton 157

Chenier, Lucille
Voodoo River - Robert Crais 344

Cochrane, Helen
Every Breath You Take - Michelle Spring 1541

Corder, Wilson
The Deep End - Chris Crutcher 364

Dancer, Karen
The Dying Room - E.X. Giroux 599

Eton, Vic
Dark of Night - Richard Nehrbass 1200

Gallagher, Jan
Recycled - Jo Bailey 80

Greene, Charlie
Death of the Office Witch - Marlys Millhiser 1155

Halperin, Elizabeth
Mommy and the Murder - Nancy Gladstone 600

Hayle, Tamara
Devil's Gonna Get Him - Valerie Wilson Wesley 1691
When Death Comes Stealing - Valerie Wilson Wesley 1692

James, Gemma
A Share in Death - Deborah Crombie 358

Jeffry, Jane
From Here to Paternity - Jill Churchill 246

Lacey, Meg
No Forwarding Address - Elisabeth Bowers 161

Lord, Emma
The Alpine Advocate - Mary Daheim 370

MacGowen, Maggie
Telling Lies - Wendy Hornsby 809

Michaels, Laura
A Permanent Retirement - John Miles 1153

Mitchell, Michelle "Mitch"
Icewater Mansions - Douglas Allyn 48

Ness, Lydia
Undue Influence - Miriam Borgenicht 153

Page, Gideon
Probable Cause - Griff Stockley 1577

Rosen, Lucy
Turtle Moon - Alice Hoffman 795

Rowe, Valerie
The Suitor - Michael Allegretto 43

Terranova, Marie
Room 9 - Soledad Santiago 1435

Travis, Melanie
A Pedigree to Die For - Laurien Berenson 121

Walsh, Jackie
A Tail of Two Murders - Melissa Cleary 259

SMUGGLER

Lopez, Rebecca
The Quality of Mercy - Faye Kellerman 883

SOCIAL WORKER

Bradley, Barbara "Bo"
Child of Silence - Abigail Padgett 1251
Strawgirl - Abigail Padgett 1252

Davison, Molly
The Harbinger Effect - S.K. Wolf 1746

Eltern, Anna
Nightside - Soledad Santiago 1434

Magill, Margo
Wild Again - Kathrin King Segal 1471

Socialite

Newman, Victor
Dead Men Don't Marry - Dorothy Sucher 1588
Stewart, Ada Chan
The Heaven Stone - David Daniel 386
Swift, Sabrina
Dead Men Don't Marry - Dorothy Sucher 1588

SOCIALITE

Bennett, Mildred
The Pumpkin-Shell Wife - Susanna Hofmann McShea 1138

SPINSTER

Borden, Lizzie
Miss Lizzie - Walter Satterthwait 1441
Clively, Miranda
Clively Close: Dead as Dead Can Be - Ann Crowleigh 361
Fry, Esmerelda
Murder, Mystery and Mayhem - Jennifer Carnell 220

SPORTS FIGURE

Arkwright, Santa
First and Ten - Douglas Anderson 50
Arnold, Jessie
Murder on the Iditarod Trail - Sue Henry 775
Bannion, Rick
The Man Offside - A.W. Gray 652
Barzeny, Jakob
Furnished for Murder - Richard Barth 101
Baskin, David
Play Dead - Harlan Coben 266
Brogan, Jerry
Hot Air - Jon L. Breen 170
Loose Lips - Jon L. Breen 171
Carpenter, Scott
The Only Good Priest - Mark Richard Zubro 1795
Cochran, William "Bull"
Strikezone - David F. Nighbert 1206
Eagle, Ken
Dead Fix - Michael Geller 573
Farrell, Jack
The Fall Line - Mark T. Sullivan 1589
Franklin, Derek
Straight - Dick Francis 541
Martin, Tricia
Dead Fix - Michael Geller 573
Myles, Jordan
The Total Zone - Martina Navratilova 1195
Ofsted, Lee
Rotten Lies - Charlotte Elkins 481
A Wicked Slice - Aaron Elkins 480
Pedersen, Gun
Strike - L.L. Enger 492
Swing - L.L. Enger 493
Rawlings, Mickey
Murder at Fenway Park - Troy Soos 1536
Reeves, Townsend
Final Dictation - L.M. Vincent 1655
Pas De Death - L.M. Vincent 1656
Smith, Brad
Dropshot: A Brad Smith Novel - Jack Bickham 129
Straun, Angus
Unnatural Hazard - Barry Cork 317
Winter Rules - Barry Cork 318

Wylie, Eva
Bucket Nut - Liza Cody 270
Monkey Wrench - Liza Cody 271

SPOUSE

Bartholomew, Connie
Rough Water - Sally Gunning 687
Bowman, Lee
Killer in Paradise - John Leslie 1011
Cadette, Sandy
Act of Faith - Michael Bowen 158
Fielder's Choice - Michael Bowen 160
Decker, Rina
Grievous Sin - Faye Kellerman 880
Fairchild, Tom
The Body in the Belfry - Katherine Hall Page 1255
The Body in the Bouillon - Katherine Hall Page 1256
The Body in the Vestibule - Katherine Hall Page 1258
Forbes, Molly
Treasure by Post - David Williams 1730
Fredrick, Kay
In Blacker Moments - S.E. Schenkel 1451
Hickey, Wendy
The Angel Gang - Ken Kuhlken 956
Lazarus, Rina
False Prophet - Faye Kellerman 879
Justice - Faye Kellerman 881
Sanctuary - Faye Kellerman 884
Miyomoto, Hatsue
Snow Falling on Cedars - David Guterson 692
Pitt, Charlotte
Farrier's Lane - Anne Perry 1294
Rhys, Jenny
The Wrong Rite - Alisa Craig 334
St. James, Deborah
Missing Joseph - Elizabeth George 575
Slater, Faith
Bad Desire - Gary Devon 417
Stock, Joan
Frobisher's Savage - Leonard Tourney 1624
Tibbet, Emmy
Black Girl, White Girl - Patricia Moyes 1179
Tracer, Chris
Tracer, Inc. - Jeff Andrus 58
Van Der Valk, Arlette
Sand Castles - Nicholas Freeling 549
Vernet, Victoire
Napoleon Must Die - Quinn Fawcett 519

SPY

Alexeyev, Gennadi
A Black Legend - John Horton 810
Archer, Owen
The Apothecary Rose - Candace M. Robb 1375
The Nun's Tale - Candace M. Robb 1377
Bailey, Nick
The Lantern Network - Ted Allbeury 37
Bond, James
Win, Lose or Die - John Gardner 567
Chapman, Harry
A Time Without Shadows - Ted Allbeury 38
Chernov, Yuri
Crossed Swords - Sean Flannery 528
Connor, Ned
The Hawthorne Group - Thomas Hauser 756

What Mystery Do I Read Next?

Croft, Tom
Winter of the Wolves - James N. Frey 552
Defoe, Chase
August Ice - Deforest Day 399
DePalrey, Horatio
The Russia House - John Le Carre 995
Devereaux
The Last Good German - Bill Granger 647
Dillon, Sean
Angel of Death - Jack Higgins 786
Fairweather, Theodore
Winter of the Wolves - James N. Frey 552
Frost, Leslie
Frost the Fiddler - Janice Weber 1681
Gillard, Patrick
Rook-Shoot - Margaret Duffy 452
Who Killed Cock Robin? - Margaret Duffy 453
Hamilton, Carl
Enemy's Enemy - Jan Guillou 685
Heinemann, Kurt
The Last Good German - Bill Granger 647
Hildreth, Jane
Cotswold Moles - Michael Spicer 1539
Holland, Mark
Deadly Sonata - Paul Myers 1192
Huntington, Patricia
Cotswold Moles - Michael Spicer 1539
James, Ken
Day of the Cheetah - Dale Brown 179
Kaplin, Anatoli
Moving Targets - Sean Flannery 529
Koenig, Paul
The Faust Conspiracy - James Baddock 78
Lang, John
Thunder - James Grady 633
Langley, Ingrid
Rook-Shoot - Margaret Duffy 452
Who Killed Cock Robin? - Margaret Duffy 453
Lawford, Tom
Pillars of Fire - Steve Shagan 1473
Mahoney, Wallace
Crossed Swords - Sean Flannery 528
McGuire, Madison
A Singular Spy - Amanda Kyle Williams 1727
Montana, Tucker
Tucker's Last Stand - William F. Buckley Jr. 188
Muffin, Charlie
The Run Around - Brian Freemantle 550
Oakes, Blackford
Tucker's Last Stand - William F. Buckley Jr. 188
Oliver, Ted
A Black Legend - John Horton 810
Parker, Charles
The Lantern Network - Ted Allbeury 37
Pollifax, Emily
Mrs. Pollifax and the Whirling Dervish - Dorothy Gilman 588
Quiller
Quiller KGB - Adam Hall 706
Ryan, Jack
The Sum of All Fears - Tom Clancy 248
Sparks, Jack
The 6 Messiahs - Mark Frost 560
Stark, Robert
Gunpower - Mark Schorr 1456
Stern, Jonas
Spandau Phoenix - Greg Iles 824

Character Description Index

Stuart, Jud
River of Darkness - James Grady 632

Tristram, James
Spy Shadow - Tim Sebastian 1466

Turner, Derek
A Clinic for Murder - Marsha Landreth 974
Vial Murders - Marsha Landreth 976

STOCK BROKER

Kelly, Virginia
In the Game - Nikki Baker 82
The Lavender House Murder - Nikki Baker 83

Kiehl, Felix
Disassociated States - Leonard Simon 1499

Spencer, Warren
The Garden Club - Muriel Resnick Jackson 836

STORE OWNER

Darling, Annie Laurance
The Christie Caper - Carolyn G. Hart 741
Mint Julep Murder - Carolyn G. Hart 744

Flagg, Conan
Dead Matter - M.K. Wren 1764
King of the Mountain - M.K. Wren 1765

Janeway, Cliff
Booked to Die - John Dunning 466

Jasper, Kate
Adjusted to Death - Jaqueline Girdner 593
The Last Resort - Jaqueline Girdner 594
A Stiff Critique - Jaqueline Girdner 595
Tea-Totally Dead - Jaqueline Girdner 596

Rhodenbarr, Bernie
The Burglar Who Traded Ted Williams - Lawrence Block 145

STREETPERSON

Freeman, Jefferson "Free"
Free - Todd Komarnicki 952

Ledbetter, Romulus
The Caveman's Valentine - George Dawes Green 662

Skink
Stormy Weather - Carl Hiaasen 784

Spadafino, Joey
Felony Murder - Joseph T. Klempner 940

Sullivan, Liz
Murder in a Nice Neighborhood - Lora Roberts 1388

STRIPPER

Grant, Erin
Strip Tease - Carl Hiaasen 785

Mothersill, Sylvia
Death of a Fantasy Life - T.G. Gilpin 590

STUDENT

Barlow, Hannah
Murder in Brief - Carrol Lachint 963

Biggers, Petrinella
Murder in Wrigley Field - Crabbe Evers 507

Blake, Meredith
Crossover - Judith Eubank 502

Boatwright, Thomas
Passion Play - W. Edward Blain 140

Bone, Charlotte
A Knife at the Opera - Susannah Stacey 1555

Bow, April
Monkey on a Chain - Harlen Campbell 211

Brocato, Melody
Jazz Funeral - Julie Smith 1526

Bush, Beth
Sweet Death - Bill Waggoner 1657

Carey, Neal
A Cool Breeze on the Underground - Don Winslow 1743
The Trail to Buddha's Mirror - Don Winslow 1744

Carmody, Lorelei
Fatal Obsession - D.B. Taylor 1606

Cooper, Iris
Peril under the Palms - K.K. Beck 117

Ellis, Sairey
Dream of Darkness - Patrick Ruell 1412

Fran
Killing Time in Buffalo - Deidre S. Laiken 964

James, Nora
Night Butterfly - Patricia McFall 1127

Karr, Ginny
Monday's Child Is Dead - James Elward 484

Keane, Owen
Die Dreaming - Terence Faherty 514
The Lost Keats - Terence Faherty 515

Kendricks, Lucas
Death Qualified: A Mystery of Chaos - Kate Wilhelm 1723

Kenyon, Laurie
All Around the Town - Mary Higgins Clark 252

Kimura, Patti
Kimura - Robert Davis 395

Knowles, Richard
Hide and Seek - Barry Berg 122

Leigh, Petra
The Ransom of Black Stealth One - Dean Ing 825

LeVender, Catherine
Death Comes as Epiphany - Sharan Newman 1203

MacKenzie, Christabel
Death Wore a Diadem - Iona McGregor 1133

McGill, Susannah
The Scarred Man - Keith Peterson 1310

McGrail, Nuala
Irish Gold - Andrew M. Greeley 657

Newman, Cassie
A Brush with Death - Joan Smith 1519

Prescott, Brie
Berlin Covenant - Celeste Paul 1278

Renee
Killing Time in Buffalo - Deidre S. Laiken 964

Russell, Mary
The Beekeeper's Apprentice - Laurie R. King 924
A Monstrous Regiment of Women - Laurie R. King 926

Shaw, Darby
The Pelican Brief - John Grisham 681

Shea, Kevin
A Certain Justice - John T. Lescroart 1008

Stevens, Janet
Quaker Witness - Irene Allen 46

Tallis, John
Rat's Nest - Charles West 1694

Tracer, Shorty
Tracer, Inc. - Jeff Andrus 58

Tullis, Faye
In the Dead of Winter - Abbey Penn Baker 81

Vogler, Deena
Till Death Do Us Part - Rochelle Majer Krich 955

Whitcomb, Leah
Paws Before Dying - Susan Conant 290

Winfield, Jane
Murder in Burgundy - Audrey Peterson 1305

STUDENT—HIGH SCHOOL

McLaughlin, Teresa
Justice - Faye Kellerman 881

STUNTMAN

Hallam, Lucas
Dead-Stick - L.J. Washburn 1674
Dog Heavies - L.J. Washburn 1675

TAXI DRIVER

Carlyle, Carlotta
Coyote - Linda Barnes 92
Steel Guitar - Linda Barnes 94

MacLeish, Cooper
Get What's Coming - Sam Reaves 1354
A Long Cold Fall - Sam Reaves 1355

TEACHER

Black, Steven
The Judas Pool - George Owens 1250

Bone, Grizel
Bone Idle - Susannah Stacey 1553

Brett, David
Long Chain of Death - S.K. Wolf 1747

Buckland, Casey
Blood Marks - Bill Crider 349

Counsel, Colin
Unknown Hand - Gillian Linscott 1031

Deane, Sarah
The Bridled Groom - J.S. Borthwick 154

Evron, Ronit
Cover Story - Robert Cullen 365

Falconer, William
Falconer's Crusade - Ian Morson 1175

Halloran, Meg
Children's Games - Janet LaPierre 982

Joan
A Vow of Chastity - Veronica Black 136

Lake, Barrett
Interview with Mattie - Shelley Singer 1504
Picture of David - Shelley Singer 1505
Searching for Sara - Shelley Singer 1506

Levity, Thomas More
The Lynching - Bennie Lee Sinclair 1503

Markem, Julia
Love Lies - Fern Kupfer 960

Mason, Tom
The Only Good Priest - Mark Richard Zubro 1795
Why Isn't Becky Twitchell Dead? - Mark Richard Zubro 1797

McQuaid, Mike
Hangman's Root - Susan Wittig Albert 32

Meltzer, Fran
Love Lies - Fern Kupfer 960

Mitchell, Cassandra
Mother Love - L.R. Wright 1774

Morton, Lana
Follow That Blonde - Joan Smith   1521

Murphy, Gordon
A Touch of Panic - L.R. Wright   1776

Pepper, Amanda
I'd Rather Be in Philadelphia - Gillian Roberts   1378
Philly Stakes - Gillian Roberts   1379
With Friends Like These - Gillian Roberts   1380

Southgate, Carol
A City of Strangers - Robert Barnard   88

Stewart, Eleanor
Death Wore a Diadem - Iona McGregor   1133

Travis, Melanie
A Pedigree to Die For - Laurien Berenson   121

Veryan, Ann
Skylark - Sheila Simonson   1501

Walsh, Jackie
First Pedigree Murder - Melissa Cleary   257
The Maltese Puppy - Melissa Cleary   258

Welles, Sarah
Criminal Conversation - Evan Hunter   820

Winston, Stoney
Truck Shot - Jim Stinson   1574

TEENAGER

Anders, Sally
A Death in a Town - Hillary Waugh   1678

Baker, Wellesley
Clearwater Summer - John E. Keegan   876

Bradford, Will
Clearwater Summer - John E. Keegan   876

Burton, Amanda
Miss Lizzie - Walter Satterthwait   1441

Clark, Taylor
Clearwater Summer - John E. Keegan   876

Ebinger, Mariah
Blood Relative - Carolyn Hougan   811

Farrady, Rowena
Never Walk Behind Me - Lin Summerfield   1593

Frank, Lisa
Hide and Seek - Barry Berg   122

Heenan, Annie
The Masters of the House - Robert Barnard   90

Heenan, Matthew
The Masters of the House - Robert Barnard   90

Hudson, Jane
To Die Like a Gentleman - Bernard Bastable   103

Knowles, Richard
Hide and Seek - Barry Berg   122

Mendoza, Mariana
The Kingsbridge Plot - Maan Meyers   1148

TELEVISION

Abagnard, Abby
Until Death - Polly Whitney   1709

Abagnaro, Abby
Until the End of Time - Polly Whitney   1710

Manwaring, Kevin
Barking Dogs - R.R. Irvine   827

Rune
Hard News - Jeffrey Wilds Deaver   403

Tygart, Mary "Ike"
Until Death - Polly Whitney   1709
Until the End of Time - Polly Whitney   1710

TELEVISION PERSONALITY

Collier, Alex
Savage Justice - Ron Handberg   721

TERRORIST

Kort, Anthony
Hard Fall - Ridley Pearson   1284

Mannion, Billy
19th Precinct - Christopher Newman   1202

THIEF

Dortmunder, John
Don't Ask - Donald E. Westlake   1697
Drowned Hopes - Donald E. Westlake   1698

Reno
Edge City - Sin Soracco   1537

TOUR GUIDE

Rover, Rowan
Missing Susan - Sharyn McCrumb   1118

TROUBLESHOOTER

Carey, Neal
A Cool Breeze on the Underground - Don Winslow   1743
The Trail to Buddha's Mirror - Don Winslow   1744

Demarkian, Gregor
Not a Creature Was Stirring - Jane Haddam   695
Quoth the Raven - Jane Haddam   696

Doll
A Small and Incidental Murder - John Walter Putre   1337

Trent, Wendell
Bright Shark - Robert Ballard   85

TWIN

Thomas, Ike
Box Nine - Jack O'Connell   1223

Thomas, Lenore
Box Nine - Jack O'Connell   1223

UNDERTAKER

Hawley, Bill
Double Plot - Leo Axler   70
Grave Matters - Leo Axler   71

Humberstone, Hubert
Deadly Errand - Christine Green   659

UNEMPLOYED

Amiss, Robert
Clubbed to Death - Ruth Dudley Edwards   472

Phelan, Jack
A City of Strangers - Robert Barnard   88

Radkin, Joseph
The Genesis Files - Bob Biderman   130

VETERAN

Bosch, Harry
The Black Echo - Michael Connelly   292
The Black Ice - Michael Connelly   293
The Concrete Blonde - Michael Connelly   294

Boyd, Orin
Exit Wounds - John Westermann   1696

Chambers, Ishmael
Snow Falling on Cedars - David Guterson   692

Demming, Walter
Under the Beetle's Cellar - Mary Willis Walker   1660

Devlin, Mac
Eagles Die Too - Meg O'Brien   1215

Doll
Death Among the Angels - John Walter Putre   1336
A Small and Incidental Murder - John Walter Putre   1337

Dunn, Micah
The Caesar Clue - M.K. Shuman   1491
Deep Kill - M.K. Shuman   1492
The Last Man to Die - M.K. Shuman   1493
The Maya Stone Murders - M.K. Shuman   1494

Elliot, David
Vertical Run - Joseph R. Garber   566

Hooper, B.F.
Saint Louie Blues - Jake Tanner   1601

Lewis, Dowdy Jr.
A Gypsy Good Time - Gustav Hasford   755

MacLeish, Cooper
A Long Cold Fall - Sam Reaves   1355

McCleet, Adam
Mortal Remains - Rick Hanson   728

Murdock, Matt
Merry Christmas, Murdock - Robert J. Ray   1352
Murdock Cracks Ice - Robert J. Ray   1353

Odum, Glenn
Hard Guy - Thorton Elliott   482

Porter, Rainbow
Monkey on a Chain - Harlen Campbell   211

Rawlins, Easy
Devil in a Blue Dress - Walter Mosley   1176

Robicheaux, Dave
Black Cherry Blues - James Lee Burke   193

Rodrigue, John
Big Fish - Ken Grissom   682
Drowned Man's Key - Ken Grissom   683

Storme, Wyatt
Dreamsicle - W.L. Ripley   1370

Sughrue, C.W.
The Mexican Tree Duck - James Crumley   363

Swagger, Bob Lee
Point of Impact - Stephen Hunter   822

Tyler, Hap
Hard Aground - James W. Hall   709

VETERINARIAN

Alexeyev, Nina
Murder Most Grizzly - Elizabeth Quinn   1340

Augustin, Louis
Copy Cat Crimes - Karen Ann Wilson   1733
Eight Dogs Flying - Karen Ann Wilson   1734

Borden, Liza
Forty Whacks - Sheila MacGill Callahan   207

Holt, Samantha
Copy Cat Crimes - Karen Ann Wilson   1733
Eight Dogs Flying - Karen Ann Wilson   1734

MacIntire, Carlson "Mac"
The Lion's Share - Kelly A. Tate   1605

McCarthy, Gail
Cutter - Laura Crum   362

Character Description Index

Nightingale, Deirdre "Didi" Quinn
Dr. Nightingale Goes the Distance - Lydia Adamson 21
Dr. Nightingale Rides the Elephant - Lydia Adamson 22

WAITER/WAITRESS

Chadwick, Maud
The End of the Pier - Martha Grimes 674

WEALTHY

Conrad, Claire
Beauty Dies - Melodie Johnson Howe 813

Phipps, Howard
Elsinore - Jerome Charyn 238

WIDOW(ER)

Bone, Robert
Grave Responsibility - Susannah Stacey 1554

Caliban, Catherine "Cat"
Four Elements of Murder - D.B. Borton 155
Three Is a Crowd - D.B. Borton 156

Cardenas, Vic
Death of a DJ - Jane Rubino 1411

Clively-Murdoch, Clare
Clively Close: Dead as Dead Can Be - Ann Crowleigh 361

Collins, Henrietta O'Dwyer
Dead Man's Island - Carolyn G. Hart 742

Daniels, Charmian
Dead Set - Jennie Melville 1141

Dann, Peaches
Who Killed What's-Her-Name? - Elizabeth Daniels Squire 1548

Drexler, Sarah
Justice for Some - Kate Wilhelm 1724

Elliot, Elizabeth
Quaker Silence - Irene Allen 45
Quaker Witness - Irene Allen 46

Gastner, Bill
Heartshot - Steven F. Havill 758

Harper, Benni
Fool's Puzzle - Earlene Fowler 536
Irish Chain - Earlene Fowler 537

Harris, Liana
Kingdom Road - K. Patrick Conner 295

Howard, Vivien
A Temporary Ghost - Mickey Friedman 556

Jacobs, Calista
Mortal Words - Kathryn Lasky Knight 945

Jeffry, Jane
The Class Menagerie - Jill Churchill 244
A Farewell to Yarns - Jill Churchill 245
From Here to Paternity - Jill Churchill 246
A Quiche Before Dying - Jill Churchill 247

Kettler, Jane
The Texas Capitol Murders - Bill Crider 353

Ladd, Diana
Hour of the Hunter - J.A. Jance 843

Lashley, Mavis
Death Beneath the Christmas Tree - Robert Nordan 1208
Death on Wheels - Robert Nordan 1209

Lazarus, Rina
Day of Atonement - Faye Kellerman 878
Milk and Honey - Faye Kellerman 882

MacAlister, Marti
Dead Time - Eleanor Taylor Bland 141

MacIntire, Carlson "Mac"
The Lion's Share - Kelly A. Tate 1605

Malory, Sheila
The Cruellest Month - Hazel Holt 800
Mrs. Malory Investigates - Hazel Holt 802

Martin, Dorothy
The Body in the Transept - Jeanne M. Dams 385

Mulcay, Kate
Ah, Sweet Mystery - Celestine Sibley 1495
Dire Happenings at Scratch Ankle - Celestine Sibley 1496
Straight as an Arrow - Celestine Sibley 1498

Nesbitt, Alan
The Body in the Transept - Jeanne M. Dams 385

Nolan, Maeve
The Gombeen Man - Randy Lee Eickoff 474

Pargeter, Melita
Mrs. Pargeter's Package - Simon Brett 175

Pickett, Mel
Buried in Stone - Eric Wright 1766

Potter, Eugenia
The 27 Ingredient Chili Con Carne Murders - Nancy Pickard 1315

Rhodes, Frank
Love Lies - Fern Kupfer 960

Ross, Hubert
The Killing of Ellis Martin - Lucretia Grindle 677
So Little to Die For - Lucretia Grindle 678

Serian, Lenore
Criminal Seduction - Darian North 1211

Shapiro, Desiree
Murder Can Kill Your Social Life - Selma Eichler 473

Steele, Jack
When Reason Sleeps - Tom Sehler 1472

Stewart, Blaine
Dancing in the Dark - Sharon Zukowski 1798
Leap of Faith - Sharon Zukowski 1799

Trask, Ginny
Cold Tracks - Lee Wallingford 1668

Travis, Sheila
Deadly Secrets on the St. Johns - Patricia Houck Sprinkle 1542

Turner, Samantha
A Clinic for Murder - Marsha Landreth 974
The Holiday Murders - Marsha Landreth 975

West, Delilah
Set-Up - Maxine O'Callaghan 1220

Wren, Susan
Consider the Crows - Charlene Weir 1685

WORKER

Andrews, Jessie
The Chesapeake Project - Phyllis Horn 806

Flannery, Jimmy
The Gift Horse's Mouth - Robert Campbell 212

Indermill, Bonnie
Island Girl - Carole Berry 127

Mitchell, Michelle "Mitch"
Icewater Mansions - Douglas Allyn 48

Rawlins, Easy
Devil in a Blue Dress - Walter Mosley 1176

Stone, Lucy
Mail-Order Murder - Leslie Meier 1140

WRITER

Alexander, Tess
Deadline - D.F. Mills 1157

Ardleigh, Kathryn "Kate"
Death at Bishop's Keep - Robin Paige 1259
Death at Gallows Green - Robin Paige 1260

Atwood, Diane
Writers of the Purple Sage - Barbara Burnett Smith 1517

Austen, Cat
Death of a DJ - Jane Rubino 1411

Baker, Anne
The Last Page - Bob Fenster 524

Blue, Royal
Blood of Poets - Kenn Davis 393

Bradley, Mark
Shot on Location - Stan Cutler 369

Brown, Cordelia
Report for Murder - Val McDermid 1126

Bryce, Kevin
A Collector of Photographs - Deborah Valentine 1645

Byman, Luke
The Forever Beat - John Cline 262

Byrne, Owen
Criminal Seduction - Darian North 1211

Camden, Claire
Shroud for a Scholar - Audrey Peterson 1306

Carter, Jack "the Poacher"
Screaming Bones - Pat Burden 191

Christie, Agatha
Dorothy and Agatha - Gaylord Larsen 984

Cochran, William "Bull"
Shutout - David F. Nighbert 1204
Squeezeplay - David F. Nighbert 1205

Cohen, Magaret Midge
Date with a Dead Doctor - Toni Brill 177

Craig, Melissa
Exhaustive Enquiries - Betty Rowlands 1408
Over the Edge - Betty Rowlands 1409

Dalrymple, Daisy
The Winter Garden Mystery - Carola Dunn 465

Dann, Peaches
Memory Can Be Murder - Elizabeth Daniels Squire 1547
Who Killed What's-Her-Name? - Elizabeth Daniels Squire 1548

Davilov, Queenie
Cut To—Murder - Denise Osborne 1247
Murder Offscreen - Denise Osborne 1248

Dean, Sam
Blood Rights - Mike Phillips 1314

Doyle, Arthur Conan
Escapade - Walter Satterthwait 1438

Fixx, Raleigh
Flamingo - Bob Reiss 1359

Griffin, Lew
Moth - James Sallis 1422

Hammett, Dashiell
The Black Mask Murders - William F. Nolan 1207

Hannaford, Bennis
Not a Creature Was Stirring - Jane Haddam 695

Hannigan, Dev
In the Dark - Carol Brennan 173

Hastings, Stanley
Strangler - Parnell Hall 715

Hawkins, Jack
Paint It Black - W.R. Philbrick 1313

Young Woman

Heller, Tom
True Crime - Michael Mewshaw 1145

Helmers, Jack
A Country of Old Men - Joseph Hansen 727

Hill, Maggie
The Mother Shadow - Melodie Johnson Howe 814

Hoag, Stewart
The Man Who Cancelled Himself - David Handler 722
The Man Who Would Be F. Scott Fitzgerald - David Handler 723
The Woman Who Fell From Grace - David Handler 724

Ivory, Kate
Death and the Oxford Box - Veronica Stallwood 1557
Oxford Exit - Veronica Stallwood 1559

Kelly, Nick
River of Darkness - James Grady 632

Kendall, John
Longshot - Dick Francis 540

King, Willow
Bitter Herbs - Natasha Cooper 307
Bloody Roses - Natasha Cooper 308
Rotten Apples - Natasha Cooper 309

Kirby, Jacqueline
Naked Once More - Elizabeth Peters 1300

Lacey, James
Agatha Raisin and the Vicious Vet - M.C. Beaton 108

Langley, Ingrid
Rook-Shoot - Margaret Duffy 452
Who Killed Cock Robin? - Margaret Duffy 453

Lisle, Darina
Recipe for Death - Janet Laurence 990

Malory, Sheila
The Cruellest Month - Hazel Holt 800
Mrs. Malory and the Festival Murders - Hazel Holt 801

Maltravers, Augustus
The Book of the Dead - Robert Richardson 1365
The Dying of the Light - Robert Richardson 1366
Murder in Waiting - Robert Richardson 1367

Maxwell, Georgia Lee
A Temporary Ghost - Mickey Friedman 556

McFarland, Fowler
Sweet Death - Bill Waggoner 1657

McIntyre, Urbino
Death in a Serene City - Edward Sklepowich 1510

McKenna, Patience
Once and Always Murder - Orania Papazoglou 1263

Metcalf, Pamela
Night Vision - Paul Levine 1015

Omega, Jay
Zombies of the Gene Pool - Sharyn McCrumb 1121

Pamplemousse
Monsieur Pamplemousse Investigates - Michael Bond 151
Pamplemousse Rests His Case - Michael Bond 152

Perkins, Oliver
The Animal Hour - Andrew Klavan 935

Pink, Melinda
Rage - Gwen Moffat 1162
The Stone Hawk - Gwen Moffat 1163

Pratt, Tony
Murder at Musket Beach - Bernie Lee 998
Murder Without Reservation - Bernie Lee 999

Rafferty, Madeline
A Deep Disturbance - Constance Rauch 1351

Reilly, Cassandra
Gaudi Afternoon - Barbara Wilson 1731

Roper, Taggert
The Next Victim - William Sanders 1423

Saldinger, Byron
Shooting Script - Gordon Cotler 332

Sasser, Jim
He's Dead-She's Dead: Details at Eleven - John Bartholomew Tucker 1635

Sayers, Dorothy L.
Dorothy and Agatha - Gaylord Larsen 984

Shakespeare, William
The Quality of Mercy - Faye Kellerman 883

Shaw, Emma
Death and the Trumpets of Tuscany - Hazel Wynn Jones 847

Shaw, Galen
Love Lies Slain - L.L. Blackmur 139

Shaw, George Bernard
Stage Fright - Gillian Linscott 1030

Sherman, Winston
Deception Island - M.K. Lorens 1043
Dreamland - M.K. Lorens 1044
Sweet Narcissus - M.K. Lorens 1045

Spencer, Warren
The Garden Club - Muriel Resnick Jackson 836

Springer, Dan
Hollywood Requiem - Peter Freeborn 546

Starkey, Dan
Divorcing Jack - Colin Bateman 104

Stein, Gertrude
The Caravaggio Shawl - Samuel M. Steward 1573

Stone, Belinda
Coronation - W.J. Weatherby 1679

Tallis, John
Rat's Nest - Charles West 1694

Toklas, Alice B.
The Caravaggio Shawl - Samuel M. Steward 1573

Valencia, Fermin
The Shadow of the Shadow - Paco Ignacio Taibo II 1598

Ward, Emerson
Death Came Dressed in White - Michael W. Sherer 1481
Little Use for Death - Michael W. Sherer 1482

Wentworth, Lyon
Death on the Mississippi - Richard Forrest 535

Woodruff, Bernard
Friends till the End - Gloria Dank 387

Wyatt, Jolie
Dust Devils of the Purple Sage - Barbara Burnett Smith 1516
Writers of the Purple Sage - Barbara Burnett Smith 1517

YOUNG WOMAN

Hitchcock, Martha
Hot Water - Sally Gunning 686

McIntyre, Marie
Shadow Queen - Tony Gibbs 583

Vereker, Lucy
The Yellow Room Conspiracy - Peter Dickinson 420

Westerland, Sally
The Tijuana Bible - Ron Goulart 630

Author Index

This index is an alphabetical listing of the authors of books featured in entries and those listed under "Other books you might like." For each author, the titles of books written and entry numbers are also provided. Bold numbers indicate a featured main entry; other numbers refer to books recommended for further reading.

A

Aaron, David
State Scarlet 1473

Abbott, Jeff
Do Unto Others **1**, 70, 415, 744, 1319
The Jordan Poteet Series 71, 688, 1242, 1464
The Only Good Yankee **2**

Abel, Kenneth
Bait **3**, 294, 1210, 1514, 1672

Abrahams, Peter
Hard Rain 823
Lights Out **4**
Pressure Drop **5**, 602, 848, 1174
Revolution #9 **6**, 406, 809

Abshire, Richard
The Dallas Deception **7**, 1753
Dallas Drop 352, 458
Turnaround Jack **8**, 354

Adams, Bronte
Margin for Murder **9**

Adams, Cleve F.
Shady Lady 1307

Adams, Deborah
All the Great Pretenders **10**, 374, 457, 989, 1115, 1119
The Jesus Creek Series 2, 1464, 1516, 1517

Adams, George
Swindle **11**

Adams, Harold
The Carl Wilcox Series 212, 213, 956, 958, 1583, 1584, 1625, 1674
The Ditched Blonde **12**
The Man Who Missed the Party **13**
The Man Who Was Taller than God 742
Paint the Town Red 501
A Perfectly Proper Murder **14**

Adamson, Lydia
The Alice Nestleton Series 180, 251, 414, 438, 1391, 1783
A Cat in a Glass House **15**
A Cat in Fine Style **16**
A Cat in the Manger **17**, 167, 169, 181, 182, 443, 516
A Cat in the Wings **18**
A Cat in Wolf's Clothing **19**
A Cat of a Different Color 1782
A Cat on a Winning Streak 1065
A Cat on the Cutting Edge **20**
Dr. Nightingale Comes Home 362, 372
Dr. Nightingale Goes the Distance **21**

Dr. Nightingale Goes to the Dogs 121
Dr. Nightingale Rides the Elephant **22**
The Dr. Nightingale Series 1733, 1734

Adamson, M.J.
Not Till a Hot January 845

Adcock, Thomas
Dark Maze 1623
Drown All the Dogs **23**, 104, 657, 786
Thrown Away Child 881

Adey, R.C.S.
Death Locked In 221
Murder Impossible 221

Adkins, Jan
Cookie 1232

Adrian, Jack
Detective Stories from the Strand **24**

Aird, Catherine
The Body Politic **25**, 203, 911
Harm's Way 1253
Henrietta Who? 260, 1168
The Inspector Sloane Series 366, 469, 472, 790, 912, 1159
Passing Strange 753, 789
Some Die Eloquent 470

Albert, Marvin
The Riviera Contract **26**
The Stone Angel Series 327, 329, 1488
The Zig-Zag Man **27**, 328

Albert, Neil
Burning March **28**
Cruel April **29**
The Dave Garrett Series 669, 818
The February Trouble **30**, 1110
The January Corpse **31**, 164

Albert, Susan Wittig
The China Bayles Series 115, 377, 422, 596, 944, 1516
Death at Bishop's Keep **1259**
Death at Gallows Green **1260**
Hangman's Root **32**
Thyme of Death **33**, 172, 198, 375, 389, 390, 959, 1155, 1156, 1333, 1401, 1567

Albert, William J.
Death at Bishop's Keep **1259**
Death at Gallows Green **1260**

Aldyne, Nathan
Cobalt 1588
The Daniel Valentine Series 1150, 1151, 1572, 1795, 1796
Vermillion 726, 727

Alexander, Gary
Kiet Goes West **34**, 297, 616
Pigeon Blood 874

Unfunny Money **35**

Alexander, Lawrence
The Big Stick 1079
The Strenuous Life **36**

Allbeury, Ted
The Lantern Network **37**, 420, 584, 787, 1278
The Other Side of Silence 1466
Shadow of Shadows 995
A Time Without Shadows **38**, 824

Allegretto, Michael
Blood Relative **39**, 1110, 1688
The Dead of Winter **40**
Dead of Winter 1364
Death on the Rocks 200
Grave Doubt **41**, 830
Night of Reunion **42**, 899, 937, 1310, 1762
The Suitor **43**, 673
The Watchers 843
The Watchman **44**, 252

Allen, Irene
Quaker Silence **45**
Quaker Witness **46**

Allen, Karen
Give My Secrets Back 1356

Allen, Steve
The Talk Show Murders 75, 1635

Allyn, Douglas
The Cheerio Killings **47**, 447, 555, 833
Icewater Mansions **48**

Ambler, Eric
Epitaph for a Spy 37

Amis, Kingsley
The Alteration 419

Amo, Gary
Silent Night 43, **49**, 149, 253, 893, 899, 937

Anderson, Douglas
First and Ten **50**

Anderson, J.R.L.
A Sprig of Sea Lavender 1168

Anderson, Jack Albin
The Society Ball Murders **51**, 603

Anderson, James
The Affair of the Blood-Stained Egg Cosy 103, 220, 401, 695

Anderson, Virginia
Blood Lies 21, **52**, 538, 540, 541, 839
King of the Roses 170, 171, 1172, 1190
Storm Front **53**

Andreae, Christine
Grizzly **54**, 1341, 1625, 1784

Trail of Murder **55**, 57, 1233, 1234, 1607, 1626, 1667

Andrews, Sarah
A Fall in Denver **56**
Tensleep 48, **57**, 605

Andrus, Jeff
Tracer, Inc. **58**, 71, 870

Angus, John
The Monster Squad **59**

Angus, Sylvia
Dead to Rites 1163

Anthony, Michael David
The Becket Factor **60**, 1429, 1706
Dark Provenance **61**

Appel, William
Whisper.He Might Hear You **62**, 976
Widowmaker **63**

Appiah, Anthony
Avenging Angel **64**, 235, 598

Ardies, Tom
Balboa Firefly **1633**

Armistead, John
A Homecoming for Murder **65**

Arnold, Margot
Exit Actors Dying 174, 176

Arnston, Harrison
Act of Passion 1015
Trade-Off **66**, 216, 240, 446, 1092, 1357, 1401, 1640, 1723, 1724, 1780

Ashford, Jeffrey
The Honourable Detective **67**, 451
Hostage to Death 1149

Asimov, Isaac
Murder at the A.B.A. 524

Atherton, Nancy
Aunt Dimity and the Duke **68**, 385
Aunt Dimity's Death **69**, 795, 959, 1065

Auster, Paul
City of Glass 238

Avallone, Michael
Shoot It Again, Sam 1574

Axler, Leo
The Bill Hawley Series 2, 688, 1021, 1242, 1464
Double Plot **70**
Final Viewing 1
Grave Matters **71**

Ayres, E.C.
Eye of the Gator **72**
Hour of the Manatee **73**, 211, 336, 344, 870, 1596

Ayres, Noreen
Carcass Trade **74**

Azolakov, Antoinette
The Smokey Brandon Series 325
A World the Color of Salt 322, 324, 1527

Azolakov, Antoinette
The Contactees Die Young 533

B

Babbin, Jacqueline
Bloody Soaps: A Tale of Love and Death in the Afternoon **75**, 1121

Babson, Marian
The Cruise of a Deathtime 117
Encore Murder **76**
Murder, Murder, Little Star 1034

Babson, Marion
Dangerous to Know 1149
Death Warmed Up 729, 988
The Twelve Days of Christmas 220

Babula, William
According to St. John **77**, 1716
The St. John Series 907
St. John's Baptism 511, 1352, 1414, 1781

Bachman, Richard
Roadwork 1617

Bacon, Gail
The Bishop's Tale 544
The Boy's Tale 545

Baddock, James
The Faust Conspiracy **78**, 410, 787

Bahadur, K.P.
Murder in the Dehli Mail 35

Bailey, Jo
Bagged **79**, 302, 448, 659, 660, 931, 932, 934, 968, 970, 1130, 1656
Recycled **80**

Baker, Abbey Penn
In the Dead of Winter **81**, 400, 560, 835, 924, 926, 1259

Baker, Nikki
In the Game **82**, 1198, 1323, 1356, 1410
The Lavender House Murder **83**, 761
The Virginia Kelly Series 142, 1691, 1692

Baker, Richard M.
The Drood Murder Case 1407

Baker, Susan
My First Murder **84**, 771, 947, 1121

Ball, Brian
Death of a Low-Handicap Man 480

Ball, John
Chief Tallon and the S.O.R. 1712
In the Heat of the Night 393, 1314

Ballard, Robert
Bright Shark **85**

Ballard, W.T.
Pretty Miss Murder 132

Ballinger, Bill S.
The Tooth and the Nail 704

Bandy, Franklin
Deceit and Deadly Lies 105

Banks, Carolyn
Death by Dressage 1487

Banks, Oliver
The Caravaggio Obsession 1573
The Rembrandt Panel 1180, 1211, 1243, 1521, 1666

Bannister, Jo
Death and Other Lovers **86**, 893
Gilgamesh 1645
The Going Down of the Sun **87**, 581

Barber, Willetta
The Christopher Storm Series 999

Barnao, Jack
Hammerlocke 1472
The John Locke Series 26, 486
Locke Step 300, 684
Timelocke 1682

Barnard, Robert
Bodies 754
The Cherry Blossom Corpse 1050
A City of Strangers **88**
Death and the Chaste Apprentice **89**
Death by Sheer Torture 472, 1063, 1322
Death of a Literary Widow 402
Death of a Mystery Writer 307, 695
Death on the High C's 609, 1191, 1192
The Masters of the House **90**
Out of the Blackout 994
A Scandal in Belgravia **91**
The Skeleton in the Grass 385
To Die Like a Gentleman 103

Barnes, Linda
Bitter Finish 569, 908, 1713
Blood Will Have Blood 174, 176, 1346
The Carlotta Carlyle Series 378, 379, 380, 381, 383, 398, 638, 639, 837, 917, 918, 921, 1099, 1182, 1185, 1266, 1489, 1490
Coyote **92**, 161, 364, 636, 972, 1093, 1220, 1251, 1252, 1265, 1355, 1410, 1504, 1505
The Snake Tattoo 274, 1702
Snapshot **93**, 808
Steel Guitar **94**, 637, 1076
A Trouble of Fools 384, 919, 920, 1264, 1271

Barnes, Trevor
A Midsummer Night's Killing 1141, 1144
A Pound of Flesh **95**

Barr, Nevada
The Anna Pigeon Series 1649
Firestorm 1552
A Superior Death **96**, 1428
Track of the Cat 48, 54, **97**, 605, 792, 842, 1137, 1234, 1268, 1332, 1340, 1341, 1605, 1652, 1784

Barre, Richard
The Innocents 164, 1325

Barrett, Neal Jr.
Pink Vodka Blues **98**, 147, 164, 935, 1038, 1763

Barrow, Adam
Flawless **99**

Barth, Richard
The Condo Kill 588
Deathics **100**, 977
The Final Shot 968
Furnished for Murder 70, **101**, 1112, 1240, 1463, 1777, 1778
The Margaret Binton Series 45, 654, 978, 1138, 1171, 1246, 1445, 1446, 1447, 1485, 1571
The Rag Bag Clan 286, 1063

Bartlett, James Y.
Death Is a Two-Stroke Penalty 318, 481

Barton, Frederick
With Extreme Prejudice **102**, 592

Bass, Milton
The Moving Finger 231

Bastable, Bernard
To Die Like a Gentleman 103

Bateman, Colin
Divorcing Jack **104**, 786

Baty, Linda Thrasher
Cat's Paw, Inc. **1618**

Bay, Austin
The Coyote Cried Twice 350

Bayer, William
Blind Side 11, **105**, 192, 227, 262, 295, 421, 842, 1562, 1732
Switch 306, 750, 858, 1193, 1249, 1533

Beal, M.F.
Angel Dance 523

Bean, Gregory
No Comfort in Victory **106**, 1788

Beaton, M.C.
Agatha Raisin and the Quiche of Death 100, **107**, 145, 389
Agatha Raisin and the Vicious Vet **108**
Death of a Charming Man **109**, 740
Death of a Gossip 317, 719, 948, 1639
Death of a Hussy **110**
Death of a Nag **111**
Death of a Perfect Wife **112**, 191
Death of a Traveling Man **113**
The Hamish MacBeth Series 249, 720, 912, 943

Beck, K.K.
Amateur Night **114**, 770
The Body in the Cornflakes 145
The Body in the Volvo 1121
Death in a Deck Chair 250, 1519
Electric City **115**, 372, 774
A Hopeless Case 69, **116**, 198, 312, 503, 795, 959, 1076, 1697, 1743
The Iris Cooper Series 465
The Jane Silva Series 251
Murder in a Mummy Case 1320
Peril under the Palms **117**, 834, 835
Unwanted Attentions 798
Young Mrs. Cavendish and the Kaiser's Men 1028, 1049

Becklund, Jack
Golden Fleece **118**

Beinhart, Larry
You Get What You Pay For 184

Belfort, Sophie
The Lace Curtain Murders 120, 882, 982
The Marvell College Murders **119**, 960, 1196

Bellairs, George
All Roads to Sospel 87

Belsky, Dick
The Jenny McKay Series 1568
One for the Money 1214, 1636
South Street Confidential **120**

Benjamin, Paul
Squeeze Play 510, 574, 1205, 1206

Benke, Patricia D.
False Witness 1268
Guilty by Choice 1465

Bennett, Liza
Madison Avenue Murder 11, 346, 347, 1543
Seventh Avenue Murder 403, 404

Berenson, Laurien
A Pedigree to Die For **121**, 258, 288

Berg, Barry
Hide and Seek **122**, 403, 404, 848, 1558, 1592, 1593

Berger, Thomas
Who Is Teddy Villinova? 238

Bergman, Andrew
The Big Kiss-Off of 1944 1270
Hollywood and LeVine 860

Berlinski, David
A Clean Sweep **123**, 906

Berne, Karin
Bare Acquaintances 208, 274, 346, 405
False Impressions 347, 1316, 1650

Bernhardt, William
Perfect Justice 940
Primary Justice 333, 666, 1022, 1357

Berrenson, Marc
Perfection 62, 980

Berry, Carole
The Bonnie Indermill Series 56, 347, 403, 596, 1155
Death of a Dancing Fool **124**
The Death of a Difficult Woman **125**
Good Night, Sweet Prince 18, **126**, 346, 1319
Island Girl **127**, 989
The Letter of the Law 1333
Nightmare Point **128**
The Year of the Monkey 1543, 1545

Bickham, Jack
Dropshot: A Brad Smith Novel **129**
A Permanent Retirement **1153**

Biderman, Bob
The Genesis Files **130**

Biederman, Marcia
Post No Bonds 1512

Biggle, Lloyd Jr.
The Glendower Conspiracy **131**, 440
The Glendower Conspiracy: A Memoir of Sherlock Holmes 442
A Hazard of Losers **132**

Birkett, John
The Last Private Eye 1755
The Queen's Mare **133**, 170

Bishop, Claudia
A Dash of Death **134**
The Sarah Quilliam Series 377, 699
A Taste for Murder 32, **135**, 375, 1289, 1291

Bishop, Michael
The Secret Ascension 419

Black, Ian Stuart
The Man on the Bridge 647

Black, Lionel
Death by Hoax 1034
The Eve of the Wedding 87

Black, Veronica
The Sister Joan Series 1237, 1239, 1339
A Vow of Chastity **136**, 1591
A Vow of Obedience **137**
A Vow of Sanctity **138**
A Vow of Silence 670, 671, 672
Vow of Silence 1238

Author Index

Blackmur, L.L.
Love Lies Slain 21, 52, **139**, 539, 546, 1676

Blackstock, Charity
Dewey Death 416, 611, 1031, 1559

Blain, W. Edward
Passion Play **140**, 468, 515, 1250, 1593

Blake, Nicholas
End of the Chapter 224
The Nigel Strangeways Series 471, 1366
The Whisper in the Gloom 368

Bland, Eleanor Taylor
Dead End 1198
Dead Time **141**, 840, 953, 954, 1222, 1452
The Marti MacAlister Series 1691, 1692
Slow Burn **142**

Blank, Martin
Shadowchase **143**, 1683

Blauner, Peter
Slow Motion Riot **144**, 292, 293, 1000, 1067, 1152, 1199, 1623

Bloch, Robert
Psycho 1013, 1606

Blochman, Lawrence G.
Red Snow at Darjeeling 35

Block, Lawrence
After the First Death 98, 1763
The Bernie Rhodenbarr Series 210, 714
The Burglar Series 402
The Burglar Who Studied Spinoza 1745
The Burglar Who Traded Ted Williams **145**, 169, 467, 494, 1697
Burglars Can't Be Choosers 178, 715, 1698
A Dance at the Slaughterhouse **146**, 196, 292, 750, 1067
The Devil Knows You're Dead 147
Make Out with Murder 607, 1047
The Matt Scudder Series 73, 195, 495, 1012, 1039, 1075, 1422, 1458, 1585, 1640, 1646
Out on the Cutting Edge **148**, 1455, 1532
The Thief Who Couldn't Sleep 1697
A Ticket to the Boneyard **149**, 767, 1010, 1347
The Topless Tulip Caper 237, 585, 608
A Walk Among the Tombstones **150**

Blodgett, Michael
Hero and the Terror 840

Blum, Bill
Prejudicial Error 1280

Bohan, Becky
Fertile Betrayal 812

Bond, Larry
Red Phoenix 248

Bond, Michael
Monsieur Pamplemousse Investigates **151**
The Monsieur Pamplemousse Series 389, 390, 768, 988, 1061
Pamplemousse Rests His Case **152**

Borgenicht, Marian
Undue Influence 848

Borgenicht, Miriam
No Duress 1022

Undue Influence 66, **153**

Borthwick, J.S.
The Bridled Groom **154**
The Down-East Murders 120, 1063, 1140, 1255, 1588
The Student Body 892, 1256, 1520, 1767, 1797

Borton, D.B.
The Cat Caliban Series 1185, 1489, 1506
Four Elements of Murder **155**
One for the Money 503
Three Is a Crowd **156**, 1065
Two Points for Murder **157**

Boucher, Anthony
The Case of the Baker Street Irregulars 1365
Nine Times Nine 1238

Bourgeau, Art
The Seduction 187, 208

Bowen, John
The McGuffin 1630

Bowen, Michael
Act of Faith **158**
Faithfully Executed **159**
Fielder's Choice **160**, 1201
The Richard Michaelson Series 509
Washington Deceased 353, 1312, 1613

Bowers, Elisabeth
No Forwarding Address **161**, 947

Bowker, Richard
Marlborough Street 241

Bowman, Robert J.
The House of Blue Lights 222, 397, 920, 972, 1116, 1379, 1579

Box, Edgar
Death in the Fifth Position 18, 126, 1346

Boyer, Rick
Billingsgate Shoal 233, 340, 683, 686, 1602, 1779
The Doc Adams Series 336, 688, 764, 1604, 1615
The Giant Rat of Sumatra 131
The Penny Ferry 335, 922, 1074
The Whale's Footprints 339, 687, 765, 850, 903, 904, 1324
Yellow Bird 58, **162**

Boylan, Eleanor
The Clara Gamadge Series 46, 284, 285
Murder Machree 801
Working Murder 711, 712, 1171, 1245, 1406

Boyle, Gerry
Deadline 154, **163**, 467, 1590

Boyle, Thomas
Only the Dead Know Brooklyn 754, 890, 1628

Bradford, Kelly
Footprints 444, 533

Bradley, Lynn
Stand-In for Murder **164**

Brand, Christianna
Fog of Doubt 576, 586
Green for Danger 471, 579

Brandon, Jay
Deadbolt 617
Fade the Heat 557, 1016, 1090
Loose Among the Lambs 592
Predator's Waltz 42, **165**, 1106

Brandt, Nat
A Death in Bulloch Parish 1496
Land Kills 166, 1720, 1721

Brandt, Yanna
Land Kills 166

Branson, H.C.
The John Bent Series 1373

Brashler, William
Bleeding Dodger Blue **505**
Fear in Fenway **506**
Murder in Wrigley Field **507**
Tigers Burning **508**

Braun, Lilian Jackson
The Cat Who Moved a Mountain **167**
The Cat Who Series 15, 16, 17, 19, 20, 180, 181, 182, 438, 439, 443, 620, 950, 1733
The Cat Who Talked to Ghosts **168**
The Cat Who Went into the Closet **169**
The Cats Who Series 619

Breen, Jon L.
The Gathering Place 743, 1300
Hot Air **170**
The Jerry Brogan Series 1190
Listen for the Click 133, 573, 1172
Loose Lips **171**, 871
Touch of the Past 466, 535, 611, 1054, 1055, 1500, 1764

Brennan, Carol
Full Commission **172**
Headhunt 347
In the Dark **173**, 1514
The Liz Wareham Series 32, 124

Brett, John
Who'd Hire Brett? 1645

Brett, Simon
The Charles Paris Series 76, 1064, 1131
Corporate Bodies **174**
The Mrs. Pargeter Series 1246, 1483
Mrs. Pargeter's Package **175**, 1171
Mrs., Presumed Dead 1594
Murder Unprompted 1173
A Scandal in Belgravia 696, 697
A Series of Murders **176**
So Much Blood 1707
Star Trap 1768

Brewer, Steve
Lonely Street 1755

Brightwell, Emily
The Mrs. Jeffries Series 929

Brill, Toni
Date with a Dead Doctor 127, **177**, 312, 423, 1501

Brix, Alexi
Blood Ties 1471

Brock, Stuart
Killer's Choice 491

Brod, D.C.
Murder in Store **178**, 1345

Brooks, Janice Young
The Class Menagerie **244**
A Farewell to Yarns **245**
From Here to Paternity **246**
A Quiche Before Dying **247**

Brown, Dale
Day of the Cheetah **179**, 409, 825, 1513

Brown, John
Zaibatsu 348

Brown, R.D.
Hazzard 350, 352

Brown, Rita Mae
The Mrs. Murphy Series 20
Murder at Monticello 121, **180**
Rest in Pieces **181**, 443
Sudden Death 1195
Wish You Were Here 15, 17, 19, 167, 169, **182**, 258, 438, 439, 619, 983

Browne, Howard
Halo in Blood 1270
Pork City 276, 277, 279, 501, 1207, 1609
Scotch on the Rocks **183**, 1583

Bruce, Leo
The Carolus Deene Series 1366
The Sergeant Beef Series 109, 912

Bruno, Anthony
Bad Apple **184**
Bad Blood **185**, 348, 1128, 1363
Bad Guys 273, 1188, 1199, 1202, 1362, 1433, 1622, 1672
Bad Moon **186**
The Tozzi and Gibbons Series 1760

Buchanan, Edna
Contents under Pressure 1641
Nobody Lives Forever **187**, 1011
Suitable for Framing 275, 615

Buckley, Christopher
Wet Work 437

Buckley, William F. Jr.
The Blackford Oakes Series 647, 810
Saving the Queen 419
Tucker's Last Stand **188**

Buckstaff, Kathryn
No One Dies in Branson 902, 1755

Bunn, Thomas
Closing Costs **189**, 1023, 1436
Worse than Death **190**, 500

Burden, Pat
Screaming Bones **191**, 645

Burke, Alan Dennis
Dead Wrong **192**, 475, 653, 1463, 1562, 1683, 1694, 1732

Burke, J.F.
Death Trick 762, 1314
Location Shots 1005, 1693

Burke, James Lee
Black Cherry Blues **193**, 1025, 1307, 1327, 1329, 1603
Burning Angel **194**
The Dave Robicheaux Series 147, 344, 1026, 1039, 1218, 1422
Dixie City Jam **195**
Heaven's Prisoners 1672
In the Electric Mist with Confederate Dead **196**
A Morning for Flamingos **197**, 1038, 1308, 1492, 1738
The Neon Rain 272, 273, 399, 844, 981, 1024, 1421, 1491, 1494, 1704
A Stained White Radiance 454, 869, 1000, 1493
To the Bright and Shining Sun 1584

Burke, Jan
Goodnight, Irene **198**, 1332, 1659

Burkey, Dave
Rain Lover 52, 171

Burley, W.J.
Death in the Willow Pattern 1729
Guilt Edged 748
To Kill a Cat 260, 1001

Burns, Rex
Wycliffe and the Beales 1253
Wycliffe and the Scapegoat 89, 759

Burns, Rex
The Alvarez Journal 40, 844, 1570
The Avenging Angel 1018
Body Guard **199**
The Gabe Wager Series 1711, 1715, 1717
Parts Unknown 39, 41, **200**, 1439
Suicide Season 871
When Reason Sleeps **1472**

Burns, Ron
The Livinius Severus Series 1450
Roman Nights **201**, 1390, 1448
The Strange Death of Meriweather Lewis 1164

Bushnell, Agnes
Shadow Dance **202**, 1460, 1689

Butler, Gwendoline
Coffin on Murder Street **203**
Coffin Underground **204**
The Dull Dead 1592
Murder Has a Pretty Face **1142**
Witching Murder **1144**

Byrd, Max
California Thriller 1455
Fuse Time **205**, 684

C

Cahill, Mary
Carpool 244, 315, 1749

Cail, Carol
The Maxey Burnell Series 373
Private Lies 1586
Unsafe Keeping **206**

Cain, James M.
The Postman Always Rings Twice 295, 773, 1562

Callahan, Sheila MacGill
Death in a Far Country 23, 331
Forty Whacks **207**

Callahan, Sheila McGill
Death in a Far Country 104

Cambray, C.K.
Personal **208**

Cameron, Sara
Natural Enemies **209**, 225

Camp, John
The Empress File **210**, 388, 1538
The Fool's Run 145, 437, 622, 1100
Rules of Prey **1425**
Shadow Prey **1426**
Silent Prey **1427**
Winter Prey **1428**

Campbell, Harlen
Monkey on a Chain **211**, 294, 341, 618, 796, 822, 1210, 1272, 1370, 1436, 1790

Campbell, R. Wright
Killer of Kings 1574
The Spy Who Sat and Waited 37, 78

Campbell, Robert
Alice in La-La Land 148, 254, 886, 1217
The Gift Horse's Mouth **212**
In La-La Land We Trust 717, 718
The Jake Hatch Series 212, 213
The Jimmy Flannery Series 353
Juice 184, 783, 1152
The La-La Land Series 292
Nibbled to Death by Ducks **213**

Red Cent 13
Sweet La-La Land 888
The Whistler Series 1643

Cannell, Dorothy
The Ellie Haskell Series 422
Femmes Fatal **214**, 423, 1557
How to Murder Your Mother-in-Law **215**
Mum's the Word 1061
The Thin Woman 151, 152, 374, 390, 988, 989, 990, 1097, 1098, 1257, 1290, 1291

Cannon, Taffy
A Pocketful of Karma **216**

Cape, Tony
The Cambridge Theorem 91, **217**, 330

Carl, Lillian Stewart
Ashes to Ashes 502

Carlson, P.M.
Audition for Murder 1707
Bad Blood **218**
Bloodstream 1686
Gravestone **219**, 1685
The Maggie Ryan Series 76, 593, 1117, 1254
The Marty Hopkins Series 970, 1099
Murder Is Academic 351, 891, 1797
Murder Misread 359, 979
Rehearsal for Murder 414, 641, 1391

Carmichael, Harry
Naked to the Grave 1055

Carnell, Jennifer
Murder, Mystery and Mayhem **220**

Carr, A.Z.H.
Finding Maubee 845

Carr, Caleb
The Alienist 400, 560, 1787

Carr, Glyn
Swing Away, Climber 1163

Carr, John Dickson
The Burning Court 103
Captain Cutthroat 519
Fell and Foul Play **221**
The Gideon Fell Series 471

Carter, Noel Vreeland
The Mooncalf Murders 130, **222**

Carter, Robert
Final Slaughter 580

Carter, Robert A.
Casual Slaughters 9, **223**, 467
Final Edit **224**
The Nicholas Barlow Series 484

Carvic, Heron
The Miss Seeton Series 175

Casberg, Melvin A.
Death Stalks the Punjab 875

Casley, Dennis
Death Underfoot **225**

Catanach, J.N.
Brideprice 158, **226**
The Last Rite of Hugo T **227**

Caudwell, Sarah
The Hilary Tamar Series 597, 598
The Sirens Sang of Murder **228**, 763
Thus Was Adonis Murdered 561, 979, 1002, 1003, 1004, 1118, 1187, 1243, 1501, 1510, 1642, 1658

Caunitz, William J.
Exceptional Clearance **229**, 1534, 1535
One Police Plaza 306, 348, 1070, 1344, 1443, 1533
Suspects 750, 840, 1067, 1202

Caxton, Tony
Murder in a Quiet Place **230**

Chafets, Zev
Inherit the Mob **231**, 355, 606

Chais, Pamela
Final Cut 332, 1574

Chandler, Raymond
The Philip Marlowe Series 1176, 1177

Chapman, Sally
Love Bytes **232**, 1489

Chaput, W.J.
Dead in the Water **233**, 475, 689

Charbonneau, Louis
The Ice **234**, 725

Charles, Kate
A Drink of Deadly Wine 61, **235**

Charnee, David
Party Till You Die **236**
To Kill a Clown **237**

Charyn, Jerome
Blue Eyes 554
Elsinore **238**
The Good Policeman 1663
Montezuma's Man 580

Chase, Elaine Raco
Dangerous Places 1214, 1759

Chase, Samantha
Needlepoint 798

Chastain, Thomas
Pandora's Box 1684
Perry Mason in The Case of Too Many Murders **239**
The Prosecutor **240**
Spanner 840
Vital Statistics 1585

Chesbro, George C.
The Beasts of Valhalla 238
The Fear in Yesterday's Rings 429
In the House of Secret Enemies **241**, 283
An Incident at Bloodtide 554
The Language of Cannibals **242**
Shadow of a Broken Man 1371

Cheyney, Peter
Lady Beware 1629

Chisholm, P.F.
A Famine of Horses **243**, 1377, 1468, 1624

Chiu, Tony
Bright Shark 85

Christie, Agatha
And Then There Were None 220, 742
Evil under the Sun 225
The Miss Marple Series 385, 1097, 1098, 1406, 1484

Christmas, Joyce
The Lady Margaret Priam Series 214, 813, 1098, 1209
Simply to Die For 1097
Suddenly in Her Sorbet 51, 449

Churchill, Jill
The Class Menagerie **244**, 698
A Farewell to Yarns 215, **245**, 1208, 1256, 1750

From Here to Paternity **246**
Grime and Punishment 594, 990, 1146, 1255, 1258, 1748
The Jane Jeffry Series 155, 157, 422, 595, 600, 1254, 1749
A Quiche Before Dying 214, **247**, 423, 968

Clancy, Tom
The Hunt for Red October 85, 179, 825, 1513, 1530
Patriot Games 474, 684, 685, 1284
The Sum of All Fears **248**

Claridge, Marten
Nobody's Fool 111, **249**, 591, 1134

Clark, Carol Higgins
Decked 68, **250**
Snagged **251**

Clark, Dick
Murder on Tour 1587

Clark, Douglas
Dead Letter 789
Death After Evensong 1502
The Masters and Green Series 366, 470, 504, 1159, 1160, 1454, 1479
Premedicated Murder 1402
Sick to Death 576
Storm Center 368

Clark, Mary Higgins
All Around the Town **252**, 843, 1157
The Cradle Will Fall 5, 93, 462, 602
A Cry in the Night 44, 899, 1453
Loves Music, Loves to Dance 43, 49, **253**, 275, 673, 769, 821, 1761
Remember Me 1791
Stillwatch 1062
A Stranger Is Watching 1046
Weep No More, My Lady 173, 665, 879, 990, 1097
Where Are the Children? 128, 794, 1062, 1351, 1664
While My Pretty One Sleeps 139, 770

Clarkson, John
And Justice for One 195, 196, **254**, 421, 518, 1039, 1211, 1370, 1585
One Man's Law 363, 1152

Cleary, Jon
Babylon South **255**
Murder Song **256**
The Scobie Malone Series 328, 329, 1695

Cleary, Melissa
First Pedigree Murder **257**
The Jackie Walsh Series 121, 288, 291, 1734
The Maltese Puppy **258**
A Tail of Two Murders **259**, 289

Cleeves, Ann
A Day in the Death of Dorothea Cassidy 203, 230, **260**, 677

Cline, Edward
Whisper the Guns **261**, 1744

Cline, John
The Forever Beat **262**

Clinton-Baddeley, V.C.
The Dr. Davie Series 330, 331, 590
Only a Matter of Time 609, 1043
To Study a Long Silence 1045

Clothier, Peter
Chiaroscuro 477, 1180, 1211, 1507, 1521, 1645, 1666

Author Index

Dirty-Down 1509, 1676

Cluster, Dick
Obligations of the Bone 93, **263**

Clynes, Michael
The Poisoned Chalice **264**, 426
The Roger Shallot Series 1468
The White Rose Murders **265**, 1375, 1376, 1377, 1469

Coben, Harlan
Dropshot 1195
Play Dead **266**

Coburn, Andrew
Company Secrets 647
Goldilocks 842
No Way Home **267**, 1230, 1758
Voices in the Dark **268**, 626, 1774, 1776

Cochran, Molly
End Game **1585**
The Temple Dogs **1188**

Cockburn, Sarah
The Sirens Sang of Murder **228**

Cody, Liza
The Anna Lee Series 304, 428, 455, 456, 1094, 1125, 1143, 1338, 1541
Backhand **269**
Bucket Nut **270**, 751, 1125
Dupe 95, 1141, 1144, 1181, 1630
Monkey Wrench **271**

Coe, Tucker
A Jade in Aries 148
The Mitch Tobin Series 1532

Cohen, Anthea
Angel of Death 1321

Cohen, Stephen Paul
Heartless 1602
Island of Steel 1532
Night Launch 179

Coker, Carolyn
The Balmoral Nude 345, 477, 1216, 1521
The Hand of the Lion 1676
The Other David 1180, 1211, 1343

Colbert, James
All I Have Is Blue **272**
Skinny Man **273**, 910, 1416

Cole, Jameson
A Killing in Quail County 106, 1788

Collins, Anna Ashwood
Deadly Resolutions **274**

Collins, Eliza G.C.
Going, Going, Gone 570, 572, 729, 1240, 1565

Collins, Judy
Shameless **275**

Collins, Max Allan
The Baby Blue Rip Off 459
Blood and Thunder **276**
Carnal Hours **277**
The Dark City 501
Dying in the Post-War World 283
Kill Your Darlings 623, 668, 715, 1263
The Million-Dollar Wound 957
Murder by the Numbers **278**
Murder in the Post-War World **279**
The Nate Heller Series 183, 498, 956, 1177, 1207, 1609, 1674
A Nice Weekend for Murder 741, 1364
The Nolan Series 210
The Quarry Series 238
Stolen Away **280**, 958

True Crime 278
True Detective 483, 501, 1161, 1176

Collins, Michael
Cassandra in Red **281**
Chasing Eights **282**
Crime, Punishment and Resurrection **283**
The Dan Fortune Series 343, 486, 1491, 1492, 1493, 1684
Freak 1494
Minnesota Strip 242, 1371

Comfort, B.
The Cashmere Kid **284**
Elusive Quarry **285**
Grave Consequences **286**, 361, 711, 713, 765, 1069, 1103, 1105, 1246, 1445, 1571
Phoebe's Knee 801
The Tish McWhinney Series 978, 1446, 1483, 1548

Comfort, Barbara
The Cashmere Kid **284**
Elusive Quarry **285**
Grave Consequences **286**

Conant, Susan
A Bite of Death **287**
Black Ribbon 121, **288**
Bloodlines **289**
Gone to the Dogs 722
The Holly Winter Series 127, 257, 258, 259, 1734
A New Leash on Death 17, 116
Paws Before Dying **290**
Ruffly Speaking **291**

Conley, Martha
Growing Light 821

Connelly, Michael
The Black Echo 211, **292**, 363, 618, 1436, 1623, 1672
The Black Ice 3, **293**, 910, 1210, 1534
The Concrete Blond 1067
The Concrete Blonde **294**, 580, 909, 1025
The Harry Bosch Series 1026, 1424, 1585
The Last Coyote 881, 1008

Conner, K. Patrick
Kingdom Road **295**, 854, 1562

Connor, K. Patrick
Kingdom Road 4, 653, 855

Conroy, Richard Timothy
The India Exhibition **296**
Mr. Smithson's Bones 207, **297**

Constantine, K.C.
Always a Body to Trade 1712
The Blank Page 1678
Bottom-Feeder Blues 1104, 1105
A Fix Like This 1135
The Man Who Liked Slow Tomatoes 1231
The Mario Balzac Series 65, 1230, 1776
The Rocksburg Railroad Murders 1070, 1740, 1741
Sunshine Enemies **298**, 1103

Cook, Bruce
Death as a Career Move **299**, 665, 1587
Rough Cut **300**, 332, 369, 1007, 1096, 1200, 1575
The Sidewalk Hilton **301**

Cook, Robin
Blindsight 80, **302**
Coma 659, 888, 965, 1262

Fatal Cure 1130, 1656
Harmful Intent 5, 602
Outbreak 976, 1321
Vital Signs **303**, 448, 934, 1799

Cook, Stephen
Dead Fit **304**, 661, 778

Cook, Thomas
Sacrificial Lamb 1279

Cook, Thomas H.
The City When It Rains **305**
Evidence of Blood 1726
Flesh and Blood 184, 186, 1532
Night Secrets 1023
Sacrificial Ground 1533
Streets of Fire **306**, 498, 910, 1503, 1535
Tabernacle 509, 827, 828, 829, 830, 1018

Cooke, John Peyton
Torsos 278

Cooney, Caroline
Sand Trap 480

Coonts, Stephen
Minotaur 409, 825

Cooper, Natasha
Bitter Herbs **307**, 1306
Bloody Roses **308**, 1411
Poison Flowers 107
Rotten Apples **309**
The Willow King Series 108

Cooper, Susan Rogers
Chasing Away the Devil 626, 1742
Dead Moon on the Rise **310**, 1766
Doctors, Lawyers and Such **311**
Funny as a Dead Comic 125, **312**, 770
Funny as a Dead Relative **313**, 902, 1204, 1517
Houston in the Rearview Mirror **314**, 1103, 1775
The Man in the Green Chevy 1739, 1740, 1772
The Milt Kovack Series 1776
The Milt Kovak Series 65, 1230, 1756, 1758, 1774
One, Two, What Did Daddy Do? **315**, 849
Other People's Houses 267, 268, **316**, 1231

Cores, Lucy
Corpse de Ballet 18, 126, 1346

Cork, Barry
The Angus Straum Series 109, 111
Dead Ball 110, 112, 113, 719, 720
Unnatural Hazard **317**, 1134
Winter Rules **318**

Cormany, Michael
Lost Daughter 826
Red Winter **319**, 1281, 1345
Skin Deep Is Fatal **320**

Cornwell, Bernard
Killer's Wake 541, 582, 1037

Cornwell, David
The Russia House 995

Cornwell, Patricia D.
All That Remains 80, **321**, 1736
The Body Farm **322**
Body of Evidence **323**, 448, 463
Cruel and Unusual 294, **324**, 1737
From Potter's Field **325**
The Kay Scarpetta Series 63, 74, 430, 476, 774, 974, 975, 976, 1051

Crichton, Michael

Postmortem 49, 62, 79, 216, 253, 302, 303, **326**, 429, 431, 478, 1027, 1285, 1321, 1405

Corris, Peter
The Cliff Hardy Series 26, 27, 1694, 1695
The Dying Trade 255, 256
The Green Apartments 1693
Matrimonial Causes **327**
O'Fear **328**
Wet Graves **329**

Cory, Desmond
The Catalyst 207, **330**, 590
The Dobie Paradox **331**
The John Dobie Series 484
The Mask of Zeus 1488

Cotler, Gordon
Shooting Script **332**

Coughlin, William J.
Death Penalty 730
Shadow of a Doubt **333**, 666

Coyne, P.J.
Manuscript for Murder 723

Craig, Alisa
The Madoc Rhys Series 1785
Murder Goes Mumming 220, 627, 1417, 1418, 1419, 1770
A Pint of Murder 896, 898
The Terrible Tide 763
Trouble in the Brasses 1305, 1420, 1769
The Wrong Rite **334**

Craig, Philip R.
A Beautiful Place to Die 96, 233, **335**, 386, 686, 689, 903, 905, 922, 1074, 1463
A Case of Vineyard Poisoning **336**
Cliff Hanger **337**, 1099
The Double Minded Men **338**
The J.W. Jackson Series 72, 687
Off Season **339**
The Woman Who Walked into the Sea **340**, 904, 1078

Crais, Robert
The Elvis Cole Series 764, 791, 1272, 1385, 1400, 1440, 1646
Free Fall 294, **341**, 454, 1269
Lullaby Town 199, **342**, 369, 432, 765, 1110, 1200, 1413
The Monkey's Raincoat 301, 433, 435, 634, 766, 815, 1271, 1313, 1352, 1383, 1387, 1459, 1575, 1616
Stalking the Angel **343**, 434, 716, 717, 718, 766, 1000
Voodoo River 194, **344**, 1596

Crane, Caroline
The Girls Are Missing 44

Crespi, Camilla T.
The Trouble with Going Home **345**

Crespi, Trella
The Simona Griffo Series 56, 124, 596
The Trouble with a Small Raise 125, 1155
The Trouble with Moonlighting **346**, 413, 517, 992, 1247, 1248, 1290, 1782, 1783
The Trouble with Too Much Sun **347**, 1485

Crews, Lary
Extreme Close-up 11

Crichton, Michael
Disclosure 1615
Jurassic Park 1405

Crider, Bill
Rising Sun **348**, 750, 1127, 1742
Sphere 85
Crider, Bill
Blood Marks **349**, 651
The Carl Burns Series 622
The Dan Rhodes Series 1111
A Dangerous Thing 1275
Dead on the Island 8, **350**, 1007, 1096, 1347, 1472
Dying Voices **351**, 722, 744, 776, 1512, 1657, 1735, 1797
Gator Kill **352**
One Dead Dean 359, 696, 714, 715, 776, 1136, 1482, 1767
The Sheriff Dan Rhodes Series 12, 14, 106, 310, 311, 700, 757, 780, 781, 1086, 1087, 1138, 1153, 1431, 1788
Shotgun Saturday Night 1105, 1108, 1739, 1741
The Texas Capitol Murders **353**, 1435
Too Late to Die 298, 316, 1740
The Truman Smith Series 1032
When Old Men Die **354**, 906

Criscuolo, C. Clark
Wiseguys in Love **355**

Crispin, Edmund
Beware of Trains 221
The Gervase Fen series 228, 330, 331, 590, 1366, 1367
The Moving Toyshop 763

Crombie, Deborah
All Shall Be Well 95, **356**, 644, 1132, 1396
The Duncan Kincaid Series 1397
The Kincaid and James Series 643
Leave the Grave Green **357**, 1553
A Share in Death **358**, 640, 642, 678, 740, 897, 1141, 1143, 1408, 1556

Crosby, Virginia
The Fast-Death Factor **359**, 977, 983

Crosland, Susan
Dangerous Games 1608

Cross, Amanda
Death in a Tenured Position 892, 1520, 1522
An Imperfect Spy **360**, 1196
In the Last Analysis 1136
The James Joyce Murder 583, 1045, 1512
The Kate Fansler Series 1511
The Players Come Again 979, 1187
The Question of Max 359, 745

Crowleigh, Ann
Clively Close: Dead as Dead Can Be **361**, 928, 929

Crum, Laura
Cutter 21, **362**, 536, 537, 538, 839
The Gail McCarthy Series 1733

Crumley, James
Dancing Bear 164, 1601, 1677
The Last Good Kiss 148, 193, 554, 736, 791, 1096, 1455, 1580, 1618
The Mexican Tree Duck **363**, 1370
The Wrong Case 193, 273, 319, 320, 342, 1307

Crutcher, Chris
The Deep End **364**, 879, 885, 887, 1791

Cullen, Robert
Cover Story **365**
Soviet Sources 913

Cummings, Barbara
Clively Close: Dead as Dead Can Be **361**

Cunningham, E.V.
The Case of the Kidnapped Angel 1712
The Case of the One-Penny Orange 548

Curran, Terrie
All Booked Up 416, 1275, 1559

Curzon, Clare
Cat's Cradle **366**
Death Prone **367**
Three-Core Lead **368**, 1682
The Yeadings and Mott Series 469, 504

Cussler, Clive
Night Probe 179, 1456
Raise the Titanic! 1513

Cutler, Stan
The Face on the Cutting Room Floor 722
Shot on Location 332, **369**, 1411

D

Daheim, Mary
The Alpine Advocate 14, 163, **370**, 383, 868, 1041, 1156
The Alpine Betrayal 520
The Alpine Christmas **371**
The Alpine Decoy **372**, 1065
The Alpine Fury **373**
The Alpine Series 206, 1497
Auntie Mayhem 385
Bantam of the Opera **374**, 744
The Bed-and-Breakfast Series 134, 135, 698, 699
The Emma Lord Series 22, 115
A Fit of Tempera **375**
Fowl Prey 145
Holy Terrors **376**, 1061
Murder, My Suite **377**, 1289

Dain, Catherine
Bet Against the House **378**
The Freddie O'Neal Series 398, 917, 921, 1266, 1700
Lay It on the Line 251, **379**
Sing a Song of Death **380**, 542
Walk a Crooked Mile **381**

Daley, Robert
Hands of a Stranger 1070
Wall of Brass 940

D'Amato, Barbara
The Cat Marsala Series 93, 141, 603, 604, 610, 637, 1052, 1182, 1215, 1266, 1388, 1398
Hard Tack **382**, 401, 1647
Hard Women **383**, 615, 760, 808, 1659
Hardball 161, **384**, 569, 636, 893, 894, 895, 1113, 1265, 1476, 1636, 1759

Dams, Jeanne M.
The Body in the Transept **385**

Daniel, David
The Heaven Stone **386**

Daniel, Mark
The Devil to Pay 538, 839, 1486, 1487

Dank, Gloria
Friends till the End 51, **387**

Danks, Denise
User Deadly 232, **388**, 610, 694, 1753

Davey, Jocelyn
The Ambrose Usher Series 228, 1366
A Capitol Offense 1043

Davidson, Diane Mott
Catering to Nobody 214, 245, 247, 374, 989, 1061, 1256, 1342
The Cereal Murders **389**
Dying for Chocolate 32, **390**, 1257, 1258, 1290
The Goldy Bear Series 244, 422, 698, 849, 1289, 1291

Davis, Dorothy Salisbury
A Death in the Life 404, 556, 713, 1300, 1638
Lullaby of Murder 814, 890
Scarlet Night 1519

Davis, J. Madison
Red Knight **391**
White Rook 197, **392**, 973, 1281, 1738

Davis, Kenn
As October Dies 788
Blood of Poets **393**
The Carver Bascombe Series 1178
The Forza Trap 589, 609
Melting Point 1010
Words Can Kill 762

Davis, Lindsey
The Marcus Didius Series 1390, 1448, 1450
The Silver Pigs 201, **394**, 1382, 1449

Davis, Robert
Kimura **395**, 1161, 1503

Davis, Thomas D.
Suffer Little Children **396**

Dawkins, Cecil
Clay Dancers 702
The Santa Fe Rembrandt 803

Dawson, Janet
The Jeri Howard Series 638, 639, 649, 921, 1182, 1185, 1490, 1506, 1700
Kindred Crimes 116, **397**, 648, 1183, 1184, 1505, 1701, 1702
Nobody's Child **398**

Day, Deforest
August Ice **399**, 624, 1472

Day, Dianne
The Strange Files of Fremont Jones **400**, 465

De Felitta, Frank
Funeral March 49, 62

Dean, S.F.X.
By Frequent Anguish 140, 178, 515, 1250, 1657, 1694
It Can't Be My Grave 1020
The Neil Kelly Series 1673
Such Pretty Toys 1043

Dean, Spencer
Credit for a Murder 178

DeAndrea, William L.
Cronus 528
Five O'Clock Lightning 160, 507
Killed in the Act 760
Killed in the Ratings 75, 1212, 1635, 1709
Killed on the Ice 872
Killed on the Rocks **401**, 1771
The Lunatic Fringe 36, 400, 560, 1079, 1654, 1787

The Manx Murders **402**
The Matt Cobb Series 1413

Deaver, Jeffrey Wilds
Death of a Blue Movie Star 1782
Hard News **403**, 760, 1671
The Lesson of Her Death 1531
Manhattan Is My Beat 19, 126, 127, 271, 312, **404**, 749, 755, 1434
Mistress of Justice **405**, 851, 852, 853, 963
Praying for Sleep 796, 1499

Debin, David
Nice Guys Finish Dead 211, **406**

DeBrosse, Jim
Hidden City **407**
Southern Cross **408**

DeFelice, Jim
Coyote Bird **409**

Deford, Frank
The Spy on the Deuce Court 129

Deighton, Len
The Bernard Samson Series 647
Catch a Falling Spy 995
City of Gold **410**
The Harry Palmer Series 188
The Ipcress File 567
SS-GB 38, 78, 419, 579, 824, 861, 1066
XPD 1466

Delahaye, Michael
Stalking-Horse 1466

Delman, David
The Last Gambit **411**, 1419

Delving, Michael
The Devil Finds Work 1031
Smiling, the Boy Fell Dead 1673

DeMarco, Gordon
October Heat 1583

DeMille, Nelson
By the Waters of Babylon 1473
Cathedral 1344
The Gold Coast **412**

Dentinger, Jane
Dead Pan **413**, 517, 1257
Death Mask 19, 1173, 1783
First Hit of the Season 15, 641, 1219
The Jocelyn O'Roarke Series 1782
Murder on Cue 174, 176, 516, 713, 1707
The Queen Is Dead 16, **414**, 1391

Dereske, Jo
Miss Zukas and the Island Murders **415**, 699
Miss Zukas and the Library Murders 1, **416**
The Miss Zukas Series 732

Devine, D.M.
The Devil at Your Elbow 941

Devon, Gary
Bad Desire 262, **417**, 1360, 1471

Dewey, Thomas B.
The "Mac" Series 667, 1326, 1327, 1328, 1329

Dexter, Colin
The Dead of Jericho 260, 1168, 1189, 1253, 1392
The Inspector Morse Series 25, 109, 1394, 1396, 1397
Last Bus to Woodstock 110
Service of All the Dead 89, 841, 1001, 1502
The Wench Is Dead **418**, 800

Author Index

Dibdin, Michael
The Tryst 1412

Dick, Philip K.
The Man in the High Castle 419

Dickens, Charles
The Mystery of Edwin Drood 1407

Dickinson, Peter
The Glass-Sided Ant's Nest 586
King & Joker 1697
The Last House-Party 402
Skeleton-in-Waiting 419
The Yellow Room Conspiracy 420

Dickson, Carter
He Wouldn't Kill Patience 1605
The Sir Henry Merrivale Series 471

Diehl, William
Hooligans 1344, 1611, 1612, 1613
Primal Fear **421**, 651, 1014, 1283
Sharky's Machine 306, 1696

Dietz, Denise
Beat Up a Cookie **422**
The Ellie Bernstein Series 849
Throw Darts at a Cheesecake 135, **423**, 457, 959, 1290

Dillon, Ellis
Death at Crane's Court 530

Dobyns, Stephen
The Charlie Bradshaw Series 495
Saratoga Longshot 133, 1190
Saratoga Swimmer 171, 540, 573

Doherty, P.C.
The Crown in Darkness 265, 1302, 1303
The Death of a King 1376, 1467
The Fate of Princes **424**, 1375, 1469
The Hugh Corbett Series 243, 512, 1404
The Masked Man **425**
Murder Wears a Cowl **426**
The Prince of Darkness **427**, 1624
Satan in St. Mary's 883, 1081, 1082, 1084
Tapestry of Murders 1175

Dolittle, Jerome
Body Scissors 1613

Dominic, R.B.
Epitaph for a Lobbyist 1634
Murder in High Places 1169

Donald, Anabel
The Glass Ceiling **428**

Donaldson, D.J.
Blood on the Bayou **429**, 476, 478, 974, 975, 1499
Cajun Nights 303, 391
The Kit Franklin/Andy Broussard Series 976
New Orleans Requiem **430**
No Mardi Gras for the Dead **431**, 1493, 1726

Doody, Margaret
Aristotle, Detective 201, 394, 883, 1382, 1449

Doolittle, Jerome
Bear Hug 344, **432**, 1753
Body Scissors 263, **433**, 521, 939, 1000, 1100, 1312, 1472
Kill Story **434**
Stranglehold 159, 388, **435**, 539, 850, 1353
The Tom Bethany Series 485, 764, 864, 1423

Dorner, Marjorie
Blood Kin 252, **436**, 1637, 1724
Family Closets 694, 959, 1157

Freeze Frame 502, 563, 1471

Doss, James D.
The Shaman Sings 1680

Dougherty, Kathleen
Moth to the Flame **437**, 756, 1174

Douglas, Carole Nelson
Cat on a Blue Monday **438**
Catnap 167, 181, **439**, 1733
Good Morning, Irene **440**, 519, 1029, 1164, 1298
Good Night, Mr. Holmes 131, **441**, 834, 926
The Irene Adler Series 400, 465, 835, 924, 930, 1028, 1030, 1259, 1260
Irene at Large **442**
Irene's Last Waltz 81
The Midnight Louie Series 20, 169, 180
Pussyfoot **443**

Douglas, Lauren Wright
The Daughters of Artemis 1356
Ninth Life **444**, 946, 1461, 1462

Downing, Warwick
A Clear Case of Murder 199, 240, **445**
The Mountains West of Town 793, 1570
The Player 200
The Water Cure 240, 391, **446**, 1582

Drake, Alison
Black Moon 1058
High Strangeness **447**
Tango Key 96, 804, 1088

Dreyer, Eileen
Bad Medicine 1051
A Man to Die For **448**, 658, 931, 932, 934, 974

Drummond, John Keith
Mass Murder **449**
The Matilda Worthing Series 1112
'Tis the Season to Be Dying 1208

Drummond, June
Junta 1114
The Saboteurs 1114

Du Maurier, Daphne
Rebecca 502

Ducker, Bruce
Bankroll **450**, 1040

Duffy, James
A Very Venetian Murder **1187**

Duffy, Margaret
The Lanley and Gillard Series 1539
Man of Blood **451**
A Murder of Crows 1518, 1681
Rook-Shoot **452**
Who Killed Cock Robin? **453**, 1420

Dukthas, Anne
A Time for the Death of a King 243

Dulaney, Harris
One Kiss Led to Another **454**

Dumas, Alexandre
The Man in the Iron Mask 425

Dunant, Sarah
Birthmarks 304, 308, 428, **455**, 1125, 1143, 1541
Fatlands 1094
Under My Skin 309, **456**

Dunbar, Sophie
Behind Eclaire's Doors **457**

Dunbar, Tony
Crooked Man 194

Duncan, W. Glenn
Rafferty: Fatal Sisters **458**
The Rafferty Series 7, 352, 354
Rafferty's Rules 8, 1616

Dundee, Wayne
The Burning Season 141, 319, 1384, 1386
The Joe Hannibal Series 862
The Skintight Shroud 190, **459**

Dundee, Wayne D.
The Skintight Shroud 500, 1019, 1648

Dunham, Mikel
Casting for Murder 1003

Dunlap, Susan
As a Favor 771, 772, 1089, 1528, 1687
The Bohemian Connection 966
Death and Taxes **460**, 1087
Diamond in the Buff **461**
The Jill Smith Series 59, 219, 447, 804, 925, 927, 967, 968, 969, 970, 971, 1077, 1086, 1222, 1225, 1226, 1452, 1504, 1515, 1523, 1525, 1526
The Kiernan O'Shaughnessy Series 774, 1051, 1490
Not Exactly a Brahmin 1170, 1180
Pious Deception 79, 92, 323, 326, 397, **462**, 634, 1795
Rogue Wave 80, 302, 321, 322, 324, 430, 431, **463**, 478, 974, 975
Time Expired **464**

Dunn, Carola
The Winter Garden Mystery **465**

Dunne, Colin
Retrieval 1456

Dunning, John
Booked to Die 9, 223, 224, **466**, 611, 1054, 1764
The Bookman's Wake **467**

E

Early, Jack
A Creative Kind of Killer 40, 146, 282, 703, 1350, 1663, 1684
Donato and Daughter 1227
Donato and Daughter 150, 805, 858, 1077, 1222, 1224, 1443
Razzamatazz 1663

Eastburn, Joseph
Kiss Them Goodbye **468**

Ebersohn, Wessel
Divide the Night 1114
A Lonely Place to Die 1114

Eccles, Marjorie
Death of a Good Woman 230
The Gil Mayo Series 1479
The Inspector Gil Mayo Series 367, 678
Late of This Parish **469**
The Mayo and Kite Series 504
More Deaths than One **470**, 1708

Eco, Umberto
The Name of the Rose 544, 545, 1203, 1301, 1302, 1303, 1467, 1470

Eddenden, A.E.
Murder on the Thirteenth **471**

Edwards, Ruth Dudley
Clubbed to Death **472**, 911, 912

The English School of Murder 451

Eichler, Selma
Murder Can Kill Your Social Life 16, **473**

Eickoff, Randy Lee
The Gombeen Man **474**, 657

Eidson, Bill
Dangerous Waters **475**

Elkins, Aaron
Dead Men's Hearts **476**
A Deceptive Clarity 1568
Fellowship of Fear 351
The Gideon Oliver Series 430, 1071, 1579
A Glancing Light 345, **477**, 1508, 1509, 1714
Make No Bones 431, **478**, 1726
Old Bones 1409, 1493
Old Scores **479**
Rotten Lies 481
A Wicked Slice **480**

Elkins, Charlotte
Rotten Lies **481**, 1195
A Wicked Slice 317, 318, **480**, 614, 1405

Ellin, Stanley
The Bind 1612
The Dark Fantastic 1633
The Luxembourg Run 3, 617
Mirror on the Wall 105

Elliott, Thornton
Hard Guy 1288, 1589, 1677

Elliott, Thorton
Hard Guy **482**, 1210

Ellison, Harlan
Mefisto in Onyx 1276
No Doors, No Windows 241

Ellroy, James
American Tabloid 276, 277, 1421
The Big Nowhere 498, 1161, 1177
The Black Dahlia 278, 279, 280, 1422, 1609
Blood on the Moon 185, 292, 1193, 1433
Brown's Requiem 717
L.A. Confidential **483**, 1025
White Jazz 1644

Elward, James
Monday's Child Is Dead **484**

Ely, Ron
East Beach **485**
Night Shadows 164, **486**

Emerson, Earl
Fat Tuesday 819
Help Wanted: Orphans Preferred **487**
Morons and Madmen **488**
The Portland Laugher **489**
The Thomas Black Series 39, 815, 818, 863, 865, 869, 1384, 1386, 1604, 1754, 1765
The Vanishing Smile **490**
Yellow Dog Party **491**

Engel, Howard
The Benny Cooperman Series 1766
A City Called July 1757
Murder on Location 992, 1131, 1519, 1684, 1768, 1770

Enger, L.L.
Comeback 118, 624, 1145, 1204, 1206
Strike **492**
Swing 58, 162, **493**, 505, 574, 613, 1205, 1718

Enger, Leif
Strike **492**
Swing **493**

Enger, Len
Strike **492**

Enger, Lin
Swing **493**

Engleman, Paul
Catch a Fallen Angel 1350
Dead in Center Field 50, 160, 493, 505, 507, 508, 510, 574, 613, 1205
The Man with My Name **494**
The Mark Renzler Series 1206, 1684
Who Shot Longshot Sam? **495**

Epperson, S.K.
Dumford Blood 267, 268

Epstein, Charlotte
Murder at the Friendship Hotel 261, **496**, 1743

Erskine, Margaret
The Septimus Finch Series 204, 1179

Estleman, Loren D.
Amos Walker 1060
The Amos Walker Series 41, 147, 190, 833, 862, 863, 865, 1019, 1056, 1059, 1347, 1373, 1374, 1384, 1386, 1440, 1646, 1648
Downriver 1647
Kill Zone 238
King of the Corner **497**
The Macklin Series 1297
Motor City Blues 282
Motown **498**, 1178, 1421
P.I. Files 1348
Peeper 494, **499**, 1697
Red Highway 183
Roses Are Red 553
Sherlock Holmes vs. Dracula 440, 1407, 1654
Sugartown 319
Sweet Women Lie **500**
Whiskey River 276, 277, 279, **501**, 1207, 1536, 1609

Eubank, Judith
Crossover 68, 69, **502**

Evanovich, Janet
One for the Money 155, **503**, 1413

Evans, Geraldine
Dead Before Morning **504**

Evelyn, John Michael
Seeds of Murder **1642**

Evers, Crabbe
Bleeding Dodger Blue **505**
The Duffy House Series 613
Fear in Fenway **506**, 1536
Murder in Wrigley Field 493, **507**, 510, 646, 871
Murderer's Row 1718
Tigers Burning **508**

Everson, David
False Profits **509**
Rebound 646
Recount 1752
Suicide Squeeze 493, 506, 508, **510**, 574, 613, 646, 1205, 1400

Eversz, Robert
The Bottom Line Is Murder 986
False Profit **511**, 565

Eyre, Elizabeth
Death of the Duchess **512**, 1403, 1404

F

Fackler, Elizabeth
Barbed Wire 612

Faherty, Terence
Deadstick **513**
Die Dreaming **514**
Live to Regret 12
The Lost Keats **515**, 1250

Fairleigh, Runa
An Old-Fashioned Mystery 220, 401

Falkirk, Richard
Blackstone 941, 1083, 1404
The Blackstone Series 1403

Farrell, Gillian B.
Alibi for an Actress 15, 20, 413, **516**, 770, 1228, 1247, 1248, 1391, 1782, 1783
Murder and a Muse 16, 414, **517**, 1465

Farris, John
The Trouble at Harrison High 144

Faust, Ron
Fugitive Moon 271
In the Forest of the Night 1589
When She Was Bad **518**

Fawcett, Bill
Cats in Space 619

Fawcett, Quinn
Napoleon Must Die **519**

Feddersen, Connie
Dead in the Water 900

Feddersen, Connie
The Amanda Hazard Series 902
Dead in the Cellar 313, **520**, 1516
Dead in the Water 1517

Feegel, John R.
Death Sails the Bay 462

Feilstrup, Margaret
Sweet Narcissus 1045

Feinstein, John
Running Mates **521**

Feldmeyer, Dean
Viper Quarry **522**

Femling, Jean
Hush, Money **523**

Fenady, Andrew J.
The Man with Bogart's Face 860

Fennelly, Tony
The Glory Hole Murders 726, 1150, 1151, 1572

Fenster, Bob
The Last Page 119, 177, 223, **524**, 882, 895, 1379

Ferrars, E.X.
The Crime and the Crystal 255

Ferrigno, Robert
The Cheshire Moon 102, 408, 518, **525**, 710, 1561
The Horse Latitudes 227, 295, **526**, 653, 709, 755, 854, 1006, 1152

Fielding, Joy
Don't Cry Now 275
Kiss Mommy Goodbye 128
Tell Me No Secrets 769

Fieldstrup, Margaret
Deception Island 1043
Dreamland 1044

Filson, Sidney
Nightwalker **527**

Fink, John
The Leaf Boat 1277

Finney, Jack
Time and Again 1536

Fish, Robert L.
The Murder League 1518

Fisher, David E.
Hostage One 825

Fiske, Dorothy
Bound to Murder 1275, 1559

Flannery, Sean
Broken Idols 706
Counterstrike 248
Crossed Swords **528**
False Prophets 1278
The Hollow Men 550, 685, 810
Moving Targets 365, **529**

Fleming, Ian
The James Bond Series 188, 567, 996

Fleming, Joan
Kill or Cure 587

Fliegal, Richard
The Allerton Avenue Precinct Series 856

Flood, Norman
To Killashea 23, 104, 474, **530**, 657

Flora, Kate Clark
Chosen for Death 803
Death in a Funhouse Mirror **531**

Fluke, Joanne
Video Kill 749

Flusfeder, D.L.
Man Kills Woman 935

Flynn, Don
Ed Fitzgerald Series 130, 1309
Murder Isn't Enough 1053, 1719
Murder on the Hudson 166, 1261, 1368, 1369
A Suitcase in Berlin 86, **532**

Follett, Ken
Eye of the Needle 78, 410, 579, 787, 1679, 1746
Night over Water 584

Forbes, Colin
Target Five 1530

Ford, G.M.
Who the Hell Is Wanda Fuca? 728

Forrest, Katherine V.
The Beverly Malibu 47, 202, **533**, 634, 1126, 1323, 1796
The Kate Delafield Series 927, 1170
Murder at the Nightwood Bar 83
Murder by Tradition **534**

Forrest, Richard
Bea and Lyon Wentworth Series 162
A Child's Garden of Death 384, 387, 1634, 1678
Death on the Mississippi **535**, 693, 836, 901, 1108, 1725

Forster, R.A.
Keeping Counsel 940, 1465

Forsyth, Frederick
The Day of the Jackal 60, 78, 786, 1679

Foster, Marion
The Monarchs Are Flying 202

Fowler, Earlene
The Benni Harper Series 1516
Fool's Puzzle 362, **536**, 559
Irish Chain **537**

Fox, Peter
The Trail of the Reaper 1606

Foy, George
Coaster 1037

Foy, Peter
Challenge 582

Francis, Dick
Blood Sport 573
Bolt 52
Come to Grief **538**
Comeback **539**
Dead Cert 133
Flying Finish 1037, 1486
Longshot **540**, 1068, 1172, 1190
Straight **541**
Whip Hand 839, 1487

Francome, John
Outsider 538, 839, 1486
Stone Cold 1487

Frankel, Valerie
A Body to Die For 554
Deadline for Murder 473
Prime Time for Murder 380, **542**

Frankos, Laura
St. Oswald's Niche 250

Fraser, Antonia
The Cavalier Case **543**, 1144
The Jemima Shore Series 269, 1399
Oxford Blood 1142
A Splash of Red 729

Frazer, Margaret
The Bishop's Tale **544**
The Boy's Tale **545**
The Sister Frevisse Series 631, 1203, 1301

Freeborn, Peter
Hollywood Requiem **546**

Freedman, J.F.
Against the Wind 102, 333, **547**, 651, 666, 1331, 1577, 1640, 1649

Freeling, Nicholas
Inspector Van Der Valk Series 204
Not as Far as Velma **548**
Sand Castles **549**

Freeman, Gillian
Diary of a Nazi Lady 584

Freemantle, Brian
Charlie M 995
The Run Around **550**, 706

Freidman, Philip
Reasonable Doubt 412

Frey, James N.
Came a Dead Cat **551**
A Long Way to Die 1010
Winter of the Wolves **552**, 553, 728, 822

Friedman, Gary
Gun Men **553**, 618, 822

Friedman, Harry
Deadly Stakes **1745**

Friedman, Kinky
God Bless John Wayne **554**
The Kinky Friedman Series 320, 1423, 1587
Musical Chairs **555**

Friedman, Linda
Deadly Stakes **1745**

Friedman, Mickey
A Temporary Ghost **556**, 724, 1300, 1476, 1671
Venetian Mask 1002, 1004

Friedman, Philip
Inadmissible Evidence **557**
Reasonable Doubt 66, 445, **558**, 1016, 1090, 1106, 1577, 1640

Frommer, Sara Hoskinson
Buried in Quilts 536, **559**
Murder in C Major 1304, 1305

Frost, Mark
The 6 Messiahs **560**
The List of 7 400, 924, 926, 1438, 1787

Furst, Alan
Night Soldiers 584

Fyfield, Frances
Deep Sleep 308, **561**, 642
A Question of Guilt **562**, 598, 1343
Shadows on the Mirror 436, **563**, 751

G

Gage, Edwin
Phoenix No More 262, 1794

Gallison, Kate
Bury the Bishop **564**
Jersey Monkey **565**
The Nick Magaracz Series 869

Garber, Joseph R.
Vertical Run **566**

Gardner, Erle Stanley
The Perry Mason Series 239, 704, 1135

Gardner, John
The Moriarty Series 1403
The Return of Moriarty 131, 441, 1404
Win, Lose or Die **567**

Garfield, Brian
Fear in a Handful of Dust 1152
Hopscotch 550, 633, 706
Manifest Destiny 36
Necessity 5, 1128, 1351, 1381, 1746, 1762
The Paladin 37, 38, 410, 680
Recoil 395
Relentless 793
The Threepersons Hunt 700, 701, 792, 793

Garton, Ray
Trade Secrets **568**

Garwood, Judith
Bet Against the House 378
Lay It on the Line 379
Make Friends with Murder 371, **569**, 603, 894, 908, 1245
Sing a Song of Death 380
Walk a Crooked Mile 381

Gash, Joe
The El Murders 1425
Newspaper Murders 143

Gash, Jonathan
The Gondola Scam 1004, 1510
The Great California Game **570**, 616, 791
Jade Woman 296, 1243, 1743, 1744
The Judas Pair 1241, 1563, 1630
The Lies of Fair Ladies **571**, 1722
The Lovejoy Series 1068, 1069, 1240, 1564, 1565, 1566
The Sin Within Her Smile **572**
The Very Last Gambado 479, 1036

Gat, Dimitri
Personal **208**

Gault, William Campbell
Blood on the Boards 174, 176

Geddes, Paul
Codename Hangman 1456

Geller, Michael
Dead Fix 541, **573**, 871
Dead Last 170, 171, 1190
Major League Murder 493, 505, 506, 507, 508, 612, 652, 1205
Three Strikes, You're Dead **574**, 1059

George, Elizabeth
For the Sake of Elena 677, 1141
A Great Deliverance 191, 358, 366, 586, 676, 751, 841, 1132, 1143, 1343, 1392, 1393, 1395, 1554, 1556
The Inspector Lynley Series 356, 357, 1361, 1394, 1396, 1454, 1670, 1773
Missing Joseph **575**
Payment in Blood **576**, 644, 675, 898, 1197
Playing for the Ashes **577**
A Suitable Vengeance 417, **578**
Well-Schooled in Murder 563, 790

Gerson, Jack
Death Squad London **579**, 1161
Death's Head Berlin 787, 914
Deathwatch '39 1792

Gertsner, Nickolae
Dark Veil 139

Gibbs, Tony
Capitol Offense **580**
Landfall 48, **581**
Running Fix **582**, 1037
Shadow Queen 69, 252, 513, **583**, 1115

Gidel, Daranna
Criminal Seduction **1211**

Gifford, Thomas
The Assassini 60, 1429
The Cavanaugh Quest 105, 823
The Glendower Legacy 583
Hollywood Gothic 1574
The Man from Lisbon 129
Praetorian 410, **584**
The Suspense Is Killing Me **1102**
Wind Chill Factor 1428

Gilbert, Anthony
The Arthur Crook Series 597, 598

Gilbert, Dale
The Black Star Murders 607

Gilbert, Dale L.
The Black Star Murders 814, 1047, 1048
The Carter Winfield Series 608
Murder Begins at Home **585**

Gilbert, Michael
The Black Seraphim 587
Blood and Judgement 1402, 1502, 1639
The Body of a Girl 563
The Doors Open 1367
End-Game 451, 961
The Killing of Katie Steelstock 576
Paint, Gold and Blood 1507
Smallbone Deceased 228, 1139

Gilbertod, Michael
Death Has Deep Roots 562

Giles, Kenneth
Murder Pluperfect 738

Gill, B.M.
Death Drop 228
The Fifth Rapunzel 586
Time and Time Again 587

Gill, Bartholomew
Death of a Joyce Scholar 360, 1134
The Inspector McGarr Series 549
McGarr and the Method of Descartes 530
The McGarr Series 23
Neon Caesar **1128**

Gilman, Dorothy
The Amazing Mrs. Pollifax 1163
Caravan 1298
Mrs. Pollifax and the Whirling Dervish **588**, 1518
Mrs. Pollifax on the China Station 496
The Mrs. Pollifax Series 45, 175, 1098, 1112, 1246, 1571, 1594
The Unexpected Mrs. Pollifax 996

Gilpatrick, Noreen
The Piano Man **589**, 816, 951, 1732

Gilpin, T.G.
Death of a Fantasy Life **590**
Is Anybody There? **591**, 1036

Girard, James Preston
The Late Man **592**, 1590

Girdner, Jacqueline
Adjusted to Death 51

Girdner, Jaqueline
Adjusted to Death 214, 215, 245, 423, **593**, 1255, 1258, 1543, 1748
Fat-Free and Fatal 1065
The Kate Jasper Series 115, 155, 246, 1117, 1388, 1749
The Last Resort **594**, 990, 1146, 1256
A Stiff Critique **595**, 600, 744
Tea-Totally Dead **596**

Giroux, E.X.
A Death for a Dancing Doll **597**
A Death for a Dodo **598**
A Death for Adonis 1658
The Dying Room **599**

Gladstone, Nancy
Mommy and the Murder 246, 595, **600**

Glass, Leslie
Burning Time 887
Hanging Time **601**
To Do No Harm **602**, 1699, 1799

Glen, Alison
Showcase 297, 373, **603**, 1641
Trunk Show **604**

Godard, Kenneth W.
Balefire 1344

Goddard, Kenneth W.
Wildfire **605**

Goldberg, Lee
My Gun Has Bullets **606**

Goldman, William
The Color of Light 546
Heat 132
Marathon Man 1188, 1456

Goldsborough, Robert
Fade to Black **607**, 1047
Silver Spire **608**

Goldstein, Arthur D.
Nobody's Sorry He Got Killed 1447, 1621

Gollin, James
Broken Consort 589, **609**, 1191, 1192, 1304
The Philomel Foundation 1192
The Verona Passamezzo 1020

Gonzalez, Gloria
The Thirteenth Apostle **610**

Goodrum, Charles A.
The Best Cellar 1275
Carnage of the Realm 1186
Dewey Decimated 1031, 1627
A Slip of the Tong 296, 297, 479, **611**, 1559
The Werner-Bok Library Series 416

Gordon, Alison
The Dead Pull Hitter 160, 505, 506, 507, **612**, 1053, 1718
The Kate Henry Series 1195
Night Game 481, **613**
Safe at Home **614**
Striking Out **615**

Gordon, Deborah
Beating the Odds 446

Gores, Joe
32 Cadillacs **616**, 736
The D.K.A. Series 123
Dead Man 3, **617**, 1354, 1760
Dead Skip 266
The DKA Series 199
Gone, No Forwarding 213
Hammett 860, 1207, 1270, 1674, 1675
Interface 1010
Menaced Assassin **618**
A Time of Predators 165, 1457, 1747
Wolf Time 433, 632, 823, 1188, 1312

Gorman, Ed
The Autumn Dead 1355, 1457, 1579, 1653
The Black Lizard Anthology of Crime Fiction 1122
Cat Crimes 167, **619**, 1299
Cat Crimes II **620**
Dark Crimes: Great Noir Fiction From the '50's to the '90's **621**
Invitation to Murder 1348
Night Kills **622**, 1072, 1121
The Night Remembers 305, 396, **623**, 1326, 1327, 1329, 1619, 1620

Gosling, Paula
The Body in Blackwater Bay **624**
Death Penalties 328, 366, **625**, 1159, 1244, 1480, 1669, 1670, 1708
A Few Dying Words 268, **626**
Solo Blues 609
The Wychford Murders 367

Gottesfeld, Gary
White Angel 1051

Gough, Laurence
Hot Shots 334, **627**, 1417

Goulart, Ron
Even the Butler Was Poor **628**
Now He Thinks He's Dead **629**, 1710
The Tijuana Bible **630**

Grace, C.L.
The Eye of God 426, **631**
The Fate of the Princes 265
The Katherine Swinbrooke Series 545
A Shrine of Murders 544, 1203, 1301

Grady, James
River of Darkness **632**, 811, 823, 1109
Runner in the Street 189
Six Days of the Condor 1284
Thunder **633**

Grafton, Sue
F Is for Fugitive **634**, 1180, 1219, 1265
G Is for Gumshoe **635**, 1181, 1229, 1264
H Is for Homicide 396, **636**, 1269, 1798
I Is for Innocent **637**, 837
#A Is for Alibi 919
K Is for Killer **638**
The Kinsey Millhone Series 92, 94, 96, 161, 323, 378, 486, 917, 918, 920, 921, 1183, 1184, 1220, 1569
L Is for Lawless **639**

Graham, Caroline
Death in Disguise 358, **640**
Death of a Hollow Man 76, 357, **641**, 1707, 1768, 1769
The Inspector Barnaby Series 356, 385, 469, 575, 577, 1397, 1480
The Killings at Badger's Drift 578, 1393, 1395, 1556

Graham, James
The Run to Morning 474, 657, 961, 1760

Graham, Mark
The Harbinger 1633

Granger, Ann
Cold in the Earth 358, 640, **642**, 897, 1408
A Fine Place for Death 357, **643**
The Meredith Mitchell/Allan Markby Series 307
Murder Among Us **644**, 1553
Say It with Poison 896
A Season for Murder 107, 308, **645**

Granger, Bill
The British Cross 37, 38, 824, 1278
Drover and the Zebras **646**
The Last Good German **647**
The November Man Series 528, 552, 810
Public Murders 306, 580, 1628, 1712
Schism 188

Grant, Linda
Blind Trust 511, 986, 1701
The Catherine Saylor Series 918, 921, 1182, 1184, 1185, 1489, 1490, 1506, 1700, 1798
Love nor Money 637, **648**, 1220, 1702
Random Access Murder 84, 397, 919, 1183, 1703
A Woman's Place 232, **649**

Grant-Adamson, Lesley
Curse the Darkness 561, 1145, 1642, 1658
Guilty Knowledge 1126
The Rain Morgan Series 382
Threatening Eye 1730
Too Many Questions 269, 308, 455
Wild Justice 168, 1369

Gray, A.W.
Bino 1280, 1357
The Bino Phillips Series 1576
Bino's Blues **650**
In Defense of Judges 1015
Killings **651**
The Man Offside **652**, 1596

Prime Suspect **653**

Gray, Gallagher
Hubbert and Lil: Partners in Crime **654**

Grayson, Richard
Death Off Stage **655**
The Inspector Gautier Series 519, 943
The Murders at Impasse Louvain 942, 1049

Greber, Judith
I'd Rather Be in Philadelphia **1378**
Philly Stakes **1379**
With Friends Like These **1380**

Greeley, Andrew M.
The Blackie Ryan Series 1101
Happy Are the Merciful **656**
Happy Are Those Who Thirst for Justice 916
Irish Gold **657**
Virgin and Martyr 915

Green, Christine
Deadly Admirer **658**
Deadly Errand **659**, 931, 934, 1130, 1656
Deadly Practice **660**
Die in My Dreams **661**
The Kate Kinsella Series 932, 1129

Green, George Dawes
The Caveman's Valentine 271, **662**, 952, 993, 1578
The Juror 794, 1623

Green, Jen
Reader, I Murdered Him **663**, 1073, 1267, 1299

Green, Kate
Black Dreams 993
Night Angel 91, 253, 514, **664**, 674, 746, 767, 937, 964, 1092, 1102, 1183, 1355, 1453, 1579, 1665, 1683
Shattered Moon 811, 846, 1062, 1308
Shooting Star 173, 252, 332, **665**, 769, 1247, 1248, 1514, 1763

Green, Vincent
The Price of Victory **666**

Greenberg, Martin H.
Cat Crimes 619
Cat Crimes II **620**

Greene, Hugh
The Rivals of Sherlock Holmes 24

Greenleaf, Stephen
Blood Type 263, **667**, 906
Book Case 31, 281, 623, **668**, 723, 816
Death Bed 819, 1019
The John Marshall Tanner Series 28, 29, 30, 818, 877, 1648
Southern Cross **669**
State's Evidence 704, 1662, 1688

Greenwood, D.M.
Clerical Errors 61, 136, 137, 138, 235, **670**, 1706, 1730
Idol Bones **671**
The Theodora Braithwaite Series 564, 799, 1239, 1339
Unholy Ghosts **672**

Greenwood, L.B.
Sherlock Holmes and the Thistle of Scotland 131, 440, 441, 442, 1654

Grice, Julia
The Cutting Hours **673**

Grimes, Martha
The Anodyne Necklace 562
The Dirty Duck 1343
The End of the Pier 599, **674**
Help the Poor Struggler 640
The Inspector Jury Series 356, 575, 577, 578, 790, 1361
The Man with a Load of Mischief 1393, 1669
The Old Contemptibles **675**
The Old Fox Deceiv'd 25, 576, 1197, 1554, 1555
The Old Silent 191, **676**, 1395
The Richard Jury Series 563

Grimes, Terris McMahan
Somebody Else's Child 761

Grindle, Lucretia
The Killing of Ellis Martin 230, **677**
So Little to Die For **678**

Grisham, John
The Chamber 650, **679**
The Client 680, 1724
The Firm 333, 547, 1015, 1110, 1531
The Pelican Brief 102, 405, 553, 633, **681**, 852, 1312, 1435
The Rainmaker 985
A Time to Kill 1017

Grissom, Ken
Big Fish 616, **682**, 687, 904, 1324
Drop-Off 905, 1336
Drowned Man's Key **683**

Gross, Ken
Hell Bent 23, 104, **684**, 1008

Gruenfeld, Lee
All Fall Down 1633

Guillou, Jan
Enemy's Enemy **685**

Gunning, Sally
Hot Water 70, **686**, 696, 1722
Ice Water 337, 1099
The Peter Bartholomew Series 2, 336, 339, 1464
Rough Water **687**
Still Water **688**
Troubled Water **689**
Underwater 1078

Gur, Batya
Murder on a Kibbutz **690**
The Saturday Morning Murder **691**

Gurr, David
A Woman Called Scylla 1746

Guterson, David
Snow Falling on Cedars **692**, 1218

Guthrie, A.B. Jr.
The Chick Charleston Series 777, 779, 780, 1584
No Second Wind 13
Playing Catch-Up 757, 758, 1307

Guthrie, Al
Grave Murder 1430, 1725
Murder by Tarot 629, **693**, 1431
Private Murder 101

H

Haddad, C.A.
Caught in the Shadows 232, **694**, 1665

Haddam, Jane
Not a Creature Was Stirring **695**
Quoth the Raven 696
A Stillness in Bethlehem **697**

Hadley, Joan
The Night-Blooming Cereus 1484, 1485
The Theo Bloomer Series 1064

Hagberg, David
Countdown 756
Crossed Swords **528**
Crossfire 685
Moving Targets **529**

Hager, Jean
Blooming Murder 135, 244, 375, **698**
Dead and Buried 415, 595, **699**, 803
Ghostland **700**
The Grandfather Medicine 1232, 1430, 1437, 1781
The Grandmother Medicine 1153
The Iris House Series 134, 377
The Mitch Bushyhead Series 310, 311
The Molly Bearpaw Series 778, 1680, 1686
Night Walker 1431, 1739, 1742, 1756
Ravenmocker **701**, 1086, 1087, 1332, 1550, 1607, 1625, 1626
The Redbird's Cry **702**

Haggard, H. Rider
King Solomon's Mines 1298
She 1298

Haiblum, Isidore
Bad Neighbors **703**

Hailey, J.P.
The Baxter Trust 877
Juror **714**
The Naked Typist 236, **704**, 1022
The Steve Winslow Series 237, 923
Strangler **715**
The Underground Man 144, **705**

Hall, Adam
Quiller KGB **706**

Hall, James W.
Bones of Coral 98, 408, 525, 632, 682, **707**, 784, 785, 823, 1204, 1560, 1763
Gone Wild **708**, 1137
Hard Aground 4, **709**, 952, 1012, 1014, 1024, 1325, 1561
Mean High Tide **710**
Tropical Freeze 72, 653, 683, 854, 973
Tropical Heat 1058
Under Cover of Daylight 981, 1747

Hall, Mary Bowen
Emma Chizzit and the Mother Lode Marauder **711**
Emma Chizzit and the Napa Nemesis **712**, 739, 1245, 1790
Emma Chizzit and the Queen Anne Killer 376, **713**, 1235, 1661
Emma Chizzit and the Sacramento Stalker 972
The Emma Chizzit Series 284, 285, 761, 1234, 1446

Hall, Parnell
Actor 1387, 1714
Juror 236, **714**
Murder 1616
The Naked Typist **704**
The Stanley Hastings Series 494
Strangler **715**
The Underground Man **705**

Hall, Patricia
The Poison Pool 308

Hall, Robert Lee
The Benjamin Franklin Series 1148

Hallahan, William H.
The Search for Joseph Tully 266
The Trade 1456

Halleran, Tucker
A Cool Clear Death 872, 1005

Halliday, Brett
She Woke to Darkness 984, 1044

Halliday, Fred
Murder in the Kitchen 151, 152

Hallinan, Timothy
Everything but the Squeal 262, **716**, 1217
Incinerator **717**
The Simeon Grist Series 301
Skin Deep **718**

Hamill, Pete
Dirty Laundry 1350
The Guns of Heaven 961

Hamilton, Donald
Death of a Citizen 567

Hammett, Dashiell
The Thin Man 630, 999

Hammond, Gerald
A Brace of Skeet **719**
Home to Roost **720**
The Keith Calder Series 109, 113
Whose Dog Is It? 287, 290

Handberg, Ron
Cry Vengeance 812, 1276, 1641
Savage Justice 492, **721**, 1428

Handler, David
The Man Who Cancelled Himself **722**
The Man Who Series 546
The Man Who Would Be F. Scott Fitzgerald 259, 287, **723**, 1358
The Stewart Hoag Series 257, 484, 1100, 1464
The Woman Who Fell From Grace **724**

Hanlon, Sean
The Cold Front 407, 775, 950, 1261, 1549, 1580
The Frozen Franklin **725**
The Prestor John Riordan Series 1581

Hanna, Edward B.
The Whitechapel Horrors 442

Hanna, Jack
The Lion's Share **1605**

Hansen, Joseph
The Boy Who Was Buried This Morning **726**
A Country of Old Men **727**
The Dave Brandstetter Series 1054, 1150, 1151, 1194, 1572, 1795, 1796

Hanson, Rick
Mortal Remains **728**
Spare Parts 708

Harcourt, Palma
Dance for Diplomats 453

Harding, Paul
The Brother Athelstan Series 544, 545, 1376, 1470
The Fate of Princes 424
The Masked Man 425
Murder Wears a Cowl 426
The Nightingale Gallery 265, 1303, 1377
The Prince of Darkness 427

Hardwick, Mollie
The Bandersnatch **729**, 801

Hare, Cyril
Tragedy at Law 228, 1139
The Wind Blows Death 1366

Harper, Brian
Deadly Pursuit 728

Harrington, William
Town on Trial **730**

Harris, Charlaine
The Aurora Teagarden Series 156, 416, 1516
A Bone to Pick 69, 457, **731**, 742, 801, 1409, 1569
The Julius House **732**
Real Murders 1, 415, 711
A Secret Rage 42
Sweet and Deadly 222

Harris, John
Pel and the Missing Persons **768**

Harris, Lee
The Christening Day Murder 138, **733**, 1451
The Christine Bennett Series 564, 1239, 1339
The Christmas Night Murder **734**, 799, 1237
The Good Friday Murder 1434, 1591
The Saint Patrick's Day Murder 137
The Yom Kippur Murder 136

Harris, Richard
Enemies 935
Honor Bound 66, 421, 547, 557, 558, 592, 735, 923, 1016, 1022, 1023, 1090, 1280, 1590, 1662

Harris, Robert
Enigma 994

Harris, Thomas
Black Sunday 248
Red Dragon 53, 229, 846, 980, 1154, 1165, 1166, 1279, 1425, 1427, 1737
The Silence of the Lambs 62, 99, 321, 323, 326, 651, 937, 1279, 1736

Harris, Timothy
Kyd for Hire 148, 342, 938, 1270

Harris, Will
Timor Mortis 1673

Harrison, Colin
Break and Enter 66, **735**, 1106, 1357

Harrison, Jamie
The Edge of the Crazies **736**

Harrison, Payne
Storming Intrepid 1513

Harrison, Ray
The Bragg and Morton Series 655, 943
Death of a Dancing Lady 1028, 1296
Death of an Honourable Member 942
Deathwatch 1292, 1293, 1294, 1295
Patently Murder **737**
Tincture of Death **738**, 1029, 1403
Why Kill Arthur Potter? 1049

Harriss, Will
The Bay Psalm Book Murder 223, 611, 1020, 1031, 1627
Noble Rot **739**, 1451, 1790

Harrod-Eagles, Cynthia
Death Watch **740**
The Inspector Slider Series 469

Hart, Carolyn G.
The Annie Laurance/Max Darling Series 334, 747, 983, 1064
The Annie Laurance Series 218, 376, 836, 1117, 1661
The Annie Laurence Series 732
The Christie Caper **741**
Dead Man's Island **742**, 1078
Death on Demand 160, 535, 777, 779, 1263
The Henrietta O'Dwyer Series 1497, 1547
Honeymoon with Murder 1120
A Little Class on Murder 119, 168, 387, **743**, 1379
Mint Julep Murder **744**
A Settling of Accounts 1565
Something Wicked 776, 781, 1500
Southern Ghost 1451

Hart, Ellen
Hallowed Murder 83, **745**, 971, 1042, 1133, 1194, 1323, 1461, 1797
Vital Lies 82, 516, **746**, 967

Hart, Jeanne
Some Die Young 889, 1664
Threnody for Two **747**

Hart, Roy
Breach of Promise **748**
A Pretty Place for a Murder 1555

Hartzmark, Gini
Final Option 1268
The Katherine Milholland Series 852
Principal Defense 405, 851, 1780

Harvester, Simon
Assassins Road 1473

Harvey, James Neal
By Reason of Insanity **749**
Flesh and Blood 940
Painted Ladies **750**, 1717

Harvey, John
The Charlie Resnick Series 643
Cold Light **751**
Cold Night 1050
Cutting Edge **752**
The Inspector Resnick Series 356, 678
Off Minor 740, **753**
The Wasted Years **754**

Hasford, Gustav
A Gypsy Good Time **755**

Hastings, Beverly
Don't Look Back 128

Hastings, Laura
The Peacock's Secret 68

Hastings, Michael
The Devil's Spy 1028, 1746

Hauser, Thomas
The Beethoven Conspiracy 609, 1304
The Hawthorne Group **756**

Hautman, Pete
Drawing Dead 855, 1672

Havill, Steven F.
Bitter Recoil **757**, 1021
Heartshot **758**, 1108, 1111
The Sheriff Bill Gastner Series 65

Haymon, S.T.
A Very Particular Murder **759**

Haynes, Conrad
Bishop's Gambit, Declined 1043, 1045, 1657

Hayter, Sparkle
What's a Girl Gotta Do? **760**, 1201, 1709, 1710

Haywood, Gar Anthony
The Aaron Gunner Series 1176, 1177, 1178, 1691
Bad News Travels Fast **761**
Fear of the Dark 393, 788, 938, 1481
Not Long for This World **762**

Head, Matthew
The Cabinda Affair 226

Heald, Tim
Business Unusual **763**, 1034, 1035, 1730
Murder at Moose Jaw 1418, 1770
The Simon Bogner Series 1036

Healy, Jeremiah
Act of God 93, **764**
Blunt Darts 938, 1326, 1328, 1602
Foursome **765**
The John Francis Cuddy Series 28, 29, 30, 94, 337, 341, 343, 344, 386, 432, 669, 816, 818, 863, 864, 939, 1269, 1271, 1272, 1327, 1400, 1440, 1615, 1646, 1703
Right to Die 435, 695, 850, 1329
So Like Sleep 1000, 1313
Yesterday's News 40, 335, 340, 668, 686, **766**, 922, 1074, 1358

Hearn, Daniel
Black Light 6, 406, **767**, 1202

Hebden, Mark
The Inspector Pel Series 549
Pel and the Bombers 548
Pel and the Missing Persons **768**

Heckler, Jonellen
Circumstances Unknown **769**
Final Tour **770**

Heffernan, William
Blood Rose 1165

Hegerty, Frances
Deep Sleep 561
A Question of Guilt **562**
Shadows on the Mirror **563**

Helgerson, Joel
Slow Burn 622

Heller, Keith
Man's Illegal Life 1083
Man's Storm 1083

Hendricks, Michael
Friends in High Places 542, **771**, 1799
Money to Burn 614, **772**, 1219, 1228, 1631, 1638

Hendricks, Vicki
Miami Purity **773**, 1560

Hendricksen, Louise
The Amy Prescott Series 325, 1129
Grave Secrets **774**
Lethal Legacy 1262
With Deadly Intent 322, 476, 658

Hendryx, James B.
All Titles 1785

Henry, Sue
Murder on the Iditarod Trail 725, **775**, 1549, 1550, 1551, 1580, 1581, 1786
Termination Dust 1552

Hensley, Joe L.
Color Him Guilty 558, 730, 1576, 1577, 1794
The Don Roback Series 704, 705, 777, 779, 780, 923, 1281
The Don Robak Series 1135
Fort's Law 1111, 1662

Hentoff, Nat
Robak's Cross 239
Song of Corpus Juris 1602

Hentoff, Nat
Blues for Charlie Darwin 856, 857, 1158
Internal Affairs 1362, 1363
The Man From Internal Affairs 1249, 1535, 1628, 1696

Hervey, Evelyn
The Man of Gold 737, 1295

Hess, Joan
The Arly Hanks Series 1111
The Claire Malloy Series 218, 593, 731, 732, 836, 967, 991, 1153, 1661
A Diet to Die For 215, **776**, 1118, 1147
Madness in Maggody **777**
The Maggody Series 22, 219, 970, 971, 983, 1153, 1432, 1685, 1687
Malice in Maggody 298, 143.1, 1741
Miracles in Maggody **778**
Mortal Remains in Maggody **779**
Murder at the Mimosa Inn 741, 746, 1316
O Little Town of Maggody **780**
A Really Cute Corpse 1477
Roll Over and Play Dead 522, **781**
Strangled Prose 119, 743, 803, 933, 1120, 1232, 1263, 1379, 1500

Hiaasen, Carl
Double Whammy 682, 707, 709, 949, 951, 1012, 1058, 1475, 1560, 1704
Native Tongue 34, 98, 102, 408, 525, 708, 710, **782**, 903, 1006, 1014, 1474, 1561, 1611
Skin Deep 568
Skin Tight 632, 707, **783**, 854, 1474
Stormy Weather **784**
Strip Tease 231, 606, 773, **785**
Tourist Season 707, 1015, 1475, 1582, 1612, 1613

Higgins, George V.
The Friends of Eddie Coyle 831

Higgins, Jack
Angel of Death 104, **786**
The Eagle Has Flown **787**
The Eagle Has Landed 37, 78, 410, 1679
Night of the Fox 584
Touch the Devil 474, 657, 1381

Higgins, Joan
A Little Death Music 559, 1304, 1305

Highsmith, Patricia
People Who Knock on the Door 88, 90, 1277, 1478
Strangers on a Train 1360, 1761
The Talented Mr. Ripley 450

Hilary, Richard
Behind the Fact 565, **788**
The Easy Barnes Series 1176
Snake in the Grasses 762

Hill, Peter
The Liars 1189

Hill, R. Lance
The Evil That Men Do 632, 1284, 1704

Hill, Reginald
Another Death in Venice 1004
Bones and Silence 675, 754, **789**
Child's Play 368
The Collaborators 420
The Dalziel and Pascoe Series 366, 470, 504, 625, 678, 752, 1160, 1322, 1361, 1394, 1454, 1479
Dream of Darkness **1412**
A Killing Kindness 260
A Pinch of Snuff 676, 1132
Recalled to Life 753, **790**
Ruling Passion 89, 1392, 1502
A Very Good Hater 1367

Hill, Richard
Shoot the Piper **791**

Hillerman, Tony
The Blessing Way 700, 1570
Coyote Waits 843
The Dark Wind 874
The Ghostway 1162
The Joe Leaphorn and Jim Chee Series 1649
The Joe Leaphorn Series 701, 702, 1273, 1437, 1439, 1781
Sacred Clowns **792**
Talking God 758, **793**

Hilton, John Buxton
Passion in the Peak 1614
The Quiet Stranger 1292, 1293, 1294, 1295
Some Run Crooked 1502

Himes, Chester
Blind Man with a Pistol 1314
A Rage in Harlem 1177, 1178
The Real Cool Killers 788

Hinkemeyer, Michael T.
The Fields of Eden 1135, 1584
Fourth Down, Death 140, 314, 515, 1250
A Time to Reap 757, 758, 966, 1108

Hjortsberg, William
Nevermore 81, 926, 1438, 1787

Hoag, Tami
Night Sins **794**

Hoch, Edward D.
Murder Most Sacred 1299
The Shattered Raven 524, 984, 1044

Hoffman, Alice
Turtle Moon 147, **795**, 808

Hogan, Chuck
The Standoff 566, **796**

Holden, Craig
The Last Sanctuary 566, 1788
The River Sorrow 842, 1218

Holland, Isabelle
The Claire Aldington Series 564, 671, 672, 733, 734, 799, 1239, 1339
A Death at St. Anselm's 60, 136, 449, 670, 1124
A Fatal Advent **797**, 916, 1048, 1123, 1442
The Long Search 436, **798**
The Lost Madonna 1243, 1508

Hollingsworth, Gerelyn
Murder at St. Adelaide's **799**, 1237

Holt, Hazel
The Cruellest Month **800**, 1275
The Mavis Lashley Series 1446
Mrs. Malory and the Festival Murders **801**
Mrs. Malory Investigates 107, 361, **802**, 1246, 1445, 1485
The Mrs. Malory Series 108, 978, 1571

Holton, Leonard
The Father Bredder Series 916

Holtzer, Susan
Curly Smoke **803**

Homes, Geoffrey
The Man Who Murdered Goliath 1309

Hone, Joseph
The Oxford Gambit 217

Hoof, David L.
Sight Unseen **1046**

Hooper, Kay
Crime of Passion 17, 19, 116, 251, 1631

Horansky, Ruby
Dead Ahead 447, **804**, 969, 1222, 1226, 1452, 1523, 1527
Dead Center **805**, 909, 1224

Horn, Phyllis
The Chesapeake Project **806**

Hornig, Doug
Deep Dive 905, 1336
Foul Shot 871, 872
Waterman 13, 475, 539, 806, 1078, 1757

Hornsby, Wendy
Bad Intent 881
Half a Mind 218, **807**, 1334, 1335
Midnight Baby 531, 615, 778, **808**, 880, 1317, 1380, 1451
No Harm 889, 890, 1318, 1419, 1420, 1728
Telling Lies 610, **809**, 1637

Horton, John
A Black Legend **810**

Hougan, Carolyn
Blood Relative **811**, 1724

Hough, S.B.
Dear Daughter Dead 1614

Housewright, David
Penance **812**

Howe, Melodie Johnson
Beauty Dies 275, **813**
The Mother Shadow 177, 417, 449, 556, 607, 608, 695, **814**, 1120, 1300

Hoyt, Richard
30 for a Harry 819
Bigfoot **815**
Decoys 487, 491, 1212, 1350
The John Denson Series 488, 489, 490, 1751, 1754, 1765
Whoo? **816**

Huber, Frederic
Axx Goes South 624, **817**, 1011

Huebner, Frederick D.
The Joshua Sequence 6, 1603
Judgement by Fire 193, 488
The Matt Riordan Series 28, 31, 489, 490, 815, 1604
Methods of Execution 650, **818**, 1765

Huebner, Fredrick D.
Picture Postcard 445, 491, **819**, 1216

Hugo, Richard
Death and the Good Life 491, 736, 815, 1273, 1618, 1668

Hull, J.H.
Nicole 581, 1337

Hume, Fergus
The Mystery of a Hansom Cab 1293

Hunsburger, H. Edward
Death Signs 1414

Hunter, Alan
Gently Through the Woods 67
The Scottish Decision 948

Hunter, Evan
The Blackboard Jungle 144
Criminal Conversation **820**, 1531
Three Blind Mice **1106**
Vespers **1107**

Hunter, Jessie Prichard
Blood Music **821**

Hunter, Stephen
Dirty White Boys 708, 796
Point of Impact 553, 618, **822**, 1210

Huxley, Elspeth
The African Poison Murders 226
Murder on Safari 158

Hyde, Anthony
China Lake **823**

I

Iles, Greg
Spandau Phoenix **824**

Ing, Dean
The Ransom of Black Stealth One 179, 409, **825**, 1513

Innes, Michael
The Case of the Journeying Boy 530
Hamlet, Revenge! 174, 176
Paper Thunderbolt 1031

Irvine, R.R.
The Angel's Share **826**, 1678
Barking Dogs **827**
Called Home **828**
The Great Reminder **829**
The Moroni Traveler Series 509, 1018
Pillar of Fire 41, **830**
Ratings Are Murder 75, 1574

Irvine, Robert R.
The Moroni Traveler Series 490, 1032

Irwin, Wallace
The Julius Caesar Murder Case 394

Isaacs, Susan
Compromising Positions 448, 593, 594, 1146, 1415, 1748, 1750

Izzi, Eugene
King of the Hustlers **831**, 832, 1311, 1444, 1537
The Prime Roll 1128, 1286
Prowlers 1416
The Take 185, 526, 1622

J

Jackson, Basil
Crooked Flight 179, 409

Jackson, Jon A.
The Blind Pig 254, 498, 1421
Grootka 272, 497, **832**, 910
Hit on the House **833**

Jackson, Marian J.A.
The Abigail Danforth Series 465, 924, 930, 1259, 1260
Diamond Head **834**, 1030
The Punjat's Ruby 1298

Author Index

The Sunken Treasure 835

Jackson, Muriel Resnick
The Garden Club 33, 698, **836**, 900, 901, 1517, 1544, 1548

Jacobs, Nancy Baker
The Devon MacDonald Series 380, 381, 1490
The Silver Scapel **837**, 1041
Slash of Scarlet 521
The Turquoise Tattoo 116, 263, **838**, 1504, 1505

Jaffe, Jody
Horse of a Different Killer **839**

Jahn, Michael
City of God **840**, 1585, 1692

James, P.D.
The Cordelia Gray Series 304, 1125, 1338
Cover Her Face 260, 677, 1343, 1555
Death of an Expert Witness 576, 1139
Devices and Desires **841**
The Inspector Adam Dalgliesh Series 578, 1773
The Inspector Dagliesh Series 575, 577
Shroud for a Nightingale 1479
A Taste for Death 1554
Unnatural Cause 759
An Unsuitable Job for a Woman 95, 269, 456, 1141, 1142, 1143

Jance, J.A.
Desert Heat **842**, 1233, 1649
Hour of the Hunter 673, **843**
The J.P. Beaumont Series 488, 815, 1353, 1711, 1715
Minor in Possession **844**
Until Proven Guilty 487

Janeschutz, Trish
High Strangeness 447

Janeshutz, Trish
Hidden Lake 208
Shadow 844

Jeffers, H. Paul
The Adventure of the Stalwart Companions 36, 131, 441, 1654

Jeffreys, J.G.
The Thief Taker 941, 942

Jeffries, Roderic
The Honourable Detective **67**
The Inspector Alvarez Series 1002
Three and One Make Five 67
Too Clever by Half **845**

Jerina, Carol
The Tall Dark Alibi 411

Jevons, Marshall
The Fatal Equilibrium 1482

Johnson, Diane
The Shadow Knows 43, 673

Johnson, E. Richard
The Inside Man 652

Johnson, Martha
Deadly Secret 794

Johnston, Velda
Flight to Yesterday 139
Shadow Behind the Curtain 436, 798
The Underground Stream 502

Jones, Bruce
In Deep 293, 525, 710, **846**

Jones, Cleo
Prophet Motive 826, 828, 1018, 1124

Jones, Hazel Wynn
Death and the Trumpets of Tuscany **847**, 1003

Jones, Madison
Season of the Strangler 964

Jones, Margaret
The Confucious Enigma 496

Jordan, Cathleen
Carol in the Dark 967

Jordan, Lee
The Toy Cupboard **848**

Jorgensen, Christine T.
A Love to Die For **849**, 1094

Joshee, O.K.
Mr. Surie 874, 875

Juniper, Alex
A Very Proper Death **850**

K

Kahn, James
The Echo Vector 1321, 1372

Kahn, Michael A.
Death Benefits **851**, 963, 1529
Due Diligence **852**
Firm Ambitions 650, **853**, 1780
Grave Designs 405, 1333

Kakonis, Michael
Double-Cross 1005

Kakonis, Tom
Criss Cross 482, 755, 1288, 1589
Double Down 295, 709, 710, **854**
Michigan Roll 4, 497, 622, 773, 1416, 1444, 1690
Shadow Counter **855**

Kallen, Lucille
The C.B. Greenfield Series 813, 1304
C.B. Greenfield: The Tanglewood Murder 1305
Introducing C.B. Greenfield 120, 814, 866, 1309
No Lady in the House 168
The Tanglewood Murder 559, 609, 814, 1191

Kaminsky, Stuart
When the Dark Man Calls 1351

Kaminsky, Stuart M.
Black Knight in Red Square 1066
Bullet for a Star 276
Death of a Dissident 1066
Exercise in Terror 1351
The Inspector Rostnikov Series 365, 913
Lieberman's Choice **856**
Lieberman's Day **857**
Lieberman's Folly **858**
The Man Who Shot Lewis Vance 1675
The Man Who Walked Like a Bear **859**, 1793
The Melting Clock **860**
Opening Shots 1330
Poor Butterfly 957
Rostnikov's Vacation **861**
The Toby Peters Series 277, 956, 958, 1207
When the Dark Man Calls 384

Kantner, Rob
The Back Door Man 459, 500, 1384, 1386
The Ben Perkins Series 489, 490, 833, 1059, 1373, 1374, 1385, 1458

Concrete Hero 232, **862**, 870
Hell's Only Half Full 826
Made in Detroit 497
The Quick and the Dead **863**
The Red, White, and Blues **864**
The Thousand Yard Stare **865**

Karl, M.S.
Death Notice **866**, 1261, 1721, 1722
Deerslayer **867**, 949, 1109, 1720
Killer's Ink 371, 951, 1368, 1369, 1495
The Last Man to Die **1493**
The Maya Stone Murders **1494**

Karr, Leona
Murder in Bandora 206, 373, **868**

Katz, Jon
Death by Station Wagon 58, 157, **869**, 1463
The Family Stalker 794, **870**
The Kit Deleeuw Series 71
The Last Housewife 722

Katz, Michael J.
The Big Freeze 827, **871**, 1771
Last Dance in Redondo Beach 120, 718, **872**, 1005, 1109
Murder Off the Glass 646, 1655

Katzenbach, John
Day of Reckoning 42, 513, 1091, 1093, 1308, 1310
In the Heat of the Summer 53, 707, 937, 1011, 1014, 1057, 1166, 1279, 1285, 1297, 1425, 1427
Just Cause 656, 709, 710, **873**, 1007, 1659
The Traveler 99, 326, 349, 1027, 1282

Kavanagh, Dan
Duffy 726, 1573

Kavanagh, Paul
The Triumph of Evil 1284

Kavanaugh, Paul
Not Comin' Home to You 183
Such Men are Dangerous 1704

Kaye, M.M.
Death in Zanzibar 158, 226

Kaye, Marvin
My Brother, the Druggist 1698
The Soap Opera Slaughters 75

Keating, H.R.F.
Dead on Time **874**
The Iciest Sin **875**
The Inspector Ghote Series 34, 35, 845
Mrs. Craggs: Crimes Cleaned Up 1484

Keegan, John E.
Clearwater Summer 692, **876**

Keeling, Douglas J.
A Case of Innocence 445, **877**

Kellerman, Faye
Day of Atonement **878**, 955
False Prophet 173, 364, **879**
Grievous Sin **880**
Justice **881**
Milk and Honey 807, **882**
The Quality of Mercy 264, 425, 427, 512, **883**, 1081, 1082, 1083, 1084, 1376, 1624
The Ritual Bath 208, 890, 955, 1457
Sacred and Profane 953
Sanctuary **884**

Kellerman, Jonathan
The Alex Delaware Series 364, 1251, 1252, 1499, 1747
Bad Love **885**
Blood Test 879
The Butcher's Theater 690, 691, 884
Private Eyes **886**, 1791
Self-Defense **887**
Silent Partner 1457
Time Bomb 144, **888**, 1276
The Web 708
When the Bough Breaks 1643

Kelley, Patrick
Sleight of Hand 1595

Kelley, Susan
The Liz Connors Series 411

Kelly, Mary Anne
Foxglove 599, **889**
Park Lane South, Queens 315, 807, 878, **890**, 1664

Kelly, Nora
Bad Chemistry **891**, 1196, 1274, 1306
The Gillian Adams Series 1511
My Sister's Keeper 428, **892**, 960, 1522, 1767

Kelly, Susan
And Soon I'll Come to Kill You 119, 889, **893**, 1401
The Gemini Man 798, 882, 890, 982, 1046, 1214, 1318, 1476
The Liz Connors Series 154, 382, 383, 581, 603, 610, 944, 1041, 1215, 1317, 1378, 1380, 1388, 1636, 1637
Out of the Darkness 173, 880, **894**, 1496, 1514, 1659, 1660, 1671
The Summertime Soldiers 1420, 1498
Trail of the Dragon 222
Until Proven Innocent 114, **895**, 1362, 1759, 1771

Kelly, Susan B.
Hope Against Hope 642, 645, **896**, 1244, 1408, 1419, 1728
Hope Will Answer 357, 644
Kid's Stuff **897**
Kidstuff 643
Time of Hope 677, **898**, 1553

Kelman, Judith
The House on the Hill 128, **899**
Hush Little Darlings 1643
While Angels Sleep 769

Kelner, Toni L.P.
Dead Ringer 313, **900**, 1544
Down Home Murder 520, **901**, 1517
The Laura Fleming Series 1542, 1547
Trouble Looking for a Place to Happen **902**, 1204

Kemelman, Harry
Monday the Rabbi Took Off 690
The Rabbi Small Series 656, 878, 915, 916, 955, 1101

Kemp, Sarah
No Escape 321
What Dread Hand 303

Kemprecos, Paul
The Aristotle Socarides Series 336, 339, 687
Cool Blue Tomb 233, 683, 689, 1336
Death in Deep Water **903**, 1324
Feeding Frenzy **904**
Neptune's Eye 337, 338, **905**, 1099, 1353

Kennealy, Jerry

Kennealy, Jerry
Beggar's Choice 354, **906**
The Nick Polo Series 1688, 1714
Polo Solo 77, 1713, 1716
Special Delivery **907**
Vintage Polo **908**, 1245

Kenney, Charles
Hammurabi's Code **909**, 1660

Kenney, Susan
Garden of Malice 892, 1520, 1522
Graves in Academe 1140, 1196, 1274
The Roz Howard Series 960, 1511

Kent, Bill
Down by the Sea 293, **910**

Kent, Winona
Skywatcher 528

Kenyon, Michael
Kill the Butler! **911**
Peckover Joins the Choir **912**

Keppel, Charlotte
The Villains 1083

Kerr, Philip
The Bernie Gunther Series 994
Dead Meat 365, **913**
The Grid 566
March Violets 27, 957, 1792
The Pale Criminal 690, 691, 754, **914**, 958

Key, Samuel M.
I'll Be Watching You 673

Kienzle, William
The Father Koesler Series 1101

Kienzle, William X.
Chameleon **915**
Deathbed 797, 1048, 1123
Masquerade **916**

Kijewski, Karen
Alley Kat Blues **917**, 1227
Copy Kat **918**, 1607
The Kat Colorado Series 378, 379, 380, 381, 398, 637, 639, 649, 1009, 1182, 1266, 1398, 1506, 1700
Katapult 94, 397, **919**
Katwalk 92, 116, 161, 384, 551, 636, 648, **920**, 1052, 1265, 1410, 1701
Wild Kat **921**

Kiker, Douglas
Death at the Cut 950, 951, 998, 1111, 1359, 1368, 1720
Death Below Deck 338, 904, **922**
Death on Clam Pond 1074
The Mac McFarland Series 724
Murder on Clam Pond 166, 335, 340, 532, 686, 866, 867, 949, 1231, 1719, 1721
Murder on the Cut 1719

Kincaid, D.
A Lawyer's Tale **923**, 1014

Kincaid, Nell
To the Fourth Generation 1157

King, Charles
Mama's Boy 525, 846

King, Laurie R.
The Beekeeper's Apprentice 835, **924**, 1259, 1260
A Grave Talent **925**, 946, 1042, 1222, 1452, 1461, 1462, 1515, 1526, 1527
The Kate Martinelli Series 1525
A Monstrous Regiment of Women **926**

To Play the Fool 927

Kingsbury, Kate
Check-out Time **928**
Eat, Drink and Be Buried **929**
The Pennyfoot Hotel Series 134, 1030, 1292
Room with a Clue **930**, 1294
Service for Two 103

Kirk, Michael
The Interface Man 948

Kirst, Hans Hellmut
The Night of the Generals 579

Kittredge, Mary
The Charlotte Kent Series 1378
Desperate Remedy **931**
The Edwina Crusoe Series 658, 660, 774, 1129, 1130
Fatal Diagnosis 79, 448, 659
Kill or Cure **932**
Murder in Mendocino 10, 370, 1235, 1495, 1498
Poison Pen 172, 206, 594, 723, 868, **933**, 1146, 1215, 1636
Rigor Mortis 79, 302
Walking Dead Man **934**

Klaich, Delores
Heavy Gilt 83

Klaich, Dolores
Heavy Gilt 1689

Klavan, Andrew
The Animal Hour **935**
Corruption 163, 467, 592, **936**, 1109, 1578, 1590
Don't Say a Word 150, 773, 885, 899, **937**, 1297, **1308**, 1622
Rough Justice 1309
The Scarred Man 1075, **1310**
True Crime 679

Klein, Dave
Blind Side 50, 652, 872

Klein, Zachary
The Matt Jacob Series 669, 864
Still Among the Living 386, 446, 454, **938**, 1481
Two Way Toll **939**, 1353

Klempner, Joseph T.
Felony Murder **940**

Kline, Christina Baker
Sweet Water 592

Knebel, Fletcher
Seven Days in May 681

Knickmeyer, Steve
Cranmer 1056
Straight 817, 1060

Knight, Alanna
Blood Line **941**
Deadly Beloved **942**
The Inspector Faro Series 655, 929
Killing Cousins **943**

Knight, Katherine Lasky
Trace Elements 1156

Knight, Kathryn Lasky
The Calista Jacobs Series 372, 604, 991, 1388
Dark Swan **944**
Mortal Words 603, 838, 893, **945**, 1636
Mumbo Jumbo 1138
Trace Elements 1232, 1332, 1405

Knight, Phyllis
Shattered Rhythms **946**
Switching the Odds **947**, 1042, 1462

Knox, Bill
The Colin Thane Series 111, 113, 249, 719, 720, 943
The Interface Man 948
Who Shot the Bull 112

Koenig, Joseph
Floater 617, 1026, 1103, 1104, 1105, 1582
Smuggler's Notch 568, 1757

Kohler, Vince
Banjo Boy 606, **949**
Rainy North Woods 12, 14, 163, 166, 370, 376, 407, 827, **950**, 1072, 1145, 1261, 1368, 1477, 1721
Rising Dog 408, **951**, 1474, 1475, 1722

Komarnicki, Todd
Free 662, **952**, 1578

Komo, Dolores
Clio Browne, Private Investigator 523

Kosak, Carl
Sunshine Enemies 298

Kraft, Gabrielle
Screwdriver 51

Krich, Rochelle Majer
Angel of Death 74, 881, 884, **953**, 1515
Fair Game 63, 324, 325, 805, **954**, 1221, 1526
The Jessica Drake Series 1525
Till Death Do Us Part 879, 880, 884, **955**
Where's Mommy Now 275
Where's Mommy Now? 945

Kuhfeld, Mary Monica
The Boy's Tale 545

Kuhlken, Ken
The Angel Gang **956**
The Loud Adios **957**
The Venus Deal **958**

Kunz, Kathleen
Murder Once Removed **959**, 1155

Kupfer, Fern
Love Lies 960

Kupfer, Fran
Love Lies 1511

L

La Barre, Harriet
The Florentine Win 139

Lacey, Peter
The Bag Man **961**

Lacey, Sarah
File Under: Arson 309
File Under: Deceased **962**
File Under: Missing 1094

Lachint, Carrol
Murder in Brief **963**

Lacy, Ed
Breathe No More, My Lady 705
Room to Swing 762, 788, 1314

Laiken, Deidre S.
Killing Time in Buffalo 664, 674, **964**, 1102

Laing, David
Double Blind **965**

Lake, M.D.
Amends for Murder 351, 461, 777, **966**, 1528

Cold Comfort 417, 746, 779, **967**, 1089
A Gift for Murder 247, 360, 595, 600, 744, **968**, 1044, 1764
Murder by Mail 960, **969**, 1331
Once upon a Crime 970
The Peggy O'Neill Series 80, 219, 460, 464, 778, 780, 1380
Poisoned Ivy 119, 696, **971**, 1482

Lamb, J.J.
Nickel Straight 132
The Zach Rolfe Series 379

Lambert, Mercedes
Dogtown 852, **972**, 1435, 1524, 1529

Landers, Gunnard
The Deer Killers 96, **973**

Landreth, Marsha
A Clinic for Murder **974**
The Holiday Murders 63, 80, 322, 324, 660, **975**
The Samantha Turner Series 325, 774, 1129
Vial Murders **976**

Landrum, Graham
The Famous DAR Murder Mystery **977**, 1209
The Rotary Club Mystery **978**

Langley, Bob
Precipice 234

Langton, Jane
The Dante Game **979**, 1187
The Homer Kelly Series 747, 1136

Lansdale, Joe R.
Act of Love 99, 349, **980**, 1154, 1165, 1166, 1279, 1282, 1285
Cold in July 292, 622, 1287, 1596
Mucho Mojo 211, 1677
The Savage Season 102, 149, 482, 682, 1024, 1288, 1589
Stories by Mama Lansdale's Youngest Boy 1330

Lantigua, John
Burn Season **981**

LaPierre, Janet
Children's Games 10, 807, 945, **982**, 991, 1120, 1378, 1668
The Cruel Mother 1235
Grandmother's House **983**, 1156, 1317
Old Enemies 599
Unquiet Grave 1728

LaPlante, Lydia
Prime Suspect 754, 1132
The Prime Suspect Series 95, 661

LaPlante, Richard
Mantis 468, 1736

Larsen, Gaylord
Dorothy and Agatha **984**

Lashner, William
Hostile Witness **985**

Lathen, Emma
East Is East **986**
The John Putnam Thatcher Series 654, 1186
John Putnam Thatcher Series 1729
The John Putnam Thatcher Series 1730
Murder Against the Grain 1040
Right on the Money **987**

Latimer, Jonathan
Headed for a Hearse 1038
Solomon's Vineyard 1540

Author Index

Laurence, Janet
The Darina Lisle Series 389, 390, 698
A Deepe Coffyn 127, 151, **988**, 1034, 1035, 1342
Hotel Morgue 135, 374, 375, 377, 699, **989**, 1557
Recipe for Death **990**
A Tasty Way to Die 1289, 1290, 1291

Law, Alexander
To an Easy Grave 612, 1546, 1757

Law, Janice
The Anna Peters Series 1799
Backfire 1227
The Big Payoff 1228
Death under Par 480, 614
Infected Be the Air 315, 976, **991**
A Safe Place to Die 1568
The Shadow of the Palms 635
Time Lapse 542, **992**, 1257

Lawrence, Martha C.
Murder in Scorpio **993**

Lawton, John
Black Out **994**
Blackout 420

Le Carre, John
Call for the Dead 217
The Little Drummer Girl 1284
The Russia House 38, 824, **995**, 1508
The Spy Who Came in from the Cold 706
Tinker, Tailor, Soldier, Spy 453, 550

Leasor, James
Frozen Assets 571, **996**, 1564

Leather, Stephen
The Fireman 261, 811, **997**, 1673, 1743, 1744
Pay Off 1134

Lee, Bernie
Murder at Musket Beach 693, 741, 747, **998**, 1064, 1147, 1430, 1725
Murder Without Reservation 376, 629, 951, **999**, 1608
The Toni and Pat Pratt Series 1201

Lee, Gypsy Rose
The G-String Murders 1346

Lee, Harper
To Kill a Mockingbird 876

Lee, Wendi
The Good Daughter 503

Lehane, Dennis
A Drink Before the War **1000**, 1218

Lemarchand, Elizabeth
Alibi for a Corpse 675
Buried in the Past 841
The Glade Manor Murder 191, 676, 789, **1001**
Nothing to Do with the Case 752
Troubled Waters 67
Unhappy Returns 759

Leon, Donna
Death and Judgment **1002**
Death at La Fenice **1003**
Death in a Strange Country **1004**

Leonard, Elmore
The Big Bounce 1677
City Primeval 497, 831, 833, 1199, 1311, 1374, 1433, 1622
Get Shorty **1005**, 1128
Glitz 185
Killshot 1531

La Brava 526, 1212
Maximum Bob 721, 785, **1006**, 1561
Rum Punch 355, 855, **1007**
Split Images 1058
Stick 434, 482, 854, 1288, 1349, 1416, 1444
Unknown Man #89 500
Unknown Man No. 89 266

Lescroart, John T.
The 13th Juror 730, 985, 1576, 1724
A Certain Justice **1008**
Dead Irish 906, 907, 1161, 1713, 1716, 1779
The Dismas Hardy Series 123, 908
Hard Evidence **1009**
Rasputin's Revenge 1438
Son of Holmes 81
The Vig **1010**

Leslie, John
Killer in Paradise 53, 187, 1007, **1011**, 1608
Killing Me Softly 123, **1012**, 1714

Leuci, Bob
Odessa Beach 1793

Levin, Donna
California Street 364, 885, 886, 887, 888

Levin, Ira
Sliver **1013**
The Stepford Wives 568

Levine, Paul
Mortal Sin 650, **1014**
Night Vision 63, **1015**
To Speak for the Dead 66, 72, 73, 153, 254, 557, 558, 651, 985, **1016**, 1023, 1090, 1106, 1280, 1349, 1577, 1677

Levitsky, Ronald
The Love That Kills 445, 446, 1576, 1582, 1600
Stone Boy 1009, **1017**

Levitt, J.R.
Carnivores 828
Ten of Swords 624, 827, 829, 830, **1018**, 1472, 1505

Lewin, Michael Z.
The Albert Samson Series 71, 494, 1060, 1085, 1383, 1385, 1386, 1751, 1754
And Baby Will Fall 58
Ask the Right Question 459, 826
Called by a Panther **1019**, 1056

Lewis, Roy
Bloodeagle 1726

Lewis, Roy Harley
A Cracking of Spines 571
Death in Verona 979, **1020**, 1069, 1187
The Matthew Coll Series 1673
Where Agents Fear to Tread 1043

Lewis, Sherry
No Place for Secrets **1021**, 1586

Lewis, Stephen
And Baby Makes None 602, **1022**
Cowboy Blues 1573
The Monkey Rope **1023**

Lieberman, Herbert
City of the Dead 323, 326, 463
Nightbloom 749

Lindsay, Jeffry P.
Tropical Depression **1024**

Lindsay, Paul
Gentkill: A Novel of the FBI **1025**

Lindsey, David L.
An Absence of Light 909, 1025, **1026**
Black Gold, Red Death 1596
A Cold Mind 53, 165, 253, 844, 1425, 1427
Heat From Another Sun 229, 1426, 1644
In the Lake of the Moon 1006
Mercy 49, 63, 99, 321, 322, 324, 325, 349, 954, 975, 980, **1027**, 1033, 1154, 1166, 1221, 1282, 1283, 1534, 1736, 1737
Spiral 186, 1533
The Stuart Haydon Series 1095, 1711, 1715

Linscott, Gillian
Hanging on the Wire **1028**
The Nell Bray Series 519, 835, 928, 1259, 1260
Sister Beneath the Sheet 930, **1029**
Stage Fright **1030**
Unknown Hand 64, 611, 800, 891, **1031**, 1306

Linzee, David
Death in Connecticutt 1634

Lipinski, Thomas
The Fall-Down Artist **1032**

Littell, Robert
The Defection of A.J. Lewinter 995

Little, Constance
The Black Paw 168

Livingston, Jack
The Joe Binney Series 1414
The Nightmare File 242
A Piece of the Silence 281, 282, 1494

Livingston, Jayson
Point Blank **1033**, 1715

Livingston, Nancy
Death in Close-Up 763, **1034**
The G.D.H. Pringle Series 591, 962
Mayhem in Parva **1035**
Unwillingly to Vegas **1036**

Llewellyn, Caroline
The Masks of Rome 1521

Llewellyn, Sam
Blood Orange 541
Dead Reckoning 539, 540, 581, 582
Deadeye **1037**

Lochte, Dick
Blue Bayou 231, **1038**, 1059
Laughing Dog 680, 945, 1705
The Neon Smile **1039**
Sleeping Dog 122, 403, 499, 680, 1558, 1592

Lockridge, Frances and Richard
The Mr. and Mrs. North Series 387, 999

Lockridge, Richard and Frances
The Mr. and Mrs. North Series 160

Logan, Chuck
Hunter's Moon 566, 796

Logan, Margaret
Deathampton Summer 286, 686, 1777
A Killing in Venture Capital **1040**, 1778

Logue, John
Follow the Leader 317, 318
Murder on the Links 481

Logue, Mary
Red Lake of the Heart 966
Still Explosion 521, 615, 837, 936, **1041**, 1590

Lordon, Randye
Brotherly Love 946, 1462
Sister's Keeper **1042**

Lorens, M.K.
Deception Island **1043**
Dreamland **1044**
Sweet Narcissus 9, 223, **1045**
The Winston Sherman Series 484

Lorne, David
Sight Unseen **1046**

Love, William F.
The Bishop Regan Series 608
Bloody Ten **1047**
The Chartreuse Clue 60, 607, 656, 915, **1048**

Lovell, Marc
Good Spies Don't Grow on Trees 550
Spy on the Run 996
The Spy with His Head in the Clouds 706

Lovesey, Peter
Abracadaver 942
Bertie and the Seven Bodies 103, **1049**
The False Inspector Dew 117
Keystone 117, 860, 1674, 1675
The Prince of Wales Series 655, 929
The Sergeant Cribb Series 655, 737
The Summons **1050**
Waxwork 1292, 1293, 1294, 1296, 1610
Wobble to Death 738, 1295

Lovett, Sarah
Dangerous Attachments **1051**

Lowry, Cheryl Meredith
Showcase 603
Trunk Show 604

Luce, Carol Davis
Night Prey 821

Lucke, Margaret
A Relative Stranger 251, 379, 648, 649, **1052**

Ludlum, Robert
The Bourne Identity 552

Lundy, Mike
Raven 1311

Lupica, Mike
Dead Air 1635, 1709
Limited Partner 721, **1053**, 1481, 1718, 1771

Lupoff, Richard A.
The Classic Car Killer **1054**, 1564
The Comic Book Killer 630, **1055**
The Cover Girl Killer 467
The Hobart Lindsey Series 1242

Lustbader, Eric Van
The Ninja 527

Lutz, John
The Alo Nudger Series 71, 1326, 1327, 1329, 1374, 1688, 1754
Better Mousetraps 1330
The Carver Series 1705
Diamond Eyes **1056**
Flame 784, 1011, **1057**
The Fred Carver Series 72, 73, 817, 1349, 1492, 1560
Hot 1006
Nightlines 1527
Ride the Lightning 1659

The Right to Sing the Blues 319, 459, 497, 500
S.W.F. Seeks Same 1514, 1761
Scorcher 1313, 1371, 1422
The Shadow Man 1286, 1634
Single White Female 821, 1791
Spark **1058**
Thicker than Blood **1059**
Time Exposure **1060**

Lyall, Gavin
Shooting Script 847

Lynch, Jack
Bragg's Hunch 1616

Lynds, Dennis
Cassandra in Red **281**
Chasing Eights **282**
Crime, Punishment and Resurrection **283**

Lyons, Arthur
Fast Fade 299, 300, 369, 665, 1200, 1575
Hard Trade 726, 727
The Jacob Asch Series 29, 30, 31, 301, 342, 667, 862, 1269, 1271, 1413, 1440, 1458
Three with a Bullet 511

Lyons, Ivan
Someone Is Killing the Great Chefs of America **1061**

Lyons, Nan
Sold! 570
Someone Is Killing the Great Chefs of America **1061**
Someone Is Killing the Great Chefs of Europe 151, 152

Lysaght, Brian
Special Circumstances 105, 192, 682, 735

M

MacCahery, James
The Lavinia London Series 1021

MacDonald, John D.
Barrier Island 1608
The Deep Blue Goodbye 1337
Dress Her in Indigo 1653
The Drowner 973
A Flash of Green 782, 1359
The Last One Left 783
Nightmare in Pink 568
Pale Gray for Guilt 1349
The Travis McGee Series 73, 432, 485, 817, 1057, 1336, 1352

MacDonald, Patricia
No Way Home 848, **1062**, 1664
Stranger in the House 43

Macdonald, Ross
The Lew Archer Series 396

MacGregor, T.J.
On Ice 84, 807
The St. James and McCleary Series 411

MacInnes, Helen
The Venetian Affair 1510

MacLean, Alistair
Ice Station Zebra 234, 725, 1530

MacLeod, Charlotte
The Bilbao Looking Glass 1430
The Family Vault 117, 286, 1447
The Gladstone Bag **1063**
The Grub-and-Stakers Series 977
An Owl Too Many **1064**
The Peter Shandy Series 776, 971
Rest You Merry 697, 1045, 1208
The Sarah Kelling Series 154, 155, 284, 693, 743, 781
The Silver Ghost 629
Something in the Water **1065**
Something the Cat Dragged In 387
The Wrong Rite 334

MacLeod, Robert
The Interface Man 948

Madsen, David
U.S.S.A. 861, **1066**, 1530

Maguire, Michael
Scratchproof 573
Shot Silk 540

Mahoney, Don
Detective First Grade **1067**

Maiman, Jaye
Someone to Watch 1356

Maiman, Joyce
Left My Heart 1731

Malcolm, John
A Back Room in Somers Town 477, 1563
The Godwin Sideboard 1565
Sheep, Goats and Soap **1068**
The Tim Simpson Series 570, 571, 572, 1242, 1564, 1566
Whistler in the Dark 1507, 1508
The Wrong Impression **1069**, 1509

Mallory, Drew
Target Manhattan 205, 1633

Malone, Michael
Time's Witness 735, 1006, **1070**, 1281
Uncivil Seasons 795

Maner, William
Die of a Rose 140

Mann, Jessica
Faith, Hope and Homicide **1071**, 1162

Mann, Paul
Season of the Monsoon 1137

Mano, D. Keith
Topless 355, 590, **1072**

Manson, Cynthia
Women of Mystery **1073**

Margolis, Seth Jacob
False Faces **1074**
Vanishing Act **1075**

Mariz, Linda
Body English 476, 583, 702
Snake Dance 1137

Maron, Margaret
Baby Doll Games 47, 1088
Bloody Kin 1687
Bootlegger's Daughter 900, 901, 936, **1076**, 1637, 1685
Corpus Christmas 1113
Death of a Butterfly 461
One Coffee With 460, 1087, 1089
Past Imperfect **1077**
Shooting at Loons **1078**, 1119
The Sigrid Harald Series 141, 142, 447, 464, 534, 804, 805, 925, 954, 969, 1086, 1224, 1225, 1226, 1523

Marris, Kathrine
Amateur Night 114
Electric City 115
A Hopeless Case 116
Peril under the Palms 117

Marsh, Ngaio
Killer Dolphin 641
Night of the Vulcan 1173
Overture to Death 609, 1191

Marshall, William
Faces in the Crowd **1079**
The New York Detective **1080**
Yellowthread Street 34, 35

Marston, Edward
The Mad Courtesan **1081**, 1164
The Nicholas Bracewell Series 264, 426, 512, 1375, 1377, 1468, 1469, 1470
The Nine Giants **1082**
The Queen's Head 427, **1083**, 1467
The Trip to Jerusalem 425, **1084**

Martin, A.E.
Death in the Limelight 1693

Martin, David
Lie to Me 267

Martin, George R.R.
The Armageddon Rag 299, 406, 1102

Martin, James E.
The Flip Side of Life **1085**, 1647, 1751
The Gil Disbro Series 1385
The Mercy Trap 1383

Martin, Lee
Bird in a Cage **1086**
The Buzzards Must Also Be Fed 1739
The Day That Dusty Died **1087**
The Deb Ralston Series 142, 219, 464, 778, 779, 780, 969, 1224, 1225, 1226, 1452, 1523, 1525, 1685, 1686
Deficit Ending 47, 460, **1088**, 1095
The Eye of Anna **1741**
Hacker 1113
Hal's Own Murder Case 534
The Mensa Murders **1089**
Too Sane a Murder 1170, 1687
Yakuza, Go Home **1742**

Martin, Robert
To Have and to Kill 1085

Martini, Steve
Compelling Evidence 557, **1090**, 1577, 1600
Undue Influence 820, 1599

Matera, Lia
The Good Fight 153, 809, **1091**, 1650, 1651
A Hard Bargain 514, **1092**, 1529
Hidden Agenda 216
The Laura Di Palma Series 852, 1699, 1780
Prior Convictions 436, 851, 972, 1076, **1093**, 1167, 1357, 1599
A Radical Departure 6, 767, 1320
The Smart Money 986, 1524
Where Lawyers Fear to Tread 237, 963
The Willa Jansson Series 853

Mather, Linda
Blood of an Aries 849, **1094**

Matheson, Don
Ninth Life 338, 819, 1509
Stray Cat 475, 1337

Mathewson, Joseph
Alicia's Trump 404

Mathis, Edward
Another Path, Another Dragon 165
The Dan Roman Series 7, 8, 352, 458, 877
Dark Streets and Empty Places 353

From a High Place 84, 350, 1741
Natural Prey 354
See No Evil **1095**
September Song 1007, **1096**

Matteson, Stefanie
The Charlotte Graham Series 214, 712
Murder at the Spa **1097**
Murder on the Cliff 516, **1098**

Matteson, Stephanie
The Charlotte Graham Series 284, 285, 1245

Matthews, Francine
Death on Rough Water **1099**

Maxwell, A.E.
The Fiddler Series 434, 485
Gatsby's Vineyard 511, 569, 908
Just Another Day in Paradise 392
Money Burns **1100**

Maxwell, Ann
Money Burns **1100**

Maxwell, Evan
Money Burns **1100**

Maxwell, Jan
Baptism for Murder **1101**

Maxwell, Thomas
Kiss Me Once 279
The Saberdene Variations 105
The Suspense Is Killing Me 227, 299, 406, 1072, **1102**, 1587

Mayor, Archer
Borderlines 1092, **1103**, 1436
Fruits of the Poisonous Tree **1104**
The Joe Gunther Series 1230, 1717
Open Season 765, 1231, 1578
Scent of Evil 936, **1105**, 1776

McBain, Ed
The 87th Precinct Series 199, 856, 857, 1033, 1077
Cinderella 1022
Lizzie 1441
The Matthew Hope Series 73, 818, 1057, 1603, 1604
Three Blind Mice **1106**
Vespers **1107**

McBriarty, Douglas
Carolina Gold **1108**

McCabe, Peter
City of Lies **1109**
Wasteland **1110**

McCafferty, Taylor
Pet Peeves **1111**
Ruffled Feathers 1751

McCaffrey, Anne
Ring of Fear 52

McCahery, James
Grave Undertaking 1097, **1112**, 1171, 1172, 1442

McCall, Thomas
A Wide and Capable Revenge **1113**

McCammon, Robert R.
Mine 843, 1091

McCarry, Charles
The Paul Christopher Series 647
The Tears of Autumn 188

McCloy, Helen
Two Thirds of a Ghost 556, 1300

McClure, James
The Artful Egg 226
The Song Dog **1114**
The Steam Pig 226

McConnell, Frank
Liar's Poker 734, 1591
Murder Among Friends 1745

McConnell, Vicki
Double Daughter 444, 533

McConnor, Vincent
The Man Who Knew Hammett 858, 1619, 1620, 1621

McCrumb, Sharyn
The Elizabeth MacPherson Series 10, 114, 218, 731, 732, 977, 1318, 1335
The Hangman's Beautiful Daughter 267, 522, 742, 936, **1115**, 1665
Highland Laddie Gone 1316
If Ever I Return, Pretty Peggy-O 42, 242, 314, 316, 514, 664, 674, 811, 1078, 1091, 1092, **1116**, 1334, 1367, 1392, 1742
Lovely in Her Bones 522
MacPherson's Lament **1117**
Missing Susan **1118**
She Walks These Hills 626, **1119**
Sick of Shadows 933
The Spencer Arrowood Series 311, 1774
The Windsor Knot 334, **1120**
Zombies of the Gene Pool **1121**

McCullough, David Willis
City Sleuths and Tough Guys **1122**
Point No-Point **1123**
Think on Death 137, **1124**
The Ziza Todd Series 138, 564, 671, 672, 733

McDermid, Val
Crack Down 456, **1125**
Report for Murder **1126**

McDonald, Gregory
Fletch 532, 1698
The Fletch Series 714, 1309
Who Took Toby Rinaldi? 1046

McEwan, Ian
The Innocent 914

McFall, Patricia
Night Butterfly **1127**

McGarrity, Mark
Neon Caesar **1128**, 1537

McGiffin, Janet
The Dr. Maxene St. Clair Series 660
Elective Murder **1129**
Emergency Murder 658, 1656
The Maxene St. Clair Series 932
Prescription for Death 931, 974, **1130**

McGill, E.J.
Immaculate in Black 1342, 1430, 1627, 1725

McGinley, Patrick
Goosefoot 530

McGown, Jill
The Inspector Lloyd & Judy Hill Series 357, 661
Murder Movie **1131**
The Other Woman **1132**, 1670

McGrady, Sean
Sealed with a Kiss 1331

McGraw, Lee
Hatchett 1264

McGregor, Iona
Death Wore a Diadem **1133**

McGuire, Christine
Until Proven Guilty 820

McIlvanney, William
Laidlaw 112, 249, 720, 948, 1639
Strange Loyalties 113, **1134**

McInerny, Ralph
The Andrew Broome Series 236, 237
Body and Soil **1135**, 1603
The Father Dowling Series 656, 916, 1101
The Noonday Devil 1429
Nun Plussed **1339**
The Search Committee **1136**, 1482
Second Vespers 915

McKittrick, Molly
The Medium Is Murder 591

McNab, Claire
Cop-Out 83, 256, 534, 1170
Death Down Under 1528
Lessons in Murder 533

McNamara, Joseph
The First Directive 1070, 1193, 1249, 1712, 1715

McQuillan, Karin
The Cheetah Chase 225, 362, **1137**
Deadly Safari 54, 55, 158, 209

McRae, Diana
All the Muscle You Need 806, 1460, 1689

McRae, Diane
All the Muscle You Need 533

McShea, Susanna Hofmann
The Pumpkin-Shell Wife 100, 361, 1021, **1138**, 1446

Meek, M.R.D.
A Loose Connection **1139**

Meier, Leslie
Mail-Order Murder 22, 312, 457, **1140**, 1254, 1258, 1378, 1567

Melville, Jennie
The Charmian Daniels Series 95, 304, 455, 661, 1125, 1338
Coffin Underground **204**
Dead Set **1141**, 1670
Murder Has a Pretty Face **1142**
Whoever Has the Heart **1143**
Witching Murder 203, **1144**

Meredith, D.R.
The Homefront Murders 106
Murder by Deception 353
Murder by Impulse 1741
Murder by Masquerade 354
The Sheriff and the Branding Iron Murders 353
The Sheriff and the Panhandle Murders 316, 1086, 1739, 1740
The Sheriff Charles Matthews Series 65, 310, 311, 1087, 1153, 1756, 1758

Mertz, Barbara
The Last Camel Died at Noon **1298**
Naked Once More **1300**

Mewshaw, Michael
True Crime **1145**, 1638, 1726

Meyer, Lawrence
A Capitol Crime 159, 1169, 1286, 1389

Meyer, Nicholas
The Seven-Percent Solution 440, 441, 442, 1407

Meyers, Annette
The Big Killing 986, 1040, 1186, 1389
Blood on the Street **1146**
The Deadliest Option **1147**
The Kingsbridge Plot **1148**

The Smith and Wetzon Series 172, 654, 987, 1333

Meyers, Maan
The Kingsbridge Plot **1148**

Meyers, Martin
The Kingsbridge Plot **1148**

Meynell, Laurence
The Hooky Heffernan Series 1695

Michael, Simon
The Cut Throat **1149**

Michaels, Barbara
Ammie, Come Home 502
Black Rainbow 68
Search the Shadows 769, 1453

Michaels, Grant
A Body to Dye For 727, **1150**, 1194, 1572, 1795, 1796
Love You to Death **1151**

Mickleson, Monty
Purgatory **1152**

Miles, John
A Permanent Retirement 701, **1153**, 1209

Miles, Keith
Bullet Hole 317, 318, 480
Double Eagle 480

Miller, Geoffrey
The Black Glove 1459

Miller, Judy
Murder of the Soap Opera 75

Miller, Rex
Slob 1027, 1425
Stone Shadow 229, **1154**, 1308, 1426

Millhiser, Marlys
The Charlie Green Series 115, 124
Death of the Office Witch 56, 125, **1155**
Murder at Moot Point 33, 128, 172, 370, 371, 372, 376, 944, **1156**, 1401, 1567

Mills, D.F.
Deadline 599, 694, 894, **1157**

Milne, A.A.
The Red House Mystery 1365

Milne, John
Dead Birds 27, 327, 1371, 1488, 1630
The Moody Man 1629

Minahan, John
The Great Grave Robbery **1158**, 1362
The Great Hotel Robbery 1363

Miner, Valerie
Murder in the English Department 891, 892, 1133, 1520, 1522

Mitchell, Gladys
The Saltmarsh Murders 1484

Mitchell, Kay
In Stoney Places **1159**, 1479, 1670
The Inspector Morrissey Series 367
A Lively Form of Death 230, **1160**, 1454
The Morrissey and Barrett Series 504

Mitchell, Kirk
High Desert Malice 106
With Siberia Comes a Chill 957, **1161**

Moffat, Gwen
Grizzly Trail 1651
The Miss Pink Series 1071, 1594

Over the Sea to Death 802
Rage **1162**, 1549
The Stone Hawk **1163**

Monfredo, Miriam Grace
The Glynis Tryon Series 1260
North Star Conspiracy **1164**

Monniger, Joseph
Incident at Potter's Bridge **1165**

Montanari, Richard
Deviant Way **1166**

Montecino, Marcel
The Cross Killer 62

Montgomery, Yvonne
Obstacle Course 880, **1167**
Scavengers 33, 1333, 1543, 1545

Moody, Susan
Penny Dreadful 1144
The Penny Wanawake Series 455

Moore, Barbara
The Doberman Wore Black 17, 257, 258, 259, 288, 289, 290, 291, 1241, 1734
The Wolf Whispered Death 290

Moore, Margaret
Dangerous Conceits **1168**

Moore, Rayanne
Bagels for Tea **1571**

Moore, William
The Last Surprise **1169**

Morel, Mary
The Lucia Ramos Series 927

Morell, Mary
Final Session 925, **1170**

Morgan, D. Miller
A Lovely Night to Kill 274
Money Leads to Murder 84

Morgan, Kate
The Dewey James Series 1406, 1547
Home Sweet Homicide **1171**
A Slay at the Races **1172**

Morice, Anne
Death in the Round 87
Fatal Charm 516, **1173**
Scared to Death 729
Sleep of Death 1707
The Tessa Crichton Series 76, 414, 543, 1071, 1131, 1179, 1213, 1391, 1399

Morison, B.J.
Beer and Skittles 1140

Morrell, David
Assumed Identity 518, 633
Blood Oath 1531
The Brotherhood of the Rose 552
The Covenant of the Flame 681, 756, **1174**, 1381, 1727
The Fifth Profession 348
First Blood 527
Testament 5, 395, 822, 1188

Morse, L.A.
The Big Enchilada 1540
The Old Dick 1619, 1620, 1621

Morson, Ian
Falconer's Crusade 243, **1175**, 1468

Mortimer, John
Rumpole of the Bailey 705
The Rumpole Series 923

Mosley, Walter
Black Betty 833
Devil in a Blue Dress 277, 279, 280, 393, 498, 958, **1176**, 1609

497

Moyes, Patricia
The Easy Rawlins Series 956
A Red Death 276, **1177**
White Butterfly **1178**, 1421

Moyes, Patricia
Angel Death 543, 1594
Black Girl, White Girl **1179**
Death on the Agenda 1409
Down Among the Dead Men 87
Falling Star 76, 641, 1131, 1768
A Six-Letter Word for Death 368
Who Is Simon Warwick? 1173

Muller, Marcia
The Cavalier in White 1521, 1645
The Cheshire Cat's Eye 982
Dark Star 436, 479, 848, 1093, **1180**, 1410, 1789
Deceptions 1330
Edwin of the Iron Shoes 919
The Elena Oliverez Series 1569
Eye of the Storm 947
The Joanna Stark Series 1052, 1216, 1398
The Shape of Dread 461, 462, 634, **1181**, 1219, 1229, 1264
The Sharon McCone Series 92, 397, 398, 551, 635, 638, 639, 649, 837, 838, 917, 918, 920, 1009, 1052, 1220, 1266
Sharon McCone Series 1328
The Sharon McCone Series 1332, 1506, 1569, 1700, 1701, 1702
There Hangs the Knife 1507, 1666
There's Something About a Sunday 772
Till The Butchers Cut Him Down **1182**
The Tree of Death 523, 536, 537
Trophies and Dead Things 6, 94, 514, 636, 637, 648, 767, 771, 809, 1092, **1183**, 1326, 1579
Where Echoes Live 463, 1115, 1119, 1162, **1184**, 1265, 1607
A Wild and Lonely Place **1185**

Munro, Hugh
The Man Who Sold Death 550
Who Told Clutha? 1629

Munson, Ronald
Nothing Human 1165

Murphy, Dallas
Lover Man 257, 287, 288, 290, 724

Murphy, Haughton
Murder for Lunch 713
Murder Times Two **1186**
Murders and Acquisitions 986, 987
The Reuben Frost Series 236, 654, 1778
A Very Venetian Murder **1187**

Murphy, Warren
Digger Smoked Out 554
End Game **1585**
Jericho Day 633, 681, 756, 1174
Leonardo's Law 207, 402
The Temple Dogs 1127, **1188**
The Trace Series 212, 213, 499, 723, 724

Murphy, Warren B.
The Red Moon 1595

Murray, Stephen
The Noose of Time **1189**, 1555

Murray, William
I'm Getting Killed Right Here **1190**
The Shifty Anderson Series 1486
Tip on a Dead Crab 170, 171, 495, 540, 541

Myers, Amy
The August Didier Series 928
Murder in the Limelight 1030

Myers, Paul
Deadly Cadenza 589
Deadly Crescendo **1191**, 1681
Deadly Sonata **1192**
The Mark Holland Series 452, 1071

Myers, Tamar
Too Many Cooks Spoil the Broth 134, 1289
Too Many Crooks Spoil the Broth 375

N

Nabb, Magdalen
Death of a Dutchman 845, 1003
The Marshall Guarnaccia Series 549, 1002

Naha, Ed
On the Edge **1193**, 1249

Nash, Jay Robert
A Crime Story 1443

Nasland, Sena Jeter
Sherlock in Love 926

Nastase, Ilie
Break Point 1195
Tie-Break 129

Natsuki, Shizuko
Innocent Journey 1127

Nava, Michael
How Town 727, **1194**
Little Death 395
The Little Death 1150, 1797

Navratilova, Martina
The Total Zone 481, **1195**

Neel, Janet
Death Among the Dons 428, 891, **1196**, 1274, 1306, 1522
Death of a Partner 203, 643, 897, **1197**, 1393, 1395, 1454
Death on Site 309, 644, 898, 1553
Death's Bright Angel 307, 642, 645, 896, 1399, 1408, 1419, 1669, 1671
The McLeish and Wilson Series 1361

Neely, Barbara
Blanche Among the Talented Tenth 761, 1691
Blanche on the Lam 141, 142, **1198**, 1692

Neely, Richard
The Plastic Nightmare 1149

Nehrbass, Arthur F.
Dead Easy **1199**, 1561

Nehrbass, Richard
Dark of Night 1110, **1200**
A Perfect Death for Hollywood 332

Nessen, Ron
Knight & Day **1201**, 1710

Neuman, Johanna
Knight & Day **1201**

Neville, Katherine
The Eight 1539, 1681

Newman, Christopher
19th Precinct **1202**

Newman, Sharan
The Cathe LeVendeur Series 545
Death Comes as Epiphany 427, 544, 631, 1164, **1203**, 1301, 1375, 1377, 1624
The Devil's Door 1175

Nickles, Liz
The Total Zone 1195

Niesewand, Peter
A Member of the Club 1114

Nighbert, David F.
Shutout **1204**
Squeezeplay 506, **1205**
Strikezone 493, 574, 613, **1206**

Noguchi, Thomas T.
Unnatural Causes 478, 1285

Nolan, William F.
The Black Mask Boys 283, 1122
The Black Mask Murders **1207**
The Boys in the Black Mask 621

Nordan, Robert
All Dressed Up to Die 45
Death Beneath the Christmas Tree 245, **1208**, 1750
Death on Wheels **1209**
The Mavis Lashley Series 46

Norman, Geoffrey
Deep End **1210**
Sweetwater Ranch 1072

North, Darian
Criminal Seduction 518, 1104, **1211**

Norwood, Frank
The Man in the Moon **1212**

Nusser, Richard
Walking After Midnight 412

O

O'Brien, Maureen
Close-Up on Death 346, 413, 517, 992, **1213**, 1247, 1248

O'Brien, Meg
The Daphne Decisions 569, 1167, **1214**, 1476, 1638
Eagles Die Too **1215**, 1641
Hare Today, Gone Tomorrow **1216**, 1474, 1475
The Jessica James Series 127, 155, 156, 177, 373, 382, 383, 813, 868, 1398, 1632
The Keeper **1217**
Salmon in the Soup 1477

O'Brien, Tim
In the Lake of the Woods **1218**

O'Callaghan, Maxine
Death Is Forever 274, 1227
The Delilah West Series 379, 380, 381, 398, 638, 917, 1052, 1569, 1798
Hit and Run 771, 772, **1219**, 1264
Set-Up **1220**, 1228

O'Connell, Carol
Killing Critics 601
Mallory's Oracle 805, 857, 953, **1221**, 1224, 1515, 1686
The Man Who Cast Two Shadows 1660

O'Connell, Catherine
Skins 59, **1222**, 1526

O'Connell, Jack
Box Nine 59, 74, 293, 1202, 1221, **1223**

O'Cork, Shannon
Sports Freak 614

O'Donnell, Lillian
Casual Affairs 1077
Cop Without a Shield 1687, 1789
A Good Night to Kill 47, 533, 771, 1241, 1528
The Gwen Ramadge Series 473, 542, 1798, 1799
The Kate Mulcahaney Series 954
Lockout **1224**
The Mici Anhalt Series 968
No Business Being a Cop 460, 1088, 1089
The Norah Mulcahaney Series 142, 464, 601, 804, 805, 1523
A Private Crime **1225**
Pushover **1226**
The Raggedy Man **1227**
Used to Kill **1228**
A Wreath for the Bride **1229**

O'Donnell, Peter
The Modesty Blaise Series 452, 1727

Olcott, Anthony
Murder at the Red October 365, 859, 861, 913, 1066, 1793

Olden, Marc
Poe Must Die 984

Oleksiw, Susan
Double Take 626
Family Album **1230**
The Joe Silva Series 65
Murder in Mellingham 268, **1231**, 1758

Oliphant, B.J.
A Ceremonial Death 106, 1788
Dead in the Scrub 55, 57, 315, 983, 999, **1232**, 1340, 1495, 1498, 1605, 1650, 1652, 1661, 1668
Death and the Delinquent 33, **1233**, 1496, 1667
Death Served Up Cold **1234**
The Shirley McClintock Series 156, 537, 711, 1483, 1497, 1551
The Unexpected Corpse 97, 746, **1235**, 1784

Oliver, Anthony
The Pew Group 1035, 1478

Oliver, Maria-Antonia
Antipodes **1236**, 1731
Study in Lilac 1126

Olshaker, Mark
The Edge 1424

O'Marie, Carol Anne
Advent of Dying 449, 670, 797, 1123, 1124, 1442
Advent of Silence 136
Death Goes on Retreat **1237**
The Missing Madonna 1591
Murder in Ordinary Time **1238**
Murder Makes a Pilgrimage **1239**
Novena for Murder 286
The Sister Mary Helen Series 137, 138, 564, 672, 733, 799, 1339

Orde, A.J.
Death and the Dogwalker **1240**
The Jason Lynx Series 70, 572
A Little Neighborhood Murder 100, 101, 192, 696, 977, 1138, 1167, **1241**, 1415, 1683, 1777, 1778
A Long Time Dead **1242**

Orenstein, Frank
The Man in the Gray Flannel Shroud 1040

Ormerod, Roger
By Death Possessed **1243**
Hung in the Balance 625, 645, 962, **1244**, 1708

Orum, Paul
Scapegoat 548

Osborn, David
The Margaret Barlow Series 46, 100, 284, 285, 978, 1138, 1406, 1483
Murder in the Napa Valley 711, **1245**
Murder on Martha's Vineyard 108, 1445, 1485
Murder on the Chesapeake 45, **1246**

Osborne, Denise
Cut To—Murder **1247**, 1488
Murder Offscreen 517, **1248**, 1411

Oster, Jerry
Fixing to Die 186, 391, **1249**
The Joe Cullen Series 1711
Violent Love 254

Owens, George
The Judas Pool **1250**

P

Pace, Tom
Fisherman's Luck 817

Padgett, Abigail
Child of Silence 97, **1251**, 1331
Strawgirl **1252**, 1504

Page, Emma
Last Walk Home 1035
A Violent End **1253**, 1592

Page, Jake
The Stolen Gods 1017, 1273

Page, Katherine Hall
The Body in the Basement 536, 537, 559, **1254**
The Body in the Belfry 157, 245, 247, 734, **1255**, 1315, 1545, 1748, 1750
The Body in the Bouillon 135, 697, **1256**, 1317
The Body in the Cast **1257**, 1291
The Body in the Vestibule 345, **1258**
The Faith Fairchild Series 244, 246, 531, 1749

Paige, Robin
Death at Bishop's Keep 68, **1259**
Death at Gallows Green 465, **1260**

Paisner, Daniel
Obit **1261**

Palmer, Michael
Natural Causes **1262**

Palmer, William J.
The Detective and Mr. Dickens 984, 1030

Papazoglou, Orania
Charisma 580, 1428
Death's Savage Passion 250
Not a Creature Was Stirring **695**
Once and Always Murder **1263**
The Patience McKenna Series 1477, 1567
Quoth the Raven **696**
A Stillness in Bethlehem **697**
Wicked, Loving Murder 933

Papazoulou, Orania
Sweet, Savage Death 1500

Paretsky, Sara
Bitter Medicine 93, 263, 659, 837, 1219
Blood Shot 634, 1355
Burn Marks 143, 161, 202, 459, 636, 1181, 1229, **1264**
Deadlock 382, 1638

Guardian Angel 781, 1251, 1252, **1265**, 1504
Indemnity Only 919, 1113
Killing Orders 1429, 1795
Tunnel Vision **1266**, 1410
The V.I. Warshawski Series 82, 92, 190, 381, 635, 638, 639, 918, 920, 1184, 1185, 1345, 1398, 1702
A Woman's Eye 1073, **1267**, 1299

Pargeter, Edith
Brother Cadfael's Penance 1301

Parker, Barbara
Suspicion of Guilt 784, **1268**, 1465
Suspicion of Innocence 1280

Parker, Percy Spurlark
Good Girls Don't Get Murdered 762, 832, 1314

Parker, Robert B.
Ceremony 716
Crimson Joy 187, 1313
Double Deuce **1269**
Early Autumn 1355, 1364
God Save the Child 1384, 1643
The Godwulf Manuscript 360, 1602
The Judas Goat 791
Mortal Stakes 507, 510, 1358, 1718
Perchance to Dream **1270**
Playmates 646, 765, 1655
Poodle Springs 956
Promised Land 40, 458, 850
The Spenser Series 190, 341, 342, 343, 344, 386, 432, 764, 1400, 1615
Stardust 403, **1271**
Valediction 766
Walking Shadow **1272**
The Widening Gyre 1745

Parker, T. Jefferson
Laguna Heat 1352
Little Saigon 165, 1106

Parrish, Frank
The Dan Mallett Series 109
Snare in the Dark 110

Parrish, Richard
The Dividing Line 692, 1017, 1251, **1273**, 1325, 1331, 1599, 1649

Patillo, James
Skim 707, 785

Paton Walsh, Jill
A Piece of Justice **1274**
The Wyndham Case **1275**, 1559

Patterson, James
Along Came a Spider 468, **1276**, 1434
Kiss the Girls 1424
The Thomas Berryman Number 392, 1623

Patterson, Richard North
Degree of Guilt 1576
Escape the Night 1762
The Lasko Tangent 1443
Private Screening 526

Paul, Barbara
A Cadenza for Caruso 117
The Fourth Wall 641
In-laws and Outlaws **1277**

Paul, Celeste
Berlin Covenant **1278**

Paul, Raymond
The Thomas Street Horror 1403, 1404

Paulsen, Gary
Night Rituals 200, 229, 873, 980, **1279**, 1282

Peak, John A.
Spare Change **1280**

Pearce, Gerald
Orphans **1281**

Pearson, Ridley
The Angel Maker 1276, **1282**, 1737
Chain of Evidence **1283**
Hard Fall 248, 521, 684, 1199, 1202, **1284**, 1499, 1633, 1690
No Witnesses 1424
Probable Cause 53, **1285**, 1286, 1427
Undercurrents 1644

Pease, William D.
Playing the Dozens 159, 1249, **1286**

Pedneau, Dave
A.P.B. 807, 1759
D.O.A. 1546

Pedrazas, Allan
The Harry Chronicles **1287**

Pelecanos, George
Shoedog **1288**

Pelecanos, George P.
Nick's Trip 1075

Pence, Joanne
Cooking Up Trouble 377, **1289**
Something's Cooking 134, **1290**
Too Many Cooks **1291**

Perry, Anne
Belgrave Square 930, 1029
Cain His Brother **1292**
The Cater Street Hangman 738, 942
A Dangerous Mourning **1293**
Farrier's Lane **1294**
Highgate Rise **1295**
The Inspector Monk Series 737
Paragon Walk 1049
Resurrection Row 738
Silence in Hanover Close 941, 1610
A Sudden, Fearful Death **1296**
The Thomas and Charlotte Pitt Series 655, 737, 834, 928, 929, 943

Perry, Thomas
The Butcher's Boy 981
Island 782, 783, 1608, 1762
Metzger's Dog 363, 432, 433, 434, 435, 525, 606, 782, 783, 785, 949, 1611, 1612, 1613, 1698
Sleeping Dogs 3, 486, **1297**

Perry, Will
The Kremlin Watcher 1466

Peters, Elizabeth
The Amelia Peabody Series 440, 441, 442, 476, 519, 834, 928, 930, 1029, 1071, 1118
Die for Love 250, 1263
The Last Camel Died at Noon **1298**
Malice Domestic #1 **1299**
The Murders of Richard III 424
Naked Once More 177, 546, 556, 724, **1300**
Street of the Five Moons 479
Trojan Gold 1409

Peters, Ellis
The Brother Cadfael Series 544, 545, 631, 1175, 1203, 1467, 1470
Brother Cadfael's Penance 1301
Dead Man's Ransom 883
The Grass-Widow's Tale 802, 1484
The Potter's Field **1302**

The Summer of the Danes **1303**

Peters, Ralph
Flames of Heaven 529

Peterson, Audrey
Deadly Rehearsal 559
Death Too Soon 309
Elegy in a Country Graveyard **1304**
Murder in Burgundy **1305**
The Nocturne Murder 1191, 1192
Shroud for a Scholar **1306**, 1586

Peterson, Geoff
Medicine Dog 492, 772, 1281, **1307**, 1719, 1751

Peterson, Keith
Don't Say a Word **1308**
The John Wells Series 163, 222, 305, 407, 997, 1109, 1578, 1771
The Rain 86, 144, 950
Rough Justice 130, 146, 532, 873, 1053, **1309**
The Scarred Man 513, 664, 721, 811, 964, **1310**, 1747, 1792
There Fell a Shadow 1719
The Trapdoor 166, 679, 838, 866, 867, 1261, 1368, 1369, 1546

Petievich, Gerald
Earth Angels 1193, **1311**, 1426
Paramour 186, 632, 633, 681, 822, **1312**
The Quality of the Informant 981
Shakedown 254
To Live and Die in L.A. 185, 831, 832, 1433

Philbin, Tom
Precinct Siberia Series 1033

Philbrick, W.R.
The Crystal Blue Persuasion 683, 905, 1337
Paint It Black 359, 873, **1313**, 1362, 1363, 1705
Shadow Kills 938
Slow Dancer 77
The T.D. Stash Series 1336

Philips, Judson
The Peter Styles Series 1309

Phillips, Mike
Blood Rights 86, 130, 721, 788, 1053, **1314**

Pickard, Nancy
The 27 Ingredient Chili Con Carne Murders 389, 1257, **1315**
Bum Steer 10, 55, 868, 1120, 1147, 1172, 1235, **1316**, 1432
But I Wouldn't Want to Die There **1317**, 1451
Confession 808, 880
Generous Death 535, 933, 966, 1118, 1167, 1379
I.O.U. 218, 599, 694, **1318**, 1334, 1661, 1665
The Jenny Cain Series 114, 120, 531, 991, 1064, 1117, 1335, 1380
Marriage Is Murder 387, 772, 1378
Say No to Murder 126, 895, 945, 982, 1543

Pierce, David M.
Write Me a Letter 123

Piesman, Marissa
Close Quarters **1319**
Unorthodox Practices 473, 879, **1320**, 1783

Pike, Robert L.
The Lieutenant Reardon Series 1158

Pirincci, Akif
Felidae 180, 438, 439

Platt, Kin
Dead as They Come 524
The Princess Stakes Murder 133

Platt, Orah
Letting Blood **1321**

Platt, Richard
Letting Blood 303, **1321**

Pollack, J.C.
Centrifuge 1116

Porter, Anna
Hidden Agenda 1435

Porter, Joyce
Dover and the Claret Tappers **1322**
The Inspector Dover Series 472, 768

Pottinger, Stanley
The Fourth Procedure 1262

Powell, Deborah
Bayou City Secrets 82, **1323**

Power, Jo-Ann
Clively Close: Dead as Dead Can Be 361

Powers, Elizabeth
On Account of Murder 126, 346

Powers, Tim
Last Call 855

Poyer, David
Louisiana Blue **1324**

Price, Anthony
The Labyrinth Makers 995
Sion Crossing 38, 824

Pronzini, Bill
Blue Lonesome **1325**
Bones 766
Breakdown **1326**
Casefile 283
Epitaphs 1269, **1327**
The Eye 99
Games 526, 589
Hoodwink 668, 1055
Jackpot 282, **1328**, 1353
The Nameless Detective Series 77, 281, 341, 343, 396, 489, 551, 623, 667, 906, 907, 908, 1009, 1075
Nameless Detective Series 1181
The Nameless Detective Series 1272, 1347, 1350, 1414, 1713, 1714, 1716
Quarry **1329**, 1647
Quincannon 1675
The Running of Beasts 187, 349, 618, 980
Stacked Deck **1330**
A Treasury of Detective and Mystery Stories from the Great Pulps 1122
With an Extreme Burning **1331**

Prowell, Sandra West
By Evil Means 97, 736, 1268, **1332**, 1680
The Killing of Monday Brown 792, 1017

Pugh, Dianne G.
Cold Call 56, 125, 531, **1333**
The Iris Thorne Series 124
Slow Squeeze 1413

Pulver, Mary Monica
Ashes to Ashes 897, 1769
The Bishop's Tale 544
The Kori and Peter Brichter Series 154, 1380
Murder at the War 25, 1118
Original Sin 898, **1334**, 1432

Show Stopper **1335**
The Unforgiving Minutes 162, 1420

Purtre, John Walter
Down Among the Angels 905

Putre, John Walter
Death Among the Angels 339, 435, 682, 683, 904, **1336**, 1373
A Small and Incidental Murder 233, 338, 340, 399, 433, 475, 689, 806, 903, 1324, **1337**, 1704

Q

Queen, Ellery
A Study in Terror 1365

Quest, Erica
Cold Coffin 661
The Kate Maddox Series 455
Model Murder 304, **1338**
The October Cabaret 729

Quill, Monica
Body and Soil **1135**
Nun Plussed **1339**
Sine Qua Nun 136, 670, 797, 1123, 1124
Sister Hood 1591
The Sister Mary Teresa Series 137, 138, 1237, 1238, 1239

Quinn, Elizabeth
Murder Most Grizzly 54, 198, **1340**, 1551, 1626
A Wolf in Death's Clothing **1341**, 1552

Quinnell, A.J.
The Mahdi 248, 1473

Quittner, Joshua
Shoofly Pie to Die 629, **1342**, 1710

R

Radley, Sheila
The Chief Inspector's Daughter 1669
Death in the Morning 677, 1179, 1244
The Inspector Quantrill Series 575, 577, 578, 790
The Quiet Road to Death 1253
A Talent for Destruction 1035
This Way Out 841, **1343**
Who Saw Him Die? 676, 759

Raines, Jeff
Unbalanced Acts **1344**

Raleigh, Michael
Death in Uptown **1345**

Ramsay, Diana
Four Steps to Death 18, **1346**

Ramsey, Diana
Four Steps to Death 798

Randisi, Robert J.
The Dead of Brooklyn **1347**
Deadly Allies **1348**
The Disappearance of Penny 133, 170, 573, 1487
Full Contact 873, 1313
The Ham Reporter 36, 1079, 1080, 1654, 1787
Hard Look **1349**
The Miles Jacoby Series 565, 1423
No Exit From Brooklyn 40, 703, 1532
Separate Cases 551, **1350**

The Steinway Collection 282, 630, 1054, 1055

Rankin, Ian
The Inspector John Rebus Series 113
The Inspector Rebus Series 111, 1050

Rauch, Constance
A Deep Disturbance 794, **1351**

Ray, Robert J.
Bloody Murdock 300
Cage of Mirrors 8, 458, 1096
The Matt Murdock Series 486
Merry Christmas, Murdock **1352**
Murdock Cracks Ice **1353**

Raymond, Derek
I Was Dora Suarez 1598

Reasoner, James
Texas Wind 7, 8, 14, 352, 458, 1096

Reasoner, Livia
Dead-Stick **1674**
Dog Heavies **1675**

Reaves, Sam
Get What's Coming **1354**
A Long Cold Fall 305, 767, 1287, 1308, 1345, **1355**, 1644

Redmann, J.M.
The Intersection of Law and Desire **1356**

Reed, Barry
The Choice **1357**, 1600
The Indictment 820

Reed, Christopher
The Big Scratch 180, 181, 182, 438, 439, 443

Rees, Dilwyn
The Cambridge Murders 64

Reeves, Robert
Doubting Thomas 1486, 1657, 1735
Peeping Thomas 590, 850, **1358**

Reid, Robert Sims
Big Sky Blues 193

Reiss, Bob
Flamingo **1359**
The Last Spy 529

Rendell, Ruth
The Best Man to Die 751
Death Notes 143
From Doon with Death 841
Gallowsglass 1277
Going Wrong 417, **1360**
A Guilty Thing Surprised 748
The Inspector Wexford Series 575, 578, 586, 675, 1343, 1393, 1394, 1395, 1396, 1397, 1773
A Judgement in Stone 1062
Kissing the Gunner's Daughter 420, 790, **1361**
The Lake of Darkness 587
Live Flesh 88, 1453
A Sleeping Life 358
Speaker of Mandarin 676
An Unkindness of Ravens 759, 1168

Renfroe, Martha Kay
Dead Matter **1764**
King of the Mountain **1765**

Reno, Marie
Final Proof 384, 524

Resnicow, Herbert
The Gold Deadline 1729
The Gold Solution 607, 608, 1047

Reuben, Shelly
Julian Solo 1372

Reynolds, John Lawrence
And Leave Her Lay Dying **1362**, 1534
The Man Who Murdered God 1705
Whisper Death 272, **1363**

Reynolds, William J.
The Naked Eye **1364**, 1423
Nebraska 1060
The Nebraska Quotient 189, 1056
The Nebraska Series 39, 509, 865, 877, 1754

Rich, Virginia
The Baked Bean Supper Murders 1063, 1140, 1315
The Cooking School Murders 151, 152, 286, 989, 1061, 1255, 1315, 1588, 1594
The Mrs. Potter Series 390, 1445, 1571
The Nantucket Diet Murders 449, 1315

Richardson, Robert
The Augustus Maltravers Series 235, 331
The Book of the Dead 1044, **1365**
The Dying of the Light 110, **1366**
The Latimer Mercy 61, 1050, 1706
Murder in Waiting **1367**

Rider, J.W.
Jersey Tomatoes 77, 189, 565, 703, 1436

Riggs, John R.
A Dragon Lives Forever **1368**
The Garth Ryland Series 166, 922, 1720
Hunting Ground 371, 1722
Let Sleeping Dogs Lie 163
Wolf in Sheep's Clothing 130, 867, **1369**, 1546, 1721

Ripley, W.L.
Dreamsicle **1370**

Ritchie, Simon
The Hollow Woman 242, 1491
Work for a Dead Man **1371**, 1492, 1494

Rivers, Caryl
Indecent Behavior 401, **1372**

Roat, Ronald Clair
Close Softly the Doors **1373**
A Still and Icy Silence 1032, **1374**

Robb, Candace M.
The Apothecary Rose 264, 265, **1375**, 1469
The Lady Chapel 1175, **1376**
The Nun's Tale **1377**
The Owen Archer Series 243

Roberts, Carey
Pray God to Die 734

Roberts, Gillian
The Amanda Pepper Series 114, 154, 246, 596, 991, 1117, 1254, 1567, 1749
Caught Dead in Philadelphia 247, 515, 593, 594, 895, 933, 945, 982, 1136, 1140, 1250, 1316, 1318, 1415, 1748, 1750
I'd Rather Be in Philadelphia 808, **1378**
Philly Stakes 10, 423, 697, **1379**
With Friends Like These **1380**

Roberts, Jan
A Blood Affair **1381**

Roberts, John Maddox
SPQR **1382**, 1449

Author Index

The SPQR Series 201, 1390, 1448, 1450

Roberts, Keith
Pavane 419

Roberts, Les
The Cleveland Connection **1383**
Deep Shaker **1384**
The Duke of Cleveland **1385**
Full Cleveland 1085, **1386**
An Infinite Number of Monkeys 300, 717, 718
The Milan Jacovich Series 39, 41, 407, 565, 791, 869, 1032, 1059, 1345, 1646, 1648
Not Enough Horses 715, 1200, 1575
Pepper Pike 189, 1056, 1060, 1647
The Saxon Series 301, 369
Seeing the Elephant **1387**

Roberts, Lora
Murder in a Nice Neighborhood 422, 596, **1388**

Roberts, Nora
Brazen Virtue 1263

Robin, Robert
Above the Law 820, 1599

Robinett, Stephen
Final Option 86, 755, **1389**
Unfinished Business 1072

Robinson, Kevin
Split Seconds 359

Robinson, Leah Ruth
Blood Run 302, 1321, 1372

Robinson, Lynda S.
Murder in the Place of Anubis **1390**, 1450

Robinson, Patricia
A Trick of Light **1391**

Robinson, Peter
The Alan Banks Series 1050, 1480
A Dedicated Man 203, **1392**, 1556
Gallows View 625, 645, 1197, **1393**, 1669, 1769
The Hanging Valley 358, 640, **1394**, 1767
The Inspector Banks Series 356, 577, 643, 678, 752, 1361
A Necessary End **1395**
Past Reason Hated 230, **1396**
Wednesday's Child 740, **1397**

Robinson, Robert
Landscape with Dead Dons 64, 1045

Robitaille, Julie
Jinx 868, **1398**, 1568

Roe, C.F.
The Jean Montrose Series 660, 932, 1129
A Nasty Bit of Murder 658, 931, 934, 1130, 1656
A Torrid Piece of Murder 1262

Roe, Francis
Dangerous Practices 1283

Ronns, Edward
The Art Studio Murders 628

Roome, Annette
A Second Shot in the Dark 741, 894, **1399**, 1557, 1671

Roosevelt, Elliott
Murder and the First Lady 1634

Rosen, Dorothy & Sidney
Death and Blintzes 1588

Rosen, Richard
Fadeaway 1655

Saturday Night Dead 652, 1709
Strike Three, You're Dead 505, 506, 508, 872, 1206, 1271, 1536
World of Hurt **1400**

Rosenberg, Nancy Taylor
Interest of Justice 216
Mitigating Circumstances 421, 1381, **1401**, 1465, 1780

Rosenblum, Robert
The Good Thief 1429

Ross, Jonathan
Burial Deferred 789, 1639
Daphne Dead and Done For 753
Dark Blue and Dangerous 748, 1001
Dropped Dead 1168
A Rattling of Old Bones 1614
A Time for Dying **1402**

Ross, Kate
A Broken Vessel **1403**
Cut to the Quick 103, **1404**

Rossiter, John
A Time for Dying **1402**

Rostand, Robert
The Killer Elite 552

Rothenberg, Rebecca
The Bulrush Murders 1234, **1405**

Rovin, Jeff
Hollywood Detective: Garrison 1674

Rowe, Jennifer
Death in Store **1406**
Grim Pickings 46
Murder by the Book 9, 224, 307, 583
The Verity Birdwood Series 156

Rowland, Peter
The Disappearance of Edwin Drood 1164, **1407**

Rowlands, Betty
Exhaustive Enquiries **1408**
Finishing Touch 1557
A Little Gentle Sleuthing 107, 361
The Melissa Craig Series 108
Over the Edge **1409**

Royce, Kenneth
The XYZ Man 567

Rozan, S.J.
China Trade 601, **1410**

Rubino, Jane
Death of a DJ **1411**

Ruell, Patrick
Dream of Darkness **1412**, 1593

Russell, Alan
The Hotel Detective **1413**
No Sign of Murder **1414**, 1439
The Rivals of Sherlock Holmes 24

Russell, E.S.
Dead Easy **1415**

Russell, Randy
Caught Looking **1416**
Hot Wire 952, 1444, 1537, 1690

Ryan, Conall
Black Gravity 1478

Ryan, J.M.
Brooks Wilson Ltd. 628

S

Sale, Medora
The Inspector Sanders Series 1396, 1397

Murder in a Good Cause 642, 644, 1197, 1334, 1408, **1417**, 1768
Murder in Focus 896, 898, 1132, **1418**, 1772
Pursued by Shadows **1419**
Short Cut to Santa Fe 884, **1420**, 1766
Sleep of the Innocent 897, 1767, 1769

Sallis, James
Black Hornet **1421**
The Lew Griffin Series 1691
The Long-Legged Fly 194
Moth 1325, **1422**

Sanders, Lawrence
Capital Crimes 1169
The First Deadly Sin 1158, 1344, 1533

Sanders, William
The Next Victim **1423**
The Taggert Roper Series 485

Sandford, John
Eyes of Prey 623, 1095, 1381
Fool's Run 566
The Lucas Davenport Series 1008
Night Prey 1026, **1424**
Rules of Prey 149, 196, 812, 846, 1039, **1425**
Shadow Prey **1426**, 1534
Silent Prey 229, 840, 873, 1363, **1427**, 1600, 1736, 1737
Sudden Prey 1025
Winter Prey 195, **1428**

Sandom, J.G.
Gospel Truths 61, 235, **1429**

Sandstrom, Eve K.
Death Down Home 522, 693, 889, 1334, 1335, 1399, **1430**, 1627, 1637
The Devil Down Home 520, 902, **1431**, 1685, 1740
The Down Home Heifer Heist **1432**

Sanford, Jerome
Miami Heat 1286, **1433**

Santiago, Soledad
Nightside **1434**
Room 9 1317, **1435**
Undercover 59, 74, 1221, 1223

Sarazen, Nicholas
Family Reunion 49

Sarrantonio, Al
Summer Cool 211, **1436**

Satterthwait, Walter
At Ease with the Dead 478, 1233, **1437**, 1781
Escapade 560, **1438**
A Flower in the Desert 41, 830, 1200, 1217, 1252, 1423, **1439**, 1505, 1581
The Hanged Man **1440**
The Joshua Croft Series 490, 1458
Miss Lizzie 207, **1441**
Wall of Glass 757, 758, 1162, 1601, 1650, 1688, 1794

Saum, Karen
Murder Is Germane **1442**
Murder Is Relative 82

Sauter, Eric
Hunter 1352
Predators 553
Skeletons 205, 1427, **1443**

Savage, Marc
Flamingos 1370, **1444**, 1537, 1690

Sawyer, Corinne Holt
The Benbow and Wingate Series 285, 361
The J. Alfred Prufrock Murders 712, 1098, 1112, 1315
Murder by Owl Light 1209, **1445**
Murder Has No Calories **1446**
Murder in Gray and White **1447**

Sayers, Dorothy L.
Busman's Honeymoon 800
Gaudy Night 64
Strong Poison 543, 1417

Saylor, Steven
Arms of Nemesis 1175
Catalina's Riddle 1390, **1448**
Roman Blood 201, **1449**
The Venus Throw **1450**

Schenkel, S.E.
In Blacker Moments **1451**

Schermerhorn, James
Night of the Cat 59, 954, 970, **1452**, 1526, 1717

Schneider, Joyce Anne
Darkness Falls 79, 323, 326, 463, 602, 886, 975, 1062, **1453**, 1699, 1761

Scholefield, Alan
Never Die in January 1708
Thieftaker **1454**

Schopen, Bernard
The Big Silence 1437, 1439
The Desert Look 97, 132, **1455**

Schorr, Mark
Ace of Diamonds 132
Bully! 1049
Gunpower **1456**

Schow, David J.
The Kill Riff 1102

Schutz, Benjamin M.
Embrace the Wolf 146, 150, 716
A Fistful of Empty 149, 305, 454, 623, 1104, **1457**, 1481, 1765
The Leo Haggerty Series 28, 29, 30, 489, 667, 862, 863, 864, 865, 939, 1272, 1648
Mexico Is Forever 485, **1458**
A Tax in the Blood 1601
The Things We Do for Love 1358, 1587

Schwartz, Richard B.
Frozen Stare **1459**

Scoppettone, Sandra
Everything You Have Is Mine 1442, **1460**
I'll Be Leaving You Always 1042, **1461**
The Lauren Laurano Series 927, 946
My Sweet Untraceable You **1462**

Scott, Jack S.
The View from Deacon Hill 112, 1189

Scott, Justin
The Ben Abbott Series 2, 72, 688
Hardscape 1, 70, 336, 337, 339, 687, **1463**
StoneDust **1464**

Scott, Rosie
Glory Days 533, 806, 1731

Scottoline, Lisa
Running From the Law **1465**

Sebastian, Tim
The Spy in Question 529
Spy Shadow **1466**

Sedley, Kate
Death and the Chapman 265, 427, 512, 1375, **1467**
The Holy Innocents **1468**
The Plymouth Cloak **1469**
The Roger the Chapman Series 243, 264, 631, 1376
The Weaver's Tale 426, **1470**, 1624

Segal, Kathrin King
Wild Again **1471**

Sehler, Tom
When Reason Sleeps **1472**

Selwyn, Francis
Cracksman on Velvet 1610

Serafin, David
The Body in Cadiz Bay 1236, 1731

Shagan, Steve
Pillars of Fire 1174, **1473**

Shah, Diane K.
As Crime Goes By 1323

Shames, Laurence
Florida Straits 231, 784, 1024, 1560
Scavenger Reef 1012

Shankman, Sarah
First Kill All the Lawyers 198, 894, 1041, 1399, 1498, 1545
He Was Her Man 313, 522, **1474**
The King Is Dead **1475**
Now Let's Talk of Graves 215, 569, 1145, 1215, 1216, **1476**
The Samantha Adams Series 382, 383, 604, 1542, 1544, 1632
She Walks in Beauty 1119, **1477**, 1495
Then Hang All the Liars 731, 1496, 1631

Shannon, Dell
Case Pending 1107
The Luis Mendoza Series 747

Shannon, Doris
A Death for a Dancing Doll 597
A Death for a Dodo 598
The Dying Room 599

Shaw, Howard
Death of a Don 64

Shaw, P.B.
The Seraphim Kill 1231

Shaw, Simon
Killer Cinderella **1478**

Shepherd, Stella
Nurse Dawes Is Dead **1479**
Thinner than Blood **1480**, 1556

Sherburne, James
Death's Clenched Fist 36
Death's Pale Horse 1079, 1080

Sherer, Michael W.
Death Came Dressed in White **1481**
Little Use for Death 207, 330, 484, 869, 1044, **1482**, 1735

Sherwood, John
Bones Gather No Moss **1483**
A Bouquet of Thorns **1484**
The Celia Grant Series 46, 107, 108, 802, 1406
Flowers of Evil 562
The Hanging Garden **1485**

Shoemaker, Bill
Fire Horse **1486**
Stalking Horse 538, **1487**

Shone, Anna
Mr. Donaghue Investigates **1488**

Short, Sharon Gwyn
Angel's Bidding **1489**
The Death We Share **1490**

Shuman, M.K.
The Caesar Clue **1491**, 1694
Death Notice 866
Deep Kill 272, **1492**
Deerslayer 867
The Last Man to Die 431, 829, **1493**
The Maya Stone Murders 1371, **1494**, 1738
The Micah Dunn Series 281

Sibley, Celestine
Ah, Sweet Mystery 100, 206, 371, 731, 742, 867, 1208, 1209, 1409, **1495**, 1545, 1631, 1632
Dire Happenings at Scratch Ankle **1496**, 1542, 1544
The Kate Mulcay Series 373, 1483, 1548
A Plague of Kinfolks **1497**
Straight as an Arrow 624, 674, 1315, **1498**, 1547

Siciliano, Sam
The Angel of the Opera 81

Sidwa, B.N.
The Crow Eaters 35, 874, 875

Silliphant, Stirling
Steel Tiger 581, 1337

Silver, Victoria
Death of a Harvard Freshman 140, 745, 1519

Silvis, Randall
An Occasional Hell 1283, 1325

Simenon, Georges
The Inspector Maigret Series 548, 690, 768

Simmons, Dan
Summer of Night 935

Simon, Leonard
Disassociated States **1499**

Simon, Roger L.
The Big Fix 1102
California Roll 7, 511, 1703, 1753
Raising the Dead 878

Simonson, Sheila
Larkspur **1500**, 1764
Mudlark 1432
Skylark 345, 962, **1501**

Simpson, Dorothy
Dead by Morning 800, 1001, **1502**
Element of Doubt 1555
The Inspector Luke Thanet Series 25, 367, 1160, 1213
The Inspector Thanet Series 1394, 1480
Last Seen Alive 748
Puppet for a Corpse 470, 1554
Six Feet Under 1392

Simpson, J.A.
Cold Comfort 967
A Gift for Murder 968
Murder by Mail 969
Once upon a Crime 970
Poisoned Ivy 971

Sims, L.V.
Murder Is Only Skin Deep 47, 1088, 1089

Sinclair, Bennie Lee
The Lynching 669, 1178, **1503**, 1538

Singer, Shelley
The Barrett Lake Series 156, 378
Following Jane 157, 503, 1701

Free Draw 462, 1573
Interview with Mattie **1504**
The Jake Samson Series 907, 1414
Picture of David **1505**
Samson's Deal 1009
Searching for Sara 1434, **1506**

Sjowall, Maj
The Martin Beck Series 690, 691

Skeggs, Douglas
The Estuary Pilgrim **1507**
The Talinin Madonna 365, **1508**, 1744
The Triumph of Bacchus **1509**

Sklepowich, Edward
Death in a Serene City 1002, 1003, 1004, 1187, **1510**

Skom, Edith
The George Eliot Murders **1511**
The Mark Twain Murders 535, 583, 712, 1136, 1167, **1512**, 1627

Slade, Michael
Headhunter 1027

Slatalla, Michelle
Shoofly Pie to Die 1342

Slater, Ian
Deep Chill **1513**

Slesar, Henry
The Gray Flannel Shroud 1040

Sloan, Susan R.
Guilt by Association 985, **1514**

Slovo, Gillian
The Kate Baeier Series 1541

Slusher, William S.
Shepherd of the Wolves 736

Smilgis, Martha
Fame's Peril 770

Smith, April
North of Montana 881, 953, 1221, 1268, **1515**, 1525, 1527, 1660

Smith, Barbara Burnett
Dust Devils of the Purple Sage 537, **1516**, 1586
Writers of the Purple Sage 224, 595, 600, 1411, **1517**

Smith, Charles Merrill
Reverend Randollph and the Avenging Angel 1124
The Reverend Randollph Series 797, 1101, 1706

Smith, Dennis
Glitter and Ash 487

Smith, Evelyn
Miss Melville Regrets 1063
The Miss Melville Series 813

Smith, Evelyn E.
Miss Melville Regrets 1478
Miss Melville Rides a Tiger **1518**
The Miss Melville Series 786, 1539
Miss Melville's Revenge 1681

Smith, Janet L.
The Annie MacPherson Series 115
Practice to Deceive 216, 853, 963

Smith, Joan
A Brush with Death 1216, 1509, **1519**
Don't Leave Me This Way 269, 307, 801, 1306, **1520**, 1586
Follow That Blonde 345, 477, **1521**
The Loretta Lawson Series 1511, 1541
A Masculine Ending 892, 962, 1305, 1501, 1557

What Men Say 309, 960, 1196, 1274, **1522**
Why Aren't They Screaming? 891

Smith, Julie
The Axeman's Jazz 321, 1515, **1523**
Dead in the Water **1524**
Death Turns a Trick 462, 1183, 1651
House of Blues **1525**
Huckleberry Fiend 712, 1512
Jazz Funeral **1526**, 1632
New Orleans Beat **1527**
New Orleans Mourning 194, 195, 196, 197, 391, 429, 430, 925, 953, 1038, 1039, 1170, 1225, 1422, 1476, 1491, **1528**
Other People's Skeletons **1529**
The Rebecca Schwartz Series 851, 853
The Skip Langdon Series 447, 601, 927, 969, 1226, 1686
The Sourdough Wars 153, 988, 1320
Tourist Trap 1316, 1716
True-Life Adventure 1241

Smith, Kay Nolte
Catching Fire 487, 488

Smith, Marie
More Ms. Murder 1267, 1348
Ms. Murder 663, 1073, 1267

Smith, Martin Cruz
Gorky Park 859, 861, 1066, 1793
Polar Star 234, 725, 913, **1530**

Smith, Mitchell
Karma 1354, **1531**

Smith, Richard C.
A Secret Singing 1703

Smith, Scott
A Simple Plan 363, 1354

Smith, Terrence Lore
Yours Truly, From Hell 1610

Smoke, Stephen
Pacific Coast Highway 1282

Smolens, John
Winter by Degrees 233, 689

Solomita, Stephen
Bad to the Bone 149, 150, **1532**
Force of Nature 186, 197, **1533**
A Good Day to Die 147, **1534**
A Piece of the Action 910, 1008, **1535**
The Stanley Moodrow Series 1024
A Twist of the Knife 146, 306, 749, 1075, 1644, 1696

Solomon, Brad
The Open Shadow 1745

Soos, Troy
Murder at Ebbets Field 12
Murder at Fenway Park 508, **1536**

Soracco, Sin
Edge City 4, 270, 271, 952, 1370, 1444, **1537**

Sorrells, Walter
Will to Murder 985

Specht, Robert
The Soul of Betty Fairchild 69, 665, 1503, **1538**

Spencer, Ross H.
The Missing Bishop 499

Spicer, Michael
Cotswold Moles **1539**

Spikol, Art
The Physalia Incident 1779

Spillane, Mickey
The Killing Man **1540**

Spring, Michelle
Every Breath You Take 428, 1094, **1541**

Sprinkle, Patricia Houck
Deadly Secrets on the St. Johns **1542**
Death of a Dunwoody Matron 313
Murder in the Charleston Manner 457, 731, 1315, 1547
Murder on Peachtree Street 347, **1543**, 1631, 1632, 1635
A Mystery Bred in Buckhead 900, 1204, **1544**
The Sheila Travis Series 32, 1497, 1548
Somebody's Dead in Snellville 22, 836, 901, 1496, **1545**

Squire, Elizabeth Daniels
Kill the Messenger 836, 900, 1503, **1546**
Memory Can Be Murder 803, **1547**
The Peaches Dann Series 732, 1411, 1542
Who Killed What's-Her-Name? 520, **1548**

Stabenow, Dana
A Cold-Blooded Business 56, 57, **1550**
A Cold Day for Murder 259, 289, 291, 492, 1341, **1549**, 1580, 1581, 1607, 1784, 1786
Dead in the Water **1551**
The Kate Shugak Series 48, 701, 702, 1340, 1625, 1626
Play with Fire **1552**

Stacey, Susannah
Bone Idle 111, **1553**
Death of the Duchess 512
Goodbye, Nanny Gray 25, 110, 1160
Grave Responsibility 470, **1554**, 1708
A Knife at the Opera **1555**
The Late Lady **1556**
The Superintendent Bone Series 469, 1159, 1480

Stallwood, Veronica
Death and the Oxford Box 1274, **1557**
Deathspell **1558**, 1593
Oxford Exit **1559**

Standiford, Les
Deal to Die For **1560**
Done Deal 3, 617, 1012, **1561**
Raw Deal 1354
Spill 605

Stanford, Jerome
Miami Heat 98

Stansberry, Dominic
The Spoiler 612

Stanton, Mary
A Dash of Death 134

Stark, Richard
Butcher's Moon 1297
The Grofield Series 1387
The Parker Series 1690

Starrett, Vincent
Murder in Peking 496

Stashower, Daniel
The Adventure of the Ectoplasmic Man 560

Staynes, Jill
Bone Idle **1553**
Grave Responsibility **1554**

A Knife at the Opera **1555**
The Late Lady **1556**

Stearn, Martha
Deadly Diagnosis 1262

Stebel, S.L.
The Boss's Wife 987, **1562**

Steed, Neville
Black Eye **1563**, 1695
Boxed In **1564**
Clockwork 1069, **1565**
The Peter Marklin Series 570, 571, 572, 1068, 1242
Wind-Up **1566**

Stein, Benjamin
Her Only Sin 546

Stein, Triss
Murder at the Class Reunion 206, 360, 415, 604, 699, 944, **1567**

Steinberg, Janice
Death of a Postmodernist 360, **1568**

Steiner, Susan
Library: No Murder Aloud 1, 415, 416, **1569**

Stephens, Reed
The Man Who Killed His Brother 262

Stephenson, Neal
Zodiac 335, 340

Stern, Richard Martin
Death in the Snow 793
The Johnny Ortiz Series 1437, 1781
Missing Man **1570**

Stevens, Serita
Bagels for Tea 978, **1571**

Stevens, Shane
By Reason of Insanity 1027, 1154

Stevenson, Richard
The Donald Strachey Series 1151
Ice Blues 727, 1796
On the Other Hand, Death 726
Third Man Out **1572**

Steward, Samuel M.
The Caravaggio Shawl **1573**

Stewart, Gary
The Tenth Virgin 828, 1018
The Zarahembla Vision 509, 828, 829, 830

Stinson, Jim
Double Exposure 413, 847, 992
Low Angles 299, 300
The Stoney Winston Series 301, 369, 1247
Truck Shot 718, **1574**
TV Safe **1575**

Stockley, Grif
Expert Testimony 923
Illegal Motion **1576**

Stockley, Griff
Probable Cause **1577**

Storey, Alice
First Kill All the Lawyers 612, 1318
Then Hang All the Lawyers 866
Then Hang All the Liars 867

Storey, Margaret
Bone Idle **1553**
Grave Responsibility **1554**
A Knife at the Opera **1555**
The Late Lady **1556**

Story, William L.
Final Thesis 1482, 1735

Stout, David
Carolina Skeletons 13, 669, 939, 1503, 1538, 1583, 1683

The Dog Hermit 1287, **1578**, 1720
Night of the Ice Storm 1095, 1215, **1579**, 1665

Stout, Rex
Gambit 411
The League of Frightened Men 1095
Murder by the Book 668
The Nero Wolfe Series 402, 585, 814, 1048
Too Many Cooks 988
Where There's a Will 695

Straley, John
The Curious Eat Themselves **1580**
The Curious Eat Themsleves 708
The Woman Who Married a Bear 492, 1137, 1354, 1374, 1549, 1550, 1551, 1552, **1581**, 1786

Strange, John Stephen
Murder on the Ten-Yard Line 50

Strieber, Whitley
The Wolfen 1426

Stroud, Carsten
Lizardskin **1582**

Strunk, Frank C.
Jordon's Showdown **1583**
Jordon's Wager 757, 758, 1108, **1584**

Stryker, Dev
End Game **1585**

Stuyck, Karen Hanson
Cry for Help 1021, **1586**

Sublett, Jesse
Boiled in Concrete 406, **1587**
The Martin Fender Series 320, 1755
Rock Critic Murders 555
Tough Baby 350, 555

Sucher, Dorothy
Dead Men Don't Give Seminars 776
Dead Men Don't Marry **1588**
The Vic Newman/Sabina Swift Series 813

Sullivan, Mark T.
The Fall Line 518, **1589**
Hard News **1590**

Sullivan, Winona
A Sudden Death at the Norfolk Cafe 671, 734, 799, 1237, 1434, **1591**

Summerfield, Lin
Count the Days **1592**
Never Walk Behind Me 1558, **1593**

Sutton, Remar
Boiling Rock **1594**
Long Lines 175, 1112

Swain, James
The Man Who Walked Through Walls **1595**

Swanson, Doug J.
Dreamboat **1596**

Swarthout, Glendon
Skeletons 1653

Sylvester, Martin
A Dangerous Age 739
A Lethal Vintage 571, 739, 1563, 1566, 1790
The William Warner Series 1564

Symons, Julian
The Blackheath Poisonings 1292, 1293, 1294, 1296
Bland Beginning 1028
Death's Darkest Face 1412
The Kentish Manor Murders 1365

Something Like a Love Affair 90
A Three-Pipe Problem 1365

T

Taibo, Paco Ignacio II
An Easy Thing 27, 327, **1597**
The Shadow of the Shadow **1598**

Takagi, Akimitsu
No Patent on Death 1127

Tanenbaum, Robert K.
Depraved Indifference 184
Immoral Certainty 333, 1015, 1640
Justice Denied 650, 820, **1599**
Material Witness 940
Reversible Error **1600**

Tanner, Jake
Saint Louie Blues **1601**

Tapply, William G.
The Brady Coyne Series 28, 162, 236, 764, 1615
Dead Winter 766, **1602**
Follow the Sharks 1358
Spotted Cats 31, 337, 338, 445, 922, **1603**
Tight Lines **1604**
A Void in Hearts 819

Tarkenton, Fran
Murder at the Superbowl 50

Tartt, Donna
The Secret History 90

Tate, Kelly A.
The Lion's Share **1605**

Taylor, Bonnie
Neon Dancers **1608**

Taylor, D.B.
Fatal Obsession 893, 1360, **1606**

Taylor, Domoni
Praying Mantis 1157

Taylor, Elizabeth Atwood
The Northwest Murders 57, 370, 1119, **1607**, 1667

Taylor, L.A.
Footnote to Murder 556, 745
A Murder Waiting to Happen 966
Poetic Justice 1121, 1359, 1588

Taylor, Matt
Neon Dancers **1608**, 1710
Neon Flamingos 1201

Telushkin, Joseph
The Unorthodox Murder of Rabbi Wahl 878

Tepper, Sheri S.
Dead in the Scrub **1232**
Death and the Delinquent **1233**
Death and the Dogwalker **1240**
Death Served Up Cold **1234**
A Little Neighborhood Murder **1241**
A Long Time Dead **1242**
The Unexpected Corpse **1235**

Terman, Douglas
Free Flight 409, 825

Tey, Josephine
The Daughter of Time 418, 424

Thall, Michael
Let Sleeping Afghans Lie 629, 723

Tharp, Jeffrey
A Killing in Kansas 592

Thayer, Steve
Saint Mudd 280, **1609**

Thomas, Donald
The Weatherman 812, 1641

Thomas, Donald
The Ripper's Apprentice **1610**

Thomas, Ross
Ah, Treachery **1611**
Briarpatch 395, 435, 1312, 1617, 1762
The Cold War Swap 981
The Fools in Town Are on Our Side 159, 210, 616, 1752, 1760
The Fourth Durango 433, 483, 782, 785, 1100, **1612**
The Mordida Man 434
Out on the Rim 783
The Porkchoppers 184
Twilight at Mac's Place **1613**

Thompson, Earl
Caldo Largo 1598

Thompson, J.A.
Amends for Murder **966**

Thompson, Jim
The Grifters 773
Nothing More Than Murder 295

Thompson, Joyce
Bones 430, 431

Thompson, Thomas
Celebrity 1662

Thomson, June
Death Cap 1402
Dying Fall 67
The Habit of Loving 748, 1253, 1554
The Inspector Rudd Series 367, 1139, 1159
The Long Revenge 368
Not One of Us 1160
A Question of Identity 204
Rosemary for Remembrance 753
The Spoils of Time 675, 752, **1614**

Thomson, Maynard F.
Trade Secrets 232, 386, 1400, **1615**

Thoreau, David
The Book of Numbers **1616**

Thornburg, Newton
The Lion at the Door **1617**

Thorp, Roderick
Rainbow Drive 293, 832, 1311
River 1166

Thrasher, L.L.
Cat's Paw, Inc. **1618**

Tierney, Ronald
The Iron Glove **1619**
The Steel Web **1620**
The Stone Veil **1621**

Tobin, Brian
The Missing Person 514
The Ransom 1199, **1622**

Togawa, Masako
The Lady Killer 1127

Tolkin, Michael
The Player 847

Topol, Edward
Red Snow 1530

Topor, Roland
The Tenant 1013

Topor, Tom
The Codicil **1623**

Tourney, Leonard
Frobisher's Savage **1624**
Low Treason 883, 1084

The Matthew Stock Series 264, 426, 512, 631, 1467, 1468, 1469, 1470
The Player's Boy Is Dead 427, 1081, 1082, 1295

Townsend, Guy M.
To Prove a Villain 424

Tracy, Margaret
Mrs. White 1116

Trainor, J.F.
The Angela Biwaban Series 702, 1550, 1551, 1680
Corona Blue **1625**
Dynamite Pass 1017, 1273, 1340, 1341, **1626**, 1667

Traver, Robert
Anatomy of a Murder 558

Travis, Elizabeth
Finders Keepers 223, 224, 1501, **1627**
Under the Influence 9, 162, 693, 1342, 1725

Trevanian
The Loo Sanction 552
Shibumi 527

Trevor, Elleston
Quiller KGB **706**

Trigoboff, Joseph
The Bone Orchard 1535, **1628**

Trimble, Barbara
The Fifth Rapunzel **586**
Time and Time Again **587**

Tripp, Miles
The Cords of Vanity **1629**
The John Samson Series 26, 27, 327, 329, 1488
Video Vengeance **1630**

Trocheck, Kathy Hogan
The Callahan Garrity Series 1542, 1548
Every Crooked Nanny 125, 312, 374, **1631**
To Live and Die in Dixie 503, 1544, **1632**

Trolley, Jack
Balboa Firefly **1633**

Trott, Susan
The Housewife and the Assassin 44
Pursued by the Crooked Man 713

Troy, Simon
Swift to Its Close 1614

Truman, Margaret
Murder at the Kennedy Center 1169, **1634**
Murder at the Smithsonian 296, 297

Tryon, Thomas
The Night of the Moonbow 935

Tucker, John Bartholomew
He's Dead-She's Dead: Details at Eleven 760, 1475, 1477, **1635**, 1709

Tucker, Kerry
Cold Feet 124, 615, **1636**
Death Echo 372, 1497, **1637**
The Libby Kincaid Series 944, 1388
Still Waters 198, 313, 520, 610, 809, 901, 1041, 1145, 1498, **1638**, 1723

Turnbull, Peter
Condition Purple **1639**
Dead Knock 948
The "P" Division Series 249

Turow, Scott
The Burden of Proof 1723
Pleading Guilty **1640**
Presumed Innocent 239, 333, 412, 421, 547, 557, 558, 1016, 1023, 1600, 1662

Tyre, Peg
Strangers in the Night **1641**

U

Uhnak, Dorothy
The Bait 1077, 1789
The Christie Opera Series 601
The Ledger 141, 1088, 1225
Policewoman 804

Underwood, Michael
A Compelling Case 543
Double Jeopardy 1651
The Hidden Man 153
Rosa's Dilemma 562, 1658
Seeds of Murder 561, 598, **1642**

Upfield, Arthur W.
The Inspector Napoleon Bonaparte Series 255, 328, 329, 874, 1695
The Scribner Crime Classic Series 256, 875

Upton, Robert
Dead on the Stick 317, 318, 481
Fade Out 728, 1010, 1575

V

Vachss, Andrew
Blossom 716, **1643**
Flood 527, 888
Footsteps of the Hawk **1644**
Hard Candy 831
Sacrifice 1217, 1252
Shella 755
Strega 526, 886, 1251

Valentine, Deborah
A Collector of Photographs **1645**

Valin, Jonathan
Day of Wrath 1540
Extenuating Circumstances 150, 1601
Fire Lake 189, 1093
The Harry Stoner Series 29, 30, 31, 39, 342, 343, 407, 667, 862, 863, 864, 865, 1019, 1085, 1347, 1373, 1383, 1385, 1458, 1765
Life's Work 50, 196, 319, 652
The Lime Pit 146, 668, 716, 826, 1618, 1619
Missing **1646**
The Music Lovers **1647**
Second Chance 717, 1287, **1648**

Van De Wetering, Janwillem
The Rattle-Rat 548

Van Gieson, Judith
The Lies That Bind **1649**
The Neil Hamel Series 1076, 1625, 1699
North of the Border 97, 1320, 1439
The Other Side of Death 33, 851, 1401, 1437, 1440, 1529, **1650**
Raptor 55, 972, 1234, 1235, 1524, 1570, 1603, 1604, 1626, **1651**, 1668
The Wolf Path 32, 54, 1233, 1340, **1652**, 1667

Van Gulik, Robert
The Judge Dee Series 875

Van Meter, David A.
Body of Evidence **1653**

Van Til, Reinder
Bleeding Dodger Blue **505**
Fear in Fenway **506**
Tigers Burning **508**

Vance, John Holbrook
The Fox Valley Murders 298

Vazquez Montalban, Manuel
Murder in the Central Committee 1236
Murder in the Central Committee 1597

Vetter, Louise
Showcase **603**
Trunk Show **604**

Victor, Daniel D.
The Seventh Bullet 81, **1654**

Vincent, L.M.
Final Dictation **1655**
Pas De Death **1656**

Vine, Barbara
The Dark-Adapted Eye 90, 587, 1360
A Fatal Inversion 1310, 1367

Viorst, Judith
Murdering Mr. Monti 1319

W

Wade, Henry
A Dying Fall 191

Waggoner, Bill
Sweet Death **1657**, 1735

Wainwright, John
All on a Summer's Day 112, 1001
All Through the Night 1639
The Man Who Wasn't There 1189
The Venus Fly Trap 1402

Wakefield, Hannah
The Price You Pay 269, 561, 1529, 1642
A Woman's Own Mystery 962, 1501, 1541, **1658**

Walker, Mary Willis
The Red Scream 194, 679, 909, **1659**
Under the Beetle's Cellar 796, 1051, **1660**
Zero at the Bone 21, 22, 96, 362, 604, 903, 1605, 1652, **1661**, 1733, 1734

Walker, Walter
A Dime to Dance By 735
The Immediate Prospect of Being Hanged 240, 547, **1662**
Two Dude Defense 1016, 1090

Wall, David Cooper
One Cried Murder **1663**

Wallace, Marilyn
A Case of Loyalties 593
Deadly Allies **1348**
A Single Stone 252, 1217, **1664**
Sisters in Crime 663
Sisters in Crime 2 663
The Sisters in Crime Series 1073, 1267
So Shall You Reap **1665**

Wallace, Robert
To Catch a Forger **1666**

Wallingford, Lee
Clear-Cut Murder 57, 605, 1341, **1667**, 1784

Author Index

Cold Tracks 54, 55, 370, 492, 1652, **1668**, 1728

Walters, Minette
The Ice House **1669**
The Scold's Bridle 1660, **1670**
The Sculptress 114, 909, **1671**

Wambaugh, Joseph
The Blue Knight 1067
The Delta Star 1033, 1311
The Glitter Dome 1426, 1696

Ward, E.C.
A Nice Little Beach Town 1777

Ward, Robert
The Cactus Garden 784, **1672**

Warfield, Gallatin
Silent Son 1599

Warga, Wayne
Fatal Impressions 477, 479, 532, 1068, 1507, 1508, 1666, 1676
Hardcover 341, 466, 1020, 1054, 1055, 1387, 1500, 1764
Singapore Transfer 261, **1673**, 1744

Warmbold, Jean
June Mail 1435

Warner, Mignon
A Medium for Murder 591

Washburn, L.J.
Dead-Stick 501, 847, 860, **1674**
Dog Heavies **1675**
Wild Night 299

Washburn, Stan
Intent to Harm 1424

Watson, Clarissa
The Fourth Stage of Gainsborough Brown 1666

Watson, Colin
Charity Ends at Home 752, 753, 789
Hopjoy was Here 1189
The Inspector Purbright Series 472, 911
Lonelyheart 4122 89
Plaster Sinners 204
Six Nuns and a Shotgun 1322

Watson, Peter
Landscape of Lies **1676**

Watts, Timothy
Cons 482, 1288, 1589, **1677**, 1760

Waugh, Carol-Lynn Rossel
Purrfect Crime 619, 620

Waugh, Hillary
A Death in a Town **1678**
Last Seen Wearing. . . 1107

Weatherby, W.J.
Coronation 787, **1679**

Weaver, Michael
Impulse 468

Webb, Jack
The Bad Blonde 915
The Father Shanley Series 656

Webb, Lise McClendon
The Bluejay Shaman **1680**

Webb, Martha G.
Bird in a Cage 1086
The Buzzards Must Also Be Fed **1739**
Darling Corey's Dead 350, 460, 461, 464
The Day That Dusty Died 1087
Deficit Ending **1088**
Exception to Murder **1740**
The Eye of Anna **1741**

The Mensa Murders **1089**
White Male Running 1135
Yakuza, Go Home **1742**

Weber, Janice
Frost the Fiddler 1539, **1681**

Webster, Noah
The Jonathan Gaunt Series 451
The Spanish Maze Game **1682**

Weikart, Jim
Casualty Loss 6, 809, **1683**

Weinman, Irving
The Lenny Schwartz Series 1711, 1717
Virgil's Ghost **1684**

Weir, Charlene
Consider the Crows 219, 1432, **1685**
Family Practice **1686**
The Winter Widow 536, 925, **1687**

Weiss, Mike
The Ben Henry Series 907
A Dry and Thirsty Ground **1688**

Welch, Pat
Murder by the Book 82, 947, 1042, 1126, 1356, 1442, 1460, 1461, **1689**

Wellen, Edward
An Hour to Kill **1690**

Wender, Theodora
Knight Must Fall 1520

Wentworth, Patricia
The Miss Silver Series 175, 802, 1163, 1171

Werry, Richard
Casket for a Lying Lady 1745

Wesley, Valerie Wilson
Devil's Gonna Get Him **1691**
When Death Comes Stealing **1692**

West, Charles
Funnelweb 256, **1693**
Rat's Nest **1694**
Stonefish 327, 328, 329, **1695**

West, Chassie
Sunrise 761

Westbrook, Robert
Nostalgia Kills 1696

Westermann, John
Exit Wounds 1535, **1696**
High Crimes 185, 1433

Westlake, Donald E.
Baby Would I Lie 1755
Butcher's Moon 210
Don't Ask 616, **1697**
The Dortmunder Series 145
Drowned Hopes **1698**
The Fugitive Pigeon 355
God Save the Mark 11, 628, 714, 715
Levine 856, 857, 858
A Likely Story 524
Trust Me on This 401

Wetherby, W.J.
Coronation 60

Whalley, Peter
Robbers 1629, 1630

Wheat, Carolyn
Dead Man's Thoughts 1524
Fresh Kills **1699**
Where Nobody Dies 1076, 1650

White, Gloria
Charged with Guilt **1700**
Money to Burn **1701**

Murder on the Run 94, 648, 649, 1220, **1702**, 1798
The Ronnie Ventana Series 378

White, Ned
The Very Bad Thing 7, 330, 939, **1703**, 1753

White, Randy Wayne
Sanibel Flats 1011, **1704**

White, Stephen
The Alan Gregory Series 1499
Private Practices 364, 885, 887, 1276

White, Teri
Fault Lines 1455
Thursday's Child **1705**
Tightrope 483, 1664
Triangle 1116

Whitehead, Barbara
The Dean It Was That Died 61, 670, 671, 672, 733, **1706**, 1730
Playing God 235, **1707**
Sweet Death, Come Softly **1708**

Whitelaw, Stella
The Cat That Wasn't There 619

Whitney, Phyllis
Rainbow in the Mist 1453
The Singing Stones 139

Whitney, Polly
Until Death 760, **1709**
Until the End of Time 1201, **1710**

Whitten, Les
Moon of the Wolf 429

Whittingham, Richard
Their Kind of Town 1287

Wilcox, Collin
Dead Center **1711**
A Death Before Dying **1712**
Except for the Bones 1387, **1713**
Full Circle **1714**
Hire a Hangman **1715**
The Lieutenant Hastings Series 856, 857, 858, 1008, 1033, 1107, 1158
Silent Witness 123, **1716**
Switchback **1717**

Wilcox, Stephen F.
All the Dead Heroes 408, **1718**
The Dry White Tear 721, 1053, **1719**
The Elias Hackshaw Series 688, 1032
The Green Mosaic **1720**
The NIMBY Factor 2, 949, **1721**
The Painted Lady **1722**

Wilhelm, Kate
Death Qualified: A Mystery of Chaos 240, **1723**
The Hamlet Trap 728, 870
Justice for Some 730, **1724**
Seven Kinds of Death **1725**

Willeford, Charles
Cockfighter 482
Miami Blues 855, 1057, 1058, 1416
New Hope for the Dead 1349
Sideswipe 653, 709, 938

Willey, Gordon Randolph
Selena **1726**

Williams, Amanda Kyle
A Singular Spy **1727**

Williams, Ann M.
Flowers for the Dead 172, 849, 1156, 1668, **1728**

Williams, Charles
Dead Calm 973, 1057

Williams, David
Holy Treasure! 1069, **1729**
The Mark Treasure Series 452, 1068, 1179
Treasure by Post 1706, **1730**

Williams, Philip Lee
Slow Dance in Autumn 148, 320, 454, 1457, 1481

Willocks, Tim
Green River Rising 4

Wilson, Barbara
The Dog Collar Murders 533, 534, 1323
Gaudi Afternoon **1731**
Murder in the Collective 745
Sisters of the Road 947

Wilson, Charles
Nightwatcher 1165
Silent Witness 1538, 1562, **1732**

Wilson, F. Paul
Dydeetown World 241

Wilson, Karen Ann
Copy Cat Crimes **1733**
Eight Dogs Flying 121, 257, 258, 288, 291, 362, **1734**
The Samantha Holt Series 21

Wilson, Robin
Death by Degrees **1735**

Wilson, Tom
Black Wolf 786

Wiltse, David
The Edge of Sleep **1736**
The Fifth Angel 205
Into the Fire 1283, **1737**
Prayer for the Dead 468
The Serpent 1628

Wiltz, Chris
A Diamond Before You Die 1752
The Emerald Lizard 197, 273, 1038, 1492, **1738**
The Killing Circle 1491, 1493, 1494

Winder, Robert
No Admission 11

Wingate, Anne
The Buzzards Must Also Be Fed **1739**
Death by Deception 267, 298, 314, 316, 626, 1431, 1775
Deficit Ending **1088**
Exception to Murder **1740**
The Eye of Anna **1741**
The Mark Shigata Series 311, 1230, 1756
Yakuza, Go Home **1742**

Wingfield, R.D.
The Frost Series 472, 911, 912
A Touch of Frost 740, 751

Wings, Mary
She Came in a Flash 202, 274
She Came Too Late 1460, 1461, 1462

Winslow, Don
A Cool Breeze on the Underground 227, **1743**
The Trail to Buddha's Mirror 261, 952, **1744**

Wiser, H. Fred
Deadly Stakes **1745**

Wolf, S.K.
The Harbinger Effect 86, 453, 685, 756, 1727, **1746**

Wolfe, Susan
Long Chain of Death 305, 513, 842, 886, 1582, **1747**, 1791

Wolfe, Susan
The Last Billable Hour 51, 237, 405, 963, 1093, 1155, 1524

Wolzien, Valerie
All Hallows Evil **1748**
A Good Year for a Corpse 215, **1749**
Murder at the PTA Luncheon 101, 594, 1255, 1258, 1415
A Star-Spangled Murder 1319
The Susan Henshaw Series 157, 244, 246, 247, 600, 1254
We Wish You a Merry Murder 245, 1146, 1208, 1256, 1315, **1750**

Womack, Steven
Dead Folks' Blues 870, **1751**
Murphy's Fault 494, 513, 1738, **1752**, 1777, 1778
The Software Bomb **1753**
Torch Town Boogie 1474, **1754**
Way Past Dead 902, 1104, **1755**

Wood, Ted
Dead in the Water 316, 1418
Flashback **1756**
An Inside Job 627
Live Bait 13, 314, 1739
On the Inside 539, 1103, 1105, 1417, 1601, **1757**, 1770
The Reid Bennett Series 259, 291, 310, 775, 1549, 1580, 1766, 1773, 1774, 1776, 1785, 1786
Snow Job 294, **1758**
When the Killing Starts 1742, 1775

Woodrell, Daniel
Under the Bright Lights 193, 197, 272, 273, 973, 1738

Woods, Sara
The Anthony Maitland Series 563
The Case Is Altered 1729
The Law's Delay 562
Nor Live So Long 561, 1642, 1658

Woods, Sherryl
Reckless 1214
Ties That Bind **1759**

Woods, Stuart
Chiefs 1070, 1546
Deep Lie 85

Grass Roots 936, 1169
Heat **1760**
Imperfect Strangers **1761**
Palindrome 1351, **1762**
Run Before the Wind 582, 1037
Santa Fe Rules 98, 173, 547, 665, 1297, **1763**
White Cargo 363, 581, 582, 1188

Woolrich, Cornell
The Bride Wore Black 1606

Wouk, Herman
The Caine Mutiny 666

Wozencraft, Kim
Rush 74, 1223

Wren, M.K.
The Conan Flagg Series 167, 169, 182, 998, 999
Curiosity Didn't Kill the Cat 1020, 1618
Dead Matter **1764**
King of the Mountain **1765**

Wright, Daphne
Bitter Herbs 307
Bloody Roses 308
Rotten Apples 309

Wright, Eric
A Body Surrounded by Water 1772
Buried in Stone **1766**, 1774
The Charlie Salter Series 1773
Death by Degrees 1767
Final Cut 992, **1768**
A Fine Italian Hand **1769**
The Man Who Changed His Name 1418
A Question of Guilt 334, 627
A Question of Murder 1417
A Sensitive Case 614, **1770**

Wright, Jim
The Last Man Standing **1771**

Wright, L.R.
A Chill Wind in January **1772**
Fall From Grace 268, **1773**
The Karl Alberg Series 310, 1756, 1758
Mother Love 1766, **1774**
Prized Possessions **1775**
The Suspect 314, 1418, 1785
A Touch of Panic **1776**

Wuamett, Victor
Artichoke Hearts 1463, 1732, **1777**
Deeds of Trust **1778**
Teardown 101, 192, 1240, **1779**

Wynn Jones, Hazel
Death and the Trumpets of Tuscany 979, 1510

Wyrick, E.L.
A Strange and Bitter Crop 1699, **1780**
A Strange and Bitter Fruit 853

Y

Yaffe, James
Mom Among the Liars 722
Mom Meets Her Maker 697
The Mom Series 45, 175, 177, 411

Yarbro, Chelsea Quinn
The Charlie Moon Series 701
Ogilvie, Tallant, and Moon 77, 793
Poison Fruit **1781**

Yeager, Dorian
Cancellation by Death 15, 20, 413, 414, 1248, **1782**
Eviction by Death 16, 473, 517, **1783**
Murder Will Out 48, 1568, **1784**

York, Andrew
The Eliminator 567

Yorke, Margaret
Admit to Murder 640, 1412
Intimate Kill 67

Young, Scott
Murder in a Cold Climate 775, 1550, 1552, 1775, **1785**
The Shaman's Knife 1680, **1786**

Yount, Steven
Wandering Star 90, 876

Z

Zackel, Fred
Cinderella After Midnight 816
Cocaine and Blue Eyes 1618

Zahava, Irene
The Womansleuth Anthology Series 663, 1267

Zannos, Susan
Trust the Liar 1558

Zaremba, Eve
Beyond Hope 83, 444, 533, 534, 1460, 1689, 1731
A Reason to Kill 806
Work for a Million 202, 533, 746, 946, 1236, 1573

Zencey, Eric
Panama **1787**

Zigal, Thomas
Into Thin Air **1788**

Zimmelman, Lue
Honolulu Red 1005, 1223, **1789**

Zimmerman, Bruce
Blood under the Bridge 1713, 1779
Full-Bodied Red 739, **1790**

Zimmerman, R.D.
Blood Trance 887, **1791**
Closet 812
Deadfall in Berlin 914, 1113, 1278, 1747, **1792**
Death Trance 993
Mindscream 303, 965
Red Trance **1793**

Zochert, Donald
Another Weeping Woman 1307
The Man of Glass 199, 200
Murder in the Hellfire Club 883

Zollinger, Norman
Lautrec **1794**

Zubro, Mark Richard
The Only Good Priest **1795**
A Simple Suburban Murder 1194, 1415
Sorry Now? **1796**
The Tom Mason Series 1150, 1151, 1572
Why Isn't Becky Twitchell Dead? **1797**

Zukowski, Sharon
Dancing in the Dark 320, 473, 542, 1227, 1228, 1319, **1798**
Leap of Faith **1799**

Title Index

This index alphabetically lists all titles featured in entries and those listed under "Other books you might like." Each title is followed by the author's name and the number of the entry of that title. Bold numbers indicate featured main entries; other numbers refer to books recommended for further reading.

A

The 6 Messiahs
Frost, Mark **560**

The 13th Juror
Lescroart, John T. 730, 985, 1576, 1724

19th Precinct
Newman, Christopher **1202**

The 27 Ingredient Chili Con Carne Murders
Pickard, Nancy 389, 1257, **1315**

30 for a Harry
Hoyt, Richard 819

32 Cadillacs
Gores, Joe **616**, 736

The 87th Precinct Series
McBain, Ed 199, 856, 857, 1033, 1077

A.P.B.
Pedneau, Dave 807, 1759

The Aaron Gunner Series
Haywood, Gar Anthony 1176, 1177, 1178, 1691

The Abigail Danforth Series
Jackson, Marian J.A. 465, 924, 930, 1259, 1260

Above the Law
Robin, Robert 820, 1599

Abracadaver
Lovesey, Peter 942

An Absence of Light
Lindsey, David L. 909, 1025, **1026**

According to St. John
Babula, William **77**, 1716

Ace of Diamonds
Schorr, Mark 132

Act of Faith
Bowen, Michael **158**

Act of God
Healy, Jeremiah 93, **764**

Act of Love
Lansdale, Joe R. 99, 349, **980**, 1154, 1165, 1166, 1279, 1282, 1285

Act of Passion
Arnston, Harrison 1015

Actor
Hall, Parnell 1387, 1714

Adjusted to Death
Girdner, Jacqueline 51

Adjusted to Death
Girdner, Jaquelin 214, 215, 245, 423, **593**, 1255, 1258, 1543, 1748

Admit to Murder
Yorke, Margaret 640, 1412

Advent of Dying
O'Marie, Carol Anne 449, 670, 797, 1123, 1124, 1442

Advent of Silence
O'Marie, Carol Anne 136

The Adventure of the Ectoplasmic Man
Stashower, Daniel 560

The Adventure of the Stalwart Companions
Jeffers, H. Paul 36, 131, 441, 1654

The Affair of the Blood-Stained Egg Cosy
Anderson, James 103, 220, 401, 695

The African Poison Murders
Huxley, Elspeth 226

After the First Death
Block, Lawrence 98, 1763

Against the Wind
Freedman, J.F. 102, 333, **547**, 651, 666, 1331, 1577, 1640, 1649

Agatha Raisin and the Quiche of Death
Beaton, M.C. 100, **107**, 145, 389

Agatha Raisin and the Vicious Vet
Beaton, M.C. **108**

Ah, Sweet Mystery
Sibley, Celestine 100, 206, 371, 731, 742, 867, 1208, 1209, 1409, **1495**, 1545, 1631, 1632

Ah, Treachery
Thomas, Ross **1611**

The Alan Banks Series
Robinson, Peter 1050, 1480

The Alan Gregory Series
White, Stephen 1499

The Albert Samson Series
Lewin, Michael Z. 71, 494, 1060, 1085, 1383, 1385, 1386, 1751, 1754

The Alex Delaware Series
Kellerman, Jonathan 364, 1251, 1252, 1499, 1747

Alibi for a Corpse
Lemarchand, Elizabeth 675

Alibi for an Actress
Farrell, Gillian B. 15, 20, 413, **516**, 770, 1228, 1247, 1248, 1391, 1782, 1783

Alice in La-La Land
Campbell, Robert 148, 254, 886, 1217

The Alice Nestleton Series
Adamson, Lydia 180, 251, 414, 438, 1391, 1783

Alicia's Trump
Mathewson, Joseph 404

The Alienist
Carr, Caleb 400, 560, 1787

All Around the Town
Clark, Mary Higgins **252**, 843, 1157

All Booked Up
Curran, Terrie 416, 1275, 1559

All Dressed Up to Die
Nordan, Robert 45

All Fall Down
Gruenfeld, Lee 1633

All Hallows Evil
Wolzien, Valerie **1748**

All I Have Is Blue
Colbert, James **272**

All on a Summer's Day
Wainwright, John 112, 1001

All Roads to Sospel
Bellairs, George 87

All Shall Be Well
Crombie, Deborah 95, **356**, 644, 1132, 1396

All That Remains
Cornwell, Patricia D. 80, **321**, 1736

All the Dead Heroes
Wilcox, Stephen F. 408, **1718**

All the Great Pretenders
Adams, Deborah **10**, 374, 457, 989, 1115, 1119

All the Muscle You Need
McRae, Diana 806, 1460, 1689

All the Muscle You Need
McRae, Diane 533

All Through the Night
Wainwright, John 1639

All Titles
Hendryx, James B. 1785

The Allerton Avenue Precinct Series
Fliegal, Richard 856

Alley Kat Blues
Kijewski, Karen **917**, 1227

The Alo Nudger Series
Lutz, John 71, 1326, 1327, 1329, 1374, 1688, 1754

Along Came a Spider
Patterson, James 468, **1276**, 1434

The Alpine Advocate
Daheim, Mary 14, 163, **370**, 383, 868, 1041, 1156

The Alpine Betrayal
Daheim, Mary 520

The Alpine Christmas
Daheim, Mary **371**

The Alpine Decoy
Daheim, Mary **372**, 1065

The Alpine Fury
Daheim, Mary **373**

The Alpine Series
Daheim, Mary 206, 1497

The Alteration
Amis, Kingsley 419

The Alvarez Journal
Burns, Rex 40, 844, 1570

Always a Body to Trade
Constantine, K.C. 1712

The Amanda Hazard Series
Fedderson, Connie 902

The Amanda Pepper Series
Roberts, Gillian 114, 154, 246, 596, 991, 1117, 1254, 1567, 1749

Amateur Night
Beck, K.K. **114**, 770

The Amazing Mrs. Pollifax
Gilman, Dorothy 1163

The Ambrose Usher Series
Davey, Jocelyn 228, 1366

The Amelia Peabody Series
Peters, Elizabeth 440, 441, 442, 476, 519, 834, 928, 930, 1029, 1071, 1118

507

Amends for Murder
Lake, M.D. 351, 461, 777, **966**, 1528

American Tabloid
Ellroy, James 276, 277, 1421

Ammie, Come Home
Michaels, Barbara 502

Amos Walker
Estleman, Loren D. 1060

The Amos Walker Series
Estleman, Loren D. 41, 147, 190, 833, 862, 863, 865, 1019, 1056, 1059, 1347, 1373, 1374, 1384, 1386, 1440, 1646, 1648

The Amy Prescott Series
Hendricksen, Louise 325, 1129

Anatomy of a Murder
Traver, Robert 558

And Baby Makes None
Lewis, Stephen 602, **1022**

And Baby Will Fall
Lewin, Michael Z. 58

And Justice for One
Clarkson, John 195, 196, **254**, 421, 518, 1039, 1211, 1370, 1585

And Leave Her Lay Dying
Reynolds, John Lawrence **1362**, 1534

And Soon I'll Come to Kill You
Kelly, Susan 119, 889, **893**, 1401

And Then There Were None
Christie, Agatha 220, 742

The Andrew Broome Series
McInerny, Ralph 236, 237

Angel Dance
Beal, M.F. 523

Angel Death
Moyes, Patricia 543, 1594

The Angel Gang
Kuhlken, Ken **956**

The Angel Maker
Pearson, Ridley 1276, **1282**, 1737

Angel of Death
Cohen, Anthea 1321

Angel of Death
Higgins, Jack 104, **786**

Angel of Death
Krich, Rochelle Majer 74, 881, 884, **953**, 1515

The Angel of the Opera
Siciliano, Sam 81

The Angela Biwaban Series
Trainor, J.F. 702, 1550, 1551, 1680

Angel's Bidding
Short, Sharon Gwyn **1489**

The Angel's Share
Irvine, R.R. **826**, 1678

The Angus Straum Series
Cork, Barry 109, 111

The Animal Hour
Klavan, Andrew 935

The Anna Lee Series
Cody, Liza 304, 428, 455, 456, 1094, 1125, 1143, 1338, 1541

The Anna Peters Series
Law, Janice 1799

The Anna Pigeon Series
Barr, Nevada 1649

The Annie Laurance/Max Darling Series
Hart, Carolyn G. 334, 747, 983, 1064

The Annie Laurance Series
Hart, Carolyn G. 218, 376, 836, 1117, 1661

The Annie Laurence Series
Hart, Carolyn G. 732

The Annie MacPherson Series
Smith, Janet L. 115

The Anodyne Necklace
Grimes, Martha 562

Another Death in Venice
Hill, Reginald 1004

Another Path, Another Dragon
Mathis, Edward 165

Another Weeping Woman
Zochert, Donald 1307

The Anthony Maitland Series
Woods, Sara 563

Antipodes
Oliver, Maria-Antonia **1236**, 1731

The Apothecary Rose
Robb, Candace M. 264, 265, **1375**, 1469

Aristotle, Detective
Doody, Margaret 201, 394, 883, 1382, 1449

The Aristotle Socarides Series
Kemprecos, Paul 336, 339, 687

The Arly Hanks Series
Hess, Joan 1111

The Armageddon Rag
Martin, George R.R. 299, 406, 1102

Arms of Nemesis
Saylor, Steven 1175

The Art Studio Murders
Ronns, Edward 628

The Artful Egg
McClure, James 226

The Arthur Crook Series
Gilbert, Anthony 597, 598

Artichoke Hearts
Wuamett, Victor 1463, 1732, **1777**

As a Favor
Dunlap, Susan 771, 772, 1089, 1528, 1687

As Crime Goes By
Shah, Diane K. 1323

As October Dies
Davis, Kenn 788

Ashes to Ashes
Carl, Lillian Stewart 502

Ashes to Ashes
Pulver, Mary Monica 897, 1769

Ask the Right Question
Lewin, Michael Z. 459, 826

The Assassini
Gifford, Thomas 60, 1429

Assassins Road
Harvester, Simon 1473

Assumed Identity
Morrell, David 518, 633

At Ease with the Dead
Satterthwait, Walter 478, 1233, **1437**, 1781

Audition for Murder
Carlson, P.M. 1707

The August Didier Series
Myers, Amy 928

August Ice
Day, Deforest **399**, 624, 1472

The Augustus Maltravers Series
Richardson, Robert 235, 331

Aunt Dimity and the Duke
Atherton, Nancy **68**, 385

Aunt Dimity's Death
Atherton, Nancy **69**, 795, 959, 1065

Auntie Mayhem
Daheim, Mary 385

The Aurora Teagarden Series
Harris, Charlaine 156, 416, 1516

The Autumn Dead
Gorman, Ed 1355, 1457, 1579, 1653

Avenging Angel
Appiah, Anthony **64**, 235, 598

The Avenging Angel
Burns, Rex 1018

The Axeman's Jazz
Smith, Julie 321, 1515, **1523**

Axx Goes South
Huber, Frederic 624, **817**, 1011

B

The Baby Blue Rip Off
Collins, Max Allan 459

Baby Doll Games
Maron, Margaret 47, 1088

Baby Would I Lie
Westlake, Donald E. 1755

Babylon South
Cleary, Jon **255**

The Back Door Man
Kantner, Rob 459, 500, 1384, 1386

A Back Room in Somers Town
Malcolm, John 477, 1563

Backfire
Law, Janice 1227

Backhand
Cody, Liza **269**

Bad Apple
Bruno, Anthony **184**

The Bad Blonde
Webb, Jack 915

Bad Blood
Bruno, Anthony **185**, 348, 1128, 1363

Bad Blood
Carlson, P.M. **218**

Bad Chemistry
Kelly, Nora **891**, 1196, 1274, 1306

Bad Desire
Devon, Gary 262, **417**, 1360, 1471

Bad Guys
Bruno, Anthony 273, 1188, 1199, 1202, 1362, 1433, 1622, 1672

Bad Intent
Hornsby, Wendy 881

Bad Love
Kellerman, Jonathan **885**

Bad Medicine
Dreyer, Eileen 1051

Bad Moon
Bruno, Anthony **186**

Bad Neighbors
Haiblum, Isidore **703**

Bad News Travels Fast
Haywood, Gar Anthony **761**

Bad to the Bone
Solomita, Stephen 149, 150, **1532**

The Bag Man
Lacey, Peter **961**

Bagels for Tea
Stevens, Serita 978, **1571**

Bagged
Bailey, Jo **79**, 302, 448, 659, 660, 931, 932, 934, 968, 970, 1130, 1656

Bait
Abel, Kenneth **3**, 294, 1210, 1514, 1672

The Bait
Uhnak, Dorothy 1077, 1789

The Baked Bean Supper Murders
Rich, Virginia 1063, 1140, 1315

Balboa Firefly
Trolley, Jack **1633**

Balefire
Godard, Kenneth W. 1344

The Balmoral Nude
Coker, Carolyn 345, 477, 1216, 1521

The Bandersnatch
Hardwick, Mollie **729**, 801

Banjo Boy
Kohler, Vince 606, **949**

Bankroll
Ducker, Bruce **450**, 1040

Bantam of the Opera
Daheim, Mary **374**, 744

Baptism for Murder
Maxwell, Jan **1101**

Barbed Wire
Fackler, Elizabeth 612

Bare Acquaintances
Berne, Karin 208, 274, 346, 405

Barking Dogs
Irvine, R.R. 827

The Barrett Lake Series
Singer, Shelley 156, 378

Barrier Island
MacDonald, John D. 1608

The Baxter Trust
Hailey, J.P. 877

The Bay Psalm Book Murder
Harriss, Will 223, 611, 1020, 1031, 1627

Bayou City Secrets
Powell, Deborah 82, **1323**

Bea and Lyon Wentworth Series
Forrest, Richard 162

Bear Hug
Doolittle, Jerome 344, **432**, 1753

The Beasts of Valhalla
Chesbro, George C. 238

Beat Up a Cookie
Dietz, Denise **422**

Beating the Odds
Gordon, Deborah 446

A Beautiful Place to Die
Craig, Philip R. 96, 233, **335**, 386, 686, 689, 903, 905, 922, 1074, 1463

Beauty Dies
Howe, Melodie Johnson 275, **813**

The Becket Factor
Anthony, Michael David **60**, 1429, 1706

The Bed-and-Breakfast Series
Daheim, Mary 134, 135, 698, 699

The Beekeeper's Apprentice
King, Laurie R. 835, **924**, 1259, 1260

Beer and Skittles
Morison, B.J. 1140

The Beethoven Conspiracy
Hauser, Thomas 609, 1304

Beggar's Choice
Kennealy, Jerry 354, **906**

Behind Eclaire's Doors
Dunbar, Sophie **457**

Behind the Fact
Hilary, Richard 565, **788**

Belgrave Square
Perry, Anne 930, 1029

The Ben Abbott Series
Scott, Justin 2, 72, 688

The Ben Henry Series
Weiss, Mike 907

The Ben Perkins Series
Kantner, Rob 489, 490, 833, 1059, 1373, 1374, 1385, 1458

The Benbow and Wingate Series
Sawyer, Corinne Holt 285, 361

The Benjamin Franklin Series
Hall, Robert Lee 1148

The Benni Harper Series
Fowler, Earlene 1516

The Benny Cooperman Series
Engel, Howard 1766

Berlin Covenant
Paul, Celeste **1278**

The Bernard Samson Series
Deighton, Len 647

The Bernie Gunther Series
Kerr, Philip 994

The Bernie Rhodenbarr Series
Block, Lawrence 210, 714

Bertie and the Seven Bodies
Lovesey, Peter 103, **1049**

The Best Cellar
Goodrum, Charles A. 1275

The Best Man to Die
Rendell, Ruth 751

Bet Against the House
Dain, Catherine 378

Better Mousetraps
Lutz, John 1330

The Beverly Malibu
Forrest, Katherine V. 47, 202, **533**, 634, 1126, 1323, 1796

Beware of Trains
Crispin, Edmund 221

Beyond Hope
Zaremba, Eve 83, 444, 533, 534, 1460, 1689, 1731

The Big Bounce
Leonard, Elmore 1677

The Big Enchilada
Morse, L.A. 1540

Big Fish
Grissom, Ken 616, **682**, 687, 904, 1324

The Big Fix
Simon, Roger L. 1102

The Big Freeze
Katz, Michael J. 827, **871**, 1771

The Big Killing
Meyers, Annette 986, 1040, 1186, 1389

The Big Kiss-Off of 1944
Bergman, Andrew 1270

The Big Nowhere
Ellroy, James 498, 1161, 1177

The Big Payoff
Law, Janice 1228

The Big Scratch
Reed, Christopher 180, 181, 182, 438, 439, 443

The Big Silence
Schopen, Bernard 1437, 1439

Big Sky Blues
Reid, Robert Sims 193

The Big Stick
Alexander, Lawrence 1079

Bigfoot
Hoyt, Richard 815

The Bilbao Looking Glass
MacLeod, Charlotte 1430

The Bill Hawley Series
Axler, Leo 2, 688, 1021, 1242, 1464

Billingsgate Shoal
Boyer, Rick 233, 340, 683, 686, 1602, 1779

The Bind
Ellin, Stanley 1612

Bino
Gray, A.W. 1280, 1357

The Bino Phillips Series
Gray, A.W. 1576

Bino's Blues
Gray, A.W. **650**

Bird in a Cage
Martin, Lee **1086**

Birthmarks
Dunant, Sarah 304, 308, 428, **455**, 1125, 1143, 1541

The Bishop Regan Series
Love, William F. 608

Bishop's Gambit, Declined
Haynes, Conrad 1043, 1045, 1657

The Bishop's Tale
Frazer, Margaret **544**

A Bite of Death
Conant, Susan **287**

Bitter Finish
Barnes, Linda 569, 908, 1713

Bitter Herbs
Cooper, Natasha **307**, 1306

Bitter Medicine
Paretsky, Sara 93, 263, 659, 837, 1219

Bitter Recoil
Havill, Steven F. **757**, 1021

Black Betty
Mosley, Walter 833

Black Cherry Blues
Burke, James Lee **193**, 1025, 1307, 1327, 1329, 1603

The Black Dahlia
Ellroy, James 278, 279, 280, 1422, 1609

Black Dreams
Green, Kate 993

The Black Echo
Connelly, Michael 211, **292**, 363, 618, 1436, 1623, 1672

Black Eye
Steed, Neville **1563**, 1695

Black Girl, White Girl
Moyes, Patricia **1179**

The Black Glove
Miller, Geoffrey 1459

Black Gold, Red Death
Lindsey, David L. 1596

Black Gravity
Ryan, Conall 1478

Black Hornet
Sallis, James **1421**

The Black Ice
Connelly, Michael 3, **293**, 910, 1210, 1534

Black Knight in Red Square
Kaminsky, Stuart M. 1066

A Black Legend
Horton, John 810

Black Light
Hearn, Daniel 6, 406, **767**, 1202

The Black Lizard Anthology of Crime Fiction
Gorman, Ed 1122

The Black Mask Boys
Nolan, William F. 283, 1122

The Black Mask Murders
Nolan, William F. **1207**

Black Moon
Drake, Alison 1058

Black Out
Lawton, John 994

The Black Paw
Little, Constance 168

Black Rainbow
Michaels, Barbara 68

Black Ribbon
Conant, Susan 121, **288**

The Black Seraphim
Gilbert, Michael 587

The Black Star Murders
Gilbert, Dale 607

The Black Star Murders
Gilbert, Dale L. 814, 1047, 1048

Black Sunday
Harris, Thomas 248

Black Wolf
Wilson, Tom 786

The Blackboard Jungle
Hunter, Evan 144

The Blackford Oakes Series
Buckley, William F. Jr. 647, 810

The Blackheath Poisonings
Symons, Julian 1292, 1293, 1294, 1296

The Blackie Ryan Series
Greeley, Andrew M. 1101

Blackout
Lawton, John 420

Blackstone
Falkirk, Richard 941, 1083, 1404

The Blackstone Series
Falkirk, Richard 1403

Blanche Among the Talented Tenth
Neely, Barbara 761, 1691

Blanche on the Lam
Neely, Barbara 141, 142, **1198**, 1692

Bland Beginning
Symons, Julian 1028

The Blank Page
Constantine, K.C. 1678

Bleeding Dodger Blue
Evers, Crabbe **505**

The Blessing Way
Hillerman, Tony 700, 1570

Blind Man with a Pistol
Himes, Chester 1314

The Blind Pig
Jackson, Jon A. 254, 498, 1421

Blind Side
Bayer, William 11, **105**, 192, 227, 262, 295, 421, 842, 1562, 1732

Blind Side
Klein, Dave 50, 652, 872

Blind Trust
Grant, Linda 511, 986, 1701

Blindsight
Cook, Robin 80, **302**

A Blood Affair
Roberts, Jan **1381**

Blood and Judgement
Gilbert, Michael 1402, 1502, 1639

Blood and Thunder
Collins, Max Allan **276**

Blood Kin
Dorner, Marjorie 252, **436**, 1637, 1724

Blood Lies
Anderson, Virginia 21, **52**, 538, 540, 541, 839

Blood Line
Knight, Alanna **941**

Blood Marks
Crider, Bill **349**, 651

Blood Music
Hunter, Jessie Prichard **821**

Blood Oath
Morrell, David 1531

Blood of an Aries
Mather, Linda 849, **1094**

Blood of Poets
Davis, Kenn **393**

Blood on the Bayou
Donaldson, D.J. **429**, 476, 478, 974, 975, 1499

Blood on the Boards
Gault, William Campbell 174, 176

Blood on the Moon
Ellroy, James 185, 292, 1193, 1433

Blood on the Street
Meyers, Annette **1146**

Blood Orange
Llewellyn, Sam 541

Blood Relative
Allegretto, Michael **39**, 1110, 1688

Blood Relative
Hougan, Carolyn **811**, 1724

Blood Rights
Phillips, Mike 86, 130, 721, 788, 1053, **1314**

Blood Rose
Heffernan, William 1165

Blood Run
Robinson, Leah Ruth 302, 1321, 1372

Blood Shot
Paretsky, Sara 634, 1355

Blood Sport
Francis, Dick 573

Blood Test
Kellerman, Jonathan 879

Blood Ties
Brix, Alexi 1471

Blood Trance
Zimmerman, R.D. 887, **1791**

Blood Type
Greenleaf, Stephen 263, **667**, 906

Blood under the Bridge
Zimmerman, Bruce 1713, 1779

Blood Will Have Blood
Barnes, Linda 174, 176, 1346

Bloodeagle
Lewis, Roy 1726

Bloodlines
Conant, Susan **289**

Bloodstream
Carlson, P.M. 1686

Bloody Kin
Maron, Margaret 1687

Bloody Murdock
Ray, Robert J. 300

Bloody Roses
Cooper, Natasha **308**, 1411

Bloody Soaps: A Tale of Love and Death in the Afternoon
Babbin, Jacqueline **75**, 1121

Bloody Ten
Love, William F. **1047**

Blooming Murder
Hager, Jean 135, 244, 375, **698**

Blossom
Vachss, Andrew 716, **1643**

Blue Bayou
Lochte, Dick 231, **1038**, 1059

Blue Eyes
Charyn, Jerome 554

The Blue Knight
Wambaugh, Joseph 1067

Blue Lonesome
Pronzini, Bill **1325**

The Bluejay Shaman
Webb, Lise McClendon **1680**

Blues for Charlie Darwin
Hentoff, Nat 856, 857, 1158

Blunt Darts
Healy, Jeremiah 938, 1326, 1328, 1602

Bodies
Barnard, Robert 754

Body and Soil
McInerny, Ralph **1135**, 1603

Body English
Mariz, Linda 476, 583, 702

The Body Farm
Cornwell, Patricia D. **322**

Body Guard
Burns, Rex **199**

The Body in Blackwater Bay
Gosling, Paula **624**

The Body in Cadiz Bay
Serafin, David 1236, 1731

The Body in the Basement
Page, Katherine Hall 536, 537, 559, **1254**

The Body in the Belfry
Page, Katherine Hall 157, 245, 247, 734, **1255**, 1315, 1545, 1748, 1750

The Body in the Bouillon
Page, Katherine Hall 135, 697, **1256**, 1317

The Body in the Cast
Page, Katherine Hall **1257**, 1291

The Body in the Cornflakes
Beck, K.K. 145

The Body in the Transept
Dams, Jeanne M. **385**

The Body in the Vestibule
Page, Katherine Hall 345, **1258**

The Body in the Volvo
Beck, K.K. 1121

The Body of a Girl
Gilbert, Michael 563

Body of Evidence
Cornwell, Patricia D. **323**, 448, 463

Body of Evidence
Van Meter, David A. **1653**

The Body Politic
Aird, Catherine **25**, 203, 911

Body Scissors
Dolittle, Jerome 1613

Body Scissors
Doolittle, Jerome 263, **433**, 521, 939, 1000, 1100, 1312, 1472

A Body Surrounded by Water
Wright, Eric 1772

A Body to Die For
Frankel, Valerie 554

A Body to Dye For
Michaels, Grant 727, **1150**, 1194, 1572, 1795, 1796

The Bohemian Connection
Dunlap, Susan 966

Boiled in Concrete
Sublett, Jesse 406, **1587**

Boiling Rock
Sutton, Remar **1594**

Bolt
Francis, Dick 52

Bone Idle
Stacey, Susannah 111, **1553**

The Bone Orchard
Trigoboff, Joseph 1535, **1628**

A Bone to Pick
Harris, Charlaine 69, 457, **731**, 742, 801, 1409, 1569

Bones
Pronzini, Bill 766

Bones
Thompson, Joyce 430, 431

Bones and Silence
Hill, Reginald 675, 754, **789**

Bones Gather No Moss
Sherwood, John **1483**

Bones of Coral
Hall, James W. 98, 408, 525, 632, 682, **707**, 784, 785, 823, 1204, 1560, 1763

The Bonnie Indermill Series
Berry, Carole 56, 347, 403, 596, 1155

Book Case
Greenleaf, Stephen 31, 281, 623, **668**, 723, 816

The Book of Numbers
Thoreau, David **1616**

The Book of the Dead
Richardson, Robert 1044, **1365**

Booked to Die
Dunning, John 9, 223, 224, **466**, 611, 1054, 1764

The Bookman's Wake
Dunning, John **467**

Bootlegger's Daughter
Maron, Margaret 900, 901, 936, **1076**, 1637, 1685

Borderlines
Mayor, Archer 1092, **1103**, 1436

The Boss's Wife
Stebel, S.L. 987, **1562**

Bottom-Feeder Blues
Constantine, K.C. 1104, 1105

The Bottom Line Is Murder
Eversz, Robert 986

Bound to Murder
Fiske, Dorothy 1275, 1559

A Bouquet of Thorns
Sherwood, John **1484**

The Bourne Identity
Ludlum, Robert 552

Box Nine
O'Connell, Jack 59, 74, 293, 1202, 1221, **1223**

Boxed In
Steed, Neville **1564**

The Boy Who Was Buried This Morning
Hansen, Joseph **726**

The Boys in the Black Mask
Nolan, William F. 621

The Boy's Tale
Frazer, Margaret **545**

A Brace of Skeet
Hammond, Gerald **719**

The Brady Coyne Series
Tapply, William G. 28, 162, 236, 764, 1615

The Bragg and Morton Series
Harrison, Ray 655, 943

Bragg's Hunch
Lynch, Jack 1616

Brazen Virtue
Roberts, Nora 1263

Title Index

Breach of Promise
Hart, Roy **748**

Break and Enter
Harrison, Colin 66, **735**, 1106, 1357

Break Point
Nastase, Ilie 1195

Breakdown
Pronzini, Bill **1326**

Breathe No More, My Lady
Lacy, Ed 705

Briarpatch
Thomas, Ross 395, 435, 1312, 1617, 1762

The Bride Wore Black
Woolrich, Cornell 1606

Brideprice
Catanach, J.N. 158, **226**

The Bridled Groom
Borthwick, J.S. **154**

Bright Shark
Ballard, Robert **85**

The British Cross
Granger, Bill 37, 38, 824, 1278

Broken Consort
Gollin, James 589, **609**, 1191, 1192, 1304

Broken Idols
Flannery, Sean 706

A Broken Vessel
Ross, Kate **1403**

Brooks Wilson Ltd.
Ryan, J.M. 628

The Brother Athelstan Series
Harding, Paul 544, 545, 1376, 1470

The Brother Cadfael Series
Peters, Ellis 544, 545, 631, 1175, 1203, 1467, 1470

Brother Cadfael's Penance
Peters, Ellis **1301**

The Brotherhood of the Rose
Morrell, David 552

Brotherly Love
Lordon, Randye 946, 1462

Brown's Requiem
Ellroy, James 717

A Brush with Death
Smith, Joan 1216, 1509, **1519**

Bucket Nut
Cody, Liza **270**, 751, 1125

Bullet for a Star
Kaminsky, Stuart M. 276

Bullet Hole
Miles, Keith 317, 318, 480

Bully!
Schorr, Mark 1049

The Bulrush Murders
Rothenberg, Rebecca 1234, **1405**

Bum Steer
Pickard, Nancy 10, 55, 868, 1120, 1147, 1172, 1235, **1316**, 1432

The Burden of Proof
Turow, Scott 1723

The Burglar Series
Block, Lawrence 402

The Burglar Who Studied Spinoza
Block, Lawrence 1745

The Burglar Who Traded Ted Williams
Block, Lawrence **145**, 169, 467, 494, 1697

Burglars Can't Be Choosers
Block, Lawrence 178, 715, 1698

Burial Deferred
Ross, Jonathan 789, 1639

Buried in Quilts
Frommer, Sara Hoskinson 536, **559**

Buried in Stone
Wright, Eric **1766**, 1774

Buried in the Past
Lemarchand, Elizabeth 841

Burn Marks
Paretsky, Sara 143, 161, 202, 459, 636, 1181, 1229, **1264**

Burn Season
Lantigua, John **981**

Burning Angel
Burke, James Lee **194**

The Burning Court
Carr, John Dickson 103

Burning March
Albert, Neil **28**

The Burning Season
Dundee, Wayne 141, 319, 1384, 1386

Burning Time
Glass, Leslie 887

Bury the Bishop
Gallison, Kate **564**

Business Unusual
Heald, Tim **763**, 1034, 1035, 1730

Busman's Honeymoon
Sayers, Dorothy L. 800

But I Wouldn't Want to Die There
Pickard, Nancy **1317**, 1451

The Butcher's Boy
Perry, Thomas 981

Butcher's Moon
Stark, Richard 1297

Butcher's Moon
Westlake, Donald E. 210

The Butcher's Theater
Kellerman, Jonathan 690, 691, 884

The Buzzards Must Also Be Fed
Wingate, Anne **1739**

By Death Possessed
Ormerod, Roger **1243**

By Evil Means
Prowell, Sandra West 97, 736, 1268, **1332**, 1680

By Frequent Anguish
Dean, S.F.X. 140, 178, 515, 1250, 1657, 1694

By Reason of Insanity
Harvey, James Neal **749**

By Reason of Insanity
Stevens, Shane 1027, 1154

By the Waters of Babylon
DeMille, Nelson 1473

C

The C.B. Greenfield Series
Kallen, Lucille 813, 1304

C.B. Greenfield: The Tanglewood Murder
Kallen, Lucille 1305

The Cabinda Affair
Head, Matthew 226

The Cactus Garden
Ward, Robert 784, **1672**

A Cadenza for Caruso
Paul, Barbara 117

The Caesar Clue
Shuman, M.K. **1491**, 1694

Cage of Mirrors
Ray, Robert J. 8, 458, 1096

Cain His Brother
Perry, Anne **1292**

The Caine Mutiny
Wouk, Herman 666

Cajun Nights
Donaldson, D.J. 303, 391

Caldo Largo
Thompson, Earl 1598

California Roll
Simon, Roger L. 7, 511, 1703, 1753

California Street
Levin, Donna 364, 885, 886, 887, 888

California Thriller
Byrd, Max 1455

The Calista Jacobs Series
Knight, Kathryn Lasky 372, 604, 991, 1388

Call for the Dead
Le Carré, John 217

The Callahan Garrity Series
Trocheck, Kathy Hogan 1542, 1548

Called by a Panther
Lewin, Michael Z. **1019**, 1056

Called Home
Irvine, R.R. 828

The Cambridge Murders
Rees, Dilwyn 64

The Cambridge Theorem
Cape, Tony 91, **217**, 330

Came a Dead Cat
Frey, James N. **551**

Cancellation by Death
Yeager, Dorian 15, 20, 413, 414, 1248, **1782**

Capital Crimes
Sanders, Lawrence 1169

A Capitol Crime
Meyer, Lawrence 159, 1169, 1286, 1389

A Capitol Offense
Davey, Jocelyn 1043

Capitol Offense
Gibbs, Tony **580**

Captain Cutthroat
Carr, John Dickson 519

The Caravaggio Obsession
Banks, Oliver 1573

The Caravaggio Shawl
Steward, Samuel M. **1573**

Caravan
Gilman, Dorothy 1298

Carcass Trade
Ayres, Noreen **74**

The Carl Burns Series
Crider, Bill 622

The Carl Wilcox Series
Adams, Harold 212, 213, 956, 958, 1583, 1584, 1625, 1674

The Carlotta Carlyle Series
Barnes, Linda 378, 379, 380, 381, 383, 398, 638, 639, 837, 917, 918, 921, 1099, 1182, 1185, 1266, 1489, 1490

Carnage of the Realm
Goodrum, Charles A. 1186

Carnal Hours
Collins, Max Allan **277**

Carnivores
Levitt, J.R. 828

Carol in the Dark
Jordan, Cathleen 967

Carolina Gold
McBriarty, Douglas **1108**

Carolina Skeletons
Stout, David 13, 669, 939, 1503, 1538, 1583, 1683

The Carolus Deene Series
Bruce, Leo 1366

Carpool
Cahill, Mary 244, 315, 1749

The Carter Winfield Series
Gilbert, Dale L. 608

The Carver Bascombe Series
Davis, Kenn 1178

The Carver Series
Lutz, John 1705

The Case Is Altered
Woods, Sara 1729

A Case of Innocence
Keeling, Douglas J. 445, **877**

A Case of Loyalties
Wallace, Marilyn 593

The Case of the Baker Street Irregulars
Boucher, Anthony 1365

The Case of the Journeying Boy
Innes, Michael 530

The Case of the Kidnapped Angel
Cunningham, E.V. 1712

The Case of the One-Penny Orange
Cunningham, E.V. 548

A Case of Vineyard Poisoning
Craig, Philip R. **336**

Case Pending
Shannon, Dell 1107

Casefile
Pronzini, Bill 283

The Cashmere Kid
Comfort, B. **284**

Casket for a Lying Lady
Werry, Richard 1745

Cassandra in Red
Collins, Michael **281**

Casting for Murder
Dunham, Mikel 1003

Casual Affairs
O'Donnell, Lillian 1077

Casual Slaughters
Carter, Robert A. 9, **223**, 467

Casualty Loss
Weikart, Jim 6, 809, **1683**

The Cat Caliban Series
Borton, D.B. 1185, 1489, 1506

Cat Crimes
Gorman, Ed 167, **619**, 1299

Cat Crimes II
Gorman, Ed **620**

A Cat in a Glass House
Adamson, Lydia 15

A Cat in Fine Style
Adamson, Lydia 16

A Cat in the Manger
Adamson, Lydia **17**, 167, 169, 181, 182, 443, 516

A Cat in the Wings
Adamson, Lydia **18**

A Cat in Wolf's Clothing
Adamson, Lydia **19**

The Cat Marsala Series
D'Amato, Barbara 93, 141, 603, 604, 610, 637, 1052, 1182, 1215, 1266, 1388, 1398

A Cat of a Different Color
Adamson, Lydia 1782

Cat on a Blue Monday
Douglas, Carole Nelson **438**

A Cat on a Winning Streak
Adamson, Lydia 1065

A Cat on the Cutting Edge
Adamson, Lydia **20**

The Cat That Wasn't There
Whitelaw, Stella 619

The Cat Who Moved a Mountain
Braun, Lilian Jackson 167

The Cat Who Series
Braun, Lilian Jackson 15, 16, 17, 19, 20, 180, 181, 182, 438, 439, 443, 620, 950, 1733

The Cat Who Talked to Ghosts
Braun, Lilian Jackson 168

The Cat Who Went into the Closet
Braun, Lilian Jackson **169**

Catalina's Riddle
Saylor, Steven 1390, **1448**

The Catalyst
Cory, Desmond 207, **330**, 590

Catch a Fallen Angel
Engleman, Paul 1350

Catch a Falling Spy
Deighton, Len 995

Catching Fire
Smith, Kay Nolte 487, 488

The Cater Street Hangman
Perry, Anne 738, 942

Catering to Nobody
Davidson, Diane Mott 214, 245, 247, 374, 989, 1061, 1256, 1342

The Cathe LeVendeur Series
Newman, Sharan 545

Cathedral
DeMille, Nelson 1344

The Catherine Saylor Series
Grant, Linda 918, 921, 1182, 1184, 1185, 1489, 1490, 1506, 1700, 1798

Catnap
Douglas, Carole Nelson 167, 181, **439**, 1733

Cat's Cradle
Curzon, Clare 366

Cats in Space
Fawcett, Bill 619

Cat's Paw, Inc.
Thrasher, L.L. **1618**

The Cats Who Series
Braun, Lilian Jackson 619

Caught Dead in Philadelphia
Roberts, Gillian 247, 515, 593, 594, 895, 933, 945, 982, 1136, 1140, 1250, 1316, 1318, 1415, 1748, 1750

Caught in the Shadows
Haddad, C.A. 232, **694**, 1665

Caught Looking
Russell, Randy **1416**

The Cavalier Case
Fraser, Antonia **543**, 1144

The Cavalier in White
Muller, Marcia 1521, 1645

The Cavanaugh Quest
Gifford, Thomas 105, 823

The Caveman's Valentine
Green, George Dawes 271, **662**, 952, 993, 1578

Celebrity
Thompson, Thomas 1662

The Celia Grant Series
Sherwood, John 46, 107, 108, 802, 1406

Centrifuge
Pollack, J.C. 1116

The Cereal Murders
Davidson, Diane Mott 389

A Ceremonial Death
Oliphant, B.J. 106, 1788

Ceremony
Parker, Robert B. 716

A Certain Justice
Lescroart, John T. **1008**

Chain of Evidence
Pearson, Ridley **1283**

Challenge
Foy, Peter 582

The Chamber
Grisham, John 650, **679**

Chameleon
Kienzle, William X. **915**

Charged with Guilt
White, Gloria **1700**

Charisma
Papazoglou, Orania 580, 1428

Charity Ends at Home
Watson, Colin 752, 753, 789

The Charles Paris Series
Brett, Simon 76, 1064, 1131

The Charlie Bradshaw Series
Dobyns, Stephen 495

The Charlie Green Series
Millhiser, Marlys 115, 124

Charlie M
Freemantle, Brian 995

The Charlie Moon Series
Yarbro, Chelsea Quinn 701

The Charlie Resnick Series
Harvey, John 643

The Charlie Salter Series
Wright, Eric 1773

The Charlotte Graham Series
Matteson, Stefanie 214, 712

The Charlotte Graham Series
Matteson, Stephanie 284, 285, 1245

The Charlotte Kent Series
Kittredge, Mary 1378

The Charmian Daniels Series
Melville, Jennie 95, 304, 455, 661, 1125, 1338

The Chartreuse Clue
Love, William F. 60, 607, 656, 915, **1048**

Chasing Away the Devil
Cooper, Susan Rogers 626, 1742

Chasing Eights
Collins, Michael **282**

Check-out Time
Kingsbury, Kate 928

The Cheerio Killings
Allyn, Douglas **47**, 447, 555, 833

The Cheetah Chase
McQuillan, Karin 225, 362, **1137**

The Cherry Blossom Corpse
Barnard, Robert 1050

The Chesapeake Project
Horn, Phyllis **806**

The Cheshire Cat's Eye
Muller, Marcia 982

The Cheshire Moon
Ferrigno, Robert 102, 408, 518, **525**, 710, 1561

Chiaroscuro
Clothier, Peter 477, 1180, 1211, 1507, 1521, 1645, 1666

The Chick Charleston Series
Guthrie, A.B. Jr. 777, 779, 780, 1584

The Chief Inspector's Daughter
Radley, Sheila 1669

Chief Tallon and the S.O.R.
Ball, John 1712

Chiefs
Woods, Stuart 1070, 1546

Child of Silence
Padgett, Abigail 97, **1251**, 1331

Children's Games
LaPierre, Janet 10, 807, 945, **982**, 991, 1120, 1378, 1668

A Child's Garden of Death
Forrest, Richard 384, 387, 1634, 1678

Child's Play
Hill, Reginald 368

A Chill Wind in January
Wright, L.R. **1772**

The China Bayles Series
Albert, Susan Wittig 115, 377, 422, 596, 944, 1516

China Lake
Hyde, Anthony 823

China Trade
Rozan, S.J. 601, **1410**

The Choice
Reed, Barry **1357**, 1600

Chosen for Death
Flora, Kate Clark 803

The Christening Day Murder
Harris, Lee 138, **733**, 1451

The Christie Caper
Hart, Carolyn G. **741**

The Christie Opera Series
Uhnak, Dorothy 601

The Christine Bennett Series
Harris, Lee 564, 1239, 1339

The Christmas Night Murder
Harris, Lee **734**, 799, 1237

The Christopher Storm Series
Barber, Willetta 999

Cinderella
McBain, Ed 1022

Cinderella After Midnight
Zackel, Fred 816

Circumstances Unknown
Heckler, Jonellen **769**

A City Called July
Engel, Howard 1757

City of Glass
Auster, Paul 238

City of God
Jahn, Michael **840**, 1585, 1692

Title Index

City of Gold
Deighton, Len **410**

City of Lies
McCabe, Peter **1109**

A City of Strangers
Barnard, Robert **88**

City of the Dead
Lieberman, Herbert 323, 326, **463**

City Primeval
Leonard, Elmore 497, 831, 833, 1199, 1311, 1374, 1433, 1622

City Sleuths and Tough Guys
McCullough, David Willis **1122**

The City When It Rains
Cook, Thomas H. **305**

The Claire Aldington Series
Holland, Isabelle 564, 671, 672, 733, 734, 799, 1239, 1339

The Claire Malloy Series
Hess, Joan 218, 593, 731, 732, 836, 967, 991, 1153, 1661

The Clara Gamadge Series
Boylan, Eleanor 46, 284, 285

The Class Menagerie
Churchill, Jill **244**, 698

The Classic Car Killer
Lupoff, Richard A. **1054**, 1564

Clay Dancers
Dawkins, Cecil 702

A Clean Sweep
Berlinski, David **123**, 906

A Clear Case of Murder
Downing, Warwick 199, 240, **445**

Clear-Cut Murder
Wallingford, Lee 57, 605, 1341, **1667**, 1784

Clearwater Summer
Keegan, John E. 692, **876**

Clerical Errors
Greenwood, D.M. 61, 136, 137, 138, 235, **670**, 1706, 1730

The Cleveland Connection
Roberts, Les **1383**

The Client
Grisham, John **680**, 1724

Cliff Hanger
Craig, Philip R. **337**, 1099

The Cliff Hardy Series
Corris, Peter 26, 27, 1694, 1695

A Clinic for Murder
Landreth, Marsha **974**

Clio Browne, Private Investigator
Komo, Dolores 523

Clively Close: Dead as Dead Can Be
Crowleigh, Ann **361**, 928, 929

Clockwork
Steed, Neville 1069, **1565**

Close Quarters
Piesman, Marissa **1319**

Close Softly the Doors
Roat, Ronald Clair **1373**

Close-Up on Death
O'Brien, Maureen 346, 413, 517, 992, **1213**, 1247, 1248

Closet
Zimmerman, R.D. 812

Closing Costs
Bunn, Thomas **189**, 1023, 1436

Clubbed to Death
Edwards, Ruth Dudley **472**, 911, 912

Coaster
Foy, George 1037

Cobalt
Aldyne, Nathan 1588

Cocaine and Blue Eyes
Zackel, Fred 1618

Cockfighter
Willeford, Charles 482

Codename Hangman
Geddes, Paul 1456

The Codicil
Topor, Tom **1623**

Coffin on Murder Street
Butler, Gwendoline **203**

Coffin Underground
Butler, Gwendoline **204**

A Cold-Blooded Business
Stabenow, Dana 56, 57, **1550**

Cold Call
Pugh, Dianne G. 56, 125, 531, **1333**

Cold Coffin
Quest, Erica 661

Cold Comfort
Lake, M.D. 417, 746, 779, **967**, 1089

A Cold Day for Murder
Stabenow, Dana 259, 289, 291, 492, 1341, **1549**, 1580, 1581, 1607, 1784, 1786

Cold Feet
Tucker, Kerry 124, 615, **1636**

The Cold Front
Hanlon, Sean 407, 775, 950, 1261, 1549, 1580

Cold in July
Lansdale, Joe R. 292, 622, 1287, 1596

Cold in the Earth
Granger, Ann 358, 640, **642**, 897, 1408

Cold Light
Harvey, John **751**

A Cold Mind
Lindsey, David L. 53, 165, 253, 844, 1425, 1427

Cold Night
Harvey, John 1050

Cold Tracks
Wallingford, Lee 54, 55, 370, 492, 1652, **1668**, 1728

The Cold War Swap
Thomas, Ross 981

The Colin Thane Series
Knox, Bill 111, 113, 249, 719, 720, 943

The Collaborators
Hill, Reginald 420

A Collector of Photographs
Valentine, Deborah **1645**

Color Him Guilty
Hensley, Joe L. 558, 730, 1576, 1577, 1794

The Color of Light
Goldman, William 546

Coma
Cook, Robin 659, 888, 965, 1262

Come to Grief
Francis, Dick **538**

Comeback
Enger, L.L. 118, 624, 1145, 1204, 1206

Comeback
Francis, Dick **539**

The Comic Book Killer
Lupoff, Richard A. 630, **1055**

Company Secrets
Coburn, Andrew 647

A Compelling Case
Underwood, Michael 543

Compelling Evidence
Martini, Steve 557, **1090**, 1577, 1600

Compromising Positions
Isaacs, Susan 448, 593, 594, 1146, 1415, 1748, 1750

The Conan Flagg Series
Wren, M.K. 167, 169, 182, 998, 999

The Concrete Blond
Connelly, Michael 1067

The Concrete Blonde
Connelly, Michael **294**, 580, 909, 1025

Concrete Hero
Kantner, Rob 232, **862**, 870

Condition Purple
Turnbull, Peter **1639**

The Condo Kill
Barth, Richard 588

Confession
Pickard, Nancy 808, 880

The Confucious Enigma
Jones, Margaret 496

Cons
Watts, Timothy 482, 1288, 1589, **1677**, 1760

Consider the Crows
Weir, Charlene 219, 1432, **1685**

The Contactees Die Young
Azolakov, Antoinette 533

Contents under Pressure
Buchanan, Edna 1641

Cookie
Adkins, Jan 1232

The Cooking School Murders
Rich, Virginia 151, 152, 286, 989, 1061, 1255, 1315, 1588, 1594

Cooking Up Trouble
Pence, Joanne 377, **1289**

Cool Blue Tomb
Kemprecos, Paul 233, 683, 689, 1336

A Cool Breeze on the Underground
Winslow, Don 227, **1743**

A Cool Clear Death
Halleran, Tucker 872, 1005

Cop-Out
McNab, Claire 83, 256, 534, 1170

Cop Without a Shield
O'Donnell, Lillian 1687, 1789

Copy Cat Crimes
Wilson, Karen Ann **1733**

Copy Kat
Kijewski, Karen **918**, 1607

The Cordelia Gray Series
James, P.D. 304, 1125, 1338

The Cords of Vanity
Tripp, Miles **1629**

Corona Blue
Trainor, J.F. **1625**

Coronation
Weatherby, W.J. 787, **1679**

Coronation
Wetherby, W.J. 60

Corporate Bodies
Brett, Simon **174**

Corpse de Ballet
Cores, Lucy 18, 126, 1346

Corpus Christmas
Maron, Margaret 1113

Corruption
Klavan, Andrew 163, 467, 592, **936**, 1109, 1578, 1590

Cotswold Moles
Spicer, Michael **1539**

Count the Days
Summerfield, Lin **1592**

Countdown
Hagberg, David 756

Counterstrike
Flannery, Sean 248

A Country of Old Men
Hansen, Joseph **727**

The Covenant of the Flame
Morrell, David 681, 756, **1174**, 1381, 1727

The Cover Girl Killer
Lupoff, Richard A. 467

Cover Her Face
James, P.D. 260, 677, 1343, 1555

Cover Story
Cullen, Robert **365**

Cowboy Blues
Lewis, Stephen 1573

Coyote

Coyote
Barnes, Linda 92, 161, 364, 636, 972, 1093, 1220, 1251, 1252, 1265, 1355, 1410, 1504, 1505

Coyote Bird
DeFelice, Jim 409

The Coyote Cried Twice
Bay, Austin 350

Coyote Waits
Hillerman, Tony 843

Crack Down
McDermid, Val 456, **1125**

A Cracking of Spines
Lewis, Roy Harley 571

Cracksman on Velvet
Selwyn, Francis 1610

The Cradle Will Fall
Clark, Mary Higgins 5, 93, 462, 602

Cranmer
Knickmeyer, Steve 1056

A Creative Kind of Killer
Early, Jack 40, 146, 282, 703, 1350, 1663, 1684

Credit for a Murder
Dean, Spencer 178

The Crime and the Crystal
Ferrars, E.X. 255

Crime of Passion
Hooper, Kay 17, 19, 116, 251, 1631

Crime, Punishment and Resurrection
Collins, Michael 283

A Crime Story
Nash, Jay Robert 1443

Criminal Conversation
Hunter, Evan 820, **1531**

Criminal Seduction
North, Darian 518, 1104, **1211**

Crimson Joy
Parker, Robert B. 187, 1313

Criss Cross
Kakonis, Tom 482, 755, 1288, 1589

Cronus
DeAndrea, William L. 528

Crooked Flight
Jackson, Basil 179, 409

Crooked Man
Dunbar, Tony 194

The Cross Killer
Montecino, Marcel 62

Crossed Swords
Flannery, Sean 528

Crossfire
Hagberg, David 685

Crossover
Eubank, Judith 68, 69, **502**

The Crow Eaters
Sidwa, B.N. 35, 874, 875

The Crown in Darkness
Doherty, P.C. 265, 1302, 1303

Cruel and Unusual
Cornwell, Patricia D. 294, **324**, 1737

Cruel April
Albert, Neil 29

The Cruel Mother
LaPierre, Janet 1235

The Cruellest Month
Holt, Hazel **800**, 1275

The Cruise of a Deathtime
Babson, Marian 117

Cry for Help
Stuyck, Karen Hanson 1021, **1586**

A Cry in the Night
Clark, Mary Higgins 44, 899, 1453

Cry Vengeance
Handberg, Ron 812, 1276, 1641

The Crystal Blue Persuasion
Philbrick, W.R. 683, 905, 1337

Curiosity Didn't Kill the Cat
Wren, M.K. 1020, 1618

The Curious Eat Themselves
Straley, John **1580**

The Curious Eat Themsleves
Straley, John 708

Curly Smoke
Holtzer, Susan **803**

Curse the Darkness
Grant-Adamson, Lesley 561, 1145, 1642, 1658

The Cut Throat
Michael, Simon **1149**

Cut To—Murder
Osborne, Denise **1247**, 1488

Cut to the Quick
Ross, Kate 103, **1404**

Cutter
Crum, Laura 21, **362**, 536, 537, 538, 839

Cutting Edge
Harvey, John **752**

The Cutting Hours
Grice, Julia **673**

D

The D.K.A. Series
Gores, Joe 123

D.O.A.
Pedneau, Dave 1546

The Dallas Deception
Abshire, Richard **7**, 1753

Dallas Drop
Abshire, Richard 352, 458

The Dalziel and Pascoe Series
Hill, Reginald 366, 470, 504, 625, 678, 752, 1160, 1322, 1361, 1394, 1454, 1479

The Dan Fortune Series
Collins, Michael 343, 486, 1491, 1492, 1493, 1684

The Dan Mallett Series
Parrish, Frank 109

The Dan Rhodes Series
Crider, Bill 1111

The Dan Roman Series
Mathis, Edward 7, 8, 352, 458, 877

A Dance at the Slaughterhouse
Block, Lawrence **146**, 196, 292, 750, 1067

Dance for Diplomats
Harcourt, Palma 453

Dancing Bear
Crumley, James 164, 1601, 1677

Dancing in the Dark
Zukowski, Sharon 320, 473, 542, 1227, 1228, 1319, **1798**

A Dangerous Age
Sylvester, Martin 739

Dangerous Attachments
Lovett, Sarah **1051**

Dangerous Conceits
Moore, Margaret **1168**

Dangerous Games
Crosland, Susan 1608

A Dangerous Mourning
Perry, Anne **1293**

Dangerous Places
Chase, Elaine Raco 1214, 1759

Dangerous Practices
Roe, Francis 1283

A Dangerous Thing
Crider, Bill 1275

Dangerous to Know
Babson, Marion 1149

Dangerous Waters
Eidson, Bill **475**

The Daniel Valentine Series
Aldyne, Nathan 1150, 1151, 1572, 1795, 1796

The Dante Game
Langton, Jane **979**, 1187

Daphne Dead and Done For
Ross, Jonathan 753

The Daphne Decisions
O'Brien, Meg 569, 1167, **1214**, 1476, 1638

The Darina Lisle Series
Laurence, Janet 389, 390, 698

The Dark-Adapted Eye
Vine, Barbara 90, 587, 1360

Dark Blue and Dangerous
Ross, Jonathan 748, 1001

The Dark City
Collins, Max Allan 501

Dark Crimes: Great Noir Fiction From the '50's to the '90's
Gorman, Ed **621**

The Dark Fantastic
Ellin, Stanley 1633

Dark Maze
Adcock, Thomas 1623

Dark of Night
Nehrbass, Richard 1110, **1200**

Dark Provenance
Anthony, Michael David **61**

Dark Star
Muller, Marcia 436, 479, 848, 1093, **1180**, 1410, 1789

Dark Streets and Empty Places
Mathis, Edward 353

Dark Swan
Knight, Kathryn Lasky **944**

Dark Veil
Gertsner, Nickolae 139

The Dark Wind
Hillerman, Tony 874

Darkness Falls
Schneider, Joyce Anne 79, 323, 326, 463, 602, 886, 975, 1062, **1453**, 1699, 1761

Darling Corey's Dead
Webb, Martha G. 350, 460, 461, 464

A Dash of Death
Bishop, Claudia **134**

Date with a Dead Doctor
Brill, Toni 127, **177**, 312, 423, 1501

The Daughter of Time
Tey, Josephine 418, 424

The Daughters of Artemis
Douglas, Lauren Wright 1356

The Dave Brandstetter Series
Hansen, Joseph 1054, 1150, 1151, 1194, 1572, 1795, 1796

The Dave Garrett Series
Albert, Neil 669, 818

The Dave Robicheaux Series
Burke, James Lee 147, 344, 1026, 1039, 1218, 1422

A Day in the Death of Dorothea Cassidy
Cleeves, Ann 203, 230, **260**, 677

Day of Atonement
Kellerman, Faye **878**, 955

Day of Reckoning
Katzenbach, John 42, 513, 1091, 1093, 1308, 1310

Day of the Cheetah
Brown, Dale **179**, 409, 825, 1513

The Day of the Jackal
Forsyth, Frederick 60, 78, 786, 1679

Day of Wrath
Valin, Jonathan 1540

The Day That Dusty Died
Martin, Lee **1087**

Dead Ahead
Horansky, Ruby 447, **804**, 969, 1222, 1226, 1452, 1523, 1527

Dead Air
Lupica, Mike 1635, 1709

Dead and Buried
Hager, Jean 415, 595, **699**, 803

Dead as They Come
Platt, Kin 524

Title Index — Death by Degrees

Dead Ball
Cork, Barry   110, 112, 113, 719, 720

Dead Before Morning
Evans, Geraldine   **504**

Dead Birds
Milne, John   27, 327, 1371, 1488, 1630

Dead by Morning
Simpson, Dorothy   800, 1001, **1502**

Dead Calm
Williams, Charles   973, 1057

Dead Center
Horansky, Ruby   **805**, 909, 1224

Dead Center
Wilcox, Collin   **1711**

Dead Cert
Francis, Dick   133

Dead Easy
Nehrbass, Arthur F.   **1199**, 1561

Dead Easy
Russell, E.S.   **1415**

Dead End
Bland, Eleanor Taylor   1198

Dead Fit
Cook, Stephen   **304**, 661, 778

Dead Fix
Geller, Michael   541, **573**, 871

Dead Folks' Blues
Womack, Steven   870, **1751**

Dead in Center Field
Engleman, Paul   50, 160, 493, 505, 507, 508, 510, 574, 613, 1205

Dead in the Cellar
Fedderson, Connie   313, **520**, 1516

Dead in the Scrub
Oliphant, B.J.   55, 57, 315, 983, 999, **1232**, 1340, 1495, 1498, 1605, 1650, 1652, 1661, 1668

Dead in the Water
Chaput, W.J.   **233**, 475, 689

Dead in the Water
Feddersen, Connie   900

Dead in the Water
Fedderson, Connie   1517

Dead in the Water
Smith, Julie   **1524**

Dead in the Water
Stabenow, Dana   **1551**

Dead in the Water
Wood, Ted   316, 1418

Dead Irish
Lescroart, John T.   906, 907, 1161, 1713, 1716, 1779

Dead Knock
Turnbull, Peter   948

Dead Last
Geller, Michael   170, 171, 1190

Dead Letter
Clark, Douglas   789

Dead Man
Gores, Joe   3, **617**, 1354, 1760

Dead Man's Island
Hart, Carolyn G.   **742**, 1078

Dead Man's Ransom
Peters, Ellis   883

Dead Man's Thoughts
Wheat, Carolyn   1524

Dead Matter
Wren, M.K.   **1764**

Dead Meat
Kerr, Philip   365, **913**

Dead Men Don't Give Seminars
Sucher, Dorothy   776

Dead Men Don't Marry
Sucher, Dorothy   **1588**

Dead Men's Hearts
Elkins, Aaron   **476**

Dead Moon on the Rise
Cooper, Susan Rogers   **310**, 1766

The Dead of Brooklyn
Randisi, Robert J.   **1347**

The Dead of Jericho
Dexter, Colin   260, 1168, 1189, 1253, 1392

The Dead of Winter
Allegretto, Michael   **40**

Dead of Winter
Allegretto, Michael   1364

Dead on the Island
Crider, Bill   8, **350**, 1007, 1096, 1347, 1472

Dead on the Stick
Upton, Robert   317, 318, 481

Dead on Time
Keating, H.R.F.   **874**

Dead Pan
Dentinger, Jane   **413**, 517, 1257

The Dead Pull Hitter
Gordon, Alison   160, 505, 506, 507, **612**, 1053, 1718

Dead Reckoning
Llewellyn, Sam   539, 540, 581, 582

Dead Ringer
Kelner, Toni L.P.   313, **900**, 1544

Dead Set
Melville, Jennie   **1141**, 1670

Dead Skip
Gores, Joe   266

Dead-Stick
Washburn, L.J.   501, 847, 860, **1674**

Dead Time
Bland, Eleanor Taylor   **141**, 840, 953, 954, 1222, 1452

Dead to Rites
Angus, Sylvia   1163

Dead Winter
Tapply, William G.   766, **1602**

Dead Wrong
Burke, Alan Dennis   **192**, 475, 653, 1463, 1562, 1683, 1694, 1732

Deadbolt
Brandon, Jay   617

Deadeye
Llewellyn, Sam   **1037**

Deadfall in Berlin
Zimmerman, R.D.   914, 1113, 1278, 1747, **1792**

The Deadliest Option
Meyers, Annette   **1147**

Deadline
Boyle, Gerry   154, **163**, 467, 1590

Deadline
Mills, D.F.   599, 694, 894, **1157**

Deadline for Murder
Frankel, Valerie   473

Deadlock
Paretsky, Sara   382, 1638

Deadly Admirer
Green, Christine   **658**

Deadly Allies
Randisi, Robert J.   **1348**

Deadly Beloved
Knight, Alanna   **942**

Deadly Cadenza
Myers, Paul   589

Deadly Crescendo
Myers, Paul   **1191**, 1681

Deadly Diagnosis
Stearn, Martha   1262

Deadly Errand
Green, Christine   **659**, 931, 934, 1130, 1656

Deadly Practice
Green, Christine   **660**

Deadly Pursuit
Harper, Brian   728

Deadly Rehearsal
Peterson, Audrey   559

Deadly Resolutions
Collins, Anna Ashwood   **274**

Deadly Safari
McQuillan, Karin   54, 55, 158, 209

Deadly Secret
Johnson, Martha   794

Deadly Secrets on the St. Johns
Sprinkle, Patricia Houck   **1542**

Deadly Sonata
Myers, Paul   **1192**

Deadly Stakes
Wiser, H. Fred   **1745**

Deadstick
Faherty, Terence   **513**

Deal to Die For
Standiford, Les   **1560**

The Dean It Was That Died
Whitehead, Barbara   61, 670, 671, 672, 733, **1706**, 1730

Dear Daughter Dead
Hough, S.B.   1614

Death After Evensong
Clark, Douglas   1502

Death Among the Angels
Putre, John Walter   339, 435, 682, 683, 904, **1336**, 1373

Death Among the Dons
Neel, Janet   428, 891, **1196**, 1274, 1306, 1522

Death and Blintzes
Rosen, Dorothy & Sidney   1588

Death and Judgment
Leon, Donna   **1002**

Death and Other Lovers
Bannister, Jo   **86**, 893

Death and Taxes
Dunlap, Susan   **460**, 1087

Death and the Chapman
Sedley, Kate   265, 427, 512, 1375, **1467**

Death and the Chaste Apprentice
Barnard, Robert   **89**

Death and the Delinquent
Oliphant, B.J.   33, **1233**, 1496, 1667

Death and the Dogwalker
Orde, A.J.   **1240**

Death and the Good Life
Hugo, Richard   491, 736, 815, 1273, 1618, 1668

Death and the Oxford Box
Stallwood, Veronica   1274, **1557**

Death and the Trumpets of Tuscany
Jones, Hazel Wynn   **847**, 1003

Death and the Trumpets of Tuscany
Wynn Jones, Hazel   979, 1510

Death as a Career Move
Cook, Bruce   **299**, 665, 1587

Death at Bishop's Keep
Paige, Robin   68, **1259**

Death at Crane's Court
Dillon, Ellis   530

Death at Gallows Green
Paige, Robin   465, **1260**

Death at La Fenice
Leon, Donna   **1003**

A Death at St. Anselm's
Holland, Isabelle   60, 136, 449, 670, 1124

Death at the Cut
Kiker, Douglas   950, 951, 998, 1111, 1359, 1368, 1720

Death Bed
Greenleaf, Stephen   819, 1019

A Death Before Dying
Wilcox, Collin   **1712**

Death Below Deck
Kiker, Douglas   338, 904, **922**

Death Beneath the Christmas Tree
Nordan, Robert   245, **1208**, 1750

Death Benefits
Kahn, Michael A.   **851**, 963, 1529

Death by Deception
Wingate, Anne   267, 298, 314, 316, 626, 1431, 1775

Death by Degrees
Wilson, Robin   **1735**

Death by Degrees
Wright, Eric **1767**

Death by Dressage
Banks, Carolyn 1487

Death by Hoax
Black, Lionel 1034

Death by Sheer Torture
Barnard, Robert 472, 1063, 1322

Death by Station Wagon
Katz, Jon 58, 157, **869**, 1463

Death Came Dressed in White
Sherer, Michael W. **1481**

Death Cap
Thomson, June 1402

Death Comes as Epiphany
Newman, Sharan 427, 544, 631, 1164, **1203**, 1301, 1375, 1377, 1624

Death Down Home
Sandstrom, Eve K. 522, 693, 889, 1334, 1335, 1399, **1430**, 1627, 1637

Death Down Under
McNab, Claire 1528

Death Drop
Gill, B.M. 228

Death Echo
Tucker, Kerry 372, 1497, **1637**

A Death for a Dancing Doll
Giroux, E.X. 597

A Death for a Dodo
Giroux, E.X. 598

A Death for Adonis
Giroux, E.X. 1658

Death Goes on Retreat
O'Marie, Carol Anne **1237**

Death Has Deep Roots
Gilbertod, Michael 562

Death in a Deck Chair
Beck, K.K. 250, 1519

Death in a Far Country
Callahan, Sheila MacGill 23, 331

Death in a Far Country
Callahan, Sheila McGill 104

Death in a Funhouse Mirror
Flora, Kate Clark **531**

Death in a Serene City
Sklepowich, Edward 1002, 1003, 1004, 1187, **1510**

Death in a Strange Country
Leon, Donna **1004**

Death in a Tenured Position
Cross, Amanda 892, 1520, 1522

A Death in a Town
Waugh, Hillary **1678**

A Death in Bulloch Parish
Brandt, Nat 1496

Death in Close-Up
Livingston, Nancy 763, **1034**

Death in Connecticutt
Linzee, David 1634

Death in Deep Water
Kemprecos, Paul **903**, 1324

Death in Disguise
Graham, Caroline 358, **640**

Death in Store
Rowe, Jennifer **1406**

Death in the Fifth Position
Box, Edgar 18, 126, 1346

A Death in the Life
Davis, Dorothy Salisbury 404, 556, 713, 1300, 1638

Death in the Limelight
Martin, A.E. 1693

Death in the Morning
Radley, Sheila 677, 1179, 1244

Death in the Round
Morice, Anne 87

Death in the Snow
Stern, Richard Martin 793

Death in the Willow Pattern
Burley, W.J. 1729

Death in Uptown
Raleigh, Michael **1345**

Death in Verona
Lewis, Roy Harley 979, **1020**, 1069, 1187

Death in Zanzibar
Kaye, M.M. 158, 226

Death Is a Two-Stroke Penalty
Bartlett, James Y. 318, 481

Death Is Forever
O'Callaghan, Maxine 274, 1227

Death Locked In
Adey, R.C.S. 221

Death Mask
Dentinger, Jane 19, 1173, 1783

Death Notes
Rendell, Ruth 143

Death Notice
Karl, M.S. **866**, 1261, 1721, 1722

Death of a Blue Movie Star
Deaver, Jeffrey Wilds 1782

Death of a Butterfly
Maron, Margaret 461

Death of a Charming Man
Beaton, M.C. **109**, 740

Death of a Citizen
Hamilton, Donald 567

Death of a Dancing Fool
Berry, Carole 124

Death of a Dancing Lady
Harrison, Ray 1028, 1296

The Death of a Difficult Woman
Berry, Carole **125**

Death of a Dissident
Kaminsky, Stuart M. 1066

Death of a DJ
Rubino, Jane **1411**

Death of a Don
Shaw, Howard 64

Death of a Dunwoody Matron
Sprinkle, Patricia Houck 313

Death of a Dutchman
Nabb, Magdalen 845, 1003

Death of a Fantasy Life
Gilpin, T.G. **590**

Death of a Good Woman
Eccles, Marjorie 230

Death of a Gossip
Beaton, M.C. 317, 719, 948, 1639

Death of a Harvard Freshman
Silver, Victoria 140, 745, 1519

Death of a Hollow Man
Graham, Caroline 76, 357, **641**, 1707, 1768, 1769

Death of a Hussy
Beaton, M.C. **110**

Death of a Joyce Scholar
Gill, Bartholomew 360, 1134

The Death of a King
Doherty, P.C. 1376, 1467

Death of a Literary Widow
Barnard, Robert 402

Death of a Low-Handicap Man
Ball, Brian 480

Death of a Mystery Writer
Barnard, Robert 307, 695

Death of a Nag
Beaton, M.C. **111**

Death of a Partner
Neel, Janet 203, 643, 897, **1197**, 1393, 1395, 1454

Death of a Perfect Wife
Beaton, M.C. **112**, 191

Death of a Postmodernist
Steinberg, Janice 360, **1568**

Death of a Traveling Man
Beaton, M.C. **113**

Death of an Expert Witness
James, P.D. 576, 1139

Death of an Honourable Member
Harrison, Ray 942

Death of the Duchess
Eyre, Elizabeth **512**, 1403, 1404

Death of the Office Witch
Millhiser, Marlys 56, 125, **1155**

Death Off Stage
Grayson, Richard **655**

Death on Clam Pond
Kiker, Douglas 1074

Death on Demand
Hart, Carolyn G. 160, 535, 777, 779, 1263

Death on Rough Water
Matthews, Francine **1099**

Death on Site
Neel, Janet 309, 644, 898, 1553

Death on the Agenda
Moyes, Patricia 1409

Death on the High C's
Barnard, Robert 609, 1191, 1192

Death on the Mississippi
Forrest, Richard 535, 693, 836, 901, 1108, 1725

Death on the Rocks
Allegretto, Michael 200

Death on Wheels
Nordan, Robert **1209**

Death Penalties
Gosling, Paula 328, 366, **625**, 1159, 1244, 1480, 1669, 1670, 1708

Death Penalty
Coughlin, William J. 730

Death Prone
Curzon, Clare **367**

Death Qualified: A Mystery of Chaos
Wilhelm, Kate 240, **1723**

Death Sails the Bay
Feegel, John R. 462

Death Served Up Cold
Oliphant, B.J. **1234**

Death Signs
Hunsburger, H. Edward 1414

Death Squad London
Gerson, Jack **579**, 1161

Death Stalks the Punjab
Casberg, Melvin A. 875

Death Too Soon
Peterson, Audrey 309

Death Trance
Zimmerman, R.D. 993

Death Trick
Burke, J.F. 762, 1314

Death Turns a Trick
Smith, Julie 462, 1183, 1651

Death under Par
Law, Janice 480, 614

Death Underfoot
Casley, Dennis **225**

Death Warmed Up
Babson, Marion 729, 988

Death Watch
Harrod-Eagles, Cynthia **740**

The Death We Share
Short, Sharon Gwyn **1490**

Death Wore a Diadem
McGregor, Iona **1133**

Deathampton Summer
Logan, Margaret 286, 686, 1777

Deathbed
Kienzle, William X. 797, 1048, 1123

Deathics
Barth, Richard **100**, 977

Death's Bright Angel
Neel, Janet 307, 642, 645, 896, 1399, 1408, 1419, 1669, 1671

Death's Clenched Fist
Sherburne, James 36

Death's Darkest Face
Symons, Julian 1412

Death's Head Berlin
Gerson, Jack 787, 914

Death's Pale Horse
Sherburne, James 1079, 1080

Death's Savage Passion
Papazoglou, Orania 250

Title Index — Dortmunder Series

Deathspell
Stallwood, Veronica **1558**, 1593

Deathwatch
Harrison, Ray 1292, 1293, 1294, 1295

Deathwatch '39
Gerson, Jack 1792

The Deb Ralston Series
Martin, Lee 142, 219, 464, 778, 779, 780, 969, 1224, 1225, 1226, 1452, 1523, 1525, 1685, 1686

Deceit and Deadly Lies
Bandy, Franklin 105

Deception Island
Lorens, M.K. **1043**

Deceptions
Muller, Marcia 1330

A Deceptive Clarity
Elkins, Aaron 1568

Decked
Clark, Carol Higgins 68, **250**

Decoys
Hoyt, Richard 487, 491, 1212, 1350

A Dedicated Man
Robinson, Peter 203, **1392**, 1556

Deeds of Trust
Wuamett, Victor **1778**

The Deep Blue Goodbye
MacDonald, John D. 1337

Deep Chill
Slater, Ian **1513**

A Deep Disturbance
Rauch, Constance 794, **1351**

Deep Dive
Hornig, Doug 905, 1336

The Deep End
Crutcher, Chris **364**, 879, 885, 887, 1791

Deep End
Norman, Geoffrey **1210**

Deep Kill
Shuman, M.K. 272, **1492**

Deep Lie
Woods, Stuart 85

Deep Shaker
Roberts, Les **1384**

Deep Sleep
Fyfield, Frances 308, **561**, 642

A Deepe Coffyn
Laurence, Janet 127, 151, **988**, 1034, 1035, 1342

The Deer Killers
Landers, Gunnard 96, **973**

Deerslayer
Karl, M.S. **867**, 949, 1109, 1720

The Defection of A.J. Lewinter
Littell, Robert 995

Deficit Ending
Martin, Lee 47, 460, **1088**, 1095

Degree of Guilt
Patterson, Richard North 1576

The Delilah West Series
O'Callaghan, Maxine 379, 380, 381, 398, 638, 917, 1052, 1569, 1798

The Delta Star
Wambaugh, Joseph 1033, 1311

Depraved Indifference
Tanenbaum, Robert K. 184

Desert Heat
Jance, J.A. **842**, 1233, 1649

The Desert Look
Schopen, Bernard 97, 132, **1455**

Desperate Remedy
Kittredge, Mary **931**

The Detective and Mr. Dickens
Palmer, William J. 984, 1030

Detective First Grade
Mahoney, Don **1067**

Detective Stories from the Strand
Adrian, Jack 24

Deviant Way
Montanari, Richard **1166**

Devices and Desires
James, P.D. **841**

The Devil at Your Elbow
Devine, D.M. 941

The Devil Down Home
Sandstrom, Eve K. 520, 902, **1431**, 1685, 1740

The Devil Finds Work
Delving, Michael 1031

Devil in a Blue Dress
Mosley, Walter 277, 279, 280, 393, 498, 958, **1176**, 1609

The Devil Knows You're Dead
Block, Lawrence 147

The Devil to Pay
Daniel, Mark 538, 839, 1486, 1487

The Devil's Door
Newman, Sharan 1175

Devil's Gonna Get Him
Wesley, Valerie Wilson **1691**

The Devil's Spy
Hastings, Michael 1028, 1746

The Devon MacDonald Series
Jacobs, Nancy Baker 380, 381, 1490

Dewey Death
Blackstock, Charity 416, 611, 1031, 1559

Dewey Decimated
Goodrum, Charles A. 1031, 1627

The Dewey James Series
Morgan, Kate 1406, 1547

A Diamond Before You Die
Wiltz, Chris 1752

Diamond Eyes
Lutz, John **1056**

Diamond Head
Jackson, Marian J.A. **834**, 1030

Diamond in the Buff
Dunlap, Susan **461**

Diary of a Nazi Lady
Freeman, Gillian 584

Die Dreaming
Faherty, Terence **514**

Die for Love
Peters, Elizabeth 250, 1263

Die in My Dreams
Green, Christine **661**

Die of a Rose
Maner, William 140

A Diet to Die For
Hess, Joan 215, **776**, 1118, 1147

Digger Smoked Out
Murphy, Warren 554

A Dime to Dance By
Walker, Walter 735

Dire Happenings at Scratch Ankle
Sibley, Celestine **1496**, 1542, 1544

Dirty-Down
Clothier, Peter 1509, 1676

The Dirty Duck
Grimes, Martha 1343

Dirty Laundry
Hamill, Pete 1350

Dirty White Boys
Hunter, Stephen 708, 796

The Disappearance of Edwin Drood
Rowland, Peter 1164, **1407**

The Disappearance of Penny
Randisi, Robert J. 133, 170, 573, 1487

Disassociated States
Simon, Leonard **1499**

Disclosure
Crichton, Michael 1615

The Dismas Hardy Series
Lescroart, John T. 123, 908

The Ditched Blonde
Adams, Harold **12**

Divide the Night
Ebersohn, Wessel 1114

The Dividing Line
Parrish, Richard 692, 1017, 1251, **1273**, 1325, 1331, 1599, 1649

Divorcing Jack
Bateman, Colin **104**, 786

Dixie City Jam
Burke, James Lee **195**

The DKA Series
Gores, Joe 199

Do Unto Others
Abbott, Jeff **1**, 70, 415, 744, 1319

The Doberman Wore Black
Moore, Barbara 17, 257, 258, 259, 288, 289, 290, 291, 1241, 1734

The Dobie Paradox
Cory, Desmond **331**

The Doc Adams Series
Boyer, Rick 336, 688, 764, 1604, 1615

The Dr. Davie Series
Clinton-Baddeley, V.C. 330, 331, 590

The Dr. Maxene St. Clair Series
McGiffin, Janet 660

Dr. Nightingale Comes Home
Adamson, Lydia 362, 372

Dr. Nightingale Goes the Distance
Adamson, Lydia **21**

Dr. Nightingale Goes to the Dogs
Adamson, Lydia 121

Dr. Nightingale Rides the Elephant
Adamson, Lydia **22**

The Dr. Nightingale Series
Adamson, Lydia 1733, 1734

Doctors, Lawyers and Such
Cooper, Susan Rogers **311**

The Dog Collar Murders
Wilson, Barbara 533, 534, 1323

Dog Heavies
Washburn, L.J. **1675**

The Dog Hermit
Stout, David 1287, **1578**, 1720

Dogtown
Lambert, Mercedes 852, **972**, 1435, 1524, 1529

The Don Roback Series
Hensley, Joe L. 704, 705, 777, 779, 780, 923, 1281

The Don Robak Series
Hensley, Joe L. 1135

The Donald Strachey Series
Stevenson, Richard 1151

Donato and Daugher
Early, Jack 1227

Donato and Daughter
Early, Jack 150, 805, 858, 1077, 1222, 1224, 1443

Done Deal
Standiford, Les 3, 617, 1012, **1561**

Don't Ask
Westlake, Donald E. 616, **1697**

Don't Cry Now
Fielding, Joy 275

Don't Leave Me This Way
Smith, Joan 269, 307, 801, 1306, **1520**, 1586

Don't Look Back
Hastings, Beverly 128

Don't Say a Word
Klavan, Andrew 150, 773, 885, 899, **937**, 1297, 1622

Don't Say a Word
Peterson, Keith **1308**

The Doors Open
Gilbert, Michael 1367

Dorothy and Agatha
Larsen, Gaylord **984**

The Dortmunder Series
Westlake, Donald E. 145

Double Blind

Double Blind
Laing, David **965**

Double-Cross
Kakonis, Michael 1005

Double Daughter
McConnell, Vicki 444, 533

Double Deuce
Parker, Robert B. **1269**

Double Down
Kakonis, Tom 295, 709, 710, **854**

Double Eagle
Miles, Keith 480

Double Exposure
Stinson, Jim 413, 847, 992

Double Jeopardy
Underwood, Michael 1651

The Double Minded Men
Craig, Philip R. **338**

Double Plot
Axler, Leo **70**

Double Take
Oleksiw, Susan 626

Double Whammy
Hiaasen, Carl 682, 707, 709, 949, 951, 1012, 1058, 1475, 1560, 1704

Doubting Thomas
Reeves, Robert 1486, 1657, 1735

Dover and the Claret Tappers
Porter, Joyce **1322**

Down Among the Angels
Purtre, John Walter 905

Down Among the Dead Men
Moyes, Patricia 87

Down by the Sea
Kent, Bill 293, **910**

The Down-East Murders
Borthwick, J.S. 120, 1063, 1140, 1255, 1588

The Down Home Heifer Heist
Sandstrom, Eve K. **1432**

Down Home Murder
Kelner, Toni L.P. 520, **901**, 1517

Downriver
Estleman, Loren D. 1647

A Dragon Lives Forever
Riggs, John R. **1368**

Drawing Dead
Hautman, Pete 855, 1672

Dream of Darkness
Ruell, Patrick **1412**, 1593

Dreamboat
Swanson, Doug J. **1596**

Dreamland
Lorens, M.K. **1044**

Dreamsicle
Ripley, W.L. **1370**

Dress Her in Indigo
MacDonald, John D. 1653

A Drink Before the War
Lehane, Dennis **1000**, 1218

A Drink of Deadly Wine
Charles, Kate 61, **235**

The Drood Murder Case
Baker, Richard M. 1407

Drop-Off
Grissom, Ken 905, 1336

Dropped Dead
Ross, Jonathan 1168

Dropshot
Coben, Harlan 1195

Dropshot: A Brad Smith Novel
Bickham, Jack **129**

Drover and the Zebras
Granger, Bill **646**

Drown All the Dogs
Adcock, Thomas **23**, 104, 657, 786

Drowned Hopes
Westlake, Donald E. **1698**

Drowned Man's Key
Grissom, Ken **683**

The Drowner
MacDonald, John D. 973

A Dry and Thirsty Ground
Weiss, Mike **1688**

The Dry White Tear
Wilcox, Stephen F. 721, 1053, **1719**

Due Diligence
Kahn, Michael A. **852**

Duffy
Kavanagh, Dan 726, 1573

The Duffy House Series
Evers, Crabbe 613

The Duke of Cleveland
Roberts, Les **1385**

The Dull Dead
Butler, Gwendoline 1592

Dumford Blood
Epperson, S.K. 267, 268

The Duncan Kincaid Series
Crombie, Deborah 1397

Dupe
Cody, Liza 95, 1141, 1144, 1181, 1630

Dust Devils of the Purple Sage
Smith, Barbara Burnett 537, **1516**, 1586

Dydeetown World
Wilson, F. Paul 241

Dying Fall
Thomson, June 67

A Dying Fall
Wade, Henry 191

Dying for Chocolate
Davidson, Diane Mott 32, **390**, 1257, 1258, 1290

Dying in the Post-War World
Collins, Max Allan 283

The Dying of the Light
Richardson, Robert 110, **1366**

The Dying Room
Giroux, E.X. **599**

The Dying Trade
Corris, Peter 255, 256

Dying Voices
Crider, Bill **351**, 722, 744, 776, 1512, 1657, 1735, 1797

Dynamite Pass
Trainor, J.F. 1017, 1273, 1340, 1341, **1626**, 1667

E

The Eagle Has Flown
Higgins, Jack **787**

The Eagle Has Landed
Higgins, Jack 37, 78, 410, 1679

Eagles Die Too
O'Brien, Meg **1215**, 1641

Early Autumn
Parker, Robert B. 1355, 1364

Earth Angels
Petievich, Gerald 1193, **1311**, 1426

East Beach
Ely, Ron **485**

East Is East
Lathen, Emma **986**

The Easy Barnes Series
Hilary, Richard 1176

The Easy Rawlins Series
Mosley, Walter 956

An Easy Thing
Taibo, Paco Ignacio II 27, 327, **1597**

Eat, Drink and Be Buried
Kingsbury, Kate **929**

The Echo Vector
Kahn, James 1321, 1372

Ed Fitzgerald Series
Flynn, Don 130, 1309

The Edge
Olshaker, Mark 1424

Edge City
Soracco, Sin 4, 270, 271, 952, 1370, 1444, **1537**

The Edge of Sleep
Wiltse, David **1736**

The Edge of the Crazies
Harrison, Jamie **736**

Edwin of the Iron Shoes
Muller, Marcia 919

The Edwina Crusoe Series
Kittredge, Mary 658, 660, 774, 1129, 1130

The Eight
Neville, Katherine 1539, 1681

Eight Dogs Flying
Wilson, Karen Ann 121, 257, 258, 288, 291, 362, **1734**

The El Murders
Gash, Joe 1425

Elective Murder
McGiffin, Janet 1129

Electric City
Beck, K.K. **115**, 372, 774

Elegy in a Country Graveyard
Peterson, Audrey **1304**

Element of Doubt
Simpson, Dorothy 1555

The Elena Oliverez Series
Muller, Marcia 1569

The Elias Hackshaw Series
Wilcox, Stephen F. 688, 1032

The Eliminator
York, Andrew 567

The Elizabeth MacPherson Series
McCrumb, Sharyn 10, 114, 218, 731, 732, 977, 1318, 1335

The Ellie Bernstein Series
Dietz, Denise 849

The Ellie Haskell Series
Cannell, Dorothy 422

Elsinore
Charyn, Jerome **238**

Elusive Quarry
Comfort, B. **285**

The Elvis Cole Series
Crais, Robert 764, 791, 1272, 1385, 1400, 1440, 1646

Embrace the Wolf
Schutz, Benjamin M. 146, 150, 716

The Emerald Lizard
Wiltz, Chris 197, 273, 1038, 1492, **1738**

Emergency Murder
McGiffin, Janet 658, 1656

Emma Chizzit and the Mother Lode Marauder
Hall, Mary Bowen **711**

Emma Chizzit and the Napa Nemesis
Hall, Mary Bowen **712**, 739, 1245, 1790

Emma Chizzit and the Queen Anne Killer
Hall, Mary Bowen 376, **713**, 1235, 1661

Emma Chizzit and the Sacramento Stalker
Hall, Mary Bowen 972

The Emma Chizzit Series
Hall, Mary Bowen 284, 285, 761, 1234, 1446

The Emma Lord Series
Daheim, Mary 22, 115

The Empress File
Camp, John **210**, 388, 1538

Encore Murder
Babson, Marian **76**

End-Game
Gilbert, Michael 451, 961

End Game
Stryker, Dev **1585**

End of the Chapter
Blake, Nicholas 224

The End of the Pier
Grimes, Martha 599, **674**

Title Index — File Under: Deceased

Enemies
Harris, Richard 935

Enemy's Enemy
Guillou, Jan **685**

The English School of Murder
Edwards, Ruth Dudley 451

Enigma
Harris, Robert 994

Epitaph for a Lobbyist
Dominic, R.B. 1634

Epitaph for a Spy
Ambler, Eric 37

Epitaphs
Pronzini, Bill 1269, **1327**

Escapade
Satterthwait, Walter 560, **1438**

Escape the Night
Patterson, Richard North 1762

The Estuary Pilgrim
Skeggs, Douglas **1507**

The Eve of the Wedding
Black, Lionel 87

Even the Butler Was Poor
Goulart, Ron **628**

Every Breath You Take
Spring, Michelle 428, 1094, **1541**

Every Crooked Nanny
Trocheck, Kathy Hogan 125, 312, 374, **1631**

Everything but the Squeal
Hallinan, Timothy 262, **716**, 1217

Everything You Have Is Mine
Scoppettone, Sandra 1442, **1460**

Eviction by Death
Yeager, Dorian 16, 473, 517, **1783**

Evidence of Blood
Cook, Thomas H. 1726

The Evil That Men Do
Hill, R. Lance 632, 1284, 1704

Evil under the Sun
Christie, Agatha 225

Except for the Bones
Wilcox, Collin 1387, **1713**

Exception to Murder
Wingate, Anne **1740**

Exceptional Clearance
Caunitz, William J. **229**, 1534, 1535

Exercise in Terror
Kaminsky, Stuart M. 1351

Exhaustive Enquiries
Rowlands, Betty **1408**

Exit Actors Dying
Arnold, Margot 174, 176

Exit Wounds
Westermann, John 1535, **1696**

Expert Testimony
Stockley, Grif 923

Extenuating Circumstances
Valin, Jonathan 150, 1601

Extreme Close-up
Crews, Lary 11

The Eye
Pronzini, Bill 99

The Eye of Anna
Wingate, Anne **1741**

The Eye of God
Grace, C.L. 426, **631**

Eye of the Gator
Ayres, E.C. **72**

Eye of the Needle
Follett, Ken 78, 410, 579, 787, 1679, 1746

Eye of the Storm
Muller, Marcia 947

Eyes of Prey
Sandford, John 623, 1095, 1381

F

F Is for Fugitive
Grafton, Sue **634**, 1180, 1219, 1265

The Face on the Cutting Room Floor
Cutler, Stan 722

Faces in the Crowd
Marshall, William **1079**

Fade Out
Upton, Robert 728, 1010, 1575

Fade the Heat
Brandon, Jay 557, 1016, 1090

Fade to Black
Goldsborough, Robert **607**, 1047

Fadeaway
Rosen, Richard 1655

Fair Game
Krich, Rochelle Majer 63, 324, 325, 805, **954**, 1221, 1526

The Faith Fairchild Series
Page, Katherine Hall 244, 246, 531, 1749

Faith, Hope and Homicide
Mann, Jessica **1071**, 1162

Faithfully Executed
Bowen, Michael **159**

Falconer's Crusade
Morson, Ian 243, **1175**, 1468

The Fall-Down Artist
Lipinski, Thomas **1032**

Fall From Grace
Wright, L.R. 268, **1773**

A Fall in Denver
Andrews, Sarah **56**

The Fall Line
Sullivan, Mark T. 518, **1589**

Falling Star
Moyes, Patricia 76, 641, 1131, 1768

False Faces
Margolis, Seth Jacob **1074**

False Impressions
Berne, Karin 347, 1316, 1650

The False Inspector Dew
Lovesey, Peter 117

False Profit
Eversz, Robert **511**, 565

False Profits
Everson, David **509**

False Prophet
Kellerman, Faye 173, 364, **879**

False Prophets
Flannery, Sean 1278

False Witness
Benke, Patricia D. 1268

Fame's Peril
Smilgis, Martha 770

Family Album
Oleksiw, Susan **1230**

Family Closets
Dorner, Marjorie 694, 959, 1157

Family Practice
Weir, Charlene **1686**

Family Reunion
Sarazen, Nicholas 49

The Family Stalker
Katz, Jon 794, **870**

The Family Vault
MacLeod, Charlotte 117, 286, 1447

A Famine of Horses
Chisholm, P.F. **243**, 1377, 1468, 1624

The Famous DAR Murder Mystery
Landrum, Graham **977**, 1209

A Farewell to Yarns
Churchill, Jill 215, **245**, 1208, 1256, 1750

Farrier's Lane
Perry, Anne **1294**

The Fast-Death Factor
Crosby, Virginia 359, 977, 983

Fast Fade
Lyons, Arthur 299, 300, 369, 665, 1200, 1575

Fat-Free and Fatal
Girdner, Jaqueline 1065

Fat Tuesday
Emerson, Earl 819

A Fatal Advent
Holland, Isabelle **797**, 916, 1048, 1123, 1442

Fatal Charm
Morice, Anne 516, **1173**

Fatal Cure
Cook, Robin 1130, 1656

Fatal Diagnosis
Kittredge, Mary 79, 448, 659

The Fatal Equilibrium
Jevons, Marshall 1482

Fatal Impressions
Warga, Wayne 477, 479, 532, 1068, 1507, 1508, 1666, 1676

A Fatal Inversion
Vine, Barbara 1310, 1367

Fatal Obsession
Taylor, D.B. 893, 1360, **1606**

The Fate of Princes
Doherty, P.C. **424**, 1375, 1469

The Fate of the Princes
Grace, C.L. 265

The Father Bredder Series
Holton, Leonard 916

The Father Dowling Series
McInerny, Ralph 656, 916, 1101

The Father Koesler Series
Kienzle, William 1101

The Father Shanley Series
Webb, Jack 656

Fatlands
Dunant, Sarah 1094

Fault Lines
White, Teri 1455

The Faust Conspiracy
Baddock, James **78**, 410, 787

Fear in a Handful of Dust
Garfield, Brian 1152

Fear in Fenway
Evers, Crabbe **506**, 1536

The Fear in Yesterday's Rings
Chesbro, George C. 429

Fear of the Dark
Haywood, Gar Anthony 393, 788, 938, 1481

The February Trouble
Albert, Neil **30**, 1110

Feeding Frenzy
Kemprecos, Paul **904**

Felidae
Pirincci, Akif 180, 438, 439

Fell and Foul Play
Carr, John Dickson **221**

Fellowship of Fear
Elkins, Aaron 351

Felony Murder
Klempner, Joseph T. **940**

Femmes Fatal
Cannell, Dorothy **214**, 423, 1557

Fertile Betrayal
Bohan, Becky 812

A Few Dying Words
Gosling, Paula 268, **626**

The Fiddler Series
Maxwell, A.E. 434, 485

Fielder's Choice
Bowen, Michael **160**, 1201

The Fields of Eden
Hinkemeyer, Michael T. 1135, 1584

The Fifth Angel
Wiltse, David 205

The Fifth Profession
Morrell, David 348

The Fifth Rapunzel
Gill, B.M. **586**

File Under: Arson
Lacey, Sarah 309

File Under: Deceased
Lacey, Sarah **962**

File Under: Missing

File Under: Missing
Lacey, Sarah 1094

Final Cut
Chais, Pamela 332, 1574

Final Cut
Wright, Eric 992, **1768**

Final Dictation
Vincent, L.M. **1655**

Final Edit
Carter, Robert A. **224**

Final Option
Hartzmark, Gini 1268

Final Option
Robinett, Stephen 86, 755, **1389**

Final Proof
Reno, Marie 384, 524

Final Session
Morell, Mary 925, **1170**

The Final Shot
Barth, Richard 968

Final Slaughter
Carter, Robert 580

Final Thesis
Story, William L. 1482, 1735

Final Tour
Heckler, Jonellen **770**

Final Viewing
Axler, Leo 1

Finders Keepers
Travis, Elizabeth 223, 224, 1501, **1627**

Finding Maubee
Carr, A.Z.H. 845

A Fine Italian Hand
Wright, Eric **1769**

A Fine Place for Death
Granger, Ann 357, **643**

Finishing Touch
Rowlands, Betty 1557

Fire Horse
Shoemaker, Bill **1486**

Fire Lake
Valin, Jonathan 189, 1093

The Fireman
Leather, Stephen 261, 811, **997**, 1673, 1743, 1744

Firestorm
Barr, Nevada 1552

The Firm
Grisham, John 333, 547, 1015, 1110, 1531

Firm Ambitions
Kahn, Michael A. 650, **853**, 1780

First and Ten
Anderson, Douglas **50**

First Blood
Morrell, David 527

The First Deadly Sin
Sanders, Lawrence 1158, 1344, 1533

The First Directive
McNamara, Joseph 1070, 1193, 1249, 1712, 1715

First Hit of the Season
Dentinger, Jane 15, 641, 1219

First Kill All the Lawyers
Shankman, Sarah 198, 894, 1041, 1399, 1498, 1545

First Kill All the Lawyers
Storey, Alice 612, 1318

First Pedigree Murder
Cleary, Melissa **257**

Fisherman's Luck
Pace, Tom 817

A Fistful of Empty
Schutz, Benjamin M. 149, 305, 454, 623, 1104, **1457**, 1481, 1765

A Fit of Tempera
Daheim, Mary **375**

Five O'Clock Lightning
DeAndrea, William L. 160, 507

A Fix Like This
Constantine, K.C. 1135

Fixing to Die
Oster, Jerry 186, 391, **1249**

Flame
Lutz, John 784, 1011, **1057**

Flames of Heaven
Peters, Ralph 529

Flamingo
Reiss, Bob **1359**

Flamingos
Savage, Marc 1370, **1444**, 1537, 1690

A Flash of Green
MacDonald, John D. 782, 1359

Flashback
Wood, Ted **1756**

Flawless
Barrow, Adam **99**

Flesh and Blood
Cook, Thomas H. 184, 186, 1532

Flesh and Blood
Harvey, James Neal 940

Fletch
McDonald, Gregory 532, 1698

The Fletch Series
McDonald, Gregory 714, 1309

Flight to Yesterday
Johnston, Velda 139

The Flip Side of Life
Martin, James E. **1085**, 1647, 1751

Floater
Koenig, Joseph 617, 1026, 1103, 1104, 1105, 1582

Flood
Vachss, Andrew 527, 888

The Florentine Win
La Barre, Harriet 139

Florida Straits
Shames, Laurence 231, 784, 1024, 1560

A Flower in the Desert
Satterthwait, Walter 41, 830, 1200, 1217, 1252, 1423, **1439**, 1505, 1581

Flowers for the Dead
Williams, Ann M. 172, 849, 1156, 1668, **1728**

Flowers of Evil
Sherwood, John 562

Flying Finish
Francis, Dick 1037, 1486

Fog of Doubt
Brand, Christianna 576, 586

Follow That Blonde
Smith, Joan 345, 477, **1521**

Follow the Leader
Logue, John 317, 318

Follow the Sharks
Tapply, William G. 1358

Following Jane
Singer, Shelley 157, 503, 1701

The Fools in Town Are on Our Side
Thomas, Ross 159, 210, 616, 1752, 1760

Fool's Puzzle
Fowler, Earlene 362, **536**, 559

The Fool's Run
Camp, John 145, 437, 622, 1100

Fool's Run
Sandford, John 566

Footnote to Murder
Taylor, L.A. 556, 745

Footprints
Bradford, Kelly 444, 533

Footsteps of the Hawk
Vachss, Andrew **1644**

For the Sake of Elena
George, Elizabeth 677, 1141

Force of Nature
Solomita, Stephen 186, 197, **1533**

The Forever Beat
Cline, John **262**

Fort's Law
Hensley, Joe L. 1111, 1662

Forty Whacks
Callahan, Sheila MacGill **207**

The Forza Trap
Davis, Kenn 589, 609

Foul Shot
Hornig, Doug 871, 872

Four Elements of Murder
Borton, D.B. **155**

Four Steps to Death
Ramsay, Diana 18, **1346**

Four Steps to Death
Ramsey, Diana 798

Foursome
Healy, Jeremiah **765**

Fourth Down, Death
Hinkemeyer, Michael T. 140, 314, 515, 1250

The Fourth Durango
Thomas, Ross 433, 483, 782, 785, 1100, **1612**

The Fourth Procedure
Pottinger, Stanley 1262

What Mystery Do I Read Next?

The Fourth Stage of Gainsborough Brown
Watson, Clarissa 1666

The Fourth Wall
Paul, Barbara 641

Fowl Prey
Daheim, Mary 145

The Fox Valley Murders
Vance, John Holbrook 298

Foxglove
Kelly, Mary Anne 599, **889**

Freak
Collins, Michael 1494

The Fred Carver Series
Lutz, John 72, 73, 817, 1349, 1492, 1560

The Freddie O'Neal Series
Dain, Catherine 398, 917, 921, 1266, 1700

Free
Komarnicki, Todd 662, **952**, 1578

Free Draw
Singer, Shelley 462, 1573

Free Fall
Crais, Robert 294, **341**, 454, 1269

Free Flight
Terman, Douglas 409, 825

Freeze Frame
Dorner, Marjorie 502, 563, 1471

Fresh Kills
Wheat, Carolyn **1699**

Friends in High Places
Hendricks, Michael 542, **771**, 1799

The Friends of Eddie Coyle
Higgins, George V. 831

Friends till the End
Dank, Gloria 51, **387**

Frobisher's Savage
Tourney, Leonard **1624**

From a High Place
Mathis, Edward 84, 350, 1741

From Doon with Death
Rendell, Ruth 841

From Here to Paternity
Churchill, Jill **246**

From Potter's Field
Cornwell, Patricia D. **325**

The Frost Series
Wingfield, R.D. 472, 911, 912

Frost the Fiddler
Weber, Janice 1539, **1681**

Frozen Assets
Leasor, James 571, **996**, 1564

The Frozen Franklin
Hanlon, Sean **725**

Frozen Stare
Schwartz, Richard B. **1459**

Fruits of the Poisonous Tree
Mayor, Archer **1104**

Fugitive Moon
Faust, Ron 271

Title Index

The Fugitive Pigeon
Westlake, Donald E.   355

Full-Bodied Red
Zimmerman, Bruce   739, **1790**

Full Circle
Wilcox, Collin   **1714**

Full Cleveland
Roberts, Les   1085, **1386**

Full Commission
Brennan, Carol   **172**

Full Contact
Randisi, Robert J.   873, 1313

Funeral March
De Felitta, Frank   49, 62

Funnelweb
West, Charles   256, **1693**

Funny as a Dead Comic
Cooper, Susan Rogers   125, **312**, 770

Funny as a Dead Relative
Cooper, Susan Rogers   **313**, 902, 1204, 1517

Furnished for Murder
Barth, Richard   70, **101**, 1112, 1240, 1463, 1777, 1778

Fuse Time
Byrd, Max   **205**, 684

G

The G.D.H. Pringle Series
Livingston, Nancy   591, 962

G Is for Gumshoe
Grafton, Sue   **635**, 1181, 1229, 1264

The G-String Murders
Lee, Gypsy Rose   1346

The Gabe Wager Series
Burns, Rex   1711, 1715, 1717

The Gail McCarthy Series
Crum, Laura   1733

Gallows View
Robinson, Peter   625, 645, 1197, **1393**, 1669, 1769

Gallowsglass
Rendell, Ruth   1277

Gambit
Stout, Rex   411

Games
Pronzini, Bill   526, 589

The Garden Club
Jackson, Muriel Resnick   33, 698, **836**, 900, 901, 1517, 1544, 1548

Garden of Malice
Kenney, Susan   892, 1520, 1522

The Garth Ryland Series
Riggs, John R.   166, 922, 1720

The Gathering Place
Breen, Jon L.   743, 1300

Gator Kill
Crider, Bill   **352**

Gatsby's Vineyard
Maxwell, A.E.   511, 569, 908

Gaudi Afternoon
Wilson, Barbara   **1731**

Gaudy Night
Sayers, Dorothy L.   64

The Gemini Man
Kelly, Susan   798, 882, 890, 982, 1046, 1214, 1318, 1476

Generous Death
Pickard, Nancy   535, 933, 966, 1118, 1167, 1379

The Genesis Files
Biderman, Bob   **130**

Gentkill: A Novel of the FBI
Lindsay, Paul   **1025**

Gently Through the Woods
Hunter, Alan   67

The George Eliot Murders
Skom, Edith   **1511**

The Gervase Fen series
Crispin, Edmund   228, 330, 331, 590, 1366, 1367

Get Shorty
Leonard, Elmore   **1005**, 1128

Get What's Coming
Reaves, Sam   **1354**

Ghostland
Hager, Jean   **700**

The Ghostway
Hillerman, Tony   1162

The Giant Rat of Sumatra
Boyer, Rick   131

The Gideon Fell Series
Carr, John Dickson   471

The Gideon Oliver Series
Elkins, Aaron   430, 1071, 1579

A Gift for Murder
Lake, M.D.   247, 360, 595, 600, 744, **968**, 1044, 1764

The Gift Horse's Mouth
Campbell, Robert   **212**

The Gil Disbro Series
Martin, James E.   1385

The Gil Mayo Series
Eccles, Marjorie   1479

Gilgamesh
Bannister, Jo   1645

The Gillian Adams Series
Kelly, Nora   1511

The Girls Are Missing
Crane, Caroline   44

Give My Secrets Back
Allen, Karen   1356

The Glade Manor Murder
Lemarchand, Elizabeth   191, 676, 789, **1001**

The Gladstone Bag
MacLeod, Charlotte   **1063**

A Glancing Light
Elkins, Aaron   345, **477**, 1508, 1509, 1714

The Glass Ceiling
Donald, Anabel   **428**

The Glass-Sided Ant's Nest
Dickinson, Peter   586

The Glendower Conspiracy
Biggle, Lloyd Jr.   **131**, 440

The Glendower Conspiracy: A Memoir of Sherlock Holmes
Biggle, Lloyd Jr.   442

The Glendower Legacy
Gifford, Thomas   583

Glitter and Ash
Smith, Dennis   487

The Glitter Dome
Wambaugh, Joseph   1426, 1696

Glitz
Leonard, Elmore   185

Glory Days
Scott, Rosie   533, 806, 1731

The Glory Hole Murders
Fennelly, Tony   726, 1150, 1151, 1572

The Glynis Tryon Series
Monfredo, Miriam Grace   1260

God Bless John Wayne
Friedman, Kinky   **554**

God Save the Child
Parker, Robert B.   1384, 1643

God Save the Mark
Westlake, Donald E.   11, 628, 714, 715

The Godwin Sideboard
Malcolm, John   1565

The Godwulf Manuscript
Parker, Robert B.   360, 1602

The Going Down of the Sun
Bannister, Jo   **87**, 581

Going, Going, Gone
Collins, Eliza G.C.   570, 572, 729, 1240, 1565

Going Wrong
Rendell, Ruth   417, **1360**

The Gold Coast
DeMille, Nelson   **412**

The Gold Deadline
Resnicow, Herbert   1729

The Gold Solution
Resnicow, Herbert   607, 608, 1047

Golden Fleece
Becklund, Jack   **118**

Goldilocks
Coburn, Andrew   842

The Goldy Bear Series
Davidson, Diane Mott   244, 422, 698, 849, 1289, 1291

The Gombeen Man
Eickoff, Randy Lee   **474**, 657

The Gondola Scam
Gash, Jonathan   1004, 1510

Gone, No Forwarding
Gores, Joe   213

Gone to the Dogs
Conant, Susan   722

Gone Wild
Hall, James W.   **708**, 1137

The Good Daughter
Lee, Wendi   503

A Good Day to Die
Solomita, Stephen   147, **1534**

The Good Fight
Matera, Lia   153, 809, **1091**, 1650, 1651

The Good Friday Murder
Harris, Lee   1434, 1591

Good Girls Don't Get Murdered
Parker, Percy Spurlark   762, 832, 1314

Good Morning, Irene
Douglas, Carole Nelson   **440**, 519, 1029, 1164, 1298

Good Night, Mr. Holmes
Douglas, Carole Nelson   131, **441**, 834, 926

Good Night, Sweet Prince
Berry, Carole   18, **126**, 346, 1319

A Good Night to Kill
O'Donnell, Lillian   47, 533, 771, 1241, 1528

The Good Policeman
Charyn, Jerome   1663

Good Spies Don't Grow on Trees
Lovell, Marc   550

The Good Thief
Rosenblum, Robert   1429

A Good Year for a Corpse
Wolzien, Valerie   215, **1749**

Goodbye, Nanny Gray
Stacey, Susannah   25, 110, 1160

Goodnight, Irene
Burke, Jan   **198**, 1332, 1659

Goosefoot
McGinley, Patrick   530

Gorky Park
Smith, Martin Cruz   859, 861, 1066, 1793

Gospel Truths
Sandom, J.G.   61, 235, **1429**

The Grandfather Medicine
Hager, Jean   1232, 1430, 1437, 1781

The Grandmother Medicine
Hager, Jean   1153

Grandmother's House
LaPierre, Janet   **983**, 1156, 1317

Grass Roots
Woods, Stuart   936, 1169

The Grass-Widow's Tale
Peters, Ellis   802, 1484

Grave Consequences
Comfort, B.   **286**, 361, 711, 713, 765, 1069, 1103, 1105, 1246, 1445, 1571

Grave Designs
Kahn, Michael A.   405, 1333

Grave Doubt
Allegretto, Michael   **41**, 830

521

Grave Matters / **What Mystery Do I Read Next?**

Grave Matters
Axler, Leo **71**

Grave Murder
Guthrie, Al 1430, 1725

Grave Responsibility
Stacey, Susannah 470, **1554**, 1708

Grave Secrets
Hendricksen, Louise **774**

A Grave Talent
King, Laurie R. **925**, 946, 1042, 1222, 1452, 1461, 1462, 1515, 1526, 1527

Grave Undertaking
McCahery, James 1097, **1112**, 1171, 1172, 1442

Graves in Academe
Kenney, Susan 1140, 1196, 1274

Gravestone
Carlson, P.M. **219**, 1685

The Gray Flannel Shroud
Slesar, Henry 1040

The Great California Game
Gash, Jonathan **570**, 616, 791

A Great Deliverance
George, Elizabeth 191, 358, 366, 586, 676, 751, 841, 1132, 1143, 1343, 1392, 1393, 1395, 1554, 1556

The Great Grave Robbery
Minahan, John **1158**, 1362

The Great Hotel Robbery
Minahan, John 1363

The Great Reminder
Irvine, R.R. **829**

The Green Apartments
Corris, Peter 1693

Green for Danger
Brand, Christianna 471, 579

The Green Mosaic
Wilcox, Stephen F. **1720**

Green River Rising
Willocks, Tim 4

The Grid
Kerr, Philip 566

Grievous Sin
Kellerman, Faye **880**

The Grifters
Thompson, Jim 773

Grim Pickings
Rowe, Jennifer 46

Grime and Punishment
Churchill, Jill 594, 990, 1146, 1255, 1258, 1748

Grizzly
Andreae, Christine **54**, 1341, 1625, 1784

Grizzly Trail
Moffat, Gwen 1651

The Grofield Series
Stark, Richard 1387

Grootka
Jackson, Jon A. 272, 497, **832**, 910

Growing Light
Conley, Martha 821

The Grub-and-Stakers Series
MacLeod, Charlotte 977

Guardian Angel
Paretsky, Sara 781, 1251, 1252, **1265**, 1504

Guilt by Association
Sloan, Susan R. 985, **1514**

Guilt Edged
Burley, W.J. 748

Guilty by Choice
Benke, Patricia D. 1465

Guilty Knowledge
Grant-Adamson, Lesley 1126

A Guilty Thing Surprised
Rendell, Ruth 748

Gun Men
Friedman, Gary **553**, 618, 822

Gunpower
Schorr, Mark **1456**

The Guns of Heaven
Hamill, Pete 961

The Gwen Ramadge Series
O'Donnell, Lillian 473, 542, 1798, 1799

A Gypsy Good Time
Hasford, Gustav **755**

H

H Is for Homicide
Grafton, Sue 396, **636**, 1269, 1798

The Habit of Loving
Thomson, June 748, 1253, 1554

Hacker
Martin, Lee 1113

Half a Mind
Hornsby, Wendy 218, **807**, 1334, 1335

Hallowed Murder
Hart, Ellen 83, **745**, 971, 1042, 1133, 1194, 1323, 1461, 1797

Halo in Blood
Browne, Howard 1270

Hal's Own Murder Case
Martin, Lee 534

The Ham Reporter
Randisi, Robert J. 36, 1079, 1080, 1654, 1787

The Hamish MacBeth Series
Beaton, M.C. 249, 720, 912, 943

Hamlet, Revenge!
Innes, Michael 174, 176

The Hamlet Trap
Wilhelm, Kate 728, 870

Hammerlocke
Barnao, Jack 1472

Hammett
Gores, Joe 860, 1207, 1270, 1674, 1675

Hammurabi's Code
Kenney, Charles **909**, 1660

The Hand of the Lion
Coker, Carolyn 1676

Hands of a Stranger
Daley, Robert 1070

The Hanged Man
Satterthwait, Walter **1440**

The Hanging Garden
Sherwood, John **1485**

Hanging on the Wire
Linscott, Gillian **1028**

Hanging Time
Glass, Leslie **601**

The Hanging Valley
Robinson, Peter 358, 640, **1394**, 1767

The Hangman's Beautiful Daughter
McCrumb, Sharyn 267, 522, 742, 936, **1115**, 1665

Hangman's Root
Albert, Susan Wittig **32**

Happy Are the Merciful
Greeley, Andrew M. **656**

Happy Are Those Who Thirst for Justice
Greeley, Andrew M. 916

The Harbinger
Graham, Mark 1633

The Harbinger Effect
Wolf, S.K. 86, 453, 685, 756, 1727, **1746**

Hard Aground
Hall, James W. 4, **709**, 952, 1012, 1014, 1024, 1325, 1561

A Hard Bargain
Matera, Lia 514, **1092**, 1529

Hard Candy
Vachss, Andrew 831

Hard Evidence
Lescroart, John T. **1009**

Hard Fall
Pearson, Ridley 248, 521, 684, 1199, 1202, **1284**, 1499, 1633, 1690

Hard Guy
Elliott, Thornton 1288, 1589, 1677

Hard Guy
Elliott, Thorton **482**, 1210

Hard Look
Randisi, Robert J. **1349**

Hard News
Deaver, Jeffrey Wilds **403**, 760, 1671

Hard News
Sullivan, Mark T. **1590**

Hard Rain
Abrahams, Peter 823

Hard Tack
D'Amato, Barbara **382**, 401, 1647

Hard Trade
Lyons, Arthur 726, 727

Hard Women
D'Amato, Barbara **383**, 615, 760, 808, 1659

Hardball
D'Amato, Barbara 161, **384**, 569, 636, 893, 894, 895, 1113, 1265, 1476, 1636, 1759

Hardcover
Warga, Wayne 341, 466, 1020, 1054, 1055, 1387, 1500, 1764

Hardscape
Scott, Justin 1, 70, 336, 337, 339, 687, **1463**

Hare Today, Gone Tomorrow
O'Brien, Meg **1216**, 1474, 1475

Harmful Intent
Cook, Robin 5, 602

Harm's Way
Aird, Catherine 1253

The Harry Bosch Series
Connelly, Michael 1026, 1424, 1585

The Harry Chronicles
Pedrazas, Allan **1287**

The Harry Palmer Series
Deighton, Len 188

The Harry Stoner Series
Valin, Jonathan 29, 30, 31, 39, 342, 343, 407, 667, 862, 863, 864, 865, 1019, 1085, 1347, 1373, 1383, 1385, 1458, 1765

Hatchett
McGraw, Lee 1264

The Hawthorne Group
Hauser, Thomas **756**

A Hazard of Losers
Biggle, Lloyd Jr. **132**

Hazzard
Brown, R.D. 350, 352

He Was Her Man
Shankman, Sarah 313, 522, **1474**

He Wouldn't Kill Patience
Dickson, Carter 1605

Headed for a Hearse
Latimer, Jonathan 1038

Headhunt
Brennan, Carol 347

Headhunter
Slade, Michael 1027

Heartless
Cohen, Stephen Paul 1602

Heartshot
Havill, Steven F. **758**, 1108, 1111

Heat
Goldman, William 132

Heat
Woods, Stuart **1760**

Heat From Another Sun
Lindsey, David L. 229, 1426, 1644

The Heaven Stone
Daniel, David **386**

Heaven's Prisoners
Burke, James Lee 1672

Heavy Gilt
Klaich, Delores 83

Heavy Gilt
Klaich, Delores 1689

Hell Bent
Gross, Ken 23, 104, **684**, 1008

Hell's Only Half Full
Kantner, Rob 826

Help the Poor Struggler
Grimes, Martha 640

Help Wanted: Orphans Preferred
Emerson, Earl **487**

The Henrietta O'Dwyer Series
Hart, Carolyn G. 1497, 1547

Henrietta Who?
Aird, Catherine 260, 1168

Her Only Sin
Stein, Benjamin 546

Hero and the Terror
Blodgett, Michael 840

He's Dead-She's Dead: Details at Eleven
Tucker, John Bartholomew 760, 1475, 1477, **1635**, 1709

Hidden Agenda
Matera, Lia 216

Hidden Agenda
Porter, Anna 1435

Hidden City
DeBrosse, Jim **407**

Hidden Lake
Janeshutz, Trish 208

The Hidden Man
Underwood, Michael 153

Hide and Seek
Berg, Barry **122**, 403, 404, 848, 1558, 1592, 1593

High Crimes
Westermann, John 185, 1433

High Desert Malice
Mitchell, Kirk 106

High Strangeness
Drake, Alison **447**

Highgate Rise
Perry, Anne **1295**

Highland Laddie Gone
McCrumb, Sharyn 1316

The Hilary Tamar Series
Caudwell, Sarah 597, 598

Hire a Hangman
Wilcox, Collin **1715**

Hit and Run
O'Callaghan, Maxine 771, 772, **1219**, 1264

Hit on the House
Jackson, Jon A. **833**

The Hobart Lindsey Series
Lupoff, Richard A. 1242

The Holiday Murders
Landreth, Marsha 63, 80, 322, 324, 660, **975**

The Hollow Men
Flannery, Sean 550, 685, 810

The Hollow Woman
Ritchie, Simon 242, 1491

The Holly Winter Series
Conant, Susan 127, 257, 258, 259, 1734

Hollywood and LeVine
Bergman, Andrew 860

Hollywood Detective: Garrison
Rovin, Jeff 1674

Hollywood Gothic
Gifford, Thomas 1574

Hollywood Requiem
Freeborn, Peter **546**

The Holy Innocents
Sedley, Kate **1468**

Holy Terrors
Daheim, Mary **376**, 1061

Holy Treasure!
Williams, David 1069, **1729**

Home Sweet Homicide
Morgan, Kate **1171**

Home to Roost
Hammond, Gerald **720**

A Homecoming for Murder
Armistead, John **65**

The Homefront Murders
Meredith, D.R. 106

The Homer Kelly Series
Langton, Jane 747, 1136

Honeymoon with Murder
Hart, Carolyn G. 1120

Honolulu Red
Zimmelman, Lue 1005, 1223, **1789**

Honor Bound
Harris, Richard 66, 421, 547, 557, 558, 592, 735, 923, 1016, 1022, 1023, 1090, 1280, 1590, 1662

The Honourable Detective
Ashford, Jeffrey **67**, 451

Hoodwink
Pronzini, Bill 668, 1055

The Hooky Heffernan Series
Meynell, Laurence 1695

Hooligans
Diehl, William 1344, 1611, 1612, 1613

Hope Against Hope
Kelly, Susan B. 642, 645, **896**, 1244, 1408, 1419, 1728

Hope Will Answer
Kelly, Susan B. 357, 644

A Hopeless Case
Beck, K.K. 69, **116**, 198, 312, 503, 795, 959, 1076, 1697, 1743

Hopjoy was Here
Watson, Colin 1189

Hopscotch
Garfield, Brian 550, 633, 706

The Horse Latitudes
Ferrigno, Robert 227, 295, **526**, 653, 709, 755, 854, 1006, 1152

Horse of a Different Killer
Jaffe, Jody **839**

Hostage One
Fisher, David E. 825

Hostage to Death
Ashford, Jeffrey 1149

Hostile Witness
Lashner, William **985**

Hot
Lutz, John 1006

Hot Air
Breen, Jon L. **170**

Hot Shots
Gough, Laurence 334, **627**, 1417

Hot Water
Gunning, Sally 70, **686**, 696, 1722

Hot Wire
Russell, Randy 952, 1444, 1537, 1690

The Hotel Detective
Russell, Alan **1413**

Hotel Morgue
Laurence, Janet 135, 374, 375, 377, 699, **989**, 1557

Hour of the Hunter
Jance, J.A. 673, **843**

Hour of the Manatee
Ayres, E.C. **73**, 211, 336, 344, 870, 1596

An Hour to Kill
Wellen, Edward **1690**

The House of Blue Lights
Bowman, Robert J. 222, 397, 920, 972, 1116, 1379, 1579

House of Blues
Smith, Julie **1525**

The House on the Hill
Kelman, Judith 128, **899**

The Housewife and the Assassin
Trott, Susan 44

Houston in the Rearview Mirror
Cooper, Susan Rogers 314, 1103, 1775

How to Murder Your Mother-in-Law
Cannell, Dorothy **215**

How Town
Nava, Michael 727, **1194**

Hubbert and Lil: Partners in Crime
Gray, Gallagher **654**

Huckleberry Fiend
Smith, Julie 712, 1512

The Hugh Corbett Series
Doherty, P.C. 243, 512, 1404

Hung in the Balance
Ormerod, Roger 625, 645, 962, **1244**, 1708

The Hunt for Red October
Clancy, Tom 85, 179, 825, 1513, 1530

Hunter
Sauter, Eric 1352

Hunter's Moon
Logan, Chuck 566, 796

Hunting Ground
Riggs, John R. 371, 1722

Hush Little Darlings
Kelman, Judith 1643

Hush, Money
Femling, Jean **523**

I

I Is for Innocent
Grafton, Sue **637**, 837

I.O.U.
Pickard, Nancy 218, 599, 694, **1318**, 1334, 1661, 1665

I Was Dora Suarez
Raymond, Derek 1598

The Ice
Charbonneau, Louis **234**, 725

Ice Blues
Stevenson, Richard 727, 1796

The Ice House
Walters, Minette **1669**

Ice Station Zebra
MacLean, Alistair 234, 725, 1530

Ice Water
Gunning, Sally 337, 1099

Icewater Mansions
Allyn, Douglas **48**

The Iciest Sin
Keating, H.R.F. **875**

I'd Rather Be in Philadelphia
Roberts, Gillian 808, **1378**

Idol Bones
Greenwood, D.M. **671**

If Ever I Return, Pretty Peggy-O
McCrumb, Sharyn 42, 242, 314, 316, 514, 664, 674, 811, 1078, 1091, 1092, **1116**, 1334, 1367, 1392, 1742

I'll Be Leaving You Always
Scoppettone, Sandra 1042, **1461**

I'll Be Watching You
Key, Samuel M. 673

Illegal Motion
Stockley, Grif **1576**

I'm Getting Killed Right Here
Murray, William **1190**

Immaculate in Black
McGill, E.J. 1342, 1430, 1627, 1725

The Immediate Prospect of Being Hanged
Walker, Walter 240, 547, **1662**

Immoral Certainty
Tanenbaum, Robert K. 333, 1015, 1640

An Imperfect Spy
Cross, Amanda **360**, 1196

Imperfect Strangers
Woods, Stuart **1761**

Impulse
Weaver, Michael 468

In Blacker Moments | What Mystery Do I Read Next?

In Blacker Moments
Schenkel, S.E. **1451**

In Deep
Jones, Bruce 293, 525, 710, **846**

In Defense of Judges
Gray, A.W. 1015

In La-La Land We Trust
Campbell, Robert 717, 718

In-laws and Outlaws
Paul, Barbara **1277**

In Stoney Places
Mitchell, Kay **1159**, 1479, 1670

In the Dark
Brennan, Carol **173**, 1514

In the Dead of Winter
Baker, Abbey Penn **81**, 400, 560, 835, 924, 926, 1259

In the Electric Mist with Confederate Dead
Burke, James Lee **196**

In the Forest of the Night
Faust, Ron 1589

In the Game
Baker, Nikki **82**, 1198, 1323, 1356, 1410

In the Heat of the Night
Ball, John 393, 1314

In the Heat of the Summer
Katzenbach, John 53, 707, 937, 1011, 1014, 1057, 1166, 1279, 1285, 1297, 1425, 1427

In the House of Secret Enemies
Chesbro, George C. **241**, 283

In the Lake of the Moon
Lindsey, David L. 1006

In the Lake of the Woods
O'Brien, Tim **1218**

In the Last Analysis
Cross, Amanda 1136

Inadmissible Evidence
Friedman, Philip **557**

An Incident at Bloodtide
Chesbro, George C. 554

Incident at Potter's Bridge
Monniger, Joseph **1165**

Incinerator
Hallinan, Timothy **717**

Indecent Behavior
Rivers, Caryl 401, **1372**

Indemnity Only
Paretsky, Sara 919, 1113

The India Exhibition
Conroy, Richard Timothy **296**

The Indictment
Reed, Barry 820

Infected Be the Air
Law, Janice 315, 976, **991**

An Infinite Number of Monkeys
Roberts, Les 300, 717, 718

Inherit the Mob
Chafets, Zev **231**, 355, 606

The Innocent
McEwan, Ian 914

Innocent Journey
Natsuki, Shizuko 1127

The Innocents
Barre, Richard 164, 1325

An Inside Job
Wood, Ted 627

The Inside Man
Johnson, E. Richard 652

The Inspector Adam Dalgliesh Series
James, P.D. 578, 1773

The Inspector Alvarez Series
Jeffries, Roderic 1002

The Inspector Banks Series
Robinson, Peter 356, 577, 643, 678, 752, 1361

The Inspector Barnaby Series
Graham, Caroline 356, 385, 469, 575, 577, 1397, 1480

The Inspector Dagliesh Series
James, P.D. 575, 577

The Inspector Dover Series
Porter, Joyce 472, 768

The Inspector Faro Series
Knight, Alanna 655, 929

The Inspector Gautier Series
Grayson, Richard 519, 943

The Inspector Ghote Series
Keating, H.R.F. 34, 35, 845

The Inspector Gil Mayo Series
Eccles, Marjorie 367, 678

The Inspector John Rebus Series
Rankin, Ian 113

The Inspector Jury Series
Grimes, Martha 356, 575, 577, 578, 790, 1361

The Inspector Lloyd & Judy Hill Series
McGown, Jill 357, 661

The Inspector Luke Thanet Series
Simpson, Dorothy 25, 367, 1160, 1213

The Inspector Lynley Series
George, Elizabeth 356, 357, 1361, 1394, 1396, 1454, 1670, 1773

The Inspector Maigret Series
Simenon, Georges 548, 690, 768

The Inspector McGarr Series
Gill, Bartholomew 549

The Inspector Monk Series
Perry, Anne 737

The Inspector Morrissey Series
Mitchell, Kay 367

The Inspector Morse Series
Dexter, Colin 25, 109, 1394, 1396, 1397

The Inspector Napoleon Bonaparte Series
Upfield, Arthur W. 255, 328, 329, 874, 1695

The Inspector Pel Series
Hebden, Mark 549

The Inspector Purbright Series
Watson, Colin 472, 911

The Inspector Quantrill Series
Radley, Sheila 575, 577, 578, 790

The Inspector Rebus Series
Rankin, Ian 111, 1050

The Inspector Resnick Series
Harvey, John 356, 678

The Inspector Rostnikov Series
Kaminsky, Stuart M. 365, 913

The Inspector Rudd Series
Thomson, June 367, 1139, 1159

The Inspector Sanders Series
Sale, Medora 1396, 1397

The Inspector Slider Series
Harrod-Eagles, Cynthia 469

The Inspector Sloane Series
Aird, Catherine 366, 469, 472, 790, 912, 1159

The Inspector Thanet Series
Simpson, Dorothy 1394, 1480

Inspector Van Der Valk Series
Freeling, Nicholas 204

The Inspector Wexford Series
Rendell, Ruth 575, 578, 586, 675, 1343, 1393, 1394, 1395, 1396, 1397, 1773

Intent to Harm
Washburn, Stan 1424

Interest of Justice
Rosenberg, Nancy Taylor 216

Interface
Gores, Joe 1010

The Interface Man
Knox, Bill 948

Internal Affairs
Hentoff, Nat 1362, 1363

The Intersection of Law and Desire
Redmann, J.M. **1356**

Interview with Mattie
Singer, Shelley **1504**

Intimate Kill
Yorke, Margaret 67

Into the Fire
Wiltse, David 1283, **1737**

Into Thin Air
Zigal, Thomas **1788**

Introducing C.B. Greenfield
Kallen, Lucille 120, 814, 866, 1309

Invitation to Murder
Gorman, Ed 1348

The Ipcress File
Deighton, Len 567

The Irene Adler Series
Douglas, Carole Nelson 400, 465, 835, 924, 930, 1028, 1030, 1259, 1260

Irene at Large
Douglas, Carole Nelson **442**

Irene's Last Waltz
Douglas, Carole Nelson 81

The Iris Cooper Series
Beck, K.K. 465

The Iris House Series
Hager, Jean 134, 377

The Iris Thorne Series
Pugh, Dianne G. 124

Irish Chain
Fowler, Earlene **537**

Irish Gold
Greeley, Andrew M. **657**

The Iron Glove
Tierney, Ronald **1619**

Is Anybody There?
Gilpin, T.G. **591**, 1036

#A Is for Alibi
Grafton, Sue 919

Island
Perry, Thomas 782, 783, 1608, 1762

Island Girl
Berry, Carole **127**, 989

Island of Steel
Cohen, Stephen Paul 1532

It Can't Be My Grave
Dean, S.F.X. 1020

J

The J. Alfred Prufrock Murders
Sawyer, Corinne Holt 712, 1098, 1112, 1315

The J.P. Beaumont Series
Jance, J.A. 488, 815, 1353, 1711, 1715

The J.W. Jackson Series
Craig, Philip R. 72, 687

The Jackie Walsh Series
Cleary, Melissa 121, 288, 291, 1734

Jackpot
Pronzini, Bill 282, **1328**, 1353

The Jacob Asch Series
Lyons, Arthur 29, 30, 31, 301, 342, 667, 862, 1269, 1271, 1413, 1440, 1458

A Jade in Aries
Coe, Tucker 148

Jade Woman
Gash, Jonathan 296, 1243, 1743, 1744

The Jake Hatch Series
Campbell, Robert 212, 213

The Jake Samson Series
Singer, Shelley 907, 1414

The James Bond Series
Fleming, Ian 188, 567, 996

The James Joyce Murder
Cross, Amanda 583, 1045, 1512

The Jane Jeffry Series
Churchill, Jill 155, 157, 422, 595, 600, 1254, 1749

The Jane Silva Series
Beck, K.K. 251

The January Corpse
Albert, Neil **31**, 164

Title Index

The Jason Lynx Series
Orde, A.J. 70, 572

Jazz Funeral
Smith, Julie **1526**, 1632

The Jean Montrose Series
Roe, C.F. 660, 932, 1129

The Jemima Shore Series
Fraser, Antonia 269, 1399

The Jenny Cain Series
Pickard, Nancy 114, 120, 531, 991, 1064, 1117, 1335, 1380

The Jenny McKay Series
Belsky, Dick 1568

The Jeri Howard Series
Dawson, Janet 638, 639, 649, 921, 1182, 1185, 1490, 1506, 1700

Jericho Day
Murphy, Warren 633, 681, 756, 1174

The Jerry Brogan Series
Breen, Jon L. 1190

Jersey Monkey
Gallison, Kate **565**

Jersey Tomatoes
Rider, J.W. 77, 189, 565, 703, 1436

The Jessica Drake Series
Krich, Rochelle Majer 1525

The Jessica James Series
O'Brien, Meg 127, 155, 156, 177, 373, 382, 383, 813, 868, 1398, 1632

The Jesus Creek Series
Adams, Deborah 2, 1464, 1516, 1517

The Jill Smith Series
Dunlap, Susan 59, 219, 447, 804, 925, 927, 967, 968, 969, 970, 971, 1077, 1086, 1222, 1225, 1226, 1452, 1504, 1515, 1523, 1525, 1526

The Jimmy Fannery Series
Campbell, Robert 353

Jinx
Robitaille, Julie 868, **1398**, 1568

The Joanna Stark Series
Muller, Marcia 1052, 1216, 1398

The Jocelyn O'Roarke Series
Dentinger, Jane 1782

The Joe Binney Series
Livingston, Jack 1414

The Joe Cullen Series
Oster, Jerry 1711

The Joe Gunther Series
Mayor, Archer 1230, 1717

The Joe Hannibal Series
Dundee, Wayne 862

The Joe Leaphorn and Jim Chee Series
Hillerman, Tony 1649

The Joe Leaphorn Series
Hillerman, Tony 701, 702, 1273, 1437, 1439, 1781

The Joe Silva Series
Oleksiw, Susan 65

The John Bent Series
Branson, H.C. 1373

The John Denson Series
Hoyt, Richard 488, 489, 490, 1751, 1754, 1765

The John Dobie Series
Cory, Desmond 484

The John Francis Cuddy Series
Healy, Jeremiah 28, 29, 30, 94, 337, 341, 343, 344, 386, 432, 669, 816, 818, 863, 864, 939, 1269, 1271, 1272, 1327, 1400, 1440, 1615, 1646, 1703

The John Locke Series
Barnao, Jack 26, 486

The John Marshall Tanner Series
Greenleaf, Stephen 28, 29, 30, 818, 877, 1648

The John Putnam Thatcher Series
Lathen, Emma 654, 1186

John Putnam Thatcher Series
Lathen, Emma 1729

The John Putnam Thatcher Series
Lathen, Emma 1730

The John Samson Series
Tripp, Miles 26, 27, 327, 329, 1488

The John Wells Series
Peterson, Keith 163, 222, 305, 407, 997, 1109, 1578, 1771

The Johnny Ortiz Series
Stern, Richard Martin 1437, 1781

The Jonathan Gaunt Series
Webster, Noah 451

The Jordan Poteet Series
Abbott, Jeff 71, 688, 1242, 1464

Jordon's Showdown
Strunk, Frank C. **1583**

Jordon's Wager
Strunk, Frank C. 757, 758, 1108, **1584**

The Joshua Croft Series
Satterthwait, Walter 490, 1458

The Joshua Sequence
Huebner, Frederick D. 6, 1603

The Judas Goat
Parker, Robert B. 791

The Judas Pair
Gash, Jonathan 1241, 1563, 1630

The Judas Pool
Owens, George **1250**

The Judge Dee Series
Van Gulik, Robert 875

Judgement by Fire
Huebner, Frederick D. 193, 488

A Judgement in Stone
Rendell, Ruth 1062

Juice
Campbell, Robert 184, 783, 1152

Julian Solo
Reuben, Shelly 1372

The Julius Caesar Murder Case
Irwin, Wallace 394

The Julius House
Harris, Charlaine **732**

June Mail
Warmbold, Jean 1435

Junta
Drummond, June 1114

Jurassic Park
Crichton, Michael 1405

The Juror
Green, George Dawes 794, 1623

Juror
Hall, Parnell 236, **714**

Just Another Day in Paradise
Maxwell, A.E. 392

Just Cause
Katzenbach, John 656, 709, 710, **873**, 1007, 1659

Justice
Kellerman, Faye **881**

Justice Denied
Tanenbaum, Robert K. 650, 820, **1599**

Justice for Some
Wilhelm, Kate 730, **1724**

K

K Is for Killer
Grafton, Sue **638**

The Karl Alberg Series
Wright, L.R. 310, 1756, 1758

Karma
Smith, Mitchell 1354, **1531**

The Kat Colorado Series
Kijewski, Karen 378, 379, 380, 381, 398, 637, 639, 649, 1009, 1182, 1266, 1398, 1506, 1700

Katapult
Kijewski, Karen 94, 397, **919**

The Kate Baeier Series
Slovo, Gillian 1541

The Kate Delafield Series
Forrest, Katherine V. 927, 1170

The Kate Fansler Series
Cross, Amanda 1511

The Kate Henry Series
Gordon, Alison 1195

The Kate Jasper Series
Girdner, Jaqueline 115, 155, 246, 1117, 1388, 1749

The Kate Kinsella Series
Green, Christine 932, 1129

The Kate Maddox Series
Quest, Erica 455

The Kate Martinelli Series
King, Laurie R. 1525

The Kate Mulcahaney Series
O'Donnell, Lillian 954

The Kate Mulcay Series
Sibley, Celestine 373, 1483, 1548

The Kate Shugak Series
Stabenow, Dana 48, 701, 702, 1340, 1625, 1626

The Katherine Milholland Series
Hartzmark, Gini 852

The Katherine Swinbrooke Series
Grace, C.L. 545

Katwalk
Kijewski, Karen 92, 116, 161, 384, 551, 636, 648, **920**, 1052, 1265, 1410, 1701

The Kay Scarpetta Series
Cornwell, Patricia D. 63, 74, 430, 476, 774, 974, 975, 976, 1051

The Keeper
O'Brien, Meg **1217**

Keeping Counsel
Forster, R.A. 940, 1465

The Keith Calder Series
Hammond, Gerald 109, 113

The Kentish Manor Murders
Symons, Julian 1365

Keystone
Lovesey, Peter 117, 860, 1674, 1675

Kid's Stuff
Kelly, Susan B. **897**

Kidstuff
Kelly, Susan B. 643

The Kiernan O'Shaughnessy Series
Dunlap, Susan 774, 1051, 1490

Kiet Goes West
Alexander, Gary **34**, 297, 616

Kill or Cure
Fleming, Joan 587

Kill or Cure
Kittredge, Mary **932**

The Kill Riff
Schow, David J. 1102

Kill Story
Doolittle, Jerome **434**

Kill the Butler!
Kenyon, Michael **911**

Kill the Messenger
Squire, Elizabeth Daniels 836, 900, 1503, **1546**

Kill Your Darlings
Collins, Max Allan 623, 668, 715, 1263

Kill Zone
Estleman, Loren D. 238

Killed in the Act
DeAndrea, William L. 760

Killed in the Ratings
DeAndrea, William L. 75, 1212, 1635, 1709

Killed on the Ice
DeAndrea, William L. 872

Killed on the Rocks
DeAndrea, William L. **401**, 1771

Killer Cinderella
Shaw, Simon **1478**

Killer Dolphin

Killer Dolphin
Marsh, Ngaio 641

The Killer Elite
Rostand, Robert 552

Killer in Paradise
Leslie, John 53, 187, 1007, **1011**, 1608

Killer of Kings
Campbell, R. Wright 1574

Killer's Choice
Brock, Stuart 491

Killer's Ink
Karl, M.S. 371, 951, 1368, 1369, 1495

Killer's Wake
Cornwell, Bernard 541, 582, 1037

The Killing Circle
Wiltz, Chris 1491, 1493, 1494

Killing Cousins
Knight, Alanna **943**

Killing Critics
O'Connell, Carol 601

A Killing in Kansas
Tharp, Jeffrey 592

A Killing in Quail County
Cole, Jameson 106, 1788

A Killing in Venture Capital
Logan, Margaret **1040**, 1778

A Killing Kindness
Hill, Reginald 260

The Killing Man
Spillane, Mickey **1540**

Killing Me Softly
Leslie, John 123, **1012**, 1714

The Killing of Ellis Martin
Grindle, Lucretia 230, **677**

The Killing of Katie Steelstock
Gilbert, Michael 576

The Killing of Monday Brown
Prowell, Sandra West 792, 1017

Killing Orders
Paretsky, Sara 1429, 1795

Killing Time in Buffalo
Laiken, Deidre S. 664, 674, **964**, 1102

Killings
Gray, A.W. **651**

The Killings at Badger's Drift
Graham, Caroline 578, 1393, 1395, 1556

Killshot
Leonard, Elmore 1531

Kimura
Davis, Robert **395**, 1161, 1503

The Kincaid and James Series
Crombie, Deborah 643

Kindred Crimes
Dawson, Janet 116, **397**, 648, 1183, 1184, 1505, 1701, 1702

King & Joker
Dickinson, Peter 1697

The King Is Dead
Shankman, Sarah **1475**

King of the Corner
Estleman, Loren D. **497**

King of the Hustlers
Izzi, Eugene **831**, 832, 1311, 1444, 1537

King of the Mountain
Wren, M.K. **1765**

King of the Roses
Anderson, Virginia 170, 171, 1172, 1190

King Solomon's Mines
Haggard, H. Rider 1298

Kingdom Road
Conner, K. Patrick **295**, 854, 1562

Kingdom Road
Connor, K. Patrick 4, 653, 855

The Kingsbridge Plot
Meyers, Maan **1148**

The Kinky Friedman Series
Friedman, Kinky 320, 1423, 1587

The Kinsey Millhone Series
Grafton, Sue 92, 94, 96, 161, 323, 378, 486, 917, 918, 920, 921, 1183, 1184, 1220, 1569

Kiss Me Once
Maxwell, Thomas 279

Kiss Mommy Goodbye
Fielding, Joy 128

Kiss the Girls
Patterson, James 1424

Kiss Them Goodbye
Eastburn, Joseph 468

Kissing the Gunner's Daughter
Rendell, Ruth 420, 790, **1361**

The Kit Deleeuw Series
Katz, Jon 71

The Kit Franklin/Andy Broussard Series
Donaldson, D.J. 976

A Knife at the Opera
Stacey, Susannah **1555**

Knight & Day
Nessen, Ron **1201**, 1710

Knight Must Fall
Wender, Theodora 1520

The Kori and Peter Brichter Series
Pulver, Mary Monica 154, 1380

The Kremlin Watcher
Perry, Will 1466

Kyd for Hire
Harris, Timothy 148, 342, 938, 1270

L

L.A. Confidential
Ellroy, James **483**, 1025

L Is for Lawless
Grafton, Sue **639**

La Brava
Leonard, Elmore 526, 1212

The La-La Land Series
Campbell, Robert 292

The Labyrinth Makers
Price, Anthony 995

The Lace Curtain Murders
Belfort, Sophie 120, 882, 982

Lady Beware
Cheyney, Peter 1629

The Lady Chapel
Robb, Candace M. 1175, **1376**

The Lady Killer
Togawa, Masako 1127

The Lady Margaret Priam Series
Christmas, Joyce 214, 813, 1098, 1209

Laguna Heat
Parker, T. Jefferson 1352

Laidlaw
McIlvanney, William 112, 249, 720, 948, 1639

The Lake of Darkness
Rendell, Ruth 587

Land Kills
Brandt, Nat **166**, 1720, 1721

Landfall
Gibbs, Tony 48, **581**

Landscape of Lies
Watson, Peter **1676**

Landscape with Dead Dons
Robinson, Robert 64, 1045

The Language of Cannibals
Chesbro, George C. **242**

The Lanley and Gillard Series
Duffy, Margaret 1539

The Lantern Network
Allbeury, Ted **37**, 420, 584, 787, 1278

Larkspur
Simonson, Sheila **1500**, 1764

The Lasko Tangent
Patterson, Richard North 1443

The Last Billable Hour
Wolfe, Susan 51, 237, 405, 963, 1093, 1155, 1524

Last Bus to Woodstock
Dexter, Colin 110

Last Call
Powers, Tim 855

The Last Camel Died at Noon
Peters, Elizabeth **1298**

The Last Coyote
Connelly, Michael 881, 1008

Last Dance in Redondo Beach
Katz, Michael J. 120, 718, **872**, 1005, 1109

The Last Gambit
Delman, David **411**, 1419

The Last Good German
Granger, Bill **647**

The Last Good Kiss
Crumley, James 148, 193, 554, 736, 791, 1096, 1455, 1580, 1618

The Last House-Party
Dickinson, Peter 402

What Mystery Do I Read Next?

The Last Housewife
Katz, Jon 722

The Last Man Standing
Wright, Jim **1771**

The Last Man to Die
Shuman, M.K. 431, 829, **1493**

The Last One Left
MacDonald, John D. 783

The Last Page
Fenster, Bob 119, 177, 223, **524**, 882, 895, 1379

The Last Private Eye
Birkett, John 1755

The Last Resort
Girdner, Jaqueline **594**, 990, 1146, 1256

The Last Rite of Hugo T
Catanach, J.N. **227**

The Last Sanctuary
Holden, Craig 566, 1788

Last Seen Alive
Simpson, Dorothy 748

Last Seen Wearing...
Waugh, Hillary 1107

The Last Spy
Reiss, Bob 529

The Last Surprise
Moore, William **1169**

Last Walk Home
Page, Emma 1035

The Late Lady
Stacey, Susannah **1556**

The Late Man
Girard, James Preston **592**, 1590

Late of This Parish
Eccles, Marjorie **469**

The Latimer Mercy
Richardson, Robert 61, 1050, 1706

Laughing Dog
Lochte, Dick 680, 945, 1705

The Laura Di Palma Series
Matera, Lia 852, 1699, 1780

The Laura Fleming Series
Kelner, Toni L.P. 1542, 1547

The Lauren Laurano Series
Scoppettone, Sandra 927, 946

Lautrec
Zollinger, Norman **1794**

The Lavender House Murder
Baker, Nikki **83**, 761

The Lavinia London Series
MacCahery, James 1021

The Law's Delay
Woods, Sara 562

A Lawyer's Tale
Kincaid, D. **923**, 1014

Lay It on the Line
Dain, Catherine 251, **379**

The Leaf Boat
Fink, John 1277

The League of Frightened Men
Stout, Rex 1095

Title Index — MacPherson's Lament

Leap of Faith
Zukowski, Sharon **1799**

Leave the Grave Green
Crombie, Deborah **357**, 1553

The Ledger
Uhnak, Dorothy 141, 1088, 1225

Left My Heart
Maiman, Joyce 1731

The Lenny Schwartz Series
Weinman, Irving 1711, 1717

The Leo Haggerty Series
Schutz, Benjamin M. 28, 29, 30, 489, 667, 862, 863, 864, 865, 939, 1272, 1648

Leonardo's Law
Murphy, Warren 207, 402

The Lesson of Her Death
Deaver, Jeffrey Wilds 1531

Lessons in Murder
McNab, Claire 533

Let Sleeping Afghans Lie
Thall, Michael 629, 723

Let Sleeping Dogs Lie
Riggs, John R. 163

Lethal Legacy
Hendricksen, Louise 1262

A Lethal Vintage
Sylvester, Martin 571, 739, 1563, 1566, 1790

The Letter of the Law
Berry, Carole 1333

Letting Blood
Platt, Richard 303, **1321**

Levine
Westlake, Donald E. 856, 857, 858

The Lew Archer Series
Macdonald, Ross 396

The Lew Griffin Series
Sallis, James 1691

The Liars
Hill, Peter 1189

Liar's Poker
McConnell, Frank 734, 1591

The Libby Kincaid Series
Tucker, Kerry 944, 1388

Library: No Murder Aloud
Steiner, Susan 1, 415, 416, **1569**

Lie to Me
Martin, David 267

Lieberman's Choice
Kaminsky, Stuart M. **856**

Lieberman's Day
Kaminsky, Stuart M. **857**

Lieberman's Folly
Kaminsky, Stuart M. **858**

The Lies of Fair Ladies
Gash, Jonathan **571**, 1722

The Lies That Bind
Van Gieson, Judith **1649**

The Lieutenant Hastings Series
Wilcox, Collin 856, 857, 858, 1008, 1033, 1107, 1158

The Lieutenant Reardon Series
Pike, Robert L. 1158

Life's Work
Valin, Jonathan 50, 196, 319, 652

Lights Out
Abrahams, Peter **4**

A Likely Story
Westlake, Donald E. 524

The Lime Pit
Valin, Jonathan 146, 668, 716, 826, 1618, 1619

Limited Partner
Lupica, Mike 721, **1053**, 1481, 1718, 1771

The Lion at the Door
Thornburg, Newton **1617**

The Lion's Share
Tate, Kelly A. **1605**

The List of 7
Frost, Mark 400, 924, 926, 1438, 1787

Listen for the Click
Breen, Jon L. 133, 573, 1172

A Little Class on Murder
Hart, Carolyn G. 119, 168, 387, **743**, 1379

Little Death
Nava, Michael 395

The Little Death
Nava, Michael 1150, 1797

A Little Death Music
Higgins, Joan 559, 1304, 1305

The Little Drummer Girl
Le Carre, John 1284

A Little Gentle Sleuthing
Rowlands, Betty 107, 361

A Little Neighborhood Murder
Orde, A.J. 100, 101, 192, 696, 977, 1138, 1167, **1241**, 1415, 1683, 1777, 1778

Little Saigon
Parker, T. Jefferson 165, 1106

Little Use for Death
Sherer, Michael W. 207, 330, 484, 869, 1044, **1482**, 1735

Live Bait
Wood, Ted 13, 314, 1739

Live Flesh
Rendell, Ruth 88, 1453

Live to Regret
Faherty, Terence 12

A Lively Form of Death
Mitchell, Kay 230, **1160**, 1454

The Livinius Severus Series
Burns, Ron 1450

The Liz Connors Series
Kelley, Susan 411

The Liz Connors Series
Kelly, Susan 154, 382, 383, 531, 603, 610, 944, 1041, 1215, 1317, 1378, 1380, 1388, 1636, 1637

The Liz Wareham Series
Brennan, Carol 32, 124

Lizardskin
Stroud, Carsten **1582**

Lizzie
McBain, Ed 1441

Location Shots
Burke, J.F. 1005, 1693

Locke Step
Barnao, Jack 300, 684

Lockout
O'Donnell, Lillian **1224**

A Lonely Place to Die
Ebersohn, Wessel 1114

Lonely Street
Brewer, Steve 1755

Lonelyheart 4122
Watson, Colin 89

Long Chain of Death
Wolf, S.K. 305, 513, 842, 886, 1582, **1747**, 1791

A Long Cold Fall
Reaves, Sam 305, 767, 1287, 1308, 1345, **1355**, 1644

The Long-Legged Fly
Sallis, James 194

Long Lines
Sutton, Remar 175, 1112

The Long Revenge
Thomson, June 368

The Long Search
Holland, Isabelle 436, **798**

A Long Time Dead
Orde, A.J. **1242**

A Long Way to Die
Frey, James N. 1010

Longshot
Francis, Dick **540**, 1068, 1172, 1190

The Loo Sanction
Trevanian 552

Loose Among the Lambs
Brandon, Jay 592

A Loose Connection
Meek, M.R.D. **1139**

Loose Lips
Breen, Jon L. **171**, 871

The Loretta Lawson Series
Smith, Joan 1511, 1541

Lost Daughter
Cormany, Michael 826

The Lost Keats
Faherty, Terence **515**, 1250

The Lost Madonna
Holland, Isabelle 1243, 1508

The Loud Adios
Kuhlken, Ken **957**

Louisiana Blue
Poyer, David **1324**

Love Bytes
Chapman, Sally **232**, 1489

Love Lies
Kupfer, Fern **960**

Love Lies
Kupfer, Fran 1511

Love Lies Slain
Blackmur, L.L. 21, 52, **139**, 539, 546, 1676

Love nor Money
Grant, Linda 637, **648**, 1220, 1702

The Love That Kills
Levitsky, Ronald 445, 446, 1576, 1582, 1600

A Love to Die For
Jorgensen, Christine T. **849**, 1094

Love You to Death
Michaels, Grant **1151**

The Lovejoy Series
Gash, Jonathan 1068, 1069, 1240, 1564, 1565, 1566

Lovely in Her Bones
McCrumb, Sharyn 522

A Lovely Night to Kill
Morgan, D. Miller 274

Lover Man
Murphy, Dallas 257, 287, 288, 290, 724

Loves Music, Loves to Dance
Clark, Mary Higgins 43, 49, **253**, 275, 673, 769, 821, 1761

Low Angles
Stinson, Jim 299, 300

Low Treason
Tourney, Leonard 883, 1084

The Lucas Davenport Series
Sandford, John 1008

The Lucia Ramos Series
Morel, Mary 927

The Luis Mendoza Series
Shannon, Dell 747

Lullaby of Murder
Davis, Dorothy Salisbury 814, 890

Lullaby Town
Crais, Robert 199, **342**, 369, 432, 765, 1110, 1200, 1413

The Lunatic Fringe
DeAndrea, William L. 36, 400, 560, 1079, 1654, 1787

The Luxembourg Run
Ellin, Stanley 3, 617

The Lynching
Sinclair, Bennie Lee 669, 1178, **1503**, 1538

M

The Mac McFarland Series
Kiker, Douglas 724

The "Mac" Series
Dewey, Thomas B. 667, 1326, 1327, 1328, 1329

The Macklin Series
Estleman, Loren D. 1297

MacPherson's Lament
McCrumb, Sharyn **1117**

The Mad Courtesan
Marston, Edward **1081**, 1164

Made in Detroit
Kantner, Rob 497

Madison Avenue Murder
Bennett, Liza 11, 346, 347, 1543

Madness in Maggody
Hess, Joan **777**

The Madoc Rhys Series
Craig, Alisa 1785

The Maggie Ryan Series
Carlson, P.M. 76, 593, 1117, 1254

The Maggody Series
Hess, Joan 22, 219, 970, 971, 983, 1153, 1432, 1685, 1687

The Mahdi
Quinnell, A.J. 248, 1473

Mail-Order Murder
Meier, Leslie 22, 312, 457, **1140**, 1254, 1258, 1378, 1567

Major League Murder
Geller, Michael 493, 505, 506, 507, 508, 612, 652, 1205

Make Friends with Murder
Garwood, Judith 371, **569**, 603, 894, 908, 1245

Make No Bones
Elkins, Aaron 431, **478**, 1726

Make Out with Murder
Block, Lawrence 607, 1047

Malice Domestic #1
Peters, Elizabeth **1299**

Malice in Maggody
Hess, Joan 298, 1431, 1741

Mallory's Oracle
O'Connell, Carol 805, 857, 953, **1221**, 1224, 1515, 1686

The Maltese Puppy
Cleary, Melissa **258**

Mama's Boy
King, Charles 525, 846

The Man From Internal Affairs
Hentoff, Nat 1249, 1535, 1628, 1696

The Man from Lisbon
Gifford, Thomas 129

The Man in the Gray Flannel Shroud
Orenstein, Frank 1040

The Man in the Green Chevy
Cooper, Susan Rogers 1739, 1740, 1772

The Man in the High Castle
Dick, Philip K. 419

The Man in the Iron Mask
Dumas, Alexandre 425

The Man in the Moon
Norwood, Frank **1212**

Man Kills Woman
Flusfeder, D.L. 935

Man of Blood
Duffy, Margaret 451

The Man of Glass
Zochert, Donald 199, 200

The Man of Gold
Hervey, Evelyn 737, 1295

The Man Offside
Gray, A.W. **652**, 1596

The Man on the Bridge
Black, Ian Stuart 647

A Man to Die For
Dreyer, Eileen **448**, 658, 931, 932, 934, 974

The Man Who Cancelled Himself
Handler, David **722**

The Man Who Cast Two Shadows
O'Connell, Carol 1660

The Man Who Changed His Name
Wright, Eric 1418

The Man Who Killed His Brother
Stephens, Reed 262

The Man Who Knew Hammett
McConnor, Vincent 858, 1619, 1620, 1621

The Man Who Liked Slow Tomatoes
Constantine, K.C. 1231

The Man Who Missed the Party
Adams, Harold **13**

The Man Who Murdered God
Reynolds, John Lawrence 1705

The Man Who Murdered Goliath
Homes, Geoffrey 1309

The Man Who Series
Handler, David 546

The Man Who Shot Lewis Vance
Kaminsky, Stuart M. 1675

The Man Who Sold Death
Munro, Hugh 550

The Man Who Walked Like a Bear
Kaminsky, Stuart M. **859**, 1793

The Man Who Walked Through Walls
Swain, James **1595**

The Man Who Was Taller than God
Adams, Harold 742

The Man Who Wasn't There
Wainwright, John 1189

The Man Who Would Be F. Scott Fitzgerald
Handler, David 259, 287, **723**, 1358

The Man with a Load of Mischief
Grimes, Martha 1393, 1669

The Man with Bogart's Face
Fenady, Andrew J. 860

The Man with My Name
Engleman, Paul **494**

Manhattan Is My Beat
Deaver, Jeffrey Wilds 19, 126, 127, 271, 312, **404**, 749, 755, 1434

Manifest Destiny
Garfield, Brian 36

Man's Illegal Life
Heller, Keith 1083

Man's Storm
Heller, Keith 1083

Mantis
LaPlante, Richard 468, 1736

Manuscript for Murder
Coyne, P.J. 723

The Manx Murders
DeAndrea, William L. **402**

Marathon Man
Goldman, William 1188, 1456

March Violets
Kerr, Philip 27, 957, 1792

The Marcus Didius Series
Davis, Lindsey 1390, 1448, 1450

The Margaret Barlow Series
Osborn, David 46, 100, 284, 285, 978, 1138, 1406, 1483

The Margaret Binton Series
Barth, Richard 45, 654, 978, 1138, 1171, 1246, 1445, 1446, 1447, 1485, 1571

Margin for Murder
Adams, Bronte **9**

The Mario Balzac Series
Constantine, K.C. 65, 1230, 1776

The Mark Holland Series
Myers, Paul 452, 1071

The Mark Renzler Series
Engleman, Paul 1206, 1684

The Mark Shigata Series
Wingate, Anne 311, 1230, 1756

The Mark Treasure Series
Williams, David 452, 1068, 1179

The Mark Twain Murders
Skom, Edith 535, 583, 712, 1136, 1167, **1512**, 1627

Marlborough Street
Bowker, Richard 241

Marriage Is Murder
Pickard, Nancy 387, 772, 1378

The Marshall Guarnaccia Series
Nabb, Magdalen 549, 1002

The Marti MacAlister Series
Bland, Eleanor Taylor 1691, 1692

The Martin Beck Series
Sjowall, Maj 690, 691

The Martin Fender Series
Sublett, Jesse 320, 1755

The Marty Hopkins Series
Carlson, P.M. 970, 1099

The Marvell College Murders
Belfort, Sophie **119**, 960, 1196

A Masculine Ending
Smith, Joan 892, 962, 1305, 1501, 1557

The Mask of Zeus
Cory, Desmond 1488

The Masked Man
Doherty, P.C. **425**

The Masks of Rome
Llewellyn, Caroline 1521

Masquerade
Kienzle, William X. **916**

Mass Murder
Drummond, John Keith **449**

The Masters and Green Series
Clark, Douglas 366, 470, 504, 1159, 1160, 1454, 1479

The Masters of the House
Barnard, Robert **90**

Material Witness
Tanenbaum, Robert K. 940

The Matilda Worthing Series
Drummond, John Keith 1112

Matrimonial Causes
Corris, Peter **327**

The Matt Cobb Series
DeAndrea, William L. 1413

The Matt Jacob Series
Klein, Zachary 669, 864

The Matt Murdock Series
Ray, Robert J. 486

The Matt Riordan Series
Huebner, Frederick D. 28, 31, 489, 490, 815, 1604

The Matt Scudder Series
Block, Lawrence 73, 195, 495, 1012, 1039, 1075, 1422, 1458, 1585, 1640, 1646

The Matthew Coll Series
Lewis, Roy Harley 1673

The Matthew Hope Series
McBain, Ed 73, 818, 1057, 1603, 1604

The Matthew Stock Series
Tourney, Leonard 264, 426, 512, 631, 1467, 1468, 1469, 1470

The Mavis Lashley Series
Holt, Hazel 1446

The Mavis Lashley Series
Nordan, Robert 46

The Maxene St. Clair Series
McGiffin, Janet 932

The Maxey Burnell Series
Cail, Carol 373

Maximum Bob
Leonard, Elmore 721, 785, **1006**, 1561

The Maya Stone Murders
Shuman, M.K. 1371, **1494**, 1738

Mayhem in Parva
Livingston, Nancy **1035**

The Mayo and Kite Series
Eccles, Marjorie 504

McGarr and the Method of Descartes
Gill, Bartholomew 530

The McGarr Series
Gill, Bartholomew 23

The McGuffin
Bowen, John 1630

The McLeish and Wilson Series
Neel, Janet 1361

Title Index

Mean High Tide
Hall, James W. **710**

Medicine Dog
Peterson, Geoff 492, 772, 1281, **1307**, 1719, 1751

A Medium for Murder
Warner, Mignon 591

The Medium Is Murder
McKittrick, Molly 591

Mefisto in Onyx
Ellison, Harlan 1276

The Melissa Craig Series
Rowlands, Betty 108

The Melting Clock
Kaminsky, Stuart M. **860**

Melting Point
Davis, Kenn 1010

A Member of the Club
Niesewand, Peter 1114

Memory Can Be Murder
Squire, Elizabeth Daniels 803, **1547**

Menaced Assassin
Gores, Joe **618**

The Mensa Murders
Martin, Lee **1089**

Mercy
Lindsey, David L. 49, 63, 99, 321, 322, 324, 325, 349, 954, 975, 980, **1027**, 1033, 1154, 1166, 1221, 1282, 1283, 1534, 1736, 1737

The Mercy Trap
Martin, James E. **1383**

The Meredith Mitchell/Allan Markby Series
Granger, Ann 307

Merry Christmas, Murdock
Ray, Robert J. **1352**

Methods of Execution
Huebner, Frederick D. 650, **818**, 1765

Metzger's Dog
Perry, Thomas 363, 432, 433, 434, 435, 525, 606, 782, 783, 785, 949, 1611, 1612, 1613, 1698

The Mexican Tree Duck
Crumley, James **363**, 1370

Mexico Is Forever
Schutz, Benjamin M. 485, **1458**

Miami Blues
Willeford, Charles 855, 1057, 1058, 1416

Miami Heat
Sanford, Jerome 1286, **1433**

Miami Heat
Stanford, Jerome 98

Miami Purity
Hendricks, Vicki **773**, 1560

The Micah Dunn Series
Shuman, M.K. 281

Michigan Roll
Kakonis, Tom 4, 497, 622, 773, 1416, 1444, 1690

The Mici Anhalt Series
O'Donnell, Lillian 968

Midnight Baby
Hornsby, Wendy 531, 615, 778, **808**, 880, 1317, 1380, 1451

The Midnight Louie Series
Douglas, Carole Nelson 20, 169, 180

A Midsummer Night's Killing
Barnes, Trevor 1141, 1144

The Milan Jacovich Series
Roberts, Les 39, 41, 407, 565, 791, 869, 1032, 1059, 1345, 1646, 1648

The Miles Jacoby Series
Randisi, Robert J. 565, 1423

Milk and Honey
Kellerman, Faye 807, **882**

The Million-Dollar Wound
Collins, Max Allan 957

The Milt Kovack Series
Cooper, Susan Rogers 1776

The Milt Kovak Series
Cooper, Susan Rogers 65, 1230, 1756, 1758, 1774

Mindscream
Zimmerman, R.D. 303, 965

Mine
McCammon, Robert R. 843, 1091

Minnesota Strip
Collins, Michael 242, 1371

Minor in Possession
Jance, J.A. **844**

Minotaur
Coonts, Stephen 409, 825

Mint Julep Murder
Hart, Carolyn G. **744**

Miracles in Maggody
Hess, Joan **778**

Mirror on the Wall
Ellin, Stanley 105

Miss Lizzie
Satterthwait, Walter 207, **1441**

The Miss Marple Series
Christie, Agatha 385, 1097, 1098, 1406, 1484

Miss Melville Regrets
Smith, Evelyn 1063

Miss Melville Regrets
Smith, Evelyn E. 1478

Miss Melville Rides a Tiger
Smith, Evelyn E. **1518**

The Miss Melville Series
Smith, Evelyn 813

The Miss Melville Series
Smith, Evelyn E. 786, 1539

Miss Melville's Revenge
Smith, Evelyn E. 1681

The Miss Pink Series
Moffat, Gwen 1071, 1594

The Miss Seeton Series
Carvic, Heron 175

The Miss Silver Series
Wentworth, Patricia 175, 802, 1163, 1171

Miss Zukas and the Island Murders
Dereske, Jo **415**, 699

Miss Zukas and the Library Murders
Dereske, Jo 1, **416**

The Miss Zukas Series
Dereske, Jo 732

Missing
Valin, Jonathan **1646**

The Missing Bishop
Spencer, Ross H. 499

Missing Joseph
George, Elizabeth **575**

The Missing Madonna
O'Marie, Carol Anne 1591

Missing Man
Stern, Richard Martin **1570**

The Missing Person
Tobin, Brian 514

Missing Susan
McCrumb, Sharyn **1118**

Mistress of Justice
Deaver, Jeffrey Wilds **405**, 851, 852, 853, 963

The Mitch Bushyhead Series
Hager, Jean 310, 311

The Mitch Tobin Series
Coe, Tucker 1532

Mitigating Circumstances
Rosenberg, Nancy Taylor 421, 1381, **1401**, 1465, 1780

Model Murder
Quest, Erica 304, **1338**

The Modesty Blaise Series
O'Donnell, Peter 452, 1727

The Molly Bearpaw Series
Hager, Jean 778, 1680, 1686

Mom Among the Liars
Yaffe, James 722

Mom Meets Her Maker
Yaffe, James 697

The Mom Series
Yaffe, James 45, 175, 177, 411

Mommy and the Murder
Gladstone, Nancy 246, 595, **600**

The Monarchs Are Flying
Foster, Marion 202

Monday the Rabbi Took Off
Kemelman, Harry 690

Monday's Child Is Dead
Elward, James 484

Money Burns
Maxwell, A.E. **1100**

Money Leads to Murder
Morgan, D. Miller 84

Money to Burn
Hendricks, Michael 614, **772**, 1219, 1228, 1631, 1638

Money to Burn
White, Gloria **1701**

Monkey on a Chain
Campbell, Harlen **211**, 294, 341, 618, 796, 822, 1210, 1272, 1370, 1436, 1790

The Monkey Rope
Lewis, Stephen **1023**

Monkey Wrench
Cody, Liza **271**

The Monkey's Raincoat
Crais, Robert 301, 433, 435, 634, 766, 815, 1271, 1313, 1352, 1383, 1387, 1459, 1575, 1616

Monsieur Pamplemousse Investigates
Bond, Michael **151**

The Monsieur Pamplemousse Series
Bond, Michael 389, 390, 768, 988, 1061

The Monster Squad
Angus, John **59**

A Monstrous Regiment of Women
King, Laurie R. **926**

Montezuma's Man
Charyn, Jerome 580

The Moody Man
Milne, John 1629

Moon of the Wolf
Whitten, Les 429

The Mooncalf Murders
Carter, Noel Vreeland 130, **222**

The Mordida Man
Thomas, Ross 434

More Deaths than One
Eccles, Marjorie **470**, 1708

More Ms. Murder
Smith, Marie 1267, 1348

The Moriarty Series
Gardner, John 1403

A Morning for Flamingos
Burke, James Lee **197**, 1038, 1308, 1492, 1738

The Moroni Traveler Series
Irvine, R.R. 509, 1018

The Moroni Traveler Series
Irvine, Robert R. 490, 1032

Morons and Madmen
Emerson, Earl **488**

The Morrissey and Barrett Series
Mitchell, Kay 504

Mortal Remains
Hanson, Rick **728**

Mortal Remains in Maggody
Hess, Joan **779**

Mortal Sin
Levine, Paul 650, **1014**

Mortal Stakes
Parker, Robert B. 507, 510, 1358, 1718

Mortal Words | What Mystery Do I Read Next?

Mortal Words
Knight, Kathryn Lasky 603, 838, 893, **945**, 1636

Moth
Sallis, James 1325, **1422**

Moth to the Flame
Dougherty, Kathleen **437**, 756, 1174

Mother Love
Wright, L.R. 1766, **1774**

The Mother Shadow
Howe, Melodie Johnson 177, 417, 449, 556, 607, 608, 695, **814**, 1120, 1300

Motor City Blues
Estleman, Loren D. 282

Motown
Estleman, Loren D. **498**, 1178, 1421

The Mountains West of Town
Downing, Warwick 793, 1570

The Moving Finger
Bass, Milton 231

Moving Targets
Flannery, Sean 365, **529**

The Moving Toyshop
Crispin, Edmund 763

The Mr. and Mrs. North Series
Lockridge, Frances and Richard 387, 999

The Mr. and Mrs. North Series
Lockridge, Richard and Frances 160

Mr. Donaghue Investigates
Shone, Anna **1488**

Mr. Smithson's Bones
Conroy, Richard Timothy 207, **297**

Mr. Surie
Joshee, O.K. 874, 875

Mrs. Craggs: Crimes Cleaned Up
Keating, H.R.F. 1484

The Mrs. Jeffries Series
Brightwell, Emily 929

Mrs. Malory and the Festival Murders
Holt, Hazel **801**

Mrs. Malory Investigates
Holt, Hazel 107, 361, **802**, 1246, 1445, 1485

The Mrs. Malory Series
Holt, Hazel 108, 978, 1571

The Mrs. Murphy Series
Brown, Rita Mae 20

The Mrs. Pargeter Series
Brett, Simon 1246, 1483

Mrs. Pargeter's Package
Brett, Simon **175**, 1171

Mrs. Pollifax and the Whirling Dervish
Gilman, Dorothy **588**, 1518

Mrs. Pollifax on the China Station
Gilman, Dorothy 496

The Mrs. Pollifax Series
Gilman, Dorothy 45, 175, 1098, 1112, 1246, 1571, 1594

The Mrs. Potter Series
Rich, Virginia 390, 1445, 1571

Mrs., Presumed Dead
Brett, Simon 1594

Mrs. White
Tracy, Margaret 1116

Ms. Murder
Smith, Marie 663, 1073, 1267

Mucho Mojo
Lansdale, Joe R. 211, 1677

Mudlark
Simonson, Sheila 1432

Mumbo Jumbo
Knight, Kathryn Lasky 1138

Mum's the Word
Cannell, Dorothy 1061

Murder
Hall, Parnell 1616

Murder Against the Grain
Lathen, Emma 1040

Murder Among Friends
McConnell, Frank 1745

Murder Among Us
Granger, Ann **644**, 1553

Murder and a Muse
Farrell, Gillian B. 16, 414, **517**, 1465

Murder and the First Lady
Roosevelt, Elliott 1634

Murder at Ebbets Field
Soos, Troy 12

Murder at Fenway Park
Soos, Troy 508, **1536**

Murder at Monticello
Brown, Rita Mae 121, **180**

Murder at Moose Jaw
Heald, Tim 1418, 1770

Murder at Moot Point
Millhiser, Marlys 33, 128, 172, 370, 371, 372, 376, 944, **1156**, 1401, 1567

Murder at Musket Beach
Lee, Bernie 693, 741, 747, **998**, 1064, 1147, 1430, 1725

Murder at St. Adelaide's
Hollingsworth, Gerelyn **799**, 1237

Murder at the A.B.A.
Asimov, Isaac 524

Murder at the Class Reunion
Stein, Triss 206, 360, 415, 604, 699, 944, **1567**

Murder at the Friendship Hotel
Epstein, Charlotte 261, **496**, 1743

Murder at the Kennedy Center
Truman, Margaret 1169, **1634**

Murder at the Mimosa Inn
Hess, Joan 741, 746, 1316

Murder at the Nightwood Bar
Forrest, Katherine V. 83

Murder at the PTA Luncheon
Wolzien, Valerie 101, 594, 1255, 1258, 1415

Murder at the Red October
Olcott, Anthony 365, 859, 861, 913, 1066, 1793

Murder at the Smithsonian
Truman, Margaret 296, 297

Murder at the Spa
Matteson, Stefanie **1097**

Murder at the Superbowl
Tarkenton, Fran 50

Murder at the War
Pulver, Mary Monica 25, 1118

Murder Begins at Home
Gilbert, Dale L. **585**

Murder by Deception
Meredith, D.R. 353

Murder by Impulse
Meredith, D.R. 1741

Murder by Mail
Lake, M.D. 960, **969**, 1331

Murder by Masquerade
Meredith, D.R. 354

Murder by Owl Light
Sawyer, Corinne Holt 1209, **1445**

Murder by Tarot
Guthrie, Al 629, **693**, 1431

Murder by the Book
Rowe, Jennifer 9, 224, 307, 583

Murder by the Book
Stout, Rex 668

Murder by the Book
Welch, Pat 82, 947, 1042, 1126, 1356, 1442, 1460, 1461, **1689**

Murder by the Numbers
Collins, Max Allan **278**

Murder by Tradition
Forrest, Katherine V. **534**

Murder Can Kill Your Social Life
Eichler, Selma 16, **473**

Murder for Lunch
Murphy, Haughton 713

Murder Goes Mumming
Craig, Alisa 220, 627, 1417, 1418, 1419, 1770

Murder Has a Pretty Face
Melville, Jennie **1142**

Murder Has No Calories
Sawyer, Corinne Holt **1446**

Murder Impossible
Adey, R.C.S. 221

Murder in a Cold Climate
Young, Scott 775, 1550, 1552, 1775, **1785**

Murder in a Good Cause
Sale, Medora 642, 644, 1197, 1334, 1408, **1417**, 1768

Murder in a Mummy Case
Beck, K.K. 1320

Murder in a Nice Neighborhood
Roberts, Lora 422, 596, **1388**

Murder in a Quiet Place
Caxton, Tony **230**

Murder in Bandora
Karr, Leona 206, 373, **868**

Murder in Brief
Lachint, Carrol **963**

Murder in Burgundy
Peterson, Audrey **1305**

Murder in C Major
Frommer, Sara Hoskinson 1304, 1305

Murder in Focus
Sale, Medora 896, 898, 1132, **1418**, 1772

Murder in Gray and White
Sawyer, Corinne Holt **1447**

Murder in High Places
Dominic, R.B. 1169

Murder in Mellingham
Oleksiw, Susan 268, **1231**, 1758

Murder in Mendocino
Kittredge, Mary 10, 370, 1235, 1495, 1498

Murder in Ordinary Time
O'Marie, Carol Anne **1238**

Murder in Peking
Starrett, Vincent 496

Murder in Scorpio
Lawrence, Martha C. **993**

Murder in Store
Brod, D.C. **178**, 1345

Murder in the Central Commitee
Vazquez Montalban, Manuel 1236

Murder in the Central Committee
Vazquez Montalban, Manuel 1597

Murder in the Charleston Manner
Sprinkle, Patricia Houck 457, 731, 1315, 1547

Murder in the Collective
Wilson, Barbara 745

Murder in the Dehli Mail
Bahadur, K.P. 35

Murder in the English Department
Miner, Valerie 891, 892, 1133, 1520, 1522

Murder in the Hellfire Club
Zochert, Donald 883

Murder in the Kitchen
Halliday, Fred 151, 152

Murder in the Limelight
Myers, Amy 1030

Murder in the Napa Valley
Osborn, David 711, **1245**

Murder in the Place of Anubis
Robinson, Lynda S. **1390**, 1450

Murder in the Post-War World
Collins, Max Allan **279**

Murder in Waiting
Richardson, Robert **1367**

Murder in Wrigley Field
Evers, Crabbe 493, **507**, 510, 646, 871

Murder Is Academic
Carlson, P.M. 351, 891, 1797

Murder Is Germane
Saum, Karen **1442**

530

Title Index

Murder Is Only Skin Deep
Sims, L.V.   47, 1088, 1089

Murder Is Relative
Saum, Karen   82

Murder Isn't Enough
Flynn, Don   1053, 1719

The Murder League
Fish, Robert L.   1518

Murder Machree
Boylan, Eleanor   801

Murder Makes a Pilgrimage
O'Marie, Carol Anne   **1239**

Murder Misread
Carlson, P.M.   359, 979

Murder Most Grizzly
Quinn, Elizabeth   54, 198, **1340**, 1551, 1626

Murder Most Sacred
Hoch, Edward D.   1299

Murder Movie
McGown, Jill   **1131**

Murder, Murder, Little Star
Babson, Marian   1034

Murder, My Suite
Daheim, Mary   **377**, 1289

Murder, Mystery and Mayhem
Carnell, Jennifer   **220**

A Murder of Crows
Duffy, Margaret   1518, 1681

Murder of the Soap Opera
Miller, Judy   75

Murder Off the Glass
Katz, Michael J.   646, 1655

Murder Offscreen
Osborne, Denise   517, **1248**, 1411

Murder on a Kibbutz
Gur, Batya   **690**

Murder on Clam Pond
Kiker, Douglas   166, 335, 340, 532, 686, 866, 867; 949, 1231, 1719, 1721

Murder on Cue
Dentinger, Jane   174, 176, 516, 713, 1707

Murder on Location
Engel, Howard   992, 1131, 1519, 1684, 1768, 1770

Murder on Martha's Vineyard
Osborn, David   108, 1445, 1485

Murder on Peachtree Street
Sprinkle, Patricia Houck   347, **1543**, 1631, 1632, 1635

Murder on Safari
Huxley, Elspeth   158

Murder on the Chesapeake
Osborn, David   45, **1246**

Murder on the Cliff
Matteson, Stefanie   516, **1098**

Murder on the Cut
Kiker, Douglas   1719

Murder on the Hudson
Flynn, Don   166, 1261, 1368, 1369

Murder on the Iditarod Trail
Henry, Sue   725, **775**, 1549, 1550, 1551, 1580, 1581, 1786

Murder on the Links
Logue, John   481

Murder on the Run
White, Gloria   94, 648, 649, 1220, **1702**, 1798

Murder on the Ten-Yard Line
Strange, John Stephen   50

Murder on the Thirteenth
Eddenden, A.E.   **471**

Murder on Tour
Clark, Dick   1587

Murder Once Removed
Kunz, Kathleen   **959**, 1155

Murder Pluperfect
Giles, Kenneth   738

Murder Song
Cleary, Jon   **256**

Murder Times Two
Murphy, Haughton   **1186**

Murder Unprompted
Brett, Simon   1173

A Murder Waiting to Happen
Taylor, L.A.   966

Murder Wears a Cowl
Doherty, P.C.   **426**

Murder Will Out
Yeager, Dorian   48, 1568, **1784**

Murder Without Reservation
Lee, Bernie   376, 629, 951, **999**, 1608

Murderer's Row
Evers, Crabbe   1718

Murdering Mr. Monti
Viorst, Judith   1319

Murders and Acquisitions
Murphy, Haughton   986, 987

The Murders at Impasse Louvain
Grayson, Richard   942, 1049

The Murders of Richard III
Peters, Elizabeth   424

Murdock Cracks Ice
Ray, Robert J.   **1353**

Murphy's Fault
Womack, Steven   494, 513, 1738, **1752**, 1777, 1778

The Music Lovers
Valin, Jonathan   **1647**

Musical Chairs
Friedman, Kinky   **555**

My Brother, the Druggist
Kaye, Marvin   1698

My First Murder
Baker, Susan   **84**, 771, 947, 1121

My Gun Has Bullets
Goldberg, Lee   **606**

My Sister's Keeper
Kelly, Nora   428, **892**, 960, 1522, 1767

My Sweet Untraceable You
Scoppettone, Sandra   **1462**

A Mystery Bred in Buckhead
Sprinkle, Patricia Houck   900, 1204, **1544**

The Mystery of a Hansom Cab
Hume, Fergus   1293

The Mystery of Edwin Drood
Dickens, Charles   1407

N

The Naked Eye
Reynolds, William J.   **1364**, 1423

Naked Once More
Peters, Elizabeth   177, 546, 556, 724, **1300**

Naked to the Grave
Carmichael, Harry   1055

The Naked Typist
Hailey, J.P.   236, **704**, 1022

The Name of the Rose
Eco, Umberto   544, 545, 1203, 1301, 1302, 1303, 1467, 1470

The Nameless Detective Series
Pronzini, Bill   77, 281, 341, 343, 396, 489, 551, 623, 667, 906, 907, 908, 1009, 1075

Nameless Detective Series
Pronzini, Bill   1181

The Nameless Detective Series
Pronzini, Bill   1272, 1347, 1350, 1414, 1713, 1714, 1716

The Nantucket Diet Murders
Rich, Virginia   449, 1315

Napoleon Must Die
Fawcett, Quinn   **519**

A Nasty Bit of Murder
Roe, C.F.   658, 931, 934, 1130, 1656

The Nate Heller Series
Collins, Max Allan   183, 498, 956, 1177, 1207, 1609, 1674

Native Tongue
Hiaasen, Carl   34, 98, 102, 408, 525, 708, 710, **782**, 903, 1006, 1014, 1474, 1561, 1611

Natural Causes
Palmer, Michael   **1262**

Natural Enemies
Cameron, Sara   **209**, 225

Natural Prey
Mathis, Edward   354

Nebraska
Reynolds, William J.   1060

The Nebraska Quotient
Reynolds, William J.   189, 1056

The Nebraska Series
Reynolds, William J.   39, 509, 865, 877, 1754

A Necessary End
Robinson, Peter   **1395**

Necessity
Garfield, Brian   5, 1128, 1351, 1381, 1746, 1762

Nicholas Barlow Series

Needlepoint
Chase, Samantha   798

The Neil Hamel Series
Van Gieson, Judith   1076, 1625, 1699

The Neil Kelly Series
Dean, S.F.X.   1673

The Nell Bray Series
Linscott, Gillian   519, 835, 928, 1259, 1260

Neon Caesar
McGarrity, Mark   **1128**, 1537

Neon Dancers
Taylor, Matt   **1608**, 1710

Neon Flamingos
Taylor, Matt   1201

The Neon Rain
Burke, James Lee   272, 273, 399, 844, 981, 1024, 1421, 1491, 1494, 1704

The Neon Smile
Lochte, Dick   **1039**

Neptune's Eye
Kemprecos, Paul   337, 338, **905**, 1099, 1353

The Nero Wolfe Series
Stout, Rex   402, 585, 814, 1048

Never Die in January
Scholefield, Alan   1708

Never Walk Behind Me
Summerfield, Lin   1558, **1593**

Nevermore
Hjortsberg, William   81, 926, 1438, 1787

New Hope for the Dead
Willeford, Charles   1349

A New Leash on Death
Conant, Susan   17, 116

New Orleans Beat
Smith, Julie   **1527**

New Orleans Mourning
Smith, Julie   194, 195, 196, 197, 391, 429, 430, 925, 953, 1038, 1039, 1170, 1225, 1422, 1476, 1491, **1528**

New Orleans Requiem
Donaldson, D.J.   **430**

The New York Detective
Marshall, William   **1080**

Newspaper Murders
Gash, Joe   143

The Next Victim
Sanders, William   **1423**

Nibbled to Death by Ducks
Campbell, Robert   **213**

Nice Guys Finish Dead
Debin, David   211, **406**

A Nice Little Beach Town
Ward, E.C.   1777

A Nice Weekend for Murder
Collins, Max Allan   741, 1364

The Nicholas Barlow Series
Carter, Robert A.   484

Nicholas Bracewell Series — What Mystery Do I Read Next?

The Nicholas Bracewell Series
Marston, Edward 264, 426, 512, 1375, 1377, 1468, 1469, 1470

The Nick Magaracz Series
Gallison, Kate 869

The Nick Polo Series
Kennealy, Jerry 1688, 1714

Nickel Straight
Lamb, J.J. 132

Nick's Trip
Pelecanos, George P. 1075

Nicole
Hull, J.H. 581, 1337

The Nigel Strangeways Series
Blake, Nicholas 471, 1366

Night Angel
Green, Kate 91, 253, 514, **664**, 674, 746, 767, 937, 964, 1092, 1102, 1183, 1355, 1453, 1579, 1665, 1683

The Night-Blooming Cereus
Hadley, Joan 1484, 1485

Night Butterfly
McFall, Patricia **1127**

Night Game
Gordon, Alison 481, **613**

Night Kills
Gorman, Ed **622**, 1072, 1121

Night Launch
Cohen, Stephen Paul 179

Night of Reunion
Allegretto, Michael **42**, 899, 937, 1310, 1762

Night of the Cat
Schermerhorn, James 59, 954, 970, **1452**, 1526, 1717

Night of the Fox
Higgins, Jack 584

The Night of the Generals
Kirst, Hans Hellmut 579

Night of the Ice Storm
Stout, David 1095, 1215, **1579**, 1665

The Night of the Moonbow
Tryon, Thomas 935

Night of the Vulcan
Marsh, Ngaio 1173

Night over Water
Follett, Ken 584

Night Prey
Luce, Carol Davis 821

Night Prey
Sandford, John 1026, **1424**

Night Probe
Cussler, Clive 179, 1456

The Night Remembers
Gorman, Ed 305, 396, **623**, 1326, 1327, 1329, 1619, 1620

Night Rituals
Paulsen, Gary 200, 229, 873, 980, **1279**, 1282

Night Secrets
Cook, Thomas H. 1023

Night Shadows
Ely, Ron 164, **486**

Night Sins
Hoag, Tami **794**

Night Soldiers
Furst, Alan 584

Night Vision
Levine, Paul 63, **1015**

Night Walker
Hager, Jean 1431, 1739, 1742, 1756

Nightbloom
Lieberman, Herbert 749

The Nightingale Gallery
Harding, Paul 265, 1303, 1377

Nightlines
Lutz, John 1527

The Nightmare File
Livingston, Jack 242

Nightmare in Pink
MacDonald, John D. 568

Nightmare Point
Berry, Carole **128**

Nightside
Santiago, Soledad **1434**

Nightwalker
Filson, Sidney **527**

Nightwatcher
Wilson, Charles 1165

The NIMBY Factor
Wilcox, Stephen F. 2, 949, **1721**

The Nine Giants
Marston, Edward **1082**

Nine Times Nine
Boucher, Anthony 1238

The Ninja
Lustbader, Eric Van 527

Ninth Life
Douglas, Lauren Wright **444**, 946, 1461, 1462

Ninth Life
Matheson, Don 338, 819, 1509

No Admission
Winder, Robert 11

No Business Being a Cop
O'Donnell, Lillian 460, 1088, 1089

No Comfort in Victory
Bean, Gregory **106**, 1788

No Doors, No Windows
Ellison, Harlan 241

No Duress
Borgenicht, Miriam 1022

No Escape
Kemp, Sarah 321

No Exit From Brooklyn
Randisi, Robert J. 40, 703, 1532

No Forwarding Address
Bowers, Elisabeth **161**, 947

No Harm
Hornsby, Wendy 889, 890, 1318, 1419, 1420, 1728

No Lady in the House
Kallen, Lucille 168

No Mardi Gras for the Dead
Donaldson, D.J. **431**, 1493, 1726

No One Dies in Branson
Buckstaff, Kathryn 902, 1755

No Patent on Death
Takagi, Akimitsu 1127

No Place for Secrets
Lewis, Sherry **1021**, 1586

No Second Wind
Guthrie, A.B. Jr. 13

No Sign of Murder
Russell, Alan **1414**, 1439

No Way Home
Coburn, Andrew **267**, 1230, 1758

No Way Home
MacDonald, Patricia 848, **1062**, 1664

No Witnesses
Pearson, Ridley 1424

Noble Rot
Harriss, Will **739**, 1451, 1790

Nobody Lives Forever
Buchanan, Edna **187**, 1011

Nobody's Child
Dawson, Janet **398**

Nobody's Fool
Claridge, Marten 111, **249**, 591, 1134

Nobody's Sorry He Got Killed
Goldstein, Arthur D. 1447, 1621

The Nocturne Murder
Peterson, Audrey 1191, 1192

The Nolan Series
Collins, Max Allan 210

The Noonday Devil
McInerny, Ralph 1429

The Noose of Time
Murray, Stephen **1189**, 1555

Nor Live So Long
Woods, Sara 561, 1642, 1658

The Norah Mulcahaney Series
O'Donnell, Lillian 142, 464, 601, 804, 805, 1523

North of Montana
Smith, April 881, 953, 1221, 1268, **1515**, 1525, 1527, 1660

North of the Border
Van Gieson, Judith 97, 1320, 1439

North Star Conspiracy
Monfredo, Miriam Grace **1164**

The Northwest Murders
Taylor, Elizabeth Atwood 57, 370, 1119, **1607**, 1667

Nostalgia Kills
Westbrook, Robert 1696

Not a Creature Was Stirring
Haddam, Jane 695

Not as Far as Velma
Freeling, Nicholas 548

Not Comin' Home to You
Kavanaugh, Paul 183

Not Enough Horses
Roberts, Les 715, 1200, 1575

Not Exactly a Brahmin
Dunlap, Susan 1170, 1180

Not Long for This World
Haywood, Gar Anthony **762**

Not One of Us
Thomson, June 1160

Not Till a Hot January
Adamson, M.J. 845

Nothing Human
Munson, Ronald 1165

Nothing More Than Murder
Thompson, Jim 295

Nothing to Do with the Case
Lemarchand, Elizabeth 752

The November Man Series
Granger, Bill 528, 552, 810

Novena for Murder
O'Marie, Carol Anne 286

Now He Thinks He's Dead
Goulart, Ron **629**, 1710

Now Let's Talk of Graves
Shankman, Sarah 215, 569, 1145, 1215, 1216, **1476**

Nun Plussed
Quill, Monica 1339

The Nun's Tale
Robb, Candace M. **1377**

Nurse Dawes Is Dead
Shepherd, Stella **1479**

O

O Little Town of Maggody
Hess, Joan **780**

Obit
Paisner, Daniel **1261**

Obligations of the Bone
Cluster, Dick 93, **263**

Obstacle Course
Montgomery, Yvonne 880, **1167**

An Occasional Hell
Silvis, Randall 1283, 1325

The October Cabaret
Quest, Erica 729

October Heat
DeMarco, Gordon 1583

Odessa Beach
Leuci, Bob 1793

O'Fear
Corris, Peter **328**

Off Minor
Harvey, John 740, **753**

Off Season
Craig, Philip R. **339**

Ogilvie, Tallant, and Moon
Yarbro, Chelsea Quinn 77, 793

Old Bones
Elkins, Aaron 1409, 1493

Title Index

The Old Contemptibles
Grimes, Martha **675**

The Old Dick
Morse, L.A. 1619, 1620, 1621

Old Enemies
LaPierre, Janet 599

An Old-Fashioned Mystery
Fairleigh, Runa 220, 401

The Old Fox Deceiv'd
Grimes, Martha 25, 576, 1197, 1554, 1555

Old Scores
Elkins, Aaron **479**

The Old Silent
Grimes, Martha 191, **676**, 1395

On Account of Murder
Powers, Elizabeth 126, 346

On Ice
MacGregor, T.J. 84, 807

On the Edge
Naha, Ed **1193**, 1249

On the Inside
Wood, Ted 539, 1103, 1105, 1417, 1601, **1757**, 1770

On the Other Hand, Death
Stevenson, Richard 726

Once and Always Murder
Papazoglou, Orania **1263**

Once upon a Crime
Lake, M.D. 970

One Coffee With
Maron, Margaret 460, 1087, 1089

One Cried Murder
Wall, David Cooper **1663**

One Dead Dean
Crider, Bill 359, 696, 714, 715, 776, 1136, 1482, 1767

One for the Money
Belsky, Dick 1214, 1636

One for the Money
Borton, D.B. 503

One for the Money
Evanovich, Janet 155, **503**, 1413

One Kiss Led to Another
Dulaney, Harris **454**

One Man's Law
Clarkson, John 363, 1152

One Police Plaza
Caunitz, William J. 306, 348, 1070, 1344, 1443, 1533

One, Two, What Did Daddy Do?
Cooper, Susan Rogers 315, 849

Only a Matter of Time
Clinton-Baddeley, V.C. 609, 1043

The Only Good Priest
Zubro, Mark Richard **1795**

The Only Good Yankee
Abbott, Jeff **2**

Only the Dead Know Brooklyn
Boyle, Thomas 754, 890, 1628

Open Season
Mayor, Archer 765, 1231, 1578

The Open Shadow
Solomon, Brad 1745

Opening Shots
Kaminsky, Stuart M. 1330

Original Sin
Pulver, Mary Monica 898, **1334**, 1432

Orphans
Pearce, Gerald **1281**

The Other David
Coker, Carolyn 1180, 1211, 1243

Other People's Houses
Cooper, Susan Rogers 267, 268, **316**, 1231

Other People's Skeletons
Smith, Julie **1529**

The Other Side of Death
Van Gieson, Judith 33, 851, 1401, 1437, 1440, 1529, **1650**

The Other Side of Silence
Allbeury, Ted 1466

The Other Woman
McGown, Jill **1132**, 1670

Out of the Blackout
Barnard, Robert 994

Out of the Darkness
Kelly, Susan 173, 880, **894**, 1496, 1514, 1659, 1660, 1671

Out on the Cutting Edge
Block, Lawrence **148**, 1455, 1532

Out on the Rim
Thomas, Ross 783

Outbreak
Cook, Robin 976, 1321

Outsider
Francome, John 538, 839, 1486

Over the Edge
Rowlands, Betty **1409**

Over the Sea to Death
Moffat, Gwen 802

Overture to Death
Marsh, Ngaio 609, 1191

The Owen Archer Series
Robb, Candace M. 243

An Owl Too Many
MacLeod, Charlotte **1064**

Oxford Blood
Fraser, Antonia 1142

Oxford Exit
Stallwood, Veronica **1559**

The Oxford Gambit
Hone, Joseph 217

P

The "P" Division Series
Turnbull, Peter 249

P.I. Files
Estleman, Loren D. 1348

Pacific Coast Highway
Smoke, Stephen 1282

Paint, Gold and Blood
Gilbert, Michael 1507

Paint It Black
Philbrick, W.R. 359, 873, **1313**, 1362, 1363, 1705

Paint the Town Red
Adams, Harold 501

Painted Ladies
Harvey, James Neal **750**, 1717

The Painted Lady
Wilcox, Stephen F. **1722**

The Paladin
Garfield, Brian 37, 38, 410, 680

The Pale Criminal
Kerr, Philip 690, 691, 754, **914**, 958

Pale Gray for Guilt
MacDonald, John D. 1349

Palindrome
Woods, Stuart 1351, **1762**

Pamplemousse Rests His Case
Bond, Michael **152**

Panama
Zencey, Eric **1787**

Pandora's Box
Chastain, Thomas 1684

Paper Thunderbolt
Innes, Michael 1031

Paragon Walk
Perry, Anne 1049

Paramour
Petievich, Gerald 186, 632, 633, 681, 822, **1312**

Park Lane South, Queens
Kelly, Mary Anne 315, 807, 878, **890**, 1664

The Parker Series
Stark, Richard 1690

Parts Unknown
Burns, Rex 39, 41, **200**, 1439

Party Till You Die
Charnee, David **236**

Pas De Death
Vincent, L.M. **1656**

Passing Strange
Aird, Catherine 753, 789

Passion in the Peak
Hilton, John Buxton 1614

Passion Play
Blain, W. Edward **140**, 468, 515, 1250, 1593

Past Imperfect
Maron, Margaret **1077**

Past Reason Hated
Robinson, Peter 230, **1396**

Patently Murder
Harrison, Ray **737**

The Patience McKenna Series
Papazoglou, Orania 1477, 1567

Patriot Games
Clancy, Tom 474, 684, 685, 1284

The Paul Christopher Series
McCarry, Charles 647

Permanent Retirement

Pavane
Roberts, Keith 419

Paws Before Dying
Conant, Susan **290**

Pay Off
Leather, Stephen 1134

Payment in Blood
George, Elizabeth **576**, 644, 675, 898, 1197

The Peaches Dann Series
Squire, Elizabeth Daniels 732, 1411, 1542

The Peacock's Secret
Hastings, Laura 68

Peckover Joins the Choir
Kenyon, Michael **912**

A Pedigree to Die For
Berenson, Laurien **121**, 258, 288

Peeper
Estleman, Loren D. 494, **499**, 1697

Peeping Thomas
Reeves, Robert 590, 850, **1358**

The Peggy O'Neill Series
Lake, M.D. 80, 219, 460, 464, 778, 780, 1380

Pel and the Bombers
Hebden, Mark 548

Pel and the Missing Persons
Hebden, Mark 768

The Pelican Brief
Grisham, John 102, 405, 553, 633, **681**, 852, 1312, 1435

Penance
Housewright, David **812**

Penny Dreadful
Moody, Susan 1144

The Penny Ferry
Boyer, Rick 335, 922, 1074

The Penny Wanawake Series
Moody, Susan 455

The Pennyfoot Hotel Series
Kingsbury, Kate 134, 1030, 1292

People Who Knock on the Door
Highsmith, Patricia 88, 90, 1277, 1478

Pepper Pike
Roberts, Les 189, 1056, 1060, 1647

Perchance to Dream
Parker, Robert B. **1270**

A Perfect Death for Hollywood
Nehrbass, Richard 332

Perfect Justice
Bernhardt, William 940

Perfection
Berenson, Marc 62, 980

A Perfectly Proper Murder
Adams, Harold 14

Peril under the Palms
Beck, K.K. **117**, 834, 835

A Permanent Retirement
Miles, John 701, **1153**, 1209

Perry Mason in The Case of Too Many Murders — **What Mystery Do I Read Next?**

Perry Mason in The Case of Too Many Murders
Chastain, Thomas **239**

The Perry Mason Series
Gardner, Erle Stanley 239, 704, 1135

Personal
Cambray, C.K. **208**

Pet Peeves
McCafferty, Taylor **1111**

The Peter Bartholomew Series
Gunning, Sally 2, 336, 339, 1464

The Peter Marklin Series
Steed, Neville 570, 571, 572, 1068, 1242

The Peter Shandy Series
MacLeod, Charlotte 776, 971

The Peter Styles Series
Philips, Judson 1309

The Pew Group
Oliver, Anthony 1035, 1478

The Philip Marlowe Series
Chandler, Raymond 1176, 1177

Philly Stakes
Roberts, Gillian 10, 423, 697, **1379**

The Philomel Foundation
Gollin, James 1192

Phoebe's Knee
Comfort, B. 801

Phoenix No More
Gage, Edwin 262, 1794

The Physalia Incident
Spikol, Art 1779

The Piano Man
Gilpatrick, Noreen **589**, 816, 951, 1732

Picture of David
Singer, Shelley **1505**

Picture Postcard
Huebner, Fredrick D. 445, 491, **819**, 1216

A Piece of Justice
Paton Walsh, Jill **1274**

A Piece of the Action
Solomita, Stephen 910, 1008, **1535**

A Piece of the Silence
Livingston, Jack 281, 282, 1494

Pigeon Blood
Alexander, Gary 874

Pillar of Fire
Irvine, R.R. 41, **830**

Pillars of Fire
Shagan, Steve 1174, **1473**

A Pinch of Snuff
Hill, Reginald 676, 1132

Pink Vodka Blues
Barrett, Neal Jr. **98**, 147, 164, 935, 1038, 1763

A Pint of Murder
Craig, Alisa 896, 898

Pious Deception
Dunlap, Susan 79, 92, 323, 326, 397, **462**, 634, 1795

A Plague of Kinfolks
Sibley, Celestine **1497**

Plaster Sinners
Watson, Colin 204

The Plastic Nightmare
Neely, Richard 1149

Play Dead
Coben, Harlan **266**

Play with Fire
Stabenow, Dana **1552**

The Player
Downing, Warwick 200

The Player
Tolkin, Michael 847

The Player's Boy Is Dead
Tourney, Leonard 427, 1081, 1082, 1295

The Players Come Again
Cross, Amanda 979, 1187

Playing Catch-Up
Guthrie, A.B. Jr. 757, 758, 1307

Playing for the Ashes
George, Elizabeth **577**

Playing God
Whitehead, Barbara 235, **1707**

Playing the Dozens
Pease, William D. 159, 1249, **1286**

Playmates
Parker, Robert B. 646, 765, 1655

Pleading Guilty
Turow, Scott **1640**

The Plymouth Cloak
Sedley, Kate **1469**

A Pocketful of Karma
Cannon, Taffy **216**

Poe Must Die
Olden, Marc 984

Poetic Justice
Taylor, L.A. 1121, 1359, 1588

Point Blank
Livingston, Jayson **1033**, 1715

Point No-Point
McCullough, David Willis **1123**

Point of Impact
Hunter, Stephen 553, 618, **822**, 1210

Poison Flowers
Cooper, Natasha 107

Poison Fruit
Yarbro, Chelsea Quinn **1781**

Poison Pen
Kittredge, Mary 172, 206, 594, 723, 868, **933**, 1146, 1215, 1636

The Poison Pool
Hall, Patricia 308

The Poisoned Chalice
Clynes, Michael **264**, 426

Poisoned Ivy
Lake, M.D. 119, 696, **971**, 1482

Polar Star
Smith, Martin Cruz 234, 725, 913, **1530**

Policewoman
Uhnak, Dorothy 804

Polo Solo
Kennealy, Jerry 77, 1713, 1716

Poodle Springs
Parker, Robert B. 956

Poor Butterfly
Kaminsky, Stuart M. 957

Pork City
Browne, Howard 276, 277, 279, 501, 1207, 1609

The Porkchoppers
Thomas, Ross 184

The Portland Laugher
Emerson, Earl 489

Post No Bonds
Biederman, Marcia 1512

The Postman Always Rings Twice
Cain, James M. 295, 773, 1562

Postmortem
Cornwell, Patricia D. 49, 62, 79, 216, 253, 302, 303, **326**, 429, 431, 478, 1027, 1285, 1321, 1405

The Potter's Field
Peters, Ellis **1302**

A Pound of Flesh
Barnes, Trevor **95**

Practice to Deceive
Smith, Janet L. 216, 853, 963

Praetorian
Gifford, Thomas 410, **584**

Pray God to Die
Roberts, Carey 734

Prayer for the Dead
Wiltse, David 468

Praying for Sleep
Deaver, Jeffrey Wilds 796, 1499

Praying Mantis
Taylor, Domoni 1157

Precinct Siberia Series
Philbin, Tom 1033

Precipice
Langley, Bob 234

Predators
Sauter, Eric 553

Predator's Waltz
Brandon, Jay 42, **165**, 1106

Prejudicial Error
Blum, Bill 1280

Premedicated Murder
Clark, Douglas 1402

Prescription for Death
McGiffin, Janet 931, 974, **1130**

Pressure Drop
Abrahams, Peter **5**, 602, 848, 1174

The Prestor John Riordan Series
Hanlon, Sean 1581

Presumed Innocent
Turow, Scott 239, 333, 412, 421, 547, 557, 558, 1016, 1023, 1600, 1662

Pretty Miss Murder
Ballard, W.T. 132

A Pretty Place for a Murder
Hart, Roy 1555

The Price of Victory
Green, Vincent **666**

The Price You Pay
Wakefield, Hannah 269, 561, 1529, 1642

Primal Fear
Diehl, William **421**, 651, 1014, 1283

Primary Justice
Bernhardt, William 333, 666, 1022, 1357

The Prime Roll
Izzi, Eugene 1128, 1286

Prime Suspect
Gray, A.W. **653**

Prime Suspect
LaPlante, Lydia 754, 1132

The Prime Suspect Series
LaPlante, Lydia 95, 661

Prime Time for Murder
Frankel, Valerie 380, **542**

The Prince of Darkness
Doherty, P.C. **427**, 1624

The Prince of Wales Series
Lovesey, Peter 655, 929

The Princess Stakes Murder
Platt, Kin 133

Principal Defense
Hartzmark, Gini 405, 851, 1780

Prior Convictions
Matera, Lia 436, 851, 972, 1076, **1093**, 1167, 1357, 1599

A Private Crime
O'Donnell, Lillian **1225**

Private Eyes
Kellerman, Jonathan **886**, 1791

Private Lies
Cail, Carol 1586

Private Murder
Guthrie, Al 101

Private Practices
White, Stephen 364, 885, 887, 1276

Private Screening
Patterson, Richard North 526

Prized Possessions
Wright, L.R. **1775**

Probable Cause
Pearson, Ridley 53, **1285**, 1286, 1427

Probable Cause
Stockley, Griff **1577**

Promised Land
Parker, Robert B. 40, 458, 850

Prophet Motive
Jones, Cleo 826, 828, 1018, 1124

The Prosecutor
Chastain, Thomas **240**

Title Index

Prowlers
Izzi, Eugene   1416

Psycho
Bloch, Robert   1013, 1606

Public Murders
Granger, Bill   306, 580, 1628, 1712

The Pumpkin-Shell Wife
McShea, Susanna Hofmann   100, 361, 1021, **1138**, 1446

The Punjat's Ruby
Jackson, Marian J.A.   1298

Puppet for a Corpse
Simpson, Dorothy   470, 1554

Purgatory
Mickleson, Monty   **1152**

Purrfect Crime
Waugh, Carol-Lynn Rossel   619, 620

Pursued by Shadows
Sale, Medora   **1419**

Pursued by the Crooked Man
Trott, Susan   713

Pushover
O'Donnell, Lillian   **1226**

Pussyfoot
Douglas, Carole Nelson   443

Q

Quaker Silence
Allen, Irene   45

Quaker Witness
Allen, Irene   46

The Quality of Mercy
Kellerman, Faye   264, 425, 427, 512, **883**, 1081, 1082, 1083, 1084, 1376, 1624

The Quality of the Informant
Petievich, Gerald   981

Quarry
Pronzini, Bill   **1329**, 1647

The Quarry Series
Collins, Max Allan   238

The Queen Is Dead
Dentinger, Jane   16, **414**, 1391

The Queen's Head
Marston, Edward   427, **1083**, 1467

The Queen's Mare
Birkett, John   **133**, 170

A Question of Guilt
Fyfield, Frances   **562**, 598, 1343

A Question of Guilt
Wright, Eric   334, 627

A Question of Identity
Thomson, June   204

The Question of Max
Cross, Amanda   359, 745

A Question of Murder
Wright, Eric   1417

A Quiche Before Dying
Churchill, Jill   214, **247**, 423, 968

The Quick and the Dead
Kantner, Rob   863

The Quiet Road to Death
Radley, Sheila   1253

The Quiet Stranger
Hilton, John Buxton   1292, 1293, 1294, 1295

Quiller KGB
Hall, Adam   **706**

Quincannon
Pronzini, Bill   1675

Quoth the Raven
Haddam, Jane   **696**

R

The Rabbi Small Series
Kemelman, Harry   656, 878, 915, 916, 955, 1101

A Radical Departure
Matera, Lia   6, 767, 1320

Rafferty: Fatal Sisters
Duncan, W. Glenn   **458**

The Rafferty Series
Duncan, W. Glenn   7, 352, 354

Rafferty's Rules
Duncan, W. Glenn   8, 1616

The Rag Bag Clan
Barth, Richard   286, 1063

Rage
Moffat, Gwen   **1162**, 1549

A Rage in Harlem
Himes, Chester   1177, 1178

The Raggedy Man
O'Donnell, Lillian   **1227**

The Rain
Peterson, Keith   86, 144, 950

Rain Lover
Burkey, Dave   52, 171

The Rain Morgan Series
Grant-Adamson, Lesley   382

Rainbow Drive
Thorp, Roderick   293, 832, 1311

Rainbow in the Mist
Whitney, Phyllis   1453

The Rainmaker
Grisham, John   985

Rainy North Woods
Kohler, Vince   12, 14, 163, 166, 370, 376, 407, 827, **950**, 1072, 1145, 1261, 1368, 1477, 1721

Raise the Titanic!
Cussler, Clive   1513

Raising the Dead
Simon, Roger L.   878

Random Access Murder
Grant, Linda   84, 397, 919, 1183, 1703

The Ransom
Tobin, Brian   1199, **1622**

The Ransom of Black Stealth One
Ing, Dean   179, 409, **825**, 1513

Raptor
Van Gieson, Judith   55, 972, 1234, 1235, 1524, 1570, 1603, 1604, 1626, **1651**, 1668

Rasputin's Revenge
Lescroart, John T.   1438

Ratings Are Murder
Irvine, R.R.   75, 1574

Rat's Nest
West, Charles   **1694**

The Rattle-Rat
Van De Wetering, Janwillem   548

A Rattling of Old Bones
Ross, Jonathan   1614

Raven
Lundy, Mike   1311

Ravenmocker
Hager, Jean   **701**, 1086, 1087, 1332, 1550, 1607, 1625, 1626

Raw Deal
Standiford, Les   1354

Razzamatazz
Early, Jack   1663

Reader, I Murdered Him
Green, Jen   **663**, 1073, 1267, 1299

The Real Cool Killers
Himes, Chester   788

Real Murders
Harris, Charlaine   1, 415, 711

A Really Cute Corpse
Hess, Joan   1477

A Reason to Kill
Zaremba, Eve   806

Reasonable Doubt
Freidman, Philip   412

Reasonable Doubt
Friedman, Philip   66, 445, **558**, 1016, 1090, 1106, 1577, 1640

Rebecca
Du Maurier, Daphne   502

The Rebecca Schwartz Series
Smith, Julie   851, 853

Rebound
Everson, David   646

Recalled to Life
Hill, Reginald   753, **790**

Recipe for Death
Laurence, Janet   **990**

Reckless
Woods, Sherryl   1214

Recoil
Garfield, Brian   395

Recount
Everson, David   1752

Recycled
Bailey, Jo   **80**

Red Cent
Campbell, Robert   13

A Red Death
Mosley, Walter   276, **1177**

Reuben Frost Series

Red Dragon
Harris, Thomas   53, 229, 846, 980, 1154, 1165, 1166, 1279, 1425, 1427, 1737

Red Highway
Estleman, Loren D.   183

The Red House Mystery
Milne, A.A.   1365

Red Knight
Davis, J. Madison   **391**

Red Lake of the Heart
Logue, Mary   966

The Red Moon
Murphy, Warren B.   1595

Red Phoenix
Bond, Larry   248

The Red Scream
Walker, Mary Willis   194, 679, 909, **1659**

Red Snow
Topol, Edward   1530

Red Snow at Darjeeling
Blochman, Lawrence G.   35

Red Trance
Zimmerman, R.D.   **1793**

The Red, White, and Blues
Kantner, Rob   **864**

Red Winter
Cormany, Michael   **319**, 1281, 1345

The Redbird's Cry
Hager, Jean   **702**

Rehearsal for Murder
Carlson, P.M.   414, 641, 1391

The Reid Bennett Series
Wood, Ted   259, 291, 310, 775, 1549, 1580, 1766, 1773, 1774, 1776, 1785, 1786

A Relative Stranger
Lucke, Margaret   251, 379, 648, 649, **1052**

Relentless
Garfield, Brian   793

The Rembrandt Panel
Banks, Oliver   1180, 1211, 1243, 1521, 1666

Remember Me
Clark, Mary Higgins   1791

Report for Murder
McDermid, Val   **1126**

Rest in Pieces
Brown, Rita Mae   **181**, 443

Rest You Merry
MacLeod, Charlotte   697, 1045, 1208

Resurrection Row
Perry, Anne   738

Retrieval
Dunne, Colin   1456

The Return of Moriarty
Gardner, John   131, 441, 1404

The Reuben Frost Series
Murphy, Haughton   236, 654, 1778

Reverend Randollph and the Avenging Angel | | | **What Mystery Do I Read Next?**

Reverend Randollph and the Avenging Angel
Smith, Charles Merrill 1124

The Reverend Randollph Series
Smith, Charles Merrill 797, 1101, 1706

Reversible Error
Tanenbaum, Robert K. **1600**

Revolution #9
Abrahams, Peter **6**, 406, 809

The Richard Jury Series
Grimes, Martha 563

The Richard Michaelson Series
Bowen, Michael 509

Ride the Lightning
Lutz, John 1659

Right on the Money
Lathen, Emma **987**

Right to Die
Healy, Jeremiah 435, 695, 850, 1329

The Right to Sing the Blues
Lutz, John 319, 459, 497, 500

Rigor Mortis
Kittredge, Mary 79, 302

Ring of Fear
McCaffrey, Anne 52

The Ripper's Apprentice
Thomas, Donald **1610**

Rising Dog
Kohler, Vince 408, **951**, 1474, 1475, 1722

Rising Sun
Crichton, Michael 348, 750, 1127, 1742

The Ritual Bath
Kellerman, Faye 208, 890, 955, 1457

The Rivals of Sherlock Holmes
Greene, Hugh 24

The Rivals of Sherlock Holmes
Russell, Alan 24

River
Thorp, Roderick 1166

River of Darkness
Grady, James **632**, 811, 823, 1109

The River Sorrow
Holden, Craig 842, 1218

The Riviera Contract
Albert, Marvin **26**

Roadwork
Bachman, Richard 1617

Robak's Cross
Hensley, Joe L. 239

Robbers
Whalley, Peter 1629, 1630

Rock Critic Murders
Sublett, Jesse 555

The Rocksburg Railroad Murders
Constantine, K.C. 1070, 1740, 1741

The Roger Shallot Series
Clynes, Michael 1468

The Roger the Chapman Series
Sedley, Kate 243, 264, 631, 1376

Rogue Wave
Dunlap, Susan 80, 302, 321, 322, 324, 430, 431, **463**, 478, 974, 975

Roll Over and Play Dead
Hess, Joan 522, **781**

Roman Blood
Saylor, Steven 201, **1449**

Roman Nights
Burns, Ron **201**, 1390, 1448

The Ronnie Ventana Series
White, Gloria 378

Rook-Shoot
Duffy, Margaret **452**

Room 9
Santiago, Soledad 1317, **1435**

Room to Swing
Lacy, Ed 762, 788, 1314

Room with a Clue
Kingsbury, Kate 930, 1294

Rosa's Dilemma
Underwood, Michael 562, 1658

Rosemary for Remembrance
Thomson, June 753

Roses Are Red
Estleman, Loren D. 553

Rostnikov's Vacation
Kaminsky, Stuart M. **861**

The Rotary Club Mystery
Landrum, Graham **978**

Rotten Apples
Cooper, Natasha **309**

Rotten Lies
Elkins, Charlotte **481**, 1195

Rough Cut
Cook, Bruce **300**, 332, 369, 1007, 1096, 1200, 1575

Rough Justice
Peterson, Keith 130, 146, 532, 873, 1053, **1309**

Rough Water
Gunning, Sally **687**

The Roz Howard Series
Kenney, Susan 960, 1511

Ruffled Feathers
McCafferty, Taylor 1751

Ruffly Speaking
Conant, Susan **291**

Rules of Prey
Sandford, John 149, 196, 812, 846, 1039, **1425**

Ruling Passion
Hill, Reginald 89, 1392, 1502

Rum Punch
Leonard, Elmore 355, 855, **1007**

Rumpole of the Bailey
Mortimer, John 705

The Rumpole Series
Mortimer, John 923

The Run Around
Freemantle, Brian **550**, 706

Run Before the Wind
Woods, Stuart 582, 1037

The Run to Morning
Graham, James 474, 657, 961, 1760

Runner in the Street
Grady, James 189

Running Fix
Gibbs, Tony **582**, 1037

Running From the Law
Scottoline, Lisa **1465**

Running Mates
Feinstein, John **521**

The Running of Beasts
Pronzini, Bill 187, 349, 618, 980

Rush
Wozencraft, Kim 74, 1223

The Russia House
Le Carre, John 38, 824, **995**, 1508

S

S.W.F. Seeks Same
Lutz, John 1514, 1761

The Saberdene Variations
Maxwell, Thomas 105

The Saboteurs
Drummond, June 1114

Sacred and Profane
Kellerman, Faye 953

Sacred Clowns
Hillerman, Tony **792**

Sacrifice
Vachss, Andrew 1217, 1252

Sacrificial Ground
Cook, Thomas H. 1533

Sacrificial Lamb
Cook, Thomas 1279

Safe at Home
Gordon, Alison **614**

A Safe Place to Die
Law, Janice 1568

The St. James and McCleary Series
MacGregor, T.J. 411

The St. John Series
Babula, William 907

St. John's Baptism
Babula, William 511, 1352, 1414, 1781

Saint Louie Blues
Tanner, Jake **1601**

Saint Mudd
Thayer, Steve 280, **1609**

St. Oswald's Niche
Frankos, Laura 250

The Saint Patrick's Day Murder
Harris, Lee 137

Salmon in the Soup
O'Brien, Meg 1477

The Saltmarsh Murders
Mitchell, Gladys 1484

The Samantha Adams Series
Shankman, Sarah 382, 383, 604, 1542, 1544, 1632

The Samantha Holt Series
Wilson, Karen Ann 21

The Samantha Turner Series
Landreth, Marsha 325, 774, 1129

Samson's Deal
Singer, Shelley 1009

Sanctuary
Kellerman, Faye **884**

Sand Castles
Freeling, Nicholas **549**

Sand Trap
Cooney, Caroline 480

Sanibel Flats
White, Randy Wayne 1011, **1704**

The Santa Fe Rembrandt
Dawkins, Cecil 803

Santa Fe Rules
Woods, Stuart 98, 173, 547, 665, 1297, **1763**

The Sarah Kelling Series
MacLeod, Charlotte 154, 155, 284, 693, 743, 781

The Sarah Quilliam Series
Bishop, Claudia 377, 699

Saratoga Longshot
Dobyns, Stephen 133, 1190

Saratoga Swimmer
Dobyns, Stephen 171, 540, 573

Satan in St. Mary's
Doherty, P.C. 883, 1081, 1082, 1084

The Saturday Morning Murder
Gur, Batya **691**

Saturday Night Dead
Rosen, Richard 652, 1709

Savage Justice
Handberg, Ron 492, **721**, 1428

The Savage Season
Lansdale, Joe R. 102, 149, 482, 682, 1024, 1288, 1589

Saving the Queen
Buckley, William F. Jr. 419

The Saxon Series
Roberts, Les 301, 369

Say It with Poison
Granger, Ann 896

Say No to Murder
Pickard, Nancy 126, 895, 945, 982, 1543

A Scandal in Belgravia
Barnard, Robert **91**

A Scandal in Belgravia
Brett, Simon 696, 697

Scapegoat
Orum, Paul 548

Scared to Death
Morice, Anne 729

Scarlet Night
Davis, Dorothy Salisbury 1519

Title Index

The Scarred Man
Klavan, Andrew 1075

The Scarred Man
Peterson, Keith 513, 664, 721, 811, 964, **1310**, 1747, 1792

Scavenger Reef
Shames, Laurence 1012

Scavengers
Montgomery, Yvonne 33, 1333, 1543, 1545

Scent of Evil
Mayor, Archer 936, **1105**, 1776

Schism
Granger, Bill 188

The Scobie Malone Series
Cleary, Jon 328, 329, 1695

The Scold's Bridle
Walters, Minette 1660, **1670**

Scorcher
Lutz, John 1313, 1371, 1422

Scotch on the Rocks
Browne, Howard **183**, 1583

The Scottish Decision
Hunter, Alan 948

Scratchproof
Maguire, Michael 573

Screaming Bones
Burden, Pat **191**, 645

Screwdriver
Kraft, Gabrielle 51

The Scribner Crime Classic Series
Upfield, Arthur W. 256, 875

The Sculptress
Walters, Minette 114, 909, **1671**

Sealed with a Kiss
McGrady, Sean 1331

The Search Committee
McInerny, Ralph **1136**, 1482

The Search for Joseph Tully
Hallahan, William H. 266

Search the Shadows
Michaels, Barbara 769, 1453

Searching for Sara
Singer, Shelley 1434, **1506**

A Season for Murder
Granger, Ann 107, 308, **645**

Season of the Monsoon
Mann, Paul 1137

Season of the Strangler
Jones, Madison 964

Second Chance
Valin, Jonathan 717, 1287, **1648**

A Second Shot in the Dark
Roome, Annette 741, 894, **1399**, 1557, 1671

Second Vespers
McInerny, Ralph 915

The Secret Ascension
Bishop, Michael 419

The Secret History
Tartt, Donna 90

A Secret Rage
Harris, Charlaine 42

A Secret Singing
Smith, Richard C. 1703

The Seduction
Bourgeau, Art 187, 208

See No Evil
Mathis, Edward **1095**

Seeds of Murder
Underwood, Michael 561, 598, **1642**

Seeing the Elephant
Roberts, Les **1387**

Selena
Willey, Gordon Randolph **1726**

Self-Defense
Kellerman, Jonathan **887**

A Sensitive Case
Wright, Eric 614, **1770**

Separate Cases
Randisi, Robert J. 551, **1350**

September Song
Mathis, Edward 1007, **1096**

The Septimus Finch Series
Erskine, Margaret 204, 1179

The Seraphim Kill
Shaw, P.B. 1231

The Sergeant Beef Series
Bruce, Leo 109, 912

The Sergeant Cribb Series
Lovesey, Peter 655, 737

A Series of Murders
Brett, Simon 176

The Serpent
Wiltse, David 1628

Service for Two
Kingsbury, Kate 103

Service of All the Dead
Dexter, Colin 89, 841, 1001, 1502

Set-Up
O'Callaghan, Maxine **1220**, 1228

A Settling of Accounts
Hart, Carolyn G. 1565

Seven Days in May
Knebel, Fletcher 681

Seven Kinds of Death
Wilhelm, Kate **1725**

The Seven-Percent Solution
Meyer, Nicholas 440, 441, 442, 1407

Seventh Avenue Murder
Bennett, Liza 403, 404

The Seventh Bullet
Victor, Daniel D. 81, **1654**

Shadow
Janeshutz, Trish 844

Shadow Behind the Curtain
Johnston, Velda 436, 798

Shadow Counter
Kakonis, Tom 855

Shadow Dance
Bushnell, Agnes 202, 1460, 1689

Shadow Kills
Philbrick, W.R. 938

The Shadow Knows
Johnson, Diane 43, 673

The Shadow Man
Lutz, John 1286, 1634

Shadow of a Broken Man
Chesbro, George C. 1371

Shadow of a Doubt
Coughlin, William J. **333**, 666

Shadow of Shadows
Allbeury, Ted 995

The Shadow of the Palms
Law, Janice 635

The Shadow of the Shadow
Taibo, Paco Ignacio II **1598**

Shadow Prey
Sandford, John **1426**, 1534

Shadow Queen
Gibbs, Tony 69, 252, 513, **583**, 1115

Shadowchase
Blank, Martin 143, 1683

Shadows on the Mirror
Fyfield, Frances 436, **563**, 751

Shady Lady
Adams, Cleve F. 1307

Shakedown
Petievich, Gerald 254

The Shaman Sings
Doss, James D. 1680

The Shaman's Knife
Young, Scott 1680, **1786**

Shameless
Collins, Judy **275**

The Shape of Dread
Muller, Marcia 461, 462, 634, **1181**, 1219, 1229, 1264

A Share in Death
Crombie, Deborah **358**, 640, 642, 678, 740, 897, 1141, 1143, 1408, 1556

Sharky's Machine
Diehl, William 306, 1696

The Sharon McCone Series
Muller, Marcia 92, 397, 398, 551, 635, 638, 639, 649, 837, 838, 917, 918, 920, 1009, 1052, 1220, 1266

Sharon McCone Series
Muller, Marcia 1328

The Sharon McCone Series
Muller, Marcia 1332, 1506, 1569, 1700, 1701, 1702

Shattered Moon
Green, Kate 811, 846, 1062, 1308

The Shattered Raven
Hoch, Edward D. 524, 984, 1044

Shattered Rhythms
Knight, Phyllis **946**

She
Haggard, H. Rider 1298

She Came in a Flash
Wings, Mary 202, 274

She Came Too Late
Wings, Mary 1460, 1461, 1462

She Walks in Beauty
Shankman, Sarah 1119, **1477**, 1495

She Walks These Hills
McCrumb, Sharyn 626, **1119**

She Woke to Darkness
Halliday, Brett 984, 1044

Sheep, Goats and Soap
Malcolm, John **1068**

The Sheila Travis Series
Sprinkle, Patricia Houck 32, 1497, 1548

Shella
Vachss, Andrew 755

Shepherd of the Wolves
Slusher, William S. 736

The Sheriff and the Branding Iron Murders
Meredith, D.R. 353

The Sheriff and the Panhandle Murders
Meredith, D.R. 316, 1086, 1739, 1740

The Sheriff Bill Gastner Series
Havill, Steven F. 65

The Sheriff Charles Matthews Series
Meredith, D.R. 65, 310, 311, 1087, 1153, 1756, 1758

The Sheriff Dan Rhodes Series
Crider, Bill 12, 14, 106, 310, 311, 700, 757, 780, 781, 1086, 1087, 1138, 1153, 1431, 1788

Sherlock Holmes and the Thistle of Scotland
Greenwood, L.B. 131, 440, 441, 442, 1654

Sherlock Holmes vs. Dracula
Estleman, Loren D. 440, 1407, 1654

Sherlock in Love
Nasland, Sena Jeter 926

Shibumi
Trevanian 527

The Shifty Anderson Series
Murray, William 1486

The Shirley McClintock Series
Oliphant, B.J. 156, 537, 711, 1483, 1497, 1551

Shoedog
Pelecanos, George **1288**

Shoofly Pie to Die
Quittner, Joshua 629, **1342**, 1710

Shoot It Again, Sam
Avallone, Michael 1574

Shoot the Piper
Hill, Richard **791**

Shooting at Loons
Maron, Margaret **1078**, 1119

Shooting Script
Cotler, Gordon **332**

Shooting Script — **What Mystery Do I Read Next?**

Shooting Script
Lyall, Gavin 847

Shooting Star
Green, Kate 173, 252, 332, **665**, 769, 1247, 1248, 1514, 1763

Short Cut to Santa Fe
Sale, Medora 884, **1420**, 1766

Shot on Location
Cutler, Stan 332, **369**, 1411

Shot Silk
Maguire, Michael 540

Shotgun Saturday Night
Crider, Bill 1105, 1108, 1739, 1741

Show Stopper
Pulver, Mary Monica **1335**

Showcase
Glen, Alison 297, 373, **603**, 1641

A Shrine of Murders
Grace, C.L. 544, 1203, 1301

Shroud for a Nightingale
James, P.D. 1479

Shroud for a Scholar
Peterson, Audrey **1306**, 1586

Shutout
Nighbert, David F. **1204**

Sick of Shadows
McCrumb, Sharyn 933

Sick to Death
Clark, Douglas 576

Sideswipe
Willeford, Charles 653, 709, 938

The Sidewalk Hilton
Cook, Bruce **301**

Sight Unseen
Lorne, David **1046**

The Sigrid Harald Series
Maron, Margaret 141, 142, 447, 464, 534, 804, 805, 925, 954, 969, 1086, 1224, 1225, 1226, 1523

Silence in Hanover Close
Perry, Anne 941, 1610

The Silence of the Lambs
Harris, Thomas 62, 99, 321, 323, 326, 651, 937, 1279, 1736

Silent Night
Amo, Gary 43, **49**, 149, 253, 893, 899, 937

Silent Partner
Kellerman, Jonathan 1457

Silent Prey
Sandford, John 229, 840, 873, 1363, **1427**, 1600, 1736, 1737

Silent Son
Warfield, Gallatin 1599

Silent Witness
Wilcox, Collin 123, **1716**

Silent Witness
Wilson, Charles 1538, 1562, **1732**

The Silver Ghost
MacLeod, Charlotte 629

The Silver Pigs
Davis, Lindsey 201, **394**, 1382, 1449

The Silver Scapel
Jacobs, Nancy Baker **837**, 1041

Silver Spire
Goldsborough, Robert 608

The Simeon Grist Series
Hallinan, Timothy 301

The Simon Bogner Series
Heald, Tim 1036

The Simona Griffo Series
Crespi, Trella 56, 124, 596

A Simple Plan
Smith, Scott 363, 1354

A Simple Suburban Murder
Zubro, Mark Richard 1194, 1415

Simply to Die For
Christmas, Joyce 1097

The Sin Within Her Smile
Gash, Jonathan 572

Sine Qua Nun
Quill, Monica 136, 670, 797, 1123, 1124

Sing a Song of Death
Dain, Catherine **380**, 542

Singapore Transfer
Warga, Wayne 261, **1673**, 1744

The Singing Stones
Whitney, Phyllis 139

A Single Stone
Wallace, Marilyn 252, 1217, **1664**

Single White Female
Lutz, John 821, 1791

A Singular Spy
Williams, Amanda Kyle **1727**

Sion Crossing
Price, Anthony 38, 824

The Sir Henry Merrivale Series
Dickson, Carter 471

The Sirens Sang of Murder
Caudwell, Sarah **228**, 763

Sister Beneath the Sheet
Linscott, Gillian 930, **1029**

The Sister Frevisse Series
Frazer, Margaret 631, 1203, 1301

Sister Hood
Quill, Monica 1591

The Sister Joan Series
Black, Veronica 1237, 1239, 1339

The Sister Mary Helen Series
O'Marie, Carol Anne 137, 138, 564, 672, 733, 799, 1339

The Sister Mary Teresa Series
Quill, Monica 137, 138, 1237, 1238, 1239

Sisters in Crime
Wallace, Marilyn 663

Sisters in Crime 2
Wallace, Marilyn 663

The Sisters in Crime Series
Wallace, Marilyn 1073, 1267

Sister's Keeper
Lordon, Randye **1042**

Sisters of the Road
Wilson, Barbara 947

Six Days of the Condor
Grady, James 1284

Six Feet Under
Simpson, Dorothy 1392

A Six-Letter Word for Death
Moyes, Patricia 368

Six Nuns and a Shotgun
Watson, Colin 1322

The Skeleton in the Grass
Barnard, Robert 385

Skeleton-in-Waiting
Dickinson, Peter **419**

Skeletons
Sauter, Eric 205, 1427, **1443**

Skeletons
Swarthout, Glendon 1653

Skim
Patillo, James 707, 785

Skin Deep
Hallinan, Timothy **718**

Skin Deep
Hiaasen, Carl 568

Skin Deep Is Fatal
Cormany, Michael **320**

Skin Tight
Hiaasen, Carl 632, 707, **783**, 854, 1474

Skinny Man
Colbert, James **273**, 910, 1416

Skins
O'Connell, Catherine 59, **1222**, 1526

The Skintight Shroud
Dundee, Wayne 190, **459**

The Skintight Shroud
Dundee, Wayne D. 500, 1019, 1648

The Skip Langdon Series
Smith, Julie 447, 601, 927, 969, 1226, 1686

Skylark
Simonson, Sheila 345, 962, **1501**

Skywatcher
Kent, Winona 528

Slash of Scarlet
Jacobs, Nancy Baker 521

A Slay at the Races
Morgan, Kate **1172**

Sleep of Death
Morice, Anne 1707

Sleep of the Innocent
Sale, Medora 897, 1767, 1769

Sleeping Dog
Lochte, Dick 122, 403, 499, 680, 1558, 1592

Sleeping Dogs
Perry, Thomas 3, 486, **1297**

A Sleeping Life
Rendell, Ruth 358

Sleight of Hand
Kelley, Patrick 1595

A Slip of the Tong
Goodrum, Charles A. 296, 297, 479, **611**, 1559

Sliver
Levin, Ira **1013**

Slob
Miller, Rex 1027, 1425

Slow Burn
Bland, Eleanor Taylor **142**

Slow Burn
Helgerson, Joel 622

Slow Dance in Autumn
Williams, Philip Lee 148, 320, 454, 1457, 1481

Slow Dancer
Philbrick, W.R. 77

Slow Motion Riot
Blauner, Peter **144**, 292, 293, 1000, 1067, 1152, 1199, 1623

Slow Squeeze
Pugh, Dianne G. 1413

A Small and Incidental Murder
Putre, John Walter 233, 338, 340, 399, 433, 475, 689, 806, 903, 1324, **1337**, 1704

Smallbone Deceased
Gilbert, Michael 228, 1139

The Smart Money
Matera, Lia 986, 1524

Smiling, the Boy Fell Dead
Delving, Michael 1673

The Smith and Wetzon Series
Meyers, Annette 172, 654, 987, 1333

The Smokey Brandon Series
Ayres, Noreen 325

Smuggler's Notch
Koenig, Joseph 568, 1757

Snagged
Clark, Carol Higgins **251**

Snake Dance
Mariz, Linda 1137

Snake in the Grasses
Hilary, Richard 762

The Snake Tattoo
Barnes, Linda 274, 1702

Snapshot
Barnes, Linda **93**, 808

Snare in the Dark
Parrish, Frank 110

Snow Falling on Cedars
Guterson, David 692, 1218

Snow Job
Wood, Ted 294, **1758**

So Like Sleep
Healy, Jeremiah 1000, 1313

So Little to Die For
Grindle, Lucretia **678**

So Much Blood
Brett, Simon 1707

Title Index

So Shall You Reap
Wallace, Marilyn **1665**

The Soap Opera Slaughters
Kaye, Marvin 75

The Society Ball Murders
Anderson, Jack Albin **51**, 603

The Software Bomb
Womack, Steven **1753**

Sold!
Lyons, Nan 570

Solo Blues
Gosling, Paula 609

Solomon's Vineyard
Latimer, Jonathan 1540

Some Die Eloquent
Aird, Catherine 470

Some Die Young
Hart, Jeanne 889, 1664

Some Run Crooked
Hilton, John Buxton 1502

Somebody Else's Child
Grimes, Terris McMahan 761

Somebody's Dead in Snellville
Sprinkle, Patricia Houck 22, 836, 901, 1496, **1545**

Someone Is Killing the Great Chefs of America
Lyons, Nan **1061**

Someone Is Killing the Great Chefs of Europe
Lyons, Nan 151, 152

Someone to Watch
Maiman, Jaye 1356

Something in the Water
MacLeod, Charlotte **1065**

Something Like a Love Affair
Symons, Julian 90

Something the Cat Dragged In
MacLeod, Charlotte 387

Something Wicked
Hart, Carolyn G. 776, 781, 1500

Something's Cooking
Pence, Joanne 134, **1290**

Son of Holmes
Lescroart, John T. 81

The Song Dog
McClure, James **1114**

Song of Corpus Juris
Hensley, Joe L. 1602

Sorry Now?
Zubro, Mark Richard **1796**

The Soul of Betty Fairchild
Specht, Robert 69, 665, 1503, **1538**

The Sourdough Wars
Smith, Julie 153, 988, 1320

South Street Confidential
Belsky, Dick **120**

Southern Cross
DeBrosse, Jim **408**

Southern Cross
Greenleaf, Stephen **669**

Southern Ghost
Hart, Carolyn G. 1451

Soviet Sources
Cullen, Robert 913

Spandau Phoenix
Iles, Greg **824**

The Spanish Maze Game
Webster, Noah **1682**

Spanner
Chastain, Thomas 840

Spare Change
Peak, John A. **1280**

Spare Parts
Hanson, Rick 708

Spark
Lutz, John **1058**

Speaker of Mandarin
Rendell, Ruth 676

Special Circumstances
Lysaght, Brian 105, 192, 682, 735

Special Delivery
Kennealy, Jerry **907**

The Spencer Arrowood Series
McCrumb, Sharyn 311, 1774

The Spenser Series
Parker, Robert B. 190, 341, 342, 343, 344, 386, 432, 764, 1400, 1615

Sphere
Crichton, Michael 85

Spill
Standiford, Les 605

Spiral
Lindsey, David L. 186, 1533

A Splash of Red
Fraser, Antonia 729

Split Images
Leonard, Elmore 1058

Split Seconds
Robinson, Kevin 359

The Spoiler
Stansberry, Dominic 612

The Spoils of Time
Thomson, June 675, 752, **1614**

Sports Freak
O'Cork, Shannon 614

Spotted Cats
Tapply, William G. 31, 337, 338, 445, 922, **1603**

SPQR
Roberts, John Maddox **1382**, 1449

The SPQR Series
Roberts, John Maddox 201, 1390, 1448, 1450

A Sprig of Sea Lavender
Anderson, J.R.L. 1168

The Spy in Question
Sebastian, Tim 529

The Spy on the Deuce Court
Deford, Frank 129

Spy on the Run
Lovell, Marc 996

Spy Shadow
Sebastian, Tim **1466**

The Spy Who Came in from the Cold
Le Carre, John 706

The Spy Who Sat and Waited
Campbell, R. Wright 37, 78

The Spy with His Head in the Clouds
Lovell, Marc 706

Squeeze Play
Benjamin, Paul 510, 574, 1205, 1206

Squeezeplay
Nighbert, David F. 506, **1205**

SS-GB
Deighton, Len 38, 78, 419, 579, 824, 861, 1066

Stacked Deck
Pronzini, Bill **1330**

Stage Fright
Linscott, Gillian **1030**

A Stained White Radiance
Burke, James Lee 454, 869, 1000, 1493

Stalking-Horse
Delahaye, Michael 1466

Stalking Horse
Shoemaker, Bill 538, **1487**

Stalking the Angel
Crais, Robert **343**, 434, 716, 717, 718, 766, 1000

Stand-In for Murder
Bradley, Lynn **164**

The Standoff
Hogan, Chuck 566, **796**

The Stanley Hastings Series
Hall, Parnell 494

The Stanley Moodrow Series
Solomita, Stephen 1024

A Star-Spangled Murder
Wolzien, Valerie 1319

Star Trap
Brett, Simon 1768

Stardust
Parker, Robert B. 403, **1271**

State Scarlet
Aaron, David 1473

State's Evidence
Greenleaf, Stephen 704, 1662, 1688

The Steam Pig
McClure, James 226

Steel Guitar
Barnes, Linda **94**, 637, 1076

Steel Tiger
Silliphant, Stirling 581, 1337

The Steel Web
Tierney, Ronald **1620**

The Steinway Collection
Randisi, Robert J. 282, 630, 1054, 1055

The Stepford Wives
Levin, Ira 568

The Steve Winslow Series
Hailey, J.P. 237, 923

The Stewart Hoag Series
Handler, David 257, 484, 1100, 1464

Stick
Leonard, Elmore 434, 482, 854, 1288, 1349, 1416, 1444

A Stiff Critique
Girdner, Jaqueline **595**, 600, 744

Still Among the Living
Klein, Zachary 386, 446, 454, **938**, 1481

A Still and Icy Silence
Roat, Ronald Clair 1032, **1374**

Still Explosion
Logue, Mary 521, 615, 837, 936, **1041**, 1590

Still Water
Gunning, Sally **688**

Still Waters
Tucker, Kerry 198, 313, 520, 610, 809, 901, 1041, 1145, 1498, **1638**, 1723

A Stillness in Bethlehem
Haddam, Jane **697**

Stillwatch
Clark, Mary Higgins 1062

Stolen Away
Collins, Max Allan **280**, 958

The Stolen Gods
Page, Jake 1017, 1273

The Stone Angel Series
Albert, Marvin 327, 329, 1488

Stone Boy
Levitsky, Ronald 1009, **1017**

Stone Cold
Francome, John 1487

The Stone Hawk
Moffat, Gwen **1163**

Stone Shadow
Miller, Rex 229, **1154**, 1308, 1426

The Stone Veil
Tierney, Ronald **1621**

StoneDust
Scott, Justin **1464**

Stonefish
West, Charles 327, 328, 329, **1695**

The Stoney Winston Series
Stinson, Jim 301, 369, 1247

Stories by Mama Lansdale's Youngest Boy
Lansdale, Joe R. 1330

Storm Center
Clark, Douglas 368

Storm Front
Anderson, Virginia **53**

Storming Intrepid
Harrison, Payne 1513

Stormy Weather
Hiaasen, Carl **784**

Straight
Francis, Dick **541**

Straight
Knickmeyer, Steve 817, 1060

Straight as an Arrow
Sibley, Celestine 624, 674, 1315, **1498**, 1547

A Strange and Bitter Crop
Wyrick, E.L. 1699, **1780**

A Strange and Bitter Fruit
Wyrick, E.L. 853

The Strange Death of Meriweather Lewis
Burns, Ron 1164

The Strange Files of Fremont Jones
Day, Dianne **400**, 465

Strange Loyalties
McIlvanney, William 113, **1134**

Stranger in the House
MacDonald, Patricia 43

A Stranger Is Watching
Clark, Mary Higgins 1046

Strangers in the Night
Tyre, Peg **1641**

Strangers on a Train
Highsmith, Patricia 1360, 1761

Strangled Prose
Hess, Joan 119, 743, 803, 933, 1120, 1232, 1263, 1379, 1500

Stranglehold
Doolittle, Jerome 159, 388, **435**, 539, 850, 1353

Strangler
Hall, Parnell **715**

Strawgirl
Padgett, Abigail **1252**, 1504

Stray Cat
Matheson, Don 475, 1337

Street of the Five Moons
Peters, Elizabeth 479

Streets of Fire
Cook, Thomas H. **306**, 498, 910, 1503, 1535

Strega
Vachss, Andrew 526, 886, 1251

The Strenuous Life
Alexander, Lawrence **36**

Strike
Enger, L.L. **492**

Strike Three, You're Dead
Rosen, Richard 505, 506, 508, 872, 1206, 1271, 1536

Strikezone
Nighbert, David F. 493, 574, 613, **1206**

Striking Out
Gordon, Alison **615**

Strip Tease
Hiaasen, Carl 231, 606, 773, **785**

Strong Poison
Sayers, Dorothy L. 543, 1417

The Stuart Haydon Series
Lindsey, David L. 1095, 1711, 1715

The Student Body
Borthwick, J.S. 892, 1256, 1520, 1767, 1797

Study in Lilac
Oliver, Maria-Antonia 1126

A Study in Terror
Queen, Ellery 1365

Such Men are Dangerous
Kavanaugh, Paul 1704

Such Pretty Toys
Dean, S.F.X. 1043

Sudden Death
Brown, Rita Mae 1195

A Sudden Death at the Norfolk Cafe
Sullivan, Winona 671, 734, 799, 1237, 1434, **1591**

A Sudden, Fearful Death
Perry, Anne **1296**

Sudden Prey
Sandford, John 1025

Suddenly in Her Sorbet
Christmas, Joyce 51, 449

Suffer Little Children
Davis, Thomas D. **396**

Sugartown
Estleman, Loren D. 319

Suicide Season
Burns, Rex 871

Suicide Squeeze
Everson, David 493, 506, 508, **510**, 574, 613, 646, 1205, 1400

Suitable for Framing
Buchanan, Edna 275, 615

A Suitable Vengeance
George, Elizabeth 417, **578**

A Suitcase in Berlin
Flynn, Don 86, **532**

The Suitor
Allegretto, Michael 43, 673

The Sum of All Fears
Clancy, Tom **248**

Summer Cool
Sarrantonio, Al 211, **1436**

Summer of Night
Simmons, Dan 935

The Summer of the Danes
Peters, Ellis **1303**

The Summertime Soldiers
Kelly, Susan 1420, 1498

The Summons
Lovesey, Peter **1050**

The Sunken Treasure
Jackson, Marian J.A. **835**

Sunrise
West, Chassie 761

Sunshine Enemies
Constantine, K.C. **298**, 1103

The Superintendent Bone Series
Stacey, Susannah 469, 1159, 1480

A Superior Death
Barr, Nevada **96**, 1428

The Susan Henshaw Series
Wolzien, Valerie 157, 244, 246, 247, 600, 1254

The Suspect
Wright, L.R. 314, 1418, 1785

Suspects
Caunitz, William J. 750, 840, 1067, 1202

The Suspense Is Killing Me
Maxwell, Thomas 227, 299, 406, 1072, **1102**, 1587

Suspicion of Guilt
Parker, Barbara 784, **1268**, 1465

Suspicion of Innocence
Parker, Barbara 1280

Sweet and Deadly
Harris, Charlaine 222

Sweet Death
Waggoner, Bill **1657**, 1735

Sweet Death, Come Softly
Whitehead, Barbara **1708**

Sweet La-La Land
Campbell, Robert 888

Sweet Narcissus
Lorens, M.K. 9, 223, **1045**

Sweet, Savage Death
Papazoulou, Orania 1500

Sweet Water
Kline, Christina Baker 592

Sweet Women Lie
Estleman, Loren D. **500**

Sweetwater Ranch
Norman, Geoffrey 1072

Swift to Its Close
Troy, Simon 1614

Swindle
Adams, George **11**

Swing
Enger, L.L. 58, 162, **493**, 505, 574, 613, 1205, 1718

Swing Away, Climber
Carr, Glyn 1163

Switch
Bayer, William 306, 750, 858, 1193, 1249, 1533

Switchback
Wilcox, Collin **1717**

Switching the Odds
Knight, Phyllis **947**, 1042, 1462

T

The T.D. Stash Series
Philbrick, W.R. 1336

Tabernacle
Cook, Thomas H. 509, 827, 828, 829, 830, 1018

The Taggert Roper Series
Sanders, William 485

A Tail of Two Murders
Cleary, Melissa **259**, 289

The Take
Izzi, Eugene 185, 526, 1622

A Talent for Destruction
Radley, Sheila 1035

The Talented Mr. Ripley
Highsmith, Patricia 450

The Talinin Madonna
Skeggs, Douglas 365, **1508**, 1744

The Talk Show Murders
Allen, Steve 75, 1635

Talking God
Hillerman, Tony 758, **793**

The Tall Dark Alibi
Jerina, Carol 411

The Tanglewood Murder
Kallen, Lucille 559, 609, 814, 1191

Tango Key
Drake, Alison 96, 804, 1088

Tapestry of Murders
Doherty, P.C. 1175

Target Five
Forbes, Colin 1530

Target Manhattan
Mallory, Drew 205, 1633

A Taste for Death
James, P.D. 1554

A Taste for Murder
Bishop, Claudia 32, **135**, 375, 1289, 1291

A Tasty Way to Die
Laurence, Janet 1289, 1290, 1291

A Tax in the Blood
Schutz, Benjamin M. 1601

Tea-Totally Dead
Girdner, Jaqueline **596**

Teardown
Wuamett, Victor 101, 192, 1240, **1779**

The Tears of Autumn
McCarry, Charles 188

Tell Me No Secrets
Fielding, Joy 769

Telling Lies
Hornsby, Wendy 610, **809**, 1637

The Temple Dogs
Murphy, Warren 1127, **1188**

A Temporary Ghost
Friedman, Mickey **556**, 724, 1300, 1476, 1671

Ten of Swords
Levitt, J.R. 624, 827, 829, 830, **1018**, 1472, 1505

The Tenant
Topor, Roland 1013

Tensleep
Andrews, Sarah 48, **57**, 605

The Tenth Virgin
Stewart, Gary 828, 1018

Termination Dust
Henry, Sue 1552

The Terrible Tide
Craig, Alisa 763

Title Index

The Tessa Crichton Series
Morice, Anne 76, 414, 543, 1071, 1131, 1179, 1213, 1391, 1399

Testament
Morrell, David 5, 395, 822, 1188

The Texas Capitol Murders
Crider, Bill **353**, 1435

Texas Wind
Reasoner, James 7, 8, 14, 352, 458, 1096

Their Kind of Town
Whittingham, Richard 1287

Then Hang All the Lawyers
Storey, Alice 866

Then Hang All the Liars
Shankman, Sarah 731, 1496, 1631

Then Hang All the Liars
Storey, Alice 867

The Theo Bloomer Series
Hadley, Joan 1064

The Theodora Braithwaite Series
Greenwood, D.M. 564, 799, 1239, 1339

There Fell a Shadow
Peterson, Keith 1719

There Hangs the Knife
Muller, Marcia 1507, 1666

There's Something About a Sunday
Muller, Marcia 772

Thicker than Blood
Lutz, John **1059**

The Thief Taker
Jeffreys, J.G. 941, 942

The Thief Who Couldn't Sleep
Block, Lawrence 1697

Thieftaker
Scholefield, Alan **1454**

The Thin Man
Hammett, Dashiell 630, 999

The Thin Woman
Cannell, Dorothy 151, 152, 374, 390, 988, 989, 990, 1097, 1098, 1257, 1290, 1291

The Things We Do for Love
Schutz, Benjamin M. 1358, 1587

Think on Death
McCullough, David Willis 137, **1124**

Thinner than Blood
Shepherd, Stella **1480**, 1556

Third Man Out
Stevenson, Richard **1572**

The Thirteenth Apostle
Gonzalez, Gloria **610**

This Way Out
Radley, Sheila 841, **1343**

The Thomas and Charlotte Pitt Series
Perry, Anne 655, 737, 834, 928, 929, 943

The Thomas Berryman Number
Patterson, James 392, 1623

The Thomas Black Series
Emerson, Earl 39, 815, 818, 863, 865, 869, 1384, 1386, 1604, 1754, 1765

The Thomas Street Horror
Paul, Raymond 1403, 1404

The Thousand Yard Stare
Kantner, Rob **865**

Threatening Eye
Grant-Adamson, Lesley 1730

Three and One Make Five
Jeffries, Roderic 67

Three Blind Mice
McBain, Ed **1106**

Three-Core Lead
Curzon, Clare **368**, 1682

Three Is a Crowd
Borton, D.B. **156**, 1065

A Three-Pipe Problem
Symons, Julian 1365

Three Strikes, You're Dead
Geller, Michael **574**, 1059

Three with a Bullet
Lyons, Arthur 511

The Threepersons Hunt
Garfield, Brian 700, 701, 792, 793

Threnody for Two
Hart, Jeanne **747**

Throw Darts at a Cheesecake
Dietz, Denise 135, **423**, 457, 959, 1290

Thrown Away Child
Adcock, Thomas 881

Thunder
Grady, James **633**

Thursday's Child
White, Teri **1705**

Thus Was Adonis Murdered
Caudwell, Sarah 561, 979, 1002, 1003, 1004, 1118, 1187, 1243, 1501, 1510, 1642, 1658

Thyme of Death
Albert, Susan Wittig **33**, 172, 198, 375, 389, 390, 959, 1155, 1156, 1333, 1401, 1567

A Ticket to the Boneyard
Block, Lawrence **149**, 767, 1010, 1347

Tie-Break
Nastase, Ilie 129

Ties That Bind
Woods, Sherryl **1759**

Tigers Burning
Evers, Crabbe **508**

Tight Lines
Tapply, William G. **1604**

Tightrope
White, Teri 483, 1664

The Tijuana Bible
Goulart, Ron **630**

Till Death Do Us Part
Krich, Rochelle Majer 879, 880, 884, **955**

Till The Butchers Cut Him Down
Muller, Marcia **1182**

The Tim Simpson Series
Malcolm, John 570, 571, 572, 1242, 1564, 1566

Time and Again
Finney, Jack 1536

Time and Time Again
Gill, B.M. **587**

Time Bomb
Kellerman, Jonathan 144, **888**, 1276

Time Expired
Dunlap, Susan **464**

Time Exposure
Lutz, John **1060**

A Time for Dying
Ross, Jonathan **1402**

A Time for the Death of a King
Dukthas, Anne 243

Time Lapse
Law, Janice 542, **992**, 1257

Time of Hope
Kelly, Susan B. 677, **898**, 1553

A Time of Predators
Gores, Joe 165, 1457, 1747

A Time to Kill
Grisham, John 1017

A Time to Reap
Hinkemeyer, Michael T. 757, 758, 966, 1108

A Time Without Shadows
Allbeury, Ted **38**, 824

Timelocke
Barnao, Jack 1682

Time's Witness
Malone, Michael 735, 1006, **1070**, 1281

Timor Mortis
Harris, Will 1673

Tincture of Death
Harrison, Ray **738**, 1029, 1403

Tinker, Tailor, Soldier, Spy
Le Carre, John 453, 550

Tip on a Dead Crab
Murray, William 170, 171, 495, 540, 541

'Tis the Season to Be Dying
Drummond, John Keith 1208

The Tish McWhinney Series
Comfort, B. 978, 1446, 1483, 1548

To an Easy Grave
Law, Alexander 612, 1546, 1757

To Catch a Forger
Wallace, Robert **1666**

To Die Like a Gentleman
Bastable, Bernard **103**

To Do No Harm
Glass, Leslie **602**, 1699, 1799

To Have and to Kill
Martin, Robert 1085

To Kill a Cat
Burley, W.J. 260, 1001

To Kill a Clown
Charnee, David **237**

To Kill a Mockingbird
Lee, Harper 876

To Killashea
Flood, Norman 23, 104, 474, **530**, 657

To Live and Die in Dixie
Trocheck, Kathy Hogan 503, 1544, **1632**

To Live and Die in L.A.
Petievich, Gerald 185, 831, 832, 1433

To Play the Fool
King, Laurie R. **927**

To Prove a Villain
Townsend, Guy M. 424

To Speak for the Dead
Levine, Paul 66, 72, 73, 153, 254, 557, 558, 651, 985, **1016**, 1023, 1090, 1106, 1280, 1349, 1577, 1677

To Study a Long Silence
Clinton-Baddeley, V.C. 1045

To the Bright and Shining Sun
Burke, James Lee 1584

To the Fourth Generation
Kincaid, Nell 1157

The Toby Peters Series
Kaminsky, Stuart M. 277, 956, 958, 1207

The Tom Bethany Series
Doolittle, Jerome 485, 764, 864, 1423

The Tom Mason Series
Zubro, Mark Richard 1150, 1151, 1572

The Toni and Pat Pratt Series
Lee, Bernie 1201

Too Clever by Half
Jeffries, Roderic **845**

Too Late to Die
Crider, Bill 298, 316, 1740

Too Many Cooks
Pence, Joanne **1291**

Too Many Cooks
Stout, Rex 988

Too Many Cooks Spoil the Broth
Myers, Tamar 134, 1289

Too Many Crooks Spoil the Broth
Myers, Tamar 375

Too Many Questions
Grant-Adamson, Lesley 269, 308, 455

Too Sane a Murder
Martin, Lee 1170, 1687

The Tooth and the Nail
Ballinger, Bill S. 704

Topless
Mano, D. Keith 355, 590, **1072**

The Topless Tulip Caper
Block, Lawrence 237, 585, 608

Torch Town Boogie
Womack, Steven 1474, **1754**

A Torrid Piece of Murder
Roe, C.F. 1262

Torsos
Cooke, John Peyton 278

The Total Zone
Navratilova, Martina 481, **1195**

A Touch of Frost
Wingfield, R.D. 740, 751

A Touch of Panic
Wright, L.R. **1776**

Touch of the Past
Breen, Jon L. 466, 535, 611, 1054, 1055, 1500, 1764

Touch the Devil
Higgins, Jack 474, 657, 1381

Tough Baby
Sublett, Jesse 350, 555

Tourist Season
Hiaasen, Carl 707, 1015, 1475, 1582, 1612, 1613

Tourist Trap
Smith, Julie 1316, 1716

Town on Trial
Harrington, William 730

The Toy Cupboard
Jordan, Lee 848

The Tozzi and Gibbons Series
Bruno, Anthony 1760

Trace Elements
Knight, Katherine Lasky 1156

Trace Elements
Knight, Kathryn Lasky 1232, 1332, 1405

The Trace Series
Murphy, Warren 212, 213, 499, 723, 724

Tracer, Inc.
Andrus, Jeff 58, 71, 870

Track of the Cat
Barr, Nevada 48, 54, **97**, 605, 792, 842, 1137, 1234, 1268, 1332, 1340, 1341, 1605, 1652, 1784

The Trade
Hallahan, William H. 1456

Trade-Off
Arnston, Harrison 66, 216, 240, 446, 1092, 1357, 1401, 1640, 1723, 1724, 1780

Trade Secrets
Garton, Ray 568

Trade Secrets
Thomson, Maynard F. 232, 386, 1400, **1615**

Tragedy at Law
Hare, Cyril 228, 1139

Trail of Murder
Andreae, Christine 55, 57, 1233, 1234, 1607, 1626, 1667

Trail of the Dragon
Kelly, Susan 222

The Trail of the Reaper
Fox, Peter 1606

The Trail to Buddha's Mirror
Winslow, Don 261, 952, **1744**

The Trapdoor
Peterson, Keith 166, 679, 838, 866, 867, 1261, 1368, 1369, 1546

The Traveler
Katzenbach, John 99, 326, 349, 1027, 1282

The Travis McGee Series
MacDonald, John D. 73, 432, 485, 817, 1057, 1336, 1352

Treasure by Post
Williams, David 1706, **1730**

A Treasury of Detective and Mystery Stories from the Great Pulps
Pronzini, Bill 1122

The Tree of Death
Muller, Marcia 523, 536, 537

Triangle
White, Teri 1116

A Trick of Light
Robinson, Patricia **1391**

The Trip to Jerusalem
Marston, Edward 425, **1084**

The Triumph of Bacchus
Skeggs, Douglas **1509**

The Triumph of Evil
Kavanagh, Paul 1284

Trojan Gold
Peters, Elizabeth 1409

Trophies and Dead Things
Muller, Marcia 6, 94, 514, 636, 637, 648, 767, 771, 809, 1092, **1183**, 1326, 1579

Tropical Depression
Lindsay, Jeffry P. **1024**

Tropical Freeze
Hall, James W. 72, 653, 683, 854, 973

Tropical Heat
Hall, James W. 1058

The Trouble at Harrison High
Farris, John 144

Trouble in the Brasses
Craig, Alisa 1305, 1420, 1769

Trouble Looking for a Place to Happen
Kelner, Toni L.P. **902**, 1204

A Trouble of Fools
Barnes, Linda 384, 919, 920, 1264, 1271

The Trouble with a Small Raise
Crespi, Trella 125, 1155

The Trouble with Going Home
Crespi, Camilla T. **345**

The Trouble with Moonlighting
Crespi, Trella **346**, 413, 517, 992, 1247, 1248, 1290, 1782, 1783

The Trouble with Too Much Sun
Crespi, Trella **347**, 1485

Troubled Water
Gunning, Sally **689**

Troubled Waters
Lemarchand, Elizabeth 67

Truck Shot
Stinson, Jim 718, **1574**

True Crime
Collins, Max Allan 278

True Crime
Klavan, Andrew 679

True Crime
Mewshaw, Michael **1145**, 1638, 1726

True Detective
Collins, Max Allan 483, 501, 1161, 1176

True-Life Adventure
Smith, Julie 1241

The Truman Smith Series
Crider, Bill 1032

Trunk Show
Glen, Alison **604**

Trust Me on This
Westlake, Donald E. 401

Trust the Liar
Zannos, Susan 1558

The Tryst
Dibdin, Michael 1412

Tucker's Last Stand
Buckley, William F. Jr. **188**

Tunnel Vision
Paretsky, Sara **1266**, 1410

Turnaround Jack
Abshire, Richard **8**, 354

The Turquoise Tattoo
Jacobs, Nancy Baker 116, 263, 838, 1504, 1505

Turtle Moon
Hoffman, Alice 147, **795**, 808

TV Safe
Stinson, Jim **1575**

The Twelve Days of Christmas
Babson, Marion 220

Twilight at Mac's Place
Thomas, Ross **1613**

A Twist of the Knife
Solomita, Stephen 146, 306, 749, 1075, 1644, 1696

Two Dude Defense
Walker, Walter 1016, 1090

Two Points for Murder
Borton, D.B. **157**

Two Thirds of a Ghost
McCloy, Helen 556, 1300

Two Way Toll
Klein, Zachary **939**, 1353

U

U.S.S.A.
Madsen, David 861, **1066**, 1530

Unbalanced Acts
Raines, Jeff **1344**

Uncivil Seasons
Malone, Michael 795

Under Cover of Daylight
Hall, James W. 981, 1747

Under My Skin
Dunant, Sarah 309, **456**

Under the Beetle's Cellar
Walker, Mary Willis 796, 1051, **1660**

Under the Bright Lights
Woodrell, Daniel 193, 197, 272, 273, 973, 1738

Under the Influence
Travis, Elizabeth 9, 162, 693, 1342, 1725

Undercover
Santiago, Soledad 59, 74, 1221, 1223

Undercurrents
Pearson, Ridley 1644

The Underground Man
Hailey, J.P. 144, **705**

The Underground Stream
Johnston, Velda 502

Underwater
Gunning, Sally 1078

Undue Influence
Borgenicht, Marian 848

Undue Influence
Borgenicht, Miriam 66, **153**

Undue Influence
Martini, Steve 820, 1599

The Unexpected Corpse
Oliphant, B.J. 97, 746, **1235**, 1784

The Unexpected Mrs. Pollifax
Gilman, Dorothy 996

Unfinished Business
Robinett, Stephen 1072

The Unforgiving Minutes
Pulver, Mary Monica 162, 1420

Unfunny Money
Alexander, Gary **35**

Unhappy Returns
Lemarchand, Elizabeth 759

Unholy Ghosts
Greenwood, D.M. **672**

An Unkindness of Ravens
Rendell, Ruth 759, 1168

Unknown Hand
Linscott, Gillian 64, 611, 800, 891, **1031**, 1306

Unknown Man #89
Leonard, Elmore 500

Unknown Man No. 89
Leonard, Elmore 266

Unnatural Cause
James, P.D. 759

Unnatural Causes
Noguchi, Thomas T. 478, 1285

Unnatural Hazard
Cork, Barry **317**, 1134

The Unorthodox Murder of Rabbi Wahl
Telushkin, Joseph 878

Title Index

Unorthodox Practices
Piesman, Marissa 473, 879, **1320**, 1783

Unquiet Grave
LaPierre, Janet 1728

Unsafe Keeping
Cail, Carol **206**

An Unsuitable Job for a Woman
James, P.D. 95, 269, 456, 1141, 1142, 1143

Until Death
Whitney, Polly 760, **1709**

Until Proven Guilty
Jance, J.A. 487

Until Proven Guilty
McGuire, Christine 820

Until Proven Innocent
Kelly, Susan 114, **895**, 1362, 1759, 1771

Until the End of Time
Whitney, Polly 1201, **1710**

Unwanted Attentions
Beck, K.K. 798

Unwillingly to Vegas
Livingston, Nancy **1036**

Used to Kill
O'Donnell, Lillian **1228**

User Deadly
Danks, Denise 232, **388**, 610, 694, 1753

V

The V.I. Warshawski Series
Paretsky, Sara 82, 92, 190, 381, 635, 638, 639, 918, 920, 1184, 1185, 1345, 1398, 1702

Valediction
Parker, Robert B. 766

Vanishing Act
Margolis, Seth Jacob **1075**

The Vanishing Smile
Emerson, Earl **490**

The Venetian Affair
MacInnes, Helen 1510

Venetian Mask
Friedman, Mickey 1002, 1004

The Venus Deal
Kuhlken, Ken **958**

The Venus Fly Trap
Wainwright, John 1402

The Venus Throw
Saylor, Steven **1450**

The Verity Birdwood Series
Rowe, Jennifer 156

Vermillion
Aldyne, Nathan 726, 727

The Verona Passamezzo
Gollin, James 1020

Vertical Run
Garber, Joseph R. **566**

The Very Bad Thing
White, Ned 7, 330, 939, **1703**, 1753

A Very Good Hater
Hill, Reginald 1367

The Very Last Gambado
Gash, Jonathan 479, 1036

A Very Particular Murder
Haymon, S.T. **759**

A Very Proper Death
Juniper, Alex **850**

A Very Venetian Murder
Murphy, Haughton **1187**

Vespers
McBain, Ed **1107**

Vial Murders
Landreth, Marsha **976**

The Vic Newman/Sabina Swift Series
Sucher, Dorothy 813

Video Kill
Fluke, Joanne 749

Video Vengeance
Tripp, Miles **1630**

The View from Deacon Hill
Scott, Jack S. 112, 1189

The Vig
Lescroart, John T. **1010**

The Villains
Keppel, Charlotte 1083

Vintage Polo
Kennealy, Jerry **908**, 1245

A Violent End
Page, Emma **1253**, 1592

Violent Love
Oster, Jerry 254

Viper Quarry
Feldmeyer, Dean **522**

Virgil's Ghost
Weinman, Irving **1684**

Virgin and Martyr
Greeley, Andrew M. 915

The Virginia Kelly Series
Baker, Nikki 142, 1691, 1692

Vital Lies
Hart, Ellen 82, 516, **746**, 967

Vital Signs
Cook, Robin **303**, 448, 934, 1799

Vital Statistics
Chastain, Thomas 1585

Voices in the Dark
Coburn, Andrew **268**, 626, 1774, 1776

A Void in Hearts
Tapply, William G. 819

Voodoo River
Crais, Robert 194, **344**, 1596

A Vow of Chastity
Black, Veronica **136**, 1591

A Vow of Obedience
Black, Veronica **137**

A Vow of Sanctity
Black, Veronica **138**

A Vow of Silence
Black, Veronica 670, 671, 672

Vow of Silence
Black, Veronica 1238

W

Walk a Crooked Mile
Dain, Catherine **381**

A Walk Among the Tombstones
Block, Lawrence **150**

Walking After Midnight
Nusser, Richard 412

Walking Dead Man
Kittredge, Mary **934**

Walking Shadow
Parker, Robert B. **1272**

Wall of Brass
Daley, Robert 940

Wall of Glass
Satterthwait, Walter 757, 758, 1162, 1601, 1650, 1688, 1794

Wandering Star
Yount, Steven 90, 876

Washington Deceased
Bowen, Michael 353, 1312, 1613

The Wasted Years
Harvey, John **754**

Wasteland
McCabe, Peter **1110**

The Watchers
Allegretto, Michael 843

The Watchman
Allegretto, Michael **44**, 252

The Water Cure
Downing, Warwick 240, 391, **446**, 1582

Waterman
Hornig, Doug 13, 475, 539, 806, 1078, 1757

Waxwork
Lovesey, Peter 1292, 1293, 1294, 1296, 1610

Way Past Dead
Womack, Steven 902, 1104, **1755**

We Wish You a Merry Murder
Wolzien, Valerie 245, 1146, 1208, 1256, 1315, **1750**

The Weatherman
Thayer, Steve 812, 1641

The Weaver's Tale
Sedley, Kate 426, **1470**, 1624

The Web
Kellerman, Jonathan 708

Wednesday's Child
Robinson, Peter 740, **1397**

Weep No More, My Lady
Clark, Mary Higgins 173, 665, 879, 990, 1097

Well-Schooled in Murder
George, Elizabeth 563, 790

The Wench Is Dead
Dexter, Colin **418**, 800

The Werner-Bok Library Series
Goodrum, Charles A. 416

Wet Graves
Corris, Peter **329**

Wet Work
Buckley, Christopher 437

The Whale's Footprints
Boyer, Rick 339, 687, 765, 850, 903, 904, 1324

What Dread Hand
Kemp, Sarah 303

What Men Say
Smith, Joan 309, 960, 1196, 1274, **1522**

What's a Girl Gotta Do?
Hayter, Sparkle **760**, 1201, 1709, 1710

When Death Comes Stealing
Wesley, Valerie Wilson **1692**

When Old Men Die
Crider, Bill **354**, 906

When Reason Sleeps
Sehler, Tom **1472**

When She Was Bad
Faust, Ron **518**

When the Bough Breaks
Kellerman, Jonathan 1643

When the Dark Man Calls
Kaminsky, Stuart 1351

When the Dark Man Calls
Kaminsky, Stuart M. 384

When the Killing Starts
Wood, Ted 1742, 1775

Where Agents Fear to Tread
Lewis, Roy Harley 1043

Where Are the Children?
Clark, Mary Higgins 128, 794, 1062, 1351, 1664

Where Echoes Live
Muller, Marcia 463, 1115, 1119, 1162, **1184**, 1265, 1607

Where Lawyers Fear to Tread
Matera, Lia 237, 963

Where Nobody Dies
Wheat, Carolyn 1076, 1650

Where There's a Will
Stout, Rex 695

Where's Mommy Now
Krich, Rochelle Majer 275

Where's Mommy Now?
Krich, Rochelle Majer 945

While Angels Sleep
Kelman, Judith 769

While My Pretty One Sleeps
Clark, Mary Higgins 139, 770

Whip Hand
Francis, Dick 839, 1487

Whiskey River ... What Mystery Do I Read Next?

Whiskey River
Estleman, Loren D. 276, 277, 279, **501**, 1207, 1536, 1609

Whisper Death
Reynolds, John Lawrence 272, **1363**

Whisper.He Might Hear You
Appel, William **62**, 976

The Whisper in the Gloom
Blake, Nicholas 368

Whisper the Guns
Cline, Edward **261**, 1744

Whistler in the Dark
Malcolm, John 1507, 1508

The Whistler Series
Campbell, Robert 1643

White Angel
Gottesfeld, Gary 1051

White Butterfly
Mosley, Walter **1178**, 1421

White Cargo
Woods, Stuart 363, 581, 582, 1188

White Jazz
Ellroy, James 1644

White Male Running
Webb, Martha G. 1135

White Rook
Davis, J. Madison 197, **392**, 973, 1281, 1738

The White Rose Murders
Clynes, Michael **265**, 1375, 1376, 1377, 1469

The Whitechapel Horrors
Hanna, Edward B. 442

Who Is Simon Warwick?
Moyes, Patricia 1173

Who Is Teddy Villinova?
Berger, Thomas 238

Who Killed Cock Robin?
Duffy, Margaret **453**, 1420

Who Killed What's-Her-Name?
Squire, Elizabeth Daniels 520, **1548**

Who Saw Him Die?
Radley, Sheila 676, 759

Who Shot Longshot Sam?
Engleman, Paul **495**

Who Shot the Bull
Knox, Bill 112

Who the Hell Is Wanda Fuca?
Ford, G.M. 728

Who Told Clutha?
Munro, Hugh 1629

Who Took Toby Rinaldi?
McDonald, Gregory 1046

Who'd Hire Brett?
Brett, John 1645

Whoever Has the Heart
Melville, Jennie **1143**

Whoo?
Hoyt, Richard **816**

Whose Dog Is It?
Hammond, Gerald 287, 290

Why Aren't They Screaming?
Smith, Joan 891

Why Isn't Becky Twitchell Dead?
Zubro, Mark Richard **1797**

Why Kill Arthur Potter?
Harrison, Ray 1049

Wicked, Loving Murder
Papazoglou, Orania 933

A Wicked Slice
Elkins, Aaron **480**

A Wicked Slice
Elkins, Charlotte 317, 318, 614, 1405

A Wide and Capable Revenge
McCall, Thomas **1113**

The Widening Gyre
Parker, Robert B. 1745

Widowmaker
Appel, William **63**

Wild Again
Segal, Kathrin King **1471**

A Wild and Lonely Place
Muller, Marcia **1185**

Wild Justice
Grant-Adamson, Lesley 168, 1369

Wild Kat
Kijewski, Karen **921**

Wild Night
Washburn, L.J. 299

Wildfire
Goddard, Kenneth W. **605**

Will to Murder
Sorrells, Walter 985

The Willa Jansson Series
Matera, Lia 853

The William Warner Series
Sylvester, Martin 1564

The Willow King Series
Cooper, Natasha 108

Win, Lose or Die
Gardner, John 567

The Wind Blows Death
Hare, Cyril 1366

Wind Chill Factor
Gifford, Thomas 1428

Wind-Up
Steed, Neville **1566**

The Windsor Knot
McCrumb, Sharyn 334, **1120**

The Winston Sherman Series
Lorens, M.K. 484

Winter by Degrees
Smolens, John 233, 689

The Winter Garden Mystery
Dunn, Carola **465**

Winter of the Wolves
Frey, James N. **552**, 553, 728, 822

Winter Prey
Sandford, John 195, **1428**

Winter Rules
Cork, Barry **318**

The Winter Widow
Weir, Charlene 536, 925, **1687**

Wiseguys in Love
Criscuolo, C. Clark **355**

Wish You Were Here
Brown, Rita Mae 15, 17, 19, 167, 169, **182**, 258, 438, 439, 619, 983

Witching Murder
Melville, Jennie 203, **1144**

With an Extreme Burning
Pronzini, Bill **1331**

With Deadly Intent
Hendricksen, Louise 322, 476, 658

With Extreme Prejudice
Barton, Frederick **102**, 592

With Friends Like These
Roberts, Gillian **1380**

With Siberia Comes a Chill
Mitchell, Kirk 957, **1161**

Wobble to Death
Lovesey, Peter 738, 1295

A Wolf in Death's Clothing
Quinn, Elizabeth **1341**, 1552

Wolf in Sheep's Clothing
Riggs, John R. 130, 867, **1369**, 1546, 1721

The Wolf Path
Van Gieson, Judith 32, 54, 1233, 1340, **1652**, 1667

Wolf Time
Gores, Joe 433, 632, 823, 1188, 1312

The Wolf Whispered Death
Moore, Barbara 290

The Wolfen
Strieber, Whitley 1426

A Woman Called Scylla
Gurr, David 1746

The Woman Who Fell From Grace
Handler, David **724**

The Woman Who Married a Bear
Straley, John 492, 1137, 1354, 1374, 1549, 1550, 1551, 1552, **1581**, 1786

The Woman Who Walked into the Sea
Craig, Philip R. **340**, 904, 1078

A Woman's Eye
Paretsky, Sara 1073, **1267**, 1299

A Woman's Own Mystery
Wakefield, Hannah 962, 1501, 1541, **1658**

A Woman's Place
Grant, Linda 232, **649**

The Womansleuth Anthology Series
Zahava, Irene 663, 1267

Women of Mystery
Manson, Cynthia **1073**

Words Can Kill
Davis, Kenn 762

Work for a Dead Man
Ritchie, Simon **1371**, 1492, 1494

Work for a Million
Zaremba, Eve 202, 533, 746, 946, 1236, 1573

Working Murder
Boylan, Eleanor 711, 712, 1171, 1245, 1406

World of Hurt
Rosen, Richard **1400**

A World the Color of Salt
Ayres, Noreen 322, 324, 1527

Worse than Death
Bunn, Thomas **190**, 500

A Wreath for the Bride
O'Donnell, Lillian **1229**

Write Me a Letter
Pierce, David M. 123

Writers of the Purple Sage
Smith, Barbara Burnett 224, 595, 600, 1411, **1517**

The Wrong Case
Crumley, James 193, 273, 319, 320, 342, 1307

The Wrong Impression
Malcolm, John **1069**, 1509

The Wrong Rite
Craig, Alisa **334**

The Wychford Murders
Gosling, Paula 367

Wycliffe and the Beales
Burley, W.J. 1253

Wycliffe and the Scapegoat
Burley, W.J. 89, 759

The Wyndham Case
Paton Walsh, Jill **1275**, 1559

X

XPD
Deighton, Len 1466

The XYZ Man
Royce, Kenneth 567

Y

Yakuza, Go Home
Wingate, Anne **1742**

The Yeadings and Mott Series
Curzon, Clare 469, 504

The Year of the Monkey
Berry, Carole 1543, 1545

Yellow Bird
Boyer, Rick 58, **162**

Yellow Dog Party
Emerson, Earl **491**

The Yellow Room Conspiracy
Dickinson, Peter **420**

Yellowthread Street
Marshall, William 34, 35

Yesterday's News
Healy, Jeremiah 40, 335, 340, 668, 686, **766**, 922, 1074, 1358

Title Index

The Yom Kippur Murder
Harris, Lee 136

You Get What You Pay For
Beinhart, Larry 184

Young Mrs. Cavendish and the Kaiser's Men
Beck, K.K. 1028, 1049

Yours Truly, From Hell
Smith, Terrence Lore 1610

Z

The Zach Rolfe Series
Lamb, J.J. 379

Zaibatsu
Brown, John 348

The Zarahembla Vision
Stewart, Gary 509, 828, 829, 830

Zero at the Bone
Walker, Mary Willis 21, 22, 96, 362, 604, 903, 1605, 1652, **1661**, 1733, 1734

The Zig-Zag Man
Albert, Marvin **27**, 328

The Ziza Todd Series
McCullough, David Willis 138, 564, 671, 672, 733

Zodiac
Stephenson, Neal 335, 340

Zombies of the Gene Pool
McCrumb, Sharyn **1121**